한 권으로 끝내는
해커스 토익 700+

LC+RC+ VOCA

KB169987

200% 활용법

🎧 교재 MP3 `FREE`

해커스인강(HackersIngang.com) 접속 ▶
상단 메뉴 **[토익 → MP3/자료 → 문제풀이 MP3]** 클릭하여 다운받기

* QR코드로 [교재 MP3] 바로 가기

📋 들으면서 외우는 단어암기자료 `FREE`

✏️ 받아쓰기&쉐도잉 워크북 `FREE`

해커스인강(HackersIngang.com) 접속 ▶
상단 메뉴 **[토익 → MP3/자료 → 무료 MP3/자료]** 클릭하여 다운받기

* QR코드로 [MP3/자료] 바로 가기

🖥 온라인 토익 실전모의고사 `FREE`

해커스인강(HackersIngang.com) 접속 ▶
상단 메뉴 **[토익 → MP3/자료 → 온라인 모의고사]** 클릭하여 이용하기

📚 교재 해설 `FREE`

해커스토익(Hackers.co.kr) 접속 ▶ 상단 메뉴 **[교재/무료 MP3** →
해커스 토익 책 소개 → 한 권으로 끝내는 해커스 토익 700+ (LC+RC+VOCA)] 클릭 ▶
[RC 무료해설] 클릭하여 이용하기

* QR코드로 [교재 해설] 바로 가기

한 권으로 끝내는

해커스
토익
700+

LC+RC+ VOCA

해커스 어학연구소

토익
이제는 **빠르게**
끝내세요.

취업, 졸업, 공무원 시험, 승진...

여러분의 멋진 꿈을 위해 해야 할 다른 중요한 일들도 참 많은데,
토익 점수가 여러분의 꿈에 걸림돌이 되어서는 안 되겠죠?

그래서 《해커스 토익 700+》는 여러분이 중요한 일들에 더 오래 집중할 수 있도록,
꼭 필요한 내용만으로 토익 목표 점수를 빠르게 달성할 수 있도록 구성되었습니다.

한 권으로		빠르게		확실하게
LC, RC, VOCA를 한 권으로 끝낼 수 있습니다.		기초부터 실전까지 빠르게 끝낼 수 있습니다.		다양한 부가 학습자료와 상세한 해설로 확실하게 끝낼 수 있습니다.

가장 빠른 토익 목표 달성!
《해커스 토익 700+》로 가능합니다!

목차

 리스닝

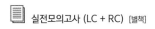 실전모의고사 (LC + RC) [별책]   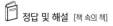 정답 및 해설 [책 속의 책]

 리딩

책의 특징 및 구성

LC + RC + VOCA를

한 권으로

+

기초부터 실전까지

빠르게

+

다양한 부가 학습자료와 상세한 해설로

확실하게

목표 달성 700+

《해커스 토익 700+》는 여러분이 목표 점수를 단 **한 권으로 빠르고 확실하게** 달성하여 더 중요한 일들에 집중할 수 있도록 꼭 필요한 내용만을 엄선하여 수록하였습니다.

01 LC + RC + VOCA 구성
LC, RC, VOCA를 한 번에 끝내 한 권으로 목표를 달성하세요.

700+의 목표 점수를 빠르게 달성하기 위해서는 무엇보다 LC와 RC의 모든 파트, 그리고 VOCA에 익숙해져야 합니다. 《해커스 토익 700+》에는 LC, RC, VOCA가 한 권에 구성되어 있어 LC, RC, VOCA를 한 번에 완성하여 더 빠르게 목표를 달성할 수 있습니다.

LC

RC

VOCA

기초 + 실전 통합 구성

02 기초와 실전을 함께 학습하여 빠르게 목표를 달성하세요.

토익 기초가 부족해도 걱정하지 않아도 됩니다. 《해커스 토익 700+》는 본격적인 학습을 시작하기 위한 기초 내용을 정리한 기초 다지기 코너가 구성되어 있어, 토익 기초부터 쉽게 학습할 수 있습니다.

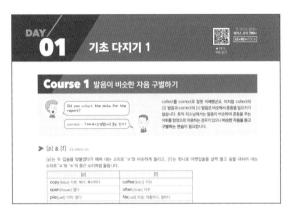

리스닝 기초 다지기

리스닝 학습에 꼭 필요한 혼동하기 쉬운 자음·모음 발음 구별부터 연음 및 끊어 듣기까지 확실하게 정복할 수 있습니다.

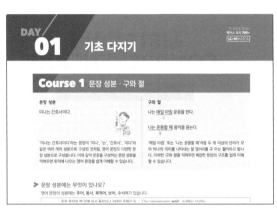

리딩 기초 다지기

리딩 학습에 꼭 필요한 문장 구조에 대해 이해하고 패러프레이징 방법에 대해 확실하게 익힐 수 있습니다.

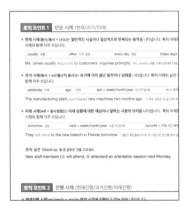

포인트 학습

포인트 학습으로 토익에 출제되는 핵심 포인트와 문제 풀이에 필요한 전략을 빠르게 학습할 수 있습니다.

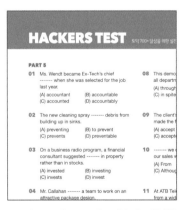

HACKERS PRACTICE & TEST

앞서 학습한 핵심 포인트와 전략을 연습 문제를 통해 점검해 보고, 실전 문제를 통해 토익 실전에 필요한 실력을 다질 수 있습니다.

실전모의고사 [별책]

토익 경향이 완벽히 반영된 실전모의고사(별책)를 통해 실전 감각을 키울 수 있습니다.

책의 특징 및 구성

03 다양한 부가 학습자료와 상세한 해설
실력을 키워주는 부가 학습자료와 해설집**으로** 확실하게 **목표를 달성하세요.**

토익 온라인 모의고사

토익 시험의 유형과 난이도를 완벽하게 반영한 토익 온라인 모의고사를 추가로 풀어보며 목표 점수를 획득할 수 있는지 여부를 점검하고 실전 감각을 키울 수 있습니다.

* 토익 온라인 모의고사는 해커스인강 사이트(HackersIngang.com)에서 무료로 제공됩니다.

단어암기자료 (PDF & MP3)

실제 토익 리스닝 시험에 자주 출제되는 주제별 핵심 어휘와 예문을 정리한 단어장과 MP3로, 이동할 때나 자투리 시간에 효율적으로 단어를 암기하고 토익 리스닝 발음에 익숙해질 수 있습니다.

* 단어암기자료(PDF & MP3)는 해커스인강 사이트(HackersIngang.com)에서 무료로 다운로드할 수 있습니다.

받아쓰기 & 쉐도잉 워크북 (PDF)

교재에 수록된 핵심 문장을 복습할 수 있는 받아쓰기 & 쉐도잉 워크북으로, 토익 리스닝 점수를 단기에 대폭 향상할 수 있는 기본 실력을 갖출 수 있습니다.

* 받아쓰기 & 쉐도잉 워크북(PDF & MP3)은 해커스인강 사이트(HackersIngang.com)에서 무료로 다운로드할 수 있습니다.

한 권으로 끝내는
해커스 토익 700+
LC+RC+VOCA

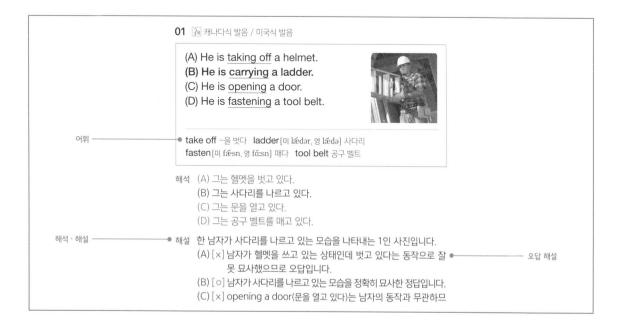

01 🔊 캐나다식 발음 / 미국식 발음

(A) He is <u>taking off</u> a helmet.
(B) He is <u>carrying</u> a ladder.
(C) He is <u>opening</u> a door.
(D) He is <u>fastening</u> a tool belt.

어휘 ── take off ~을 벗다 ladder[미 lǽdər, 영 lǽdə] 사다리
fasten[미 fǽsn, 영 fɑ́ːsn] 매다 tool belt 공구 벨트

해석 (A) 그는 헬멧을 벗고 있다.
(B) 그는 사다리를 나르고 있다.
(C) 그는 문을 열고 있다.
(D) 그는 공구 벨트를 매고 있다.

해석 · 해설 ── 해설 한 남자가 사다리를 나르고 있는 모습을 나타내는 1인 사진입니다.
(A) [×] 남자가 헬멧을 쓰고 있는 상태인데 벗고 있다는 동작으로 잘 ●──── 오답 해설
못 묘사했으므로 오답입니다.
(B) [○] 남자가 사다리를 나르고 있는 모습을 정확히 묘사한 정답입니다.
(C) [×] opening a door(문을 열고 있다)는 남자의 동작과 무관하므

해석 · 해설

모든 문제에 대한 정확한 해석을 통해 해석이 잘 되지 않는 문장의 구조를 확실하게 익힐 수 있으며, 실제 문제를 푸는 순서와 문제
풀이 전략을 적용한 해설을 통해 모든 문제를 확실하게 이해하고 이론을 다시 한번 복습할 수 있습니다.

오답 해설

오답 보기가 오답이 되는 이유까지 상세하게 설명하여 틀렸던 문제의 원인을 파악하고 보완할 수 있습니다.

어휘

지문 및 문제에서 사용된 단어와 표현의 뜻을 함께 수록하여 문제를 복습할 때 일일이 사전을 찾는 불편을 덜 수 있습니다.

토익 소개

토익(TOEIC)이란?

TOEIC은 Test Of English for International Communication의 약자로 영어가 모국어가 아닌 사람들을 대상으로 언어 본래의 기능인 '커뮤니케이션' 능력에 중점을 두고 일상생활 또는 국제 업무 등에 필요한 실용영어 능력을 평가하는 시험입니다. 토익은 일상생활 및 비즈니스 현장에서 필요로 하는 내용을 평가하기 위해 개발되었으며, 다음과 같은 실용적인 주제들을 주로 다루고 있습니다.

- 협력 개발: 연구, 제품 개발
- 재무 회계: 대출, 투자, 세금, 회계, 은행 업무
- 일반 업무: 계약, 협상, 마케팅, 판매
- 기술 영역: 전기, 공업 기술, 컴퓨터, 실험실
- 사무 영역: 회의, 서류 업무
- 물품 구입: 쇼핑, 물건 주문, 대금 지불

- 식사: 레스토랑, 회식, 만찬
- 문화: 극장, 스포츠, 피크닉
- 건강: 의료 보험, 병원 진료, 치과
- 제조: 생산 조립 라인, 공장 경영
- 직원: 채용, 은퇴, 급여, 진급, 고용 기회
- 주택: 부동산, 이사, 기업 부지

토익 시험의 구성

구성	내용		문항 수	시간	배점
Listening Test	PART 1	사진 묘사	6문항(1번-6번)	45분	495점
	PART 2	질의 응답	25문항(7번-31번)		
	PART 3	짧은 대화	39문항, 13지문(32번-70번)		
	PART 4	짧은 담화	30문항, 10지문(71번-100번)		
Reading Test	PART 5	단문 빈칸 채우기(문법/어휘)	30문항(101번-130번)	75분	495점
	PART 6	장문 빈칸 채우기(문법/어휘/문장 고르기)	16문항, 4지문(131번-146번)		
	PART 7	지문 읽고 문제 풀기(독해)	54문항, 15지문(147번-200번)		
		– 단일 지문(Single Passage)	– 29문항, 10지문(147번-175번)		
		– 이중 지문(Double Passages)	– 10문항, 2지문(176번-185번)		
		– 삼중 지문(Triple Passages)	– 15문항, 3지문(186번-200번)		
Total	7 PARTS		200문항	120분	990점

토익, 접수부터 성적 확인까지

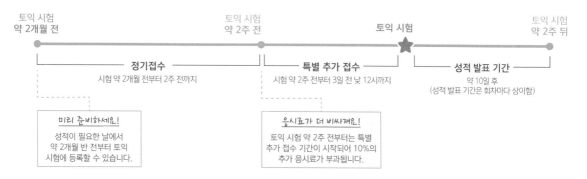

1. 토익 접수

- 인터넷 접수 기간을 TOEIC위원회 인터넷 사이트(www.toeic.co.kr) 혹은 공식 애플리케이션에서 확인하세요. 정기 토익은 시험 약 2개월 전부터 접수가 가능하며, 특별추가 접수 기간에는 정기접수 기간 응시료에서 10%가 추가된 응시료로 접수할 수 있습니다.
- 추가 토익 시험은 2월과 8월에 있으며 이외에도 연중 상시로 시행되니 인터넷으로 확인하고 접수해야 합니다.
- 접수 시, jpg 형식의 사진 파일이 필요하므로 미리 준비해야 합니다.

2. 토익 응시

- 토익 응시일 이전에 시험 장소 및 수험번호를 미리 확인합니다.
- 시험 당일 신분증이 없으면 시험에 응시할 수 없으므로, 반드시 ETS에서 요구하는 신분증(주민등록증, 운전면허증, 공무원증 등)을 지참해야 합니다.
  ETS에서 인정하는 신분증 종류는 TOEIC위원회 인터넷 사이트(www.toeic.co.kr)에서 확인 가능합니다.

3. 성적 확인

성적 발표일	시험일로부터 약 10일 이후 (성적 발표 기간은 회차마다 상이함)
성적 확인 방법	TOEIC위원회 인터넷 사이트(www.toeic.co.kr) 혹은 공식 애플리케이션
성적표 수령 방법	우편 수령 또는 온라인 출력 (시험 접수 시 선택) *온라인 출력은 성적 발표 즉시 발급 가능하나, 우편 수령은 약 7일가량의 발송 기간이 소요될 수 있음

파트별 출제 유형 및 전략

PART 1 사진 묘사 (6문제)

- PART 1은 주어진 4개의 보기 중에서 사진의 상황을 가장 잘 묘사한 보기를 선택하는 파트입니다.
- 문제지에는 사진만 제시되고 음성에서는 4개의 보기를 들려줍니다.

문제 형태

[문제지]

1.

[음성]

Number One.

Look at the picture marked number one in your test book.

(A) A woman is serving a meal.
(B) A woman is washing a bowl.
(C) A woman is pouring some water.
(D) A woman is preparing some food.

문제 풀이 전략

전략 1 | 보기를 듣기 전에 사진 유형을 확인하고 관련 표현을 미리 연상해야 합니다.

보기를 듣기 전에 사람의 유무 및 수에 따라 사진 유형을 확인하고, 사람의 동작/상태 또는 사물의 상태/위치와 관련된 표현들을 미리 연상하면 보기를 훨씬 명확하게 들을 수 있어 정답 선택이 쉬워집니다.

전략 2 | ○, ×, △를 표시하면서 오답을 걸러내야 합니다.

○, ×, △ 표시를 하지 않으면 다른 보기 내용과 혼동하기 쉬우므로, 보기를 듣고 ○, ×, △ 를 표시하면서 문제를 풀어야 헷갈리는 오답 보기를 확실히 제거하고 정답을 정확하게 선택할 수 있습니다.

전략 3 | PART 1에 자주 출제되는 오답 유형을 알아두어야 합니다.

PART 1에서 자주 출제되는 오답 유형을 알아두면 보기의 일부만 듣고도 오답을 골라낼 수 있어 정확하게 정답을 선택하는 데 큰 도움이 됩니다.

PART 1 빈출 오답 유형
- 사진 속 사람의 동작을 잘못 묘사한 오답
- 사진 속 사물의 상태나 위치를 잘못 묘사한 오답
- 사진에 없는 사람이나 사물을 언급한 오답
- 완료된 상태를 진행중인 것으로 잘못 묘사한 오답
- 사진에서는 확인할 수 없는 사실을 진술한 오답

PART 2 질의 응답 (25문제)

- PART 2는 주어진 질문이나 진술에 가장 적절한 응답을 선택하는 파트입니다.
- 문제지에는 질문과 보기가 제시되지 않으며 음성에서는 질문과 3개의 보기를 들려줍니다.

문제 형태

[문제지]

7. Mark your answer on your answer sheet.

[음성]

Number Seven.

Where is the nearest park?

(A) There's one on Lincoln Avenue.
(B) No, I don't drive.
(C) I'm nearly finished.

문제 풀이 전략

전략 1 | 질문의 첫 단어를 반드시 들어 질문 유형을 확인해야 합니다.

PART 2에서 평균 11문제가 출제되는 의문사 의문문은 첫 단어인 의문사만 들으면 대부분 정답을 선택할 수 있습니다. 단, 부가 의문문은 평서문 뒤에 덧붙여진 'doesn't he?'나 'right?'와 같은 형태를 듣고, 선택 의문문은 질문의 중간에 접속사 'or'를 듣고서 유형을 파악해야 합니다.

전략 2 | ○, ×, △를 표시하면서 오답을 걸러내야 합니다.

○, ×, △ 표시를 하지 않으면 다른 보기 내용과 혼동하기 쉬우므로, 보기를 듣고 ○, ×, △를 표시하면서 문제를 풀어야 헷갈리는 오답 보기를 확실히 제거하고 정답을 정확하게 선택할 수 있습니다.

전략 3 | PART 2에 자주 출제되는 오답 유형을 파악해야 합니다.

PART 2에서 자주 출제되는 오답 유형을 알아두면 보기의 일부만 듣고도 오답을 골라낼 수 있어 정확하게 정답을 선택하는 데 큰 도움이 됩니다.

PART 2 빈출 오답 유형

- 질문에 등장한 단어를 반복하거나, 발음이 유사한 어휘를 사용한 오답
  ex) Where is the **nearest** park? - I'm **nearly** finished.

- 관련 어휘, 동의어, 반의어, 다의어를 사용한 오답
  ex) How's the **book** review going? - That's my favorite **author**.

- 정보를 묻는 의문사 의문문에 Yes/No로 응답한 오답
  ex) **Who** is the man next to the manager? - **Yes**, he is out of town.

- 질문의 내용과 전혀 관계없는 응답을 한 오답
  ex) Do you **have a key** to the supply room? - **I visited my parents in Canada.**

PART 3 짧은 대화 (39문제)

- PART 3는 두세 사람의 대화를 듣고 이와 관련된 3개의 문제의 정답을 선택하는 파트입니다.
- 문제지에는 하나의 질문과 4개의 보기로 구성된 39개의 문제가 제시되고, 일부 문제는 시각 자료가 함께 제시되기도 합니다. 음성으로는 대화와 이에 대한 3문제의 질문을 들려줍니다.

문제 형태

[문제지]

32. Why does the woman say, "But I have to meet with a Sorel representative on Friday"?

    (A) To confirm an appointment
    (B) To explain a mistake
    (C) **To express concern**
    (D) To change a deadline

[음성]

Questions 32 through 34 refer to the following conversation with three speakers.

W: George, Jerry . . . I'm sorry I couldn't make it for lunch today. My boss wanted to talk with me about the advertising campaign for Sorel Incorporated. This is a big project, and I'm a little nervous about it.

M1: Don't worry. You're a hard worker. And our clients never complain about your work.

W: But I have to meet with a Sorel representative on Friday. I'm not sure if I'll be able to create a proposal in time.

M2: Why don't we all go to a café after work? We can help you come up with some ideas.

M1: Yeah. We're happy to help.

Number 32. Why does the woman say, "But I have to meet with a Sorel representative on Friday"?

문제 풀이 전략

전략 1 | 대화를 듣기 전에 반드시 문제를 먼저 읽어야 합니다.

질문의 핵심 어구를 미리 읽으면 대화의 어느 부분을 중점적으로 들어야 할지 전략을 세울 수 있습니다. 시각 자료가 제시된 문제라면, 문제와 시각 자료를 함께 확인하면서 시각 자료의 종류와 내용을 파악합니다.

전략 2 | 대화를 들으면서 동시에 정답을 선택해야 합니다.

문제를 읽을 때 세워놓은 전략에 따라, 대화를 들으면서 3문제의 정답을 선택해야 합니다. 즉, 대화를 들려주는 음성이 끝날 때에는 3문제의 정답 선택도 완료되어 있어야 합니다.

전략 3 | 대화의 초반은 반드시 들어야 합니다.

PART 3에서는 대화의 초반에 언급된 내용 중 80% 이상이 문제로 출제되며, 특히 주제 및 목적 문제나 화자 및 장소 문제처럼 전체 대화 관련 문제에 대한 정답의 단서는 대부분 대화의 초반에 언급됩니다. 대화 초반의 내용을 듣지 못하면 대화 후반에서 언급된 특정 표현을 사용한 오답을 정답으로 선택하는 오류를 범할 수 있으므로 주의해야 합니다.

PART 4 짧은 담화 (30문제)

- PART 4는 하나의 담화를 듣고 이와 관련된 3개의 문제의 정답을 선택하는 파트입니다.
- 문제지에는 하나의 질문과 4개의 보기로 구성된 30개의 문제가 제시되고, 일부 문제는 시각 자료가 함께 제시되기도 합니다. 음성으로는 담화와 이에 대한 3문제의 질문을 들려줍니다.

문제 형태

[문제지]

Lunch Specials	
Item	Price
Panini Sandwich	$7
Spaghetti	$6
Dinner Specials	
Item	Price
Lasagna	$9
Grilled Chicken	$11

73. Look at the graphic. Which meal will come with a complimentary beverage?

(A) Panini Sandwich
(B) Spaghetti
(C) Lasagna
(D) Grilled Chicken

[음성]

Questions 71 through 73 refer to the following talk and menu.

As many of you already know, our restaurant's menu will be updated soon. I sent everyone an e-mail with the details yesterday, but I'll go over the main changes quickly now. First, the prices of our dinner menu items have been reduced by 10 percent to attract more evening customers. Also, we will provide a complimentary coffee or soft drink with one of our lunch specials . . . uh, the cheaper one. Some new dishes will be offered as well. I will now pass around a list of these dishes and the ingredients they will contain. Please study it so you'll be able to answer diners' questions.

Number 73. Look at the graphic. Which meal will come with a complimentary beverage?

문제 풀이 전략

전략 1 | 지문을 듣기 전에 반드시 문제를 먼저 읽어야 합니다.

질문의 핵심 어구를 미리 읽으면 담화의 어느 부분을 중점적으로 들어야 할지 전략을 세울 수 있습니다. 시각 자료가 제시된 문제라면, 문제와 시각 자료를 함께 확인하면서 시각 자료의 종류와 내용을 파악합니다.

전략 2 | 지문을 들으면서 동시에 정답을 선택해야 합니다.

문제를 읽을 때 세워놓은 전략에 따라, 지문을 들으면서 3문제의 정답을 선택해야 합니다. 즉, 지문을 들려주는 음성이 끝날 때에는 3문제의 정답 선택도 완료되어 있어야 합니다.

전략 3 | 지문의 초반은 반드시 들어야 합니다.

PART 4에서는 지문의 초반에 언급된 내용 중 80% 이상이 문제로 출제되며, 특히 주제 및 목적 문제나 화자·청자 및 장소 문제처럼 전체 지문 관련 문제에 대한 정답의 단서는 대부분 지문의 초반에 언급됩니다. 지문 초반의 내용을 듣지 못할 경우, 더 이상 문제와 관련된 내용이 언급 되지 않아 정답 선택이 어려워질 수 있으므로 주의해야 합니다.

파트별 출제 유형 및 전략

PART 5 단문 빈칸 채우기 (30문제)

- PART 5는 한 문장의 빈칸에 알맞은 어휘나 문법 사항을 4개의 보기 중에서 골라 채우는 파트입니다.
- 총 30개의 문제 중 문법 문제가 평균 20개, 어휘 문제가 평균 10개 출제됩니다.
- PART 7 문제 풀이에 시간이 모자라지 않으려면 각 문제를 20~22초 내에, 총 30문제를 약 11분 내에 끝내야 합니다.

문제 형태

문법

> **101.** Kathleen Wilson is a recent graduate who ------- three months ago to help the marketing team with graphic design.
>
> (A) hired
> (B) hiring
> **(C) was hired**
> (D) is hiring

어휘

> **102.** In spite of the bad weather and traffic delays, Mr. Chandra showed up ------- for his coworker's housewarming party.
>
> (A) gradually
> (B) intensely
> (C) considerably
> **(D) punctually**

문제 풀이 전략

전략 1 | 보기를 보고 문법 문제인지, 어휘 문제인지를 파악합니다.

hired, hiring, was hired, is hiring처럼 보기가 어근은 같지만 형태가 다른 단어들로 구성되어 있으면 문법 문제이고, 보기가 gradually, intensely, considerably, punctually처럼 같은 품사의 다양한 어휘들로 구성되어 있으면 어휘 문제입니다.

전략 2 | 파악한 문제 유형에 따라 빈칸 주변이나 문장의 전체적인 구조 및 문맥을 통해 정답을 선택합니다.

문법 문제는 문제 유형에 따라 빈칸 주변이나 문장의 전체적인 구조를 통해 빈칸에 적합한 문법적 요소를 정답으로 선택합니다. 만약 구조만으로 풀 수 없는 경우, 문맥을 확인하여 정답을 선택합니다. 어휘 문제는 문맥을 확인하여 그 문맥에 가장 적합한 어휘를 정답으로 선택합니다.

PART 6 장문 빈칸 채우기 (16문제)

- PART 6는 한 지문 내의 4개 빈칸에 알맞은 문법 사항이나 어휘 및 문장을 4개의 보기 중에서 골라 채우는 파트입니다.
- 총 4개 지문, 16문제 중 문법 문제가 평균 7개, 어휘 문제가 평균 5개, 문장 고르기 문제가 4개 출제됩니다.
- PART 7 문제 풀이에 시간이 모자라지 않으려면 각 문제를 25~30초 내에, 총 16문제를 약 8분 내에 끝내야 합니다.

문제 형태

Questions 131-134 refer to the following e-mail.

-------. As you know, you are in charge of driving our visitor from Fennel Corporation, Mr. Palmer. He will be here as
   131
scheduled from May 16 to 20. However, his arrival time from Dublin has been moved back four hours because he

------- a quick stop in New York. This means you do not need to be at the airport until 2 P.M. on the 16th.
   132

Also, the factory tour ------- he was supposed to take on Monday morning has been canceled. He'll have a breakfast
                        133
meeting with the plant manager instead at the Oberlin Hotel. Attached is a revised -------. Please let me know as
                                                                                    134
soon as you've confirmed these adjustments.

Helen Cho, Client relations

Ctrek Apparel

131. (A) Regretfully, Mr. Palmer will no longer be needing our services.
   (B) I'm writing to inform you of a few changes concerning our client.
   (C) The following are some details about the new factory manager.
   (D) Finally, I have received the new schedule for your flight to Dublin.

132. (A) will be made   **(B) is making**
   (C) had made   (D) has been making

133. (A) this   (B) what
   (C) when   **(D) that**

134. **(A) itinerary**   (B) estimate
   (C) transcript   (D) inventory

문제 풀이 전략

전략 1 | 보기를 보고 문제 유형을 파악합니다.
will be made, is making, had made, has been making처럼 보기가 어근은 같지만 형태가 다른 단어들로 구성되어 있으면 문법 문제, 보기가 itinerary, estimate, transcript, inventory처럼 같은 품사의 다양한 어휘들로 구성되어 있으면 어휘 문제이며, 보기가 문장으로 되어 있으면 문장 고르기 문제입니다.

전략 2 | 파악한 문제 유형에 따라 빈칸이 포함된 문장, 또는 앞뒤 문장이나 전체 지문의 구조 및 문맥을 통해 정답을 선택합니다.
PART 6에서는 앞뒤 문맥이나 전체 지문의 문맥을 파악해야 정답을 선택할 수 있는 문제도 출제됩니다. 따라서 먼저 빈칸이 포함된 문장의 구조만으로 정답 선택이 어려울 경우, 반드시 앞뒤 문장이나 전체 지문의 구조 및 문맥을 파악하여 문맥에 가장 잘 어울리는 보기를 정답으로 선택해야 합니다.

PART 7 지문 읽고 문제 풀기 (54문제)

- PART 7은 제시된 지문과 관련된 질문들에 대해 4개의 보기 중에서 적절한 답을 선택하는 파트입니다.
- 독해 지문은 단일 지문(Single Passage), 이중 지문(Double Passages), 삼중 지문(Triple Passages)으로 나뉘며, 단일 지문에서 29문제, 이중 지문에서 10문제, 삼중 지문에서 15문제가 출제됩니다.
- PART 7의 모든 문제를 제한 시간 내에 풀려면 한 문제를 1분 내에 풀어야 합니다.

문제 형태

단일 지문 (Single Passage)

Questions 147-148 refer to the following text message chain.

Natasha Walla	4:08 P.M.
Robert, about the sponsorship packages for the Shoreland Music Festival, do you want to go for the Platinum package? It allows us to broadcast commercials during the event.	
Robert Fish	4:09 P.M.
That would give us good exposure. Plus, we can put up company banners at the venue.	
Natasha Wallace	4:10 P.M.
That's right. So, should I go ahead and sign us up? The deadline is this Friday.	
Robert Fish	4:10 P.M.
Well, we can't spend any more than $6,000 on this, you know. How much is it?	
Natasha Wallace	4:12 P.M.
More than that. How about the Gold sponsorship package then? It costs $5,250, and festival announcers will mention our company over the loudspeakers throughout the day.	
Robert Fish	4:13 P.M.
That sounds OK to me. Send me all the details once you're done.	

147. In which department do the speakers most likely work?
  (A) Accounting
  (B) Marketing
  (C) Customer service
  (D) Human resources

148. At 4:12 P.M., what does Ms. Wallace mean when she writes, "More than that"?
  (A) She believes that registering after the deadline is acceptable.
  (B) She acknowledges that a cost exceeds a budgeted amount.
  (C) She would like to receive some additional sponsorship benefits.
  (D) She doubts that $6,000 is their maximum spending allowance.

이중 지문 (Double Passages)

Questions 176-180 refer to the following e-mail and Web form.

To	Jennifer Ellis <jenniferellis@jagmail.com>
From	Travis Whitman <traviswhitman@mywebpress.com>
Date	November 1
Subject	Action Needed on Your Account

Dear Ms. Ellis,

Your MyWebPress account is due to renew in 10 days. You have the option to pay for another year at the rate of $29.99, or you may choose the three-year option at $79.99. We also offer a premium version of MyWebPress that enables many more features and design templates. One year of the higher level software costs $49.99 while the three-year package price is $129.99.

These special prices are only available if your renewal form is received by November 10.

Thank you,

Travis Whitman

MyWebPress Subscription Renewal Form   Date: November 8

Please fill out all information to process your renewal request and payment.

Account Name	Jennifer Ellis		Account Number	83402839

Please choose your renewal option:

	One Year	Three Years
MyWebPress Standard	☐ $29.99	☐ $79.99
MyWebPress Premium	■ $49.99	☐ $129.99
Pre-made Forms Add-On	☐ $5.99	☐ $8.99
Graphic Design Add-On	☐ $12.99	☐ $18.99

Payment Information:

Credit Card Type	☐ Bankster ■ SureCredit ☐ YPay	Card Number	2934 4992 0041
Expiration Date	November 30	Security Code	557

176. What is indicated about Ms. Ellis?

(A) She is using a new credit card for payment.

(B) She failed to meet a deadline set by MyWebPress.

(C) She chose an upgraded version of her original plan.

(D) She added some security features to her package.

파트별 출제 유형 및 전략

삼중 지문 (Triple Passages)

Questions 186-190 refer to the following Web page, form, and e-mail.

Laurel Art Center

Upcoming Events

Summer Sounds Fest • Concert featuring local musicians • June 5, from noon to 10 P.M. • Tickets go on sale May 15	**Spectacular Vistas** • Exhibit of watercolor paintings by local landscape artist Samantha Davey • Opens 6 P.M., July 3, at the Campbell Gallery • Refreshments provided by Gordon's Café
Exploring Wood • Seminar conducted by Paula Sue • Thursday July 6 from 10:00 A.M. to 4 P.M. • $25 for eight classes (participants must bring safety glasses and a pair of work gloves)	**Annual Craft Show** • Our biggest event of the year, featuring handicrafts made by talented local artists • August 5, 10 A.M. to 4 P.M. • Admission is $5 for adults and $2 for seniors • Includes a buffet lunch from Kostas Mediterranean Kitchen

To join our mailing list, click here.

Laurel Art Center

Registration Form

Name	Ella Chung	Date	June 12
Telephone	555-3205	Address	108 Spruce Drive
E-mail	ellachung@mymail.net		Hendersonville, TN 37075
Event title	Exploring Wood		
Payment method			

☐ Cash (Please pay two weeks in advance to reserve your slot)
■ Credit card: Liberty Bancard 2347-8624-5098-5728

To	Melissa Hamada <m.hamada@laurelart.org>
From	Hector Villa <h.villa@laurelart.org>
Subject	Catering
Date	June 21

Dear Melissa,

As we discussed yesterday afternoon, Kostas Mediterranean Kitchen had to back out of catering our August 5 event due to a scheduling conflict. However, I've received confirmation that Asian Flavors can take their place. Please update our Web site to reflect this change.

Hector Villa
Activities director, Laurel Art Center

186. What is suggested about Ms. Chung?
(A) She is a member of the Laurel Art Center.
(B) She will be attending an upcoming exhibit.
(C) She is expected to bring gear to an activity.
(D) She will be charged $5 for admission to an event.

187. Which event will Asian Flavors be catering?
(A) Summer Sounds Fest
(B) Spectacular Vistas
(C) Exploring Wood
(D) Annual Craft Show

문제 풀이 전략

전략 1 | 지문의 종류나 글의 제목을 먼저 확인하여 지문의 개괄적인 내용을 추측해야 합니다.
지문 맨 위에 지문을 소개하는 문장을 통해 언급된 지문의 종류를 확인하거나 글의 제목을 읽어서 지문이 어떤 내용을 담고 있을지 추측하며 문제를 풀도록 합니다.

전략 2 | 질문을 읽고, 질문의 핵심 어구와 관련된 정답의 단서를 지문에서 확인해야 합니다.
질문을 읽고 질문의 핵심 어구를 파악한 후, 핵심 어구와 관련된 내용이 언급된 부분을 지문에서 찾아 정답의 단서를 확인합니다. 이중 지문이나 삼중 지문과 같은 연계 지문의 경우, 처음 확인한 단서만으로 정답을 선택할 수 없으면 첫 번째 단서와 관련된 두 번째 단서를 다른 지문에서 찾아야 합니다.

전략 3 | 정답의 단서를 그대로 언급했거나 바꾸어 표현한 보기를 정답으로 선택해야 합니다.
정답의 단서를 그대로 언급했거나 바꾸어 표현한 보기를 정답으로 선택해야 합니다. 이중 지문이나 삼중 지문과 같은 연계 지문의 경우에는 두 개의 지문에 언급된 각각의 단서를 종합하여 정답을 선택해야 하는 경우도 있습니다.

700+ 정복 학습 플랜

나에게 딱 맞는 학습 플랜 고르는 법

학습 플랜 A

학습 플랜 A는 20일간 매일 리스닝 DAY 1개와 리딩 DAY 1개를 학습하는 코스로, 토익 시험 경험이 없거나 단계적으로 학습하여 목표 점수를 취득하길 원하는 학습자에게 추천합니다.

· 하루 학습량: 적당한 수준
· 학습 기간: 20일

학습 플랜 B

학습 플랜 B는 점수가 쉽게 오르는 리스닝부터 집중 공략하는 코스로, 토익 시험 경험이 있거나 짧은 기간에 집중하여 목표 점수를 취득하길 원하는 학습자에게 추천합니다.

· 하루 학습량: 도전적인 수준
· 학습 기간: 10일

학습 플랜 A 매일 LC, RC, VOCA 1일치씩 학습하여 20일 만에 700+를 정복하는 플랜

		1st Day	2nd Day	3rd Day	4th Day	5th Day
1st week	리스닝	DAY 01	DAY 02	DAY 03	DAY 04	DAY05
	리딩	DAY 01	DAY 02	DAY 03	DAY 04	DAY05
2nd week	리스닝	DAY 06	DAY 07	DAY 08	DAY09	DAY10
	리딩	DAY 06	DAY 07	DAY 08	DAY09	DAY10
3rd week	리스닝	DAY 11	DAY 12	DAY 13	DAY 14	DAY 15
	리딩	DAY 11	DAY 12	DAY 13	DAY 14	DAY 15
4th week	리스닝	DAY 16	DAY 17	DAY18	DAY 19	DAY 20, 실전모의고사 (별책)
	리딩	DAY 16	DAY 17	DAY18	DAY 19	DAY 20, 실전모의고사 (별책)

* VOCABULARY는 하루에 DAY 1개를 학습합니다.

학습 플랜 B 점수가 쉽게 오르는 리스닝부터 집중 공략하여 10일 만에 700+를 정복하는 플랜

		1st Day	2nd Day	3rd Day	4th Day	5th Day
1st week	리스닝	DAY 01~04	DAY 05~08	DAY 09~12	DAY 13~16	DAY 17~20
2nd week	리딩	DAY 01~04	DAY 05~08	DAY 09~12	DAY 13~16	DAY 17~20, 실전모의고사 (별책)

* VOCABULARY는 하루에 DAY 2개를 학습합니다.

해커스는 더 높은 목표를 꿈꾸는 여러분을 응원합니다.

토익 목표 점수 700+를 달성한 이후, 더 높은 점수를 목표로 공부하실 계획이 있으신가요? 아래 해커스 교재로 여러분들의 목표하는 바를 달성할 수 있습니다.

	750~850점 목표	850점 이상 목표
기본서	《해커스 토익 750+ LC》 《해커스 토익 750+ RC》	《해커스 토익 Listening》 《해커스 토익 Reading》
실전서	《해커스 토익 실전 1200제 Listening》 《해커스 토익 실전 1200제 Reading》 《해커스 토익 실전 1000제 1 Listening》 《해커스 토익 실전 1000제 1 Reading》	《해커스 토익 실전 1000제 1 Listening》 《해커스 토익 실전 1000제 1 Reading》 《해커스 토익 실전 1000제 2 Listening》 《해커스 토익 실전 1000제 2 Reading》
VOCA	《해커스 토익 기출 보카》	

한 권으로 끝내는
해커스 토익 **700+**
LC+RC+VOCA

LISTENING 리스닝

한 권으로 끝내는
해커스 토익 700+
LC+RC+VOCA

리스닝
기초 다지기

토익에 나오는 문장을 듣고 쉽게 이해할 수 있도록 발음이 비슷한 자음과 모음을 구별하고, 연음에 유의하며 긴 문장을 끊어 듣는 연습을 합니다.

DAY 01 기초 다지기 1

DAY 02 기초 다지기 2

DAY
01 / 기초 다지기 1

▲ MP3
바로 듣기

한 권으로 끝내는
해커스 토익 700+
LC+RC+VOCA

Course 1 발음이 비슷한 자음 구별하기

Did you collect the data for the report?

correct ...? 데이터 수정했냐고 묻는 건가?

collect를 correct로 잘못 이해했군요. 이처럼 collect의 [l] 발음과 correct의 [r] 발음은 비슷해서 혼동을 일으키기 쉽습니다. 토익 리스닝에서는 발음이 비슷하여 혼동을 주는 어휘를 함정으로 이용하는 경우가 있으니 **비슷한 자음을 듣고 구별하는 연습**이 필요합니다.

➤ [p] & [f] ∩ DAY01_01

[p]는 두 입술을 맞붙였다가 떼며 내는 소리로 'ㅍ'와 비슷하게 들리고, [f]는 윗니로 아랫입술을 살짝 물고 숨을 내쉬어 내는 소리로 'ㅍ'와 'ㅎ'의 중간 소리처럼 들립니다.

[p]	[f]
copy[kápi] 사본, 복사; 복사하다	coffee[kɔ́:fi] 커피
open[óupən] 열다	often[ɔ́:fən] 자주
pile[pail] 더미; 쌓다	file[fail] 파일; 제출하다, 철하다
pound[paund] 영국의 화폐 단위	found[faund] 찾았다(find의 과거형), 설립하다

➤ [b] & [v] ∩ DAY01_02

[b]는 두 입술을 맞붙였다가 떼며 내는 소리로 'ㅂ'와 비슷하게 들리고, [v]는 윗니로 아랫입술을 살짝 물었다 놓으며 내는 소리로 'ㅂ'보다 바람 새는 소리가 더 많이 들립니다.

[b]	[v]
base[beis] 기초	vase[veis] 꽃병
bend[bend] 구부리다, 숙이다	vend[vend] 팔다, 행상하다
bow[bau] 인사하다, 허리를 굽히다	vow[vau] 다짐하다, 맹세하다
curb[kə:rb] 연석; 억제하다	curve[kə:rv] 곡선; 구부리다

➤ [l] & [r] ∩ DAY01_03

[l]는 혀끝을 앞니 뒤에 대었다가 떼며 내는 소리로 '(을)르'와 비슷하게 들리고, [r]는 혀를 둥글게 말아 입천장 가까이 가져가며 내는 소리로 '(우)르'와 비슷하게 들립니다.

[l]	[r]
collect[kəlékt] 모으다	correct[kərékt] 수정하다, 고치다
lack[læk] 부족; 모자라다	rack[ræk] 걸이, 선반
lake[leik] 호수, 연못	rake[reik] 갈퀴; 긁어모으다
late[leit] 늦은	rate[reit] 요금

HACKERS PRACTICE

유사 발음에 유의하여 음성을 듣고 빈칸에 알맞은 단어를 고르세요. (음성은 두 번 들려줍니다.)

01 I need to _____ the application forms.
    (A) file   (B) pile

02 People sometimes _____ in order to show respect.
    (A) bow   (B) vow

03 The charity organization is concerned about the _____ of donations.
    (A) lack   (B) rack

04 The _____ machine isn't working properly.
    (A) coffee   (B) copy

05 _____ your knees, lifting your arms over your head.
    (A) Bend   (B) Vend

음성을 들으면서 빈칸을 채우세요. (음성은 두 번 들려줍니다.)

06 This shop won't _____.

07 I _____ to rent on Oak Street.

08 Do you offer _____ for children under school age?

09 This _____ tourist destination during the summer.

10 You may park your vehicle in a _____.

DAY 01 기초 다지기 1 | Course 1 발음이 비슷한 자음 구별하기 **29**

Course 2 발음이 비슷한 모음 구별하기

The plane will leave for New York at 1 P.M.

live . . .? 뉴욕에 산다는 건가?

leave를 live로 잘못 이해했군요. 이처럼 leave의 [iː] 발음과 live의 [i] 발음은 비슷해서 혼동을 일으키기 쉽습니다. 토익 리스닝에서는 발음이 비슷하여 혼동을 주는 어휘를 함정으로 이용하는 경우가 있으니 **비슷한 모음을 듣고 구별하는 연습**이 필요합니다.

➤ [i] & [iː] ∩ DAY01_05

[i]는 짧게 끊어서 내는 소리로 '이'처럼 들리고, [iː]는 입술을 옆으로 크게 벌리고 길게 내는 소리로 '이-'와 비슷하게 들립니다.

[i]	[iː]
fit[fit] 꼭 맞다	feet[fiːt] 발
live[liv] 살다	leave[liːv] 떠나다
pick[pik] 선택하다, 줍다	peak[piːk] 정상; 최고의
pill[pil] 알약	peel[piːl] 껍질을 벗기다

➤ [ou] & [ɔː] ∩ DAY01_06

[ou]는 입을 동그랗게 해서 내는 소리로 '오우'처럼 들리고, [ɔː]는 '오'와 '아'의 중간 소리처럼 들립니다.

[ou]	[ɔː]
cold[kould] 추운	called[kɔːld] 전화했다(call의 과거형)
coast[koust] 해안, 연안	cost[kɔːst] 비용; (비용이) ~이다
row[rou] 줄, 열; 노를 젓다	raw[rɔː] 날것의, 익히지 않은
whole[houl] 전체; 전체의	hall[hɔːl] 복도, 넓은 방

유사 발음에 유의하여 음성을 듣고 빈칸에 알맞은 단어를 고르세요. (음성은 두 번 들려줍니다.)

01 Did you _____ how soft the fabric is?

(A) fill   (B) feel

02 You can use the computers in the room down the _____ on the right.

(A) hall   (B) whole

03 Mr. Collins _____ close to Waterfront station.

(A) leaves   (B) lives

04 The storm has destroyed many buildings on the east _____.

(A) cost   (B) coast

05 I need to exchange these shoes for larger ones. They don't _____ me well.

(A) fit   (B) feet

음성을 들으면서 빈칸을 채우세요. (음성은 두 번 들려줍니다.)

06 One of the managers _____.

07 Traveling to Rome will _____.

08 Do you mean the woman wearing a blue dress _____?

09 I asked my assistant to _____ for the staff party.

10 The doctor told me to _____ for two weeks.

정답·스크립트 **p.2**

리스닝 기초 다지기

DAY 01 기초 다지기 1

한 권으로 끝내는 해커스 토익 **700+** (LC+RC+VOCA)

음성을 듣고 사진을 가장 알맞게 묘사한 보기를 고르세요.

01

(A)   (B)

02

(A)   (B)

03

(A)   (B)

음성을 듣고 질문에 가장 알맞은 응답을 고르세요.

04 Who can reach the top shelf?　　　　　　　　　　(A)　　　　(B)

05 Where is the law office?　　　　　　　　　　　　(A)　　　　(B)

06 Are you fine with going on Friday?　　　　　　　(A)　　　　(B)

07 Will you apply for the bank loan?　　　　　　　(A)　　　　(B)

08 Why do you collect stamps?　　　　　　　　　　(A)　　　　(B)

09 Didn't you want to purchase a fan?　　　　　　(A)　　　　(B)

10 Why don't we order some cold drinks?　　　　　(A)　　　　(B)

11 Should I print the list or e-mail it?　　　　　　(A)　　　　(B)

12 I bought a loaf of bread at the bakery.　　　　　(A)　　　　(B)

정답·스크립트·해설 p.3

한 권으로 끝내는
해커스 토익 700+
LC+RC+VOCA

▲ MP3
바로 듣기

Course 1 연음 듣기

Where is the nearest gas station?

게스테이션이 어디냐고? 그게 뭐지?

gas와 station이 연이어 발음되어 [게스테이션]으로 들리는 것을 이해하지 못했군요. 이처럼 두 발음이 이어질 때 상호 간의 간섭으로 발음이 변하거나 탈락하는 현상을 연음 현상이라고 합니다. 연음 현상으로 문장의 내용을 이해하지 못 하는 일이 없도록 **연음 듣기 연습**이 필요합니다.

➤ 연음 시 탈락되는 소리 🎧 DAY02_01

두 단어 사이에 발음이 같거나 유사한 자음이 나란히 나오면 앞의 자음이 탈락되고, 뒤의 자음만 들립니다.

accustomed[əkʌ́stəmd] + to[tu] ⟶ [əkʌ́stəmtu]	hard[hɑːrd] + time[taim] ⟶ [hɑ́ːrtaim]
cold[kould] + day[dei] ⟶ [kouldéi]	health[helθ] + center[séntər] ⟶ [hélsentər]
front[frʌnt] + desk[desk] ⟶ [frʌndésk]	last[læst] + time[taim] ⟶ [læstáim]
gas[gæs] + station[stéiʃən] ⟶ [gǽstèiʃən]	used[juːst] + to[tu] ⟶ [júːstu]

➤ 연음 시 하나 되는 소리 🎧 DAY02_02

앞 단어의 마지막 자음과 뒷 단어의 첫 번째 모음이 이어져 하나의 소리로 들립니다.

checked[tʃekt] + out[aut] ⟶ [tʃéktaut]	for[fɔːr] + a[ə] + break[breik] ⟶ [fɔ́ːrəbréik]
depend[dipénd] + on[ən] ⟶ [dipéndən]	give[giv] + up[ʌp] ⟶ [gívʌp]
fill[fil] + out[aut] ⟶ [fílaut]	pick[pik] + up[ʌp] ⟶ [píkʌp]
find[faind] + out[aut] ⟶ [faindáut]	placed[pleist] + on[ən] ⟶ [pléistən]

➤ 연음 시 변화되는 소리 🎧 DAY02_03

모음과 모음 사이에 [t]가 오면 우리말 'ㄹ'와 비슷한 소리로 들립니다.

a[ə] + lot[lɑt] + of[əv] ⟶ [əlɑ́r*əv]	make[meik] + it[it] + easy[íːzi] ⟶ [meikir*íːzi]
about[əbáut] + an[ən] + hour[auər] ⟶ [əbáur*ənàuər]	meet[miːt] + a[ə] + client[kláiənt] ⟶ [mìːr*əkláiənt]
at[æt] + all[ɔːl] + times[taimz] ⟶ [ær*ɔ́ːltaimz]	pick[pik] + it[it] + up[ʌp] ⟶ [pikir*ʌ́p]
cut[kʌt] + out[aut] ⟶ [kʌr*áut]	put[put] + on[ən] ⟶ [pur*ɔ́n]

※ 변화된 [t]를 편의상 [r*]로 표기하였으나, 정확한 [r] 발음과는 다른 [d]와 [r]의 중간 소리입니다.
※ 영국식 발음과 호주식 발음에서는 두 모음 사이에 [t]가 와도 소리가 변하지 않습니다.

HACKERS PRACTICE

연음에 유의하여 음성을 들으면서 빈칸을 채우세요. (음성은 두 번 들려줍니다.)

01 _____

02 _____

03 _____

04 _____

05 _____

06 Children have to _____.

07 I will _____.

08 We _____ at 11 A.M.

09 Let's go to the _____.

10 Employees must _____.

정답·스크립트 p.5

Course 2 끊어 듣기

> I want to let customers know about some service issues. First of all . . .

> 무슨 말이지? 길어서 못 알아듣겠어...

문장이 길어져서 내용을 파악하지 못했군요. 긴 문장을 통째로 듣고 이해하려 하지 않고 의미 덩어리로 끊어 들으면 내용을 쉽게 이해할 수 있습니다. 토익 리스닝에서는 한 문장이 긴 대화나 지문이 출제되므로, **긴 문장을 구와 절 등의 의미 덩어리로 끊어서 듣는 연습**이 필요합니다.

➤ 구로 끊어 듣기 ∩ DAY02_05

주어와 동사를 포함하지 않은 두 단어 이상의 의미 덩어리를 '구'라고 합니다. 구를 하나로 묶어 끊어 들으면 화자가 전달하는 의미를 쉽게 파악할 수 있습니다.

> For its 100th anniversary, / the company had a large celebration.
> 　　100주년 기념일이어서　　　　　　그 회사는 큰 기념행사를 열었습니다
>
> By the museum's main entrance, / there is a huge stone statue.
> 　　　박물관의 정문 옆에　　　　　　　큰 석상이 있습니다
>
> Please pick up a brochure / from the front desk.
> 　소책자를 가지고 가시기 바랍니다　　안내 데스크에서
>
> She bought a plane ticket / for New York.
> 　그녀는 비행기 티켓을 샀습니다　　뉴욕으로 가는

➤ 절로 끊어 듣기 ∩ DAY02_06

주어와 동사를 포함한 두 단어 이상의 의미 덩어리를 '절'이라고 합니다. 절을 하나로 묶어 끊어 들으면 화자가 전달하는 의미를 쉽게 파악할 수 있습니다.

> Mr. Gould requested / that a receptionist be hired.
> 　Mr. Gould는 요청했습니다　　접수원을 고용해야 한다고
>
> If you have any questions, / please raise your hand.
> 　　질문이 있으시면　　　　　　손을 들어 주세요
>
> Please give a round of applause, / when the winner is announced.
> 　　박수를 보내주시기 바랍니다　　　　　우승자가 발표되면
>
> While driving to work, / I listened to the traffic report.
> 　직장까지 운전하는 동안　　저는 교통 방송을 들었습니다

끊어 듣기에 유의하여 음성을 들으면서 빈칸을 채우세요. (음성은 두 번 들려줍니다.)

01 I bought snacks _____.

02 He will arrive _____.

03 It is obvious _____.

04 _____, the meeting will begin.

05 _____, let's go on a picnic.

06 _____, I stood _____.

07 _____, he wakes up _____.

08 _____, he walked _____.

09 _____, I shared one _____.

10 _____, the train arrived _____ on time.

정답·스크립트 p.6

음성을 듣고 사진을 가장 알맞게 묘사한 보기를 고르세요.

01

(A)　　　　(B)

02

(A)　　　　(B)

03

(A)　　　　(B)

음성을 듣고 질문에 가장 알맞은 응답을 고르세요.

04 Who owns that gas station?   (A)   (B)

05 Where's your office building?   (A)   (B)

06 When will your friend arrive?   (A)   (B)

07 Could you call me back once you decide?   (A)   (B)

08 How can we get to the mall?   (A)   (B)

09 Did you park by the entrance?   (A)   (B)

10 Which subway station is closest to city hall?   (A)   (B)

11 We can order now since everyone's here, right?   (A)   (B)

12 I assume you made an airline reservation for tomorrow.   (A)   (B)

정답·스크립트·해설 **p.6**

한 권으로 끝내는
해커스 토익 700+
LC+RC+VOCA

PART 1

PART 1은 1번부터 6번까지 총 6문제로, 네 개의 보기 중에서 주어진 사진을 가장 적절하게 묘사한 보기를 선택하는 유형입니다.

DAY 03 사람 중심 사진

DAY 04 사물·풍경 중심 사진

한 권으로 끝내는
해커스 토익 700+
LC+RC+VOCA

▲ MP3
바로 듣기

Course 1 1인 사진

한 여자가 현미경을 들여다보고 있어요.

현미경을 들여다보고 있는 한 여자의 사진을 잘 묘사했네요. 이처럼 PART 1에서는 **사람이 한 명밖에 없는 1인 사진**이 출제됩니다. 주로 사진 속 사람의 동작, 시선, 옷차림 등을 묘사하는 문제가 출제됩니다.

핵심 POINT

1. 보기의 주어로 사람을 나타내는 표현(He, She, A man, A woman 등)이 주로 출제됩니다.

   ex) **A woman** is looking into a microscope. 한 여자가 현미경을 들여다보고 있다.

2. 보기에는 '~하고 있는' 사람의 동작이나 상태를 묘사하기 위해 현재 진행형(be + -ing) 동사가 자주 출제됩니다.

   ex) **He** is answering the phone. 그는 전화를 받고 있다.

3. 정답의 단서는 사람의 동작을 묘사하는 동사 부분에서 주로 출제됩니다.

Example ∩ DAY03_01

[캐나다식 발음]

(A) He is washing a dish.
(B) He is holding a knife.
(C) He is facing the window.
(D) He is opening a bottle.

(A) 그는 그릇을 닦고 있다.
(B) 그는 칼을 잡고 있다.
(C) 그는 창문 쪽을 보고 있다.
(D) 그는 병을 열고 있다.

정답 (B)

해설 한 남자가 칼을 사용하여 무언가를 썰고 있는 모습을 나타내는 1인 사진입니다.

(A) [×] washing(닦고 있다)은 남자의 동작과 무관하므로 오답입니다.
(B) [○] 남자가 칼을 잡고 무언가를 썰고 있는 모습을 가장 잘 묘사한 정답입니다.
(C) [×] 남자가 창문을 등지고 있는데 창문 쪽을 보고 있다고 잘못 묘사했으므로 오답입니다.
(D) [×] opening(열고 있다)은 남자의 동작과 무관하므로 오답입니다.

어휘 face[feis] ~쪽을 보다, ~쪽을 향하다 bottle[미 bάtl, 영 bɔ́tl] 병

음성을 듣고 사진에 대한 묘사가 맞으면 ○, 틀리면 ×, 헷갈리는 보기에는 △를 표시하면서 정답을 선택해 보세요. 음성을 다시 들으면서 빈칸을 채우세요. (음성은 두 번 들려줍니다.)

01

(A) _____ (B) _____ (C) _____ (D) _____

(A) He is _____ a helmet.
(B) He is _____ a ladder.
(C) He is _____ a door.
(D) He is _____ a tool belt.

02

(A) _____ (B) _____ (C) _____ (D) _____

(A) He is _____ a power tool.
(B) He is _____ a tire.
(C) He is _____ the scenery.
(D) He is _____ a car.

03

(A) _____ (B) _____ (C) _____ (D) _____

(A) Some flowerpots are _____.
(B) She is _____ her _____.
(C) Some plants are _____.
(D) She is _____ a watering can.

04

(A) _____ (B) _____ (C) _____ (D) _____

(A) The man is _____ a newspaper.
(B) A book is _____ on the table.
(C) A waiter is _____ a cup.
(D) The man is _____ a pair of glasses.

정답·스크립트·해설 **p.9**

PART 1

DAY 03 사람 중심 사진

한 권으로 끝내는 해커스 토익 700+ (LC+RC+VOCA)

Course 2 2인 이상 사진

사람들이 우산을 들고 있어요.

우산을 들고 걸어가는 여러 사람들의 사진을 잘 묘사했네요. 이처럼 PART 1에서는 **두 명 이상의 사람이 등장하는 2인 이상 사진**이 출제됩니다. 주로 사람들의 공통 동작, 개인의 동작이나 옷차림 등을 묘사하는 문제가 출제됩니다.

핵심 POINT

1. 보기의 주어로 여러 사람을 나타내는 표현(They, People, Some people 등)이나 한 사람을 나타내는 표현 (One of the men, One of the women, One man, One woman 등)이 주로 출제됩니다.
   ex) People are holding umbrellas. 사람들이 우산을 들고 있다.

2. 보기에는 사람의 동작이나 상태를 묘사하기 위해 현재 진행형(be + -ing) 동사가 자주 출제됩니다.
   ex) They are smiling at each other. 그들은 서로를 향해 미소를 짓고 있다.

3. 사물의 상태를 묘사하기 위해 수동형(be + p.p., be + being + p.p., have + been + p.p.) 동사가 출제되기도 합니다. ※ 수동형(be + p.p.): ~되다, 진행 수동형(be + being + p.p.): ~되고 있다, 완료 수동형(have + been + p.p.): ~되어 있다
   ex) A building is being repaired. 한 건물이 수리되고 있다.

Example 　∩ DAY03_03

3॥ 미국식 발음

(A) Some people are shaking hands.
(B) A clock has been placed on the wall.
(C) Some people are carrying a sofa.
(D) A woman is handing some papers.

(A) 몇몇 사람들이 악수를 하고 있다.
(B) 시계가 벽에 걸려 있다.
(C) 몇몇 사람들이 소파를 옮기고 있다.
(D) 한 여자가 서류를 건네주고 있다.

정답 (A)

해설　몇몇 사람들이 소파에 앉아 있는 모습을 나타내는 2인 이상 사진입니다.
   (A) [○] 두 남자가 악수를 하고 있는 모습을 정확히 묘사한 정답입니다.
   (B) [×] 사진에서 시계(clock)를 확인할 수 없으므로 오답입니다.
   (C) [×] 사람들이 소파에 앉아 있는 상태인데 소파를 옮기고 있다고 잘못 묘사했으므로 오답입니다.
   (D) [×] handing(건네주고 있다)은 여자의 동작과 무관하므로 오답입니다.

어휘　shake hands 악수하다　hand[hænd] 건네주다

음성을 듣고 사진에 대한 묘사가 맞으면 ○, 틀리면 ×, 헷갈리는 보기에는 △를 표시하면서 정답을 선택해 보세요. 음성을 다시 들으면서 빈칸을 채우세요. (음성은 두 번 들려줍니다.)

01

(A) _____ (B) _____ (C) _____ (D) _____

(A) People are _____ indoors.
(B) A lamppost has been _____ near some trees.
(C) Bushes are _____ in the woods.
(D) People are _____ a bench.

02

(A) _____ (B) _____ (C) _____ (D) _____

(A) One of the men is _____ a cash register.
(B) One of the men is _____ an apron.
(C) One of the men is _____ some groceries.
(D) One of the men is _____ some products.

03

(A) _____ (B) _____ (C) _____ (D) _____

(A) A woman is _____ a glass.
(B) A woman is _____ food.
(C) A server is _____ a table.
(D) A man is _____.

04

(A) _____ (B) _____ (C) _____ (D) _____

(A) They are _____ a piece of paper.
(B) They are _____ next to each other.
(C) They are _____ a document.
(D) They are _____ safety gear.

정답·스크립트·해설 **p.10**

01

(A)   (B)   (C)   (D)

02

(A)   (B)   (C)   (D)

03

(A)   (B)   (C)   (D)

04

(A)   (B)   (C)   (D)

05

(A)　　　　(B)　　　　(C)　　　　(D)

06

(A)　　　　(B)　　　　(C)　　　　(D)

정답·스크립트·해설 **p.10**

DAY 04 사물 · 풍경 중심 사진

한 권으로 끝내는
해커스 토익 700+
LC+RC+VOCA

▲ MP3
바로 듣기

Course 1 사물 중심 사진

컴퓨터가 책상 위에 놓여 있어요.

컴퓨터가 책상 위에 놓여 있는 사진을 잘 묘사했네요. 이처럼 PART 1에서는 **사람이 없고, 사물을 가까이에서 찍은 사물 중심 사진**이 출제됩니다. 주로 사진 속 사물의 위치, 상태를 묘사하는 문제가 출제됩니다.

핵심 POINT

1. 보기에는 사물의 위치나 상태를 묘사하기 위해 수동형(be + p.p., be + being + p.p., have + been + p.p.) 동사나 현재 진행형(be + ~ing) 동사가 자주 출제됩니다.

   ex) A computer has been placed on the desk. 컴퓨터가 책상 위에 놓여 있다.

2. 사물의 위치를 묘사하기 위해 on(~의 위에), beside(~의 옆에), in(~의 안에), between(~의 사이에)과 같은 전치사가 자주 출제됩니다.

   ex) Some plants are beside a window. 몇몇 식물들이 창문 옆에 있다.

3. 사람이 없는 사물 중심 사진에서, 주어가 사람인 보기가 오답으로 출제되기도 합니다.

Example 🎧 DAY04_01

🇦 호주식 발음

(A) A mop is leaning against a wall.
(B) A bottle is being filled with water.
(C) The stairs are being washed.
(D) Some gloves are on the floor.

(A) 대걸레가 벽에 기대 있다.
(B) 병에 물이 채워지고 있다.
(C) 계단이 닦이고 있다.
(D) 몇몇 장갑들이 바닥 위에 있다.

정답 (A)

해설 장갑, 대걸레, 바구니 등이 놓여 있는 모습을 나타내는 사물 중심 사진입니다.

　(A) [○] 대걸레가 벽에 기대 있는 모습을 가장 잘 묘사한 정답입니다.

　(B) [×] 사진에서 병은 보이지만 물이 채워지고 있는(is being filled) 모습은 아니므로 오답입니다.

　(C) [×] 사진에서 계단은 보이지만 닦이고 있는(are being washed) 모습은 아니므로 오답입니다.

　(D) [×] 장갑들이 바구니 위에 놓여 있는데 바닥 위에 있다고 잘못 묘사했으므로 오답입니다.

어휘 mop [미 mɑp, 영 mɔp] 대걸레, 자루걸레　lean against ~에 기대다

음성을 듣고 사진에 대한 묘사가 맞으면 ○, 틀리면 ×, 헷갈리는 보기에는 △를 표시하면서 정답을 선택해 보세요. 음성을 다시 들으면서 빈칸을 채우세요. (음성은 두 번 들려줍니다.)

01

(A) _____ (B) _____ (C) _____ (D) _____

(A) A wall is _____ with artwork.
(B) Some cushions are _____.
(C) The floor is _____ with a carpet.
(D) Some books are _____ on the windowsill.

02

(A) _____ (B) _____ (C) _____ (D) _____

(A) Towels are _____ on a shelf.
(B) Forks have been _____ in a jar.
(C) The table has been _____ for a meal.
(D) A napkin has been _____.

03

(A) _____ (B) _____ (C) _____ (D) _____

(A) A cabinet door has been _____.
(B) Papers are _____ on a desk.
(C) A computer monitor has been _____.
(D) Binders are _____ on the shelves.

04

(A) _____ (B) _____ (C) _____ (D) _____

(A) Workers are _____ a sidewalk.
(B) The cart has _____.
(C) Workers are _____ a hole with shovels.
(D) A wheelbarrow has been _____ some bricks.

정답·스크립트·해설 **p.12**

PART 1

DAY 04 사물·풍경 중심 사진

한 권으로 끝내는 해커스 토익 **700+** (LC+RC+VOCA)

Course 2 풍경 중심 사진

분수가 몇몇 빌딩 가까이에 위치해 있어요.

빌딩 근처에 분수가 있는 사진을 잘 묘사했네요. 이처럼 PART 1에서는 **사람이 없고, 강이나 호수 주변, 건물 외관 등의 야외 풍경이나 주변 환경을 넓게 찍은 풍경 중심 사진**이 출제됩니다. 주로 사진 속 사물의 위치 및 상태, 전반적인 풍경을 묘사하는 문제가 출제됩니다.

핵심 POINT

1. 보기에는 전반적인 풍경이나 사물의 위치 및 상태를 묘사하기 위해 수동형(be + p.p., be + being + p.p., have + been + p.p.) 동사가 자주 출제됩니다.

   ex) A fountain is located near some buildings. 분수가 몇몇 빌딩 가까이에 위치해 있다.

2. 전반적인 풍경을 묘사하기 위해 'There + be동사 + 명사' 형태의 문장이 출제되기도 합니다.

   ex) There are trees on a hill. 언덕 위에 나무들이 있다.

3. 어떤 동작이 이미 완료된 상태인데, 진행 수동형(be + being + p.p.) 동사를 사용하여 동작이 현재 진행 중인 상태로 묘사하는 보기가 오답으로 자주 출제됩니다.

Example 🎧 DAY04_03

🎙 영국식 발음

(A) People are drinking outside the hut.
(B) Trees are being cut down.
(C) There is a boat on a beach.
(D) Swimmers are passing a yacht.

(A) 사람들이 오두막집 밖에서 음료를 마시고 있다.
(B) 나무들이 베어지고 있다.
(C) 해변에 보트 한 척이 있다.
(D) 수영하는 사람들이 요트를 지나치고 있다.

정답 (C)

해설 해변에 보트가 놓여 있는 모습과 주변 풍경을 나타내는 풍경 중심 사진입니다.
   (A) [×] 사람이 없는 사진에 사람을 나타내는 People(사람들)을 사용했으므로 오답입니다.
   (B) [×] 사진에서 나무들은 보이지만 베어지고 있는(are being cut down) 모습은 아니므로 오답입니다.
   (C) [○] 보트 한 척이 해변에 있는 모습을 가장 잘 묘사한 정답입니다.
   (D) [×] 사람이 없는 사진에 사람을 나타내는 Swimmers(수영하는 사람들)를 사용했으므로 오답입니다.

어휘 hut[hʌt] 오두막집   cut down ~을 베다   yacht[미 jɑːt, 영 jɔt] 요트

음성을 듣고 사진에 대한 묘사가 맞으면 ○, 틀리면 ×, 헷갈리는 보기에는 △를 표시하면서 정답을 선택해 보세요. 음성을 다시 들으면서 빈칸을 채우세요. (음성은 두 번 들려줍니다.)

01

(A) _____ (B) _____ (C) _____ (D) _____

(A) Some boats are _____ on the water.
(B) Some passengers are _____ a ship.
(C) Some people are _____ into the river.
(D) Some houses are _____.

02

(A) _____ (B) _____ (C) _____ (D) _____

(A) Umbrellas have been _____.
(B) Chairs are being _____ near the water.
(C) A building is _____ in the pool.
(D) Trees are being _____.

03

(A) _____ (B) _____ (C) _____ (D) _____

(A) A sign is _____.
(B) Some workers are _____ a window.
(C) A vehicle is _____ in front of a structure.
(D) Some bushes _____ a balcony.

04

(A) _____ (B) _____ (C) _____ (D) _____

(A) People are _____ outdoors.
(B) The chairs are being _____ in the corner.
(C) Some musical instruments have been _____.
(D) Some steps _____ a seating area.

정답·스크립트·해설 **p.13**

01

(A)　　　(B)　　　(C)　　　(D)

02

(A)　　　(B)　　　(C)　　　(D)

03

(A)　　　(B)　　　(C)　　　(D)

04

(A)　　　(B)　　　(C)　　　(D)

05

(A)　　　(B)　　　(C)　　　(D)

06

(A)　　　(B)　　　(C)　　　(D)

정답·스크립트·해설 **p.14**

PART 2

PART 2는 7번부터 31번까지 총 25문제로, 하나의 질문에 대한 세 개의 응답을 들은 후 질문에 가장 자연스러운 응답을 한 보기를 선택하는 유형입니다.

DAY 05

의문사 의문문 1

▲ MP3
바로 듣기

한 권으로 끝내는
해커스 토익 700+
LC+RC+VOCA

Course 1 Who 의문문

누가(Who) 우편물 배달을 책임지나요?

제 비서요.

남자가 여자에게 우편물 배달을 누가 책임지는지를 물었네요. 그럼 여자는 우편물 배달을 책임지는 사람을 말해줘야 하겠죠? 이처럼 PART 2에서는 특정 행동이나 업무 등에 관련된 당사자를 묻는 Who 의문문이 출제됩니다.

핵심 POINT

1. 직책/부서/회사명이나 사람 이름을 포함한 응답이 정답으로 자주 출제됩니다.

   Q. Who is responsible for delivering the mail? 누가 우편물 배달을 책임지나요?
   A. My assistant is. 제 비서요. [직책]

   Q. Who is in charge of hiring staff? 누가 직원 고용을 담당하고 있나요?
   A. Contact the human resources department. 인사부서에 연락해 보세요. [부서]

   Q. Who has been recording sales? 누가 매출액을 기록해 왔나요?
   A. Mr. Costa, I think. Mr. Costa인 것 같아요. [사람 이름]

2. I/We/You와 같은 인칭대명사를 포함한 응답도 정답이 될 수 있습니다.

   Q. Who is supposed to edit these files? 누가 이 파일들을 수정하기로 되어 있나요?
   A. I am. 저요. [인칭대명사]

Example 🎧 DAY05_01

🔊 호주식 발음 → 영국식 발음

Who is designing our business brochures?

(A) Tony is making them.

(B) Yes, I'll ask him.

(C) Business is a bit slow right now.

누가 우리 회사의 안내 책자를 디자인하고 있나요?

(A) Tony가 그것들을 만들고 있어요.

(B) 네, 제가 그에게 물어볼게요.

(C) 사업이 요즘 좀 부진해요.

정답 (A)

해설 누가 회사의 안내 책자를 디자인하고 있는지를 묻는 Who 의문문입니다.

(A) [ㅇ] Tony가 그것들을 만들고 있다며 회사의 안내 책자를 디자인하고 있는 인물을 언급했으므로 정답입니다.

(B) [×] 의문사 의문문에 Yes로 응답했으므로 오답입니다.

(C) [×] 질문의 business(회사)를 '사업'이라는 의미로 반복 사용하여 혼동을 준 오답입니다.

어휘 brochure[미 brouʃúər, 영 bróuʃə] 안내 책자 slow[미 slou, 영 sləu] 부진한, 불경기의

음성을 듣고 질문에 대한 응답이 맞으면 ○, 틀리면 ×, 헷갈리는 보기에는 △를 표시하면서 정답을 선택해 보세요. 음성을 다시 들으면서 빈칸을 채우세요. (음성은 두 번 들려줍니다.)

01 (A) _____ (B) _____ (C) _____

Q. _____ the event invitations?
(A) Mr. Ross, I think.
(B) You can lend it to him.
(C) Thanks, I can take it.

02 (A) _____ (B) _____ (C) _____

Q. _____ the city film festival?
(A) Green Tech supported the event.
(B) They're all the same.
(C) About $2 each.

03 (A) _____ (B) _____ (C) _____

Q. _____ the shop today?
(A) At 8:00 A.M.
(B) Mr. Harper.
(C) I will buy some socks.

04 (A) _____ (B) _____ (C) _____

Q. _____ is writing our monthly _____?
(A) No, they're quite economical.
(B) Isn't it the finance department?
(C) I am writing a story now.

05 (A) _____ (B) _____ (C) _____

Q. _____ Julia and Karl's wedding?
(A) They got married on Wednesday.
(B) We are planning to attend.
(C) I'm not sure.

06 (A) _____ (B) _____ (C) _____

Q. _____ is in charge of _____ new employees?
(A) There's a $25 application fee.
(B) The HR manager.
(C) Here's a job description.

07 (A) _____ (B) _____ (C) _____

Q. _____ has already _____ the assignment?
(A) I'm competing for the prize.
(B) A ten-page essay.
(C) I finished it yesterday.

정답·스크립트·해설 p.16

Course 2 Where 의문문

어디에서(Where) 오늘 점심을 드셨나요?

구내식당에서요.

여자가 남자에게 어디에서 점심을 먹었는지를 물었네요. 그럼 남자는 점심을 먹은 장소를 말해줘야 하겠죠? 이처럼 PART 2에서는 장소나 위치, 방향, 정보나 사물의 출처 등을 묻는 **Where 의문문**이 출제됩니다.

핵심 POINT

1. 장소, 위치, 방향 등을 나타내는 전치사(in, at, on, to 등)를 사용한 응답이 정답으로 자주 출제됩니다.

   Q. Where did you have lunch today? 어디에서 오늘 점심을 드셨나요?
   A. In the cafeteria. 구내식당에서요. [장소]

   Q. Where is Click Boutique located? Click 부티크는 어디에 위치해 있나요?
   A. On the next corner. 다음 코너에요. [위치]

   Q. Where is Rodney traveling in May? Rodney는 5월에 어디로 가나요?
   A. To Hong Kong for a lecture. 강의를 위해 홍콩으로요. [방향]

2. 정보나 사물의 출처를 묻는 경우, 사람 이름을 포함한 응답도 정답이 될 수 있습니다.

   Q. Where did this letter come from? 이 편지는 어디서 왔나요?
   A. Regina sent it. Regina가 보냈어요. [출처]

Example 🎧 DAY05_03

📖 미국식 발음 → 캐나다식 발음

Where will the marketing conference be held?

(A) On the third floor of the hotel.
(B) I registered today.
(C) A marketing expert.

마케팅 회의는 어디에서 열릴 예정인가요?

(A) 호텔 3층에서요.
(B) 저는 오늘 등록했어요.
(C) 마케팅 전문가요.

정답 (A)

해설 마케팅 회의가 어디에서 열릴 예정인지를 묻는 Where 의문문입니다.
(A) [ㅇ] 호텔 3층에서라는 말로 마케팅 회의가 열릴 장소를 언급했으므로 정답입니다.
(B) [×] 마케팅 회의가 열릴 장소를 물었는데, 이와 관련이 없는 오늘 등록했다는 내용으로 응답했으므로 오답입니다.
(C) [×] 질문의 marketing을 반복 사용하여 혼동을 준 오답입니다.

어휘 conference[미 kánfərəns, 영 kɔ́nfərəns] 회의 register[미 rédʒistər, 영 rédʒistə] 등록하다 expert[미 ékspəːrt, 영 ékspəːt] 전문가

음성을 듣고 질문에 대한 응답이 맞으면 ○, 틀리면 ×, 헷갈리는 보기에는 △를 표시하면서 정답을 선택해 보세요. 음성을 다시 들으면서 빈칸을 채우세요. (음성은 두 번 들려줍니다.)

01 (A) _____ (B) _____ (C) _____

Q. _____ are you _____ tonight?
(A) Tomorrow, most likely.
(B) At my brother's apartment.
(C) Just a while longer.

02 (A) _____ (B) _____ (C) _____

Q. _____ is the _____?
(A) I like my new office.
(B) Yes, inform the teller.
(C) There's one three blocks south.

03 (A) _____ (B) _____ (C) _____

Q. _____ should we _____ the TV?
(A) Next to the stereo.
(B) It has a clear image.
(C) I will wait as long as I can.

04 (A) _____ (B) _____ (C) _____

Q. _____ did you get _____?
(A) Actually, I made them myself.
(B) I think there are a dozen.
(C) It has a large snack selection.

05 (A) _____ (B) _____ (C) _____

Q. _____ did these magazines _____?
(A) The feature article is interesting.
(B) Sarah brought them.
(C) I'd like to get a copy.

06 (A) _____ (B) _____ (C) _____

Q. _____ is bus 28's _____?
(A) The bus is still running now.
(B) I caught it on Main Street.
(C) I'll have to check.

07 (A) _____ (B) _____ (C) _____

Q. _____ are you and Maria going _____?
(A) Pasta salad, please.
(B) We are planning to launch it tomorrow.
(C) The restaurant across the street.

정답·스크립트·해설 **p.17**

01 Mark your answer.　　(A)　　(B)　　(C)

02 Mark your answer.　　(A)　　(B)　　(C)

03 Mark your answer.　　(A)　　(B)　　(C)

04 Mark your answer.　　(A)　　(B)　　(C)

05 Mark your answer.　　(A)　　(B)　　(C)

06 Mark your answer.　　(A)　　(B)　　(C)

07 Mark your answer.　　(A)　　(B)　　(C)

08 Mark your answer.　　(A)　　(B)　　(C)

09 Mark your answer.　　(A)　　(B)　　(C)

10 Mark your answer.　　(A)　　(B)　　(C)

11 Mark your answer.　　(A)　　(B)　　(C)

12 Mark your answer.　　(A)　　(B)　　(C)

13 Mark your answer.　　(A)　　(B)　　(C)

14 Mark your answer.   (A)   (B)   (C)

15 Mark your answer.   (A)   (B)   (C)

16 Mark your answer.   (A)   (B)   (C)

17 Mark your answer.   (A)   (B)   (C)

18 Mark your answer.   (A)   (B)   (C)

19 Mark your answer.   (A)   (B)   (C)

20 Mark your answer.   (A)   (B)   (C)

21 Mark your answer.   (A)   (B)   (C)

22 Mark your answer.   (A)   (B)   (C)

23 Mark your answer.   (A)   (B)   (C)

24 Mark your answer.   (A)   (B)   (C)

25 Mark your answer.   (A)   (B)   (C)

정답·스크립트·해설 **p.18**

DAY
06
의문사 의문문 2

한 권으로 끝내는
해커스 토익 700+
LC+RC+VOCA

▲ MP3
바로 듣기

Course 1 When 의문문

토익 출제경향
평균 2문제 정도 출제

언제(When) 새집으로 이사를 가세요?

10월 14일에요.

남자가 여자에게 언제 이사 가는지를 물었네요. 그럼 여자는 이사를 가는 시점을 말해줘야 하겠죠? 이처럼 PART 2에서는 특정 사건과 관련된 시점을 묻는 **When 의문문**이 출제됩니다.

핵심 POINT

1. 날짜/요일/시간 등 특정 시점을 사용한 응답이 정답으로 자주 출제됩니다.

Q. When are you moving into your new house? 언제 새집으로 이사를 가세요?
A. On October 14. 10월 14일에요. [날짜]

2. 구체적인 시점이 정해지지 않은 불확실한 시점을 사용한 응답도 정답이 될 수 있습니다.

Q. When is the meeting going to start? 회의는 언제 시작할 건가요?
A. Once Mr. Grundy arrives. Mr. Grundy가 도착하면요. [불확실한 시점]

3. When 의문문의 응답으로 숫자가 자주 등장하는 것을 이용하여, 기간이나 가격을 언급한 응답처럼 숫자를 함정으로 사용한 보기가 오답으로 자주 출제됩니다.

Q. When is the seminar going to start? 세미나는 언제 시작할 건가요?
A. For two weeks. 2주 동안이요. [숫자를 함정으로 사용한 오답]

Example ∩ DAY06_01

🔊 호주식 발음 → 영국식 발음

When will the museum reopen?

(A) In two weeks.
(B) He's visiting on Saturday.
(C) The main exhibition.

박물관이 언제 문을 다시 열 예정인가요?

(A) 2주 후에요.
(B) 그는 토요일에 방문할 거예요.
(C) 주요 전시회요.

정답 (A)

해설 박물관이 언제 문을 다시 열 예정인지를 묻는 When 의문문입니다.
　　 (A) [○] 2주 후에라는 말로 박물관이 다시 문을 열 시점을 언급했으므로 정답입니다.
　　 (B) [×] 박물관이 문을 다시 열 시점을 물었는데, 이와 관련이 없는 그가 토요일에 방문할 거라는 내용으로 응답했으므로 오답입니다.
　　 (C) [×] 질문의 museum(박물관)과 관련 있는 exhibition(전시회)을 사용하여 혼동을 준 오답입니다.

어휘 museum[mjuːzíːəm] 박물관　exhibition[미 èksəbíʃən, 영 èksibíʃən] 전시회

음성을 듣고 질문에 대한 응답이 맞으면 ○, 틀리면 ×, 헷갈리는 보기에는 △를 표시하면서 정답을 선택해 보세요. 음성을 다시 들으면서 빈칸을 채우세요. (음성은 두 번 들려줍니다.)

01 (A) _____ (B) _____ (C) _____

Q. _____ does your train _____?
(A) At Penn Station.
(B) At 9:45 P.M.
(C) It's $125 per ticket.

02 (A) _____ (B) _____ (C) _____

Q. _____ is the annual _____?
(A) Next Thursday afternoon.
(B) It's in the main auditorium.
(C) I had to meet the deadline.

03 (A) _____ (B) _____ (C) _____

Q. _____ the awards ceremony _____?
(A) It's arriving at 7 P.M.
(B) Once the guest speaker finishes.
(C) It's a great honor.

04 (A) _____ (B) _____ (C) _____

Q. _____ is the store's _____?
(A) August 9.
(B) Over a week.
(C) They're already on sale.

05 (A) _____ (B) _____ (C) _____

Q. _____ is the seminar _____?
(A) 200 participants.
(B) Yes, it's in Helsinki.
(C) Around noon.

06 (A) _____ (B) _____ (C) _____

Q. _____ did you _____ working here?
(A) You mean, in this department?
(B) I'm a secretary.
(C) I work until 9 P.M. every day.

07 (A) _____ (B) _____ (C) _____

Q. _____ I _____ the furniture I ordered?
(A) Your order will be discounted.
(B) Five chairs and a table.
(C) Let me ask the shipping department.

정답·스크립트·해설 **p.23**

Course 2 What · Which 의문문

토익 출제경향
평균 1~2문제 정도 출제

어떤(What) 종류의 음악을 좋아하세요?

저는 재즈 음악을 좋아해요.

여자가 남자에게 좋아하는 음악에 대한 정보를 물었네요. 그럼 남자는 좋아하는 음악이 무엇인지 말해줘야 하겠죠? 이처럼 PART 2에서는 종류, 날씨, 시간, 의견 등 다양한 정보를 묻는 What · Which 의문문이 출제됩니다.

핵심 POINT

1. What · Which 뒤에 나오는 명사나 동사를 들으면 질문이 무엇에 관한 정보를 묻고 있는지 쉽게 파악할 수 있습니다.

   Q. **What kind of music** do you like? 어떤 종류의 음악을 좋아하세요? [음악 종류 묻기]
   A. I like jazz music. 저는 재즈 음악을 좋아해요.

   Q. **What is the weather** for tomorrow? 내일 날씨는 어때요? [날씨 묻기]
   A. Rain is expected. 비가 올 것으로 예상돼요.

   Q. **What time will the conference call begin?** 전화 회의가 몇 시에 시작되나요? [시간 묻기]
   A. At 9:30 A.M. 오전 9시 30분에요.

   Q. **What will you have for dinner?** 저녁으로 무엇을 드실 건가요? [식사 메뉴 묻기]
   A. I'll skip dinner. 저는 저녁 식사를 거를 거예요.

2. What ~ like? 형태의 의문문은 의견을 물을 때 자주 사용되는 표현입니다.

   Q. **What was Vancouver like?** 밴쿠버는 어땠어요? [의견 묻기]
   A. It was very clean and beautiful. 굉장히 깨끗하고 아름다웠어요.

3. Which 의문문에는 The one을 포함하여 다수 중 하나를 선택하는 응답이 정답으로 자주 출제됩니다.

   Q. **Which of the advertisements do you prefer?** 광고들 중 어느 것을 선호하시나요?
   A. The one Matt made. Matt가 만든 것이요. [다수 중 하나를 선택]

Example 🎧 DAY06_03

🎤) 미국식 발음 → 캐나다식 발음

What are you **working on** this morning?

(A) I'm editing a research proposal.
(B) Yes, I will do that later.
(C) Probably tomorrow afternoon.

당신은 오늘 오전에 무엇을 작업하고 있나요?

(A) 저는 연구 제안서를 수정하고 있어요.
(B) 네, 제가 나중에 할게요.
(C) 아마 내일 오후에요.

정답 (A)

해설 오늘 오전에 무엇을 작업하고 있는지를 묻는 What 의문문입니다.

(A) [o] 연구 제안서를 수정하고 있다는 말로 작업하고 있는 것을 언급했으므로 정답입니다.
(B) [×] 의문사 의문문에 Yes로 응답했으므로 오답입니다.
(C) [×] 질문의 this morning(오늘 오전)과 관련 있는 tomorrow afternoon(내일 오후)을 사용하여 혼동을 준 오답입니다.

어휘 edit[édit] 수정하다 proposal[미 prəpóuzəl, 영 prəpáuzəl] 제안서

음성을 듣고 질문에 대한 응답이 맞으면 ○, 틀리면 ×, 헷갈리는 보기에는 △를 표시하면서 정답을 선택해 보세요. 음성을 다시 들으면서 빈칸을 채우세요. (음성은 두 번 들려줍니다.)

01 (A) _____ (B) _____ (C) _____

Q. _____ will tomorrow's _____ be like?

(A) I like sunny days.
(B) It's on September 24.
(C) It's supposed to rain.

02 (A) _____ (B) _____ (C) _____

Q. _____ do you think I should _____?

(A) They all look good on you.
(B) I'm wearing a blue suit.
(C) Can you tie it?

03 (A) _____ (B) _____ (C) _____

Q. _____ can we go skiing _____?

(A) The mountains are covered in snow.
(B) We are staying at Henson Resort.
(C) I'm free on Thursday.

04 (A) _____ (B) _____ (C) _____

Q. _____ is the most expensive?

(A) About $8,500.
(B) The one in this case.
(C) The doorbell is ringing.

05 (A) _____ (B) _____ (C) _____

Q. _____ should we _____ after dinner?

(A) It's your choice.
(B) Around 8, probably.
(C) I'd like to go for pizza.

06 (A) _____ (B) _____ (C) _____

Q. _____ would you like to _____?

(A) Are any of them on sale?
(B) I will pay with a credit card.
(C) I'll return your call soon.

07 (A) _____ (B) _____ (C) _____

Q. _____ is the company banquet scheduled to _____?

(A) About two hours.
(B) At 6:30 P.M.
(C) She's always on time.

정답·스크립트·해설 **p.24**

01   Mark your answer.   (A)   (B)   (C)

02   Mark your answer.   (A)   (B)   (C)

03   Mark your answer.   (A)   (B)   (C)

04   Mark your answer.   (A)   (B)   (C)

05   Mark your answer.   (A)   (B)   (C)

06   Mark your answer.   (A)   (B)   (C)

07   Mark your answer.   (A)   (B)   (C)

08   Mark your answer.   (A)   (B)   (C)

09   Mark your answer.   (A)   (B)   (C)

10   Mark your answer.   (A)   (B)   (C)

11   Mark your answer.   (A)   (B)   (C)

12   Mark your answer.   (A)   (B)   (C)

13   Mark your answer.   (A)   (B)   (C)

14 Mark your answer.   (A)   (B)   (C)

15 Mark your answer.   (A)   (B)   (C)

16 Mark your answer.   (A)   (B)   (C)

17 Mark your answer.   (A)   (B)   (C)

18 Mark your answer.   (A)   (B)   (C)

19 Mark your answer.   (A)   (B)   (C)

20 Mark your answer.   (A)   (B)   (C)

21 Mark your answer.   (A)   (B)   (C)

22 Mark your answer.   (A)   (B)   (C)

23 Mark your answer.   (A)   (B)   (C)

24 Mark your answer.   (A)   (B)   (C)

25 Mark your answer.   (A)   (B)   (C)

정답·스크립트·해설 **p.25**

한 권으로 끝내는
해커스 토익 700+
LC+RC+VOCA

▲ MP3
바로 듣기

Course 1 Why 의문문

왜(Why) 약속에 늦었어요?

버스를 놓쳐서요.

남자가 여자에게 왜 약속에 늦었는지를 물었네요. 그럼 여자는 늦은 이유를 말해줘야 하겠죠? 이처럼 PART 2에서는 특정 상황이나 행동에 대한 이유나 목적을 묻는 Why 의문문이 출제됩니다.

핵심 POINT

1. Because, For, To를 사용하여 이유를 나타내는 응답이 정답으로 자주 출제됩니다.

Q. Why were you late for the appointment? 약속에 왜 늦었어요?
A. Because I missed my bus. 버스를 놓쳐서요.

Q. Why did Jason buy that suit? Jason은 왜 그 정장을 구입했나요?
A. For a job interview tomorrow. 내일 있을 면접 때문에요.

Q. Why has the board of directors called a meeting? 이사회가 왜 회의를 소집했나요?
A. To discuss the upcoming merger. 곧 있을 합병을 논의하기 위해서요.

2. Because, For, To가 없이 이유를 나타내는 응답도 정답이 될 수 있습니다.

Q. Why did you go to the manager's office? 부장님 사무실에 왜 갔었나요?
A. We talked about my report. 우리는 제 보고서에 대해 이야기했어요.

3. Why don't you(we) ~로 시작하는 의문문은 이유를 묻는 것이 아니라 제안을 할 때 자주 사용되는 표현입니다.

Q. Why don't we go to the zoo today? 오늘 동물원에 가는 게 어때요? [제안]
A. OK, that would be fun. 좋아요, 재미있을 것 같아요.

Example 🎧 DAY07_01

🔊 미국식 발음 → 호주식 발음

Why are you going to Seattle?

(A) He's flying by business class.
(B) I'll return in four days.
(C) For a conference.

시애틀에 왜 가나요?

(A) 그는 비즈니스석을 타고 가요.
(B) 저는 4일 후에 돌아올 거예요.
(C) 회의 때문에요.

정답 (C)

해설 시애틀에 가는 이유를 묻는 Why 의문문입니다.
　(A) [×] 시애틀에 가는 이유를 물었는데, 이와 관련이 없는 그는 비즈니스석을 타고 간다는 내용으로 응답했으므로 오답입니다.
　(B) [×] 질문의 going(가다)과 관련 있는 return(돌아오다)을 사용하여 혼동을 준 오답입니다.
　(C) [○] 회의 때문이라는 말로 시애틀에 가는 이유를 언급했으므로 정답입니다.

어휘 conference[미 kánfərəns, 영 kɔ́nfərəns] 회의

음성을 듣고 질문에 대한 응답이 맞으면 ○, 틀리면 ×, 헷갈리는 보기에는 △를 표시하면서 정답을 선택해 보세요. 음성을 다시 들으면서 빈칸을 채우세요. (음성은 두 번 들려줍니다.)

01 (A) _____ (B) _____ (C) _____

Q. _____ did you _____ Friday _____?

(A) To visit the doctor.
(B) I'm bringing it on Monday.
(C) I don't know why he did.

02 (A) _____ (B) _____ (C) _____

Q. _____ is Beth _____ our meeting?

(A) Because her schedule changed.
(B) Orders must be canceled by phone.
(C) I discussed them with our boss.

03 (A) _____ (B) _____ (C) _____

Q. _____ is the new CEO _____ the office?

(A) Yes, it's a special offer.
(B) To see the board of directors.
(C) He should be arriving soon.

04 (A) _____ (B) _____ (C) _____

Q. _____ are there _____ in the break room?

(A) Sure, that'll be fine.
(B) I go to lunch at 11.
(C) They are for Simone's birthday.

05 (A) _____ (B) _____ (C) _____

Q. _____ are you _____ here on the corner, Jane?

(A) I am waiting for my friend.
(B) Milton Street and Vine Avenue.
(C) Just around the corner.

06 (A) _____ (B) _____ (C) _____

Q. _____ is the printer in the copy room _____?

(A) It's next to the conference room.
(B) The printer is broken?
(C) Since sometime last week.

07 (A) _____ (B) _____ (C) _____

Q. _____ see Ms. Park in the payroll department?

(A) I'm going to pay for that item.
(B) She's not here today.
(C) Yes, I can see quite well.

정답·스크립트·해설 **p.30**

Course 2 How 의문문

토익 출제경향
평균 2문제 정도 출제

어떻게(How) 출퇴근하시나요?

지하철로요.

여자가 남자에게 출퇴근하는 방법에 대한 정보를 물었네요. 그럼 남자는 출퇴근하는 방법에 대해 말해줘야 하겠죠? 이처럼 PART 2에서는 방법, 기간, 가격, 수량, 의견 등 다양한 정보를 묻는 How 의문문이 출제됩니다.

핵심 POINT

1. How 뒤에 나오는 형용사/부사나 동사를 들으면 질문이 무엇에 관한 정보를 묻고 있는지 쉽게 파악할 수 있습니다.

   Q. How do you commute to work? 어떻게 출퇴근하시나요? [방법 묻기]
   A. By subway. 지하철로요.

   Q. How long were you at the bank? 당신은 은행에 얼마나 오래 있었나요? [기간 묻기]
   A. About half an hour. 30분 정도요.

   Q. How much is this camera? 이 카메라는 얼마인가요? [가격 묻기]
   A. It costs $200. 200달러예요.

   Q. How many people are attending the party? 파티에 얼마나 많은 사람들이 참석하나요? [수량 묻기]
   A. Around 50. 50명 정도요.

2. How do(would) you like ~?, How ~ go? 형태의 의문문은 의견을 물을 때 자주 사용됩니다.

   Q. How do you like your new office? 당신의 새로운 사무실은 어때요? [의견 묻기]
   A. It's very spacious and bright. 굉장히 넓고 밝아요.

3. How about ~? 형태의 의문문은 제안을 할 때 자주 사용되는 표현입니다.

   Q. How about inviting Jihye to the party? Jihye를 파티에 초대하는 게 어때요? [제안하기]
   A. I'll call her right away. 제가 그녀에게 바로 전화할게요.

Example 🎧 DAY07_03

[3회] 영국식 발음 → 캐나다식 발음

How do we **book** a room for an event?

(A) There was enough room.
(B) It starts tomorrow.
(C) By speaking to the receptionist.

행사를 위한 방을 어떻게 예약하나요?

(A) 충분한 공간이 있었어요.
(B) 그것은 내일 시작해요.
(C) 접수원에게 말을 해서요.

정답 (C)

해설 행사를 위한 방을 예약하는 방법을 묻는 How 의문문입니다.
    (A) [×] 질문의 room(방)을 '공간'이라는 의미로 반복 사용하여 혼동을 준 오답입니다.
    (B) [×] 행사를 위한 방을 예약하는 방법을 물었는데, 이와 관련이 없는 그것은 내일 시작한다는 내용으로 응답했으므로 오답입니다.
    (C) [○] 접수원에게 말을 해서라는 말로 행사를 위한 방을 예약하는 방법을 언급했으므로 정답입니다.

어휘 receptionist[risépʃənist] 접수원

음성을 듣고 질문에 대한 응답이 맞으면 ○, 틀리면 ×, 헷갈리는 보기에는 △를 표시하면서 정답을 선택해 보세요. 음성을 다시 들으면서 빈칸을 채우세요. (음성은 두 번 들려줍니다.)

01 (A) _____ (B) _____ (C) _____

Q. _____ can I make _____?

(A) It's the most famous kind of Japanese food.
(B) Just follow this recipe.
(C) I'll wash the dishes later.

02 (A) _____ (B) _____ (C) _____

Q. _____ did your piano class _____?

(A) Many students study music.
(B) It went well.
(C) I've played for years.

03 (A) _____ (B) _____ (C) _____

Q. _____ will _____ the conference?

(A) It's on September 21.
(B) Seven from each department.
(C) Around $200.

04 (A) _____ (B) _____ (C) _____

Q. _____ does this phone _____?

(A) OK, I'll call you back.
(B) How did you know?
(C) It is $125.

05 (A) _____ (B) _____ (C) _____

Q. _____ the new Thai restaurant downtown?

(A) I'm going there tonight.
(B) I've visited Bangkok many times.
(C) I couldn't get it untied.

06 (A) _____ (B) _____ (C) _____

Q. _____ will we have to _____ for a table?

(A) It seats seven.
(B) Ask the person at the counter.
(C) The five-course meal.

07 (A) _____ (B) _____ (C) _____

Q. _____ to the gas station?

(A) About 60 liters.
(B) It costs nearly $40.
(C) Once a week.

정답·스크립트·해설 p.31

01 Mark your answer.　　　　(A)　　　(B)　　　(C)

02 Mark your answer.　　　　(A)　　　(B)　　　(C)

03 Mark your answer.　　　　(A)　　　(B)　　　(C)

04 Mark your answer.　　　　(A)　　　(B)　　　(C)

05 Mark your answer.　　　　(A)　　　(B)　　　(C)

06 Mark your answer.　　　　(A)　　　(B)　　　(C)

07 Mark your answer.　　　　(A)　　　(B)　　　(C)

08 Mark your answer.　　　　(A)　　　(B)　　　(C)

09 Mark your answer.　　　　(A)　　　(B)　　　(C)

10 Mark your answer.　　　　(A)　　　(B)　　　(C)

11 Mark your answer.　　　　(A)　　　(B)　　　(C)

12 Mark your answer.　　　　(A)　　　(B)　　　(C)

13 Mark your answer.　　　　(A)　　　(B)　　　(C)

14 Mark your answer.　　　(A)　　(B)　　(C)

15 Mark your answer.　　　(A)　　(B)　　(C)

16 Mark your answer.　　　(A)　　(B)　　(C)

17 Mark your answer.　　　(A)　　(B)　　(C)

18 Mark your answer.　　　(A)　　(B)　　(C)

19 Mark your answer.　　　(A)　　(B)　　(C)

20 Mark your answer.　　　(A)　　(B)　　(C)

21 Mark your answer.　　　(A)　　(B)　　(C)

22 Mark your answer.　　　(A)　　(B)　　(C)

23 Mark your answer.　　　(A)　　(B)　　(C)

24 Mark your answer.　　　(A)　　(B)　　(C)

25 Mark your answer.　　　(A)　　(B)　　(C)

정답·스크립트·해설 **p.33**

DAY

08 일반 의문문 및 평서문

한 권으로 끝내는
해커스 토익 **700+**
LC+RC+VOCA

▲ MP3
바로 듣기

Course 1 일반 의문문

토익 출제경향
평균 6~8문제 정도 출제

> 마케팅 세미나에 오실 건가요?

> 네, 참석할 계획이에요.

남자가 여자에게 세미나에 참석하는지를 물었네요. 그럼 여자는 세미나 참석 여부를 말해줘야 하겠죠? 이처럼 PART 2 에서는 조동사(Do, Have, Can/Will/Should 등)나 Be동사 (Is, Are 등)로 시작되며, 특정 사실이나 의견을 확인하는 **일반 의문문**이 출제됩니다.

핵심 POINT

1. 확인하는 사실이 참이거나 의견에 동의하면 Yes로, 사실을 부인하거나 의견에 동의하지 않으면 No로 답한 후, 부연 설명을 하는 응답이 정답으로 자주 출제됩니다.

Q. Will you come to the marketing seminar? 마케팅 세미나에 오실 건가요?
A. Yes, I'm planning to attend. 네, 참석할 계획이에요.

2. Yes/No를 생략한 응답도 정답이 될 수 있습니다.

Q. Is Andy Dayton still working for your company? Andy Dayton은 여전히 당신의 회사에서 일을 하나요?
A. (No,) He retired last year. (아니요,) 그는 지난해에 은퇴했어요. [No를 생략한 응답]

3. '조동사/Be동사 + not' 형태로 시작하는 부정 의문문도 출제됩니다.

Q. Isn't Mr. Johnson a little late? Mr. Johnson이 조금 늦지 않나요?
A. Yes, he should be here by now. 네, 그는 지금쯤 와 있어야 해요.

4. 질문의 중간에 의문사가 포함된 경우, 해당 의문사에 알맞게 응답한 보기가 정답으로 출제됩니다.

Q. Can you tell me where the workshop is taking place? 워크숍이 어디에서 열리는지 말해 줄래요?
A. It'll be held at the Hamilton building. Hamilton 빌딩에서 열릴 거예요.

5. Could you ~?, Would you ~? 형태로 요청을 나타내는 의문문이 출제되기도 합니다.

Q. Could you drive me home? 저를 집까지 태워 주실 수 있나요? [요청하기]
A. Sure, wait a moment. 물론이죠, 잠시만 기다리세요.

Example | ∩ DAY08_01

🎧 미국식 발음 → 호주식 발음

Do we have an extra projector?

(A) I had some as well.
(B) There's one in the stockroom.
(C) The project is completed.

우리에게 여분의 프로젝터가 있나요?

(A) 저도 몇 개 가지고 있었어요.
(B) 창고에 하나 있어요.
(C) 그 프로젝트는 완료되었어요.

정답 (B)

해설 여분의 프로젝터가 있는지를 묻는 일반 의문문입니다.
  (A) [×] 질문의 have(가지고 있다)를 had로 반복 사용하여 혼동을 준 오답입니다.
  (B) [○] 창고에 하나 있다는 말로 여분의 프로젝터가 있음을 전달했으므로 정답입니다.
  (C) [×] projector – project의 유사 발음 어휘를 사용하여 혼동을 준 오답입니다.

어휘 extra[ékstrə] 여분의 complete[kəmplíːt] 완료하다, 마치다

음성을 듣고 질문에 대한 응답이 맞으면 ○, 틀리면 ×, 헷갈리는 보기에는 △를 표시하면서 정답을 선택해 보세요. 음성을 다시 들으면서 빈칸을 채우세요. (음성은 두 번 들려줍니다.)

01 (A) _____ (B) _____ (C) _____

Q. _____ to go to lunch?

(A) We go there often.
(B) I'd love to.
(C) She is taking a cooking class.

02 (A) _____ (B) _____ (C) _____

Q. _____ the seminar?

(A) Yes, I'll be there.
(B) The workshop was informative.
(C) In Spencer Auditorium.

03 (A) _____ (B) _____ (C) _____

Q. _____ our contact lists?

(A) Yes, they need to be revised.
(B) He will sign the contract.
(C) That date should work.

04 (A) _____ (B) _____ (C) _____

Q. _____ my phone?

(A) Yes, I just called.
(B) Certainly.
(C) No, I didn't.

05 (A) _____ (B) _____ (C) _____

Q. Do you know _____?

(A) Have you checked the closet?
(B) I'll move it for you.
(C) It looks very warm.

06 (A) _____ (B) _____ (C) _____

Q. Will you _____ for a moment?

(A) I already have one.
(B) Here you go.
(C) Buy more pencils also.

07 (A) _____ (B) _____ (C) _____

Q. Is the history museum _____ today?

(A) An event on October 22.
(B) It was in the past.
(C) No, it's closed on Mondays.

정답·스크립트·해설 p.37

Course 2 평서문

이 프린터의 사용 방법을 모르겠어요.

제가 도와 드릴게요.

여자가 프린터의 사용 방법을 모른다며 도움을 요청하고 있네요. 그럼 남자는 요청을 수락하거나 거절해야 하겠죠? 이처럼 PART 2에서는 요청, 의견·정보 제공, 문제점 언급 등 다양한 의도를 전달하는 **평서문**이 출제됩니다.

핵심 POINT

1. 평서문은 문장의 초점이 되는 부분이 없으므로 문장 전체를 놓치지 않고 들어야 문장의 의도를 파악할 수 있습니다.

2. 평서문의 의도에 따라 수락/거절, 동의/반대하거나, 추가로 정보를 제공하는 응답이 정답이 될 수 있습니다.

   Q. I don't know how to use this printer. 이 프린터의 사용 방법을 모르겠어요. [요청]
   A. I can help you with that. 제가 도와 드릴게요. [수락]

   Q. Helen has been an excellent team leader. Helen은 훌륭한 팀장이었어요. [의견 제공]
   A. I think she's too strict. 저는 그녀가 너무 엄격하다고 생각해요. [반대]

   Q. I heard the employee manual was revised. 직원 안내서가 수정되었다고 들었어요. [정보 제공]
   A. New policies were added. 새로운 정책들이 추가되었어요. [추가 정보 제공]

3. 의문문을 사용하여 추가 정보를 요구하는 응답도 정답이 될 수 있습니다.

   Q. I'm late because my car broke down on the way here.
   여기 오는 길에 제 차가 고장이 나서 늦었어요. [문제점 언급]
   A. What's wrong with it? 차에 무슨 문제가 있나요? [추가 정보 요구]

Example   ∩ DAY08_03

[3·W] 영국식 발음 → 캐나다식 발음

Mr. Thompson is out of the office at the moment.

(A) I'll leave a message for him then.
(B) We'll be there shortly.
(C) It's quite cold outside.

Mr. Thompson은 현재 사무실에 안 계세요.

(A) 그러면 그에게 메시지를 남길게요.
(B) 우리는 곧 그곳에 도착할 거예요.
(C) 밖은 꽤 추워요.

정답 (A)

해설 Mr. Thompson이 현재 사무실에 없다는 문제점을 언급하는 평서문입니다.
   (A) [○] 그러면 그에게 메시지를 남기겠다는 말로 Mr. Thompson이 사무실에 없다는 문제점에 대한 대응 방안을 제시했으므로 정답입니다.
   (B) [×] 질문의 at the moment(현재)와 관련 있는 shortly(곧)를 사용하여 혼동을 준 오답입니다.
   (C) [×] 질문의 out(~ 밖)과 관련 있는 outside(밖)를 사용하여 혼동을 준 오답입니다.

어휘 shortly [미 ʃɔ́ːrtli, 영 ʃɔ́ːtli] 곧

음성을 듣고 질문에 대한 응답이 맞으면 ○, 틀리면 ×, 헷갈리는 보기에는 △를 표시하면서 정답을 선택해 보세요. 음성을 다시 들으면서 빈칸을 채우세요. (음성은 두 번 들려줍니다.)

01 (A) _____ (B) _____ (C) _____

Q. _____ at 11:45 P.M.

(A) I'll pick you up then.
(B) You're an excellent pilot.
(C) The flight is full.

02 (A) _____ (B) _____ (C) _____

Q. The new TV model is _____.

(A) It has many new features.
(B) I didn't know you were a model.
(C) It's on a different channel.

03 (A) _____ (B) _____ (C) _____

Q. Clarkson Industries' _____ 200 percent.

(A) I'll let you know when I get it.
(B) These roses are very expensive.
(C) That's impressive.

04 (A) _____ (B) _____ (C) _____

Q. _____ anything about the job I applied for.

(A) They'll contact you soon.
(B) I am looking for a job.
(C) The president's interview was brief.

05 (A) _____ (B) _____ (C) _____

Q. It's going to be _____ in Beijing _____.

(A) I'll have to pack some shorts, then.
(B) We visited your family.
(C) I can't eat spicy food.

06 (A) _____ (B) _____ (C) _____

Q. _____ a copy of the training schedule.

(A) Wasn't it e-mailed to you?
(B) The trainer is very popular.
(C) Yes, it's interesting.

07 (A) _____ (B) _____ (C) _____

Q. I suggest _____ for the workshop.

(A) Many people attended.
(B) He's in the IT department.
(C) OK, I will do that right now.

정답·스크립트·해설 **p.39**

01 Mark your answer.   (A)   (B)   (C)

02 Mark your answer.   (A)   (B)   (C)

03 Mark your answer.   (A)   (B)   (C)

04 Mark your answer.   (A)   (B)   (C)

05 Mark your answer.   (A)   (B)   (C)

06 Mark your answer.   (A)   (B)   (C)

07 Mark your answer.   (A)   (B)   (C)

08 Mark your answer.   (A)   (B)   (C)

09 Mark your answer.   (A)   (B)   (C)

10 Mark your answer.   (A)   (B)   (C)

11 Mark your answer.   (A)   (B)   (C)

12 Mark your answer.   (A)   (B)   (C)

13 Mark your answer.   (A)   (B)   (C)

14 Mark your answer. (A) (B) (C)

15 Mark your answer. (A) (B) (C)

16 Mark your answer. (A) (B) (C)

17 Mark your answer. (A) (B) (C)

18 Mark your answer. (A) (B) (C)

19 Mark your answer. (A) (B) (C)

20 Mark your answer. (A) (B) (C)

21 Mark your answer. (A) (B) (C)

22 Mark your answer. (A) (B) (C)

23 Mark your answer. (A) (B) (C)

24 Mark your answer. (A) (B) (C)

25 Mark your answer. (A) (B) (C)

정답·스크립트·해설 p.40

DAY 09
선택 의문문 및 부가 의문문

한 권으로 끝내는
해커스 토익 700+
LC+RC+VOCA

▲ MP3
바로 듣기

Course 1 선택 의문문

토익 출제경향
평균 2문제 정도 출제

사무실까지 버스를 타고 왔나요, 아니면 (or) 걸어왔나요?

버스를 탔어요.

남자가 여자에게 버스를 타고 왔는지, 아니면 걸어왔는지를 물었네요. 그럼 여자는 둘 중 어느 방법으로 왔는지를 말해 줘야 하겠죠? 이처럼 PART 2에서는 or로 연결된 두 가지 사항 중 하나를 선택하도록 요구하는 **선택 의문문**이 출제됩니다.

핵심 POINT

1. 두 가지 선택 사항 중 하나를 선택하거나, either/neither/whichever/both 등을 사용하여 둘 다 선택하거나 둘 다 선택하지 않는 응답이 정답으로 자주 출제됩니다.

Q. Did you take the bus or walk to the office? 사무실까지 버스를 타고 왔나요, 아니면 걸어왔나요?
A. I took the bus. 버스를 탔어요. [둘 중 하나를 선택함]

Q. Are you available to come in for an interview on Monday or Tuesday?
월요일이나 화요일 중에 면접을 보러 올 시간이 있나요?
A. Both work for me. 저는 둘 다 괜찮아요. [둘 다 선택함]

Q. Would you like to have a coffee or a tea? 커피나 차를 좀 드시겠어요?
A. Neither, thanks. 감사하지만, 둘 다 사양할게요. [둘 다 선택하지 않음]

2. 보통 Yes/No로 시작된 응답은 정답이 되지 않지만, 두 개의 의문문이 or로 연결된 경우 Yes/No로 시작된 응답도 정답이 될 수 있습니다.

Q. Can you help me move this table, or are you in a hurry?
이 테이블을 옮기는 것을 도와주실 수 있나요, 아니면 바쁘신가요?
A. Yes, I can help. 네, 도와드릴 수 있어요.

Example   ∩ DAY09_01

🔊 호주식 발음 → 미국식 발음

Have you met the new receptionist, **or** should I introduce you to him?

(A) I met him this morning.
(B) Yes, the first shelf.
(C) The front desk in the lobby.

새로 온 접수원을 만났나요, 아니면 제가 당신을 그에게 소개할까요?

(A) 저는 오늘 아침에 그를 만났어요.
(B) 네, 첫 번째 선반이요.
(C) 로비의 안내 데스크요.

정답 (A)

해설 새로 온 접수원을 만났는지 아니면 자신이 소개할지를 묻는 선택 의문문입니다.
(A) [o] 자신은 오늘 아침에 그를 만났다는 말로 새로 온 접수원을 만났다는 것을 선택했으므로 정답입니다.
(B) [×] 새로 온 접수원을 만났는지 아니면 자신이 소개할지를 물었는데, 이와 관련이 없는 첫 번째 선반이라는 내용으로 응답했으므로 오답입니다.
(C) [×] 질문의 receptionist(접수원)와 관련 있는 front desk(안내 데스크)를 사용하여 혼동을 준 오답입니다.

어휘 receptionist[risépʃənist] 접수원   front desk (호텔·사무실 등의) 안내 데스크

음성을 듣고 질문에 대한 응답이 맞으면 ○, 틀리면 ×, 헷갈리는 보기에는 △를 표시하면서 정답을 선택해 보세요. 음성을 다시 들으면서 빈칸을 채우세요. (음성은 두 번 들려줍니다.)

01 (A) _____ (B) _____ (C) _____

Q. _____ London or Brighton?

(A) They're both lovely places.
(B) Brighton isn't a large city.
(C) My apartment is in London.

02 (A) _____ (B) _____ (C) _____

Q. Do you want to _____?

(A) I want the newer device.
(B) Either would be fine with me.
(C) The snow is perfect today.

03 (A) _____ (B) _____ (C) _____

Q. _____, or can I cross it?

(A) Our office closes at 5 P.M.
(B) It crosses the Han River.
(C) No, it's open now.

04 (A) _____ (B) _____ (C) _____

Q. Do you want to _____ or _____?

(A) I'll have whichever is healthier.
(B) Your order will be $12.
(C) We eat here a lot.

05 (A) _____ (B) _____ (C) _____

Q. Are you going on vacation _____ or _____?

(A) At the Grand Canyon Resort.
(B) I will go with my family.
(C) I leave this Saturday.

06 (A) _____ (B) _____ (C) _____

Q. Should I _____ or just this one?

(A) You don't have to fill out both.
(B) Near the top of the form.
(C) My insurance agent.

07 (A) _____ (B) _____ (C) _____

Q. _____, or are you going to have lunch?

(A) The mall has three floors.
(B) I have to buy some shoes.
(C) He'd rather stay home.

정답·스크립트·해설 **p.45**

Course 2 부가 의문문

그 회의실은 아직 수리 중이죠, 그렇지 않나요 (isn't it)?

네, 다음 주부터 이용할 수 있어요.

여자가 회의실이 아직 수리 중이라고 말한 뒤, 사실이 맞는지 남자에게 확인하고 있네요. 이처럼 PART 2에서는 평서문 뒤에 덧붙여 사실을 확인하거나 의견에 동의를 구하는 **부가 의문문**이 출제됩니다.

핵심 POINT

1. 부가 의문문 앞의 평서문이 전달하는 사실이 참이거나 의견에 동의하면 Yes로, 사실을 부인하거나 의견에 반대하면 No로 답한 후 부연 설명을 추가한 응답이 정답으로 자주 출제됩니다.

   Q. The conference room is still being renovated, isn't it? 그 회의실은 아직 수리 중이죠, 그렇지 않나요?
   A. Yes, it will be available next week. 네, 다음 주부터 이용할 수 있어요.

   Q. You called the client, didn't you? 당신이 고객에게 전화했죠, 안 그랬나요?
   A. No, I've been busy. 아니요, 저는 바빴어요.

2. Yes/No를 생략한 응답도 정답이 될 수 있습니다.

   Q. You have time to help me with my speech, right? 제가 연설 준비하는 걸 도와줄 시간이 있죠, 그렇죠?
   A. (Yes,) I'm free all afternoon. (네,) 전 오후 내내 한가해요. [Yes를 생략한 응답]

   Q. You've not read that book, have you? 당신은 그 책을 읽지 않았죠, 그렇죠?
   A. (No,) I don't like mystery novels. (아니요,) 저는 추리 소설을 좋아하지 않아요. [No를 생략한 응답]

Example ∩ DAY09_03

3╗) 영국식 발음 → 캐나다식 발음

Debra is on a business trip this week, **isn't she**?

(A) Yes, I think she is.
(B) She had a wonderful time.
(C) The weekly timetable.

Debra는 이번 주에 출장 중이죠, 안 그런가요?

(A) 네, 그런 것 같아요.
(B) 그녀는 멋진 시간을 보냈어요.
(C) 주간 계획표요.

정답 (A)

해설 Debra가 이번 주에 출장 중인지를 묻는 부가 의문문입니다.
(A) [o] 그런 것 같다는 말로 Debra가 출장 중임을 전달했으므로 정답입니다.
(B) [×] 질문의 business trip(출장)에서 trip(여행)과 관련 있는 wonderful time(멋진 시간)을 사용하여 혼동을 준 오답입니다.
(C) [×] week - weekly의 유사 발음 어휘를 사용하여 혼동을 준 오답입니다.

어휘 business trip 출장   timetable[미 táimteibl, 영 táimtèibl] 계획표

음성을 듣고 질문에 대한 응답이 맞으면 ○, 틀리면 ×, 헷갈리는 보기에는 △를 표시하면서 정답을 선택해 보세요. 음성을 다시 들으면서 빈칸을 채우세요. (음성은 두 번 들려줍니다.)

01 (A) _____ (B) _____ (C) _____

Q. You've _____ Seattle, _____?

(A) No, I'll be in Chicago.
(B) Yes, actually I used to live there.
(C) She's never seen it.

02 (A) _____ (B) _____ (C) _____

Q. We should _____, _____?

(A) I'll print out the receipt.
(B) Yes, the old one is broken.
(C) Toner is very expensive.

03 (A) _____ (B) _____ (C) _____

Q. Your department _____ now, _____?

(A) Yes, he's great.
(B) No, I'm a full-time employee.
(C) My internship will begin tomorrow.

04 (A) _____ (B) _____ (C) _____

Q. The business lounge is _____, isn't it?

(A) She'll repair it soon.
(B) I am starting a new business.
(C) You should ask one of the staff members.

05 (A) _____ (B) _____ (C) _____

Q. Patty will _____, won't she?

(A) Yes, on April 1.
(B) No, she just opened an account.
(C) That department is on the third floor.

06 (A) _____ (B) _____ (C) _____

Q. Mark is _____ this year, isn't he?

(A) I met him last month in Prague.
(B) I heard he is in charge of it.
(C) Organizational skills are very important.

07 (A) _____ (B) _____ (C) _____

Q. You don't need any help _____ for our next project, _____?

(A) I don't have any money.
(B) The projector isn't working right now.
(C) Could you give me a hand?

정답·스크립트·해설 **p.46**

PART 2

DAY 09 선택 의문문 및 부가 의문문

한 권으로 끝내는 해커스 토익 **700+** (LC+RC+VOCA)

01   Mark your answer.   (A)   (B)   (C)

02   Mark your answer.   (A)   (B)   (C)

03   Mark your answer.   (A)   (B)   (C)

04   Mark your answer.   (A)   (B)   (C)

05   Mark your answer.   (A)   (B)   (C)

06   Mark your answer.   (A)   (B)   (C)

07   Mark your answer.   (A)   (B)   (C)

08   Mark your answer.   (A)   (B)   (C)

09   Mark your answer.   (A)   (B)   (C)

10   Mark your answer.   (A)   (B)   (C)

11   Mark your answer.   (A)   (B)   (C)

12   Mark your answer.   (A)   (B)   (C)

13   Mark your answer.   (A)   (B)   (C)

14 Mark your answer.   (A)   (B)   (C)

15 Mark your answer.   (A)   (B)   (C)

16 Mark your answer.   (A)   (B)   (C)

17 Mark your answer.   (A)   (B)   (C)

18 Mark your answer.   (A)   (B)   (C)

19 Mark your answer.   (A)   (B)   (C)

20 Mark your answer.   (A)   (B)   (C)

21 Mark your answer.   (A)   (B)   (C)

22 Mark your answer.   (A)   (B)   (C)

23 Mark your answer.   (A)   (B)   (C)

24 Mark your answer.   (A)   (B)   (C)

25 Mark your answer.   (A)   (B)   (C)

정답·스크립트·해설 p.47

PART 3

PART 3는 32번부터 70번까지 총 39문제(13대화)로, 2~3 사람이 주고받는 짧은 대화를 듣고 제시된 질문과 시각 자료에 가장 적절한 답을 선택하는 유형입니다.

DAY 10

전체 대화 관련 문제

한 권으로 끝내는
해커스 토익 **700+**
LC+RC+VOCA

▲ MP3
바로 듣기

Course 1 주제 및 목적 문제

토익 출제경향
평균 2문제 정도 출제

Jane, 컴퓨터에 무슨 문제가 있나요?

컴퓨터가 켜지지 않아요.

음... 제가 바로 점검해 드릴게요.

Q. 화자들은 주로 무엇에 대해 이야기하고 있는가?
A. 컴퓨터 고장

화자들이 주로 무엇에 대해 이야기하고 있는지를 묻고 있습니다. 이처럼 PART 3에서는 대화의 핵심 내용인 **주제**나 **목적**을 묻는 문제가 출제됩니다.

핵심 POINT

1. 대화의 주제나 목적을 나타내는 핵심어구는 주로 대화의 초반에 언급됩니다.

2. 대화의 후반에 언급된 명사를 직접 사용하거나 발음이 유사한 단어를 사용하여 혼란을 주는 보기가 오답으로 출제되기도 합니다.

3. 주로 다음과 같은 질문을 사용하여 대화의 주제나 목적을 묻습니다.

주제   What **are the speakers** mainly discussing?   화자들은 주로 무엇에 대해 이야기하고 있는가?
          What **is the conversation** mainly about?   대화는 주로 무엇에 대한 것인가?

목적   Why **is the man** calling?   남자는 왜 전화를 하고 있는가?
          What **is the** purpose **of the call**?   전화의 목적은 무엇인가?

Example   ∩ DAY10_01

1. What are the speakers mainly discussing? (A) Planning a summer vacation (B) Arranging a staff party (C) Taking part of the day off (D) Meeting with a manager	1. 화자들은 주로 무엇에 대해 이야기하고 있는가? (A) 여름 휴가 계획하기 (B) 직원 파티 준비하기 (C) 하루의 일부 쉬기 (D) 부장과 만나기

---

③ 호주식 발음 → 미국식 발음

Question 1 refers to the following conversation.

M: **I'd like to take some time off next Friday.**
W: James is going on vacation then. That means we will be a bit shorthanded.
M: I have an appointment with my dentist at 1 P.M., so I just need the afternoon off.
W: That should be fine. We can manage without you for a few hours.

1번은 다음 대화에 관한 문제입니다.

남: 다음 주 금요일에 휴가를 좀 내고 싶어요.
여: James가 그때 휴가를 가요. 그래서 우리는 일손이 조금 모자라게 될 거예요.
남: 치과 진료가 오후 1시에 있어서, 저는 오후 휴무만 필요해요.
여: 그건 괜찮을 것 같네요. 몇 시간 만이라면 당신 없이도 그럭저럭할 수 있어요.

정답 (C)

해설 대화의 주제를 묻는 문제입니다. 남자가 "I'd like to take some time off next Friday."라며 다음 주 금요일에 휴가를 좀 내고 싶다고 한 뒤, 오후 휴무를 사용하는 것에 관한 내용으로 대화가 이어지고 있습니다. 따라서 정답은 (C) Taking part of the day off입니다.

어휘 take time off 휴가를 내다   shorthanded [미 ʃɔ́ːrthǽndid, 영 ʃɔ́ːthǽndid] 일손이 모자란

질문과 보기를 먼저 읽은 후 음성을 들으며 정답을 선택하세요. 이후 음성을 다시 들으면서 빈칸을 채우세요.
(음성은 두 번 들려줍니다.)

01 What is the purpose of the call?

(A) To request assistance
(B) To ask for an opinion
(C) To offer advice
(D) To submit a complaint

02 What does the woman ask the man to do?

(A) Purchase some furniture
(B) Contact a caterer
(C) Mail some documents
(D) Change a dinner menu

W: Hi, Mark. This is Donna. I'd like to
_____ for our boss.
He became the department head last
week. Can you _____
the preparations?
M: I'd be happy to. What should I do?
W: Could you _____
that _____ you
organized last year? I need to know
how much dinner for 50 people costs.

03 What is the conversation mainly about?

(A) A ticket discount
(B) A film review
(C) A theater opening
(D) A movie release

04 What does the man mean when he says,
"Especially when you consider that Bill Waters
wrote it"?

(A) He is critical of a work.
(B) He will revise a script.
(C) He respects a writer.
(D) He will request a copy.

W1: I just _____ of
our movie, *Cosmos*. Have either of
you seen it yet?
W2: I read it this morning. Overall, it is really
positive. Right, Steve?
M: Yeah. I'm happy with it. Especially
when you consider that Bill Waters
wrote it. He is a _____
_____, and thousands of
people read his articles.
W1: Right. I'm sure it will _____
higher ticket sales at theaters.

Course 2 화자 및 장소 문제

주문하시겠어요?

오늘의 특별 요리는 무엇인가요?

호박을 곁들인 스테이크예요.

Q. 남자는 누구인 것 같은가?

A. 종업원

남자가 누구인 것 같은지를 묻고 있습니다. 이처럼 PART 3 에서는 **화자의 신분이나 대화가 이루어지고 있는 장소**를 묻는 문제가 출제됩니다.

핵심 POINT

1. 화자의 신분이나 대화가 이루어지는 장소와 관련된 내용은 주로 대화의 초반에 언급됩니다.

2. 특정 직업이나 장소와 관련된 여러 표현들을 통해 화자의 신분이나 대화가 이루어지는 장소를 유추할 수 있습니다.

3. 주로 다음과 같은 질문을 사용하여 대화의 화자나 대화가 이루어지는 장소를 묻습니다.

화자　Who **most likely is** the man/the woman? 남자/여자는 누구인 것 같은가?
　　　Who **are** the speakers? 화자들은 누구인가?
　　　Where do the speakers **most likely** work? 화자들은 어디에서 일하는 것 같은가?

장소　Where **most likely are** the speakers? 화자들은 어디에 있는 것 같은가?
　　　Where **does this** conversation **(probably)** take place? 이 대화는 어디에서 일어나는가?

Example　⌒ DAY10_03

1. Who most likely is the woman? (A) A real estate agent (B) A public official (C) A maintenance worker (D) A financial consultant	1. 여자는 누구인 것 같은가? (A) 부동산 중개인 (B) 공무원 (C) 보수 관리 직원 (D) 재무 상담사

영국식 발음 → 캐나다식 발음

Question 1 refers to the following conversation. W: **Thank you for coming to my real estate office** today, Mr. Goodman. **What type of property would you like to purchase?** M: I'm interested in a two-bedroom house located near a major subway station. I work in the downtown area, so access to public transportation is important to me. W: I'm sure I can find something that meets those requirements. In fact, some new properties were recently built close to . . . um . . . to Center Station. I'll show you photos of them now.	1번은 다음 대화에 관한 문제입니다. 여: 오늘 저의 부동산 중개 사무소에 와주셔서 감사합니다, Mr. Goodman. 어떤 종류의 부동산을 구매하고 싶으신가요? 남: 주요 지하철역 가까이에 있는 방 2개짜리 집에 관심이 있어요. 저는 도심 지역에서 근무해서, 대중교통으로의 접근성이 중요해요. 여: 그 요건들을 충족하는 곳을 분명히 찾을 수 있을 거예요. 사실, 최근에 새 건물들이... 음... 중앙역 근처에 지어졌어요. 지금 그것들의 사진을 보여드릴게요.

정답 (A)

해설 여자의 신분을 묻는 문제입니다. 여자가 "Thank you for coming to my real estate office"라며 자신의 부동산 중개 사무소에 와주어 고맙다고 한 뒤, "What type of property would you like to purchase?"라며 어떤 종류의 부동산을 구매하고 싶은지 물은 것을 통해 여자가 부동산 중개인임을 알 수 있습니다. 따라서 정답은 (A) A real estate agent입니다.

어휘 real estate office 부동산 중개 사무소　property [미 prápərti, 영 prɔ́pəti] 부동산, 건물　access to ~로의 접근성
public transportation 대중교통　requirement [미 rikwáiərmənt, 영 rikwáiəmənt] 요건, 요구

질문과 보기를 먼저 읽은 후 음성을 들으며 정답을 선택하세요. 이후 음성을 다시 들으면서 빈칸을 채우세요.
(음성은 두 번 들려줍니다.)

01 Where most likely are the speakers?

(A) At a travel agency
(B) At a retail store
(C) At a gym
(D) At a hotel

02 According to the woman, what can be made available?

(A) A different room
(B) A free membership
(C) A discounted price
(D) An instruction manual

M: Hello. I'm _____ Suite 107, and the air conditioner in here _____.

W: Really? Have you tried _____ _____ and then back on?

M: I already did that, but it's still not working.

W: All right. I'll tell a technician to go up and look at it immediately. If he can't get it working right away, we'll move you to _____ on the same floor.

03 Where does the man most likely work?

(A) At a post office
(B) At an online store
(C) At a credit card company
(D) At an investment firm

04 What is mentioned about the replacement?

(A) It will contain more information.
(B) It will be sent in the mail.
(C) It will involve an additional fee.
(D) It will include improved features.

M: Kenwood Financial. How may I help you?

W: Hello. I'm calling because I . . . uh . . . I _____ yesterday. I need to cancel it and _____.

M: Can you provide your name and address?

W: My name is Martina Rhodes and I live at 5001 Selah Way, Danville, Vermont.

M: OK, Ms. Rhodes. Your request will _____ to process. The _____ then.

정답·스크립트·해설 **p.54**

01 Where does the man most likely work?

(A) At an educational institute
(B) At an art gallery
(C) At a concert hall
(D) At a real estate agency

02 What does the woman inquire about?

(A) Where an office is located
(B) Why she didn't receive an e-mail
(C) What requirements should be met
(D) When she will be contacted

03 What does the man mention about the president?

(A) She attends a weekly meeting.
(B) She intends to be at an interview.
(C) She made an announcement.
(D) She has reviewed a proposal.

04 What are the speakers mainly discussing?

(A) Policy changes
(B) Technical errors
(C) Customer complaints
(D) Sales results

05 What does the woman say about a competitor?

(A) It has well-trained staff.
(B) It uses online marketing.
(C) It sells expensive products.
(D) It is not popular.

06 What suggestion does the woman make?

(A) Speaking to a manager
(B) Offering discounts online
(C) Conducting customer surveys
(D) Hiring a consultant

07 What is the woman's job?

(A) Personal driver
(B) Rental agent
(C) Event planner
(D) Airline ticketing agent

08 Why is the man traveling to New York City?

(A) To meet some clients
(B) To go to a conference
(C) To visit an old friend
(D) To celebrate a marriage

09 What does the woman ask the man about?

(A) The location of a hotel
(B) The dates of a trip
(C) The distance to an airport
(D) The cost of a service

10 Where most likely are the speakers?

(A) At an office building
(B) At a recreation center
(C) At an academy
(D) At an accommodation facility

11 Why does the man say, "The interior is more spacious than I thought it would be"?

(A) To indicate he agrees with an opinion
(B) To suggest an alternative to a plan
(C) To imply an area is too large
(D) To reassure his colleague about a task

12 What will the man most likely do next?

(A) Attend a ceremony
(B) Choose a meal option
(C) Pay for a service
(D) Approach a manager

13 Why is the man calling?

(A) To give some feedback
(B) To offer an apology
(C) To seek some assistance
(D) To report a damaged device

14 What problem does the woman mention?

(A) Some technicians are unavailable.
(B) A repair cannot be made.
(C) A phone has not been installed.
(D) Some staff members require more training.

15 How can the man schedule an appointment?

(A) By e-mailing a receptionist
(B) By filling out a form
(C) By visiting an office
(D) By calling a worker

Maple Street	Spot A	Harris Park	Spot B	Vince Street
	Washburn Avenue			
	Spot C	Parking Lot	Spot D	

16 What are the speakers mainly discussing?

(A) Checking traffic conditions
(B) Traveling to the city center
(C) Visiting a local park
(D) Buying a bus pass

17 Where will the woman meet her friend?

(A) At an art gallery
(B) At a city park
(C) At a museum
(D) At a mall

18 Look at the graphic. Where is the subway station?

(A) At Spot A
(B) At Spot B
(C) At Spot C
(D) At Spot D

정답·스크립트·해설 p.55

PART 3

DAY 10 전체 대화 관련 문제

한 권으로 끝내는 해커스 토익 700+ (LC+RC+VOCA)

Course 1 요청 · 제안 문제

토익 출제경향
평균 3~5문제 정도 출제

이번 회사 연회의 사회를 맡아 줄래요?

물론이죠. 영광이에요.

당신이 적임자라고 생각했어요.

Q. 남자는 여자에게 무엇을 해달라고 요청하는가?
A. 행사의 사회를 맡는다.

남자가 여자에게 무엇을 요청하는지를 묻고 있습니다. 이처럼 PART 3에서는 화자가 다른 화자에게 요청 또는 제안한 내용을 묻는 문제가 출제됩니다.

핵심 POINT

1. 질문에 언급된 화자가 남자와 여자 중 누구인지 확인한 후, 해당 화자의 말을 주의 깊게 들어야 합니다.

2. 세 명의 대화인 경우, 남자들(men) 또는 여자들(women)과 같이 같은 성별을 가진 화자들에 대한 질문이 출제되기도 합니다.

3. 요청하는 내용은 Can(Could) you ~, I'd like you to ~와 같은 표현 다음에 자주 언급되고, 제안하는 내용은 Why don't we ~, I suggest/recommend ~, You should ~와 같은 표현 다음에 자주 언급됩니다.

4. 주로 다음과 같은 질문을 사용하여 요청 또는 제안한 내용을 묻습니다.

요청　What does the man ask the woman to do?　남자는 여자에게 무엇을 해달라고 요청하는가?

제안　What does the woman suggest/recommend?　여자는 무엇을 제안하는가?
　　　What do the men offer to do?　남자들은 무엇을 해주겠다고 제안하는가?

Example　🎧 DAY11_01

1. What does the man suggest?

(A) Extend a project deadline
(B) Review a financial report
(C) Meet with him next week
(D) Contact a head designer

1. 남자는 무엇을 제안하는가?

(A) 프로젝트 마감기한을 연장한다.
(B) 재무 보고서를 검토한다.
(C) 그와 다음 주에 회의를 한다.
(D) 수석 설계사에게 연락한다.

🎙 캐나다식 발음 → 미국식 발음

Question 1 refers to the following conversation.

M: As a reminder, the initial blueprints for the Stanton Office Building need to be ready before the end of the month.
W: That won't be a problem. My team will complete the first draft by next Monday.
M: Oh, really? Then, **why don't we have a meeting regarding the blueprints next Tuesday?**

1번은 다음 대화에 관한 문제입니다.

남: 상기시켜 드리자면, Stanton 사무소 건물의 설계도 초안은 이달 말 전에 준비가 되어야 해요.
여: 문제없을 거예요. 저희 팀은 다음 주 월요일까지 초안을 완성할 거거든요.
남: 아, 정말요? 그렇다면, 다음 주 화요일에 설계도에 관해 회의를 하는 게 어때요?

정답 (C)

해설 남자가 제안하는 것을 묻는 문제입니다. 남자가 여자에게 "why don't we have a meeting regarding the blueprints next Tuesday?"라며 다음 주 화요일에 설계도에 관해 회의를 할 것을 제안하였습니다. 따라서 정답은 (C) Meet with him next week입니다.

어휘 meet with (특히 논의를 위해) ~와 만나다　initial[iníʃəl] 초기의　blueprint[blú:print] 설계도, 계획　draft[미 dræft, 영 drɑ:ft] 초안

질문과 보기를 먼저 읽은 후 음성을 들으며 정답을 선택하세요. 이후 음성을 다시 들으면서 빈칸을 채우세요.
(음성은 두 번 들려줍니다.)

01 What is the conversation mainly about?

(A) Taking a weekend trip
(B) Organizing an upcoming concert
(C) Attending a musical performance
(D) Taking an online class

02 What does the man offer to do?

(A) Print some posters
(B) Purchase some tickets
(C) Change a schedule
(D) Drive to a venue

M: Hi, Alexandra. Do you want to go to the Blue Tiger _____ next weekend? _____ on both days.
W: Definitely. I'm busy on Saturday, but I can go on Sunday.
M: OK. _____ for us online after I return home tonight.
W: Thanks. Oh, and by the way, could you get me an extra ticket? My sister would love to come with us, too.

03 What is Paula Schwartz planning to do?

(A) Call a customer
(B) Update an order
(C) File a complaint
(D) Request a refund

04 What does the woman ask the man to do?

(A) Provide contact details
(B) Save a computer file
(C) Search a database
(D) Edit sales numbers

M: Could you answer any phone calls from Paula Schwartz while I'm on a business trip next week?
W: Sure, Brad. What will she call about?
M: Well, she's planning to _____ _____ of T-shirts in her order. She'll call when she knows how many she requires.
W: OK. But could you send me her _____ _____? I need to save it to my list of _____.
M: Just give me a minute.

정답·스크립트·해설 **p.58**

Course 2 언급 문제

주변에 차를 댈 만한 곳이 있나요?

이 건물 지하 1층에 주차장이 있어요.

그렇군요. 감사합니다.

Q. 여자는 건물에 대해 무엇을 언급하는가?
A. 주차할 공간이 있다.

여자가 건물에 대해 무엇을 언급하는지를 묻고 있습니다.
이처럼 PART 3에서는 **화자가 언급한 내용을 묻는 문제**
가 출제됩니다.

핵심 POINT

1. 질문에 언급된 화자가 남자와 여자 중 누구인지 확인한 후, 해당 화자의 말을 주의 깊게 들어야 합니다.

2. 세 명의 대화인 경우, 남자들(men) 또는 여자들(women)과 같이 같은 성별을 가진 화자들이 언급한 내용을
   묻는 질문이 출제되기도 합니다.

3. 정답의 단서는 질문의 say/mention(mentioned) about 뒤에 나오는 핵심어구가 언급된 부분과 그 주변
   에서 주로 등장합니다.

4. 주로 다음과 같은 질문을 사용하여 언급된 내용을 묻습니다.
   What **does the woman** mention about the building? 여자는 건물에 대해 무엇을 언급하는가?
   What **does the man** say about the credit card? 남자는 신용카드에 대해 무엇을 말하는가?
   What **is** mentioned about the presentation? 발표에 대해 무엇이 언급되는가?

Example ∩ DAY11_03

1. What does the man say about the credit card? (A) It was approved a week ago. (B) It will be automatically renewed. (C) It has to be signed before use. (D) It is not working correctly.	1. 남자는 신용카드에 대해 무엇을 말하는가? (A) 일주일 전에 승인되었다. (B) 자동으로 교체될 것이다. (C) 사용 전에 서명되어야 한다. (D) 제대로 작동하지 않고 있다.

3ᵈ 영국식 발음 → 호주식 발음 Question 1 refers to the following conversation. W: Hello. I need to renew my credit card. My current one expires in three weeks. M: Yes, ma'am. But, actually, **you don't have to request a new card. The bank automatically sends one to your home address** two weeks before the expiry date. W: I know. But I am going on a business trip next Friday for almost a month. So, I want to renew my card before then.	1번은 다음 대화에 관한 문제입니다. 여: 안녕하세요. 제 신용카드를 새로 교체해야 해요. 제 기존 카드가 3주 뒤에 만료될 거예요. 남: 네, 고객님. 그런데, 사실, 새 카드를 신청하지 않으셔도 됩니다. 은행에서 만료일 2주 전에 고객님의 자택 주소로 자동으로 신용카드를 보내드리거든요. 여: 알아요. 하지만 저는 다음 주 금요일부터 거의 한 달 동안 출장을 갈 예정이에요. 그래서, 저는 제 카드를 그 전에 새로 교체했으면 해요.

정답 (B)

해설 남자가 신용카드에 대해 언급하는 것을 묻는 문제입니다. 남자가 "you don't have to request a new card. The bank automatically sends one [credit card] to your home address"라며 새 카드를 신청하지 않아도 된다고 한 뒤 은행에서 여자의 자택 주소로 자동으로 신용카드를 보내준다고 하였습니다. 따라서 정답은 (B) It will be automatically renewed입니다.

어휘 automatically[ɔ̀ːtəmǽtikəli] 자동으로 renew[rinjúː] 새로 교체하다, 새롭게 하다 current[미 kə́ːrənt, 영 kʌ́rənt] 기존의, 현재의
expire[미 ikspáiər, 영 ikspáiə] 만료되다, 끝나다 business trip 출장

질문과 보기를 먼저 읽은 후 음성을 들으며 정답을 선택하세요. 이후 음성을 다시 들으면서 빈칸을 채우세요.
(음성은 두 번 들려줍니다.)

01 What is mentioned about Oliver Yates?

(A) He will book a flight.
(B) He will attend a conference.
(C) He arrived early in Dallas.
(D) He changed an appointment time.

02 What does the man offer to do?

(A) Review some documents
(B) Schedule a meeting
(C) Notify staff members
(D) Fix a technical issue

W: Hi, Paul. It's Sandra. I have to stay in Dallas for an extra day . . . until Wednesday. The author I'm getting together with, Oliver Yates, suddenly _____.
Could you contact Alliance Airlines and change my departure date?

M: Absolutely. Would you also like me to _____ the editorial staff that _____ Tuesday's meeting?

W: Oh, I completely forgot about that. Yes, please _____ about that as well.

03 What is the problem?

(A) A complaint was submitted.
(B) A report contains errors.
(C) A business has few customers.
(D) A company requires more personnel.

04 What does the man say about the rooms?

(A) They have modern artwork.
(B) They have outdated furnishings.
(C) They are too small.
(D) They were inspected by a supervisor.

W1: There are _____ at our resort these days. What do you two think we should do to bring in more guests?

W2: Well, there are many online reviews stating that our _____ _____.

M: To be honest, I agree. In particular, the tables and chairs in the rooms are a bit _____.

W1: All right. Thanks for your feedback. I'll discuss this with our supervisor when we meet this afternoon.

정답·스크립트·해설 p.59

01 What does the man mention about a camera?

(A) It is too small.
(B) It is hard to use.
(C) It is on sale.
(D) It is damaged.

02 What does the woman ask for?

(A) A price tag
(B) A shipping document
(C) A purchase receipt
(D) Another product

03 What will the woman most likely do next?

(A) Get an item from a storeroom
(B) Order a device from a Web site
(C) Take a camera to a repair shop
(D) Send a shipment to the man

04 Why is the man calling?

(A) To learn about a menu
(B) To revise an order
(C) To confirm a reservation
(D) To ask about a fee

05 What does the man say about the banquet?

(A) It will be held in a couple of weeks.
(B) It was promoted on the Internet.
(C) It will be catered at no charge.
(D) It was announced last week.

06 What does the woman offer to do?

(A) Provide an address
(B) Pay for extra dishes
(C) E-mail a receipt
(D) Compare restaurant prices

07 What is the woman's problem?

(A) She needs help leading a class.
(B) She is not feeling well.
(C) She forgot to sign up for an orientation.
(D) She is unable to locate some items.

08 Who is Sally Reynolds?

(A) A training instructor
(B) A department head
(C) A personal assistant
(D) A front desk worker

09 What does the woman request?

(A) A product price
(B) A shipping date
(C) A phone number
(D) An office address

10 How is the woman going to Myrtle Beach?

(A) By car
(B) By train
(C) By airplane
(D) By bus

11 What is mentioned about Rachel?

(A) She will be moving this weekend.
(B) She will be working overtime.
(C) She lives in the Myrtle Beach area.
(D) She plans to go on a vacation.

12 Why does the woman say, "Well, Thomas is driving down on Sunday morning"?

(A) To explain the reason for a delay
(B) To express uncertainty about a plan
(C) To indicate when she will leave
(D) To suggest a transportation option

13 What are the speakers mainly discussing?

(A) Beverage sales
(B) Research project deadlines
(C) Design job openings
(D) Product packaging

14 What is mentioned about customers?

(A) They offered negative feedback.
(B) They received a newsletter.
(C) They tried free samples.
(D) They voted on different designs.

15 Why are some colleagues working together?

(A) To respond to questions
(B) To review a document
(C) To acquire more funding
(D) To improve a design

Model Number	Weight
150A	5.3 kg
172E	5.0 kg
530R	4.8 kg
200B	4.5 kg

16 According to the man, what will take place tomorrow?

(A) A product demonstration
(B) An electronics trade show
(C) An executive gathering
(D) A training workshop

17 What does the man recommend?

(A) Fixing some malfunctioning devices
(B) Reserving a different conference room
(C) Taking speakers from another room
(D) Contacting a new electronics supplier

18 Look at the graphic. Which model will the man order?

(A) 150A
(B) 172E
(C) 530R
(D) 200B

정답·스크립트·해설 **p.60**

▲ MP3
바로 듣기

한 권으로 끝내는
해커스 토익 **700+**
LC+RC+VOCA

Course 1 이유·방법·정도 문제

토익 출제경향
평균 2~4문제 정도 출제

최송해요. 오래 기다리셨어요?

오늘 왜 지각했어요?

늦잠을 자서 지각했어요.

Q. 여자는 왜 늦었는가?
A. 그녀는 늦잠을 잤다.

여자가 왜 늦었는지를 묻고 있습니다. 이처럼 PART 3에서는 특정 상황과 관련된 이유, 방법, 정도를 묻는 문제가 출제됩니다.

핵심
POINT

1. 이유를 나타내는 내용은 because(~ 때문에), since(~이므로), so(따라서) 주변에서 자주 언급됩니다.

2. 교통/통신 수단이나 문제 해결 방법 등을 묻는 방법 문제에서는 대화에 언급된 여러 수단이 오답 보기로 출제되기도 합니다.

3. 기간, 빈도, 수량 등을 묻는 정도 문제에서는 대화에 언급된 여러 수치가 오답 보기로 출제되기도 합니다.

4. 주로 다음과 같은 질문을 사용하여 이유나 방법, 정도와 관련된 내용을 묻습니다.

이유 Why is the woman late? 여자는 왜 늦었는가?
Why is the delivery delayed? 배송은 왜 늦어졌는가?

방법 How does the woman plan to get to city hall? 여자는 어떻게 시청에 갈 계획인가?

정도 How long will Mr. Blackhill stay in China? Mr. Blackhill은 중국에 얼마나 머무를 것인가?

Example ⌂ DAY12_01

1. Why is the delivery delayed?

(A) A payment was not made.
(B) A system error occurred.
(C) A company changed its mailing address.
(D) Items are out of stock.

1. 배송은 왜 늦어졌는가?

(A) 금액이 지불되지 않았다.
(B) 시스템 오류가 발생했다.
(C) 회사가 우편 주소를 변경했다.
(D) 물품의 재고가 없다.

[3에] 영국식 발음 → 호주식 발음

Question 1 refers to the following conversation.

W: You've reached Delight Office Goods. How can I help you?
M: My company ordered 25 boxes of printer paper on June 23. But we haven't received anything yet. The order number is 45837.
W: I'm sorry about the delay. **We are having issues with handling existing orders because of a system error.** Your shipment should arrive later today.

1번은 다음 대화에 관한 문제입니다.

여: Delight 사무용품점입니다. 무엇을 도와드릴까요?
남: 저희 회사에서 6월 23일에 인쇄용지 25박스를 주문했어요. 그런데 아직 아무것도 받지 못했어요. 주문 번호는 45837입니다.
여: 지연되어서 죄송합니다. 저희는 시스템 오류로 인해 기존 주문들을 처리하는 데 문제를 겪고 있어요. 고객님의 물품은 오늘 늦게 도착할 거예요.

정답 (B)

해설 배송이 늦어진 이유를 묻는 문제입니다. 여자가 "We are having issues with handling existing orders because of a system error."라며 시스템 오류로 인해 기존 주문들을 처리하는 데 문제를 겪고 있다고 하였습니다. 따라서 정답은 (B) A system error occurred입니다.

어휘 handle[hǽndl] 처리하다 existing[igzístiŋ] 기존의 shipment[ʃípmənt] 물품, 배송품

질문과 보기를 먼저 읽은 후 음성을 들으며 정답을 선택하세요. 이후 음성을 다시 들으면서 빈칸을 채우세요.
(음성은 두 번 들려줍니다.)

01 Why does the man say, "I forgot I have a doctor's appointment tomorrow morning"?

(A) He cannot attend an event.
(B) He didn't check an e-mail.
(C) He wants to change a booking.
(D) He needs to request a refund.

02 How much will the man be charged?

(A) $5
(B) $7
(C) $8
(D) $9

M: Hello. I'm supposed to take the 8 A.M. train to Boston tomorrow. But I forgot I have a doctor's appointment tomorrow morning. Are there _____ _____ in the evening?

W: We have a few _____ _____ leaving at five. Will that work?

M: I'll still arrive in Boston before nine, so that's fine.

W: OK. There is a _____ _____ your reservation.

03 Why is an event going to take place next Friday evening?

(A) To give out an award
(B) To welcome a new employee
(C) To celebrate a retirement
(D) To announce a promotion

04 How will the woman make an inquiry?

(A) By calling an assistant
(B) By sending an e-mail
(C) By holding a meeting
(D) By posting a notice

M: As you know, Mr. Johnson is _____ _____. We're going to _____ for him next Friday evening. Could you help me prepare for it?

W: Certainly. I'm not very busy today.

M: Great. I'm hoping you can find out which staff members will be coming to the party. That way, I'll be able to know _____ should be.

W: OK. I'll _____ _____ right now.

정답·스크립트·해설 p.64

Course 2 문제점 문제

무엇을 도와드릴까요?

금요일에 회의실을 예약하려고요.

그날은 회의실 예약이 다 찼어요.

Q. 무엇이 문제인가?
A. 이용 가능한 회의실이 없다.

무엇이 문제인지를 묻고 있습니다. 이처럼 PART 3에서는 화자가 겪고 있는 문제점이나 걱정하고 있는 사항을 묻는 문제가 출제됩니다.

핵심 POINT

1. 질문에 특정 화자가 언급된 경우, 해당 화자의 말을 주의 깊게 들어야 합니다.

2. 세 명의 대화인 경우, 남자들(men) 또는 여자들(women)과 같이 같은 성별을 가진 화자들이 겪고 있는 문제점에 대한 질문이 출제되기도 합니다.

3. 문제점과 관련된 내용은 however(하지만), but(그러나), unfortunately(안타깝게도), sorry(죄송합니다), worried(걱정스러운)와 같은 부정적인 표현 다음에 자주 언급됩니다.

4. 주로 다음과 같은 질문을 사용하여 문제점을 묻습니다.
What is the problem? 무엇이 문제인가?
What problem does the man mention? 남자는 어떤 문제를 언급하는가?
What is the woman concerned/worried about? 여자는 무엇을 걱정하는가?

Example 〇 DAY12_03

1. What is the problem? (A) A logo was misprinted on items. (B) A field day was canceled. (C) A purchase cannot be returned. (D) A supplier cannot meet a deadline.	1. 무엇이 문제인가? (A) 로고가 제품에 잘못 인쇄되었다. (B) 운동회가 취소되었다. (C) 구매한 물건이 반품될 수 없다. (D) 공급업체가 기한을 맞출 수 없다.

3㎞ 캐나다식 발음 → 미국식 발음

Question 1 refers to the following conversation.

M: The speakers and microphones I ordered for our upcoming company field day will arrive this Thursday.

W: Thanks for doing that. But did you place an order for the T-shirts with our company logo?

M: Not yet. Actually, I contacted a clothing supplier yesterday. **But they have several orders right now, so they can't complete our request in time.** I will contact other suppliers this afternoon.

1번은 다음 대화에 관한 문제입니다.

남: 우리 회사의 다가오는 운동회를 위해 제가 주문한 스피커와 마이크가 이번 주 목요일에 도착할 거예요.

여: 주문해 주셔서 감사해요. 그런데 우리 회사의 로고가 있는 티셔츠들은 주문하셨나요?

남: 아직이요. 실은, 어제 한 의류 공급업체에 연락했어요. 하지만 그들은 지금 몇 건의 주문들이 있어서, 우리의 주문을 시간에 맞춰 완성할 수가 없대요. 오늘 오후에 다른 공급업체들에 연락해보려고요.

정답 (D)

해설 문제점을 묻는 문제입니다. 남자가 "But they[clothing supplier] have several orders right now, so they can't complete our request in time." 이라며 의류 공급업체에 지금 몇 건의 주문들이 있어서 주문을 시간에 맞춰 완성할 수가 없다고 하였습니다. 따라서 정답은 (D) A supplier cannot meet a deadline입니다.

어휘 upcoming[ʌ́pkʌmiŋ] 다가오는   field day 운동회   supplier[미 səpláiər, 영 səpláiə] 공급업체

질문과 보기를 먼저 읽은 후 음성을 들으며 정답을 선택하세요. 이후 음성을 다시 들으면서 빈칸을 채우세요.
(음성은 두 번 들려줍니다.)

01 What problem does the woman mention?

(A) An instrument was damaged.
(B) A refund policy has changed.
(C) A type of item is not in stock.
(D) A performance has been canceled.

02 What will happen on Thursday?

(A) A discount will be offered.
(B) A receipt will be provided.
(C) Some tickets will be sold.
(D) Some merchandise will arrive.

M: Excuse me. I'm looking for a new electric guitar. Do you have any here?
W: Yes, but only secondhand instruments. _____ any new electric guitars in stock.
M: Hmm . . . I'd prefer a new instrument. When do you expect to _____?
W: Our next delivery is Thursday. I'll post details about the _____ on our Web site once it's here, so you'll _____ in advance.
M: Thanks. That would be great.

03 What is the problem?

(A) An offer was refused.
(B) A document was left behind.
(C) A meeting was postponed.
(D) A client is dissatisfied.

04 What is mentioned about the contract?

(A) It needs to be copied.
(B) It was recently edited.
(C) It has to be mailed out.
(D) It will be signed today.

M1: Harriett, _____ _____ for the Bluejay Incorporated merger?
W: Oh, no! It's in my briefcase. And _____.
M2: Please go and get it, then. Our supervisor wants to see it before the management meeting in 30 minutes. Right, Craig?
M1: Yeah. And we also have to _____ the contract before that meeting.

정답·스크립트·해설 **p.65**

01 What is the main purpose of the call?

(A) To arrange an early arrival
(B) To request a room upgrade
(C) To reserve an outdoor activity
(D) To check on a booking

02 Why is the man visiting Interlaken?

(A) To tour a facility
(B) To ski with his family
(C) To go hiking
(D) To meet a friend

03 According to the woman, where can luggage be stored?

(A) By the dining hall
(B) Behind the front desk
(C) In the lobby
(D) Next to the stairs

04 What is the problem?

(A) Some equipment is not working.
(B) Some supplies are missing.
(C) A videoconference was delayed.
(D) A cable is not long enough.

05 What is mentioned about the man's laptop?

(A) It has a built-in camera.
(B) It has a small screen.
(C) It is out of power.
(D) It is an old model.

06 What does the man ask the woman to do?

(A) Give him a different model
(B) Find an instruction manual
(C) Set up an Internet connection
(D) Turn on a desktop computer

07 Why is the book signing being held?

(A) To advertise a sale
(B) To promote an expansion
(C) To celebrate an anniversary
(D) To increase novel sales

08 What does the woman say about Edward Swift?

(A) He will hand out free gifts.
(B) He is a local resident.
(C) He visited the store before.
(D) He wrote a book.

09 How can people sign up for the event?

(A) By sending an e-mail
(B) By calling a hot line
(C) By going to a Web site
(D) By speaking with a representative

10 How many items will most likely be purchased?

(A) 10
(B) 15
(C) 20
(D) 50

11 According to the woman, what is on sale?

(A) Gift cards
(B) Wrapping supplies
(C) Some plates
(D) Some cups

12 What problem does the woman mention?

(A) A product is sold out.
(B) A system is having errors.
(C) A service is unavailable.
(D) A staff member is on leave.

13 What is the man's problem?

(A) He lost a registration form.
(B) He is late for a conference call.
(C) He cannot go to a seminar.
(D) He finished a task late.

14 How will the woman correct a billing error?

(A) By revising an order
(B) By making a phone call
(C) By visiting a supplier
(D) By submitting a document

15 What does the man imply when he says, "An experienced accountant will be leading the event"?

(A) A colleague will also be going.
(B) A presentation will be well attended.
(C) A class will require a fee.
(D) A session will be informative.

16 Where most likely are the speakers?

(A) In a manufacturing facility
(B) In an appliance store
(C) In a service center
(D) In a company headquarters

17 Look at the graphic. Which location do the speakers work at?

(A) Sacramento
(B) San Diego
(C) Los Angeles
(D) Oakland

18 Why will the woman be busy in the afternoon?

(A) She will be giving an inspector a tour.
(B) She will be visiting a local branch.
(C) She will be leading a seminar.
(D) She will be working to meet a deadline.

정답·스크립트·해설 p.66

한 권으로 끝내는
해커스 토익 **700+**
LC+RC+VOCA

▲ MP3
바로 듣기

Course 1 특정 세부 사항 문제

토익 출제경향
최대 17문제까지 출제

Sarah, 어제 어디에 있었나요?

덴버로 출장을 가서 고객과 만났어요.

아... 지난주에 제게 말해줬었죠?

Q. 여자는 어제 무엇을 했는가?
A. 고객을 만났다.

여자가 어제 무엇을 했는지를 묻고 있습니다. 이처럼 PART 3에서는 특정 시간이나 장소, 화자가 아닌 특정 인물 등에 대한 내용을 묻는 문제가 출제됩니다.

핵심 POINT

1. 질문의 핵심어구를 미리 확인하여 무엇을 묻고 있는지를 정확히 파악해야 합니다.

2. 세 명의 대화인 경우, 남자들(men) 또는 여자들(women)과 같이 같은 성별을 가진 화자들에게 공통으로 해당되는 내용을 묻는 질문이 출제되기도 합니다.

3. 특정 시간, 장소, 인물에 대해 묻는 문제에서는 대화에서 언급된 시간, 장소, 인물이 그대로 오답 보기로 출제되기도 합니다.

4. 주로 다음과 같은 질문을 사용하여 특정 세부 사항을 묻습니다.

What **did the woman** do yesterday? 여자는 어제 무엇을 했는가?
Where **did the man** just return from? 남자는 어디에서 막 돌아왔는가?
Who **is** Mr. Carter? Mr. Carter는 누구인가?
What **will** class participants receive? 수업 참여자들은 무엇을 받을 것인가?

Example ∩ DAY13_01

1. What will class participants receive? (A) A discount (B) A membership card (C) An extra lesson (D) A free item	1. 수업 참여자들은 무엇을 받을 것인가? (A) 할인 (B) 회원권 (C) 추가 수업 (D) 무료 물품

🎙️ 호주식 발음 → 영국식 발음

Question 1 refers to the following conversation.

M: Welcome to Fieldstone Community Center. What can I do for you?
W: I'd like to take the beginner cooking class in June.
M: OK . . . The fee is $65. And **everyone who participates will receive a complimentary cookbook at the first class**.
W: Great. Here's my credit card.

1번은 다음 대화에 관한 문제입니다.

남: Fieldstone 시민 문화 회관에 오신 것을 환영합니다. 무엇을 도와드릴까요?
여: 저는 6월에 초급 요리 수업을 듣고 싶어요.
남: 알겠습니다... 수강료는 65달러입니다. 그리고 참여하시는 모든 분들은 첫 수업에서 무료 요리책을 받으실 거예요.
여: 좋네요. 여기 제 신용카드예요.

정답 (D)

해설 수업 참여자들이 받을 것을 묻는 문제입니다. 남자가 "everyone who participates will receive a complimentary cookbook at the first class"라며 참여하는 모든 사람들은 첫 수업에서 무료 요리책을 받을 것이라고 하였습니다. 따라서 정답은 (D) A free item입니다.

어휘 participate[미 pɑːrtísəpèit, 영 pɑːtísipèit] 참여하다 complimentary[미 kàːmpləméntəri, 영 kɔ̀mpliméntəri] 무료의

질문과 보기를 먼저 읽은 후 음성을 들으며 정답을 선택하세요. 이후 음성을 다시 들으면서 빈칸을 채우세요.
(음성은 두 번 들려줍니다.)

01   Who is Michaela Hernandez?

(A) A board member
(B) An investor
(C) An advertiser
(D) A branch manager

02   Where did the woman work last year?

(A) In Los Angeles
(B) In Boston
(C) In Portland
(D) In New York

W: I heard Mr. Jensen will retire next year. Do you know who is going to replace him?

M: Apparently, Michaela Hernandez will. She's been _____ the Los Angeles branch for three years. But I guess _____ to New York to be closer to her family in Boston.

W: Really? I met her _____ _____ last year. She visited our branch to give a presentation.

03   According to the man, what is made at the factory?

(A) Office equipment
(B) Sports gear
(C) Building materials
(D) Clothing

04   What do the women mention about the new supplier?

(A) It has helped increase production.
(B) It is displeased with a contract.
(C) It dropped off materials today.
(D) It has raised its prices.

W1: Bill and Margaret, could one of you give me a copy of our factory's production report?

M: Here you go. I noticed that the plant produced considerably _____ _____ this quarter. But I'm not sure why.

W1: Yes, that's because we contracted a _____.

W2: Exactly. The new one delivers materials more regularly and reliably. As a result, we've seen a 15 percent _____.

M: That's quite impressive.

W2: Yeah. Changing suppliers was the right decision.

정답·스크립트·해설 **p.70**

Course 2 다음에 할 일 문제

Tim, 사내 연락망을 업데이트했나요?

지금 바로 업데이트하겠습니다.

네, 서둘러 작업해 주세요.

Q. 남자는 다음에 무엇을 할 것 같은가?
A. 사내 연락망을 업데이트한다.

남자가 다음에 무엇을 할 것 같은지를 묻고 있습니다. 이처럼 PART 3에서는 화자가 다음에 할 일이나 다음에 일어날 일을 묻는 문제가 출제됩니다.

핵심 POINT

1. 정답의 단서는 대화의 마지막 부분이나, will/be going to 등의 미래 시제 또는 now, next, after, before 등의 미래를 나타내는 표현이 포함된 문장에서 자주 언급됩니다.

2. 주로 다음과 같은 질문을 사용하여 다음에 할 일이나 다음에 일어날 일을 묻습니다.

What **will the man most likely** do next? 남자는 다음에 무엇을 할 것 같은가?
What **will happen** next Friday? 다음 주 금요일에 무슨 일이 일어날 것인가?
What **does the man/woman** say he/she will do? 남자/여자는 다음에 무엇을 하겠다고 말하는가?

Example   ∩ DAY13_03

1. What will the man most likely do next?	1. 남자는 다음에 무엇을 할 것 같은가?
(A) Go to another department (B) Contact another employee (C) Reboot a computer (D) Write an e-mail	(A) 다른 부서로 간다. (B) 다른 직원에게 연락한다. (C) 컴퓨터를 재시작한다. (D) 이메일을 작성한다.

[3] 캐나다식 발음 → 미국식 발음

Question 1 refers to the following conversation.

M: My computer has been running slowly this week. It's really making it hard to get work done.
W: You should contact the IT department and ask for some assistance.
M: I think the IT staff are undergoing off-site training this week. Are some of the personnel available now?
W: Mr. Cowan is in the office, I believe. **Try calling him now.**

1번은 다음 대화에 관한 문제입니다.

남: 이번 주에 제 컴퓨터가 계속 느리게 작동하고 있어요. 그게 업무를 완료하는 것을 정말 어렵게 하고 있어요.
여: IT 부서에 연락해서 도움을 좀 청하는 게 좋겠어요.
남: IT 부서의 직원들은 이번 주에 사외 교육을 받는 것 같아요. 몇몇 직원들은 지금 시간이 괜찮은가요?
여: Mr. Cowan이 사무실에 있는 것 같아요. 그에게 지금 전화해 보세요.

정답 (B)

해설 남자가 다음에 할 일을 묻는 문제입니다. 여자가 남자에게 "Try calling him[Mr. Cowan] now."라며 IT 부서의 직원인 Mr. Cowan에게 지금 전화해 보라고 하였습니다. 따라서 정답은 (B) Contact another employee입니다.

어휘 assistance[əsístəns] 도움, 지원   undergo[미 ʌndərgóu, 영 ʌndəgə́u] 받다, 겪다   off-site[미 ɔ́ːfsàit, 영 ɔ́fsàit] (어느 특정한 장소에서) 떨어진 personnel[미 pə̀ːrsənél, 영 pə̀ːsənél] 직원, 인원

질문과 보기를 먼저 읽은 후 음성을 들으며 정답을 선택하세요. 이후 음성을 다시 들으면서 빈칸을 채우세요.
(음성은 두 번 들려줍니다.)

01 What problem does the man mention?

(A) A shipment did not arrive.
(B) A package was damaged.
(C) A customer representative was not available.
(D) A box was mailed to the wrong address.

02 What will the woman probably do next?

(A) Check a schedule
(B) Update an inventory list
(C) Explain a shipping fee
(D) Approve a delivery

W: Thank you for calling Nexus Electronics. How can I help you?
M: I ordered a laptop from you last Thursday. However, when it arrived at my house, _____ _____. Moreover, the keyboard was _____.
W: I'm sorry to hear that. I can mail you a replacement laptop for no extra charge. I'll _____ _____ right away.
M: Great. I'd appreciate that.

03 Who most likely is the man?

(A) A travel agent
(B) A tour guide
(C) An airline employee
(D) A security official

04 What does the man say he will do next?

(A) Make an announcement
(B) Check a system
(C) Print another ticket
(D) Post flight information

W: Hello. An announcement was made _____. What's the new _____?
M: Ah . . . You mean Flight 345 to Philadelphia?
W: Yes. I'm concerned because I have a meeting there at 1 P.M.
M: That flight's departure has been moved to noon because of engine problems. But maybe I can _____ you to another flight. Let me check our _____.

정답·스크립트·해설 p.71

01 Where most likely are the speakers?

(A) At a retail store
(B) At a bicycle factory
(C) At a corporate office
(D) At a trade show

02 Why does the man suggest a hybrid product?

(A) It is faster than other models.
(B) It is within the woman's budget.
(C) It is very durable.
(D) It is suited for short distances.

03 What will the man most likely do next?

(A) Test out a product
(B) Repair some equipment
(C) Enter a building
(D) Show some merchandise

04 What kind of event is the man preparing for?

(A) A company seminar
(B) An executive meeting
(C) A charity event
(D) An international conference

05 What problem does the man mention?

(A) A document is incomplete.
(B) A device is not working.
(C) A meeting was delayed.
(D) A staff member is absent.

06 What does the woman suggest?

(A) Ordering additional paper
(B) Calling the maintenance team
(C) Using different equipment
(D) Resetting the machine

07 What are the speakers mainly discussing?

(A) A staff training session
(B) A hiring process
(C) An accounting system
(D) An expense report

08 What is mentioned about the meeting?

(A) It will include a presentation.
(B) It will not be taking place.
(C) It will last for more than an hour.
(D) It will concern an employee review.

09 What does the woman say she will do?

(A) Print some notes
(B) Contact some meeting attendees
(C) Review a financial report
(D) Change a project deadline

10 What happened last Sunday?

(A) A restaurant was newly opened.
(B) An additional server was hired.
(C) New dishes became available.
(D) Opening hours were extended.

11 What have customers complained about?

(A) The quality of a service
(B) The number of options available
(C) The length of opening hours
(D) The price of some items

12 What will probably happen next?

(A) Food items will be sampled.
(B) Different beverages will be selected.
(C) Workers will receive information.
(D) A dinner banquet will be held.

13 What will the man attend?

(A) A client meeting
(B) A trade fair
(C) A museum exhibit
(D) A company retreat

14 What does the man mean when he says, "I'm not doing anything this afternoon"?

(A) He has not checked his schedule.
(B) He has taken the day off.
(C) He has time to work on a task.
(D) He canceled an appointment.

15 What will the man most likely do next?

(A) Pick up a car
(B) Contact a rental company
(C) Cancel a booking
(D) Look over some documents

Coupon Code: 472A

**Lyle Concert Hall
Discount Coupon**

$10 off one performance ticket
For use on orchestra seats only

Expires on March 10

16 What does the man want to do?

(A) Change a booking
(B) Buy a ticket
(C) Confirm a schedule
(D) Request a refund

17 What does the woman say about tomorrow's performance?

(A) It is sold out.
(B) It has been canceled.
(C) It features a dance.
(D) It was advertised online.

18 Look at the graphic. Why is the coupon rejected?

(A) It is for a different center.
(B) It can only be used for one ticket.
(C) It is for another seating section.
(D) It has already expired.

정답·스크립트·해설 **p.72**

한 권으로 끝내는
해커스 토익 700+
LC+RC+VOCA

▲ MP3
바로 듣기

Course 1 의도 파악 문제

토익 출제경향
2문제 출제

오늘 저녁 식사를 같이 할까요?

저는... 선약이 있어요.

그럼 내일 점심은 어때요?

Q. 여자가 **"선약이 있어요"**라고 말할 때 의도하는 것은 무엇인가?
A. **그녀는 제안을 수락할 수 없다.**

여자가 한 말의 의도를 묻고 있습니다. 이처럼 PART 3에서는 대화에서 언급된 특정 문장에 담긴 화자의 의도를 묻는 문제가 출제됩니다.

핵심 POINT

1. 대화를 듣기 전 질문에 언급된 화자와 인용어구가 무엇인지를 미리 확인하면, 대화를 들으며 정답의 단서를 쉽게 파악할 수 있습니다.

2. 인용어구 일부 단어의 일차적인 의미를 이용한 오답이나, 제시된 대화 상황과 다른 상황에서 정답이 될 법한 오답이 출제되기도 합니다.

3. 주로 다음과 같은 질문을 사용하여 언급된 말의 의도를 묻습니다.

What **does the woman** mean/imply **when she** says, "I have another appointment"?
여자가 "선약이 있어요"라고 말할 때 의도하는 것은 무엇인가?
Why **does the man** say, "My sister said it was worth a visit"?
남자는 왜 "제 여동생이 그곳은 방문할 가치가 있었다고 해서"라고 말하는가?

Example 🎧 DAY14_01

1. Why does the man say, "My sister said it was worth a visit"? (A) To recommend a family member (B) To accept an invitation (C) To volunteer for an event (D) To suggest a destination	1. 남자는 왜 "제 여동생이 그곳은 방문할 가치가 있었다고 해서"라고 말하는가? (A) 가족 구성원을 추천하기 위해 (B) 초대를 받아들이기 위해 (C) 행사에서 자원봉사를 하기 위해 (D) 행선지를 제안하기 위해

🎙️ 미국식 발음 → 캐나다식 발음 Question 1 refers to the following conversation. W: I've got two tickets for the Wolford Museum's exhibit on Ancient Egypt. Do you want to go on Saturday? M: My sister said it was worth a visit, so **I definitely want to go**. W: Oh, yes. I'd forgotten that Jenna saw it with your parents.	1번은 다음 대화에 관한 문제입니다. 여: 저는 Wolford 박물관의 고대 이집트 전시회 티켓이 두 장 있어요. 토요일에 가실래요? 남: 제 여동생이 그곳은 방문할 가치가 있었다고 해서, 저는 정말 가고 싶어요. 여: 아, 맞아요. 저는 Jenna가 당신의 부모님과 함께 전시회를 봤다는 걸 잊고 있었네요.

정답 (B)
해설 남자가 하는 말(My sister said it was worth a visit)의 의도를 묻는 문제입니다. 전시회에 가자고 제안하는 여자에게 남자가 "I definitely want to go"라며 정말 가고 싶다고 한 말을 통해 초대를 받아들이려는 의도임을 알 수 있습니다. 따라서 정답은 (B) To accept an invitation입니다.

질문과 보기를 먼저 읽은 후 음성을 들으며 정답을 선택하세요. 이후 음성을 다시 들으면서 빈칸을 채우세요.
(음성은 두 번 들려줍니다.)

01 What does the man imply when he says, "How about Gino's Diner in Little Italy"?

(A) He disagrees with a suggestion.
(B) He believes the woman is mistaken.
(C) He thinks a restaurant is closed.
(D) He cannot make a decision.

02 What does the woman suggest?

(A) Using a delivery app
(B) Ordering takeout
(C) Leaving work early
(D) Meeting at a café

W: Would you like to eat at the Indian buffet on 12th Street tonight? It's quite _____.

M: How about Gino's Diner in Little Italy? I'd _____. Plus, Gino's offers a three-course dinner special for $40 on Fridays.

W: All right. I get off work at 4 P.M. _____ next to Gino's first.

03 Why does the woman say, "There's a construction site nearby"?

(A) To provide the reason for a client request
(B) To point out a potential safety issue
(C) To indicate the location of a mall
(D) To suggest a task was not done properly

04 What will the woman most likely do next?

(A) Visit a window supplier
(B) Contact a department store
(C) Meet with a cleaning crew
(D) Confirm a job's completion

W: Jonathan, which worksite are you _____ today?

M: Belleview Department Store. I clean the windows there _____ Thursday of the month. Why?

W: Well . . . the manager at Sellers Mall just called. He asked me to send someone immediately. There's a construction site nearby, so the building's windows are really dusty.

M: Understood. But what about Belleview Department Store?

W: Don't worry about it. I'll _____ _____.

정답·스크립트·해설 **p.76**

PART 3

DAY 14 세부 사항 관련 문제 4

한 권으로 끝내는 해커스 토익 **700+** (LC+RC+VOCA)

Course 2 추론 문제

Kim, Min! 제품 기획안을 제출했나요?

저희는 오전 내내 회의가 있었어요.

얼른 마무리할게요.

Q. 기획안에 대해 무엇이 암시되는가?

A. 아직 제출되지 않았다.

기획안에 대해 무엇이 암시되는지를 묻고 있습니다. 이처럼 PART 3에서는 대화 내용을 통해 추론할 수 있는 것을 묻는 문제가 출제됩니다.

핵심 POINT

1. 세 명의 대화인 경우, 남자들(men) 또는 여자들(women)과 같이 같은 성별을 가진 화자들이 언급한 내용을 통해 추론할 수 있는 것을 묻는 질문이 출제되기도 합니다.

2. 정답의 단서는 질문의 suggest(suggested)/imply about 뒤에 나오는 핵심어구가 언급된 부분과 그 주변에서 주로 등장합니다.

3. 정답의 단서는 분산되어 나올 수 있으며, 주로 패러프레이징되어 정답으로 출제됩니다.

4. 주로 다음과 같은 질문을 사용하여 추론할 수 있는 내용을 묻습니다.

What **is** suggested **about the proposal?** 기획안에 대해 무엇이 암시되는가?
What **does the man** suggest **about the receipt?** 남자는 영수증에 대해 무엇을 암시하는가?
What **do the women** imply **about the new staff?** 여자들은 신규 직원들에 대해 무엇을 암시하는가?

Example ∩ DAY14_03

1. What do the women imply about the new staff? (A) They will deal with customers. (B) They have met with a supervisor. (C) They have already been trained. (D) They will only work part-time.	1. 여자들은 신규 직원들에 대해 무엇을 암시하는가? (A) 그들은 고객들을 상대할 것이다. (B) 그들은 관리자와 만난 적이 있다. (C) 그들은 이미 교육을 받았다. (D) 그들은 시간제로만 근무할 것이다.

🔊 미국식 발음 → 호주식 발음 → 영국식 발음

Question 1 refers to the following conversation with three speakers. W1: Harvey, I heard that the next hiring process will start in August. Is that right? M: Yes. We'll begin accepting applications at that time. Then, interviews will be held at the end of September. W1: OK. So, that means the new staff will start in October. **That's good to know since we've been getting a lot of calls from customers** recently. W2: I agree. **We really need some more people on our team to respond to their complaints and questions.**	1번은 다음 세 명의 대화에 관한 문제입니다. 여1: Harvey, 다음 채용 절차가 8월에 시작할 거라고 들었어요. 맞나요? 남: 네. 우리는 그때 지원서를 받기 시작할 거예요. 그러면, 9월 말에는 면접이 있을 거예요. 여1: 그렇군요. 그러면, 신규 직원들은 10월에 근무를 시작하게 되겠네요. 최근에 고객들로부터 많은 전화를 받고 있으니 그건 좋은 일이네요. 여2: 동의해요. 우리 팀에는 그들의 불만과 문의에 응대해줄 더 많은 사람이 꼭 필요해요.

정답 (A)

해설 여자들이 신규 직원들에 대해 암시하는 것을 묻는 문제입니다. 여자 1이 "That's good to know since we've been getting a lot of calls from customers"라며 고객들로부터 많은 전화를 받고 있으므로 신규 직원들이 10월에 근무를 시작하는 것은 좋은 일이라고 하자, 여자 2가 "We really need ~ to respond to their[customers] complaints and questions."라며 고객들의 불만과 문의에 응대해줄 더 많은 사람들이 꼭 필요하다며 동의하였습니다. 이를 통해 신규 직원들이 고객들을 상대할 것임을 알 수 있습니다. 따라서 정답은 (A) They will deal with customers입니다.

어휘 hiring process 채용 절차 application[미 æ̀pləkéiʃən, 영 æ̀plikéiʃən] 지원서, 신청서

질문과 보기를 먼저 읽은 후 음성을 들으며 정답을 선택하세요. 이후 음성을 다시 들으면서 빈칸을 채우세요.
(음성은 두 번 들려줍니다.)

01 Who most likely is the man?

(A) A cook
(B) A salesperson
(C) A server
(D) A designer

02 What does the man imply about the discount?

(A) It is not available on weekdays.
(B) It applies to desserts.
(C) It is only for large groups.
(D) It requires a coupon.

M: Welcome to Green's Restaurant.
_____ now?
W: Yes. Can you tell me _____
_____ today?
M: Certainly. We have the chef's recommended grilled fish. And we always offer a 25 percent discount on any beverage _____
_____.
W: I'll take the grilled fish to begin with, then, and just a _____ to drink.

03 What is implied about the menswear department?

(A) Its sales have increased.
(B) It needs additional staff training.
(C) It will hold a promotion.
(D) Its manager was recently hired.

04 What does the woman mention about the new clothing line?

(A) It was announced recently.
(B) It will become available next month.
(C) It consists of a variety of business outfits.
(D) It will include casual items.

W: What did you think of Bill's presentation this morning?
M: Oh, I didn't realize our menswear department _____
last quarter.
W: Yeah. The suits we introduced were _____ with our customers.
_____
even more when we launch our new clothing line this spring.
M: That's great. I'm assuming it will be _____ as well?
W: Actually, it's a _____
_____ . . . like summer shirts and shorts.

정답·스크립트·해설 **p.77**

01 Why does the woman say, "the service has always been perfect"?

(A) To explain a change
(B) To recommend a business
(C) To express surprise
(D) To show gratitude

02 According to the man, what will the woman receive?

(A) A full refund
(B) A warranty card
(C) A set of samples
(D) A discount code

03 What does the woman ask the man to do?

(A) Set an arrival date
(B) Send an additional item
(C) Change a delivery location
(D) Provide contact information

---

04 Where do the speakers most likely work?

(A) At a publishing company
(B) At an electronics retailer
(C) At a marketing firm
(D) At a camera manufacturer

05 What does the woman mean when she says "a lot of people are out of the office at the moment"?

(A) A video conference is a better option.
(B) A meeting should be scheduled later.
(C) A client's request cannot be granted.
(D) More customer opinions are needed.

06 What will the woman probably do next?

(A) Give a presentation
(B) Contact a colleague
(C) Take a survey
(D) Make a reservation

---

07 What problem does the woman mention?

(A) An applicant is unavailable.
(B) A printer is malfunctioning.
(C) An account is inaccessible.
(D) An order is on hold.

08 What does the woman ask the man to do?

(A) Forward some e-mails
(B) Attend an interview
(C) Print out some documents
(D) Contact an applicant

09 What does the man imply about the documents?

(A) They are brief.
(B) They contain errors.
(C) They have been revised.
(D) They are hard to understand.

---

10 Why did Mark call the technician last week?

(A) A power outage stopped production.
(B) A piece of equipment stopped functioning properly.
(C) Some routine maintenance was scheduled.
(D) Some factory machinery was installed incorrectly.

11 What does the woman imply when she says, "And tomorrow is a national holiday"?

(A) An order may be delayed.
(B) A celebration may be held.
(C) A repair may not be necessary.
(D) A delivery may not be made.

12 According to the woman, what might staff need to do?

(A) Work extra hours
(B) Conduct an inspection
(C) Use a different device
(D) Contact a technician

---

13 Where does this conversation most likely take place?

(A) At a home goods shop
(B) At a post office
(C) At a laundry facility
(D) At a clothing store

14 What is suggested about the business?

(A) It is closed on weekends.
(B) It stays open late on Fridays.
(C) It will hire a new worker.
(D) It has multiple branches.

15 What does the woman offer to do?

(A) Talk to her supervisor
(B) Deliver an order
(C) Demonstrate a product
(D) Contact a customer

16 Who is Benjamin Baxter?

(A) A professor
(B) An editor
(C) An executive
(D) An author

17 According to the man, what is the most important advice for business owners?

(A) Increasing advertising budgets
(B) Offering products at lower prices
(C) Conducting frequent customer surveys
(D) Focusing on improving products

18 What is suggested about social media campaigns?

(A) They attract fewer older customers.
(B) They are cheaper than other forms of advertising.
(C) They require more effort than television marketing.
(D) They do not make a company more memorable.

정답·스크립트·해설 p.78

세부 사항 관련 문제 5

Course 1 시각 자료 문제 1 (표 및 그래프)

> 토익 출제경향
> 최대 3문제까지 출제

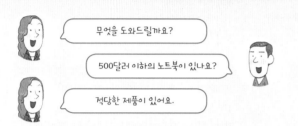

무엇을 도와드릴까요?

500달러 이하의 노트북이 있나요?

적당한 제품이 있어요.

모델명	XD101	XD201
금액	480달러	550달러

Q. 시각 자료를 보아라. 어떤 제품이 구매될 것 같은가?
A. XD101

어떤 제품이 구매될 것 같은지를 묻고 있습니다. 이처럼 PART 3에서는 대화 내용과 함께 표 및 그래프의 내용을 묻는 문제가 출제됩니다.

핵심 POINT

1. 대화를 듣기 전에 제시된 표나 그래프를 보고 무엇에 관한 내용인지를 미리 확인하면, 대화를 들으며 정답의 단서를 쉽게 파악할 수 있습니다.

2. 정답의 단서는 대화에서 변동 사항, 최고·최저 항목, 특정 수치 이상·이하 등의 특이 사항이 언급되는 부분에서 주로 등장합니다.

3. 주로 다음과 같은 질문을 사용하여 시각 자료와 관련된 내용을 묻습니다.

   Look at the graphic. What product will probably be purchased?
   시각 자료를 보아라. 어떤 제품이 구매될 것 같은가?
   Look at the graphic. When was a new product released?
   시각 자료를 보아라. 신제품은 언제 출시되었는가?
   Look at the graphic. Who will be the first presenter?
   시각 자료를 보아라. 누가 첫 번째 발표자가 될 것인가?
   Look at the graphic. Which product does the woman say she prefers?
   시각 자료를 보아라. 여자는 어떤 제품이 좋다고 말하는가?

4. 제품 가격표, 행사 일정표, 매출 그래프, 월별 고객 항의 건수 그래프 등의 시각 자료가 출제됩니다.

Item	Price
Recycled Copy Paper (1 box)	$45
Glossy Copy Paper (1 box)	$55
Plastic File Folders (1 box)	$60
Printer toner (1 cartridge)	$65

제품	가격
재생 복사 용지 (1 상자)	45달러
광택 복사 용지 (1 상자)	55달러
비닐 파일 폴디 (1 상지)	60달러
프린터 토너 (1 카트리지)	65달러

1. Look at the graphic. Which product does the woman say she prefers?

(A) Recycled Copy Paper
(B) Glossy Copy Paper
(C) Plastic File Folders
(D) Printer Toner

1. 시각 자료를 보아라. 여자는 어떤 제품이 좋다고 말하는가?

(A) 재생 복사 용지
(B) 광택 복사 용지
(C) 비닐 파일 폴더
(D) 프린터 토너

🔊 미국식 발음 → 호주식 발음

Question 1 refers to the following conversation and list.

W: Thank you for meeting with me today to sign our agreement, Mr. Dwyer.
M: I'm pleased to supply your firm with what you need.
W: We appreciate your high quality products. **I especially like this copy paper you provide, since it's under $50 a box.**

1번은 다음 대화와 표에 관한 문제입니다.

여: 우리의 계약을 체결하기 위해 오늘 저와 만나주셔서 감사합니다, Mr. Dwyer.
남: 귀사에 필요한 물건을 공급하게 되어 기쁩니다.
여: 저희는 당신 회사의 품질 좋은 제품들을 높이 평가해요. 저는 특히 당신의 회사가 제공하는 이 복사 용지가 좋은데, 상자당 50달러 이하이기 때문이에요.

정답 (A)

해설 여자가 좋다고 말한 제품을 묻는 문제입니다. 여자가 "I especially like this copy paper you provide, since it's under $50 a box."라며 상자당 50달러 이하인 복사 용지가 특히 좋다고 하였으므로, 여자가 좋다고 말하는 제품이 재생 복사 용지임을 표에서 알 수 있습니다. 따라서 정답은 (A) Recycled Copy Paper입니다.

어휘 sign an agreement 계약을 체결하다 supply[səplái] 공급하다 appreciate[미 əprí:ʃièit, 영 əprí:ʃièit] 높이 평가하다, 인정하다

시각 자료, 질문과 보기를 먼저 읽은 후 음성을 들으며 정답을 선택하세요. 이후 음성을 다시 들으면서 빈칸을 채우세요.
(음성은 두 번 들려줍니다.)

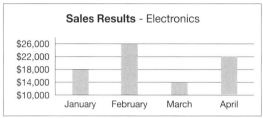

Sales Results - Electronics

01 What did the woman do this morning?

(A) Submitted a financial report
(B) Worked on a presentation
(C) Created a budget
(D) Reviewed a sales goal

02 Look at the graphic. Which month's sales results are inaccurate?

(A) January
(B) February
(C) March
(D) April

M: _____
    for Tuesday's sales strategy presentation?
W: Not yet. When I was working on them this morning, I realized that the monthly electronics sales figures are _____.
M: So, the graph you showed me this morning has an error?
W: That's right. _____,
    which is $14,000, is actually incorrect. I'm _____.

Name	Time	Specialty
Robert Como	10:00 A.M.-10:50 A.M.	Italian
Janet Durand	11:00 A.M.-11:50 A.M.	French
Lunch		
Susan Mori	1:00 P.M.-1:50 P.M.	Japanese
Daniel Chavez	2:00 P.M.–2:50 P.M.	Mexican

03 What are the speakers mainly discussing?

(A) Choosing a catering company
(B) Rescheduling a cooking class
(C) Finding a new employee
(D) Training an academy instructor

04 Look at the graphic. Who will the speakers meet at 2:00 P.M.?

(A) Robert Como
(B) Janet Durand
(C) Susan Mori
(D) Daniel Chavez

M: Hi, Janet. Are you ready for the _____ _____ tomorrow? We need to _____ for our cooking academy.
W: Yes. I was just looking over the applicants' résumés. We've got several qualified chefs to choose from.
M: That's true. Oh, before I forget . . . I need to revise the schedule. The applicant who specializes in Italian food will come in right after lunch. As a result, all the other afternoon appointments have been _____ _____.

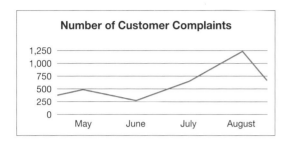

Number of Customer Complaints

	May	June	July	August
1,250				
1,000				
750				
500				
250				
0				

05 Look at the graphic. When was the last software update released?

(A) May
(B) June
(C) July
(D) August

06 What does the woman request the man do?

(A) Contact some customers
(B) Change a feature
(C) Review some feedback
(D) Send a report

Brady Furniture Office Chair Inventory

Item Number	Amount in Stock
A3349	12
E2128	8
R7550	13
V6200	10

07 Look at the graphic. Which item did the woman order?

(A) A3349
(B) E2128
(C) R7550
(D) V6200

08 What will happen next?

(A) A chair will be repaired.
(B) An announcement will be made.
(C) Staff will attend a presentation.
(D) Office supplies will be restocked.

W: Steven, there have been multiple _____ about our most recent smartphone model. It's a bit concerning.

M: Yeah. The problem is the last software update. The number of complaints has

_____ since its release. I'm reviewing this summary of the new software features to figure out which one might be causing the issues.

W: Hmm . . . I'd better help out to speed things up. Could you _____ a copy of that document?

M: _____.

M: Did you order the chairs for the new staff lounge?

W: I did, but the chairs we chose are almost _____. We need 10, but they don't have that many _____ _____ right now.

M: That's unfortunate. I guess we'll just have to wait for them to be restocked, right?

W: Well, they'll receive more chairs next Wednesday and deliver them on Thursday. So, we can finish _____ _____ on Friday as planned.

M: Great. Then can you notify the staff that the lounge will be open on Monday?

W: I'll make an announcement now.

정답·스크립트·해설 **p.82**

Course 2 시각 자료 문제 2 (약도 및 기타)

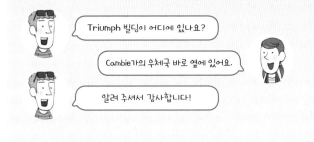

Triumph 빌딩이 어디에 있나요?

Cambie가의 우체국 바로 옆에 있어요.

알려 주셔서 감사합니다!

우체국	건물 A	건물 B
	Cambie가	

Q. 시각 자료를 보아라. Triumph 빌딩은 어느 것인가?

A. 건물 A

Triumph 빌딩이 어느 것인지를 묻고 있습니다. 이처럼 PART 3에서는 대화 내용과 함께 약도나 기타 시각 자료의 내용을 묻는 문제가 출제됩니다.

핵심 POINT

1. 대화를 듣기 전에 제시된 약도나 기타 시각 자료를 보고 무엇에 관한 내용인지를 미리 확인하면, 대화를 들으며 정답의 단서를 쉽게 파악할 수 있습니다.

2. 약도가 제시된 문제에서 정답의 단서는 between(~와 ‒의 사이에), next to(~ 옆에), opposite(~ 맞은편에), in front of(~ 앞에)와 같이 위치나 방향을 나타내는 표현과 함께 자주 등장합니다.

3. 주로 다음과 같은 질문을 사용하여 시각 자료와 관련된 내용을 묻습니다.

Look at the graphic. Which is the Triumph Building?
시각 자료를 보아라. Triumph 빌딩은 어느 것인가?

Look at the graphic. Where will the speakers most likely set up the stand?
시각 자료를 보아라. 화자들은 어디에 진열대를 설치할 것 같은가?

Look at the graphic. Where is the sign most likely located?
시각 자료를 보아라. 표지판은 어디에 위치해 있을 것 같은가?

Look at the graphic. What information is inaccurate?
시각 자료를 보아라. 어느 정보가 잘못되었는가?

4. 약도나 평면도, 메뉴, 영수증, 표지판 등의 다양한 시각 자료가 출제됩니다.

Dairy Products		Entrance
		Area D
Area A		Baked Goods
Area B	Snack Food	Area C

유제품		입구
		D 구역
A 구역		제과류
B 구역	스낵류	C 구역

1. Look at the graphic. Where will the speakers most likely set up the stand?

(A) In Area A
(B) In Area B
(C) In Area C
(D) In Area D

1. 시각 자료를 보아라. 화자들은 어디에 진열대를 설치할 것 같은가?

(A) A 구역에
(B) B 구역에
(C) C 구역에
(D) D 구역에

3ᵐ 영국식 발음 → 캐나다식 발음

Question 1 refers to the following conversation and map.

W: Charles, where should we put our Sunfresh Crackers samples?
M: How about next to the dairy section? There's already another promotion stand by the snack food. So we shouldn't set up there.
W: But that's a bit far from the entrance. **What about between the baked goods section and the entrance?** That way, customers will see the stand right after they come in.
M: **OK. Let's try that.**

1번은 다음 대화와 약도에 관한 문제입니다.

여: Charles, 우리는 Sunfresh Crackers사의 샘플들을 어디에 두어야 할까요?
남: 유제품 구역 옆이 어때요? 스낵류 옆에는 이미 다른 홍보 진열대가 있어요. 그래서 그곳에 설치할 수는 없어요.
여: 하지만 그곳은 입구에서 좀 멀잖아요. 제과류 구역과 입구 사이는 어떤가요? 그렇게 하면, 고객들이 들어오자마자 진열대를 보게 될 거예요.
남: 그래요. 그렇게 합시다.

정답 (D)

해설 화자들이 진열대를 설치할 위치를 묻는 문제입니다. 여자가 "What about between the baked goods section and the entrance?"라며 제과류 구역과 입구 사이가 어떤지를 묻자, 남자가 "OK. Let's try that."이라며 그렇게 하자고 하였으므로, 화자들이 제과류 구역과 입구 사이인 D 구역에 진열대를 설치할 것임을 약도에서 알 수 있습니다. 따라서 정답은 (D) In Area D입니다.

어휘 dairy[미 déəri, 영 déəri] 유제품   section[sékʃən] (백화점 등의) 구역, 매장   promotion[미 prəmóuʃən, 영 prəmə́uʃən] 홍보, 판촉   stand[stænd] 진열대   set up ~을 설치하다   entrance[éntrəns] 입구

시각 자료, 질문과 보기를 먼저 읽은 후 음성을 들으며 정답을 선택하세요. 이후 음성을 다시 들으면서 빈칸을 채우세요.
(음성은 두 번 들려줍니다.)

MENU

1 Black Bean Soup	$7.99
2 Buffalo Chicken Sandwich	$9.25
3 Chips and Guacamole	$8.99
4 Steak Tacos	$9.99

01 Look at the graphic. Which menu item is sold out?

(A) Item 1
(B) Item 2
(C) Item 3
(D) Item 4

02 What does the woman offer to do?

(A) Provide a free item
(B) Update a dessert menu
(C) Get a to-go container
(D) Reduce the price of a meal

W: Pardon me. There's an issue with your order. Unfortunately, we're out of black bean soup. Is there something else _____?
M: That's a shame. I really want to order _____. Hmm . . . I guess I'll try your other vegetarian dish.
W: I'll put the order in right away. Do you want something else while you wait? I can _____
—free of charge, of course.
M: OK. Thanks.

Exchange Slip

Product Name	Purchase Date	Return Code

<Return Codes>
01 – Wrong size   02 – Wrong color
03 – Damaged item   04 – Incorrect item

03 What did the woman do last week?

(A) Returned an item
(B) Made an online purchase
(C) Printed out a form
(D) Tried on some clothes

04 Look at the graphic. Which return code should the woman use?

(A) 01
(B) 02
(C) 03
(D) 04

W: Hello. I'd like to _____ a wool sweater I purchased from your online store last week.
M: Certainly. What seems to be the _____? Is it the wrong size?
W: No, that's not it. There is a _____ _____ in the left sleeve.
M: We'd be happy to _____ _____. Just mail it back to us with a completed exchange slip in the next two weeks. You can download the form from our Web site.

Fresno Furniture	
Receipt #: 847573	Date of purchase: June 14
Item	**Price**
Coffee table	$150
Standing lamp	$50
Table lamp	$30
Book shelf	$300

05 What problem does the woman mention?

(A) Some merchandise was broken.
(B) A payment was declined.
(C) A mistake cannot be determined.
(D) Some items cannot be returned.

06 Look at the graphic. Which amount will the woman adjust?

(A) $150
(B) $50
(C) $30
(D) $300

Air Conditioner Cleaning - June 3	
1st Floor	9:00 A.M. – 11:00 A.M.
2nd Floor	11:00 A.M. – 1:00 P.M.
3rd Floor	1:00 P.M. – 3:00 P.M.
4th Floor	3:00 P.M. – 5:00 P.M.

07 Look at the graphic. On what floor will the man's meeting take place?

(A) On the 1st floor
(B) On the 2nd floor
(C) On the 3rd floor
(D) On the 4th floor

08 What does the woman suggest the man do?

(A) Call a manager
(B) Attend a presentation
(C) Reschedule a meeting
(D) Speak with some clients

W: Oh, Josh, can you look at this electronic receipt? A customer just e-mailed it to me saying that _____. But I can't _____ the exact problem.

M: Sure. Well, our tables were on sale when the customer made this purchase. It looks like _____.

W: Ah . . . you're right. We charged full price for everything. So, I just need to _____ for this one item.

M: Did you _____ in the break room?

W: Yeah. I heard that while the filters are being cleaned, the air conditioning will need to be shut off.

M: That's going to be a problem. I'm meeting with an important client at 1 P.M. He'll be uncomfortable if the _____ during our meeting.

W: Right . . . I can see why that's an issue. Um, why don't you _____ of maintenance? He might change the schedule.

정답·스크립트·해설 p.84

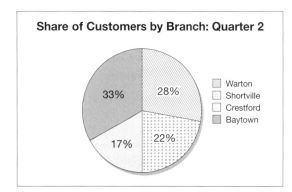

Share of Customers by Branch: Quarter 2

- Warton 28%
- Shortville 22%
- Crestford 17%
- Baytown 33%

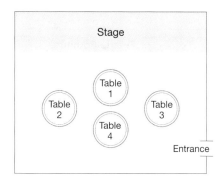

01 What does the man say about the meeting?

(A) It was attended by executives.
(B) It required sound equipment.
(C) It has been rescheduled.
(D) It happened over videoconference.

02 What did the company recently do?

(A) Booked a local venue
(B) Held a promotional event
(C) Hired a sales manager
(D) Launched a product line

03 Look at the graphic. Which branch opened in January?

(A) Warton
(B) Shortville
(C) Crestford
(D) Baytown

04 Look at the graphic. Where is the man's seat?

(A) At Table 1
(B) At Table 2
(C) At Table 3
(D) At Table 4

05 What does the man say he needs to do?

(A) Meet a colleague
(B) Make a call
(C) Present an award
(D) Create a chart

06 What is available in the lobby?

(A) A phone charger
(B) A parking permit
(C) A directory
(D) A schedule

To	Edward Coyle
From	Patricia Wilkins
Subject	Electronics Trade Show

Company Name: Coretek Incorporated
Payment Date: May 2
Reservation Date: May 11
Booth Number: 117

Bike Lane Closed

Road Construction Ahead

07 What is the purpose of the call?

(A) To encourage participation in an event
(B) To promote an upcoming exhibition
(C) To confirm receipt of payment
(D) To request some feedback

08 Look at the graphic. Which information was changed?

(A) Coretek Incorporated
(B) May 2
(C) May 11
(D) 117

09 What does the man ask about?

(A) An extra charge
(B) A start time
(C) A contact number
(D) A manager's name

10 Why was the man late?

(A) He took an alternative route.
(B) A train broke down.
(C) A meeting was delayed.
(D) He was stuck in traffic.

11 Look at the graphic. Where is the sign most likely located?

(A) On Rye Street
(B) On Granger Road
(C) On Morrison Avenue
(D) On Carter Way

12 What will the speakers probably do next?

(A) Lock up a bicycle
(B) Return a purchase
(C) Review a city map
(D) Enter a dining establishment

정답·스크립트·해설 **p.86**

PART 4

PART 4는 71번부터 100번까지 총 30문제(10지문)로, 짧은 담화를 듣고 제시된 질문과 시각 자료에 가장 적절한 답을 선택하는 유형입니다.

Course 1 주제 및 목적 문제

토익 출제경향
평균 2~3문제 정도 출제

여러분께 회사의 창립 기념일 저녁 만찬에 대한 정보를 알려드리고자 합니다. 우리는 Vancity 호텔에서 행사를 열 것을 고려하고 있습니다...

Q. 담화는 주로 무엇에 대한 것인가?
A. 행사 계획

담화가 주로 무엇에 대한 것인지를 묻고 있습니다. 이처럼 PART 4에서는 지문의 주제나 목적을 묻는 문제가 출제됩니다.

핵심 POINT

1. 지문의 주제나 목적을 나타내는 핵심어구는 주로 지문의 초반에 언급됩니다.

2. 지문의 후반에 언급된 명사를 직접 사용하여 혼란을 주는 보기가 오답으로 출제되기도 합니다.

3. 주로 다음과 같은 질문을 사용하여 지문의 주제나 목적을 묻습니다.

주제　What is the talk mainly about? 담화는 주로 무엇에 대한 것인가?
　　　What is the speaker mainly discussing? 화자는 주로 무엇에 대해 이야기하고 있는가?
　　　What is being advertised? 무엇이 광고되고 있는가?

목적　What is the purpose of the talk? 담화의 목적은 무엇인가?
　　　Why is the speaker calling? 화자는 왜 전화를 하고 있는가?

Example 🎧 DAY16_01

1. What is the talk mainly about? (A) A client request (B) A job opening (C) A financial expert (D) A sales report	1. 담화는 주로 무엇에 대한 것인가? (A) 고객 요청 (B) 채용 공고 (C) 재무 전문가 (D) 매출 보고서

🎧 미국식 발음

Question 1 refers to the following talk.

Good morning, everyone. **I want to briefly introduce Simon Hendrie. Mr. Hendrie is a tax consultant** who has been hired to manage this year's business taxes. Over the next two weeks, he will be calculating our revenues and expenses. So, Mr. Hendrie may ask for expense reports and, um, and other financial documents from some of you. Please make him feel welcome.

1번은 다음 담화에 관한 문제입니다.

안녕하세요, 여러분. 저는 Simon Hendrie를 짧게 소개해 드리고자 합니다. Mr. Hendrie는 올해의 영업세를 관리하기 위해 고용된 세금 컨설턴트입니다. 앞으로 2주 동안, 그는 우리의 수익과 지출을 결산할 것입니다. 그래서, Mr. Hendrie가 여러분 중 몇몇 분들로부터 지출 결의서와, 음, 다른 회계 자료들을 요청할 수도 있습니다. 그를 환영해 주시기 바랍니다.

정답 (C)

해설 담화의 주제를 묻는 문제입니다. "I want to briefly introduce Simon Hendrie, Mr. Hendrie is a tax consultant"라며 Simon Hendrie를 짧게 소개하겠다고 한 뒤, 세금 컨설턴트인 Mr. Hendrie를 소개하는 내용이 이어지고 있습니다. 따라서 정답은 (C) A financial expert입니다.

어휘 briefly [brí:fli] 짧게, 간단히　introduce [미 ìntrədjú:s, 영 ìntrədʒú:s] 소개하다　calculate [미 kǽlkjulèit, 영 kǽlkjəlèit] 결산하다, 계산하다
revenue [미 révənjù:, 영 révənjù:] 수익　expense [ikspéns] 지출

질문과 보기를 먼저 읽은 후 음성을 들으며 정답을 선택하세요. 이후 음성을 다시 들으면서 빈칸을 채우세요.
(음성은 두 번 들려줍니다.)

01 What is the speaker mainly discussing?

(A) An overtime policy
(B) A payment delay
(C) A schedule change
(D) An employee orientation

02 Why should listeners e-mail Minjoo?

(A) To request another shift
(B) To confirm their attendance
(C) To make further inquiries
(D) To share project details

Attention, everyone. _____
_____ is going to be changed
next month. Currently, _____
_____ for working more than
50 hours in one week. However, the number
of hours needed for overtime pay will be
lowered to 45 hours per week. If you have

_____,
please send an e-mail to Minjoo in the
human resources department. OK, you
may return to work.

03 What is the purpose of the message?

(A) To verify a meeting schedule
(B) To request a coworker's assistance
(C) To change a presentation topic
(D) To check a project's status

04 What does the speaker say about the sales conference?

(A) It was organized by the board.
(B) It was very successful.
(C) It will be held in another town.
(D) It finishes tomorrow.

Alison, this is Henry. I'm calling to
_____. Um . . . can
you _____ to the
board of directors this afternoon on our
project's status? Unfortunately, I'm away
at a sales conference today. It doesn't
_____, so I will not
be able to make it to the meeting myself.
Please call me back as soon as possible
to let me know _____.
Thanks!

정답·스크립트·해설 **p.90**

PART 4

DAY 16 전체 지문 관련 문제

한 권으로 끝내는 해커스 토익 **700+** (LC+RC+VOCA)

Course 2 화자·청자 및 장소 문제

아침 교통 정보입니다. 어젯밤 경기 지방에 내린 폭우로 인해 발생한 홍수가 3번 고속도로의 통행을 막고 있어, 현재 정체가 발생하고 있습니다...

Q. 화자는 누구인 것 같은가?
A. 라디오 뉴스 리포터

화자가 누구인 것 같은지를 묻고 있습니다. 이처럼 PART 4에서는 화자나 청자, 지문을 들을 수 있는 장소를 묻는 문제가 출제됩니다.

핵심 POINT

1. 화자·청자의 신분이나 직업, 지문을 들을 수 있는 장소와 관련된 내용은 주로 지문의 초반에 언급됩니다.

2. 화자의 신분이나 직업은 I am(저는 ~입니다)이나 As(~로서)와 같은 표현 다음에 자주 언급되고, 청자의 신분이나 직업은 Attention(주목해 주십시오)과 같은 표현 다음에 자주 언급됩니다.

3. 장소와 관련된 단서는 Welcome to(~에 오신 것을 환영합니다), Thank you for coming to(~에 와주셔서 감사합니다), Here at(이곳 ~에서)과 같은 표현 다음에 자주 언급됩니다.

4. 주로 다음과 같은 질문을 사용하여 지문의 화자·청자나 지문을 들을 수 있는 장소를 묻습니다.

화자·청자	Who **most likely is** the speaker/the listener? 화자/청자는 누구인 것 같은가?
	Where **does** the speaker **probably** work? 화자는 어디에서 일하는 것 같은가?
장소	Where **is the announcement** being made? 공지는 어디에서 이루어지고 있는가?
	Where **most likely are** the listeners? 청자들은 어디에 있는 것 같은가?

Example 🎧 DAY16_03

1. Who most likely is the speaker?	1. 화자는 누구인 것 같은가?
(A) A ticket agent	(A) 승차권 판매원
(B) A train conductor	(B) 철도 기관사
(C) A restaurant employee	(C) 음식점 점원
(D) A flight attendant	(D) 비행기 승무원

🎤) 캐나다식 발음

Question 1 refers to the following announcement.	1번은 다음 공지에 관한 문제입니다.
Welcome aboard the Trans America Great Lakes Train. I'm your conductor, Gerard Hopkins, and I'll be taking you from Chicago to New York. Our total travel time will be 21 hours, with 30-minute stops every 300 miles. You may exit the train at stations along the way, but please return before we depart. As a reminder, our dining car will be open throughout the trip. Thank you, and enjoy your journey.	Trans America Great Lakes 기차에 탑승하신 것을 환영합니다. 저는 여러분의 기관사인 Gerard Hopkins이고, 시카고에서 뉴욕으로 여러분을 모실 것입니다. 우리의 총 이동 시간은 21시간이 될 것이며, 300마일마다 30분간의 정차가 있습니다. 정차 중에 열차에서 내리셔도 되지만, 출발하기 전에 돌아오시기 바랍니다. 다시 한번 말씀드리자면, 식당칸은 이동 내내 열려 있을 것입니다. 감사합니다, 즐거운 여행 되십시오.

정답 (B)

해설 화자의 신분을 묻는 문제입니다. "Welcome aboard the Trans America Great Lakes Train. I'm your conductor, Gerard Hopkins"라며 Trans America Great Lakes 기차에 탑승한 것을 환영한다고 한 뒤, 자신을 기관사인 Gerard Hopkins라고 소개하였습니다. 따라서 정답은 (B) A train conductor입니다.

어휘 aboard [미 əbɔ́ːrd, 영 əbɔ́ːd] 탑승하여, 승선하여   conductor [미 kəndʌ́ktər, 영 kəndʌ́ktə] 기관사   dining car (기차의) 식당칸

질문과 보기를 먼저 읽은 후 음성을 들으며 정답을 선택하세요. 이후 음성을 다시 들으면서 빈칸을 채우세요.
(음성은 두 번 들려줍니다.)

01 Who is the announcement intended for?

(A) Bookstore customers
(B) Publishing firm staff
(C) Science fiction authors
(D) Conference attendees

02 What will take place this weekend?

(A) A store renovation
(B) A book signing event
(C) A writing workshop
(D) A promotional offer

> Attention all London Books _____!
> We're currently having a huge sale on
> _____. All books in
> this genre _____
> 25 percent. This is the perfect opportunity
> to add to your collection. We're also
> _____ on recipe
> books this weekend. If you buy two
> cookbooks, one will be _____.
> Be sure to take advantage of this great offer
> while it's available!

03 Where most likely are the listeners?

(A) At a high school
(B) At a sports complex
(C) At an art museum
(D) At a daycare center

04 Why does the speaker say, "Many of our graduates are accepted into top universities"?

(A) To justify a program's length
(B) To encourage greater diligence
(C) To explain an option
(D) To highlight an institution's reputation

> Thank you for visiting Bridgeport Academy.
> Today, I'll discuss some of the reasons to
> _____.
> First of all, _____ is
> well known for its _____.
> Many of our graduates are accepted into
> top universities. In addition, we offer
> various sports and arts programs. We are
> particularly proud of our basketball team,
> which _____
> in the tournament last week. Now, let me
> show you around our facilities.

정답·스크립트·해설 **p.91**

01 What is the purpose of the talk?

(A) To thank a business partner
(B) To introduce a new employee
(C) To announce a project
(D) To ask for advice from staff

02 What is mentioned about Mr. Schiller?

(A) He has founded a magazine.
(B) He is a professional photographer.
(C) He used to work for the company.
(D) He will manage a team.

03 What are listeners asked to do?

(A) Create some new images
(B) Make the new worker feel welcome
(C) Share some of their opinions
(D) Hold another meeting

04 Who most likely are the listeners?

(A) Accountants
(B) University lecturers
(C) Conference organizers
(D) Lawyers

05 According to the speaker, what has been set up?

(A) Company booths
(B) Display posters
(C) Safety equipment
(D) Additional seating

06 What does the speaker suggest?

(A) Listening to a special lecture
(B) Updating a schedule
(C) Registering for an event
(D) Getting a program

07 Where is this announcement most likely being made?

(A) At a bakery
(B) At a restaurant
(C) At a catering company
(D) At a grocery store

08 What is the purpose of the announcement?

(A) To describe lost property
(B) To advertise a sales event
(C) To introduce a new item
(D) To explain a company policy

09 According to the speaker, what will happen on Friday?

(A) A product will be launched.
(B) An announcement will be made.
(C) A store will close early.
(D) A promotion will conclude.

10 Where does the speaker most likely work?

(A) At an advertising firm
(B) At a service center
(C) At a financial company
(D) At an electronics retailer

11 What is mentioned about a payment?

(A) It has not been received.
(B) It was made on a Web site.
(C) It cannot be fully refunded.
(D) It was sent last Friday.

12 What is the speaker curious about?

(A) Why some devices are not working
(B) When a shipment will arrive
(C) Whether a purchase will be made
(D) Who will receive a delivery

13 What is the speaker mainly discussing?

(A) A leave system
(B) A refund process
(C) A training program
(D) A safety procedure

14 What does the speaker emphasize?

(A) An item must be from the store.
(B) An employee's signature is needed.
(C) All purchases should have been recent.
(D) Some merchandise is only available online.

15 Why does the speaker say, "At least one floor manager will always be on duty"?

(A) To introduce a new policy
(B) To update some information
(C) To provide reassurance
(D) To proceed to the next step

Room 201	Conference Room	Room 202
Room 203	Elevator	Room 204	Staff Lounge

16 Who most likely are the listeners?

(A) Technicians
(B) Marketing assistants
(C) Receptionists
(D) Sales representatives

17 Why will the new employees start later than planned?

(A) A work area is too small.
(B) A project has been delayed.
(C) An office is under construction.
(D) A team has been reassigned.

18 Look at the graphic. Which room will be occupied by the marketing team?

(A) Room 201
(B) Room 202
(C) Room 203
(D) Room 204

정답·스크립트·해설 **p.92**

세부 사항 관련 문제 1

한 권으로 끝내는
해커스 토익 700+
LC+RC+VOCA

▲ MP3
바로 듣기

Course 1 요청 · 제안 · 언급 문제

토익 출제경향
평균 3문제 정도 출제

안녕하세요, Mr. Brian. 새 전화기에 대한 주문서를 받았는데, 어떤 색상인지가 빠져 있네요. 구매하시려는 제품의 색상을 알려 주시기 바랍니다...

Q. 화자는 무엇을 요청하는가?
A. 제품의 색상

화자가 무엇을 요청하는지를 묻고 있습니다. 이처럼 PART 4에서는 청자에게 요청 또는 제안한 내용과 언급한 내용을 묻는 문제가 출제됩니다.

핵심 POINT

1. 요청이나 제안하는 내용은 Please로 시작하는 명령문이나, Why don't you, must, should, ask와 같은 표현 다음에 자주 언급됩니다.

2. 언급 문제에서 정답의 단서는, 질문의 say/mention about 뒤에 나오는 핵심어구가 언급된 부분과 그 주변에서 주로 등장합니다.

3. 주로 다음과 같은 질문을 사용하여 요청 · 제안 · 언급한 내용을 묻습니다.

요청　What does the speaker request? 화자는 무엇을 요청하는가?
　　　What does the speaker ask the listener to do? 화자는 청자에게 무엇을 해달라고 요청하는가?

제안　What does the speaker suggest? 화자는 무엇을 제안하는가?

언급　What does the speaker say about the sale? 화자는 할인 판매에 대해 무엇을 말하는가?
　　　What does the speaker mention about the orientation? 화자는 오리엔테이션에 대해 무엇을 언급하는가?
　　　What is mentioned about the clients? 고객들에 대해 무엇이 언급되는가?

Example ∩ DAY17_01

1. What does the speaker say about the sale? (A) It will begin in December. (B) It is available online. (C) It will last for a month. (D) It is only for members.	1. 화자는 할인 판매에 대해 무엇을 말하는가? (A) 12월에 시작할 것이다. (B) 온라인으로 이용할 수 있다. (C) 한 달 동안 지속될 것이다. (D) 회원들만을 위한 것이다.
영국식 발음 Question 1 refers to the following advertisement. Don't let winter keep you from being active. Come to Adrenaline Sports Warehouse today! **Throughout the month of November, we are holding a special sale** on winter sports equipment and clothing. Whether you are looking for snowboards, ice skates, or simply warm winter jackets, we have what you need. So be sure to visit us soon. You won't regret it!	1번은 다음 광고에 관한 문제입니다. 겨울이 여러분을 활동적이지 못하게 하도록 두지 마세요. 오늘 Adrenaline 스포츠용품 도매점으로 오세요! 11월 한 달 내내, 저희는 겨울 스포츠용품과 의류에 대해 특별 할인 판매를 하고 있습니다. 여러분이 스노보드, 아이스 스케이트, 혹은 그저 따뜻한 겨울 재킷을 찾고 있든 간에, 저희는 여러분에게 필요한 것을 가지고 있습니다. 그러니 어서 저희를 방문하세요. 후회하지 않으실 것입니다!

정답 (C)

해설 화자가 할인 판매에 대해 언급하는 것을 묻는 문제입니다. "Throughout the month of November, we are holding a special sale"이라며 11월 한 달 내내 특별 할인 판매를 하고 있다고 하였습니다. 따라서 정답은 (C) It will last for a month입니다.

어휘 active[æktiv] 활동적인, 적극적인　warehouse[미 wérhaus, 영 wéəhaus] 도매점, 큰 상점　regret[rigrét] 후회하다

질문과 보기를 먼저 읽은 후 음성을 들으며 정답을 선택하세요. 이후 음성을 다시 들으면서 빈칸을 채우세요.
(음성은 두 번 들려줍니다.)

01 What does the speaker say about the apartment building?

(A) It will be demolished on September 10.
(B) Its outside walls will be painted.
(C) Its parking area will be expanded.
(D) It limits access for delivery vehicles.

02 What does the speaker ask the listeners to do?

(A) Enter through a side entrance
(B) Park in a certain area
(C) Stop by a management office
(D) Check a schedule for updates

Thank you for coming to this meeting. I want to provide an update on the _____ _____ to the apartment building since _____ _____. All that's left to do is _____ _____. This will happen on September 10. On that day, do not leave your vehicle along the side of the building. Paint might fall on your car. Please make use of the _____ _____.

03 What does the speaker mention about Pine Forest Park?

(A) It is very crowded.
(B) It has steep trails.
(C) It has a large lake.
(D) It is hard to reach.

04 What does the speaker offer to do?

(A) Postpone a departure
(B) Pass out drinks
(C) Take photographs
(D) Find another route

May I please have everyone's attention? We'll reach Pine Forest Park very shortly. Many of the trails in the park are _____ _____, so please be careful during the hike. I also recommend _____ _____ for protection against the sun. Oh . . . and halfway through our hike, we'll rest at a natural spring, where you can _____. If you did not bring a camera, I'll gladly _____.

정답·스크립트·해설 **p.95**

PART 4

DAY 17 세부 사항 관련 문제 1

한 권으로 끝내는 해커스 토익 **700+** (LC+RC+VOCA)

Course 2 이유 · 방법 · 정도 문제

Louis 식당에서 신메뉴를 출시했습니다. 무료 시식을 원하는 분들은 저희의 웹사이트 Louisisbest.com으로 접속하셔서 신청할 수 있습니다...

Q. 일부 청자들은 왜 웹사이트를 방문할 것인가?
A. 무료 시식을 신청하기 위해

청자들이 왜 웹사이트를 방문할 것인지를 묻고 있습니다. 이처럼 PART 4에서는 **특정 상황과 관련된 이유, 방법, 정도를 묻는 문제**가 출제됩니다.

핵심 POINT

1. 이유를 나타내는 내용은 due to(~ 때문에), because(~ 때문에), since(~이므로), so(따라서) 주변이나 to 부정사구에서 자주 언급됩니다.

2. 추가 정보를 얻는 방법을 묻는 문제에서 정답의 단서는 주로 지문의 후반에서 언급됩니다.

3. 기간, 빈도, 수량 등을 묻는 정도 문제에서는 지문에서 언급된 여러 수치가 오답 보기로 자주 등장합니다.

4. 주로 다음과 같은 질문을 사용하여 이유나 방법, 또는 정도와 관련된 내용을 묻습니다.

   이유   Why should some listeners visit the Web site? 일부 청자들은 왜 웹사이트를 방문할 것인가?

   방법   How can listeners cast a vote? 청자들은 어떻게 투표할 수 있는가?

   정도   How many people will attend the party? 얼마나 많은 사람들이 파티에 참석할 것인가?

Example 🎧 DAY17_03

1. How can listeners cast a vote? (A) By filling out a paper form (B) By raising their hands (C) By using a computer (D) By placing a phone call	1. 청자들은 어떻게 투표할 수 있는가? (A) 서면 양식을 작성함으로써 (B) 손을 들어 올림으로써 (C) 컴퓨터를 사용함으로써 (D) 전화를 함으로써

🎙 호주식 발음

Question 1 refers to the following speech. Thank you for attending this shareholders' meeting for Benton Automotive. I look forward to discussing our accomplishments from the first quarter of the year. But before we start, I'd like to remind you that a vote to select the next CFO will be held today. Uh, **you can cast an electronic ballot before leaving on any of the computers set up near the back doors**. Now, let's start the meeting.	1번은 다음 연설에 관한 문제입니다. Benton 자동차 회사의 이번 주주 회의에 참석해 주신 여러분께 감사드립니다. 저는 올해 일사분기부터의 우리의 성과에 대해 이야기하는 것을 고대하고 있습니다. 하지만 시작하기 전에, 다음 최고 재무 책임자를 선출하기 위한 투표가 오늘 열릴 것임을 여러분께 상기시켜드리고 싶습니다. 어, 여러분께서는 나가시기 전에 뒷문 옆에 설치된 컴퓨터들 중 어느 것에서든 전자 투표를 하실 수 있습니다. 이제, 회의를 시작합시다.

정답 (C)

해설 청자들이 투표를 할 수 있는 방법을 묻는 문제입니다. "you can cast an electronic ballot ~ on any of the computers set up near the back doors"라며 뒷문 옆에 설치된 컴퓨터들 중 어느 것에서든 전자 투표를 할 수 있다고 하였습니다. 따라서 정답은 (C) By using a computer입니다.

어휘 shareholder[미 ʃéərhòuldər, 영 ʃéəhəuldə] 주주 accomplishment[미 əkámpliʃmənt, 영 əkʌ́mpliʃmənt] 성과, 업적 CFO 최고 재무 책임자
cast a ballot 투표하다

질문과 보기를 먼저 읽은 후 음성을 들으며 정답을 선택하세요. 이후 음성을 다시 들으면서 빈칸을 채우세요.
(음성은 두 번 들려줍니다.)

01 Why did the speaker change his plans?

(A) To extend a personal vacation
(B) To fulfill a client's request
(C) To make time for a presentation
(D) To avoid missing a conference call

02 What does the speaker mean when he says, "there's no need to reschedule"?

(A) Another person will replace him.
(B) The presentation will be canceled.
(C) A meeting is unimportant.
(D) An event can start late.

Albert, it's Vincent Shell calling. There has been an unexpected change to my plans. Our client _____ in France for two extra days for _____ _____. Consequently, I'll miss our three o'clock presentation on Thursday. I'm _____. However, there's no need to reschedule. I'm sure one of our other team members _____ for me. I've already e-mailed you the slideshow that I created for the presentation. Thank you.

03 How can diners place orders?

(A) By talking to a robot
(B) By sending a text message
(C) By using a mobile application
(D) By calling a phone number

04 How long is the average customer wait time?

(A) 5 minutes
(B) 10 minutes
(C) 20 minutes
(D) 30 minutes

This is Carol Ward. I'm here at one of Detroit's most unique dining establishments, Fig Leaf. Here, customers _____ with a _____ right from their table. Then, a robot delivers their food from the kitchen! Owner David Maggio says this unusual style of service has many benefits. In addition to reducing the average customer wait time to _____, it also has resulted in 30 percent fewer mistakes with orders.

정답·스크립트·해설 **p.96**

01 Where is the announcement being made?

(A) At a sports stadium
(B) At a concert hall
(C) At an art gallery
(D) At a movie cinema

02 According to the speaker, what can listeners do during the intermission?

(A) Purchase some drinks
(B) Meet some of the musicians
(C) Make reservations for future shows
(D) Request a performance program

03 What does the speaker ask listeners to do?

(A) Present their tickets when returning
(B) Turn off their mobile phones
(C) Leave beverages in a lobby
(D) Keep their valuables with them

04 What is the speaker mainly discussing?

(A) A new product
(B) A store opening
(C) A movie release
(D) A rental contract

05 According to the speaker, what will be offered until June 15?

(A) A discount
(B) A gift card
(C) An extended warranty
(D) A membership

06 What is mentioned about Jensen Technologies?

(A) It has released several new TV models this year.
(B) Its devices are sold by multiple companies.
(C) It operates retail outlets across the country.
(D) Its online games are popular with consumers.

07 How can listeners complete employee evaluations?

(A) By using a mobile application
(B) By filling out a paper form
(C) By placing a call
(D) By visiting an online page

08 Who is Roger Tan?

(A) A sales manager
(B) A security officer
(C) A guest speaker
(D) A technical worker

09 Why should listeners enter an ID code?

(A) To provide verification
(B) To save an electronic file
(C) To register for a session
(D) To participate in a forum

10 Why are the listeners gathered at the academy?

(A) To participate in some training
(B) To enroll in courses
(C) To take part in a celebration
(D) To view a presentation

11 What does the speaker suggest?

(A) Picking up a business card
(B) Providing contact information
(C) Turning off camera flashes
(D) Checking a facility's Web site

12 What will listeners most likely do next?

(A) Exit an auditorium
(B) View a video
(C) Approach a stage
(D) Listen to a speech

13 What is the purpose of the talk?

(A) To update a project schedule
(B) To remind listeners of a training session
(C) To explain a marketing campaign
(D) To notify listeners of a company expansion

14 Why does the speaker say, "Now, I know that it's on a Saturday"?

(A) To suggest an alternative
(B) To emphasize a deadline
(C) To complain about a date
(D) To express sympathy

15 How many people have registered for the event next Saturday?

(A) 10
(B) 15
(C) 20
(D) 30

16 What did the store recently do?

(A) Hired more cashiers
(B) Moved to a new location
(C) Conducted a survey
(D) Held a sales event

17 What does the man say about the fitting rooms?

(A) They were expanded.
(B) They are close to the entrance.
(C) They were shut down temporarily.
(D) They are too few in number.

18 Look at the graphic. When was the new loyalty program introduced?

(A) In March
(B) In April
(C) In May
(D) In June

PART 4

DAY 17 세부 사항 관련 문제 1

한 권으로 끝내는 **해커스 토익 700+** (LC+RC+VOCA)

정답·스크립트·해설 **p.97**

DAY
18
세부 사항 관련 문제 2

한 권으로 끝내는
해커스 토익 **700+**
LC+RC+VOCA
▲ MP3
바로 듣기

Course 1 특정 세부 사항 문제

토익 출제경향
평균 9~11문제 정도 출제

사무실 출입 시스템이 이번 주에 업데이트될 예정입니다. 시스템 업데이트 후에는 기존 출입증을 사용할 수 없습니다. 모든 직원들은 이번 주 목요일에 새로운 출입증을 받을 것입니다...

Q. 직원들은 언제 새 출입증을 받을 것인가?
A. 목요일에

직원들이 언제 새 출입증을 받을 것인지를 묻고 있습니다. 이처럼 PART 4에서는 **특정 시간이나 장소, 인물, 문제점 등을 묻는 문제**가 출제됩니다.

핵심 POINT

1. 질문의 핵심어구를 미리 확인하여 무엇을 묻고 있는지를 정확히 파악해야 합니다.

2. 문제점과 관련된 내용은 unavailable(이용할 수 없는), lack(~이 없다), late(늦은) 등의 부정적인 표현과 함께 자주 언급됩니다.

3. 특정 시간, 장소, 인물에 대해 묻는 문제에서는 지문에서 언급된 시간, 장소, 인물이 그대로 오답 보기에 등장하기도 합니다.

4. 주로 다음과 같은 질문을 사용하여 특정 세부 사항을 묻습니다.

   When will the listeners receive a new pass? 청자들은 언제 새 출입증을 받을 것인가?
   What event will take place at Greenly Field? Greenly Field에서 어떤 행사가 열릴 것인가?
   Who is Malcolm Mendez? 누가 Malcolm Mendez인가?
   What is the problem? 무엇이 문제인가?

Example ∩ DAY18_01

1. What event will take place at Greenly Field? (A) A city festival (B) A grand opening sale (C) A sports competition (D) A public concert	1. Greenly Field에서 어떤 행사가 열릴 것인가? (A) 시 축제 (B) 개점 할인 판매 (C) 스포츠 경기 (D) 공공 콘서트
3•)) 캐나다식 발음 Question 1 refers to the following broadcast. It's time for 107.6 XDFM's news update. This Sunday, the subway's Red Line will close for repairs between Poundstone Station and Pleasantville Station. Additional city buses will be operating to make up for the closure. So if you're going to **Sunday's baseball game at Greenly Field**, you'll have to travel by car or bus. Now stay tuned for the 9 P.M. local news.	1번은 다음 방송에 관한 문제입니다. 107.6 XDFM의 뉴스 속보 시간입니다. 이번 주 일요일, Poundstone 역과 Pleasantville 역 사이에서 지하철 빨강 노선이 수리를 위해 폐쇄될 예정입니다. 이 폐쇄를 보완하기 위해 추가적인 시내버스들이 운행될 것입니다. 따라서 Greenly Field에서 열리는 일요일의 야구 경기에 가실 예정 이라면, 자동차나 버스로 이동하셔야 할 것입니다. 이제 오후 9시 지역 뉴스를 위해 채널을 고정해 주세요.

정답 (C)

해설 Greenly Field에서 열릴 행사를 묻는 문제입니다. "Sunday's baseball game at Greenly Field"라며 Greenly Field에서 열리는 일요일의 야구 경기라고 하였습니다. 따라서 정답은 (C) A sports competition입니다.

어휘 repair[미 ripέər, 영 ripéə] 수리, 보수 operate[미 ά:pərèit, 영 ɔ́pərèit] 운행하다, 작동하다 make up for ~을 보완하다, ~을 만회하다

질문과 보기를 먼저 읽은 후 음성을 들으며 정답을 선택하세요. 이후 음성을 다시 들으면서 빈칸을 채우세요.

(음성은 두 번 들려줍니다.)

01 Where most likely are the listeners?

(A) At a gym
(B) At a store
(C) At a warehouse
(D) At a factory

02 What can the listeners do in the next room?

(A) Try some sample drinks
(B) Purchase some gifts
(C) Pick up a pamphlet
(D) Watch a video

On this stop of the tour, we'll see the _____ where bottles are filled with soft drinks. When operating at full capacity, _____ _____ 10,000 containers every day. If you look to your right, you'll see empty bottles entering the room on the conveyor belt and being filled. Now, we'll move to the next room, where you can

_____.

Please follow me.

03 What is the problem?

(A) An event was canceled.
(B) A brochure has errors.
(C) A colleague is unavailable.
(D) A client made a complaint.

04 What does the speaker ask the listener to do?

(A) Provide a business card
(B) Print some posters
(C) Reserve a bigger booth
(D) Create some handouts

Hello, Frank. It's Marcie calling. I'm attending the Calvin University Career Fair on Friday, and one of my team members was supposed to _____ _____ for the event. Unfortunately, _____ for an urgent client meeting. So, uh, could you possibly _____ instead? I'd like to use something similar to the promotional materials you created for last fall's sales expo. Please let me know sometime today whether you can complete this task.

정답·스크립트·해설 p.101

Course 2 다음에 할 일 문제

토익 출제경향
평균 2~3문제 정도 출제

Thompson사의 창립 10주년 기념 만찬에 오신 모든 분들을 환영합니다. 본사 CEO인 Jane Thompson의 연설이 곧 시작되오니 모두 착석해 주시기 바랍니다...

Q. 청자들은 다음에 무엇을 할 것 같은가?
A. 연설을 들을 것이다.

청자들이 다음에 무엇을 할 것 같은지를 묻고 있습니다. 이처럼 PART 4 에서는 **청자들이 다음에 할 일이나 다음에 일어날 일을 묻는 문제**가 출제됩니다.

핵심 POINT

1. 정답의 단서는 지문의 마지막 부분이나, will/be going to 등의 미래 시제 또는 now, next, after, before 등의 미래를 나타내는 표현이 포함된 문장에서 자주 언급됩니다.

2. 주로 다음과 같은 질문을 사용하여 다음에 할 일이나 다음에 일어날 일을 묻습니다.

   What **will the listeners probably** do next? 청자들은 다음에 무엇을 할 것 같은가?
   What **will** happen next week? 다음 주에 무슨 일이 일어날 것인가?
   What **does the speaker say** will take place in May? 화자는 5월에 무슨 일이 일어날 것이라고 말하는가?

Example ∩ DAY18_03

1. What will happen next week?

   (A) A shop will be relocated.
   (B) Regular hours will resume.
   (C) Visitors will receive gifts.
   (D) A holiday sale will begin.

1. 다음 주에 무슨 일이 일어날 것인가?

   (A) 가게가 이전할 것이다.
   (B) 정상 영업시간이 재개될 것이다.
   (C) 방문객들이 선물을 받을 것이다.
   (D) 휴일 할인 판매가 시작될 것이다.

[미국식 발음]

Question 1 refers to the following announcement.

Attention Southfield Shopping Mall visitors. Our hours of operation will be adjusted this upcoming holiday weekend. Instead of being open from 9 A.M. to 9 P.M. on Saturday, we will shut down at seven o'clock. And the mall will be closed all day Sunday. **Normal business hours will resume next Monday.** We apologize for the inconvenience and thank you for visiting Southfield Mall.

1번은 다음 공지에 관한 문제입니다.

Southfield 쇼핑몰을 방문해주신 분들은 주목해 주십시오. 다가오는 이번 주말 연휴에 저희 쇼핑몰의 영업시간이 조정될 것입니다. 토요일에 오전 9시부터 오후 9시까지 문을 여는 대신에, 저희는 7시에 문을 닫을 것입니다. 그리고 저희 쇼핑몰은 일요일에는 하루 종일 문을 닫을 것입니다. 정상 영업시간은 다음 주 월요일에 재개될 것입니다. 불편에 대해 사과드리며 Southfield 쇼핑몰을 찾아주셔서 감사드립니다.

정답 (B)

해설 다음 주에 일어날 일을 묻는 문제입니다. "Normal business hours will resume next Monday."라며 정상 영업시간이 다음 주 월요일에 재개될 것이라고 하였습니다. 따라서 정답은 (B) Regular hours will resume입니다.

어휘 hours of operation 영업시간 adjust[ədʒʌ́st] 조정하다 shut down 문을 닫다 resume[미 rizúːm, 영 rizjúːm] 재개하다

질문과 보기를 먼저 읽은 후 음성을 들으며 정답을 선택하세요. 이후 음성을 다시 들으면서 빈칸을 채우세요.
(음성은 두 번 들려줍니다.)

01 Who is Shawn Jameson?

    (A) A company executive
    (B) A technology consultant
    (C) A marketing manager
    (D) An application designer

02 What will the speaker probably do tomorrow?

    (A) Stop by another branch
    (B) Talk about a budget
    (C) Make changes to a document
    (D) Reorganize an office space

> Jason, this is Kara. I won't be at the office until 4 P.M. I'm meeting with Shawn Jameson, the _____ of Landlow Clothing. He wants to discuss the mobile application that our firm is creating for his company. I'm hoping to meet with their marketing manager as well. I know we planned to _____ over lunch, but we'll have to _____ _____. Sorry for the unexpected schedule change.

03 Who most likely is the speaker?

    (A) A restaurant manager
    (B) A ship captain
    (C) A taxi driver
    (D) A flight attendant

04 What will most likely happen in five minutes?

    (A) Staff members will check tickets.
    (B) Passengers will board a ship.
    (C) A cruise ship will reach a port.
    (D) A meal will be served.

> Good morning, Global Cruise Line passengers. _____ _____. In one hour, _____ in Tunis. For those interested, there are many beautiful beaches and outdoor markets that are accessible by taxi. In addition, _____ in the main dining area in five minutes. Please head there now if you want to eat before we dock. Thank you for traveling with Global Cruise Line.

정답·스크립트·해설 **p.102**

01 What problem does the speaker mention?

(A) A warranty is expired.
(B) A computer is malfunctioning.
(C) A laptop accessory is missing.
(D) A screen is cracked.

02 According to the speaker, what is included with the product?

(A) A free carrying case
(B) A trial membership
(C) An extra power cord
(D) A one-year warranty

03 Why does the speaker want the listener to return his call?

(A) He needs to obtain a mailing address.
(B) He wants to confirm shipping rates.
(C) He has a question about a product.
(D) He would like to order a new monitor.

04 Who most likely is the speaker?

(A) A weather reporter
(B) A bus driver
(C) A city employee
(D) A Web site developer

05 What does the speaker suggest?

(A) Driving on a highway
(B) Preparing flood barriers
(C) Tuning in again later
(D) Avoiding certain areas

06 According to the speaker, what is available on the Web site?

(A) Safety tips
(B) Video clips
(C) Downloadable maps
(D) News updates

07 What is the purpose of the speech?

(A) To describe a charity dinner
(B) To thank vendors for their services
(C) To introduce a local businessperson
(D) To describe a yearly event

08 What is available at the market?

(A) A gift-wrapping service
(B) A special discount
(C) A facility for children
(D) A brochure for local businesses

09 What will most likely happen next?

(A) A stage will be prepared for a concert.
(B) Some gifts will be distributed to guests.
(C) Beverages and snacks will be served.
(D) A brief speech will be given.

10 Who is Malcolm Mendez?

(A) A film actor
(B) An award presenter
(C) A movie director
(D) An event host

11 What problem does the speaker mention?

(A) A guest must leave early.
(B) A movie review was negative.
(C) A screening is fully booked.
(D) An auditorium will be closed.

12 What will the listeners probably do next?

(A) Fill out a questionnaire
(B) Write a review
(C) View a film
(D) Have some refreshments

13 What does the speaker mean when she says, "We have only 25 rooms"?

(A) Tour groups may not visit the resort.
(B) Guests should have a peaceful stay.
(C) Advance reservations are needed.
(D) Certain rooms will be renovated.

14 What will happen in May?

(A) A discount will be applied.
(B) A resort will reopen.
(C) A pamphlet will be published.
(D) A spa will relocate.

15 How can people get more information about the Shore Resort?

(A) By sending a text message
(B) By calling a hotline
(C) By writing an e-mail
(D) By going to a Web page

Extension Number	Name
100	Jerry Chow
110	Melinda Bright
120	Edward Klein
130	Claire Preston

16 What does the speaker ask the listener to do?

(A) Confirm a requested amount
(B) Enter a coupon code
(C) Select a shipping date
(D) Make a bill payment

17 What will happen this afternoon?

(A) Some items will be returned.
(B) An order will be shipped.
(C) Some notepads will be made.
(D) A schedule will be changed.

18 Look at the graphic. Who should the listener call after 1 P.M.?

(A) Jerry Chow
(B) Melinda Bright
(C) Edward Klein
(D) Claire Preston

정답·스크립트·해설 p.103

PART 4

DAY 18 세부 사항 관련 문제 2

한 권으로 끝내는 **해커스 토익 700+** (LC+RC+VOCA)

DAY / 19

세부 사항 관련 문제 3

한 권으로 끝내는
해커스 토익 **700+**
LC+RC+VOCA

▲ MP3
바로 듣기

Course 1 의도 파악 문제

토익 출제경향
3문제 출제

Jeremy Collins가 Walter 소설상 분야의 수상자가 되었습니다. 이는 놀라운 결과가 아닌데요. 그의 최신 소설은 평론가들의 대단한 찬사를 받아왔습니다...

Q. 화자가 "이는 놀라운 결과가 아닌데요"라고 말할 때 의도하는 것은 무엇인가?

A. 그녀는 작가의 능력을 인정한다.

화자가 한 말의 의도를 묻고 있습니다. 이처럼 PART 4에서는 지문에서 언급된 특정 문장에 담긴 화자의 의도를 묻는 문제가 출제됩니다.

핵심 POINT

1. 지문을 듣기 전 질문의 인용어구가 무엇인지를 미리 확인하면, 지문을 들으며 정답의 단서를 쉽게 파악할 수 있습니다.

2. 인용어구 일부 단어의 일차적인 의미를 이용한 오답이나, 제시된 지문 상황과 다른 상황에서 정답이 될 법한 오답이 자주 출제됩니다.

3. 주로 다음과 같은 질문을 사용하여 언급된 말의 의도를 묻습니다.

What **does the speaker** mean/imply **when she says,** "This is not a surprising result"?
화자가 "이는 놀라운 결과가 아닌데요"라고 말할 때 의도하는 것은 무엇인가?

Why **does the speaker** say, "Still not convinced"? 화자는 왜 "아직 확신이 들지 않나요"라고 말하는가?

Example ∩ DAY19_01

1. Why does the speaker say, "Still not convinced"? (A) To introduce another reason (B) To express frustration (C) To suggest an alternative (D) To describe a location	1. 화자는 왜 "아직 확신이 들지 않나요"라고 말하는가? (A) 다른 이유를 소개하기 위해 (B) 실망감을 표현하기 위해 (C) 대안을 제시하기 위해 (D) 위치를 설명하기 위해

🎧 영국식 발음

Question 1 refers to the following advertisement.

Instead of gift shopping at the mall this holiday season, come to the Winter Charity Fair! It will be held at the Metro Center from December 3 to 5. **A variety of donated goods will be sold at incredible prices**, including electronics, clothing, and more. **Still not convinced?** **All money raised will be given to local non-profit organizations.** So it's your best choice for Christmas shopping!

1번은 다음 광고에 관한 문제입니다.

이번 축제 시즌에는 쇼핑몰에서 선물을 구매하는 대신, 겨울 자선 바자회로 오세요! 바자회는 12월 3일부터 5일까지 Metro 센터에서 열릴 것입니다. 전자제품, 의류 등을 포함하여, 다양한 기부된 물품들이 놀라운 가격에 판매될 것입니다. 아직 확신이 들지 않나요? 모든 수익금은 지역의 비영리 단체들로 전달될 것입니다. 그러므로 이곳은 크리스마스 쇼핑을 위한 최고의 선택입니다!

정답 (A)

해설 화자가 하는 말(Still not convinced)의 의도를 묻는 문제입니다. "A variety of donated goods will be sold at incredible prices"라며 다양한 기부된 물품들이 놀라운 가격에 판매될 것이라며 바자회에 와야 할 이유를 언급한 뒤, "All money raised will be given to local non-profit organizations."라며 모든 수익금은 지역의 비영리 단체들로 전달될 것이라고 한 말을 통해 화자가 또 다른 이유를 소개하려는 의도임을 알 수 있습니다. 따라서 정답은 (A) To introduce another reason입니다.

어휘 **charity**[tʃǽrəti] 자선   **donate**[미 dóuneit, 영 dəunéit] 기부하다   **convince**[kənvíns] 확신시키다   **non-profit organization** 비영리 단체

질문과 보기를 먼저 읽은 후 음성을 들으며 정답을 선택하세요. 이후 음성을 다시 들으면서 빈칸을 채우세요.
(음성은 두 번 들려줍니다.)

01 Where is the talk taking place?

(A) At a retail branch
(B) At a manufacturing plant
(C) At a research facility
(D) At a science museum

02 What does the speaker imply when he says,
"He isn't always able to meet with tour groups"?

(A) A laboratory will open for a test.
(B) A tour will run longer than expected.
(C) An engineer was recently promoted.
(D) An employee's time should be appreciated.

My name is Jeff, and I'll be your guide today here at Lexington Incorporated's _____. We'll start our tour by looking at some sketches in our design team's office. Then, we'll go to the lab for computer, phone, and tablet testing. While there, you'll have a _____ _____ to our head engineer, David Tao. He isn't always able to meet with tour groups. So make sure to _____ this rare opportunity.

03 What happened last week?

(A) An award was given.
(B) An album was released.
(C) An academy was opened.
(D) A performance was recorded.

04 Why does the speaker say, "Official live recordings will be available on Mr. Peterson's Web site"?

(A) To advertise a social media site
(B) To give an alternative
(C) To explain a venue's schedule
(D) To provide reasons for a delay

Joining us next is William Peterson. Peterson has been performing as _____ for 20 years now. Just last week, he received the prestigious _____ from the Academy of Music. But before he begins . . . he asked us to mention one thing. Throughout the performance, please do not _____. Official live recordings will be available on Mr. Peterson's Web site. Thank you for understanding.

정답·스크립트·해설 **p.106**

Course 2 추론 문제

Central 자동차 수리점입니다. 고객님께서 오늘 오전 10시에 차량 점검 예약을 하셨으나, 예약 시간 30분이 지나도록 아무런 연락 없이 도착하지 않으셨어요...

Q. 자동차 수리점에 대해 무엇이 암시되는가?
A. 예약제가 운영되고 있다.

자동차 수리점에 대해 무엇이 암시되는지를 묻고 있습니다. 이처럼 PART 4에서는 **지문 내용을 통해 추론할 수 있는 것을 묻는** 문제가 출제됩니다.

핵심 POINT

1. 정답의 단서는 질문의 suggest(suggested)/imply about 뒤에 나오는 핵심어구가 언급된 부분과 그 주변에서 주로 등장합니다.

2. 정답의 단서는 주로 패러프레이징되고, must, may, might, probably와 같이 추측을 나타내는 표현이 포함된 문장에서 자주 언급됩니다.

3. 주로 다음과 같은 질문을 사용하여 추론할 수 있는 내용을 묻습니다.

What **is** suggested about **the car repair shop?** 자동차 수리점에 대해 무엇이 암시되는가?
What **does the speaker** imply about **the task?** 화자는 업무에 대해 무엇을 암시하는가?
What **does the speaker** suggest about **the West Coast Auto?**
화자는 West Coast 자동차 회사에 대해 무엇을 암시하는가?

Example 　🎧 DAY19_03

1. What does the speaker suggest about West Coast Auto? (A) It is providing discounts to customers. (B) It has expanded its local branch. (C) It will increase its rates in June. (D) It has a new reservation system.	1. 화자는 West Coast 자동차 회사에 대해 무엇을 암시하는가? (A) 고객들에게 할인을 제공하고 있다. (B) 지방 지점을 확장했다. (C) 6월에 요금을 인상할 것이다. (D) 새로운 예약 시스템을 갖추고 있다.

🇦🇺 호주식 발음

Question 1 refers to the following telephone message. Hello, Ms. Vinar. This is Kenneth Dryden from West Coast Auto returning your call. In your message, you asked if there was a van available from May 29 to June 3. There are several vans for those dates. Plus, **we are holding a promotional event now, so you will be able to get a good rate**. Just visit our Web site to make a reservation. Thanks.	1번은 다음 전화 메시지에 관한 문제입니다. 안녕하세요, Ms. Vinar. 저는 고객님께 답변 전화를 드리는 West Coast 자동차 회사의 Kenneth Dryden입니다. 메시지에서, 고객님께서는 5월 29일부터 6월 3일까지 이용 가능한 승합차가 있는지 문의하셨습니다. 그 날짜에 몇 대의 승합차들이 있습니다. 또한, 저희는 지금 판촉 행사를 진행하고 있으므로, 괜찮은 가격에 이용하실 수 있을 것입니다. 예약하시려면 저희 웹사이트를 방문해 주세요. 감사합니다.

정답 (A)

해설 화자가 West Coast 자동차 회사에 대해 암시하는 것을 묻는 문제입니다. "we[West Coast Auto] are holding a promotional event now, so you will be able to get a good rate"라며 West Coast 자동차 회사가 지금 판촉 행사를 진행하고 있어서 괜찮은 가격에 이용할 수 있을 것이라고 한 말을 통해, 고객들에게 할인을 제공하고 있음을 알 수 있습니다. 따라서 정답은 (A) It is providing discounts to customers입니다.

어휘 local branch 지방 지점　rate[reit] 가격, 요금　return a call 답변 전화를 하다　promotional[미 prəmóuʃənəl, 영 prəmóuʃənəl] 판촉의, 홍보의 make a reservation 예약하다

질문과 보기를 먼저 읽은 후 음성을 들으며 정답을 선택하세요. 이후 음성을 다시 들으면서 빈칸을 채우세요.

(음성은 두 번 들려줍니다.)

01 What does the speaker suggest about the Hamilton Art Festival?

(A) It is almost sold out.
(B) It supports local organizations.
(C) It has few participants.
(D) It has been postponed.

02 How can listeners sign up as volunteers?

(A) By logging in to a Web site
(B) By calling a hotline
(C) By visiting a store
(D) By e-mailing a form

> And now for the local news . . . The Hamilton Art Festival will begin on Friday, July 12. This year's festival will be the largest ever, with 35 artists from the region participating.
>
> _____
> will go to _____. Oh . . . and keep in mind that _____
>
> _____ .
>
> If you would like to help out, _____ Riverside Art Supplies to fill out a registration form.

03 Why is the speaker calling?

(A) To change a data plan
(B) To follow up on a request
(C) To inquire about a bill
(D) To ask for a list of services

04 What does the speaker imply about TeleComm?

(A) It no longer offers an unlimited plan.
(B) It increased cell phone package rates.
(C) It provided refunds in the past.
(D) It overcharged him for a service.

> This is Dean Saunders. I'm calling regarding my latest phone bill. It says that I have to pay $60, but my cell phone package is usually only _____. I'm certain this is a mistake because I chose one of TeleComm's plans with _____
> _____. What's more, I didn't
> _____ .
> So, I'd like someone to _____
> _____ and see what the problem is.

정답·스크립트·해설 **p.107**

01 Who is Ms. Lopez?

(A) An art professor
(B) A chef
(C) A restaurant reviewer
(D) An interior decorator

02 What will Ms. Lopez be doing this weekend?

(A) Catering some events
(B) Hosting a charity gala
(C) Renovating a kitchen
(D) Conducting a workshop

03 What does the speaker imply when he says, "Her devoted fans are likely to be interested, though"?

(A) A restaurant is expected to be popular.
(B) Products will be in high demand.
(C) An interview will appeal to some fans.
(D) Passes could sell out quickly.

04 Who most likely is the speaker?

(A) A store manager
(B) A delivery person
(C) A secretary
(D) A publisher

05 What does the speaker mean when he says, "we only make deliveries in the mornings on weekends"?

(A) A customer will be charged additional fees.
(B) A request cannot be fulfilled.
(C) A schedule was misprinted.
(D) An order has not been sent.

06 What does the speaker ask the listener to do?

(A) Contact a driver
(B) Return a call
(C) Visit a Web site
(D) Drop by a store

07 Where most likely are the listeners?

(A) At a talent competition
(B) At a theater production
(C) At a school performance
(D) At a charity concert

08 Who is Merle Collins?

(A) A show organizer
(B) A musician
(C) A foundation member
(D) An educator

09 Why does the speaker say, "That's 20 percent of our total today"?

(A) She needs to confirm the accuracy of an amount.
(B) She hopes to show the importance of an event.
(C) She wishes to stress the number of participants.
(D) She wants to emphasize the size of a contribution.

10 What is being announced?

(A) A facility tour
(B) A staffing policy
(C) A government inspection
(D) An employee evaluation

11 What is implied about the factory?

(A) Its machinery can be dangerous.
(B) It can produce food for animals.
(C) It must remain clean.
(D) Its products are sold internationally.

12 What will the speaker most likely do next?

(A) Put on a safety hat
(B) Provide a demonstration
(C) Clean his hands
(D) Greet a visiting group

13 What is the advertisement mainly about?

(A) An electronics repair shop
(B) A shopping center
(C) A computer retailer
(D) An Internet service provider

14 What does the speaker imply about Digital Solutions?

(A) It will extend its hours.
(B) It will open another branch.
(C) It will develop a new service.
(D) It will relocate.

15 What does the speaker mention about a Web site?

(A) It will launch in July.
(B) It will offer a discount.
(C) It will sell exclusive items.
(D) It will feature free shipping.

16 Who is Mr. Hoffman?

(A) A freelance editor
(B) A company manager
(C) A financial analyst
(D) A course instructor

17 What does the speaker mention about Mr. Hoffman?

(A) He will transfer to South America.
(B) He worked for the government.
(C) He wrote a popular book.
(D) He owns a large company.

18 What is suggested about the workshop?

(A) It has more than one presenter.
(B) It lasts for several days.
(C) It deals with a variety of topics.
(D) It includes many participants.

정답·스크립트·해설 p.108

세부 사항 관련 문제 4

한 권으로 끝내는
해커스 토익 700+
LC+RC+VOCA

▲ MP3
바로 듣기

Course 1 시각 자료 문제 1 (표 및 그래프)

토익 출제경향
최대 2문제까지 출제

King's 미술관에 오신 것을 환영합니다.
1층의 Luna 전시관부터 가장 먼저 둘러보실
것이고, 투어가 끝나면 기념품 구매 상점으로
이동할 것입니다...

장소	Luna 전시관	Star 전시관
전시	고전주의 작품 전시	초현실주의 작품 전시

Q. 시각 자료를 보아라. 청자들은 어떤 전시를 가장 먼저 볼 것인가?
A. 고전주의 작품 전시

청자들이 어떤 전시를 가장 먼저 볼 것인지를 묻고 있습니다. 이처럼 PART 4에서는 **지문 내용과 함께 표 및 그래프의 내용을 묻는 문제**가 출제됩니다.

핵심 POINT

1. 지문을 듣기 전에 제시된 표나 그래프를 보고 무엇에 관한 내용인지를 미리 확인하면, 지문을 들으며 정답의 단서를 쉽게 파악할 수 있습니다.

2. 정답의 단서는 변동 사항, 최고·최저 항목, 특정 수치 이상·이하 등의 특이 사항이 언급되는 부분에서 주로 등장합니다.

3. 주로 다음과 같은 질문을 사용하여 시각 자료와 관련된 내용을 묻습니다.

Look at the graphic. Which exhibit will the listeners view first?
시각 자료를 보아라. 청자들은 어떤 전시를 가장 먼저 볼 것인가?

Look at the graphic. When will the awards ceremony take place?
시각 자료를 보아라. 시상식은 언제 열릴 것인가?

Look at the graphic. Which store will the speaker go to?
시각 자료를 보아라. 화자는 어느 가게로 갈 것인가?

Look at the graphic. Where will the conference be held?
시각 자료를 보아라. 회의는 어디에서 열릴 것인가?

4. 행사 시간표, 업무 진행표, 회사의 매출 그래프, 강설량 그래프 등의 시각 자료가 출제됩니다.

Pearson Design's 50th Anniversary Celebration	
Opening Remarks	4:00 P.M. – 4:50 P.M.
Speech by CEO	5:00 P.M. – 5:50 P.M.
Dinner	6:00 P.M. – 7:50 P.M.
Employee Awards	8:00 P.M. – 8:50 P.M.

Pearson Design사 50주년 기념행사	
개회사	오후 4시 – 오후 4시 50분
CEO 연설	오후 5시 – 오후 5시 50분
만찬	오후 6시 – 오후 7시 50분
직원 시상식	오후 8시 – 오후 8시 50분

1. Look at the graphic. When will the awards ceremony take place?

(A) 4:00 P.M. – 4:50 P.M.
(B) 5:00 P.M. – 5:50 P.M.
(C) 6:00 P.M. – 7:50 P.M.
(D) 8:00 P.M. – 8:50 P.M.

1. 시각 자료를 보아라. 시상식은 언제 열릴 것인가?

(A) 오후 4시 – 오후 4시 50분
(B) 오후 5시 – 오후 5시 50분
(C) 오후 6시 – 오후 7시 50분
(D) 오후 8시 – 오후 8시 50분

🇨🇦 캐나다식 발음

Question 1 refers to the following talk and schedule.

Welcome to Pearson Design's 50th anniversary celebration. Over the years, this design firm has grown into a multinational company. It's all thanks to our hard-working and dedicated staff. Now, before we get started, I need to mention one schedule change. **Our CEO, Mr. Pearson, will give his speech right after dinner, and the awards ceremony will move to his original time slot.**

1번은 다음 담화와 일정표에 관한 문제입니다.

Pearson Design사의 50주년 기념행사에 오신 것을 환영합니다. 수년간, 이 디자인 회사는 다국적 기업으로 성장했습니다. 이는 모두 근면하고 헌신적인 우리 직원들 덕분입니다. 이제, 시작하기 전에, 한 가지 일정 변경 사항을 말씀드려야 할 것 같습니다. 우리 회사의 CEO이신 Mr. Pearson은 만찬이 끝난 직후 연설을 하시기로 했으며, 시상식은 그의 원래 연설 시간대로 옮겨질 것입니다.

정답 (B)

해설 언제 시상식이 열릴 것인지를 묻는 문제입니다. "Our CEO, Mr. Pearson, will give his speech right after dinner, and the awards ceremony will move to his original time slot."이라며 회사의 CEO인 Mr. Pearson이 만찬이 끝난 직후 연설을 하기로 했으며 시상식은 그의 원래 연설 시간대로 옮겨질 것이라고 하였으므로, 시상식이 열릴 시간은 오후 5시 – 오후 5시 50분임을 일정표에서 알 수 있습니다. 따라서 정답은 (B) 5:00 P.M. – 5:50 P.M.입니다.

어휘 opening remarks 개회사 multinational[mʌ̀ltinǽʃənəl] 다국적의 hard-working[미 hàːrdwə́ːrkiŋ, 영 kàːdwə́ːkiŋ] 근면한 dedicated[미 dédikèitid, 영 dédikèitid] 헌신적인 time slot 시간대

PART 4

DAY 20 세부 사항 관련 문제 4

한 권으로 끝내는 해커스 토익 700+ (LC+RC+VOCA)

시각 자료, 질문과 보기를 먼저 읽은 후 음성을 들으며 정답을 선택하세요. 이후 음성을 다시 들으면서 빈칸을 채우세요.
(음성은 두 번 들려줍니다.)

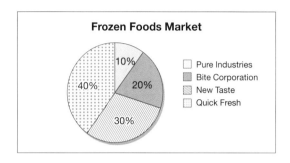

Frozen Foods Market

10%
40%
20%
30%

☐ Pure Industries
▨ Bite Corporation
▨ New Taste
▧ Quick Fresh

01 Look at the graphic. Where does the speaker work?

(A) At Pure Industries
(B) At Bite Corporation
(C) At New Taste
(D) At Quick Fresh

02 What does the speaker ask listeners to do?

(A) Reserve a meeting room
(B) Attend a sales conference
(C) Order some equipment
(D) Conduct some research

This graph represents companies' shares in the _____.
I'm pleased that we've achieved the _____ among frozen foods brands. But we still have progress to make to pass the current leader, Quick Fresh. Quick Fresh has recently launched a TV advertising campaign to increase its sales. I suggest we consider doing this as well. So, could you all _____ so that we can create an ad concept? I'll _____ what you've found at Friday's staff meeting.

Tour Schedule	
European Landscapes	10:00 A.M. – 10:50 A.M.
Still Life	11:00 A.M. – 11:50 A.M.
Lunch	
Modern Sculpture	1:00 P.M. – 1:50 P.M.
Abstract Art	2:00 P.M. – 2:50 P.M.

03 Where is the talk most likely taking place?

(A) At a train station
(B) At a gallery
(C) At a hotel
(D) At an art academy

04 Look at the graphic. Which exhibit will include an autograph signing?

(A) European Landscapes
(B) Still Life
(C) Modern Sculpture
(D) Abstract Art

We'll now _____ for the National Gallery. It will take about 20 minutes to reach the gallery _____. That will give you some time to look over this brochure about the exhibits that I will hand out. Oh . . . and a famous artist, Linda Newman, is at the museum today. She will be _____.
We'll have a chance to see her at the first exhibit after lunch, at 1 P.M. Alright, let's get on the bus.

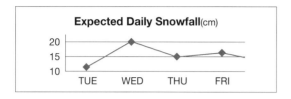

Expected Daily Snowfall(cm)

	TUE	WED	THU	FRI
20				
15				
10				

05 What does the speaker mention about Toronto?

(A) It will hire temporary workers.

(B) It will buy snow removal equipment.

(C) It will close several highways.

(D) It will provide assistance to drivers.

06 Look at the graphic. When is freezing rain expected?

(A) On Tuesday

(B) On Wednesday

(C) On Thursday

(D) On Friday

The National Weather Service has issued _____ for Toronto. Heavy snow is expected over the next four days. The Toronto City Council will _____ _____ for snow removal. Nevertheless, residents should avoid driving unless absolutely necessary. If you must drive, please note that freezing rain is expected the day after we _____. Road conditions will be extremely hazardous.

Team Name	Employee Count
Web design	10
Support	20
Engineering	25
Mobile software	15

07 Why was RidgeFX upgraded?

(A) To fix some errors

(B) To address some complaints

(C) To create a mobile version

(D) To add new features

08 Look at the graphic. Which team will be trained in the afternoon?

(A) Web design

(B) Support

(C) Engineering

(D) Mobile software

Can I have your attention, please? RidgeFX, a program that many of you use, was recently upgraded to _____ _____. The IT department head will lead _____ _____ on the new software for everyone next Monday. You'll be divided into training groups according to team. All teams will have a training session in the morning, except for the one _____ _____. That team will be trained in the afternoon. I will _____ later today.

정답·스크립트·해설 **p.112**

Course 2 시각 자료 문제 2(약도 및 기타)

Arizona 스포츠용품점이 2호점을 냈습니다. 가게는 Veronica 쇼핑몰 3층에 위치해 있고, 에스컬레이터 좌측에 있으므로 쉽게 찾아오실 수 있습니다.

복도		
장소 A	에스컬레이터	장소 B

Q. 시각 자료를 보아라. 가게는 어디에 위치해 있는가?
A. 장소 A

가게가 어디에 위치해 있는지를 묻고 있습니다. 이처럼 PART 4에서는 지문 내용과 함께 약도나 기타 시각 자료의 내용을 묻는 문제가 출제됩니다.

핵심 POINT

1. 지문을 듣기 전에 제시된 약도나 기타 시각 자료를 보고 무엇에 관한 내용인지를 미리 확인하면, 지문을 들으며 정답의 단서를 쉽게 파악할 수 있습니다.

2. 약도가 제시된 문제에서 정답의 단서는 between(~와 –의 사이에), next to(~ 옆에), opposite(~ 맞은편에), in front of(~ 앞에)와 같이 위치나 방향을 나타내는 표현과 함께 자주 등장합니다.

3. 주로 다음과 같은 질문을 사용하여 시각 자료와 관련된 내용을 묻습니다.

Look at the graphic. Where is the store located?
시각 자료를 보아라. 가게는 어디에 위치해 있는가?
Look at the graphic. Where will the listeners eat lunch?
시각 자료를 보아라. 청자들은 어디에서 점심을 먹을 것인가?
Look at the graphic. How much of a discount will the speaker receive?
시각 자료를 보아라. 화자는 얼만큼의 할인을 받게 될 것인가?
Look at the graphic. What information is inaccurate?
시각 자료를 보아라. 어느 정보가 잘못되었는가?

4. 약도나 평면도, 좌석 배치도, 할인 쿠폰, 영수증 등의 다양한 시각 자료가 출제됩니다.

Example

Fruit Stand	Area B	Parking Lot
Area A	Area C	
Packaging Facility		Area D

과일 가판대	B 구역	주차장
A 구역	C 구역	
포장시설		D 구역

1. Look at the graphic. Where will the listeners eat lunch?

(A) Area A
(B) Area B
(C) Area C
(D) Area D

1. 시각 자료를 보아라. 청자들은 어디에서 점심을 먹을 것인가?

(A) A 구역
(B) B 구역
(C) C 구역
(D) D 구역

🔊 영국식 발음

Question 1 refers to the following talk and map.

Welcome to the Shady Valley Orchard. We produce 12 varieties of apples here. During the tour this morning, you will get a chance to pick some apples and learn how we package fruit for shipment. After that, **we will have lunch in the area next to the parking lot, the one right beside the fruit stand**. Now, let's begin.

1번은 다음 담화와 약도에 관한 문제입니다.

Shady Valley 과수원에 오신 것을 환영합니다. 저희는 이곳에서 12 종류의 사과를 재배합니다. 오늘 오전에 견학하시는 동안, 여러분들은 사과를 딸 기회를 가질 것이고 배송을 위해 저희가 과일을 포장하는 방법을 알게 되실 겁니다. 그 후에, 우리는 주차장 옆, 과일 가판대 바로 옆의 구역에서 점심을 먹을 것입니다. 이제, 시작해 보겠습니다.

정답 (B)

해설 청자들이 점심을 먹을 장소를 묻는 문제입니다. "we will have lunch in the area next to the parking lot, the one right beside the fruit stand" 라며 주차장 옆, 과일 가판대 바로 옆의 구역에서 점심을 먹을 것이라고 하였으므로, 청자들이 주차장 옆이면서 과일 가판대 옆에 있는 B 구역에서 점심을 먹을 것임을 알 수 있습니다. 따라서 정답은 (B) Area B입니다.

어휘 orchard [미 ɔ́ːrtʃərd, 영 ɔ́ːtʃəd] 과수원 package [pǽkidʒ] 포장하다 shipment [ʃípmənt] 배송 beside [bisáid] ~의 옆에

시각 자료, 질문과 보기를 먼저 읽은 후 음성을 들으며 정답을 선택하세요. 이후 음성을 다시 들으면서 빈칸을 채우세요.
(음성은 두 번 들려줍니다.)

Burger Palace Coupon

One Free Sundae
Purchase of a meal combo required

|||||||||||||||||||||||||
12345678901234

Expires on July 3   Valid only at the Portland location

---

01 According to the speaker, what did the company recently do?

(A) Opened a new restaurant
(B) Added menu items
(C) Expanded a facility
(D) Reduced meal prices

02 Look at the graphic. Which information is incorrect?

(A) Required purchase
(B) Expiration date
(C) Free item
(D) Location validity

Mammal Exhibit		Bird Exhibit
Reptile Exhibit	Gift Shop	Fish Exhibit
Ticket Booth		Entrance

---

03 Who is the speaker addressing?

(A) Guides
(B) Tourists
(C) Students
(D) Professors

04 Look at the graphic. Which exhibit will the groups view first?

(A) The mammal exhibit
(B) The bird exhibit
(C) The reptile exhibit
(D) The fish exhibit

Looking for a way to beat the heat? Then visit Burger Palace Restaurant. We're offering several _____

_____ to celebrate summer. And for a limited time, when you purchase one of our meal combos, you'll receive a free sundae. To take advantage of this offer, _____ from our Web site. Note that this promotion is only valid at our Portland location and

_____.

Thank you!

OK . . . Several student organizations are _____ tomorrow, so you'll be busy. To prevent overcrowding, please spend no more than 20 minutes at each exhibit. Also, start with the exhibit _____ the gift shop, _____ the ticket booth. Then, lead your group clockwise, ending with the one closest to the entrance. Oh, and the mammal exhibit was recently updated. _____ on the displays now for you to review.

Janice Walker - Credit Card Statement

Merchant	Amount
Bartleby's Books	$125.00
Hart & Crane	$325.00
Maria's Market	$65.00
Wentworth Clothing	$75.00

My name is Janice Walker, and I signed up for the Wentworth Mall Rewards Club that _____. Joining this loyalty program was supposed to qualify me for 10 percent off all purchases. But looking at my credit card statement, I see that I was charged full price at one store. And it was for the _____ I made. I'd like you to correct this error. I'll be _____ starting tomorrow, so please call me back this afternoon.

05 What is mentioned about the Wentworth Mall Rewards Club?

(A) It is a new program.
(B) It has not been launched yet.
(C) It includes a membership fee.
(D) It does not provide cards to members.

06 Look at the graphic. At which store was the speaker charged the incorrect amount?

(A) Bartleby's Books
(B) Hart & Crane
(C) Maria's Market
(D) Wentworth Clothing

Westfield Hotel Directory

Conference Room	5th Floor
Regina Kitchen	4th Floor
Hailey Hall	3rd Floor
Francesca Ballroom	2nd Floor

Thank you for coming to the annual International Advertising Conference. We'll have events _____ at Westfield Hotel today. The highlight of our day will be a speech from Melissa Grand, the CEO of Bellow Advertising Corporation. _____ at 5 P.M. in the Francesca Ballroom. After that, there will be a _____ _____ at the hotel's restaurant, Regina Kitchen. Those interested in attending should _____ by writing their names on the form outside Hailey Hall now.

07 Look at the graphic. Where will Melissa Grand give her speech?

(A) On the 5th floor
(B) On the 4th floor
(C) On the 3rd floor
(D) On the 2nd floor

08 What will some of the listeners do next?

(A) Place a dinner order
(B) Visit a social media site
(C) Register for an event
(D) Head to a restaurant

정답·스크립트·해설 p.114

Condo Prices at Driftwood Estates

CATEGORY 1	CATEGORY 2
Under $400,000	$400,000 to $599,000
CATEGORY 3	**CATEGORY 4**
$600,000 to $799,000	over $800,000

01 What will happen on June 1?

(A) A sports tournament will get underway.
(B) Some neighbors will attend a party.
(C) A charity auction will be held.
(D) Some homeowners will move in.

02 Look at the graphic. What type of units are available?

(A) Category 1
(B) Category 2
(C) Category 3
(D) Category 4

03 What can the listeners do at the reception office?

(A) Consult with a salesperson
(B) Pick up a brochure
(C) Register for a tour
(D) Look at a model

Pearson Beverages

Bottled Water

Quantity	Price per Unit
1-99	$1.75
100-199	$1.50
200-299	$1.25
Over 300	$1.00

04 Why is the speaker calling?

(A) To report that he made a reservation
(B) To invite the listener to attend an event
(C) To explain why he rescheduled a seminar
(D) To ask the listener to contact a center

05 What does the speaker mention about the room?

(A) It is available at a discount.
(B) It has limited seating.
(C) It comes with free equipment.
(D) It is larger than expected.

06 Look at the graphic. How much will the listener most likely pay per unit?

(A) $1.75
(B) $1.50
(C) $1.25
(D) $1.00

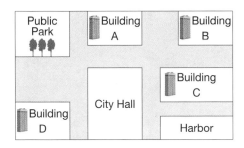

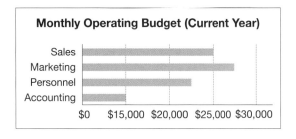

07 Look at the graphic. Which building did Rosalyn Gonzalez design?

(A) Building A
(B) Building B
(C) Building C
(D) Building D

08 What is mentioned about Rosalyn Gonzalez?

(A) She currently works for the city.
(B) She teaches an architecture course.
(C) She won an award for a design.
(D) She graduated more than a decade ago.

09 What does the speaker encourage the listeners to do?

(A) Sign up for a program
(B) Think of a question
(C) Make a recording
(D) Visit a landmark

10 Who most likely are the listeners?

(A) Sales assistants
(B) Company interns
(C) Department heads
(D) Board members

11 Look at the graphic. Which department will not have its budget reduced?

(A) Sales
(B) Marketing
(C) Personnel
(D) Accounting

12 What does the speaker suggest the listeners do?

(A) Arrange a meeting
(B) Read a report
(C) Contact a manager
(D) Give a presentation

정답·스크립트·해설 **p.116**

한 권으로 끝내는
해커스 토익 700+
LC+RC+VOCA

READING **리딩**

리딩
기초 다지기

토익에 나오는 문장을 읽고 쉽게 이해할 수 있도록 문장
성분과 구와 절을 익히고, 패러프레이징 연습을 합니다.

DAY 01 기초 다지기

Course 1 문장 성분 · 구와 절

문장 성분

미나는 간호사이다.

'미나는 간호사이다'라는 문장이 '미나', '는', '간호사', '이다'와 같은 여러 개의 성분으로 구성된 것처럼, 영어 문장도 다양한 문장 성분으로 구성됩니다. 이와 같이 문장을 구성하는 문장 성분을 익혀두면 토익에 나오는 영어 문장을 쉽게 이해할 수 있습니다.

구와 절

나는 <u>매일 아침</u> 운동을 한다.
        구

나는 <u>운동할 때</u> 음악을 듣는다.
        절

'매일 아침' 또는 '나는 운동할 때'처럼 두 개 이상의 단어가 모여 하나의 의미를 나타내는 말 덩어리를 **구** 또는 **절**이라고 합니다. 이러한 구와 절을 익혀두면 복잡한 문장의 구조를 쉽게 이해할 수 있습니다.

➤ 문장 성분에는 무엇이 있나요?

영어 문장의 성분에는 **주어, 동사, 목적어, 보어, 수식어**가 있습니다.

주어	주로 문장의 맨 앞에 와서 동작이나 상태의 주체가 되는 말입니다.	The passengers **wait**. 승객들이 기다린다. The students **study**. 학생들은 공부한다.
동사	주로 주어 뒤에 와서 주어의 동작이나 상태를 나타내는 말입니다.	I drive. 나는 운전한다. We agree. 우리는 동의한다.
목적어	주로 동사 뒤에 와서 동작이나 상태의 대상이 되는 말입니다.	**Tom bought** a watch. Tom은 손목시계를 샀다. **They like** hamburgers. 그들은 햄버거를 좋아한다.
보어	주로 동사 뒤 또는 목적어 뒤에 와서 주어나 목적어를 보충 설명해주는 말입니다.	**Mina is** a nurse. Mina는 간호사이다. **My friends make me** happy. 내 친구들은 나를 행복하게 만든다.
수식어	문장에 꼭 필요한 요소는 아니지만 다른 문장 성분을 꾸며주는 역할을 하는 말입니다.	**Mr. Wright saw the concert** yesterday. Mr. Wright는 어제 콘서트를 봤다.

➤ 구와 절은 어떻게 다른가요?

첫 번째 문장의 'every morning(매일 아침)'처럼 둘 이상의 단어로 이루어진 말 덩어리에 <주어 + 동사>가 없을 경우 **구**라고 하고, 두 번째 문장의 'when I exercise(나는 운동할 때)'처럼 <주어 + 동사>가 포함되어 있을 경우 **절**이라고 합니다.

I exercise every morning. 나는 매일 아침 운동을 한다.

I listen to music when I exercise. 나는 운동할 때 음악을 듣는다.
                         주어   동사

HACKERS PRACTICE

밑줄 친 부분에 해당되는 문장 성분이 무엇인지 고르세요.

01 The director is here.

    (A) 주어   (B) 동사   (C) 목적어   (D) 보어   (E) 수식어

02 My uncle is a scientist.

    (A) 주어   (B) 동사   (C) 목적어   (D) 보어   (E) 수식어

03 Mr. Jones needs a ticket.

    (A) 주어   (B) 동사   (C) 목적어   (D) 보어   (E) 수식어

04 The staff works daily.

    (A) 주어   (B) 동사   (C) 목적어   (D) 보어   (E) 수식어

05 The client signed the agreement.

    (A) 주어   (B) 동사   (C) 목적어   (D) 보어   (E) 수식어

밑줄 친 부분이 구와 절 중 어떤 것에 해당되는지 고르세요.

06 A nearby coffee shop is offering discounts on drinks.

    (A) 구   (B) 절

07 Mr. Quince does not know where Ms. White lives.

    (A) 구   (B) 절

08 The train to Topeka has been delayed by 20 minutes.

    (A) 구   (B) 절

09 The audience applauded when the speech was over.

    (A) 구   (B) 절

10 If you order within the week, the delivery will be free.

    (A) 구   (B) 절

정답·해석 **p.120**

Course 2 패러프레이징

나는 오렌지와 사과를 샀다(bought). = 나는 오렌지와 사과를 샀다(purchased).

위 두 문장에서 bought와 purchased는 표현은 다르지만 동일한 의미(샀다)를 전달하고 있습니다. 이처럼 어떤 말을 의미가 같거나 비슷한 다른 말로 표현하는 것을 **패러프레이징**이라고 합니다. 이와 같은 패러프레이징의 종류를 익혀두면 독해 문제의 정답을 쉽게 찾을 수 있습니다.

➤ 패러프레이징에는 어떤 종류가 있나요?

패러프레이징에는 크게 네 가지의 경우가 있습니다.

(1) 지문에 쓰인 표현을 같거나 비슷한 의미의 다른 어구로 바꾸는 경우

지문의 특정 단어, 구, 절과 같거나 비슷한 의미의 표현을 사용하는 방법입니다.

> I bought oranges and apples. 나는 오렌지와 사과를 샀다.
> = I purchased oranges and apples. 나는 오렌지와 사과를 샀다.
>
> → '샀다'라는 의미의 bought를 같은 의미의 purchased로 패러프레이징하였습니다.

(2) 지문에 쓰인 표현을 일반화하는 경우

한 개 이상의 단어나 구를 대표할 수 있는 범주의 표현으로 일반화하는 방법입니다.

> Bus and subway information is available on the city's Web site. 버스와 지하철 정보는 시의 웹사이트에서 구하실 수 있습니다.
> = Public transportation information is available on the city's Web site. 대중교통 정보는 시의 웹사이트에서 구하실 수 있습니다.
>
> → '버스와 지하철(Bus and subway)'을 일반화하여 '대중교통(Public transportation)'이라고 패러프레이징하였습니다.

(3) 지문에 쓰인 표현을 요약하는 경우

지문의 특정 절이나 문장을 요약하여 표현하는 방법입니다.

> Peter's Catering and Enchanting Meals are the most famous catering companies in town, but only Enchanting Meals has vegetarian options.
> Peter's Catering사와 Enchanting Meals사는 마을에서 가장 유명한 출장 요리 업체인데, 오직 Enchanting Meals사에만 채식주의자 선택권이 있다.
> = Peter's Catering does not have vegetarian options. Peter's Catering사에는 채식주의자 선택권이 없다.
>
> → 'Peter's Catering사와 Enchanting Meals사는 마을에서 가장 유명한 출장 요리 업체인데, 오직 Enchanting Meals사에만 채식주의자 선택권이 있다'라는 문장을 'Peter's Catering사에는 채식주의자 선택권이 없다'고 요약하여 패러프레이징하였습니다.

(4) 지문에 쓰인 표현을 바탕으로 새로운 사실을 추론하는 경우

지문의 내용을 근거로 새로운 사실을 추론하는 방법입니다.

> The library will be closed for a month while it is being renovated. 도서관은 보수 공사가 진행되는 한 달간 문을 닫을 것이다.
> = The renovation of the library will take around a month to finish. 도서관의 보수 공사는 완료되는 데 한 달 정도 걸릴 것이다.
>
> → '도서관은 보수 공사가 진행되는 한 달간 문을 닫을 것이다'라는 내용을 근거로 '도서관의 보수 공사는 완료되는 데 한 달 정도 걸릴 것이다'라는 새로운 사실을 추론하여 패러프레이징하였습니다.

HACKERS PRACTICE

지문의 일부 또는 전체 내용이 올바르게 패러프레이징된 문장을 고르세요.

01

> The annual agricultural trade show will be held at the Prembleton Convention Center on June 5. It will be attended by over 150 producers and manufacturers in the region.

(A) Producers from international companies are attending.
(B) An agricultural trade show is held once a year.

02

> The accounting staff has been asked to analyze and review last quarter's earnings. They have to submit a report by the end of the week.

(A) The accounting department made a big profit last quarter.
(B) Employees need to complete an assignment by the end of the week.

03

> The Bartletville Central Library opens at 9:00 A.M. and closes at 10:00 P.M. from Monday to Friday. On Saturdays, Sundays, and public holidays, however, it opens at 10:00 A.M. and closes at 6:00 P.M.

(A) The Bartletville Central Library is open to the public every day of the year.
(B) On weekends, certain facilities at the Bartletville Central Library are closed.

04

> Many hotels try to make themselves stand out with a theme, and the newly opened Book & Bed is no exception. Stocked with over 2,000 novels, Book & Bed caters to those who enjoy literature.

(A) Famous authors have visited the newly opened hotel.
(B) The Book & Bed is a hotel targeting a specific market.

정답·해석·해설 **p.120**

[01-04] 지문을 읽고 패러프레이징에 유의하여 각 문제의 답을 고르세요.

Seasonal Hiring Up

September—Drummond plans to hire more than 35,000 additional workers for the upcoming holiday season to meet demand at its department stores around the country. Drummond spokesperson Miriam Flacks said the company actually began hiring in August and expects most jobs to be filled by mid-November.

Several other businesses have also scaled up their hiring. Postal carrier Parcelfast will hire about 45,000 people nationwide to help it deliver large numbers of holiday orders to customers. Home-appliance retailer Tickit has said it will recruit more than 20,000 seasonal store workers. Meanwhile, Randon Toys has not given a final hiring figure, but expects to add at least 10,000 workers in five of its biggest markets.

According to Mark Arnott of Lindsay Capital, the increase in hiring has a simple explanation. "More people shop around the holidays than at any other time of the year. Still, another factor could be the wage rises we've seen over the past year. People now also have more money to spend."

---

01 What is expected to happen in November?

(A) Several retailers will announce plans for the coming year.
(B) A sale will be launched throughout a store's network of branches.
(C) Several key positions will be filled at a retailer's head office.
(D) A department store will have hired thousands of temporary staff.

02 Why is Parcelfast planning to hire more workers?

(A) It is opening offices in new cities.
(B) It wants to keep up with competitors.
(C) It expects shipping demand to rise.
(D) It recently merged with another firm.

03 What is indicated about Randon Toys?

(A) It operates in a limited number of locations.
(B) It could hire more than 10,000 new workers.
(C) It has not altered its plans from the year before.
(D) It sells most of its products through an online shop.

04 According to Mr. Arnott, what could be behind a recent trend in hiring?

(A) The increase in employees' salaries
(B) The growing popularity of online shopping
(C) The availability of capital for expansion
(D) The success of seasonal advertising efforts

[05-08] 지문을 읽고 패러프레이징에 유의하여 각 문제의 답을 고르세요.

TO: Ray Douglas <r.douglas@douglasbros.com>
FROM: Amber Hughes <a.hughes@snippets.org>
DATE: May 3
SUBJECT: Work and shop with Snippets

Dear Mr. Douglas,

I am writing to tell you that we are opening a new nonprofit store in town called Snippets. We are asking residents, community groups, and businesses for donations of undamaged buttons, string, scrap paper, and cardboard. We plan to resell them as craft supplies at our store. All the money we earn will be put toward environmental and educational projects here in town.

We ask you to collect items at your office that you would normally throw away and donate them to our store. We can arrange to pick up anything you may have at a location that's convenient for you.

Our grand opening will be on May 20. Come visit the store to see what is available at Snippets!

Sincerely,

Amber Hughes
Snippets General Manager

---

05 What is true about the items people donate?

(A) They will be recycled at a nearby plant.
(B) They should not be damaged.
(C) They will be sold in an online store.
(D) They should still be in their packaging.

06 What is indicated about Snippets?

(A) It opened for business last month.
(B) It is funded by the government.
(C) It will use earnings for the community.
(D) It was founded by a local artist.

07 What does Ms. Hughes ask Mr. Douglas to do?

(A) Gather items at a workplace
(B) Work on a project proposal
(C) Contribute to a local school
(D) Apply for a volunteer position

08 What is suggested about Mr. Douglas?

(A) He has shopped at a local craft store.
(B) He has contributed to Snippets before.
(C) He will not have to drop off donations.
(D) He works for a nonprofit organization.

정답·해석·해설 p.120

GRAMMAR

PART 5, 6

PART 5는 101번부터 130번까지 총 30문제로, 한 문장의 빈칸에 알맞은 어휘나 문법 사항을 고르는 유형이고, PART 6는 131번 부터 146번까지 총 16문제로, 각 지문마다 4개의 빈칸에 알맞은 문법 사항이나 어휘 및 문장을 고르는 유형입니다.

Course 1 주어 · 동사

토익 출제경향
최대 2문제까지 출제

<u>그녀는</u> <u>노래한다</u>.
　주어　　　동사

'그녀는 노래한다'에서 '그녀'와 같이 동작의 주체를 나타내는 말을 **주어**, '노래한다'와 같이 주어의 동작이
나 상태를 나타내는 말을 **동사**라고 합니다.

기초문법 잡기

1 주어와 동사는 문장에서 꼭 있어야 하나요?

영어에서 주어와 동사는 문장을 만들기 위해 꼭 필요한 요소입니다. 즉, 최소한 한 개의 주어와 한 개의 동사가 있어야 문장이 될
수 있습니다.

<u>She</u> <u>sings</u>. (○) 그녀는 노래한다.
주어　동사

<u>She</u> <u>happy</u> (×) 그녀는 행복한
주어　동사 X

2 문장에서 주어 자리는 어디인가요?

주어는 주로 문장 맨 앞에 옵니다.

<u>David</u> wrote a letter. David는 편지를 썼다.
주어

3 문장에서 동사 자리는 어디인가요?

동사는 주로 주어 다음에 옵니다.

The train <u>stopped</u>. 기차가 멈췄다.
　　　　　동사

토익 포인트 1   주어 자리에 올 수 있는 것

✱ 주어 자리에 올 수 있는 것은 **명사 역할을 하는 것들**입니다. 명사 역할을 하는 것에는 **명사구**나 **대명사**, 그리고 '**~하는 것**'으로 해석되는 **동명사구, to 부정사구, 명사절**이 있습니다.

명사구	The television commercial **attracted many customers.**	그 텔레비전 광고는 많은 고객들을 끌어들였다.
대명사	He **sent an e-mail to Mr. Baker this morning.**	그는 오늘 아침 Mr. Baker에게 이메일을 보냈다.
동명사구	Maintaining a professional image **is a key requirement.**	전문적인 이미지를 유지하는 것은 핵심 요구 사항이다.
to 부정사구	To arrive on time **might be impossible.**	제시간에 도착하는 것은 불가능할 수도 있다.
명사절	What the manager ordered **was printer paper.**	담당자가 주문한 것은 프린터 용지였다.

토익 실전 Check-up 둘 중 알맞은 것을 고르세요.

The (ⓐ regulate, ⓑ regulation) will be reviewed by the manager.   정답·해석·해설 **p.123**

토익 포인트 2   가짜 주어 it / there

✱ it은 to 부정사구, that절 같은 긴 주어를 대신하여 주어 자리에 쓰입니다. 이때, it을 **가짜 주어**, 문장 뒤로 간 긴 주어를 **진짜 주어**라고 합니다.

It is essential to respond to customer inquiries promptly.   고객 문의에 즉시 답변하는 것은 필수적이다.
가짜 주어   진짜 주어

It is expected that all staff complete their training this week.   모든 직원들은 이번 주에 교육을 완료할 것으로 예상된다.
가짜 주어   진짜 주어

✱ 가짜 주어 there는 '**~이 있다**'를 의미하며, '**there + 동사(be, remain ⋯) + 진짜 주어(명사)**' 형태를 이룹니다.

There is an office space on Grant Avenue that will be available in June.
가짜 주어   진짜 주어
6월에 이용 가능할 사무실 공간이 Grant가에 있다.

There remain several issues to discuss.   논의해야 할 몇 가지 문제들이 남아 있다.
가짜 주어   진짜 주어

토익 실전 Check-up 둘 중 알맞은 것을 고르세요.

(ⓐ He, ⓑ It) is mandatory to turn off all electronic devices in the laboratory.   정답·해석·해설 **p.123**

동사 자리에 올 수 있는 것

★ 동사 자리에 올 수 있는 것은 **동사** 또는 '**조동사 + 동사원형**'입니다.

| 동사 | The machine produces 200 units per hour. 그 기계는 한 시간에 200개의 제품을 생산한다. |
| 조동사 + 동사원형 | The machine can produce 200 units per hour. 그 기계는 한 시간에 200개의 제품을 생산할 수 있다. |

토익 실전 Check-up 둘 중 알맞은 것을 고르세요.

Ms. Kennedy (ⓐ evaluates, ⓑ evaluating) her staff each year.

정답·해석·해설 **p.123**

토익 포인트 4 동사로 시작되는 명령문

★ 명령문은 일반적인 문장과 달리 주어 없이 **동사로 시작**됩니다. 이때 명령문의 동사 자리에는 **동사원형**이 와야 합니다.

Visit our downtown branch for a consultation. 상담을 받으시려면 저희의 시내 지점을 방문하세요.

Please provide your phone number when placing an order. 주문하실 때 귀하의 전화번호를 제공해 주십시오.

→ 공손함을 나타내는 표현인 please가 명령문의 동사 앞에 쓰이기도 합니다.

토익 실전 Check-up 둘 중 알맞은 것을 고르세요.

(ⓐ To ask, ⓑ Ask) any of our salespeople about the promotions this month.

정답·해석·해설 **p.123**

HACKERS PRACTICE 토익 700+ 달성을 위한 연습 문제

다음 문장에서 알맞은 것을 고르세요.

01 The (ⓐ supervisor, ⓑ supervise) will review the project proposal next week.

02 (ⓐ They, ⓑ It) was recommended that human resources develop a new employee manual.

03 Mr. Thompson will (ⓐ to decide, ⓑ decide) later who will manage the Drayvon project.

04 (ⓐ Increasingly, ⓑ Increasing) the size of the company logo on staff uniforms will make it clearer.

05 If the client (ⓐ accepts, ⓑ accepting) the conditions, we will send the contracts today.

06 (ⓐ He, ⓑ It) is necessary that all managers conduct employee performance evaluations.

07 (ⓐ To install, ⓑ Install) a new security system on all staff computers is our assignment.

08 (ⓐ Register, ⓑ Registering) now to get daily updates delivered to your inbox.

다음 문장에서 밑줄 친 곳을 문법에 맞게 고치세요.

09 Please to verify that you have received your shipment by signing the delivery form.

10 Guests who wish to reserve a table at the hotel's restaurant should contacting the front desk.

11 According to market forecasts, any is possible that the price of oil will increase this year.

12 Ms. Hemwood can reserved tickets in advance because she is a theater member.

13 This is hard to find a parking space on Grove Road.

14 Find a reasonably priced office space in this town is becoming very difficult.

15 Customers can accumulation points each time they use their MogiShop Rewards Card.

16 Employee badges permission staff to park anywhere on Mason Street.

무료 해설 ▶
바로 보기 정답·해석 **p.123**

Course 2 목적어 · 보어 · 수식어

목적어 · 보어

나는 책상을 샀다.
　　　目的語(목적어)

이것은 책상이다.
　　　보어

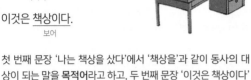

첫 번째 문장 '나는 책상을 샀다'에서 '책상을'과 같이 동사의 대상이 되는 말을 **목적어**라고 하고, 두 번째 문장 '이것은 책상이다'에서 '책상이다'와 같이 주어나 목적어를 보충 설명해주는 말을 **보어**라고 합니다.

수식어

우리는 어제 책상을 정리했다.
　　　　수식어

'우리는 어제 책상을 정리했다'에서 '어제'는 '우리는 책상을 정리했다'라는 문장에 의미를 더해주는 말로, '어제'가 없어도 문장을 만들 수 있습니다. 이처럼 문장에 꼭 필요한 부분은 아니지만 문장에 의미를 더해주는 말을 **수식어**라고 합니다.

기초문법 잡기

1 문장에서 목적어 자리는 어디인가요?

목적어는 주로 동사 뒤에 옵니다.

I **bought** a desk. 나는 책상을 샀다.
　　동사　목적어

2 문장에서 보어 자리는 어디인가요?

보어는 무엇을 보충 설명하는지에 따라 자리가 달라집니다. 주어를 보충 설명하는 주격 보어는 동사 뒤에, 목적어를 보충 설명하는 목적격 보어는 목적어 뒤에 옵니다.

This is a desk. 이것은 책상이다.
　　동사 주격 보어

I find the chair comfortable. 나는 그 의자가 편안하다고 생각한다.
　　　목적어　　목적격 보어

3 문장에서 수식어 자리는 어디인가요?

수식어는 문장 앞, 문장 중간, 문장 뒤 어디에나 올 수 있고, 한 문장에 여러 개가 올 수도 있습니다.

The desk arrived at my office yesterday. 그 책상은 어제 내 사무실에 도착했다.
　　　　　　　　수식어　　　수식어

토익 포인트 1 목적어 자리에 올 수 있는 것

✱ 목적어 자리에 올 수 있는 것은 **명사 역할을 하는 것들**입니다. 명사 역할을 하는 것에는 **명사구**나 **대명사**, 그리고 '**~하는 것**'으로 해석되는 **동명사구, to 부정사구, 명사절**이 있습니다.

명사구	Brenton Corporation announced several changes to its incentive policy.
	Brenton사는 장려금 정책에 대한 몇몇 변경 사항을 발표했다.
대명사	I met him in the library this morning. 나는 오늘 아침 도서관에서 그를 만났다.
동명사구	The supervisor considered hiring a programmer. 관리자는 프로그래머를 고용하는 것을 고려했다.
to 부정사구	Playtron hopes to release 10 new video games within the next three years.
	Playtron사는 다음 3년 안에 10개의 새로운 비디오 게임을 출시하기를 희망한다.
명사절	Keller Company reports how much it earns yearly to shareholders worldwide.
	Keller사는 전 세계 주주들에게 매년 얼마나 버는지를 보고한다.

토익 실전 Check-up 둘 중 알맞은 것을 고르세요.

Frameworks Inc. has a lot of (ⓐ competition, ⓑ competitive) from other interior design firms.

정답·해석·해설 p.123

토익 포인트 2 보어 자리에 올 수 있는 것

✱ 보어 자리에 올 수 있는 것은 **명사 역할을 하는 것들**과 **형용사 역할을 하는 것들**입니다.

• 명사 역할을 하는 것들

명사구	Peaceful Borough is an apartment complex in downtown Newton.
	Peaceful Borough는 Newton 시내에 있는 아파트 단지이다.
동명사구	Mr. Lee's favorite pastime after work is watching movies.
	Mr. Lee가 퇴근 후에 하는 가장 좋아하는 취미는 영화를 보는 것이다.
to 부정사구	The purpose of the meeting is to review the survey results.
	회의의 목적은 설문 조사 결과를 검토하는 것이다.
명사절	The issue is that the customer was put on hold for more than 30 minutes.
	문제는 고객이 30분 이상 통화 대기 상태에 놓여있었다는 것이다.

• 형용사 역할을 하는 것들

형용사	Jembot Electronics' appliance division was profitable last quarter.
	Jembot Electronics사의 가전기기 부서는 지난 분기에 수익성이 있었다.
분사	The museum's exhibition of modern art was inspiring to those who viewed it.
	박물관의 현대 미술 전시회는 그것을 관람한 사람들에게 영감을 주었다.

토익 실전 Check-up 둘 중 알맞은 것을 고르세요.

Laptops sold online are (ⓐ afford, ⓑ affordable) compared to similar items in mall stores. 정답·해석·해설 p.123

✴ **보어가 주어나 목적어와 동격 관계를 이루면 보어 자리에 명사가 옵니다.**

주어와 동격   The researchers at NR Laboratories are experts.   NR 실험실의 연구원들은 전문가들이다.
                                 주어   보어

목적어와 동격   The board of directors elected Mr. Bauer president.   이사회는 Mr. Bauer를 회장으로 선출했다.
                                       목적어   보어

→ 주어(The researchers ~ Laboratories)와 목적어(Mr. Bauer)가 보어(experts/president)와 동격 관계를 이루므로 명사가 보어 자리에 와야 합니다.

✴ **보어가 주어나 목적어를 설명해주면 보어 자리에 형용사가 옵니다.**

주어 설명   The location of the bank is convenient.   그 은행의 위치는 편리하다.
                        주어   보어

목적어 설명   Our designers made the Web site easy to use.   우리의 디자이너들이 웹사이트를 사용하기 쉽게 만들었다.
                              목적어   보어

→ 주어(The location ~ bank)와 목적어(the Web site)를 보어(convenient/easy)가 설명해주므로 형용사가 보어 자리에 와야 합니다.

토익 실전 Check-up 둘 중 알맞은 것을 고르세요.

Mr. Stein's commitment to the organization is (ⓐ admiration, ⓑ admirable).   정답·해석·해설 **p.123**

✴ **동사가 없는 수식어 거품을 거품구라고 합니다. 거품구가 될 수 있는 것은 전치사구, to 부정사구, 분사(구문)입니다.**

전치사구   Within the hour, visitors from an overseas branch will arrive.
            한 시간 내에, 해외 지사로부터의 방문객들이 도착할 것이다.

to 부정사구   Invitees should contact Ms. Davis to confirm their attendance.
            초청객들은 참석을 확정하기 위해 Ms. Davis에게 연락해야 한다.

분사(구문)   Applicants accepted for the position will be called shortly.
            일자리에 합격한 지원자들은 곧 전화를 받을 것이다.

✴ **동사가 있는 수식어 거품을 거품절이라고 합니다. 거품절이 될 수 있는 것은 관계절, 부사절입니다.**

관계절   The event will be held at the Rotterdam Park, which is close to the hotel.
            행사는 호텔에서 가까운 로테르담 공원에서 열릴 것이다.

부사절   Once the supervisor returns from his trip, we can discuss the issue.
            관리자가 출장에서 돌아오면, 우리는 그 문제를 논의할 수 있다.

토익 실전 Check-up 둘 중 알맞은 것을 고르세요.

All travelers (ⓐ arriving, ⓑ arrive) at International Terminal 2 have to pass through Immigration.   정답·해석·해설 **p.123**

다음 문장에서 알맞은 것을 고르세요.

01 Ms. Alvan referred to notes as she delivered her (ⓐ speech, ⓑ speaks) to the crowd.

02 The long delay of the parts shipment creates (ⓐ difficult, ⓑ difficulties) for the manufacturing plant.

03 Mr. Loren is an experienced (ⓐ professional, ⓑ profess) who will be a good addition to the team.

04 A visit to the Pearson Museum is (ⓐ advice, ⓑ advisable), according to guidebooks.

05 The cleaning service promises that all of its employees are (ⓐ thorough, ⓑ thoroughly).

06 Evening staff at Bron's Diner may leave for the night (ⓐ once, ⓑ in) the kitchen has been cleaned.

07 Mr. Powell will be a (ⓐ speaker, ⓑ speak) at our next product release.

08 Relocating to Louisiana was an (ⓐ adjustment, ⓑ adjustable) for many staff members.

다음 문장에서 밑줄 친 곳을 문법에 맞게 고치세요.

09 The addition of a new wing could be <u>expensively</u> for Sacred Heart Hospital.

10 Hanson gallery expects <u>receive</u> government funding for the project.

11 The baseball team's chances of winning the championship are <u>promise</u>.

12 All staff <u>interest</u> in taking professional development classes can sign up with human resources.

13 The Layton Community Center offers residents free yoga and meditation <u>sessional</u>.

14 Mr. Bryant is considering adding some tables to his restaurant now that he is making a <u>profitable</u>.

15 Being able to eat outdoors is a <u>beneficial</u> of The Petunia Bar and Grill.

16 The most important quality for potential candidates is <u>diligent</u>.

무료 해설 ▶ 바로 보기

정답·해석 **p.124**

PART 5

01 Ms. Wendt became Ex-Tech's chief ------- when she was selected for the job last year.

(A) accountant   (B) accountable
(C) accounted   (D) accountably

02 The new cleaning spray ------- debris from building up in sinks.

(A) preventing   (B) to prevent
(C) prevents   (D) preventable

03 On a business radio program, a financial consultant suggested ------- in property rather than in stocks.

(A) invested   (B) investing
(C) invests   (D) invest

04 Mr. Callahan ------- a team to work on an attractive package design.

(A) to organize   (B) organized
(C) organizing   (D) organization

05 Business management students appreciate taking marketing courses as they are -------.

(A) benefit   (B) beneficial
(C) beneficially   (D) can benefit

06 The schedule for the final exam is available ------- the department's Web site.

(A) yet   (B) but
(C) on   (D) still

07 According to the finance team, the newly introduced ------- seems practical.

(A) systematically   (B) systemized
(C) systematic   (D) system

08 This demonstration will commence ------- all department managers arrive.

(A) throughout   (B) meanwhile
(C) in spite of   (D) as soon as

09 The client's ------- of the proposal has made the firm's executives very happy.

(A) accept   (B) acceptance
(C) accepted   (D) accepts

10 ------- we did not advertise on television, our sales were very high this year.

(A) From   (B) Both
(C) Although   (D) Regarding

11 At ATB Telecom, customers can ------- from a wide range of mobile phone data plans.

(A) chosen   (B) to choose
(C) choosing   (D) choose

12 The cleaning services provided by Maids For Moving are generally -------.

(A) satisfy   (B) satisfies
(C) satisfactory   (D) satisfaction

13 The information on this Web site is ------- to those who want to purchase a home in Detroit.

(A) help   (B) helpful
(C) helpfulness   (D) helpfully

14 ------- to and from work can be pleasant if it is less than 30 minutes each way.

(A) Commuters   (B) Commuted
(C) Commutable   (D) Commuting

15 ------- at the entrance, shoppers hoped to be the first to purchase the latest model of a popular mobile phone.

(A) Gather   (B) Gatherable
(C) Gathers   (D) Gathering

16 To prevent loss of data, ------- your computer with a program that protects against intrusion.

(A) securing   (B) secure
(C) secures   (D) secured

17 An experienced ------- was hired to recommend new marketing strategies.

(A) advised   (B) to advise
(C) advise   (D) adviser

18 The decision to merge was ------- to the company as its survival depended on it.

(A) importantly   (B) important
(C) importance   (D) import

PART 6

Questions 19-22 refer to the following memo.

Hello Everyone,

It has been reported to me by several team leaders ------- there have been instances of staff logging in on the attendance board via mobile devices over the past few months. Staff must sign in using their workplace computers. Only those who are traveling for business may sign in with their phones. -------. In the future, mobile access to the site will be restricted to those who have received a special code from management. Any ------- attempts to log in from a mobile device will be rejected.

If you have questions on this matter, please ------- them to me at jamste@zencorp.com.

19 (A) their   (B) that
(C) then   (D) therefore

20 (A) The company Intranet will no longer be accessible from today.
(B) All reports should be submitted by the indicated deadline.
(C) Create an account to keep track of your mobile phone activity.
(D) This is the only exception permitted by the administration.

21 (A) unused   (B) repeated
(C) unauthorized   (D) random

22 (A) directing   (B) director
(C) directly   (D) direct

정답·해석·해설 p.124

Course 1 동사의 형태와 종류

토익 출제경향
최대 2문제까지 출제

동사의 형태

walk
walk<u>s</u>
walk<u>ed</u>

'walk(걷다)'라는 동사의 기본형은 'walks, walked'처럼 모양을 바꾸어 나타낼 수 있습니다. 이러한 동사의 형태는 크게 5가지로, 기본형, 3인칭 단수형, 과거형, 현재분사형, 과거분사형이 있습니다.

동사의 종류

동사
├─ 자동사
└─ 타동사

기초문법 잡기

1 동사의 5가지 형태는 어떻게 생겼나요?

(1) 기본형(동사원형)

I walk to school every day. 나는 매일 학교에 걸어간다.

(2) 3인칭 단수형(동사원형 + (e)s)

The contract ends in January. 계약은 1월에 끝난다.

(3) 과거형(동사원형 + ed / 불규칙 변화)

The director asked for an update. 관리자는 최신 정보를 요청했다.

Mr. Holloway sent the bill yesterday. Mr. Holloway는 어제 청구서를 발송했다.

(4) 현재분사형(동사원형 + ing)

Management is reviewing the proposal. 경영진은 제안서를 검토하는 중이다.

(5) 과거분사형(동사원형 + ed / 불규칙 변화)   * 과거분사형(past participle)은 약자 p.p.로 표기합니다.

Profits have increased over the past few years. 수익이 지난 수년간 증가해왔다.

They have recently rebuilt the damaged bridge. 그들은 최근에 훼손된 다리를 다시 지었다.

2 자동사와 타동사는 무엇인가요?

'그녀는 걷는다'라는 문장에서 '걷는다'처럼 그 자체로 의미가 통해 목적어 없이 쓰는 동사를 자동사라고 부릅니다. 그러나 '그녀는 사과를 먹는다'라는 문장에서 '먹는다'처럼 동작의 대상인 목적어가 반드시 필요한 동사를 타동사라고 부릅니다.

자동사   She walks. 그녀는 걷는다.

타동사   She eats an apple. 그녀는 사과를 먹는다.

토익 포인트 1　조동사 + 동사원형

✱ **조동사**(will/would, may/might, can/could, must, should) **뒤에는 동사원형**이 와야 합니다.

The vacation policy <u>will</u> (~~to take~~, take) effect as of March 20.　휴가 정책은 3월 20일부터 효력을 발휘할 것이다.
→ 조동사(will) 다음에는 to 부정사(to take)가 올 수 없고 동사원형(take)이 와야 합니다.

The server shutdown <u>may</u> (~~lasts~~, last) several more hours.　서버 정지는 몇 시간 더 지속될 수 있다.
→ 조동사(may) 다음에는 3인칭 단수형(lasts)이 올 수 없고 동사원형(last)이 와야 합니다.

✱ **조동사처럼 쓰이는 표현 뒤에도 동사원형**이 와야 합니다.

ought to ~해야 한다	had better ~하는 게 좋다	would like to ~하고 싶다	be able to ~할 수 있다
have to ~해야 한다	be going to ~할 것이다	used to ~했었다, ~하곤 했다	

I <u>ought to</u> (~~am~~, be) careful with my personal information.　나는 내 개인 정보를 조심히 다루어야 한다.

Mr. Douglas <u>used to</u> (~~worked~~, work) in this office.　Mr. Douglas는 이 사무실에서 일했었다.
→ 조동사처럼 쓰이는 표현(ought to/used to) 뒤에는 동사원형(be/work)이 와야 합니다.

> **토익 실전 Check-up** 둘 중 알맞은 것을 고르세요.
>
> Employees can (ⓐ register, ⓑ registered) for the workshop online.　정답·해석·해설 p.126

토익 포인트 2　진행형(be + -ing) / 수동형(be + p.p.) / 완료형(have + p.p.)

✱ **동사의 -ing/p.p. 형태는 be동사/have동사와 결합하여 진행형, 수동형, 완료형**이 됩니다.

진행형(be + -ing)　The inspector is checking the new machinery to make sure it is functional.
조사관이 새 기계가 작동하는지를 확인하기 위해 점검하고 있다.

수동형(be + p.p.)　A tour of the Museum of Natural History is scheduled for this afternoon.
자연사 박물관 관람이 오늘 오후에 예정되어 있다.

완료형(have + p.p.)　The managers have asked all staff to meet their deadlines.
관리자들은 모든 직원들에게 마감기한을 지킬 것을 요청했다.

> **토익 실전 Check-up** 둘 중 알맞은 것을 고르세요.
>
> Mr. Creston and his team have (ⓐ opened, ⓑ open) three new offices in the last month.　정답·해석·해설 p.126

토익 포인트 3 자동사와 타동사

✱ 자동사는 뒤에 목적어를 갖기 위해 반드시 '전치사'가 있어야 하지만, 타동사는 전치사 없이 목적어를 바로 갖습니다.

자동사 Mr. Janicki will also (**participate**, participate in) the shareholders' meeting this year.
Mr. Janicki도 올해 주주 총회에 참석할 것이다.
→ participate는 자동사이므로 목적어(the shareholders' meeting)를 갖기 위해서는 전치사(in)가 함께 쓰여야 합니다.

타동사 Many jobseekers (**attended to**, attended) the career fair at Chester Convention Hall.
Chester Convention Hall에서 열린 취업 박람회에 많은 구직자들이 참석했다.
→ attend는 타동사이므로 전치사 없이 바로 목적어(the career fair)가 와야 합니다.

토익 실전 Check-up 둘 중 알맞은 것을 고르세요.

The supervisor (ⓐ mentioned, ⓑ mentioned about) some important news during the conversation.

정답·해석·해설 **p.126**

토익 포인트 4 혼동하기 쉬운 자동사와 타동사

✱ 의미가 비슷하여 혼동하기 쉬운 자동사와 타동사

의미	자동사 + 전치사 + 목적어	타동사 + 목적어
말하다	speak to the audience 관객들에게 말하다 talk to the technician 기술자에게 말하다 talk about staff orientation 직원 오리엔테이션에 대해 이야기하다 account for the revenue decrease 수익 감소에 대해 설명하다	tell the customer 고객에게 말하다 discuss the issue 사안을 논의하다 mention the special promotion 특별 홍보 행사를 언급하다 explain the changes 변경 사항을 설명하다 address the crowd 군중에게 말을 하다
답하다	respond to the request 요청에 응답하다 reply to the correspondence 서신에 답장하다	answer the question 질문에 대답하다
동의하다	agree with/to/on a schedule change 일정 변경에 동의하다 consent to the proposal 제안에 동의하다	approve the plan 계획을 승인하다
반대하다	object to the idea 의견에 반대하다	oppose the deal 거래에 반대하다
기타	participate in the seminar 세미나에 참가하다 arrive at the hotel 호텔에 도착하다 wait for the call 전화를 기다리다	attend the meeting 미팅에 참석하다 reach the office building 사무실 건물에 도착하다 await the results 결과를 기다리다

토익 실전 Check-up 둘 중 알맞은 것을 고르세요.

They made an appointment to (ⓐ talk, ⓑ discuss) the impact of the sale.

정답·해석·해설 **p.126**

HACKERS PRACTICE 토익 700+ 달성을 위한 연습 문제

다음 문장에서 알맞은 것을 고르세요.

01 Customers will (ⓐ receive, ⓑ received) a discount if they buy the software within 48 hours.

02 The advertiser has (ⓐ promoted, ⓑ promoting) the tablet computer since January.

03 The warehouse is (ⓐ process, ⓑ processing) a large order that will be shipped tomorrow.

04 Mr. Bowman plans to (ⓐ speak, ⓑ explain) investment options to the client.

05 The memo (ⓐ announced about, ⓑ announced) Mr. Anderson's promotion.

06 It is (ⓐ recommend, ⓑ recommended) that adults get six to eight hours of sleep a night.

07 Subscribers must (ⓐ consent, ⓑ approve) to having their visits to the *Daily News* Web site monitored.

08 (ⓐ Advertise, ⓑ Advertising) a newly opened business can be challenging for the owners.

다음 문장에서 밑줄 친 곳을 문법에 맞게 고치세요.

09 <u>To notify</u> the appropriate supervisors in case of an illness-related absence.

10 Eckert Corporation is <u>study</u> how to expand their operations into Asia.

11 She <u>completion</u> the report as requested and left it on Mr. Hartman's desk to review.

12 Mr. Jackson ordered office furniture, which will be <u>deliver</u> next week.

13 The accountant <u>talked</u> how overspending was hurting the company.

14 <u>Inspirational</u> for the author's latest novel comes from her own personal experience.

15 Jeff Kinsey has <u>lead</u> the public relations division since last year.

16 Employment advisors say jobseekers should <u>practicing</u> how they will answer interview questions.

무료 해설 ▶
바로 보기

정답·해설 **p.127**

Course 2 주어와의 수일치

A girl laughs. 한 소녀가 웃는다.
단수 주어 단수 동사

Girls laugh. 소녀들이 웃는다.
복수 주어 복수 동사

주어가 단수인 A girl일 때에는 동사도 단수인 laughs를 쓰고, 주어가 복수인 Girls일 때에는 동사도 복수인 laugh를 씁니다. 이와 같이 주어에 따라 동사의 수를 일치시켜야 하는데, 이를 **수일치**라고 합니다.

기초문법 잡기

1 단수 주어와 복수 주어란 무엇인가요?

단수 주어란 하나의 사람이나 사물이 주어인 경우를 말하며, 앞에 관사 a/an을 붙입니다. 반면 복수 주어는 둘 이상의 사람이나 사물이 주어인 경우를 말하며, 뒤에 (e)s를 붙입니다.

단수 주어	하나의 사람/사물	an artist, a computer
복수 주어	둘 이상의 사람/사물	artists, computers

An artist **is painting** a picture. 한 예술가가 그림을 그리고 있다.
Computers **require updates.** 컴퓨터들은 업데이트가 필요하다.

2 단수 동사와 복수 동사란 무엇인가요?

단수 동사는 단수 주어가 나올 때 쓰는 동사로 동사원형에 (e)s를 붙인 3인칭 단수형을 쓰고, 복수 동사는 복수 주어가 나올 때 쓰는 동사로 동사원형 그대로 씁니다. 그러나 단수 동사와 복수 동사의 구분은 현재형일 때에만 해당되고, 과거형의 경우는 동일합니다.

단수 주어	3인칭 단수형	expects, shows
복수 주어	동사원형	expect, show

Mr. Fender **expects** fast service. Mr. Fender는 빠른 서비스를 기대한다.
단수 주어

Photos **show** available products. 사진들은 구입 가능한 상품들을 보여준다.
복수 주어

✴ **단수 주어** 뒤에는 **단수 동사**를, **복수 주어** 뒤에는 **복수 동사**를 씁니다.

A bus arrives every 10 minutes at this stop.   이 정거장에서는 10분마다 버스 한 대가 정차한다.
<u>단수 주어</u>

The new products need to be tested.   그 신제품들은 검사를 받아야 한다.
        <u>복수 주어</u>

✴ 주어와 동사 사이에 있는 **수식어 거품**은 동사의 수 결정에 아무런 영향을 주지 않습니다.

Researchers [in the marketing department] (~~gathers~~, gather) information.   마케팅 부서에 있는 연구원들은 정보를 수집한다.

→ 동사(gather) 바로 앞에 있는 수식어 거품(in the marketing department) 속의 the marketing department를 주어로 혼동하여 단수 동사를
   쓰는 일이 없도록 주의해야 합니다.

> **토익 실전 Check-up** 둘 중 알맞은 것을 고르세요.
>
> The video game from LS Softworks (ⓐ demonstrates, ⓑ demonstrate) the superiority of the new
> technology.   정답·해석·해설 p.127

✴ **단수 취급되는 수량 표현** 뒤에는 **단수 동사**를, **복수 취급되는 수량 표현** 뒤에는 **복수 동사**를 씁니다.

단수 취급되는 수량 표현	복수 취급되는 수량 표현
one (+ 단수 명사), each (+ 단수 명사), every + 단수 명사 the number of + 복수 명사 somebody, someone, something anybody, anyone, anything everybody, everyone, everything nobody, no one, nothing	many/several/few/both + (of the) + 복수 명사 a number of + 복수 명사 a couple/variety of + 복수 명사

Each volunteer has received an assignment.   각각의 자원봉사자들은 임무를 받았다.

A couple of chairs are missing from the conference room.   의자 몇 개가 회의실에서 없어졌다.

✴ **부분이나 전체**를 나타내는 표현이 주어로 쓰이면 **of 뒤의 명사**에 동사를 수일치시킵니다.

all, most, any, some, half, a lot (lots) part, the rest, the bulk, percent, 분수	+ of +	단수 명사 + 단수 동사 복수 명사 + 복수 동사

Most of the lobby requires renovations.   로비의 대부분은 수리가 필요하다.

→ Most of 뒤의 명사가 단수 명사(the lobby)이므로, 단수 동사(requires)를 씁니다.

Most of the team members agree with the plan.   팀원들 대부분은 계획에 동의한다.

→ Most of 뒤의 명사가 복수 명사(the team members)이므로, 복수 동사(agree)를 씁니다.

> **토익 실전 Check-up** 둘 중 알맞은 것을 고르세요.
>
> Part of the problem (ⓐ were, ⓑ was) a lack of government funding for social services.   정답·해석·해설 p.127

✱ **접속사 and로 연결된 주어**는 복수 취급하여 뒤에 **복수 동사**를 씁니다.

Ms. Ross <u>and</u> her former coworker meet every month for lunch.
Ms. Ross와 그녀의 전 동료는 점심 식사를 하기 위해 매달 만난다.

✱ **접속사 or로 연결된 주어(A or B)**는 **B에 동사를 수일치**시킵니다.

Your college transcripts <u>or</u> a letter of reference is necessary to apply.
지원하기 위해서는 귀하의 대학 성적 증명서들 또는 추천서가 필요합니다.
→ 복수 명사(Your college transcripts)와 단수 명사(a letter of reference)가 접속사 or로 연결되어 있으므로, or 뒤에 오는 명사(a letter of reference)에 맞추어 단수 동사(is)를 씁니다.

토익 실전 Check-up 둘 중 알맞은 것을 고르세요.

Some chairs or a sofa (ⓐ are, ⓑ is) needed for the employee break room.   정답·해석·해설 **p.127**

✱ **주격 관계절의 동사**는 **선행사와 수일치**시킵니다. 선행사가 단수이면 단수 동사, 복수이면 복수 동사를 씁니다.

단수 선행사 복수 선행사	+	주격 관계사(who, which, that)	+	단수 동사 복수 동사

The new product requires a marketing campaign that attracts consumers.
새 상품은 소비자들을 끌어들이는 마케팅 캠페인을 필요로 한다.
→ 선행사(a marketing campaign)가 단수이므로 주격 관계절에는 단수 동사(attracts)를 씁니다.

City Hall offers many youth programs, which are managed by members of the community.
시청은 많은 청소년 프로그램들을 제공하는데, 그것들은 지역 사회의 구성원들에 의해 운영된다.
→ 선행사(youth programs)가 복수이므로 주격 관계절에는 복수 동사(are)를 씁니다.

토익 실전 Check-up 둘 중 알맞은 것을 고르세요.

A password is required to open documents that (ⓐ contain, ⓑ contains) confidential information.
                                    정답·해석·해설 **p.127**

다음 문장에서 알맞은 것을 고르세요.

01 Make sure no carry-on luggage (ⓐ has, ⓑ have) been left behind before exiting the aircraft.

02 The committee head (ⓐ expression, ⓑ expressed) appreciation to the volunteers for all their hard work.

03 Employee surveys and feedback (ⓐ provide, ⓑ provides) the company with valuable insights.

04 Mr. Pitt was (ⓐ familiar, ⓑ familiarize) with the new software, so he did not attend training.

05 A number of requirements (ⓐ need, ⓑ needs) to be satisfied before a work visa can be granted.

06 Credit cards or cash (ⓐ is, ⓑ are) accepted at Juno Foods.

07 More than 50 percent of consumers (ⓐ trusts, ⓑ trust) the information found on company Web sites.

08 The researchers were reminded about (ⓐ getting, ⓑ get) permits to operate some of their equipment.

다음 문장에서 밑줄 친 곳을 문법에 맞게 고치세요.

09 Staff members with unused vacation time <u>qualifies</u> for additional pay at the end of the year.

10 Ms. Taft often visits the Brennan Art Gallery, which <u>allow</u> people to enter for free on Sundays.

11 Nobody <u>were</u> selected for the general manager position until yesterday.

12 The contestant who <u>take</u> the best picture will win a cash prize.

13 Discounts that <u>applies</u> to subscribers will automatically go into effect when a purchase is made.

14 Mr. Tang made a <u>modify</u> to the schedule for the upcoming board meeting.

15 Ms. Garcia and Mr. Torres <u>is</u> working on the firm's upcoming advertising campaign.

16 Mr. Bing will install cabinets in the kitchen while the rest of the workers <u>paints</u> the walls.

무료 해설 ▶
바로 보기

정답·해석 **p.127**

GRAMMAR PART 5, 6

DAY 03 동사 1

한 권으로 끝내는 해커스 토익 **700+** (LC+RC+VOCA)

PART 5

01 Mr. Peters ------- out invitations to everyone on his contact list whenever he organizes a fundraising event.

(A) sending
(B) sends
(C) to send
(D) send

02 The bus driver announced that they would ------- at Frankfurt Airport at 3 P.M., half an hour earlier than expected.

(A) reach
(B) arrive
(C) occur
(D) follow

03 Technicians are given advanced training so that they are able to ------- equipment problems quickly and fix them.

(A) locate
(B) locates
(C) located
(D) location

04 Marketing team is participating in an exercise in which each team member ------- a personal weakness.

(A) admittance
(B) admit
(C) admittedly
(D) admits

05 A number of staff members ------- the company at the trade exposition that is held in Morel Falls each year.

(A) representative
(B) represent
(C) represents
(D) representing

06 Mr. Harrison did a very good job of negotiating an outcome that was ------- to the parties involved.

(A) have desired
(B) desires
(C) desirability
(D) desirable

07 The Ultracorp conglomerate grew rapidly, ------- smaller companies with similar operations.

(A) will absorb
(B) absorbing
(C) has absorbed
(D) was absorbing

08 Many trees in the Hamilton park were severely ------- by the powerful thunderstorm that occurred last night.

(A) damages
(B) damage
(C) damaged
(D) damageable

09 Please ------- the invitation by June 1st so that event organizers can make arrangements accordingly.

(A) respond
(B) respond to
(C) responding
(D) response

10 ------- the software has increased the laptop's speed and improved the battery life considerably.

(A) Updating
(B) Updated
(C) Updates
(D) Update

11 This year's community carnival is ------- by soft drink company BubbleFizz and the local chamber of commerce.

(A) fund
(B) funding
(C) funds
(D) funded

12 The structural ------- taking place in the lobby are likely to be finished before the deadline.

(A) renovations
(B) renovating
(C) renovation
(D) renovated

13 Teaching the new employees how the packaging system works in just one day could ------- them.

(A) confused
(B) confusing
(C) confusion
(D) confuse

14 Programs ------- the physical fitness and wellbeing of employees are becoming popular at a number of companies.

(A) will encourage
(B) encourage
(C) are encouraged
(D) encouraging

15 Periodically ------- your password to improve the security of your online account.

(A) change
(B) changed
(C) changes
(D) changing

16 Ms. Denton is ------- a city tour for a group of visitors that will stay at the hotel next week.

(A) arrange
(B) arranges
(C) arrangement
(D) arranging

17 After the inspection is done, the mechanic will let us know whether the tires or the steering wheel ------- to be replaced.

(A) needing
(B) needs
(C) need
(D) to need

18 The sharp decline of oil prices is a problem that ------- practically everyone in the industry.

(A) affect
(B) affecting
(C) affects
(D) affection

PART 6

Questions 19-22 refer to the following notice.

Abandoned dogs have become a problem on the streets of the city, and this has caused residents to demand that the local government take action.

Officials have ------- by providing a dual solution. First, they have ------- an existing law on the
      19   **20**
deliberate abandonment of animals, increasing the fine for such acts to $2,000 and allowing for jail time of up to 90 days. In addition, all pets now require electronic tags. -------. An authorized agency
                                                                                          21
will be ------- these tags for a fee.
         22

These measures are expected to drastically reduce the stray dog population. Meanwhile, the government's animal services will continue to have them sheltered and placed in permanent homes.

19 (A) declined
(B) objected
(C) addressed
(D) responded

20 (A) revision
(B) revising
(C) revised
(D) revise

21 (A) These contain GPS devices that allow owners to track them.
(B) These will get veterinarians to help us further reduce the number of strays.
(C) There is a growing need for animal shelters in the city.
(D) The penalty will increase for second-time offenders.

22 (A) issued
(B) issuing
(C) issuance
(D) issue

정답·해석·해설 **p.128**

Course 1 능동태 · 수동태

지훈이가 문을 <u>열었다</u>.
능동태

<u>문이 열렸다</u>.
수동태

'지훈이가 문을 열었다'라는 문장처럼 주어가 행위의 주체가 되는 것을 **능동태**라고 하고, '문이 열렸다'처럼 주어가 행위의 대상이 되는 것을 **수동태**라고 합니다.

기초문법 잡기

1 수동태는 어떻게 생겼나요?

수동태의 기본 형태는 'be동사 + p.p.'입니다.

능동태	Jihoon opened the door. 지훈이가 문을 열었다.
수동태	The door <u>was opened</u> by Jihoon. 지훈이에 의해 문이 열렸다.

be동사 + p.p.

2 능동태 문장을 수동태 문장으로 어떻게 바꾸나요?

능동태 문장의 목적어는 수동태 문장에서 주어가 되고, 능동태 문장의 주어는 수동태 문장에서 보통 'by + 목적격'으로 바뀝니다.

능동태 He <u>signed</u> <u>the contracts</u>. 그는 계약서에 서명했다.
주어 능동태 동사 목적어

수동태 <u>The contracts</u> <u>were signed</u> <u>by him</u>. 계약서는 그에 의해 서명되었다.
주어 수동태 동사 by + 목적격

3 모든 동사가 수동태가 될 수 있나요?

능동태 문장의 목적어가 수동태 문장의 주어가 되므로, 반드시 목적어를 가지는 타동사만 수동태가 될 수 있습니다. arrive(도착하다), occur(발생하다)와 같은 자동사는 목적어를 갖지 않기 때문에 수동태가 될 수 없습니다.

The train was arrived on time. (×)

The train arrived on time. (○)
→ 자동사(arrive)는 목적어를 갖지 않기 때문에 수동태가 될 수 없습니다.

토익 포인트 1 능동태와 수동태 구별

✽ 동사 뒤에 **목적어가 있으면 능동태**를, **목적어가 없으면 수동태**를 씁니다.

능동태 The city (~~was fined~~, fined) the company $10,000. 시는 회사에 1만 달러를 부과했다.

→ 반드시 목적어를 가지는 타동사(fine) 뒤에 목적어가 있으므로, **능동**태 동사(fined)를 써야 합니다.

수동태 He (fined, was fined) for speeding. 그는 과속으로 벌금을 부과받았다.

→ 반드시 목적어를 가지는 타동사(fine) 뒤에 목적어가 없으므로, 수동태 동사(was fined)를 써야 합니다.

토익 실전 Check-up 둘 중 알맞은 것을 고르세요.

The tourists (ⓐ visited, ⓑ were visited) several famous landmarks. 정답·해석·해설 p.130

토익 포인트 2 감정을 나타내는 동사의 능동태와 수동태 구별

✽ 감정을 나타내는 타동사는 **주어가 감정의 원인**이면 **능동태**를, **주어가 감정을 느끼면 수동태**를 씁니다.

흥미·만족	interest 흥미를 일으키다	excite 흥분시키다	satisfy 만족시키다
	fascinate 매료시키다	please 기쁘게 하다	amuse 즐겁게 하다
실망·좌절	disappoint 실망시키다	frustrate 좌절시키다	discourage 낙담시키다
놀람·걱정	surprise 놀라게 하다	shock 충격을 주다	concern 걱정시키다

능동태 The discovery of the new species (~~was fascinated~~, fascinated) biologists.

새로운 종의 발견은 생물학자들을 매료시켰다.

→ 주어(The discovery of the new species)가 매료시키는 원인이므로, 능동태 동사(fascinated)를 씁니다.

수동태 Biologists (~~fascinated~~, were fascinated) by the discovery of the new species.

생물학자들은 새로운 종의 발견에 매료되었다.

→ 주어(Biologists)가 매료됨을 느끼므로, 수동태 동사(were fascinated)를 씁니다.

토익 실전 Check-up 둘 중 알맞은 것을 고르세요.

People at the gallery (ⓐ interested, ⓑ were interested) in the new exhibit. 정답·해석·해설 p.130

토익 포인트 3 　수동태 동사 + 전치사

∗ by가 아닌 다른 전치사와 함께 쓰이는 수동태 동사 표현

be satisfied with ~에 만족하다	be worried about ~을 걱정하다
be pleased with ~으로 기뻐하다	be concerned about ~을 걱정하다
be amused at ~을 즐거워하다	be disappointed in ~에 실망하다
be surprised at ~에 놀라다	be shocked at ~에 충격을 받다
be alarmed at ~에 놀라다	be interested in ~에 관심이 있다
be frightened of ~에 놀라다	be convinced of ~을 확신하다
be related to ~과 관련되어 있다	be covered with ~으로 덮이다
be associated with ~과 관련되다	be absorbed in ~에 열중하다
be based on ~에 기반하다, 근거하다	be divided into ~으로 나뉘다
be equipped with ~을 갖추고 있다	be assigned to ~에 배정되다

The movie is based on a bestselling novel.　그 영화는 베스트셀러 소설을 기반으로 한다.

토익 실전 Check-up 둘 중 알맞은 것을 고르세요.

The consumption of soda is related (ⓐ at, ⓑ to) a high risk of diabetes.　　정답·해석·해설 p.130

토익 포인트 4 　수동태 동사 + to 부정사

∗ '수동태 동사 + to 부정사' 형태로 자주 쓰이는 표현

be asked to ~하라고 요청받다	be allowed to ~하도록 허가받다
be requested to ~하라고 요청받다	be permitted to ~하도록 허가받다
be required to ~하도록 요구받다	be entitled to ~할 자격이 있다
be reminded to ~하라는 말을 듣다	be prepared to ~할 준비가 되다
be encouraged to ~하라고 권고받다	be scheduled to ~할 예정이다
be advised to ~하라고 충고받다	be supposed to ~하기로 되어 있다
be warned to ~하라고 경고받다	be expected to ~할 것으로 기대되다

Mr. Dalton is prepared to deliver his speech tomorrow.　Mr. Dalton은 내일 연설을 할 준비가 되었다.

토익 실전 Check-up 둘 중 알맞은 것을 고르세요.

Presto Airline passengers are allowed (ⓐ to use, ⓑ use) electronic devices during flights.

정답·해석·해설 p.130

HACKERS PRACTICE 토익 700+ 달성을 위한 연습 문제

다음 문장에서 알맞은 것을 고르세요.

01 Membership fees at Navid's Gym are (ⓐ charging, ⓑ charged) every month.

02 The speaker (ⓐ amused, ⓑ was amused) the audience with stories about his first job.

03 The board (ⓐ is, ⓑ has) decided to nominate Maria Alexi as the next company president.

04 Most city residents are satisfied (ⓐ at, ⓑ with) the newly expanded public transit system.

05 Junior associates (ⓐ are required, ⓑ require) to submit progress reports at least once a week.

06 Community residents (ⓐ object, ⓑ oppose) the construction of the nuclear reactor.

07 The company (ⓐ produces, ⓑ is produced) a wide range of greeting cards.

08 This year's trade conference (ⓐ is scheduled, ⓑ schedules) to take place on February 7th.

다음 문장에서 밑줄 친 곳을 문법에 맞게 고치세요.

09 Participants of yesterday morning's workshop session <u>bored</u> as they only watched a technical video.

10 The accounting department <u>are</u> recruiting temporary assistants for the busy tax payment period.

11 For his contribution to the book, Mr. Avery <u>entitles</u> to receive one percent of the profits.

12 Blake Inc. <u>was disappointed</u> many of its investors as the profits were lower than anticipated.

13 Ms. Cartwright <u>was hiring</u> as manager because of her extensive experience in the industry.

14 Passengers <u>permit</u> to keep one personal item and a carry-on bag in the cabin of the plane.

15 The credit card offered by HTI Solutions <u>accumulate</u> points that can be redeemed for air travel.

16 We had better <u>paid</u> the bill or our cable access might be cut off.

무료 해설 ▶
바로 보기

정답·해석 **p.131**

GRAMMAR PART 5, 6

DAY 04 동사 2

한 권으로 끝내는 해커스 토익 700+ (LC+RC+VOCA)

Course 2 시제 · 가정법

토익 출제경향
평균 1~2문제 정도 출제

시제

버스가 **출발했다**.
　　　동사(과거)

버스가 **출발할 것이다**.
　　　동사(미래)

동사는 '출발했다', '출발할 것이다'와 같이 시간의 변화에 따라 다양하게 나타낼 수 있습니다. 이와 같이 동사의 형태를 바꾸어 어떤 행동이나 사건을 시간의 흐름에 따라 표현할 수 있는데, 이를 동사의 **시제**라고 합니다.

가정법

오늘이 일요일이라면,
늦게까지 잘 수 있을 텐데.

'오늘이 일요일이라면 늦게까지 잘 수 있을 텐데'라는 문장은 오늘은 일요일이 아니지만 일요일이라고 가정하여 말하고 있습니다. 이와 같이 현재나 과거의 반대 상황을 가정하여 말하는 것을 **가정법**이라고 합니다.

기초문법 잡기

1 시제의 종류에는 어떤 것이 있나요?

동사의 시제에는 단순, 진행, 완료 시제가 있습니다.

(1) 단순 시제: 특정한 시간에 발생한 일이나 상태를 나타내는 시제입니다.

현재	The bus leaves at 7 A.M. every day. 버스는 매일 오전 7시에 출발한다.
과거	The bus left at 7 A.M. yesterday. 버스는 어제 오전 7시에 출발했다.
미래	The bus will leave at 7 A.M. tomorrow. 버스는 내일 오전 7시에 출발할 것이다.

(2) 진행 시제: 주어진 시점에 동작이 계속 진행 중임을 나타내는 시제입니다.

현재진행	Ms. Jenner is running in the marathon now. Ms. Jenner는 지금 마라톤을 뛰고 있다.
과거진행	Ms. Jenner was running in the marathon last year. Ms. Jenner는 작년에 마라톤을 뛰었다.
미래진행	Ms. Jenner will be running in the marathon next year. Mr. Jenner는 내년에 마라톤을 뛸 것이다.

(3) 완료 시제: 기준 시점보다 앞선 시점부터 발생한 일이나 상태가 기준 시점까지 계속되는 것을 나타내는 시제입니다.

현재완료	My neighbor has lived in Boston for five years. 내 이웃은 보스턴에 5년째 살고 있다.
과거완료	My neighbor had lived in Chicago for five years before moving to Boston. 내 이웃은 보스턴으로 이사 오기 전까지 시카고에서 5년 동안 살았었다.
미래완료	My neighbor will have lived in Boston for five years by next month. 내 이웃은 다음 달쯤에는 보스턴에서 5년째 살아온 것이 될 것이다.

2 가정법의 종류에는 어떤 것이 있나요?

가정법에는 가정법 과거, 가정법 과거완료, 가정법 미래가 있습니다.

(1) 가정법 과거: 현재 상황을 반대로 가정하여 표현할 때 씁니다.

If today were Sunday, I would not have to go to school. 오늘이 일요일이라면, 학교에 안 가도 됐을 텐데.

(2) 가정법 과거완료: 과거의 사실이나 상황을 반대로 가정하여 표현할 때 씁니다.

If I had taken a taxi, I would have gotten home earlier. 만약 택시를 탔더라면, 집에 더 일찍 도착했을 텐데.

(3) 가정법 미래: 가능성이 희박한 미래나 미래에 일어날 법한 일을 가정하여 표현할 때 씁니다.

If it should snow tomorrow, we will postpone the trip. 만약 내일 눈이 온다면, 우리는 소풍을 연기할 텐데.

토익 포인트 1   단순 시제 (현재/과거/미래)

✴ **현재 시제(동사/동사 + (e)s)는 일반적인 사실이나 일상적으로 반복되는 동작을 나타냅니다.** 특히 아래와 같은 표현들이 현재 시제와 함께 자주 쓰입니다.

usually 보통	often 자주, 종종	every day 매일	these days 요즘

Ms. Jones usually responds to customers' inquiries promptly. Ms. Jones는 보통 고객의 문의에 지체 없이 답변한다.

✴ **과거 시제(동사 + ed/불규칙 동사)는 과거에 이미 끝난 동작이나 상태를 나타냅니다.** 특히 아래와 같은 표현들이 과거 시제와 함께 자주 쓰입니다.

yesterday 어제	ago ~ 전에	last + week/month/year 지난주/달/해	in + 과거 연도 ~년에

The manufacturing plant purchased new machines two months ago. 그 제조 공장은 두 달 전에 새 기계들을 구매했다.

✴ **미래 시제(will + 동사원형)는 미래 상황에 대한 예상이나 말하는 사람의 의지를 나타냅니다.** 특히 아래와 같은 표현들이 미래 시제와 함께 자주 쓰입니다.

tomorrow 내일	next + week/month/year 다음 주/달/해	by/until + 미래 시간 표현 ~까지

They will drive to the new branch in Florida tomorrow. 그들은 내일 플로리다의 새 지점으로 운전을 해서 갈 것이다.

> **토익 실전 Check-up** 둘 중 알맞은 것을 고르세요.
> New staff members (ⓐ will attend, ⓑ attended) an orientation session next Monday.   정답·해석·해설 p.131

토익 포인트 2   진행 시제 (현재진행/과거진행/미래진행)

✴ **현재진행 시제(am/are/is + -ing)는 현재 시점에 진행되고 있는 일을 나타냅니다.**

Mr. Rogers is inspecting some factory equipment at the moment.
Mr. Rogers는 현재 몇몇 공장 기기들을 검사하고 있다.

✴ **과거진행 시제(was/were + -ing)는 과거 특정 시점에 진행되고 있던 일을 나타냅니다.**

The workers were packing the order when their supervisor arrived yesterday.
어제 감독관이 도착했을 때 직원들은 주문품을 포장하고 있었다.

✴ **미래진행 시제(will be + -ing)는 미래 특정 시점에 진행되고 있을 일을 나타냅니다.**

Mr. Nathans will be speaking with a potential investor at this time tomorrow.
Mr. Nathans는 내일 이때쯤이면 잠재 투자자와 이야기하고 있을 것이다.

> **토익 실전 Check-up** 둘 중 알맞은 것을 고르세요.
> A technician (ⓐ was, ⓑ is) fixing the broken photocopier now.   정답·해석·해설 p.131

토익 포인트 3 **완료 시제** (현재완료/과거완료/미래완료)

✱ **현재완료 시제(have/has + p.p.)는 과거에 시작된 일이 현재 시점까지 계속되고 있는 것을 나타냅니다.** 특히 아래와 같은 표현들이 현재완료 시제와 함께 자주 쓰입니다.

since + 과거 시점 ~이래로	over the last/past + 기간 지난 ~ 동안	for + 기간 ~ 동안

Some customers have waited for an hour already. 몇몇 고객들은 이미 한 시간 동안 기다려왔다.

✱ **과거완료 시제(had + p.p.)는 과거의 특정 시점을 기준으로 그보다 더 이전에 일어난 일을 나타냅니다.**

The committee had consulted an expert before it made its decision. 위원회는 결정을 내리기 전에 전문가에게 자문을 구했다.

✱ **미래완료 시제(will have + p.p.)는 현재나 과거에 발생한 동작이 미래의 특정 시점에 완료될 것임을 나타냅니다.** 특히 아래와 같은 표현들이 미래완료 시제와 함께 자주 쓰입니다.

by next + 시간 표현 다음 ~쯤에는	by the end of + 시간 표현 ~ 말까지	next + 시간 표현 다음 ~에

Mr. Ben will have studied English for five years by next month. Mr. Ben은 다음 달쯤에는 영어를 5년째 공부해온 것이 된다.

토익 실전 Check-up 둘 중 알맞은 것을 고르세요.

Ms. Petrov (ⓐ will have moved, ⓑ moved) to Lennoxville by the end of the week. 정답·해석·해설 p.131

토익 포인트 4 **가정법 과거/가정법 과거완료/가정법 미래**

✱ **가정법 과거와 가정법 과거완료는 현재나 과거 사실을 반대로 가정하여 말할 때 씁니다.**

과거	If + 주어 + 과거동사(be동사의 경우 were), 주어 + would(could, might, should) + 동사원형	현재의 반대를 가정
	만약 ~이라면,　　　　　　　　　　　　　　　　~할 텐데	
과거완료	If + 주어 + had p.p., 주어 + would(could, might, should) have p.p.	과거의 반대를 가정
	만약 ~했었더라면,　　　　　　~했을 텐데	

If Mr. Levine checked the manual, he would know how to use the equipment.
만약 Mr. Levine이 설명서를 확인한다면, 그 장비를 어떻게 사용하는지 알 텐데.
→ 현재 Mr. Levine이 설명서를 확인하지 않아서 장비를 사용할 줄 모른다는 사실의 반대를 가정하고 있습니다.

If Mr. Alberici had been on time for work, he would have attended the meeting.
만약 Mr. Alberici가 회사에 제시간에 왔더라면, 회의에 참석했을 텐데.
→ 과거에 Mr. Alberici가 회사에 제시간에 오지 않아서 회의에 참석하지 못했다는 사실의 반대를 가정하고 있습니다.

✱ **가정법 미래는 일어날 가능성이 적은 미래의 일을 가정하거나 미래에 일어날 법한 일을 염려하거나 대비할 때 씁니다.**

If + 주어 + should + 동사원형, 주어 + will(can, may, should) + 동사원형
혹시 ~한다면,　　　　　　　　~할 텐데

If stock market prices should drop overnight, investors will lose a significant amount of money.
혹시라도 주가가 하룻밤 사이에 떨어진다면, 투자자들은 상당한 양의 돈을 잃을 텐데.
→ 주가가 하룻밤 사이에 떨어질 것이라는 일어날 가능성이 적은 미래의 일을 가정하고 있습니다.

토익 실전 Check-up 둘 중 알맞은 것을 고르세요.

If the company (ⓐ had, ⓑ should) change suppliers, it may lose customers. 정답·해석·해설 p.131

다음 문장에서 알맞은 것을 고르세요.

01 The professor often (ⓐ participates, ⓑ was participating) in after-school programs for teens.

02 The Pierson Clinic (ⓐ provides, ⓑ has provided) free medical services to the poor since 2005.

03 On Monday, Mr. Shaffer (ⓐ will be reporting, ⓑ has reported) for work as the new manager.

04 The (ⓐ instructions, ⓑ instruction) for putting together the furniture are too complex.

05 Camberton Corp.'s main cement supplier (ⓐ has been renewing, ⓑ will renew) its contract soon.

06 Before the financial report was printed, it (ⓐ is revised, ⓑ had been revised) several times.

07 Currently, the studio's programmers (ⓐ are developing, ⓑ will develop) a new video game.

08 If Fortune-Tech (ⓐ had invested, ⓑ invests) in the project, they would have made a profit.

다음 문장에서 밑줄 친 곳을 문법에 맞게 고치세요.

09 Ms. Neely has taught accounting courses at the training institute for 10 years by next month.

10 If the firm had made a reasonable offer on the property, the owner might accept it.

11 Mr. Rogers will meet with a client when I arrived at the office.

12 Half of the participants in the marketing study rates the product very highly.

13 Mr. Klaxton is a famous chef whose dishes has received numerous positive reviews.

14 If the event was promoted more, it would attract a larger number of attendees.

15 Two years ago, Mr. Jackson will leave for Spain to work as a diplomat for the British government.

16 Ms. Dobbs has complete her training and will begin working soon.

무료 해설 ▶
바로 보기

정답·해석 p.131

PART 5

01 Many people ------- by the council's announcement that the city planned to build a new baseball stadium.

(A) surprises
(B) surprised
(C) were surprised
(D) has surprised

02 As of now, Bastion Incorporated ------- one floor of the Wasser building, but they will eventually expand.

(A) occupies
(B) occupied
(C) had occupied
(D) were occupying

03 Residents of Cowansville hope that the local government ------- plans for the new housing development next week.

(A) will approve
(B) had approved
(C) has approved
(D) to approve

04 Mr. Quesada ------- the number of attendees at the architects' convention by the time a venue for the event is reserved.

(A) confirmed
(B) will have confirmed
(C) was confirming
(D) confirmation

05 Urban planners expect ------- the amount of traffic on the city's streets through the construction of a new subway line.

(A) reduces
(B) to reduce
(C) have reduced
(D) were reduced

06 Mr. Gallagher contacted his attorney since he wasn't certain that he ------- the agreement accurately.

(A) interpreting
(B) had interpreted
(C) have interpreted
(D) interprets

07 Mr. Brookside was ------- to notify his clients that he will be absent next week due to the trade exhibition.

(A) reminding
(B) reminded
(C) reminder
(D) reminds

08 The digital library ------- considerably over the past three years and now offers a much wider range of materials.

(A) is expanding
(B) has expanded
(C) will expand
(D) expands

09 Mr. Campbell noticed a problem with the revolving door as he ------- yesterday.

(A) enters
(B) was entering
(C) is entering
(D) has entered

10 If the quality of the new products had been better, the company ------- fewer customer complaints.

(A) is having
(B) might have had
(C) to have had
(D) will have

11 Only job applications that ------- by March 9 will be reviewed by Bradbury & Associates' hiring committee.

(A) are submitted
(B) being submitted
(C) is submitted
(D) has been submitted

12 The crew ------- the tiles to the bathroom later today and installing the fixtures on Thursday.

(A) will be adding
(B) has been added
(C) has added
(D) addition

13 If the city's population should continue to grow, Vero-Build ------- even more residential complexes.

(A) constructs
(B) had constructed
(C) will construct
(D) constructed

14 Ms. Taylor ------- on a Web site design for a large corporate client this month, so she is unavailable now.

(A) had worked
(B) working
(C) was working
(D) is working

15 If Ms. Scott ------- in charge of the marketing team, she would manage it efficiently.

(A) has been   (B) is
(C) were   (D) is being

16 A new office tower ------- in the heart of the financial district.

(A) will build   (B) has been building
(C) was built   (D) will be building

17 Ms. Aileen will resign next month ------- she receives a salary raise or not.

(A) there   (B) probably
(C) whether   (D) regarding

18 A poll shows that the gap between the rich and the poor has ------- this decade.

(A) wide   (B) wider
(C) widening   (D) widened

PART 6

Questions 19-22 refer to the following e-mail.

To: <chris_rivers@globex.com>

From: <b.andreson@radeelectronics.com >

Dear Mr. Rivers,

Thank you for your e-mail. I am glad you are pleased ------- your new phone. Unfortunately, Rade
    19
Electronics does not stock cases for your phone.

In order to obtain the ------- smartphone cases for the model, I suggest you visit your local Wallaby
                        20
Telecom branch. For your convenience, I ------- up the store locations on their Web site. -------. As
                                          21   22
you can see, the closest store to your location is on 350 Harold Street.

If you need further assistance, please let me know.

Sincerely,

Bethany Anderson, Rade Electronics

---

19 (A) of   (B) to
(C) in   (D) with

20 (A) imported   (B) appropriate
(C) colorful   (D) expensive

21 (A) look   (B) looked
(C) will look   (D) had looked

22 (A) I believe you will be satisfied with our service.
(B) You'll find the map as an attachment to this e-mail.
(C) It features all of their products.
(D) Please refer to the user manual.

정답·해석·해설 **p.132**

Course 1 to 부정사와 동명사

토익 출제경향
최대 2문제까지 출제

나는 그림을 <u>그리기 위해</u> 스케치북을 샀다.
　　　　　부사 역할

나는 그림 <u>그리는 것</u>을 좋아한다.
　　　　명사 역할

동사 '그리다'가 '그리기 위해', '그리는 것'으로 형태가 바뀌어 동사가 아닌 다른 품사의 역할을 하고 있습니다. 영어에서도 동사 앞에 to가 붙은 **to 부정사**와 동사 뒤에 ing가 붙은 **동명사**가 문장 속에서 여러 역할을 할 수 있습니다.

기초문법 잡기

1 to 부정사는 어떤 형태를 가지고 있나요?

to 부정사의 형태는 'to + 동사원형'입니다.

I bought a sketchbook <u>to draw</u> pictures.　나는 그림을 그리기 위해 스케치북을 샀다.
　　　　　　　　　　　to 부정사

2 동명사는 어떤 형태를 가지고 있나요?

동명사의 형태는 '동사원형 + ing'입니다.

I like <u>drawing</u> pictures.　나는 그림 그리는 것을 좋아한다.
　　　　동명사

3 to 부정사와 동명사는 동사의 성질을 가지고 있나요?

to 부정사와 동명사는 문장에서 동사의 역할을 하지는 않지만 동사의 성질을 그대로 가지고 있습니다. 그래서 to 부정사와 동명사, 그리고 다음 Course에서 배울 분사를 동사에 준한다는 의미로 **준동사**라고 부릅니다. 예를 들어, 준동사는 to thank his teacher처럼 뒤에 목적어나 보어를 가질 수 있고, exercising regularly처럼 부사의 꾸밈을 받기도 합니다.

Mr. Jensen wants <u>to thank</u> <u>his teacher</u>.　Mr. Jensen은 그의 선생님께 감사드리고 싶어 한다.
　　　　　　　　　to 부정사　　목적어

Karen enjoys <u>exercising</u> <u>regularly</u>.　Karen은 규칙적으로 운동하는 것을 좋아한다.
　　　　　　　동명사　　　부사

✱ to 부정사는 **명사 역할**을 하여 문장의 **주어, 목적어, 보어 자리**에 오며, '**~하는 것, ~하기**'로 해석합니다.

주어	To promote the fundraising event **is Layla's responsibility.** 기금 모금 행사를 홍보하는 것은 Layla의 책무이다.
목적어	**Dr. Simons decided** to redecorate his waiting room. Dr. Simons는 그의 대기실을 재단장하기로 결정했다.
주격 보어	**My advice is** to send an e-mail to customer service. 내 조언은 고객 서비스에 이메일을 보내는 것이다
목적격 보어	**The secretary wants staff members** to submit their insurance forms. 비서는 직원들이 보험 신청서를 제출하기를 바란다.

✱ to 부정사는 **형용사 역할**을 하여 **명사 뒤에서 명사를 수식**하며, '**~해야 할, ~할**'로 해석합니다.

명사 수식	**There is not enough time** to complete the project today. 오늘 프로젝트를 완료할 만한 시간이 충분히 없다.

✱ to 부정사는 **부사 역할**을 하여 **목적, 이유, 결과** 등의 의미를 나타냅니다.

목적	To expand, **the organization may require additional financial backing.** 확장하기 위해서, 조직은 추가적인 자금 지원이 필요할 수도 있다.
이유	**Mr. Fabian was happy** to accept an invitation to the opening ceremony. Mr. Fabian은 개회식 초청을 승낙하게 되어 기뻤다.
결과	**Ms. Ren went to refill her cup only** to notice the coffee pot was empty. Ms. Ren은 그녀의 컵을 리필하러 갔으나 주전자가 빈 것을 알게 되었을 뿐이었다.

토익 실전 Check-up 둘 중 알맞은 것을 고르세요.

People must register with the Web site (ⓐ apply, ⓑ to apply) for jobs. 정답·해석·해설 p.134

✱ to 부정사를 목적어로 취하는 동사

want to ~하는 것을 원하다	**need to** ~하는 것을 필요로 하다	**expect to** ~하는 것을 기대하다	**decide to** ~하기로 결정하다
ask to ~하는 것을 요청하다	**agree to** ~하는 것에 동의하다	**refuse to** ~하는 것을 거절하다	**try to** ~하는 것을 시도하다

They **decided** to submit **the proposal today.** 그들은 제안서를 오늘 제출하기로 결정했다.

✱ to 부정사를 취하는 형용사

be able to ~할 수 있다	**be ready to** ~할 준비가 되어 있다
be eager to 몹시 ~하고 싶다	**be difficult to** ~하기 어렵다
be delighted to ~하는 것을 기쁘게 생각하다	**be pleased to** ~하는 것을 기쁘게 생각하다

Employees are **able** to reserve **conference rooms.** 직원들은 회의실을 예약할 수 있다.

토익 실전 Check-up 둘 중 알맞은 것을 고르세요.

The customer refused (ⓐ paying, ⓑ to pay) for the unsatisfactory service. 정답·해석·해설 p.134

GRAMMAR PART 5, 6

DAY 05 준동사

한 권으로 끝내는 해커스 토익 700+ (LC+RC+VOCA)

✱ **동명사는 명사 역할**을 하여 문장의 **주어, 목적어, 보어** 자리에 오며, '**~하는 것, ~하기**'로 해석합니다.

주어	Launching a new product **requires effective marketing.**
	새로운 제품을 출시하는 것은 효과적인 마케팅을 필요로 한다.
동사의 목적어	**The client appreciates** receiving a discount coupon.
	그 고객은 할인 쿠폰을 받은 것을 고맙게 생각한다.
전치사의 목적어	**The waitress apologized for** making a mistake with the order.
	그 여종업원은 주문에 대해 실수를 한 것에 대해 사과했다.
보어	**The sales representative's goal is** meeting his monthly quota.
	영업 직원의 목표는 월별 할당량을 달성하는 것이다.

토익 실전 Check-up 둘 중 알맞은 것을 고르세요.

(ⓐ Speaking, ⓑ Speak) in front of a large crowd can be stressful.

정답·해석·해설 **p.134**

✱ **동명사를 포함하는 표현**

go -ing ~하러 가다	be busy -ing ~하느라 바쁘다
be worth -ing ~할 가치가 있다	keep -ing 계속 ~하다
spend + 시간/돈 + -ing 시간/돈을 ~하는 데 쓰다	cannot help -ing ~하지 않을 수 없다
have difficulty(trouble, a problem) -ing ~하는 데 어려움을 겪다	

Ms. Martinez is busy preparing **for the presentation.** Ms. Martinez는 발표를 준비하느라 바쁘다.

✱ **'전치사 to + 동명사'를 포함하는 표현**

contribute to -ing ~에 공헌하다	be committed to -ing ~에 전념하다
look forward to -ing ~하기를 고대하다	be dedicated to -ing ~에 전념하다, ~에 헌신적이다
object to -ing ~에 반대하다, ~에 이의를 제기하다	be devoted to -ing ~에 헌신적이다
lead to -ing ~의 원인이 되다	be used to -ing ~에 익숙하다

* 전치사 to를 to 부정사의 to로 착각하여 to 뒤에 동사원형을 쓰지 않도록 주의합니다.

The group is dedicated to collecting **items for charity.** 단체는 자선을 위한 물품들을 모으는 것에 전념한다.

토익 실전 Check-up 둘 중 알맞은 것을 고르세요.

Some of the computers are having difficulty (ⓐ to connect, ⓑ connecting) to the Internet. 정답·해석·해설 **p.134**

HACKERS PRACTICE 토익 700+ 달성을 위한 연습 문제

다음 문장에서 알맞은 것을 고르세요.

01 Mr. Jan called the manager (ⓐ briefed, ⓑ to brief) her on a customer complaint.

02 Most participants enjoyed (ⓐ attending, ⓑ attend) the seminar and speaking with others.

03 Ms. Harrington is in charge of (ⓐ organized, ⓑ organizing) the end-of-year staff party.

04 Mr. Rio is currently unavailable as he (ⓐ is preparing, ⓑ was preparing) for a presentation.

05 The best way (ⓐ to learn, ⓑ learns) a new language is to practice it with other people.

06 Ms. Dingman is busy (ⓐ to respond, ⓑ responding) to a customer's inquiry at the moment.

07 Because no local bookstores carried the novel, Ms. Jones ultimately decided (ⓐ to order, ⓑ ordered) it online.

08 We (ⓐ will resolve, ⓑ resolving) any product flaws mentioned in the report by next month.

다음 문장에서 밑줄 친 곳을 문법에 맞게 고치세요.

09 Mr. Kensington is used to <u>eat</u> at a nearby restaurant for lunch during the workweek.

10 Ms. Reece worked very hard <u>succeed</u> in her role as operations manager.

11 Ms. Gable wants <u>continuing</u> subscribing to *PhotoLite Magazine*.

12 Many residents in the Bay Area <u>concern</u> about the conditions of nearby beaches.

13 Tomorrow is the deadline <u>choose</u> courses for the new semester.

14 Ms. Lambert visited Dauphine Furnishings <u>buy</u> new office furniture for her workspace.

15 The producer has <u>cancel</u> the event suddenly without giving an explanation.

16 Mr. Lee expects <u>receiving</u> a copy of the budget report.

무료 해설 ▶
바로 보기

정답·해석 p.135

Course 2 분사

달리는 자동차
형용사 역할

'달리는'은 자동차가 달리고 있다는 동작의 의미를 담고 있습니다. 이와 같이 동사의 성격을 가지고 있으면서 명사를 수식하는 형용사 역할을 하는 것을 **분사**라고 합니다.

기초문법 잡기

1 분사는 어떤 형태를 가지고 있나요?

분사에는 현재분사와 과거분사가 있는데 이 둘은 다른 형태를 갖습니다. 현재분사는 '동사원형 + ing'로 능동의 의미를 나타내고, 과거분사는 '동사원형 + ed'로 수동의 의미를 나타냅니다.

Please watch out for <u>falling</u> objects.　떨어지는 물체에 주의하시기 바랍니다.
　　　　　　　　　　　현재분사 (능동의 의미)

Ms. Nam spent 400 dollars fixing the <u>broken</u> windows.　Ms. Nam은 깨진 유리창을 수리하는 데 400달러를 썼다.
　　　　　　　　　　　　　　　　　　　과거분사 (수동의 의미)

2 분사도 동사의 성질을 가지고 있나요?

분사도 to 부정사와 동명사처럼, 문장에서 동사의 역할을 하지는 않지만 동사의 성질을 그대로 가지고 있습니다. 따라서 teaching the course처럼 분사 뒤에 목적어나 보어를 가질 수도 있고, announced yesterday처럼 부사의 꾸밈을 받기도 합니다.

The instructor <u>teaching</u> <u>the course</u> is Ms. Rosen.　수업을 가르치는 강사는 Ms. Rosen이다.
　　　　　　　　분사　　　목적어

The news <u>announced</u> <u>yesterday</u> surprised us.　어제 발표된 뉴스는 우리를 놀라게 했다.
　　　　　　分사　　　　부사

토익 포인트 1   분사의 역할과 자리

✱ 분사는 문장에서 **형용사 역할**을 하여, **명사 앞**이나 **뒤**에서 **명사를 수식**하거나 **보어 자리**에 옵니다.

명사 앞	The company offers existing customers a discount on bulk orders.
	그 회사는 기존의 고객들에게 대량 주문에 대한 할인을 제공한다.
명사 뒤	These are the documents required to apply for a passport. 이것들이 여권을 신청하기 위해 필요한 서류들이다.
주격 보어	The assembly instructions for the desk were confusing. 그 책상의 조립 설명서는 헷갈렸다.
목적격 보어	The comedian kept the audience entertained. 그 코미디언은 관객들을 계속해서 즐겁게 했다.

토익 실전 Check-up 둘 중 알맞은 것을 고르세요.

The contributors were thanked for their (ⓐ continue, ⓑ continued) support.   정답·해석·해설 **p.135**

토익 포인트 2   분사구문

✱ 분사구문은 '**(접속사 +) 분사**'의 형태로, '**부사절 접속사 + 주어 + 동사 ~**' 형태의 부사절을 축약한 구문입니다. 부사절이 분사구문으로 바뀌는 과정은 아래와 같습니다.

부사절 접속사 생략 (단, 접속사를 생략했을 때 의미가 모호해질 경우, 생략하지 않습니다.)	As he checked his messages, he saw that Ms. Myers had called.
▼	
부사절 주어 생략 (주절의 주어와 같은 경우에만 생략합니다.)	As he checked his messages, he saw that Ms. Myers had called.
▼	
부사절 동사를 현재분사 또는 과거분사로 교체	Checking his messages, he saw that Ms. Myers had called. 메시지를 확인했을 때, 그는 Ms. Myers가 전화했었다는 것을 보았다.

✱ 분사구문에서 주절의 주어와 분사구문의 관계가 **능동**이면 **현재분사**, **수동**이면 **과거분사**를 씁니다.

(Inspected, Inspecting) the factory, they detected a critical flaw with a machine.
공장을 점검할 때, 그들은 기계에서 치명적인 결함을 발견했다.
→ 주절의 주어(they)와 분사구문이 '그들이 점검하다'라는 의미의 능동 관계이므로 현재분사(Inspecting)를 씁니다.

(Alarming, Alarmed) by the news, investors are selling the stock rapidly.
뉴스로 인해 불안해졌기 때문에, 투자자들은 주식을 빠르게 팔고 있다.
→ 주절의 주어(investors)와 분사구문이 '투자자들이 불안해졌다'라는 의미의 수동 관계이므로 과거분사(Alarmed)를 씁니다.

토익 실전 Check-up 둘 중 알맞은 것을 고르세요.

(ⓐ Speaking, ⓑ Spoke) to potential clients, Mr. Gore always emphasizes the quality of his products.
    정답·해석·해설 **p.135**

✱ 분사가 명사를 수식하는 경우, **수식을 받는 명사와 분사의 관계가 능동**이면 **현재분사**, **수동**이면 **과거분사**를 씁니다.

Students studying abroad need to learn the local language. 해외에서 공부하는 학생들은 현지 언어를 배울 필요가 있다.
→ 수식을 받는 명사(Students)와 분사가 '공부하는 학생들'이라는 의미의 능동 관계이므로 현재분사(studying)를 씁니다.

According to the label, the paper is made entirely from recycled materials.
라벨에 따르면, 그 종이는 전부 재활용된 물질로 만들어졌다.
→ 수식을 받는 명사(materials)와 분사가 '재활용된 물질'이라는 의미의 수동 관계이므로 과거분사(recycled)를 씁니다.

✱ 분사가 보어로 쓰이는 경우, **주어와 보어 또는 목적어와 보어의 관계가 능동**이면 **현재분사**, **수동**이면 **과거분사**를 씁니다.

The mayor's speech at the trade fair was inspiring. 무역 박람회에서 시장의 연설은 고무적이었다.
→ 주어(The mayor's speech)와 보어의 관계가 '시장의 연설은 고무적이었다'라는 의미의 능동 관계이므로 현재분사(inspiring)를 씁니다.

Learning about the merger left some employees concerned. 합병에 대해 알게 된 것은 몇몇 직원들을 염려되게 했다.
→ 목적어(some employees)와 보어의 관계가 '몇몇 직원들이 염려되게 했다'라는 의미의 수동 관계이므로 과거분사(concerned)를 씁니다.

토익 실전 Check-up 둘 중 알맞은 것을 고르세요.

Noticing a mistake, Ms. Roberts had her order (ⓐ canceled, ⓑ canceling).　　　정답·해석·해설 p.135

✱ 명사와 함께 쓰일 때 현재분사와 과거분사를 혼동하기 쉬운 표현

현재분사 + 명사	과거분사 + 명사
leading hotel 일류 호텔	preferred option 선호되는 선택권
opening statement 개회사	proposed change 제안된 변경 사항
promising opportunity 유망한 기회	experienced professional 숙련된 전문가
existing manual 기존 설명서	detailed description 자세한 설명
lasting effect 지속적인 영향	limited budget 제한된 예산
improving market 발전하는 시장	attached file 첨부된 파일
missing information 누락된 정보	damaged appliance 손상된 기기

The economic crisis had a lasting effect on many countries. 경제 공황은 많은 국가에 지속적인 영향을 끼쳤다.

토익 실전 Check-up 둘 중 알맞은 것을 고르세요.

Mr. Hopps performs repairs on a number of (ⓐ damaged, ⓑ damaging) appliances.　　　정답·해석·해설 p.135

HACKERS PRACTICE 토익 700+ 달성을 위한 연습 문제

다음 문장에서 알맞은 것을 고르세요.

01 Many workers are qualified to take (ⓐ advanced, ⓑ advanced) courses in industrial technology.

02 Candidates (ⓐ looking, ⓑ looked) to apply should have work experience in related fields.

03 Critics found the story (ⓐ exaggerated, ⓑ exaggerating) and largely inaccurate.

04 The staff was inspired by their manager's (ⓐ encouragement, ⓑ encouraging) words.

05 The National Air Authority (ⓐ was postponed, ⓑ postponed) all flights to and from Denver until tomorrow morning.

06 (ⓐ Accessed, ⓑ Accessing) thousands of times a day, Leeds' online store is very popular.

07 After moving to a different office, Mr. Castro (ⓐ ordering, ⓑ ordered) some furniture.

08 *The Black Moon* is an (ⓐ excited, ⓑ exciting) action film with some impressive special effects.

다음 문장에서 밑줄 친 곳을 문법에 맞게 고치세요.

09 Electronic Superstore products will <u>discount</u> by up to 70 percent this weekend.

10 <u>Returning</u> late, the book was unavailable for other library members to borrow.

11 The band <u>performed</u> at the concert hall right now was famous in the 1990s.

12 By the end of last month, the Chicago factory <u>has succeeded</u> in achieving its production quotas.

13 For many new entrepreneurs, purchasing a franchise can be a <u>promised</u> opportunity.

14 <u>This</u> is Ms. Ogawa's responsibility to record all transactions in an electronic database.

15 JK Consulting is seeking an <u>experiencing</u> professional for a management position.

16 Banquet guests were asked to let organizers know their <u>preferring</u> meal option.

무료 해설 ▶
바로 보기

정답·해석 **p.135**

PART 5

01 Though it was a ------- day on the stock market, most analysts agreed that prices would soon recover.

(A) disappoints
(B) disappointed
(C) disappointing
(D) disappointment

02 Because the representative spoke primarily in Arabic, management hired someone ------- what he was saying.

(A) interpretation
(B) interprets
(C) interpretative
(D) to interpret

03 The ------- that Mr. Craig hired offered suggestions on how to keep his staff motivated.

(A) consultative
(B) consulted
(C) will consult
(D) consultant

04 The hospital has adopted a computer program ------- for the purpose of better maintaining patient records.

(A) develop
(B) has developed
(C) develops
(D) developed

05 The conference kits ------- accommodation and transport information were distributed to the participants.

(A) holding
(B) holds
(C) hold
(D) will hold

06 Hoping to create more jobs, the government has proposed legislation ------- the official working week to 35 hours.

(A) shortened
(B) shortens
(C) shorten
(D) to shorten

07 The Pembleton Transit Service is devoted to ------- customers a safe and comfortable alternative to driving.

(A) provide
(B) provider
(C) providing
(D) provides

08 All tenants must agree ------- the rules of the building outlined in the rental agreement.

(A) follow
(B) to follow
(C) be followed
(D) following

09 The workshops that Ms. Rodriguez gives on accounting practices for small businesses are very highly -------.

(A) regarding
(B) regards
(C) regarded
(D) regard

10 The greatest challenge many companies face is a ------- budget.

(A) limited
(B) limitation
(C) limits
(D) limit

11 After several failed attempts to contact Mr. Vaughn, Ms. Dean managed ------- a message to his assistant.

(A) conveyed
(B) to convey
(C) convey
(D) conveys

12 The annual report is being proofread for the final time ------- it is printed.

(A) although
(B) by
(C) during
(D) before

13 Because of heavy traffic and narrow sidewalks, the area around the train station can become ------- during peak hours.

(A) crowds
(B) crowding
(C) crowdedly
(D) crowded

14 The head of the engineering department recently ------- his team by suggesting a practical solution for a product design flaw.

(A) assisted
(B) assisting
(C) assist
(D) assists

한 권으로 끝내는
해커스 토익 700+
LC+RC+VOCA

GRAMMAR PART 5, 6

DAY 05 준동사

한 권으로 끝내는 해커스 토익 700+ (LC+RC+VOCA)

15 A variety of preexisting theories ------- the current research on consumer behavior.

(A) guides (B) guide
(C) is guided (D) to guide

16 The store will close early on Monday evening ------- new windows at the front of the building.

(A) to install (B) install
(C) installed (D) will install

17 Football fans need ------- if they want to buy tickets to tomorrow night's game.

(A) to hurry (B) have hurried
(C) hurries (D) hurried

18 A package ------- an antique vase was delivered directly to the curator of the museum.

(A) contain (B) containing
(C) containment (D) container

PART 6

Questions 19-22 refer to the following letter.

Enclosed is your requested replacement card for the Gespanzo Center for the Arts. The card affirms your membership -------. Your new Diamond status entitles you to discounted admission to our exhibitions. Additionally, you may reserve seats in advance for all performances ------- in our Grand Hall.
19   **20**

To show how much we appreciate your support, we would like to invite you to our annual benefit that ------- this Saturday, January 25. -------.
21   **22**

If you have any questions regarding your card, please contact our Patron Relations Center at 555-6293.

19 (A) renewal (B) registration
(C) period (D) upgrade

20 (A) presented (B) presenting
(C) presents (D) are presented

21 (A) will be held (B) have been held
(C) are holding (D) are held

22 (A) Our Web site lists a number of ways you can donate.
(B) Your application was missing some essential information.
(C) We ask that you submit payment for your reservation.
(D) You may bring one guest to the event for free.

정답·해석·해설 p.136

Course 1 명사

토익 출제경향
평균 3문제 정도 출제

남자, 강아지, 불, 행복

'남자', '강아지', '불', '행복'처럼 사람이나 사물, 추상적인 개념 등을 가리키는 것을 **명사**라고 합니다.
명사에는 가산 명사와 불가산 명사가 있습니다.

기초문법 잡기

1 가산 명사와 불가산 명사는 무엇인가요?

가산 명사는 man, dog처럼 개수를 셀 수 있는 명사이고, 불가산 명사는 fire, happiness, history처럼 개수를 셀 수 없는 명사입니다.

가산 명사 (= 셀 수 있는 명사)	일반적인 사물이나 사람	man, friend, dog, pencil
불가산 명사 (= 셀 수 없는 명사)	세상에 하나밖에 없는 지명이나 인명	London, Germany, David, Ms. Reed
	형태가 분명치 않은 것	fire, air, water, oil
	추상적인 개념	history, happiness, success, honesty

Mr. Kim met a <u>friend</u> at a nearby restaurant. Mr. Kim은 근처 식당에서 친구 한 명을 만났다.
　　　　　　　　가산 명사

The interviewer was impressed by the applicant's <u>honesty</u>. 면접관은 지원자의 정직함에 좋은 인상을 받았다.
　　　　　　　　　　　　　　　　　　　　　불가산 명사

2 명사는 주로 어떤 형태를 가지고 있나요?

명사는 주로 -tion/-sion/-ion, -ness, -ance/-ence, -ment, -ty와 같은 꼬리말로 끝납니다.

-tion	emo**tion**	감정
-ness	happi**ness**	행복
-ance	import**ance**	중요성
-ment	develop**ment**	개발
-ty	abili**ty**	능력

토익 포인트 1 명사 자리

★ 명사는 문장에서 **주어, 목적어, 보어** 자리에 옵니다.

주어 자리	**Registration** must be completed by Friday afternoon. 등록은 금요일 오후까지 완료되어야만 한다.
동사의 목적어 자리	Please make a **reservation** as soon as possible. 가능한 한 빨리 예약해 주십시오.
전치사의 목적어 자리	The CEO talked about **attendance** at the last assembly. 최고경영자는 지난 회의에서 출석에 대해 이야기했다.
보어 자리	The e-mail was **confirmation** of Ms. Wilson's purchase. 그 이메일은 Ms. Wilson의 구매에 대한 확인이었다.

★ 명사는 주로 **관사, 소유격, 형용사** 뒤에 옵니다.

관사 뒤	Ms. Stewart checked the **availability** of the auditorium. Ms. Stewart는 강당의 이용 가능 여부를 확인했다.
소유격 뒤	Mr. Gates was told that filing was his **responsibility**. Mr. Gates는 파일 정리가 그의 책임이라고 들었다.
형용사 뒤	Meritt Electronics is hiring people to write short **descriptions** of its products. Meritt Electronics사는 회사의 상품들에 대한 짧은 설명을 쓸 사람들을 고용하고 있다.

> **토익 실전 Check-up** 둘 중 알맞은 것을 고르세요.
>
> The (ⓐ advertisement, ⓑ advertise) is popular with viewers. 정답·해석·해설 **p.138**

토익 포인트 2 가산 명사와 불가산 명사

★ **부정관사 a/an**은 단수 가산 명사 앞에만 오며, 복수 가산 명사나 불가산 명사 앞에는 올 수 없습니다.

The clerk received a (requests, request) from a customer. 직원은 고객으로부터 요청을 받았다.

★ 셀 수 없는 것처럼 보이는 **가산 명사**와 셀 수 있는 것처럼 보이는 **불가산 명사**를 구분하여 알아둡니다.

가산 명사		불가산 명사	
a detail 세부 사항	an account 계좌	information 정보	access 접근, 출입, 이용
a discount 할인	a suggestion 제안	approval 승인	advice 조언, 충고
a reservation 예약	a request 요청	confirmation 확인	satisfaction 만족
an increase 증가	a profit 이익	participation 참가	construction 건설
a requirement 요구 사항	an approach 접근법	furniture 가구	appreciation 감사

(An information, Information) about the fundraiser can be found online. 모금 행사에 대한 정보는 온라인에서 찾을 수 있다.

> **토익 실전 Check-up** 둘 중 알맞은 것을 고르세요.
>
> (ⓐ A construction, ⓑ Construction) of the new baseball stadium was announced yesterday.
>
> 정답·해석·해설 **p.138**

사람명사 vs. 사물/추상명사

🔹 사람명사와 사물/추상명사는 모두 명사 자리에 올 수 있는데, 이 중 문장 안에서 자연스러운 의미를 만드는 명사가 와야 합니다.

attendee 참석자 - attention 주의 - attendance 출석	licensor 검열관 - license 면허, 자격증
producer 생산자 - production 생산 - product 생산품	instructor 강사 - instruction 지시
architect 건축가 - architecture 건축(술)	investor 투자자 - investment 투자
beneficiary 수혜자 - benefit 이익	manufacturer 제조자 - manufacture 제조
applicant 지원자 - application 지원, 신청서	negotiator 협상가 - negotiation 협상
contributor 공헌자 - contribution 공헌	participant 참가자 - participation 참가
developer 개발자 - development 개발	resident 거주자 - residence 거주
distributor 분배자 - distribution 분배	reviewer 비평가 - review 평론
donor 기증자 - donation 기증	subscriber 구독자 - subscription 구독, 가입

The (~~donation~~, donor) wishes to remain unknown. 그 기증자는 익명으로 남기를 원한다.
→ '기증자는 익명으로 남기를 원한다'라는 의미가 되어야 하므로, '기증'이라는 의미의 추상명사(donation)가 아닌, '기증자'라는 의미의 사람명사 (donor)가 와야 합니다.

(~~Participant~~, Participation) in the team building exercise is encouraged. 팀 빌딩 훈련 참가는 장려된다.
→ '팀 빌딩 훈련 참가'라는 의미가 되어야 하므로, '참가자'라는 의미의 사람명사(Participant)가 아닌, '참가'라는 의미의 추상명사(Participation)가 와야 합니다.

토익 실전 Check-up 둘 중 알맞은 것을 고르세요.

Defective items can be returned to the (ⓐ manufacturer, ⓑ manufacture). 정답·해석·해설 p.138

복합 명사

🔹 '명사 + 명사' 형태의 복합 명사

application form 지원서	reception desk 접수처
arrival date 도착일	registration form 등록 양식, 신청서
assembly line 조립 라인	retail sales 소매 판매
confirmation number 예약 확인 번호	retirement celebration 퇴직 기념 축하연
customer satisfaction 고객 만족	safety regulations 안전 규정
sales quota 판매 할당량	travel arrangements 여행(출장) 준비

The staff organized a memorable (~~retired~~, retirement) celebration for Mr. Downing.
직원들은 Mr. Downing을 위해 기억에 남을 퇴직 기념 축하연을 준비했다.

토익 실전 Check-up 둘 중 알맞은 것을 고르세요.

Hotel guests may leave their room keys at the (ⓐ reception, ⓑ receptive) desk when they go out.
정답·해석·해설 p.138

다음 문장에서 알맞은 것을 고르세요.

01 The instructor chose Ms. Kang's essay for (ⓐ submitted, ⓑ submission) to the contest.

02 The (ⓐ importance, ⓑ importantly) of showing up to work on time cannot be overstated.

03 A passport (ⓐ application, ⓑ applicant) form can be downloaded from the Internet.

04 The store set up a new (ⓐ display, ⓑ displays) in its windows for the holiday season.

05 (ⓐ Maintaining, ⓑ Maintain) factory equipment helps prevent breakdowns.

06 If you cannot decide what color to paint your house, our staff would be happy to provide (ⓐ suggestion, ⓑ suggestions).

07 The bank always tries (ⓐ to respond, ⓑ responsible) to any complaints within a day.

08 New employees received a lot of valuable (ⓐ advice, ⓑ advices) from the senior staffs.

다음 문장에서 밑줄 친 곳을 문법에 맞게 고치세요.

09 Ms. Terrence said that it was a <u>pleasurably</u> working with Mr. Harper.

10 Mr. Johnson has provided the directors with a detailed budget, which they <u>reviewed</u> right now.

11 The staff at Gaynor Corp. have a <u>challenger</u> schedule next month.

12 <u>Sale</u> quotas at Preston Industries are rarely met in the early winter season.

13 Only three <u>instructions</u> will be available to teach classes in the summer.

14 The government has announced a new <u>regulate</u> regarding the acquisition of a driver's license.

15 Next week, a new <u>architecture</u> will join the team, so everyone should be ready to welcome her.

16 <u>Construct</u> on the employee parking lot will commence later this week.

무료 해설 ▶
바로 보기

정답·해석 **p.138**

Course 2 대명사

토익 출제경향
평균 2~3문제 정도 출제

준우는 수의사이다. <u>그는</u> 동물을 좋아한다.
대명사(= 준우)

두 번째 문장에서 '준우'라는 명사를 다시 쓰지 않기 위해 '그'라는 표현을 썼습니다. 이처럼 앞에 쓴 명사의 반복을 피하기 위해 해당 명사를 대신해서 쓰는 말을 **대명사**라고 합니다. 대명사에는 인칭대명사, 지시대명사, 부정대명사가 있습니다.

기초문법 잡기

1 인칭대명사는 무엇인가요?

인칭대명사는 '그', '그녀', '그것'처럼 사람이나 사물을 가리키는 대명사로 인칭, 수, 성, 격에 따라 형태가 달라집니다. 인칭대명사에는 '소유격 + 명사'를 대신하는 소유대명사와 -self (-selves)가 붙는 재귀대명사가 있습니다.

인칭/수/성	격		주격 (-은, -는, -이, -가)	소유격 (-의)	목적격 (-을, -를)	소유대명사 (-의 것)	재귀대명사 (- 자신)
1인칭	단수		I	my	me	mine	myself
	복수		we	our	us	ours	ourselves
2인칭	단수		you	your	you	yours	yourself
	복수						yourselves
3인칭	단수	남성	he	his	him	his	himself
		여성	she	her	her	hers	herself
		사물	it	its	it	-	itself
	복수		they	their	them	theirs	themselves

2 지시대명사는 무엇인가요?

지시대명사는 '이것(들)', '저것(들)'처럼 특정 사람이나 사물을 가리킬 때 쓰는 대명사입니다. 가리키는 대상이 단수일 때는 this(이것)/that(저것)을, 복수일 때는 these(이것들)/those(저것들)를 씁니다. 이러한 지시대명사는 뒤에 나온 명사를 수식하는 지시형용사로도 사용합니다.

<u>This</u> is my book. 이것은 나의 책이다.
지시대명사

<u>That</u> book is hers. 저 책은 그녀의 것이다.
지시형용사

3 부정대명사는 무엇인가요?

부정대명사는 '모든 사람', '몇 개'처럼 정확한 대상이나 수, 양을 알 수 없어서 막연하게 말할 때 쓰는 대명사입니다. 즉, 부정대명사의 '부정'은 '아니다'라는 뜻이 아니라 '정확히 정할 수 없다'는 뜻입니다. 이러한 부정대명사는 뒤에 나온 명사를 수식하는 부정형용사로도 사용합니다.

| **all** 모든 것, 모든 사람 | **both** 둘 다 | **each** 각각 | **some** 몇 개, 몇 명, 약간 |

<u>Some</u> of the students studied in the library. 학생들 중 몇 명은 도서관에서 공부했다.
부정대명사

The society received <u>some</u> donation last year. 협회는 지난해에 약간의 기부를 받았다.
부정형용사

토익 포인트 1 인칭대명사

★ 인칭대명사의 주격은 주어 자리, 목적격은 목적어 자리, 소유격은 명사 앞에 오고, '~의 것'으로 해석하는 소유대명사는 주어, 목적어, 보어 자리에 옵니다.

주격 He replied to the e-mail immediately. 그는 즉시 이메일에 답장을 보냈다.

목적격 The coupons will expire tomorrow, so use them at our store today.
그 쿠폰들은 내일 만료될 것이므로, 그것들을 오늘 저희 매장에서 사용하세요.

소유격 Judy canceled her appointment. Judy는 그녀의 약속을 취소했다.

소유대명사 My idea was good, but yours was much better. 제 아이디어는 좋았지만, 당신의 것이 훨씬 더 좋았어요.

★ 재귀대명사는 주어와 목적어가 같은 대상일 때 목적어 자리에 옵니다. 주어나 목적어를 강조하기 위해 쓰기도 하는데, 이때는 생략 가능합니다.

주어 = 목적어 Mr. Trent considers himself a competent employee. Mr. Trent는 그 자신을 능력 있는 직원이라고 생각한다.

강조 The programmers themselves were responsible for the security violation.
프로그래머들 그들 자신들은 그 보안 침입에 책임이 있었다.

★ '전치사 + 재귀대명사' 표현

by oneself(=on one's own) 혼자서, 혼자 힘으로	for oneself 혼자 힘으로
of itself 저절로	in itself 자체로, 본질적으로

Ms. Peters was unable to finish the work by herself. Ms. Peters는 혼자서 업무를 완료할 수 없었다.

토익 실전 Check-up 둘 중 알맞은 것을 고르세요.

Mr. Allen completed the project, so the supervisor asked (ⓐ him, ⓑ he) to write a report. 정답·해석·해설 p.139

토익 포인트 2 지시대명사/지시형용사

★ 지시대명사 that은 앞에서 언급된 **단수 명사**를, those는 **복수 명사**를 대신해서 사용합니다.

Ms. Wendt bought the printer, because that was the only one she could afford.
Ms. Wendt는 그 프린터를 구매했는데, 그것이 그녀가 유일하게 살 수 있는 것이었기 때문이다.

These samples are from India, and those in the back are from Taiwan.
이 샘플들은 인도에서 온 것이고 저 뒤의 것들은 대만에서 온 것이다.

★ 지시대명사 those는 '~한 사람들'이라는 의미로도 쓰이는데, 이때 분사, 전치사구, 관계절의 수식을 받습니다.

The new headphones target those who lead an active life style. 최신 헤드폰은 활동적인 생활을 하는 이들을 대상으로 한다.

★ 지시형용사 this/that은 **단수 명사**를, these/those는 **복수 명사**를 수식하여 '이 ~', '저 ~'를 의미합니다.

Mr. Kim has already read this report. Mr. Kim은 이미 이 보고서를 읽었다.

Those cars will be repaired by tomorrow. 저 차들은 내일까지는 수리될 것이다.

토익 실전 Check-up 둘 중 알맞은 것을 고르세요.

The most expensive shoes in our shop are (ⓐ those, ⓑ that) from Italian makers. 정답·해석·해설 p.139

부정대명사/부정형용사 1: some, any

✱ some과 any는 '몇몇(의), 약간(의)'이라는 의미의 부정대명사와 부정형용사로, some은 주로 **긍정문**에 쓰이고 any는 주로 **부정문, 의문문, 조건문**에 쓰입니다.

부정대명사 some	Some of the photographs had to be retaken.
	사진들 중 몇몇은 다시 촬영되어야 했다.
부정형용사 some	Mr. Schmidt asked for some help rearranging the furniture.
	Mr. Schmidt는 가구를 재배치하는 것에 약간의 도움을 요청했다.
부정대명사 any	The CEO doesn't like any of the proposed logos.
	최고 경영자는 제안된 로고 중 어느 것도 마음에 들어 하지 않는다.
부정형용사 any	Are there any extra charges for overnight delivery?
	익일 배달에 대해 조금의 추가 요금이라도 있습니까?

토익 실전 Check-up 둘 중 알맞은 것을 고르세요.

Mr. Watts has asked for (ⓐ them, ⓑ some) feedback on his work.

정답·해석·해설 p.139

부정대명사/부정형용사 2: one, another, other

✱ one은 정해지지 않은 단수 가산 명사를 대신하고, another는 '(이미 언급된 것 이외의) 또 다른 하나'의 의미로 단수 가산 명사를 대신하거나 수식합니다.

부정대명사 one	Ms. Patrick enjoyed her cup of coffee, so she purchased a second one.
	Ms. Patrick은 커피 한 잔을 맛있게 마셔서, 그녀는 두 번째 잔을 구매했다.
부정대명사 another	Mr. Becker had a question earlier, and now he wants to ask another.
	Mr. Becker는 이전에 질문 하나를 했고, 지금 그는 또 다른 하나를 물어보고 싶어 한다.
부정형용사 another	One of the copies is on your desk. Another copy has been sent to your e-mail address.
	사본 중 한 개는 당신의 책상 위에 있습니다. 또 다른 하나의 사본은 당신의 이메일 주소로 보내졌습니다.

✱ other/others는 '(이미 언급된 것 이외의) 다른 몇몇'이라는 의미로, the other(s)는 '나머지 전부'라는 의미로 쓰입니다.

부정형용사 other	The software prevents computer crashes and other problems.
	그 소프트웨어는 컴퓨터 고장과 다른 문제들을 예방한다.
부정대명사 others	This resort is considered the best in the area, but others are catching up.
	이 리조트는 이 지역에서 최고로 여겨지지만, 다른 리조트들이 따라잡고 있다.
부정대명사 the others	The first proposal was rejected, but the others are being considered.
	첫 번째 제안은 거절되었지만, 나머지 제안들은 전부 고려되고 있다.

토익 실전 Check-up 둘 중 알맞은 것을 고르세요.

This assignment is harder than all (ⓐ another, ⓑ the others) you have done before.

정답·해석·해설 p.139

HACKERS PRACTICE 토익 700+ 달성을 위한 연습 문제

다음 문장에서 알맞은 것을 고르세요.

01 (ⓐ We, ⓑ Our) have gone over your résumé carefully and would like to interview you.

02 Ms. Anderson had forgotten (ⓐ her, ⓑ hers) laptop at the airport.

03 (ⓐ Another, ⓑ Some) of the most brilliant engineers in the industry formed a team to create the new sports car.

04 The visiting clients will arrive today, so a car has been sent to pick (ⓐ they, ⓑ them) up.

05 Volart's Jazz Troupe has (ⓐ talked, ⓑ discussed) about their inspiration.

06 Mr. Paulson stayed at the checkout counter while (ⓐ one, ⓑ the other) employees stocked the shelves.

07 (ⓐ Presenting, ⓑ Present) business cards to potential clients is often done at sales conferences.

08 None of the audience members had (ⓐ they, ⓑ any) questions for the speaker.

다음 문장에서 밑줄 친 곳을 문법에 맞게 고치세요.

09 When he was asked whose laptop was on the table, Mr. Lewis said that it was <u>him</u>.

10 With nearly 50 years of experience, Borton Inc. prides <u>it</u> on guaranteeing customer satisfaction.

11 Please come to <u>mine</u> office sometime this week to collect copies of the annual report.

12 Successful since opening two years ago, HNT Consulting has had <u>other</u> great quarter.

13 Mr. Wynn is eager <u>for</u> relocate to headquarters at the end of the year.

14 When <u>any</u> employees were on leave last month, the office clerk left their mail on their desks.

15 Some Web sites provide guidance to <u>these</u> pursuing careers in business.

16 The main building at the Museum of Fine Arts in Canberra is <u>on</u> itself a work of art.

무료 해설 ▶
바로 보기

정답·해석 **p.139**

PART 5

01 Mr. Jameson is a renowned ------- who has won multiple international awards with his innovative designs.

(A) architect
(B) architecture
(C) architectural
(D) architecturally

02 Members of the O'Grady family have set up social networking accounts so that ------- can find one another online.

(A) the others
(B) themselves
(C) the one
(D) they

03 ------- basic graphic design and desktop publishing techniques would be an asset for any candidate applying for this position.

(A) Knowingly
(B) Know
(C) Knowledge
(D) Knowing

04 Ms. Henderson will have a meeting with ------- lawyers at Hartford Convention Center.

(A) some
(B) its
(C) others
(D) the others

05 Tourists seem to enjoy photographing ------- next to the many historical sites and attractions found in the area.

(A) their
(B) they
(C) themselves
(D) them

06 Two unknown authors claimed that the idea for the famous writer's published novel had originally been -------.

(A) ours
(B) us
(C) theirs
(D) they

07 The first sponsorship package is too expensive, so the company will have to consider a cheaper -------.

(A) one
(B) all
(C) less
(D) as

08 ------- hoping to attend the strategic marketing class need to register for it on our Web site before April 15.

(A) Other
(B) Who
(C) Them
(D) Those

09 Having a degree in computer science is a ------- for the job.

(A) requirements
(B) requirement
(C) requiring
(D) required

10 The first topic that managers need to discuss before the workshop is -------.

(A) attendance
(B) attend
(C) attended
(D) be attended

11 If you would like an estimate for the cost of your project, call to book an appointment with ------- today.

(A) us
(B) we
(C) our
(D) ours

12 To accommodate growth, the Hepburn Department Store plans to purchase ------- floor of the building where it is located.

(A) several
(B) another
(C) other
(D) both

13 Mr. Fields does not have ------- objection to postponing the appointment until Thursday.

(A) both
(B) all
(C) some
(D) any

14 Ms. Oliver accepted the job due to the many benefits, the flexible work schedule and the generous pay among -------.

(A) others
(B) none
(C) other
(D) either

15 Arlington Business Association is looking for an experienced Web designer ------- a new Web site for them.

(A) to create   (B) created
(C) creator   (D) has created

16 Committee members were asked to submit ------- for their chairperson's replacement following his resignation announcement.

(A) nominate   (B) nominations
(C) nominates   (D) nominated

17 Mr. Smith asked to borrow Ms. Vargas's mobile phone charger because he had forgotten ------- at home.

(A) hers   (B) his
(C) him   (D) her

18 New workers are not permitted to operate the factory machinery on ------- until after they have been certified to do so.

(A) themselves   (B) their own
(C) theirs   (D) their

PART 6

Questions 19-22 refer to the following notice.

Expanded Public Transit Service

-------. The council has decided that our transportation system is in need of an upgrade in order to meet the needs of Glenwood's population. One way this can be accomplished is by creating new bus routes. This means revising some of the old routes as well. The ------- are scheduled to be completed by October 1. Furthermore, the city will be creating a new subway line and expanding two ------- lines.

Unfortunately, this work will interrupt normal traffic as roads may need to be torn up. Advance notice will be given of any street ------- that occur because of line construction.

---

19 (A) A new airport will be built near the outskirts of the city.
(B) The city of Glenwood is growing, and public transit must expand with it.
(C) Increased number of cars is creating parking problems.
(D) More transit routes will temporarily be added, and hours will be extended.

20 (A) changeable   (B) changed
(C) change   (D) changes

21 (A) tentative   (B) inaccessible
(C) existing   (D) inoperative

22 (A) closures   (B) will close
(C) closers   (D) closed

정답·해석·해설 p.139

Course 1 형용사

토익 출제경향
평균 2~3문제 정도 출제

비싼 신발
형용사

신발이 비싸다.
형용사

'비싼' 또는 '비싸다'가 신발의 성질에 대해 구체적으로 표현하고 있습니다. 이와 같이 명사의 성질이나 모양, 상태 등을 설명해주는 것을 **형용사**라고 합니다.

기초문법 잡기

1 '비싼'과 '비싸다' 모두 형용사인가요?

'비싼'과 '비싸다'는 모두 형용사입니다. 형용사는 크게 두 가지 역할을 하는데, '비싼 신발'에서처럼 명사 앞에서 꾸며주기도 하고, '신발이 비싸다'에서처럼 be동사 뒤에서 주어를 설명해주기도 합니다.

<u>expensive</u> shoes 비싼 신발
형용사

The shoes are <u>expensive</u>. 그 신발은 비싸다.
형용사

2 형용사는 주로 어떤 형태를 가지고 있나요?

형용사는 주로 –tive, –able, –ous, –sive, –tic, –y와 같은 꼬리말로 끝납니다.

-tive	posi**tive**	긍정적인
-able	comfort**able**	편안한
-ous	seri**ous**	심각한
-sive	impres**sive**	인상적인
-tic	fantas**tic**	아주 멋진
-y	happ**y**	행복한

* likely(~할 것 같은), timely(시기적절한), costly(값비싼)와 같이 –ly로 끝나는 형용사도 있으며, 이 형용사를 부사로 혼동하지 않도록 해야 합니다.

토익 포인트 1 형용사 자리

✦ 형용사는 주로 **명사 앞**이나 **보어 자리**에 옵니다.

명사 앞	The new product received positive reviews from customers. 새 제품은 소비자들로부터 긍정적인 평가를 받았다.
주격 보어 자리	The company is close to City Hall. 그 회사는 시청에서 가깝다.
목적격 보어 자리	The manager considers Ms. Lewis capable. 그 관리자는 Ms. Lewis가 유능하다고 생각한다.

토익 실전 Check-up 둘 중 알맞은 것을 고르세요.

Schools and government offices were closed due to the (ⓐ heaviness, ⓑ heavy) snowstorm.

정답·해석·해설 **p.142**

토익 포인트 2 수량 형용사

✦ 가산 명사 · 불가산 명사 앞에 올 수 있는 수량 형용사를 구분하여 알아둡니다.

가산 명사 앞		불가산 명사 앞	가산 · 불가산 명사 모두의 앞
단수 명사 앞	복수 명사 앞		
one 하나의 each 각각의 every 모든 another 또 다른	(a) few 몇 개의 many 많은 several 몇몇의	(a) little 적은 less 더 적은 much 많은	all 모든 most 대부분의 some 몇몇의, 어떤

Real estate agents earn commissions on (a̶ ̶f̶e̶w̶, each) house they sell.
부동산 중개인은 그들이 파는 각각의 집에 대해 수수료를 받는다.
→ house는 가산 명사인데 단수형으로 쓰였으므로, 복수 가산 명사 앞에 오는 수량 형용사(a few)가 아니라 단수 가산 명사 앞에 오는 수량 형용사
   (each)가 와야 합니다.

There has been (m̶a̶n̶y̶, much) interest in the new sports car lately. 최근 새로운 스포츠카에 대한 많은 관심이 있었다.
→ interest는 불가산 명사이므로, 가산 명사 앞에 오는 수량 형용사(many)가 아니라 불가산 명사 앞에 오는 수량 형용사(much)가 와야 합니다.

토익 실전 Check-up 둘 중 알맞은 것을 고르세요.

Mr. Conrad has to take the subway to work (ⓐ many, ⓑ every) day, so he bought an annual travel pass.

정답·해석·해설 **p.142**

✱ 형태가 비슷해 혼동하기 쉬운 형용사들을 구분하여 알아둡니다.

careful 세심한, 조심스러운 – caring 보살피는	persuasive 설득력 있는 – persuaded 확신하고 있는
considerable 상당한, 중요한 – considerate 사려 깊은	profitable 유리한, 이익이 있는 – proficient 능숙한
comparable 필적할 만한 – comparative 비교의	prospective 장래의 – prosperous 번영하는
dependent ~에 좌우되는, 의존적인 – dependable 믿을 수 있는	reliable 믿을 수 있는 – reliant 의지하는
economic 경제의 – economical 경제적인, 절약하는	respectable 존경할 만한 – respective 각자의
favorable 호의적인, 유리한 – favorite 가장 좋아하는	seasonal 계절적인 – seasoned 경험이 많은
impressive 인상적인 – impressed 감명받은	successful 성공한, 성공의 – successive 연속의
informed 정통한, 알고 있는 – informative 유익한	understanding 이해심 있는 – understandable 이해할 만한
managerial 경영의 – manageable 관리할 수 있는	

The Westend Animal Shelter received a (~~considerate~~, considerable) amount of donation last year.
Westend 동물 보호소는 지난해에 상당한 액수의 기부금을 받았다.
→ '상당한 액수'라는 의미이므로, considerate(사려 깊은)이 아닌 considerable(상당한)이 와야 합니다.

토익 실전 Check-up 둘 중 알맞은 것을 고르세요.
Critics wrote (ⓐ favorable, ⓑ favorite) reviews about Tia's Café.
정답·해석·해설 **p.142**

✱ 'be + 형용사' 형태로 자주 쓰이는 표현

be about to + 동사 막 ~하려고 하다	be available to + 동사 ~할 수 있다
be capable of -ing ~할 수 있다	be eligible for ~할 자격이 있다, ~에 대한 자격이 있다
be responsible for ~에 책임이 있다	be likely to + 동사 ~할 것 같다
be willing to + 동사 기꺼이 ~할 의향이 있다	be skilled in/at ~에 능력이 있다

The CEO of GrivTek is about to make an announcement. GrivTek사의 최고 경영자는 막 발표를 하려고 한다.
Government employees are eligible for promotion after a year of work. 공무원들은 일 년 근무 후 승진할 자격이 있다.

토익 실전 Check-up 둘 중 알맞은 것을 고르세요.
Many companies are (ⓐ willing, ⓑ will) to offer discounts on bulk purchases.
정답·해석·해설 **p.142**

HACKERS PRACTICE
토익 700+ 달성을 위한 연습 문제

다음 문장에서 알맞은 것을 고르세요.

01 The manager said that Ms. Kovac was (ⓐ diligent, ⓑ diligence) in her annual performance review.

02 Visitors to the Colton Museum can view (ⓐ attractively, ⓑ attractive) collections of modern art.

03 The basketball player received harsh (ⓐ criticism, ⓑ critical) for his mistakes during the last game.

04 (ⓐ Much, ⓑ Many) customers complain about the company's service.

05 Mr. Brown is an (ⓐ understandable, ⓑ understanding) person, so he will forgive you.

06 All rights to the images belong to their (ⓐ respective, ⓑ respectable) owners.

07 Prize winners of the contest are chosen (ⓐ every, ⓑ a few) week.

08 Only those who have a passport will be (ⓐ eligibly, ⓑ eligible) for an assignment overseas.

다음 문장에서 밑줄 친 곳을 문법에 맞게 고치세요.

09 Ms. Jones provided a <u>thoroughly</u> explanation of the recent changes in development policy.

10 There was <u>few</u> ink left in the printer cartridge, so the clerk brought another one.

11 The building materials were not only <u>economic</u> but durable as well.

12 Mr. Chang is <u>hesitantly</u> to hire any more staff until the recession is over.

13 Buzz Corporation has recently begun advertising for several new <u>manageable</u> positions.

14 The professor encourages students <u>ask</u> relevant questions throughout his lecture.

15 Their retail strategy could <u>providing</u> the company with an advantage over its rivals.

16 The director is <u>will</u> to approve the accounting team's revisions to the budget.

무료 해설 ▶
바로 보기

정답·해석 **p.142**

Course 2 부사

토익 출제경향
평균 4~5문제 정도 출제

나는 음식을 <u>천천히</u> 먹는다.
　　　　　　부사

'천천히'가 '먹는다'라는 동작을 더 분명하고 자세하게 표현해주고 있습니다. 이와 같이 동사나 형용사 등을 수식하여 의미를 강조하거나 풍부하게 하는 것을 **부사**라고 합니다.

기초문법 잡기

1 부사는 동사와 형용사 말고 다른 것도 수식할 수 있나요?

부사는 명사를 제외한 나머지 품사들, 즉 형용사, 부사, 동사 및 준동사(to 부정사, 동명사, 분사)를 수식하거나 구, 절, 문장 전체를 수식할 수 있습니다.

형용사 수식	The room is completely <u>full</u>.　그 방은 완전히 꽉 찼다.
부사 수식	She speaks very <u>softly</u>.　그녀는 매우 부드럽게 말한다.
동사 수식	Mr. Francis frequently <u>takes</u> the subway.　Mr. Francis는 종종 지하철을 탄다.
to 부정사 수식	Students are expected <u>to listen</u> carefully during lectures. 학생들은 강의 동안 주의 깊게 듣는 것이 기대된다.
동명사 수식	<u>Talking</u> slowly will help the audience understand.　천천히 말하는 것은 청중이 이해하는 데 도움이 될 것이다.
분사 수식	The new manager recently <u>transferred</u> to our branch will be here tomorrow. 최근 우리 지사로 전근을 온 새로운 매니저가 내일 여기에 있을 것이다.
구 수식	Mr. Larkin went to see a movie just <u>after dinner</u>.　Mr. Larkin은 저녁 식사 바로 후에 영화를 보러 갔다.
절 수식	Ms. Clark left immediately <u>after she finished work</u>.　Ms. Clark은 업무를 마치고 바로 떠났다.
문장 전체 수식	Fortunately, <u>she arrived on time</u>.　다행히도, 그녀는 제시간에 도착했다.

2 부사는 어떤 형태를 가지고 있나요?

부사는 주로 형용사 뒤에 꼬리말 –ly가 붙은 '형용사 + ly' 형태를 가지고 있습니다.

형용사	부사
careful	carefully
slow	slowly
quick	quickly
exact	exactly

토익 포인트 1   부사 자리

✱ 부사가 동사를 수식하는 경우, [(준)동사 + 목적어] 앞이나 뒤, [be동사/조동사 + -ing/p.p.] 사이 또는 뒤에 옵니다.

동사 + 목적어 앞	The accountant carefully examined the financial statements.
	그 회계사는 재무제표를 신중히 검토했다.
준동사 + 목적어 뒤	Our sales representative plans to contact the client directly by phone.
	우리 영업사원이 고객에게 직접 전화로 연락할 계획이다.
be동사와 -ing 사이 또는 뒤	The inspector is already driving to the office and should be here soon.
	조사관은 이미 사무실로 운전하고 있고 이곳에 곧 도착할 것이다.
조동사와 p.p. 사이 또는 뒤	Ms. Duncan has checked thoroughly to make sure the article is free of mistakes.
	Ms. Duncan은 기사에 오류가 없도록 하기 위해 철저하게 확인했다.

✱ 부사가 동사 이외의 것을 수식하는 경우, **수식 받는 것 앞에** 옵니다.

Wearing professional clothing for an interview is very important. 면접을 위해 정장을 입는 것은 매우 중요하다.

Very surprisingly, the famous CEO of NL Investments announced his retirement.
매우 놀랍게도, NL 투자회사의 유명한 최고 경영자는 그의 은퇴를 발표했다.

토익 실전 Check-up 둘 중 알맞은 것을 고르세요.

The photocopier needs to be maintained (ⓐ regularly, ⓑ regular).   정답·해석·해설 p.143

토익 포인트 2   부사의 종류 1: 빈도 부사

✱ 빈도 부사는 '얼마나 자주' 일이 발생하는지를 표현하는 부사입니다.

always 항상	frequently 종종	usually 보통	once 한 번
sometimes 때때로	hardly/rarely/seldom/scarcely/barely 거의 ~ 않다		never 결코 ~ 않다

Rooms at the hotel are sometimes available at a discount. 호텔의 객실들은 때때로 할인된 가격에 이용 가능하다.

✱ hardly, rarely, seldom, scarcely, barely(거의 ~ 않다)는 부정의 의미를 담고 있어서, not과 같은 다른 부정어와 함께 올 수 없습니다.

Ms. Lane is (rarely not, rarely) late for work. Ms. Lane은 거의 회사에 지각하지 않는다.

토익 실전 Check-up 둘 중 알맞은 것을 고르세요.

Mr. Keith hardly (ⓐ never, ⓑ ever) travels overseas for business.   정답·해석·해설 p.143

부사의 종류 2: 접속부사

★ 접속부사는 **앞뒤 절의 의미를 연결**해주는 부사입니다.

besides 게다가	moreover 더욱이	furthermore 더욱이	accordingly 그러므로
therefore 그러므로	however 그러나	meanwhile 그동안	consequently 결과적으로
otherwise 그렇지 않으면	then 그리고 나서	nevertheless/nonetheless 그럼에도 불구하고	

Mr. Wood broke sales records every year and is therefore worthy of a promotion.
Mr. Wood는 매년 판매 기록을 깼고 그러므로 승진을 할 만하다.

★ 접속부사는 콤마와 함께 문장의 맨 앞에 위치하여 두 개의 문장을 의미적으로 연결합니다.

Ms. Hall started working on the report. Meanwhile, her assistant continued gathering data.
Ms. Hall은 보고서를 작성하기 시작했다. 그동안, 그녀의 조수는 계속해서 자료를 수집했다.

토익 실전 Check-up 둘 중 알맞은 것을 고르세요.

EM Development owns a number of hotels around the country. (ⓐ Therefore, ⓑ Moreover), it manages multiple shopping centers.

정답·해석·해설 p.143

혼동하기 쉬운 부사

★ 형태가 비슷하지만 의미가 달라 혼동하기 쉬운 부사를 구분하여 알아둡니다.

late 늦게 lately 최근에	The concert started nearly an hour late. 콘서트는 거의 한 시간 늦게 시작했다. Mr. Lawrence has been a little unwell lately. Mr. Lawrence는 최근에 건강이 약간 좋지 않다.
hard 열심히, 힘들게 hardly 거의 ~않다	The crew worked hard to complete the repairs. 그 직원들은 수리를 완료하기 위해 열심히 일했다. Joseph hardly got any sleep last night. Joseph은 어젯밤에 거의 잠을 못 잤다.
high (높이, 목표가) 높이 highly (위상, 평가가) 매우	Fragile items are placed high on the shelves. 깨지기 쉬운 물품들은 선반 높이 놓여져 있다. The computer course is highly recommended. 그 컴퓨터 수업은 매우 추천된다.
most 가장/매우 mostly 주로/대체로	All of the audience members cheered, but Susan applauded most. 모든 청중들이 환호했지만, Susan이 가장 많이 갈채를 보냈다. The company makes products mostly for young people. 그 회사는 주로 젊은 사람들을 위해 제품을 만든다.

토익 실전 Check-up 둘 중 알맞은 것을 고르세요.

The residents of this neighborhood are (ⓐ mostly, ⓑ most) immigrants.

정답·해석·해설 p.143

HACKERS PRACTICE 토익 700+ 달성을 위한 연습 문제

다음 문장에서 알맞은 것을 고르세요.

01 Our operating hours have been extended until 10 P.M. this week, and (ⓐ furthermore, ⓑ consequently), we will be open on the holiday.

02 Rising unemployment has (ⓐ often, ⓑ almost) been cited in the news since last year.

03 The mall was (ⓐ completion, ⓑ completely) rebuilt to be more modern and welcoming.

04 Ms. Rogers has agreed to stay (ⓐ late, ⓑ lately) at work tonight to finish her assignment.

05 The staff at the nursing home help (ⓐ residentially, ⓑ residents) with their medical needs.

06 Ms. Cole (ⓐ once, ⓑ seldom) leaves for work after 8 A.M. because she doesn't want to be late.

07 Most advertising staff members have desks on the 2nd floor, but (ⓐ yours, ⓑ your) will be on the 3rd.

08 Tourists (ⓐ hard, ⓑ usually) visit the locations that are historically significant.

다음 문장에서 밑줄 친 곳을 문법에 맞게 고치세요.

09 Poor communication is the <u>mostly</u> problematic issue in office settings.

10 The applicants need <u>submitting</u> writing samples with their résumés.

11 Bowman City has become <u>increasing</u> popular with tourists in recent years.

12 A reader sent a very <u>strong</u> written letter of complaint to the magazine.

13 It is <u>high</u> likely that Mr. Fournier will be promoted to a management role in the next few weeks.

14 Someone from Keller Books called Mr. Yates to tell him that <u>he</u> order had been delayed.

15 The Tricourt Society has very <u>generous</u> provided a large grant to the hospital.

16 Mr. Gordon read the newspaper as he waited <u>patience</u> for the train to New York to arrive.

무료 해설 ▶
바로 보기

정답·해석 **p.143**

PART 5

01 A number of residents are ------- to the city's proposal to construct new condominiums in the community.

(A) opposing   (B) opposition
(C) opposed   (D) opposingly

02 The transition to a new hardware system was ------- handled by everyone in the information technology department.

(A) effectively   (B) effectual
(C) effective   (D) effect

03 To the disappointment of its organizers, attendance at the Atlanta Motor Show fell short of -------.

(A) expectedly   (B) expectations
(C) expectant   (D) expectable

04 While it is not ------- to purchase insurance for a rental vehicle, it is strongly recommended.

(A) necessitate   (B) necessary
(C) necessity   (D) necessarily

05 Hiring highly qualified staff could be very ------- for the company in the long run.

(A) proficient   (B) profitable
(C) profit   (D) proficiently

06 With major branches ------- in New York and San Francisco, Kinsi Tech serves clients from coast to coast.

(A) locating   (B) are located
(C) been located   (D) located

07 To increase effectiveness, the Hudson Department Store ------- its marketing department into two separate units.

(A) will divide   (B) was divided
(C) is divided   (D) has been divided

08 Engineers warn that it is not a good idea to launch the satellite unless weather conditions are -------.

(A) favorite   (B) favoring
(C) favorably   (D) favorable

09 The new dormitory will include several recreational ------- for students to enjoy.

(A) facilitating   (B) facility
(C) facilitated   (D) facilities

10 It is essential to comply with federal regulations when importing ------- goods from a foreign country.

(A) commerce   (B) commercial
(C) commercials   (D) commercialize

11 Mr. Scranton ------- received his order, so he called the customer service center to ask for a refund.

(A) once   (B) ever
(C) never   (D) after

12 ClearSkin offers a wide variety of ------- anti-aging products.

(A) affordability   (B) affordably
(C) affordable   (D) afford

13 The new concert hall being constructed on Harley Lane is still only ------- complete.

(A) partially   (B) partial
(C) partiality   (D) parts

14 A city planner will visit ------- site individually to ensure that all of the relevant building codes have been met.

(A) each   (B) much
(C) many   (D) a few

한 권으로 끝내는
해커스 토익 700+
LC+RC+VOCA

GRAMMAR PART 5, 6

DAY 07 형용사와 부사

한 권으로 끝내는 해커스 토익 700+ (LC+RC+VOCA)

15 Since he was offered a contract with increased benefits, Mr. Park is ------- to sign on for another year.

(A) likely   (B) like
(C) liking   (D) liked

16 If Mr. Andrews ------- of the schedule change, he would not have missed the board meeting.

(A) is notified   (B) notification
(C) had been notified (D) be notified

17 Ms. Richards says she can take ------- employees to the restaurant in her minivan, and the rest can travel in a taxi.

(A) all   (B) some
(C) much   (D) little

18 Mr. Chen made more sales than any other employee and was ------- promoted and awarded with a raise.

(A) however   (B) consequently
(C) meanwhile   (D) otherwise

PART 6

Questions 19-22 refer to the following advertisement.

Martello's bread is now available at your local Price-Time Food Market! -------. The famous bakery
         19
uses the finest, most wholesome ingredients and fortifies its goods with vitamins and minerals.
-------, Martello's products are the most nutritious available.
20
Martello's also offers an ------- of cookies, cakes, and pies that are baked fresh daily. And we
        21
welcome your family to try our newest selections of tortillas, sweet rolls, and buns as well. They
are the ------- complement to any meal. Visit the nearest Price-Time Food Market and stock up on
     22
Martello's items today.

---

19 (A) The store will begin operations at the end of next month.
     (B) Check out white, wheat, and Italian-style breads on your next visit.
     (C) You'll find easy recipes for all your favorite baked goods.
     (D) Visit during this time to receive a special offer on their products.

20 (A) Nonetheless   (B) Subsequently
     (C) Therefore   (D) However

21 (A) enhancement   (B) accumulation
     (C) assortment   (D) organization

22 (A) perfect   (B) perfection
     (C) perfectly   (D) perfects

정답·해석·해설 **p.143**

Course 1 시간·시점·위치·방향 전치사

<u>on</u> the table 탁자 위에
전치사

<u>under</u> the table 탁자 아래에
전치사

'on'과 'under'가 탁자 '위'와 '아래'라는 위치를 나타내고 있습니다. 이와 같이 명사나 대명사 앞에서 시간, 장소, 방향 등을 나타내는 것을 **전치사**라고 합니다.

기초문법 잡기

1 전치사의 자리는 어디인가요?

전치사는 명사나 대명사, 동명사, 명사절과 같은 명사 역할을 하는 것 앞에 옵니다. 이때 전치사 뒤에 온 명사 역할을 하는 것을 전치사의 목적어라고 하며, '전치사 + 전치사의 목적어'를 합쳐 '전치사구'라고 합니다.

명사 앞   The report was finished before <u>the deadline</u>. 그 보고서는 마감 전에 완료되었다.
명사

대명사 앞   Mr. Jackson sits next to <u>me</u> at the office. Mr. Jackson은 사무실에서 내 옆자리에 앉는다.
대명사

동명사 앞   Ms. Kelly had some tea instead of <u>drinking</u> coffee. Ms. Kelly는 커피를 마시는 대신 차를 마셨다.
동명사

명사절 앞   Ms. Li sent the package to <u>where Mr. Tremblay lives</u>. Ms. Li는 소포를 Mr. Tremblay가 사는 곳으로 보냈다.
명사절

2 전치사구는 무슨 역할을 하나요?

'전치사 + 전치사의 목적어' 형태의 전치사구는 문장에서 형용사나 부사 역할을 하여, 명사나 동사 등을 수식할 수 있습니다.

The box by the bookcase **is very heavy.** 책장 옆에 있는 상자는 매우 무겁다.
→ 전치사구(by the bookcase)가 형용사처럼 명사(The box)를 수식하고 있습니다.

I walked for two hours. 나는 두 시간 동안 걸었다.
→ 전치사구(for two hours)가 부사처럼 동사(walked)를 수식하고 있습니다.

토익 포인트 1 　전치사의 종류 1: 시간과 장소 in/at/on

✱ 시간을 나타내는 전치사 in/at/on

전치사	쓰임	예	
in	월 · 연도 계절 · 세기 ~시간 후에	in July 7월에 in summer 여름에 in five days 5일 후에	in 2005 2005년에 in the 18th century 18세기에
at	시각 · 시점	at 4 o'clock 4시 정각에 at the beginning/end of the year 연초에/연말에	at noon 정오에
on	날짜 · 요일	on January 22 1월 22일에	on Thursday 목요일에

The article was printed on Monday, March 5.　그 기사는 3월 5일 월요일에 발행되었다.

✱ 장소를 나타내는 전치사 in/at/on

전치사	쓰임	예	
in	큰 공간 내 장소	in Asia 아시아에서	in Colorado 콜로라도 주에서
at	지점 · 번지	at home 집에서 at the mall 쇼핑몰에서	at the cinema 극장에서 at 21 Elm Street Elm가 21번지에서
on	표면 위 · 일직선 상의 지점	on the third floor 3층에서	on the desk 책상 위에

Conference attendees will meet at the airport.　회의 참석자들은 공항에서 만날 것이다.

> **토익 실전 Check-up** 둘 중 알맞은 것을 고르세요.
>
> The training is conducted (ⓐ in, ⓑ on) the fifth floor.　　　　정답 · 해석 · 해설 **p.146**

토익 포인트 2 　전치사의 종류 2: 시점과 기간

✱ 시점을 나타내는 전치사

before/prior to ~ 전에	after ~ 후에	
since ~ 이래로	toward ~ 무렵	+ 시점 표현 (11 A.M., July, this afternoon 등)
until/by ~까지	from ~부터	

All application forms must be submitted before 3 P.M.　모든 신청서는 오후 3시 전에 제출되어야 한다.

✱ 기간을 나타내는 전치사

for/during ~ 동안	
throughout ~하는 내내	+ 기간 표현 (the vacation, five years, a decade 등)
within ~ 이내에	

Tom visited many interesting places during his vacation.　Tom은 휴가 동안 많은 흥미로운 장소들을 방문했다.

> **토익 실전 Check-up** 둘 중 알맞은 것을 고르세요.
>
> Mr. Logan will be moving to France (ⓐ from, ⓑ within) three years.　　　정답 · 해석 · 해설 **p.146**

전치사의 종류 3: 위치

✱ **위치를** 나타내는 전치사

전치사	예문
above/over ~ 위에, ~보다 위에	He stays in a room above/over a garage. 그는 차고 위에 있는 방에 머문다.
below/under ~ 아래에	Mr. Conrad's office is a floor below/under Ms. Green's. Mr. Conrad의 사무실은 Ms. Green의 사무실 한 층 아래에 있다.
beside/next to/by ~ 옆에	Tim will wait beside/next to/by the station entrance. Tim은 역 입구 옆에서 기다릴 것이다.
behind ~ 뒤에	There are more parking spaces behind the restaurant. 식당 뒤에 더 많은 주차 공간이 있다.
near ~ 근처에	Mr. Brady lives near Logan International Airport. Mr. Brady는 Logan 국제공항 근처에 산다.
around ~ 여기저기에, ~ 주위에	We hired a gardener to plant some trees around the yard. 우리는 마당 여기저기에 몇몇 나무들을 심기 위해 정원사를 고용했다.

토익 실전 Check-up 둘 중 알맞은 것을 고르세요.

The warehouse is (ⓐ behind, ⓑ before) the main building.

정답·해석·해설 **p.146**

전치사의 종류 4: 방향

✱ **방향을** 나타내는 전치사

전치사	예문
from ~에서, ~로부터	I came here from Chicago yesterday morning. 나는 어제 아침 시카고에서 이곳으로 왔다.
to ~로, ~쪽으로	The items were delivered to his home. 물품들이 그의 집으로 배달되었다.
across ~을 가로질러, 건너서 through ~을 통과하여 along ~을 따라서	We drove the truck across the bridge. 우리는 다리를 가로질러 트럭을 운전했다. You must go through a tunnel to reach Highway 17. 17번 고속도로에 가려면 반드시 터널을 통과해야 한다. Streetlamps have been installed along the path. 가로등이 길을 따라서 설치되었다.
for ~로 향해	Jane boarded a train leaving for Montreal. Jane은 몬트리올로 향해 떠나는 기차에 탑승했다.
into ~ 안으로 out of ~ 밖으로	Ms. Moore placed her belongings into a box. Ms. Moore는 그녀의 소지품을 상자 안으로 넣었다. Mr. Adams pulled several bills out of his wallet. Mr. Adams는 지폐 몇 장을 지갑 밖으로 꺼냈다.

토익 실전 Check-up 둘 중 알맞은 것을 고르세요.

The employee transferring (ⓐ from, ⓑ along) the Munich branch will arrive tomorrow.

정답·해석·해설 **p.146**

HACKERS PRACTICE 토익 700+ 달성을 위한 연습 문제

다음 문장에서 알맞은 것을 고르세요.

01 The boxes in the storage area must be kept (ⓐ out of, ⓑ above) the damp floor.

02 A number of online courses at Humbert College are offered (ⓐ into, ⓑ throughout) the year.

03 The annual street festival will close down Bay Street (ⓐ for, ⓑ until) six hours.

04 The entrance to the office is (ⓐ between, ⓑ across) the street from a subway station.

05 Tickets for the musical performance can be purchased online or (ⓐ at, ⓑ on) the box office.

06 Applicants must answer (ⓐ every, ⓑ all) questions on the form.

07 Mr. Ross installed a roof (ⓐ between, ⓑ over) the front door of his shop.

08 The city is constructing a new pedestrian trail that runs (ⓐ during, ⓑ along) Highway 23.

다음 문장에서 밑줄 친 곳을 문법에 맞게 고치세요.

09 Regina Corp. will be closed <u>at</u> the next four days.

10 The researchers thought the evidence was <u>convince</u>.

11 The supervisor would like to know how many employees are going <u>in</u> the workshop.

12 Several coal <u>mine</u> have been closed over the past 4 years.

13 Three years <u>before</u> the earthquake, most of the buildings were rebuilt.

14 The television commercial will air on several channels <u>since</u> May 1 to May 21.

15 The author of *Mind Games* will hold a book signing event <u>on</u> Kendall Bookstore.

16 GW Group is seeking private investors to fund its <u>proposing</u> project.

무료 해설 ▶
바로 보기

정답·해석 **p.146**

<u>except</u> Sunday 일요일을 제외하고
전치사

'except Sunday'에서 'except'는 제외의 의미를 나타내고 있습니다. 이와 같이 전치사는 시간, 시점, 위치, 방향 외에도 다양한 의미를 나타낼 수 있습니다.

기초문법 잡기

1 전치사는 시간, 시점, 위치, 방향 외에 또 어떤 의미를 나타낼 수 있나요?

전치사는 제외, 이유, 양보, 수단과 같은 다양한 의미를 나타낼 수 있습니다.

They go to the gym every day except Sunday. 그들은 일요일을 제외하고 매일 체육관에 간다.

Joanne cannot concentrate because of the noise. Joanne은 소음 때문에 집중할 수가 없다.

The soccer game continued despite the heavy rain. 축구 경기는 폭우에도 불구하고 계속되었다.

Gordon became a good pianist by practicing. Gordon은 연습함으로써 뛰어난 피아노 연주자가 되었다.

2 전치사는 꼭 한 단어로만 이루어지나요?

전치사는 한 단어로만 이루어질 수도 있고, 두 개 이상의 단어로 이루어질 수도 있습니다.

Mr. Kane will be the new manager as of next week. Mr. Kane은 다음 주부터 새로운 관리자가 될 것이다.

Ms. Morris is in charge of purchasing food for the party. Ms. Morris는 파티를 위해 음식을 구매하는 것을 책임지고 있다.

Mr. Crane attended the conference on behalf of his company. Mr. Crane은 그의 회사를 대표하여 회의에 참석했다.

★ **제외·이유·목적·양보·부가를 나타내는 전치사**

구분	전치사	의미	예문
제외	except (for) without	~을 제외하고 ~ 없이	Except for a couple of issues, the event was a success. 몇몇 문제들을 제외하면, 행사는 성공적이었다.
이유	due to because of	~ 때문에	Ms. Cruz will not be attending the party due to other commitments. Ms. Cruz는 다른 약속들 때문에 파티에 참석하지 않을 것이다.
목적	for	~을 위해서	Submit proposals for the board's approval. 이사회의 승인을 위해 제안서를 제출하십시오.
양보	despite in spite of notwithstanding	~에도 불구하고	Ms. Conn walks to work despite the long distance. Ms. Conn은 먼 거리에도 불구하고 직장까지 걸어간다.
부가	besides in addition to	~ 외에도, ~에 더하여	Besides writing books, he also enjoys directing films. 책을 쓰는 것 외에도, 그는 영화를 감독하는 것 또한 좋아한다.

토익 실전 Check-up 둘 중 알맞은 것을 고르세요.

Sadly, we have no rooms available (ⓐ because of, ⓑ without) the holiday rush.

정답·해석·해설 p.146

★ **기타 전치사**

전치사	의미	예문
by	~힘으로써, ··에 의해	You can change your reservation by calling this number. 이 번호로 전화함으로써 예약을 변경하실 수 있습니다.
through	~을 통해서	I learned programming through watching videos on the Internet. 나는 인터넷에서 동영상을 보는 것을 통해 프로그래밍을 배웠다.
throughout	~ 전역에, 도처에 ~ 전반에 걸친	The supermarket has several branches throughout the city. 그 슈퍼마켓은 도시 전역에 몇 개의 지점이 있다.
with	~과 함께, ~을 가지고	The researchers reviewed the survey results with management. 연구자들은 설문 조사 결과를 경영진과 함께 검토했다.
as	~으로서	She worked part-time as an editor for Hartman Publications. 그녀는 Hartman 출판사에서 편집자로서 시간제 근무를 했다.
following	~에 이어	Following the talk, there will be a catered lunch. 연설에 이어, 출장 요리 점심 식사가 있을 것이다.
amid	~ 가운데, ~으로 에워싸인	The old monument stands amid newly constructed skyscrapers. 그 오래된 기념물은 새로 건설된 고층 건물들 가운데에 있다.
about regarding	~에 관하여	Qualified applicants can inquire about the open position at PNB Inc. 자격을 갖춘 지원자들은 PNB사의 비어 있는 일자리에 관하여 문의할 수 있다.

토익 실전 Check-up 둘 중 알맞은 것을 고르세요.

There are many famous landmarks (ⓐ throughout, ⓑ as) the region.

정답·해석·해설 p.146

● 두 개 이상의 단어가 함께 묶여 쓰이는 전치사

contrary to ~과 반대로	on behalf of ~을 대표하여, 대신하여	in exchange for ~의 대신으로
as of + 시간 ~부터, ~부로	in place of ~을 대신하여	in excess of ~을 초과하여
in case of ~할 경우에	in preparation for ~에 대비하여	in response to ~에 응하여
regardless of ~에 상관없이	in charge of ~을 책임지고 있는	in keeping with ~과 어울려

The new parking policies will go into effect as of next Monday.　새 주차 정책은 다음 주 월요일부터 효력이 발생될 것이다.

토익 실전 Check-up 둘 중 알맞은 것을 고르세요.
Mr. Tate is in charge (ⓐ of, ⓑ for) the office in the director's absence.　　　정답·해석·해설 **p.146**

● '동사 + 전치사' 표현

register for ~에 등록하다	depend on(=rely on, count on) ~에 의존하다	contribute to ~에 기여하다
wait for ~을 기다리다	congratulate A on B A에게 B를 축하하다	advertise on ~에 광고하다
add to ~을 더하다	keep track of ~을 계속 알고 있다	account for ~을 설명하다

You may register for the exam online or by telephone.　온라인 또는 전화로 시험에 등록할 수 있습니다.

● '형용사 + 전치사' 표현

equivalent to ~과 동일한	identical to ~과 동일한	consistent with ~과 일치하는
similar to ~과 비슷한	absent from ~에 불참한	responsible for ~에 책임이 있는
comparable to ~에 필적하는	comparable with ~과 비교되는	

Mr. Corden will be absent from tomorrow's meeting with the client.　Mr. Corden은 내일 고객과의 회의에 불참할 것이다.

● '명사 + 전치사' 표현

a solution to ~에 대한 해결책	concern over/about ~에 대한 걱정	a lack of ~의 부족
access to ~에의 접근, 출입	permission from ~로부터의 허가	an advocate for(of) ~의 옹호자
a problem with ~의 문제	a cause/reason for ~의 원인/이유	respect for ~에 대한 존경

The project was not completed due to a lack of funding.　프로젝트는 자금의 부족으로 인해 완료되지 못했다.

토익 실전 Check-up 둘 중 알맞은 것을 고르세요.
A council member suggested a solution (ⓐ with, ⓑ to) the overspending problem.　　　정답·해석·해설 **p.146**

다음 문장에서 알맞은 것을 고르세요.

01 The software tutorial was postponed (ⓐ because of, ⓑ contrary to) an urgent assignment.

02 (ⓐ Without, ⓑ As) a good advertising campaign, the new line of sneakers is likely to sell poorly.

03 (ⓐ Due to, ⓑ In spite of) its advanced security system, the computer may still be vulnerable to attack.

04 Staff will be handing out (ⓐ specific, ⓑ specification) instructions on how to register for courses.

05 Most travel Web sites allow people to book flights (ⓐ in addition to, ⓑ between) hotel rooms.

06 (ⓐ Continue, ⓑ Continuously) encouraging professional development helps improve the staff's skills.

07 (ⓐ Besides, ⓑ Through) answering calls, receptionists are responsible for maintaining files.

08 You can reach the train station quickly (ⓐ over, ⓑ by) taking Route 45.

다음 문장에서 밑줄 친 곳을 문법에 맞게 고치세요.

09 Contrary <u>in</u> one critic's opinion, most people found the play interesting and enjoyable.

10 Lucy's Bar and Grill is open every day of the week <u>throughout</u> Monday.

11 Employees were reminded to register <u>to</u> the workshop before the deadline.

12 Dr. Hammerstein's presentation was met with an enthusiastic <u>respond</u> from the audience.

13 Employees may use their corporate credit cards <u>to</u> business-related expenses only.

14 Ms. Roberts will accept the award on behalf <u>from</u> her team at the ceremony tonight.

15 Bexler Co. manufactures several product lines, but each brand is <u>promote</u> separately.

16 Documentation is necessary if employees are absent <u>for</u> work for three consecutive days.

무료 해설 ▶
바로 보기

정답·해석 **p.147**

PART 5

01 The renovations to the Haddad Art Gallery should be completed ------- August.

(A) of
(B) on
(C) in
(D) at

02 Mr. Wang's work performance has not been consistent ------- his skill level.

(A) as
(B) through
(C) under
(D) with

03 ------- the company's announcement that they would be restructuring, Mr. Glass decided to update his résumé.

(A) On behalf of
(B) In response to
(C) As of
(D) In exchange for

04 ------- working at investment firm Frazier Finance, Jack Harper was employed as an advisor to several banks in the region.

(A) Along
(B) Prior to
(C) Near
(D) Across from

05 A recently opened museum exhibition that is ------- to the history of video games has been receiving lots of media attention.

(A) devoting
(B) devotion
(C) devotedly
(D) devoted

06 ------- Ms. Garner, Alex also came to the office this weekend.

(A) Ahead
(B) Within
(C) Besides
(D) Over

07 ------- an initial 10 percent drop in its stock value, the company's expansion overseas has been successful overall.

(A) In charge of
(B) Due to
(C) In case of
(D) Except for

08 A notice was posted reminding residents to sort their recyclable items before placing them ------- the bins.

(A) into
(B) in addition to
(C) since
(D) in excess of

09 Mr. Blanchard was able to form several promising business relationships ------- his attendance at the networking event.

(A) as a result
(B) as well as
(C) regarding
(D) due to

10 The new trainees were provided with printed ------- on proper workplace conduct as part of their orientation.

(A) guides
(B) guided
(C) will guide
(D) to guide

11 The software ------- the office computers should be installed by the end of the day.

(A) outside
(B) for
(C) because
(D) even though

12 The reality TV show *SongStar* was canceled last week after 10 seasons ------- its popularity.

(A) yet
(B) although
(C) despite
(D) however

13 The satellite dish installed ------- the home's second-story windows was badly damaged in the storm.

(A) without
(B) following
(C) above
(D) about

14 Most of the staff was interested in taking professional development classes, contrary ------- the director's expectations.

(A) to
(B) among
(C) against
(D) from

15 ------- the objections of several key committee members, the proposed cuts to the budget were approved.

(A) Near
(B) Regardless
(C) Notwithstanding
(D) In addition to

16 Electronic devices, such as laptops and mobile phones, should be turned off ------- takeoff and landing.

(A) during
(B) behind
(C) among
(D) into

17 ------- experience in the service industry is necessary to apply for the position.

(A) Each
(B) Some
(C) Either
(D) Both

18 Mr. Felding handed out coupons and flyers for his business ------- the crowd of office workers heading to lunch.

(A) until
(B) throughout
(C) below
(D) amid

PART 6

Questions 19-22 refer to the following instructions.

Your new Schmidt-Carr washing machine is a high-performance piece of equipment. To ensure the best results, ------- is important to use and care for your machine properly. One important aspect
19
to consider is safety. -------, all users should follow a few basic guidelines to avoid hazardous
20
situations.

First, never put items stained ------- gasoline, cooking oil, or alcohol in the machine. The action of
21
washing these can produce toxic vapors. In addition, as these are flammable substances, there is a risk of explosion or fire. -------.
22

19 (A) that
(B) it
(C) he
(D) any

20 (A) Instead
(B) Meanwhile
(C) Accordingly
(D) Otherwise

21 (A) for
(B) with
(C) below
(D) through

22 (A) For such items, hand washing is the best solution.
(B) Once the cycle is over, they should be removed immediately.
(C) This will ensure that your clothing does not shrink.
(D) Therefore, you may want to use a fabric softener or stain remover.

정답·해석·해설 p.147

한 권으로 끝내는
해커스 토익 700+
LC+RC+VOCA

GRAMMAR PART 5, 6

DAY 08 전치사

한 권으로 끝내는 해커스 토익 700+ (LC+RC+VOCA)

Course 1 등위접속사와 상관접속사

토익 출제경향
최대 2문제까지 출제

이 소파는 푹신하다, 그리고 편안하다.
       접속사

'이 소파는 푹신하다'와 '편안하다'라는 문장이 '그리고'로 연결되어 있는데, 이와 같이 단어와 단어, 구와
구 또는 절과 절을 연결하는 것을 **접속사**라고 합니다. 단어나 구, 절을 대등하게 연결해주는 접속사에는
등위접속사와 상관접속사가 있습니다.

기초문법 잡기

1 등위접속사는 무엇인가요?

등위접속사는 단어와 단어, 구와 구, 절과 절을 대등하게 연결하는 접속사입니다.

This sofa is <u>soft</u> and <u>comfortable</u>. 이 소파는 푹신하고 편안하다.
         단어(형용사)   단어(형용사)

I can meet you <u>at 2:00 P.M. on Monday</u> or <u>before noon on Friday</u>.
              구(전치사구)   구(전치사구)

월요일 오후 2시 또는 금요일 정오 이전에 당신을 만날 수 있습니다.

<u>John left earlier than usual</u>, but <u>he was still late</u>. John은 평소보다 더 일찍 나왔지만, 여전히 늦었다.
        절   절

2 상관접속사는 무엇인가요?

상관접속사도 단어와 단어, 구와 구, 절과 절을 대등하게 연결하는 접속사로, 두 단어가 서로 짝을 이루어 함께 쓰입니다.

The store sells both <u>clothing</u> and <u>shoes</u>. 그 상점은 옷과 신발 모두를 판다.
               단어(명사)   단어(명사)

The box office is not <u>at the entrance</u> but <u>inside the building</u>. 매표소는 입구에 있는 것이 아니라 건물 안에 있다.
                    구(전치사구)   구(전치사구)

We can either <u>have dinner</u> or <u>go to the art gallery</u>. 우리는 저녁 식사를 하거나 또는 미술관에 갈 수 있다.
            절   절

토익 포인트 1   등위접속사

✽ 등위접속사는 문맥에 알맞은 것을 사용해야 합니다.

and 그리고	or 또는	but 그러나	yet 그러나	so 그래서	for 왜냐하면

Ms. Lee ordered a few pizzas (~~yet~~, and) some chicken wings for the staff.

Ms. Lee는 직원들을 위해 피자 몇 판과 치킨윙을 주문했다.

→ 피자 몇 판과 치킨윙을 주문했다는 문맥이 되어야 하므로, yet이 아니라 and를 써야 합니다.

You can park the car yourself (~~and~~, or) have the valet do it for you.

직접 주차하거나 또는 주차 요원이 대신하게 할 수 있습니다.

→ 직접 주차하거나 또는 주차 요원이 대신하게 할 수 있다는 문맥이 되어야 하므로, and가 아니라 or를 써야 합니다.

Mr. Booth is on leave, (~~for~~, but) he should be returning next week.

Mr. Booth는 휴가 중이지만, 다음 주에 돌아올 것이다.

→ Mr. Booth가 휴가 중이지만 다음 주에는 돌아올 것이라는 문맥이 되어야 하므로, for가 아니라 but을 써야 합니다.

Mr. Young was concerned about traffic, (~~but~~, so) he left home early.

Mr. Young은 교통량이 걱정되어서, 집에서 일찍 출발했다.

→ 교통량이 걱정되어서 집에서 일찍 출발했다는 문맥이 되어야 하므로, but이 아니라 so를 써야 합니다.

토익 실전 Check-up 둘 중 알맞은 것을 고르세요.

Mr. Taylor didn't answer his phone, (ⓐ or, ⓑ so) the caller left a message.

정답·해석·해설 p.150

토익 포인트 2   등위접속사로 연결된 주어의 수일치

✽ and로 연결된 주어는 복수 취급하여 뒤에 복수 동사를 쓰고, or로 연결된 주어(A or B)는 B에 수를 일치시킵니다.

<u>The CEO and the board</u> are going to approve the expansion plans.   최고경영자와 이사회는 확장 계획을 승인할 것이다.

→ 주어(The CEO, the board)가 and로 연결되었으므로 복수 동사(are)를 써야 합니다.

<u>Major credit cards or cash</u> is accepted at the store.   그 상점에서는 주요 신용카드 또는 현금이 받아들여진다.

→ or로 연결된 주어 A or B(Major credit cards or cash)의 B(cash)가 단수이므로 단수 동사(is)를 써야 합니다.

토익 실전 Check-up 둘 중 알맞은 것을 고르세요.

His tickets and hotel room (ⓐ have, ⓑ has) been booked.

정답·해석·해설 p.150

★ 상관접속사는 서로 짝이 맞는 것끼리 사용해야 합니다.

both A and B A와 B 모두	either A or B A 또는 B 중 하나
neither A nor B A도 B도 아닌	not A but B A가 아닌 B
not only A but (also) B = B as well as A A뿐 아니라 B도	

Both the tenant (or, and) the landlord may cancel the rental agreement. 세입자와 임대주는 모두 임대차 계약을 취소할 수 있다.
→ 상관접속사 both의 맞는 짝은 or가 아니고 and입니다.

Lunch will be served either at 1 P.M. (nor, or) after the next session. 점심 식사는 오후 1시 또는 다음 순서 후에 제공될 것이다.
→ 상관접속사 either의 맞는 짝은 nor가 아니고 or입니다.

Sarah (either, neither) plays a musical instrument nor sings. Sarah는 악기를 연주하지도 노래를 부르지도 않는다.
→ 상관접속사 nor의 맞는 짝은 either가 아니고 neither입니다.

Not only employees (and, but also) their families are invited to the event. 직원뿐 아니라 그들의 가족들도 행사에 초대된다.
→ 상관접속사 not only의 맞는 짝은 and가 아니고 but also입니다.

토익 실전 Check-up 둘 중 알맞은 것을 고르세요.

He speaks not one language (ⓐ but, ⓑ and) three.

정답·해석·해설 p.150

★ 상관접속사로 연결된 주어는 상관접속사의 종류에 따라 수일치를 다르게 합니다.

B에 일치시키는 경우	either A or B	neither A nor B	not A but B	not only A but (also) B
항상 복수 동사를 쓰는 경우	both A and B			

Neither shareholders nor management wants to comment on the report.
주주들도 경영진도 보고서에 대해 의견을 말하고 싶어 하지 않는다.
→ Neither A nor B에서는 B에 동사를 일치시키므로, B인 단수 명사 management에 일치시켜 단수 동사 wants를 써야 합니다.

Both food and accommodation are included in the price. 음식과 숙박 시설 모두 가격에 포함되어 있다.
→ Both A and B 뒤에는 항상 복수 동사를 쓰므로 복수 동사 are를 써야 합니다.

토익 실전 Check-up 둘 중 알맞은 것을 고르세요.

Either posters or a banner (ⓐ come, ⓑ comes) with sponsorship.

정답·해석·해설 p.150

HACKERS PRACTICE 토익 700+ 달성을 위한 연습 문제

다음 문장에서 알맞은 것을 고르세요.

01 Incoming passengers can take a taxi (ⓐ or, ⓑ nor) rent a car at the airport.

02 A factory manager must ensure (ⓐ both, ⓑ either) the safety and the productivity of his workers.

03 The report was due today, (ⓐ yet, ⓑ even) there has been too much other work to finish first.

04 Ms. Bouma is a communications expert (ⓐ but also, ⓑ as well as) an excellent programmer.

05 The speaker asked that everyone save their questions (ⓐ until, ⓑ since) the end of his lecture.

06 The tourism industry is booming, (ⓐ for, ⓑ yet) hotel occupancy rates are on the decline.

07 Rent must be paid on the first day of (ⓐ much, ⓑ each) month.

08 Mr. Hinkley will continue to work for Lapis, Inc. (ⓐ still, ⓑ but) will transfer to its headquarters.

다음 문장에서 밑줄 친 곳을 문법에 맞게 고치세요.

09 Library users have to speak <u>silent</u> while they are in the building.

10 The proprietor of the apartment building will rent to neither pet owners <u>or</u> smokers.

11 Users were unable to access the Web site <u>about</u> at least four hours.

12 Paris and Marseille <u>is</u> captivating cities, but Paris receives more visitors each year.

13 There are not one <u>then</u> two marketing staff members who will be away for training this month.

14 Neither magazines nor television <u>are</u> available to clients in the dentist's waiting room.

15 Employees receive not only incentive bonuses <u>and</u> also benefits, like health insurance.

16 Departmental supervisors or the general manager <u>need</u> to approve requests for vacation.

무료 해설 ▶
바로 보기

정답·해석 **p.150**

Course 2 관계절

토익 출제경향
평균 1문제 정도 출제

<u>지윤이가 신고 있는</u> 운동화
　　　　관계절

'지윤이가 신고 있는'이 명사인 '운동화'를 꾸며주고 있습니다. 이와 같이 명사를 수식해주는 형용사 역할
을 하는 절을 **관계절**이라고 합니다.

기초문법 잡기

1 관계절은 어떤 형태를 가지고 있나요?

관계절의 형태는 '관계대명사 + (주어) + 동사 ~' 또는 '관계부사 + 주어 + 동사 ~'입니다.

Customers <u>who sign up</u> receive a discount.　등록하는 고객들은 할인을 받는다.
　　　　　관계대명사(who) + 동사(sign up)

The sneakers <u>which she is wearing</u> are too big for her.　그녀가 신고 있는 운동화는 그녀에게 너무 크다.
　　　　　　관계대명사(which) + 주어(she) + 동사(is wearing)

2 관계절은 어떻게 만드나요?

두 문장에서 공통되는 것을 가리키는 명사 중 하나를 관계사(관계대명사 또는 관계부사)로 바꾸어 두 문장을 한 문장으로 만들면
관계절을 포함한 문장을 만들 수 있습니다. 이때 관계사는 두 문장을 연결하는 접속사 역할을 하는 동시에 앞에 나온 명사를 대신
하는 대명사 역할을 합니다.

Leonard has a sister. + The sister is a singer.
Leonard에게는 여자 형제가 있다. + 그 여자 형제는 가수이다. (a sister = The sister)

→ **Leonard has <u>a sister</u> who is a singer.**　Leonard에게는 가수인 여자 형제가 있다.
　　　　　　　명사　　관계사

참고로, a sister와 같이 관계절의 꾸밈을 받는 명사를 선행사라고 합니다.

토익 포인트 1 관계절의 자리와 쓰임

✦ 관계절은 문장에서 형용사 역할을 하는 수식어절이며, **수식하는 명사(선행사) 뒤**에 옵니다.

<u>The client</u> who requested a meeting is here. 회의를 요청한 고객이 도착했다.
　선행사

✦ 관계절을 이끄는 관계대명사나 관계부사 자리에 **대명사**나 **부사**는 올 수 없습니다.

The firm hired Ms. Anderson (~~she~~, who) resigned from Parker Holdings.

그 회사는 Parker Holdings사에서 사퇴한 Ms. Anderson을 고용했다.

→ Ms. Anderson을 꾸며주기 위한 관계절을 이끄는 자리이므로 대명사(she)가 아닌 관계대명사(who)가 와야 합니다.

Ms. Smith forgot the name of the store (~~there~~, where) she bought her laptop.

Ms. Smith는 그녀가 노트북을 샀던 상점의 이름을 잊어버렸다.

→ the store를 수식하기 위한 관계절을 이끄는 자리이므로 부사(there)가 아닌 관계부사(where)가 와야 합니다.

토익 실전 Check-up 둘 중 알맞은 것을 고르세요.

We ask customers (ⓐ who, ⓑ they) buy the product to fill out a survey. 　정답·해석·해설 **p.150**

토익 포인트 2 관계대명사

✦ 관계대명사는 **선행사**가 **사람**인지 **사물**인지, 그리고 관계절 내에서 **주격, 목적격, 소유격**으로 쓰이는지에 따라 알맞은 관계대명사를 사용해야 합니다.

선행사 ＼ 격	주격	목적격	소유격
사람	who	whom, who	whose
사물·동물	which	which	whose, of which
사람·사물·동물	that	that	-

<u>The hotel</u> that was reserved for conference members is conveniently located.

회의 구성원들을 위해 예약된 그 호텔은 편리한 위치에 있다.

→ 선행사(The hotel)가 사물이고 관계대명사가 관계절 안에서 주어 역할을 하고 있으므로 관계대명사 that이 쓰였습니다.

Ms. Atkins tries to be a <u>leader</u> (whom/who) her employees admire.

Ms. Atkins는 그녀의 직원들이 존경하는 리더가 되려고 노력한다.

→ 선행사(a leader)가 사람이고 관계대명사가 관계절 안에서 목적어 역할을 하고 있으므로 관계대명사 whom/who가 쓰였습니다. 목적격 관계대명사는 생략할 수 있고, whom 대신 who를 쓰기도 합니다.

Ms. Turner will attend the seminar with Mr. Moore, whose <u>car</u> they will take.

Ms. Turner는 Mr. Moore와 함께 세미나에 참여할 것인데, 그들은 그의 자동차를 탈 것이다.

→ 소유격 관계대명사(whose)는 관계절 안에서 '~의'를 의미하며 명사(car)를 꾸며 주는 소유격 역할을 합니다.

토익 실전 Check-up 둘 중 알맞은 것을 고르세요.

The applicant (ⓐ whom, ⓑ whose) we selected turned down our offer. 　정답·해석·해설 **p.150**

토익 포인트 3 관계부사

✹ 관계부사는 **선행사의 종류**에 따라 알맞은 것을 사용해야 합니다.

선행사의 종류	관계부사	예문
시간을 나타내는 선행사 day, year, time	when	Mr. Miles remembers the day when he first opened his restaurant. Mr. Miles는 처음으로 그의 식당을 개업한 날을 기억한다.
이유를 나타내는 선행사 the reason	why	The memo included the reason why the company was restructuring. 그 회람은 회사가 구조 조정을 하는 이유를 포함했다.
장소를 나타내는 선행사 place	where	The resort aims to be a place where families can have a good time together. 그 리조트는 가족들이 함께 좋은 시간을 보내는 곳이 되는 것을 목표로 한다.
방법을 나타내는 선행사 the way	how	Mr. Jung explained the way he plans to make the company profitable. Mr. Jung은 그가 어떻게 회사를 수익성이 있도록 만들 계획인지 설명했다. The survey measures how customers evaluate quality. 설문 조사는 고객들이 어떻게 품질을 평가하는지를 판단한다. *the way와 how는 함께 쓰이지 않으므로 한 가지만 써야 합니다.

토익 실전 Check-up 둘 중 알맞은 것을 고르세요.

Mr. Sosa received the email on the day (ⓐ why, ⓑ when) he came back from the business trip.

정답·해석·해설 p.150

토익 포인트 4 관계대명사 vs. 관계부사

✹ **관계대명사 뒤**에는 주어나 목적어가 빠진 **불완전한 절**이 오고, **관계부사 뒤**에는 **완전한 절**이 옵니다.

The promotion only applies to customers who shop on the Web site.
그 판촉 행사는 웹사이트에서 쇼핑하는 고객들에게만 해당되는 것이다.
→ 관계대명사(who) 뒤에 주어가 없는 불완전한 절이 왔습니다.

The new project is the reason why AMR Construction is hiring more architects.
그 새로운 프로젝트는 AMR 건설사가 더 많은 건축가들을 고용하는 이유이다.
→ 관계부사(why) 뒤에 주어(AMR Construction)와 목적어(more architects)가 모두 갖춰진 완전한 절이 왔습니다.

토익 실전 Check-up 둘 중 알맞은 것을 고르세요.

The new park, (ⓐ where, ⓑ which) includes several sports fields, will open next month.   정답·해석·해설 p.150

HACKERS PRACTICE
토익 700+ 달성을 위한 연습 문제

다음 문장에서 알맞은 것을 고르세요.

01 The candidate (ⓐ who, ⓑ whose) wins the mayoral election will take office in early January.

02 The company (ⓐ that, ⓑ whom) Mr. Gaines founded, is now making a big profit.

03 The fundraising event was successful (ⓐ despite, ⓑ within) the lack of volunteers.

04 Starbound Travel provides tour packages (ⓐ where, ⓑ that) truly exceed expectations.

05 Fans are eager to see Lucas Wright's latest painting, (ⓐ who, ⓑ which) is being exhibited at the Connhurst Gallery.

06 Mr. Kent thanked Ms. Meyers, (ⓐ whom, ⓑ whose) he received his training from.

07 Ms. Savic was quick at (ⓐ respond, ⓑ responding) to the interview questions.

08 The number of animals (ⓐ they, ⓑ that) live in the zoo has decreased considerably.

다음 문장에서 밑줄 친 곳을 문법에 맞게 고치세요.

09 The building <u>what</u> Mr. Wallace works houses a number of clothing companies.

10 The workers painted white lines <u>from</u> the pavement of the parking lot.

11 Tuesday morning is the time <u>why</u> Ms. Williams would most prefer to be interviewed.

12 The survey <u>this</u> was conducted last Monday shows that most citizens are happy about the economy.

13 The client did not give a reason <u>whom</u> he decided to cancel his contract.

14 The home, which <u>is</u> built last year, is decorated tastefully and modernly.

15 The business journal had an article on Mr. Orville, <u>who</u> shop has been open for 50 years.

16 The instructor is teaching the trainees <u>which</u> the equipment can be operated.

무료 해설 ▶
바로 보기

정답·해석 **p.151**

PART 5

01 As long as they have access to the Internet, staff members are permitted to work from home ------- the office.

(A) otherwise (B) or
(C) on (D) over

02 The benefits offered by Dale Airways, ------- are only available to members, include access to VIP lounges.

(A) whom (B) they
(C) which (D) them

03 Upper management at *Gram Magazine* will ------- hire more designers or outsource artwork entirely.

(A) each (B) another
(C) either (D) much

04 Mr. Baxter has just returned from Norwich, ------- he had gone on a business trip.

(A) how (B) when
(C) why (D) where

05 Neither the instructions nor the user guide ------- enough information to properly assemble the computer.

(A) containing (B) contain
(C) contains (D) container

06 *Bizweek* published a story about Mr. Greer, ------- restaurant has managed to thrive despite the economic recession.

(A) his (B) other
(C) he (D) whose

07 Quik Movers offers a range of options for ------- domestic ground service and international freight shipments.

(A) also (B) where
(C) both (D) neither

08 VNT Labs decided to recall all of its smartphones from stores after discovering a critical bug in ------- units.

(A) any (B) every
(C) less (D) some

09 Most guests at the Kriya Hotel are satisfied with the service ------- find the facilities to be outdated.

(A) meanwhile (B) yet
(C) for (D) while

10 After the seminar is complete, the conference hall will be ------- rearranged in preparation for the evening's banquet.

(A) quicken (B) quicker
(C) quickening (D) quickly

11 Thomas often thinks of the time ------- his family traveled to Hawaii.

(A) when (B) about
(C) which (D) where

12 The firm has just accepted a major commission from Johnson and Partners, and all staff will ------- be asked to work some extra hours next week.

(A) similarly (B) besides
(C) because (D) therefore

13 Many citizens agree that either real estate prices or the average cost of rent ------- to decrease.

(A) needing (B) need
(C) needful (D) needs

14 Ms. Topham has requested an ------- for why the Shipton Shopping Mall building designs are so far behind schedule.

(A) explanation (B) explain
(C) explanatory (D) explains

15 The man ------- Ms. Neilson met at the networking event gave her his business card and suggested she contact him.

(A) them   (B) those
(C) whose   (D) whom

16 Passengers ------- check in on the Internet before arriving at the airport will be able to go straight to the security gate.

(A) when   (B) what
(C) whose   (D) who

17 Newbrook catering ------- turned up late to the event but also failed to make enough food for all the guests.

(A) rather   (B) neither
(C) not only   (D) in addition

18 The customer service workshop, ------- takes place this Friday, is mandatory for all sales representatives.

(A) it   (B) which
(C) what   (D) this

PART 6

Questions 19-22 refer to the following advertisement.

Every day, businesses across the nation hold amazing sales. -------. That's where Bargain-A-Day
                                          19
comes in. Our state-of-the-art algorithm locates the best deals in your city. We then automatically
send notifications about ------- to you. The bargains are organized into categories that help you
                          20
find whatever you need. We also have a price match guarantee policy ------- the lowest price
                                                    21
available.

We hope you take ------- of this opportunity to enjoy the best prices in your city. Visit www.
                      22
bargainaday.com to get started.

19 (A) Nevertheless, it is necessary for members to pay a small annual fee.
(B) Please remember that the offer is available for a limited time only.
(C) However, consumers often miss them if they're not widely advertised.
(D) Our coupons can be redeemed at Bargain-A-Day locations everywhere.

20 (A) it   (B) them
(C) this   (D) which

21 (A) to be ensured   (B) are ensured
(C) that ensures   (D) it ensured

22 (A) benefit   (B) assurance
(C) advantage   (D) exception

정답·해석·해설 **p.151**

Course 1 부사절

<u>외출하기 전에</u> 삼촌은 머리를 빗는다.
부사절

문장에서 주절은 '삼촌은 머리를 빗는다'입니다. 앞에 있는 '외출하기 전에'는 언제 머리를 빗는지를 나타
내는 종속절입니다. 이와 같이 주절을 수식하여 이유, 조건, 시간 등의 부가적인 정보를 제공해주는 절을
부사절이라고 합니다.

기초문법 잡기

1 부사절은 어떤 형태를 가지고 있나요?

부사절의 형태는 '부사절 접속사 + 주어 + 동사 ~'입니다.

My uncle always combs his hair <u>before he goes out</u>. 외출하기 전에 삼촌은 항상 머리를 빗는다.
부사절 접속사(before) + 주어(he) + 동사(goes) ~ = 부사절

2 부사절은 앞에서 배운 관계절과 어떻게 다른가요?

부사절은 문장에서 시간이나 이유 등 부가적 의미를 더해주는 부사 역할을 하는 반면, 관계절은 명사를 뒤에서 꾸며주는 형용사
역할을 합니다.

부사절 Ms. Thurman went to a resort when she was on vacation. Ms. Thurman은 휴가 동안 리조트에 갔다.

관계절 9:30 A.M. is <u>the time</u> when the stores in the mall open. 오전 9시 30분은 쇼핑몰의 가게들이 개점하는 시간이다.

명사

토익 포인트 1　부사절의 자리와 쓰임

☀ 부사절은 문장에서 **주절의 앞**이나 **뒤**에 옵니다.

Because Mr. Quinn will be away on business, <u>he will not be able to attend the meeting</u>.
Mr. Quinn은 출장으로 인해 부재중일 것이기 때문에, 회의에 참식할 수 없을 것이다.
→ 부사절(Because ~ business)이 주절(he ~ meeting) 앞에 왔습니다.

<u>BR, Inc. has already hired staff for its new factory</u> even though it is still being built.
BR사는 비록 새 공장이 여전히 지어지고 있지만 그곳을 위한 직원들을 이미 채용했다.
→ 부사절(even though ~ built)이 주절(BR, Inc. ~ factory) 뒤에 왔습니다.

☀ 부사절을 이끄는 부사절 접속사 자리에 **전치사**는 올 수 없습니다. 의미가 비슷한 부사절 접속사와 전치사를 혼동하지 않도록
주의합니다.

부사절 접속사	전치사
while ~하는 동안	during, for ~ 동안
because, since ~이기 때문에	because of, due to ~ 때문에
although, even though 비록 ~이지만	in spite of, despite ~에도 불구하고

Ms. Grey reads the newspaper (~~during~~, while) she commutes to work.　Ms. Grey는 회사로 통근하는 동안 신문을 읽는다.

토익 실전 Check-up 둘 중 알맞은 것을 고르세요.
Ms. Patterson cannot do the assignment (ⓐ because, ⓑ because of) she has a full schedule.

정답·해석·해설 p.154

토익 포인트 2　부사절 접속사 1: 시간

☀ 시간을 나타내는 부사절 접속사

until ~할 때까지	as ~할 때, ~함에 따라	when ~할 때
before ~하기 전에	while ~하는 동안	after ~한 이후에
since ~한 이래로	as soon as ~하자마자 (=immediately after)	once 일단 ~하면, ~하는 대로

Three weeks remain until Giftek releases its newest programming software.
Giftek사가 최신 프로그래밍 소프트웨어를 출시할 때까지 3주 남았다.

Mr. Bailey's phone rang as he was leaving for work.
Mr. Bailey가 출근하려고 나갈 때 전화가 울렸다.

Once their payments are completed, customers receive order confirmation e-mails.
일단 지불이 완료되면, 고객들은 주문 확인 이메일을 받는다.

Ms. Brown's secretary contacted her as soon as the delivery arrived.
Ms. Brown의 비서는 배달 물품이 도착하자마자 그녀에게 연락했다.

토익 실전 Check-up 둘 중 알맞은 것을 고르세요.
Mr. Azarov received several calls (ⓐ while, ⓑ once) he was out.

정답·해석·해설 p.154

✦ **조건을 나타내는 부사절 접속사**

if 만약 ~이라면	unless ~하지 않는 한	in case (that), in the event (that) ~에 대비하여 (~의 경우)
as long as, providing/provided (that), only if, on condition that 오직 ~하는 경우에만		

Unless Ms. Gordon pays her parking tickets, she will not be permitted to drive.
Ms. Gordon이 그녀의 주차 위반 딱지에 대한 벌금을 내지 않는 한, 그녀는 운전하도록 허락되지 않을 것이다.

✦ **양보를 나타내는 부사절 접속사**

although, though, even if, even though 비록 ~이지만	whereas, while ~한 반면에

Although sales improved in the fourth quarter, this will be the company's least profitable year.
비록 4분기에 매출이 나아졌지만, 올해는 회사가 수익을 가장 내지 못한 해일 것이다.

토익 실전 Check-up 둘 중 알맞은 것을 고르세요.

Demand for local real estate is high (ⓐ when, ⓑ even though) prices are increasing.   정답·해석·해설 **p.154**

✦ **이유, 목적, 결과, 제외를 나타내는 부사절 접속사**

이유	because, as, since ~이기 때문에	now that ~이니까	in that ~이라는 점에서
목적	so that, in order that ~할 수 있도록		
결과	so/such ~ that - 매우 ~해서 ~하다		
제외	except that ~을 제외하고는		

Now that the store has reopened, we need to hire more staff.
상점이 다시 개점했으니까, 우리는 더 많은 직원을 고용해야 한다.

Ms. Quentin has installed her company's software on her laptop so that she can work from home.
Ms. Quentin은 그녀가 재택근무를 할 수 있도록 그녀의 노트북에 회사 소프트웨어를 설치했다.

The interviewer was so impressed with Ms. Parker that he offered her a job right away.
그 면접관은 Ms. Parker에게 매우 좋은 인상을 받아서 그녀에게 곧바로 일자리를 제안했다.

Mr. Trenton's holiday in France was lovely except that it was unusually cold.
몹시 추웠다는 것을 제외하고는 프랑스에서의 Mr. Trenton의 휴가는 아주 좋았다.

토익 실전 Check-up 둘 중 알맞은 것을 고르세요.

The company made (ⓐ such, ⓑ as) a good profit that it was able to open several new branches.
정답·해석·해설 **p.154**

HACKERS PRACTICE 토익 700+ 달성을 위한 연습 문제

다음 문장에서 알맞은 것을 고르세요.

01 The next meeting's agenda will be distributed (ⓐ within, ⓑ before) it takes place.

02 The Helmsburg Center will remain open (ⓐ unless, ⓑ as long as) it continues to receive funding.

03 The speaker will begin his presentation (ⓐ as soon as, ⓑ even though) everyone is seated.

04 The first candidate is already fully certified (ⓐ so that, ⓑ whereas) the second is still in training.

05 Mr. Collins will be in charge of the department (ⓐ although, ⓑ while) the director is away.

06 Ms. Kim offers regular incentives (ⓐ accordingly, ⓑ in order that) her employees stay motivated.

07 The convention will continue (ⓐ even if, ⓑ once) one of the speakers doesn't show up.

08 Upon arriving at the hotel, Ms. Quincy was (ⓐ much, ⓑ so) tired that she went to bed right away.

다음 문장에서 밑줄 친 곳을 문법에 맞게 고치세요.

09 Hiring more staff for the busy holiday season would be helpful except <u>they</u> it would cost a lot of money.

10 The editor discovered a <u>mistakenly</u> while he was proofreading the document for the final time.

11 Since the merger, the company's stock price has <u>drops</u> even lower than market specialists' predictions.

12 After Mr. Willis promoted <u>him</u> store on the radio, the sales increased by 70 percent.

13 The housing council is <u>responsibility</u> for clearing away any tree that falls during a storm.

14 Almost all participants <u>whom</u> attended Mr. Jones' seminar responded positively to it.

15 Employees may leave early today <u>in</u> condition that they stay late tomorrow.

16 The conference room is being expanded <u>even</u> that more staff can fit in it comfortably.

무료 해설 ▶
바로 보기

정답·해석 **p.154**

<u>그는 옷이 작다는 것을 알지 못했다.</u>
　　　명사절

'옷이 작다는 것'이라는 절이 '그는 알지 못했다'라는 문장에 포함되어 목적어 자리에 왔습니다. 이와 같이
명사가 오는 자리에 와서 명사 역할을 하는 절을 **명사절**이라고 합니다.

기초문법 잡기

1 명사절은 어떤 형태를 가지고 있나요?

명사절의 형태는 '명사절 접속사 + 주어 + 동사 ~'입니다.

He didn't know that the shirt was so small. 그는 셔츠가 그렇게 작았다는 것을 알지 못했다.
　　　　　　　명사절 접속사(that) + 주어(the shirt) + 동사(was) ~ = 명사절

2 명사절 접속사에는 어떤 것이 있나요?

명사절을 이끄는 명사절 접속사는 의미에 따라 크게 세 가지로 나뉩니다.

명사절 접속사	의미		
that	~라는 것		
whether/ if	~인지 아닌지		
의문사	who 누가 ~하는지	when 언제 ~하는지	where 어디서 ~하는지
	what 무엇이(을) ~하는지	how 어떻게 ~하는지	why 왜 ~하는지
	which 어느 것이(을) ~하는지		

* 의문사는 문장에서 의문대명사, 의문형용사, 의문부사 역할을 할 수 있습니다.

Ms. Santos asked if she could reschedule the meeting. Ms. Santos는 회의의 일정을 다시 잡을 수 있는지 없는지를 물었다.

Where the event will be held has still not been decided. 어디에서 행사가 열릴지는 여전히 결정되지 않았다.

토익 포인트 1   명사절의 자리와 쓰임

✱ 명사절은 문장에서 명사 역할을 하므로 명사처럼 **주어, 목적어, 보어 자리**에 옵니다.

주어	How to assemble the desk **is described in the manual.** 어떻게 책상을 조립하는지가 설명서에 기술되어 있다.
동사의 목적어	**Ms. Scott forgot** when the appointment is. Ms. Scott은 약속이 언제인지를 잊어버렸다.
전치사의 목적어	**Mr. Gerard thought about** where he should take his guests to dinner. Mr. Gerard는 그의 손님들을 저녁 식사에 어디로 데려갈지에 대해 생각했다.
보어	**Cutting costs is** what we need to discuss today. 비용 절감이 우리가 오늘 논의해야 하는 것이다.

✱ 명사절을 이끄는 명사절 접속사 자리에 **전치사, 대명사**는 올 수 없습니다.

The director announced (~~during, them,~~ where) the annual holiday party will happen.
관리자는 어디서 연례 공휴일 파티가 열릴지를 발표했다.

→ 전치사(during)나 대명사(them)는 절(the annual holiday party will happen)을 이끌 수 없으므로 접속사가 와야 합니다. 그리고 동사 (announced)의 목적어가 될 수 있는 명사절이 와야 하므로 명사절 접속사(where)가 와야 합니다.

토익 실전 Check-up 둘 중 알맞은 것을 고르세요.

The supervisor asked (ⓐ what, ⓑ about) Mr. Kline was working on.   정답·해석·해설 **p.154**

토익 포인트 2   명사절 접속사 1: that

✱ that이 이끄는 명사절은 '**~라는 것**'을 의미하며, 문장에서 **주어, 동사의 목적어, 보어, 동격절**로 쓰입니다.

주어	That some machinery malfunctioned **delayed production considerably.** 몇몇 기계가 제대로 작동하지 않은 것이 생산을 상당히 지체시켰다.
동사의 목적어	**Ms. Bowen realized** that the article contained several technical errors. Ms. Bowen은 기사가 몇 가지 기술적인 오류를 포함하고 있다는 것을 알아차렸다.
보어	**The argument against the merger is** that some jobs will be cut. 합병에 반대하는 주장은 몇몇 일자리가 줄어들 것이라는 것이다.
동격절	**The fact** that a subway station is close to the office **is convenient.** 지하철역이 사무실에서 가깝다는 사실은 편리하다.

토익 실전 Check-up 둘 중 알맞은 것을 고르세요.

The idea (ⓐ it, ⓑ that) people learn in different ways is generally accepted.   정답·해석·해설 **p.154**

* **whether**가 이끄는 명사절은 '~인지 아닌지'를 의미하며, 문장에서 **주어, 동사의 목적어, 전치사의 목적어, 보어**로 쓰입니다.

주어	Whether the company expands this year or not **is uncertain.** 회사가 올해 확장할지 아닐지는 불확실하다.
동사의 목적어	**The researchers must determine** whether they will discontinue the product. 연구가들은 상품을 단종시킬지 아닐지를 결정해야만 한다.
전치사의 목적어	**The shareholders will vote on** whether they need to change the CEO. 주주들은 최고 경영자를 바꿔야 할지 아닐지에 대해 투표할 것이다.
보어	**The topic of the meeting is** whether the budget should be cut or not. 회의의 주제는 예산을 삭감해야 할지 아닐지이다.

* **if**가 이끄는 명사절도 '~인지 아닌지'를 의미하는데, whether가 이끄는 명사절과는 달리 문장에서 **동사의 목적어와 보어로만** 쓰입니다.

동사의 목적어	**We can check** if our flight will depart on schedule. 우리는 우리의 항공편이 일정대로 출발할지 아닐지를 확인할 수 있다.
보어	**Our concern is** if we can catch the train. 우리의 걱정은 기차를 시간에 맞춰 탈 수 있을지 아닐지이다.

토익 실전 Check-up 둘 중 알맞은 것을 고르세요.

(ⓐ Whether, ⓑ If) employees are eligible for a bonus depends on their performance. 정답·해석·해설 **p.154**

---

* **의문대명사** who, whom, whose, what, which는 명사절을 이끌며, 명사절 내에서 주어나 목적어 역할을 합니다. 따라서 뒤에 **주어나 목적어가 없는 불완전한 절**이 옵니다.

What worried us was the client's slow response to our proposal.
우리를 걱정시켰던 것은 우리의 제안에 대한 고객의 늦은 답변이었다.

* **의문형용사** whose, what, which는 명사를 수식하면서 명사절을 이끌며, '의문형용사 + 명사'가 명사절 내에서 주어, 목적어, 보어 역할을 합니다. 따라서 **뒤에 주어나 목적어, 보어가 없는 불완전한 절**이 옵니다.

Which booth we rent for the exposition will be decided tomorrow.
박람회를 위해 우리가 어떤 부스를 대여할 것인지는 내일 결정될 것이다.

* **의문부사** when, where, how, why는 명사절을 이끌며, **뒤에 빠지는 것 없는 완전한 절**이 옵니다.

When the company event starts will be announced this afternoon.
사내 행사가 언제 시작하는지는 오늘 오후에 공지될 것이다.

토익 실전 Check-up 둘 중 알맞은 것을 고르세요.

The memo explains (ⓐ why, ⓑ what) the building is inaccessible today. 정답·해석·해설 **p.154**

HACKERS PRACTICE 토익 700+ 달성을 위한 연습 문제

다음 문장에서 알맞은 것을 고르세요.

01 A factory inspector found out (ⓐ why, ⓑ about) the plant's machines haven't been working properly.

02 A customer called to ask (ⓐ who, ⓑ if) shirts ordered online could be returned.

03 In his speech, Mr. Tenzig talked about (ⓐ by, ⓑ how) he built the company from the ground up.

04 The firm was confident (ⓐ that, ⓑ because of) its new weight loss drug would be successful.

05 The statues (ⓐ that, ⓑ them) were erected downtown are monuments to the city's founders.

06 Mr. Crane forgot (ⓐ at, ⓑ where) he parked his car.

07 The company will continue to innovate regardless of (ⓐ either, ⓑ whether) the market remains favorable.

08 An applicant is inquiring (ⓐ what, ⓑ if) his scheduled interview can be postponed until Monday.

다음 문장에서 밑줄 친 곳을 문법에 맞게 고치세요.

09 Your ticket contains information about <u>how</u> airport terminal the flight will be departing from.

10 <u>Who</u> the spokesperson said tonight will be featured on tomorrow's newspaper.

11 Mr. Johansson will contact us <u>what</u> the chief executive arrives at the Los Angeles branch.

12 The committee chooses <u>why</u> will give the welcoming speech at the opening ceremony.

13 A hotel room will be arranged for the visiting client, <u>his</u> flight will be arriving this afternoon.

14 A science documentary explains in detail how the caves <u>was</u> formed.

15 Customers placing orders of more than $100 would not only receive a discount <u>besides</u> a free gift.

16 Survey respondents were asked about <u>which</u> they support the government's new policies or not.

무료 해설 ▶ 바로 보기

정답·해설 **p.155**

PART 5

01 Residents of Fulton Towers are expected to keep quiet after 11 P.M. ------- they do not disturb their neighbors.

(A) so that
(B) such as
(C) but also
(D) instead of

02 The consultant recommended ------- the administration implement a new data management system to improve efficiency.

(A) about
(B) if
(C) that
(D) while

03 The human resources department wants to determine ------- job incentives will spur the office staff to become more productive.

(A) those
(B) as
(C) all
(D) if

04 Ms. Paulson looked at Mr. Vega's workshop schedule and realized that it was nearly the same as -------.

(A) hers
(B) her
(C) herself
(D) she

05 Mr. Jenkins ------- for 4 years by the time he becomes a senior analyst.

(A) will have worked
(B) has worked
(C) worked
(D) will work

06 Employee satisfaction surveys have shown a marked improvement ------- the new benefits package was implemented.

(A) in the event
(B) within
(C) since
(D) during

07 All PINOX staff can go on a vacation any time of the year ------- their supervisor has been notified in advance.

(A) as much as
(B) except that
(C) so that
(D) as long as

08 Belmont Corporation is certain ------- it will be able to acquire a small technology firm with innovative business ideas.

(A) who
(B) yet
(C) but
(D) that

09 The radio commentator interviewed an author ------- wrote a best-selling book about his experiences living in Asia.

(A) whom
(B) whose
(C) whoever
(D) who

10 Ms. Patterson has an allergy to nuts, so she asked the waiter ------- her dish contained any.

(A) which
(B) whether
(C) however
(D) either

11 Mr. Sean received a great performance evaluation ------- he was late several times.

(A) in order that
(B) even though
(C) in preparation for
(D) as of

12 The culinary instructor showed the students ------- cheese is made.

(A) how
(B) who
(C) about
(D) on

13 Mr. Marcus is ------- sure of the project's success that he has invested his own money in it.

(A) even
(B) so
(C) who
(D) as

14 ------- borrowers fail to repay their short-term loans by the due date, they will be charged late fees and interest.

(A) Otherwise
(B) If
(C) Following
(D) Thus

15 The report on the firm's current marketing projects ------- various advertising strategies that have proven successful.

(A) describes   (B) describe
(C) are described   (D) descriptively

16 The manager didn't know ------- cell phone rang during the meeting, so she reminded everyone to silence their phones at work.

(A) any   (B) whose
(C) that   (D) other

17 ------- Ms. Hill left for Thailand, she ensured that her passport and tourist visa were valid.

(A) Unless   (B) Before
(C) While   (D) Although

18 The Carson Hotel continues to charge its standard rates, ------- the others have instituted summer prices.

(A) why   (B) rather than
(C) whereas   (D) despite

PART 6

Questions 19-22 refer to the following announcement.

It's our pleasure to announce that the Fall Ready-to-Wear Fashion event will take place in Camden Building's rooftop garden. The program is being promoted as this year's big fashion affair ------- it
    19
was last season's most-talked-about show.

We ------- fall clothing lines by both new designers and veterans, such as Ann Mobley and Peter
    20
Wells. -------. Moreover, you'll have the opportunity to mingle with some of the biggest names in
    21
the industry.

The show will be held on October 15. Tickets to the event are being ------- now, starting at $30.
    22
Visit our Web site and click "Fall Fashion Event" to reserve a seat today.

19 (A) until   (B) because of
     (C) even though   (D) since

20 (A) presented   (B) will present
     (C) have presented   (D) present

21 (A) This includes a full list of participants and an event schedule.
(B) The collection will be available in selected retail outlets on October 1.
(C) His award-winning work is a major influence on younger designers.
(D) You'll also see many of today's most promising fashion models.

22 (A) sold   (B) selling
     (C) sell   (D) to sell

정답·해석·해설 p.155

Course 1 비교 구문

토익 출제경향
최대 2문제까지 출제

언니는 나보다 키가 크다.
　　　　비교

우리 가족 중에서 언니가 가장 크다.
　　　　　　　　　　비교

'언니는 나보다 키가 크다', '우리 가족 중에서 언니가 가장 크다'와 같이 두 가지 이상의 대상을 서로 견주
어 비교하는 구문을 **비교 구문**이라고 합니다.

기초문법 잡기

1 비교 구문에는 어떤 것들이 있나요?

비교 구문에는 원급 구문, 비교급 구문, 최상급 구문이 있습니다.

(1) 원급: 두 대상이 동등함을 나타낼 때 씁니다.

My sister is as tall as me. 언니는 나만큼 키가 크다.

(2) 비교급: 두 대상 중 하나가 더 우월함을 나타낼 때 씁니다.

My sister is taller than me. 언니는 나보다 키가 크다.

(3) 최상급: 셋 이상의 대상 중 하나가 가장 우월함을 나타낼 때 씁니다.

My sister is the tallest in my family. 언니는 우리 가족 중에서 가장 키가 크다.

2 비교급과 최상급은 어떻게 만드나요?

비교급과 최상급은 형용사와 부사의 형태를 변화시켜서 만드는데, 이때 규칙 변화와 불규칙 변화가 있습니다.

규칙 변화			
비교급	1음절 또는 2음절(-er, -y , -ow, -some 등으로 끝나는)	(e)r를 붙인다.	fast → faster
	2음절(-able, -ful, -ous 등으로 끝나는) 또는 3음절 이상	앞에 more를 붙인다.	delicious → more delicious
최상급	1음절 또는 2음절(-er, -y , -ow, -some 등으로 끝나는)	(e)st를 붙인다.	fast → fastest
	2음절(-able, -ful, -ous 등으로 끝나는) 또는 3음절 이상	앞에 most를 붙인다.	delicious → most delicious

불규칙 변화		
원급	비교급	최상급
good/well 좋은/잘	better 더 좋은/더 잘	best 가장 좋은/가장 잘
bad 나쁜	worse 더 나쁜	worst 가장 나쁜
many/much 많은	more 더 많은	most 가장 많은
little 적은	less 더 적은	least 가장 적은

BHM Company is more successful than Lemieux Corp. BHM사는 Lemieux사보다 더 잘 되고 있다.

Nota Telecom offers the fastest Internet service in the area.
Nota Telecom은 그 지역에서 가장 빠른 인터넷 서비스를 제공한다.

토익 포인트 1   원급 구문

☀ '~만큼 -한'이라는 의미로 두 대상의 동등함을 나타내는 원급 구문은 'as + 형용사/부사 + as'를 씁니다.

The company is as popular as its primary competitors.
그 회사는 주요 경쟁사들만큼 잘 알려져 있다.

The tablet was rated as positively as our best-selling laptop.
그 태블릿 컴퓨터는 우리의 가장 잘 팔리는 노트북만큼 긍정적으로 평가되었다.

☀ '~만큼 많은/적은 명사'라는 의미를 나타내는 원급 구문은 'as + many/much/few/little 명사 + as'를 씁니다.

You can have as much time as you need to finish.   당신은 완료하기 위해 필요한 만큼 많은 시간을 가질 수 있습니다.

토익 실전 Check-up 둘 중 알맞은 것을 고르세요.

Mr. Jenkins is (ⓐ more, ⓑ as) professional as he sounded on the phone.   정답·해석·해설 **p.158**

토익 포인트 2   비교급 구문

☀ '~보다 -한'이라는 의미로 두 대상 중 한쪽이 우월함을 나타내는 비교급 구문은 '형용사/부사의 비교급 + than'을 씁니다.

Beta Corporation is bigger than Alego Inc.   Beta사는 Alego사보다 크다.

Ms. Maxwell completed her work more quickly than her teammates.
Ms. Maxwell은 그녀의 팀원들보다 더 빨리 작업을 완료했다.

☀ '~보다 더 많은/적은 명사'라는 의미를 나타내는 비교급 구문은 'more/fewer/less 명사 + than'을 씁니다.

More people than we expected applied for the position.   우리가 예상했던 것보다 더 많은 사람들이 일자리에 지원했다.

There is less money in the budget than last year.   예산에 작년보다 더 적은 돈이 있다.

☀ '훨씬'이라는 의미로 비교급을 강조하는 표현에는 much, even, still, far 등이 있습니다.

The lecture was much <u>longer than</u> we thought.   강의는 우리가 생각했던 것보다 훨씬 더 길었다.

The revised draft is far <u>better than</u> the previous version.   수정된 원고는 이전 버전보다 훨씬 더 낫다.

토익 실전 Check-up 둘 중 알맞은 것을 고르세요.

Mr. Smith's business is much (ⓐ more profitable, ⓑ profitable) than before.   정답·해석·해설 **p.158**

최상급 구문

✱ '~ 중에 가장 -한'이라는 의미로 셋 이상의 대상들 중 하나가 우월함을 나타내는 최상급 구문은 **'형용사/부사의 최상급 + of ~/in ~/that절'**을 씁니다.

Janet is the most recently hired employee <u>of Myers & Son's</u>. Janet은 Myers & Son's사의 가장 최근에 고용된 직원이다.

This smartphone is the cheapest model <u>in the store</u>. 이 스마트폰은 그 상점에서 가장 저렴한 모델이다.

The Grey Land is the best movie <u>that I've ever watched</u>. *The Grey Land*는 내가 봤던 것 중 최고의 영화이다.

✱ **'최상급 + 명사'** 앞에는 주로 **the**가 옵니다. 이때, the가 아닌 **소유격**이 올 수도 있습니다.

Ms. Grenich rented an office space in the busiest part of town.
Ms. Grenich는 도시의 가장 바쁜 지역에 있는 사무실 공간을 임대했다.

The company president is proud of her most recent accomplishment.
그 회사의 회장은 그녀의 가장 최근의 성과를 자랑스러워한다.

토익 실전 Check-up 둘 중 알맞은 것을 고르세요.

Ms. Alvares is the (ⓐ most, ⓑ much) qualified candidate of the group. 정답·해석·해설 p.158

비교급 표현

✱ 비교급이 포함된 표현

표현	예문
more than + 명사 ~ 이상	More than 100 flights were canceled because of the storm. 폭풍 때문에 100편 이상의 항공편이 취소되었다.
less than + 명사 ~ 이하	The discussion lasted less than an hour. 회의는 한 시간 이하로 지속되었다.
no later than 늦어도 ~까지	Applicants must submit their résumés no later than tomorrow. 지원자들은 늦어도 내일까지 이력서를 제출해야 한다.
no longer 더 이상 ~ 않다	Several items in the catalogue are no longer available. 카탈로그의 몇몇 물품들은 더 이상 구매가 가능하지 않다.
no sooner ~ than - ~하자마자 -하다	No sooner had Ms. Harris graduated university than she found a job. Ms. Harris는 대학을 졸업하자마자 일자리를 구했다.
other than ~ 이외에	Other than a couple of convenience stores, there are no shops nearby. 두어 개의 편의점 이외에, 근처에 상점은 없다.
rather than ~보다는	Mr. Bueller bought the blue suit rather than the black one. Mr. Bueller는 검정색 양복보다는 파란색을 샀다.

토익 실전 Check-up 둘 중 알맞은 것을 고르세요.

Construction on the shopping center will start no (ⓐ late, ⓑ later) than June 3. 정답·해석·해설 p.158

HACKERS PRACTICE 토익 700+ 달성을 위한 연습 문제

다음 문장에서 알맞은 것을 고르세요.

01 Customers agree that Yerba Market sells the (ⓐ freshly, ⓑ freshest) tomatoes in the city.

02 The board is as (ⓐ positivity, ⓑ positive) as the CEO about the new business venture.

03 Property prices in the area are much higher (ⓐ than, ⓑ that) they were several years ago.

04 Customers returning clothes must have a receipt (ⓐ before, ⓑ and) ensure that tags are attached.

05 According to the news, it will rain (ⓐ as, ⓑ much) heavily this week as it did during last year's storm.

06 We will arrange a video conference rather (ⓐ than, ⓑ more) meet in person.

07 Ms. Kim is currently (ⓐ in, ⓑ to) London on business, but she should be back by Friday.

08 (ⓐ Until, ⓑ As soon as) management hires some new employees, the office will be understaffed.

다음 문장에서 밑줄 친 곳을 문법에 맞게 고치세요.

09 Mr. Adams is the <u>harder</u> worker in his department, so he deserves a promotion.

10 The advertising manager is seeking candidates who are <u>imaginative</u> than others.

11 After the renovation, the hotel was as <u>elegance</u> as a palace.

12 This year's parade attracted as <u>much</u> tourists as it did last year.

13 Workers with flexible schedules are more productive <u>and</u> those without them.

14 The weather forecaster said that today will be the <u>hotter</u> day the city has had in over a decade.

15 The delivery receipt cannot be signed by anyone <u>another</u> than Ms. Clowery.

16 The Cavalier Islands are a popular tourist destination regardless <u>with</u> the time of the year.

무료 해설 ▶
바로 보기

정답·해석 **p.158**

병치

작고 귀여운 아기
형용사 형용사

'작은 아기'와 '귀여운 아기'는 연결어 '그리고'를 이용해서 '작고 귀여운 아기'라고 말할 수 있습니다. 연결어로 이어진 '작은(형용사)'과 '귀여운(형용사)'은 같은 품사로 이루어져 있는데, 이와 같이 연결어 앞뒤가 서로 균형을 이루는 것을 **병치**라고 합니다.

도치

She is seldom late. 그녀는 거의 지각하지 않는다.

Seldom is she late. 거의 그녀는 지각하지 않는다.

She is seldom late(그녀는 거의 지각하지 않는다)에서 seldom(거의)을 강조하기 위해 문장의 앞으로 보내면, 주어 she와 동사 is의 순서가 바뀌는데, 이를 **도치**라고 합니다.

기초문법 잡기

1 병치는 어떤 연결어를 쓸 때 일어나나요?

병치는 단어, 구, 절 등이 등위접속사나 상관접속사로 연결될 때 일어납니다. 이때 연결된 항목들은 서로 같은 품사, 구조를 취해야 합니다.

The baby is small and cute. 그 아기는 작고 귀엽다.
형용사   형용사

The customer has neither answered our call nor replied to our e-mail.
분사구   분사구

고객은 우리의 전화를 받지도 않았고 이메일에 회신하지도 않았다.

2 도치는 언제, 어떻게 일어나나요?

강조하고자 하는 말(부정어, 'only + 부사' 등)이 문장 앞으로 나올 때, 주어와 동사의 순서가 바뀌는 도치가 일어납니다. 문장에 be/have/조동사가 있는 경우와 일반동사가 있는 경우에 도치 후의 동사 형태가 각각 달라집니다.

(1) be/have/조동사가 있는 경우: be/have/조동사가 주어 앞으로 옵니다.

A security guard should never leave his post. 경비원은 절대 근무 지역을 떠나서는 안 된다.
주어   조동사 부정어 일반동사

Never should a security guard leave his post.
[강조된 말] 조동사   주어   일반동사

(2) 일반동사가 있는 경우: do동사(do, does, did)가 주어 앞으로 오고, 일반동사는 원래 자리에 동사원형으로 남습니다.

Ms. Park hardly spoke during the meeting. Ms. Park은 회의 동안 거의 말을 하지 않았다.
주어   부정어 일반동사(과거)

Hardly did Ms. Park speak during the meeting.
[강조된 말] do동사 주어   일반동사
        (과거)   (동사원형)

토익 포인트 1 병치 구문

✱ 병치 구문에서는 **같은 품사끼리 연결**되어야 합니다. 즉, 등위접속사와 상관접속사의 앞, 뒤에 **동일한 품사**가 와야 합니다.

The presenter spoke slowly <u>and</u> clearly to the employees. 발표자는 직원들에게 천천히 그리고 명확하게 말했다.
→ 등위접속사 and가 부사(slowly)와 부사(clearly)를 연결해주고 있습니다.

<u>Both</u> the tires <u>and</u> the battery in Ms. Kwan's truck were replaced. Ms. Kwan의 트럭의 타이어와 배터리가 모두 교체되었다.
→ 상관접속사 both ~ and가 명사(the tires)와 명사(the battery)를 연결해주고 있습니다.

✱ 병치 구문에서는 **같은 구조끼리 연결**되어야 합니다. 즉, 등위접속사와 상관접속사의 앞, 뒤에 **동일한 구조**가 와야 합니다.

Working hard <u>but</u> seeing no results can be very frustrating.
열심히 일하지만 아무 결과를 내지 못하는 것은 매우 좌절스러울 수 있다.
→ 등위접속사 but이 동명사구(Working hard)와 동명사구(seeing no results)를 연결해주고 있습니다.

Janet is <u>either</u> in her office <u>or</u> at the cafeteria. Janet은 그녀의 사무실에 있거나 구내식당에 있다.
→ 상관접속사 either ~ or가 전치사구(in her office)와 전치사구(at the cafeteria)를 연결해주고 있습니다.

토익 실전 Check-up 둘 중 알맞은 것을 고르세요.

Reviews say the hotel's staff is attentive and (ⓐ hospitably, ⓑ hospitable). 정답·해석·해설 p.159

토익 포인트 2 부정어 도치

✱ 부정어(never, nor, hardly, seldom, rarely, little 등)가 강조되어 절의 맨 앞으로 나오면 도치가 일어납니다.

Ms. Fender is seldom late for the morning meeting. Ms. Fender는 아침 회의에 거의 늦지 않는다.
⇨ <u>Seldom</u> <u>is</u> <u>Ms. Fender</u> late for the morning meeting.
　　부정어　be동사　주어
› 부정어(Seldom)가 절의 맨 앞으로 나오면 주어(Ms. Fender)와 be동사(is)가 도치됩니다.

Mr. Conway never drives his car to work. Mr. Conway는 절대 직장에 그의 자동차를 운전해서 가지 않는다.
⇨ <u>Never</u> <u>does</u> <u>Mr. Conway</u> <u>drive</u> his car to work.
　　부정어　do동사　　주어　　　동사
→ 부정어(Never)가 절의 맨 앞으로 나오면 주어(Mr. Conway)와 do동사(does)가 도치됩니다.

토익 실전 Check-up 둘 중 알맞은 것을 고르세요.

(ⓐ Never, ⓑ Ever) had Ms. Campbell visited such a beautiful hotel. 정답·해석·해설 p.159

✱ [only + 부사(구, 절)]가 강조되어 문장의 맨 앞으로 나오면 도치가 일어납니다.

Mr. Jones has only once traveled abroad for business. Mr. Jones는 사업차 딱 한 번 해외로 출장을 간 적이 있다.

⇨ Only once has Mr. Jones traveled abroad for business.

→ 'Only + 부사(once)'가 문장 앞으로 나오면 주어(Mr. Jones)와 have동사(has)가 도치됩니다.

Employees may use the fire exits only in the event of an emergency. 직원들은 비상사태에만 화재용 비상구를 이용할 수 있다.

⇨ Only in the event of an emergency may employees use the fire exits.

→ 'Only + 부사구(in the event of an emergency)'가 문장 앞으로 나오면 주어(employees)와 조동사(may)가 도치됩니다.

Ms. Kent received her business card only after she had completed the probationary period.

⇨ Only after she had completed the probationary period did Ms. Kent receive her business card.

Ms. Kent는 수습 기간을 완료한 후에야 명함을 받았다.

→ 'Only + 부사절(after she had completed the probationary period)'이 문장 앞으로 나오면 주어(Ms. Kent)와 do동사(did)가 도치됩니다.

토익 실전 Check-up 둘 중 알맞은 것을 고르세요.

Only after returning home did Mr. Carter (ⓐ check, ⓑ checked) his e-mail. 정답·해석·해설 **p.159**

✱ '~도 역시 그러하다/그렇지 않다'라는 의미의 so, neither가 절의 맨 앞으로 나오면 도치가 일어납니다.

Ms. Roy was pleased with the sales figures, and her employees were pleased with the sales figures.

⇨ Ms. Roy was pleased with the sales figures, and so were her employees.

Ms. Roy는 판매액에 만족했고, 그녀의 직원들도 역시 그랬다.

→ '~도 역시 그러하다'라는 의미의 so가 절의 맨 앞으로 나오면 주어(her employees)와 be동사(were)가 도치됩니다.

Mr. Winston did not go to the workshop, and his colleagues did not go to the workshop.

⇨ Mr. Winston did not go to the workshop, and neither did his colleagues.

Mr. Winston은 워크숍에 가지 않았고, 그의 동료들도 역시 그렇지 않았다.

→ '~도 역시 그렇지 않다'는 의미의 neither가 절의 맨 앞으로 나오면 주어(his colleagues)와 do동사(did)가 도치됩니다.

토익 실전 Check-up 둘 중 알맞은 것을 고르세요.

Mr. Sanchez is willing to stay late, and (ⓐ so, ⓑ then) is Ms. Benoit. 정답·해석·해설 **p.159**

HACKERS PRACTICE 토익 700+ 달성을 위한 연습 문제

다음 문장에서 알맞은 것을 고르세요.

01 During the holidays, the store (ⓐ reduces, ⓑ reduced) prices and extends operating hours.

02 (ⓐ When, ⓑ Never) has the company experienced so much growth.

03 Most find the hiking trail (ⓐ difficult, ⓑ difficulty) but worthwhile.

04 (ⓐ More, ⓑ Only) after the new software was installed could Ms. Howell begin her work.

05 The fastest way to reach the sports arena is to take (ⓐ either, ⓑ both) a cab or the subway.

06 Those registering for the workshop and (ⓐ requiring, ⓑ to require) transportation there should speak to Mr. Dillan.

07 The morning meeting was delayed (ⓐ rarely, ⓑ because) the manager was stuck in traffic.

08 (ⓐ Hardly, ⓑ Very) had Mr. Kim begun his lecture when someone asked a question.

다음 문장에서 밑줄 친 곳을 문법에 맞게 고치세요.

09 Only recently did the company <u>becomes</u> a top retailer of portable computers.

10 Spring has arrived, and <u>such</u> have the latest fashion designs for warmer weather.

11 Seldom is a board meeting <u>cancel</u> on account of the absence of some members.

12 Landcom's new mobile phones are similar <u>by</u> those of Bridge Mobile when it comes to price.

13 Only after Ms. Sullivan came back to the office <u>she did</u> want us to call the caterer.

14 Mr. Ramirez has not tried the new sushi restaurant yet, and <u>either</u> has Ms. Powell.

15 Mr. Larson <u>apologizes</u> for being tardy and promised that it would not happen again.

16 The most common complaint of customers <u>are</u> that there aren't enough sales staff.

무료 해설 ▶
바로 보기

정답·해석 **p.159**

PART 5

01 Dozier Technology plans to release a new smartphone model in order to get a ------- share of the market than it has now.

(A) large
(B) largely
(C) larger
(D) largest

02 When designing a structure, it is the responsibility of the architect to ensure that all dimensions are as ------- as possible.

(A) accurately
(B) accuracy
(C) accurate
(D) accurateness

03 The blueprints for the Shen Building have not been e-mailed to the director, ------- have they been scanned into the system.

(A) nor
(B) yet
(C) even
(D) either

04 Establishing a strategic partnership with Gren Co. has had a ------- impact on the company's performance.

(A) measurement
(B) measurably
(C) measurable
(D) measure

05 Hardly had Ms. Fox ------- her baggage when she noticed a driver holding a sign with her name on it.

(A) collect
(B) to collect
(C) collecting
(D) collected

06 Mr. Saucedo not only writes articles for the magazine ------- edits those outsourced to contributing writers.

(A) nor
(B) and
(C) or
(D) but

07 After over a week of practice, Mr. Bennet decided that he was as ------- for the interview as he would ever be.

(A) preparation
(B) preparedly
(C) prepared
(D) prepare

08 Researchers have discovered that most high-achieving university students tend to study ------- than many of their peers.

(A) independent
(B) more independently
(C) independence
(D) independently

09 Most runners participating in the marathon consider the 10-mile mark to be the ------- part of the race, as it is mostly downhill.

(A) ease
(B) easiness
(C) easily
(D) easiest

10 The CEO will give the keynote speech ------- the business professor introduces him.

(A) after
(B) since
(C) in order that
(D) during

11 Mr. Donati wants to know ------- he can get a full refund if he cancels his registration a week before the convention.

(A) on
(B) about
(C) once
(D) whether

12 Every year, *Turner Business Journal* holds an awards ceremony to honor the top three ------- startups of the year.

(A) more successful
(B) successes
(C) most successful
(D) success

13 Due to a construction delay, the hotel pool will not be ready by June 1 and ------- will the fitness center.

(A) none
(B) as
(C) so
(D) neither

14 The tourist recorded over two hours of footage, ------- she shared with her friends upon returning home.

(A) how
(B) which
(C) what
(D) who

15 Ms. Bergmann is an extremely ------- salesperson who always surpasses her coworkers.

(A) competitive   (B) competes
(C) to compete   (D) competitor

16 From October 1, Beta Airlines will no ------- offer direct flights from Tokyo to Berlin.

(A) long   (B) longer
(C) length   (D) longest

17 Only in the last year did Bonnie's Bakery ------- staying open 24 hours a day.

(A) began   (B) begun
(C) beginning   (D) begin

18 GC Telecom has lowered its prices by 10 percent, and ------- has Telelink.

(A) such   (B) so
(C) why   (D) he

PART 6

Questions 19-22 refer to the following advertisement.

Leganza Linens is ------- for its Comfabulous line of cozy blankets, sheets, and other bedding
      19
supplies. The products are famous for being made from 100 percent, extra-fine Egyptian cotton,

guaranteed to be both ------- and easy to maintain. -------.
        20   **21**

Now, Leganza is pleased to introduce the Comfabulous electric blanket. This comforter offers all

the luxurious smoothness of the other items in the series, with the addition of electric heat. -------,
             22

it features a removable cover that can be machine-washed. Try our Comfabulous electric blanket

today!

19 (A) relevant   (B) receptive
    (C) renowned   (D) reasonable

20 (A) soft   (B) softly
    (C) softer   (D) softest

21 (A) This special offer is available throughout the month of December.
    (B) As the grey and black blankets are sold out, red is the only option available.
    (C) In short, the line has been redesigned with a more contemporary style.
    (D) Still, some of our customers have been asking for something even warmer.

22 (A) Instead   (B) Furthermore
    (C) Next   (D) Consequently

정답·해석·해설 **p.160**

READING

PART 6

PART 6는 131번부터 146번까지 총 16문제로, 각 지문마다 4개의
빈칸에 알맞은 단어나 문장을 고르는 유형입니다. 그 중, 지문을
읽고 주변 문맥과 일치하는 단어를 고르는 문제가 평균 6~7문제,
문장을 고르는 문제가 총 4문제 출제됩니다.

DAY 12 문맥 파악 문제

Course 1 단어 고르기 문제

토익 출제경향
평균 6~7문제 정도 출제

> 귀하께서 지원하신 그 직위는 이미 채용되었습니다. _____, 저희는 귀하께서 관심 있어 하실 만한 또 다른 직위가 있습니다. 관심이 있으시다면, 연락 주세요.

> 그러나

내용이 일부 빠져 있는 이메일과 그 부분에 들어갈 알맞은 단어입니다. 이처럼 PART 6에서는 지문의 빈칸에 들어갔을 때 문맥이 자연스럽게 연결되는 **단어를 고르는 문맥 파악 문제**가 출제됩니다.

📋 문제 유형

문법 문제

주변 또는 전체 문맥을 파악하여 빈칸에 들어갈 알맞은 시제, 대명사, 접속부사를 묻는 문제가 출제됩니다.

어휘 문제

주변 또는 전체 문맥을 파악하여 빈칸에 들어갈 알맞은 어휘를 고르는 문제로, 주로 명사 어휘를 묻는 문제가 출제됩니다.

📋 문제 풀이 전략

STEP 1 빈칸이 있는 문장의 내용을 파악한 후 빈칸 주변 문장에서 단서를 찾습니다.

[문법 문제]

시제 문제: 빈칸 주변 문장에 쓰인 동사의 시제를 확인하여 빈칸에 들어갈 동사의 시제를 예상합니다. 주변 문장이나 지문 상단에 날짜가 언급되어 있다면 함께 확인하여 시간의 흐름을 파악합니다.

대명사 문제: 빈칸에서 가리키는 대상은 주로 빈칸 앞 문장에 언급되어 있으므로 앞 문장에서 언급된 명사들을 먼저 확인합니다. 이때, 빈칸에서 가리키는 대상의 수(단수/복수), 인칭 등을 중점적으로 확인합니다.

접속부사 문제: 빈칸이 있는 문장과 그 앞 문장의 의미 관계를 파악합니다. 두 문장이 서로 상반되는 내용을 설명하는지, 추가적인 내용을 전달하는지, 순차적인 일을 설명하는지 등 두 문장의 의미가 어떻게 연결되는지를 파악합니다.

[어휘 문제]

주로 빈칸의 주변 문장에 단서가 되는 어휘나 표현이 포함되어 있으므로 빈칸 주변 문장을 확인합니다. 참고로, 명사 어휘 문제에서 빈칸 앞에 정관사, 지시어, 소유격이 있으면 가리키는 대상이 앞 문장에 언급되어 있으므로 빈칸 앞 문장을 먼저 확인합니다.

STEP 2 지문의 흐름에 자연스러운 보기를 정답으로 선택합니다.

전략 적용

[문법 문제] 접속부사

Ms. Furness께,

저는 귀하의 입사 지원 진행 상황에 대한 최신 정보를 알려드리기 위해 편지를 씁니다. 안타깝게도, 그 직위는 이미 채용되었습니다. -------, 저희는 귀하께서 관심 있어 하실 만한 또 다른 직위가 있습니다. 저는 금융 업계에서의 귀하의 경력이 귀하를 신용 등급 조사원직에 대해 매우 적합한 후보자로 만든다고 생각합니다. 만약 관심이 있으시다면, 저는 다음 주에 언제든 면접을 할 수 있습니다.

Q. (A) 마찬가지로
   (B) 결과적으로
   (C) 그러나
   (D) 상당히

Dear Ms. Furness,

I am writing to update you on the status of your job application. Unfortunately, the position has already been filled. -------, we do have another job you may be interested in. I think your experience in the finance industry makes you a highly suitable candidate for the credit analyst position. If you're interested, I can arrange for an interview sometime next week.

Q. (A) Similarly
   (B) Consequently
   (C) However
   (D) Rather

STEP 1
빈칸이 있는 문장의 내용을 파악한 후 빈칸 주변 문장에서 단서를 찾습니다.

STEP 2
지문의 흐름에 자연스러운 보기를 정답으로 선택합니다.

해설 STEP 1 빈칸이 있는 문장에서 상대방이 관심 있어 할 만한 또 다른 직위가 있다고 했고, 빈칸 앞 문장에서 안타깝게도 상대방이 지원한 직위는 이미 채용되었다고 했으므로 빈칸 앞뒤 문장이 서로 상반되는 내용을 설명하고 있음을 확인합니다.

STEP 2 서로 상반되는 두 문장을 연결하는 접속부사 (C) However(그러나)가 정답입니다.

[어휘 문제] 명사 어휘

Odin Organic Cosmetics사가 Gainesville에 올 예정이다. 새로운 곳은 Banff와 Lake Louise 상점에 이어, 체인점 중 세 번째이다. 소유주 Sean Erasmus는 기존 두 -------의 성공에 의해 자극을 받았다고 말했다. 두 도시 모두 번창하는 관광 산업을 누리고 있다. 또한 Gainesville이 그만큼 유명한 것은 아니지만, 인기 있는 행선지로 빠르게 변화하고 있다. 그러므로 Mr. Erasmus는 그의 세 번째 상점이 번창할 것이라고 확신한다. 업계 전문가들은 Gainesville이 훌륭한 선택이라는 데 동의한다.

Q. (A) 분점
   (B) 매출
   (C) 제품
   (D) 공장

Odin Organic Cosmetics is coming to Gainesville. The new location is the third of the franchise, alongside its Banff and Lake Louise stores. Owner Sean Erasmus said he was inspired by the success of the two existing -------. Both cities enjoy thriving tourism industries. And while Gainesville is not quite as popular, it is quickly becoming a sought-after destination. Mr. Erasmus thus feels assured that his third store will prosper. Industry experts agree that Gainesville is an excellent choice.

Q. (A) branches
   (B) sales
   (C) products
   (D) plants

STEP 1
빈칸이 있는 문장의 내용을 파악한 후 빈칸 주변 문장에서 단서를 찾습니다.

STEP 2
지문의 흐름에 자연스러운 보기를 정답으로 선택합니다.

해설 STEP 1 빈칸 앞에 정관사(the)가 있으므로 빈칸 앞 문장을 먼저 확인합니다. 빈칸 앞 문장에서 새로운 곳은 Banff와 Lake Louise 상점에 이어, 체인점 중 세 번째라고 했고, 빈칸이 있는 문장에서 소유주는 기존 두 빈칸의 성공에 의해 자극을 받았다고 했음을 확인합니다.

STEP 2 빈칸 앞 문장에 언급된 상점(stores)과 가장 비슷한 의미인 (A) branches(분점)가 정답입니다.

Questions 01-04 refer to the following e-mail.

To: Adrian Korlova <a.korlova@forwardcookware.com>

From: Julia Morgan <j.morgan@forwardcookware.com>

Subject: Event with Keith Andreas

Date: April 22

Dear Adrian,

You may remember that when we last spoke, I told you I would be going to a talk given by the famous business speaker Keith Andreas. It ------- on Wednesday at 7:30 P.M. at the Haverford Arts
01
Center downtown. However, I don't think I'll be able to make it. -------. Unfortunately, there's no
02
way -------. Would you like to take my ticket to the event instead?
03

Mr. Andreas has written a number of books on business leadership and has given numerous lectures targeted at mid-level managers, such as you and me. Therefore, I believe the speech would be -------.
04

If you are able to attend the event, would you mind taking some notes so that I can read what was covered? Let me know if you're available that evening.

Best wishes,

Julia Morgan

---

01 (A) happened
(B) to happen
(C) will have happened
(D) will happen

02 (A) Perhaps you would be interested in accompanying me to the event.
(B) Tickets to the lecture are still available for purchase on the Web site.
(C) I have to take an important client out for dinner that evening.
(D) I am confident that you will be interested in attending the event.

03 (A) rescheduled
(B) to reschedule
(C) rescheduling
(D) reschedules

04 (A) worthwhile
(B) lengthy
(C) improvised
(D) exclusive

한 권으로 끝내는
해커스 토익 700+
LC+RC+VOCA

READING PART 6

DAY 12 문맥 파악 문제

한 권으로 끝내는 해커스 토익 700+ (LC+RC+VOCA)

Questions 05-08 refer to the following article.

Madgerville Transportation Department will offer a more ------- rush hour subway and bus service.
Starting in November, trains will arrive at stations on the Red and Blue lines every two and a half
minutes instead of every three minutes. -------, bus availability will increase by 7 percent during
peak hours.

To make the changes, the city is purchasing additional vehicles. ------- will include eight new trains
from rail equipment firm Falu Incorporated and 125 new buses. This will call for an expansion of
the department's garages. -------.

05 (A) affordable
(B) precise
(C) frequent
(D) uniform

06 (A) Likewise
(B) Nevertheless
(C) Specifically
(D) Accordingly

07 (A) These
(B) Such
(C) Most
(D) Any

08 (A) Several seldom-used routes will be
changed or canceled entirely.
(B) The cost of a monthly transit pass will
therefore be lowered.
(C) Many city residents have stated the
differences are already noticeable.
(D) Approximately $250 million has been
budgeted for the project.

정답·해석·해설 p.163

Course 2 문장 고르기 문제

케어테이커 운송 회사
최고의 운송 회사

12월 1일부터 15퍼센트 할인을 제공
합니다.

이 기간 내에 기회를 잡으세요!

할인은 12월 31일에 종료됩니다.

내용이 일부 빠져 있는 광고지와 그 부분에 들어갈 알맞은 문장입니다. 이처럼
PART 6에서는 지문의 빈칸에 들어갔을 때 문맥이 자연스럽게 연결되는 **문장을
고르는 문맥 파악 문제**가 출제됩니다.

📋 문제 유형

빈칸이 지문 초반에 제시되는 경우
지문 초반에는 주로 주제 문장이 언급되므로, 빈칸에는 지문의 주제나 목적을 나타내는 문장이 오는 경우가 많습니다.

빈칸이 지문 중간이나 뒷부분에 제시되는 경우
지문의 흐름상 적절한 세부 내용이 빈칸에 들어가야 하므로, 빈칸에는 앞뒤 내용에 대한 첨가, 부연 설명이나 요약, 강조, 이유, 결과와 관련된 내용이 오는 경우가 많습니다.

📋 문제 풀이 전략

STEP 1 빈칸의 주변 문맥을 파악하여 빈칸에 들어갈 내용을 예상합니다.
빈칸의 앞뒤 문장을 확인하되, 주변 문맥 파악만으로는 빈칸에 들어갈 내용을 예상하기 어렵다면 지문 전체를 확인합니다.

STEP 2 파악한 지문 문맥을 바탕으로 각 보기의 내용을 확인하며 빈칸에 알맞은 내용을 선택합니다.
· 보기 또는 앞뒤 문장 내에 대명사(this, we, it 등)가 있다면 대명사가 가리키는 부분과 일치하는지 확인합니다.
· 보기 또는 앞뒤 문장 내에 연결어(for example, moreover, however 등)가 있다면 빈칸과 앞뒤 문맥이 올바르게 연결되는지 확인합니다.

STEP 3 선택한 보기를 빈칸에 넣었을 때, 문맥이 자연스러운지 확인합니다.

전략 적용

<table>
<tr>
<td>
Caretaker 운송 회사

시내 최고의 운송 회사

집과 사무실의 이사가 필요하시든지 포장 및 창고 보관에 관한 해결책이 필요하시든지, Caretaker 운송 회사가 도와드릴 수 있습니다!

12월 1일부터, 모든 서비스에 대해 15퍼센트 할인을 제공합니다. ------. 연말 전에 기회를 잡으세요. 자세한 내용을 알아보시려면 555-0440으로 전화하십시오.

Q. (A) 성대한 개업식에 모두를 초대합니다.
　 (B) 이 할인은 12월 31일에 종료됩니다.
　 (C) 추가 요금을 내면 이사 보험이 이용 가능합니다.
　 (D) 다음 달에 본사가 이전될 것입니다.
</td>
<td>
Caretaker Transporting

The best mover in town

Whether you need home and office relocation or packing and storage solutions, Caretaker Transporting can help!

Starting December 1, we are offering 15 percent off all our services. -------.Take advantage before the end of the year. **Call 555-0440 for details.**

Q. (A) Everyone is invited to our grand opening.
　 (B) This offer ends on December 31.
　 (C) Moving insurance is available for an additional fee.
　 (D) Our headquarters will be relocated next month.
</td>
</tr>
</table>

STEP 1 빈칸의 주변 문맥을 파악하여 빈칸에 들어갈 내용을 예상합니다.

STEP 3 선택한 보기를 빈칸에 넣었을 때, 문맥이 자연스러운지 확인합니다.

STEP 2 파악한 지문 문맥을 바탕으로 각 보기의 내용을 확인하며 빈칸에 알맞은 내용을 선택합니다.

해설 **STEP 1** 빈칸의 앞 문장인 'Starting December 1, we are offering 15 percent off ~ services.'에서 12월 1일부터 15퍼센트 할인을 제공한다고 했고, 빈칸의 뒤 문장인 'Take advantage before the end of the year.'에서 연말 전에 기회를 잡으라고 했으므로, 빈칸에는 할인이 진행되는 기간과 관련된 내용이 들어가야 함을 예상할 수 있습니다.

STEP 2 할인이 12월 31일에 종료된다는 보기 (B)가 예상한 내용과 일치하고, 보기에 있는 대명사 This offer가 앞 문장에서 나온 명사(15 percent off)와 일치하므로 보기 (B)를 선택합니다.

STEP 3 선택한 보기 (B)를 빈칸에 넣었을 때, 할인이 12월 31일에 종료되니 연말 전에 기회를 잡으라는 자연스러운 문맥이 되므로 (B)가 정답입니다.

Questions 01-04 refer to the following article.

Huntington's 3rd Annual Independent Publishing Fair

Huntington—More than 100 writers, graphic novelists, and literary agencies ------- in Huntington's
01
3rd Annual Independent Publishing Fair. Scheduled to take place from May 3 to 7 at the Moira
Lambert Cultural Center, the fair will be an opportunity for the public to meet self-published authors
and purchase ------- copies of their books.
02

The ------- should also prove useful to aspiring writers. Well-known figures in the self-publishing
03
world, such as author of the bestselling *Stolen Knight* series Tara Holten, will give presentations on
how to succeed without the assistance of an established publishing house.

-------. For the full program schedule, visit www.huntingtonipf.com.
04

01 (A) participated
(B) participate
(C) will participate
(D) have been participating

02 (A) signature
(B) signed
(C) signing
(D) sign

03 (A) policy
(B) manual
(C) event
(D) video

04 (A) The fair is the first of its kind to be held
in the area.
(B) A sequel to the book will be published
this summer.
(C) Tickets are available at the Lambert
Center box office.
(D) Posters, comics, and stationery have
already sold out.

Questions 05-08 refer to the following notice.

Bentworth Condominium

Notice to Residents

Building management was ------- by the water company this morning. They notified us that the
05
building's water supply will be suspended tomorrow from 9 A.M. to 4 P.M. Utility workers will be
replacing a section of pipe to improve the flow of water. I realize that the building's plumbing
was already ------- last year. However, this failed to resolve the problem completely. In any case,
06
everyone should probably do their best to get ready. -------. We understand that this situation may
07
be -------, but I'm sure the increased water pressure will make it rewarding.
08

---

05 (A) contact
(B) contacted
(C) contacting
(D) contacts

06 (A) updated
(B) situated
(C) proposed
(D) initiated

07 (A) It is recommended that you fill water
containers for your use.
(B) The building will open and close at the
usual time after that.
(C) They will look for what is causing the
leaks in the building.
(D) New measures will be implemented to
lower levels of water usage.

08 (A) inconveniences
(B) inconvenienced
(C) inconvenient
(D) inconveniently

READING

PART 7

PART 7은 147번부터 200번까지 총 54문제로, 지문을 읽고 지문과 관련된 질문들에 대해 가장 적절한 보기를 정답으로 고르는 유형입니다. 단일 지문에서 29문제, 이중 지문에서 10문제, 삼중 지문에서 15문제가 출제됩니다.

Course 1 주제 찾기 문제

토익 출제경향
최대 4문제까지 출제

공고

건물의 대회의실에서 신입 사원을 환영하기 위한 모임이 열릴 예정입니다.

Q. 공고는 무엇에 대한 것인가?
A. 신입 사원 환영회

공고가 무엇에 대한 것인지를 묻고 있습니다. 이처럼 PART 7에서는 지문의 가장 핵심이 되는 내용, 즉 글의 주제가 무엇인지 묻는 **주제 찾기 문제**가 출제됩니다.

빈출 질문 유형

What **is the notice** (mainly) about? 공고는 (주로) 무엇에 대한 것인가?
What **is being** advertised/announced? 광고되고/공고되고 있는 것은 무엇인가?
What **is** discussed in the article? 기사에서 논의되는 것은 무엇인가?

문제 풀이 전략

STEP 1 지문의 주제를 나타내는 주제 문장을 찾습니다.

주제 문장은 주로 지문의 앞부분에 있습니다. 앞부분에 글의 주제가 나타나 있지 않거나 지문 전체를 통해 주제를 파악해야 하는 경우 지문 전체를 빠르게 훑어 읽으면서 주제를 파악합니다.

STEP 2 주제 문장 또는 지문 전체의 내용을 읽고 글의 주제를 파악합니다.

STEP 3 글의 주제를 패러프레이징하거나 바르게 요약한 보기를 선택합니다.

전략 적용

[공고]

NOTICE

A meeting will be held in the building's main conference room to welcome the newly hired staff. This will take place on Saturday, May 10, from 11:30 A.M. to 1:00 P.M. While attendance is optional, we encourage everyone to participate. The company will provide lunch.

Q. What is the notice about?

(A) A policy on staff attendance
(B) A celebration in honor of top executives
(C) A welcome ceremony for new employees

해석 **p.166**

STEP 1
지문의 주제를 나타내는 주제 문장은 주로 지문의 앞부분에 있으므로 공고의 앞부분을 확인합니다.

STEP 2
지문의 첫 문장 'A meeting will be held ~ to welcome the newly hired staff.'에서 글의 주제가 새로 채용된 사원들을 환영하기 위한 모임이라는 것을 파악합니다.

STEP 3
글의 주제를 패러프레이징한 보기인 (C)를 정답으로 선택합니다.

HACKERS PRACTICE 토익 700+ 달성을 위한 연습 문제

패러프레이징 연습 | 주어진 문장과 가까운 의미를 가진 문장을 고르세요.

01

> Miller & Sons provides an overview of policies in its corporate manual. However, it also recognizes that giving each employee personalized training is vital to its success.

(A) Miller & Sons believes in addressing each worker's individual need for instruction.
(B) Following the corporate manual is the key to success at Miller & Sons.

02

> East Sky Airlines experienced a boost in sales when it reduced fares for round-trip tickets. Since then, other airlines have done the same in an effort to remain competitive.

(A) East Sky Airlines has partnered with other airlines to offer discounted fares.
(B) Airlines began lowering prices in order to keep up with the competition.

유형 연습 | 주어진 지문을 읽고 문제를 풀어보세요.

03 [이메일]

> Congratulations! I showed your proposal to the board and they accepted it. It wasn't hard to convince them. They liked the studies you included that describe the advantages of employee wellness programs. You can start working on them for the staff from today. Just make sure to keep track of any results as the board will want a report on the programs in six months.

Q. What is mainly discussed in the e-mail?

    (A) A board member's proposal
    (B) A staff wellness program
    (C) A customer service report

04 [광고]

> ### Executive Club Investment Seminar
>
> - Thursday November 18 at 7:00 P.M.
> - Elroy Convention Hall, Room 322
>
> At this award-winning seminar, we'll teach you the fundamentals of investing in the stock market and how to maintain a strong and stable portfolio that builds wealth over the long term. Using these techniques, you will be able to maximize your retirement savings.

Q. What is being advertised?

    (A) A retirement plan
    (B) A stock market lesson
    (C) A real estate workshop

정답·해석·해설 **p.166**

수신: Jasper Conway
발신: Excel 문구사

주문 물품의 배송 일자를 알려드리려고 합니다. 물품은 3월 14일에 배송 완료될 예정입니다.

Q. 이메일의 목적은 무엇인가?
A. 배송 정보를 제공하기 위해

판매자가 구매자에게 보낸 이메일의 목적이 무엇인지를 묻고 있습니다. 이처럼 PART 7에서는 지문을 쓴 목적을 묻는 **목적 찾기 문제**가 출제됩니다.

빈출 질문 유형

글의 목적
What is the (main) purpose of the e-mail? 이메일의 (주)목적은 무엇인가?
What is one purpose of the memo? 회람의 한 가지 목적은 무엇인가?

글을 쓴 이유
Why was the letter written? 편지는 왜 쓰였는가?
Why did Ms. Ellis write to Mr. Roberts? Ms. Ellis는 왜 Mr. Roberts에게 글을 썼는가?

문제 풀이 전략

STEP 1 지문의 목적을 나타낸 문장을 찾습니다.

목적을 나타낸 문장은 주로 지문의 앞부분에 있습니다. 앞부분에 지문의 목적이 나타나 있지 않거나 지문 전체를 통해 목적을 파악해야 하는 경우 지문 전체를 빠르게 훑어 읽으면서 목적을 파악합니다.

STEP 2 목적을 나타낸 문장 또는 지문 전체를 읽고 글을 쓴 목적을 파악합니다.

STEP 3 글을 쓴 목적을 정확히 나타내거나 패러프레이징한 보기를 선택합니다.

전략 적용

[이메일]

To: Jasper Conway <j.conway@zumail.com>
From: Excel Office Supplies <orders@excel.com>

Dear Mr. Conway,

I'm writing to notify you of the arrival date of your order. The Hillman standing desk you purchased last Friday will be shipped today. Delivery is expected to be completed on March 14. You may track the shipment using this code: TS441928.

Q. What is the purpose of the e-mail?

(A) To follow up on a payment
(B) To provide shipping information
(C) To recommend a service provider

STEP 1
지문의 목적을 나타낸 문장은 주로 지문의 앞부분에 있으므로 이메일의 앞부분을 확인합니다.

STEP 2
지문의 첫 문장 'I'm writing to notify you of the arrival date of your order.'에서 글의 목적이 주문한 물품이 도착하는 날짜를 알리기 위함이라는 것을 파악합니다.

STEP 3
글을 쓴 목적을 패러프레이징한 보기인 (B)를 정답으로 선택합니다.

해석 p.167

HACKERS PRACTICE 토익 700+ 달성을 위한 연습 문제

패러프레이징 연습 주어진 문장과 가까운 의미를 가진 문장을 고르세요.

01

> I regret to inform you that the accountant role has been filled. I will hold on to your application in case a similar position opens up later.

(A) An applicant may be considered for a future job in accounting.
(B) An applicant will be notified further about a scheduled job interview.

02

> On Wednesday, Avery announced it had bought Turkish steel producer Zorko. As a result, Avery's stock price increased to $67.20 per share.

(A) A firm is moving its headquarters to Turkey.
(B) Company share values rose after news of a purchase went public.

유형 연습 주어진 지문을 읽고 문제를 풀어보세요.

03 [광고]

> Gregor Diamante has opened a new restaurant on LaSalle Street called Diamante's. Offering authentic Italian cuisine—from pizza to pasta—the restaurant is perfect for those seeking a relaxing night out at an affordable price. Reservations are permitted, and the dress code is semi-formal.

Q. What is the purpose of the advertisement?

(A) To publicize an Italian restaurant
(B) To describe a neighborhood grocery store
(C) To introduce a vineyard tour

04 [편지]

> On behalf of the Regional Realtors Association, we are delighted that you have decided to join our group. As a member, you will gain access to an array of services designed to help you succeed in this profession, including learning opportunities and discount programs from partner firms. Please see the enclosed document for detailed information about these and other benefits.

Q. Why was the letter written?

(A) To introduce some membership benefits
(B) To promote a company's services
(C) To explain a corporate policy

정답·해석·해설 p.167

Questions 01-03 refer to the following e-mail.

TO: Ricardo Flores <rflores@learnspanish.org>
FROM: Brenda Dean <bdean@fastmail.com>
DATE: March 2
SUBJECT: Question

Dear Mr. Flores,

My name is Brenda Dean, and I'm an employee of Penbrook Financial Analysts. My company works with many foreign clients, so I sometimes have to fly overseas to meet with them in person.

On April 1, I'm going to Colombia to speak with several of our partners there, and I'll need to know how to speak fluent Spanish in order to communicate effectively with them. I know a fair amount of Spanish, but I'd like to improve my skills before flying over there.

I saw your advertisement for Spanish tutoring in the newspaper, *The Long Island Gazette*, and I'm writing to see if your services are still available. If possible, I'd like to take a two-week intensive course in conversational Spanish. I'm available in the evenings, from 6 P.M., and all day on the weekends. If you're interested, please e-mail me back.

I look forward to hearing from you.

Sincerely,
Brenda Dean

---

01 Why did Ms. Dean write to Mr. Flores?

(A) To screen an applicant for a position
(B) To get financial assistance for a project
(C) To ask about the services of a language instructor
(D) To organize the schedule for an overseas trip

02 What will Ms. Dean do next month?

(A) Write an evaluation report
(B) Go on a business trip
(C) Reserve a hotel room
(D) Enroll in a language class

03 Where did Ms. Dean see Mr. Flores' advertisement?

(A) On a Web site
(B) On a local TV commercial
(C) In a publication
(D) On a bulletin board

Questions 04-07 refer to the following announcement.

RIVERDALE PET HOSPITAL

Summer is here and it's time to enjoy some fun in the sun with your pets! But before you go outside, make sure you and your pets are safe. High temperatures caused by the heat of the sun can harm your pets' health. Learn how to protect them by joining an Animal Health Seminar.

Riverdale Pet Hospital regularly holds Animal Health Seminars every Saturday from 10:00 A.M. to 12:00 P.M. They cover a variety of important and relevant topics. Entrance is free and each participant is given a printed guide to basic animal health care. Plus, participants are entered into a monthly draw to win one of several exciting prizes. This month, we are giving away a Travel Pet Water Bottle with a handy wrist strap!

If you would like to take part, register online at www.riverdalepet. com.

04 What is the announcement mainly about?

(A) A monthly adoption campaign
(B) A facility's newest services
(C) A talk about caring for pets
(D) A sickness affecting animals

05 According to the announcement, what can pose a hazard to pets?

(A) Infrequent exercise
(B) Poor nutrition
(C) Inadequate rest
(D) Extreme heat

06 What is given away each week at Riverdale Pet Hospital?

(A) A free brochure
(B) A box of medicine
(C) A discount coupon
(D) A bag of pet food

07 For whom is the monthly draw being held?

(A) Customers with membership cards
(B) Volunteers at a local facility
(C) Participants in a seminar
(D) Sponsors of a pet program

정답·해석·해설 p.168

Course 1 육하원칙 문제

> **회람**
>
> 최신 휴가 정책이 인트라넷에 게시되었습니다. 질문이 있으시다면, 인사 부서의 Mr. Stanley에게 연락하십시오.

Q. Mr. Stanley는 누구인가?

A. 인사부서 직원

지문의 세부 내용인 Mr. Stanley가 누구인지를 묻고 있습니다. 이처럼 PART 7에서는 무엇, 왜, 어떻게, 언제, 누가, 어디서 등 지문의 세부 내용에 대해 묻는 **육하원칙 문제**가 출제됩니다.

📄 빈출 질문 유형

무엇	What **does the product feature?**	제품은 무엇을 특징으로 포함하는가?
왜	Why **should Ms. Lee pay an additional fee?**	Ms. Lee는 왜 추가 요금을 지불해야 하는가?
어떻게	How **can employees register?**	직원들은 어떻게 등록할 수 있는가?
언제	When **will the event take place?**	행사는 언제 개최될 것인가?
누가	Who **is Mr. Bennett?**	Mr. Bennett은 누구인가?
어디서	Where **will the awards ceremony be held?**	시상식은 어디에서 열릴 것인가?

📄 문제 풀이 전략

STEP 1 질문을 읽고 의문사와 핵심 어구를 확인합니다.

STEP 2 지문에서 질문의 핵심 어구와 관련된 정답의 단서를 찾습니다.
질문의 핵심 어구를 그대로 언급하거나 패러프레이징한 부분의 주변에서 정답의 단서를 찾습니다.

STEP 3 정답의 단서를 그대로 언급하거나 패러프레이징한 보기를 선택합니다.

📄 전략 적용

[회람]

MEMO

An updated vacation policy has been uploaded on the company Intranet. It includes changes to the number of days employees are entitled to and guidelines about the notice period. If you have any questions, please contact Mr. Stanley in the human resources department.

Q. Who is Mr. Stanley?

(A) A business consultant
(B) A customer service representative
(C) A human resources employee

STEP 2
질문의 핵심 어구 Mr. Stanley를 그대로 언급한 부분인 'Mr. Stanley in the human resources department'에서 Mr. Stanley가 인사 부서 소속이라는 정답의 단서를 찾습니다.

STEP 1
질문을 읽고 의문사 Who와 핵심 어구 Mr. Stanley를 확인합니다.

STEP 3
정답의 단서를 패러프레이징한 보기인 (C)를 정답으로 선택합니다.

해석 p.169

HACKERS PRACTICE 토익 700+ 달성을 위한 연습 문제

패러프레이징 연습 | 주어진 문장과 가까운 의미를 가진 문장을 고르세요.

01

> As stated in the lease, keeping pets and smoking inside the premises are strictly prohibited. Disregarding these regulations will result in fines.

(A) Residents will pay for breaking the rules of a rental contract.
(B) Tenants may pay extra to be allowed to smoke or have pets.

02

> On May 11, BGR Bank will be completing its merger with Gitwoll Financial. During this period, debit cards and Internet banking services will be unavailable.

(A) BGR Bank's services will no longer be available once it merges with Gitwoll Financial.
(B) BGR Bank is temporarily suspending some services while finalizing a business deal.

유형 연습 | 주어진 지문을 읽고 문제를 풀어보세요.

03 [주문서]

Name	Marianne Verns	Address	#321, 355 Haskill Avenue, Ripley, MI 43159		
Order Date	April 25				
Items	Size	Quantity	Price per unit		Total
Amore T-Shirt	Medium	1	$20.00		$20.00
Additional Requests	Your Web site mentions that some items can be gift-wrapped, but I could not find the option on the order page. I'd like to have the item wrapped.				

Q. What problem did Ms. Verns have with her order?

(A) A packaging option was not visible to her.
(B) The transaction could not be completed.
(C) Her delivery address was not saved.

04 [광고지]

> Starting this Thursday, March 10, we invite you to enjoy 20 percent off our new 60-minute spa packages listed below (promotional prices are shown).
>
> **Tranquility Package:** Facial Treatment and Sage Body Scrub for $180
> **Soul Package:** Full-body Massage, Manicure, and Pedicure for $250
>
> Offer is available through April 30. To take advantage of this promotion, register online at www.tsdspas.com or call our main Kendall Square branch at 555-0767.

Q. According to the flyer, how can customers obtain a discount?

(A) By visiting the Kendall Square branch
(B) By sending an e-mail to the main office
(C) By signing up on a Web site

정답·해석·해설 **p.169**

사무용품 세일

– 모든 연필과 펜 25퍼센트 할인
– 접착식 메모지 20퍼센트 할인
– 모든 봉투 15퍼센트 할인

Q. 연필에 대해 언급된 것은?
A. 할인된 가격에 판매될 것이다.

연필에 대해 언급된 것을 묻고 있습니다. 이처럼 PART 7에서는 지문의 내용과 일치하지 않거나 일치하는 내용을 묻는 **Not/True 문제**가 출제됩니다.

빈출 질문 유형

Not 문제
What is NOT mentioned/stated/indicated **about the event?** 행사에 대해 언급되지 않은 것은?
What is NOT true **about Joe's Restaurant?** Joe's 식당에 대해 사실이 아닌 것은?
What is NOT provided/included **in the letter?** 편지에 제공되지/포함되지 않은 것은?

True 문제
What is mentioned/stated/indicated **about Mr. Wood?** Mr. Wood에 대해 언급된 것은?
What is true **about Ms. Burnes?** Ms. Burnes에 대해 사실인 것은?

문제 풀이 전략

STEP 1 질문 또는 보기를 읽고 핵심 어구를 확인합니다.

STEP 2 지문에서 질문 또는 보기의 핵심 어구와 관련된 내용을 찾습니다.
질문의 핵심 어구를 그대로 언급하거나 패러프레이징한 부분의 주변에서 정답의 단서를 찾습니다.

STEP 3 핵심 어구와 관련된 지문의 내용을 보기와 하나씩 대조하여 정답을 선택합니다.

전략 적용

[광고]

OFFICE SUPPLIES SALE

Ben's Office Supplies is holding a sale. Find great deals on selected items. Sale ends June 30.

- 25% off all pencils and pens
- 20% off sticky notes
- 15% off all envelopes

Q. What is stated about pencils?

(A) They will no longer be stocked after June 30.
(B) They will be sold at reduced prices.
(C) They will be given to customers for free.

해석 p.170

STEP 2
질문의 핵심 어구 pencils를 그대로 언급한 부분인 '25% off all pencils'에서 연필을 25퍼센트 할인한다는 정답의 단서를 찾습니다.

STEP 1
질문을 읽고 핵심 어구 pencils를 확인합니다.

STEP 3
핵심 어구와 관련된 지문의 내용을 보기와 하나씩 대조하여, 연필을 25퍼센트 할인한다는 지문의 내용과 일치하는 보기인 (B)를 정답으로 선택합니다.

HACKERS PRACTICE 토익 700+ 달성을 위한 연습 문제

패러프레이징 연습 | 주어진 문장과 가까운 의미를 가진 문장을 고르세요.

01

> Specializing in lessons for the guitar, musician Corey Lermin opened a studio last week to teach newcomers how to play the instrument. To make inquiries, call 555-6892.

(A) Corey Lermin gave his first musical performance at a studio last week.
(B) Beginners can learn to play the guitar at Corey Lermin's new studio.

02

> Ms. Phelps finished updating the Web site like you asked. It shows the final list of speakers for this weekend's event. She will add pictures from the event next week.

(A) Ms. Phelps needs one more week to finalize a list of speakers.
(B) Photographs taken during an event will be posted online next week.

유형 연습 | 주어진 지문을 읽고 문제를 풀어보세요.

03 [공고]

> A gathering with land developer Handley has been organized for locals. It will concern an apartment complex that Handley will be building in the area. At the meeting, Handley plans to discuss several topics related to the work, including the location of the buildings. The meeting will be held on Sunday, February 8, at 7 P.M. in Harmony Memorial Center. Everyone attending is welcome to ask questions about the proposed project.

Q. What is NOT mentioned about the meeting?

   (A) It will take place during a weekend.
   (B) It will include discussions about building sites.
   (C) It will be attended by every resident in the area.

04 [편지]

> Dear Mr. Gresham,
>
> Thank you for your donation to the Australian Wildlife Conservancy. Our organization could not exist without the support of dedicated members like you. Because you are a regular donor to our organization, we are enclosing a free Australian Wildlife Conservancy calendar with this letter.
>
> Bruce Niles, Australian Wildlife Conservancy

Q. What is stated about Mr. Gresham?

   (A) He ordered a calendar recently.
   (B) He donates regularly to a group.
   (C) He is a well-known scientist.

정답·해석·해설 **p.170**

Questions 01-04 refer to the following letter.

Chiaroscuro Photography Club
#85, 377 Westminster Road
Lancaster, England, LE5109

June 1

Dear Members,

The next two months promise to be very exciting for our members. The city's tourism office is hosting a photography competition. For the contest, both professional and non-professional photographers from Lancaster are invited to take promotional pictures of the city. As entries are received, the best ones will be put on display in the Fulmore Gallery next to City Hall. In connection with this event, several past winners have agreed to deliver lectures at the art gallery, giving aspiring photographers an opportunity to improve their skills. Below is the schedule:

Topic	Speaker	Date & Time
Travel photography	Isabelle Robey	Tuesday, June 15, 7 P.M.
Portraits in outdoor settings	Jeanette Dennis	Thursday, June 24, 7 P.M.
Composing a scene	Wilbur Smithey	Saturday, July 3, 2 P.M.
Using natural lighting	Hana Takagi	Monday, July 12, 8 P.M.

Of course, I hope everyone will be able to attend the awards ceremony on July 26 at the gallery. Starting at 1 P.M., winners' names will be announced. Each of them will participate in a question-and-answer session at 2:30 P.M. The entire awards show will end by 4 P.M. I will send further details to members as they are announced.

Best wishes,
Alvin Markham, President
Chiaroscuro Photography Club

01 What is true about the photography competition?

(A) Participation is open to amateurs.
(B) There is a small entrance fee.
(C) Awards will take the form of cash prizes.
(D) Winners will be notified by mail.

02 Who will give a lecture on taking pictures of people?

(A) Isabelle Robey
(B) Jeanette Dennis
(C) Wilbur Smithey
(D) Hana Takagi

03 When will the awards show be held?

(A) On June 15
(B) On June 24
(C) On July 12
(D) On July 26

04 What is NOT mentioned about the Fulmore Art Gallery?

(A) It is located near City Hall.
(B) It will host lectures from past contest winners.
(C) It will feature a local photography exhibit.
(D) It offers free entrance to its members.

Questions 05-08 refer to the following brochure.

Baylor Aquarium

Ventura Travel is a proud partner of the Baylor Aquarium. This facility is the largest aquarium in the Louisville area. It is also the only one in Kentucky to feature both saltwater and freshwater fish. Our agency recommends that you stop by with your family to learn more about the fascinating world of aquatic animals.

Attractions

Shark Tank: View the ocean's fiercest predators. The tank includes tiger sharks, blue sharks, and hammerhead sharks.

Amazon River Adventure: Explore the unique species and rich diversity of freshwater wildlife that populates the world's largest river.

Submarine: Be sure to sign up ahead of time for a tour of the aquarium's full-scale reproduction of an American World War II submarine.

Regular Hours:
Monday-Friday: 9 A.M. to 5 P.M.
Saturday-Sunday: 8 A.M. to 6 P.M.

Special Events:
Mondays at 2 P.M.: Otter Show
Wednesdays and Fridays at 1 P.M.: Submarine Tours
Saturdays at 4 P.M.: Dolphin Show

Entrance Fees:
General admission: $10
Students: $8 with identification
Seniors: $7

Aquarium members and children under four are admitted for free.

For more information, e-mail us at inquiries@venturatrav.com.

---

05 What is indicated about the Baylor Aquarium?

(A) It is the most popular destination in the region.
(B) It showcases animals that live in the sea.
(C) It has recently added new attractions.
(D) It sells snacks at a cafeteria.

06 When can visitors see the dolphin show?

(A) On Mondays
(B) On Wednesdays
(C) On Fridays
(D) On Saturdays

07 What is NOT provided in the brochure?

(A) Admission prices
(B) Opening hours
(C) Directions to a facility
(D) Descriptions of attractions

08 How can people get more information about Baylor Aquarium?

(A) By logging into an establishment's Web site
(B) By visiting a tourist information center
(C) By calling a facility during business hours
(D) By sending a message to Ventura Travel

정답·해석·해설 **p.171**

Course 1 추론 문제

토익 출제경향
평균 9~13문제 정도 출제

> 저희 회사는 휴대전화 부품 공급업체를 새로 찾고 있는데, 그 중 Mervone사의 제품이 가장 적합한 것 같습니다.

Q. Mervone사에 대해 암시되는 것은?
A. 휴대전화 부품을 만든다.

회사에 대해 암시되는 것을 묻고 있습니다. 이처럼 PART 7에서는 지문에서 직접 언급되지 않은 사항을 지문의 내용을 바탕으로 유추하는 **추론 문제**가 출제됩니다.

📋 빈출 질문 유형

글의 대상 추론   For whom **is the information** (most likely) intended? 안내문은 누구를 대상으로 하는 (것 같은)가?

글의 출처 추론   Where **would the notice** most likely **be found?** 공고는 어디에서 볼 수 있을 것 같은가?

세부 정보 추론   What is suggested/indicated/implied **about Ms. Vanessa?** Ms. Vanessa에 대해 암시/추론되는 것은?
         What will probably **happen next Friday?** 다음 주 금요일에 무슨 일이 일어날 것 같은가?

📋 문제 풀이 전략

STEP 1 질문을 읽고 핵심 어구를 확인합니다.

질문에 핵심 어구가 없는 경우 각 보기의 핵심 어구를 확인합니다.

STEP 2 지문에서 핵심 어구와 관련된 정답의 단서를 찾습니다.

질문의 핵심 어구를 그대로 언급하거나 패러프레이징한 부분의 주변에서 정답의 단서를 찾습니다. 질문에 핵심 어구가 없는 경우, 지문 전체를 읽으며 대상이나 출처를 암시하는 단서를 찾습니다.

STEP 3 지문의 단서를 바탕으로 올바르게 추론한 보기를 선택합니다.

📋 전략 적용

[이메일]

Dear Mr. Pugsley,

My company was looking for a new supplier of cell phone microchips, and we've concluded that Mervone's R5G chip has the specifications we require. We would like to place a large order. If you are interested, please contact me at 555-2323 as soon as possible to set up a meeting.

Sincerely,

Joan Marshfield, Research director, Saxonia

Q. What is suggested about Mervone?

(A) It makes parts for mobile devices.
(B) It recently entered a new market.
(C) It mailed a product catalog to Saxonia.

STEP 2
질문의 핵심 어구 Mervone이 언급된 'My company was looking for a new supplier of cell phone microchips and ~ Mervone's ~ chip has the specifications we require.'에서 회사가 휴대전화 마이크로칩 공급업체를 찾고 있었는데, Mervone사의 칩이 적합하다는 정답의 단서를 확인합니다.

STEP 1
질문을 읽고 질문의 핵심 어구 Mervone을 확인합니다.

STEP 3
지문의 단서를 바탕으로 Mervone사가 무선 단말기 부품을 만든다는 것을 올바르게 추론한 보기인 (A)를 정답으로 선택합니다.

해석 p.173

패러프레이징 연습 | 주어진 문장과 가까운 의미를 가진 문장을 고르세요.

01

> Please note that you should include your complete address on the order form. Otherwise, you will have to collect the package at the nearest post office.

(A) A package with an incomplete address will be sent to the closest post office.
(B) Order forms for parcels can be collected at any nearby post office.

02

> If you are a resident interested in lending a hand at the Tourist Bureau, please fill out an application. You should list any of your relevant experience and skills.

(A) An application for membership to the Tourist Bureau is available.
(B) Residents may apply by completing a form that includes relevant background information.

유형 연습 | 주어진 지문을 읽고 문제를 풀어보세요.

03 [공고]

> In celebration of Children's Day, the Mariposa Cultural Center will be holding a seminar on November 20 at 4 P.M. The seminar, entitled "How to Talk to Your Kids: Conversational Skills Every Parent Should Have," will be led by famous psychologist Dr. Marsha Peterson. To reserve a seat, please call the center at 555-3209.

Q. For whom is the announcement most likely intended?

(A) Child psychology professionals
(B) Parents of young children
(C) Center staff working with children

04 [이메일]

> Dear Ms. Ming,
>
> I see you want my opinion about the Vermillion Red graphics card I recently bought. The graphics card has excellent value considering its performance. With the video editing software you use on your home PC for work, I think that the card can give you the quality that you are looking for. Let me know if you have any other questions.
>
> Best,
> John Cortes

Q. What is implied about Ms. Ming?

(A) She uses her computer to edit videos.
(B) She has never purchased a graphics card before.
(C) She is a successful movie producer.

정답·해석·해설 **p.173**

Course 2 문장 위치 찾기 문제

> 실내 테니스 코트가 수리로 인해 임시 폐쇄될 예정입니다. ― [1] ―. 그동안에는 야외 코트를 이용해주시기 바랍니다. ― [2] ―.

Q. [1], [2]로 표시된 위치 중, 다음 문장이 들어갈 곳으로 가장 적절한 곳은?
"그래서, 이번 주 동호회 대회는 다음 주로 미뤄졌습니다."
A. [1]

실내 테니스 코트 사용에 관해 알리는 공고에서 주어진 문장이 들어갈 적절한 위치를 묻고 있습니다. 이처럼 PART 7에서는 지문의 흐름을 파악하여 주어진 문장이 들어가기에 가장 알맞은 위치를 선택하는 **문장 위치 찾기 문제**가 출제됩니다.

빈출 질문 유형

In which of the positions marked [1], [2], [3], and [4] does the following sentence best belong?
[1], [2], [3], [4]로 표시된 위치 중, 다음 문장이 들어갈 곳으로 가장 적절한 것은?

문제 풀이 전략

STEP 1 주어진 문장을 읽고 문장이 들어갈 위치의 앞뒤 내용을 예상합니다.

STEP 2 예상한 내용을 바탕으로 지문에서 문장이 들어가기에 적합한 위치를 선택합니다.
· 숫자로 표시된 부분의 앞, 뒤 문장 중에 예상한 내용과 일치하거나 관련 있는 부분을 찾아 적합한 위치를 선택합니다.
· 주어진 문장에 지시대명사(it, that 등)가 있다면 지문에서 지시대명사가 가리키는 부분 뒤에 주어진 문장을 삽입해봅니다.
· 문장 내에 연결어(therefore, however 등)가 있다면 빈칸의 앞뒤 문맥을 파악하여 주어진 문장을 삽입해봅니다.

STEP 3 선택한 위치에 주어진 문장을 넣었을 때 문맥이 자연스럽게 연결되는지 확인합니다.

전략 적용

[공고]

Attention, all club members! ― [1] ―. The indoor tennis courts will be closed for repairs from May 12 to 18. ― [2] ―. In the meantime, everyone is advised to use the outdoor courts. ― [3] ―.

Q. In which of the positions marked [1], [2], and [3] does the following sentence best belong?

"Therefore, this week's club competition has been moved to next week."

(A) [1]
(B) [2]
(C) [3]

해석 **p.174**

STEP 2
[2]의 앞 'The indoor tennis courts will be closed for repairs'에서 실내 테니스 코트가 수리로 인해 폐쇄될 것이라고 했으므로, 예상한 내용과 관련이 있는 부분인 [2]에 주어진 문장을 삽입합니다.

STEP 1
주어진 문장은 그래서 이번 주 동호회 대회가 다음 주로 미뤄졌다는 내용이므로, 그 앞에는 미뤄진 이유에 대한 내용이 나올 것을 예상할 수 있습니다.

STEP 3
[2]에 주어진 문장을 넣었을 때 실내 테니스 코트가 수리로 폐쇄될 예정이기 때문에 이번 주 동호회 대회가 미뤄질 것이라는 문맥이 자연스럽게 연결되므로 (B)를 정답으로 선택합니다.

HACKERS PRACTICE 토익 700+ 달성을 위한 연습 문제

패러프레이징 연습 | 주어진 문장과 가까운 의미를 가진 문장을 고르세요.

01

> If your credit card is lost, inform the bank as soon as possible to prevent its unauthorized use. Otherwise, you may be required to pay for charges you did not make.

(A) It is necessary to call the bank to activate a new credit card.
(B) Card owners may be responsible for charges made on lost credit cards.

02

> Herqwell's filtered water bottle is popular because each replacement filter costs a mere $2. But over time, its costs add up quickly because the filters frequently need to be replaced.

(A) Herqwell's filtered water bottles are ultimately more expensive than they seem.
(B) Of all the water pitchers on the market, Herqwell's is the most affordable.

유형 연습 | 주어진 지문을 읽고 문제를 풀어보세요.

03 [기사]

> Earlier this week, Fontaineville's fire department received a delivery of two new fire trucks and an equipment van purchased by the city. — [1] —. The trucks are part of an effort to update the fire department's fleet of emergency vehicles, many of which are outdated. — [2] —. Currently, the department's staff members need to take training courses for the new vehicles. — [3] —.

Q. In which of the positions marked [1], [2], and [3] does the following sentence best belong?

"Once that is complete, the vehicles will begin to be used."

(A) [1]
(B) [2]
(C) [3]

04 [공고]

> NOTE: Sheridan Concert Hall is not responsible for the loss or theft of any items brought to the facility. — [1] —. Guests are kindly asked to take care of their own valuables. Should you misplace anything, check with our lost-and-found counter in the lobby. — [2] —. For bulky items, the hall does offer a coat-check service. — [3] —. Give your items to our staff, and you'll be provided with a ticket to retrieve your belongings after a performance.

Q. In which of the positions marked [1], [2], and [3] does the following sentence best belong?

"You may leave outerwear, umbrellas, and large bags or packages there."

(A) [1]
(B) [2]
(C) [3]

정답·해석·해설 p.174

Questions 01-03 refer to the following article.

The Next Big Thing for Mark Timan

Mark Timan's financial empire began in real estate with the development of resorts in Florida and Hawaii. However, a severe drop in land values led him to invest in an Internet company called Partizone. — [1] —. Partizone's Web site became the leading booking tool for flights, hotels, and rental cars. With a tie-in to Mr. Timan's resorts, both businesses soon flourished. They became industry leaders and made Mr. Timan a billionaire. — [2] —.

Given this history of success, the business community was surprised when Mr. Timan announced that he was selling everything. — [3] —. He said, "I am getting older, and I'd like to spend more time with my children. But as the business gets bigger, it takes up more of my time."

— [4] —. However, that does not mean he is completely retiring. "No, I want to stay active in the business world," said the still energetic Timan. "I've started to focus on financing. I'd like to invest in fresh start-up companies. There are a few promising ones I've reached out to about that possibility already. However, I'll be less involved, giving advice from a distance."

01 What is indicated about Partizone?

(A) It is mainly for business people.
(B) It was awarded for its service.
(C) It is used for making travel bookings.
(D) It was originally for selling real estate.

02 What will Mr. Timan most likely do in the near future?

(A) Invest in housing abroad
(B) Teach a business course
(C) Become a corporate chairperson
(D) Fund a new business

03 In which of the positions marked [1], [2], [3], and [4] does the following sentence best belong?

"Though reluctant to discuss his reasons, Mr. Timan explained his decision during an interview."

(A) [1]
(B) [2]
(C) [3]
(D) [4]

Questions 04-07 refer to the following memo.

To: Community outreach department
From: Kevin Miles, AAHS President
Date: June 22
Subject: Banquet

As you know, the AAHS annual banquet is approaching. At this event, all of our major donors will be treated to a three-course meal while listening to a series of talks about the progress our historical society has made.

In order to ensure that our donors can make it to this event, we need to send them invitations by mail. — [1] —. Over the next couple of days, I'd like you to send personal letters to each of them. — [2] —. I have provided you with a list of all the people who donated $500 or more to our society over the past year. — [3] —.

In your letters, please include the following information: The banquet will be held on July 10. The dress code is formal. The main speech will be delivered by a member of our historical society's board of trustees and will focus on how we've expanded our collection of early American antiques. — [4] —. Along with each letter, please enclose a stamped envelope addressed to the society and a card allowing donors to indicate their dinner preference and how many guests they will bring. Donors should fill out this card and mail it back to us in the envelope we provide them with.

04 For whom is the memo most likely intended?

(A) Donors to a cultural society
(B) Members of a board of trustees
(C) Staff at a history society
(D) Clients of a catering service

05 What are the invited donors required to do?

(A) Wear suitable clothing for the occasion
(B) Confirm attendance with a phone call
(C) Arrive at the venue by six in the evening
(D) Bring a card to an event

06 What is indicated about the organization?

(A) It gathers antiques.
(B) It holds a banquet quarterly.
(C) It recently hired a new president.
(D) It rotates exhibits on a monthly basis.

07 In which of the positions marked [1], [2], [3], and [4] does the following sentence best belong?

"Their addresses are also included on it."

(A) [1]
(B) [2]
(C) [3]
(D) [4]

정답·해석·해설 p.175

Course 1 의도 파악 문제

Leo Rossi	오전 11:01
배송 요청하신 소포를 어떻게 할까요?	
Cathy Schneider	오전 11:05
건물 관리인에게 맡겨주시겠어요?	
Leo Rossi	오전 11:06
알겠어요. 그렇게 해드릴게요.	
	Send

Q. 오전 11시 6분에, Mr. Rossi가 "그렇게 해드릴게요"라고 썼을 때, 그가 의도한 것은?

A. 소포를 건물 관리인에게 맡길 것이다.

Mr. Rossi와 주고받은 문자 메시지 중 마지막 메시지의 의미를 묻고 있습니다. 이처럼 PART 7에서는 지문의 내용을 바탕으로 언급된 문구가 어떤 의도로 쓰였는지를 파악하는 **의도 파악 문제**가 출제됩니다.

빈출 질문 유형

At 11:23 A.M., what does **Ms. Miller** most likely mean when she writes, "I'll do that as well"?
오전 11시 23분에, Ms. Miller가 "I'll do that as well"이라고 썼을 때, 그녀가 의도한 것 같은 것은?

At 10:33 A.M., what does **Ms. Graham** mean when she writes, "But we are open until 8 P.M."?
오전 10시 33분에, Ms. Graham이 "But we are open until 8 P.M."이라고 썼을 때, 그녀가 의도한 것은?

문제 풀이 전략

STEP 1 질문을 읽고 인용구가 지문의 어디에서 언급되었는지를 확인합니다.

STEP 2 지문에서 인용구의 앞뒤 대화 내용을 읽고 인용구의 문맥상 의미를 파악합니다.
주변 문맥으로는 정답을 찾기 어렵다면 지문 전체의 흐름을 파악해야 합니다.

STEP 3 인용구가 쓰인 의도를 가장 잘 나타낸 보기를 선택합니다.

전략 적용

[메시지 대화문]

Leo Rossi	11:01 A.M.
Mr. Holbrook is not at home. What should I do with the parcel you asked me to deliver?	
Cathy Schneider	11:05 A.M.
Could you leave it with the building manager? He can take care of it.	
Leo Rossi	11:06 A.M.
OK. I can do that for you.	

Q. At 11:06 A.M., what does Mr. Rossi mean when he writes, "I can do that for you"?

(A) He will leave a parcel at Ms. Schneider's home.
(B) He will drop off a package with the building manager.
(C) He will wait in Mr. Holbrook's office.

STEP 2
인용구 앞의 'Could you leave it with the building manager?'에서 Cathy Schneider가 배송될 소포를 건물 관리인에게 맡겨달라고 했고, 이에 Leo Rossi가 I can do that for you(그렇게 해드릴게요)라고 대답한 것을 통해, Mr. Rossi가 소포를 건물 관리인에게 맡기겠다고 의미한 것임을 파악합니다.

STEP 1
질문을 읽고 인용구 'I can do that for you'가 지문의 어디에서 언급되었는지를 확인합니다.

STEP 3
인용구가 쓰인 의도를 가장 잘 나타낸 보기인 (B)를 정답으로 선택합니다.

해석 p. 177

패러프레이징 연습 | 주어진 문장과 가까운 의미를 가진 문장을 고르세요.

01

> The central bank announced that it may lower interest rates further to stimulate the economy. Last week's reports of poor earnings by several major firms contributed to this decision.

(A) Disappointing earnings results could prompt lower interest rates.
(B) Decisions about interest rates have prevented the economy from improving.

02

> The news that a Luxen Motors factory will open in Gerringville was welcomed by local residents. They expect it will create quite a few jobs in the economically weak area.

(A) Gerringville locals think Luxen Motors' new factory will benefit their region.
(B) A welcome celebration will be held for Luxen Motors in Gerringville.

유형 연습 | 주어진 지문을 읽고 문제를 풀어보세요.

03 [메시지 대화문]

Linda Graham	10:28 A.M.	The cake you ordered for your staff party is ready. You can pick it up at any time.
Dave Poplar	10:32 A.M.	I'm at work at the moment. You don't offer a delivery service, do you?
Linda Graham	10:33 A.M.	I'm afraid not. But we are open until 8 P.M.
Dave Poplar	10:34 A.M.	OK. I'll stop by early this afternoon.

Q. At 10:33 A.M., what does Ms. Graham mean when she writes, "But we are open until 8 P.M."?

(A) There will be enough time to visit after work.
(B) An additional cake can be purchased later.
(C) Delivery will be the best option for a customer.

04 [메시지 대화문]

Cindy Kane	4:20 P.M.	Mr. Wilson wants to have a consultation on Tuesday morning. Could either of you meet him? He is one of our biggest clients.
Kathy Jones	4:23 P.M.	I have an appointment that morning, so I can't do it.
James Wong	4:25 P.M.	I should be able to manage that. I don't have anything else scheduled until 11.
Cindy Kane	4:26 P.M.	Thanks, Mr. Wong.

Q. At 4:25 P.M., what does Mr. Wong mean when he writes, "I don't have anything else scheduled until 11"?

(A) He will be able to attend a conference.
(B) He can meet a client for a consultation.
(C) He will manage an office while Ms. Kane is away.

정답·해석·해설 **p.177**

Course 2 동의어 문제

Nevertire사의 위기

당국은 Nevertire사의 자동차 타이어가 더운 날씨에서 변형된다고 결론을 내렸다. 이 **사태**에 대한 Nevertire사의 대응이 그 명성에 매우 중요할 것으로 보인다.

Q. 1문단 세 번째 줄의 단어 "사태"는 의미상 -와 가장 가깝다.

A. 상황

Nevertire사의 자동차 타이어와 관련한 신문 기사에 쓰인 단어의 의미를 묻고 있습니다. 이처럼 PART 7에서는 지문 내에 있는 한 단어와 가장 유사한 의미의 단어를 고르는 **동의어 문제**가 출제됩니다.

📋 빈출 질문 유형

단일 지문

The word "maintain" in paragraph 1, line 5, is closest in meaning to
1문단 다섯 번째 줄의 단어 "maintain"은 의미상 -와 가장 가깝다.

다중 지문

In the letter, the word "drew" in paragraph 2, line 3, is closest in meaning to
편지에서, 2문단 세 번째 줄의 단어 "drew"는 의미상 -와 가장 가깝다.

📋 문제 풀이 전략

STEP 1 질문을 읽고 단어의 위치를 확인합니다.

STEP 2 지문에서 해당 단어가 포함된 문장을 읽고 문맥을 통해 단어의 의미를 파악합니다.

해당 단어의 동의어이지만 문맥에 어울리지 않는 단어가 오답 보기로 출제되므로 반드시 문맥을 통해 단어의 의미를 파악해야 합니다.

STEP 3 문맥상 가장 비슷한 의미를 갖는 보기를 정답으로 선택합니다.

📋 전략 적용

[기사]

Nevertire's Crisis

Authorities have determined that Nevertire's all-weather wheels do indeed have a tendency to deform in hot weather. So, they have the potential to cause car accidents. Nevertire's response to this matter is expected to be critical to its reputation.

Q. The word "matter" in paragraph 1, line 3 is closest in meaning to

(A) object
(B) element
(C) situation

해석 p.178

STEP 2
해당 단어가 포함된 문장 'Nevertire's response to this matter is expected to be critical to its reputation.'에서 이 사태에 대한 Nevertire사의 대응이 회사의 명성에 매우 중요할 것으로 예상된다는 문맥을 통해 matter가 '사태'라는 뜻으로 사용되었음을 확인합니다.

STEP 1
질문을 읽고 matter의 위치가 1문단 세 번째 줄임을 확인합니다.

STEP 3
문맥상 '사태'와 가장 비슷한 의미인 '상황'이라는 뜻을 가진 보기인 (C)를 정답으로 선택합니다.

HACKERS PRACTICE 토익 700+ 달성을 위한 연습 문제

패러프레이징 연습 | 주어진 문장과 가까운 의미를 가진 문장을 고르세요.

01

> Held annually, the Fabric Trade Fair offers clothing retailers a chance to meet with suppliers from around the world. Deals totaling millions of dollars are often made at the event.

(A) A trade fair attracts the fashion industry's top models every two years.
(B) The combined value of the deals made at the fair usually totals millions of dollars.

02

> Under Mr. Tim's leadership, West Pharma grew into a profitable company. Mark Metzner, the former head of global operations, will succeed him as the CEO.

(A) Mr. Metzner will replace Mr. Tim as the head of a successful company.
(B) Mr. Tim was extremely productive as West Pharma's head of global operations.

유형 연습 | 주어진 지문을 읽고 문제를 풀어보세요.

03 [회람]

> As you may know, employees are required to attend a one-hour training session each year on managing interoffice relationships. The session will focus on how to productively mediate conflicts and how to maintain good relations with one's colleagues.
>
> I would like each of you to bring at least two questions to the session. Our speaker this year, Harold Bridge, has been working in the IT industry for over 15 years, and I'm sure he will have compelling answers to all of your inquiries. I look forward to seeing you all there.

Q. The word "maintain" in paragraph 1, line 3, is closest in meaning to

  (A) cause
  (B) claim
  (C) keep

04 [공고]

> We are expanding our retail space to dramatically enhance the shopping experience for customers. In order to do this, we will need to temporarily close off the men's clothing and sportswear sections. For your safety, please do not enter either of these areas. Each zone will be marked by a sign and orange construction tape. Consult a store employee if you have any questions. Thank you for your support.

Q. The word "dramatically" in paragraph 1, line 1, is closest in meaning to

  (A) expressively
  (B) substantially
  (C) energetically

정답·해석·해설 **p.178**

Questions 01-04 refer to the following online chat discussion.

Hannah Miller   11:02 A.M.   I was online and found a company called Enviro-Ware. All their products are made of recycled paper materials. I'm thinking about switching from our current supplier.

Glenn Friedman   11:13 A.M.   I'm looking at the company's Web site now. They've got a wide selection as well. Using environmentally friendly cups could be a good selling point.

Olivia Liu   11:15 A.M.   But their cups cost 15 percent more than the ones we currently use.

Hannah Miller   11:17 A.M.   The site indicates that they can discuss bulk order pricing. And I agree with Glenn that it is good for marketing.

Glenn Friedman   11:18 A.M.   I see here we can also have products designed to our specifications. We should ask for some samples with our company logo.

Hannah Miller   11:19 A.M.   That's a good idea. It will give us a chance to evaluate the cups. If we like the samples, I'll see what I can do about the price.

Olivia Liu   11:22 A.M.   What about getting napkin and plate samples, too? The ones we use now aren't made of recycled material.

Hannah Miller   11:23 A.M.   I'll do that as well. Thanks, and I'll keep you updated.

[Send]

---

01 Why is Mr. Friedman interested in Enviro-Ware's cups?

(A) He is a supporter of eco-friendly firms.
(B) He thinks they could help with marketing.
(C) He believes the company would save money.
(D) He is satisfied with the product samples.

02 What is NOT indicated about Enviro-Ware?

(A) Its merchandise is made of paper.
(B) Its prices are higher than a current supplier.
(C) It customizes some items for clients.
(D) It offers only a small selection of products.

03 What most likely does Ms. Miller intend to do?

(A) Request a discount on an order
(B) Cancel a recent online order
(C) Alter a corporate logo design
(D) Submit a review of a service

04 At 11:23 A.M., what does Ms. Miller mean when she writes, "I'll do that as well"?

(A) She will purchase some cups with logos.
(B) She will send order forms to Ms. Liu.
(C) She will ask for other types of product samples.
(D) She will provide updates on negotiations.

한 권으로 끝내는
해커스 토익 700+
LC+RC+VOCA

READING PART 7

DAY 16 질문 유형 4

한 권으로 끝내는 해커스 토익 700+ (LC+RC+VOCA)

Questions 05-07 refer to the following brochure.

Proship Luxury Cruises

At Proship, we have a reputation for providing the highest quality cruises to people from across the USA and beyond. We've been taking honeymooners, retirees, and vacationers to the Caribbean islands for 30 years. We also started to do tours of the Mediterranean in the mid-1990s, and we've even begun taking cruises to Antarctica to explore the last great wilderness on our planet.

Now we're expanding yet again. Starting in April, Proship will be arranging short chartered business cruises to the Caribbean. Leaving from our port in Miami, we can take you to the Bahamas, Turks and Caicos, Jamaica, the Dominican Republic, and Puerto Rico. These cruises will be perfect for any company whether your aim is to hold an unforgettable staff retreat or to entertain and make a presentation to potential clients.

The perfect itinerary can be arranged through consultation with our staff, ensuring you get enough time for both business and pleasure. Your leisure time could include visiting seaside towns, scuba diving off the coast, or simply relaxing on the beach. When it's time to get serious again, our cruise ships have several options for meeting spaces. The boats are also equipped with wireless Internet and projector systems. Meanwhile, our chefs will be cooking up some delicious meals, including local seafood, to keep you well-fueled for negotiations, discussions, teambuilding exercises, or whatever you want to do.

So call us at 555-9682 to discuss options and pricing, and make your next business meeting the trip of a lifetime.

05 What is being advertised?

(A) A travel agency's new cruises
(B) An exhibit at a ship museum
(C) A Web site for booking a boat tour
(D) A store selling boat equipment

06 The word "aim" in paragraph 2, line 4, is closest in meaning to

(A) design
(B) belief
(C) course
(D) intention

07 What is stated about the ships?

(A) They offer 24-hour dining facilities.
(B) They are equipped for presentations.
(C) Their exercise rooms have been upgraded.
(D) Their routes start in the Bahamas.

정답·해석·해설 **p.179**

Course 1 이메일 및 편지 (E-mail & Letter)

토익 출제경향
평균 2~3지문 정도 출제

수신: Kyle Taylor
발신: Teal 출판사

수신·발신자

귀하의 구독이 3월 31일에 종료됨을 알려드리고 자 합니다. 6개월을 더 연장하고 싶으시다면 첨부된 양식을 작성해서 회신해주시기 바랍니다.

목적

세부 사항

잡지 구독 연장에 관해 안내하는 이메일입니다. 이처럼 PART 7에서는 일상생활 또는 비즈니스와 관련된 여러 정보를 주고받는 **이메일 및 편지**가 출제됩니다.

📋 빈출 지문

단일 지문

일상생활	호텔, 학교, 병원 등의 시설 또는 각종 업체의 담당자와 고객이 주고받는 이메일/편지
비즈니스	회사 동료들 혹은 서로 다른 회사의 직원들이 업무와 관련된 내용을 주고받는 이메일

다중 지문

이메일 & 이메일	주문 담당자가 결제를 안내하는 이메일 & 주문에 대한 변경 사항을 알리는 이메일
이메일 & 양식 & 이메일	고객 만족에 관한 설문 조사 참여 요청 이메일 & 설문 조사지 양식 & 설문 조사 결과에 관해 보고하는 직원의 이메일

📋 빈출 문제 유형

주제/목적 찾기 문제	이메일/편지의 목적을 묻습니다. **What is the purpose of the e-mail/letter?** 이메일/편지의 목적은 무엇인가? **Why did Ms. Collins write the e-mail/letter?** Ms. Collins는 왜 이메일/편지를 썼는가?
육하원칙 문제	이메일/편지의 수신자가 요청받는 사항 또는 기타 세부 사항을 주로 묻습니다. **What is Mr. Marshall asked to do?** Mr. Marshall은 무엇을 하기를 요청받는가? **How can customers receive a discount?** 고객들은 어떻게 할인을 받을 수 있는가?
Not/True 문제	이메일/편지에 언급된 사람이나 회사 등에 관해 일치하거나 일치하지 않는 것을 주로 묻습니다. **What is indicated about Ms. Rochefort?** Ms. Rochefort에 대해 언급된 것은? **What is NOT true about TN Bank?** TN 은행에 대해 사실이 아닌 것은?
추론 문제	이메일/편지에 언급된 사람, 회사, 제품 등의 특정 사항에 대해 추론할 수 있는 것을 주로 묻습니다. **Who most likely is Mr. Hawthorne?** Mr. Hawthorne은 누구일 것 같은가? **What is suggested about the subscription?** 구독권에 대해 암시되는 것은?

[이메일]

수신: Kyle Taylor <taylor@mesamail.com>
발신: Teal 출판사 <cs@tealmags.com>
제목: 구독 연장
날짜: 6월 10일
첨부: 연장 양식

*Brand Magazine*의 구독자가 되어 주셔서 감사합니다. 저희의 기록은 귀하의 구독이 6월 30일에 종료된다는 것을 보여줍니다. ^A6개월 더 연장하고 싶으시다면, 첨부된 양식을 작성하셔서 6월 28일까지 저희에게 회신해주시기 바랍니다. 10퍼센트 추가 할인을 받으시려면, 1년 구독을 신청하십시오. ^B저희의 다른 잡지들에도 좋은 혜택들이 있습니다. 이 출판물들을 보시려면 <u>여기</u>를 클릭하셔서 온라인 카탈로그를 이용하십시오.

Q. Teal 출판사에 대해 사실이 아닌 것은?

(A) 반년 구독권을 제공한다.
(B) 여러 잡지들을 발행한다.
(C) 6월에 세일을 한다.

To: Kyle Taylor <taylor@mesamail.com>
From: Teal Publications <cs@tealmags.com>
Subject: Subscription renewal
Date: June 10
Attachment: Renewal form

Thank you for being a subscriber to *Brand Magazine*. Our records show that your subscription ends on June 30. ^AIf you'd like to renew it for another six months, fill out the attached form and send it back to us by June 28. To get an additional 10 percent savings, sign up for a one-year subscription. ^BWe also have great offers on our other magazines. To view these titles, click <u>here</u> to access our online catalog.

Q. What is NOT true about Teal Publications?

(A) It offers half-year subscriptions.
(B) It publishes several magazines.
(C) It is holding a sale in June.

수신·발신자

목적

세부 사항

해설 Not/True 문제 질문의 핵심 어구인 Teal Publications와 관련된 내용을 지문에서 찾아 각 보기와 대조하는 Not/True 문제입니다. (A)는 'If you'd like to renew it for another six months, fill out the attached form'에서 구독을 6개월 더 연장하고 싶으면 첨부된 양식을 작성하라고 했으므로 지문의 내용과 일치하고, (B)는 'We also have great offers on our other magazines.'에서 Teal 출판사의 다른 잡지들에도 좋은 혜택이 있다고 했으므로 지문의 내용과 일치합니다. (C)는 지문에 언급되지 않은 내용입니다. 따라서 (C) It is holding a sale in June이 정답입니다.

Questions 01-03 refer to the following letter.

Grandmercia International

Suite #402A, 100 Upscale Boulevard, Milwaukee, MN
Phone: 555-2344 Fax: 555-2343 http://www.grandmercia.com/

April 18

Crystal Rose Investments Inc.
Mr. Bernard O'Donnell
Human Resources Managing Director
87 Werchester Drive, Saint Paul, MN

Dear Mr. O'Donnell,

Ms. Katherine Coolidge has asked that I write to you in regard to her application for employment with your esteemed organization. Ms. Coolidge and I have worked together for over 10 years, and I can enthusiastically testify to her competence and work ethic. She started out at Grandmercia with me in financial product sales and then quickly rose to a position in client research in the automotive industry. During the entire time I worked with her, she never missed a day of work, being characteristically punctual and diligent.

I am aware that she is leaving her current position here at Grandmercia of her own accord in order to seek further career advancement at Crystal Rose Investments. I am confident that she will be able to carry out any task required of her. Please feel free to contact me at 555-2348 with any inquiries in regard to this recommendation.

Sincerely,

Caleb Thickett

Senior analyst, Grandmercia International, Inc.

---

01 What is the purpose of the letter?

(A) To provide interview results
(B) To apply for a vacant position
(C) To recommend a job candidate
(D) To inquire about salary details

02 The phrase "carry out" in paragraph 2, line 3, is closest in meaning to

(A) bring
(B) complete
(C) order
(D) divert

03 What is suggested about the position at Crystal Rose Investments?

(A) It requires five years of prior work experience.
(B) It offers better opportunities for Ms. Coolidge.
(C) It is in a very demanding company division.
(D) It pays a higher wage than Mr. Thickett's job.

한 권으로 끝내는
해커스 토익 700+
LC+RC+VOCA

READING PART 7

DAY 17 지문 유형 1

한 권으로 끝내는 해커스 토익 700+ (LC+RC+VOCA)

Questions 04-05 refer to the following e-mails.

TO	Maureen Huddleston <huddleston@midproductions.com>
FROM	Abed Khan <abed_khan@uni-direct.com>
SUBJECT	Final Designs
DATE	April 4
ATTACHMENT	Uniform Designs

Dear Ms. Huddleston,

Thank you for choosing Uni-direct. I've attached the designs for your recreational baseball team's uniforms. As with previous years' orders, the team's red-and-blue logo will appear on the right sleeve of the jersey. Also, we're happy to make them out of the new sweat-resistant fabric that you requested.

The uniforms will cost $95 each. We'll start making them as soon as you pay the 50 percent deposit. Also, for a $60 fee, we can deliver. Let me know if you have further questions.

Abed Khan

TO	Abed Khan <abed_khan@uni-direct.com>
FROM	Maureen Huddleston <huddleston@midproductions.com>
SUBJECT	my order
DATE	April 5

Dear Mr. Khan,

I placed an order for uniforms yesterday. I have to say that I was very pleased with the designs your company came up with.

However, I've just learned that two more people are joining our team for the upcoming season. Could I add two large uniforms to the order? I can make another deposit. Or, you can add the cost to my balance, which I'll pay when I pick up the items at your store on May 6. Thank you.

Best,
Maureen Huddleston

04 What is a feature of the uniforms?

(A) A long-sleeved shirt
(B) A team logo on the back
(C) A special material
(D) A red-and-blue cap

05 What is suggested about Ms. Huddleston?

(A) She wants a refund.
(B) She will not pay a $60 service fee.
(C) She wears a large uniform.
(D) She paid an additional deposit.

정답·해석·해설 p.181

Course 2 메시지 대화문 (Text Message Chain)

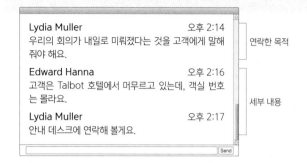

Lydia Muller	오후 2:14

우리의 회의가 내일로 미뤄졌다는 것을 고객에게 말해 줘야 해요.

Edward Hanna	오후 2:16

고객은 Talbot 호텔에서 머무르고 있는데, 객실 번호는 몰라요.

Lydia Muller	오후 2:17

안내 데스크에 연락해 볼게요.

연락한 목적

세부 내용

고객에게 회의 연기를 알리기 위해 문자를 주고받는 두 직원 간의 메시지 대화문입니다. 이처럼 PART 7에서는 업무와 관련된 정보를 모바일이나 온라인 메신저상에서 2인 이상이 논의하는 **메시지 대화문**이 출제됩니다.

▨ 빈출 지문

메시지 대화문   작업 현장에 나가 있거나 외근 중인 직원과 사무실에서 근무하는 직원 간의 업무 관련 대화

온라인 채팅 대화문   팀장과 팀원들 또는 동료들 간의 업무 진행 상황을 공유하는 대화

▨ 빈출 문제 유형

의도 파악 문제   대화문에서 특정 어구가 어떤 의도로 쓰였는지를 묻습니다.

At 11:44 A.M., what does Mr. Nielsen mean when he writes, "That's what I think"?
오전 11시 44분에, Mr. Nielsen이 "That's what I think"라고 썼을 때, 그가 의도한 것은?

육하원칙 문제   대화자의 문의 사항이나 요청 사항, 제안 사항 등을 주로 묻습니다.

What does Ms. Park ask Mr. Dukas to do? Ms. Park은 Mr. Dukas에게 무엇을 하기를 요청하는가?
What problem does Mr. Hanna have? Mr. Hanna는 어떤 문제를 갖고 있는가?

Not/True 문제   메시지 대화문에 언급된 사람 및 회사 등에 대해 일치하거나 일치하지 않는 것을 주로 묻습니다.

What is true about Mr. Kaur? Mr. Kaur에 대해 사실인 것은?
What is NOT indicated about QP Corporation? QP사에 대해 언급되지 않은 것은?

추론 문제   대화자가 일하는 회사의 종류, 메시지 대화문에 언급된 사람이나 특정 사항에 대해 추론할 수 있는 것을 주로 묻습니다.

Where does Mr. Scott most likely work? Mr. Scott은 어디에서 일할 것 같은가?
What is suggested about Ms. Davis? Ms. Davis에 대해 암시되는 것은?

예제

[메시지 대화문]

Lydia Muller 오후 2:14 우리 고객이 머무르고 있는 호텔의 이름이 뭐죠? 저는 그에게 우리의 회의가 내일로 미뤄졌다는 것을 말해줘야 해요. **Edward Hanna** 오후 2:16 Talbot International이에요. 하지만, 그가 어느 객실에 있는지는 모르겠네요. **Lydia Muller** 오후 2:17 고마워요. 안내 데스크를 통해 그에게 연락할 수 있을 거예요. Q. Ms. Muller는 무엇을 하기를 원하는가? (A) 회의를 위해 방을 예약한다 (B) 그녀의 고객에게 지연에 대해 알린다 (C) 호텔로의 길 안내를 받는다	**Lydia Muller** 2:14 P.M. What's the name of the hotel where our client is staying? I need to tell him that our meeting has been pushed back to tomorrow. ——— 연락한 목적 **Edward Hanna** 2:16 P.M. It's the Talbot International. However, I don't remember which room he's in. ——— 세부 내용 **Lydia Muller** 2:17 P.M. Thanks. I'm sure I can reach him through the front desk. Q. What does Ms. Muller want to do? (A) Reserve a room for a meeting (B) Notify her client of a delay (C) Get directions to a hotel

해설 **육하원칙 문제** Ms. Muller가 무엇(What)을 하기 원하는지를 묻는 육하원칙 문제입니다. 질문의 핵심 어구인 Ms. Muller want to do와 관련하여, 'I need to tell him that our meeting has been pushed back to tomorrow.'에서 회의가 내일로 미뤄졌다는 것을 그녀의 고객에게 말해줘야 한다고 했으므로 (B) Notify her client of a delay가 정답입니다.

Questions 01-02 refer to the following text-message chain.

Samson Pandia	4:22 P.M.

Did you catch this morning's news report on Channel 22? It seems that Membangan has decided not to offer a quote for the government's new construction project.

Micah Lesmono	4:24 P.M.

Yes, I saw. That's good news. That leaves only one other company that we need to compete with.

Samson Pandia	4:26 P.M.

That's right, but they've been in this industry for a long time—over 45 years.

Micah Lesmono	4:27 P.M.

Still, I'm confident about our chances. T.M. Construction has developed a reputation for being too slow for today's fast-paced environment.

Samson Pandia	4:28 P.M.

I agree. They also have not been able to integrate new building technologies like we have.

Micah Lesmono	4:29 P.M.

Given your design proposal and our company's track record for completing projects on time, our overall chances are very good indeed.

Samson Pandia	4:30 P.M.

Well, we shall find out soon enough!

01 Where do the writers most likely work?

(A) At a television station
(B) At a government office
(C) At a construction firm
(D) At a transportation agency

02 At 4:24 P.M., what does Ms. Lesmono mean when she writes, "That's good news"?

(A) One of her coworkers is being promoted.
(B) A project was assigned to her group.
(C) Some colleagues will be awarded at a ceremony.
(D) A firm's withdrawal benefits her company.

Questions 03-06 refer to the following online chat discussion.

Alfreda Hailey	11:38 A.M.	What did you think of the final applicants we interviewed for the research manager job? I'd like to give them an answer by tomorrow.
Jerome Bartha	11:40 A.M.	I thought Ben Trenton had the stronger educational qualifications, but Stefania Lucci handled the questions we asked her better. She would be my choice.
Dane Nielsen	11:41 A.M.	I agree. Stefania was also friendly and simple to communicate with during the meeting. Those are good qualities for a leader.
Alfreda Hailey	11:43 A.M.	Thanks for the input. I agree with you both. I'll notify the human resources department that we'd like to make her an official offer.
Jerome Bartha	11:43 A.M.	I think she'd be a great addition to the company.
Dane Nielsen	11:44 A.M.	That's what I think. Also, Ben Trenton is currently working, but she is not. She could start at any time.
Alfreda Hailey	11:45 A.M.	Okay. But in case she doesn't accept the offer, are you both fine with Ben Trenton instead?
Dane Nielsen	11:46 A.M.	That's fine by me.
Jerome Bartha	11:47 A.M.	Same here.

Send

03 What does Ms. Hailey hope to do?

(A) Select some final applicants during a morning meeting
(B) Promote a staff member to a research position
(C) Notify candidates of a decision by tomorrow
(D) Drop off some contracts at the human resources department

04 What is suggested about Mr. Trenton?

(A) He was involved in an employee referral program.
(B) He has a better academic background than Ms. Lucci.
(C) He was late for the interview this morning.
(D) He graduated at the top of his class.

05 What is NOT indicated about Ms. Lucci?

(A) She has qualities appropriate for a management job.
(B) She is applying for a position in research department.
(C) She will receive an official employment offer.
(D) She is currently employed at another company.

06 At 11:44 A.M., what does Mr. Nielsen mean when he writes, "That's what I think"?

(A) He believes Mr. Trenton should be appointed to the position.
(B) He wants to have follow-up interviews with some candidates.
(C) He agrees that Ms. Lucci is the ideal candidate for the job.
(D) He is satisfied with an offer made to an applicant.

정답·해석·해설 p.182

지문 유형 2

한 권으로 끝내는
해커스 토익 700+
LC+RC+VOCA

Course 1 양식 (Forms)

토익 출제경향
평균 1~2지문 정도 출제

고객 영수증 Cutler 가구점		
품명	수량	가격
Arma 식탁 의자	6	$600

교환 가능 기한: 11월 15일

☐ 양식 종류

세부 사항

☐ 참고 사항

주문한 가구에 관한 영수증입니다. 이처럼 PART 7에서는 제품 및 서비스의 요금에 대한 영수증, 청구서, 웹페이지, 일정표, 전단지, 후기 등 생활 속에서 볼 수 있는 다양한 **양식**이 출제됩니다.

빈출 지문

단일 지문

영수증	물품 구매를 증명하는 영수증
청구서	물품 대금 또는 작업비를 청구하는 송장
웹페이지	인터넷상에서 회사의 제품 및 서비스를 소개하는 웹페이지
일정표	회의, 행사, 강연 등의 일정 또는 개인 업무 일정을 나타내는 표
전단지	시설, 행사, 제품, 서비스 등을 광고하는 전단지
후기	업체에서 제공하는 제품, 서비스, 시설 등에 대한 고객의 이용 후기

다중 지문

양식 & 이메일	주제 및 일정 등을 포함한 강의 소개 웹페이지 & 강의에 대해 문의하는 이메일
양식 & 양식 & 이메일	행사의 일정표 & 행사 참여 신청서 & 행사의 변동 사항을 참가자들에게 알리는 이메일

빈출 문제 유형

육하원칙 문제

행사의 참가자나 주최 측과 관련된 사항 또는 양식에 언급된 제품에 대한 세부 사항을 주로 묻습니다.

What must guests do to attend? 손님들은 참석하기 위해 무엇을 해야 하는가?

How much are the T-shirts? 티셔츠의 가격은 얼마인가?

Not/True 문제

양식에 언급된 행사나 사람에 대해 일치하거나 일치하지 않는 것을 주로 묻습니다.

What is stated about the conference? 회의에 대해 언급된 것은?

What is NOT true about Mr. Edwards? Mr. Edwards에 대해 사실이 아닌 것은?

추론 문제

양식에 언급된 회사나 사람의 특정 사항에 대해 추론할 수 있는 것을 주로 묻습니다.

What kind of business most likely is EUB Corporation? EUB사는 어떤 종류의 사업체일 것 같은가?

Who most likely is Mr. Carter? Mr. Carter는 누구일 것 같은가?

◢ 예제

고객 영수증

Cutler 가구점

130번지 Ellington가

555-6874

날짜: 10월 15일

거래: 3496

고객 이름: James Howard

계산대: 02

품목	수량	가격
Arma 식탁 의자	6	$600
	세금	$60
	C총액	$660

(영수증을 지참한) 교환 가능 기한: 11월 15일.

C500달러 이상의 주문은 무료 배송됩니다.

Q. Mr. Howard에 대해 사실인 것은?

(A) 몇 개의 제품을 온라인으로 샀다.

(B) 물품을 그의 사무실로 배달되게 할 것이다.

(C) 무료 배송을 받을 자격이 있다.

CUSTOMER RECEIPT

Cutler Furniture Store

130 Ellington Avenue

555-6874

Date: October 15

Transaction: 3496

Customer name: James Howard

Register: 02

Item	Quantity	Price
Arma dining chairs	6	$600
	Tax	$60
	CTOTAL	$660

Returns accepted (with receipt) until: November 15.

COrders over $500 qualify for free shipping.

Q. What is true about Mr. Howard?

(A) He bought some merchandise online.

(B) He will have items shipped to his office.

(C) He is eligible for free delivery.

양식 종류

세부 사항

참고 사항

해설 Not/True 문제 질문의 핵심 어구인 Mr. Howard와 관련된 내용을 지문에서 찾아 각 보기와 대조하는 Not/True 문제입니다. (A)와 (B)는 지문에 언급되지 않은 내용입니다. (C)는 'Orders over $500 qualify for free shipping.'에서 500달러 이상의 주문은 무료 배송된다고 했고, 'TOTAL: $660'에서 총액이 660달러, 즉 500달러 이상임을 알 수 있으므로 지문의 내용과 일치합니다. 따라서 (C) He is eligible for free delivery가 정답입니다.

Questions 01-04 refer to the following schedule.

Join us at the
25th Graceville Sports Celebrity Dinner and Auction
August 16 at the Meadows Civic Center

The Graceville Sports Celebrity Dinner and Auction is a volunteer-organized event celebrating sports. It is held each year in support of the Graceville Children's Center. The Graceville Children's Center provides access to vital care for disabled youth.

6:00 P.M.	**Catered Dinner**	
	Dinner will be provided by The Commons restaurant.	
7:00 P.M.	**Speaker Presentations**	
	Including Baseball Hall of Fame pitcher Stephen Fisher and captain of the Olympic national hockey team Hal Wheaton.	
7:30 P.M.	**Auction**	
	Preview items for sale at www.gracevillescda.com.	

Standard tickets cost $20 and include general seating in the gallery area.
Premier tickets cost $30 and includes seating on the main floor.
Tickets for the event are available exclusively at www.gracevillscda.com/events.

To learn more, call 555-5782.

Sponsored by: Ingram Bank I Mason Publications I Sport Select I Allied Groceries

---

01 Who will benefit from the event?

(A) Local sports teams
(B) Sports award winners
(C) Students in high schools
(D) Kids with disabilities

02 What is indicated about the invited speakers?

(A) They will be giving away sports memorabilia.
(B) They have spoken at the event in the past.
(C) They will be conducting free demonstrations.
(D) They are well-known sports personalities.

03 What will probably happen during the event?

(A) Performances will be given.
(B) Farewell speeches will be held.
(C) Awards will be given out.
(D) Items will be put up for sale.

04 What must guests do to attend?

(A) Make a charitable donation
(B) Send in a confirmation card
(C) Phone an association's office
(D) Visit an establishment's Web page

Questions 05-06 refer to the following Web page and e-mail.

| Home | Info | Enroll Now | Locations |

Are you interested in gaining marketable business skills but don't have the time to go back to college? Kinski Institute is here to help. We offer a range of certificate programs that will ensure you can compete in today's global marketplace.

Our upcoming classes are as follows:

PROGRAM	INSTRUCTOR	DATES	PRICE
Business Communication	Franklin Ward	October 31-December 2	$250
Nonprofit Management	Toby French	November 1-December 6	$280
Marketing Management	Melinda Jackson	November 5-January 11	$310
Financial Accounting	Emily Pearce	January 2-January 27	$340

To sign up, click HERE. We only accept credit cards. We do not offer refunds. If you have any questions, e-mail customersupport@kinski.com or call 555-1412.

TO   Customer Support <customersupport@kinski.com>
FROM   Bill Dixon <bdixon@fastmail.com>
DATE   August 12
SUBJECT   Recent payment

Dear Support Staff,

My name is Bill Dixon, and I'm an IT specialist looking to gain nonprofit management experience. Yesterday, I signed up for one of your classes, but I just received an e-mail informing me that my payment did not go through due to an expired credit card. However, my credit card does not expire until December. Could you check again and let me know how to proceed? Also, my friend Erin Johnson wants to sign up for the business communication course, but she doesn't have her own credit card. Is it all right if I pay for her instead?

Thanks for your help.

Sincerely,
Bill Dixon

05 Whose class did Mr. Dixon probably sign up for?

(A) Franklin Ward
(B) Toby French
(C) Melinda Jackson
(D) Emily Pearce

06 What is indicated about Ms. Johnson?

(A) She wants to take the same course as Mr. Dixon.
(B) Her payment information was updated.
(C) She does not possess a credit card.
(D) Her work background is in business communication.

정답·해석·해설 **p.184**

Course 2 광고 (Advertisement)

Elite 믹서 1000으로 손쉬운 블렌딩을 경험하세요!

업그레이드된 Elite 믹서 1000은 가볍지만 강력합니다.

· 800와트 모터
· 스테인리스 날

주문하시려면 1-800-555-8994로 전화하세요!

광고되는 것

장점

연락처

믹서기를 홍보하는 광고입니다. 이처럼 PART 7에서는 상품이나 서비스를 홍보하거나 직원을 모집하는 **광고**가 출제됩니다.

빈출 지문

단일 지문

일반 광고	행사, 공연, 강의, 회사의 제품 및 서비스 등을 홍보하는 광고
구인 광고	회사 및 기관에서 한 개 또는 여러 개의 직무별로 직원들을 모집하는 공고

다중 지문

광고 & 이메일	여행 상품 광고 & 여행 상품 예약 확인 이메일
광고 & 양식 & 양식	제품 광고 & 구매한 제품에 대한 송장 & 제품을 구매한 고객의 이용 후기

빈출 문제 유형

주제/목적 찾기 문제	광고되고 있는 것이나 광고의 목적을 묻습니다.
	What is being advertised? 광고되고 있는 것은 무엇인가?
	What is the purpose of the advertisement? 광고의 목적은 무엇인가?
육하원칙 문제	구매자가 제품을 구매할 수 있는 방법 또는 광고되는 제품 및 서비스에 대한 세부 사항을 주로 묻습니다.
	How can customers order the product? 고객들은 어떻게 제품을 주문할 수 있는가?
	When will the lecture start? 강의는 언제 시작할 것인가?
Not/True 문제	광고되는 회사 또는 제품의 특징에 대해 언급되거나 언급되지 않은 것을 주로 묻습니다.
	What is mentioned about RunIt sneakers? RunIt사 운동화에 대해 언급된 것은?
	What is NOT stated about the tour packages? 여행 패키지에 대해 언급되지 않은 것은?
추론 문제	광고에 언급된 업체나 제품의 특정 사항에 대해 추론할 수 있는 것을 주로 묻습니다.
	What is indicated about H&J Financials? H&J 금융 회사에 대해 암시되는 것은?
	What is suggested about the refund policy? 환불 정책에 대해 암시되는 것은?

[광고]

Nuvee사의 Elite 믹서 1000으로 손쉬운 블렌딩을 경험하세요!

완전히 새롭게 업그레이드된 Nuvee사의 Elite 믹서 1000은 가볍지만 강력합니다. 이 믹서기의 특징은 다음과 같습니다:

· 800와트 모터
· 스테인리스 날
· 안전 잠금장치와 속도 조절기

*Kitchen Magazine*이 왜 Elite 믹서 1000을 지난달 최고의 주방용품으로 선정했는지 알아보십시오.

주문하시려면, Nuvee Kitchen Systems사에 1-800-555-8994로 전화하시거나, www.nuvee.com/shop에서 저희의 온라인 상점을 방문하세요.

Q. 고객들은 어떻게 Elite 믹서 1000을 주문할 수 있는가?

(A) 웹사이트를 방문함으로써
(B) 주소로 신청서를 보냄으로써
(C) 쇼룸이 있는 지점에 방문함으로써

Experience Easy Blending with Nuvee's Elite Mixer 1000!

The all-new upgraded Elite Mixer 1000 from Nuvee is lightweight yet powerful. It features:
• An 800-watt motor
• Stainless steel blades
• A safety lock and speed controller

Find out why *Kitchen Magazine* called the Elite Mixer 1000 their number one pick for kitchen appliances last month.

To order, contact Nuvee Kitchen Systems at 1-800-555-8994, or visit our online store **at www. nuvee.com/shop.**

Q. How can customers order an Elite Mixer 1000?

(A) By going to a Web site
(B) By mailing a form to an address
(C) By visiting a showroom location

광고되는 것

장점

연락처

해설 육하원칙 문제 고객들이 어떻게(How) Elite 믹서 1000을 주문할 수 있는지를 묻는 육하원칙 문제입니다. 질문의 핵심 어구인 customers order an Elite Mixer 1000와 관련하여, 'To order, ~ visit our online store'에서 주문하려면 온라인 상점을 방문하라고 했으므로 (A) By going to a Web site가 정답입니다.

Questions 01-03 refer to the following advertisement.

Do you have a gift for talking to people?
Put that to work!
At
ShareUs Telemarketing

ShareUs runs telemarketing campaigns for diverse companies. Our clients include, but are not limited to, Greendom Grocers, Fanatic Coffee Shops, and Huffman Department Stores.

No specialized degree or prior experience is required. All that applicants need is an outgoing personality, a positive attitude, and the ability to speak politely on the phone. Duties at the entry level are limited to handling phone calls. Employees who stay with the company for at least two years enjoy prospects for advancement, either to management in phone services, or through internal hiring to other departments such as recordkeeping.

* Places where ShareUs is currently recruiting:
Elmwood, Alberta—2 positions
Marston, Saskatchewan—5 positions
Pasquer, Ontario—4 positions

ShareUs is always willing to consider applications. Feel free to apply at any time through the company Web site, www.shareusrecruit.com. Simply fill out the application form, and you will be on your way to an interesting new career.

01 What is being advertised?

(A) A seminar about customer service
(B) A promotional offer for clients
(C) A job with a service provider
(D) A company's new locations

02 The word "prospects" in paragraph 2, line 4, is closest in meaning to

(A) views
(B) arrangements
(C) possibilities
(D) proposals

03 What is indicated about ShareUs?

(A) It plans to move its headquarters.
(B) It specializes in technical support.
(C) It is recruiting staff in different locations.
(D) It will provide a period of paid training.

Questions 04-05 refer to the following advertisement, invoice, and review.

Introducing GREEN-CARE's Newest Innovation in Lawn Care!

Green-Care's GC-24 Lawn Mower is self-propelled and has wheels that are suitable for any terrain, making it simple to cut grass on hills or other inclines. It is battery-powered and recharges quickly! Not only that, but all Green-Care products come with a six-month warranty for free repairs or replacement. Bring the coupon below to take advantage of this month's special offer.

> Discount Coupon
> **$25 off your purchase of a GC-24 Lawn Mower**
> Limit of one per customer. Offer expires on September 30.

Garrison Garden Supplies: 543 West Road, Sandpoint, ID 83864
Customer: Mr. Westley Beecher, 827 Dearborn Street, Sandpoint, ID 83864   **Order Number: B-3948374**

Product	Price	Quantity	Total
Green-Care GC-24 Lawn Mower	$375.00	1	$375.00
		Discount	-$25.00
		Total	$350.00

Product: Green-Care GC-24 Lawn Mower   **Member: Westley Beecher**

I purchased this mower four months ago. The machine is easy to operate and has a surprisingly powerful motor. The recharging process is fast, usually taking under an hour. However, when I first got it, my mower lasted only about 10 minutes per charge. I sent it back to the manufacturer, and they repaired it for me. And now the battery lasts for over an hour. Considering the low cost, the Green-Care GC-24 is a great value.

---

04 What did Mr. Beecher most likely give Garrison Garden Supplies?

(A) A customer satisfaction survey
(B) A discount coupon
(C) A membership card
(D) A product purchase receipt

05 What is NOT true about Mr. Beecher?

(A) His mower uses a rechargeable battery.
(B) He got an electronic device fixed recently.
(C) His machine runs an hour or more at a time.
(D) He has owned a lawn mower for half a year.

정답·해석·해설 p.185

Course 1 기사 및 안내문 (Article & Information)

Huxley사와 Beltway사의 합병 계획 발표

Huxley International사와 Beltway Media사가 합병 계획을 발표했다. 두 회사는 다음 주에 합동 기자 회견을 열 것이다.

☐ 제목
☐ 주제 요약
☐ 세부 내용

두 회사의 합병 계획 발표에 대한 신문 기사입니다. 이처럼 PART 7에서는 신문이나 잡지 등에 게재되는 **기사**나 일상에서 쉽게 접할 수 있는 다양한 정보를 제공하는 **안내문**이 출제됩니다.

🔲 빈출 지문

[기사]

단일 지문

비즈니스   회사를 전반적으로 소개하거나 합병, 매각, 경영진 또는 정책의 변경, 지점 확장 등 특정 소식을 알리는 기사

사회   시설의 건설 및 철거 계획, 행사의 개최 또는 결과를 알리는 기사

다중 지문

기사 & 이메일   시설 완공에 관한 기사 & 완공 일정 변경에 관한 이메일

기사 & 이메일 & 양식   행사 개최에 관한 기사 & 행사에 관해 직원이 행사 진행 업체에 보내는 이메일 & 행사 초청장

[안내문]

제품 안내   사용 설명서나 품질 보증서 등 제품과 관련된 안내문

서비스 안내   시설이나 서비스의 이용 방법, 규정, 정책 등을 설명하는 안내문

🔲 빈출 문제 유형

주제/목적 찾기 문제   기사/안내문의 주제나 목적을 묻습니다.

What is the article mainly about? 기사는 주로 무엇에 관한 것인가?

What is the purpose of the information? 안내문의 목적은 무엇인가?

육하원칙 문제   기사/안내문에 언급된 인물이나 규정 등과 같은 세부 사항을 주로 묻습니다.

Who is Ms. Parkin? Ms. Parkin은 누구인가?

What should be enclosed when an item is returned? 물품이 반송될 때 무엇이 동봉되어야 하는가?

Not/True 문제   기사/안내문에 언급된 사람이나 제품, 규정 등에 대해 일치하거나 일치하지 않는 것을 주로 묻습니다.

What is indicated about Mr. Adams? Mr. Adams에 대해 언급된 것은?

What is NOT mentioned about the printer? 프린터에 대해 언급되지 않은 것은?

추론 문제   기사/안내문에 언급된 시점이나 사물 등과 같은 세부 사항에 대해 추론할 수 있는 것을 주로 묻습니다.

When might BR Inc. make an announcement? BR사는 언제 발표를 할 것 같은가?

What can be inferred about the warranty? 품질 보증서에 대해 추론될 수 있는 것은?

예제

[기사]

Huxley사와 Beltway사의 합병 계획 발표

8월 20일에, 기대 마케팅 회사 Huxley International사와 Beltway Media사가 합병 계획을 발표했다. 그들은 다음 주 월요일에 합동 기자 회견을 열어서 계약의 세부 내용을 공개할 것이다. 이 소식에 따라 두 회사 모두의 주가가 상승했다.

Q. 기사에 따르면, 다음 주에 무슨 일이 일어날 것인가?

(A) 주주들이 회의를 위해 모일 것이다.
(B) 합병의 세부 사항이 발표될 것이다.
(C) Huxley International사가 신제품을 발표할 것이다.

Huxley-Beltway's Merger Plans Announced

On August 20, marketing giants Huxley International and Beltway Media announced plans for a merger. They will hold a joint press conference next Monday to release the specifics of the deal. Share prices in both companies rose following the news.

Q. According to the article, what is going to happen next week?

(A) Stockholders will gather for a meeting.
(B) The details of a merger will be announced.
(C) Huxley International will announce a new product.

제목

주제 요약

세부 내용

해설 **육하원칙 문제** 다음 주에 무슨(what) 일이 일어날 것인지를 묻는 육하원칙 문제입니다. 질문의 핵심 어구인 going to happen next week과 관련하여, 'They will hold a joint press conference next Monday to release the specifics of the deal.'에서 다음 주 월요일에 합동 기자 회견을 열어서 계약, 즉 합병의 세부 내용을 공개할 것이라고 했으므로 (B) The details of a merger will be announced가 정답입니다.

Questions 01-04 refer to the following information.

Information For New Tenants

As a tenant, it is important to protect yourself from any potential lease disagreements with the property owner. The Oslo Tenants Advisory Committee offers the following advice to those who are considering renting a property:

- Be sure to get a signed written contract. Make at least two copies of the document, one for you and one for the property's owner. In many cases, the terms of the contract will be used to settle disputes, so read it carefully before signing it.
- For safekeeping, the law requires that landlords keep all accommodation deposits in a separate savings account. Tenants are entitled to proof of this deposit. Accordingly, make sure to ask for a receipt upon payment.
- Ask for an inventory list and make sure that it contains accurate details about all items in the unit. Take photographs of any visible damage. They may be used at the end of the rental contract to protect you against damage claims that can be taken from your rental deposit.
- While the proprietor is present, test all plumbing and lighting fixtures to make sure they work. Additionally, ensure that the locks on all doors and windows are functional.

If you encounter any problems while renting, contact the Tenants Advisory Committee at 555-7156.

01 What is the purpose of the information?

(A) To explain a renovation project for an old building
(B) To provide advice to people planning on renting
(C) To alert tenants of a new law
(D) To announce upcoming construction work

02 What are building proprietors required to give tenants?

(A) A proof of deposit receipt
(B) An extra set of door keys
(C) A lock for a storage area
(D) An emergency contact number

03 What can be inferred about deposits?

(A) Proprietors must keep them at a local bank.
(B) They should not be greater than one month's rent.
(C) They will be used to pay for rent if a tenant leaves without notice.
(D) Building owners may use them to cover the costs of damage.

04 What does the information NOT suggest tenants check?

(A) That the ventilation system is not blocked
(B) That the property has running water
(C) That the inventory list is correctly recorded
(D) That the doors have working locks

WATER PURIFICATION PLANT NEARS COMPLETION

Elkwood's new water treatment facility, located on the outskirts of the city on Divot Road, is nearing the end of the final construction phase. Roger Hanks, whose firm, HMC Contractors, is overseeing the project, says the plant will be ready for operation by May 8. Construction of the $7.2 million facility was funded by a property tax increase and has taken over two years. The new plant will join the existing one on Blake Street in treating the city's water. Once it goes into operation, it will serve the rapidly-growing west side of Elkwood, helping to ensure a clean supply of tap water for all city residents. The city will shortly announce a date for a launch ceremony, which will include a short speech by Mayor Arlene Jennings.

TO	Leann Edison <ledison@elkwoodcity.gov>
FROM	Melvin O'Rourke <meorourke@elkwoodcity.gov>
DATE	May 2
SUBJECT	Assignment

Hi, Leann.

It sounds like we are going to launch the new treatment facility later than expected, on May 10. So we will need to reschedule system tests to May 9. That means that there will be a temporary water interruption on that date. I'll need you to prepare a public notice about this change as soon as possible. Once it's done, could you send me a copy for review? Please do this before 4:00 P.M.

Melvin

05 What is NOT indicated about the water treatment plant in the article?

(A) It will be located on the edge of the city.
(B) It is being built by HMC Contractors.
(C) It will replace an existing plant.
(D) It required raising property taxes.

06 When might Ms. Jennings give a talk?

(A) On May 2
(B) On May 8
(C) On May 9
(D) On May 10

정답·해석·해설 **p.187**

Course 2 공고 및 회람(Notice & Memo)

공 고

보수 공사로 인해 Baker역이 임시 폐쇄됩니다. 공사는 5월 10일에 이루어질 예정입니다. 문의 사항은 555-6404로 전해주십시오.

☐ 주제·목적
☐ 세부 사항
☐ 연락처

지하철 보수 공사를 알리는 공고입니다. 이처럼 PART 7에서는 공공시설 이용 관련 사항이나 각종 공지 사항을 알리는 **공고**나 사내 방침 및 업무 관련 사항을 전달하는 **회람**이 출제됩니다.

🔳 빈출 지문

[공고]

단일 지문

일반 공고	지역 행사 또는 공공시설의 이용 관련 사항에 대해 알리는 공고
사내 공고	사내 행사 또는 회사 정책 시행 및 변경에 대해 알리는 공고

다중 지문

공고 & 양식	대회 공고 & 대회 출품작 제출 양식
공고 & 이메일 & 이메일	근무 일정 변경에 대한 공고 & 변경 사항에 관한 문의 이메일 & 문의에 관한 답변 이메일

[회람]

사내 방침	새로 도입되거나 변경되는 사내 정책에 대해 공지하는 회람
업무 관련	업무 관련 공지 및 특정 안건에 대한 직원들의 의견을 요청하는 회람

🔳 빈출 문제 유형

주제/목적 찾기 문제	공고/회람의 주제나 목적을 묻습니다. **What is the main purpose of the notice?** 공고의 주 목적은 무엇인가? **What is the memo mainly about?** 회람은 주로 무엇에 관한 것인가?
육하원칙 문제	공고/회람에 언급된 추후 일정, 요청 사항이나 기타 세부 사항을 주로 묻습니다. **What are employees expected to do?** 직원들은 무엇을 할 것으로 기대되는가? **What has changed about the event?** 행사에 대해 무엇이 변경되었는가?
Not/True 문제	공고/회람에 언급된 사람, 단체 및 행사 등에 대해 일치하거나 일치하지 않는 것을 주로 묻습니다. **What is true about Chase Hospital?** Chase 병원에 대해 사실인 것은? **What is NOT mentioned about the trade fair?** 무역 박람회에 대해 언급되지 않은 것은?
추론 문제	공고/회람을 받는 대상이나 공고/회람에 언급된 특정 사항에 대해 추론할 수 있는 것을 주로 묻습니다. **For whom is the notice most likely intended?** 공고는 누구를 대상으로 하는 것 같은가? **What is indicated about Mr. Sadik?** Mr. Sadik에 대해 암시되는 것은?

예제

[공고]

공고	Notice	
보수 공사로 인해 Baker역이 임시적으로 폐쇄됩니다. 공사는 5월 10일 토요일 오전 6시부터 오후 2시까지 이루어질 예정입니다. 이 기간 동안 지하철은 역에서 정차하지 않을 것입니다. 그러므로, 승객들은 연결되는 버스편을 대신 이용하거나 이동을 위해 대안을 준비하시는 것이 권장됩니다. 문의 사항은 555-6404로 전해주시기 바랍니다.	Baker station will be temporarily shut down for maintenance work. The work will take place on Saturday, May 10, from 6:00 A.M. to 2:00 P.M. During this period, subway trains will not stop at the station. Therefore, passengers are advised to use connecting bus services instead, or make alternative arrangements for travel. Inquiries may be directed to 555-6404.	주제·목적 / 세부 사항 / 연락처
Q. 공고의 주 목적은 무엇인가? (A) 역의 폐쇄를 알리기 위해 (B) 대체할 형태의 운송 수단을 장려하기 위해 (C) 지하철 서비스 확장을 발표하기 위해	Q. What is the main purpose of the notice? (A) To announce a station's closure (B) To promote alternative forms of transport (C) To announce a subway service expansion	

해설 **주제/목적 찾기 문제** 공고의 주 목적을 묻는 목적 찾기 문제이므로 지문의 앞부분을 주의 깊게 확인합니다. 'Baker station will be temporarily shut down'에서 Baker역이 임시적으로 폐쇄될 것이라고 했으므로 (A) To announce a station's closure가 정답입니다.

Questions 01-03 refer to the following memo.

To	All staff at Karpour
From	Simone Kingsley, Administrative secretary
Date	January 10
Subject	Replacement period

The administration team has announced that it is time once again to review the office's inventory of furniture and replace items that are in disrepair. This assessment occurs every three years. Please understand that this does not mean everyone will get new furnishings. There is a process that must be followed.

First, employees must fill out a request form. This requires the employee's name, office number, and a short description of the items that need to be replaced, including their asset codes. Every piece in the office is labeled with this information. If an asset code cannot be found, then the piece was likely someone's personal purchase and is not eligible to be replaced by the company.

Once the form has been completed, it must be turned in to your department secretary, who will send it to us. Someone will then contact you to do an inspection. If an item is determined to be sufficiently worn, then the request will be approved. Because many employees are expected to make requests, the entire replacement process will take approximately one month. The deadline for completing forms is January 30.

01 What is the memo mainly about?

(A) An office leave policy for new employees
(B) A periodic replacement of office supplies
(C) An upcoming move to a nearby building
(D) A change in a security procedure

02 What are employees expected to do?

(A) Retrieve records of past purchases
(B) Put an asset code on office equipment
(C) Complete assignments before the end of the week
(D) Give completed forms to a department staff member

03 What most likely is true about Karpour?

(A) It has been in operation for over three years.
(B) It has numerous buildings in the area.
(C) It will take advantage of a bulk deal.
(D) It will replace its furniture in July.

Questions 04-05 refer to the following announcement and e-mails.

This is an announcement for all Steadfast Company guards assigned to provide security for Blaine Manufacturing. Starting November 2, the shift schedule will be changing substantially. Management at Blaine Manufacturing has asked Steadfast to extend our shifts to 10 hours per day, and we have agreed to comply in exchange for a four-day work week. Waterside Warehouse, Lockhart Industries, and Henderson Milling are also considering extending shifts, but no final plans have been made. If you have any questions, contact administrative manager Al Johnson (ajohnson@steadfast.com).

To	Al Johnson <ajohnson@steadfast.com>
From	Brian Swift <bswift@steadfast.com>
Date	October 8
Subject	Shift change

Dear Mr. Johnson,

I read the announcement about the scheduling changes at Blaine Manufacturing. I originally took the job there because the work shifts gave me time to take care of family. Of course, working four days a week for 10 hours per day has some advantages, but I prefer the original schedule. Is there any way you could assign me to work at another company?

Brian Swift

To	Brian Swift <bswift@steadfast.com>
From	Al Johnson <ajohnson@steadfast.com>
Date	October 10
Subject	RE: Shift change

Hi, Brian.

Thanks for reaching out. Per your request, I've found a possible solution. I think you can switch shifts with one of our other guards, Ahmed Sadik. He currently does five eight-hour shifts each week for Nuscope Industries at their Cannondale plant. He has expressed that he would like to switch assignments with you. Please let me know if this arrangement will work.

Al Johnson

04 What is suggested about Steadfast Company?

(A) It provides security for multiple companies.
(B) It has reduced its number of employees.
(C) It manufactures security products.
(D) Its headquarters has been relocated.

05 What is indicated about Mr. Sadik?

(A) He has a long commute to the Cannondale plant.
(B) He was recommended by a former supervisor.
(C) He does not have any family members to take care of.
(D) He prefers to have a four-day work week.

정답·해석·해설 p.189

Course 1 이중 지문(Double Passages)

토익 출제경향
2지문 출제

MORROW'S 레스토랑

이메일 또는 전화로 예약하시는 분들께 무료 음료를 드립니다.

수신: book@morrows.com
발신: Ms. Bastidas

제 이름은 Carla Bastidas이고 저는 어제 12명 테이블을 예약하기 위해 전화했습니다. 예약 확인 요청드립니다.

Q. Ms. Bastidas에 대해 암시되는 것은?
A. 무료 음료를 받을 것이다.

음식점 광고지와 그 음식점에 예약 확인을 요청하는 이메일입니다. 이처럼 PART 7에는 두 개의 지문이 서로 연계된 **이중 지문**이 출제되며, 두 개의 지문에서 각각 단서를 찾아 조합해야 정답을 찾을 수 있는 연계 문제도 출제됩니다.

📋 빈출 지문 유형

양식 & 양식	시설을 소개하는 웹페이지 & 시설 이용객의 후기
이메일 & 이메일	시설 이용 관련 사항을 안내하는 이메일 & 안내 사항에 대해 문의하는 이메일
광고 & 이메일	업체 광고 & 예약 문의 이메일

📋 연계 문제 풀이 전략

이중 지문에서 두 개의 지문에서 각각 단서를 찾아 조합해야 정답을 찾을 수 있는 연계 문제는 아래와 같이 푸세요.

STEP 1 질문의 핵심 어구를 통해 먼저 확인할 지문을 결정합니다.
질문을 읽고 핵심 어구를 확인한 다음, 핵심 어구가 있는 지문부터 먼저 확인합니다.

STEP 2 핵심 어구를 포함한 지문에서 첫 번째 단서를 찾고, 나머지 지문에서 그 단서와 관련된 두 번째 단서를 찾습니다.
핵심 어구가 있는 지문을 읽으며 정답의 단서를 찾습니다. 첫 번째 단서로는 정답을 찾기는 어려우므로, 다른 지문에서 두 번째 단서를 찾습니다.

STEP 3 단서들을 조합한 내용과 부합하는 보기를 정답으로 선택합니다.
첫 번째 단서와 두 번째 단서를 조합하여 말하거나, 그 내용을 패러프레이징한 보기를 정답으로 선택합니다.

전략 적용

[광고 & 이메일]

MORROW'S 레스토랑	**MORROW'S RESTAURANT**
즐겁고 편안한 분위기에서 제공되는 맛있는 가정식 식사를 찾고 계십니까? Morrow's 레스토랑에 방문하십시오. 555-5789로 전화하시거나 book@morrows.com으로 이메일을 보내주셔서 예약하시고 무료 음료를 즐기십시오!	Looking for delicious, family-style meals served in a fun and casual atmosphere? Visit Morrow's restaurant. Call 555-5789 or send an e-mail to • book@morrows.com to make a reservation and enjoy a free beverage!

> **STEP 2-2**
> 다른 지문에서 두 번째 단서를 찾습니다.

수신: <book@morrows.com> 발신: <c.bastidas@kna.com> 첨부: 메뉴 항목	To: <book@morrows.com> From: <c.bastidas@kna.com> Attachment: Menu Items
제 이름은 Carla Bastidas이고, 저는 어제 12명을 위한 테이블을 예약하기 위해 전화했습니다. 다음 주 월요일 저녁 식사를 위한 주문을 첨부하였습니다. 감사합니다.	My name is Carla Bastidas, and I called • yesterday to book a table for 12. I have attached our order for next Monday's dinner. Thank you.

> **STEP 2-1**
> 핵심 어구를 포함한 지문에서 첫 번째 단서를 찾습니다.

Q. Ms. Bastidas에 대해 암시되는 것은? (A) 다음 주 월요일에 연설을 할 것이다. (B) 이전에 Morrow's 레스토랑에서 식사를 해본 적이 있다. (C) 무료 음료를 받을 것이다.	Q. What is suggested about Ms. Bastidas? • (A) She will give a speech next Monday. (B) She has eaten at Morrow's Restaurant in the past. (C) She will receive a complimentary drink. •

> **STEP 1**
> 질문의 핵심 어구를 통해 먼저 확인할 지문을 결정합니다.

> **STEP 3**
> 단서들을 조합한 내용과 부합하는 보기를 정답으로 선택합니다.

해설

STEP 1 질문을 읽고 질문의 핵심 어구인 Ms. Bastidas가 작성한 두 번째 지문인 이메일부터 확인합니다.

STEP 2-1 이메일의 'My name is Carla Bastidas, and I called ~ to book a table'에서 Ms. Bastidas가 테이블을 예약하기 위해 전화했다는 첫 번째 단서를 찾을 수 있습니다. 하지만 예약에 대한 세부 정보가 제시되지 않았으므로 다른 지문에서 두 번째 단서를 찾습니다.

STEP 2-2 광고의 'Call ~ to make a reservation and enjoy a free beverage!'에서 전화로 예약하면 무료 음료를 즐길 수 있다는 두 번째 단서를 찾을 수 있습니다.

STEP 3 Ms. Bastidas가 테이블을 예약하기 위해 전화했다는 첫 번째 단서와 전화로 예약하면 무료 음료를 즐길 수 있다는 두 번째 단서를 종합할 때, Ms. Bastidas가 무료 음료를 받을 것임을 추론할 수 있습니다. 따라서 두 가지 단서들을 조합한 내용과 부합하는 보기인 (C)를 정답으로 선택합니다.

Questions 01-05 refer to the following e-mails.

TO   Lucy Cruz <lcruz@carlington.edu.au>
FROM   Andrea Goodman <agoodman@carlington.edu.au>
SUBJECT Books to Collect
DATE   November 12

Dear Ms. Cruz,

I'm writing to let you know that the following books you reserved are now available.

- Barbara Mahoney, *Modern Human Behavior*
- Stanley Bradburn, *An Introduction to Psychology*
- Robert Chin, *Statistical Methods in Sociology*

These books can be collected from the front desk of the Carlington University library building any time between 9 A.M. and 6 P.M. If you cannot pick up the reserved books by tomorrow, we can hold them for one week at a cost of 50 cent per book. If they are not collected in that time, we will make them available to other borrowers.

Our records also show you have a book that is overdue with a 60 cent fine, so far. The title is *The Politics of Globalization* by Thomas Sanderson, and it was due on Friday, November 9th. Please bring this book with you when you come to pick up your reserved titles.

Please let me know if you have any further questions.

Regards,
Andrea Goodman
Library Services, Carlington University of Canberra

TO   Andrea Goodman <agoodman@carlington.edu.au>
FROM   Lucy Cruz <lcruz@carlington.edu.au>
SUBJECT Re: Books to Collect
DATE   November 12

Dear Ms. Goodman,

Thank you for letting me know that the titles I reserved are ready for collection. However, I must object to the claim that I have an overdue book. I am sure that I returned it on the date it was due, which was the last time I was at the library. I put it in the book return box just inside the main door. Perhaps it was not scanned correctly when staff emptied the box, and that is why it is reflected as overdue on my account.

I would appreciate it if a member of staff would take the time to double-check whether the book is currently on the shelf. I will be coming in to the library to collect the reserved books tomorrow afternoon, and I hope this situation can be resolved by then.

Yours truly,
Lucy Cruz

01 What is one purpose of the first e-mail?

(A) To announce the availability of some publications
(B) To ask a member for a donation
(C) To invite library users to an event
(D) To explain changes in late fee amounts

02 What is stated about library books?

(A) They were recently moved to another floor.
(B) They can be placed on hold for a small fee.
(C) They can be borrowed for up to one week.
(D) They cannot be returned on weekends.

03 In the second e-mail, the word "reflected" in paragraph 1, line 4, is closest in meaning to

(A) thought
(B) shown
(C) accompanied
(D) repeated

04 What is indicated about Ms. Cruz?

(A) She is majoring in psychology at college.
(B) She last visited the library on Friday.
(C) She usually goes to the library in the afternoon.
(D) She works at the university library part-time.

05 What does Ms. Cruz ask the library staff to do?

(A) Search for a book she returned
(B) Send her a reminder tomorrow
(C) Reserve an additional book for her
(D) Cancel one of her reservations

정답·해석·해설 p.191

Course 2 삼중 지문(Triple Passages)

영화제에서 출품 신청을 받습니다.

참가 신청서를 다운로드해서 주최자에게 이메일로 보내주세요.

영화제 출품 신청서

영화 제목: *The River*
감독 이름: Julie Hong
이메일: jhong@wall.com

영화 뉴스

이번 주 일요일 영화제 작품상 수상작인 *The River*가 개봉한다. 영화 개봉에 감독이 참석할 예정이다.

Q. 영화 개봉에 누가 참석할 것인가?
A. Julie Hong

영화제 출품에 대한 공고와 출품 신청서 양식, 수상작 개봉에 관한 기사입니다. 이처럼 PART 7에서는 세 개의 지문이 서로 연계된 **삼중 지문**이 출제되며, 두 개 이상의 지문에서 각각 단서를 찾아 조합해야 정답을 찾을 수 있는 연계 문제도 출제됩니다.

◪ 빈출 지문 유형

양식 & 양식 & 이메일   유람선 여행 관련 브로슈어 & 고객의 이용 후기 & 후기를 작성한 고객에게 직원이 보내는 이메일

이메일 & 양식 & 이메일   서비스 이용 관련 문의 이메일 & 서비스 이용 내역 양식 & 문의에 대한 답변 이메일

공고 & 양식 & 기사   행사 공고 & 행사 참가 양식 & 행사 관련 기사

◪ 연계 문제 풀이 전략

삼중 지문에서 두 개의 지문에서 각각 단서를 찾아 조합해야 정답을 찾을 수 있는 연계 문제는 아래와 같이 푸세요.

STEP 1 질문의 핵심 어구를 통해 먼저 확인할 지문을 결정합니다.

질문을 읽고 핵심 어구를 확인한 다음, 핵심 어구가 있는 지문부터 먼저 확인합니다.

STEP 2 핵심 어구를 포함한 지문에서 첫 번째 단서를 찾고, 나머지 지문 중 첫 번째 단서와 관련된 내용이 있는 지문을 먼저 확인해서 두 번째 단서를 찾습니다.

첫 번째 단서로만 정답을 찾기는 어려우므로 다른 지문에서 추가 단서를 찾습니다. 이때, 나머지 두 지문 중에서 첫 번째 단서와 관련된 내용이 있는 지문을 먼저 확인하여 단서를 찾습니다.

STEP 3 단서들을 조합한 내용과 부합하는 보기를 정답으로 선택합니다.

첫 번째 단서와 두 번째 단서를 조합하여 말하거나, 그 내용을 패러프레이징한 보기를 정답으로 선택합니다.

전략 적용

[공고 & 양식 & 기사]

<table>
<tr>
<td>

제14회 EyeCreate 영화제에서 출품 신청을 받습니다!

출품 신청서를 www.ecff.org에서 다운로드해서 1월 31일까지 주최자 Nadia Kahn에게 kahn@ecff.org로 이메일을 보내주십시오.

</td>
<td>

14th EyeCreate Film Festival Calls for Submissions!

Download an entry form at www.ecff.org and e-mail it to organizer Nadia Kahn at kahn@ecff.org by January 31.

</td>
</tr>
<tr>
<td>

제14회 EyeCreate 영화제
출품 신청서
영화 제목: *The River*
감독 이름: Julie Hong
이메일: jhong@wall.com

</td>
<td>

14th EyeCreate Film Festival
Entry Form
Film title: *The River* •
Director's name: Julie Hong
E-mail: jhong@wall.com

</td>
</tr>
<tr>
<td>

영화 뉴스
Jeff Oxley 작성

제14회 EyeCreate 영화제의 수상작 *The River*가 이번 주 일요일 샌프란시스코 Don Ericsson 영화관에서 개봉할 것이다. 감독과 주연 배우들이 참석할 것이다.

Q. 영화 개봉에 누가 참석할 것인가?

(A) Nadia Kahn
(B) Julie Hong
(C) Jeff Oxley

</td>
<td>

Film News
by Jeff Oxley

The winner of the 14th EyeCreate Film Festival, *The River*, will premiere this Sunday at the Don Ericsson Theater in San Francisco. The director and main cast members will be present.

Q. Who will be attending the movie premiere? •

(A) Nadia Kahn
(B) Julie Hong •
(C) Jeff Oxley

</td>
</tr>
</table>

> **STEP 2-2**
> 다른 지문에서 두 번째 단서를 찾습니다.

> **STEP 2-1**
> 핵심 어구를 포함한 지문에서 첫 번째 단서를 찾습니다.

> **STEP 1**
> 질문의 핵심 어구를 통해 먼저 확인할 지문을 결정합니다.

> **STEP 3**
> 단서들을 조합한 내용과 부합하는 보기를 정답으로 선택합니다.

해설 **STEP 1** 질문을 읽고, 질문의 핵심 어구인 attending the movie premiere가 언급된 기사부터 확인합니다.

STEP 2-1 기사의 'The winner of the 14th EyeCreate Film Festival, *The River*, will premiere'에서 영화제의 수상작인 *The River*가 개봉할 것이라고 했고, 'The director ~ will be present.'에서 감독이 참석할 것이라고 했으므로, 영화 개봉에 *The River*의 감독이 참석할 예정이라는 첫 번째 단서를 찾을 수 있습니다. 하지만 감독의 이름이 제시되지 않았으므로 다른 지문에서 추가 단서를 찾습니다. 이때, 나머지 두 지문 중에서 첫 번째 단서인 영화 제목 *The River*가 언급된 지문인 양식을 확인합니다.

STEP 2-2 양식의 'Film title: *The River*, Director's name: Julie Hong'에서 *The River*의 감독 이름이 Julie Hong이라는 두 번째 단서를 찾을 수 있습니다.

STEP 3 영화 개봉에 *The River*의 감독이 참석할 예정이라는 첫 번째 단서와 영화의 감독 이름이 Julie Hong이라는 두 번째 단서를 조합하면 영화 개봉에 참석하는 사람은 영화의 감독인 Julie Hong이라는 것을 알 수 있습니다. 따라서 두 가지 단서들을 조합한 내용과 부합하는 보기인 (B)를 정답으로 선택합니다.

한 권으로 끝내는 해커스 토익 700+ (LC+RC+VOCA)

Questions 01-05 refer to the following brochure, customer review, and e-mail.

Treat yourself to a Merrytime Cruise. To book, visit www.mtcruises.com.

Route	Cabin Type		
	Deluxe	Vista View	Suite
Merrytime Blue Seattle to Anchorage, Alaska	From $200	From $410	From $560
Merrytime Beachcomber Miami to Nassau, Bahamas	From $250	From $400	From $620
Merrytime Sky San Diego to Mazatlan, Mexico	From $180	From $380	From $580
Merrytime Salsa Miami to Ponce, Puerto Rico	From $250	From $400	From $620

*Book by April 1 for 5 percent off

---

https://www.cruisebeat.com

DEAL FINDER | **TRAVELER REVIEWS** | BLOG

Name: Maxine Roscoe
Review date: April 21
Rating: ★★★★☆

Review

We went on our first Merrytime Cruise last week thanks to Trip Away Travel (www.tripaway.com). The food on board was excellent and got even better in Mexico. My biggest complaint would be that the public areas got too loud at night. Luckily, our comfortable cabin ensured we slept undisturbed. I would happily do it again.

SUBMIT

To: Maxine Roscoe <m.roscoe@happymail.com>
From: Cruise Beat <moderator@cruisebeat.com>
Subject: Your review
Date: April 22

Dear Ms. Roscoe,

Thanks for submitting your cruise review. Unfortunately, it cannot be posted because it violated our site's rules. Please review the following.

All reviews must be:
• Relevant: Do not include information unrelated to the cruise.
• Firsthand: The review should be about your personal experience.
• Non-commercial: Reviews should not include recommendations of any outside services.
• Current: Reviews should be made within three months of the cruise.

Michael Miranda, Cruise Beat Moderator

---

01 What is NOT true about Merrytime Cruises?

(A) It travels to at least four different destinations.
(B) It has two journeys originating from the same city.
(C) It charges a fee of $200 or more for each cabin.
(D) It is running a limited-time promotional offer.

02 On which ship did Ms. Roscoe probably travel?

(A) *Merrytime Blue*
(B) *Merrytime Beachcomber*
(C) *Merrytime Sky*
(D) *Merrytime Salsa*

03 What is mentioned about Ms. Roscoe?

(A) She was pleased with the ship's accommodations.
(B) She traveled on a cruise as part of a business trip.
(C) She has taken a Merrytime Cruise once before.
(D) She was unhappy with the ship's entertainment options.

04 What most likely was the issue with Ms. Roscoe's review?

(A) It did not contain relevant information.
(B) It did not refer to her own vacation.
(C) It recommended a third-party business.
(D) It was posted too long after a cruise.

05 What does Mr. Miranda ask Ms. Roscoe to do?

(A) Close an account
(B) Sign a form
(C) Include an image
(D) Review a policy

정답·해석·해설 p.192

한 권으로 끝내는
해커스 토익 700+
LC+RC+VOCA

VOCABULARY

PART 5, 6

핵심 단어 리스트

01 **promotion** [prəmóuʃən] 승진, 홍보

earn a **promotion** to a management position
관리직으로의 승진을 얻다

02 **personnel** [pə̀:rsənél] 직원들, 인원

create a training program for all **personnel**
전 직원들을 위한 교육 프로그램을 만들다

03 **subscriber** [səbskráibər] 구독자, 가입자

deliver the magazine to the **subscriber**
구독자에게 잡지를 배달하다

04 **retirement** [ritáiərmənt] 은퇴, 퇴직

consider **retirement** after 30 years of service
30년의 근무 끝에 은퇴를 고려하다

05 **employment** [implɔ́imənt] 직장, 고용

look for **employment** in the engineering field
공학 분야에서 직장을 구하다

06 **refund** [rí:fʌnd] 환불

request a **refund** for a defective item
불량품에 대해 환불을 요청하다

07 **project** [prɑ́:dʒekt] 프로젝트, 계획(기획)된 일

set a deadline for a **project**
프로젝트를 위한 마감 기한을 설정하다

08 **construction** [kənstrʌ́kʃən] 건축, 공사

visit a **construction** site
건축 현장을 방문하다

09 **outlook** [áutluk] 관점, 전망

share the long-term **outlook** for growth
성장에 대한 장기적인 관점을 공유하다

10 **comparison** [kəmpǽrisn] 비교

make a **comparison** between the two products
두 제품을 비교하다

11 **relocation** [rì:loukéiʃən] 이전, 재배치

prepare for an upcoming office **relocation**
다가오는 사무실 이전을 준비하다

12 **career** [kəríər] 경력, 이력

advance one's **career** by taking relevant courses
관련 강습을 받음으로써 경력을 쌓다

13 **extent** [ikstént] 정도, 범위

agree to compromise to a certain **extent**
어느 정도까지 타협하는 데 동의하다

14 **reception** [risépʃən] 수령

confirm the **reception** of the package
소포의 수령을 확인하다

15 **greeting** [grí:tiŋ] 인사, 환영

receive a warm **greeting** from hotel staff
호텔 직원들로부터 따뜻한 인사를 받다

16 **separation** [sèpəréiʃən] 분리

discuss the **separation** of duties
직무의 분리에 대해 논의하다

17 **occupation** [ɑ̀:kjupéiʃən] 직업

decide to pursue a different **occupation**
다른 직업에 종사하기로 결정하다

18 **appliance** [əpláiəns] 가전기기

sell refrigerators and other kitchen **appliances**
냉장고와 다른 주방 가전기기를 팔다

19-20 **volume** [vɑ́:lju:m] 양 : **size** [saiz] 크기

volume은 분량이나 수량 등을 의미하고, size는 치수나 규모를 의미합니다.

increase the **volume** of sales 판매량을 증가시키다
measure the **size** of the room 방의 크기를 측정하다

토익 실전 문제

01 Stop-Mart does not provide ------- to customers wishing to return items, but it does offer store credit.

(A) proof
(B) condition
(C) instructions
(D) refunds

02 ------- has risen dramatically nationwide thanks to growth in the tourism industry.

(A) Announcement
(B) Employment
(C) Arrangement
(D) Treatment

03 Mr. Anderson's accountant warned him that he needs ------- between his business and personal financial accounts.

(A) devotion
(B) separation
(C) continuation
(D) deposit

04 CableTyme's ------- may change the settings on their accounts if they want to receive their bills electronically.

(A) subscribers
(B) manufacturers
(C) monitors
(D) programmers

05 More than 1,000 new ------- are expected to be hired for Frenton Industries' latest factory before the end of the summer.

(A) positions
(B) personnel
(C) components
(D) improvements

06 Many financial experts say that putting money into a savings account each month can help people prepare for -------.

(A) comparison
(B) implementation
(C) appreciation
(D) retirement

07 According to the memo released last week, the ------- of company headquarters to California will likely take place next year.

(A) outcome
(B) relocation
(C) warranty
(D) compensation

08 The ------- for Ms. Jonson's new bakery is positive as it is already becoming a popular lunch spot.

(A) force
(B) registration
(C) tradition
(D) outlook

09 Passenger ------- is expected to double once the new train terminal is completed.

(A) increase
(B) volume
(C) belief
(D) size

10 Ms. Weller has been in the same position for nearly six years and feels she deserves a -------.

(A) combination
(B) location
(C) distribution
(D) promotion

정답·해석·해설 **p.194**

핵심 단어 리스트

01 estimate [éstəmət] 견적, 추정(액)

request a price **estimate**
가격 견적을 요청하다

02 reminder [rimáindər] 상기시켜 주는 메모, 독촉장

receive a **reminder** about the event via e-mail
이메일로 행사에 대해 상기시켜 주는 메모를 받다

03 procedure [prəsí:dʒər] 절차, 방법

follow the accounting **procedures** closely
회계 절차를 충실히 따르다

04 asset [ǽset] 자산, 재산

have cash and other **assets** worth over $1 million
현금과 백만 달러가 넘는 가치의 자산을 갖고 있다

05 transaction [trænsǽkʃən] 거래, 처리

record all business **transactions** carefully
모든 사업 거래를 신중히 기록하다

06 enhancement [inhǽnsmənt] 향상, 증대

focus on the **enhancement** of the customer experience
고객 경험의 향상에 주력하다

07 challenge [tʃǽlindʒ] 도전

present a **challenge** for inexperienced designers
경험이 부족한 디자이너에게 도전이 되다

08 accomplishment [əkά:mpliʃmənt] 성과, 업적

celebrate a major **accomplishment**
중대한 성과를 축하하다

09 objection [əbdʒékʃən] 반대

raise an **objection** to the policy
정책에 반대하다

10 convenience [kənví:njəns] 편의, 편리

have several locations for the **convenience** of customers
고객의 편의를 위해 여러 장소에 소재하다

11 fee [fi:] 수수료, 요금

charge a **fee** for overweight baggage
중량 초과 수하물에 대해 수수료를 부과하다

12 publicity [pʌblísəti] 언론의 주목, 관심

attract media **publicity** with an exciting promotion
흥미로운 홍보 활동으로 언론의 주목을 끌다

13 composition [kὰmpəzíʃən] 구성 (요소)

change the **composition** of the committee
위원회의 구성을 변경하다

14 development [divéləpmənt] 개발, 발달

announce the **development** of a new medicine
신약의 개발을 발표하다

15 discretion [diskréʃən] 재량(권), 신중함

use their **discretion** to select a candidate
재량권을 사용하여 후보자를 선발하다

16 billing [bíliŋ] 청구서 발송, 거래 총액

confirm an address for **billing**
청구서 발송을 위해 주소를 확인하다

17 retention [riténʃən] (어떤 것을 잃지 않는) 유지, 보유

attempt to improve the **retention** of employees
직원 유지를 개선하는 것을 시도하다

18 candidate [kǽndidèit] 후보자, 지원자

interview a prospective **candidate**
유망한 후보자의 면접을 보다

19-20 recognition [rèkəgníʃən] 인정 : **permission** [pərmíʃən] 허가, 승인

recognition은 공로 등에 대한 인정을 의미하고, permission은 행동 등에 대한 허락을 의미합니다.

receive **recognition** for their work 일에 대해 인정을 받다
obtain **permission** from authorities 당국으로부터 허가를 받다

01 JenTel sends ------- to customers with overdue accounts, urging them to pay before interest is applied.

(A) benefits
(B) souvenirs
(C) reminders
(D) favors

02 First National Bank charges a fee for certain -------, such as the transfer of currency overseas.

(A) statements
(B) quarters
(C) transactions
(D) analyses

03 The property Bertel Corp. acquired last year is a valuable ------- as it will be profitable once it is developed.

(A) asset
(B) charge
(C) lease
(D) reward

04 During training, the supervisor explained the ------- for selling merchandise over the telephone.

(A) relationship
(B) loyalty
(C) recruitment
(D) procedure

05 The Web site states that Crystal Construction can provide on-site price ------- for residential work.

(A) estimates
(B) conflicts
(C) donations
(D) creations

06 To gain insight into potential employees, interviewers often ask them what their greatest ------- has been.

(A) background
(B) operation
(C) accomplishment
(D) effect

07 A gradual ------- in the value of PanAmerican Publishing over the years made investing in its stock worthwhile.

(A) calculation
(B) classification
(C) appearance
(D) enhancement

08 Ms. Bueller attained ------- as a professional photographer by working hard and creating a strong online presence.

(A) description
(B) permission
(C) recognition
(D) communication

09 Nobody on the board had an ------- to the expansion proposal, so the project may begin as soon as this summer.

(A) indication
(B) elevation
(C) objection
(D) aspiration

10 Factory managers can hire temporary staff workers at their own ------- rather than go through human resources.

(A) observation
(B) resistance
(C) dependence
(D) discretion

정답·해석·해설 **p.195**

핵심 단어 리스트

01 **performance**[pərfɔ́ːrməns] 공연, 수행

attend an award-winning **performance**
상을 받은 공연에 참석하다

02 **issue**[íʃuː] (출판물의) 호, 발행물

receive monthly **issues** of *Highlighter Gazette*
*Highlighter Gazette*지의 월간호를 받다

03 **process**[prάːses] 절차, 과정

begin the candidate selection **process**
후보자 선발 절차를 시작하다

04 **transfer**[trǽnsfəːr] 이동, 전근

make a money **transfer** from one account to another
한 계좌에서 다른 계좌로 자금을 이동시키다

05 **feasibility**[fìːzəbíləti] 실행 가능성, 실현 가능성

assess the project's **feasibility**
프로젝트의 실행 가능성을 평가하다

06 **flavor**[fléivər] 맛, 풍미

add a new strawberry **flavor** to the menu
메뉴에 새로운 딸기 맛을 추가하다

07 **discrepancy**[diskrépənsi] 불일치, 차이

discover a **discrepancy** with the sales figures
매출액에서 불일치를 발견하다

08 **article**[άːrtikəl] 기사

read a business **article** online
온라인으로 사업 관련 기사를 읽다

09 **celebration**[sèləbréiʃən] 축하 행사

hold a **celebration** of the victory
우승 축하 행사를 개최하다

10 **priority**[praiɔ́ːrəti] 우선순위

give emergency cases a higher **priority**
위급 상황들에 더 높은 우선순위를 두다

11 **handbook**[hǽndbùk] 안내서

consult the employee **handbook**
직원 안내서를 참고하다

12 **transformation**[trǽnsfɔːrméiʃən] 변화

witness an incredible **transformation**
놀라운 변화를 목격하다

13 **confirmation**[kὰːnfərméiʃən] 확인

send **confirmation** of the order within 24 hours
24시간 내에 주문 확인을 보내다

14 **allowance**[əláuəns] 수당

provide a travel **allowance** for business trips
출장을 위한 출장 수당을 제공하다

15 **competitor**[kəmpétətər] 경쟁사

beat a tough **competitor**
강력한 경쟁사를 이기다

16 **instruction**[instrʌ́kʃən] 사용 설명서

read the easy-to-follow assembly **instructions**
따라 하기 쉬운 조립 사용 설명서를 읽다

17 **background**[bǽkgràund] (예비) 지식, 배경

prefer a candidate with a **background** in accounting
회계의 지식을 가지고 있는 지원자를 선호하다

18 **misconception**[mìskənsépʃən] 오해

correct common myths and **misconceptions**
통속적인 미신과 오해를 바로잡다

19-20 **barrier**[bǽriər] 장벽, 장애물 : **restraint**[ristréint] 규제

barrier는 어떠한 일을 하는 데 있어 방해가 되는 장애물이나 문제 등을 의미하고, restraint는 제한하거나 통제하는 것을 의미합니다.
remove all trade **barriers** 모든 무역 장벽을 없애다
impose **restraints** on competition 경쟁에 규제를 가하다

🕐 제한 시간 5분

01 All those wishing to apply for a position with Mercer Corporation must follow the ------- outlined on its Web site.

(A) management
(B) exhibition
(C) process
(D) objective

02 City officials rejected Peterson Electrical's expansion plan, saying that protecting the local ecosystem was their top -------.

(A) space
(B) proposition
(C) foundation
(D) priority

03 Guests of the Dairy Farmers' Conference should contact the organizers to provide ------- of their attendance.

(A) consideration
(B) confirmation
(C) involvement
(D) realization

04 Ms. Pullman accepted the ------- to Devplan's London office in exchange for a substantial increase in her pay package.

(A) revision
(B) factor
(C) transfer
(D) itinerary

05 Despite the language -------, Mr. Vaughn believed his meeting with members of the Chinese branch went smoothly.

(A) expression
(B) development
(C) restraint
(D) barrier

06 Signing up for *Wildflower Today* during the month of April will earn new subscribers a free ------- of the magazine.

(A) exception
(B) application
(C) issue
(D) installation

07 Employees who notice a ------- between the hours they work and the money they earn should inform accounting immediately.

(A) discrepancy
(B) collaboration
(C) translation
(D) supplement

08 Rambat University invites all faculty, students, and alumni to a special ------- by the school's musical theater club.

(A) adjustment
(B) performance
(C) negotiation
(D) attachment

09 The ------- of completing construction on the museum by June 1 is in doubt as deadlines have already been missed.

(A) function
(B) assembly
(C) occupation
(D) feasibility

10 Bouvier Telecommunications provides a living ------- to all employees assigned to overseas branches.

(A) admission
(B) allowance
(C) demand
(D) purpose

정답·해석·해설 p.196

VOCABULARY PART 5, 6

DAY 03 [어휘] 명사 3

한 권으로 끝내는 해커스 토익 700+ (LC+RC+VOCA)

DAY 04 [어휘] 명사 4

핵심 단어 리스트

01 maintenance [méintənəns] 정비, 보수 관리

conduct **maintenance** on machinery
기계에 정비를 실시하다

02 progress [prá:gres] 진행 상황, 진전

provide an update on the assignment's **progress**
업무의 진행 상황에 대한 최신 정보를 제공하다

03 resolution [rèzəlú:ʃən] 결심, 결정, 결단력

make a **resolution** to improve performance
실적을 개선하기로 결심하다

04 specification [spèsəfikéiʃən] 세부 항목, 내역

list the **specifications** for the job
직무에 대한 세부 항목들을 나열하다

05 variation [vɛəriéiʃən] 차이, 변형(시킨 것)

notice a slight **variation** in color
색깔에 대한 약간의 차이를 알아채다

06 authority [əθɔ́:rəti] 당국, 권한

contact the relevant **authorities**
관련 당국에 연락을 취하다

07 disclosure [disklóuʒər] 공개

demand full **disclosure** of financial transactions
금융 거래의 완전한 공개를 요구하다

08 coverage [kʌ́vəridʒ] 보도, 범위

broadcast live **coverage** of an awards ceremony
시상식의 실시간 보도를 방송하다

09 interruption [ìntərʌ́pʃən] 중단, 방해

experience an **interruption** of services
서비스의 중단을 겪다

10 factor [fǽktər] 요인, 요소

consider economic **factors** before making a decision
결정을 내리기 전에 경제적인 요인들을 고려하다

11 premises [prémisiz] 구내, 토지

offer security for the factory's **premises**
공장 구내에 대한 안전을 제공하다

12 collaboration [kəlæbəréiʃən] 협력, 공동 작업

work in **collaboration** with a famous artist
유명한 예술가와 협력하여 작업하다

13 inquiry [inkwáiəri] 문의

submit an **inquiry** online
온라인으로 문의를 제출하다

14 attendee [ətèndí:] 참석자

give handouts to **attendees**
참석자들에게 유인물을 주다

15 timeline [táimlàin] 시간표

develop a **timeline** for a project
프로젝트를 위한 시간표를 만들다

16 reversal [rivə́:rsəl] 전환, 역전

cause a **reversal** of the company's poor sales
회사의 저조한 판매의 전환을 야기하다

17 complaint [kəmpléint] 불평, 불만

receive **complaints** about poor service
나쁜 서비스에 대한 불평을 접수하다

18 agenda [ədʒéndə] 안건, 의제

write an **agenda** for a meeting
회의를 위한 안건을 작성하다

19-20 replacement [ripléismənt] 대체(품), 교체(품) : **renovation** [renəvéiʃən] 수리, 수선

replacement는 기존의 것을 새로운 것으로 바꾸는 것을 의미하고, renovation은 기존의 것을 더 좋게 보수하고 고치는 것을 의미합니다.
request a **replacement** 대체품을 요청하다
pass a lobby under **renovation** 수리 중인 로비를 통과하다

01 As well as running a live chat service, Zap Electronics provides responses to typical ------- on its FAQ page.

(A) notifications
(B) examples
(C) behaviors
(D) inquiries

02 Local vegetable producers have had smaller harvests than usual this summer due to unseasonable ------- in temperature.

(A) rewards
(B) validations
(C) variations
(D) exchanges

03 The elevator in the Sutton Building will be unavailable until later this afternoon as staff members are performing ------- on it.

(A) advancement
(B) maintenance
(C) direction
(D) appreciation

04 Anyone wishing to operate a restaurant must undergo a thorough inspection by the city's -------.

(A) evaluations
(B) authorities
(C) availabilities
(D) quotations

05 Arva Manufacturing's executive committee made a ------- to reduce production costs by 20 percent this year.

(A) resolution
(B) situation
(C) transition
(D) reservation

06 Applicants are advised to consult the company Web site for the ------- of the position.

(A) implications
(B) assortments
(C) specifications
(D) occasions

07 Because Ms. Petraki is a new employee, the manager still regularly checks on the ------- she is making with her projects.

(A) progress
(B) condition
(C) production
(D) environment

08 NTTV, a 24-hour news channel, achieved record ratings for its detailed ------- of the provincial election.

(A) storage
(B) engagement
(C) combination
(D) coverage

09 Due to a lack of inventory, ------- of faulty or malfunctioning merchandise may be delayed for up to one week.

(A) discharge
(B) replacement
(C) recommendation
(D) renovation

10 Hollman's Store guarantees that there will be no ------- of information provided by shoppers to any third parties.

(A) disclosure
(B) caution
(C) execution
(D) measure

정답·해석·해설 p.196

VOCABULARY PART 5, 6

DAY 04 [어휘] 명사 4

한 권으로 끝내는 해커스 토익 700+ (LC+RC+VOCA)

핵심 단어 리스트

01 **contract**[kántrækt] 계약(서)

sign a temporary employment **contract**
임시 고용 계약서에 서명하다

02 **submission**[səbmíʃən] 제출, 제기

write a proposal for **submission** to the board of directors
이사회에 제출할 제안서를 쓰다

03 **shortage**[ʃɔ́ːrtidʒ] 부족

deal with a **shortage** of capital
자금의 부족에 대처하다

04 **capacity**[kəpǽsəti] (생산) 능력, 수용력

grow beyond its **capacity** to supply food
식량을 공급할 능력 이상으로 증대하다

05 **distribution**[dìstrəbjúːʃən] 유통, 배부, 분포

supervise **distribution** of the merchandise
상품의 유통을 감독하다

06 **safety**[séifti] 안전, 치안

ensure the **safety** of workers
직원들의 안전을 보장하다

07 **facility**[fəsíləti] 시설, 기관

renovate a healthcare **facility**
의료 시설을 보수하다

08 **contestant**[kəntéstənt] (대회 등의) 참가자

introduce this year's **contestants** for the *Bookman Prize*
Bookman 상을 위한 올해의 참가자들을 소개하다

09 **reputation**[rèpjutéiʃən] 평판

establish a **reputation** for reliable service
신뢰할 수 있는 서비스로 평판을 쌓다

10 **excellence**[éksələns] 우수성, 탁월함

aim to achieve **excellence**
우수성을 성취하는 것을 목표로 하다

11 **assignment**[əsáinmənt] 과제, 업무, 임무

work on a major **assignment**
중요한 과제를 하다

12 **proposal**[prəpóuzəl] 제안(서)

accept a project **proposal**
프로젝트 제안서를 수락하다

13 **entrance**[éntrəns] 입구

buy a ticket at the **entrance**
입구에서 표를 사다

14 **negotiator**[nigóuʃièitər] 협상가

require a skilled **negotiator**
노련한 협상가를 필요로 하다

15 **shareholder**[ʃέərhòuldər] 주주

meet with **shareholders** annually
매년 주주들과 만나다

16 **norm**[nɔːrm] 규범

go against the **norm**
규범에 위배되다

17 **delight**[diláit] 기쁨, 즐거움

watch the city's firework display with **delight**
시의 불꽃놀이를 기쁘게 보다

18 **petition**[pətíʃən] 청원서, 탄원서

submit a **petition** to change a policy
정책을 변경하기 위해 청원서를 제출하다

19-20 **request**[rikwést] 요청 : **claim**[kleim] 청구, 신청

request는 상대방에게 무엇을 해 달라는 요청을 의미하고, claim은 보상금 등에 대한 청구나 신청을 의미합니다.

make a **request** for time off 휴가를 위한 요청을 하다
file an insurance **claim** 보험 청구를 제기하다

제한 시간 5분

01 Ms. Stein's professionalism and excellent performance have contributed to her positive ------- among clients.

(A) characteristic
(B) selection
(C) expectation
(D) reputation

02 Anyone interested in becoming a ------- in the upcoming Drummondville Cooking Challenge can register online.

(A) symbol
(B) reference
(C) specialist
(D) contestant

03 *The Impreda Gazette*, a daily newspaper, does not have wide -------, so many people read the articles online.

(A) exclusion
(B) inspiration
(C) transportation
(D) distribution

04 When reserving her ticket, Ms. Lucas made a special ------- to the airline for a vegetarian in-flight meal.

(A) claim
(B) problem
(C) request
(D) policy

05 The deadline for the ------- of applications for the position of regional director at Hall Advertising is October 5.

(A) motivation
(B) satisfaction
(C) promotion
(D) submission

06 Students who need help completing the final ------- may consult Professor Oldman for clarification and advice at any time.

(A) commitment
(B) assignment
(C) appointment
(D) incident

07 The machinery is currently operating at full ------- and could malfunction if it is programmed to produce more.

(A) defect
(B) report
(C) capacity
(D) addition

08 A ------- of housing in Abiline led City Council to approve the new residential development.

(A) portion
(B) separation
(C) shortage
(D) prediction

09 Shelby Corp and Entemann Associates hired a professional ------- to develop a solution for their ongoing dispute.

(A) debater
(B) negotiator
(C) supplier
(D) patron

10 Local environmental groups have written a ------- to stop the construction of a dam along the Wahatchee River.

(A) contribution
(B) memorial
(C) preference
(D) petition

정답·해석·해설 **p.197**

DAY 06 [어휘] 동사 1

핵심 단어 리스트

01 **remain** [riméin] 계속 ~이다, 남아 있다

remain seated until the plane comes to a full stop
비행기가 완전히 멈출 때까지 계속 앉아 있다

02 **address** [ədrés] (문제 등을) 다루다

address any concerns that arise
발생하는 모든 문제를 다루다

03 **accelerate** [æksélərèit] 가속화하다

accelerate the growth of the business with investment
투자로 사업의 성장을 가속화하다

04 **commence** [kəméns] 시작하다

wait for the ceremony to **commence**
식이 시작하기를 기다리다

05 **join** [dʒɔin] 가입하다, 합류하다

join a trade union
노동 조합에 가입하다

06 **maximize** [mǽksəmàiz] 극대화하다

maximize opportunities for publicity
홍보를 위한 기회를 극대화하다

07 **memorize** [méməràiz] 암기하다

memorize the entrance code for the store's back door
상점 뒷문의 출입 암호를 암기하다

08 **prove** [pruːv] 증명하다, 입증하다

prove a theory with evidence
증거를 가지고 이론을 증명하다

09 **strive** [straiv] 노력하다, 분투하다

strive to overcome obstacles
장애물을 극복하기 위해 노력하다

10 **grant** [grænt] 승인하다, 수여하다

grant access to a database
데이터베이스로의 접근을 승인하다

11 **recycle** [riːsáikəl] 재활용하다, 재사용하다

recycle all metal and cardboard containers
모든 금속과 판지 용기들을 재활용하다

12 **acquire** [əkwáiər] 획득하다, 얻다

acquire additional property to develop
개발할 추가적인 토지를 획득하다

13 **alert** [əlɔ́ːrt] 알리다, 경고하다

alert the public about the change
대중에게 변경에 대해 알리다

14 **redeem** [ridíːm] (상품권 등을) 현금으로 바꾸다

redeem reward points
보상 포인트를 현금으로 바꾸다

15 **endure** [indjúər] 견디다

endure a long meeting
긴 회의를 견디다

16 **ship** [ʃip] 운송하다

ship an item overseas
물품을 해외로 운송하다

17 **guarantee** [gærəntíː] 보장하다

guarantee a product's quality
제품의 품질을 보장하다

18 **visualize** [víʒuəlàiz] 예상하다, 시각화하다

visualize the future of the area's changing landscape
지역의 변화하는 풍경의 미래를 예상하다

19-20 **purchase** [pə́ːrtʃəs] 구매하다 : **renew** [rinjúː] 갱신하다

purchase는 물건 등을 새로 사는 것을 의미하고, renew는 이미 갖고 있던 것을 새롭게 하는 것을 의미합니다.
purchase the latest model 최신 모델을 구매하다
renew the lease for another year 임대차 계약을 1년 갱신하다

01 Although most employees leave the office at 6:00 P.M., a few ------- for a while to get ahead on the next day's work.

(A) pause
(B) occupy
(C) remain
(D) result

02 As rumors about Diablo Holdings' problems spread, the decline of its stock price ------- greatly.

(A) released
(B) motivated
(C) accelerated
(D) integrated

03 The Wallaceburg Transit Company has been granted approval to ------- construction on a new subway line.

(A) trust
(B) collect
(C) embark
(D) commence

04 State-of-the-art machinery was ordered for the factory in an effort to ------- production.

(A) alternate
(B) inspire
(C) maximize
(D) designate

05 Ms. Morrison was determined to ------- to her boss that she could handle more responsibility at work.

(A) prove
(B) fulfill
(C) hire
(D) reform

06 During the conference call, the CEO ------- the challenges that all oil and natural gas companies are currently facing.

(A) restricted
(B) obliged
(C) addressed
(D) retained

07 The representative from Frampton Construction ------- that the renovation would be finished by the end of the week.

(A) guaranteed
(B) nominated
(C) eliminated
(D) advised

08 Mr. Pelton and his wife hope to ------- their first home with money they have saved up over the last 20 years.

(A) acquire
(B) compose
(C) elevate
(D) insert

09 ------- items over the Internet using a credit card has become more popular thanks to improved online security.

(A) Renewing
(B) Purchasing
(C) Recording
(D) Portraying

10 All runners at the Busan Marathon should be prepared to ------- heat and strong wind on the marathon course.

(A) endure
(B) initiate
(C) pressure
(D) persist

정답·해석·해설 p.198

핵심 단어 리스트

01 **deliver** [dilívər] 배달하다

deliver the package to the address provided
제공된 주소로 소포를 배달하다

02 **expire** [ikspáiər] 만료되다

renew a membership card that is about to **expire**
곧 만료될 회원증을 갱신하다

03 **undergo** [ʌndərgóu] 받다, 경험하다

undergo a major renovation
큰 수리를 받다

04 **consent** [kənsént] 동의하다, 허락하다

consent to a thorough background check
철저한 배경 조사에 동의하다

05 **assure** [əʃúər] 보장하다, 안심시키다

assure clients of the product's quality
고객들에게 제품의 품질을 보장하다

06 **increase** [inkrí:s] 증가시키다, 인상되다

increase the budget for the new construction project
새로운 건설 프로젝트의 예산을 증가시키다

07 **indicate** [índikèit] 명시하다, 나타내다

indicate preferences on the form
양식에 선호도를 명시하다

08 **rate** [reit] 평가하다

rate an experience at a hotel
호텔에서의 경험을 평가하다

09 **reclaim** [rikléim] 되찾다

reclaim a lost item from the Lost and Found Office
분실물 보관소에서 잃어버린 물품을 되찾다

10 **tolerate** [tá:lərèit] 용인하다, 견디다

tolerate a moderate amount of risk while investing
투자하는 동안 적당한 정도의 위험을 용인하다

11 **divide** [diváid] 나누다

divide the participants into groups of four
참여자들을 4명의 그룹으로 나누다

12 **affect** [əfékt] ~에 영향을 미치다

affect national economy positively
국가 경제에 긍정적으로 영향을 미치다

13 **depart** [dipá:rt] 출발하다, 떠나다

depart promptly at 7:30 A.M.
정확히 오전 7시 30분에 출발하다

14 **eliminate** [ilímənèit] 제거하다, 없애다

eliminate environmental pollution
환경 오염을 제거하다

15 **reject** [ridʒékt] 거절하다, 거부하다

reject a loan application
대출 신청을 거절하다

16 **attract** [ətrǽkt] 끌어모으다, 유인하다

attract many tourists to the area
지역에 많은 관광객들을 끌어모으다

17 **classify** [klǽsəfài] 분류하다, 구분하다

classify clothing according to size
사이즈에 따라 옷을 분류하다

18 **withdraw** [wiðdrɔ́:] (계좌에서 돈을) 인출하다

withdraw funds from an ATM
현금 자동 입출금기에서 돈을 인출하다

19-20 **donate** [dóuneit] 기부하다 : **support** [səpɔ́:rt] 지지하다, 후원하다

donate는 기부하는 돈이나 물건을 목적어로 취하고, support는 지지하는 대상을 목적어로 취합니다.
donate money to a charitable organization 자선 단체에 돈을 기부하다
support the construction project 건설 프로젝트를 지지하다

01 Before proceeding to the immigration area, passengers are required to ------- their luggage in the arrivals terminal.

(A) refund
(B) reduce
(C) reflect
(D) reclaim

02 Customers must ------- to allow any personal information they reveal to be used by a third party.

(A) regard
(B) assess
(C) handle
(D) consent

03 Designer handbags are ------- as luxury items and are therefore subject to additional taxes.

(A) classified
(B) compensated
(C) substituted
(D) adopted

04 The subway operator ------- passengers that the train would begin running again after a brief delay.

(A) forecast
(B) assured
(C) recruited
(D) deviated

05 Under the new attendance policy at Thompson Furniture, tardiness will not be ------- more than twice per month.

(A) tolerated
(B) attempted
(C) misplaced
(D) innovated

06 All industrial plants in the Harper Valley will ------- inspections after the new environmental law is passed.

(A) enroll
(B) submit
(C) undergo
(D) attach

07 Potential candidates for the position are asked to ------- their availability on the application form.

(A) entitle
(B) propose
(C) negotiate
(D) indicate

08 Ms. Connors decided to watch *The Floodgates* because it was one of this year's most highly ------- films.

(A) rated
(B) meant
(C) summarized
(D) solved

09 The Web site for the Mowatsville town hall lists a number of charitable organizations in the community that people can ------- to.

(A) donate
(B) obtain
(C) support
(D) invite

10 Your Freebird Airways membership will ------- and become unusable unless the fee is paid within 14 days.

(A) succeed
(B) expire
(C) decrease
(D) extend

정답·해석·해설 **p.199**

VOCABULARY PART 5, 6

DAY 07 [어휘] 동사 2

한 권으로 끝내는 해커스 토익 700+ (LC+RC+VOCA)

핵심 단어 리스트

01 **exceed**[iksíːd] 초과하다, 넘다

exceed the budget for the construction project
건축 프로젝트의 예산을 초과하다

02 **finalize**[fáinəlàiz] 완성하다, 마무리하다

finalize plans for the reconstruction of the lobby
로비의 재건축을 위한 설계도를 완성하다

03 **present**[prizént] 수여하다, 주다

present an award to the winner
승자에게 상을 수여하다

04 **disrupt**[disrʌ́pt] 지장을 주다, 방해하다

disrupt service temporarily
일시적으로 서비스에 지장을 주다

05 **argue**[áːrgjuː] 주장하다, 언쟁하다

argue in favor of the new policy
새로운 정책을 지지하는 주장을 하다

06 **assess**[əsés] 평가하다

assess the value of the jewelry
보석의 가치를 평가하다

07 **divert**[divə́ːrt] 다른 곳으로 돌리다, 우회시키다

divert the phone call to another line
전화를 다른 곳으로 돌리다

08 **establish**[istǽbliʃ] 설립하다, 수립하다

establish an organization for local farmers
지역 농부들을 위한 단체를 설립하다

09 **suspect**[səspékt] 의심하다

suspect someone of cheating on an exam
시험에서 부정 행위를 했다고 누군가를 의심하다

10 **rephrase**[riːfréiz] 바꾸어 말하다

rephrase the question for clarity
명확성을 위해 질문을 바꾸어 말하다

11 **expand**[ikspǽnd] 확장시키다

expand the business into Europe
사업을 유럽으로 확장시키다

12 **enclose**[inklóuz] 동봉하다

enclose the application form with the letter
편지에 신청서를 동봉하다

13 **verify**[vérəfài] 확인하다, 증명하다

verify the validity of a license
자격증의 유효성을 확인하다

14 **omit**[oumít] 생략하다, 누락하다

omit the introductions and begin the presentation
도입부를 생략하고 발표를 시작하다

15 **capture**[kǽptʃər] 획득하다, 포획하다

capture the majority of the votes
투표수의 대부분을 획득하다

16 **cite**[sait] 인용하다

cite the findings from a recent study
최근 연구로부터 결과를 인용하다

17 **appoint**[əpɔ́int] 임명하다, 지명하다

appoint a new head of security
새로운 보안 부장을 임명하다

18 **demonstrate**[démənstrèit] 시연하다, 설명하다

demonstrate a technique to trainees
교육생들에게 기술을 시연하다

19-20 **cancel**[kǽnsəl] 취소하다 : **suspend**[səspénd] 중단하다, 정지하다

cancel은 어떠한 일이 더는 일어나거나 연장되지 않도록 취소하는 것을 의미하고, suspend는 임시로 중단하는 것을 의미합니다.
cancel the magazine subscription 잡지 구독을 취소하다
suspend telephone service for a month 한 달 동안 전화 서비스를 중단하다

01 Some members of the Transportation Authority ------- that building a new subway line will be too costly.

(A) execute
(B) generate
(C) reserve
(D) argue

02 The CEO of Candy Clothing ------- Ms. Jones as the board of directors' new chairperson.

(A) discovered
(B) appointed
(C) achieved
(D) influenced

03 Signs were placed by the side of Florin Avenue to ------- traffic away from some ongoing roadwork.

(A) reveal
(B) expend
(C) divert
(D) affiliate

04 Mr. Harris is in a very important meeting with a client at the moment and must not be ------- for any reason.

(A) corrupted
(B) complained
(C) disrupted
(D) reminded

05 Several nonessential parts of the new film may be ------- during the editing process if it proves to be too long.

(A) catered
(B) omitted
(C) deserved
(D) afforded

06 Vermaco may hire a consultant to ------- the overall efficiency of employees in the next quarter.

(A) minimize
(B) commit
(C) assess
(D) abolish

07 Alida Technologies will hold an information session for potential clients in order to ------- its products and services.

(A) dedicate
(B) demonstrate
(C) house
(D) allocate

08 The corporate budget was adjusted when the cost of manufacturing ------- the amount that had been designated for it.

(A) examined
(B) emerged
(C) expected
(D) exceeded

09 Manuel Rivera ------- the city's first Mexican restaurant at the Northside Mall nearly 50 years ago.

(A) established
(B) deposited
(C) decided
(D) incurred

10 Due to the occurrence of suspicious transactions, several accounts at Herald Bank have been ------- until further notice.

(A) canceled
(B) suspended
(C) moved
(D) formalized

정답·해석·해설 **p.200**

VOCABULARY PART 5, 6

DAY 08 [어휘] 동사 3

한 권으로 끝내는 해커스 토익 700+ (LC+RC+VOCA)

DAY 09 [어휘] 동사 4

핵심 단어 리스트

01 **access** [ǽkses] 접근하다, 들어가다

access confidential medical records
기밀 진료 기록에 접근하다

02 **ensure** [inʃúər] 반드시 ~하게 하다, 보장하다

ensure that all the doors are locked
모든 문이 반드시 잠기게 하다

03 **feature** [fíːtʃər] (특별히) 포함하다, 특징으로 삼다

feature several exciting upgrades
몇 가지 흥미로운 개선을 포함하다

04 **contend** [kənténd] 주장하다, 다투다

contend that more staff is required
더 많은 직원이 필요하다고 주장하다

05 **determine** [ditə́ːrmin] 알아내다, 결정하다

determine the cause of the delay
지연의 원인을 알아내다

06 **award** [əwɔ́ːrd] 주다, 수여하다

award compensation for a defective item
결함이 있는 물품에 대해 보상을 주다

07 **decline** [dikláin] 거부하다, 감소하다

decline an invitation for dinner
저녁 식사 초대를 거부하다

08 **discuss** [diskʌ́s] 논의하다

meet to **discuss** hiring plans
채용 계획을 논의하기 위해 만나다

09 **review** [rivjúː] 검토하다, 확인하다

review a budget before submission
제출 전에 예산을 검토하다

10 **serve** [səːrv] 봉사하다, (음식 등을) 제공하다

serve the city as the mayor
시장으로서 시에 봉사하다

11 **obtain** [əbtéin] 입수하다, 획득하다

obtain materials from the supplier
공급업자로부터 재료를 입수하다

12 **minimize** [mínəmàiz] 최소화하다

minimize environmental impacts
환경 영향을 최소화하다

13 **merge** [məːrdʒ] 합병하다, 통합하다

merge the two companies
두 회사를 합병하다

14 **duplicate** [djúːpləkèit] 복사하다, 복제하다

duplicate an important document
중요한 문서를 복사하다

15 **pursue** [pərsúː] 추구하다, 계속하다

vigorously **pursue** policy changes
정책 변경을 강력하게 추구하다

16 **host** [houst] 주최하다

host a small gathering for friends
친구들을 위해 작은 모임을 주최하다

17 **gather** [gǽðər] 수집하다, 모으다

use a survey to **gather** information
정보를 수집하기 위해 설문 조사를 이용하다

18 **reset** [risét] 재설정하다

reset a password once a month
한 달에 한 번씩 비밀번호를 재설정하다

19-20 **inform** [infɔ́ːrm] 알려주다 : **announce** [ənáuns] 발표하다, 공지하다

inform은 바로 뒤에 알려주는 대상이 오고, announce는 바로 뒤에 알리는 내용이 옵니다.

inform voters about where to register 투표자들에게 어디에서 등록해야 하는지 알려주다
announce plans for a new community center 새로운 시민 문화 회관에 관한 계획을 발표하다

토익 실전 문제

01 Although sales of the XCR smartphone were initially strong, they have begun to ------- in recent months.

(A) expand
(B) decline
(C) forward
(D) supplement

02 The Lennox Foundation has been ------- the Brownsville community through its various fundraising efforts for 50 years.

(A) achieving
(B) serving
(C) organizing
(D) operating

03 Walvington's new park will ------- hiking trails and an orchard when it opens to the public this fall.

(A) feature
(B) decorate
(C) realize
(D) envision

04 Sanger Manufacturing will save a lot of money if every department ------- its operating costs.

(A) acclaims
(B) intensifies
(C) minimizes
(D) calculates

05 The human resources department ------- a ban on the use of the office photocopier for personal documents.

(A) descended
(B) announced
(C) utilized
(D) informed

06 The addition of a new conference room to the third floor will ------- there is enough space for meetings.

(A) enlarge
(B) ensure
(C) accomplish
(D) permit

07 The BGW Industrial Bank and National One ------- last year after several months of intense negotiation.

(A) modified
(B) acquired
(C) accumulated
(D) merged

08 Despite strong resistance from the general public, the countries decided to ------- a more open trade network.

(A) pursue
(B) conform
(C) suspect
(D) exchange

09 After examining the stock list, Mr. Jacobs ------- that there was a problem with the inventory system.

(A) proceeded
(B) used
(C) spent
(D) determined

10 In her book *Stacked*, Ms. Atwood ------- that the country's financial crisis is a result of government policies from decades ago.

(A) founds
(B) reduces
(C) contends
(D) guarantees

정답·해석·해설 p.201

VOCABULARY PART 5, 6

DAY 09 [어휘] 동사 4

한 권으로 끝내는 해커스 토익 700+ (LC+RC+VOCA)

핵심 단어 리스트

01 **diverse**[divə́:rs] 다양한, 여러 가지의

have a culturally **diverse** population
문화적으로 다양한 인구를 가지고 있다

02 **excessive**[iksésiv] 매우 많은, 과도한

receive an **excessive** amount of mail
매우 많은 양의 편지를 받다

03 **prestigious**[prestídʒəs] 일류의, 명망 있는

attend a **prestigious** educational institution
일류의 교육 기관에 다니다

04 **comprehensive**[kàːmprihénsiv] 종합적인, 포괄적인

create a **comprehensive** evaluation system
종합적인 평가 시스템을 구축하다

05 **resistant**[rizístənt] ~에 강한, 저항하는

be **resistant** to minor climate change
작은 기후 변화에 강하다

06 **elaborate**[ilǽbərət] 복잡한, 공을 들인

follow a long and **elaborate** procedure
길고 복잡한 절차를 따르다

07 **current**[kə́:rənt] 현재의

address **current** concerns first
현재의 걱정거리들을 먼저 다루다

08 **revised**[riváizd] 수정된, 변경된

release a **revised** price estimate
수정된 가격 견적서를 공개하다

09 **affordable**[əfɔ́:rdəbəl] 가격이 알맞은, 저렴한

seek **affordable** housing in the city center
도심에서 가격이 알맞은 주택을 찾다

10 **practical**[prǽktikəl] 실용적인

offer trainees **practical** advice
교육생들에게 실용적인 조언을 제공하다

11 **time-consuming**[táimkənsùːmiŋ] 시간이 걸리는

work on a **time-consuming** task
시간이 걸리는 업무를 하다

12 **relevant**[réləvənt] 관련 있는, 적절한

discover information **relevant** to the investigation
조사에 관련 있는 정보를 발견하다

13 **adequate**[ǽdikwət] 충분한, 적절한

prepare an **adequate** amount of food
충분한 양의 음식을 준비하다

14 **minor**[máinər] 가벼운, 중요치 않은

experience a **minor** setback
가벼운 차질을 겪다

15 **productive**[prədʌ́ktiv] 생산적인

reward the highly **productive** team
매우 생산적인 팀에게 보상하다

16 **flexible**[fléksəbəl] 유동적인

prefer to have **flexible** working hours
유동적인 근무 시간을 선호하다

17 **loyal**[lɔ́iəl] 충성스러운, 충실한

offer special deals to **loyal** customers
충성스러운 고객들에게 특별한 거래를 제공하다

18 **fertile**[fə́:rtl] 비옥한, 기름진

plant crops in **fertile** soil
비옥한 토지에 작물을 심다

19-20 **vacant**[véikənt] 빈, 사람이 없는 : **hollow**[hά:lou] 속이 빈

vacant는 방, 좌석, 자리 등과 같은 곳에 사람이 없다는 것을 의미하고, hollow는 사물의 속이 텅 비어 있다는 것을 의미합니다.
book a **vacant** hotel room 빈 호텔 방을 예약하다
manufacture **hollow** pipes for plumbing systems 배수 설비를 위해 속이 빈 파이프를 제조하다

01 The building contractor quoted his price for Mr. Norman, who found it to be unreasonably -------.

(A) attentive
(B) excessive
(C) verifiable
(D) spacious

02 NRT Agricultural is developing new technologies that will make crops more ------- to pests and disease.

(A) significant
(B) acceptable
(C) thorough
(D) resistant

03 The ------- proposal includes all of the changes that were agreed upon with the client at the last meeting.

(A) acute
(B) revised
(C) aspiring
(D) domestic

04 The genetic research team received a ------- award that included a generous grant from Cardinal University.

(A) prestigious
(B) grateful
(C) keen
(D) complicated

05 Attendees of the accounting symposium should arrive at the lecture hall early or else there may not be any ------- seats left.

(A) hollow
(B) insincere
(C) vacant
(D) updated

06 The ------- car insurance policy covers theft as well as any damage caused by another driver or natural disasters.

(A) fortunate
(B) incoming
(C) wholesome
(D) comprehensive

07 Customers on a budget will enjoy shopping at Slick World as the clothing it sells is both fashionable and -------.

(A) former
(B) affordable
(C) receptive
(D) instant

08 A ------- selection of foods from around the world will be on sale at the Blumburg International Culinary Festival.

(A) positive
(B) diverse
(C) correct
(D) technical

09 The biggest problem with the ------- filing system is that it takes too long to find documents.

(A) steady
(B) eager
(C) captivating
(D) current

10 All candidates must undergo an ------- hiring procedure that includes several rounds of interviews and tests.

(A) accountable
(B) invalid
(C) elaborate
(D) interested

정답·해석·해설 **p.202**

핵심 단어 리스트

01 **renowned**[rináund] 유명한, 명성 있는

visit a region **renowned** for its vineyards
포도밭으로 유명한 지역을 방문하다

02 **valid**[vǽlid] 유효한, 타당한

show a **valid** piece of identification
유효한 신분증을 보여주다

03 **frustrating**[frʌ́streitiŋ] 불만스러운, 좌절스러운

experience a **frustrating** shipping delay
불만스러운 배송 지연을 겪다

04 **sole**[soul] 유일한, 혼자의

select a **sole** winner from the ten finalists
10명의 최종 후보 중에서 유일한 우승자를 선택하다

05 **proficient**[prəfíʃənt] 능숙한, 숙달한

become **proficient** in multiple languages
다양한 언어에 능숙하게 되다

06 **lively**[láivli] 활기찬, 강렬한

participate in a **lively** debate
활기찬 토론에 참석하다

07 **economic**[èkəná:mik] 경제적인, 경제성이 있는

discuss the **economic** impact of a tax cut
감세의 경제적인 영향을 논하다

08 **relaxing**[rilǽksiŋ] 나른한

enjoy a **relaxing** day off
나른한 휴일을 즐기다

09 **profitable**[prá:fitəbl] 수익성 있는

operate a **profitable** franchise
수익성 있는 가맹점을 운영하다

10 **wasteful**[wéistfəl] 낭비적인, 소모적인

eliminate **wasteful** spending
낭비적인 지출을 없애다

11 **alternative**[ɔːltə́ːrnətiv] 다른, 대안적인

take an **alternative** route
다른 길로 가다

12 **domestic**[dəméstik] 국내의

anticipate an increase in **domestic** demand
국내 수요 증가를 예상하다

13 **respectful**[rispéktfəl] 존중하는, 공손한

be **respectful** of others' opinions
다른 사람들의 의견을 존중하다

14 **sizable**[sáizəbl] 상당한

maintain a **sizable** lead over competitors
경쟁자들보다 상당한 우위를 유지하다

15 **disappointing**[dìsəpɔ́intiŋ] 실망스러운

report **disappointing** earnings results
실망스러운 수익 결과를 보고하다

16 **conventional**[kənvénʃənəl] 관습적인, 전통적인

apply **conventional** monetary policies
관습적인 화폐 정책을 적용하다

17 **fair**[fɛər] 공정한, 공평한

charge a **fair** price for the used car
중고차에 대해 공정한 가격을 매기다

18 **distinctive**[distíŋktiv] 독특한

feature a **distinctive** pattern
독특한 무늬를 특징으로 하다

19-20 **original**[ərídʒənəl] 원래의, 최초의 : **introductory**[ìntrədʌ́ktəri] 입문의, 서론의

original은 대상이 변경 또는 수정되기 전의 최초 또는 원래의 것을 의미하고, introductory는 처음 또는 맨 앞에 오는 것을 의미합니다.

be more popular than the **original** version of the song 원래 버전의 노래보다 더 유명하다
attend an **introductory** class for computer science 컴퓨터 공학의 입문 수업을 듣다

01 Mr. Brooks became the ------- owner of Vera Travel after his partner left the company last year.

(A) idle
(B) sole
(C) ample
(D) complex

02 The new tax legislation is expected to provide low-income families with greater ------- security.

(A) statistical
(B) hesitant
(C) mechanical
(D) economic

03 Each of the coupons is ------- for 50 percent off admission at Fountain Park.

(A) legitimate
(B) definite
(C) valid
(D) popular

04 It was very ------- for Mr. Philips to do poorly on his accounting test because he studied very hard for it.

(A) frustrating
(B) hopeful
(C) negligible
(D) bright

05 In addition to credit cards, many businesses accept ------- payment methods via smartphone applications.

(A) coordinated
(B) alternative
(C) admirable
(D) insistent

06 Internationally ------- violinist Margaret Collins will have a special performance this Friday.

(A) renowned
(B) immediate
(C) modest
(D) parallel

07 Management hopes its new training program will make employees more ------- at their jobs.

(A) advisable
(B) solid
(C) considerate
(D) proficient

08 Critics were overwhelmingly positive in their praise of singer Colin Wench after his ------- performance at the Pewter Center.

(A) present
(B) flawed
(C) remote
(D) lively

09 All new staff will attend an ------- meeting to learn about the history of the company and tour the facilities.

(A) original
(B) obvious
(C) introductory
(D) authentic

10 Kaplan Architecture is known for producing highly innovative work that differs sharply from ------- standards of design.

(A) double
(B) intense
(C) voluntary
(D) conventional

정답·해석·해설 **p.203**

핵심 단어 리스트

01 **reliable** [riláiəbl] 신뢰할 수 있는, 믿을 만한

find a **reliable** form of transportation
신뢰할 수 있는 교통수단을 찾다

02 **potential** [pəténʃəl] 잠재적인, 가능성 있는

interview **potential** candidates for the job
직무에 대한 잠재적인 후보자들의 면접을 보다

03 **efficient** [ifíʃənt] 효율적인, 능률적인

adopt an **efficient** means of production
효율적인 생산 수단을 채택하다

04 **unanticipated** [ʌnæntísəpèitid] 예상 밖의

surprised by the **unanticipated** test results
예상 밖의 실험 결과에 놀라다

05 **prominent** [prɑ́:mənənt] 유명한, 탁월한

invite **prominent** local business owners
유명한 현지 사업주들을 초대하다

06 **knowledgeable** [nɑ́:lidʒəbəl] 아는 것이 많은, 총명한

be **knowledgeable** about a broad range of topics
폭넓은 주제에 대해 아는 것이 많다

07 **appropriate** [əpróupriət] 적절한, 적당한

wear **appropriate** office attire
적절한 근무 복장을 입다

08 **combustible** [kəmbʌ́stəbl] 가연성의

avoid dangerous **combustible** chemicals
위험한 가연성 화학 물질들을 피하다

09 **equivalent** [ikwívələnt] 동등한, 상당하는

select an item of **equivalent** value
동등한 가치의 물품을 선택하다

10 **residential** [rèzədénʃəl] 주거의, 거주의

purchase a **residential** property
주거용 부동산을 구입하다

11 **deliberate** [dilíbərət] 신중한, 의도적인

make a **deliberate** decision
신중한 결정을 하다

12 **frequent** [frí:kwənt] 빈번한, 잦은

make **frequent** stops to drop off passengers
승객들을 내려주기 위해 빈번한 정차를 하다

13 **standard** [stǽndərd] 표준의, 보통의

charge the **standard** rate
표준 요금을 부과하다

14 **insistent** [insístənt] 주장하는

remain **insistent** on getting a refund
환불받는 것을 계속해서 주장하다

15 **commercial** [kəmə́:rʃəl] 상업의

lease a **commercial** space to set up a store
상점을 설립할 수 있는 상업 공간을 임대하다

16 **legitimate** [lidʒítəmət] 합법적인, 합리적인

set up a **legitimate** business
합법적인 사업을 시작하다

17 **punctual** [pʌ́ŋktʃuəl] 시간을 엄수하는

require **punctual** attendance
시간을 엄수하는 출근을 요구하다

18 **decisive** [disáisiv] 결단력 있는, 결정적인

take **decisive** action on the matter
그 일에 대해 결단력 있는 행동을 취하다

19-20 **cautious** [kɔ́:ʃəs] 주의하여, 조심스러운 : **delicate** [délikət] 다루기 어려운, 세심한, 까다로운

cautious는 행동이나 생각이 조심스럽고 신중한 것을 의미하고, delicate는 일이나 상황이 다루기 어렵고 까다로운 것을 의미합니다.
urge drivers to be **cautious** on icy roads 운전자들에게 빙판길에서 주의할 것을 촉구하다
bring up a **delicate** subject 다루기 어려운 주제를 꺼내다

토익 실전 문제

01 Ms. Morrell expects her staff to complete their assignments within an ------- time frame.

(A) esteemed
(B) undecided
(C) imaginary
(D) appropriate

02 A committee has identified several ------- candidates to replace outgoing CEO Charles Bayliss.

(A) continuous
(B) adverse
(C) potential
(D) upcoming

03 Reading online reviews has made many consumers extremely ------- about products currently on the market.

(A) unconscious
(B) knowledgeable
(C) valuable
(D) impressive

04 Tristream Laboratory is used by many medical facilities in Detroit because it is ------- in reporting its test results.

(A) evident
(B) undetermined
(C) deficient
(D) punctual

05 The highly advanced robotic equipment can help doctors perform even the most ------- surgical procedures.

(A) perceptive
(B) delicate
(C) cautious
(D) noble

06 After much consideration, Tyvercorp's board of directors made a ------- choice to close all of its overseas offices.

(A) fragile
(B) vast
(C) sociable
(D) deliberate

07 All the light bulbs in the office will be replaced with ones that are more ------- when it comes to energy use.

(A) pleasurable
(B) efficient
(C) decent
(D) hospitable

08 As one of the oldest newspapers in the nation, *The Porter Gazette* is considered by most to be a ------- source of information.

(A) reluctant
(B) reliant
(C) relative
(D) reliable

09 Ms. Bloom's incentive bonus this quarter was ------- to two weeks' pay.

(A) equivalent
(B) average
(C) advantageous
(D) composed

10 The construction firm called Mr. Harper to apologize about an ------- delay in the conference room renovation.

(A) accurate
(B) unanticipated
(C) advisory
(D) optional

정답·해석·해설 **p.204**

핵심 단어 리스트

01 **previous**[príːviəs] 이전의

   own a **previous** version of the product
   상품의 이전 버전을 소유하다

02 **sensitive**[sénsətiv] 민감한

   restrict access to **sensitive** information
   민감한 정보에 대해 접근을 제한하다

03 **substantial**[səbstǽnʃəl] 상당한, 튼튼한

   require a **substantial** amount of time to finish the project
   프로젝트를 끝내는 데 상당한 양의 시간을 필요로 하다

04 **convincing**[kənvínsiŋ] 설득력 있는, 확실한

   need a **convincing** argument to get funding for the venture
   벤처 사업을 위한 자금을 받기 위해 설득력 있는 주장이 필요하다

05 **diligent**[dílədʒənt] 성실한, 부지런한

   praise a **diligent** employee
   성실한 직원을 칭찬하다

06 **promising**[práːmisiŋ] 유망한, 전망이 밝은

   receive many **promising** candidates for the vacant position
   공석에 대해 많은 유망한 지원자들을 받다

07 **comfortable**[kʌ́mfərtəbl] 안락한, 편안한

   buy a **comfortable** sofa for the living room
   거실에 놓을 안락한 소파를 구매하다

08 **available**[əvéiləbəl] 구할 수 있는

   make **available** at department stores
   백화점에서 구할 수 있게 만들다

09 **impressive**[imprésiv] 인상적인

   have a lot of **impressive** features
   많은 인상적인 기능들을 가지고 있다

10 **direct**[dirékt] 직접적인

   receive **direct** orders from a supervisor
   감독관으로부터 직접적인 지시를 받다

11 **credible**[krédəbəl] 신뢰할 수 있는

   present **credible** evidence for the claim
   주장에 대해 신뢰할 수 있는 근거를 제시하다

12 **lengthy**[léŋkθi] 장황한, 지루한

   give a **lengthy** speech at the opening ceremony
   개막식에서 장황한 연설을 하다

13 **preferred**[priːfə́ːrd] 선호하는, 선호되는

   select one's **preferred** meal option
   선호하는 식사 선택권을 고르다

14 **rigorous**[rígərəs] 엄격한, 철저한

   implement **rigorous** regulations
   엄격한 규정을 시행하다

15 **mundane**[mʌndéin] 일상적인, 따분한

   handle **mundane** affairs
   일상적인 일을 처리하다

16 **overpriced**[òuvərpráist] 너무 비싼

   refuse to buy **overpriced** goods
   너무 비싼 상품을 구매하는 것을 거부하다

17 **conclusive**[kənklúːsiv] 결정적인

   be **conclusive** proof that the new policy is a success
   새로운 정책이 성공적이라는 결정적인 증거이다

18 **imaginary**[imǽdʒənèri] 가상의

   provide an **imaginary** scenario
   가상의 시나리오를 제공하다

19-20 **recent**[ríːsnt] 최근의 : **late**[leit] 늦은

   recent는 기간이 얼마 되지 않은 것을 의미하고, late는 예정이나 보통 때보다 늦은 것을 의미합니다.
   discuss the **recent** policy 최근의 정책을 논의하다
   cause a **late** arrival 늦은 도착을 야기하다

01 The value of HRS Bank's stock decreased by a ------- amount the day after it reported poor quarterly results.

(A) vague
(B) substantial
(C) selective
(D) frequent

02 After months of ------- effort, Ms. Parker was able to set up her first online business.

(A) tender
(B) diligent
(C) remote
(D) capable

03 Mr. Jensen thought his job as a filing clerk was ------- and decided to look for more fulfilling work.

(A) mundane
(B) confident
(C) sensational
(D) duplicate

04 Out of all the applicants, Mr. Nolan was the ------- candidate for the job.

(A) rewarding
(B) exhibited
(C) comparable
(D) preferred

05 Residents complained that the national park's ------- regulations prevented them from enjoying the area.

(A) rigorous
(B) cooperative
(C) productive
(D) durable

06 Customers who fail to pay their bill on time will be subject to a fine for the ------- payment.

(A) financial
(B) late
(C) reasonable
(D) recent

07 HL Laboratories' research is ------- as it may lead to the development of important new medications.

(A) visible
(B) revolving
(C) promising
(D) preliminary

08 Certain commodity crops, including sugar, are highly ------- to weather conditions like prolonged drought.

(A) coherent
(B) applicable
(C) sensitive
(D) mature

09 FGP Group's sales for the first quarter exceeded the expectations of analysts when it broke all ------- records.

(A) imminent
(B) conclusive
(C) massive
(D) previous

10 Although the food served at El Señor is quite good, it is far too ------- for the neighborhood it is in.

(A) indirect
(B) active
(C) overpriced
(D) liberal

정답·해석·해설 **p.205**

핵심 단어 리스트

01 **accurately**[ǽkjurətli] 정확히, 정밀하게

predict stock trends **accurately**
주식 동향을 정확히 예측하다

02 **routinely**[ruːtíːnli] 일상적으로, 언제나

routinely check the e-mail to ensure fast response
빠른 답변을 보장하기 위해 일상적으로 이메일을 확인하다

03 **markedly**[máːrkidli] 현저하게, 두드러지게

increase **markedly** from previous years
이전 해들에 비해 현저하게 증가하다

04 **superbly**[supə́ːrbli] 훌륭하게, 최상으로

develop a **superbly** designed product
훌륭하게 디자인된 제품을 개발하다

05 **closely**[klóusli] 면밀히, 유심히

analyze the results **closely**
결과를 면밀히 분석하다

06 **intentionally**[inténʃənəli] 의도적으로, 고의로

drive the car at a slow speed **intentionally**
의도적으로 차를 느린 속도로 운전하다

07 **merely**[míərli] 단지, 그저

merely provide a light snack
단지 가벼운 간식을 제공하다

08 **acceptably**[ækséptəbli] 만족스럽게

perform **acceptably** in daily use
일상적인 사용 시 만족스럽게 작동하다

09 **probably**[prɑ́ːbəbli] 아마도

be **probably** more dangerous than expected
아마도 예상보다 더 위험할 것이다

10 **gradually**[grǽdʒuəli] 서서히, 차츰

reduce interest rates **gradually**
이자율을 서서히 줄이다

11 **namely**[néimli] 다시 말해, 즉

hold a meeting on the 2nd floor, **namely** in Room 206
회의를 2층에서, 다시 말해 206호에서 열다

12 **primarily**[praimérəli] 주로

upgrade software **primarily** used by the accounting department
주로 회계 부서에 의해 사용되는 소프트웨어를 업그레이드하다

13 **aboard**[əbɔ́ːrd] 탑승하여

have 120 passengers **aboard**
120명의 승객이 탑승하여 있다

14 **occasionally**[əkéiʒənəli] 종종, 가끔

host staff outings **occasionally**
직원 야유회를 종종 주최하다

15 **completely**[kəmplíːtli] 완전히, 전적으로

have a **completely** different opinion
완전히 다른 의견을 가지다

16 **understandably**[ʌndərstǽndəbli] 당연히

feel **understandably** pleased about a promotion
승진에 대해 당연히 기뻐하다

17 **apparently**[əpǽrəntli] 보아하니, 분명히

be **apparently** more expensive than it looks
보아하니 보기보다 더 비싸다

18 **necessarily**[nèsəsérəli] (부정문에서) 반드시 ~은 아니다

do not **necessarily** apply to all applicants
반드시 모든 지원자에게 해당되는 것은 아니다

19-20 **immediately**[imíːdiətli] 즉시 : **briefly**[bríːfli] 간략하게, 잠시

immediately는 어떠한 행동을 시간의 지체 없이 바로 하는 것을 의미하고, briefly는 상황이나 사실을 요약하여 간단하고 짧게 줄이는 것을 의미합니다.

announce the news **immediately** 소식을 즉시 발표하다
explain the issue **briefly** 문제를 간략하게 설명하다

01 The last few pages of the Jones Brothers Department Store training manual are ------- left blank for note-taking.

(A) fluently
(B) incorrectly
(C) intentionally
(D) casually

02 Delivery people ------- drop packages off at the reception desk but only do so when the recipient is unavailable.

(A) virtually
(B) initially
(C) occasionally
(D) publicly

03 The real estate agent from Gulfstate Homes showed some potential buyers around a ------- decorated townhouse.

(A) vacantly
(B) consequently
(C) jealously
(D) superbly

04 The consultant ------- predicted that productivity at JN Inc. would improve thanks to the new office system.

(A) inconclusively
(B) commonly
(C) accurately
(D) vastly

05 Mr. Roberts follows a number of stocks ------- to monitor any fluctuations in their price.

(A) expensively
(B) accidentally
(C) closely
(D) rightly

06 Ms. Hymer was told to start working on the customer satisfaction report ------- because it was due at the end of the week.

(A) immediately
(B) clearly
(C) briefly
(D) seemingly

07 Weather forecasters say that the sky will be cloudy through the afternoon but then ------- clear up in the evening.

(A) knowingly
(B) internally
(C) smoothly
(D) gradually

08 The value of a new automobile drops ------- after it is used by its first owner.

(A) markedly
(B) strictly
(C) densely
(D) independently

09 Sensenet's help center handles technical problems and ------- receives hundreds of calls a day from customers.

(A) routinely
(B) severely
(C) carefully
(D) securely

10 It was later revealed that the activation of the fire alarm at Wentfield Tower was ------- part of a drill.

(A) supremely
(B) merely
(C) openly
(D) solidly

정답·해석·해설 p.206

DAY 15 [어휘] 부사 2

핵심 단어 리스트

01 exclusively[iksklú:sivli] 오직 ~만, 독점적으로

sell **exclusively** to overseas clients
오직 해외 고객에게만 판매하다

02 promptly[prá:mptli] 지체 없이, 신속히

respond to all inquiries **promptly**
모든 문의에 지체 없이 응대하다

03 relatively[rélətivli] 비교적, 상대적으로

attend a **relatively** crowded workshop
비교적 혼잡한 워크숍에 참가하다

04 periodically[pìəriá:dikəli] 정기적으로

scan computers for viruses **periodically**
바이러스에 대비하여 정기적으로 컴퓨터를 점검하다

05 elsewhere[élshwɛər] 다른 곳에서

search for assistance **elsewhere**
다른 곳에서 도움을 찾아보다

06 barely[béərli] 거의 ~하지 않은, 가까스로

introduce people who **barely** know each other
서로 거의 알지 못하는 사람들을 소개하다

07 justly[dʒʌ́stli] 정당하게, 바르게

justly claim credit for the invention
발명에 대한 공적을 정당하게 주장하다

08 inseparably[insépərəbli] 밀접하게

inseparably connected with the consumer's perception
소비자의 인식과 밀접하게 연관되어 있다

09 largely[lá:rdʒli] 대부분, 주로

largely consists of sugar and flour
대부분 설탕과 밀가루로 이루어져 있다

10 slightly[sláitli] 약간, 조금

perform **slightly** better than last quarter
지난 분기보다 약간 더 잘 수행하다

11 virtually[və́:rtʃuəli] 거의, 사실상

vote for a **virtually** unknown politician
거의 알려지지 않은 정치인에게 투표하다

12 precisely[prisáisli] 정확하게, 신중하게

arrive **precisely** at 9 o'clock
9시 정각에 정확하게 도착하다

13 evenly[í:vənli] 공평하게, 고르게

divide tasks **evenly** among staff
업무를 직원들 간에 공평하게 나누다

14 tediously[tí:diəsli] 지루하게, 따분하게

speak long and **tediously** on a subject
주제에 대해 길고 지루하게 말하다

15 consistently[kənsístəntli] 지속적으로

consistently provide good service
좋은 서비스를 지속적으로 제공하다

16 densely[dénsli] 밀집하여, 빽빽하게

move to a **densely** populated area
인구가 밀집하여 있는 지역으로 이사하다

17 initially[iníʃəli] 초기에, 처음에

initially focus on basic staff training
초기에 기본 직원 훈련에 초점을 두다

18 loosely[lú:sli] 막연하게, 느슨하게

be **loosely** based on a true event
실제 사건에 막연하게 기반을 두다

19-20 generally[dʒénərəli] 일반적으로 : **totally**[tóutəli] 완전히, 모두

generally는 대부분의 상황 및 경우에 일반적으로 적용된다는 것을 의미하고, totally는 부족하거나 빠진 부분 없이 전적임을 의미합니다.

generally pay high rent in cities 도시에서는 일반적으로 높은 임차료를 내다
totally redo the assignment 업무를 완전히 다시 하다

01 Hooper Tech ------- asks employees to complete surveys to assess their level of job satisfaction.

(A) periodically
(B) significantly
(C) rigidly
(D) truthfully

02 In the minds of Averco's employees, the company's success is ------- linked with the contributions made by the former CEO.

(A) inseparably
(B) accidentally
(C) artificially
(D) repeatedly

03 The temperature does not ------- begin to rise until March, but spring appears to have come early this year.

(A) totally
(B) deliberately
(C) generally
(D) conditionally

04 There was so much work that the team ------- finished the project before the deadline.

(A) calmly
(B) extremely
(C) gratefully
(D) barely

05 The donated funds must be used ------- for specified activities and for no other purpose.

(A) impressively
(B) exclusively
(C) reluctantly
(D) decently

06 Studies have shown that drivers who ------- follow traffic rules have far fewer accidents than those who do not.

(A) precisely
(B) outwardly
(C) tentatively
(D) courteously

07 Although several volunteers helped her, Ms. Knight was ------- responsible for organizing the anniversary banquet.

(A) gently
(B) slightly
(C) largely
(D) plentifully

08 It is advisable to pay all credit card bills ------- in order to avoid late charges.

(A) promptly
(B) primarily
(C) financially
(D) temporarily

09 Hiring more staff is ------- high on our list of priorities, so interviews will be held soon.

(A) successfully
(B) relatively
(C) separately
(D) expertly

10 Valeville residents believe that building a golf course in town is unnecessary and that the funds should be spent -------.

(A) excessively
(B) sometimes
(C) elsewhere
(D) considerably

정답·해석·해설 **p.207**

VOCABULARY PART 5, 6

DAY 15 [어휘] 부사 2

한 권으로 끝내는 해커스 토익 **700+** (LC+RC+VOCA)

핵심 단어 리스트

01 **reasonably** [rí:zənəbli] 적절히, 알맞게

   buy a **reasonably** priced car
   가격이 적절히 책정된 자동차를 구매하다

02 **gently** [dʒéntli] 천천히, 부드럽게, 약하게

   place the glass bowl **gently** on the table
   유리그릇을 천천히 탁자 위에 놓다

03 **nearly** [níərli] 거의, ~할 뻔하다

   check a **nearly** finished assignment
   거의 완료된 업무를 확인하다

04 **regularly** [régjulərli] 정기적으로, 자주

   receive medical checkups **regularly**
   정기적으로 건강 검진을 받다

05 **exactly** [igzǽktli] 정확히, 바로, 틀림없이

   cost **exactly** $100 to get the car repaired
   차를 수리하는 데 정확히 100달러가 들다

06 **overly** [óuvərli] 지나치게, 과도하게

   be **overly** dependent on the survey results
   설문 조사 결과에 지나치게 의존하다

07 **immeasurably** [iméʒərəbli] 잴 수 없을 만큼

   be **immeasurably** better than other products on the market
   시중의 다른 제품들보다 잴 수 없을 만큼 더 좋다

08 **successfully** [səksésfəli] 성공적으로

   show how **successfully** the plan worked
   계획이 어떻게 성공적으로 실행되었는지를 보여주다

09 **regretfully** [rigrétfəli] 유감스럽게도

   regretfully announce the closing of the department store
   유감스럽게도 백화점의 폐점을 발표하다

10 **formerly** [fɔ́:rmərli] 이전에, 예전에

   purchase property **formerly** owned by a corporation
   이전에 기업에 의해 소유되었던 부동산을 구매하다

11 **rapidly** [rǽpidli] 급속히, 빠르게

   experience **rapidly** dropping temperatures
   급속히 떨어지는 온도를 경험하다

12 **considerably** [kənsídərəbli] 훨씬, 상당히

   do **considerably** better than before
   이전보다 훨씬 더 잘하다

13 **typically** [típikəli] 일반적으로, 전형적으로

   typically produce high quality items
   일반적으로 고품질의 물품들을 생산하다

14 **chiefly** [tʃí:fli] 주로, 대개

   be **chiefly** used to produce electrical components
   전자 부품을 생산하는 데 주로 사용되다

15 **rightfully** [ráitfəli] 마땅히, 정당하게

   rightfully demand an apology
   마땅히 사과를 요구하다

16 **recently** [rí:sntli] 최근에

   review a **recently** opened restaurant
   최근에 개업한 식당을 논평하다

17 **entirely** [intáiərli] 완전히, 전부

   begin an **entirely** new assignment
   완전히 새로운 업무를 시작하다

18 **continually** [kəntínjuəli] 계속적으로, 끊임없이

   occur **continually** throughout the year
   연중 내내 계속적으로 발생하다

19-20 **once** [wʌns] 한 번 : **first** [fəːrst] 첫 번째로, 최초로

   once는 어떠한 사건이나 행동 등이 1회 일어나는 것을 의미하고, first는 처음이라는 순서를 의미합니다.

   go at least **once** a month   최소한 한 달에 한 번은 가다
   finish **first** in the race   경주에서 첫 번째로 도착하다

토익 실전 문제

01 Melman's Supermarket, ------- called
Second Street Grocery, is the city's largest
supplier of fresh fruit and vegetables.

(A) distinctly
(B) strictly
(C) regularly
(D) formerly

02 Great technological strides have been
made since the personal computer was
------- introduced a few decades ago.

(A) always
(B) first
(C) lately
(D) once

03 Ms. Sullivan's retirement speech lasted
------- longer than she had planned as she
didn't expect to receive so much applause.

(A) readily
(B) carelessly
(C) considerably
(D) traditionally

04 The report was written ------- in German,
so it was necessary for Ms. Vine to have it
translated.

(A) deeply
(B) honestly
(C) entirely
(D) continually

05 Although the shoes fit ------- well,
Mr. Perkins chose not to buy them.

(A) reasonably
(B) constantly
(C) previously
(D) numerously

06 Mr. Hawthorne's missing wallet was found
------- where he thought it would be.

(A) frankly
(B) exactly
(C) mostly
(D) sharply

07 Ms. Rivers ------- does not work on
weekends but took a Saturday shift to fill in
for an ill coworker.

(A) utterly
(B) correctly
(C) typically
(D) potentially

08 Whereas diners used to complain about
Mamma Mia's food being ------- seasoned,
now they say that it is too bland.

(A) secretly
(B) gladly
(C) purposefully
(D) overly

09 Parking spots will fill up -------, so be sure
to arrive at the conference venue early in
the morning.

(A) rapidly
(B) rarely
(C) belatedly
(D) curiously

10 Inclement weather ------- caused the
cancelation of Cincinnati's upcoming music
festival in the park.

(A) perfectly
(B) realistically
(C) majorly
(D) nearly

정답·해석·해설 **p.208**

VOCABULARY PART 5, 6   DAY 16 [어휘] 부사 3   한 권으로 끝내는 해커스 토익 **700+** (LC+RC+VOCA)

핵심 단어 리스트

01 be subject to ~의 대상이다

Factories **are subject to** random inspections.
공장들은 불시 점검의 대상이다.

02 be similar to ~과 비슷하다

The sequel **was similar to** the original film.
그 속편은 원작 영화와 비슷했다.

03 be pertinent to ~과 관련 있다

The memo **is pertinent to** sales department staff.
회람은 영업부 직원과 관련 있다.

04 be unable to ~할 수 없다

Mr. Quentin **was unable to** find his briefcase.
Mr. Quentin은 그의 서류 가방을 찾을 수 없었다.

05 be likely to ~할 것 같다

Ms. Fielding's home **is likely to** sell fast.
Ms. Fielding의 집은 빠르게 팔릴 것 같다.

06 be popular with ~에게 인기가 있다

The clothing line **is popular with** young adults.
그 의류 라인은 젊은 성인층에게 인기가 있다.

07 be familiar with ~을 잘 알고 있다

Applicants must **be familiar with** the word processing software.
지원자들은 문서 작성 소프트웨어를 잘 알고 있어야 한다.

08 be eligible to ~할 자격이 있다

Club members **are eligible to** receive a 25 percent discount on all purchases.
클럽 회원들은 모든 구매에 대해 25퍼센트 할인을 받을 자격이 있다.

09 be intended for ~을 대상으로 하다

The game **is intended for** children between the ages of 8 and 12.
그 게임은 8세에서 12세 사이의 어린이들을 대상으로 한다.

10 be dedicated to ~에 전념하다

The factory **is dedicated to** the production of BNT Co. vehicle parts.
그 공장은 BNT사의 차량 부품 생산에 전념한다.

11 be adequate for ~에 적합하다, ~에 충분하다

Ms. Patraki's skills **are adequate for** the position.
Ms. Patraki의 능력은 그 직책에 적합하다.

12 be equipped with ~을 갖추고 있다

The laboratory **is equipped with** a 3D printer.
그 실험실은 3D 프린터를 갖추고 있다.

13 be suitable for ~에 알맞다, ~에 어울리다

The apartment **is suitable for** tenants with pets.
그 아파트는 반려동물이 있는 세입자들에게 알맞다.

14 be skilled at ~에 능숙하다, ~에 노련하다

Ms. Groves **is skilled at** writing press releases.
Ms. Groves는 보도 자료를 쓰는 것에 능숙하다.

15 be willing to ~할 용의가 있다

Management **is willing to** negotiate on salaries.
경영진은 급여에 대해 협상할 용의가 있다.

16 be unaware of ~에 대해 알지 못하다

Some customers **were unaware of** the price increase.
일부 고객들은 가격 인상에 대해 알지 못했다.

17 be bound to 틀림없이 ~할 것이다

The product **is bound to** sell well with enough advertising.
그 제품은 충분한 광고가 된다면 틀림없이 잘 팔릴 것이다.

18 be exempt from ~이 면제되다

Non-profit organizations **are exempt from** paying income tax.
비영리 단체들은 소득세를 내는 것이 면제된다.

19 be pleased to ~하게 되어 기쁘다

The Newred Gallery **is pleased to** present an exhibit by sculptor Horatio P. Quinn.
Newred 미술관은 조각가 Horatio P. Quinn에 의한 전시회를 진행하게 되어 기쁘다.

20 be selected for ~에 뽑다, ~에 선발되다

The most qualified candidate will **be selected for** the job.
가장 자격이 있는 지원자가 직무에 뽑힐 것이다.

토익 실전 문제

01 Customers who spend $100 or more during Thompson's online sale will be ------- to receive free shipping.

(A) complimentary
(B) eligible
(C) standard
(D) productive

02 VTV Internet's least costly service is ------- for basic Web surfing and sending e-mail but not downloading videos.

(A) elaborate
(B) skilled
(C) unable
(D) adequate

03 Having been granted the consent of the government, Grayson & Kline Inc. is ------- from import taxes.

(A) fulfilled
(B) unique
(C) exempt
(D) proper

04 Santos Industries claimed that it was ------- of the environmental laws that it had supposedly broken.

(A) unanimous
(B) absolute
(C) negative
(D) unaware

05 If demand for natural gas increases, the stock value of companies that produce it is ------- to rise as well.

(A) likely
(B) detailed
(C) slight
(D) active

06 EZ-Grabs convenience store employees must be ------- to work night shifts on occasion.

(A) lasting
(B) ongoing
(C) similar
(D) willing

07 Caterers that fail to follow safety guidelines are ------- to fines and possible closure by the state's food inspection board.

(A) worthy
(B) questionable
(C) subject
(D) important

08 Longtime fans of the *Ghost Hunter* movie series are ------- to see the new film in theaters this week.

(A) impartial
(B) bound
(C) serious
(D) absent

09 The accounting team asked the division secretary to collect all financial records that were ------- to the annual audit.

(A) pertinent
(B) patient
(C) precious
(D) pleased

10 Fanli Electronics is ------- to the manufacture of high-quality, reasonably priced LED TVs.

(A) exclusive
(B) duplicate
(C) dedicated
(D) concentrated

정답·해석·해설 **p.209**

DAY 18 [어구] 동사 관련 어구

핵심 단어 리스트

01 acknowledge A for B A에게 B에 대해 감사하다

In his speech, the CEO **acknowledged** the sales team **for** their hard work.
연설에서 최고 경영자는 영업팀에게 그들의 노고에 대해 감사했다.

02 associate A with B A를 B와 관련시켜 생각하다

People often **associate** high-paying jobs **with** success.
사람들은 종종 돈을 많이 받는 직업을 성공과 관련시켜 생각한다.

03 participate in ~에 참석하다, ~에 참여하다

The employees will **participate in** a team-building exercise.
직원들은 팀워크 향상 훈련에 참석할 것이다.

04 designate A for B B에 A를 지정하다, 할당하다

Mr. Owens has already **designated** the advertising team **for** the assignment.
Mr. Owens는 이미 그 업무에 광고팀을 지정했다.

05 depend on ~에 달려 있다

Whether the firm gets the contract **depends on** its presentation.
그 회사가 계약을 따낼 것인지의 여부는 발표에 달려 있다.

06 result in ~을 낳다, ~을 야기하다

Regular incentives **result in** higher employee satisfaction.
정기적인 인센티브는 더 높은 직원 만족도를 낳는다.

07 notify A of B A에게 B를 알리다

The radio broadcast **notified** drivers **of** a road closure.
라디오 방송은 운전자들에게 도로 폐쇄를 알렸다.

08 come in (상품 등이 여러 종류로) 나오다

The ice cream bars **come in** three popular flavors.
그 막대 아이스크림은 세 가지 인기 있는 맛으로 나온다.

09 recommend A for B A를 B에 추천하다

Ms. Clarice **recommended** Sanjay Patel **for** a managerial position.
Ms. Clarice는 Sanjay Patel을 관리직에 추천했다.

10 proceed with ~을 진행하다, ~을 처리하다

The council **proceeded with** the original plan after all.
의회는 결국 원래 계획을 진행했다.

11 provide A with B A에게 B를 제공하다

The museum will **provide** visitors **with** headsets for the guided tour.
박물관은 방문객들에게 가이드 관광을 위한 헤드셋을 제공할 것이다.

12 prevent A from B A가 B하는 것을 막다, 예방하다

Heavy traffic **prevented** Ms. Kim **from** arriving on time.
극심한 교통량은 Ms. Kim이 제시간에 도착하는 것을 막았다.

13 preside over ~을 주재하다, 사회를 보다

Ms. Roberts will **preside over** the meeting.
Ms. Roberts가 회의를 주재할 것이다.

14 ask A for B A에게 B를 요청하다

Ms. Turner **asked** her boss **for** a raise.
Ms. Turner는 상사에게 급여 인상을 요청했다.

15 specialize in ~을 전문으로 하다

Ms. Torres **specializes in** corporate law.
Ms. Torres는 회사법을 전문으로 한다.

16 substitute A for B A로 B를 대신하다

The baker **substituted** honey **for** sugar.
제빵사는 꿀로 설탕을 대신했다.

17 lead to ~으로 이어지다

The store's promotion campaign **led to** increased profits.
상점의 홍보 캠페인은 증가된 수익으로 이어졌다.

18 commend A for B A를 B에 대해 칭찬하다

Mayor Brown **commended** citizens **for** their efforts.
Brown 시장은 시민들을 그들의 노력에 대해 칭찬했다.

19 search for ~을 찾아보다

Ms. Lucas **searched for** her keys in her bag.
Ms. Lucas는 그녀의 가방에서 열쇠를 찾아보았다.

20 split up 나누다, 분리되다

The corporation was **split up** into smaller companies.
그 기업은 더 작은 회사들로 나뉘어졌다.

01 The goal of TK Watches' marketing plan was to get consumers to ------- their timepieces with high-end jewelry.

(A) appreciate
(B) cooperate
(C) associate
(D) imitate

02 Most of the wedding dresses stocked by Bridal Heaven ------- a wide variety of sizes.

(A) get across
(B) move on
(C) add up
(D) come in

03 Yeats Petrochemicals has ------- $50 million dollars for the construction of its new headquarters.

(A) served
(B) implied
(C) adapted
(D) designated

04 It has been reported that President Wilson himself will ------- over the inaugural ceremony for the national park.

(A) preside
(B) perceive
(C) foresee
(D) reach

05 The success of the tourism industry ------- the government's ability to attract foreign visitors.

(A) meets with
(B) depends on
(C) narrows down
(D) carries out

06 At the awards banquet, Senator Freya Jones ------- District Attorney Harold Moffat for his years of service.

(A) commended
(B) assumed
(C) specified
(D) stimulated

07 Sweet Sensations Bakery sells all sorts of goods, but it ------- in French pastries.

(A) specializes
(B) offers
(C) improves
(D) deserves

08 Seminar attendees are encouraged to ------- in the discussion by posing questions.

(A) divide
(B) participate
(C) conform
(D) deny

09 Online security programs have been installed to ------- cyber criminals from stealing confidential information.

(A) guarantee
(B) describe
(C) challenge
(D) prevent

10 Starting next month, NFRNews.com will begin ------- readers with high-resolution weather maps.

(A) interfering
(B) developing
(C) accepting
(D) providing

정답·해석·해설 **p.210**

DAY 19 [어구] 명사 관련 어구

핵심 단어 리스트

01 attention to ~에 대한 주의

The painter's **attention to** detail was remarkable.
세부 사항에 대한 그 화가의 주의는 놀라웠다.

02 a portion of ~의 일부, 약간의

A portion of the profits will go to charity.
수익의 일부는 자선 단체에 기부될 것이다.

03 compliance with ~의 준수, ~의 지킴

Compliance with health and safety regulations is necessary for restaurants.
보건 안전 규정의 준수는 식당들에게 필수적이다.

04 identification badge 신분 확인 명찰

Employees must wear **identification badges** at all times.
직원들은 항상 신분 확인 명찰을 차고 있어야 한다.

05 concerns about ~에 대한 우려, 걱정

There are some **concerns about** the side effects of the medication.
약물의 부작용에 대한 우려가 있다.

06 intent to ~할 의사, 의도, 목적

The prime minister announced his **intent to** retire from his position.
총리는 그의 직책에서 사임하겠다는 의사를 발표했다.

07 effect on ~에 대한 효과

Exercise has a great **effect on** wellbeing.
운동은 건강에 대해 탁월한 효과가 있다.

08 admiration for ~에 대한 존경, 감탄

Mr. Jonson expressed **admiration for** his mentor.
Mr. Jonson은 그의 멘토에 대한 존경을 표했다.

09 shift in ~의 변화

A **shift in** the stock market can have a great impact on the economy.
주식 시장의 변화는 경제에 큰 영향을 줄 수 있다.

10 restrictions on ~에 대한 규제, 제한

The city government implemented new **restrictions on** weekend parking.
시 정부는 주말 주차에 대한 새로운 규제를 시행했다.

11 perspective on ~에 대한 관점

The film reviewer had a unique **perspective on** the movie's deeper meaning.
그 영화 평론가는 영화의 더 깊은 의미에 대해 독특한 관점을 갖고 있었다.

12 observation on ~에 대한 논평, 의견

The writer's **observation on** the election was entertaining.
선거에 대한 작가의 논평은 재미있었다.

13 commitment to ~에 대한 헌신, 전념

Our **commitment to** customers never weakens.
우리의 고객에 대한 헌신은 결코 약해지지 않는다.

14 requirement for ~을 위한 요건, 필요 조건

Consulting experience is a **requirement for** this position.
상담 경력은 이 일자리를 위한 요건이다.

15 transition from A to B A에서 B로의 변화, 이행

The **transition from** university life **to** the world of work can be difficult.
대학 생활에서 직장 세계로의 변화는 어려울 수 있다.

16 investment in ~에 대한 투자

Investment in overseas companies increased 17 percent last year.
해외 기업들에 대한 투자가 작년에 17퍼센트 증가했다.

17 a source of ~의 원천, 근원

Real estate rentals are a **source of** income for investors.
부동산 임대는 투자자들에게 수입의 원천이다.

18 preparation for ~을 위한 준비

Preparations for the book launch are already finished.
그 책의 출간을 위한 준비는 이미 완료되었다.

19 report for ~를 위한 보고

The **report for** the board of directors should be as thorough as possible.
이사회를 위한 보고는 최대한 상세해야 한다.

20 a consequence of ~의 결과

The store closed as a **consequence of** poor sales.
그 상점은 판매 부진의 결과로 문을 닫았다.

01 The high unemployment rate in Grettington is a ------- of the recent closure of several large factories in the area.

(A) practice
(B) consequence
(C) reinforcement
(D) suggestion

02 Mandatory ------- on water usage have been in effect since the drought began last month.

(A) invitations
(B) restrictions
(C) differences
(D) organizations

03 Known for its ------- to detail, Technica Gear manufactures apparel of incomparable quality.

(A) potential
(B) contribution
(C) decrease
(D) attention

04 Getting a master's degree would allow Ms. Vega to attempt a ------- from development to project management.

(A) transition
(B) statement
(C) measurement
(D) discussion

05 The marketing team conducts surveys to get the customer's ------- on the quality of the company's products.

(A) perspective
(B) accessibility
(C) similarity
(D) referral

06 Security upgrades, including the obligatory wearing of ------- badges, will be implemented this year.

(A) transportation
(B) interaction
(C) accommodation
(D) identification

07 ------- with the company's corporate credit card policy is expected of all employees.

(A) Preference
(B) Expansion
(C) Compliance
(D) Estimation

08 Critics have expressed ------- for singer Tara Queen's latest album, calling it her best work to date.

(A) comparison
(B) admiration
(C) influence
(D) reception

09 The CEO addressed ------- about the stock's declining value at the shareholder's meeting.

(A) procedures
(B) experiments
(C) collections
(D) concerns

10 Fremway Manufacturing plans to purchase a ------- of the property where Millville Mall used to be.

(A) division
(B) formation
(C) portion
(D) trade

정답·해석·해설 **p.211**

DAY 20 [어구] 짝을 이루는 표현

핵심 단어 리스트

01 make arrangements 준비하다

Ms. Lee **made arrangements** to meet the client.
Ms. Lee는 고객을 만나기 위해 준비했다.

02 open space 공터

The park was designed with a lot of **open spaces**.
그 공원은 많은 공터를 포함하도록 설계되었다.

03 work environment 근무 환경

A positive **work environment** keeps employees motivated.
적극적인 근무 환경은 직원들이 동기 부여가 되도록 한다.

04 concentrated effort 집중적인 노력

The team made a **concentrated effort** to finish its work for the day.
그 팀은 그날의 업무를 끝내기 위해 집중적인 노력을 했다.

05 follow the regulations 규정을 따르다

Drivers must **follow the regulations** to avoid accidents.
운전자들은 사고를 방지하기 위해 규정을 따라야 한다.

06 selling point 장점

The phone's biggest **selling point** is its long battery life.
그 핸드폰의 가장 큰 장점은 긴 배터리 수명이다.

07 warm welcome 따뜻한 환영

Seminar attendees gave the speaker a **warm welcome**.
세미나 참석자들은 연설자에게 따뜻한 환영을 해주었다.

08 thorough analysis 철저한 분석

A **thorough analysis** of the budget is necessary to prevent overspending.
예산안의 철저한 분석은 과도한 지출을 예방하기 위해 필수적이다.

09 eagerly await 간절히 기다리다

Citizens of Frankton are **eagerly awaiting** the grand opening of the new subway line.
Frankton의 시민들은 새로운 지하철 노선의 개통을 간절히 기다리고 있다.

10 mutually beneficial 상호적으로 이득이 되는

Internship programs are **mutually beneficial** to businesses and students.
인턴십 프로그램은 회사와 학생들에게 상호적으로 이득이 된다.

11 strong performer 경쟁력 있는 회사·사람

GlobalGo is a **strong performer** in the tourism industry.
GlobalGo사는 관광 산업에서 경쟁력 있는 회사이다.

12 take measures 조치를 취하다

Korincorp **took measures** to protect its computer network.
Korincorp사는 컴퓨터 네트워크를 보호하기 위한 조치를 취했다.

13 quicken the pace 속도를 높이다

Mr. Jones must **quicken the pace** of his work to meet his deadline.
Mr. Jones는 마감 기한을 맞추기 위해 업무 속도를 높여야만 한다.

14 heavy usage 과다 사용

The battery of the new smartphone lasts for 10 hours, even with **heavy usage**.
그 새로운 스마트폰의 배터리는 과다 사용 시에도 10시간 동안 지속된다.

15 display initiative 주도성을 발휘하다

The performance review will reflect whether employees **display initiative** at work.
업무 수행 평가는 직원들이 직장에서 주도성을 발휘하는지를 반영할 것이다.

16 conveniently located 편리하게 위치한

The company is **conveniently located** near a subway station.
그 회사는 지하철역 근처에 편리하게 위치해 있다.

17 steady growth 꾸준한 성장

Because of the firm's **steady growth**, it had to expand its headquarters.
그 회사의 꾸준한 성장으로 인해, 그곳은 본사를 확장해야 했다.

18 cease operations 영업을 중단하다

The company had to **cease operations** last year due to poor management.
그 회사는 형편없는 경영으로 인해 작년에 영업을 중단해야만 했다.

19 sales performance 판매 실적

The company's **sales performance** has improved.
회사의 판매 실적이 개선되었다.

20 conduct an inspection 점검을 실시하다

Technicians will **conduct an inspection** of the equipment.
기술자들은 장비에 대한 점검을 실시할 것이다.

01 The organic food industry is experiencing steady ------- thanks to an increase in demand for chemical-free produce.

(A) reach
(B) extension
(C) range
(D) growth

02 When Mr. Goldfinch asked his assistant to make ------- for some visiting investors, she booked a hotel for them downtown.

(A) assemblies
(B) arrangements
(C) speculations
(D) contributions

03 After weeks of negotiations, the two CEOs agreed to a partnership that would be ------- beneficial for both companies.

(A) skillfully
(B) fluently
(C) mutually
(D) tightly

04 The work ------- has been unpleasant as a result of ongoing renovations, so employees are permitted to work from home.

(A) machine
(B) payment
(C) environment
(D) constraint

05 The executives at Mercer Pharmaceuticals endeavor to boost sales ------- by offering attractive incentives to their staff.

(A) functions
(B) correspondence
(C) performance
(D) endorsement

06 Management will hire professionals to conduct an ------- on the building and to repair any defects they might find.

(A) interruption
(B) application
(C) inspection
(D) admission

07 Mr. Gordon is being considered for a promotion to a managerial position because he consistently displays -------.

(A) initiative
(B) exhibition
(C) quantity
(D) system

08 The efficiency consultant advised the factory manager to take ------- that would improve working conditions for workers.

(A) facilities
(B) measures
(C) sections
(D) designs

09 Fans of acclaimed singer Lawrence Stevens ------- await his next album, which is set to be released in a week.

(A) eagerly
(B) visually
(C) loosely
(D) defiantly

10 Wentworth Natural Gas must quicken the ------- and begin securing long-term contracts faster to compete with other suppliers.

(A) quest
(B) pace
(C) march
(D) lead

정답·해석·해설 **p.212**

점수 환산표

아래는 별책으로 수록된 실전모의고사를 위한 점수 환산표입니다. 문제 풀이 후, 정답 개수를 세어 자신의 토익 리스닝/리딩 점수를 예상해봅니다.

정답 수	리스닝 점수	리딩 점수	정답 수	리스닝 점수	리딩 점수	정답 수	리스닝 점수	리딩 점수
100	495	495	66	305	305	32	135	125
99	495	495	65	300	300	31	130	120
98	495	495	64	295	295	30	125	115
97	495	485	63	290	290	29	120	110
96	490	480	62	285	280	28	115	105
95	485	475	61	280	275	27	110	100
94	480	470	60	275	270	26	105	95
93	475	465	59	270	265	25	100	90
92	470	460	58	265	260	24	95	85
91	465	450	57	260	255	23	90	80
90	460	445	56	255	250	22	85	75
89	455	440	55	250	245	21	80	70
88	450	435	54	245	240	20	75	70
87	445	430	53	240	235	19	70	65
86	435	420	52	235	230	18	65	60
85	430	415	51	230	220	17	60	60
84	425	410	50	225	215	16	55	55
83	415	405	49	220	210	15	50	50
82	410	400	48	215	205	14	45	45
81	400	390	47	210	200	13	40	40
80	395	385	46	205	195	12	35	35
79	390	380	45	200	190	11	30	30
78	385	375	44	195	185	10	25	30
77	375	370	43	190	180	9	20	25
76	370	360	42	185	175	8	15	20
75	365	355	41	180	170	7	10	20
74	355	350	40	175	165	6	5	15
73	350	345	39	170	160	5	5	15
72	340	340	38	165	155	4	5	10
71	335	335	37	160	150	3	5	5
70	330	330	36	155	145	2	5	5
69	325	320	35	150	140	1	5	5
68	315	315	34	145	135	0	5	5
67	310	310	33	140	130			

※ 점수 환산표는 해커스토익 사이트 유저 데이터를 근거로 제작되었으며, 주기적으로 업데이트되고 있습니다. 해커스토익 사이트(Hackers.co.kr)에서 최신 경향을 반영하여 업데이트된 점수환산기를 이용하실 수 있습니다. (토익 > 토익게시판 > 토익점수환산기)

한 권으로 끝내는

해커스 토익

700+

LC+RC+ VOCA

실전모의고사

+정답·해석·해설

III 해커스 어학연구소

* 토익 온라인 모의고사 추가 1회분은 해커스인강 사이트(HackersIngang.com)에서 제공됩니다.

한 권으로 끝내는

해커스 토익 700+

LC+RC+ VOCA

실전모의고사

+정답·해석·해설

ⓗ 해커스 어학연구소

LISTENING TEST

In this section, you must demonstrate your ability to understand spoken English. This section is divided into four parts and will take approximately 45 minutes to complete. Do not mark the answers in your test book. Use the answer sheet that is provided separately.

PART 1

Directions: For each question, you will listen to four short statements about a picture in your test book. These statements will not be printed and will only be spoken one time. Select the statement that best describes what is happening in the picture and mark the corresponding letter (A), (B), (C) or (D) on the answer sheet.

Sample Answer

The statement that best describes the picture is (B), "The man is sitting at the desk." So, you should mark letter (B) on the answer sheet.

1.

2.

GO ON TO THE NEXT PAGE ➡

실전모의고사

한 권으로 끝내는 **해커스 토익 700+** (LC+RC+VOCA)

3.

4.

5.

6.

GO ON TO THE NEXT PAGE ▶

PART 2

Directions: For each question, you will listen to a statement or question followed by three possible responses spoken in English. They will not be printed and will only be spoken one time. Select the best response and mark the corresponding letter (A), (B), or (C) on your answer sheet.

7. Mark your answer on your answer sheet.

8. Mark your answer on your answer sheet.

9. Mark your answer on your answer sheet.

10. Mark your answer on your answer sheet.

11. Mark your answer on your answer sheet.

12. Mark your answer on your answer sheet.

13. Mark your answer on your answer sheet.

14. Mark your answer on your answer sheet.

15. Mark your answer on your answer sheet.

16. Mark your answer on your answer sheet.

17. Mark your answer on your answer sheet.

18. Mark your answer on your answer sheet.

19. Mark your answer on your answer sheet.

20. Mark your answer on your answer sheet.

21. Mark your answer on your answer sheet.

22. Mark your answer on your answer sheet.

23. Mark your answer on your answer sheet.

24. Mark your answer on your answer sheet.

25. Mark your answer on your answer sheet.

26. Mark your answer on your answer sheet.

27. Mark your answer on your answer sheet.

28. Mark your answer on your answer sheet.

29. Mark your answer on your answer sheet.

30. Mark your answer on your answer sheet.

31. Mark your answer on your answer sheet.

PART 3

Directions: In this part, you will listen to several conversations between two or more speakers. These conversations will not be printed and will only be spoken one time. For each conversation, you will be asked to answer three questions. Select the best response and mark the corresponding letter (A), (B), (C), or (D) on your answer sheet.

32. According to the man, what will Brian Oliver receive?

(A) A consultation
(B) An ID card
(C) A report
(D) An award

33. What does the woman suggest?

(A) Giving a sales presentation
(B) Buying a small gift
(C) Visiting a coworker's desk
(D) Attending a company event

34. What does the man say about the accounting report?

(A) It contains a calculation error.
(B) It should be submitted to a supervisor.
(C) It needs to be printed out.
(D) It was distributed at a meeting.

35. What are the speakers mainly discussing?

(A) A farmers' market
(B) An online promotion
(C) An art class
(D) A charitable event

36. What does the Gresham Foundation do?

(A) Host dinners
(B) Organize competitions
(C) Support artists
(D) Provide scholarships

37. What does the man suggest?

(A) Collecting an event ticket
(B) Taking public transportation
(C) Reserving a parking space
(D) Traveling as a group

38. Where do the speakers most likely work?

(A) At a financial institution
(B) At a construction corporation
(C) At a publishing company
(D) At a Web design firm

39. What will happen next week?

(A) A trade show will end.
(B) A management meeting will take place.
(C) A Web site will be shut down.
(D) A new service will be offered.

40. What will the man prepare?

(A) An agenda
(B) A presentation
(C) A budget
(D) An invoice

41. What is the woman's problem?

(A) A document is difficult to complete.
(B) An employee is late for work.
(C) A meeting was canceled.
(D) An evaluation was negative.

42. What does the woman ask the man to do?

(A) Speak with a team leader
(B) Assist with a task
(C) Sign a form
(D) Write down some instructions

43. What does the woman say she will do?

(A) Meet a client
(B) Send an e-mail
(C) Reserve a table
(D) Copy a report

GO ON TO THE NEXT PAGE

44. Where do the speakers most likely work?

(A) At a construction firm
(B) At a sporting goods store
(C) At a real estate office
(D) At a government agency

45. What did the man discuss with the supervisor?

(A) Project deadlines
(B) Material expenses
(C) Building locations
(D) Facility features

46. What will most likely happen on Wednesday?

(A) A supply order will be placed.
(B) A design plan will be released.
(C) An estimate will be submitted.
(D) A presentation will be revised.

47. Where most likely are the speakers?

(A) At a medical school
(B) At a hospital
(C) At a bank
(D) At a fitness center

48. What problem does the man mention?

(A) He needs to leave in a few minutes.
(B) He has lost a file.
(C) He wrote down incorrect information.
(D) He injured his back.

49. What does the woman tell the man to do?

(A) Fill out a form
(B) Pay for a service
(C) Schedule an appointment
(D) Contact a manager

50. What is the conversation mainly about?

(A) A software installation
(B) An office closure
(C) A broken computer
(D) A training session

51. Why is the task scheduled for the evening?

(A) To ensure a technician is available
(B) To prevent a meeting delay
(C) To avoid interrupting work
(D) To allow for a shift change

52. What does the man mention about the team members?

(A) They should hand in a document.
(B) They should save some files.
(C) They should receive some training.
(D) They should send some e-mails.

53. Where most likely are the speakers?

(A) At a jewelry shop
(B) At an office supply store
(C) At a clothing factory
(D) At a hardware store

54. What does the woman suggest?

(A) Sending back some goods
(B) Changing a supplier
(C) Recommending some merchandise
(D) Placing a display in a window

55. What problem does the woman mention?

(A) Some boxes need to be unpacked.
(B) An item must be repaired.
(C) Some areas should be cleaned.
(D) A delivery has not yet arrived.

56. What was the woman asked to do on Friday?

(A) Talk to a manager
(B) Deliver a presentation
(C) Meet with a consultant
(D) Work overtime

57. Why does the woman say, "Johnson Construction is a major client"?

(A) To indicate interest in a workshop
(B) To show excitement about a transfer
(C) To stress the importance of a task
(D) To express admiration for a company

58. What will the woman most likely do next?

(A) Print some documents
(B) Attend a meeting
(C) E-mail a request form
(D) Talk to a contractor

---

59. Why is the man calling?

(A) To ask about a schedule
(B) To inquire about a ticket
(C) To request a refund
(D) To confirm a seat number

60. What information does the woman ask the man for?

(A) Contact details
(B) Promotional codes
(C) A confirmation number
(D) A home address

61. What does the man mean when he says, "But the show is in two days"?

(A) He forgot about a performance.
(B) He has a tight budget.
(C) He might miss an event.
(D) He needs more practice time.

Bay City Technology Convention
Event Directory
Hall A: Artificial Intelligence Lecture
Hall B: Innovation Seminar
Hall C: Robotics Presentation
Hall D: Employment Fair

62. What are the speakers mainly discussing?

(A) A request from an executive
(B) An issue with some speakers
(C) A reason for a cancellation
(D) A change to a schedule

63. What does the woman say she will do?

(A) Make an announcement
(B) Arrange a meeting space
(C) Repair a malfunctioning device
(D) Get some refreshments

64. Look at the graphic. Where will the man wait for the woman?

(A) In Hall A
(B) In Hall B
(C) In Hall C
(D) In Hall D

GO ON TO THE NEXT PAGE

Flight Number	Departure Time
AE880	7:00 A.M.
AE890	9:30 A.M.
AE900	1:45 P.M.
AE910	4:30 P.M.

65. What does the woman ask about?

(A) Flight changes
(B) Ticket availability
(C) Check-in times
(D) Gate access

66. What does the woman say about the direct flight?

(A) It is not very affordable.
(B) It has no economy seats.
(C) It leaves too late.
(D) It lands in Minneapolis.

67. Look at the graphic. Which flight will the woman probably take?

(A) AE880
(B) AE890
(C) AE900
(D) AE910

Winston Recline - $190	Finnly A34 - $225
Posture Pro - $275	WellMont Glider - $315

68. What did the man do earlier?

(A) Attended a meeting
(B) Approved a budget
(C) Listened to a voice mail
(D) Sent out a memo

69. Look at the graphic. How much will the chair the woman intends to order cost?

(A) $190
(B) $225
(C) $275
(D) $315

70. What does the man ask the woman to do?

(A) Sign an invoice form
(B) Send tracking information
(C) Provide a credit card number
(D) Choose a shipping option

Directions: In this part, you will listen to several short talks by a single speaker. These talks will not be printed and will only be spoken one time. For each talk, you will be asked to answer three questions. Select the best response and mark the corresponding letter (A), (B), (C), or (D) on your answer sheet.

71. Where is the announcement most likely being made?

(A) At a subway station
(B) At a shopping complex
(C) At a government office
(D) At a construction firm

72. Why will there be a closure?

(A) Bad weather is expected.
(B) Repairs must be made.
(C) An expansion is underway.
(D) An inspection must be carried out.

73. What does the speaker suggest?

(A) Talking to an employee
(B) Arriving earlier than usual
(C) Walking to a location
(D) Catching a shuttle bus

74. What is being advertised?

(A) A product launch
(B) A clearance sale
(C) A store grand opening
(D) A celebrity appearance

75. What will be available at the event?

(A) Merchandise samples
(B) Store flyers
(C) Free refreshments
(D) Half-price items

76. What is mentioned about the Kansas branch?

(A) It has been renovated.
(B) It is near public transportation.
(C) It provides free parking to customers.
(D) It has been advertised online.

77. What is the topic of the seminar?

(A) Reducing workers' stress
(B) Planning for corporate mergers
(C) Analyzing research results
(D) Following company regulations

78. Why does the speaker say, "I'm certain you've had similar experiences yourselves"?

(A) To show the need for cooperation
(B) To indicate that stress is manageable
(C) To emphasize a shared feeling
(D) To encourage the development of goals

79. What does the speaker want to do during the seminar?

(A) Distribute staff handbooks
(B) Discuss a recent study
(C) Provide listeners with techniques
(D) Present a slide show

80. What is mentioned about Trax Corporation?

(A) Its representatives are running late.
(B) It is an educational software company.
(C) It is considering a partnership deal.
(D) Its office is located in a nearby building.

81. What problem does the speaker mention?

(A) A document is missing.
(B) An office was closed.
(C) A seminar is lasting too long.
(D) A business trip was canceled.

82. Why should the listener call back?

(A) To provide a recommendation
(B) To make a cancellation
(C) To ask for advice
(D) To respond to a request

GO ON TO THE NEXT PAGE

83. What is the purpose of the talk?

    (A) To introduce a staff member
    (B) To notify workers of a promotion
    (C) To organize a ceremony
    (D) To announce a retirement

84. According to the speaker, what did Ms. Franklin recently do?

    (A) Earned a degree
    (B) Received an award
    (C) Set up a computer network
    (D) Achieved a sales goal

85. What will Ms. Franklin do next?

    (A) Make a call
    (B) Prepare a presentation
    (C) Give a talk
    (D) Go to the airport

---

86. What most likely is the speaker's job?

    (A) Musician
    (B) Film producer
    (C) Event planner
    (D) Radio show host

87. Why does the speaker say, "and there's one more person I can't forget about"?

    (A) He will introduce a performer.
    (B) He will invite a guest to the stage.
    (C) He will acknowledge a teacher.
    (D) He will congratulate a winner.

88. What is mentioned about *Daytime Variety Show*?

    (A) The speaker has performed on the show.
    (B) It only features young musicians.
    (C) The program's viewership has dropped.
    (D) Its format has recently changed.

---

89. What is the talk mainly about?

    (A) Guidelines for a party
    (B) Rules for a tour
    (C) Changes to a facility
    (D) Directions to an attraction

90. What does the speaker ask the listeners to do?

    (A) Check event details
    (B) Tidy up a room
    (C) Use an alternate exit
    (D) Avoid touching furniture

91. What will the listeners most likely do next?

    (A) View a short video
    (B) Enter a gift shop
    (C) Head to another area
    (D) Purchase some tickets

---

92. According to the speaker, what does Mary Swan want to do?

    (A) Transfer to a new office
    (B) Post a job advertisement
    (C) Start a business
    (D) Attend a concert

93. Why does the speaker say, "He has been a vice president for over a decade"?

    (A) To thank a colleague for his service
    (B) To explain an employee's qualifications
    (C) To indicate why an award was given
    (D) To stress the importance of a position

94. What does the speaker say he will do?

    (A) Provide information about a replacement
    (B) Review guidelines for hiring new staff
    (C) Distribute application forms to workers
    (D) Give feedback on job performance

Broadcast Program – *Culture Break*	
Interview with Marla Heinz	3:00 P.M. - 3:40 P.M.
Commercial Break	3:40 P.M. - 3:50 P.M.
Spotlight on the Arts	3:50 P.M. - 4:30 P.M.
Traffic Report	4:30 P.M. - 4:40 P.M.

Trends Anniversary Event

Visit us from June 2-5 for savings
of up to 10 percent!

Located at the corner of Green St.
and Center Ave.

95. According to the speaker, what happened five years ago?

(A) A radio show was launched.
(B) A musical performance was held.
(C) A dance director was promoted.
(D) A ballet company was established.

96. How did Marla Heinz raise funds for student art programs?

(A) By applying for a grant
(B) By organizing an event
(C) By selling items
(D) By doing volunteer work

97. Look at the graphic. What time will the interview begin?

(A) At 3:00 P.M.
(B) At 3:40 P.M.
(C) At 3:50 P.M.
(D) At 4:30 P.M.

98. What kind of business is the speaker advertising?

(A) A clothing store
(B) A furniture shop
(C) A jewelry retailer
(D) A hair salon

99. Look at the graphic. When will customers be offered a free product?

(A) On June 2
(B) On June 3
(C) On June 4
(D) On June 5

100. According to the advertisement, why should listeners visit the company's Web site?

(A) To read customer reviews
(B) To make a reservation
(C) To check event dates
(D) To download a coupon

This is the end of the Listening test. Turn to PART 5 in your test book.

GO ON TO THE NEXT PAGE

READING TEST

In this section, you must demonstrate your ability to read and comprehend English. You will be given a variety of texts and asked to answer questions about these texts. This section is divided into three parts and will take 75 minutes to complete.

Do not mark the answers in your test book. Use the answer sheet that is separately provided.

PART 5

Directions: In each question, you will be asked to review a statement that is missing a word or phrase. Four answer choices will be provided for each statement. Select the best answer and mark the corresponding letter (A), (B), (C), or (D) on the answer sheet.

🕐 **PART 5** 권장 풀이 시간   11분

101. ------- the water in the vases daily so that the flowers on display stay fresh and healthy.

(A) Change
(B) Changed
(C) Changes
(D) Changing

102. The community ------- by the owner's decision to close his plastic container manufacturing facility.

(A) surprises
(B) surprised
(C) was surprised
(D) has surprised

103. ------- Mr. Tan is flying a short or long distance, he always brings his inflatable neck pillow.

(A) Anywhere
(B) Perhaps
(C) Whether
(D) Regarding

104. The report on Bawdry's current marketing projects ------- various advertising strategies that are proving successful.

(A) describes
(B) describe
(C) are described
(D) descriptively

105. Mr. Turner learned more ------- one year of working than from four years of college.

(A) during
(B) by
(C) since
(D) between

106. Ms. Landry ------- the sales projections for the next quarter at yesterday's presentation.

(A) discusses
(B) will discuss
(C) discussing
(D) discussed

107. Although the X70 camera is more ------- than many competitors', its image resolution is one of the highest on the market.

(A) expenses
(B) expensive
(C) expense
(D) expend

108. Membership to the software program is ------- renewed monthly for a period of a year.

(A) respectively
(B) occasionally
(C) automatically
(D) severely

109. According to critic Louis Arnold, nearly everything about the Big River Hotel was impressive ------- the breakfast buffet.

(A) as soon as
(B) among
(C) except for
(D) provided that

110. The applicant selected for the copy editor position must have the capacity to pay close attention to -------.

(A) approach
(B) detail
(C) privilege
(D) profession

111. An unexpected setback forced Ms. Lupo to reschedule the ribbon cutting ceremony for her new restaurant, now set to open ------- January.

(A) of
(B) on
(C) in
(D) at

112. Throughout the training session, the safety instructor ------- the need to regularly clean and inspect the equipment.

(A) launched
(B) emphasized
(C) corrected
(D) performed

113. As computers are ------- to a number of security issues, it is essential that they be routinely scanned for viruses.

(A) wary
(B) vulnerable
(C) requisite
(D) critical

114. First-week ticket sales for the movie *Autumn Winds* were ------- high enough to break the current record.

(A) around
(B) heavily
(C) frequently
(D) almost

115. Yardley Fashions has purchased a warehouse in Chester Road, which it will use as a ------- center for its goods.

(A) distribution
(B) distributed
(C) distributor
(D) distributable

116. The legal firm reported that last quarter's ------- grew primarily due to a partnership with a new corporate client.

(A) inflation
(B) revenue
(C) frequency
(D) representative

117. Ms. Adams ------- to Swarthmore University if she had gotten better grades in her senior year of high school.

(A) is going
(B) had gone
(C) could have gone
(D) would be gone

118. Before booking her literature convention tickets, Ms. Jackson looked for ------- hotels that still had rooms available.

(A) instant
(B) extended
(C) mandatory
(D) nearby

119. At the end of the year, a bonus amount will be decided upon by the board and ------- appropriately among the employees.

(A) divided
(B) division
(C) to divide
(D) divide

120. After the committee members reviewed design proposals, they chose Pendant Architects ------- on the new bank building.

(A) to work
(B) worker
(C) works
(D) has worked

GO ON TO THE NEXT PAGE

121. As part of a joint venture, HLN Co. is marketing phones ------- with Fleischman computer chips.

(A) demonstrated
(B) founded
(C) equipped
(D) recruited

122. The home team faced strong ------- from its opponents, but the players managed to secure a victory in the end.

(A) competition
(B) competitive
(C) competitor
(D) compete

123. The restructuring of Founder Chemicals was extensive, but it ------- the need for a major reduction of the company's operating budget.

(A) is not being eliminated
(B) was not eliminated
(C) did not eliminate
(D) has not been eliminated

124. Mr. Snead ------- the figures he quoted in the article to a well-known environmental research firm.

(A) attributed
(B) calculated
(C) augmented
(D) established

125. Mr. Cane ------- $50,000 from the bank to get his business started, but he did not settle the loan until recently.

(A) had borrowed
(B) borrowing
(C) will be borrowing
(D) was borrowing

126. The Ogichi 560 car has been called one of the nation's most ------- family vehicles by *Consumer Times Magazine*.

(A) popularize
(B) popularity
(C) popular
(D) popularly

127. Despite years of experience as a public speaker, Mr. Carroll still gets nervous when he ------- in front of a large audience.

(A) was standing
(B) stands
(C) would have stood
(D) had been standing

128. Coulier Fine Jewelry inspects all its merchandise with the utmost expertise to make certain no ------- are found.

(A) expenditures
(B) interruptions
(C) evaluations
(D) imperfections

129. Passengers on the delayed plane were told to go ------- to their departure gates in order to make their connecting flights.

(A) eventually
(B) directly
(C) tirelessly
(D) previously

130. There are already two OrganiFoods outlets located downtown and ------- is set to open by the end of the year.

(A) another
(B) others
(C) none
(D) some

PART 6

Directions: In this part, you will be asked to read four English texts. Each text is missing a word, phrase, or sentence. Select the answer choice that correctly completes the text and mark the corresponding letter (A), (B), (C), or (D) on the answer sheet.

🕐 **PART 6** 권장 풀이 시간　8분

Questions 131-134 refer to the following letter.

Polstar-Direct Retailer
350 50th Avenue, New York, NY

Dear Madam or Sir,

I received an e-mail from your company in regard to my recent purchase. It stated that the monitor I ordered from your online store was delivered. The tracking link in your e-mail directed me to a Web page, which indicated the place ------- was sent to. I was surprised
131.
to see that the monitor was delivered not to my home in New York ------- to a location in
132.
Kentucky.

The invoice you sent me clearly lists my actual address, so I am unsure why the purchased monitor was delivered elsewhere. I hope you can ------- this as soon as possible. -------.
133. 134.
You can reimburse the money to the credit card I used.

Sincerely,
Ruth Adams

131. (A) theirs
(B) it
(C) each
(D) what

132. (A) and
(B) for
(C) but
(D) so

133. (A) approve
(B) resolve
(C) dispute
(D) replace

134. (A) Unfortunately, I have yet to receive the item I ordered from your online store.
(B) This should be the correct information that is needed for the shipment.
(C) However, if the package can't be delivered to my address, I'd like a refund.
(D) It lists the merchandise I selected and confirms that payment has been made.

GO ON TO THE NEXT PAGE

Questions 135-138 refer to the following article.

FluDown Brings Promise

Ferminex Medical announced today that trials for a new over-the-counter flu medication, FluDown, have concluded with promising results.

According to doctors at PhysRec Labs, FluDown significantly ------- symptoms related
135.
to the illness in trial participants. More than 90 percent of the test patients said they experienced fewer instances of coughing, sneezing, and headache. Many ------- to feel
136.
better in less than 24 hours. Dr. Heather Stanbrow, head of Ferminex Medical, believes the results are incredibly encouraging. And although some patients reported negative side effects, their number falls within an expected and acceptable range. -------.
137.

"Our research teams have been developing FluDown for two years now and are thrilled by the results," Stanbrow said.

If ------- tests of the drug go similarly well, Ferminex Medical believes the medication could
138.
be available at drug stores around the country by late November.

---

135. (A) stimulated
(B) reduced
(C) rejected
(D) increased

136. (A) claims
(B) claiming
(C) will be claimed
(D) claimed

137. (A) The application to experiment with the drug on humans requires approval.
(B) Around 3 percent of participants said they had a minor upset stomach.
(C) Approximately 500 volunteers are needed to begin the trial.
(D) The drug can only be obtained with a prescription from a physician.

138. (A) initial
(B) further
(C) former
(D) contrary

Questions 139-142 refer to the following e-mail.

TO: Sarita Ravia <sarvia@indothreads.co.in>
FROM: June Shin <junes@brendanclothiers.com>
DATE: November 22
SUBJECT: Request
ATTACHMENT: Details

Dear Ms. Ravia,

I enjoyed meeting with you at the trade fair last week and seeing some of the many ------- **139.** your company manufactures.

I showed the fabric sample you gave me to Brendan Clothiers' creative director, Fiona Tyler, and she ------- how impressed she was with its high quality. We are optimistic about forming **140.** a business arrangement with your company. -------. **141.**

We understand that your schedule may be hectic. Should you be unable to fulfill our request at this time, please let us know ------- it would be more convenient for you. **142.**

Sincerely,
June Shin

---

139. (A) machines
(B) garments
(C) textiles
(D) accessories

140. (A) has mentioned
(B) was mentioned
(C) is being mentioned
(D) had been mentioned

141. (A) Regrettably, we could not locate the samples you sent.
(B) We appreciate your feedback on the design for our summer line.
(C) Our designers are graduates of highly prestigious schools.
(D) We also hope to place a large order with you in the near future.

142. (A) yet
(B) when
(C) though
(D) unless

GO ON TO THE NEXT PAGE

Questions 143-146 refer to the following information.

Thank you for ------- up for the Columbia River Adventure Tour! If you have trouble deciding
143.
what to bring with you, here are some important things to be aware of.

We will provide tents and sleeping bags as well as cooking and camping equipment.

-------, first aid and emergency kits will be supplied to those who need them. Meals,
144.
drinking water, and beverages will also be provided.

Remember that ------- it may be very warm during the daytime, temperatures can become
145.
chilly at night. Layered clothing is therefore recommended. -------. Finally, we advise
146.
participants to bring hats, sunglasses, sunscreen, and toiletries.

143. (A) to sign
    (B) had signed
    (C) signing
    (D) will be signing

144. (A) In addition
    (B) However
    (C) If so
    (D) Otherwise

145. (A) because
    (B) despite
    (C) while
    (D) rather than

146. (A) The tour will be restricted to
       designated areas.
    (B) Keep this in mind when packing for
       the trip.
    (C) So, it is essential to reserve your
       space in advance.
    (D) These units can be rented for a small
       fee.

PART 7

Directions: In this part, you will be asked to read several texts, such as advertisements, articles, instant messages, or examples of business correspondence. Each text is followed by several questions. Select the best answer and mark the corresponding letter (A), (B), (C), or (D) on your answer sheet.

🕐 **PART 7** 권장 풀이 시간   54분

Questions 147-148 refer to the following announcement.

A Night of Irish Folk Music

Keller and the Gang
With a special guest appearance by **Suzie McGregor**

Join us next Friday to celebrate the release of Keller and the Gang's third album, *High Tide*. The Irish folk group will play selections from their new album as well as classic favorites including "When I Went Down to the Sea" and "Fair-Eyed Lady." Also, Suzie McGregor, winner of the prestigious Goldy Award for music, will be present, and she will join the group in a vocal performance of three songs from *High Tide*.

Time: Friday, September 3rd, at 8 p.m. (doors open at 7:30)
Tickets: $10 at the door, $7 if purchased online
Location: The Horn of Plenty Ballroom, 917 Golden Lane, Dublin

Visit www.hornofplenty.com for more information.

---

147. What is the purpose of the announcement?

(A) To advertise a concert hall opening
(B) To promote an album release event
(C) To publicize an instrument sale
(D) To announce a Web site launch

148. What is suggested about Suzie McGregor?

(A) She joined a band last year.
(B) She plays classical music.
(C) She is a famous singer.
(D) She will be given an award.

GO ON TO THE NEXT PAGE

Watersports Kingdom
Get-Ready Sale

Watersports Kingdom has everything you need for fun in and on the water. We carry a range of equipment for fishing, sailing, and motorsports, not to mention all the gear you'll need to guarantee your safety. We also supply the most popular wakeboard and water ski brands on the market. And if you're interested in surfing, check out our new Watersports Kingdom-brand surfboards.

April is the month of our Get-Ready Sale. Starting this week, all of our swimwear from the previous year will be 10 to 30 percent off. Also, purchase any of lifejackets and goggles at a 50 percent discount. These deals are available throughout the month of April. So, stop by and get yourself ready for the start of the summer season.

149. What is true about Watersports Kingdom?

(A) It is a sponsor of major sporting events.
(B) It offers surfing classes for all levels.
(C) It sells various kinds of recreational gear.
(D) It will open for the first time next week.

150. What is NOT mentioned about the sale?

(A) It will be held during April.
(B) It features discounts of up to half off.
(C) It is exclusive to store members.
(D) It includes apparel from last year.

Mel Engle   12:12 P.M.
How did the meeting with Ms. Cantwell go this morning?

Edward Hale   12:15 P.M.
Really well, actually. I think she is going to give us the capital we need for our store. I showed her our business plan, and she seemed impressed.

Mel Engle   12:16 P.M.
Do you have any idea when we will know for sure?

Edward Hale   12:17 P.M.
She will contact me by tomorrow afternoon to inform me. However, she would like to own 20 percent of our business.

Mel Engle   12:19 P.M.
That is higher than the 15 percent we were offering. But we need the funds for our extra stock. And she has good connections in the local retail sector.

Edward Hale   12:20 P.M.
I feel the same way. Anyhow, I'll text you as soon as I hear anything from her. She seemed very positive about the opportunity.

Mel Engle   12:22 P.M.
Good to hear. At the same time, I think we are offering her a very solid investment. Sales continue to climb, so she will make a good profit.

151. Who most likely is Ms. Cantwell?

(A) An owner of a retail outlet
(B) A potential investor in a business
(C) A representative from a supplier
(D) A business planning consultant

152. At 12:20 P.M., what does Mr. Hale mean when he writes, "I feel the same way"?

(A) He thinks that giving up a larger share would be worthwhile.
(B) He believes there is too much competition in the retail sector.
(C) He doubts that stock shares will continue to go up.
(D) He agrees that business plans seem very impressive.

GO ON TO THE NEXT PAGE

Questions 153-154 refer to the following notice.

VISIT US AT OUR NEW WEB SITE, WWW.SEATTLEART.COM

SeattleArt, the best destination for in-depth local arts coverage, has acquired a new domain name as well as a whole new look. Instead of www.seart.com, you can visit us at www.seattleart.com. From now on, all our new stories will be posted to that site, and all the content from the old site will be transferred to the new one.

When we started this Web site five years ago, our objective was to give residents as clear an overview as possible of the local arts scene. Now, we're striving to realize that aim with all-new features, such as video clips and blogs by our staff of writers. This additional content will be complemented by a modern design and an improved search engine.

Over the coming months, we'll be publishing several noteworthy multimedia stories, including a visual summary of the city's annual arts festival and a video essay on a recent exhibit at the Burle Gallery.

As always, if you have any suggestions on how to improve the site, don't hesitate to contact the Web administrator, Jenny Lin, at jlin@seattleart.com. We view our site as a community-run endeavor, and we couldn't operate without your feedback.

153. What is indicated about SeattleArt?

(A) It has been running for a decade.
(B) It accepts customer feedback.
(C) It is looking for new staff writers.
(D) It offers old content upon request.

154. What is different about the new Web site?

(A) It features content from more writers.
(B) It includes articles from neighboring cities.
(C) It has more stories about local exhibits.
(D) It incorporates more visual media.

Questions 155-157 refer to the following information.

Morris Sherman is an American photographer best known for his conceptual portraits. He first became interested in the visual arts while a student at Eckhart College in Buffalo, New York. Though he began his studies in painting, he soon switched his major to photography. As Sherman himself said, "Painting takes too long. Using a camera allows me to devote more time to developing artistic ideas." Sherman was also a founding member of the Buffalo Photographers Society. He has cited as inspirations the photographic works of Edwin Miller, Ingrid Floss, and Hal Getty, among others.

Sherman always works in series, photographing himself in a range of costumes. In the process, he must take on multiple roles as author, director, stylist, and model. His photographs, which others have described as being both challenging and humorous, offer a view into the artist's perspectives on various social issues. The pieces in this exhibit explore notions of wealth and inequality in Western society. They also touch on the concepts of class, race, and religion.

155. Why did Morris Sherman stop studying painting?

(A) He did not have a talent for it.
(B) He had to interrupt his schooling.
(C) He found it too time-consuming.
(D) He did not earn enough to continue.

156. What is suggested about Ingrid Floss?

(A) She started a camera club.
(B) She attended Eckhart College.
(C) She currently lives in Buffalo.
(D) She is a photographer.

157. What is true about the photographs in the exhibit?

(A) They will be on display for about a month.
(B) They depict Mr. Sherman as the subject.
(C) They were taken by university students.
(D) They have been criticized for lacking humor.

GO ON TO THE NEXT PAGE

Questions 158-160 refer to the following form.

National Association of Town Planners (NATP) Membership Form

Please complete the form below, beginning with your personal information. Next, select the appropriate membership level based on your qualifications and experience. Note that for a degree to be recognized by NATP, it must focus on general planning principles and policies, with a specialization. If you are unsure about whether your qualifications are recognized, contact NATP for clarification. Lastly, list any relevant work experience. Start with your most recent and include a brief description and the length of time you were employed.

Name: Rachel Douglas	**E-mail:** rachel.douglas@directmail.com

Address: 243 65th Avenue, Queens, New York City, NY 11032

Membership level:
☐ Affiliate: Interested in planning but lack the required education and experience
☐ Student: Currently studying for a recognized degree in planning
☑ Associate: Hold a recognized degree in planning, but have less than two years of work experience
☐ Full: Hold a recognized planning degree, have two or more years of work experience, and currently work as a planner
☐ Retired: Meet the criteria for full membership but have retired from working

Qualifications:
Master's degree in Planning, specializing in Urban Studies, Raleigh University, NC

Work experience:
Project Assistant (1 year, 6 months); New York City Planning Department, Waterfront Regeneration Program; Assisted with the creation of zoning and building policies for the waterfront and organized community meetings to discuss plans.

Intern (3 months); Chapel Hill Transit Authority, North Carolina; While studying in nearby Raleigh, edited and fact-checked reports, took minutes at meetings, and responded to comments and concerns from local residents.

---

158. Why is Ms. Douglas unqualified to apply for a full membership?

(A) She is not a resident of New York City.
(B) She does not meet the age requirement.
(C) She has an unrecognized college degree.
(D) She lacks sufficient work experience.

159. What does the form suggest about Ms. Douglas?

(A) She is conducting a study on the city's water supply.
(B) She worked on a project for a planning department.
(C) She currently works for a transit authority.
(D) She will receive an associate membership card in two weeks.

160. What task did Ms. Douglas perform during her internship?

(A) Organizing consultations
(B) Scheduling upcoming meetings
(C) Confirming information
(D) Writing reports

Questions 161-163 refer to the following memo.

TO: All Miller Laundry Employees
FROM: James Miller, Owner of Miller Laundry
DATE: February 10
SUBJECT: An update

I'm writing to inform you that, starting next week, we're instituting a new policy here at Miller Laundry. Going forward, all clothing articles that customers drop off by noon must be cleaned and ready to be picked up by the end of the day. This includes blouses, dresses, dress shirts, coats, as well as difficult-to-wash items.

I'm instituting this policy because numerous customers have told me that it has taken employees two, or sometimes even three days to finish washing the clothing they've dropped off. Having worked in laundry business for over 10 years, I know that no clothing takes that long to clean, even on a busy day. So, next week, we're going to start telling customers that any clothes turned in by noon will be cleaned by the end of that same workday. If their clothes are not cleaned by then, customers will receive a $10 coupon.

I will therefore be counting on you to clean clothes on time. To help you, I will be hiring two more employees and installing several new machines that work more efficiently. Finally—as always—remember to be courteous to customers. The nicer you are, the kinder they will be in return, and the more likely they will be to come to our laundry again.

161. What is the memo mainly about?

(A) The implementation of a new rule
(B) A facility's forthcoming relocation
(C) The results of a customer survey
(D) A plan to increase a service fee

162. What did Mr. Miller mention about the customers?

(A) Some requested $10 discounts on their bills.
(B) Many had to wait a few days to receive clean clothes.
(C) Most dropped off difficult-to-wash items.
(D) Some received refunds for damaged garments.

163. What does Mr. Miller say he will do?

(A) Open another branch next week
(B) Post a revised regulation on a bulletin board
(C) Employ more staff for the laundry
(D) Provide training to a facility's employees

GO ON TO THE NEXT PAGE

Higher Education No Guarantee of Jobs

A new report from Rose Education Institute indicates that nearly 80 percent of high school graduates were admitted to four-year diploma programs at universities last year. Furthermore, the report shows that, in the last 10 years, significantly more people have pursued master's or doctorate degrees.

Following the recent economic recession, many college graduates returned to school immediately after receiving their degrees. — [1] —. As a result, a large number of job candidates possess advanced degrees, making applying for positions much more competitive.

In connection with this increased competition, many universities nationwide are now taking measures to provide assistance to those with a master's or doctorate degree. — [2] —. Eastforth University in Detroit, Michigan, for example, is recommending that individuals working toward advanced degrees speak with a program advisor at its graduate office for personalized assistance. — [3] —. And for those students experiencing hardships in the current job market, counselors at the university's career center are available by appointment to help with résumé writing and techniques for answering interview questions. — [4] —.

Those looking to advance their educations can learn more about Eastforth University and similar colleges offering such guidance on our publication's Web site at www. worldinbizmag.com.

164. What is the article mainly about?

(A) An innovative employment system
(B) Recent trends in education
(C) The advantages of studying abroad
(D) A newly constructed school

165. According to the article, what can Eastforth University's counselors offer?

(A) Evaluations for personal aptitude
(B) Assistance with interview skills
(C) References for potential employers
(D) Advice for university admissions

166. What is suggested about advanced degree holders?

(A) They accumulate large amounts of debt.
(B) They go on to become college professors.
(C) They work for government organizations.
(D) They are experiencing difficulties finding jobs.

167. In which of the positions marked [1], [2], [3], and [4] does the following sentence best belong?

"They did this in the hopes of gaining an advantage over other jobseekers."

(A) [1]
(B) [2]
(C) [3]
(D) [4]

Questions 168-171 refer to the following online chat discussion.

Nadia Pinsky	9:39 A.M.	I have an estimate request for a fencing project. The house is located at 354 Lexington Road. Would either of you be able to take care of that tomorrow?
Glenn Patten	9:41 A.M.	I'm completely booked with installations. I won't be able to manage it.
Hank Louis	9:42 A.M.	I have the same issue. I've got time on Friday morning, though.
Nadia Pinsky	9:43 A.M.	Understood. The client is leaving for Florida on Friday, so that's too late. Glenn, is there any possibility you can do the estimate on Wednesday?
Glenn Patten	9:43 A.M.	If it is after 5 P.M., yes.
Nadia Pinsky	9:47 A.M.	Thanks, Glenn. That shouldn't be a problem. Her name is Gloria Filmore, and she wants to install a fence around her yard.
Hank Louis	9:48 A.M.	When does she need it installed? Our schedules are so busy these days.
Nadia Pinsky	9:50 A.M.	Not until she returns from her trip. She's staying there for a week, so there isn't a big rush.
Glenn Patten	9:51 A.M.	OK. Just let me know once the appointment is confirmed.

[Send]

168. Who most likely are the writers?

(A) Travel agents
(B) Financial advisors
(C) Fencing contractors
(D) Interior decorators

169. When will Ms. Filmore return from Florida?

(A) On Wednesday
(B) Over the weekend
(C) On next Monday
(D) The following Friday

170. Why is Mr. Louis unable to meet Ms. Filmore tomorrow?

(A) He will be away on a holiday in Florida.
(B) His schedule is filled with appointments.
(C) He is doing other estimates for clients.
(D) His other project is taking longer than expected.

171. At 9:47 A.M., what does Ms. Pinsky mean when she writes, "That shouldn't be a problem"?

(A) A project will not require much effort.
(B) A specified time is likely suitable for a client.
(C) A trip schedule can easily be changed.
(D) A leave request will not create any conflict.

GO ON TO THE NEXT PAGE

How to Get the Best Results out of Staff Training
by Tom Caldwell

These days, supervisors are increasingly being made responsible for the training and development of their staff members. In fact, many corporations set aside funds for just this purpose. However, I always found it difficult to determine how these resources could actually be used to benefit the employees I managed. According to research, there are three important points to consider when choosing the best course of action. — [1] —. First, ask your workforce what they would like. — [2] —. Too many companies forget that their employees can be a key source of information. Next, conduct regular performance evaluations of your staff. Be sure to document the results so that you can track each person's development over time. — [3] —. This helps reveal areas that need attention. — [4] —. Finally, establish specific targets before doing any training and decide what you hope to achieve with your staff. By going through these simple steps, supervisors can save a great deal of time. Not only that, they will avoid wasting company funds on training sessions that have negligible results.

172. What recommendation is made in the article?

(A) Keeping a record of staff development
(B) Collecting feedback from instructors
(C) Asking staff to evaluate trainers
(D) Spending a lot of time on planning

173. What is stated as a possible outcome of following the steps outlined in the article?

(A) Increased worker satisfaction
(B) Faster project completion times
(C) More cost-efficient training
(D) Higher productivity levels

174. What is suggested about Mr. Caldwell?

(A) He used to work as a supervisor.
(B) He owns a human resources company.
(C) He recently conducted a survey.
(D) He teaches courses in training.

175. In which of the positions marked [1], [2], [3], and [4] does the following sentence best belong?

"They know best what type of training will benefit them the most."

(A) [1]
(B) [2]
(C) [3]
(D) [4]

GO ON TO THE NEXT PAGE

실전모의고사

한 권으로 끝내는 해커스 토익 **700+** (LC+RC+VOCA)

Questions 176-180 refer to the following letter and e-mail.

October 20

Martin Vesper
Raymond Development
53 Longhorn Way
Athens, GA 31444

Dear Mr. Vesper,

My name is Andrea Glick. We first met at the Hufford Business Convention following your impressive talk on Raymond Development's ecological approach to landscaping. My company, SureGreen Construction, is interested in working with yours on a major upcoming project.

I am not sure if you know about our company. SureGreen Construction is committed to building homes that are environmentally friendly. We construct our buildings with recycled or alternative materials as often as possible and design structures that efficiently incorporate different power options, like solar or wind energy. So far, our projects have been fairly small-scale and mostly limited to designing homes. However, we have a contract to create the new headquarters for Ophelia Incorporated in Atlanta, Georgia, including doing the landscaping for the project. We need your expertise and this is why I have written to you.

If you would be interested in joining us on this, please feel free to contact me by phone at 555-2358 or e-mail at andrea_glick@suregreen.com. We hope to hear from you soon.

Andrea Glick
SureGreen Construction Project Manager

To	Andrea Glick <andrea_glick@suregreen.com>
From	Martin Vesper <vesper@raymonddev.com>
Date	November 2
Subject	Ophelia Project

Dear Ms. Glick,

I am glad you enjoyed my talk back in August, and I thank you for inviting us to join SureGreen on this project. Ophelia Incorporated is well-known for its initiatives to improve environmental conditions and sustainability, so we are very interested in assisting with creating a new headquarters for them.

Before we come together to discuss the project in person, we will need more details about it. Most importantly, we will need to know where exactly the construction site is and what the conditions there are like. After that, we will want to send some technicians to look at the area, check the drainage situation, and measure soil acidity levels. Once we know what we are dealing with, we will be better able to move ahead on designs with your architects.

Best wishes,
Martin Vesper

176. Why did Ms. Glick contact Mr. Vesper?

(A) To invite his firm to take part in a project
(B) To thank him for a presentation
(C) To describe a new conservation plan
(D) To recommend a construction company

177. What is NOT mentioned about SureGreen Construction?

(A) It tries to use recovered materials.
(B) Its headquarters is in Atlanta.
(C) Its structures use alternative power sources.
(D) It has mainly designed houses.

178. What does Mr. Vesper want to do before a meeting?

(A) Talk to the architects
(B) Draw a few design ideas
(C) Find out other details
(D) Review terms of a contract

179. When did Mr. Vesper and Ms. Glick first meet?

(A) In August
(B) In September
(C) In October
(D) In November

180. Why is Mr. Vesper interested in working with Ophelia Incorporated?

(A) He has a former colleague who works at the company.
(B) He appreciates that their activities benefit the environment.
(C) He is in the process of expanding his network of contacts.
(D) He has never worked on a similar project before.

GO ON TO THE NEXT PAGE

Questions 181-185 refer to the following e-mails.

To: Melissa Ortiz <melissa@firstrunaustin.com>
From: Oliver Keller <oliver.keller@dakotashalegas.com>
Subject: Printing
Date: August 20

Dear Ms. Ortiz,

I recently came across your Web site and would like to inquire about your prices. Every year, we print an annual report focusing on our work in Argentina. As the coordinator, I have been disappointed in the quality of materials produced by our regular supplier and hope to get better results with your firm.

I understand you offer packages that include design, printing, and shipping. This is useful to us because we would not have to hire designers. We could also use the help mailing the finished reports. We've had to pay our administrative staff overtime just to take care of this in the past.

Could you tell me how much you would charge to design a 32-page color report, print 1,500 copies, and mail them to addresses we provide? 900 addresses are in the US. Of the remaining ones, 300 are in Canada, 220 in Germany, France, and Belgium, and 80 in China, South Korea, and Japan.

I look forward to hearing from you soon.

Thank you,

Oliver Keller
Dakota Shale Gas

To: Oliver Keller <oliver.keller@dakotashalegas.com>
From: Melissa Ortiz <melissa@firstrunaustin.com>
Date: August 23
Subject: Re: Printing

Dear Mr. Keller,

We would be pleased to help you with your report and hope that the information below will assist you in coming to a decision. To give you an accurate quote, we will need to know what type of paper you prefer, as prices may differ between plain paper and premium paper. Equally, there is an additional charge for different paper sizes.

Assuming you choose our standard package, design costs will be around $1,200, with a printing cost per copy of around 90 cents. This comes to $1,350 for the quantity you specified. Shipping costs are estimated to be $250 for the first 900 reports and then around $350 each for the other countries.

I hope this information helps. Let me know if you have any further questions.

Sincerely,

Melissa Ortiz
First Run Printing

181. Why is Mr. Keller looking for a printing service?

(A) He has a device that is not functioning.
(B) He is not satisfied with the current provider.
(C) His company is creating a travel pamphlet.
(D) His regular printer is too busy to take on an order.

182. What is stated about Dakota Shale Gas?

(A) They opened for business earlier this year.
(B) They have a graphic designer as a member of staff.
(C) Their administrative staff usually post the annual reports.
(D) They need a Web site to be designed as well.

183. What country will Dakota Shale Gas NOT ship reports to?

(A) Argentina
(B) Canada
(C) China
(D) France

184. What does Ms. Ortiz need to estimate prices?

(A) A copy of the previous year's report
(B) The number of images in a document
(C) The completed text of a report
(D) Information about paper size and type

185. What does Ms. Ortiz imply about costs?

(A) They decrease per piece as quantities go up.
(B) They are lower if a deposit is paid in advance.
(C) They include a discount for new customers.
(D) They cost less for delivery within the US than outside of it.

GO ON TO THE NEXT PAGE

Questions 186-190 refer to the following text message, e-mail, and agenda.

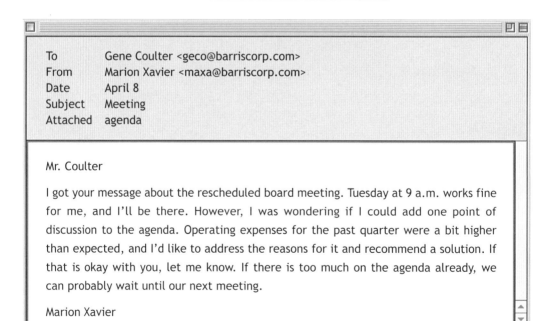

I wanted to let you all know that tomorrow morning's board meeting has been canceled. Unfortunately, too many members will be away or unavailable. As board policy requires that at least half of our members be present to make any executive decisions, we will not be able to proceed. As I need to present our quarterly report, and the board does have some pressing items on the agenda to discuss, we will reschedule as soon as possible. I will notify you all by Friday of the new date and time. I apologize for any inconvenience but kindly ask that all members prioritize our gatherings as they are important.

- Gene Coulter

To   Gene Coulter <geco@barriscorp.com>
From   Marion Xavier <maxa@barriscorp.com>
Date   April 8
Subject   Meeting
Attached   agenda

Mr. Coulter

I got your message about the rescheduled board meeting. Tuesday at 9 a.m. works fine for me, and I'll be there. However, I was wondering if I could add one point of discussion to the agenda. Operating expenses for the past quarter were a bit higher than expected, and I'd like to address the reasons for it and recommend a solution. If that is okay with you, let me know. If there is too much on the agenda already, we can probably wait until our next meeting.

Marion Xavier

AGENDA: Monthly Executive Board Meeting, Barris Corporation, April 11	
9:00 A.M.	Call to order, reading of minutes from last month's meeting by board secretary
9:15 A.M.	Reading of quarterly general report by board chair
9:45 A.M.	Reading of monthly financial report by board treasurer
10:15 A.M.	Points of discussion: 1. Progress of office expansion at Cleveland branch 2. Supply partnership proposal from Hugh & Bosch Equipment 3. Feedback from marketing survey 4. Increase in company operating expenses
12:30 P.M.	Meeting concludes

186. According to Mr. Coulter, why has the board meeting been rescheduled?

(A) A quarterly report is not yet ready to present.
(B) An agenda had insufficient points for discussion.
(C) A requirement regarding attendance will not be met.
(D) An event in the morning conflicts with its scheduled time.

187. In the text message, the word "prioritize" in paragraph 1, line 15 is closest in meaning to

(A) reevaluate
(B) put first
(C) categorize
(D) take better care of

188. Who most likely is Mr. Coulter?

(A) The chairperson of an executive board
(B) The secretary of an administrative group
(C) The finance officer of a company
(D) The operations manager of a firm

189. Why did Ms. Xavier contact Mr. Coulter?

(A) She wants to reschedule a Tuesday appointment.
(B) She would like to bring up a topic at a meeting.
(C) She has questions about the content of a report.
(D) She requires some information on operational expenses.

190. What will Ms. Xavier do after the discussion on the marketing survey?

(A) Summarize the main points of an agreement
(B) Give her recommendation to the board
(C) Present an agenda for the next meeting
(D) Distribute financial reports to the attendees

GO ON TO THE NEXT PAGE

Questions 191-195 refer to the following e-mails and schedule.

To   Jonathan Ingram <jingram@lwmail.com>
From   Geena Harris <gharris@mccloughinc.com>
Subject   Important details
Attached training schedule
Date   October 29

Hello, Jonathan.

On behalf of McClough Incorporated, I would like to welcome you to the company. As you were informed before, all new staff go through one week of training prior to starting their official duties. Attached, you will find a schedule for next week's activities. Please note that one hour, from 12:30 to 1:30, will be provided for lunch.

There are a few things you'll need to take care of next week also. The firm's accounting department asks that you bring one piece of photo identification and your social security card. Copies of these documents will be made for our records. Also, please arrive early on Monday morning and proceed immediately to the security department so that you can be issued a staff pass card and receive guidelines for handling sensitive data. At the same time, a security staff member will assign you a space for your vehicle if you need one.

If you have any questions about the training period, you may address them to me or call the human resources department at extension 38.

Geena Harris, Human Resources Director
McClough Incorporated

Training Schedule   McClough Incorporated

MONDAY, November 1, 9 A.M. – 5 P.M.	General orientation, corporate overview
TUESDAY, November 2, 9 A.M. – 5 P.M.	Office/administrative system, corporate system
WEDNESDAY, November 3, 9 A.M. – 5 P.M.	McClough Inc.'s clients and financial data
THURSDAY, November 4, 9 A.M. – 5 P.M.	Departmental training
FRIDAY, November 5, 10 A.M. – 3 P.M.	Departmental training

To   Geena Harris <gharris@mccloughinc.com>
From   Jeremy Vincent <jvincent@mccloughinc.com>
Subject   Trainee documentation
Date   November 4

Hi Geena,

Could you remind the trainees this morning to come by my department with their ID and social security card? None of them have dropped by so far. Let them know that we need the information on their cards tomorrow in order to set up salary and benefits payments. I am here until 6 P.M., but I would prefer if they came as soon as their training session ends for the day.

Thanks!
Jeremy Vincent

191. Why did Ms. Harris write the first e-mail?

(A) To describe scheduling changes to a trainee
(B) To outline new staff activities and requirements
(C) To announce some new corporate security policies
(D) To discuss a new department member's background

192. What is suggested about Mr. Ingram?

(A) He will learn about different systems on his second day of training.
(B) He will pick up a visitor's pass on Monday.
(C) He will be assigned an official duty on October 29.
(D) He will start his departmental duties on November 4.

193. What is indicated about McClough Incorporated?

(A) It outsources security to another firm.
(B) It provides employees with parking.
(C) It will offer new staff midday meals.
(D) It conducts monthly training sessions.

194. In the first e-mail, the word "sensitive" in paragraph 2, line 5, is closest in meaning to

(A) sensible
(B) thoughtful
(C) confidential
(D) responsive

195. When would Mr. Vincent prefer that the trainees visit his office?

(A) At 9 A.M.
(B) At 10 A.M.
(C) At 3 P.M.
(D) At 5 P.M.

GO ON TO THE NEXT PAGE

WILLARDS HONORS

925 48th Street, San Diego, CA 92120

For the best selection of trophies, plaques, medals, and other assorted tributes, visit Willards Honors in downtown San Diego. We sell awards of all shapes and sizes for any type of event, ceremony, or presentation. If it is official certificates you're looking for, we can custom design the perfect one for you. But that's not all. We have a generous array of gift items including high-end pens, business card holders, and key chains. And Willards will also inscribe text onto any purchased item free of charge. Or, get your company or group logo engraved for only $5 per item!

To see samples of the merchandise we carry and to get details on our costs and services, visit www.willardshonors.com. Or, drop by our store and showroom. We are open daily from 10 A.M. to 6 P.M.

WILLARDS HONORS   *Customized Order Form*

Name	Kathleen Benedict
Company/Group	Schumann Music Academy
Phone	555-9283
E-mail	benkat@schumannmusic.edu
Product	Sullivan medals, model #SM-409

Engraving

On rear of medals: "Winner, Schumann Music Academy Annual Student Performance Competition" along with school logo.

Special instructions

The medals will be awarded to winners of our event on June 27. "First Place" should be engraved on the front of the gold medal, "Second Place" on the silver medal, and "Runner-Up" on the three bronze medals.

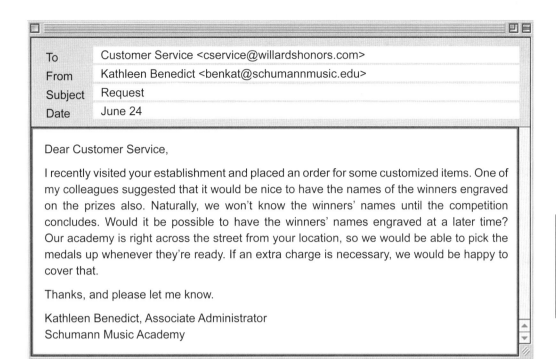

To: Customer Service <cservice@willardshonors.com>
From: Kathleen Benedict <benkat@schumannmusic.edu>
Subject: Request
Date: June 24

Dear Customer Service,

I recently visited your establishment and placed an order for some customized items. One of my colleagues suggested that it would be nice to have the names of the winners engraved on the prizes also. Naturally, we won't know the winners' names until the competition concludes. Would it be possible to have the winners' names engraved at a later time? Our academy is right across the street from your location, so we would be able to pick the medals up whenever they're ready. If an extra charge is necessary, we would be happy to cover that.

Thanks, and please let me know.

Kathleen Benedict, Associate Administrator
Schumann Music Academy

196. What is being advertised?

(A) A local printing company
(B) An awards and gift shop
(C) A graphic design firm
(D) A stationery store

197. What is indicated about Ms. Benedict's order?

(A) It will be delivered on June 27.
(B) Each item will incur an extra charge.
(C) It has been paid for in full.
(D) All selections were bought online.

198. What has Willards Honors been instructed to do?

(A) Prepare a trophy for the first-place winner
(B) Write "Runner-up" on three medals
(C) Supply certificates along with some prizes
(D) Delay production by a month

199. What does Ms. Benedict want to do?

(A) Invite a colleague to a competition
(B) Change the names on some prizes
(C) Have awards sent to the winners
(D) Add extra engravings to awards

200. What is suggested about Ms. Benedict?

(A) She was recently appointed to an administrative position.
(B) She feels that the academy was charged more than necessary.
(C) She works at an academy in a city center.
(D) She must keep the names of winners private.

This is the end of the test. You may review Parts 5, 6, and 7 if you finish the test early.

PART 1

1. (D)	2. (D)	3. (C)	4. (D)	5. (A)	6. (C)

PART 2

7. (C)	8. (B)	9. (C)	10. (A)	11. (B)	12. (A)	13. (B)	14. (A)	15. (A)	16. (C)
17. (C)	18. (C)	19. (B)	20. (C)	21. (A)	22. (A)	23. (C)	24. (A)	25. (C)	26. (C)
27. (B)	28. (B)	29. (C)	30. (A)	31. (B)					

PART 3

32. (D)	33. (C)	34. (B)	35. (D)	36. (C)	37. (D)	38. (A)	39. (B)	40. (B)	41. (A)
42. (B)	43. (A)	44. (A)	45. (B)	46. (C)	47. (B)	48. (D)	49. (A)	50. (A)	51. (C)
52. (B)	53. (A)	54. (D)	55. (B)	56. (B)	57. (C)	58. (A)	59. (B)	60. (C)	61. (C)
62. (D)	63. (D)	64. (B)	65. (B)	66. (A)	67. (B)	68. (A)	69. (C)	70. (B)	

PART 4

71. (A)	72. (B)	73. (C)	74. (C)	75. (C)	76. (B)	77. (A)	78. (C)	79. (C)	80. (C)
81. (C)	82. (D)	83. (A)	84. (B)	85. (C)	86. (A)	87. (C)	88. (A)	89. (B)	90. (C)
91. (C)	92. (C)	93. (B)	94. (A)	95. (D)	96. (B)	97. (C)	98. (D)	99. (D)	100. (B)

PART 5

101. (A)	102. (C)	103. (C)	104. (A)	105. (A)	106. (D)	107. (B)	108. (C)	109. (C)	110. (B)
111. (C)	112. (B)	113. (B)	114. (D)	115. (A)	116. (B)	117. (C)	118. (D)	119. (A)	120. (C)
121. (C)	122. (A)	123. (C)	124. (A)	125. (A)	126. (C)	127. (B)	128. (D)	129. (B)	130. (A)

PART 6

131. (B)	132. (C)	133. (B)	134. (C)	135. (B)	136. (D)	137. (B)	138. (B)	139. (C)	140. (A)
141. (D)	142. (B)	143. (C)	144. (A)	145. (C)	146. (B)				

PART 7

147. (B)	148. (C)	149. (C)	150. (C)	151. (B)	152. (A)	153. (B)	154. (D)	155. (C)	156. (D)
157. (B)	158. (D)	159. (B)	160. (C)	161. (A)	162. (B)	163. (C)	164. (B)	165. (B)	166. (D)
167. (A)	168. (C)	169. (D)	170. (B)	171. (B)	172. (A)	173. (C)	174. (A)	175. (B)	176. (A)
177. (B)	178. (C)	179. (A)	180. (B)	181. (B)	182. (C)	183. (A)	184. (D)	185. (D)	186. (C)
187. (B)	188. (A)	189. (B)	190. (B)	191. (B)	192. (A)	193. (B)	194. (C)	195. (D)	196. (B)
197. (B)	198. (B)	199. (D)	200. (C)						

PART 1

1. 🔊 호주식 발음

(A) She is tasting a cookie.
(B) She is carrying a pot.
(C) She is filling a kettle with water.
(D) She is holding a tray.

taste[teist] 맛을 보다　kettle[kétl] 주전자　tray[trei] 접시

해석　(A) 그녀는 쿠키의 맛을 보고 있다.
　　　(B) 그녀는 냄비를 옮기고 있다.
　　　(C) 그녀는 주전자에 물을 채우고 있다.
　　　(D) 그녀는 접시를 잡고 있다.

해설　한 여자가 한 손으로 접시를 잡고 있는 모습을 나타내는 1인 사진입니다.
　　　(A) [×] tasting(맛을 보고 있다)은 여자의 동작과 무관하므로 오답입니다.
　　　(B) [×] carrying a pot(냄비를 옮기고 있다)은 여자의 동작과 무관하므로 오답입니다. 사진에 있는 냄비(pot)를 사용하여 혼동을 주었습니다.
　　　(C) [×] 사진에서 물(water)을 확인할 수 없으므로 오답입니다. 사진에 있는 주전자(kettle)를 사용하여 혼동을 주었습니다.
　　　(D) [○] 여자가 접시를 잡고 있는 모습을 정확히 묘사한 정답입니다.

2. 🔊 미국식 발음

(A) The woman is listening to headphones.
(B) They are unpacking a picnic basket.
(C) They are lying on a blanket.
(D) The man is playing an instrument.

unpack[ʌnpǽk] (짐을) 풀다, 꺼내다　lie[lai] 누워 있다, 눕다
blanket[blǽŋkit] 담요　instrument[ínstrəmənt] 악기, 도구

해석　(A) 여자는 헤드폰으로 듣고 있다.
　　　(B) 그들은 소풍 바구니를 풀고 있다.
　　　(C) 그들은 담요 위에 누워 있다.
　　　(D) 남자는 악기를 연주하고 있다.

해설　두 남녀가 잔디 위에 앉아 있는 모습을 나타내는 2인 이상 사진입니다.
　　　(A) [×] 사진에 헤드폰(headphones)이 없으므로 오답입니다. The woman is listening(여자는 듣고 있다)까지만 듣고 정답으로 선택하지 않도록 주의합니다.
　　　(B) [×] unpacking(풀고 있다)은 사람들의 동작과 무관하므로 오답입니다. 사진에 있는 소풍 바구니(picnic basket)를 사용하여 혼동을 주었습니다.
　　　(C) [×] lying(누워 있다)은 사람들의 동작과 무관하므로 오답입니다.
　　　(D) [○] 남자가 악기를 연주하고 있는 모습을 가장 잘 묘사한 정답입니다.

3. 🔊 호주식 발음

(A) She is riding a passenger train.
(B) She is searching through her purse.
(C) She is going up the stairs.
(D) She is getting off a subway.

purse[미 pəːrs, 영 pəːs] 핸드백, 지갑　get off ~에서 내리다

해석　(A) 그녀는 여객 열차를 타고 있다.
　　　(B) 그녀는 핸드백을 뒤지고 있다.
　　　(C) 그녀는 계단을 오르고 있다.
　　　(D) 그녀는 지하철에서 내리고 있다.

해설　한 여자가 핸드백을 들고 계단을 올라가고 있는 모습을 나타내는 1인 사진입니다.
　　　(A) [×] riding(타고 있다)은 여자의 동작과 무관하므로 오답입니다. 사진에 있는 여객 열차(passenger train)를 사용하여 혼동을 주었습니다.
　　　(B) [×] searching through(~을 뒤지고 있다)는 여자의 동작과 무관하므로 오답입니다.
　　　(C) [○] 여자가 계단을 오르고 있는 모습을 정확히 묘사한 정답입니다.
　　　(D) [×] getting off(~에서 내리고 있다)는 여자의 동작과 무관하므로 오답입니다. 사진에 있는 지하철(subway)을 사용하여 혼동을 주었습니다.

4. 🔊 미국식 발음

(A) Ships are floating on the sea.
(B) A bridge stretches over a waterway.
(C) A crane is loading a boat with cargo.
(D) Containers are stacked in piles.

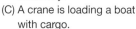

float[미 flout, 영 fləut] 뜨다　stretch[stretʃ] 뻗어 있다
waterway[미 wɔ́ːtərwèi, 영 wɔ́ːtəwei] 항로, 수로
load[미 loud, 영 ləud] 싣다　cargo[káːrgou, 영 káːgəu] 화물, 짐
stack[stæk] 쌓다　in a pile 더미로

해석　(A) 배들이 바다에 떠 있다.
　　　(B) 다리가 항로에 걸쳐 뻗어 있다.
　　　(C) 크레인이 배에 화물을 싣고 있다.
　　　(D) 컨테이너들이 더미로 쌓여 있다.

해설　컨테이너들이 쌓여 있는 항구의 전반적인 풍경을 나타내는 풍경 중심 사진입니다.
　　　(A) [×] 사진에서 바다에 떠 있는 배들(Ships)을 확인할 수 없으므로 오답입니다.
　　　(B) [×] 사진에서 다리(bridge)를 확인할 수 없으므로 오답입니다.
　　　(C) [×] 사진에서 배(boat)를 확인할 수 없으므로 오답입니다. 사진에 있는 화물(cargo)을 사용하여 혼동을 주었습니다.
　　　(D) [○] 컨테이너들이 쌓여 있는 모습을 가장 잘 묘사한 정답입니다.

정답·해석·해설

한 권으로 끝내는 해커스 토익 700+ (LC+RC+VOCA)

5. 🔊 캐나다식 발음

(A) One of the women is making a purchase.
(B) One of the women is folding an item of clothing.
(C) One of the women is browsing around the shop.
(D) One of the women is reaching over a small bag.

make a purchase 구매하다   fold[미 fould, 영 fəuld] 접다
browse[brauz] 둘러보다

해석 (A) 여자들 중 한 명이 구매를 하고 있다.
(B) 여자들 중 한 명이 옷 한 점을 접고 있다.
(C) 여자들 중 한 명이 상점 안을 둘러보고 있다.
(D) 여자들 중 한 명이 작은 가방에 손을 뻗고 있다.

해설 가게에서 구매가 이루어지고 있는 모습을 나타내는 2인 이상 사진입니다.
(A) [○] 한 여자가 구매를 하고 있는 모습을 가장 잘 묘사한 정답입니다.
(B) [×] folding(접고 있다)은 여자들의 동작과 무관하므로 오답입니다.
(C) [×] browsing around the shop(상점 안을 둘러보고 있다)은 여자들의 동작과 무관하므로 오답입니다.
(D) [×] 사진에 가방에 손을 뻗고 있는(reaching over) 여자가 없으므로 오답입니다.

6. 🔊 영국식 발음

(A) A path leads through a forest.
(B) Cyclists have stopped for a break.
(C) People are casting shadows on the ground.
(D) People are traveling in different directions.

path[미 pæθ, 영 pɑːθ] 길   lead[liːd] 이어지다
cast a shadow 그림자를 드리우다
direction[미 dirékʃən, 영 dairékʃən] 방향

해석 (A) 길이 숲을 지나 이어져 있다.
(B) 자전거를 타는 사람들이 휴식을 위해 멈춰 있다.
(C) 사람들이 땅 위에 그림자를 드리우고 있다.
(D) 사람들이 다른 방향으로 이동하고 있다.

해설 사람들이 자전거를 타고 있는 모습을 나타내는 2인 이상 사진입니다.
(A) [×] 사진에서 길이 숲을 지나 이어져 있는지 알 수 없으므로 오답입니다.
(B) [×] 사람들이 자전거를 타고 가고 있는데 멈춰 있다고 잘못 묘사했으므로 오답입니다. 사진에 있는 자전거를 타는 사람들(Cyclists)을 사용하여 혼동을 주었습니다.
(C) [○] 사람들이 땅 위에 그림자를 드리우고 있는 모습을 가장 잘 묘사한 정답입니다. 동사 cast가 그림자를 드리운 모습을 묘사할 때 사용됨을 알아둡니다.
(D) [×] 사람들이 같은 방향으로 이동하고 있는데 다른 방향으로 이동하고 있다고 잘못 묘사했으므로 오답입니다.

PART 2

7. 🔊 미국식 발음 → 호주식 발음

Who is Mr. Taylor talking with?
(A) Yes, I heard his speech too.
(B) To renew the contract.
(C) Ms. Daly, the head designer.

speech[spiːtʃ] 연설   renew[rinjúː] 갱신하다
contract[kɔ́ntrækt] 계약서

해석 Mr. Taylor는 누구와 이야기하고 있나요?
(A) 네, 저도 그의 연설을 들었어요.
(B) 계약서를 갱신하기 위해서요.
(C) 수석 디자이너인 Ms. Daly요.

해설 Mr. Taylor가 누구와 이야기하고 있는지를 묻는 Who 의문문입니다.
(A) [×] 의문사 의문문에 Yes로 응답했으므로 오답입니다.
(B) [×] Mr. Taylor가 누구와 이야기하고 있는지를 물었는데, 이와 관련이 없는 계약서를 갱신하기 위해서라는 내용으로 응답했으므로 오답입니다.
(C) [○] 수석 디자이너인 Ms. Daly라며 Mr. Taylor와 이야기하고 있는 인물을 언급했으므로 정답입니다.

8. 🔊 캐나다식 발음 → 미국식 발음

Why is the store closed so early?
(A) I'm buying some shoes.
(B) Because it's the holiday season.
(C) It's quite close to here.

holiday[미 hálədèi, 영 hɔ́lədei] 휴가   season[síːzːən] 철, 계절

해석 그 가게가 왜 이렇게 일찍 문을 닫았나요?
(A) 저는 신발을 사고 있어요.
(B) 휴가철이기 때문에요.
(C) 그곳은 여기에서 꽤 가까워요.

해설 가게가 왜 일찍 문을 닫았는지를 묻는 Why 의문문입니다.
(A) [×] 질문의 store(가게)와 관련 있는 buying some shoes(신발을 사고 있다)를 사용하여 혼동을 준 오답입니다.
(B) [○] 휴가철이기 때문이라며 가게가 일찍 문을 닫은 이유를 언급했으므로 정답입니다.
(C) [×] 질문의 closed(닫다)를 '가까운'이라는 의미의 형용사 close로 반복 사용하여 혼동을 준 오답입니다.

9. 🔊 호주식 발음 → 영국식 발음

When will the new president be appointed?
(A) I am volunteering for the campaign.
(B) Carol Johnson, I believe.
(C) At the next board meeting.

appoint[əpɔ́int] 임명하다
volunteer[미 vàːləntíər, 영 vɔ̀ləntíə] 자원봉사하다
campaign[kæmpéin] 선거 운동   board[미 bɔːrd, 영 bɔːd] 이사회

해석 새로운 사장은 언제 임명될 예정인가요?
(A) 저는 선거 운동을 위해 자원봉사를 하고 있어요.
(B) Carol Johnson인 것 같아요.

(C) 다음 이사회 회의에서요.

해설 새로운 사장이 언제 임명될 예정인지를 묻는 When 의문문입니다.
(A) [×] 새로운 사장이 언제 임명될 예정인지를 물었는데, 이와 관련이 없는 선거 운동을 위해 자원봉사를 하고 있다는 내용으로 응답했으므로 오답입니다.
(B) [×] 질문의 new president(새로운 사장)를 나타낼 수 있는 Carol Johnson을 사용하여 혼동을 준 오답입니다.
(C) [○] 다음 이사회 회의에서라며 새로운 사장이 임명될 시점을 언급했으므로 정답입니다.

10. 🔊 캐나다식 발음 → 영국식 발음

How do I change the ink cartridge?
(A) You should open the printer cover first.
(B) The price has changed recently.
(C) I prefer blue pens.

prefer [미 prifə́:r, 영 prifə́:] 더 좋아하다

해석 잉크 카트리지를 어떻게 교체하나요?
(A) 프린터의 덮개를 먼저 열어야 해요.
(B) 최근에 가격이 변경되었어요.
(C) 저는 파란색 펜이 더 좋아요.

해설 잉크 카트리지를 어떻게 교체하는지를 묻는 How 의문문입니다. How가 방법을 묻는 것임을 이해할 수 있어야 합니다.
(A) [○] 프린터의 덮개를 먼저 열어야 한다며 잉크 카트리지를 교체하는 방법을 언급했으므로 정답입니다.
(B) [×] 질문의 change(교체하다)를 '변경되다'라는 의미의 changed로 반복 사용하여 혼동을 준 오답입니다.
(C) [×] 잉크 카트리지를 어떻게 교체하는지를 물었는데, 이와 관련이 없는 파란색 펜이 더 좋다는 내용으로 응답했으므로 오답입니다.

11. 🔊 호주식 발음 → 미국식 발음

You're not visiting our clients today, are you?
(A) All visitors require passes.
(B) No, I'm going on Monday.
(C) That's my office.

pass [미 pæs, 영 pɑːs] 출입증

해석 당신은 오늘 우리 고객들을 방문하지 않을 거죠, 그렇죠?
(A) 모든 방문자들은 출입증이 필요해요.
(B) 아니요, 저는 월요일에 갈 거예요.
(C) 그것이 제 사무실이에요.

해설 상대방이 오늘 고객들을 방문하지 않을 것인지를 확인하는 부가 의문문입니다.
(A) [×] visiting – visitors의 유사 발음 어휘를 사용하여 혼동을 준 오답입니다.
(B) [○] No로 오늘 고객들을 방문하지 않을 것임을 전달한 후, 월요일에 갈 것이라는 부연 설명을 했으므로 정답입니다.
(C) [×] 오늘 고객들을 방문하지 않을 것인지를 물었는데, 이와 관련이 없는 그것이 자신의 사무실이라는 내용으로 응답했으므로 오답입니다.

12. 🔊 영국식 발음 → 호주식 발음

Where are the old financial reports kept?
(A) They're in the accounting department.
(B) I will be reporting my results tomorrow.
(C) Thanks for putting them away.

financial [fainǽnʃəl] 회계의, 재무의
report [미 ripɔ́:rt, 영 ripɔ́:t] 보고서; 보고하다
accounting [əkáuntiŋ] 회계 put ~ away ~을 치우다

해석 이전 회계 보고서들은 어디에 보관되어 있나요?
(A) 그것들은 회계 부서에 있어요.
(B) 저는 내일 제 결과물을 보고할 거예요.
(C) 그것들을 치워 줘서 고마워요.

해설 이전 회계 보고서들이 어디에 보관되어 있는지를 묻는 Where 의문문입니다.
(A) [○] 회계 부서에 있다며 이전 회계 보고서들이 보관되어 있는 장소를 언급했으므로 정답입니다.
(B) [×] 질문의 reports(보고서)를 '보고하다'라는 의미의 동사 reporting으로 반복 사용하여 혼동을 준 오답입니다.
(C) [×] 이전 회계 보고서들이 어디에 보관되어 있는지를 물었는데, 이와 관련이 없는 그것들을 치워 줘서 고맙다는 내용으로 응답했으므로 오답입니다.

13. 🔊 캐나다식 발음 → 미국식 발음

When does the staff cafeteria open for lunch?
(A) The café is closed.
(B) I'll check the Web site.
(C) On the ground floor.

cafeteria [미 kæ̀fətíəriə, 영 kæ̀fətíəriə] 구내식당
ground floor 1층

해석 직원 구내식당은 점심때 언제 문을 여나요?
(A) 그 카페는 문을 닫았어요.
(B) 제가 웹사이트를 확인해볼게요.
(C) 1층이에요.

해설 직원 구내식당이 점심때 언제 문을 여는지를 묻는 When 의문문입니다.
(A) [×] 질문의 cafeteria – café의 유사 발음 어휘를 사용하여 혼동을 준 오답입니다.
(B) [○] 자신이 웹사이트를 확인해보겠다는 말로 모른다는 간접적인 응답을 했으므로 정답입니다.
(C) [×] 직원 구내식당이 점심때 언제 문을 여는지를 물었는데 장소로 응답했으므로 오답입니다.

14. 🔊 호주식 발음 → 영국식 발음

Don't you take public transportation to work?
(A) No, I usually walk.
(B) He is working in the Peterson Building.
(C) The train is leaving.

public transportation 대중교통

해석 당신은 출근할 때 대중교통을 이용하지 않나요?
(A) 아니요, 저는 보통 걸어가요.
(B) 그는 Peterson 건물에서 근무하고 있어요.
(C) 기차가 떠나고 있어요.

해설 출근할 때 대중교통을 이용하지 않는지를 묻는 일반 의문문입니다.
　(A) [○] No로 출근할 때 대중교통을 이용하지 않음을 전달한 후, 보통 걸어간다는 추가 정보를 제공했으므로 정답입니다.
　(B) [×] 질문의 work(직장)를 '일하다'라는 의미의 동사 working으로 반복 사용하여 혼동을 준 오답입니다.
　(C) [×] 질문의 public transportation(대중교통)과 관련 있는 train(기차)을 사용하여 혼동을 준 오답입니다.

15. 🔊 미국식 발음 → 캐나다식 발음

Which of the book covers do you prefer?
(A) Both of them look nice.
(B) The newspaper already covered the story.
(C) Everyone enjoys reading it.

cover[미 kʌ́vər, 영 kʌ́və] 표지; 다루다, 포함시키다

해석 어느 책 표지가 더 좋으신가요?
　(A) 둘 다 좋아 보여요.
　(B) 신문에서 벌써 그 이야기를 다뤘어요.
　(C) 모두가 그것을 읽는 걸 좋아해요.

해설 어느 책 표지가 더 좋은지를 묻는 Which 의문문입니다. Which of the book covers를 반드시 들어야 합니다.
　(A) [○] 둘 다 좋아 보인다는 말로 두 책의 표지가 모두 좋음을 전달했으므로 정답입니다.
　(B) [×] 질문의 covers(표지)를 '다루다'라는 의미의 동사 covered로 반복 사용하여 혼동을 준 오답입니다.
　(C) [×] 질문의 book covers(책 표지)에서 '책'이라는 의미의 book과 관련된 reading(읽는 것)을 사용하여 혼동을 준 오답입니다.

16. 🔊 호주식 발음 → 영국식 발음

Where do you want to hang the new painting?
(A) During a recent art class.
(B) Yes, I chose it myself.
(C) On the back wall.

painting[péintiŋ] 그림 recent[ríːsnt] 최근의

해석 당신은 새 그림을 어디에 걸기를 원하나요?
　(A) 최근의 미술 수업 시간 동안에요.
　(B) 네, 제가 직접 그것을 선택했어요.
　(C) 뒤쪽의 벽에요.

해설 새 그림을 어디에 걸기를 원하는지를 묻는 Where 의문문입니다.
　(A) [×] 새 그림을 어디에 걸기를 원하는지를 물었는데 기간으로 응답했으므로 오답입니다.
　(B) [×] 의문사 의문문에 Yes로 응답했으므로 오답입니다.
　(C) [○] 뒤쪽의 벽이라며 새 그림을 걸고 싶은 위치를 언급했으므로 정답입니다.

17. 🔊 미국식 발음 → 캐나다식 발음

Would you like Indian or Chinese food tonight?
(A) I haven't tried that one yet.
(B) The screening is tonight.
(C) Anything spicy.

screening[skríːniŋ] 상영회 spicy[spáisi] 매운

해석 오늘 밤에 인도 음식이나 중국 음식을 먹으러 갈래요?
　(A) 전 그것을 아직 먹어 본 적이 없어요.
　(B) 상영회는 오늘 밤이에요.
　(C) 아무거나 매운 것으로요.

해설 오늘 밤에 인도 음식을 먹으러 갈 것인지 아니면 중국 음식을 먹으러 갈 것인지를 묻는 선택 의문문입니다.
　(A) [×] 질문의 Indian or Chinese food(인도 음식이나 중국 음식)와 관련 있는 tried(먹어 보다)를 사용하여 혼동을 준 오답입니다.
　(B) [×] 질문의 tonight을 반복 사용하여 혼동을 준 오답입니다.
　(C) [○] 아무거나 매운 것으로라는 말로 둘 중 매운 것을 먹고 싶다는 것을 전달했으므로 정답입니다.

18. 🔊 캐나다식 발음 → 영국식 발음

We have new employees starting tomorrow.
(A) The promotion was yesterday.
(B) Sales are starting to increase.
(C) That's good to know.

promotion[미 prəmóuʃən, 영 prəmáuʃən] 홍보 활동
increase[inkríːs] 증가하다

해석 내일부터 일을 시작하는 신규 직원들이 있어요.
　(A) 홍보 활동은 어제였어요.
　(B) 매출액이 증가하기 시작하고 있어요.
　(C) 알게 되어 좋네요.

해설 내일부터 일을 시작하는 신규 직원들이 있다는 객관적인 사실을 전달하는 평서문입니다.
　(A) [×] 질문의 tomorrow(내일)와 관련 있는 yesterday(어제)를 사용하여 혼동을 준 오답입니다.
　(B) [×] 질문의 starting을 반복 사용하여 혼동을 준 오답입니다.
　(C) [○] 알게 되어 좋다는 말로 내일부터 일을 시작하는 신규 직원들이 있다는 사실에 대한 의견을 제시했으므로 정답입니다.

19. 🔊 미국식 발음 → 호주식 발음

Would you like me to check the monthly budget?
(A) Does your store take checks?
(B) Yes, I'll e-mail you a copy.
(C) Our monthly meeting.

check[tʃek] 확인하다; 수표 monthly[mʌ́nθli] 월간의, 매월의
budget[bʌ́dʒit] 예산(안)

해석 제가 월 예산안을 확인해 드릴까요?
　(A) 당신의 가게는 수표를 받나요?
　(B) 네, 제가 이메일로 한 부 보내 드릴게요.
　(C) 우리의 월간 회의요.

해설 월 예산안을 확인해 주기를 원하는지를 묻는 일반 의문문입니다.
　(A) [×] 질문의 check(확인하다)를 '수표'라는 의미의 명사 checks로 반복 사용하여 혼동을 준 오답입니다.
　(B) [○] Yes로 확인해 달라고 한 후, 이메일로 예산안을 한 부 보내 주겠다는 부연 설명을 했으므로 정답입니다.
　(C) [×] 질문의 monthly를 반복 사용하여 혼동을 준 오답입니다.

20. 🎧 영국식 발음 → 캐나다식 발음

What is the marketing seminar going to be about?
(A) It is at 4 P.M.
(B) At the business school.
(C) I haven't been told yet.

business school 경영 대학원

해석 마케팅 세미나는 무엇에 대한 것인가요?
(A) 그것은 오후 4시에 해요.
(B) 경영 대학원에서요.
(C) 저는 아직 들은 바가 없어요.

해설 마케팅 세미나가 무엇에 대한 것인지를 묻는 What 의문문입니다.
(A) [×] 마케팅 세미나가 무엇에 대한 것인지를 물었는데 시점으로 응답했으므로 오답입니다.
(B) [×] 마케팅 세미나가 무엇에 대한 것인지를 물었는데 장소로 응답했으므로 오답입니다.
(C) [○] 아직 들은 바가 없다는 말로 모른다는 간접적인 응답을 했으므로 정답입니다.

21. 🎧 호주식 발음 → 영국식 발음

I'd like to book a single hotel room, please.
(A) Certainly. For how many nights?
(B) Next to the convention center.
(C) The staff will be cleaning soon.

convention center 컨벤션 센터(회의·전시 장소나 숙박 시설이 집중된 종합 빌딩)

해석 저는 1인 객실을 예약하고 싶어요.
(A) 알겠습니다. 몇 박 묵으실 건가요?
(B) 컨벤션 센터 옆이요.
(C) 직원이 곧 청소를 할 거예요.

해설 1인 객실을 예약해 달라고 요청하는 평서문입니다.
(A) [○] Certainly(알겠습니다)로 요청을 수락한 후, 숙박 기간에 대한 추가 정보를 요구하는 정답입니다.
(B) [×] 1인 객실을 예약해 달라고 요청했는데 위치로 응답했으므로 오답입니다.
(C) [×] 1인 객실을 예약해 달라고 요청했는데, 이와 관련이 없는 직원이 곧 청소를 할 것이라는 내용으로 응답했으므로 오답입니다.

22. 🎧 캐나다식 발음 → 미국식 발음

The receptionist was very friendly, don't you think?
(A) She was kind.
(B) James received it last night.
(C) My friend will be here for me.

receptionist [risépʃənist] 접수 담당자

해석 그 접수 담당자는 매우 친절했어요, 그렇게 생각하지 않으세요?
(A) 그녀는 친절했어요.
(B) James는 그것을 어젯밤에 받았어요.
(C) 제 친구가 저를 위해 이곳에 올 거예요.

해설 접수 담당자가 매우 친절했다는 의견에 동의를 구하는 부가 의문문입니다.
(A) [○] 그녀는 친절했다는 말로 상대방의 의견에 동의했으므

로 정답입니다.
(B) [×] receptionist - received의 유사 발음 어휘를 사용하여 혼동을 준 오답입니다.
(C) [×] friendly - friend의 유사 발음 어휘를 사용하여 혼동을 준 오답입니다.

23. 🎧 캐나다식 발음 → 호주식 발음

Have you been to the new history museum downtown yet?
(A) I'll ask a tour guide at the museum.
(B) Across from the museum.
(C) Do you mean the one on Gilmore Street?

downtown [dàuntáun] 시내에 있는

해석 시내에 있는 새로운 역사박물관에 벌써 가보셨나요?
(A) 제가 박물관에 있는 관광 가이드에게 문의해볼게요.
(B) 박물관 맞은편이에요.
(C) Gilmore가에 있는 것을 말씀하시는 건가요?

해설 시내에 있는 새로운 역사박물관에 가보았는지를 확인하는 일반 의문문입니다.
(A) [×] 질문의 museum을 반복 사용하여 혼동을 준 오답입니다.
(B) [×] 시내에 있는 새로운 역사박물관에 가보았는지를 물었는데 위치로 응답했으므로 오답입니다.
(C) [○] Gilmore가에 있는 것을 말하는지를 되물어 역사박물관에 대한 추가 정보를 요구하는 정답입니다.

24. 🎧 미국식 발음 → 캐나다식 발음

Are there enough cashiers to deal with all of our customers?
(A) We'd better hire more people.
(B) Yes, we take credit cards.
(C) A customer will call tomorrow.

cashier [미 kæʃíər, 영 kæʃíə] 계산원
deal with ~를 상대하다, ~을 처리하다 credit card 신용카드

해석 우리의 모든 고객들을 상대하기에 계산원이 충분한가요?
(A) 사람들을 더 고용하는 것이 좋겠어요.
(B) 네, 저희는 신용카드를 받습니다.
(C) 고객이 내일 전화할 거예요.

해설 모든 고객들을 상대하기에 계산원이 충분한지를 확인하는 일반 의문문입니다.
(A) [○] 사람들을 더 고용하는 것이 좋겠다는 말로 계산원이 충분하지 않음을 간접적으로 전달했으므로 정답입니다.
(B) [×] 질문의 cashiers(계산원)와 관련 있는 credit cards(신용카드)를 사용하여 혼동을 준 오답입니다.
(C) [×] 질문의 customers를 customer로 반복 사용하여 혼동을 준 오답입니다.

25. 🎧 호주식 발음 → 영국식 발음

Who is in charge of entering our sales records into the computer?
(A) I will be entering the competition.
(B) We've broken the record.
(C) They should be given to Ms. Rodriguez.

in charge of ~을 담당하는
enter[미 éntər, 영 éntə] 출전하다, 입력하다
competition[미 kɑ̀ːmpətíʃən, 영 kɔ̀mpətíʃən] 대회

해석 누가 우리의 매출 기록을 컴퓨터에 입력하는 것을 담당하나요?
(A) 저는 그 대회에 출전할 거예요.
(B) 우리는 그 기록을 깼어요.
(C) 그것들은 Ms. Rodriguez에게 보내져야 해요.

해설 누가 매출 기록을 컴퓨터에 입력하는 것을 담당하는지를 묻는 Who 의문문입니다.
(A) [×] 질문의 entering(입력하다)을 '출전하다'라는 다른 의미로 반복 사용하여 혼동을 준 오답입니다.
(B) [×] 질문의 records를 record로 반복 사용하여 혼동을 준 오답입니다.
(C) [○] 그것들은 Ms. Rodriguez에게 보내져야 한다며 매출 기록 입력을 담당하는 인물을 언급했으므로 정답입니다.

26. 3번 영국식 발음 → 캐나다식 발음

Wouldn't you prefer to pay a little extra for a longer warranty?
(A) You'll arrive a little bit late.
(B) Refer to the product catalog.
(C) I'm not sure if it's worth it.

extra[ékstrə] 추가 요금
warranty[미 wɔ́ːrənti, 영 wɔ́rənti] 품질 보증서
refer[미 rifə́ːr, 영 rifə́ː] 참고하다   worth[미 wəːrθ, 영 wəːθ] 가치 있는

해석 더 긴 기간의 품질 보증서를 위해 약간의 추가 요금을 지불하는 것이 낫지 않나요?
(A) 당신은 조금 늦게 도착하게 될 거예요.
(B) 제품 카탈로그를 참고하세요.
(C) 저는 그것이 그럴 가치가 있는지 모르겠어요.

해설 더 긴 기간의 품질 보증서를 위해 약간의 추가 요금을 지불하는 것이 낫지 않은지를 묻는 일반 의문문입니다.
(A) [×] 더 긴 기간의 품질 보증서를 위해 약간의 추가 요금을 더 지불하는 것이 낫지 않은지를 물었는데, 이와 관련이 없는 상대방이 조금 늦게 도착하게 될 것이라는 내용으로 응답했으므로 오답입니다.
(B) [×] prefer to – Refer to의 유사 발음 어휘를 사용하여 혼동을 준 오답입니다.
(C) [○] 그것이 그럴 가치가 있는지 모르겠다는 말로 더 긴 기간의 품질 보증서를 위해 추가 요금을 지불하지 않겠다는 것을 간접적으로 전달했으므로 정답입니다.

27. 3번 호주식 발음 → 미국식 발음

Can you ask a maintenance worker to fix our air conditioner?
(A) It's quite warm outside.
(B) I'll call right away.
(C) A couple of questions.

maintenance[méintənəns] 정비, 유지 보수

해석 정비공에게 우리 에어컨을 수리해 달라고 요청해 주시겠어요?
(A) 밖은 꽤 따뜻해요.
(B) 제가 바로 전화할게요.
(C) 몇 가지 질문들이요.

해설 정비공에게 에어컨을 수리해 달라고 요청해 달라는 일반 의문문입니다.
(A) [×] 정비공에게 에어컨을 수리해 달라는 요청을 해달라고 했는데, 이와 관련이 없는 밖은 꽤 따뜻하다는 내용으로 응답했으므로 오답입니다.
(B) [○] 자신이 바로 전화하겠다는 말로 요청을 수락한 정답입니다.
(C) [×] 질문의 ask(요청하다)의 다른 의미인 '묻다'와 관련 있는 questions(질문들)를 사용하여 혼동을 준 오답입니다.

28. 3번 캐나다식 발음 → 영국식 발음

I have to review my schedule before making plans for the vacation.
(A) Here are the building plans.
(B) That's a good idea.
(C) I will be working with the planning team.

schedule[미 skédʒuːl, 영 ʃédʒuːl] 일정, 계획
plan[plæn] 계획, 설계도; 기획하다

해석 저는 휴가 계획을 세우기 전에 제 일정을 확인해야 해요.
(A) 여기 건물 설계도가 있어요.
(B) 좋은 생각이네요.
(C) 저는 기획팀과 일할 거예요.

해설 휴가 계획을 세우기 전에 자신의 일정을 확인해야 한다는 의견을 제시하는 평서문입니다.
(A) [×] 질문의 plans(계획)를 '설계도'라는 다른 의미로 반복 사용하여 혼동을 준 오답입니다.
(B) [○] 좋은 생각이라며 상대방의 의견에 동의했으므로 정답입니다.
(C) [×] plans – planning의 유사 발음 어휘를 사용하여 혼동을 준 오답입니다.

29. 3번 미국식 발음 → 호주식 발음

Why are the computers being delivered later than expected?
(A) The bill has arrived.
(B) Try switching it off for a while.
(C) The shop is low on stock.

bill[bil] 청구서, 계산서   switch off ~을 끄다
low on stock 재고가 부족한

해석 왜 컴퓨터들이 예상보다 늦게 배송되고 있나요?
(A) 청구서가 도착했어요.
(B) 그것을 잠시 동안 꺼 보세요.
(C) 가게에 재고가 부족해요.

해설 왜 컴퓨터들이 예상보다 늦게 배송되고 있는지를 묻는 Why 의문문입니다.
(A) [×] 질문의 delivered(배송되다)와 관련 있는 arrived(도착했다)를 사용하여 혼동을 준 오답입니다.
(B) [×] 질문의 computers(컴퓨터들)와 관련 있는 switching ~ off(~을 끄다)를 사용하여 혼동을 준 오답입니다.
(C) [○] 가게에 재고가 부족하다는 말로 컴퓨터들이 예상보다 늦게 배송되고 있는 이유를 언급했으므로 정답입니다.

30. 3M 캐나다식 발음 → 미국식 발음

> Would you care to help me write my speech for the conference?
> **(A) John can give you a hand.**
> (B) Yes, it's at the Prince Hotel.
> (C) I'll listen to the president's speech tonight.

give a hand 도와주다

해석 제가 학회를 위한 연설문을 작성하는 것을 도와주실 수 있나요?
　　(A) John이 당신을 도울 수 있을 거예요.
　　(B) 네, 그것은 Prince 호텔에서 열려요.
　　(C) 저는 오늘 밤 대통령의 연설을 들을 거예요.

해설 연설문을 작성하는 것을 도와줄 수 있는지를 묻는 일반 의문문입니다.
　　(A) [o] John이 도와줄 수 있을 것이라는 말로 자신은 연설문 작성을 도와줄 수 없음을 간접적으로 전달했으므로 정답입니다.
　　(B) [x] 연설문을 작성하는 것을 도와줄 수 있는지를 물었는데 장소로 응답했으므로 오답입니다. Yes만 듣고 정답으로 고르지 않도록 주의합니다.
　　(C) [x] 질문의 speech를 반복 사용하여 혼동을 준 오답입니다.

31. 3M 영국식 발음 → 호주식 발음

> I thought the resort was a 30-minute taxi ride from the airport.
> (A) It was left in the cab.
> **(B) It takes an hour in traffic.**
> (C) At the check-in desk.

cab[kæb] 택시　check-in[tʃékin] 탑승 수속

해석 저는 그 리조트가 공항에서 택시로 30분 거리라고 생각했어요.
　　(A) 그것을 택시에 두고 왔어요.
　　(B) 교통 체증이 있을 땐 한 시간이 걸려요.
　　(C) 탑승 수속 창구에서요.

해설 리조트가 공항에서 택시로 30분 거리라고 생각했다는 의견을 제시하는 평서문입니다.
　　(A) [x] 질문의 taxi(택시)와 같은 의미인 cab(택시)을 사용하여 혼동을 준 오답입니다.
　　(B) [o] 교통 체증이 있을 땐 한 시간이 걸린다는 말로 리조트에서 공항까지의 거리에 대한 추가 정보를 제공했으므로 정답입니다.
　　(C) [x] 질문의 airport(공항)와 관련 있는 check-in desk(탑승 수속 창구)를 사용하여 혼동을 준 오답입니다.

PART 3

32-34 3M 캐나다식 발음 → 미국식 발음

Questions 32-34 refer to the following conversation.

> M: Did you hear that ³²**Brian Oliver would be receiving the Salesperson of the Year award**?
> W: Yeah. That's pretty impressive, considering that he only started working for our company last year. ³³**We should stop by his desk** ○
> **to congratulate him.**
> M: I'd like to, but first I need to finish updating this accounting report. ³⁴**I have to give it to our supervisor** in about an hour.
> W: I see. Well, let's talk to Brian before our staff meeting this afternoon, then.

salesperson[미 séilzpə̀:rsn, 영 séilzpə̀:sn] 영업사원
impressive[imprésiv] 인상적인
congratulate[미 kəngrǽtʃulèit, 영 kəngrǽtʃəlèit] 축하하다
accounting[əkáuntiŋ] 회계
supervisor[미 sú:pərvàizər, 영 sú:pəvàizə] 상사, 관리자

해석

32-34번은 다음 대화에 관한 문제입니다.

남: ³²Brian Oliver가 올해의 영업사원 상을 받을 것이라는 소식을 들었나요?
여: 네. 그가 작년에 우리 회사에서 막 일하기 시작했다는 걸 고려하면, 그건 매우 인상적이에요. ³³그를 축하해 주러 그의 자리로 가는 게 좋겠어요.
남: 저도 그러고 싶은데, 먼저 이 회계 보고서를 업데이트하는 걸 끝내야 해요. 한 시간 정도 뒤에 ³⁴저희 상사에게 그것을 제출해야 하거든요.
여: 알겠어요. 음, 그러면, 오늘 오후 직원회의 전에 Brian과 이야기해요.

32.

해석 남자에 따르면, Brian Oliver는 무엇을 받을 것인가?
　　(A) 상담
　　(B) 신분증
　　(C) 보고서
　　(D) 상

해설 Brian Oliver가 받을 것을 묻는 문제입니다. 남자가 "Brian Oliver would be receiving the Salesperson of the Year award"라며 Brian Oliver가 올해의 영업사원 상을 받을 것이라고 하였습니다. 따라서 정답은 (D) An award입니다.

어휘 consultation[미 kà:nsəltéiʃən, 영 kɔ̀nsʌltéiʃən] 상담

33.

해석 여자는 무엇을 제안하는가?
　　(A) 제품 소개하기
　　(B) 작은 선물 사기
　　(C) 동료의 자리에 찾아가기
　　(D) 사내 행사에 참석하기

해설 여자가 제안하는 것을 묻는 문제입니다. 여자가 "We should stop by his[Brian Oliver] desk to congratulate him."이라며 Brian Oliver를 축하해 주러 그의 자리로 갈 것을 제안하였습니다. 따라서 정답은 (C) Visiting a coworker's desk입니다.

어휘 sales presentation 제품 소개
coworker[미 kóuwə̀:rkər, 영 kə́uwə́:kə] 동료

34.

해석 남자는 회계 보고서에 대해 무엇을 말하는가?
　　(A) 계산 오류가 있다.
　　(B) 상사에게 제출되어야 한다.
　　(C) 인쇄되어야 한다.
　　(D) 회의에서 배부되었다.

해설 남자가 회계 보고서에 대해 언급하는 것을 묻는 문제입니

다. 남자가 "I have to give it[accounting report] to our supervisor"라며 회계 보고서를 상사에게 제출해야 한다고 하였습니다. 따라서 정답은 (B) It should be submitted to a supervisor입니다.

어휘 calculation[미 kæ̀lkjuléiʃən, 영 kæ̀lkjəléiʃən] 계산
distribute[distríbju:t] 배부하다, 나누어주다

35-37 [🔊] 영국식 발음 → 호주식 발음 → 미국식 발음

Questions 35-37 refer to the following conversation with three speakers.

W1: Hey, ³⁵would either of you be interested in volunteering at next month's community art fair with me?

M: Of course. That would be great. What about you, Lisa?

W2: Sure. Actually, I heard that ³⁵all the profits from the event will be donated to ³⁵/³⁶the Gresham Foundation, which supports local artists.

W1: That's right.

M: Um. . . But parking is a bit expensive near the event venue, so ³⁷I was thinking that it would be good to carpool together. I can pick both of you up if you like.

W1: Good idea.

W2: I think I'll just take the bus, but thanks for offering.

---

volunteer[미 và:ləntiər, 영 vɔ̀ləntíə] 자원봉사하다
community[kəmjú:nəti] 지역 사회
profit[미 prά:fit, 영 prɔ́fit] 수익, 이익
donate[미 dóuneit, 영 dəunéit] 기부하다
carpool[미 kά:rpu:l, 영 kά:pu:l] 차를 함께 타다
pick up ~를 (차에) 태워주다, 태우러 가다

해석

35-37번은 다음 세 명의 대화에 관한 문제입니다.

여1: 있잖아요, ³⁵여러분 중에 다음 달에 있을 지역 사회 미술 박람회에서 저와 함께 자원봉사를 하는 것에 관심 있는 분이 있나요?

남: 물론이죠. 재미있을 것 같아요. Lisa, 당신은 어때요?

여2: 좋아요. 사실, 저는 ³⁵Gresham 재단에 그 행사의 모든 수익금이 기부될 것이고, ³⁶그 재단은 지역 예술가들을 후원한다고 들었어요.

여1: 맞아요.

남: 음... 그런데 행사장 근처에는 주차가 좀 비싸서, ³⁷모두 차를 함께 타는 게 좋을 것 같다고 생각하고 있었어요. 여러분들이 괜찮다면 제가 두 분 다 태워드릴 수 있어요.

여1: 좋은 생각이에요.

여2: 저는 그냥 버스를 탈 생각인데, 제안은 감사해요.

35.

해석 화자들은 주로 무엇에 대해 이야기하고 있는가?
(A) 농산물 직판장
(B) 온라인 판촉 행사
(C) 미술 수업
(D) 자선 행사

해설 대화의 주제를 묻는 문제입니다. 여자 1이 "would either of you be interested in volunteering at next month's

community art fair with me?"라며 화자들 중에 다음 달에 있을 지역 사회 미술 박람회에서 자신과 함께 자원봉사를 하는 것에 관심 있는 사람이 있는지를 물었고, 여자 2가 "all the profits from the event will be donated to the Gresham Foundation"이라며 Gresham 재단에 그 행사의 모든 수익금이 기부될 것이라고 하면서, 자선 박람회에 관한 내용으로 대화가 이어지고 있습니다. 따라서 정답은 (D) A charitable event입니다.

어휘 farmers' market 농산물 직판장
promotion[미 prəmóuʃən, 영 prəmə́uʃən] 판촉 행사, 판촉 활동
charitable[tʃǽrətəbəl] 자선의, 자선 단체의

36.

해석 Gresham 재단은 무슨 일을 하는가?
(A) 만찬 행사를 주선한다.
(B) 대회를 개최한다.
(C) 예술가들을 후원한다.
(D) 장학금을 제공한다.

해설 Gresham 재단이 하는 일을 묻는 문제입니다. 여자 2가 "the Gresham Foundation, which supports local artists"라며 Gresham 재단이 지역 예술가들을 후원한다고 하였습니다. 따라서 정답은 (C) Support artists입니다.

어휘 competition[미 kà:mpətíʃən, 영 kɔ̀mpətíʃən] 대회, 시합
scholarship[미 skά:lərʃip, 영 skɔ́ləʃip] 장학금

37.

해석 남자는 무엇을 제안하는가?
(A) 행사 티켓 찾아오기
(B) 대중교통 타기
(C) 주차 공간 예약하기
(D) 단체로 이동하기

해설 남자가 제안하는 것을 묻는 문제입니다. 남자가 "I was thinking that it would be good to carpool together. I can pick both of you up if you like."라며 모두 차를 함께 타는 게 좋을 것 같다고 생각하고 있었다면서 화자들이 괜찮다면 자신이 두 명 다 태워줄 수 있다고 제안하였습니다. 따라서 정답은 (D) Traveling as a group입니다.

어휘 collect[kəlékt] 찾아오다, 모으다
public transportation 대중교통, 공공 운송 기관

38-40 [🔊] 미국식 발음 → 캐나다식 발음

Questions 38-40 refer to the following conversation.

W: Kevin, ³⁸how is the new Web site for our bank coming along?

M: My team has just finished designing the home page. And this week, we will begin working on the login system for customers who want to do their banking online.

W: Excellent! Do you think we'll have a chance to show a trial version of the site at the ³⁹executive meeting next week?

M: Ah, it won't be completely finished by then. But ⁴⁰I could prepare a basic presentation on the current design.

W: OK. Please have it ready by Friday so that I can look at it before the meeting.

---

banking[bǽŋkiŋ] 은행 업무, 은행업   trial version 시험 버전 ◐

executive [미 igzékjutiv, 영 igzékjətiv] 경영진, 경영 간부
completely [kəmplí:tli] 완전히
current [미 ká:rənt, 영 kʌ́rənt] 현재의

해석

38-40번은 다음 대화에 관한 문제입니다.

여: Kevin, ³⁸우리 은행의 새로운 웹사이트는 어떻게 되어 가고 있나요?

남: 저희 팀은 이제 막 홈페이지를 디자인하는 것을 끝냈어요. 그리고 이번 주에, 저희는 온라인으로 은행 업무를 보고 싶어 하는 고객들을 위한 로그인 시스템 작업을 시작할 거예요.

여: 훌륭해요! ³⁹다음 주에 있을 경영진 회의에서 사이트의 시험 버전을 보여줄 수 있을 것 같나요?

남: 아, 그때까지 완전히 완성되지는 않을 거예요. 하지만 ⁴⁰현재의 디자인으로 기본적인 발표를 준비할 수는 있어요.

여: 알겠어요. 제가 회의 전에 볼 수 있도록 금요일까지 그것을 준비해 주세요.

38.

해석 화자들은 어디에서 일하는 것 같은가?
(A) 금융 기관에서
(B) 건축 회사에서
(C) 출판사에서
(D) 웹디자인 회사에서

해설 화자들이 일하는 장소를 묻는 문제입니다. 여자가 "how is the new Web site for our bank coming along?"이라며 자신들의 은행의 새로운 웹사이트가 어떻게 되어 가고 있는지를 물었습니다. 이를 통해 화자들이 일하는 장소가 금융 기관임을 알 수 있습니다. 따라서 정답은 (A) At a financial institution입니다.

어휘 financial [fainǽnʃəl] 금융의, 재정의
institution [미 ìnstətjú:ʃən, 영 ìnstitjú:ʃən] 기관
publishing [pʌ́bliʃiŋ] 출판, 발행

39.

해석 다음 주에 무슨 일이 일어날 것인가?
(A) 무역 박람회가 끝날 것이다.
(B) 경영진 회의가 열릴 것이다.
(C) 웹사이트가 폐쇄될 것이다.
(D) 새로운 서비스가 제공될 것이다.

해설 다음 주에 일어날 일을 묻는 문제입니다. 여자가 "executive meeting next week"이라며 다음 주에 있을 경영진 회의를 언급했습니다. 따라서 정답은 (B) A management meeting will take place입니다.

어휘 management [mǽnidʒmənt] 경영진, 운영진
shut down 폐쇄하다, 문을 닫다

40.

해석 남자는 무엇을 준비할 것인가?
(A) 안건
(B) 발표
(C) 예산안
(D) 청구서

해설 남자가 준비할 것을 묻는 문제입니다. 남자가 "I could prepare a basic presentation on the current design"이라며 현재의 디자인으로 기본적인 발표를 준비할 수는 있다고 하였습니다. 따라서 정답은 (B) A presentation입니다.

어휘 agenda [ədʒéndə] 안건 invoice [ínvɔis] 청구서, 송장

41-43 [호주] 영국식 발음 → 호주식 발음

Questions 41-43 refer to the following conversation.

W: ⁴¹I'm having trouble completing this employee evaluation form, Ken. ⁴²Could you help me fill out the section about teamwork?

M: An e-mail was sent about that form last Tuesday. Didn't you get it? If not, I can forward the e-mail to you.

W: That'd be helpful. I think I wasn't included on the mailing list, since I was recently promoted. I'll have to check the e-mail this afternoon, though, because ⁴³I'm meeting a client for lunch in a few minutes.

---

complete [kəmplí:t] 작성하다
evaluation [미 ivæljuéiʃən, 영 ivǽljuéiʃən] 평가, 감정
fill out ~을 작성하다, ~을 기입하다 forward [미 fɔ́:rwərd, 영 fɔ́:wəd] 보내다
promote [미 prəmóut, 영 prəmə́ut] 승진하다

해석

41-43번은 다음 대화에 관한 문제입니다.

여: ⁴¹저는 이 직원 평가 양식을 작성하는 데 어려움을 겪고 있어요, Ken. ⁴²팀워크란을 작성하는 것을 도와주실 수 있나요?

남: 지난주 화요일에 그 양식에 관한 이메일이 발송되었어요. 그것을 받지 못했나요? 만약 못 받았다면, 제가 그 이메일을 당신께 보내 드릴게요.

여: 그건 도움이 되겠네요. 제가 최근에 승진을 해서, 이메일 수신자 명단에 포함되어 있지 않나 봐요. 그런데 ⁴³저는 몇 분 뒤에 점심 식사를 하러 고객과 만날 거라서, 그 이메일은 오늘 오후에 확인해야겠네요.

41.

해석 여자의 문제는 무엇인가?
(A) 서류를 작성하는 것이 어렵다.
(B) 직원이 회사에 늦었다.
(C) 회의가 취소되었다.
(D) 평가가 부정적이었다.

해설 여자의 문제점을 묻는 문제입니다. 여자가 "I'm having trouble completing this employee evaluation form"이라며 직원 평가 양식을 작성하는 데 어려움을 겪고 있다고 하였습니다. 따라서 정답은 (A) A document is difficult to complete 입니다.

어휘 negative [négətiv] 부정적인

42.

해석 여자는 남자에게 무엇을 해달라고 요청하는가?
(A) 팀장과 이야기한다.
(B) 업무를 도와준다.
(C) 양식에 서명한다.
(D) 설명을 적는다.

해설 여자가 남자에게 요청하는 것을 묻는 문제입니다. 여자가 "Could you help me fill out the section about teamwork?"라며 팀워크란을 작성하는 것을 도와줄 수 있는지를 물은 것을 통해, 업무를 도와줄 것을 요청하고 있음을 알 수 있습니다. 따라서 정답은 (B) Assist with a task입니다.

어휘 instruction [instrʌ́kʃən] 설명, 지시

43.

해석 여자는 무엇을 할 것이라고 말하는가?
(A) 고객을 만난다.
(B) 이메일을 보낸다.
(C) 테이블을 예약한다.
(D) 보고서를 복사한다.

해설 여자가 하겠다고 말한 것을 묻는 문제입니다. 여자가 "I'm meeting a client for lunch in a few minutes"라며 몇 분 뒤에 점심 식사를 하러 고객과 만날 거라고 하였습니다. 따라서 정답은 (A) Meet a client입니다.

44-46 🎧 미국식 발음 → 캐나다식 발음

Questions 44-46 refer to the following conversation.

> W: Dylan, I'm not sure if you've heard, but **⁴⁴our company was selected to construct the city's new football stadium.** The news was announced yesterday.
> M: Yes, I have. In fact, I met with our supervisor regarding the project this morning. **⁴⁵We talked about how much the building materials will likely cost.**
> W: Did you figure it out, or are you still making calculations?
> M: I came up with an estimate. **⁴⁶I'm planning to present it to officials . . . uhm . . . city council members this Wednesday.**

construct[kənstrʌ́kt] 건설하다 stadium[stéidiəm] 경기장
announce[ənáuns] 발표하다
regarding[미 rigá:rdiŋ, 영 rigá:diŋ] ~과 관련하여
material[mətíəriəl] 자재, 재료 figure out ~을 계산해 내다
calculation[미 kæ̀lkjuléiʃən, 영 kæ̀lkjəléiʃən] 계산
come up with ~을 내놓다 estimate[미 éstəmət, 영 éstimət] 견적
official[əfíʃəl] 공무원 council[káunsəl] 의회

해석
44-46번은 다음 대화에 관한 문제입니다.

여: Dylan, 당신이 들으셨는지 모르겠지만, **⁴⁴우리 회사가 시의 새로운 축구 경기장을 건설하는 것에 선정되었어요.** 그 소식은 어제 발표되었어요.
남: 네, 들었어요. 실은, 저는 오늘 오전에 그 프로젝트와 관련해서 우리 상사와 만났어요. **⁴⁵우리는 건축 자재의 비용이 얼마나 들 것인지에 대해 이야기를 했어요.**
여: 비용을 계산해 내셨나요, 아니면 아직 계산하는 중인가요?
남: 견적을 냈어요. **⁴⁶이번 주 수요일에 공무원들... 음... 시의회 의원들에게 그것을 제출할 예정이에요.**

44.

해석 화자들은 어디에서 일하는 것 같은가?
(A) 건축 회사에서
(B) 스포츠용품점에서
(C) 부동산 중개사무소에서
(D) 정부 기관에서

해설 화자들이 일하는 장소를 묻는 문제입니다. 여자가 "our company was selected to construct the city's new football stadium"이라며 자신들의 회사가 시의 새로운 축구 경기장을 건설하는 것에 선정되었다고 한 말을 통해 화자들이 일하는 장소가 건축 회사임을 알 수 있습니다. 따라서 정답은 (A) At a construction firm입니다.

어휘 real estate 부동산

45.

해석 남자는 상사와 무엇을 논의했는가?
(A) 프로젝트 마감기한
(B) 자재 비용
(C) 건물 위치
(D) 시설 특징

해설 남자가 상사와 논의한 것을 묻는 문제입니다. 남자가 "We talked about how much the building materials will likely cost."라며 상사와 건축 자재의 비용이 얼마나 들 것인지에 대해 이야기를 했다고 하였습니다. 따라서 정답은 (B) Material expenses입니다.

어휘 expense[ikspéns] 비용 facility[fəsíləti] 시설
feature[미 fí:tʃər, 영 fí:tʃə] 특징

46.

해석 수요일에 무슨 일이 일어날 것 같은가?
(A) 물품이 주문될 것이다.
(B) 설계도가 공개될 것이다.
(C) 견적이 제출될 것이다.
(D) 발표 자료가 수정될 것이다.

해설 수요일에 일어날 일을 묻는 문제입니다. 남자가 "I'm planning to present it[estimate] to officials ~ this Wednesday."라며 이번 주 수요일에 공무원들에게 견적을 제출할 예정이라고 하였습니다. 따라서 정답은 (C) An estimate will be submitted입니다.

어휘 submit[səbmít] 제출하다

47-49 🎧 호주식 발음 → 영국식 발음

Questions 47-49 refer to the following conversation.

> M: Hello. My name is Mason Taylor. **⁴⁷I have an 11 o'clock appointment with Dr. Chao.**
> W: OK . . . **⁴⁷Are you here for a regular checkup or a specific health problem?**
> M: **⁴⁸I have a pain in my back.** It started yesterday when I bent over too quickly. I thought the pain would go away, but it's getting worse.
> W: I see. I'll make a note on your file for Dr. Chao. **⁴⁹Please fill out this form,** and then take a seat in the waiting room. Your name will be called in a few minutes.

regular[미 régjulər, 영 régjələ] 정기적인, 규칙적인
checkup[tʃékʌ̀p] 건강 검진 pain[pein] 통증
bend over 허리를 굽히다

해석
47-49번은 다음 대화에 관한 문제입니다.

남: 안녕하세요. 제 이름은 Mason Taylor입니다. **⁴⁷저는 Dr. Chao와 11시 정각에 진료 예약이 되어 있어요.**
여: 알겠습니다... **⁴⁷정기 건강 검진으로 오셨나요, 아니면 특별한 건강 문제로 오셨나요?**
남: **⁴⁸등에 통증이 있어요.** 어제 너무 급하게 허리를 굽혔을 때 통증이 시작되었어요. 통증이 사라질 것이라고 생각했는데, 악화되고 있네요.
여: 그렇군요. Dr. Chao를 위해 당신의 파일에 메모해두겠습니다.

⁴⁹이 양식을 작성해 주시고, 대기실에 앉아 계세요. 잠시 후에 성함을 불러 드리겠습니다.

47.

해석 화자들은 어디에 있는 것 같은가?
(A) 의과 대학에
(B) 병원에
(C) 은행에
(D) 헬스클럽에

해설 화자들이 있는 장소를 묻는 문제입니다. 남자가 "I have an 11 o'clock appointment with Dr. Chao."라며 자신이 Dr. Chao와 11시 정각에 진료 예약이 되어 있다고 하자, 여자가 "Are you here for a regular checkup or a specific health problem?"이라며 정기 건강 검진으로 왔는지 아니면 특별한 건강 문제로 왔는지를 물은 것을 통해 화자들이 병원에 있음을 알 수 있습니다. 따라서 정답은 (B) At a hospital입니다.

48.

해석 남자는 어떤 문제를 언급하는가?
(A) 그는 잠시 후에 떠나야 한다.
(B) 그는 파일을 잃어버렸다.
(C) 그는 잘못된 정보를 기입했다.
(D) 그는 등을 다쳤다.

해설 남자가 언급하는 문제점을 묻는 문제입니다. 남자가 "I have a pain in my back."이라며 등에 통증이 있다고 하였습니다. 따라서 정답은 (D) He injured his back입니다.

어휘 injure[미 índʒər, 영 índʒə] 다치다

49.

해석 여자는 남자에게 무엇을 하라고 말하는가?
(A) 양식을 작성한다.
(B) 서비스 비용을 지불한다.
(C) 예약 일정을 잡는다.
(D) 관리자에게 연락한다.

해설 여자가 남자에게 요청하는 것을 묻는 문제입니다. 여자가 "Please fill out this form"이라며 양식을 작성해 달라고 요청하였습니다. 따라서 정답은 (A) Fill out a form입니다.

50-52 [3ｗ] 호주식 발음 → 미국식 발음

Questions 50-52 refer to the following conversation.

> M: Clara, I was just notified that ⁵⁰the IT team will install a new accounting program on our computers this week—on Friday. Could you let our team members know?
>
> W: All right. What time will the IT staff arrive?
>
> M: ⁵¹The task has been scheduled for the evening to avoid disrupting employees' work. The IT employees will arrive right after six. Oh, please also let people know ⁵²they should save their important files on a separate storage device, just to be safe.
>
> W: OK. I'll send a memo to our team right now.

notify[미 nóutəfài, 영 náutifai] 통지하다, 알리다
install[instɔ́ːl] 설치하다   disrupt[disrʌ́pt] 방해하다
separate[sépərət] 별도의, 개별적인   storage[stɔ́ːridʒ] 저장

해석

50-52번은 다음 대화에 관한 문제입니다.

남: Clara, 이번 주 금요일에 ⁵⁰IT팀이 우리 컴퓨터에 새 회계 프로그램을 설치할 것이라고 지금 막 통지를 받았어요. 우리 팀원들에게 알려 주시겠어요?

여: 알겠어요. IT 부서의 직원은 몇 시에 올 건가요?

남: ⁵¹직원들의 업무를 방해하지 않기 위해 그 작업은 저녁으로 예정되었어요. IT 부서의 직원들은 6시가 넘으면 바로 도착할 거예요. 아, 만약을 위해서, 사람들에게 ⁵²중요한 파일들을 별도의 저장 장치에 저장해야 한다는 것도 알려주세요.

여: 네. 지금 바로 우리 팀원들에게 메모를 보낼게요.

50.

해석 대화는 주로 무엇에 대한 것인가?
(A) 소프트웨어 설치
(B) 사무실 마감
(C) 고장 난 컴퓨터
(D) 교육 과정

해설 대화의 주제를 묻는 문제입니다. 남자가 "the IT team will install a new accounting program on our computers"라며 IT팀이 자신들의 컴퓨터에 새 회계 프로그램을 설치할 것이라고 한 뒤, 프로그램 설치에 관한 내용으로 대화가 이어지고 있습니다. 따라서 정답은 (A) A software installation입니다.

어휘 closure[미 klóuʒər, 영 klɔ́uʒə] 마감, 폐쇄

51.

해석 작업은 왜 저녁으로 예정되어 있는가?
(A) 기술자의 시간을 확보하기 위해
(B) 회의 지연을 방지하기 위해
(C) 업무를 방해하는 것을 피하기 위해
(D) 작업 교대를 가능하게 하기 위해

해설 작업이 저녁으로 예정된 이유를 묻는 문제입니다. 남자가 "The task has been scheduled for the evening to avoid disrupting employees' work."라며 직원들의 업무를 방해하지 않기 위해 작업이 저녁으로 예정되었다고 하였습니다. 따라서 정답은 (C) To avoid interrupting work입니다.

어휘 prevent[privént] 방지하다   interrupt[ìntərʌ́pt] 방해하다
shift change 작업 교대

52.

해석 남자는 팀원들에 대해 무엇을 언급하는가?
(A) 그들은 서류를 제출해야 한다.
(B) 그들은 몇몇 파일들을 저장해야 한다.
(C) 그들은 교육을 받아야 한다.
(D) 그들은 이메일을 보내야 한다.

해설 남자가 팀원들에 대해 언급하는 것을 묻는 문제입니다. 남자가 "they[team members] should save their important files on a separate storage device"라며 팀원들이 중요한 파일들을 별도의 저장 장치에 저장해야 한다고 하였습니다. 따라서 정답은 (B) They should save some files입니다.

53-55 [3ｗ] 캐나다식 발음 → 영국식 발음 → 호주식 발음

Questions 53-55 refer to the following conversation with three speakers.

> M1: Did you hear that ⁵³the store just received a shipment from our product supplier? ○

It's a new line of gold necklaces. They look quite nice.

W: In that case, $^{53/54}$why don't we display them in the storefront window? Maybe they'll attract people who are passing by outside.

M1: Good idea, Julie. Do you mind setting that up today?

W: ^{55}I'm afraid I won't have time. I have some repairs to do. We promised Ms. Flores her ring would be ready for pickup this evening.

M1: Ah, right. What about you, Martin?

M2: Sure. I just need to finish unloading these boxes.

M1: Great. Let me know when the display is put together. I'm interested in seeing how it looks.

M2: I'll do that.

---

supplier[미 səpláiər, 영 səpláiə] 공급업체, 공급자
storefront[미 stɔ́ːrfrʌnt, 영 stɔ́ːfrʌnt] 상점 정면의; 상점 앞 공간
attract[ətrǽkt] ~의 관심을 끌다, 끌어들이다
set up 준비하다, 설치하다
unload[미 ənlóud, 영 ənláud] (짐을) 내리다
put together 준비하다, 만들다

해석

53-55번은 다음 세 명의 대화에 관한 문제입니다.

남1: ^{53}매장이 방금 우리의 제품 공급업체에서 온 출하 물품을 받았다는 것을 들었나요? 그건 새로운 금목걸이 제품이에요. 꽤 좋아 보이던데요.

여: 그렇다면, $^{53/54}$상점 정면 창가에 그것들을 진열하는 게 어때요? 아마 밖에서 지나가는 사람들의 관심을 끌 거예요.

남1: 좋은 생각이에요, Julie. 오늘 당신이 그걸 준비해주시겠어요?

여: ^{55}저는 시간이 없을 것 같아요. 몇 가지 수리할 게 있어서요. 우리는 Ms. Flores에게 그녀의 반지가 오늘 저녁에 찾아갈 준비가 될 거라고 약속했거든요.

남1: 아, 알겠어요. 당신은 어때요, Martin?

남2: 물론 되죠. 저는 이 상자들을 내리는 것만 끝내면 돼요.

남1: 좋아요. 진열이 준비되면 제게 알려주세요. 저는 그게 어떻게 보일지에 대해 관심이 있거든요.

남2: 그렇게 할게요.

53.

해석 화자들은 어디에 있는 것 같은가?
(A) 귀금속 상점에
(B) 사무용품 상점에
(C) 의류 공장에
(D) 철물점에

해설 화자들이 있는 장소를 묻는 문제입니다. 남자 1이 "the store just received a shipment from our product supplier? It's a new line of gold necklaces."라며 화자들의 매장이 방금 제품 공급업체에서 온 출하 물품을 받았고 그건 새로운 금목걸이 제품이라고 하자, 여자가 "why don't we display them in the storefront window?"라며 상점 정면 창가에 그것들을 진열하는 게 어떤지 물은 것을 통해 화자들이 금목걸이 등의 귀금속을 파는 상점에 있음을 알 수 있습니다. 따라서 정답은 (A) At a jewelry shop입니다.

어휘 hardware store 철물점, 공구점

54.

해석 여자는 무엇을 제안하는가?
(A) 몇 가지 제품 반품하기
(B) 공급업체 바꾸기
(C) 몇 가지 상품 추천하기
(D) 진열품을 창가에 두기

해설 여자가 제안하는 것을 묻는 문제입니다. 여자가 "why don't we display them[gold necklaces] in the storefront window?"라며 상점 정면 창가에 금목걸이들을 진열하는 것을 제안하였습니다. 따라서 정답은 (D) Placing a display in a window입니다.

어휘 merchandise[미 mə́ːrtʃəndais, 영 mə́ːtʃəndais] 상품, 물품

55.

해석 여자는 어떤 문제를 언급하는가?
(A) 몇몇 상자들에서 짐을 풀어야 한다.
(B) 물건이 수리되어야 한다.
(C) 몇몇 구역들이 청소되어야 한다.
(D) 배송품이 아직 도착하지 않았다.

해설 여자가 언급하는 문제점을 묻는 문제입니다. 여자가 "I'm afraid I won't have time. I have some repairs to do."라며 시간이 없을 것 같다며 몇 가지 수리할 게 있다고 하였습니다. 따라서 정답은 (B) An item must be repaired입니다.

어휘 unpack[ʌnpǽk] (짐을) 풀다, 열다

56-58 ⟨캐⟩ 미국식 발음 → 캐나다식 발음

Questions 56-58 refer to the following conversation.

W: Andrew, it's Maria calling. Are you busy right now?

M: I'm about to head to a meeting, but I'm free for a few minutes. What's going on?

W: $^{56/57}$Our manager asked me to give a presentation at Johnson Construction headquarters on Friday. Johnson Construction is a major client. ^{57}So, I need someone to fill in for me at the sales training workshop on that date.

M: Sure. I'm happy to do it. ^{58}If you print out the training materials, I can come get them from your desk in a few minutes.

W: ^{58}Will do. Thanks, Andrew.

---

be about to 막 ~하려는 참이다
headquarters[미 hèdkwɔ́ːrtərz, 영 hèdkwɔ́ːtəz] 본사, 본부
material[미 mətíriəl, 영 mətíəriəl] 자료, 재료

해석

56-58번은 다음 대화에 관한 문제입니다.

여: Andrew, Maria예요. 지금 바쁘신가요?

남: 막 회의에 가려는 참인데, 몇 분은 괜찮아요. 무슨 일이에요?

여: $^{56/57}$부장님께서 제게 금요일에 Johnson 건설사 본사에서 발표를 해달라고 요청하셨어요. Johnson 건설사는 중요한 고객이에요. ^{57}그래서, 그날 영업 교육 워크숍에서 저를 대신할 사람이 필요해요.

남: 물론이죠. 제가 그걸 하게 되어 기쁘네요. ^{58}만약 당신이 교육 자료들을 출력해둔다면, 제가 몇 분 후에 당신의 책상에서 그것들

을 가져갈 수 있어요.

여: **58**그럴게요. 고마워요, Andrew.

56.
해석 여자는 금요일에 무엇을 해달라고 요청받는가?

    (A) 부장과 이야기를 나눈다.

    (B) 발표를 한다.

    (C) 자문 위원을 만난다.

    (D) 초과 근무를 한다.

해설 여자가 금요일에 해달라고 요청받은 것을 묻는 문제입니다. 여자가 "Our manager asked me to give a presentation ~ on Friday."라며 부장이 자신에게 금요일에 발표를 해달라고 요청했다고 하였습니다. 따라서 정답은 (B) Deliver a presentation입니다.

어휘 work overtime 초과 근무를 하다

57.
해석 여자는 왜 "Johnson 건설사는 중요한 고객이에요"라고 말하는가?

    (A) 워크숍에 대한 관심을 나타내기 위해

    (B) 전근에 대한 즐거움을 보여주기 위해

    (C) 업무의 중요성을 강조하기 위해

    (D) 회사에 대한 감탄을 표현하기 위해

해설 여자가 하는 말(Johnson Construction is a major client)의 의도를 묻는 문제입니다. 여자가 "Our manager asked me to give a presentation at Johnson Construction headquarters on Friday."라며 부장이 자신에게 금요일에 Johnson 건설사 본사에서 발표를 해달라고 요청했다고 한 뒤, "So, I need someone to fill in for me at the sales training workshop on that date."라며 그래서 그날 영업 교육 워크숍에서 자신을 대신할 사람이 필요하다고 한 것을 통해 자신이 요청받은 발표 업무의 중요성을 강조하려는 의도임을 알 수 있습니다. 따라서 정답은 (C) To stress the importance of a task입니다.

어휘 transfer[미 trænsfər, 영 trǽnsfə:] 전근, 이전
admiration[ædməréiʃən] 감탄, 칭찬

58.
해석 여자는 다음에 무엇을 할 것 같은가?

    (A) 몇몇 문서들을 출력한다.

    (B) 회의에 참석한다.

    (C) 요청서를 이메일로 보낸다.

    (D) 계약인에게 이야기한다.

해설 여자가 다음에 할 일을 묻는 문제입니다. 남자가 "If you print out the training materials, I can come get them from your desk in a few minutes."라며 만약 여자가 교육 자료들을 출력해둔다면 자신이 몇 분 후에 여자의 책상에서 그것들을 가져갈 수 있다고 하자, 여자가 "Will do."라며 그러겠다고 하였습니다. 따라서 정답은 (A) Print some documents입니다.

어휘 contractor[미 kάntræktər, 영 kəntrǽktə] 계약인, 도급업체

59-61 [캐] 캐나다식 발음 → 영국식 발음
Questions 59-61 refer to the following conversation.

M: Hello. **59**I'm calling about a ticket for an opera—*Rose Garden*. I purchased it online a week ago but haven't received it yet. ○

W: I'm sorry about that. **60**Can you tell me your confirmation number and the name it was booked under?

M: It's 2249. And it's for Scott Renfield.

W: Oh, it seems your name was not in our ticketing database for some reason. My apologies, Mr. Renfield. **61**We'll mail it immediately.

M: But the show is in two days, so **61**it probably won't arrive in time.

W: In that case, I'll send you an e-ticket that you can print out and bring on the night of the performance.

purchase[미 pə́:rtʃəs, 영 pə́:tʃəs] 구매하다
confirmation number 예약 확인 번호   in time 제시간에

해석

59-61번은 다음 대화에 관한 문제입니다.

남: 안녕하세요. **59**저는 오페라 *Rose Garden*의 입장권과 관련해서 전화드렸어요. 일주일 전에 온라인으로 구매했는데 아직도 그것을 받지 못했어요.

여: 죄송합니다. **60**고객님의 예약 확인 번호와 예약된 성함을 저에게 말씀해 주시겠어요?

남: 2249예요. 그리고 Scott Renfield를 위한 예약이고요.

여: 아, 어떤 이유에서인지 고객님의 성함이 저희의 입장권 발매 데이터베이스에 없었던 것 같아요. 죄송합니다, Mr. Renfield. **61**저희가 그것을 즉시 우편으로 보내드리겠습니다.

남: 하지만 공연이 이틀 뒤여서, **61**그것은 제시간에 도착하지 않을 것 같아요.

여: 그렇다면, 인쇄해서 공연 당일 저녁에 가져가실 수 있는 전자 티켓을 보내 드릴게요.

59.
해석 남자는 왜 전화를 하고 있는가?

    (A) 일정에 대해 문의하기 위해

    (B) 입장권에 대해 문의하기 위해

    (C) 환불을 요청하기 위해

    (D) 좌석 번호를 확인하기 위해

해설 전화의 목적을 묻는 문제입니다. 남자가 "I'm calling about a ticket for an opera ~. I purchased it online a week ago but haven't received it yet."이라며 오페라의 입장권과 관련해서 전화했다고 한 뒤, 그것을 일주일 전에 온라인으로 구매했는데 아직도 받지 못했다고 한 것을 통해 남자가 입장권에 대해 문의하기 위해 전화했음을 알 수 있습니다. 따라서 정답은 (B) To inquire about a ticket입니다.

어휘 refund[ríːfʌnd] 환불

60.
해석 여자는 어떤 정보를 남자에게 요청하는가?

    (A) 연락처

    (B) 쿠폰 번호

    (C) 예약 확인 번호

    (D) 집 주소

해설 여자가 남자에게 요청하는 정보를 묻는 문제입니다. 여자가 "Can you tell me your confirmation number ~?"라며 남자의 예약 확인 번호를 말해달라고 하였습니다. 따라서 정답은 (C) A confirmation number입니다.

어휘 promotional code 쿠폰 번호

61.

해석 남자가 "하지만 공연이 이틀 뒤여서"라고 말할 때 의도하는 것은 무엇인가?
(A) 그는 공연에 대해 잊어버렸다.
(B) 그는 예산이 빠듯하다.
(C) 그는 행사를 놓칠지도 모른다.
(D) 그는 연습 시간이 더 필요하다.

해설 남자가 하는 말(But the show is in two days)의 의도를 묻는 문제입니다. 여자가 "We'll mail it[ticket] immediately."라며 입장권을 즉시 우편으로 보내주겠다고 하자, 남자가 "it probably won't arrive in time"이라며 입장권이 제시간에 도착하지 않을 것 같다고 하였습니다. 이를 통해 남자가 자신이 행사를 놓칠지도 모른다는 것을 전달하려는 의도임을 알 수 있습니다. 따라서 정답은 (C) He might miss an event입니다.

어휘 tight[tait] 빠듯한 budget[bʌ́dʒit] 예산

62-64 〔3ₐ〕 영국식 발음 → 캐나다식 발음

Questions 62-64 refer to the following conversation and sign.

W: I just spoke to Danny Barton, the main organizer of the convention. **⁶²It turns out that we won't be able to begin our session on time** due to some mechanical issues with the projector we need to use.
M: Really? How long will we be delayed?
W: It's hard to say, but at least 30 minutes. However, **⁶³the delay will give me a chance to eat a quick snack in the cafeteria.**
M: OK. Well, **⁶⁴I suppose I'll head to the room where our Innovation Seminar is taking place. I can go over my notes while waiting for you.**
W: **⁶³I'll meet you there soon.**

organizer[미 ɔ́ːrgənàizər, 영 ɔ́ːgənàizə] 주최자, 조직자
turn out ~이 되다, 모습을 드러내다
session[séʃn] 회의, (활동) 시간
mechanical[məkǽnikəl] 기계적인, 기계로 작동되는
snack[snæk] 간식, 간단한 식사
note[미 nout, 영 nəut] (초벌) 원고, 기록

해석
62-64번은 다음 대화와 표지판에 관한 문제입니다.

여: 저는 방금 총회의 주요 주최자인 Danny Barton과 이야기를 나누었어요. 우리가 사용해야 하는 프로젝터의 기계적 문제 때문에 ⁶²우리의 회의를 제시간에 시작할 수 없게 되었어요.
남: 정말인가요? 우리는 얼마나 오래 지연될 건가요?
여: 말하기 어렵지만, 최소 30분이요. 하지만, ⁶³그 지연은 제가 구내식당에서 잠깐 간식을 먹을 기회를 줄 거예요.
남: 알겠어요. 음, ⁶⁴저는 우리의 혁신 세미나가 열릴 장소에 가야겠어요. 당신을 기다리는 동안 제 원고를 살펴보면 될 거예요.
여: ⁶³곧 거기서 만나요.

Bay City 기술 총회
행사 목록
A홀: 인공 지능 강의
⁶⁴B홀: 혁신 세미나
C홀: 로봇 공학 발표
D홀: 채용 박람회

62.

해석 화자들은 주로 무엇에 대해 이야기하고 있는가?
(A) 임원의 요청
(B) 몇몇 발표자들과 관련된 문제
(C) 취소의 이유
(D) 일정 변경

해설 대화의 주제를 묻는 문제입니다. 여자가 "It turns out that we won't be able to begin our session on time"이라며 자신들의 회의를 제시간에 시작할 수 없게 되었다고 한 뒤, 회의 일정 변경에 대한 내용으로 대화가 이어지고 있습니다. 따라서 정답은 (D) A change to a schedule입니다.

어휘 executive[igzékjətiv] 임원, 경영진

63.

해석 여자는 무엇을 할 것이라고 말하는가?
(A) 공지를 한다.
(B) 회의 장소를 마련한다.
(C) 고장 난 기기를 수리한다.
(D) 간식을 먹는다.

해설 여자가 다음에 할 일을 묻는 문제입니다. 여자가 "the delay will give me a chance to eat a quick snack in the cafeteria"라며 지연이 구내식당에서 잠깐 간식을 먹을 기회를 줄 거라고 한 뒤, "I'll meet you there[the room] soon."이라며 곧 회의 장소에서 만나자고 한 것을 통해, 여자가 간식을 먹을 것임을 알 수 있습니다. 따라서 정답은 (D) Get some refreshments입니다.

어휘 refreshment[rifréʃmənt] 간식, 다과

64.

해석 시각 자료를 보아라. 남자는 어디에서 여자를 기다릴 것인가?
(A) A홀에서
(B) B홀에서
(C) C홀에서
(D) D홀에서

해설 남자가 여자를 기다릴 곳을 묻는 문제입니다. 남자가 "I suppose I'll head to the room where our Innovation Seminar is taking place. I can go over my notes while waiting for you."라며 혁신 세미나가 열릴 장소에 가야겠다고 하면서 여자를 기다리는 동안 자신의 원고를 살펴보면 된다고 하였으므로, 남자가 혁신 세미나가 열리는 B홀에서 여자를 기다릴 것임을 표지판에서 알 수 있습니다. 따라서 정답은 (B) In Hall B입니다.

65-67 〔3ₐ〕 미국식 발음 → 캐나다식 발음

Questions 65-67 refer to the following conversation and flight schedule.

W: Excuse me. I need to book a flight from Calgary to Miami on July 1. **⁶⁵Are there any economy class tickets available?** ↻

M: There is a direct flight that costs $445 plus tax. There is also a flight with a two-hour stopover in Minneapolis. That option is $299.

W: ⁶⁶The direct flight is quite expensive. I'll reserve a ticket for the flight that stops in Minneapolis. But, um, ⁶⁷I'd prefer an early flight. Does it leave in the morning?

M: Yes. In fact, ⁶⁷it's now the earliest flight available that day because the one that departs at 7 A.M. is already sold out.

---

economy class 일반석
stopover [미 stáː,pouvər, 영 stɔ́pəuvə] 단기 체류, 도중 하차

해석

65-67번은 다음 대화와 항공편 일정표에 관한 문제입니다.

여: 실례합니다. 저는 7월 1일에 캘거리에서 마이애미로 가는 항공편을 예약해야 하는데요. ⁶⁵구매할 수 있는 일반석 티켓이 있나요?

남: 세금 별도로 445달러인 직항편이 있습니다. 미니애폴리스에서 2시간 체류하는 항공편도 있습니다. 그 선택권은 299달러입니다.

여: ⁶⁶직항편은 꽤 비싸네요. 저는 미니애폴리스에서 잠시 체류하는 항공편을 예약할게요. 하지만, 음, ⁶⁷저는 이른 시간대의 항공편이 좋아요. 그 항공편은 오전에 출발하나요?

남: 네, 사실, ⁶⁷오전 7시에 출발하는 것은 이미 매진되어서, 그것이 현재 그날 가장 이른 시간대의 이용 가능한 항공편이에요.

비행기 번호	출발 시간
AE880	오전 7:00
⁶⁷AE890	오전 9:30
AE900	오후 1:45
AE910	오후 4:30

65.

해석 여자는 무엇에 대해 문의하는가?
(A) 항공편 변경
(B) 이용 가능한 티켓
(C) 탑승 수속 시간
(D) 탑승구 출입

해설 여자가 문의하는 것을 묻는 문제입니다. 여자가 "Are there any economy class tickets available?"이라며 구매할 수 있는 일반석 티켓이 있는지를 물었습니다. 따라서 정답은 (B) Ticket availability입니다.

어휘 availability [əvèiləbíləti] 이용할 수 있는 것

66.

해석 여자는 직항편에 대해 무엇을 말하는가?
(A) 가격이 별로 적당하지 않다.
(B) 일반석 좌석이 없다.
(C) 너무 늦게 출발한다.
(D) 미니애폴리스에 착륙한다.

해설 여자가 직항편에 대해 언급하는 것을 묻는 문제입니다. 여자가 "The direct flight is quite expensive."라며 직항편이 꽤 비싸다고 하였습니다. 따라서 정답은 (A) It is not very affordable입니다.

어휘 affordable [미 əfɔ́ːrdəbl, 영 əfɔ́ːdəbl] 가격이 적당한

67.

해석 시각 자료를 보아라. 여자는 어떤 항공편을 탈 것 같은가?
(A) AE880
(B) AE890
(C) AE900
(D) AE910

해설 여자가 탈 항공편을 묻는 문제입니다. 여자가 "I'd prefer an early flight."이라며 이른 시간대의 항공편이 좋다고 하자, 남자가 "it's now the earliest flight available that day because the one that departs at 7 A.M. is already sold out"이라며 오전 7시에 출발하는 것이 이미 매진되어서 그것이 현재 그날 가장 이른 시간대의 이용 가능한 항공편이라고 하였으므로, 여자가 탈 비행편이 AE890임을 일정표에서 알 수 있습니다. 따라서 정답은 (B) AE890입니다.

68-70 🔊 캐나다식 발음 → 영국식 발음

Questions 68-70 refer to the following conversation and catalog.

M: Sophie, after ⁶⁸I met with a client this morning, I had a chance to look at the office chair catalog you left on my desk. But I'm not sure which one I like. What do you think?

W: ⁶⁹I think the Posture Pro would be the best option. The ones from WellMont and Winston look nice too, but their reviews weren't as good.

M: ⁶⁹Great. If you order it today, when can I expect to have it?

W: It should arrive sometime next week.

M: OK. ⁷⁰Would you mind forwarding me the tracking number once the chair ships? I want to follow the delivery progress through the shipping firm's Web site.

W: Of course.

---

review [rivjúː] 후기, 평가
forward [미 fɔ́ːrwərd, 영 fɔ́ːwəd] 보내다, 전송하다
tracking number 추적 번호(배송 상황을 추적할 수 있도록 부여된 번호)   progress [미 práːgres, 영 prə́ugres] 진행 (상태), 과정

해석

68-70번은 다음 대화와 카탈로그에 관한 문제입니다.

남: Sophie, ⁶⁸오늘 아침에 제가 고객과 만난 이후에 당신이 제 책상 위에 둔 사무용 의자 카탈로그를 볼 기회가 있었어요. 그런데 어떤 게 좋은지 모르겠네요. 당신은 어떻게 생각하세요?

여: ⁶⁹전 Posture Pro가 가장 좋은 것 같아요. WellMont사와 Winston사 것들도 좋아 보이지만, 후기가 그만큼 좋지는 않았어요.

남: ⁶⁹좋은데요. 만약 당신이 오늘 그걸 주문하면, 제가 언제 받을 것으로 예상할 수 있나요?

여: 다음 주 중에는 도착할 거예요.

남: ⁷⁰알겠어요. 의자가 출하되면 제게 배송 추적 번호를 보내주시겠어요? 배송업체 웹사이트에서 배송 진행 상태를 보고 싶어요.

여: 물론이죠.

Winston Recline – 190달러	Finnly A34 – 225달러
⁶⁹Posture Pro – 275달러	WellMont Glider – 315달러

68.

해석 남자는 이전에 무엇을 했는가?
(A) 회의에 참석했다.
(B) 예산을 승인했다.
(C) 음성 메시지를 들었다.
(D) 회람을 보냈다.

해설 남자가 이전에 한 일을 묻는 문제입니다. 남자가 "I met with a client this morning"에서 오늘 아침에 고객과 만났다고 한 것을 통해, 남자가 고객과의 회의에 참석했다는 것을 알 수 있습니다. 따라서 정답은 (A) Attended a meeting입니다.

어휘 approve[əprúːv] 승인하다, 인가하다 voice mail 음성 메시지

69.

해석 시각 자료를 보아라. 여자가 주문하고자 하는 의자는 얼마일 것인가?
(A) 190달러
(B) 225달러
(C) 275달러
(D) 315달러

해설 여자가 주문하고자 하는 의자의 가격을 묻는 문제입니다. 여자가 "I think the Posture Pro would be the best option."이라며 Posture Pro가 가장 좋은 것 같다고 하자 남자가 "Great."이라며 좋다고 하였으므로, 여자가 주문하고자 하는 Posture Pro는 275달러임을 카탈로그에서 알 수 있습니다. 따라서 정답은 (C) $275입니다.

70.

해석 남자는 여자에게 무엇을 해달라고 요청하는가?
(A) 송장 양식에 서명한다.
(B) 배송 추적 정보를 보낸다.
(C) 신용카드 번호를 알려준다.
(D) 배송 선택 사항을 고른다.

해설 남자가 여자에게 요청하는 것을 묻는 문제입니다. 남자가 "Would you mind forwarding me the tracking number once the chair ships?"라며 의자가 출하되면 자신에게 배송 추적 번호를 보내달라고 하였습니다. 따라서 정답은 (B) Send tracking information입니다.

어휘 invoice[ínvɔis] 송장, 청구서

PART 4

71-73 🎧 미국식 발음

Questions 71-73 refer to the following announcement.

⁷¹Attention all Paris Metro passengers. This is an important announcement. On Saturday and Sunday, ⁷²Anvers Station on Line Two will be closed for maintenance. The station will reopen at 5 A.M. on Monday morning. All other stations on the line will remain open during this time. ⁷³Passengers who wish to reach areas around Anvers Station are advised to get off at Pigal Station and walk three blocks south along St. Germaine Avenue. Thank you for your understanding.

attention[əténʃən] 주목하세요, 알립니다
metro[미 métrou, 영 métrəu] 지하철
maintenance[méintənəns] 보수 공사, 정비

해석
71-73번은 다음 공지에 관한 문제입니다.

⁷¹파리 지하철 승객 여러분께서는 주목해 주시기 바랍니다. 중요한 공지입니다. 토요일과 일요일에, ⁷²2호선의 Anvers 역이 보수 공사를 위해 폐쇄될 예정입니다. 역은 월요일 아침 오전 5시에 다시 개방될 것입니다. 이 노선의 다른 모든 역들은 이 기간에 계속 열려 있을 것입니다. ⁷³Anvers 역 주변 지역으로 가시려는 승객들께서는 Pigal 역에서 내리셔서 St. Germaine가를 따라 남쪽으로 세 블록 걸어가시기 바랍니다. 양해해 주셔서 감사드립니다.

71.

해석 공지는 어디에서 이루어지고 있는 것 같은가?
(A) 지하철역에서
(B) 쇼핑 단지에서
(C) 관공서에서
(D) 건설 회사에서

해설 공지가 이루어지는 장소를 묻는 문제입니다. "Attention all Paris Metro passengers."라며 파리 지하철 승객들은 주목해 달라고 한 말을 통해 공지가 이루어지고 있는 장소가 지하철역임을 알 수 있습니다. 따라서 정답은 (A) At a subway station입니다.

어휘 shopping complex 쇼핑 단지
construction[kənstrʌ́kʃən] 건설, 건축

72.

해석 폐쇄는 왜 이루어질 것인가?
(A) 궂은 날씨가 예상된다.
(B) 수리 작업이 이루어져야 한다.
(C) 확장 공사가 진행 중이다.
(D) 점검이 실시되어야 한다.

해설 폐쇄가 이루어질 이유를 묻는 문제입니다. "Anvers Station ~ will be closed for maintenance"라며 Anvers 역이 보수 공사를 위해 폐쇄될 예정이라고 하였습니다. 따라서 정답은 (B) Repairs must be made입니다.

어휘 underway[미 ʌ̀ndərwéi, 영 ʌ̀ndəwéi] 진행 중인
inspection[inspékʃən] 점검
carry out ~을 실시하다, ~을 수행하다

73.

해석 화자는 무엇을 제안하는가?
(A) 직원에게 이야기하기
(B) 평소보다 일찍 도착하기
(C) 징소로 걸어가기
(D) 셔틀버스 타기

해설 화자가 제안하는 것을 묻는 문제입니다. "Passengers ~ are advised to get off at Pigal Station and walk three blocks"라며 Anvers 역 주변 지역으로 가려는 승객들은 Pigal 역에서 내려 세 블록을 걸어가라고 하였습니다. 따라서 정답은 (C) Walking to a location입니다.

74-76 3ɯ 캐나다식 발음

Questions 74-76 refer to the following advertisement.

Lufthausen Department Store is famous throughout Europe for providing high-quality furniture, appliances, and clothing at affordable prices. **74Now, we're opening our first North American store in Kansas.** To celebrate, come down to our grand opening event on Friday, May 10. We'll offer 20 percent off the regular price of various products in the store. Moreover, **75free snacks and soft drinks will be provided during the event.** Lufthausen's **76Kansas branch is conveniently situated on Lynn Road, right next to the Bedford Bus Station.** Be sure to visit us soon!

appliance[əpláiəns] 가전제품
affordable[미 əfɔ́ːrdəbl, 영 əfɔ́ːdəbl] 알맞은, 적당한
situated[미 sítʃuèitid, 영 sítʃueitid] 위치해 있는, 자리 잡은

해석

74-76번은 다음 광고에 관한 문제입니다.

Lufthausen 백화점은 고급 가구, 가전제품, 그리고 의류를 알맞은 가격에 제공하는 것으로 유럽 전역에서 유명합니다. 74이제, 저희는 캔자스에 첫 번째 북아메리카 매장을 개점합니다. 축하하기 위해, 5월 10일 금요일에 저희의 개점 행사에 와 주세요. 저희는 매장 내 다양한 상품에 대해 정가에서 20퍼센트의 할인을 제공해 드릴 것입니다. 또한, 75무료 간식과 청량음료가 행사 중에 제공될 것입니다. Lufthausen의 76캔자스 지점은 Lynn로와 Bedford 버스 정류장 바로 옆에 편리하게 위치해 있습니다. 곧 저희를 방문해 주세요!

74.

해석 무엇이 광고되고 있는가?
(A) 제품 출시
(B) 재고 정리 할인 판매
(C) 매장 개점
(D) 유명인 출연

해설 광고의 주제를 묻는 문제입니다. "Now, we're opening our first North American store in Kansas."라며 이제 자신들은 캔자스에 첫 번째 북아메리카 매장을 개점한다고 한 뒤, 개점 행사에 대해 언급했습니다. 따라서 정답은 (C) A store grand opening입니다.

어휘 clearance[klíərəns] 재고 정리
appearance[əpíərəns] 출연, 출현

75.

해석 무엇이 행사에서 이용 가능할 것인가?
(A) 제품 샘플
(B) 매장 전단지
(C) 무료 다과
(D) 반값 할인 상품

해설 행사에서 이용 가능할 것을 묻는 문제입니다. "free snacks and soft drinks will be provided during the event"라며 무료 간식과 청량음료가 행사 중에 제공될 것이라고 하였습니다. 따라서 정답은 (C) Free refreshments입니다.

어휘 merchandise[미 mɔ́ːrtʃəndàiz, 영 mɔ́ːtʃəndais] 제품
flyer[미 fláiər, 영 fláiə] 전단지
refreshment[rifréʃmənt] 다과

76.

해석 캔자스 지점에 대해 무엇이 언급되는가?
(A) 수리되었다.
(B) 대중교통 가까이에 있다.
(C) 고객들에게 무료 주차를 제공한다.
(D) 온라인으로 광고되었다.

해설 캔자스 지점에 대해 언급되는 것을 묻는 문제입니다. "Kansas branch is conveniently situated ~ right next to the Bedford Bus Station"이라며 캔자스 지점은 Bedford 버스 정류장 바로 옆에 편리하게 위치해 있다고 하였습니다. 따라서 정답은 (B) It is near public transportation입니다.

어휘 transportation[미 trænspərtéiʃən, 영 trænspɔːtéiʃən] 교통, 운송

77-79 3ɯ 호주식 발음

Questions 77-79 refer to the following talk.

I'm Dr. Martin Shaw, a psychologist and researcher. **77In today's seminar, I'll provide you with information on how to lower stress levels among corporate employees.** Uhm . . . **78As managers, you must have noticed your employees feeling stressed out at times. I'm certain you've had similar experiences yourselves.** **79My goal is to teach some effective techniques that will help employees handle stress in the workplace.** By the end of the seminar, you'll hopefully know how to create a less stressful work environment. You'll also understand why this improves both worker satisfaction and productivity.

psychologist[미 saikálədʒist, 영 saikɔ́lədʒist] 심리학자
corporate[미 kɔ́ːrpərət, 영 kɔ́ːpərət] 기업의, 회사의
effective[iféktiv] 효과적인   handle[hǽndl] 다루다
improve[imprúːv] 향상하다
productivity[미 pròudʌktívəti, 영 prɔ̀dʌktívəti] 생산성

해석

77-79번은 다음 담화에 관한 문제입니다.

저는 심리학자이자 연구원인 Martin Shaw 박사입니다. 77오늘 세미나에서, 저는 여러분께 회사 직원들의 스트레스 수준을 낮추는 방법에 대한 정보를 드릴 것입니다. 음... 78경영자로서, 여러분은 직원들이 때때로 스트레스를 받는 것을 분명히 알고 계실 것입니다. 저는 여러분 또한 비슷한 경험을 했을 것이라고 확신합니다. 79제 목표는 직원들이 직장에서의 스트레스를 다루는 것을 도와줄 효과적인 기법

들을 알려드리는 것입니다. 세미나가 끝날 무렵에, 여러분이 스트레스가 적은 업무 환경을 조성하는 방법을 알게 되시길 바랍니다. 여러분은 또한 이것이 왜 직원 만족도와 생산성 모두를 향상시키는지 이해하게 되실 것입니다.

77.

해석 세미나의 주제는 무엇인가?
(A) 직원들의 스트레스 줄이기
(B) 기업 합병 계획하기
(C) 연구 결과 분석하기
(D) 사내 규정 준수하기

해설 세미나의 주제를 묻는 문제입니다. "In today's seminar, I'll provide you with information on how to lower stress levels among corporate employees."라며 오늘 세미나에서 화자는 청자들에게 회사 직원들의 스트레스 수준을 낮추는 방법에 대한 정보를 줄 것이라고 하였습니다. 따라서 정답은 (A) Reducing workers' stress입니다.

어휘 merger[미 mə́rdʒər, 영 má:dʒə] 합병
analyze[미 ǽnəlàiz, 영 ǽnəlaiz] 분석하다, 조사하다
regulation[미 règjuléiʃən, 영 règjəléiʃən] 규정, 규제

78.

해석 화자는 왜 "저는 여러분 또한 비슷한 경험을 했을 것이라고 확신합니다"라고 말하는가?
(A) 협력의 필요성을 보여주기 위해
(B) 스트레스를 관리할 수 있다는 것을 보여주기 위해
(C) 공통적인 감정을 강조하기 위해
(D) 목표의 개발을 격려하기 위해

해설 화자가 하는 말(I'm certain you've had similar experiences yourselves)의 의도를 묻는 문제입니다. "As managers, you must have noticed your employees feeling stressed out at times. I'm certain you've had similar experiences yourselves."라며 경영자로서 청자들은 직원들이 때때로 스트레스를 받는 것을 분명히 알고 있을 것이고, 청자들도 비슷한 경험을 했을 것이라고 확신한다고 한 말을 통해 청자들과 직원들의 공통적인 감정을 강조하기 위한 의도임을 알 수 있습니다. 따라서 정답은 (C) To emphasize a shared feeling입니다.

어휘 cooperation[미 kouàpəréiʃən, 영 kəuɔ̀pəréiʃən] 협력, 협조
manageable[mǽnidʒəbl] 관리할 수 있는
emphasize[미 émfəsàiz, 영 émfəsaiz] 강조하다

79.

해석 화자는 세미나 동안 무엇을 하고 싶어 하는가?
(A) 직원 안내서를 배부한다.
(B) 최근의 연구를 논의한다.
(C) 청자들에게 기법들을 제공한다.
(D) 슬라이드 쇼를 보여준다.

해설 화자가 세미나 동안 하고 싶어 하는 것을 묻는 문제입니다. "My goal is to teach some effective techniques that will help employees handle stress in the workplace."라며 화자의 목표는 직원들이 직장에서의 스트레스를 다루는 것을 도와줄 효과적인 기법들을 알려주는 것이라고 하였습니다. 따라서 정답은 (C) Provide listeners with techniques입니다.

어휘 distribute[distríbju:t] 배부하다

80-82 [3ᴍ] 영국식 발음

Questions 80-82 refer to the following telephone message.

> Alexander, this is Sandy Stewart. I'd like to ask you for a favor. **⁸⁰Can you meet with the Trax Corporation representatives when they arrive at our office at 12 P.M. today? They're coming to discuss a partnership** with our consulting firm. **⁸¹I'm supposed to meet them, but the workshop I'm leading this morning is lasting longer than expected.** So, I can't get back to the office until 1 P.M. **⁸²If you're not available, please let me know by calling back . . .** within the next 10 minutes. I'll have to find someone else if you can't help me.

---

representative[rèprizéntativ] 직원, 대표
consulting firm 컨설팅 회사
be supposed to ~하기로 되어 있다

해석

80-82번은 다음 전화 메시지에 관한 문제입니다.

Alexander, Sandy Stewart예요. 저는 당신에게 부탁이 있어요. ⁸⁰오늘 오후 12시에 Trax사의 직원들이 우리 사무실에 도착하면 그들과 만나주실 수 있나요? 그들은 우리 컨설팅 회사와의 제휴에 대해 논의하기 위해 오는 중이에요. ⁸¹제가 그들과 만나기로 되어 있었지만, 오늘 오전에 제가 진행하고 있는 워크숍이 예상보다 더 오래 계속되고 있어요. 그래서, 저는 오후 1시가 되어서야 사무실로 돌아갈 수 있어요. ⁸²만약 시간이 안 된다면, 제게 다시 전화하셔서 알려주세요... 10분 안에요. 만약 당신이 저를 도와주실 수 없다면 저는 다른 사람을 찾아야 할 거예요.

80.

해석 Trax사에 대해 무엇이 언급되는가?
(A) 직원들이 늦고 있다.
(B) 교육용 소프트웨어 회사이다.
(C) 제휴 합의를 고려하고 있다.
(D) 사무실이 근처 건물에 위치해 있다.

해설 Trax사에 대해 언급되는 것을 묻는 문제입니다. "Can you meet with the Trax Corporation representatives ~? They're coming to discuss a partnership"이라며 Trax사의 직원들과 만나줄 수 있는지 물은 뒤, 그들이 제휴에 대해 논의하기 위해 오는 중이라고 하였습니다. 따라서 정답은 (C) It is considering a partnership deal입니다.

어휘 be running late 늦어지고 있다

81.

해석 화자는 어떤 문제를 언급하는가?
(A) 서류가 분실되었다.
(B) 사무실이 문을 닫았다.
(C) 세미나가 너무 길어지고 있다.
(D) 출장이 취소되었다.

해설 화자가 언급하는 문제점을 묻는 문제입니다. "I'm supposed to meet them[Trax Corporation representatives], but the workshop ~ is lasting longer than expected."라며 Trax사의 직원들과 만나기로 되어 었었지만 워크숍이 예상보다 더 오래 계속되고 있다고 하였습니다. 따라서 정답은 (C) A seminar is lasting too long입니다.

어휘 missing[mísiŋ] 분실한, 실종된

82.

해석 청자는 왜 다시 전화해야 하는가?
(A) 추천을 하기 위해
(B) 취소를 하기 위해
(C) 조언을 구하기 위해
(D) 요청에 응답하기 위해

해설 청자가 다시 전화해야 하는 이유를 묻는 문제입니다. "If you're not available, please let me know by calling back"이라며 만약 시간이 안 된다면 다시 전화해서 알려달라고 한 것을 통해 청자가 화자의 요청에 응답하기 위해 다시 전화해야 함을 알 수 있습니다. 따라서 정답은 (D) To respond to a request입니다.

어휘 recommendation[미 rèkəməndéiʃən, 영 rèkəmendéiʃən] 추천, 권고

83-85 ③ 미국식 발음

Questions 83-85 refer to the following talk.

Can I have everyone's attention briefly, please? **83I'd like to introduce our new product design manager**, Elizabeth Franklin. Before joining us, Ms. Franklin was a manager at Ord-Tech in Switzerland. She also worked at technology companies in Boston and Vancouver prior to that. Moreover, **84she recently accepted an award** from the International Technology Committee for her tablet PC design work. Here at Networked Computing Services, she'll lead the design team, which is working on our latest Vymo laptop. **85Now, I will give Ms. Franklin a chance to say a few words** before I show her to her office.

briefly[bríːfli] 잠시, 간단히 prior to ~ 전에
accept an award 상을 받다 committee[kəmíti] 위원회

해석

83-85번은 다음 담화에 관한 문제입니다.

잠시 모두 주목해 주시겠습니까? 83우리의 새로운 제품 디자인 관리자인 Elizabeth Franklin을 소개해 드리려고 합니다. 우리 회사에 합류하기 전에, Ms. Franklin은 스위스에 있는 Ord-Tech사의 관리자였습니다. 그녀는 또한 그전에 보스턴과 밴쿠버에 있는 기술 회사들에서 근무했습니다. 게다가, 84그녀는 최근에 국제 기술 위원회로부터 그녀의 태블릿 PC 디자인 작업에 대해 상을 받았습니다. 이곳 Networked Computing Services사에서, 그녀는 디자인팀을 이끌 것인데, 이 팀은 우리의 최신 Vymo 휴대용 컴퓨터를 작업하고 있습니다. 85이제, 그녀의 사무실로 안내하기 전에, Ms. Franklin에게 몇 마디 할 기회를 드리겠습니다.

83.

해석 담화의 목적은 무엇인가?
(A) 직원을 소개하기 위해
(B) 직원들에게 승진에 대해 알리기 위해
(C) 시상식을 준비하기 위해
(D) 은퇴를 발표하기 위해

해설 담화의 목적을 묻는 문제입니다. "I'd like to introduce our new product design manager"라며 새로운 제품 디자인 관리자를 소개해 주려고 한다고 하였습니다. 따라서 정답은

(A) To introduce a staff member입니다.

어휘 notify[미 nóutəfài, 영 nə́utifài] 알리다, 통보하다
retirement[미 ritáiərmənt, 영 ritáiəmənt] 은퇴, 퇴직

84.

해석 화자에 따르면, Ms. Franklin은 최근에 무엇을 했는가?
(A) 학위를 받았다.
(B) 상을 받았다.
(C) 컴퓨터 네트워크를 설치했다.
(D) 목표 매출액을 달성했다.

해설 Ms. Franklin이 최근에 한 일을 묻는 문제입니다. "she [Ms. Franklin] recently accepted an award"라며 Ms. Franklin이 최근에 상을 받았다고 하였습니다. 따라서 정답은 (B) Received an award입니다.

어휘 degree[digríː] 학위, 등급 set up ~을 설치하다
achieve[ətʃíːv] 달성하다, 성취하다

85.

해석 Ms. Franklin은 다음에 무엇을 할 것인가?
(A) 전화를 한다.
(B) 발표를 준비한다.
(C) 이야기를 한다.
(D) 공항에 간다.

해설 Ms. Franklin이 다음에 할 일을 묻는 문제입니다. "Now, I will give Ms. Franklin a chance to say a few words"라며 이제 Ms. Franklin에게 몇 마디 할 기회를 주겠다고 하였습니다. 따라서 정답은 (C) Give a talk입니다.

86-88 ③ 캐나다식 발음

Questions 86-88 refer to the following speech.

Thank you. **86There are so many people that made it possible for me to receive the Album of the Year Award.** I'll begin by thanking my producer, Shane Lawson, for being there since I started singing for Bronze Records. Oh, and there's one more person I can't forget about—**87my vocal instructor, Catherine Holland. 88Her lessons gave me the confidence to perform on the popular** *Daytime Variety Show* at the age of 17, which brought me widespread public attention. So . . . **87thank you, Catherine.** I humbly accept this award and hope to continue to be a role model for pop music fans worldwide.

vocal[미 vóukəl, 영 váukəl] 노래의, 성악의
confidence[미 kάːnfədəns, 영 kɔ́nfidəns] 자신감, 확신
attention[əténʃən] 관심, 주목 humbly[hʌ́mbli] 겸손히, 겸허히

해석

86-88번은 다음 연설에 관한 문제입니다.

감사합니다. 86제가 올해의 앨범상을 받는 것을 가능하게 해주신 정말 많은 분들이 있습니다. 저의 음반 제작자인 Shane Lawson에게 제가 Bronze Records사를 위해 노래를 시작했던 때부터 제 곁에 있어 주신 것에 대해 감사를 표하는 것으로 시작하겠습니다. 아, 그리고 제가 잊을 수 없는 또 한 분이 있습니다—87저의 노래 선생님인 Catherine Holland입니다. 88그녀의 수업은 제가 17살의 나이로 인기 있는 *Daytime 버라이어티* 쇼에서 공연할 수 있는 자신감을 주었

는데, 이 쇼는 제게 대중의 큰 관심을 가져다주었습니다. 그러니까...
⁸⁷감사합니다, Catherine. 저는 겸손히 이 상을 받을 것이며 전 세계의 대중음악 팬들에게 계속해서 롤 모델이 될 수 있기를 바랍니다.

86.
해석 화자의 직업은 무엇인 것 같은가?
(A) 음악가
(B) 영화 제작자
(C) 행사 기획자
(D) 라디오 쇼 진행자

해설 화자의 직업을 묻는 문제입니다. "There are so many people that made it possible for me to receive the Album of the Year Award."라며 화자가 올해의 앨범상을 받는 것을 가능하게 해준 정말 많은 사람들이 있다고 한 뒤, 화자의 음반 제작자와 노래 선생님을 언급하였습니다. 이를 통해 화자가 음악가임을 알 수 있습니다. 따라서 정답은 (A) Musician입니다.

87.
해석 화자는 왜 "그리고 제가 잊을 수 없는 또 한 분이 있습니다"라고 말하는가?
(A) 그는 연주자를 소개할 것이다.
(B) 그는 특별 출연자를 무대로 초청할 것이다.
(C) 그는 선생님에게 감사를 표할 것이다.
(D) 그는 우승자를 축하해줄 것이다.

해설 화자가 하는 말(and there's one more person I can't forget about)의 의도를 묻는 문제입니다. "my vocal instructor, Catherine Holland"라며 자신의 노래 선생님이 Catherine Holland라고 한 뒤, "thank you, Catherine"이라며 Catherine에게 감사하다고 한 것을 통해 화자가 선생님에게 감사를 표하려는 의도임을 알 수 있습니다. 따라서 정답은 (C) He will acknowledge a teacher입니다.

어휘 acknowledge[미 ækná:lidʒ, 영 əknɔ́lidʒ] 감사를 표하다, 인정하다

88.
해석 *Daytime 버라이어티* 쇼에 대해 무엇이 언급되는가?
(A) 화자가 그 쇼에서 공연을 했었다.
(B) 오로지 젊은 음악가들만을 출연시킨다.
(C) 프로그램의 시청률이 떨어졌다.
(D) 구성 방식이 최근에 바뀌었다.

해설 *Daytime 버라이어티* 쇼에 대해 언급되는 것을 묻는 문제입니다. "Her[Catherine Holland] lessons gave me the confidence to perform on the popular *Daytime Variety Show*"라며 Catherine Holland의 수업은 화자가 *Daytime 버라이어티* 쇼에서 공연할 수 있는 자신감을 주었다고 한 것을 통해, 화자가 *Daytime 버라이어티* 쇼에서 공연했었음을 알 수 있습니다. 따라서 정답은 (A) The speaker has performed on the show입니다.

어휘 feature[미 fí:tʃər, 영 fí:tʃə] 출연시키다, 특징으로 삼다
viewership[미 vjú:ərʃip, 영 vjú:əʃip] 시청률, 시청자 (수·층)

89-91 🔊 영국식 발음

Questions 89-91 refer to the following talk.

Hi. I'm Stella, your guide for today. ⁸⁹**Before we begin the tour of Sharon Castle, I'd like to remind you of some rules.** First, certain areas of the castle are being tidied up for an event that will be hosted here next week. So, be ⟳

careful not to enter blocked off rooms. Also, ⁹⁰**please don't touch any of the furniture** in the rooms we'll pass through. Many items are historical artifacts and should not be damaged. Finally, please place your personal belongings in the storage lockers. They are by the front entrance. All right, ⁹¹**now let's proceed up the staircase to the grand ballroom.**

---

tidy up ~을 정돈하다 block off (출입구 등을) 차단하다
artifact[미 á:rtəfækt, 영 á:təfækt] 인공 유물, 공예품
belonging[미 bilɔ́:ŋiŋ, 영 bilɔ́ŋiŋ] 소지품, 소유물
proceed[prəsí:d] 이동하다, 나아가다

해석
89-91번은 다음 담화에 관한 문제입니다.

안녕하세요. 저는 오늘 여러분의 가이드인 Stella입니다. ⁸⁹Sharon 성의 관광을 시작하기 전에, 여러분께 몇 가지 규칙에 대해 상기시켜 드리고자 합니다. 첫 번째로, 성의 어떤 구역들은 다음 주에 이곳에서 주최될 행사를 위해 정돈되고 있는 중입니다. 그러므로, 출입이 차단된 방들에는 들어가지 않도록 조심해 주시기 바랍니다. 또한, 우리가 지나가게 될 방에 있는 ⁹⁰가구들을 건드리지 마시기 바랍니다. 많은 물건들이 역사적 유물이며 훼손되어서는 안 됩니다. 마지막으로, 여러분의 개인 소지품을 물품 보관함에 두시기 바랍니다. 그것들은 정문 옆에 있습니다. 좋습니다, ⁹¹이제 대연회장을 향해 계단 위로 이동하시겠습니다.

89.
해석 담화는 주로 무엇에 대한 것인가?
(A) 연회를 위한 지침
(B) 관광을 위한 규칙
(C) 시설의 변경 사항
(D) 명소로 가는 길 안내

해설 담화의 주제를 묻는 문제입니다. "Before we begin the tour ~, I'd like to remind you of some rules."라며 관광을 시작하기 전에 청자들에게 몇 가지 규칙에 대해 상기시키고자 한다고 하였습니다. 따라서 정답은 (B) Rules for a tour입니다.

어휘 attraction[ətrǽkʃən] 명소, 명물

90.
해석 화자는 청자들에게 무엇을 해달라고 요청하는가?
(A) 행사 세부 사항을 확인한다.
(B) 방을 정돈한다.
(C) 대체 비상구를 이용한다.
(D) 가구를 건드리지 않는다.

해설 화자가 청자들에게 요청하는 것을 묻는 문제입니다. "please don't touch any of the furniture"라며 가구들을 건드리지 말 것을 요청하였습니다. 따라서 정답은 (D) Avoid touching furniture입니다.

어휘 alternate[미 ɔ́:ltərnət, 영 ɔltɔ́:nət] 대체의, 교체의

91.
해석 청자들은 다음에 무엇을 할 것 같은가?
(A) 짧은 영상을 시청한다.
(B) 선물 가게에 들어간다.
(C) 다른 구역으로 이동한다.
(D) 입장권을 구매한다.

해설 청자들이 다음에 할 일을 묻는 문제입니다. "now let's proceed ~ to the grand ballroom"이라며 이제 대연회장을 향해 이

동하자고 하였습니다. 따라서 정답은 (C) Head to another area입니다.

92-94 [3일] 호주식 발음

Questions 92-94 refer to the following talk.

I want to take a moment to go over some staffing information. Mary Swan has announced her plan to step down from her position as the executive director. **92Mary is making this change in order to open her own advertising agency, which she's wanted to do** for quite some time. Fortunately, we have a personnel member—Carl Mendez—who is ready to assume her role. He has been a vice president for over a decade. **93That means you don't have to worry about whether he will be an effective executive director.** However, someone will need to be hired to replace Carl. I will hold interviews beginning next Friday. Once the position is filled, **94I will send everyone in the division an e-mail that includes details about the replacement.**

staffing[미 stǽfiŋ, 영 stáːfiŋ] 직원 채용
step down ~에서 물러나다, 은퇴하다
executive director 상임 이사
personnel[미 pə̀ːrsənél, 영 pə̀ːsənél] 직원
assume[미 əsúːm, 영 əsjúːm] 맡다
vice president 부사장, 부통령
replacement[ripléismənt] 후임(자)

해석

92-94번은 다음 담화에 관한 문제입니다.

직원 채용 정보에 대해 살펴보는 시간을 잠시 가지고자 합니다. Mary Swan이 상임 이사로서의 그녀의 직책에서 물러나겠다는 계획을 발표했습니다. 92Mary는 자신의 광고 대행사를 개업하기 위해 이런 변화를 단행하는 것인데, 이것은 그녀가 꽤 오랫동안 원해왔던 일입니다. 다행히도, 우리에게는 그녀의 역할을 맡을 준비가 되어 있는 직원인 Carl Mendez가 있습니다. 그는 10년이 넘는 기간 동안 부사장이었습니다. 93그것은 여러분들이 그가 유능한 상임 이사가 될지에 대해 걱정하지 않아도 된다는 것을 의미합니다. 그러나 누군가 Carl을 대신하기 위해 채용되어야 할 것입니다. 저는 다음 주 금요일부터 면접을 볼 것입니다. 그 직책이 채워지면, 94제가 부서의 모든 분들에게 후임자에 관한 상세 정보를 포함한 이메일을 보내드리겠습니다.

92.

해석 화자에 따르면, Mary Swan은 무엇을 하고 싶어 하는가?
(A) 새로운 사무실로 전근한다.
(B) 채용 공고를 게시한다.
(C) 사업을 시작한다.
(D) 콘서트에 참석한다.

해설 Mary Swan이 하고 싶어 하는 것을 묻는 문제입니다. "Mary is making this change in order to open her own advertising agency, which she's wanted to do"라며 Mary는 자신의 광고 대행사를 개업하기 위해 이런 변화를 단행하는 것인데 이것은 그녀가 원해왔던 일이라고 하였습니다. 따라서 정답은 (C) Start a business입니다.

어휘 transfer[미 trænsfə́ːr, 영 trænsfə́ː] 전근하다, 이동하다

93.

해석 화자는 왜 "그는 10년이 넘는 기간 동안 부사장이었습니다"라고 말하는가?
(A) 동료에게 그의 노고에 대해 감사하기 위해
(B) 직원의 자격을 설명하기 위해
(C) 상이 수여되는 이유를 언급하기 위해
(D) 직책의 중요성을 강조하기 위해

해설 화자가 하는 말(He has been a vice president for over a decade)의 의도를 묻는 문제입니다. "That means you don't have to worry about whether he will be an effective executive director."라며 그것은 그가 유능한 상임 이사가 될지에 대해 걱정하지 않아도 된다는 것을 의미한다고 한 말을 통해 상임 이사로 근무할 사람의 자격을 설명하기 위한 의도임을 알 수 있습니다. 따라서 정답은 (B) To explain an employee's qualifications입니다.

어휘 service[미 sə́ːrvis, 영 sə́ːvis] 노고, 봉사
qualification[미 kwɑ̀ːlifikéiʃən, 영 kwɔ̀lifikéiʃən] 자격, 자질
stress[stres] 강조하다

94.

해석 화자는 무엇을 할 것이라고 말하는가?
(A) 후임자에 대한 정보를 제공한다.
(B) 신규 직원 고용에 대한 지침을 검토한다.
(C) 직원들에게 신청서를 배부한다.
(D) 업무 성과에 대한 의견을 제공한다.

해설 화자가 다음에 할 일을 묻는 문제입니다. "I will send ~ an e-mail that includes details about the replacement"라며 후임자에 관한 상세 정보를 포함한 이메일을 보내주겠다고 하였습니다. 따라서 정답은 (A) Provide information about a replacement입니다.

어휘 distribute[distríbjuːt] 배부하다 application form 신청서
feedback[fíːdbæk] 의견
performance[미 pərfɔ́ːrməns, 영 pəfɔ́ːməns] 성과, 수행

95-97 [3일] 호주식 발음

Questions 95-97 refer to the following broadcast and program.

Thanks for tuning in to WBT 101.8's *Culture Break*. I'm Harry Schubert. This afternoon, I will be interviewing Marla Heinz, the director of the Gramercy Ballet Company. **95Today marks the fifth year since Ms. Heinz founded the company. 96She has organized 30 performances, including a charity recital last month that raised over $20,000 for student art programs.** Uh . . . I'm sure all of you are eager for the interview to begin. But due to a scheduling mix-up, **97I will be speaking with her after the commercial break** rather than at the start of the show. So, let's begin with music from her company's latest production, *Black River*.

tune in 청취하다
performance[미 pərfɔ́ːrməns, 영 pəfɔ́ːməns] 공연
charity[tʃǽrəti] 자선 recital[risáitl] 발표회, 연주회
commercial break 중간 광고
spotlight[미 spáːtlait, 영 spɔ́tlait] 집중 조명, 주목

95-97번은 다음 방송과 편성표에 관한 문제입니다.

WBT 101.8의 *Culture Break*를 청취해 주셔서 감사합니다. 저는 Harry Schubert입니다. 오늘 오후에, 저는 Gramercy 발레단의 감독인 Marla Heinz와 인터뷰를 할 것입니다. 95오늘은 Ms. Heinz가 단체를 설립한 지 5년째가 되는 날입니다. 96그녀는 지난달에 학생 예술 프로그램을 위해 20,000달러 이상을 모금했던 자선 무용 발표회를 포함하여 30편의 공연을 기획했습니다. 어... 저는 여러분 모두 인터뷰가 시작하기를 바라고 있다고 확신합니다. 하지만 일정 혼동으로 인해, 97저는 방송의 시작이 아닌 중간 광고가 끝난 후에 그녀와 이야기하게 될 것입니다. 그럼, 그녀의 발레단의 최신작 속 음악인 *Black River*를 들으시겠습니다.

방송 편성표 – *Culture Break*	
Marla Heinz와의 인터뷰	오후 3시 – 오후 3시 40분
97중간 광고	오후 3시 40분 – 오후 3시 50분
작품에 대한 집중 조명	오후 3시 50분 – 오후 4시 30분
교통 방송	오후 4시 30분 – 오후 4시 40분

95.

해석 화자에 따르면, 5년 전에 무슨 일이 일어났는가?
(A) 라디오 방송이 시작되었다.
(B) 음악 공연이 열렸다.
(C) 무용 감독이 승진했다.
(D) 발레단이 설립되었다.

해설 5년 전에 일어난 일을 묻는 문제입니다. "Today marks the fifth year since Ms. Heinz founded the company [Gramercy Ballet Company]."라며 오늘이 Ms. Heinz가 Gramercy 발레단을 설립한 지 5년째가 되는 날이라고 한 말을 통해 5년 전에 발레단이 설립되었음을 알 수 있습니다. 따라서 정답은 (D) A ballet company was established입니다.

96.

해석 Marla Heinz는 어떻게 학생 예술 프로그램을 위한 기금을 모으는가?
(A) 보조금을 신청함으로써
(B) 행사를 기획함으로써
(C) 물품을 판매함으로써
(D) 자원봉사 일을 함으로써

해설 Marla Heinz가 학생 예술 프로그램을 위한 기금을 모은 방법을 묻는 문제입니다. "She has organized ~ a charity recital last month that raised over $20,000 for student art programs."라며 지난달에 학생 예술 프로그램을 위해 20,000달러 이상을 모금했던 자선 무용 발표회를 기획했다고 하였습니다. 따라서 정답은 (B) By organizing an event입니다.

어휘 apply for ~을 신청하다, 지원하다
grant[미 grænt, 영 grɑːnt] 보조금, 허가

97.

해석 시각 자료를 보아라. 인터뷰는 언제 시작할 것인가?
(A) 오후 3시에
(B) 오후 3시 40분에
(C) 오후 3시 50분에
(D) 오후 4시 30분에

해설 인터뷰가 시작할 시간을 묻는 문제입니다. "I will be speaking with her after the commercial break"라며 중간 광고가 끝난 후에 그녀와 이야기하게 될 것이라고 하였으므로, 중간 광고가 끝난 후인 오후 3시 50분에 인터뷰를 시작할 것임을 편

성표에서 알 수 있습니다. 따라서 정답은 (C) At 3:50 P.M.입니다.

98-100 🔊 영국식 발음

Questions 98-100 refer to the following advertisement and flyer.

Want a new look? Then visit Trends! 98All of our employees have been trained in the latest cutting, coloring, and styling techniques. And you can request a free consultation if you are uncertain about what you'd like done to your hair. To celebrate our second anniversary, 99we will be holding a four-day event in June. During the first three days, a 10 percent discount will be offered. 99On the final day, customers will receive a free bottle of conditioner in addition to the discount! 100To arrange an appointment, go to www.trends.com.

train[trein] 훈련시키다, 교육을 받다
consultation[미 kɑ̀nsəltéiʃən, 영 kɔ̀nsʌltéiʃən] 상담
uncertain[미 ʌnsə́ːrtn, 영 ʌnsə́ːtn] 확신이 없는, 불확실한
celebrate[미 séləbrèit, 영 séləbrèit] 맞이하다, 기념하다

98-100번은 다음 광고와 전단지에 관한 문제입니다.

새로운 스타일을 원하시나요? 그렇다면 Trends를 방문하세요! 98저희의 모든 직원들은 최신 커팅, 염색, 그리고 스타일링 기술을 연수받았습니다. 그리고 만약 여러분이 머리에 무엇을 하고 싶은지 확신이 없으시다면 무료 상담을 요청하실 수 있습니다. 개업 2주년을 맞이하여, 99저희는 6월에 4일 동안 행사를 할 것입니다. 첫 3일 동안에는, 10퍼센트 할인이 제공될 것입니다. 99마지막 날에, 고객님들은 할인과 함께 무료 컨디셔너 한 병을 받으실 것입니다! 100예약을 하시려면, www.trends.com을 방문하세요.

Trends 기념일 행사
10퍼센트까지의 절약을 위해 996월 2일부터 5일까지 저희를 방문하세요!
Green로와 Center가가 만나는 모퉁이에 위치해 있습니다.

98.

해석 화자는 어떤 종류의 사업체를 광고하고 있는가?
(A) 의류 상점
(B) 가구점
(C) 보석 소매상
(D) 미용실

해설 광고의 주제를 묻는 문제입니다. "All of our employees have been trained in the latest cutting, coloring, and styling techniques."라며 모든 직원들이 최신 커팅, 염색, 그리고 스타일링 기술을 연수받았다고 한 뒤, 미용실의 할인 행사와 관련된 내용을 언급하였습니다. 따라서 정답은 (D) A hair salon입니다.

어휘 retailer[미 ríːteilər, 영 ríːteilə] 소매상

99.

해석 시각 자료를 보아라. 고객들은 언제 무료 제품을 받을 것인가?

(A) 6월 2일에
(B) 6월 3일에
(C) 6월 4일에
(D) 6월 5일에

해설 고객들이 무료 제품을 받을 시기를 묻는 문제입니다. "we will be holding a four-day event in June"이라며 6월에 4일 동안 행사를 할 것이라고 한 뒤, "On the final day, customers will receive a free bottle of conditioner"라며 마지막 날에 고객들은 무료 컨디셔너 한 병을 받을 것이라고 하였으므로, 고객들이 행사의 마지막 날인 6월 5일에 무료 제품을 받을 것임을 전단지에서 알 수 있습니다. 따라서 정답은 (D) On June 5입니다.

100.

해석 광고에 따르면, 청자들은 왜 업체의 웹사이트를 방문해야 하는가?
(A) 고객 후기를 읽기 위해
(B) 예약을 하기 위해
(C) 행사 날짜를 확인하기 위해
(D) 쿠폰을 다운로드하기 위해

해설 청자들이 업체의 웹사이트를 방문해야 하는 이유를 묻는 문제입니다. "To arrange an appointment, go to www.trends.com."이라며 예약을 하려면 www.trends.com을 방문하라고 하였습니다. 따라서 정답은 (B) To make a reservation입니다.

PART 5

101. 명령문의 동사 자리 채우기
해설 이 문장은 주어 없이 동사로 시작되는 명령문이므로, 명령문의 동사 자리에 올 수 있는 동사원형 (A) Change(교체하다)가 정답입니다. 동사의 과거형 또는 분사 (B), 동사의 3인칭 단수형 또는 명사 (C), 동명사 또는 분사 (D)는 명령문의 동사 자리에 올 수 없습니다.

해석 진열된 꽃이 싱싱하고 건강하게 유지되도록 매일 꽃병의 물을 교체하십시오.

어휘 on display phr. 진열된, 전시된
stay v. ~한 채로 유지되다, 머무르다

102. 태에 맞는 동사 채우기
해설 빈칸에 들어갈 동사(surprise)가 '놀라게 하다'라는 의미로 감정을 나타내는 타동사인데, 주어(The community)가 감정을 느끼므로 수동태를 써야 합니다. 따라서 수동태 (C) was surprised가 정답입니다. 능동태 (A), (B), (D)는 주어가 감정의 원인일 경우 사용됩니다.

해석 주민들은 플라스틱 용기 제조 시설의 문을 닫기로 한 소유주의 결정에 놀랐다.

어휘 community n. 주민, 지역 사회 container n. 용기, 그릇
manufacturing n. 제조(업)

103. 수식어 거품을 이끄는 것 채우기
해설 이 문장은 주어(he), 동사(brings), 목적어(his inflatable neck pillow)를 갖춘 완전한 절이므로 _____ ~ distance는 수식어 거품으로 보아야 합니다. 따라서 수식어 거품을 이끌 수 있는 부사절 접속사 (C)와 전치사 (D)가 정답의 후보입니다. 이 수식어 거품은 동사(is flying)가 있는 거품절이므로, 거품절을 이끌 수 있는 부사절 접속사 (C) Whether

(~이든지 ~이든지, ~이든지 아니든지)가 정답입니다. 전치사 (D) Regarding(~에 대한)은 거품절이 아닌 거품구를 이끕니다. 부사 또는 명사 (A) Anywhere(어디든지; 어디)와 부사 (B) Perhaps(아마, 혹시)는 수식어 거품을 이끌 수 없습니다.

해석 Mr. Tan은 단거리를 비행하든지, 장거리를 비행하든지 부풀릴 수 있는 목 베개를 항상 가지고 다닌다.

어휘 distance n. 거리, 간격 inflatable adj. (공기로) 부풀릴 수 있는
pillow n. 베개

104. 주어와 수일치하는 동사 채우기
해설 주절(The report ~ strategies)에 주어(The report)만 있고 동사가 없으므로 동사 (A), (B), (C)가 정답의 후보입니다. 주어가 단수이므로 단수 동사 (A) describes(설명하다, 묘사하다)가 정답입니다. 복수 동사 (B)와 (C)는 복수 주어와 함께 쓰입니다. 부사 (D)는 동사 자리에 올 수 없습니다. 참고로, 빈칸 앞의 on Bawdry's current marketing projects는 주어를 꾸미는 수식어 거품이므로, 수식어 거품 안의 projects만 보고 복수 동사 (B)나 (C)를 정답으로 고르지 않도록 주의합니다.

해석 Bawdry사의 현재 마케팅 프로젝트에 대한 보고서는 성공적이라고 판명되고 있는 다양한 광고 전략에 대해 설명한다.

어휘 current adj. 현재의, 지금의 strategy n. 전략
prove v. 판명되다, 증명하다 successful adj. 성공적인

105. 전치사 채우기: 기간
해설 '대학에서의 4년보다 1년간의 근무 동안 더 많이 배웠다'라는 의미가 되어야 하므로 기간을 나타내는 전치사 (A) during (~ 동안)이 정답입니다. (B) by는 '~까지', (C) since는 '~ 이래로'라는 의미로 시점을 나타냅니다. (D) between은 '~ 사이에'라는 의미로 기간이나 위치를 나타내고, 다음에 A and B의 형태나 명사의 복수형이 옵니다.

해석 Mr. Turner는 대학에서의 4년보다 1년간의 근무 동안 더 많이 배웠다.

어휘 college n. 대학

106. 올바른 시제의 동사 채우기
해설 문장에 주어(Ms. Landry)만 있고 동사가 없으므로 동사 (A), (B), (D)가 정답의 후보입니다. '어제의 발표에서 판매 전망을 논의했다'라는 의미로, 어제의 발표에서 판매 전망을 논의한 것은 과거에 일어난 일이므로 과거 시제 (D) discussed가 정답입니다. 현재 시제 (A)와 미래 시제 (B)는 과거를 나타낼 수 없고, 동명사 또는 분사 (C)는 동사 자리에 올 수 없습니다.

해석 Ms. Landry는 어제의 발표에서 다음 분기의 판매 전망을 논의했다.

어휘 sales projection phr. 판매 전망 quarter n. 분기, 3개월
presentation n. 발표, 제출

107. 보어 자리 채우기
해설 be동사(is) 다음의 보어 자리에 올 수 있는 명사 (A)와 (C), 형용사 (B)가 정답의 후보입니다. 'X70 카메라는 많은 경쟁사들의 카메라보다 더 비싸다'라는 의미가 되어야 하므로 be동사(is)의 보어 자리에 와서 주어(the X70 camera)를 설명해주는 형용사 (B) expensive(비싼)가 정답입니다. 명사 (A)와 (C)는 주어와 동격 관계가 되어 '카메라는 비용이다'라는 어색한 문맥을 만듭니다. 동사 (D)는 보어 자리에 올 수 없습니다.

해석 비록 X70 카메라는 많은 경쟁사들의 제품보다 더 비싸지만, 이미지 해상도가 시중에서 가장 높은 것 중 하나이다.

어휘 resolution n. 해상도, 결정

108. 부사 어휘 고르기

해설 '멤버십은 매달 자동으로 갱신된다'라는 문맥이므로 부사 (C) automatically(자동으로)가 정답입니다. (A) respectively는 '각기, 각자'라는 의미로 해석상 그럴듯해 보이지만, 앞서 언급된 두 가지 이상의 것들이 각각 어떠하다는 것을 나타냅니다. (B) occasionally는 '때때로'라는 의미로, 이미 빈도를 나타내는 부사(monthly)가 있으므로 답이 될 수 없습니다. (D) severely는 '엄격하게, 심하게'라는 의미입니다.

해석 소프트웨어 프로그램에 대한 멤버십은 일 년의 기간 동안 매달 자동으로 갱신된다.

어휘 membership n. 멤버십, 회원   renew v. 갱신하다
period n. 기간

109. 전치사 채우기: 제외

해설 이 문장은 주어(everything), 동사(was), 보어(impressive)를 갖춘 완전한 절이므로 _____ ~ buffet는 수식어 거품으로 보아야 합니다. 이 수식어 거품은 동사가 없는 거품구이므로, 거품구를 이끌 수 있는 전치사 (B)와 (C)가 정답의 후보입니다. '조식 뷔페를 제외한 거의 모든 것들이 인상적이었다'라는 의미가 되어야 하므로 제외를 나타내는 전치사 (C) except for(~을 제외하고)가 정답입니다. (B) among은 '~ 사이에, 중간에'라는 의미로 위치를 나타냅니다. 부사절 접속사 (A) as soon as(~하자마자)와 (D) provided that(만약 ~이라면)은 거품구가 아닌 거품절을 이끕니다.

해석 비평가 Louis Arnold에 따르면, 조식 뷔페를 제외한 Big River 호텔의 거의 모든 것들이 인상적이었다.

어휘 according to phr. ~에 따르면, ~에 따라
critic n. 비평가, 평론가   impressive adj. 인상적인

110. 명사 어휘 고르기

해설 '교열 담당자 자리에 선발되는 지원자는 세부 사항에 면밀히 주목하는 능력을 가져야 한다'라는 문맥이므로 명사 (B) detail(세부 사항)이 정답입니다. (A) approach는 '접근, 접근법', (C) privilege는 '특권, 혜택', (D) profession은 '직업, 직종'이라는 의미입니다.

해석 교열 담당자 자리에 선발되는 지원자는 세부 사항에 면밀히 주목하는 능력을 가져야 한다.

어휘 applicant n. 지원자   copy editor phr. 교열 담당자
capacity n. 능력   close adj. 면밀한, 가까운
pay attention to phr. ~에 주목하다

111. 전치사 채우기: 시간

해설 '새 레스토랑은 1월에 열 예정이다'라는 의미가 되어야 하므로 시간을 나타내는 전치사 (B), (C), (D)가 정답의 후보입니다. 빈칸 뒤에 January(1월)가 있으므로 월, 연도, 계절 등을 나타내는 표현 앞에 오는 (C) in이 정답입니다. (B) on은 날짜, 요일, 특정일을 나타내는 표현 앞에, (D) at은 시각, 시점을 나타내는 표현 앞에 옵니다. (A) of는 '~의'라는 의미입니다.

해석 예기치 않은 차질은 Ms. Lupo가 그녀의 새 레스토랑을 위한 개관식의 일정을 변경하게 만들었고, 레스토랑은 이제 1월에 열 예정이다.

어휘 unexpected adj. 예기치 않은, 뜻밖의   setback n. 차질, 방해
force v. (어쩔 수 없이) ~하게 만들다; ~을 강요하다; n. 힘
reschedule v. 일정을 변경하다
ribbon cutting ceremony phr. 개관식   set adj. 예정인, 준비된

112. 동사 어휘 고르기

해설 '안전 지도사는 정기적으로 장비를 점검해야 하는 필요성을 강조했다'라는 문맥이므로 동사 emphasize(강조하다, 역설하다)

의 과거형 (B) emphasized가 정답입니다. (A)의 launch는 '시작하다, 출시하다', (C)의 correct는 '정정하다, 수정하다', (D)의 perform은 '수행하다, 실행하다'라는 의미입니다.

해석 교육 시간 동안에, 안전 지도사는 정기적으로 장비를 청소하고 점검해야 하는 필요성을 강조했다.

어휘 instructor n. 지도사, 강사   inspect v. 점검하다, 검사하다

113. 형용사 어휘 고르기

해설 '컴퓨터는 많은 보안 문제들에 취약하기 때문에, 바이러스에 대한 정밀 검사를 받는 것이 필수적이다'라는 문맥이므로 형용사 (B) vulnerable(취약한, 연약한)이 정답입니다. (A) wary는 '경계하는', (C) requisite는 '필수의', (D) critical은 '비판적인, 중대한'이라는 의미입니다. 참고로, 주절(it is essential)의 essential(필수적인)과 같이 의무를 나타내는 형용사가 나오면 종속절에 동사원형이 와야 하므로 that절(that ~ viruses)에서 they are가 아니라 they be의 형태가 쓰인 것임을 알아둡니다.

해석 컴퓨터는 많은 보안 문제들에 취약하기 때문에, 정기적으로 바이러스에 대한 정밀 검사를 받는 것이 필수적이다.

어휘 a number of phr. 많은   security n. 보안   issue n. 문제
routinely adv. 정기적으로

114. 부사 채우기

해설 '티켓 판매가 거의 현재의 기록을 깰 만큼 충분히 높았다'라는 의미가 되어야 하므로 부사 (D) almost(거의)가 정답입니다. (A) around는 '약; ~의 주위에'라는 의미의 부사 또는 전치사입니다. 부사 (B) heavily는 '심하게, 무겁게', (C) frequently는 '종종, 빈번하게'라는 의미입니다.

해석 영화 *Autumn Winds*의 첫 주 동안의 티켓 판매는 거의 현재의 기록을 깰 만큼 충분히 높았다.

어휘 sale n. 판매, 매출(량)   record n. 기록; v. 기록하다

115. 다른 명사를 수식하는 명사 채우기

해설 '회사는 창고를 상품들의 물류 센터로 사용할 것이다'라는 의미가 되어야 하므로 빈칸 뒤의 center(센터, 중심지)와 함께 '물류 센터'라는 의미의 복합 명사 distribution center를 만드는 명사 (A) distribution(유통, 분배)이 정답입니다. 형용사 (B)와 (D)는 각각 '분포된 센터', '분배할 수 있는 센터'라는 어색한 문맥을 만듭니다. 명사 (C)는 '유통업자 센터'라는 어색한 문맥을 만듭니다.

해석 Yardley Fashions사는 Chester로에 있는 창고를 매입했는데, 회사는 이곳을 상품들의 물류 센터로 사용할 것이다.

어휘 warehouse n. 창고   goods n. 상품, 제품
distributed adj. 분포된, 광범위한
distributor n. 유통업자, 배급업자
distributable adj. 분배할 수 있는, 분류할 수 있는

116. 명사 어휘 고르기

해설 '수익이 주로 새로운 기업 고객과의 제휴 덕분에 증가했다'라는 문맥이므로 명사 (B) revenue(수익, 수입)가 정답입니다. (A) inflation은 '물가 인상', (C) frequency는 '빈도', (D) representative는 '대표, 대리'라는 의미입니다.

해석 법률 회사는 지난 분기의 수익이 주로 새로운 기업 고객과의 제휴 덕분에 증가했다고 발표했다.

어휘 quarter n. 분기, 4분의 1   primarily adv. 주로
due to phr. ~ 덕분에, ~ 때문에   partnership n. 제휴, 협력
corporate n. 기업, 회사

117. 가정법 동사 채우기

해설 두 번째 절(if ~ school)이 if로 시작되고 동사가 had p.p.(had gotten)인 것으로 보아 가정법 과거 완료 문장임을 알 수 있습니다. 따라서 주절(Ms. Adams ~ University)에는 had p.p.와 짝을 이루어 가정법 과거 완료를 만드는 would(could, might, should) have p.p.가 와야 하므로 (C) could have gone이 정답입니다. 현재 진행 시제 (A), 과거 완료 시제 (B), 과거 시제 (D)는 가정법 과거 완료의 주절의 동사로 쓰일 수 없습니다. 참고로, 가정법 과거 완료는 과거 사실의 반대를 가정하며 'If + 주어 + had p.p., 주어 + would(could, might, should) + have p.p.'의 형태로 쓰이고, 가정법 과거는 현재 사실의 반대를 가정하며 'If + 주어 + 과거동사(be동사의 경우 were), 주어 + would(could, might, should) + 동사원형'의 형태로 쓰임을 알아둡니다.

해석 Ms. Adams가 고등학교 최고 학년 동안 더 좋은 성적을 받았더라면 Swarthmore 대학교에 갈 수 있었을 것이다.

어휘 senior year phr. 최고 학년

118. 형용사 어휘 고르기

해설 '문학 컨벤션 티켓을 예약하기 전에 인근의 호텔들을 찾아보았다'라는 의미가 되어야 하므로 형용사 (D) nearby(인근의, 가까운)가 정답입니다. (A) instant는 '즉각적인, 긴박한', (B) extended는 '길어진, 늘어난', (C) mandatory는 '의무적인, 명령의'라는 의미입니다.

해석 그녀의 문학 컨벤션 티켓을 예약하기 전에, Ms. Jackson은 아직 이용 가능한 객실이 있는 인근의 호텔들을 찾아보았다.

어휘 literature n. 문학, 문헌

119. 병치 구문 채우기

해설 '보너스 액수가 결정될 것이고 직원들 사이에서 적절하게 분배될 것이다'라는 의미로, 빈칸이 등위접속사 and(그리고)로 연결되어 있습니다. 따라서 빈칸 앞의 수동형 'be+p.p.(be decided)'의 decided와 병치를 이루는 동사 divide(분배하다, 배분하다)의 p.p.형 (A) divided가 정답입니다. 명사 (B), to 부정사 (C), 동사원형 (D)는 p.p.형과 병치를 이룰 수 없습니다.

해석 연말에 이사회에 의해 보너스 액수가 결정될 것이고 직원들 사이에서 적절하게 분배될 것이다.

어휘 board n. 이사회, 위원회 appropriately adv. 적절하게

120. 수식어 거품을 이끄는 것 채우기

해설 이 문장은 주어(they), 동사(chose), 목적어(Pendant Architects)를 갖춘 완전한 절이므로, _____ ~ building은 수식어 거품으로 보아야 합니다. 이 수식어 거품은 동사가 없는 거품구이므로 거품구를 이끌 수 있는 to 부정사 (A) to work가 정답입니다. 명사 (B), 명사 또는 동사 (C), 동사 (D)는 수식어 거품을 이끌 수 없습니다. 만약 (B)를 써서 'Pendant 건축사의 직원을 선택했다'라는 문맥을 만들려면, worker는 가산 명사이므로 복수형으로 쓰이거나 앞에 관사가 와야 합니다.

해석 위원회 회원들이 디자인 제안서를 검토한 후, 그들은 새로운 은행 건물 작업을 하기 위해 Pendant 건축사를 선택했다.

어휘 committee n. 위원회

121. 동사 어휘 고르기

해설 'Fleischman사의 컴퓨터 칩이 장착된 전화기'라는 문맥이므로 동사 equip(장착하다, 장비를 갖추다)의 과거분사 (C) equipped가 정답입니다. (A)의 demonstrate는 '입증하다', (B)의 found는 '설립하다', (D)의 recruit는 '모집

하다, 뽑다'라는 의미입니다.

해석 합작 사업의 일부로, HLN사는 Fleischman사의 컴퓨터 칩이 장착된 전화기를 판매하고 있다.

어휘 joint adj. 합작의, 합동의 venture n. 사업, 모험 market v. 판매하다

122. 사람명사와 추상명사 구별하여 채우기

해설 빈칸 앞의 형용사(strong)의 꾸밈을 받을 수 있는 것은 명사이므로 명사 (A)와 (C)가 정답의 후보입니다. '홈팀은 상대와의 치열한 경쟁에 직면했다'라는 의미가 되어야 하므로 추상명사 (A) competition(경쟁, 대회)이 정답입니다. 사람명사 (C) competitor(경쟁자, 참가자)를 쓰면 '상대와의 치열한 경쟁자에 직면했다'라는 어색한 문맥이 됩니다. 형용사 (B)와 동사 (D)는 명사 자리에 올 수 없습니다.

해석 홈팀은 상대와의 치열한 경쟁에 직면했지만, 선수들은 마침내 간신히 승리를 확보했다.

어휘 opponent n. 상대, 경쟁자 manage to phr. 간신히 ~하다 secure v. 확보하다, 획득하다 victory n. 승리 in the end phr. 마침내

123. 태에 맞는 동사 채우기

해설 빈칸 뒤에 목적어(the need)가 있고, '구조 조정은 예산 삭감의 필요성을 없애지는 않았다'라는 능동의 의미이므로 능동태 (C) did not eliminate가 정답입니다. 수동태 (A), (B), (D)는 목적어 없이 사용되고 수동의 의미를 나타냅니다.

해석 Founder Chemicals사의 구조 조정은 광범위했지만, 이것은 회사 운영 예산의 대대적인 삭감의 필요성을 없애지는 않았다.

어휘 restructure v. 구조를 조정하다, 개혁하다 reduction n. 삭감, 축소 operating budget phr. 운영(영업) 예산

124. 동사 관련 어구 완성하기

해설 '인용한 수치가 유명한 환경 연구 회사에 의해 도출된 것이라고 했다'라는 문맥이므로 빈칸 뒤의 to와 함께 'A가 B에 의해 도출된 것이라고 하다, A를 B의 덕분으로 보다'라는 의미의 어구인 attribute A(the figures) to B(a well-known environmental research firm)를 만드는 동사 attribute(~의 것이리라고 보다, ~의 덕분이라고 여기다)의 과거형 (A) attributed가 정답입니다. (B)의 calculate는 '계산하다, 추정하다', (C)의 augment는 '늘리다, 증대시키다', (D)의 establish는 '설립하다, 제정하다'라는 의미입니다.

해석 Mr. Snead는 그가 기사에서 인용한 수치가 유명한 환경 연구 회사에 의해 도출된 것이라고 했다.

어휘 figure n. 수치, 숫자 quote v. 인용하다

125. 올바른 시제의 동사 채우기

해설 첫 번째 절(Mr. Cane ~ started)에 주어(Mr. Cane)만 있고 동사가 없으므로 동사 (A), (C), (D)가 정답의 후보입니다. '은행으로부터 5만 달러를 빌렸지만 최근에서야 그 대출금을 정산했다'라는 의미로, 과거의 특정 시점 즉, 대출금을 정산한 최근(did not settle the loan until recently) 이전의 일을 나타내고 있으므로 과거 완료 시제 (A) had borrowed가 정답입니다. 미래 시제 (C)는 특정 과거 시점 이전을 나타낼 수 없습니다. 과거 진행 시제 (D)는 과거의 특정 시점에 진행되는 일을 나타내고 '은행으로부터 돈을 빌리는 중이었지만, 최근에서야 정산했다'라는 어색한 문맥을 만듭니다. 동명사 또는 분사 (B)는 동사 자리에 올 수 없습니다.

해석 Mr. Cane은 그의 사업을 시작하기 위해 은행으로부터 5만 달

러를 빌렸지만, 최근에서야 그 대출금을 정산했다.

어휘 settle v. 정산하다, 지불하다 loan n. 대출(금), 대여

126. 형용사 자리 채우기

해설 빈칸 뒤의 명사구(family vehicles)를 꾸밀 수 있는 것은 형용사 사이므로, 형용사 (C) popular(인기 있는, 대중적인)가 정답입니다. 동사 (A)와 명사 (B), 부사 (D)는 명사구를 꾸밀 수 없습니다.

해석 Ogichi 560 차량은 *Consumer Times Magazine*에 의해 국내에서 가장 인기 있는 가족용 차량 중 하나로 칭해져 왔다.

어휘 nation n. 국가, 나라 vehicle n. 차량

127. 올바른 시제의 동사 채우기

해설 '다년간의 경험에도 불구하고 많은 청중들 앞에 서면 여전히 긴장한다'라는 의미로 반복되는 상태를 나타내므로 현재 시제 (B) stands(서다)가 정답입니다. 과거 진행 시제 (A), 가정법 과거 완료의 주절에서 쓰이는 would have p.p. 형태인 (C), 과거 완료 진행 시제 (D)는 반복되는 상태를 나타낼 수 없습니다.

해석 연설가로서의 다년간의 경험에도 불구하고, Mr. Carroll은 많은 청중들 앞에 서면 여전히 긴장한다.

어휘 public speaker phr. 연설가, 공술인 nervous adj. 긴장하는
audience n. 청중, 관중

128. 명사 어휘 고르기

해설 '어떤 결함도 발견되지 않는 것을 확실히 하기 위해 모든 상품을 최고의 전문 기술로 검사한다'라는 문맥이므로 명사 (D) imperfections(결함, 결점)가 정답입니다. (A)의 expenditure는 '지출', (B)의 interruption은 '중단, 방해', (C)의 evaluation은 '평가'라는 의미입니다.

해석 Coulier Fine Jewelry사는 어떤 결함도 발견되지 않는 것을 확실히 하기 위해 모든 상품을 최고의 전문 기술로 검사한다.

어휘 jewelry n. 보석 inspect v. 검사하다 merchandise n. 상품
utmost adj. 최고의 expertise n. 전문 기술
make certain phr. 확실히 하다

129. 부사 어휘 고르기

해설 '연결 항공편을 타기 위해 곧바로 출발 탑승구로 가라고 당부받았다'라는 문맥이므로 부사 (B) directly(곧바로, 곧장)가 정답입니다. (A) eventually는 '결국, 마침내', (C) tirelessly는 '끊임없이, 꾸준히', (D) previously는 '이전에, 사전에'라는 의미입니다.

해석 연착된 비행기의 승객들은 연결 항공편을 타기 위해 곧바로 출발 탑승구로 가라고 당부받았다.

어휘 be told to phr. ~하라고 당부받다 departure n. 출발
make a flight phr. 비행기를 타다, 비행하다

130. 부정대명사 채우기

해설 and 다음의 절(____ ~ year)에서 동사(is)가 단수이고 '두 군데의 할인점이 이미 시내에 위치해 있고 또 다른 하나가 연말까지 개점할 예정이다'라는 의미가 되어야 하므로, 단수 취급되는 부정대명사 (A) another(또 다른 하나/사람)가 정답입니다. (B) others(다른 것/사람들)와 (D) some(몇몇)은 복수 취급되어 복수 동사와 함께 쓰입니다. (C) none(아무것도/아무도 ~하다)은 주로 복수 취급되며, '두 군데의 할인점이 이미 시내에 위치해 있고 아무것도 연말에 개점하지 않을 예정이다'라는 어색한 문맥을 만듭니다. 만약 '더 이상의 할인점은 연말까지 개점하지 않을 예정이다'라는 문맥이 되려면 no more are

set to open과 같은 형태가 되어야 합니다.

해석 두 군데의 OrganiFoods 할인점이 이미 시내에 위치해 있고 또 다른 하나가 연말까지 개점할 예정이다.

PART 6

131-134번은 다음 편지에 관한 문제입니다.

Polstar-Direct 소매점
350번지 50번가, 뉴욕시, 뉴욕 주

관계자분께,

저는 귀사로부터 최근 제 구매에 관한 이메일을 받았습니다. 거기에는 제가 귀사의 온라인 상점에서 주문한 모니터가 배달되었다고 명시되어 있었습니다. ¹³¹이메일의 추적 링크는 저를 한 웹페이지로 연결해주었는데, 그 웹페이지는 그것이 보내진 장소를 보여주었습니다. ¹³²저는 그 모니터가 뉴욕에 있는 저희 집이 아니라 켄터키 주의 한 장소로 배달됐다는 것을 알고 놀랐습니다.

귀사가 보낸 송장은 명확히 저의 실제 주소를 기재하고 있으므로, 저는 왜 구매된 모니터가 다른 곳에 배달됐는지 모르겠습니다. ¹³³이를 가능한 한 신속히 해결해주실 수 있기를 바랍니다. ¹³⁴하지만, 소포가 저의 주소로 배달되지 못한다면, 저는 환불을 받고 싶습니다. 귀하는 제가 사용한 신용카드로 금액을 상환해주실 수 있습니다.

Ruth Adams 드림

retailer n. 소매점 in regard to phr. ~에 관한
recent adj. 최근의 purchase n. 구매
state v. 명시하다, 말하다 deliver v. 배달하다
track v. 추적하다 direct v. ~로 연결해주다, 보내다
indicate v. 보여주다, 나타내다 invoice n. 송장
clearly adv. 명확히, 분명히 unsure adj. 모르는
elsewhere adv. 다른 곳으로 reimburse v. 상환하다, 배상하다

---

131. 격에 맞는 인칭대명사 채우기 주변 문맥 파악

해설 빈칸 앞의 선행사(the place)를 뒤에서 꾸며주는 관계대명사 that이 생략된 관계절(____ was sent to)에 주어가 없으므로, 관계절의 주어 자리에 올 수 있는 모든 보기가 정답의 후보입니다. 빈칸이 있는 문장만으로 정답을 고를 수 없으므로 주변 문맥이나 전체 문맥을 파악합니다. 앞 문장에서 온라인 상점에서 주문한 모니터가 배달되었다고 명시되어 있었다고 했으므로, 빈칸에는 앞에서 언급된 모니터(the monitor)를 대신하는 대명사가 와야 합니다. 따라서 대명사 (B) it이 정답입니다. 인칭대명사 (A) theirs는 they의 소유대명사로 '그들의 것'이라는 의미를 나타내는데, they가 가리키는 대상이 지문에 언급되지 않았으므로 답이 될 수 없습니다. 부정대명사 (C) each (각기, 각자)는 그룹 안의 하나하나를 가리키는데, 주문된 모니터는 하나뿐이므로 답이 될 수 없습니다. 의문대명사 (D) what은 '무엇이 장소로 배달되었다'라는 어색한 문맥을 만듭니다. 또한, what이 명사절 접속사로 쓰일 경우 문장 내에서 주어, 목적어, 보어 역할을 하는 명사절을 이끌게 되므로 선행사를 꾸밀 수 없습니다.

132. 상관접속사 채우기

해설 빈칸 앞의 not(~이 아니다)과 함께 상관접속사 not A but B(A가 아니고 B)를 만드는 (C) but(그러나)이 정답입니다. 참고로, not A but B가 전치사구(to my home in New York)와 전치사구(to a location in Kentucky)를 연결하고 있음을 알아

됩니다. (A) and는 '그리고'라는 의미의 등위접속사이고, 상관접속사 both A and B(A와 B 모두)를 만들기도 합니다. and가 '뉴욕에 있는 집과 켄터키의 한 장소에 배달되지 않았다'라는 문맥을 만들 수도 있지만, 배송되는 모니터는 하나이므로 답이 될 수 없습니다. (B) for는 '~ 때문에'라는 의미의 등위접속사 또는 '~을 위해'라는 의미의 전치사로 쓰입니다. (D) so는 '그래서'라는 의미의 등위접속사입니다.

133. 동사 어휘 고르기 주변 문맥 파악

해설 '이를 가능한 한 신속히 ____해줄 수 있기를 바란다'라는 문맥이므로 모든 보기가 정답의 후보입니다. 빈칸이 있는 문장만으로 정답을 고를 수 없으므로 주변 문맥이나 전체 문맥을 파악합니다. 앞 문장에서 송장은 명확히 실제 주소를 기재하고 있는데도 구매한 모니터가 다른 곳으로 배달되었다고 했으므로 배송 오류 문제를 해결해주기를 바란다는 것을 알 수 있습니다. 따라서 동사 (B) resolve(해결하다)가 정답입니다. (A) approve는 '승인하다, 찬성하다', (C) dispute는 '논쟁하다', (D) replace는 '대체하다'라는 의미입니다.

134. 알맞은 문장 고르기

해석 (A) 안타깝게도, 귀하의 온라인 상점에서 주문한 물건을 아직 받지 못했습니다.
(B) 이것은 선적을 위해 필요한 올바른 정보일 것입니다.
(C) 하지만, 소포가 저의 주소로 배달되지 못한다면, 저는 환불을 받고 싶습니다.
(D) 이것은 제가 선택한 상품의 목록을 나열하고 있으며 지불이 되었음을 확인해줍니다.

해설 빈칸에 들어갈 알맞은 문장을 고르는 문제이므로 빈칸의 주변 문맥이나 전체 문맥을 파악합니다. 앞부분에서 모니터가 집이 아닌 다른 장소로 배달되었다고 했고, 뒤 문장 'You can reimburse the money to the credit card I used.'에서 제가, 즉 이메일 발신자가 사용한 신용카드로 금액을 상환해줄 수 있다고 했으므로 빈칸에는 환불을 원한다는 내용이 들어가야 함을 알 수 있습니다. 따라서 (C) However, if the package can't be delivered to my address, I'd like a refund가 정답입니다.

어휘 unfortunately adv. 안타깝게도 shipment n. 선적
package n. 소포, 포장 merchandise n. 상품
confirm v. 확인하다

135-138번은 다음 기사에 관한 문제입니다.

> ## FluDown이 밝은 전망을 가져오다
>
> Ferminex Medical사는 처방전 없이 살 수 있는 새로운 독감 치료제인 FluDown에 대한 실험이 촉망되는 결과와 함께 완료되었다고 오늘 발표했다.
>
> [135]PhysRec Labs의 박사들에 따르면, FluDown은 실험 참가자들의 질병과 관련한 증상을 상당히 감소시켰다. 실험 참가자들의 90퍼센트 이상이 더 적은 경우의 기침, 재채기, 두통을 경험했다고 말했다. [136]많은 사람들이 24시간이 안 되는 시간 후에 더 나아짐을 느꼈다고 주장했다. Ferminex Medical사의 대표인 Dr. Heather Stanbrow는 결과가 믿을 수 없을 정도로 고무적이라고 여긴다. 그리고 비록 몇몇 환자들이 부정적인 부작용을 보고했지만, 그 수는 예상되고 허용된 범위 내에 들어간다. [137]약 3퍼센트의 참가자들이 심하지 않은 배탈이 있었다고 말했다.
>
> "저희 연구팀은 현재까지 2년간 FluDown을 개발해왔고 결과에 매우 기뻐하고 있습니다"라고 Stanbrow가 말했다. [138]추가적인 약물 실험이 마찬가지로 잘 이루어진다면, 11월 말경 ○

에는 전국의 약국에서 약이 구매 가능할 것이라고 Ferminex Medical사는 생각한다.

trial n. 실험, 재판 **over-the-counter** adj. 처방전 없이 살 수 있는
medication n. 치료제, 약 **conclude** v. 완료되다, 결론을 내리다
promising adj. 촉망되는 **result** n. 결과
significantly adv. 상당히 **symptom** n. 증상
related to phr. ~과 관련한 **illness** n. 질병
participant n. 참가자 **instance** n. 경우 **cough** v. 기침하다
sneeze v. 재채기하다 **headache** n. 두통
incredibly adv. 믿을 수 없을 정도로 (놀라운)
encouraging adj. 고무적인 **negative** adj. 부정적인
side effect phr. 부작용 **fall within** phr. 범위 내에 들어가다
acceptable adj. 허용되는 **range** n. 범위
thrilled adj. 매우 기뻐하는

135. 동사 어휘 고르기 주변 문맥 파악

해설 'FluDown은 실험 참가자들의 질병과 관련한 증상을 상당히 ____시켰다'라는 문맥이므로 (A), (B), (D)가 정답의 후보입니다. 빈칸이 있는 문장만으로 정답을 고를 수 없으므로 주변 문맥이나 전체 문맥을 파악합니다. 뒤 문장에서 실험 참가자들의 90퍼센트 이상이 더 적은 경우의 기침, 재채기, 두통을 경험했다고 말했다고 했으므로 FluDown이 참가자들의 증상을 감소시켰음을 알 수 있습니다. 따라서 동사 reduce(감소시키다, 줄이다)의 과거형 (B) reduced가 정답입니다. (A)의 stimulate는 '활성화시키다, 자극하다', (C)의 reject는 '거절하다, 거부하다', (D)의 increase는 '증가시키다, 늘리다'라는 의미입니다.

136. 동사 자리 채우기

해설 문장에 주어(Many)만 있고 동사가 없으므로 동사 (A), (C), (D)가 정답의 후보입니다. 주어 자리에 온 대명사 Many(많은 사람들/것들)가 복수 취급되는 수량 표현이고, '많은 사람들이 더 나아짐을 느꼈고 ~라고 주장했다'라는 능동의 의미이므로 복수 주어와 함께 쓰일 수 있으면서 능동태를 나타내는 (D) claimed가 정답입니다. 단수 동사 (A)는 단수 주어와 함께 쓰입니다. 수동태 (C)는 수동의 의미를 나타내므로 정답이 될 수 없고, 동명사 또는 분사 (B)는 동사 자리에 올 수 없습니다.

137. 알맞은 문장 고르기

해석 (A) 인간에 대한 약물 실험의 적용은 승인이 필요하다.
(B) 약 3퍼센트의 참가자들이 심하지 않은 배탈이 있었다고 말했다.
(C) 실험을 시작하려면 약 500명의 자원자가 필요하다.
(D) 약은 의사의 처방전으로만 구할 수 있다.

해설 빈칸에 들어갈 알맞은 문장을 고르는 문제이므로 빈칸의 주변 문맥이나 전체 문맥을 파악합니다. 앞 문장 'And although some patients reported negative side effects, their number falls within an expected and acceptable range.'에서 비록 몇몇 환자들이 부정적인 부작용을 보고했지만 그 수는 예상되고 허용된 범위 내에 들어간다고 했으므로 빈칸에는 부정적인 부작용을 보고한 환자들에 관한 내용이 들어가야 함을 알 수 있습니다. 따라서 (B) Around 3 percent of participants said they had a minor upset stomach가 정답입니다.

어휘 application n. 적용, 신청, 지원 experiment n. 실험
approval n. 승인 minor adj. 심하지 않은, 경미한, 중요하지 않은
upset stomach phr. 배탈 approximately adv. 약, 대략
prescription n. 처방전 physician n. 의사

138. 형용사 어휘 고르기 주변 문맥 파악

해설 '_____한 약물 실험이 마찬가지로 잘 이루어진다면, 11월 말경에는 전국의 약국에서 약이 구매 가능할 것이다'라는 문맥이므로 (A)와 (B)가 정답의 후보입니다. 빈칸이 있는 문장만으로 정답을 고를 수 없으므로 주변 문맥이나 전체 문맥을 파악합니다. 앞 문장에서 연구팀이 FluDown을 개발해왔고 결과에 매우 기뻐하고 있다고 했으므로 앞으로 추가적인 실험 후에 약이 판매될 것임을 알 수 있습니다. 따라서 형용사 (B) further(추가적인, 여분의)가 정답입니다. (A) initial은 '처음의, 초기의', (C) former는 '이전의', (D) contrary는 '반대의, ~과는 다른'이라는 의미입니다.

139-142번은 다음 이메일에 관한 문제입니다.

수신: Sarita Ravia <sarvia@indothreads.co.in>
발신: June Shin <junes@brendanclothiers.com>
날짜: 11월 22일
제목: 요청
첨부: 세부 사항

Ms. Ravia께,

¹³⁹저는 지난주에 무역 박람회에서 귀하를 만나고 귀사에서 제조하는 많은 옷감들 중 일부를 보게 되어 즐거웠습니다.

¹⁴⁰귀하께서 제게 주신 직물 견본을 Brendan Clothiers사의 제작 책임자인 Fiona Tyler에게 보여주었고, 그녀는 높은 품질에 대해 얼마나 좋은 인상을 받았는지를 이야기했습니다. 저희는 귀사와 사업 계약을 맺는 것에 대해 낙관적입니다. ¹⁴¹저희는 또한 조만간 귀사에 대량 주문을 하기를 희망합니다.

귀사의 일정이 정신없이 바쁠 수 있음을 이해합니다. ¹⁴²만약 귀사가 이번에 저희의 요청을 이행하지 못할 것 같다면, 언제가 더 편할지 알려주십시오.

June Shin 드림

trade fair phr. 무역 박람회 manufacture v. 제조하다
fabric n. 직물, 천 impressed adj. 좋은 인상을 받은
optimistic adj. 낙관적인 form v. 맺다, 형성하다
arrangement n. 계약, 준비 hectic adj. 정신없이 바쁜
fulfill v. 이행하다 request n. 요청 convenient adj. 편한, 편리한

139. 명사 어휘 고르기 주변 문맥 파악

해설 '지난주에 무역 박람회에서 귀사에서 제조하는 많은 _____ 중 일부를 보게 되어 즐거웠다'라는 문맥이므로 모든 보기가 정답의 후보입니다. 빈칸이 있는 문장만으로 정답을 고를 수 없으므로 주변 문맥이나 전체 문맥을 파악합니다. 뒤 문장에서 상대방이 준 직물 견본을 자신의 회사의 제작 책임자에게 보여주었다고 했으므로 상대방의 회사에서 제조하는 것은 옷감이라는 것을 알 수 있습니다. 따라서 명사 (C) textiles(옷감)가 정답입니다. (A)의 machine은 '기계', (B)의 garment는 '의류', (D)의 accessory는 '장신구'라는 의미입니다.

140. 태에 맞는 동사 채우기

해설 빈칸 뒤에 목적어(how ~ quality)가 있으므로 목적어를 갖는 능동태 (A) has mentioned가 정답입니다. 수동태 (B)와 (C), (D)는 태가 맞지 않아 정답이 될 수 없습니다.

141. 알맞은 문장 고르기

해석 (A) 유감스럽게도, 저희는 귀하께서 보내주신 견본을 찾을 수 없었습니다.
　　 (B) 저희의 여름 제품 라인에 관한 귀하의 의견을 감사하게 생각합니다.

(C) 저희 디자이너들은 아주 명망 있는 학교의 졸업생들입니다.
(D) 저희는 또한 조만간 귀사에 대량 주문을 하기를 희망합니다.

해설 빈칸에 들어갈 알맞은 문장을 고르는 문제이므로 빈칸의 주변 문맥이나 전체 문맥을 파악합니다. 앞 문장 'We are optimistic about forming a business arrangement with your company.'에서 저희, 즉 Brendan Clothiers사는 상대방의 회사와 사업 계약을 맺는 것에 대해 낙관적이라고 했으므로 빈칸에는 계약을 맺어서 주문하기를 원한다는 내용이 들어가야 함을 알 수 있습니다. 따라서 (D) We also hope to place a large order with you in the near future가 정답입니다.

어휘 locate v. 찾아내다, 알아내다 appreciate v. 감사하게 생각하다
graduate n. 졸업생; v. 졸업하다
prestigious adj. 명망 있는, 일류의
place an order phr. 주문하다

142. 명사절 접속사 채우기

해설 동사 know(알다, 이해하다)의 목적어인 _____ ~ you가 동사(would be)가 있는 절이므로, 목적어 역할을 하면서 절을 이끌 수 있는 명사절 접속사 (B) when(언제 ~하는지)이 정답입니다. (A) yet(아직; 하지만)은 부사일 때 절을 이끌 수 없고, 등위접속사일 때에는 절과 절을 동등하게 연결하지만 '저희에게 알려주시지만 귀하에게 더 편할 것입니다'라는 어색한 문맥을 만듭니다. 부사절 접속사 (C) though(비록 ~하더라도)와 (D) unless(만약 ~이 아니라면)는 명사절이 아닌 부사절을 이끕니다.

143-146번은 다음 안내문에 관한 문제입니다.

¹⁴³컬럼비아 강 모험 투어에 등록해주셔서 감사합니다! 무엇을 가져와야 할지 결정하는 데 어려움을 겪고 계신다면, 여기에 알아야 할 중요한 몇 가지 사항들이 있습니다.

저희는 조리 도구와 캠핑용품뿐만 아니라 텐트와 침낭도 제공해드릴 것입니다. ¹⁴⁴게다가, 구급상자와 응급용품 세트가 필요한 분들에게 제공될 것입니다. 식사, 식수, 음료 또한 제공될 것입니다.

¹⁴⁵낮 시간 동안에는 매우 따뜻하더라도, 밤에는 기온이 쌀쌀해질 수 있다는 것을 기억하십시오. 그러므로 옷을 여러 겹 입는 것이 권장됩니다. ¹⁴⁶여행을 위해 짐을 쌀 때 이것을 명심하십시오. 마지막으로, 저희는 참가자들께 모자, 선글라스, 자외선 차단제와 세면도구를 가져오시기를 권해드립니다.

have trouble -ing phr. ~하는 데 어려움을 겪다
be aware of phr. ~을 알다 first aid kit phr. 구급상자
beverage n. 음료 chilly adj. 쌀쌀한
recommend v. 권장하다 toiletries n. 세면도구

143. 동명사 채우기

해설 전치사(for)의 목적어 자리에 올 수 있는 동사 sign(서명하다)의 동명사 (C) signing이 정답입니다. to 부정사 (A), 동사 (B)와 (D)는 전치사의 목적어 자리에 올 수 없습니다. 참고로, 동사 sign이 빈칸 뒤의 up과 함께 '~에 등록하다'라는 의미의 어구 sign up을 만들고 있는 것을 알아둡니다.

144. 접속부사 채우기 주변 문맥 파악

해설 빈칸이 콤마와 함께 문장의 맨 앞에 온 접속부사 자리이므로, 앞 문장과 빈칸이 있는 문장의 의미 관계를 파악하여 정답을 선택합니다. 앞 문장에서 조리 도구와 캠핑용품뿐만 아니라 텐트와 침낭도 제공할 것이라고 했고, 빈칸이 있는 문장에서는 구급상자와 응급용품 세트가 제공될 것이라고 했으므로 앞 내용과 이어지는 추가적인 내용을 언급할 때 쓰이는 접속부사 (A)

In addition(게다가)이 정답입니다. (B) However는 '그러나', (C) If so는 '그렇다면', (D) Otherwise는 '그렇지 않으면'이라는 의미입니다.

145. 부사절 접속사 채우기: 양보

해설 명령문의 동사 Remember의 목적어 자리에 온 명사절(that ___ ~ night)이 주어(temperatures), 동사(can become), 보어(chilly)를 갖춘 완전한 절이므로, ___ it ~ daytime은 명사절의 수식어 거품으로 보아야 합니다. 이 수식어 거품은 동사(may be)가 있는 거품절이므로 거품절을 이끌 수 있는 부사절 접속사 (A)와 (C)가 정답의 후보입니다. '낮 시간 동안에는 매우 따뜻하더라도 밤에는 쌀쌀해질 수 있다'라는 의미가 되어야 하므로 양보를 나타내는 부사절 접속사 (C) while(~하더라도, ~한 반면에)이 정답입니다. (A) because(~ 때문에)는 이유를 나타내서 어색한 문맥을 만듭니다. 전치사 (B) despite(~에도 불구하고)와 (D) rather than(~보다는, 대신에)는 거품절이 아닌 거품구를 이끕니다.

146. 알맞은 문장 고르기

해석 (A) 그 투어는 지정된 구역 내로 제한될 것입니다.
(B) 여행을 위해 짐을 쌀 때 이것을 명심하십시오.
(C) 그러므로, 미리 자리를 예약하는 것은 필수입니다.
(D) 이러한 기구들은 소정의 비용을 내면 대여될 수 있습니다.

해설 빈칸에 들어갈 알맞은 문장을 고르는 문제이므로 빈칸의 주변 문맥이나 전체 문맥을 파악합니다. 앞부분에서 투어에 무엇을 가져와야 할지 결정하는 데 어려움을 겪고 있다면 알아야 할 중요한 몇 가지 사항들이 있다고 했고, 앞 문장 'Layered clothing is ~ recommended.'에서 옷을 여러 겹 입는 것이 권장된다고 했으므로 빈칸에는 짐을 쌀 때 참고하라는 내용이 들어가야 함을 알 수 있습니다. 따라서 (B) Keep this in mind when packing for the trip이 정답입니다.

어휘 restrict v. 제한하다 designate v. 지정하다
keep in mind phr. 명심하다 pack v. 짐을 싸다, 포장하다
essential adj. 필수적인 reserve v. 예약하다, 예매하다
rent v. 대여하다

PART 7

147-148번은 다음 공고에 관한 문제입니다.

아일랜드 포크 음악의 밤

Keller and the Gang
특별 게스트 Suzie McGregor 출연

¹⁴⁷Keller and the Gang의 세 번째 앨범 *High Tide*의 발매를 축하하는 데에 다음 주 금요일에 저희와 함께해주십시오. 이 아일랜드 포크 그룹은 "When I Went Down to the Sea"와 "Fair-Eyed Lady"를 포함한 오랫동안 사랑받는 곡뿐만 아니라 그들의 새 앨범에서 선정한 곡들을 부를 것입니다. 또한, ¹⁴⁸음악 분야에서 명망 있는 Goldy상 수상자인 Suzie McGregor가 참석하여 *High Tide* 앨범의 세 곡을 부르는 것에 이 그룹과 함께할 것입니다.

시간: 9월 3일 금요일, 오후 8시 (7시 30분부터 입구 개방)
표: 입구에서 구매 시 10달러, 온라인 구매 시 7달러
장소: Horn of Plenty 연회장, 917번지 Golden로, 더블린

더 많은 정보를 위해 www.hornofplenty.com을 방문하십시오.

appearance n. 출연 release n. 발매

prestigious adj. 명망 있는 present adj. 참석한, 출석한
purchase v. 구매하다

147. 주제/목적 찾기 문제

문제 공고의 목적은 무엇인가?
(A) 공연장 개장을 광고하기 위해
(B) 앨범 발매 행사를 홍보하기 위해
(C) 악기 세일을 알리기 위해
(D) 웹사이트 출범을 발표하기 위해

해설 공고의 목적을 묻는 목적 찾기 문제이므로 지문의 앞부분을 주의 깊게 확인합니다. 'Join us ~ to celebrate the release of Keller and the Gang's third album'에서 Keller and the Gang의 세 번째 앨범의 발매를 축하하는 데에 함께해달라고 했으므로 (B) To promote an album release event가 정답입니다.

어휘 publicize v. 알리다, 공표하다 instrument n. 악기, 기구
launch n. 출범

148. 추론 문제

문제 Suzie McGregor에 대해 암시되는 것은?
(A) 지난해에 밴드에 합류했다.
(B) 클래식 음악을 연주한다.
(C) 유명한 가수이다.
(D) 상을 받을 것이다.

해설 질문의 핵심 어구인 Suzie McGregor에 대해 추론하는 문제입니다. 'Suzie McGregor, winner of the prestigious Goldy Award for music, will be present, and she will join the group in a vocal performance of three songs from *High Tide*'에서 음악 분야에서 명망 있는 Goldy상 수상자인 Suzie McGregor가 참석하여 *High Tide* 앨범의 세 곡을 부르는 것에 이 그룹과 함께할 것이라고 했으므로 Suzie McGregor가 유명한 가수라는 사실을 추론할 수 있습니다. 따라서 (C) She is a famous singer가 정답입니다.

149-150번은 다음 광고에 관한 문제입니다.

Watersports Kingdom
준비 세일

Watersports Kingdom은 물속과 물 위에서의 즐거움을 위해 당신이 필요한 모든 것을 가지고 있습니다. ¹⁴⁹⁻ᶜ저희는 당신의 안전을 보장하는 데 필요할 모든 장비는 말할 것도 없고, 낚시, 항해, 모터스포츠를 위한 다양한 장비를 취급합니다. 저희는 또한 시중에서 가장 인기 있는 웨이크보드와 수상스키 브랜드를 판매합니다. 그리고 서핑에 관심이 있으시다면, 저희의 새로운 Watersports Kingdom 브랜드의 서프보드를 확인해 보십시오.

¹⁵⁰⁻ᴬ4월은 준비 세일의 달입니다. 이번 주부터 시작해서, ¹⁵⁰⁻ᴰ지난해의 수영복은 모두 10퍼센트에서 30퍼센트 할인될 것입니다. 또한, ¹⁵⁰⁻ᴮ모든 구명복과 물안경을 50퍼센트 할인가에 구매하세요. 이 세일은 4월 내내 유효합니다. 그러니, 들르셔서 여름 시즌의 시작에 대비하십시오.

carry v. (상점에서 물건을) 취급하다
not to mention phr. ~은 말할 것도 없이 guarantee v. 보장하다
lifejacket n. 구명복 available adj. 유효한
stop by phr. 들르다

149. Not/True 문제

문제 Watersports Kingdom에 대해 사실인 것은?
(A) 주요 스포츠 행사들의 후원사이다.

(B) 모든 수준의 서핑 수업을 제공한다.
(C) 다양한 종류의 오락 장비를 판매한다.
(D) 다음 주에 처음으로 문을 열 것이다.

해설 질문의 핵심 어구인 Watersports Kingdom과 관련된 내용을 지문에서 찾아 각 보기와 대조하는 Not/True 문제입니다. (A)와 (B)는 지문에 언급되지 않은 내용입니다. (C)는 'We carry a range of equipment for fishing, sailing, and motorsports'에서 낚시, 항해, 모터스포츠를 위한 다양한 장비를 취급한다고 했으므로 지문의 내용과 일치합니다. 따라서 (C) It sells various kinds of recreational gear가 정답입니다. (D)는 지문에 언급되지 않은 내용입니다.

패러프레이징
carry a range of equipment for fishing, sailing, and motorsports 낚시, 항해, 모터스포츠를 위한 다양한 장비를 취급하다 → sells various kinds of recreational gear 다양한 종류의 오락 장비를 판매하다

어휘 sponsor n. 후원사, 후원자

150. Not/True 문제
문제 세일에 관해 언급되지 않은 것은?
(A) 4월 동안에 진행될 것이다.
(B) 50퍼센트까지의 할인을 포함한다.
(C) 매장 회원만 대상으로 한다.
(D) 지난해의 의류를 포함한다.

해설 질문의 핵심 어구인 the sale과 관련된 내용을 지문에서 찾아 각 보기와 대조하는 Not/True 문제입니다. (A)는 'April is the month of our Get-Ready Sale.'에서 4월이 준비 세일의 달이라고 했으므로 지문의 내용과 일치합니다. (B)는 'purchase any ~ at a 50 percent discount'에서 50퍼센트 할인가에 구매하라고 했으므로 지문의 내용과 일치합니다. (C)는 지문에 언급되지 않은 내용입니다. 따라서 (C) It is exclusive to store members가 정답입니다. (D)는 'all of our swimwear from the previous year will be 10 to 30 percent off'에서 지난해의 수영복은 모두 10퍼센트에서 30퍼센트 할인된다고 했으므로 지문의 내용과 일치합니다.

151-152번은 다음 메시지 대화문에 관한 문제입니다.

Mel Engle   오후 12:12
¹⁵¹오늘 아침에 Ms. Cantwell과의 회의는 어땠나요?

Edward Hale   오후 12:15
사실, 정말로 잘 됐어요. ¹⁵¹제 생각에는 그녀가 우리 상점을 위해 필요한 자금을 제공해줄 것 같아요. 그녀에게 우리의 사업 계획을 보여줬는데, 그녀는 깊은 인상을 받은 것 같아 보였어요.

Mel Engle   오후 12:16
우리가 언제 확실히 알 수 있을 것 같아요?

Edward Hale   오후 12:17
내일 오후까지 그녀가 저에게 연락해서 알려줄 거예요. 그런데, 그녀는 우리 사업의 20퍼센트를 소유하기를 원해요.

Mel Engle   오후 12:19
¹⁵²그건 우리가 제시했던 15퍼센트보다 높네요. 하지만 우리는 추가 재고품을 위한 자금이 필요해요. 그리고 그녀는 지역 소매 지구에 좋은 연고를 가지고 있어요.

Edward Hale   오후 12:20
저도 같은 생각이에요. 어쨌든, 그녀에게서 무엇이든 듣는 대로 당신에게 문자 메시지를 보낼게요. 그녀는 이 기회에 대해 매우 긍정적인 것 같았어요.

Mel Engle   오후 12:22
좋네요. 동시에, ¹⁵¹저는 우리가 그녀에게 매우 확실한 투자 대상을 제공하고 있다고 생각해요. 매출이 계속 오르고 있으니, 그녀는 꽤 이득을 볼 거예요.

---

capital n. 자금, 돈   **impressed** adj. 깊은 인상을 받은, 감명받은
contact v. 연락하다   **stock** n. 재고품
connection n. 연고, 연결   **retail** adj. 소매의   **sector** n. 지구, 부문
opportunity n. 기회   **solid** adj. 확실한, 단단한
investment n. 투자 대상   **climb** v. 오르다, 올라가다

151. 추론 문제
문제 Ms. Cantwell은 누구일 것 같은가?
(A) 소매 직판점의 소유주
(B) 사업의 잠재적인 투자자
(C) 공급업체의 직원
(D) 사업 설계 컨설턴트

해설 질문의 핵심 어구인 Ms. Cantwell에 대해 추론하는 문제입니다. 'How did the meeting with Ms. Cantwell go this morning?'에서 Mel Engle이 오늘 아침에 Ms. Cantwell과의 회의가 어땠는지 묻자, 'I think she is going to give us the capital we need for our store.'에서 Edward Hale이 그녀가 자신들의 상점을 위해 필요한 자금을 제공해줄 것 같다고 한 뒤, 'I think we are offering her a very solid investment'에서 Mel Engle이 자신들이 그녀에게 매우 확실한 투자 대상을 제공하고 있다고 했으므로 Ms. Cantwell이 Mel Engle과 Edward Hale의 사업에 투자하려는 잠재적인 투자자임을 알 수 있습니다. 따라서 (B) A potential investor in a business가 정답입니다.

어휘 potential adj. 잠재적인

152. 의도 파악 문제
문제 오후 12시 20분에, Mr. Hale이 "I feel the same way"라고 썼을 때, 그가 의도한 것은?
(A) 더 많은 지분을 포기하는 것이 가치가 있다고 생각한다.
(B) 소매 부문에서 경쟁이 너무 심하다고 생각한다.
(C) 주가가 계속 오를지에 대해 확신하지 못한다.
(D) 사업 계획이 매우 인상적으로 보인다는 것에 동의한다.

해설 Mr. Hale이 의도한 것을 묻는 문제이므로, 질문의 인용구(I feel the same way)가 언급된 주변 문맥을 확인합니다. 'That is higher than the 15 percent we were offering. But we need the funds ~ And she has good connections in the local retail sector.'에서 Mel Engle이 그것, 즉 Ms. Cantwell이 원하는 지분은 자신들이 제시했던 15퍼센트보다 높지만 자신들은 자금이 필요하고 Ms. Cantwell은 지역 소매 지구에도 좋은 연고를 가지고 있다고 하자 Mr. Hale이 'I feel the same way'(저도 같은 생각이에요)라고 한 것을 통해, Mr. Hale이 Ms. Cantwell이 원하는 더 많은 지분을 주는 것이 가치가 있다는 생각에 동의한다는 것을 알 수 있습니다. 따라서 (A) He thinks that giving up a larger share would be worthwhile이 정답입니다.

어휘 give up phr. 포기하다   share n. 지분, 주식
worthwhile adj. 가치가 있는   competition n. 경쟁

153-154번은 다음 공고에 관한 문제입니다.

새로운 웹사이트, WWW.SEATTLEART.COM으로 저희를 방문하세요

깊이 있는 지역 예술 관련 보도를 위한 최고의 목적지, SeattleArt가 완전히 새로운 외관뿐만 아니라 새로운 도메

인 이름을 획득했습니다. www.seart.com 대신에, www. seattleart.com으로 저희를 방문하실 수 있습니다. 이제부터, 저희의 모든 새로운 기사는 그 사이트에 게재될 것이며, **¹⁵³⁻ᴰ기존 사이트의 모든 콘텐츠는 새로운 사이트로 옮겨질 것입니다.**

¹⁵³⁻ᴬ저희가 이 사이트를 5년 전에 개설했을 때, 저희의 목표는 주민들에게 지역 예술계에 대한 가능한 한 명확한 개요를 제공하는 것이었습니다. 이제, 저희는 전속 작가들에 의한 영상과 블로그와 같은 완전히 새로운 특징으로, 그 목표를 실현하려고 노력하고 있습니다. 이 부가적인 콘텐츠들은 현대적인 디자인과 개선된 검색 엔진에 의해 보완될 것입니다.

¹⁵⁴앞으로 몇 개월간, 저희는 시의 연례 예술 축제에 대한 시각적 개요와 Burle 갤러리에서의 최근 전시에 관한 영상 에세이를 포함하여, 몇 가지의 주목할 만한 멀티미디어 기사를 게재할 것입니다.

언제나처럼, **¹⁵³⁻ᴮ사이트를 어떻게 개선할지에 대한 제안 사항이 있다면, 주저하지 마시고 웹 관리자 Jenny Lin에게 jlin@ seattleart.com으로 연락해주십시오.** 저희는 저희 사이트를 지역사회에 의해 운영되는 노력이라고 간주하며, **¹⁵³⁻ᴮ저희는 여러분들의 의견 없이는 운영할 수 없을 것입니다.**

---

destination n. 목적지 in-depth adj. 깊이 있는
local adj. 지역의 coverage n. 보도 acquire v. 획득하다, 얻다
post v. 게재하다 transfer v. 옮기다 objective n. 목표, 목적
resident n. 주민 overview n. 개요, 개관
scene n. 계, (활동의) 분야 realize v. 실현하다, 깨닫다
noteworthy adj. 주목할 만한 improve v. 개선하다
administrator n. 관리자 endeavor n. 노력, 시도

153. Not/True문제

문제 SeattleArt에 대해 언급된 것은?
(A) 10년간 운영해오고 있다.
(B) 고객의 의견을 수용한다.
(C) 새로운 전속 작가를 찾고 있다.
(D) 요청 시 예전 콘텐츠를 제공한다.

해설 질문의 핵심 어구인 SeattleArt와 관련된 내용을 지문에서 찾아 각 보기와 대조하는 Not/True 문제입니다. (A)는 'we started this Web site five years ago'에서 사이트를 5년 전에 개설했다고 했으므로 지문의 내용과 일치하지 않습니다. (B)는 'if you have any suggestions ~ don't hesitate to contact the Web administrator'와 'we couldn't operate without your feedback'에서 사이트를 어떻게 개선할지에 대한 제안 사항이 있다면 주저하지 말고 웹 관리자에게 연락해 달라고 했고, 고객의 의견 없이는 운영할 수 없다고 했으므로 지문의 내용과 일치합니다. 따라서 (B) It accepts customer feedback이 정답입니다. (C)는 지문에 언급되지 않은 내용입니다. (D)는 'all the content from the old site will be transferred to the new one'에서 기존 사이트의 모든 콘텐츠는 새로운 사이트로 옮겨질 것이라고 했으므로 지문의 내용과 일치하지 않습니다.

어휘 decade n. 10년 upon request phr. 요청 시

154. 육하원칙 문제

문제 새 웹사이트에 대해 무엇이 다른가?
(A) 더 많은 작가들의 콘텐츠를 포함한다.
(B) 인접한 도시들의 기사들을 포함한다.
(C) 지역 전시에 관한 더 많은 기사를 포함한다.
(D) 더 많은 시각 매체를 포함한다.

해설 새 웹사이트에 대해 무엇이(What) 다른지를 묻는 육하원칙 문제입니다. 질문의 핵심 어구인 different about the new

---

Web site와 관련하여, 'Over the coming months, we'll be publishing several noteworthy multimedia stories, including a visual summary of the city's annual arts festival and a video essay on a recent exhibit'에서 앞으로 몇 개월간 시의 연례 예술 축제에 대한 시각적 개요와 최근 전시에 관한 영상 에세이를 포함하여 몇 가지의 주목할 만한 멀티미디어 기사를 게재할 것이라고 했으므로, 새 웹사이트는 더 많은 시각 매체를 포함한다는 것을 알 수 있습니다. 따라서 (D) It incorporates more visual media가 정답입니다.

어휘 neighboring adj. 인접하는, 이웃의
incorporate v. 포함하다, 수반하다, 통합하다

155-157번은 다음 안내문에 관한 문제입니다.

Morris Sherman은 그의 개념 예술 인물 사진으로 가장 잘 알려진 미국의 사진작가이다. 그는 뉴욕주 버펄로에 있는 Eckhart 대학교의 학생일 때 처음으로 시각예술에 관심을 갖게 되었다. **¹⁵⁵그는 학업을 회화로 시작했으나, 곧 사진술로 전공을 바꾸었다.** Sherman 스스로가 말했듯이, "그림은 너무 오래 걸린다. 카메라를 이용하는 것은 내가 예술적인 아이디어들을 발전시키는 데 더 많은 시간을 전념하도록 해준다." Sherman은 또한 버펄로 사진작가 협회의 창립 위원이었다. **¹⁵⁶그는 다른 이들 중에서도 Edwin Miller, Ingrid Floss, 그리고 Hal Getty의 사진 작품들을 영감의 예로 들었다.**

¹⁵⁷⁻ᴮSherman은 늘 시리즈로 작업하고, 다양한 의상을 입은 자기 자신을 찍는다. 그 과정에서, 그는 작가, 감독, 스타일리스트, 그리고 모델로서의 여러 가지 역할들을 맡아야 한다. **¹⁵⁷⁻ᴰ그의 사진들은 도전적이면서도 해학적이라는 평을 받아왔고, 다양한 사회적 문제들을 향한 이 예술가의 시각에 대한 관점을 제공한다.** 이 전시회의 작품들은 서구 사회에서의 부와 불평등의 개념을 탐구한다. 또한 그것들은 계층, 인종, 그리고 종교의 개념에 관해 다룬다.

---

conceptual adj. 개념 예술의, 개념의
switch v. 바꾸다, 전환하다 devote v. 전념하다
founding member phr. 창립 위원 cite v. 예로 들다, 언급하다
inspiration n. 영감 take on phr. ~을 맡다
multiple adj. 여러 가지의, 복합적인 challenging adj. 도전적인
humorous adj. 해학적인, 익살스러운 view n. 관점
perspective n. 시각 various adj. 다양한 piece n. 작품
notion n. 개념 inequality n. 불평등, 불균형
touch on phr. ~을 다루다, 언급하다

155. 육하원칙 문제

문제 Morris Sherman은 왜 회화를 공부하는 것을 그만두었는가?
(A) 그것에 대한 재능이 없었다.
(B) 학교 교육을 중단해야 했다.
(C) 그것이 시간이 너무 오래 걸린다고 생각했다.
(D) 계속할 수 있을 만큼 충분히 돈을 벌지 못했다.

해설 Morris Sherman이 왜(Why) 회화를 공부하는 것을 그만두었는지를 묻는 육하원칙 문제입니다. 질문의 핵심 어구인 Morris Sherman stop studying painting과 관련하여, 'Though he began his studies in painting, he soon switched his major to photography. As Sherman himself said, ~ Painting takes too long.'에서 그, 즉 Morris Sherman은 학업을 회화로 시작했으나 곧 사진술로 전공을 바꾸었으며, 그림은 너무 오래 걸린다고 말했다고 했으므로 (C) He found it too time-consuming이 정답입니다.

패러프레이징
takes too long 너무 오래 걸리다
→ too time-consuming 시간이 너무 오래 걸리는

어휘 talent n. 재능 interrupt v. 중단하다
schooling n. 학교 교육 earn v. 돈을 벌다

156. 추론 문제

문제 Ingrid Floss에 대해 암시되는 것은?
(A) 카메라 동호회를 창립했다.
(B) Eckhart 대학교에 다녔다.
(C) 현재 버펄로에 살고 있다.
(D) 사진작가이다.

해설 질문의 핵심 어구인 Ingrid Floss에 대해 추론하는 문제입니다. 'He has cited as inspirations the photographic works of ~ Ingrid Floss'에서 그, 즉 Morris Sherman은 Ingrid Floss의 사진 작품들을 영감의 예로 들었다고 했으므로 Ingrid Floss가 사진작가라는 사실을 추론할 수 있습니다. 따라서 (D) She is a photographer가 정답입니다.

157. Not/True 문제

문제 전시회의 사진들에 대해 사실인 것은?
(A) 약 한 달 동안 전시될 것이다.
(B) Mr. Sherman을 대상으로 묘사한다.
(C) 대학생들에 의해 촬영되었다.
(D) 해학이 부족하다고 비난받았다.

해설 질문의 핵심 어구인 the photographs in the exhibit과 관련된 내용을 지문에서 찾아 각 보기와 대조하는 Not/True 문제입니다. (A)와 (C)는 지문에 언급되지 않은 내용입니다. (B)는 'Sherman always ~ photographing himself in a range of costumes.'에서 Sherman은 늘 다양한 의상을 입은 자기 자신을 찍는다고 했으므로 지문의 내용과 일치합니다. 따라서 (B) They depict Mr. Sherman as the subject가 정답입니다. (D)는 'His photographs, which others have described as being ~ humorous'에서 그, 즉 Sherman의 사진들은 해학적이라는 평을 받아왔다고 했으므로 지문의 내용과 일치하지 않습니다.

패러프레이징
Sherman ~ photographing himself Sherman이 자기 자신을 찍다 → depict Mr. Sherman as the subject Mr. Sherman을 대상으로 묘사하다

어휘 depict v. 묘사하다, 그리다 subject n. 대상, 주제
criticize v. 비난하다, 비평하다

158-160번은 다음 양식에 관한 문제입니다.

전국 도시 설계자 연합(NATP) 회원 양식

개인 정보부터 시작하여, 아래의 양식을 작성해주십시오. 그다음, 귀하의 자격 요건과 경력을 기반으로 적합한 회원 등급을 선택해주십시오. NATP에 의해 학위가 인정되기 위해서는, 학위가 하나의 전공을 포함하여, 일반적인 설계 원리와 정책에 초점을 맞춰야 한다는 것을 유념해주십시오. 귀하의 자격 요건이 인정되는지 여부에 확신이 없다면, 확인을 위해 NATP에 연락해주십시오. 마지막으로, 모든 관련된 업무 경력을 기재해주십시오. 가장 최근 경력부터 작성해주시고 간략한 설명과 귀하가 고용되었던 기간을 포함해주십시오.

성명: Rachel Douglas | 이메일: rachel.douglas@directmail.com
주소: 243번지 65번가, 퀸스, 뉴욕시, 뉴욕주 11032

회원 등급:
□ 가입자: 설계에 관심이 있지만 요구되는 교육과 경력이 부족함 ○

□ 학생: 설계 분야에서 인정되는 학위를 위해 현재 공부하고 있음
☑ 준회원: 설계 분야에서 인정되는 학위가 있으나, 2년 미만의 업무 경력을 갖고 있음
□ [158]정회원: 설계 분야에서 인정되는 학위가 있으며, 2년 이상의 업무 경력이 있고, 현재 설계자로 일하고 있음
□ 퇴직자: 정회원의 기준을 충족하지만 직장에서 퇴직했음

자격 요건:
노스캐롤라이나주 Raleigh 대학교의 설계학 석사 학위, 도시학 전공

[158/159]업무 경력:
[159]프로젝트 보조 ([158/159]1년 6개월); [159]뉴욕시 설계 부서, 해안 지역 재건 프로그램; 해안 지역의 지대 설정과 건축 규정 설정을 보조하고 설계를 논의하기 위한 지역 회의를 준비했음.

[160]인턴 ([158]3개월); 노스캐롤라이나주 Chapel Hill 교통 당국; 근처 Raleigh 대학에서 공부하는 동안 [160]보고서를 편집하고 사실 여부를 확인했으며, 회의에서 회의록을 작성하고, 지역 주민들의 의견과 우려 사항에 답변했음.

association n. 연합 complete v. (양식 등을) 작성하다
appropriate adj. 적합한, 적절한 based on phr. ~을 기반으로
qualification n. 자격 요건 degree n. 학위
recognize v. 인정하다 focus on phr. ~에 초점을 맞추다
general adj. 일반적인, 보편적인 principle n. 원리
specialization n. 전공, 전문화 unsure adj. 확신이 없는
clarification n. 확인, 설명 relevant adj. 관련된
recent adj. 최근의 brief adj. 간략한 length n. 기간, 길이
affiliate n. 가입자, 제휴 lack v. 부족하다; n. 부족, 결핍
currently adv. 현재 associate n. 준회원
retire v. 퇴직하다, 은퇴하다
meet v. (조건 등을) 충족하다, 만족하다 criteria n. 기준
master's degree phr. 석사 학위 assistant n. 보조
waterfront n. 해안 지역 regeneration n. 재건, 재생
creation n. 설정, 창작, 창조 organize v. 준비하다, 조직하다
discuss v. 논의하다 edit v. 편집하다 minutes n. 회의록
respond v. 답변하다, 응답하다 comment n. 의견
concern n. 우려 (사항)

158. 육하원칙 문제

문제 Ms. Douglas는 왜 정회원을 신청하기에 부적격한가?
(A) 뉴욕시의 주민이 아니다.
(B) 연령 요건을 충족시키지 못한다.
(C) 인정되지 않는 학위를 가지고 있다.
(D) 충분한 업무 경험이 부족하다.

해설 Ms. Douglas가 왜(Why) 정회원을 신청하기에 부적격한지를 묻는 육하원칙 문제입니다. 질문의 핵심 어구인 Ms. Douglas unqualified ~ for a full membership과 관련하여, 'Full: ~ have two or more years of work experience'에서 정회원은 2년 이상의 업무 경력이 있어야 한다고 했는데, 'Work experience:', '1 year, 6 months', '3 months'에서 Ms. Douglas의 업무 경력이 1년 6개월과 3개월로 2년을 채우지 못한다는 것을 알 수 있습니다. 따라서 (D) She lacks sufficient work experience가 정답입니다.

어휘 requirement n. 요건 unrecognized adj. 인정되지 않는
sufficient adj. 충분한

159. 추론 문제

문제 양식이 Ms. Douglas에 대해 암시하는 것은?
(A) 도시의 수도 공급에 관한 연구를 진행하고 있다.
(B) 설계 부서를 위한 프로젝트를 작업했다.

(C) 현재 교통 당국에서 근무하고 있다.
(D) 2주 이내에 준회원 회원 카드를 받을 것이다.

해설 질문의 핵심 어구인 Ms. Douglas에 대해 추론하는 문제입니다. 'Work experience: Project Assistant ~; New York City Planning Department'에서 업무 경력에 뉴욕시 설계 부서에서 프로젝트 보조로 일한 내용이 있으므로 설계 부서를 위한 프로젝트를 작업했다는 사실을 추론할 수 있습니다. 따라서 (B) She worked on a project for a planning department가 정답입니다.

160. 육하원칙 문제

문제 Ms. Douglas는 인턴십 동안에 어떤 업무를 수행했는가?
(A) 상담을 준비하는 것
(B) 다가오는 회의들의 일정을 잡는 것
(C) 정보를 확인하는 것
(D) 보고서를 작성하는 것

해설 Ms. Douglas가 인턴십 동안에 어떤(What) 업무를 수행했는지를 묻는 육하원칙 문제입니다. 질문의 핵심 어구인 Ms. Douglas perform during her internship과 관련하여, 'Intern;', 'fact-checked reports'에서 인턴십 동안에 보고서의 사실 여부를 확인했다고 했으므로 (C) Confirming information이 정답입니다.

어휘 consultation n. 상담 confirm v. 확인하다

161-163번은 다음 회람에 관한 문제입니다.

수신: 모든 Miller 세탁소 직원들
발신: 163James Miller, Miller 세탁소 사장
날짜: 2월 10일
제목: 최신 정보

161저는 다음 주부터 여기 Miller 세탁소에서 우리가 새로운 정책을 시행할 것임을 여러분에게 알리기 위해 회람을 씁니다. 앞으로, 고객들이 정오까지 맡기는 모든 옷들은 그날 저녁까지 세탁되어야 하고 가져갈 준비가 되어야 합니다. 이것은 세탁이 어려운 옷뿐만 아니라 블라우스, 드레스, 와이셔츠, 코트를 포함합니다.

162-B직원들이 맡긴 옷의 세탁을 완료하기까지 이틀이나, 가끔은 심지어 사흘도 걸린다고 많은 고객들이 제게 이야기했기 때문에 이 정책을 시행하는 것입니다. 10년 이상 세탁업에서 일해 왔기 때문에, 저는 바쁜 날에조차 그 어떤 옷도 세탁하는 데 그렇게 오래 걸리지 않는다는 것을 압니다. 그래서, 다음 주에, 고객들에게 정오까지 맡겨진 옷들은 같은 영업일 저녁까지 세탁될 것이라고 알리기 시작할 것입니다. 만약 옷들이 그때까지 세탁되지 않는다면, 고객들은 10달러의 쿠폰을 받게 될 것입니다.

따라서 저는 여러분이 제시간에 옷들을 세탁할 것이라고 기대할 것입니다. 여러분을 돕기 위해, 163저는 두 명의 직원을 더 고용하고, 더 효율적으로 작동하는 새 기계를 몇 대 설치할 것입니다. 마지막으로, 언제나처럼, 고객들을 예의 바르게 대할 것을 기억하십시오. 여러분이 더 친절할수록, 그들도 답례로 더 친절하게 대할 것이고, 그들이 우리의 세탁소에 다시 찾아올 가능성이 더 높습니다.

institute v. 시행하다 clothing article phr. 옷, 의류
drop off phr. (물건을 상점 등에) 맡기다 pick up phr. 가져가다
take v. (시간이) 걸리다 workday n. 영업일
count on phr. 기대하다, 믿다, 의지하다 on time phr. 제시간에
hire v. 고용하다 install v. 설치하다
efficiently adv. 효율적으로 courteous adj. 예의 바른
in return phr. 답례로

---

161. 주제/목적 찾기 문제

문제 회람은 주로 무엇에 대한 것인가?
(A) 새로운 규정의 시행
(B) 시설의 곧 있을 이전
(C) 고객 설문 조사의 결과
(D) 서비스 요금을 인상하려는 계획

해설 회람이 주로 무엇에 대한 것인지를 묻는 주제 찾기 문제이므로 지문의 앞부분을 주의 깊게 확인합니다. 'I'm writing to inform you that, starting next week, we're instituting a new policy'에서 다음 주부터 새로운 정책을 시행할 것임을 알리기 위해 회람을 쓴다고 했으므로 (A) The implementation of a new rule이 정답입니다.

어휘 implementation n. 시행 forthcoming adj. 곧 있을, 다가오는
relocation n. 이전, 재배치

162. Not/True 문제

문제 Mr. Miller가 고객들에 대해 언급한 것은?
(A) 몇몇 사람들이 청구서에서 10달러 할인을 요구했다.
(B) 많은 사람들이 깨끗한 옷을 받기 위해 며칠을 기다려야 했다.
(C) 대부분이 세탁이 어려운 옷을 맡겼다.
(D) 몇몇 사람들이 손상된 옷에 대해 환불을 받았다.

해설 질문의 핵심 어구인 the customers와 관련된 내용을 지문에서 찾아 각 보기와 대조하는 Not/True 문제입니다. (A), (C), (D)는 지문에 언급되지 않은 내용입니다. (B)는 'numerous customers have told me that it has taken employees two, or sometimes even three days to finish washing the clothing they've dropped off'에서 직원들이 맡긴 옷의 세탁을 완료하기까지 이틀이나 가끔은 심지어 사흘도 걸린다고 많은 고객들이 자신에게 이야기했다고 했으므로 지문의 내용과 일치합니다. 따라서 (B) Many had to wait a few days to receive clean clothes가 정답입니다.

패러프레이징
it has taken ~ two, or sometimes even three days to finish washing the clothing ~ dropped off 맡긴 옷의 세탁을 완료하기까지 이틀이나, 가끔은 심지어 사흘도 걸린다
→ wait a few days to receive clean clothes 깨끗한 옷을 받기 위해 며칠을 기다리다

어휘 refund n. 환불 damaged adj. 손상된 garment n. 옷, 의류

163. 육하원칙 문제

문제 Mr. Miller는 그가 무엇을 할 것이라고 말하는가?
(A) 다음 주에 또 다른 지점을 연다
(B) 변경된 규정을 게시판에 게시한다
(C) 세탁소에 더 많은 직원을 고용한다
(D) 시설의 직원들에게 교육을 제공한다

해설 Mr. Miller가 무엇을(What) 할 것이라고 말하는지를 묻는 육하원칙 문제입니다. 질문의 핵심 어구인 Mr. Miller ~ will do와 관련하여, 'James Miller, Owner of Miller Laundry'와 'I will be hiring two more employees'에서 Miller 세탁소의 사장인 James Miller가 두 명의 직원을 더 고용할 것이라고 했으므로 (C) Employ more staff for the laundry가 정답입니다.

패러프레이징
hiring two more employees 두 명의 직원을 더 고용하다
→ Employ more staff 더 많은 직원을 고용하다

164-167번은 다음 기사에 관한 문제입니다.

고등 교육이 일자리를 보장하지는 않는다

[164]Rose 교육 협회의 새로운 보고서는 고등학교 졸업생들의 약 80퍼센트가 작년에 대학교의 4년제 학위 프로그램에 입학이 허가되었다는 것을 보여준다. 게다가, 그 보고서는 지난 10년간 훨씬 더 많은 사람들이 석사나 박사 학위를 받으려고 해왔다는 것을 보여준다.

[167]최근의 경제 불황에 따라, 많은 대학 졸업생들이 학위를 받은 즉시 학교로 돌아갔다. ― [1] ―. 결과적으로, [166]많은 구직자들이 고급 학위를 보유하고 있고, 이는 일자리에 지원하는 것을 훨씬 더 경쟁적으로 만들었다.

이러한 심화된 경쟁과 관련하여, 전국적으로 많은 대학교들이 현재 석사나 박사 학위를 가진 사람들에게 도움을 제공해 주기 위한 조치를 취하고 있다. ― [2] ―. 예를 들어 미시간주 디트로이트의 Eastforth 대학교는 고급 학위를 얻기 위해 노력하는 사람들에게 맞춤화된 지원을 위해 대학원 사무실의 프로그램 상담사와 이야기해 보는 것을 권장하고 있다. ― [3] ―. 그리고 현재 직업 시장에서 어려움을 겪고 있는 학생들을 위해서, [165]이력서 작성과 면접 질문에 답하는 기술에 대한 도움을 주는 대학교의 직업 센터의 상담사를 예약을 통해 만날 수 있다. ― [4] ―.

교육에 있어서 좀 더 나아가기를 고려하는 사람들은 Eastforth 대학교와 그러한 안내를 제공하는 비슷한 대학교들에 관해 우리 출판물의 웹사이트 www.worldinbizmag.com에서 더 알아볼 수 있다.

guarantee n. 보장 institute n. 협회
indicate v. 보여주다, 나타내다 nearly adv. 약, 거의
admit v. 입학을 허가하다 diploma n. 학위
significantly adv. 훨씬, 상당히
pursue v. ~하려고 하다, 추구하다
doctorate degree phr. 박사 학위
recession n. 불황 immediately adv. 즉시, 바로
job candidate phr. 구직자 possess v. 보유하다
advanced adj. 고급의 apply for phr. 지원하다
position n. (일)자리 competitive adj. 경쟁적인
in connection with phr. ~과 관련하여
increase v. 심화되다, 증가시키다 nationwide adv. 전국적으로
take measure phr. 조치를 취하다 assistance n. 지원, 도움
recommend v. 권장하다, 추천하다 individual n. 사람, 개인
advisor n. 상담사, 조언가 personalized adj. 맞춤화된
hardship n. 어려움, 곤란 counselor n. 상담사
appointment n. (업무 관련) 예약, 약속 résumé n. 이력서
look to phr. 고려하다 similar adj. 비슷한 guidance n. 안내

164. 주제/목적 찾기 문제

문제 기사는 주로 무엇에 대한 것인가?
(A) 혁신적인 채용 시스템
(B) 교육계의 최신 경향
(C) 해외 유학의 장점
(D) 새로 건축된 학교

해설 기사가 주로 무엇에 대한 것인지를 묻는 주제 찾기 문제이므로 지문의 앞부분을 주의 깊게 확인합니다. 'A new report ~ indicates that nearly 80 percent of high school graduates were admitted to four-year diploma programs at universities last year.'에서 새로운 보고서는 고등학교 졸업생들의 약 80퍼센트가 작년에 대학교의 4년제 학위 프로그램에 입학이 허가되었다는 것을 보여준다고 한 후, 더 높은 학력을 추구하는 교육계의 최근 경향에 대해 설명하고 있으므로 (B) Recent trends in education이 정답입니다.

어휘 innovative adj. 혁신적인
study abroad phr. 해외 유학하다

165. 육하원칙 문제

문제 기사에 따르면, Eastforth 대학교의 상담사는 무엇을 제공할 수 있는가?
(A) 개인 적성 평가
(B) 면접 기술에 관한 도움
(C) 잠재 고용주를 위한 추천서
(D) 대학 입학에 관한 조언

해설 Eastforth 대학교의 상담사가 무엇(what)을 제공할 수 있는지를 묻는 육하원칙 문제입니다. 질문의 핵심 어구인 Eastforth University's counselors offer와 관련하여, 'counselors at the university's career center are available ~ to help with ~ techniques for answering interview questions'에서 면접 질문에 답하는 기술에 대한 도움을 주는 대학교, 즉 Eastforth 대학교의 직업 센터의 상담사를 만날 수 있다고 했으므로 (B) Assistance with interview skills가 정답입니다.

패러프레이징
help with ~ techniques for answering interview questions 면접 질문에 답하는 기술에 대한 도움을 주다
→ Assistance with interview skills 면접 기술에 관한 도움

어휘 aptitude n. 적성 reference n. 추천서 admission n. 입학

166. 추론 문제

문제 고급 학위 소지자들에 대해 암시되는 것은?
(A) 큰 빚을 축적한다.
(B) 대학교수가 되려고 나아간다.
(C) 정부 기관을 위해 일한다.
(D) 구직에 있어 어려움을 겪고 있다.

해설 질문의 핵심 어구인 advanced degree holders에 대해 추론하는 문제입니다. 'a large number of job candidates possess advanced degrees, making applying for positions much more competitive. In connection with this increased competition, many universities nationwide are now taking measures to provide assistance'에서 많은 구직자들이 고급 학위를 보유하고 있다는 것이 일자리에 지원하는 것을 훨씬 더 경쟁적으로 만들었고, 이러한 심화된 경쟁과 관련하여 전국적으로 많은 대학교들이 도움을 제공해 주기 위한 조치를 취하고 있다고 했으므로, 고급 학위를 가진 사람들이 구직에 있어 어려움을 겪고 있다는 사실을 추론할 수 있습니다. 따라서 (D) They are experiencing difficulties finding jobs가 정답입니다.

패러프레이징
advanced degree holders 고급 학위 소지자
→ possess advanced degrees 고급 학위를 보유하다

어휘 accumulate v. 축적하다, 쌓다 debt n. 빚

167. 문장 위치 찾기 문제

문제 [1], [2], [3], [4]로 표시된 위치 중, 다음 문장이 들어갈 곳으로 가장 적절한 것은?
"그들은 다른 구직자들에 비해 이점을 얻을 것이라는 희망을 가지고 이렇게 했다."
(A) [1]
(B) [2]
(C) [3]
(D) [4]

해설 지문의 흐름상 주어진 문장이 들어가기에 가장 적절한 곳을 고르는 문제입니다. They did this in the hopes of gaining an advantage over other jobseekers에서 그들은 다른 구직자들에 비해 이점을 얻을 것이라는 희망을 가지고 이렇게 했다고 했으므로, 문장이 구직자들이 이점을 위한 행동을 설명하는 부분 다음에 들어가야 함을 알 수 있습니다. [1]의 앞 문장인 'Following the recent economic recession, many college graduates returned to school immediately after receiving their degrees.'에서 최근의 경제 불황에 따라 많은 대학 졸업생들이 학위를 받은 즉시 학교로 돌아갔다고 했으므로, [1]에 제시된 문장이 들어가면 많은 대학 졸업생들이 학위를 받은 이후 학교로 돌아갔다는 상황과 그에 대한 이유를 설명하는 자연스러운 문맥이 된다는 것을 알 수 있습니다. 따라서 (A) [1]이 정답입니다.

168-171번은 다음 온라인 채팅 대화문에 관한 문제입니다.

> **Nadia Pinsky** 오전 9:39
> 168울타리 작업에 대한 견적 요청이 있어요. 그 집은 Lexington로 354번지에 위치해 있어요. 170두 분 중에 내일 그것을 처리해줄 수 있는 분이 있나요?
>
> **Glenn Patten** 오전 9:41
> 168/170저는 설치 작업으로 예약이 꽉 차 있어요. 170저는 그것을 할 수 없을 거예요.
>
> **Hank Louis** 오전 9:42
> 170저도 마찬가지예요. 금요일 오전에는 시간이 있기는 하지만요.
>
> **Nadia Pinsky** 오전 9:43
> 알겠어요. 169고객이 금요일에 플로리다로 떠나니까, 그건 너무 늦어요. 171Glenn, 혹시 수요일에 견적을 내줄 수 있나요?
>
> **Glenn Patten** 오전 9:43
> 171오후 5시 이후라면, 가능해요.
>
> **Nadia Pinsky** 오전 9:47
> 고마워요, Glenn. **그건 문제가 되지 않을 거예요.** 그녀의 이름은 Gloria Filmore이고, 168그녀는 마당 주변에 울타리를 설치하고 싶어 해요.
>
> **Hank Louis** 오전 9:48
> 그녀는 반세 그것이 보내지는 것을 피요로 하나요? 우리 일정은 요즘 너무 바쁘잖아요.
>
> **Nadia Pinsky** 오전 9:50
> 그녀가 여행에서 돌아올 때나 되어서예요. 169그녀는 그곳에서 일주일 동안 머무를 것이니까, 크게 서두르지 않아도 돼요.
>
> **Glenn Patten** 오전 9:51
> 알았어요. 예약이 확정되면 알려주기만 해주세요.

estimate n. 견적 **fence** v. 울타리를 치다; n. 울타리
take care of phr. ~을 처리하다
manage v. 하다, 처리하다, 다루다 **rush** n. 서두름
confirm v. 확정하다, 확인하다

168. 추론 문제
문제 작성자들은 누구일 것 같은가?
(A) 여행사 직원들
(B) 재정 자문가들
(C) 울타리 도급업자들
(D) 실내 장식가들

해설 질문의 핵심 어구인 the writers에 대해 추론하는 문제입니다. 'I have an estimate request for a fencing project.'에서 Nadia Pinsky가 울타리 작업에 대한 견적 요청이 있다고 하자, 'I'm completely booked with installations.'에

서 Glenn Patten이 설치 작업으로 예약이 꽉 차 있다고 했고, 'she wants to install a fence around her yard'에서 Nadia Pinsky가 그녀, 즉 고객이 마당 주변에 울타리를 설치하고 싶어 한다고 하면서 울타리 설치 작업에 대한 이야기를 하고 있으므로, 작성자들이 울타리를 설치하는 도급업자들이라는 사실을 추론할 수 있습니다. 따라서 (C) Fencing contractors가 정답입니다.

어휘 contractor n. 도급업자, 계약자

169. 육하원칙 문제
문제 Ms. Filmore는 언제 플로리다에서 돌아올 것인가?
(A) 수요일에
(B) 이번 주말에
(C) 다음 주 월요일에
(D) 다음 주 금요일에

해설 Ms. Filmore가 언제(When) 플로리다에서 돌아올 것인지를 묻는 육하원칙 문제입니다. 질문의 핵심 어구인 Ms. Filmore return from Florida와 관련하여, 'The client is leaving for Florida on Friday', 'She's staying there for a week'에서 Nadia Pinsky가 고객, 즉 Ms. Filmore가 금요일에 플로리다로 떠나서 그곳에서 일주일 동안 머무를 것이라고 했으므로 Ms. Filmore가 다음 주 금요일에 플로리다에서 돌아올 것임을 알 수 있습니다. 따라서 (D) The following Friday가 정답입니다.

170. 육하원칙 문제
문제 Mr. Louis는 왜 내일 Ms. Filmore를 만날 수 없는가?
(A) 플로리다로 휴가를 떠나 있을 것이다.
(B) 그의 일정이 예약으로 꽉 차 있다.
(C) 고객들을 위해 다른 견적을 내고 있다.
(D) 그의 다른 작업이 예상보다 오래 걸리고 있다.

해설 Mr. Louis가 왜(Why) 내일 Ms. Filmore를 만날 수 없는지를 묻는 육하원칙 문제입니다. 질문의 핵심 어구인 Mr. Louis unable to meet Ms. Filmore tomorrow와 관련하여, 'Would either of you be able to take care of that tomorrow?'에서 Nadia Pinsky가 두 사람 중에 내일 그것, 즉 Ms. Filmore의 견적을 내주는 것을 처리해줄 수 있는 사람이 있는지 묻자, 'I'm completely booked with installations. I won't be able to manage it.'에서 Glenn Patten이 자신은 설치 작업으로 예약이 꽉 차 있어서 그것을 할 수 없을 것이라고 했고, 'I have the same issue.'에서 Hank Louis가 자신도 마찬가지라고 했으므로 Glenn Patten처럼 Mr. Louis의 일정이 예약으로 꽉 차 있음을 알 수 있습니다. 따라서 (B) His schedule is filled with appointments가 정답입니다.

패러프레이징
unable 할 수 없는 → won't be able 할 수 없는
booked with installations 설치 작업으로 예약이 찬
→ filled with appointments 예약으로 꽉 찬

171. 의도 파악 문제
문제 오전 9시 47분에, Ms. Pinsky가 "That shouldn't be a problem"이라고 썼을 때, 그녀가 의도한 것은?
(A) 작업이 많은 노력을 필요로 하지 않을 것이다.
(B) 언급된 시간이 고객에게 적절할 것 같다.
(C) 여행 일정이 쉽게 변경될 수 있다.
(D) 휴가 요청이 어떤 상충도 발생시키지 않을 것이다.

해설 Ms. Pinsky가 의도한 것을 묻는 문제이므로, 질문의 인용구(That shouldn't be a problem)가 언급된 주변 문맥을 확인합니다. 'Glenn, is there any possibility you can do the estimate on Wednesday?'에서 Nadia Pinsky가 Glenn Patten에게 수요일에 견적을 내줄 수 있을지 물었고, 'If it is after 5 p.m., yes.'에서 Glenn Patten이 오후 5시 이후라면 가능하다고 하자, Nadia Pinsky가 'That shouldn't be a problem'(그건 문제가 되지 않을 거예요)이라고 한 것을 통해, 언급된 시간이 고객에게 적절할 것이라고 생각한다는 것을 알 수 있습니다. 따라서 (B) A specified time is likely suitable for a client가 정답입니다.

패러프레이징
shouldn't be a problem 문제가 되지 않다
→ suitable 적절한

어휘 specify v. 명확히 말하다, 명시하다 conflict n. 상충, 충돌

172-175번은 다음 기사에 관한 문제입니다.

직원 교육에서 최상의 결과를 얻는 방법
174Tom Caldwell 작성

요즘, 관리자들은 점점 더 그들의 직원들의 교육과 성장에 대한 책임을 맡게 되고 있다. 사실, 많은 회사들은 단지 이 목적을 위해 자금을 따로 마련해두기도 한다. 그러나, 174나는 이러한 자원들이 실제로 내가 관리했던 직원들에게 이익이 되도록 사용될 수 있는 방법을 알아내는 것이 어렵다고 항상 생각했다. 조사에 따르면, 최상의 행동 방침을 선택할 때 고려할 세 가지 중요한 점이 있다. ― [1] ―. 첫째, 175당신의 직원들이 무엇을 원하는지 그들에게 물어보아라. ― [2] ―. 175너무나 많은 회사들이 그들의 직원들이 정보의 핵심적인 출처가 될 수 있다는 것을 잊어버린다. 다음으로, 172당신의 직원들에 대한 정기적인 성과 평가를 실시하라. 그 결과를 반드시 기록해서 시간에 따른 개인의 성장을 지켜볼 수 있도록 하라. ― [3] ―. 이는 주의가 필요한 부분을 밝히는 데 도움이 된다. ― [4] ―. 마지막으로, 모든 교육을 하기 전에 구체적인 목표를 설정하고 당신이 직원들과 성취하기를 바라는 것을 정하라. 173-C이러한 간단한 단계들을 거침으로써, 관리자들은 많은 시간을 절약할 수 있다. 그뿐만 아니라, 그들은 대수롭지 않은 결과들을 낳는 교육 시간에 회사 자금을 낭비하는 것을 막을 것이다.

increasingly adv. 점점 더 responsible adj. 책임을 맡는
development n. 성장, 개발 fund n. 자금
determine v. 알아내다, 결정하다 resource n. 자원, 출처
consider v. 고려하다 course of action phr. 행동 방침
workforce n. 직원 key adj. 핵심적인 conduct v. 실시하다
regular adj. 정기적인 performance n. 성과
evaluation n. 평가 document v. 기록하다
over time phr. 시간에 따라 reveal v. 밝히다, 드러내다
attention n. 주의 establish v. 설정하다
specific adj. 구체적인 achieve v. 성취하다
go through phr. 거치다 avoid v. 막다, 피하다
waste v. 낭비하다 negligible adj. 대수롭지 않은

172. 육하원칙 문제

문제 기사에서 어떤 권고가 제시되는가?
(A) 직원 성장에 대해 기록하는 것
(B) 강사로부터 의견을 모으는 것
(C) 직원들에게 교육 진행자들을 평가해달라고 요청하는 것
(D) 계획에 많은 시간을 들이는 것

해설 기사에서 어떤(What) 권고가 제시되는지를 묻는 육하원칙 문제입니다. 질문의 핵심 어구인 recommendation is made와 관련하여, 'conduct regular performance evaluations of your staff. Be sure to document the results so that you can track each person's development over time.'에서 직원들에 대한 정기적인 성과 평가를 실시하고 그 결과를 반드

시 기록해서 시간에 따른 개인의 성장을 지켜볼 수 있도록 하라고 했으므로 (A) Keeping a record of staff development가 정답입니다.

패러프레이징
document 기록하다 → Keeping a record 기록하는 것

173. Not/True 문제

문제 기사에서 약술된 단계를 따르는 것에 대한 가능한 결과로 언급된 것은?
(A) 근로자들의 높아진 만족도
(B) 더 빠른 프로젝트 완료 시간
(C) 더 비용 효율적인 교육
(D) 더 높은 생산성 수준

해설 질문의 핵심 어구인 a possible outcome of following the steps와 관련된 내용을 지문에서 찾아 각 보기와 대조하는 Not/True 문제입니다. (A), (B), (D)는 지문에 언급되지 않은 내용입니다. (C)는 'By going through these simple steps, supervisors ~ will avoid wasting company funds on training sessions that have negligible results.'에서 이러한 간단한 단계들을 거침으로써 관리자들은 대수롭지 않은 결과들을 낳는 교육 시간에 회사 자금을 낭비하는 것을 막을 것이라고 했으므로 지문의 내용과 일치합니다. 따라서 (C) More cost-efficient training이 정답입니다.

패러프레이징
following 따르는 것 → going through 거침
avoid wasting company funds on training sessions that have negligible results 대수롭지 않은 결과들을 낳는 교육 시간에 회사 자금을 낭비하는 것을 막다
→ More cost-efficient training 더 비용 효율적인 교육

174. 추론 문제

문제 Mr. Caldwell에 대해 암시되는 것은?
(A) 관리자로서 일했었다.
(B) 인사 관련 회사를 소유하고 있다.
(C) 최근에 설문 조사를 실시했다.
(D) 교육 과정을 가르친다.

해설 질문의 핵심 어구인 Mr. Caldwell에 대해 추론하는 문제입니다. 'by Tom Caldwell'에서 기사를 작성한 사람이 Tom Caldwell이고, 'I always found it difficult to determine how ~ resources could actually be used to benefit the employees I managed'에서 자원들이 실제로 자신이 관리했던 직원들에게 이익이 되도록 사용될 수 있는 방법을 알아내는 것이 어렵다고 항상 생각했다고 했으므로 Tom Caldwell이 관리자로서 일했었다는 사실을 추론할 수 있습니다. 따라서 (A) He used to work as a supervisor가 정답입니다.

패러프레이징
managed 관리했던 → used to work as a supervisor 관리자로서 일했었다

175. 문장 위치 찾기 문제

문제 [1], [2], [3], [4]로 표시된 위치 중, 다음 문장이 들어갈 곳으로 가장 적절한 것은?

"그들은 어떤 종류의 교육이 그들에게 가장 도움이 되는지 가장 잘 알고 있다."

(A) [1]
(B) [2]
(C) [3]
(D) [4]

해설 지문의 흐름상 주어진 문장이 들어가기에 가장 적절한 곳을 고르는 문제입니다. They know best what type of training will benefit them the most에서 그들이 어떤 종류의 교육이 그들에게 가장 도움이 되는지 가장 잘 알고 있다고 했으므로, 문장이 교육 대상과 관련하여 언급하는 부분에 들어가야 함을 알 수 있습니다. [2]의 앞 문장인 'ask your workforce what they would like'에서 직원들이 무엇을 원하는지 그들에게 물어보라고 했고, [2]의 뒤 문장인 'Too many companies forget that their employees can be a key source of information.'에서 너무나 많은 회사들이 그들의 직원들이 정보의 핵심적인 출처가 될 수 있다는 것을 잊어버린다고 했으므로, [2]에 주어진 문장이 들어가면 직원들이 무엇을 원하는지 물어보면 그들이 자신들에게 가장 도움이 되는 교육이 무엇인지 가장 잘 알고 있을 것이라는 자연스러운 문맥이 된다는 것을 알 수 있습니다. 따라서 (B) [2]가 정답입니다.

176-180번은 다음 편지와 이메일에 관한 문제입니다.

10월 20일

Martin Vesper
Raymond Development사
53번지 Longhorn가
아테네, 조지아주 31444

Mr. Vesper께,

제 이름은 Andrea Glick입니다. [179]우리는 Hufford 비즈니스 협의회에서 조경에 대한 Raymond Development사의 생태학적 접근에 관한 귀하의 인상 깊은 연설 후에 처음 만났습니다. [176]저희 회사인 SureGreen 건설사는 다가오는 주요 프로젝트에 귀사와 일하는 것에 관심이 있습니다.

귀하께서 저희 회사에 관해 알고 계시는지 잘 모르겠습니다. SureGreen 건설사는 환경친화적인 주택을 건설하는 일에 헌신하고 있습니다. [177-A]저희는 가능한 한 자주, 재생 또는 대체 자재들로 집을 짓고 [177-C]태양이나 풍력 에너지처럼 다른 전력 옵션을 효과적으로 통합하는 건축물을 설계합니다. 지금까지, [177-D]저희 프로젝트는 꽤 작은 규모였고 대부분 주택을 설계하는 데에 국한되어 있었습니다. 하지만, 프로젝트를 위한 조경을 하는 것을 포함하여, 조지아주 애틀랜타에 있는 Ophelia사의 본사를 짓는 계약 건이 있습니다. 저희는 귀사의 전문 기술이 필요하며 이것이 귀하께 편지를 쓰는 이유입니다.

이 프로젝트에 저희와 함께하는 것에 관심이 있으시다면 주저 말고 전화 555-2358이나 이메일 andrea_glick@ suregreen.com으로 제게 연락해주시기 바랍니다. 귀하로부터 곧 소식을 듣기를 바랍니다.

Andrea Glick 드림
SureGreen 건설사 프로젝트 관리자

convention n. 협의회, 회의 impressive adj. 인상 깊은
talk n. 연설 ecological adj. 생태학적인
approach n. 접근(법) landscape v. 조경하다; n. 조경
be committed to phr. ~에 헌신하다
environmentally friendly phr. 환경친화적인
recycle v. 재활용하다 alternative adj. 대체의
material n. 자재, 재료 efficiently adv. 효과적으로
incorporate v. 통합하다, 혼합하다 fairly adv. 꽤, 상당히
headquarters n. 본사, 본부
expertise n. 전문 기술

수신: Andrea Glick <andrea_glick@suregreen.com>
발신: Martin Vesper <vesper@raymonddev.com>
날짜: 11월 2일
제목: Ophelia 프로젝트

Ms. Glick께,

[179]지난 8월에 제 연설을 즐겁게 들으셨다니 기쁘고, 이 프로젝트에 SureGreen 사의 참여하도록 청해주셔서 감사합니다. [180]Ophelia사는 환경 조건과 지속 가능성을 향상시키는 계획으로 잘 알려져 있으므로, 저희는 그들을 위한 새로운 본사를 만드는 것을 돕는 데에 매우 관심이 있습니다.

[178]직접 만나서 프로젝트를 논의하기 전에, 저희는 그에 대한 세부 사항이 더 필요할 것입니다. 가장 중요하게는, 건설 장소가 정확히 어디인지와 그곳의 상태가 어떤지 알 필요가 있을 것입니다. 그다음에, 저희는 그 지역에 기술자 몇몇을 보내서 배수 상태를 확인하고, 토양의 산성도를 측정하고 싶습니다. 우리가 무엇을 다루어야 하는지 알게 되면, 저희는 귀사의 건축가들과 설계를 더 잘 진행할 수 있을 것입니다.

Martin Vesper 드림

initiative n. 계획, 주도권 improve v. 향상시키다
sustainability n. 지속 가능성 assist v. 돕다
in person phr. 직접 만나서 site n. 장소 drainage n. 배수
measure v. 측정하다 soil n. 토양 acidity n. 산성도
move ahead phr. 진행하다, 전진하다

176. 주제/목적 찾기 문제
문제 Ms. Glick은 왜 Mr. Vesper에게 연락했는가?
(A) 프로젝트에 참여해달라고 그의 회사에 청하기 위해
(B) 발표에 대해 그에게 감사하기 위해
(C) 새로운 보존 계획을 설명하기 위해
(D) 건설 회사를 추천하기 위해

해설 Ms. Glick이 Mr. Vesper에게 연락한 목적을 묻는 목적 찾기 문제이므로 첫 번째 지문인 Ms. Glick이 작성한 편지의 앞부분을 주의 깊게 확인합니다. 편지의 'My company, SureGreen Construction, is interested in working with yours on a major upcoming project.'에서 SureGreen 건설사가 다가오는 주요 프로젝트에 Mr. Vesper의 회사와 일하는 것에 관심이 있다고 한 후, Ms. Glick의 회사와 프로젝트에 대해 설명하고 있으므로 (A) To invite his firm to take part in a project가 정답입니다.

어휘 take part in phr. ~에 참여하다 presentation n. 발표
conservation n. 보존, 보호 recommend v. 추천하다

177. Not/True 문제
문제 SureGreen 건설사에 대해 언급되지 않은 것은?
(A) 재생된 자재를 사용하려고 노력한다.
(B) 본사가 애틀랜타에 있다.
(C) 건축물들이 대체 에너지원을 이용한다.
(D) 주로 주택을 설계해왔다.

해설 질문의 핵심 어구인 SureGreen 건설사와 관련된 내용을 지문에서 찾아 각 보기와 대조하는 Not/True 문제이므로, 첫 번째 지문인 SureGreen 건설사의 직원이 쓴 편지에서 관련 내용을 확인합니다. (A)는 'We construct our buildings with recycled or alternative materials as often as possible'에서 가능한 한 자주, 재생 또는 대체 자재들로 집을 짓는다고 했으므로 지문의 내용과 일치합니다. (B)는 지문에 언급되지 않은 내용입니다. 따라서 (B) Its headquarters is in Atlanta가 정답입니다. (C)는 'design structures that efficiently incorporate different power options, like solar or wind energy'에서 태양이나 풍력 에너지처럼 다른 전력 옵션을 효과적으로 통합하는 건축물을 설계한다고 했으므로 지문의 내용과 일치합니다. (D)는 'our projects have been ~ mostly limited to designing homes'에서 프로젝트가 대부분 주택

을 설계하는 데에 국한되어 있었다고 했으므로 지문의 내용과 일치합니다.

패러프레이징

with recycled ~ materials 재생 자재들로 → use recovered materials 재생된 자재를 사용한다

mostly 대부분 → mainly 주로

어휘 recovered adj. 재생의, 회복된

178. 육하원칙 문제

문제 Mr. Vesper는 회의 전에 무엇을 하고 싶어 하는가?

(A) 건축가들과 이야기한다
(B) 몇 가지 설계 아이디어를 낸다
(C) 다른 세부 사항을 확인한다
(D) 계약 조건을 검토한다

해설 Mr. Vesper가 회의 전에 무엇(What)을 하고 싶어 하는지를 묻는 육하원칙 문제이므로 질문의 핵심 어구인 Mr. Vesper가 작성한 두 번째 지문인 이메일에서 관련 내용을 확인합니다. 이메일의 'Before we come together to discuss the project in person, we will need more details about it.'에서 직접 만나서 프로젝트를 논의하기 전에 그에 대한 세부 사항이 더 필요할 것이라고 했으므로 (C) Find out other details가 정답입니다.

179. 육하원칙 문제 연계

문제 Mr. Vesper와 Ms. Glick은 언제 처음 만났는가?

(A) 8월에
(B) 9월에
(C) 10월에
(D) 11월에

해설 두 지문의 내용을 종합해서 풀어야 하는 연계 문제입니다. 질문의 핵심 어구인 Mr. Vesper and Ms. Glick first meet에서 Mr. Vesper와 Ms. Glick이 언제(When) 처음 만났는지를 묻고 있으므로 first meet과 관련된 내용이 언급된 첫 번째 지문인 편지를 먼저 확인합니다.
'We first met ~ following your impressive talk'에서 귀하, 즉 Mr. Vesper의 인상 깊은 연설 후에 둘이 처음 만났다는 첫 번째 단서를 확인할 수 있습니다. 그런데 처음 만난 것이 언제인지가 제시되지 않았으므로 두 번째 지문인 이메일에서 관련 내용을 확인합니다. 'I am glad you enjoyed my talk back in August'에서 지난 8월에 자신, 즉 Mr. Vesper의 연설을 즐겁게 들었다니 기쁘다고 했으므로 Mr. Vesper가 8월에 연설을 했다는 두 번째 단서를 확인할 수 있습니다.
Mr. Vesper의 연설 후에 둘이 처음 만났다는 첫 번째 단서와 Mr. Vesper가 8월에 연설을 했다는 두 번째 단서를 종합할 때, Mr. Vesper와 Ms. Glick은 8월에 처음 만났다는 것을 알 수 있습니다. 따라서 (A) In August가 정답입니다.

180. 육하원칙 문제

문제 Mr. Vesper는 왜 Ophelia사와 함께 일하는 것에 관심이 있는가?

(A) 그 회사에서 일하는 이전 동료가 있다.
(B) 그들의 활동이 환경에 이롭다는 것을 높이 평가한다.
(C) 그는 연락망을 확대하는 과정에 있다.
(D) 그는 이전에 비슷한 프로젝트를 작업해본 적이 없다.

해설 Mr. Vesper가 왜(Why) Ophelia사와 함께 일하는 것에 관심이 있는지를 묻는 육하원칙 문제이므로 질문의 핵심 어구인 Mr. Vesper가 작성한 두 번째 지문인 이메일에서 관련 내용을 확인합니다. 이메일의 'Ophelia Incorporated is well-known for its initiatives to improve environmental conditions and sustainability, so we are very interested in assisting with creating a new headquarters for them.'에서 Ophelia사가 환경 조건과 지속 가능성을 향상시키는 계획으로 잘 알려져 있으므로 그들을 위한 새로운 본사를 만드는 것을 돕는 데에 매우 관심이 있다고 했으므로 (B) He appreciates that their activities benefit the environment가 정답입니다.

패러프레이징

improve environmental conditions and sustainability 환경 조건과 지속 가능성을 향상시키다 → benefit the environment 환경에 이롭다

어휘 former adj. 이전의 appreciate v. 높이 평가하다
benefit v. ~에 이롭다 expand v. 확대하다
similar adj. 비슷한

181-185번은 다음 두 이메일에 관한 문제입니다.

수신: Melissa Ortiz <melissa@firstrunaustin.com>
발신: Oliver Keller <oliver.keller@dakotashalegas.com>
제목: 인쇄
날짜: 8월 20일

Ms. Ortiz께,

저는 최근에 귀하의 웹사이트를 우연히 발견했고 가격에 대해 문의하고 싶습니다. 매년, 저희는 아르헨티나에서의 저희 사업에 초점을 맞춘 연례 보고서를 인쇄합니다. 책임자로서, [181]저는 저희의 고정 공급업체에서 제작된 자료의 질에 실망했고 귀사에서 더 나은 결과를 얻기를 바랍니다.

저는 귀사에서 디자인, 인쇄, 배송을 포함하는 패키지를 제공한다는 것을 알고 있습니다. 저희가 [182-B]디자이너들을 고용하지 않아도 될 것이기 때문에 이는 저희에게 유용합니다. [182-C]저희는 또한 완성된 보고서를 발송해주는 지원을 이용할 수도 있을 것입니다. 저희는 이전에는 행정 직원들에게 이것을 처리하게 하는 것만으로도 초과 근무 수당을 지급해야 했습니다.

32페이지 컬러 보고서를 디자인하고 1,500부를 인쇄해서 저희가 제공하는 주소로 발송하는 데 얼마를 부과하는지 알려주실 수 있으십니까? [185]900개의 주소는 미국에 있습니다. 나머지들 중 [183-B/C/D/185]300개는 캐나다에, 220개는 독일, 프랑스, 벨기에에, 80개는 중국, 한국, 일본에 있습니다.

귀하로부터 곧 답을 듣기를 기대하겠습니다.

감사합니다.

Oliver Keller 드림
Dakota Shale Gas사

---

come across phr. ~을 우연히 발견하다 inquire v. 문의하다
annual adj. 연례의 coordinator n. 책임자, 조정자
disappoint v. 실망시키다 administrative adj. 행정의
overtime n. 초과 근무 수당, 초과 근무

수신: Oliver Keller <oliver.keller@dakotashalegas.com>
발신: Melissa Ortiz <melissa@firstrunaustin.com>
날짜: 8월 23일
제목: 회신: 인쇄

Mr. Keller께,

저희가 귀하의 보고서와 관련하여 도와드린다면 기쁠 것이고, 아래의 정보가 귀하가 결정을 하는 데 도움이 되기를 바랍니다. [184]정확한 견적가를 알려드리려면, 일반 종이와 고급 종이 간에 가격이 다를 수 있기 때문에 저희는 귀하가 어떤 종류의 종이를 선호하는지 알아야 할 것입니다. 동일하게, 여러 가지 종이 크기들에 대한 추가 요금이 있습니다.

저희의 기본 패키지에서 선택한다고 가정했을 때, 디자인 비용은 약 1,200달러가 될 것이고 인쇄 비용은 한 부당 약 90센트입니다. 이는 귀하가 명시한 수량에 대해서는 1,350달러가 됩니다. [185]배송 비용은 첫 900부의 보고서는 250달러이고 그 다음으로 다른 국가들에 대해서는 각각 350달러씩으로 추산됩니다.

이 정보가 도움이 되기를 바랍니다. 추가 문의 사항이 있으면 제게 알려주십시오.

Melissa Ortiz 드림
First Run Printing사

come to a decision phr. 결정하다 accurate adj. 정확한
quote n. 견적가 assuming conj. ~이라고 가정했을 때
quantity n. 수량 estimate v. 추산하다, 추정하다

181. 육하원칙 문제

문제 Mr. Keller는 왜 인쇄 서비스업체를 찾고 있는가?
(A) 그가 가지고 있는 기계가 제대로 작동하지 않는다.
(B) 현재의 공급업체에 만족하지 않는다.
(C) 그의 회사가 여행 책자를 제작하고 있다.
(D) 그의 고정 인쇄소가 주문을 받기에 너무 바쁘다.

해설 Mr. Keller가 왜(Why) 인쇄 서비스업체를 찾고 있는지 묻는 육하원칙 문제이므로 질문의 핵심 어구인 Mr. Keller가 작성한 첫 번째 이메일에서 관련 내용을 확인합니다. 첫 번째 이메일의 'I have been disappointed in the quality of materials produced by our regular supplier'에서 고정 공급업체에서 제작된 자료의 질에 실망했다고 했으므로 (B) He is not satisfied with the current provider가 정답입니다.

패러프레이징
have been disappointed in the quality of materials produced by our regular supplier 고정 공급업체에서 제작된 자료의 질에 실망했다 → is not satisfied with the current provider 현재의 공급업체에 만족하지 않는다

어휘 function v. 제대로 작동하다 printer n. 인쇄소

182. Not/True 문제

문제 Dakota Shale Gas사에 대해 언급된 것은?
(A) 올해 초에 개업했다.
(B) 직원으로 그래픽 디자이너가 있다.
(C) 행정 직원들이 주로 연례 보고서를 발송한다.
(D) 웹사이트도 디자인될 필요가 있다.

해설 질문의 핵심 어구인 Dakota Shale Gas와 관련된 내용을 지문에서 찾아 각 보기와 대조하는 Not/True 문제이므로 Dakota Shale Gas사의 직원이 작성한 첫 번째 이메일에서 관련 내용을 확인합니다. (A)는 지문에 언급되지 않은 내용입니다. (B)는 'we would not have to hire designers'에서 디자이너들을 고용하지 않아도 될 것이라고 한 것에서 직원으로 일하는 디자이너가 없다는 것을 알 수 있으므로 지문의 내용과 일치하지 않습니다. (C)는 'We could also use the help mailing the finished reports. We've had to pay our administrative staff overtime just to take care of this in the past.'에서 완성된 보고서를 발송해주는 지원을 이용할 수도 있을 것이고 이전에는 행정 직원들에게 이것을 처리하게 하는 것만으로도 초과 근무 수당을 지급해야 했다고 했으므로 (C) Their administrative staff usually post the annual reports가 정답입니다. (D)는 지문에 언급되지 않은 내용입니다.

패러프레이징
mailing 발송하다 → post 발송하다

183. Not/True 문제

문제 Dakota Shale Gas사는 어느 나라에 보고서를 배송하지 않을 것인가?
(A) 아르헨티나
(B) 캐나다
(C) 중국
(D) 프랑스

해설 질문의 핵심 어구인 Dakota Shale Gas ~ ship reports to와 관련된 내용을 지문에서 찾아 각 보기와 대조하는 Not/True 문제이므로, 질문의 핵심 어구인 Dakota Shale Gas사의 직원이 작성한 첫 번째 이메일에서 관련 내용을 확인합니다. (A)는 지문에 언급되지 않은 내용입니다. 따라서 (A) Argentina가 정답입니다. (B), (C), (D)는 '300 are in Canada, 220 in ~ France, ~ and 80 in China, South Korea, and Japan'에서 발송할 보고서의 주소가 300개는 캐나다에, 220개는 프랑스에, 80개는 중국과 한국, 일본에 있다고 했으므로 지문의 내용과 일치합니다.

어휘 ship v. 배송하다

184. 육하원칙 문제

문제 Ms. Ortiz는 비용 견적을 내기 위해 무엇을 필요로 하는가?
(A) 이전 연도의 보고서 한 부
(B) 문서에 들어갈 이미지의 수
(C) 보고서의 완성된 원고
(D) 종이 크기와 종류에 대한 정보

해설 Ms. Ortiz가 비용 견적을 내기 위해 무엇을(What)을 필요로 하는지를 묻는 육하원칙 문제이므로 질문의 핵심 어구인 Ms. Ortiz가 작성한 두 번째 이메일에서 관련 내용을 확인합니다. 두 번째 이메일의 'To give you an accurate quote, we will need to know what type of paper you prefer ~ there is an additional charge for different paper sizes.'에서 정확한 견적가를 알려주려면 어떤 종류의 종이를 선호하는지 알아야 할 것이고 여러 가지 종이 크기들에 대한 추가 요금이 있다고 했으므로 (D) Information about paper size and type이 정답입니다.

어휘 previous adj. 이전의 completed adj. 완성된

185. 추론 문제 연계

문제 Ms. Ortiz가 비용에 관해 암시하는 것은?
(A) 수량이 늘어남에 따라 개당 비용이 줄어든다.
(B) 보증금이 미리 지불되면 비용이 더 낮다.
(C) 신규 고객들을 위한 할인을 포함한다.
(D) 미국 내에서의 배송이 외부보다 비용이 덜 든다.

해설 두 지문의 내용을 종합적으로 확인한 후 추론해서 풀어야 하는 연계 문제입니다. 질문의 핵심 어구인 Ms. Ortiz imply about costs와 관련된 내용이 언급된 두 번째 이메일을 먼저 확인합니다.
'Shipping costs are estimated to be $250 for the first 900 reports and then around $350 each for the other countries.'에서 배송 비용은 첫 900부의 보고서는 250달러이고 다른 국가들에 대해서는 각각 350달러씩으로 추산된다는 첫 번째 단서를 확인할 수 있습니다. 그런데 첫 900부의 보고서가 발송되는 지역이 어디인지 제시되지 않았으므로 첫 번째 이메일에서 관련 내용을 확인합니다. '900 addresses are in the US.', '300 are in Canada, 220 in Germany, France, and Belgium, and 80 in China, South Korea, and Japan'에서 900개의 발송 주소는 미국에 있고, 300개는 캐나다에, 220개는 독일, 프랑스, 벨기에에, 80개는 중국, 한국, 일본에 있다는 두 번째 단서를 확인할 수 있습니다.

배송 비용은 첫 900부의 보고서는 250달러이고 그다음으로 다른 국가들에 대해서는 각각 350달러씩으로 추산된다는 첫 번째 단서와 900개의 발송 주소는 미국에 있고, 300개는 캐나다에, 220개는 독일, 프랑스, 벨기에에, 80개는 중국, 한국, 일본에 있다는 두 번째 단서를 종합할 때, 미국 내에서의 배송이 미국 외의 나라들보다 저렴하다는 사실을 추론할 수 있습니다. 따라서 (D) They cost less for delivery within the US than outside of it이 정답입니다.

어휘 deposit n. 보증금, 예치금 in advance phr. 미리

186-190번은 다음 문자 메시지, 이메일, 안건 목록에 관한 문제입니다.

---

[186]저는 내일 아침의 이사회 회의가 취소되었음을 여러분 모두에게 알려드리고자 합니다. 안타깝게도, 너무 많은 회원들이 부재중이거나, 시간을 낼 수 없을 것 같습니다. [186]이사회의 방침이 어떠한 경영상의 결정을 내리려면 최소 반 이상의 회원들이 참석하는 것을 요구하므로, 우리는 회의를 진행할 수 없을 것입니다. [188]제가 분기 보고를 발표해야 하고, 이사회에서는 안건 목록에 논의해야 할 시급한 몇 가지 사항이 있으므로 가능한 한 빨리 일정을 다시 잡을 것입니다. 금요일까지 여러분 모두에게 새로운 날짜와 시간을 공지하겠습니다. 어떠한 불편함에도 사과드리며 [187]우리의 모임이 중요하므로 모든 회원들이 모임을 우선순위에 두길 정중히 부탁드립니다.

– Gene Coulter 드림

---

board meeting phr. 이사회 unfortunately adv. 안타깝게도
require v. 요구하다 present adj. 참석한, 출석한, 현재의
proceed v. 진행하다 quarterly adj. 분기의
pressing adj. 시급한, 긴급한 agenda n. 안건 목록, 의제
reschedule v. 일정이 변경되다 notify v. 공지하다, 알리다
apologize v. 사과하다 inconvenience n. 불편함
kindly adv. 정중히, 친절하게 prioritize v. 우선순위에 두다
gathering n. 모임

수신 Gene Coulter <geco@barriscorp.com>
발신 Marion Xavier <maxa@barriscorp.com>
날짜 4월 8일
제목 회의
첨부 안건 목록

Mr. Coulter께,

일정이 다시 잡힌 이사회 회의에 관한 당신의 메시지를 받았습니다. 화요일 오전 9시가 제게 괜찮고, 저는 그곳에 참석할 것입니다. 그런데, [189]안건 목록에 한 가지 논의 사항을 추가할 수 있을지 궁금합니다. [190]지난 분기의 운영 경비가 예상보다 약간 더 높아서, 저는 그에 대한 이유들을 다루고 해결책을 제시하고 싶습니다. 만약 괜찮다면 알려주십시오. 이미 안건 목록에 너무 많은 것들이 있다면, 아마 다음 회의까지 기다릴 수도 있을 것입니다.

Marion Xavier 드림

---

wonder v. 궁금해하다 add v. 추가하다 operating adj. 운영의
expense n. 비용 quarter n. 분기 expect v. 예상하다
address v. (문제 등을) 다루다, 말하다
recommend v. 제시하다, 권하다, 추천하다 solution n. 해결책

안건 목록: 4월 11일 Barris사 월례 이사회 회의

오전 9:00	개회 선언, 이사회 비서의 지난달 회의록 낭독
오전 9:15	[188]이사회 의장의 분기 일반 보고서 낭독
오전 9:45	이사회 재무부장의 월례 재무 보고서 낭독 ◑

	논의 사항
오전 10:15	1. Cleveland 지점의 사무실 확장 진행 상황 2. Hugh & Bosch Equipment사로부터의 공급 제휴 제안 [190]3. 마케팅 설문 조사에서 나온 의견 [190]4. 회사 운영 경비의 증가
오후 12:30	회의 종료

---

call to order phr. 개회를 선언하다 minutes n. 회의록
chair n. 의장 financial adj. 재무의, 재정의
treasurer n. 재무부장, 회계 담당자 progress n. 진행 (상황)
expansion n. 확장 partnership n. 제휴 proposal n. 제안

---

186. 육하원칙 문제

문제 Mr. Coulter에 의하면, 이사회 회의는 왜 일정이 변경되었는가?
(A) 분기 보고서가 아직 발표 준비가 되지 않았다.
(B) 안건 목록에 충분히 논의할 사항이 없다.
(C) 참석에 관한 필요조건이 충족되지 않을 것이다.
(D) 오전의 행사가 예정된 시간과 상충한다.

해설 Mr. Coulter에 의하면 이사회 회의가 왜(why) 일정이 변경되었는지를 묻는 육하원칙 문제이므로 Mr. Coulter가 작성한 첫 번째 지문인 문자 메시지를 확인합니다. 문자 메시지의 'tomorrow morning's board meeting has been canceled'와 'As board policy requires that at least half of our members be present to make any executive decisions, we will not be able to proceed.'에서 내일 아침의 이사회 회의가 취소되었는데, 이사회의 방침이 어떠한 경영상의 결정을 내리려면 최소 반 이상의 회원들이 참석하는 것을 요구해서 회의를 진행할 수 없을 것이라고 했으므로 (C) A requirement regarding attendance will not be met이 정답입니다.

어휘 present v. 발표하다, 제출하다 requirement n. 필요조건
attendance n. 참석, 출석 conflict v. 상충하다, 대립하다

187. 동의어 문제

문제 문자 메시지에서, 1문단 열다섯 번째 줄의 단어 "prioritize"는 의미상 –와 가장 가깝다.
(A) 재평가하다
(B) 우선으로 두다
(C) 분류하다
(D) 더 신경 쓰다

해설 첫 번째 지문인 문자 메시지의 prioritize를 포함하는 구절 'kindly ask that all members prioritize our gatherings as they are important'에서 prioritize가 '우선순위에 두다, 우선시하다'라는 뜻으로 사용되었습니다. 따라서 '우선으로 두다'라는 뜻을 가진 (B) put first가 정답입니다.

188. 추론 문제 연계

문제 Mr. Coulter는 누구일 것 같은가?
(A) 이사회 의장
(B) 행정부 비서
(C) 회사의 재무 관리자
(D) 회사의 운영 관리자

해설 세 지문 중 두 지문의 내용을 종합적으로 확인한 후 추론해서 풀어야 하는 연계 문제입니다. 질문의 핵심 어구인 Mr. Coulter가 작성한 첫 번째 지문인 문자 메시지를 먼저 확인합니다. 'I need to present our quarterly report'에서 Mr. Coulter가 분기 보고를 발표해야 한다는 첫 번째 단서를 확인할 수 있습니다. 그런데 분기 보고를 하는 사람의 직책이 제시되지

않았으므로 세 번째 지문인 안건 목록에서 관련 내용을 확인합니다. 'Reading of quarterly general report by board chair'에서 이사회 의장이 분기 일반 보고서를 낭독한다는 두 번째 단서를 확인할 수 있습니다.

Mr. Coulter가 분기 보고를 발표해야 한다는 첫 번째 단서와 이사회 의장이 분기 일반 보고서를 낭독한다는 두 번째 단서를 종합할 때, Mr. Coulter가 이사회의 의장이라는 사실을 추론할 수 있습니다. 따라서 (A) The chairperson of an executive board가 정답입니다.

패러프레이징

board chair 이사회 의장 → The chairperson of an executive board 이사회 의장

어휘 chairperson n. 의장 administrative adj. 행정의

189. 주제/목적 찾기 문제

문제 Ms. Xavier는 왜 Mr. Coulter에게 연락했는가?

(A) 화요일 약속을 조정하기를 원한다.
(B) 회의에 논제를 제기하기를 원한다.
(C) 보고서의 내용에 대한 질문이 있다.
(D) 운영 경비에 관한 정보가 필요하다.

해설 Ms. Xavier가 Mr. Coulter에게 연락한 목적을 묻는 목적 찾기 문제이므로 두 번째 지문인 이메일의 내용을 확인합니다. 이메일의 'I was wondering if I could add one point of discussion to the agenda'에서 Ms. Xavier가 안건 목록에 한 가지 논의 사항을 추가할 수 있을지 궁금하다고 했으므로 (B) She would like to bring up a topic at a meeting이 정답입니다.

패러프레이징

add one point of discussion to the agenda 안건 목록에 한 가지 논의 사항을 추가하다 → bring up a topic at a meeting 회의에 논제를 제기하다

어휘 bring up phr. (문제 등을) 제기하다, 상정하다

190. 육하원칙 문제 연계

문제 Ms. Xavier는 마케팅 설문 조사에 대한 논의 후에 무엇을 할 것인가?

(A) 계약의 주요 사항을 요약한다
(B) 이사회에 제안을 한다
(C) 다음 회의를 위한 안건 목록을 발표한다
(D) 참석자들에게 재무 보고서를 배부한다

해설 세 지문 중 두 지문의 내용을 종합해서 풀어야 하는 연계 문제입니다. 질문의 핵심 어구인 Ms. Xavier do after the discussion on the marketing survey에서 Ms. Xavier가 마케팅 조사에 대한 논의 후에 무엇(What)을 할 것인지를 묻고 있으므로 마케팅 조사가 언급된 세 번째 지문인 안건 목록을 먼저 확인합니다. '3. Feedback from marketing survey'와 '4. Increase in company operating expenses'에서 마케팅 설문 조사에서 나온 의견에 대한 논의 후에 회사 운영 경비의 증가에 대해 논의할 것이라는 첫 번째 단서를 확인할 수 있습니다. 그런데 회사 운영 경비의 증가에 대해 논의할 때에 Ms. Xavier가 무엇을 할 것인지는 제시되지 않았으므로 두 번째 지문인 이메일에서 관련 내용을 확인합니다. 'Operating expenses for the past quarter were a bit higher than expected, and I'd like to ~ recommend a solution.'에서 지난 분기의 운영 경비가 예상보다 약간 더 높아서, Ms. Xavier가 그에 대한 해결책을 제시하고 싶어 한다는 두 번째 단서를 확인할 수 있습니다. 마케팅 설문 조사에서의 의견에 대한 논의 후에 회사 운영 경비의 증가에 대해 논의할 것이라는 첫 번째 단서와 지난 분기의 운영 경비가 예상보다 약간 더 높았고 Ms. Xavier가 그에 대한 해결책을 제시하고 싶어 한다는 두 번째 단서를 종합할 때, Ms. Xavier가 마케팅 설문 조사에서의 의견에 대한 논의 후에

지난 분기의 운영 경비 증가에 대한 해결책을 제안할 것임을 알 수 있습니다. 따라서 (B) Give her recommendation to the board가 정답입니다.

어휘 agreement n. 계약, 합의 distribute v. 배부하다

191-195번은 다음 두 이메일과 일정표에 관한 문제입니다.

---

¹⁹²수신 Jonathan Ingram <jingram@lwmail.com>
발신 Geena Harris <gharris@mccloughinc.com>
제목 중요 세부 사항
첨부 교육 일정
날짜 10월 29일

안녕하세요, Jonathan.

McClough사를 대표하여, ¹⁹¹/¹⁹²귀하의 입사를 환영하고 싶습니다. ¹⁹²이전에 공지 받으신 대로, 모든 신입 사원들은 공식 업무를 시작하기에 앞서 일주일간의 교육을 받습니다. ¹⁹¹첨부된 것으로, 귀하께서는 다음 주의 활동에 대한 일정표를 확인하실 수 있을 것입니다. ¹⁹³⁻ᶜ12시 30분부터 1시 30분까지 한 시간은 점심시간으로 제공될 것임을 기억해주십시오.

¹⁹¹또한 귀하께서 다음 주에 처리하셔야 할 몇 가지 일들이 있습니다. 회사의 회계 부서는 귀하께서 사진이 있는 신분증 하나와 사회 보장 카드를 가져오시기를 요청합니다. 기록을 위해 이 서류들이 복사될 것입니다. 또한, ¹⁹⁴직원 출입 카드를 발급받고 민감한 정보를 다루는 것에 대한 지침을 받으실 수 있도록 ¹⁹³⁻ᴬ월요일 아침에 일찍 도착해서 보안 부서로 곧바로 가주시기 바랍니다. 동시에, ¹⁹³⁻ᴮ필요하시다면 보안 직원이 귀하께 차량을 위한 공간을 배정해드릴 것입니다.

교육 기간에 대한 질문이 있으시다면, 제게 알려주시거나 내선 번호 38번으로 인사 부서에 전화해주시기 바랍니다.

Geena Harris, 인사부장
McClough사

---

on behalf of phr. ~을 대표하여
go through phr. 받다, 겪다, 하다 prior to phr. ~에 앞서
official adj. 공식적인 duty n. 업무, 의무 attach v. 첨부하다
accounting department phr. 회계 부서 identification n. 신분증
proceed v. 가다, 전진하다 issue v. 발급하다 handle v. 다루다
period n. 기간 extension n. 내선, 구내전화, 연장

교육 일정	McClough사
11월 1일 월요일, 오전 9시-오후 5시	전체 오리엔테이션, 회사 개요
¹⁹²11월 2일 화요일, 오전 9시-오후 5시	사무실/행정 시스템, 회사 시스템
11월 3일 수요일, 오전 9시-오후 5시	McClough사의 고객과 재무 정보
¹⁹⁵11월 4일 목요일, 오전 9시-오후 5시	부서별 교육
11월 5일 금요일, 오전 10시-오후 3시	부서별 교육

orientation n. 오리엔테이션, 경향
corporate adj. 회사의, 기업의

수신 Geena Harris <gharris@mccloughinc.com>
발신 Jeremy Vincent <jvincent@mccloughinc.com>
주제 교육생 서류
¹⁹⁵날짜 11월 4일

안녕하세요 Geena,

¹⁹⁵교육생들에게 신분증과 사회 보장 카드를 가지고 저희 부서에 들러 달라고 오늘 아침에 다시 알려주시겠어요? 지금까지 아무도 들르지 않았어요. 급여와 수당 지급을 준비하려면 내일 그들의 카드에 있는 정보가 필요하다고 알려주세요. 저는 여기에 오후 6시까지 있지만, ¹⁹⁵그들이 교육 시간이 끝나자마자 오는 게 좋습니다.

고맙습니다!
Jeremy Vincent

remind v. ~하라고 다시 말하다, 상기시키다
come by phr. 들르다   set up phr. 준비하다, 세우다
benefit n. 수당, 이득   prefer v. ~을 (더) 좋아하다, 선호하다

191. 주제/목적 찾기 문제

문제 Ms. Harris는 왜 첫 번째 이메일을 썼는가?
(A) 교육생에게 일정 변경을 설명하기 위해
(B) 신입 사원 활동과 요청 사항들을 간략히 설명하기 위해
(C) 몇 가지의 새로운 회사 보안 규정을 알리기 위해
(D) 신입 부서원의 경력을 이야기하기 위해

해설 Ms. Harris가 첫 번째 이메일을 쓴 이유를 묻는 목적 찾기 문제이므로 첫 번째 이메일의 앞부분을 확인합니다. 첫 번째 이메일의 'I would like to welcome you to the company'에서 이메일 수신자에게 입사를 환영하고 싶다고 했고, 'Attached, you will find a schedule for next week's activities.', 'There are a few things you'll need to take care of next week also.'에서 첨부된 것으로 다음 주의 활동에 대한 일정표를 확인할 수 있을 것이며 다음 주에 처리해야 할 몇 가지 일들이 있다고 하면서 구체적인 세부 사항을 설명하고 있으므로 (B) To outline new staff activities and requirements가 정답입니다.

어휘 outline v. 간략히 서술하다, 약술하다   background n. 경력, 배경

192. 추론 문제 연계

문제 Mr. Ingram에 대해 암시되는 것은?
(A) 교육의 두 번째 날에 여러 가지의 시스템들에 대해 배울 것이다.
(B) 월요일에 방문객 출입증을 가지러 갈 것이다.
(C) 10월 29일에 공식 업무를 배정받을 것이다.
(D) 11월 4일에 부서 업무를 시작할 것이다.

해설 세 지문 중 두 지문의 내용을 종합적으로 확인한 후 추론해서 풀어야 하는 연계 문제입니다. 질문의 핵심 어구인 Mr. Ingram에게 보내진 첫 번째 이메일을 먼저 확인합니다. 'To, Jonathan Ingram'과 'I would like to welcome you to the company. ~ all new staff go through one week of training'에서 상대방, 즉 Mr. Ingram의 입사를 환영하고 싶고 모든 신입 사원들은 일주일간의 교육을 받는다고 했으므로, Mr. Ingram이 신입 사원으로서 교육을 받을 것이라는 첫 번째 단서를 확인할 수 있습니다. 그런데 교육 중에 무엇을 하는지가 제시되지 않았으므로 두 번째 지문인 일정표에서 관련 내용을 확인합니다. 'TUESDAY, November 2 ~, Office/administrative system, corporate system'에서 둘째 날인 11월 2일 화요일에 사무실/행정 시스템과 회사 시스템에 대한 교육이 있다는 두 번째 단서를 확인할 수 있습니다.
Mr. Ingram이 신입 사원으로서 교육을 받을 것이라는 첫 번째 단서와 둘째 날인 11월 2일 화요일에 사무실/행정 시스템과 회사 시스템에 대한 교육이 있다는 두 번째 단서를 종합할 때, Mr. Ingram은 교육 둘째 날에 여러 가지의 시스템에 대해 배울 것이라는 사실을 추론할 수 있습니다. 따라서 (A) He

will learn about different systems on his second day of training이 정답입니다.

패러프레이징
Office/administrative system, corporate system 사무실/행정 시스템, 회사 시스템 → different systems 여러 가지의 시스템들

어휘 assign v. 배정하다

193. Not/True 문제

문제 McClough사에 대해 언급된 것은?
(A) 다른 회사에 경비를 외주한다.
(B) 직원들에게 주차 장소를 제공한다.
(C) 신입 사원에게 중식을 제공할 것이다.
(D) 월례 교육을 실시한다.

해설 질문의 핵심 어구인 McClough Incorporated와 관련된 내용을 지문에서 찾아 각 보기와 대조하는 Not/True 문제이므로 McClough사의 직원이 신입 사원인 Mr. Ingram에게 작성한 첫 번째 이메일을 확인합니다. (A)는 'please arrive early ~ and proceed immediately to the security department'에서 일찍 도착해서 보안 부서로 곧바로 가라고 한 것에서 회사 내에 직접 보안 부서를 두고 운영하고 있음을 알 수 있으므로 지문의 내용과 일치하지 않습니다. (B)는 'security staff member will assign you a space for your vehicle if you need one'에서 필요하다면 보안 직원이 차량을 위한 공간을 배정해줄 것이라고 했으므로 지문의 내용과 일치합니다. 따라서 (B) It provides employees with parking이 정답입니다. (C)는 'Please note that one hour, from 12:30 to 1:30, will be provided for lunch'에서 12시 30분부터 1시 30분까지 한 시간은 점심시간으로 제공될 것임을 기억해달라고 했지만 중식을 제공한다는 것은 아니므로 지문의 내용과 일치하지 않습니다. (D)는 지문에 언급되지 않은 내용입니다.

패러프레이징
assign ~ a space for ~ vehicle 차량을 위한 공간을 배정하다 → provides ~ parking 주차 장소를 제공하다

어휘 outsource v. 외주하다   midday meal phr. 중식

194. 동의어 문제

문제 첫 번째 이메일에서, 2문단 다섯 번째 줄의 단어 "sensitive"는 의미상 -와 가장 가깝다.
(A) 분별 있는
(B) 사려 깊은
(C) 기밀의
(D) 즉각 반응하는

해설 첫 번째 이메일의 sensitive를 포함하고 있는 구절 'you can ~ receive guidelines for handling sensitive data'에서 sensitive가 '민감한, 기밀과 관련된'이라는 뜻으로 사용되었습니다. 따라서 '기밀의'라는 뜻을 가진 (C) confidential이 정답입니다.

195. 육하원칙 문제 연계

문제 Mr. Vincent는 언제 교육생들이 그의 사무실을 방문하기를 원하는가?
(A) 오전 9시에
(B) 오전 10시에
(C) 오후 3시에
(D) 오후 5시에

해설 세 지문 중 두 지문의 내용을 종합해서 풀어야 하는 연계 문제입니다. 질문의 핵심 어구인 Mr. Vincent prefer that the trainees visit his office에서 Mr. Vincent가 언제(When) 교

육생들이 그의 사무실에 방문하기를 원하는지를 묻고 있으므로 Mr. Vincent가 작성한 세 번째 지문인 이메일에서 관련 내용을 확인합니다. 'Date, November 4'에서 Mr. Vincent가 이메일을 11월 4일에 썼음을 알 수 있고, 'Could you remind the trainees this morning to come by my department'에서 교육생들에게 자신의 부서에 들러 달라고 오늘 아침에 다시 알려달라고 요청하였습니다. 또한, 'I would prefer if they came as soon as their training session ends for the day'에서 그들, 즉 교육생들이 교육 시간이 끝나자마자 오는 게 좋다고 했으므로, Mr. Vincent가 11월 4일에 교육생들이 교육 시간이 끝나자마자 그의 부서에 들르기를 원한다는 첫 번째 단서를 확인할 수 있습니다. 그런데 11월 4일에 교육 시간이 언제 끝나는지가 제시되지 않았으므로 두 번째 지문인 일정표에서 관련 내용을 확인합니다. 'November 4, 9 A.M. – 5 P.M.'에서 11월 4일에 교육이 오전 9시부터 오후 5시까지라는 두 번째 단서를 확인할 수 있습니다.

Mr. Vincent가 11월 4일에 교육생들이 교육 시간이 끝나자마자 그의 부서에 들르기를 원한다는 첫 번째 단서와 11월 4일에 교육이 오전 9시부터 오후 5시까지라는 두 번째 단서를 종합할 때, Mr. Vincent는 교육생들이 오후 5시에 들르기를 원한다는 것을 알 수 있습니다. 따라서 (D) At 5 P.M.이 정답입니다.

패러프레이징
visit 방문하다 → come by 들르다

196-200번은 다음 광고, 양식, 이메일에 관한 문제입니다.

WILLARDS HONORS
925번지 48번가, 샌디에이고, 캘리포니아주 92120

196최고의 트로피, 상패, 메달과 다른 여러 가지 증정물을 원하신다면, 196/200샌디에이고 시내의 Willards Honors를 방문하세요. 저희는 모든 종류의 행사, 의식, 또는 발표를 위한 모든 모양과 크기의 상을 판매합니다. 찾고 계신 것이 공식 증명서라면, 저희는 여러분에게 완벽한 것을 주문 제작해드릴 수 있습니다. 하지만 그게 다가 아닙니다. 저희는 고급 펜, 명함 꽂이, 열쇠고리를 포함한 많은 종류의 선물용품을 가지고 있습니다. 그리고 Willards사는 모든 구매 물품에 무료로 글씨도 새겨드립니다. 또는, 197-B물품당 단 5달러에 여러분의 회사나 단체의 로고를 새기세요!

저희가 취급하는 상품의 견본을 확인하고 비용과 서비스에 대한 세부 사항을 보시려면, www.willardshonors.com을 방문하세요. 또는, 저희 매장 및 전시관에 들르세요. 저희는 매일 오전 10시부터 오후 6시까지 영업합니다.

plaque n. 상패 assorted adj. 여러 가지의
tribute n. 증정물 an array of phr. 여러 종류의
generous adj. 많은, 후한 inscribe v. 새기다
free of charge phr. 무료로 engrave v. 새기다

WILLARDS HONORS	특별 주문 제작 양식
이름	Kathleen Benedict
회사/단체	Schumann 음악 학교
전화	555-9283
이메일	benkat@schumannmusic.edu
제품	Sullivan 메달, 모델 #SM-409

197-B새김

197-B메달 뒤: 학교 로고와 함께 "수상자, Schumann 음악 학교 연례 학생 연주 대회"

198특별 요구 사항

197-A메달은 6월 27일에 있을 저희 행사의 수상자들에게 수여될 것입니다. 198"1위"는 금메달 앞에, "2위"는 은메달에, "입상자"는 세 개의 동메달에 새겨져야 합니다.

customize v. 주문 제작하다 rear n. 뒤쪽; adj. 뒤의
award v. 수여하다 runner-up n. 입상자

수신 고객 서비스 <cservice@willardshonors.com>
발신 Kathleen Benedict <benkat@schumannmusic.edu>
제목 요청
날짜 6월 24일

고객 서비스 담당자분께,

197-D저는 최근에 귀하의 시설에 방문해서 특별 주문 제작 상품을 주문했습니다. 제 동료들 중 한 명은 상에 수상자들의 이름을 새겨도 좋을 것이라고 제안했습니다. 당연히, 저희는 대회가 끝나고 나서야 수상자들의 이름을 알 수 있을 것입니다. 199수상자들의 이름을 나중에 새기는 것이 가능할까요? 200저희 학교는 귀사의 위치로부터 바로 길 건너에 있기 때문에, 언제든 준비가 되면 메달을 가지러 갈 수 있을 것입니다. 추가 비용이 필요하다면 기꺼이 부담하겠습니다.

감사드리며, 답변해주시기 바랍니다.

Kathleen Benedict, 부관리자
Schumann 음악 학교

establishment n. 시설, 기관 colleague n. 동료
naturally adv. 당연히, 자연스레

196. 주제/목적 찾기 문제

문제 광고되고 있는 것은 무엇인가?
(A) 지역 인쇄 회사
(B) 상과 선물 상점
(C) 그래픽 디자인 회사
(D) 문구점

해설 광고되고 있는 것을 묻는 주제 찾기 문제이므로 첫 번째 지문인 광고의 내용을 확인합니다. 광고의 'For the best selection of trophies, plaques, medals, and other assorted tributes, visit Willards Honors in downtown San Diego.'에서 최고의 트로피, 상패, 메달과 다른 여러 가지 증정물을 원한다면 샌디에이고 시내의 Willards Honors를 방문하라고 했으므로 (B) An awards and gift shop이 정답입니다.

패러프레이징
trophies, plaques, medals, and other assorted tributes 트로피, 상패, 메달과 다른 여러 가지 증정물 → awards and gift 상과 선물

어휘 stationery store phr. 문구점

197. Not/True 문제 연계

문제 Ms. Benedict의 주문에 대해 언급된 것은?
(A) 6월 27일에 배달될 것이다.
(B) 각각의 품목은 추가 비용을 발생시킬 것이다.
(C) 전부 지불되었다.
(D) 선택된 모든 것은 온라인으로 구매되었다.

해설 질문의 핵심 어구인 Ms. Benedict's order와 관련된 내용을 지문에서 찾아 각 보기와 대조하는 Not/True 문제이므로, Ms. Benedict가 물품을 주문한 상점의 광고인 첫 번째 지문인 광고, Ms. Benedict의 주문서인 두 번째 지문인 양식, Ms. Benedict가 작성한 세 번째 지문인 이메일 모두를 확

한 권으로 끝내는 해커스 토익 700+ (LC+RC+VOCA)

인합니다. (A)는 양식의 'The medals will be awarded to winners of our event on June 27.'에서 메달이 6월 27일에 있을 행사의 수상자들에게 수여될 것이라고 했지만, 6월 27일에 배달될지는 알 수 없으므로 지문의 내용과 일치하지 않습니다. (B)는 양식의 'Engraving','On rear of medals: ~ along with school logo.'에서 메달 뒤에 학교 로고가 새겨질 것이라는 첫 번째 단서를 확인할 수 있습니다. 그런데 로고를 새기는 비용이 제시되지 않았으므로 광고에서 관련 내용을 확인합니다. 첫 번째 지문인 광고의 'get your company or group logo engraved for only $5 per item'에서 물품당 단 5달러에 회사나 단체의 로고를 새길 수 있다는 두 번째 단서를 확인할 수 있습니다. 메달 뒤에 학교 로고가 새겨질 것이라는 첫 번째 단서와 물품당 단 5달러에 회사나 단체의 로고를 새길 수 있다는 두 번째 단서를 종합할 때, Ms. Benedict가 주문한 각 품목은 추가 비용이 든다는 것을 알 수 있습니다. 따라서 (B) Each item will incur an extra charge가 정답입니다. (C)는 지문에 언급되지 않은 내용입니다. (D)는 이메일의 'I recently visited your establishment and placed an order for some customized items.'에서 자신, 즉 Ms. Benedict가 최근에 시설에 방문해서 특별 주문 제작 상품을 주문했다고 했으므로 지문의 내용과 일치하지 않습니다.

패러프레이징
medals 메달 → item 품목
$5 5달러 → extra charge 추가 비용

어휘 incur v. 발생시키다, (좋지 않은 결과에) 빠지다
in full phr. 전부, 완전히

198. 육하원칙 문제

문제 Willards Honors는 무엇을 하도록 지시받았는가?
(A) 1위 수상자를 위한 트로피를 준비한다
(B) 세 개의 메달에 "입상자"라고 쓴다
(C) 몇 가지 상과 함께 증명서를 제공한다
(D) 제작을 한 달 연기한다

해설 Willards Honors가 무엇(What)을 하도록 지시받았는지를 묻는 육하원칙 문제이므로 질문의 핵심 어구인 Willards Honors been instructed와 관련된 내용이 언급된 두 번째 지문인 양식을 확인합니다. 양식의 'Special instructions', '"First Place" ~ on ~ the gold medal, ~ and "Runner-Up" on the three bronze medals.'에서 특별 요구 사항으로 "1위"는 금메달에, "입상자"는 세 개의 동메달에 새겨져야 한다고 했으므로 (B) Write "Runner-up" on three medals가 정답입니다.

패러프레이징
been instructed 지시받다 → instructions 요구 사항

199. 육하원칙 문제

문제 Ms. Benedict는 무엇을 하고 싶어 하는가?
(A) 대회에 동료를 초대한다
(B) 몇몇 상에 있는 이름을 변경한다
(C) 수상자들에게 상이 보내지게 한다
(D) 상에 추가로 글씨를 새긴다

해설 Ms. Benedict가 무엇(What)을 하고 싶어 하는지를 묻는 육하원칙 문제이므로 질문의 핵심 어구인 Ms. Benedict가 작성한 세 번째 지문인 이메일을 확인합니다. 이메일의 'Would it be possible to have the winners' names engraved at a later time?'에서 수상자들의 이름을 나중에 새기는 것이 가능할지 물었으므로 (D) Add engravings to awards가 정답입니다.

패러프레이징
have ~ names engraved at a later time 이름을 나중에

새기다 → Add extra engravings 추가로 글씨를 새기다

200. 추론 문제 연계

문제 Ms. Benedict에 관해 암시되는 것은?
(A) 최근에 관리직에 임명되었다.
(B) 학교에 비용이 필요 이상으로 청구되었다고 생각한다.
(C) 도시 중심부에 있는 학교에서 일한다.
(D) 수상자들의 이름을 비밀로 유지해야 한다.

해설 세 지문 중 두 지문의 내용을 종합적으로 확인한 후 추론해서 풀어야 하는 연계 문제입니다. 질문의 핵심 어구인 Ms. Benedict가 작성한 세 번째 지문인 이메일을 먼저 확인합니다. 'Our academy is right across the street from your location'에서 자신의 학교는 귀사, 즉 Willards Honors의 위치로부터 바로 길 건너에 있다는 첫 번째 단서를 확인할 수 있습니다. 그런데 Willards Honors가 어디에 있는지가 제시되지 않았으므로 첫 번째 지문인 광고에서 관련 내용을 확인합니다. 'visit Willards Honors in downtown San Diego'에서 샌디에이고 시내의 Willards Honors를 방문하라고 했으므로 Willards Honors가 샌디에이고 시내에 있다는 두 번째 단서를 확인할 수 있습니다.
Ms. Benedict가 일하는 학교가 Willards Honors의 위치로부터 바로 길 건너에 있다는 첫 번째 단서와 Willards Honors가 시내에 있다는 두 번째 단서를 종합할 때, Ms. Benedict가 샌디에이고 시내에 있는 학교에서 일한다는 사실을 추론할 수 있습니다. 따라서 (C) She works at an academy in a city center가 정답입니다.

패러프레이징
downtown 시내의 → in a city center 도시 중심부에 있는

어휘 appoint v. 임명하다, 지명하다

Answer Sheet

LISTENING (PART 1~4)

READING (PART 5~7)

* 답안지 마킹은 **연필**을 사용하시기 바랍니다.
* 문제 풀이 후 본책 p.386에 있는 점수 **환산표**를 확인해보세요.

맞은 문제 개수: _____ /200

한 권으로 끝내는

해커스
토익
700+

LC+RC+ VOCA

실전모의고사

+정답·해석·해설

해커스인강 HackersIngang.com
본 교재 인강·무료 교재 MP3·들으면서 외우는 무료 단어암기자료·
무료 받아쓰기&쉐도잉 워크북·무료 온라인 토익 실전모의고사

해커스토익 Hackers.co.kr
교재 무료 해설·무료 매월 적중예상특강·무료 실시간 토익시험 정답확인/해설강의·무료 매일 실전 LC/RC문제

절취선

한 권으로 끝내는

해커스
토익
700+

LC+RC+ VOCA

개정 2판 7쇄 발행 2025년 1월 20일

개정 2판 1쇄 발행 2022년 1월 3일

지은이	해커스 어학연구소
펴낸곳	㈜해커스 어학연구소
펴낸이	해커스 어학연구소 출판팀

주소	서울특별시 서초구 강남대로61길 23 ㈜해커스 어학연구소
고객센터	02-537-5000
교재 관련 문의	publishing@hackers.com
동영상강의	HackersIngang.com

ISBN	978-89-6542-462-8 (13740)
Serial Number	02-07-01

외국어인강 1위, 해커스인강
HackersIngang.com

해커스인강

· 해커스 토익 스타강사의 **본 교재 인강**
· **무료 교재 MP3** 및 들으면서 외우는 **무료 단어암기자료**
· 단기 리스닝 점수 향상을 위한 **무료 받아쓰기&쉐도잉 워크북**
· 최신 기출유형이 100% 반영된 **무료 온라인 토익 실전모의고사**

영어 전문 포털, 해커스토익
Hackers.co.kr

해커스토익

· **무료 매월 적중예상특강 및 월별 모의토익 서비스**
· **무료 실시간 토익시험 정답확인 및 해설강의**
· 매일 실전 LC/RC 문제 및 토익 보카 TEST 등 **다양한 무료 학습 콘텐츠**

한 권으로 끝내는

해커스
토익
700+

LC+RC+ VOCA

| 정답 및 해설 |

해커스 어학연구소

한 권으로 끝내는
해커스 토익 700+

LC+RC+ VOCA

| 정답 및 해설 |

⛩ 해커스 어학연구소

리스닝 기초 다지기

DAY 01 기초 다지기 1

Course 1 발음이 비슷한 자음 구별하기

HACKERS PRACTICE 🎧 DAY01_04   p.29

01 (A)   **02** (A)   **03** (A)   **04** (B)   **05** (A)
06 open until next Monday
07 found an affordable apartment
08 special reduced rates
09 lake is a very popular
10 spot next to the curb

---

01 🎙️ 캐나다식 발음 / 영국식 발음

I need to <u>file</u> the application forms.

저는 지원서를 제출해야 해요.

application form 지원서, 신청서   file[fail] 제출하다   pile[pail] 쌓다

---

02 🎙️ 미국식 발음 / 호주식 발음

People sometimes <u>bow</u> in order to show respect.

사람들은 때때로 존중을 표하기 위해 인사를 한다.

in order to ~하기 위해   respect[rispékt] 존중, 경의
bow[bau] 인사하다, 허리를 굽히다   vow[vau] 다짐하다, 맹세하다

---

03 🎙️ 영국식 발음 / 캐나다식 발음

The charity organization is concerned about the <u>lack</u> of donations.

그 자선 단체는 기부금이 부족한 것에 대해 걱정한다.

charity[tʃǽrəti] 자선   organization[미 ɔ̀rgənizéiʃən, 영 ɔ̀ːgənaizéiʃən] 단체
concerned about ~에 대해 걱정하는
donation[미 dounéiʃən, 영 dəunéiʃən] 기부(금)
lack[læk] 부족; 모자라다   rack[ræk] 걸이, 선반

---

04 🎙️ 호주식 발음 / 미국식 발음

The <u>copy</u> machine isn't working properly.

그 복사기는 제대로 작동하지 않고 있어요.

properly[미 prápərli, 영 prɔ́pəli] 제대로   coffee[미 kɔ́ːfi, 영 kɔ́fi] 커피
copy[미 kápi, 영 kɔ́pi] 복사

---

05 🎙️ 캐나다식 발음 / 영국식 발음

<u>Bend</u> your knees, lifting your arms over your head.

두 팔을 머리 위로 올리면서, 무릎을 구부리세요.   ⊙

knee[niː] 무릎   lift[lift] 올리다   bend[bend] 구부리다   vend[vend] 팔다

---

06 🎙️ 미국식 발음 / 호주식 발음

This shop won't <u>open until next Monday</u>.

이 가게는 다음 주 월요일이 되어서야 문을 열 거예요.

open[미 óupən, 영 óupən] 문을 열다

---

07 🎙️ 영국식 발음 / 캐나다식 발음

I <u>found an affordable apartment</u> to rent on Oak Street.

저는 Oak가에서 임대하기에 알맞은 가격의 아파트를 찾았어요.

found[faund] 찾았다(find의 과거형), 설립하다
affordable[əfɔ́ːrdəbl] (가격이) 알맞은

---

08 🎙️ 호주식 발음 / 미국식 발음

Do you offer <u>special reduced rates</u> for children under school age?

학교에 들어가기 전 나이대의 아이들에게 특별 할인 요금을 제공하시나요?

offer[미 ɔ́ːfər, 영 ɔ́fə] 제공하다   reduced[ridjúːst] 할인된   rate[reit] 요금

---

09 🎙️ 캐나다식 발음 / 영국식 발음

This <u>lake is a very popular</u> tourist destination during the summer.

이 호수는 여름에 매우 인기 있는 관광지이다.

lake[leik] 호수, 연못   tourist destination 관광지

---

10 🎙️ 미국식 발음 / 호주식 발음

You may park your vehicle in a <u>spot next to the curb</u>.

연석 옆에 있는 자리에 주차하셔도 됩니다.

spot[미 spɑːt, 영 spɔt] 자리, 장소   curb[미 kəːrb, 영 kəːb] 연석; 억제하다

Course 2 발음이 비슷한 모음 구별하기

HACKERS PRACTICE 🎧 DAY01_07   p.31

01 (B)   **02** (A)   **03** (B)   **04** (B)   **05** (A)
06 called for you earlier
07 take the whole day
08 in the second row
09 pick a nearby restaurant
10 take one pill after every meal

DAY 01 기초 다지기 1

Course 1 발음이 비슷한 자음 구별하기

HACKERS PRACTICE 🎧 DAY01_04   p.29

01 (A)   02 (A)   03 (A)   04 (B)   05 (A)
06 open until next Monday
07 found an affordable apartment
08 special reduced rates
09 lake is a very popular
10 spot next to the curb

01 🎧 캐나다식 발음 / 영국식 발음

I need to file the application forms.
저는 지원서를 제출해야 해요.

application form 지원서, 신청서 file[fail] 제출하다 pile[pail] 쌓다

02 🎧 미국식 발음 / 호주식 발음

People sometimes bow in order to show respect.
사람들은 때때로 존중을 표하기 위해 인사를 한다.

in order to ~하기 위해 respect[rispékt] 존중, 경의
bow[bau] 인사하다, 허리를 굽히다 vow[vau] 다짐하다, 맹세하다

03 🎧 영국식 발음 / 캐나다식 발음

The charity organization is concerned about the lack of donations.
그 자선 단체는 기부금이 부족한 것에 대해 걱정한다.

charity[tʃǽrəti] 자선 organization[미 ɔ̀rgənizéiʃən, 영 ɔ̀ːgənaizéiʃən] 단체
concerned about ~에 대해 걱정하는
donation[미 dounéiʃən, 영 dəunéiʃən] 기부(금)
lack[læk] 부족; 모자라다 rack[ræk] 걸이, 선반

04 🎧 호주식 발음 / 미국식 발음

The copy machine isn't working properly.
그 복사기는 제대로 작동하지 않고 있어요.

properly[미 prάpərli, 영 prɔ́pəli] 제대로 coffee[미 kɔ́ːfi, 영 kɔ́fi] 커피
copy[미 kάpi, 영 kɔ́pi] 복사

05 🎧 캐나다식 발음 / 영국식 발음

Bend your knees, lifting your arms over your head.
두 팔을 머리 위로 올리면서, 무릎을 구부리세요.

knee[niː] 무릎 lift[lift] 올리다 bend[bend] 구부리다 vend[vend] 팔다

06 🎧 미국식 발음 / 호주식 발음

This shop won't open until next Monday.
이 가게는 다음 주 월요일이 되어서야 문을 열 거예요.

open[미 óupən, 영 ɔ́upən] 문을 열다

07 🎧 영국식 발음 / 캐나다식 발음

I found an affordable apartment to rent on Oak Street.
저는 Oak가에서 임대하기에 알맞은 가격의 아파트를 찾았어요.

found[faund] 찾았다(find의 과거형), 설립하다
affordable[əfɔ́ːrdəbl] (가격이) 알맞은

08 🎧 호주식 발음 / 미국식 발음

Do you offer special reduced rates for children under school age?
학교에 들어가기 전 나이대의 아이들에게 특별 할인 요금을 제공하시나요?

offer[미 ɔ́ːfər, 영 ɔ́fə] 제공하다 reduced[ridjúːst] 할인된 rate[reit] 요금

09 🎧 캐나다식 발음 / 영국식 발음

This lake is a very popular tourist destination during the summer.
이 호수는 여름에 매우 인기 있는 관광지이다.

lake[leik] 호수, 연못 tourist destination 관광지

10 🎧 미국식 발음 / 호주식 발음

You may park your vehicle in a spot next to the curb.
연석 옆에 있는 자리에 주차하셔도 됩니다.

spot[미 spαːt, 영 spɔt] 자리, 장소 curb[미 kəːrb, 영 kəːb] 연석; 억제하다

Course 2 발음이 비슷한 모음 구별하기

HACKERS PRACTICE 🎧 DAY01_07   p.31

01 (B)   02 (A)   03 (B)   04 (B)   05 (A)
06 called for you earlier
07 take the whole day
08 in the second row
09 pick a nearby restaurant
10 take one pill after every meal

한 권으로 끝내는

해커스 토익 700+

LC+RC+ VOCA

| 정답 및 해설 |

🎓 해커스 어학연구소

한 권으로 끝내는

해커스
토익
700+

LC+RC+ VOCA

| 정답 및 해설 |

해커스 어학연구소

01 🔊 영국식 발음 / 캐나다식 발음

> Did you <u>feel</u> how soft the fabric is?
>
> 이 천이 얼마나 부드러운지 만져보셨나요?

fabric[fǽbrik] 천   fill[fil] 채우다   feel[fiːl] (손가락으로) 만져보다, 느끼다

02 🔊 캐나다식 발음 / 미국식 발음

> You can use the computers in the room down the <u>hall</u> on the right.
>
> 복도 끝의 오른쪽에 있는 방에서 컴퓨터를 사용하실 수 있어요.

hall[hɔːl] 복도   whole[미 houl, 영 həul] 전체

03 🔊 호주식 발음 / 미국식 발음

> Mr. Collins <u>lives</u> close to Waterfront station.
>
> Mr. Collins는 Waterfront 역 근처에 살아요.

leave[liːv] 떠나다   live[liv] 살다

04 🔊 미국식 발음 / 캐나다식 발음

> The storm has destroyed many buildings on the east <u>coast</u>.
>
> 그 폭풍우는 동쪽 해안의 많은 건물들을 훼손했다.

storm[미 stɔːrm, 영 stɔːm] 폭풍우   destroy[distrɔ́i] 훼손하다
cost[미 kɔːst, 영 kɔst] 비용   coast[미 koust, 영 kəust] 해안

05 🔊 캐나다식 발음 / 영국식 발음

> I need to exchange these shoes for larger ones. They don't <u>fit</u> me well.
>
> 저는 이 신발들을 더 큰 것으로 교환해야 해요. 그것들은 저에게 잘 맞지 않아요.

exchange[ikstʃéindʒ] 교환하다   fit[fit] 잘 맞다   feet[fiːt] 발(foot의 복수형)

06 🔊 미국식 발음 / 캐나다식 발음

> One of the managers <u>called for you</u> earlier.
>
> 관리자들 중 한 명이 조금 전에 당신에게 전화했어요.

call[kɔːl] 전화하다

07 🔊 캐나다식 발음 / 미국식 발음

> Traveling to Rome will <u>take the whole day</u>.
>
> 로마로 이동하는 것은 온종일이 걸릴 거예요.

whole[미 houl, 영 həul] 전부의, 전체의

08 🔊 미국식 발음 / 캐나다식 발음

> Do you mean the woman wearing a blue dress <u>in the second row</u>?

⊙

> 두 번째 줄의 파란색 원피스를 입고 있는 여자를 말씀하시는 건가요?
>
> row[미 rou, 영 rəu] 줄, 열

09 🔊 미국식 발음 / 호주식 발음

> I asked my assistant to <u>pick a nearby restaurant</u> for the staff party.
>
> 저는 비서에게 직원 파티를 위해 근처의 음식점을 선택할 것을 요청했어요.

assistant[əsístənt] 비서   pick[pik] 선택하다, 줍다
staff[미 stæf, 영 stɑːf] 직원

10 🔊 영국식 발음 / 캐나다식 발음

> The doctor told me to <u>take one pill after every meal</u> for two weeks.
>
> 의사는 제게 2주 동안 식후에 알약 한 개를 복용할 것을 당부했어요.

pill[pil] 알약   meal[미 miːl, 영 miəl] 식사

HACKERS TEST 🎧 DAY01_08   p.32

01	(A)	02	(A)	03	(A)	04	(B)
05	(A)	06	(A)	07	(A)	08	(B)
09	(A)	10	(B)	11	(A)	12	(A)

01 🔊 호주식 발음

> (A) He is mowing the grass.
> (B) He is holding a glass.

mow[미 mou, 영 məu] (잔디를) 깎다, (풀을) 베다
grass[미 græs, 영 grɑːs] 잔디

해석　(A) 그는 잔디를 깎고 있다.
　　　(B) 그는 유리잔을 들고 있다.

해설　한 남자가 잔디를 깎고 있는 모습을 정확히 묘사한 (A)가 정답입니다. 사진에 있는 grass(잔디)와 발음이 비슷한 glass(유리잔)를 사용하여 혼동을 준 (B)는 오답입니다. 발음이 비슷한 자음인 [r]와 [l] 소리를 구별하여 알아둡니다.

02 🔊 미국식 발음

> (A) The men are pulling suitcases.
> (B) The sidewalk is full of people.

suitcase[súːtkeis] 여행 가방   sidewalk[sáidwɔːk] 보도, 인도
be full of ~으로 가득 차다

해석　(A) 남자들이 여행 가방을 끌고 있다.
　　　(B) 보도가 사람들로 가득 차 있다.

해설　남자들이 여행 가방을 끌고 있는 모습을 정확히 묘사한 (A)가 정답입니다. 사진에 있는 남자들의 동작 pulling(끌고 있다)과 발음이 비슷한 full(가득 찬)을 사용하여 혼동을 준 (B)는 오답입니다. 발음이 비슷한

자음인 [p]와 [f] 소리를 구별하여 알아둡니다.

03 🔊 미국식 발음

(A) A vase has been placed on a cabinet.
(B) Wheels are on the base of the desk.

vase[미 veis, 영 vɑːz] 꽃병　base[beis] (사물의) 맨 아랫부분

해석 (A) 꽃병이 캐비닛 위에 놓여 있다.
(B) 바퀴들이 책상의 맨 아랫부분에 있다.

해설 꽃병이 캐비닛 위에 놓여 있는 모습을 정확히 묘사한 (A)가 정답입니다. 사진에 있는 vase(꽃병)와 발음이 비슷한 base(맨 아랫부분)를 사용하여 혼동을 준 (B)는 오답입니다. 발음이 비슷한 자음인 [v]와 [b] 소리를 구별하여 알아둡니다.

04 🔊 미국식 발음 → 호주식 발음

Who can reach the top shelf?
(A) It's rich with detail.
(B) I think John can.

reach[riːtʃ] 닿다　rich[ritʃ] 풍부한, 부유한　detail[díːteil] 세부 묘사

해석 누가 선반 맨 위 칸에 손이 닿나요?
(A) 그것은 세부 묘사가 풍부해요.
(B) John이 닿는 것 같아요.

해설 선반 맨 위 칸에 손이 닿는 사람을 묻는 질문에 John이 닿는 것 같다고 응답한 (B)가 정답입니다. 질문에서 사용된 reach와 발음이 비슷한 rich를 사용하여 혼동을 준 (A)는 오답입니다. 발음이 비슷한 모음인 [iː]와 [i] 소리를 구별하여 알아둡니다.

05 🔊 캐나다식 발음 → 미국식 발음

Where is the law office?
(A) Just down the street.
(B) It's too low.

law office 법률 사무소, 변호사 사무소　low[미 lou, 영 ləu] 낮은

해석 법률 사무소는 어디에 있나요?
(A) 바로 길 아래쪽에요.
(B) 그것은 너무 낮아요.

해설 법률 사무소의 위치를 묻는 질문에 길 아래쪽에 있다고 응답한 (A)가 정답입니다. 질문에서 사용된 law와 발음이 비슷한 low를 사용하여 혼동을 준 (B)는 오답입니다. 발음이 비슷한 모음인 [ɔː]와 [ou] 소리를 구별하여 알아둡니다.

06 🔊 영국식 발음 → 캐나다식 발음

Are you fine with going on Friday?
(A) I prefer Wednesday.
(B) It is made of pine.

fine[fain] 괜찮은　prefer[미 prifɚ́r, 영 prifɔ́ː] 더 좋아하다, 선호하다
be made of ~으로 만들어지다　pine[pain] 소나무

해석 금요일에 가는 것이 괜찮은가요?
(A) 저는 수요일이 더 좋아요.
(B) 그것은 소나무로 만들어졌어요.

해설 금요일에 가는 것이 괜찮은지를 묻는 질문에 수요일이 더 좋다고 응답한 (A)가 정답입니다. 질문에서 사용된 fine과 발음이 비슷한 pine을 사용하여 혼동을 준 (B)는 오답입니다. 발음이 비슷한 자음인 [f]와 [p] 소리를 구별하여 알아둡니다.

07 🔊 캐나다식 발음 → 미국식 발음

Will you apply for the bank loan?
(A) No, I decided not to.
(B) The lawn needs to be watered.

apply for ~을 신청하다　loan[미 loun, 영 ləun] 대출　lawn[lɔːn] 잔디
water[미 wɔ́ːtər, 영 wɔ́ːtə] 물을 주다

해석 당신은 은행 대출을 신청하실 건가요?
(A) 아니요, 저는 그렇게 하지 않기로 결정했어요.
(B) 잔디에 물을 줘야 해요.

해설 은행 대출을 신청할 것인지를 묻는 질문에 하지 않기로 결정했다고 응답한 (A)가 정답입니다. 질문에서 사용된 loan과 발음이 비슷한 lawn을 사용하여 혼동을 준 (B)는 오답입니다. 발음이 비슷한 모음인 [ou]와 [ɔː] 소리를 구별하여 알아둡니다.

08 🔊 미국식 발음 → 호주식 발음

Why do you collect stamps?
(A) This is the correct address.
(B) It's my hobby.

collect[kəlékt] 수집하다　stamp[stæmp] 우표　correct[kərékt] 정확한
address[미 ǽdres, 영 ədrés] 주소

해석 당신은 왜 우표를 수집하나요?
(A) 이것은 정확한 주소예요.
(B) 그것은 제 취미예요.

해설 우표를 수집하는 이유를 묻는 질문에 그것이 자신의 취미라고 응답한 (B)가 정답입니다. 질문에서 사용된 collect와 발음이 비슷한 correct를 사용하여 혼동을 준 (A)는 오답입니다. 발음이 비슷한 자음인 [l]와 [r] 소리를 구별하여 알아둡니다.

09 🔊 영국식 발음 → 캐나다식 발음

Didn't you want to purchase a fan?
(A) Yes, but I don't need one anymore.
(B) This pan is on sale.

fan[fæn] 선풍기　pan[pæn] 프라이팬　on sale 할인 판매 중인

해석 선풍기를 사고 싶어 하지 않으셨나요?
(A) 네, 하지만 저는 더 이상 선풍기가 필요하지 않아요.
(B) 이 프라이팬은 할인 판매 중이에요.

해설 선풍기를 사고 싶어 하지 않았는지를 묻는 질문에 사고 싶었지만 더 이상 필요하지 않다고 응답한 (A)가 정답입니다. 질문에서 사용된 fan과 발음이 비슷한 pan을 사용하여 혼동을 준 (B)는 오답입니다. 발음이 비슷한 자음인 [f]와 [p] 소리를 구별하여 알아둡니다.

10 🔊 캐나다식 발음 → 미국식 발음

Why don't we order some cold drinks?
(A) No, Steve called me yesterday.
(B) Yes, let's do that.

cold[미 kould, 영 kəuld] 차가운　call[kɔːl] 전화하다

해석 차가운 음료를 좀 주문하는 게 어때요?
(A) 아니요, Steve는 어제 저에게 전화했어요.
(B) 네, 그럽시다.

해설 차가운 음료를 주문하는 게 어떤지를 묻는 질문에 그러자고 응답한 (B)가 정답입니다. 질문에서 사용된 cold와 발음이 비슷한 called를 사용하여 혼동을 준 (A)는 오답입니다. 발음이 비슷한 모음인 [ou]와 [ɔː] 소리를 구별하여 알아둡니다.

11 🎙 미국식 발음 → 호주식 발음

Should I print the list or e-mail it?
(A) Give me a hard copy.
(B) It is the least expensive item.

list[list] 목록   hard copy 출력된 자료
least[liːst] 가장 ~이 아니게, 최소로

해석 제가 목록을 인쇄해야 하나요, 아니면 그것을 이메일로 보내야 하나요?
(A) 출력된 자료로 한 부 주세요.
(B) 그것은 가장 비싸지 않은 제품이에요.

해설 목록을 인쇄해야 하는지, 아니면 이메일로 보내야 하는지를 묻는 질문에 출력된 자료로 달라고 응답한 (A)가 정답입니다. 질문에서 사용된 list와 발음이 비슷한 least를 사용하여 혼동을 준 (B)는 오답입니다. 발음이 비슷한 모음인 [i]와 [iː] 소리를 구별하여 알아둡니다.

12 🎙 캐나다식 발음 → 미국식 발음

I bought a loaf of bread at the bakery.
(A) Put it on the counter.
(B) We're going by boat.

loaf[미 louf, 영 ləuf] 덩어리   counter[미 káuntər, 영 káuntə] 조리대

해석 제가 빵집에서 빵 한 덩어리를 사 왔어요.
(A) 조리대 위에 두세요.
(B) 우리는 배로 갈 거예요.

해설 빵집에서 빵 한 덩어리를 사 왔다는 말에 조리대 위에 두라고 응답한 (A)가 정답입니다. 질문에서 사용된 bought와 발음이 비슷한 boat를 사용하여 혼동을 준 (B)는 오답입니다. 발음이 비슷한 모음인 [ɔː]와 [ou] 소리를 구별하여 알아둡니다.

DAY 02 기초 다지기 2

Course 1 연음 듣기

HACKERS PRACTICE 🎧 DAY02_04   p.35

01	hard time
02	find out
03	a lot of
04	meet a client
05	last time
06	depend on their parents
07	pick it up for you
08	checked out of the hotel
09	staff lounge for a break
10	wear a uniform at all times

01 🎙 캐나다식 발음 / 영국식 발음

hard time 어려움, 힘든 시기

02 🎙 미국식 발음 / 캐나다식 발음

find out 발견하다

03 🎙 캐나다식 발음 / 미국식 발음

a lot of 많은

04 🎙 미국식 발음 / 캐나다식 발음

meet a client 고객을 만나다

05 🎙 호주식 발음 / 미국식 발음

last time 지난번, 마지막

06 🎙 캐나다식 발음 / 영국식 발음

Children have to depend on their parents.
아이들은 부모님에게 의존해야 한다.

07 🎙 미국식 발음 / 캐나다식 발음

I will pick it up for you.
제가 당신을 위해 그것을 가져다드릴게요.

08 🎙 캐나다식 발음 / 미국식 발음

We checked out of the hotel at 11 A.M.
우리는 그 호텔에서 오전 11시에 나왔어요.

09 🔊 미국식 발음 / 캐나다식 발음

Let's go to the <u>staff lounge</u> for a break.
휴식을 위해 직원 휴게실로 갑시다.

10 🔊 캐나다식 발음 / 미국식 발음

Employees must <u>wear a uniform</u> at all times.
직원들은 항상 유니폼을 착용해야 합니다.

Course 2 끊어 듣기

HACKERS PRACTICE 🎧 DAY02_07   p.37

01 for the party
02 from Tokyo tomorrow
03 that Anne should be promoted
04 When the CEO comes
05 If the weather is nice
06 While waiting for the bus, by the bus stop
07 Since his shift starts early, at six o'clock
08 Because his car broke down, over the bridge
09 As the rooms were quite large, with my friend
10 Although it departed late, at its final destination

01 🔊 캐나다식 발음 / 영국식 발음

I bought snacks <u>for the party</u>.
저는 파티를 위해 간식을 샀어요.

02 🔊 미국식 발음 / 호주식 발음

He will arrive <u>from Tokyo tomorrow</u>.
그는 내일 도쿄에서 도착할 거예요.

03 🔊 영국식 발음 / 캐나다식 발음

It is obvious <u>that Anne should be promoted</u>.
Anne이 승진해야 한다는 것은 분명해요.

04 🔊 호주식 발음 / 미국식 발음

<u>When the CEO comes</u>, the meeting will begin.
최고 경영자가 오면, 회의가 시작될 거예요.

05 🔊 캐나다식 발음 / 영국식 발음

<u>If the weather is nice</u>, let's go on a picnic.
날씨가 좋으면, 소풍을 갑시다.

06 🔊 미국식 발음 / 호주식 발음

<u>While waiting for the bus</u>, I stood <u>by the bus stop</u>.
버스를 기다리는 동안, 저는 버스 정류장 옆에 서 있었어요.

07 🔊 영국식 발음 / 캐나다식 발음

<u>Since his shift starts early</u>, he wakes up <u>at six o'clock</u>.
그의 근무 시간은 일찍 시작되어서, 그는 6시 정각에 일어나요.

08 🔊 호주식 발음 / 미국식 발음

<u>Because his car broke down</u>, he walked <u>over the bridge</u>.
그의 차가 고장이 나서, 그는 다리 위로 걸어갔어요.

09 🔊 캐나다식 발음 / 영국식 발음

<u>As the rooms were quite large</u>, I shared one <u>with my friend</u>.
방들이 상당히 넓어서, 저는 제 친구와 하나를 같이 사용했어요.

10 🔊 미국식 발음 / 호주식 발음

<u>Although it departed late</u>, the train arrived <u>at its final destination</u> on time.
늦게 출발했음에도 불구하고, 기차는 종착역에 제시간에 도착했어요.

HACKERS TEST 🎧 DAY02_08   p.38

01 (B)	02 (A)	03 (A)	04 (A)
05 (A)	06 (A)	07 (A)	08 (A)
09 (A)	10 (A)	11 (B)	12 (A)

01 🔊 캐나다식 발음

(A) The man is carrying a toolbox up a ladder.
(B) The man is wearing a helmet at a construction site.

carry [kǽri] 나르다   **toolbox** [미 túːlbɑːks, 영 túːlbɔks] 공구 상자
construction [kənstrʌ́kʃən] 공사   **site** [sait] 현장

해석 (A) 남자는 사다리 위로 공구 상자를 나르고 있다.
　　 (B) 남자는 공사 현장에서 안전모를 쓰고 있다.

해설 공사 현장에 있는 한 남자가 안전모를 쓰고 있는 모습을 정확히 묘사한 (B)가 정답입니다. carrying(나르고 있다)은 남자의 동작과 무관하므로 (A)는 오답입니다.

02 🔊 미국식 발음

(A) A guitar has been placed on the man's leg.
(B) A woman is picking up an instrument.

be placed on ~ 위에 놓이다   **pick up** ~을 들어 올리다
instrument [ínstrəmənt] 악기

해석 (A) 기타가 남자의 다리 위에 놓여 있다.
　　 (B) 한 여자가 악기를 들어 올리고 있다.

해설 기타가 남자의 다리 위에 놓여 있는 모습을 정확히 묘사한 (A)가 정답입

니다. 사진에 기타를 들어 올리는 여자가 없으므로 (B)는 오답입니다.

03 🔊 영국식 발음

> (A) Clothing items have been put on display.
> (B) A table is leaning against a rack.

> on display 진열된, 전시된　lean against ~에 기대다
> rack[ræk] (옷 등의) 걸이, 선반

해석　(A) 의류 상품들이 진열되어 있다.
　　　(B) 탁자가 옷걸이에 기대 있다.

해설　의류 상품들이 진열되어 있는 모습을 정확히 묘사한 (A)가 정답입니다. 탁자가 옷걸이에 기대 있는 것이 아니라 바닥에 세워져 있으므로 (B)는 오답입니다.

04 🔊 캐나다식 발음 → 영국식 발음

> Who owns that gas station?
> (A) I think Bob Watson does.
> (B) I have to buy gas.

> own[미 oun, 영 əun] 소유하다　gas station 주유소

해석　그 주유소는 누구의 소유인가요?
　　　(A) Bob Watson인 것 같아요.
　　　(B) 저는 가스를 사야 해요.

해설　주유소가 누구의 소유인지를 묻는 질문에 Bob Watson인 것 같다고 응답한 (A)가 정답입니다. 질문과 관련이 없는 가스를 사야 한다는 내용으로 응답한 (B)는 오답입니다.

05 🔊 미국식 발음 → 호주식 발음

> Where's your office building?
> (A) Near Bedford Station.
> (B) At 8 A.M.

해석　당신의 사무실 건물은 어디인가요?
　　　(A) Bedford 역 근처요.
　　　(B) 오전 8시에요.

해설　사무실 건물이 어딘지를 묻는 질문에 Bedford 역 근처라고 응답한 (A)가 정답입니다. 질문과 관련이 없는 오전 8시라는 내용으로 응답한 (B)는 오답입니다.

06 🔊 캐나다식 발음 → 미국식 발음

> When will your friend arrive?
> (A) In about an hour.
> (B) He's from Boston.

> arrive[əráiv] 도착하다

해석　당신의 친구는 언제 도착하나요?
　　　(A) 한 시간쯤 뒤에요.
　　　(B) 그는 보스턴 출신이에요.

해설　친구가 언제 도착하는지를 묻는 질문에 한 시간쯤 뒤라고 응답한 (A)가 정답입니다. 질문과 관련이 없는 그가 보스턴 출신이라는 내용으로 응답한 (B)는 오답입니다.

07 🔊 캐나다식 발음 → 영국식 발음

> Could you call me back once you decide?
> (A) Of course. I'll do that.
> (B) He provided some information.

> once[wʌns] ~하면, ~하자마자　decide[disáid] 결정을 내리다

해석　결정을 내리시면 제게 다시 전화해주시겠어요?
　　　(A) 물론이죠. 그럴게요.
　　　(B) 그는 몇몇 정보를 제공했어요.

해설　결정을 내리면 다시 전화해주겠냐는 질문에 그렇게 하겠다고 응답한 (A)가 정답입니다. 질문과 관련이 없는 그가 몇몇 정보를 제공했다는 내용으로 응답한 (B)는 오답입니다.

08 🔊 미국식 발음 → 캐나다식 발음

> How can we get to the mall?
> (A) Go straight for two blocks.
> (B) We can't give up.

> give up 포기하다

해석　쇼핑몰로 어떻게 가야 하나요?
　　　(A) 두 블록 직진하세요.
　　　(B) 우리는 포기할 수 없어요.

해설　쇼핑몰로 가는 방법을 묻는 질문에 두 블록 직진하라고 응답한 (A)가 정답입니다. 질문과 관련이 없는 우리는 포기할 수 없다는 내용으로 응답한 (B)는 오답입니다.

09 🔊 호주식 발음 → 미국식 발음

> Did you park by the entrance?
> (A) Yes. Right over there.
> (B) He entered the building.

> entrance[éntrəns] 출입구, 문　enter[미 éntər, 영 éntə] 들어가다

해석　출입구 옆에 주차하셨나요?
　　　(A) 네. 바로 저쪽이요.
　　　(B) 그는 건물로 들어갔어요.

해설　출입구 옆에 주차했는지를 묻는 질문에 그렇다고 응답한 (A)가 정답입니다. 질문과 관련이 없는 그가 건물로 들어갔다는 내용으로 응답한 (B)는 오답입니다.

10 🔊 캐나다식 발음 → 영국식 발음

> Which subway station is closest to city hall?
> (A) You should get off at the next stop.
> (B) I have a long commute.

> commute[kəmjú:t] 통근 거리

해석　어느 지하철역이 시청에서 가장 가까운가요?
　　　(A) 다음 역에서 내리셔야 해요.
　　　(B) 저는 통근 거리가 멀어요.

해설　어느 지하철역이 시청에서 가장 가까운지를 묻는 질문에 다음 역에서 내려야 한다고 응답한 (A)가 정답입니다. 질문과 관련이 없는 통근 거리가 멀다는 내용으로 응답한 (B)는 오답입니다.

> We can order now since everyone's here, right?
> (A) Let me pay the bill.
> **(B) No, Beth is joining us as well.**
>
> bill[bil] 계산서, 청구서

해석 모두가 이곳에 왔으니 이제 주문을 해도 되겠네요, 그렇죠?
(A) 제가 계산서 비용을 지불할게요.
(B) 아니요, Beth도 우리와 합류할 거예요.

해설 모두 이곳에 왔으니 주문을 해도 되는지를 묻는 질문에 Beth도 합류
할 것이니 주문하면 안 된다고 응답한 (B)가 정답입니다. 질문과 관련
이 없는 자신이 계산서 비용을 지불하겠다는 내용으로 응답한 (A)는
오답입니다.

> I assume you made an airline reservation for tomorrow.
> **(A) I already have a seat on the early flight.**
> (B) I was staying at the Lamei Hotel.
>
> assume[미 əsú:m, 영 əsjú:m] 생각하다   airline[미 érlain, 영 éəlain] 항공

해석 저는 당신이 내일 항공편을 예약하셨을 거라고 생각해요.
(A) 저는 이미 이른 시간대의 비행기에 좌석이 있어요.
(B) 저는 Lamei 호텔에서 머물고 있었어요.

해설 상대방이 내일 항공편을 예약했을 거라고 생각한다는 말에 이미 이른
시간대의 비행기에 좌석이 있다고 응답한 (A)가 정답입니다. 질문과
관련이 없는 Lamei 호텔에서 머물고 있었다는 내용으로 응답한 (B)
는 오답입니다.

DAY 03 사람 중심 사진

Course 1 1인 사진

HACKERS PRACTICE 🎧 DAY03_02 p.43

01 (B)	02 (A)	03 (C)	04 (D)

01 🎧 캐나다식 발음 / 미국식 발음

(A) He is taking off a helmet.
(B) He is carrying a ladder.
(C) He is opening a door.
(D) He is fastening a tool belt.

---

take off ~을 벗다 ladder[미 lǽdər, 영 lǽdə] 사다리
fasten[미 fǽsn, 영 fáːsn] 매다 tool belt 공구 벨트

해석 (A) 그는 헬멧을 벗고 있다.
(B) 그는 사다리를 나르고 있다.
(C) 그는 문을 열고 있다.
(D) 그는 공구 벨트를 매고 있다.

해설 한 남자가 사다리를 나르고 있는 모습을 나타내는 1인 사진입니다.
(A) [×] 남자가 헬멧을 쓰고 있는 상태인데 벗고 있다는 동작으로 잘 못 묘사했으므로 오답입니다.
(B) [○] 남자가 사다리를 나르고 있는 모습을 정확히 묘사한 정답입니다.
(C) [×] opening a door(문을 열고 있다)는 남자의 동작과 무관하므 로 오답입니다.
(D) [×] fastening(매고 있다)은 남자의 동작과 무관하므로 오답입니 다. 사진에 있는 공구 벨트(tool belt)를 사용하여 혼동을 주 었습니다.

02 🎧 호주식 발음 / 영국식 발음

(A) He is using a power tool.
(B) He is holding a tire.
(C) He is looking at the scenery.
(D) He is driving a car.

---

power tool 전동 공구 scenery[síːnəri] 풍경

해석 (A) 그는 전동 공구를 사용하고 있다.
(B) 그는 타이어를 들고 있다.
(C) 그는 풍경을 바라보고 있다.
(D) 그는 차를 운전하고 있다.

해설 한 남자가 전동 공구를 사용하여 타이어를 수리하고 있는 모습을 나타 내는 1인 사진입니다.
(A) [○] 남자가 전동 공구를 사용하고 있는 모습을 정확히 묘사한 정 답입니다.
(B) [×] 남자가 타이어를 들고 있는 것이 아니라 전동 공구를 들고 있 으므로 오답입니다. 사진에 있는 타이어(tire)를 사용하여 혼 동을 주었습니다.

(C) [×] looking at the scenery(풍경을 바라보고 있다)는 남자의 동 작과 무관하므로 오답입니다.
(D) [×] driving(운전하고 있다)은 남자의 동작과 무관하므로 오답입 니다. 사진에 있는 차(car)를 사용하여 혼동을 주었습니다.

03 🎧 영국식 발음 / 캐나다식 발음

(A) Some flowerpots are being moved.
(B) She is rolling up her sleeves.
(C) Some plants are being watered.
(D) She is filling up a watering can.

---

flowerpot[fláuərpɑ̀ːt] 화분 roll up ~을 걷어 올리다
sleeve[sliːv] (옷의) 소매 plant[미 plænt, 영 plɑːnt] 식물; 심다
water[미 wɔ́ːtər, 영 wɔ́ːtə] 물을 주다
fill up ~을 채우다 watering can 물뿌리개

해석 (A) 몇몇 화분들이 옮겨지고 있다.
(B) 그녀는 소매를 걷어 올리고 있다.
(C) 몇몇 식물들에 물을 주고 있다.
(D) 그녀는 물뿌리개를 채우고 있다.

해설 한 여자가 물뿌리개로 식물들에 물을 주고 있는 모습을 나타내는 1인 사진입니다.
(A) [×] 사진에서 화분을 확인할 수 없으므로 오답입니다.
(B) [×] 사진에서 여자의 옷에 소매(sleeves)가 없고, rolling up(걷어 올리고 있다)은 여사의 동작과 무관하므로 오답입니다.
(C) [○] 식물들에 물을 주고 있는 모습을 가장 잘 묘사한 정답입니다.
(D) [×] filling up(채우고 있다)은 여자의 동작과 무관하므로 오답입니 다. 사진에 있는 물뿌리개(watering can)를 사용하여 혼동을 주었습니다.

04 🎧 호주식 발음 / 미국식 발음

(A) The man is reading a newspaper.
(B) A book is being placed on the table.
(C) A waiter is removing a cup.
(D) The man is wearing a pair of glasses.

---

place[pleis] 놓다 remove[rimúːv] 치우다

해석 (A) 남자는 신문을 읽고 있다.
(B) 책이 테이블 위에 놓여지고 있다.
(C) 종업원이 컵을 치우고 있다.
(D) 남자는 안경을 쓰고 있다.

해설 한 남자가 테이블에 앉아서 책을 들고 있는 모습을 나타내는 1인 사진 입니다.
(A) [×] 사진에 신문(newspaper)이 없으므로 오답입니다. The man is reading(남자가 읽고 있다)까지만 듣고 정답으로 선택하지 않도록 주의합니다.
(B) [×] 남자가 책을 들고 있는데 책이 테이블 위에 놓여지고 있다고 잘못 묘사했으므로 오답입니다.
(C) [×] 사진에 컵을 치우고 있는 종업원(waiter)이 없으므로 오답입 니다.

(D) [○] 남자가 안경을 쓴 모습을 정확히 묘사한 정답입니다.

Course 2 2인 이상 사진

HACKERS PRACTICE ∩ DAY03_04
p.45

01 (D)	02 (D)	03 (B)	04 (C)

01

(A) People are chatting indoors.
(B) A lamppost has been installed near some trees.
(C) Bushes are being cut in the woods.
(D) People are resting on a bench.

chat[tʃæt] 이야기하다 lamppost[미 læmppoust, 영 læmppəust] 가로등
bush[buʃ] 관목

해석 (A) 사람들이 실내에서 이야기하고 있다.
(B) 가로등이 나무들 옆에 설치되어 있다.
(C) 관목들이 숲속에서 베어지고 있다.
(D) 사람들이 벤치에서 쉬고 있다.

해설 두 여자가 야외에서 벤치에 앉아 있는 모습을 나타내는 2인 이상 사진입니다.
(A) [×] 사진의 장소가 실내(indoors)가 아니므로 오답입니다.
(B) [×] 사진에서 가로등(lamppost)을 확인할 수 없으므로 오답입니다. 사진에 있는 나무들(trees)을 사용하여 혼동을 주었습니다.
(C) [×] 사진에서 베어지고 있는 관목들(Bushes)을 확인할 수 없으므로 오답입니다.
(D) [○] 두 여자가 벤치에 앉아 쉬고 있는 모습을 가장 잘 묘사한 정답입니다.

02

(A) One of the men is approaching a cash register.
(B) One of the men is tying an apron.
(C) One of the men is selecting some groceries.
(D) One of the men is holding some products.

approach[미 əpróutʃ, 영 əpróutʃ] 다가가다, 접근하다
cash register 계산대 tie[tai] 매다 apron[éiprən] 앞치마
select[silékt] 고르다, 선택하다 grocery[미 gróusəri, 영 gróusəri] 식료품

해석 (A) 남자들 중 한 명이 계산대로 다가가고 있다.
(B) 남자들 중 한 명이 앞치마를 매고 있다.
(C) 남자들 중 한 명이 식료품을 고르고 있다.
(D) 남자들 중 한 명이 제품들을 들고 있다.

해설 두 남자가 상점에 있는 모습을 나타내는 2인 이상 사진입니다.
(A) [×] 사진에서 한 남자가 계산대로 다가가고 있는지 알 수 없으므로 오답입니다.
(B) [×] 한 남자가 이미 앞치마를 매고 있는 상태인데 매고 있다는 동작으로 잘못 묘사했으므로 오답입니다.
(C) [×] 사진에 식료품(groceries)이 없으므로 오답입니다.
(D) [○] 한 남자가 제품들을 들고 있는 모습을 정확히 묘사한 정답입니다.

03

(A) A woman is picking up a glass.
(B) A woman is ordering food.
(C) A server is wiping a table.
(D) A man is eating a meal.

pick up ~을 들어 올리다

해석 (A) 한 여자가 유리컵을 들어 올리고 있다.
(B) 한 여자가 음식을 주문하고 있다.
(C) 종업원이 테이블을 닦고 있다.
(D) 한 남자가 식사를 하고 있다.

해설 식당에 두 남녀가 앉아 있고 한 남자가 테이블 옆에 서 있는 모습을 나타내는 2인 이상 사진입니다.
(A) [×] 여자가 유리컵을 들어 올리고 있는 것이 아니라 메뉴판을 들고 있으므로 오답입니다. A woman is picking up(여자가 들어 올리고 있다)까지만 듣고 정답으로 선택하지 않도록 주의합니다.
(B) [○] 음식을 주문하고 있는 여자의 모습을 가장 잘 묘사한 정답입니다.
(C) [×] wiping a table(테이블을 닦고 있다)은 종업원의 동작과 무관하므로 오답입니다.
(D) [×] 사진에 식사를 하고 있는(eating a meal) 남자가 없으므로 오답입니다.

04

(A) They are folding a piece of paper.
(B) They are walking next to each other.
(C) They are reviewing a document.
(D) They are putting on safety gear.

fold[미 fould, 영 fəuld] 접다 review[rivjú:] 검토하다
safety gear 안전 장비

해석 (A) 그들은 종이 한 장을 접고 있다.
(B) 그들은 나란히 걷고 있다.
(C) 그들은 서류를 검토하고 있다.
(D) 그들은 안전 장비를 착용하고 있다.

해설 남자들이 안전모를 착용한 채 종이를 보고 있는 모습을 나타내는 2인 이상 사진입니다.
(A) [×] folding(접고 있다)은 남자들의 동작과 무관하므로 오답입니다.
(B) [×] walking(걷고 있다)은 남자들의 동작과 무관하므로 오답입니다.
(C) [○] 남자들이 서류를 검토하고 있는 모습을 가장 잘 묘사한 정답입니다.
(D) [×] putting on(착용하고 있다)은 남자들의 동작과 무관하므로 오답입니다. 장비를 착용한 상태를 나타내는 wearing과 착용하고 있는 동작을 나타내는 putting on을 혼동하지 않도록 주의합니다.

HACKERS TEST ∩ DAY03_05
p.46

01 (B)	02 (D)	03 (B)	04 (A)
05 (B)	06 (C)		

01 <img_1 /> 캐나다식 발음

(A) A woman is strolling in the park.
(B) A woman is painting on a pad.
(C) Pieces of wood are being thrown away.
(D) A camera is being set up on the field.

stroll[미 stroul, 영 strəul] 산책하다　pad[pæd] 판지　field[fi:ld] 들판

해석　(A) 한 여자가 공원에서 산책하고 있다.
　　　(B) 한 여자가 판지 위에 물감을 칠하고 있다.
　　　(C) 나무토막들이 버려지고 있다.
　　　(D) 카메라가 들판 위에 세워지고 있다.

해설　한 여자가 들판에서 물감을 칠하고 있는 모습을 나타내는 1인 사진입니다.
　　　(A) [×] strolling(산책하고 있다)은 여자의 동작과 무관하므로 오답입니다.
　　　(B) [○] 판지 위에 물감을 칠하고 있는 여자의 모습을 정확히 묘사한 정답입니다.
　　　(C) [×] 사진에서 나무토막들(Pieces of wood)을 확인할 수 없으므로 오답입니다.
　　　(D) [×] 사진에 카메라(camera)가 없으므로 오답입니다. 사진의 장소인 들판(field)을 사용하여 혼동을 주었습니다.

02  미국식 발음

(A) A man is organizing items on a display shelf.
(B) A woman is touching a screen.
(C) A woman is paying for merchandise.
(D) A man is handling an electronic device.

organize[미 ɔ́:rgənàiz, 영 ɔ́:gənàiz] 정리하다　display[displéi] 진열, 전시　merchandise[미 mə́:rtʃəndàiz, 영 mə́:tʃəndàiz] 제품　handle[hǽndl] 들다, 만지다　electronic[미 ilèktrá:nik, 영 èlektrɔ́nik] 전자의

해석　(A) 한 남자가 진열대 위에 제품들을 정리하고 있다.
　　　(B) 한 여자가 화면을 만지고 있다.
　　　(C) 한 여자가 제품의 비용을 지불하고 있다.
　　　(D) 한 남자가 전자 기기를 들고 있다.

해설　한 남자가 전자 기기를 들고 있고 두 남녀가 그것을 보고 있는 모습을 나타내는 2인 이상 사진입니다.
　　　(A) [×] organizing(정리하고 있다)은 남자들의 동작과 무관하므로 오답입니다.
　　　(B) [×] touching(만지고 있다)은 여자의 동작과 무관합니다. 사진에 있는 화면(screen)을 사용하여 혼동을 주었습니다.
　　　(C) [×] paying(비용을 지불하고 있다)은 여자의 동작과 무관하므로 오답입니다. 사진에 있는 제품(merchandise)을 사용하여 혼동을 주었습니다.
　　　(D) [○] 한 남자가 전자 기기를 들고 있는 모습을 정확히 묘사한 정답입니다.

03 호주식 발음

(A) She is typing on a keyboard.
(B) She is seated in front of a computer monitor.
(C) She is locking a drawer.
(D) She is writing on a notepad.

○

lock[미 lɑ:k, 영 lɔk] 잠그다　drawer[미 drɔːr, 영 drɔːr] 서랍　notepad[미 nóutpæd, 영 nə́utpæd] 메모장

해석　(A) 그녀는 키보드로 타자를 치고 있다.
　　　(B) 그녀는 컴퓨터 모니터 앞에 앉아 있다.
　　　(C) 그녀는 서랍을 잠그고 있다.
　　　(D) 그녀는 메모장에 글을 쓰고 있다.

해설　한 여자가 컴퓨터 앞에 앉아서 통화를 하고 있는 모습을 나타내는 1인 사진입니다.
　　　(A) [×] typing(타자를 치고 있다)은 여자의 동작과 무관하므로 오답입니다. 사진에 있는 keyboard(키보드)를 사용하여 혼동을 주었습니다.
　　　(B) [○] 컴퓨터 모니터 앞에 앉아 있는 여자의 모습을 정확히 묘사한 정답입니다.
　　　(C) [×] locking(잠그고 있다)은 여자의 동작과 무관하므로 오답입니다.
　　　(D) [×] writing(글을 쓰고 있다)은 여자의 동작과 무관하므로 오답입니다.

04 <img_2 /> 영국식 발음

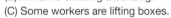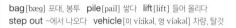

(A) Some bags are piled on top of each other.
(B) A man is entering a building.
(C) Some workers are lifting boxes.
(D) A man is stepping out of a vehicle.

bag[bæg] 포대, 봉투　pile[pail] 쌓다　lift[lift] 들어 올리다　step out ~에서 나오다　vehicle[미 víːikəl, 영 víəkəl] 차량, 탈것

해석　(A) 포대들이 차곡차곡 쌓여 있다.
　　　(B) 한 남자가 건물로 들어가고 있다.
　　　(C) 인부들이 상자들을 들어 올리고 있다.
　　　(D) 한 남자가 차량에서 나오고 있다.

해설　포대들이 쌓여 있는 곳에서 한 남자가 지게차에 타고 있는 모습을 나타내는 1인 사진입니다.
　　　(A) [○] 포대들이 차곡차곡 쌓여 있는 모습을 정확히 묘사한 정답입니다.
　　　(B) [×] entering(들어가고 있다)은 남자의 동작과 무관하므로 오답입니다.
　　　(C) [×] 남자가 지게차를 타고 있는 모습에서 연상할 수 있는 lifting boxes(상자들을 들어 올리고 있다)를 사용하여 혼동을 준 오답입니다.
　　　(D) [×] 남자가 차량 안에 있는 상태인데 차량에서 나오고 있다는 동작으로 잘못 묘사했으므로 오답입니다.

05 캐나다식 발음

(A) People are boarding an airplane.
(B) A man is pulling his luggage.
(C) A man is unpacking his suitcase.
(D) People are lined up by a plane.

board[미 bɔːrd, 영 bɔːd] 탑승하다　luggage[lʌ́gidʒ] 짐, 수화물　unpack[미 ʌ̀npǽk, 영 ʌ́npæ̀k] (짐 등을) 풀다　suitcase[súːtkeis] 여행 가방　line[lain] 줄을 서다

해석　(A) 사람들이 비행기에 탑승하고 있다.
　　　(B) 한 남자가 그의 짐을 끌고 있다.
　　　(C) 한 남자가 그의 여행 가방을 풀고 있다.
　　　(D) 사람들이 비행기 옆에 줄을 서 있다.

PART 1

한 권으로 끝내는 해커스 토익 700+ (LC+RC+VOCA)

해설 여러 사람들이 공항에 있는 모습을 나타내는 2인 이상 사진입니다.
(A) [x] 사진에 비행기(airplane)가 없으므로 오답입니다. 사람들이 공항에 있는 모습에서 연상할 수 있는 boarding an airplane (비행기에 탑승하고 있다)을 사용하여 혼동을 주었습니다.
(B) [o] 짐을 끌고 있는 남자의 모습을 정확히 묘사한 정답입니다.
(C) [x] 사진에서 여행 가방을 풀고 있는 남자를 확인할 수 없으므로 오답입니다.
(D) [x] 사진에 비행기(plane)가 없으므로 오답입니다. People are lined up(사람들이 줄을 서 있다)까지만 듣고 정답으로 선택하지 않도록 주의합니다. line이 줄지어 있는 사람 또는 사물을 묘사할 때 사용됨을 알아둡니다.

06 [3배] 미국식 발음

(A) The woman is rearranging furniture.
(B) The woman is washing a window.
(C) The woman is cleaning the floor.
(D) The woman is plugging a cord into an outlet.

rearrange[ri:əréindʒ] 재배열하다 plug[plʌg] 꽂다, 밀어 넣다
cord[미 kɔ:rd, 영 kɔ:d] (전기) 코드 outlet[áutlet] 콘센트

해석 (A) 여자는 가구를 재배열하고 있다.
(B) 여자는 창문을 닦고 있다.
(C) 여자는 바닥을 청소하고 있다.
(D) 여자는 콘센트에 전기 코드를 꽂고 있다.

해설 한 여자가 청소기로 바닥을 청소하고 있는 모습을 나타내는 1인 사진입니다.
(A) [x] rearranging(재배열하고 있다)은 여자의 동작과 무관하므로 오답입니다. 사진에 있는 가구(furniture)를 사용하여 혼동을 주었습니다.
(B) [x] 사진에서 창문(window)을 확인할 수 없으므로 오답입니다.
(C) [o] 여자가 바닥을 청소하고 있는 모습을 정확히 묘사한 정답입니다.
(D) [x] plugging(꽂고 있다)은 여자의 동작과 무관하므로 오답입니다.

DAY 04 사물·풍경 중심 사진

Course 1 사물 중심 사진

HACKERS PRACTICE ∩ DAY04_02   p.49

| 01 (B) | 02 (C) | 03 (D) | 04 (D) |

01 [3배] 캐나다식 발음 / 미국식 발음

(A) A wall is decorated with artwork.
(B) Some cushions are on a sofa.
(C) The floor is covered with a carpet.
(D) Some books are lying on the windowsill.

artwork[미 á:rtwə:rk, 영 á:twə:k] 미술품 lie on ~에 놓여 있다
windowsill[미 wíndousìl, 영 wíndəusìl] 창틀

해석 (A) 벽이 미술품으로 장식되어 있다.
(B) 몇몇 쿠션들이 소파 위에 있다.

(C) 바닥이 카펫으로 덮여 있다.
(D) 몇몇 책들이 창틀에 놓여 있다.

해설 거실에 있는 여러 사물들의 모습을 나타내는 사물 중심 사진입니다.
(A) [x] 사진에 미술품(artwork)이 없으므로 오답입니다. 사진에 있는 벽(wall)을 사용하여 혼동을 주었습니다.
(B) [o] 몇몇 쿠션들이 소파 위에 있는 모습을 정확히 묘사한 정답입니다.
(C) [x] 사진에 카펫(carpet)이 없으므로 오답입니다. 사진에 있는 바닥(floor)을 사용하여 혼동을 주었습니다.
(D) [x] 책이 소파 위에 놓여 있는데 창틀 위에 놓여 있다고 잘못 묘사했으므로 오답입니다. 창틀을 나타내는 표현 windowsill을 알아둡니다.

02 [3배] 호주식 발음 / 영국식 발음

(A) Towels are piled on a shelf.
(B) Forks have been placed in a jar.
(C) The table has been set for a meal.
(D) A napkin has been unfolded.

pile[pail] 쌓다 jar[미 dʒɑ:r, 영 dʒɑ:] 병, 단지 set[set] 준비하다, 놓다
unfold[미 ʌnfóuld, 영 ʌnfáuld] 펼치다

해석 (A) 수건들이 선반 위에 쌓여 있다.
(B) 포크들이 병 안에 있다.
(C) 테이블이 식사를 위해 준비되어 있다.
(D) 냅킨이 펼쳐져 있다.

해설 테이블 위에 있는 여러 사물들의 모습을 나타내는 사물 중심 사진입니다.
(A) [x] 사진에 선반 위에 쌓여 있는 수건들이 없으므로 오답입니다.
(B) [x] 포크가 테이블 위에 놓여 있는데 병 안에 있다고 잘못 묘사했으므로 오답입니다.
(C) [o] 테이블이 식사를 위해 준비된 모습을 가장 잘 묘사한 정답입니다.
(D) [x] 냅킨이 접혀 있는데 펼쳐져 있다고 잘못 묘사했으므로 오답입니다.

03 [3배] 영국식 발음 / 캐나다식 발음

(A) A cabinet door has been opened.
(B) Papers are filed on a desk.
(C) A computer monitor has been turned on.
(D) Binders are lined up on the shelves.

file[fail] (철하여) 정리하다 turn on ~을 켜다 line up 일렬로 정렬하다

해석 (A) 캐비닛 문이 열려 있다.
(B) 종이들이 책상 위에 정리되어 있다.
(C) 컴퓨터 모니터가 켜져 있다.
(D) 바인더들이 선반에 일렬로 정렬되어 있다.

해설 사무실에 있는 여러 사물들의 모습을 나타내는 사물 중심 사진입니다.
(A) [x] 캐비닛 문이 닫혀 있는데 열려 있다고 잘못 묘사했으므로 오답입니다.
(B) [x] 사진에서 종이들(Papers)을 확인할 수 없으므로 오답입니다.
(C) [x] 컴퓨터 모니터가 꺼져 있는데 켜져 있다고 잘못 묘사했으므로 오답입니다. 사진에 있는 컴퓨터 모니터(computer monitor)를 사용하여 혼동을 주었습니다.
(D) [o] 바인더들이 선반에 일렬로 정렬되어 있는 모습을 가장 잘 묘사한 정답입니다.

04 [호] 호주식 발음 / 미국식 발음

(A) Workers are paving a sidewalk.
(B) The cart has fallen over.
(C) Workers are digging a hole with shovels.
(D) A wheelbarrow has been loaded with some bricks.

pave[peiv] 포장하다 sidewalk[sáidwɔːk] 보도, 인도
fall over 넘어지다 dig[dig] 파다 shovel[ʃʌvl] 삽
wheelbarrow[미 wíːlbærou, 영 wíːlbærəu] 손수레
load[미 loud, 영 leud] 싣다; 짐

해석 (A) 인부들이 보도를 포장하고 있다.
(B) 손수레가 넘어져 있다.
(C) 인부들이 삽으로 구멍을 파고 있다.
(D) 벽돌들이 손수레 안에 실려 있다.

해설 벽돌들이 손수레에 실려 있는 모습을 나타내는 사물 중심 사진입니다.
(A) [×] 사람이 없는 사진에 사람을 나타내는 Workers(인부들)를 사용했으므로 오답입니다.
(B) [×] 손수레가 서 있는데 넘어져 있다고 잘못 묘사했으므로 오답입니다.
(C) [×] 사람이 없는 사진에 사람을 나타내는 Workers(인부들)를 사용했으므로 오답입니다.
(D) [○] 벽돌들이 손수레 안에 실려 있는 모습을 정확히 묘사한 정답입니다. 손수레를 나타내는 표현 wheelbarrow를 알아둡니다.

Course 2 풍경 중심 사진

HACKERS PRACTICE 🎧 DAY04_04   p.51

01 (A)	02 (C)	03 (C)	04 (C)

01 [미] 미국식 발음 / 캐나다식 발음

(A) Some boats are floating on the water.
(B) Some passengers are boarding a ship.
(C) Some people are jumping into the river.
(D) Some houses are being built.

float[미 flout, 영 fləut] 뜨다 board[미 bɔːrd, 영 bɔːd] 타다

해석 (A) 몇몇 배들이 물 위에 떠 있다.
(B) 몇몇 승객들이 배에 타고 있다.
(C) 몇몇 사람들이 강에 뛰어들고 있다.
(D) 몇몇 집들이 지어지고 있다.

해설 배들이 물 위에 떠 있는 모습과 주변 풍경을 나타내는 풍경 중심 사진입니다.
(A) [○] 배들이 물 위에 떠 있는 모습을 가장 잘 묘사한 정답입니다.
(B) [×] 사람이 없는 사진에 사람을 나타내는 passengers(승객들)를 사용했으므로 오답입니다. 사진에 있는 배(ship)를 사용하여 혼동을 주었습니다.
(C) [×] 사람이 없는 사진에 사람을 나타내는 people(사람들)을 사용했으므로 오답입니다.
(D) [×] 집들이 이미 지어진 상태인데, 진행 수동형(are being built)을 사용해 집들이 지어지고 있다고 잘못 묘사했으므로 오답입니다.

02 [영] 영국식 발음 / 호주식 발음

(A) Umbrellas have been left open.
(B) Chairs are being rearranged near the water.
(C) A building is reflected in the pool.
(D) Trees are being trimmed.

umbrella[ʌmbrélə] 파라솔, 우산 rearrange[riːəréindʒ] 다시 배열하다
reflect[riflékt] 비추다 trim[trim] 다듬다

해석 (A) 파라솔들이 펼쳐져 있다.
(B) 의자들이 물가에 다시 배열되고 있다.
(C) 건물이 수영장에 비친다.
(D) 나무들이 다듬어지고 있다.

해설 야외 수영장의 전반적인 풍경을 나타내는 풍경 중심 사진입니다.
(A) [×] 파라솔들이 접혀 있는데 펼쳐져 있다고 잘못 묘사했으므로 오답입니다.
(B) [×] 사진에서 의자들은 보이지만 다시 배열되고 있는(are being rearranged) 모습은 아니므로 오답입니다.
(C) [○] 건물이 수영장에 비치는 모습을 정확히 묘사한 정답입니다.
(D) [×] 사진에서 나무들은 보이지만 다듬어지고 있는(are being trimmed) 모습은 아니므로 오답입니다.

03 [캐] 캐나다식 발음 / 영국식 발음

(A) A sign is being posted.
(B) Some workers are installing a window.
(C) A vehicle is parked in front of a structure.
(D) Some bushes surround a balcony.

sign[sain] 표지판 post[미 poust, 영 pəust] 걸다, 붙이다
structure[미 strʌ́ktʃər, 영 strʌ́ktʃə] 건물 bush[buʃ] 덤불
surround[səráund] 둘러싸다

해석 (A) 표지판이 걸리고 있다.
(B) 몇몇 인부들이 창문을 설치하고 있다.
(C) 차량이 건물 앞에 주차되어 있다.
(D) 덤불들이 발코니를 둘러싸고 있다.

해설 건물 앞에 차량이 세워져 있는 모습과 주변 풍경을 나타내는 풍경 중심 사진입니다.
(A) [×] 사진에서 표지판(sign)을 확인할 수 없으므로 오답입니다.
(B) [×] 사람이 없는 사진에 사람을 나타내는 workers(인부들)를 사용했으므로 오답입니다. 사진에 있는 창문(window)을 사용하여 혼동을 주었습니다.
(C) [○] 건물 앞에 차량이 주차되어 있는 모습을 가장 잘 묘사한 정답입니다.
(D) [×] 사진에서 발코니를 둘러싸고 있는 덤불들(bushes)을 확인할 수 없으므로 오답입니다.

04 [미] 미국식 발음 / 호주식 발음

(A) People are performing outdoors.
(B) The chairs are being stacked in the corner.
(C) Some musical instruments have been set up.
(D) Some steps lead to a seating area.

perform[미 pərfɔ́ːrm, 영 pəfɔ́ːm] 공연하다
outdoors[미 àutdɔ́ːrz, 영 àutdɔ́ːz] 야외에서   stack[stæk] 쌓다
set up ~을 세우다   lead to ~로 이어지다

해석 (A) 사람들이 야외에서 공연을 하고 있다.
　　 (B) 의자들이 구석에 쌓이고 있다.
　　 (C) 몇몇 악기들이 세워져 있다.
　　 (D) 계단이 객석으로 이어져 있다.

해설 악기들이 세워져 있는 모습과 무대의 전반적인 풍경을 나타내는 풍경
　　 중심 사진입니다.
　　 (A) [×] 사람이 없는 사진에 사람을 나타내는 People(사람들)을 사용
　　　　 했으므로 오답입니다.
　　 (B) [×] 사진에서 의자들(chairs)을 확인할 수 없으므로 오답입니다.
　　 (C) [○] 악기들이 세워져 있는 모습을 정확히 묘사한 정답입니다.
　　 (D) [×] 사진에서 계단(steps)과 객석(seating area)을 확인할 수 없
　　　　 으므로 오답입니다.

HACKERS TEST 🎧 DAY04_05　　　　　　　p.52

01 (C)	02 (A)	03 (C)	04 (D)
05 (A)	06 (A)		

01 🔊 호주식 발음

(A) Tiles are being replaced in the hallway.
(B) Visitors are standing near an archway.
(C) Statues are being displayed.
(D) Some artworks are being removed from the wall.

replace[ripléis] 교체하다   hallway[미 hɔ́ːlwei, 영 hɔ́ːlwei] 복도
archway[미 á:rtʃwei, 영 á:tʃwei] 아치형 입구, 아치 길
statue[stǽtʃuː] 조각상   display[displéi] 전시하다
artwork[미 á:rtwəːrk, 영 á:twəːk] 미술품

해석 (A) 복도에서 타일들이 교체되고 있다.
　　 (B) 방문객들이 아치형 입구 근처에 서 있다.
　　 (C) 조각상들이 전시되고 있다.
　　 (D) 미술품들이 벽에서 치워지고 있다.

해설 복도에 전시되어 있는 여러 미술품들의 모습을 나타내는 사물 중심 사진
　　 입니다.
　　 (A) [×] 사진에서 교체되고 있는 타일들(Tiles)을 확인할 수 없으므로
　　　　 오답입니다.
　　 (B) [×] 사람이 없는 사진에 사람을 나타내는 Visitors(방문객들)를 사
　　　　 용했으므로 오답입니다.
　　 (C) [○] 조각상들이 전시되어 있는 모습을 정확히 묘사한 정답입니
　　　　 다. 참고로, 동사 display(진열하다, 전시하다)는 진행 수동형
　　　　 (is being displayed)으로 사용될 때 진열하고 있는 사람의
　　　　 동작뿐만 아니라, 진열되어 있는 상태도 나타낼 수 있음을 반
　　　　 드시 알아둡니다.
　　 (D) [×] 미술품들이 벽에 걸려 있는 상태인데, 진행 수동형(are being
　　　　 removed)을 사용해 벽에서 치워지고 있다고 잘못 묘사했으므
　　　　 로 오답입니다.

02 🔊 영국식 발음

(A) A lamp has been positioned on a dresser.
(B) Shirts are being hung on the rack.
(C) People are cleaning the fitting room.

(D) Shoes have been stored inside boxes.

position[pəzíʃən] 놓다, 두다   dresser[미 drésər, 영 drésə] 서랍장
rack[ræk] 걸이, 선반   fitting room 탈의실

해석 (A) 램프가 서랍장 위에 놓여 있다.
　　 (B) 셔츠들이 걸이에 걸리고 있다.
　　 (C) 사람들이 탈의실을 청소하고 있다.
　　 (D) 신발들이 상자 안에 보관되어 있다.

해설 방 안에 옷과 신발들이 정리되어 있는 모습을 나타내는 사물 중심 사
　　 진입니다.
　　 (A) [○] 램프가 서랍장 위에 놓여 있는 모습을 정확히 묘사한 정답입
　　　　 니다.
　　 (B) [×] 이미 셔츠들이 걸이에 걸려 있는 상태인데, 진행 수동형(are
　　　　 being hung)을 사용해 걸리고 있다고 잘못 묘사했으므로 오
　　　　 답입니다.
　　 (C) [×] 사람이 없는 사진에 사람을 나타내는 People(사람들)을 사용
　　　　 했으므로 오답입니다.
　　 (D) [×] 사진에서 상자(boxes)를 확인할 수 없으므로 오답입니다. 사
　　　　 진에 있는 신발들(Shoes)을 사용하여 혼동을 주었습니다.

03 🔊 캐나다식 발음

(A) Cooking utensils are stacked in the sink.
(B) Some seats are occupied.
(C) A counter has been cleared of objects.
(D) Cupboards are being assembled.

cooking utensil 조리 기구   sink[siŋk] 개수대
occupy[미 á:kjupài, 영 ɔ́kjəpai] 사용하다
counter[미 káuntər, 영 káuntə] 조리대
cupboard[미 kʌ́bərd, 영 kʌ́bəd] 찬장   assemble[əsémbəl] 조립하다

해석 (A) 조리 기구들이 개수대에 쌓여 있다.
　　 (B) 몇몇 의자들이 사용 중이다.
　　 (C) 조리대의 물건들이 치워져 있다.
　　 (D) 찬장이 조립되고 있다.

해설 주방의 가구들과 사물들의 모습을 나타내는 사물 중심 사진입니다.
　　 (A) [×] 사진에서 개수대에 쌓인 조리 기구들(Cooking utensils)을
　　　　 확인할 수 없으므로 오답입니다.
　　 (B) [×] 사진에 의자들(seats)이 없으므로 오답입니다.
　　 (C) [○] 조리대의 물건들이 치워져 있는 모습을 가장 잘 묘사한 정답
　　　　 입니다.
　　 (D) [×] 사진에서 찬장은 보이지만 조립되고 있는(are being
　　　　 assembled) 모습은 아니므로 오답입니다.

04 🔊 미국식 발음

(A) A swimming pool is being constructed.
(B) A worker is fixing the roof.
(C) Trees are being planted in a yard.
(D) Ladders have been placed against a board.

construct[kənstrʌ́kt] 짓다, 건축하다   plant[미 plænt, 영 plɑːnt] 심다
yard[미 jɑːrd, 영 jɑːd] 마당, 뜰   board[미 bɔːrd, 영 bɔːd] 판자, 널빤지

해석 (A) 수영장이 지어지고 있다.
　　 (B) 한 인부가 지붕을 고치고 있다.
　　 (C) 나무들이 마당에 심어지고 있다.

(D) 사다리들이 판자에 기대어져 있다.

해설 공사 중인 집과 주변 풍경을 나타내는 풍경 중심 사진입니다.
　(A) [×] 사진에서 수영장은 보이지만 지어지고 있는(is being constructed) 모습은 아니므로 오답입니다.
　(B) [×] 사람이 없는 사진에 사람을 나타내는 A worker(한 인부)를 사용했으므로 오답입니다.
　(C) [×] 사진에서 나무들은 보이지만 심어지고 있는(are being planted) 모습은 아니므로 오답입니다. 사진의 장소인 마당 (yard)을 사용하여 혼동을 주었습니다.
　(D) [o] 사다리들이 판자에 기대어져 있는 모습을 가장 잘 묘사한 정답입니다.

(B) [×] 사진에서 병은 보이지만 치워지고 있는(is being put away) 모습은 아니므로 오답입니다.
(C) [×] 사진에서 실험 기구들은 보이지만 검사되고 있는(is being examined) 모습은 아니므로 오답입니다.
(D) [×] 사진에서 용기들이 열려 있는 것이 아니라 닫혀 있으므로 오답입니다.

05 호주식 발음

(A) Cars line both sides of the road.
(B) Some bicycles are facing a walkway.
(C) Pedestrians are walking across a street.
(D) Vehicles are waiting at a traffic light.

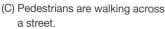

line[lain] ~을 따라 늘어서다　face[feis] ~ 쪽을 향하다
walkway[wɔ́ːkwei] 보도　pedestrian[pədéstriən] 보행자
vehicle[미 víːikəl, 영 víəkəl] 차량, 탈것　traffic light 신호등

해석 (A) 차들이 길 양쪽을 따라 늘어서 있다.
　(B) 몇몇 자전거들이 보도 쪽을 향해 있다.
　(C) 보행자들이 길을 건너고 있다.
　(D) 차량들이 신호등에서 대기하고 있다.

해설 길 위에 차들이 세워져 있는 모습과 주변 풍경을 나타내는 풍경 중심 사진입니다.
　(A) [o] 차들이 길 양쪽을 따라 늘어서 있는 모습을 정확히 묘사한 정답입니다.
　(B) [×] 사진에 자전거들(bicycles)이 없으므로 오답입니다.
　(C) [×] 사람이 없는 사진에 사람을 나타내는 Pedestrians(보행자들)를 사용했으므로 오답입니다.
　(D) [×] 사진에서 신호등(traffic light)을 확인할 수 없으므로 오답입니다. 사진에 있는 차량들(Vehicles)을 사용하여 혼동을 주었습니다.

06 🔊 영국식 발음

(A) Some test tubes have been filled with liquid.
(B) A bottle is being put away.
(C) Some laboratory equipment is being examined.
(D) Containers have been left open.

test tube 시험관　liquid[líkwid] 액체　put away ~을 치우다
laboratory[미 lǽbərətɔ̀ːri, 영 ləbɔ́rətəri] 실험
examine[igzǽmin] 검사하다, 조사하다
container[미 kəntéinər, 영 kəntéinə] 용기

해석 (A) 몇몇 시험관들이 액체로 채워져 있다.
　(B) 병이 치워지고 있다.
　(C) 몇몇 실험 기구들이 검사되고 있다.
　(D) 용기들이 열려 있다.

해설 탁자 위에 있는 실험 도구들의 모습을 나타내는 사물 중심 사진입니다.
　(A) [o] 몇몇 시험관들이 액체로 채워져 있는 모습을 정확히 묘사한 정답입니다.

PART 2

DAY 05 의문사 의문문 1

Course 1 Who 의문문

HACKERS PRACTICE ∩ DAY05_02   p.57

01 (A)	02 (A)	03 (B)	04 (B)
05 (C)	06 (B)	07 (C)	

01 ③» 캐나다식 발음 → 미국식 발음 / 호주식 발음 → 영국식 발음

> Who will send the event invitations?
> **(A) Mr. Ross, I think.**
> (B) You can lend it to him.
> (C) Thanks, I can take it.
>
> invitation[invitéiʃən] 안내장, 초대장 lend[lend] 빌려주다

해석 누가 행사 안내장을 보낼 건가요?
    (A) Mr. Ross인 것 같아요.
    (B) 당신이 그것을 그에게 빌려주면 돼요.
    (C) 고마워요, 제가 그것을 가져갈 수 있어요.

해설 누가 행사 안내장을 보낼 것인지를 묻는 Who 의문문입니다.
    (A) [o] Mr. Ross인 것 같다며 행사 안내장을 보낼 인물을 언급했으
        므로 정답입니다.
    (B) [x] send – lend의 유사 발음 어휘를 사용하여 혼동을 준 오답입
        니다.
    (C) [x] 질문의 send(보내다)와 관련 있는 take(가져가다)를 사용하여
        혼동을 준 오답입니다.

02 ③» 호주식 발음 → 영국식 발음 / 캐나다식 발음 → 미국식 발음

> Who sponsored the city film festival?
> **(A) Green Tech supported the event.**
> (B) They're all the same.
> (C) About $2 each.
>
> sponsor[미 spánsər, 영 spɔ́nsə] 후원하다
> support[미 səpɔ́ːrt, 영 səpɔ́ːt] 후원하다

해석 누가 시의 영화제를 후원했나요?
    (A) Green Tech사가 그 행사를 후원했어요.
    (B) 그것들은 모두 같아요.
    (C) 각 2달러 정도요.

해설 누가 시의 영화제를 후원했는지를 묻는 Who 의문문입니다.
    (A) [o] Green Tech사가 그 행사를 후원했다며 시의 영화제를 후원
        한 회사를 언급했으므로 정답입니다.
    (B) [x] 누가 시의 영화제를 후원했는지를 물었는데, 이와 관련 없
        는 그것들은 모두 같다는 내용으로 응답했으므로 오답입니다.
    (C) [x] 누가 시의 영화제를 후원했는지를 물었는데 가격으로 응답했
        으므로 오답입니다.

03 ③» 영국식 발음 → 캐나다식 발음 / 미국식 발음 → 호주식 발음

> Who opened the shop today?
> (A) At 8:00 A.M.
> **(B) Mr. Harper.**
> (C) I will buy some socks.

해석 누가 오늘 가게 문을 열었나요?
    (A) 오전 8시에요.
    (B) Mr. Harper요.
    (C) 저는 양말 몇 켤레를 살 거예요.

해설 누가 오늘 가게 문을 열었는지를 묻는 Who 의문문입니다.
    (A) [x] 누가 오늘 가게 문을 열었는지를 물었는데 시간으로 응답했으
        므로 오답입니다.
    (B) [o] Mr. Harper라며 가게 문을 연 인물을 언급했으므로 정답입니다.
    (C) [x] 질문의 shop(가게)과 관련 있는 buy(사다)를 사용하여 혼동
        을 준 오답입니다.

04 ③» 호주식 발음 → 미국식 발음 / 캐나다식 발음 → 영국식 발음

> Who is writing our monthly budget reports?
> (A) No, they're quite economical.
> **(B) Isn't it the finance department?**
> (C) I am writing a story now.
>
> budget[bʌ́dʒit] 예산
> economical[미 èkənámikəl, 영 ekənɔ́mikəl] 검소한, 절약하는
> finance[fáinæns] 재무, 재정

해석 누가 우리의 월례 예산 보고서를 작성하고 있나요?
    (A) 아니요, 그들은 상당히 검소해요.
    (B) 재무 부서 아닌가요?
    (C) 저는 지금 이야기를 쓰고 있어요.

해설 누가 월례 예산 보고서를 작성하고 있는지를 묻는 Who 의문문입니다.
    (A) [x] 의문사 의문문에 No로 응답했으므로 오답입니다. budget
        (예산)과 관련 있는 economical(검소한)을 사용하여 혼동을
        주었습니다.
    (B) [o] 재무 부서가 아닌지를 되물어 월례 예산 보고서를 작성하고 있
        는 부서를 전달했으므로 정답입니다.
    (C) [x] 질문의 writing을 반복 사용하여 혼동을 준 오답입니다.

05 ③» 미국식 발음 → 캐나다식 발음 / 영국식 발음 → 호주식 발음

> Who catered Julia and Karl's wedding?
> (A) They got married on Wednesday.
> (B) We are planning to attend.
> **(C) I'm not sure.**
>
> cater[미 kéitər, 영 kéitə] (행사 등에) 음식을 제공하다
> attend[əténd] 참석하다

해석 누가 Julia와 Karl의 결혼식에 음식을 제공했나요?
    (A) 그들은 수요일에 결혼했어요.
    (B) 우리는 참석할 계획이에요.
    (C) 저는 잘 모르겠어요.

해설 누가 Julia와 Karl의 결혼식에 음식을 제공했는지를 묻는 Who 의문문입니다.
- (A) [×] 질문의 wedding(결혼식)과 관련 있는 got married(결혼했다)를 사용하여 혼동을 준 오답입니다.
- (B) [×] 누가 Julia와 Karl의 결혼식에 음식을 제공했는지를 물었는데, 이와 관련이 없는 우리는 참석할 계획이라는 내용으로 응답했으므로 오답입니다.
- (C) [○] 자신은 잘 모르겠다는 말로 모른다는 간접적인 응답을 했으므로 정답입니다.

06 3째 영국식 발음 → 호주식 발음 / 미국식 발음 → 캐나다식 발음

> Who is in charge of hiring new employees?
> (A) There's a $25 application fee.
> **(B) The HR manager.**
> (C) Here's a job description.

be in charge of ~을 담당하다
application[미 æpləkéiʃən, 영 æplikéiʃən] 지원, 신청   fee[fi:] 요금
job description 직무 기술서

해석 누가 신규 직원 고용을 담당하나요?
- (A) 25달러의 지원료가 있어요.
- (B) 인사부장이요.
- (C) 직무 기술서는 여기에 있어요.

해설 누가 신규 직원 고용을 담당하는지를 묻는 Who 의문문입니다.
- (A) [×] 질문의 hiring(고용)과 관련 있는 application(지원)을 사용하여 혼동을 준 오답입니다.
- (B) [○] 인사부장이라며 신규 직원 고용을 담당하는 인물을 언급했으므로 정답입니다.
- (C) [×] 질문의 hiring(고용)과 관련 있는 job description(직무 기술서)을 사용하여 혼동을 준 오답입니다.

07 3째 캐나다식 발음 → 영국식 발음 / 호주식 발음 → 미국식 발음

> Who has already completed the assignment?
> (A) I'm competing for the prize.
> (B) A ten-page essay.
> **(C) I finished it yesterday.**

complete[kəmplí:t] 완료하다   assignment[əsáinmənt] 과제, 일
compete[kəmpí:t] 겨루다, 경쟁하다   essay[ései] 과제물

해석 누가 이미 과제를 완료했나요?
- (A) 저는 상품을 위해 겨루고 있어요.
- (B) 10페이지짜리 과제물이요.
- (C) 저는 어제 그것을 끝냈어요.

해설 누가 과제를 완료했는지를 묻는 Who 의문문입니다.
- (A) [×] completed – competing의 유사 발음 어휘를 사용하여 혼동을 준 오답입니다.
- (B) [×] 질문의 assignment(과제)와 관련 있는 essay(과제물)를 사용하여 혼동을 준 오답입니다.
- (C) [○] 자신은 어제 그것을 끝냈다며 과제를 완료한 인물을 언급했으므로 정답입니다.

Course 2 Where 의문문

HACKERS PRACTICE ∩ DAY05_04   p.59

01 (B)	02 (C)	03 (A)	04 (A)
05 (B)	06 (C)	07 (C)	

01 3째 미국식 발음 → 호주식 발음 / 영국식 발음 → 캐나다식 발음

> Where are you staying tonight?
> (A) Tomorrow, most likely.
> **(B) At my brother's apartment.**
> (C) Just a while longer.

해석 당신은 오늘 밤 어디에 머물 건가요?
- (A) 아마, 내일이요.
- (B) 제 남동생의 아파트에요.
- (C) 조금만 더 오래요.

해설 오늘 밤 어디에 머물 것인지를 묻는 Where 의문문입니다.
- (A) [×] 질문의 tonight(오늘 밤)과 관련 있는 Tomorrow(내일)를 사용하여 혼동을 준 오답입니다.
- (B) [○] 남동생의 아파트에라며 오늘 밤 머물 장소를 언급했으므로 정답입니다.
- (C) [×] 오늘 밤 어디에 머물 것인지를 물었는데, 이와 관련이 없는 조금만 더 오래라는 내용으로 응답했으므로 오답입니다.

02 3째 캐나다식 발음 → 미국식 발음 / 호주식 발음 → 영국식 발음

> Where is the nearest bank?
> (A) I like my new office.
> (B) Yes, inform the teller.
> **(C) There's one three blocks south.**

inform[미 infɔ́:rm, 영 infɔ́:m] 알리다, 공식적으로 통지하다
teller[미 télər, 영 télə] (은행의) 창구 직원

해석 가장 가까운 은행은 어디에 있나요?
- (A) 저는 제 새로운 사무실이 마음에 들어요.
- (B) 네, 창구 직원에게 알려주세요.
- (C) 남쪽으로 세 블록 가시면 한 군데가 있어요.

해설 가장 가까운 은행이 어디에 있는지를 묻는 Where 의문문입니다.
- (A) [×] 가장 가까운 은행이 어디에 있는지를 물었는데, 이와 관련이 없는 자신의 새로운 사무실이 마음에 든다는 내용으로 응답했으므로 오답입니다.
- (B) [×] 의문사 의문문에 Yes로 응답했으므로 오답입니다.
- (C) [○] 남쪽으로 세 블록 가면 한 군데가 있다며 가장 가까운 은행의 위치를 언급했으므로 정답입니다.

03 3째 호주식 발음 → 영국식 발음 / 캐나다식 발음 → 미국식 발음

> Where should we install the TV?
> **(A) Next to the stereo.**
> (B) It has a clear image.
> (C) I will wait as long as I can.

install[instɔ́:l] 설치하다

해석 우리는 텔레비전을 어디에 설치해야 할까요?
- (A) 스테레오 옆이요.
- (B) 그것은 선명한 이미지를 가지고 있어요.
- (C) 저는 가능한 한 오래 기다릴 거예요.

해설 텔레비전을 어디에 설치해야 할지를 묻는 Where 의문문입니다.
- (A) [○] 스테레오 옆이라며 텔레비전을 설치해야 하는 위치를 언급했으므로 정답입니다.
- (B) [×] 질문의 TV(텔레비전)와 관련 있는 clear image(선명한 이미지)를 사용하여 혼동을 준 오답입니다.
- (C) [×] 텔레비전을 어디에 설치해야 할지를 물었는데, 이와 관련이 없는 자신은 가능한 한 오래 기다릴 것이라는 내용으로 응답했으므로 오답입니다.

한 권으로 끝내는 해커스 토익 700+ (LC+RC+VOCA)

04 🔊 영국식 발음 → 캐나다식 발음 / 미국식 발음 → 호주식 발음

Where did you get these doughnuts?
(A) Actually, I made them myself.
(B) I think there are a dozen.
(C) It has a large snack selection.

dozen[dʌ́zn] 12개   selection[silékʃən] 종류

해석 당신은 이 도넛들을 어디에서 샀나요?
(A) 사실, 제가 그것들을 직접 만들었어요.
(B) 12개가 있는 것 같아요.
(C) 그곳은 다양한 간식 종류를 갖추고 있어요.

해설 도넛들을 어디에서 샀는지를 묻는 Where 의문문입니다.
(A) [o] 자신이 그것들을 직접 만들었다며 도넛들을 사지 않았음을 간접적으로 전달했으므로 정답입니다.
(B) [x] 도넛들을 어디에서 샀는지를 물었는데, 이와 관련이 없는 12개가 있는 것 같다는 내용으로 응답했으므로 오답입니다.
(C) [x] 질문의 doughnuts(도넛들)와 관련 있는 snack(간식)을 사용하여 혼동을 준 오답입니다.

05 🔊 호주식 발음 → 미국식 발음 / 캐나다식 발음 → 영국식 발음

Where did these magazines come from?
(A) The feature article is interesting.
(B) Sarah brought them.
(C) I'd like to get a copy.

feature[미 fíːtʃər, 영 fíːtʃə] (신문 또는 방송의) 특집

해석 이 잡지들은 어디에서 났어요?
(A) 그 특집 기사는 흥미로워요.
(B) Sarah가 그것들을 가져왔어요.
(C) 저는 한 부 갖고 싶어요.

해설 잡지들이 어디에서 났는지를 묻는 Where 의문문입니다.
(A) [x] 질문의 magazines(잡지들)와 관련 있는 feature article(특집 기사)을 사용하여 혼동을 준 오답입니다.
(B) [o] Sarah가 그것들을 가져왔다며 잡지들의 출처를 언급했으므로 정답입니다.
(C) [x] 질문의 magazines(잡지들)와 관련 있는 copy(한 부)를 사용하여 혼동을 준 오답입니다.

06 🔊 미국식 발음 → 캐나다식 발음 / 영국식 발음 → 호주식 발음

Where is bus 28's final destination?
(A) The bus is still running now.
(B) I caught it on Main Street.
(C) I'll have to check.

destination[미 dèstənéiʃən, 영 dèstinéiʃən] 목적지   run[rʌn] 운행하다

해석 28번 버스의 최종 목적지는 어디인가요?
(A) 그 버스는 지금까지도 운행 중이에요.
(B) 저는 그것을 Main가에서 탔어요.
(C) 확인해 봐야 해요.

해설 28번 버스의 최종 목적지가 어디인지를 묻는 Where 의문문입니다.
(A) [x] 질문의 bus를 반복 사용하여 혼동을 준 오답입니다.
(B) [x] 질문의 destination(목적지)과 관련 있는 Main Street(Main 가)를 사용하여 혼동을 준 오답입니다.
(C) [o] 확인해 봐야 한다는 말로 모른다는 간접적인 응답을 했으므로 정답입니다.

07 🔊 영국식 발음 → 호주식 발음 / 미국식 발음 → 캐나다식 발음

Where are you and Maria going for lunch?
(A) Pasta salad, please.
(B) We are planning to launch it tomorrow.
(C) The restaurant across the street.

launch[lɔːntʃ] (상품을) 출시하다   across[미 əkrɔ́ːs, 영 əkrɔ́s] ~의 건너편에

해석 당신과 Maria는 어디로 점심을 먹으러 가시나요?
(A) 파스타 샐러드로 주세요.
(B) 우리는 내일 그것을 출시할 계획이에요.
(C) 길 건너편의 음식점이요.

해설 상대방과 Maria가 어디로 점심을 먹으러 가는지를 묻는 Where 의문문입니다.
(A) [x] 질문의 lunch(점심)와 관련 있는 Pasta salad(파스타 샐러드)를 사용하여 혼동을 준 오답입니다.
(B) [x] lunch – launch의 유사 발음 어휘를 사용하여 혼동을 준 오답입니다.
(C) [o] 길 건너편의 음식점이라며 점심을 먹으러 가는 장소를 언급했으므로 정답입니다.

HACKERS TEST 🎧 DAY05_05   p.60

01 (C)	02 (A)	03 (C)	04 (B)
05 (C)	06 (A)	07 (B)	08 (B)
09 (A)	10 (B)	11 (A)	12 (A)
13 (C)	14 (B)	15 (A)	16 (C)
17 (B)	18 (A)	19 (C)	20 (B)
21 (B)	22 (C)	23 (C)	24 (B)
25 (A)			

01 🔊 캐나다식 발음 → 영국식 발음

Who cleaned the office?
(A) It's down the hall on the right.
(B) The project will be finished tomorrow.
(C) The company's maintenance staff.

hall[hɔːl] 복도   maintenance[méintənəns] 보수 관리

해석 누가 사무실을 청소했나요?
(A) 그것은 복도 끝 오른쪽에 있어요.
(B) 그 프로젝트는 내일 끝날 거예요.
(C) 회사의 보수 관리 직원이요.

해설 누가 사무실을 청소했는지를 묻는 Who 의문문입니다.
(A) [x] 누가 사무실을 청소했는지를 물었는데 위치로 응답했으므로 오답입니다.
(B) [x] 질문의 office(사무실)와 관련 있는 project(프로젝트)를 사용하여 혼동을 준 오답입니다.
(C) [o] 회사의 보수 관리 직원이라며 사무실을 청소한 인물을 언급했으므로 정답입니다.

02 🔊 미국식 발음 → 영국식 발음

Where should I throw away this trash?
(A) Follow me this way.
(B) We picked it up in the garage.
(C) I usually do it on Fridays.

throw away ~을 버리다   pick up ~을 줍다

해석 이 쓰레기를 어디에 버려야 하나요?
(A) 이쪽으로 저를 따라오세요.
(B) 저희는 차고에서 그것을 주웠어요.
(C) 저는 보통 금요일마다 그것을 해요.

해설 쓰레기를 어디에 버려야 하는지를 묻는 Where 의문문입니다.
(A) [o] 이쪽으로 자신을 따라오라는 말로 쓰레기를 버릴 장소를 알려 주겠다는 것을 간접적으로 전달했으므로 정답입니다.
(B) [×] 질문의 throw away(~을 버리다)와 반대 의미인 picked ~ up (~을 주웠다)를 사용하여 혼동을 준 오답입니다.
(C) [×] 쓰레기를 어디에 버려야 하는지를 물었는데 시점으로 응답했으므로 오답입니다.

03 🔊 캐나다식 발음 → 미국식 발음

Whose jacket is this?
(A) Leave your coat in the hall.
(B) Yes, I'm a bit cold.
(C) Maybe it's Anne's.

해석 이것은 누구의 재킷인가요?
(A) 코트는 현관에 두세요.
(B) 네, 저는 약간 추워요.
(C) 아마 Anne의 것인 것 같아요.

해설 이것이 누구의 재킷인지를 묻는 Who(Whose) 의문문입니다.
(A) [×] 질문의 jacket(재킷)과 관련 있는 coat(코트)를 사용하여 혼동을 준 오답입니다.
(B) [×] 의문사 의문문에 Yes로 응답했으므로 오답입니다. 질문의 jacket(재킷)과 관련 있는 cold(추운)를 사용하여 혼동을 주었습니다.
(C) [o] 아마 Anne의 것인 것 같다며 재킷의 주인인 인물을 언급했으므로 정답입니다.

04 🔊 호주식 발음 → 영국식 발음

Where will the company picnic be held?
(A) On Saturday at 11 A.M.
(B) At Central Park in Wilmington.
(C) We bought a picnic basket at the market.

company picnic 회사 야유회

해석 회사 야유회는 어디에서 열리나요?
(A) 토요일 오전 11시에요.
(B) 윌밍턴에 있는 Central 공원에서요.
(C) 우리는 시장에서 소풍 바구니를 샀어요.

해설 회사 야유회가 어디에서 열리는지를 묻는 Where 의문문입니다.
(A) [×] 회사 야유회가 어디에서 열리는지를 물었는데 시점으로 응답했으므로 오답입니다.
(B) [o] 윌밍턴에 있는 Central 공원에서라며 회사 야유회가 열리는 장소를 언급했으므로 정답입니다.
(C) [×] 회사 야유회가 어디에서 열리는지를 물었는데, 이와 관련 없는 시장에서 소풍 바구니를 샀다는 내용으로 응답했으므로 오답입니다.

05 🔊 영국식 발음 → 캐나다식 발음

Who will check the invoice?
(A) It's in my account.
(B) A 25 percent discount.
(C) Katherine in the purchasing department. 🔘

invoice[ínvɔ:s] 청구서 account[əkáunt] 계좌
purchasing department 구매 부서

해석 누가 청구서를 확인할 건가요?
(A) 그것은 제 계좌에 있어요.
(B) 25퍼센트 할인이요.
(C) 구매 부서의 Katherine이요.

해설 누가 청구서를 확인할 것인지를 묻는 Who 의문문입니다.
(A) [×] 질문의 invoice(청구서)에서 연상할 수 있는 청구 금액의 납부와 관련된 account(계좌)를 사용하여 혼동을 준 오답입니다.
(B) [×] 누가 청구서를 확인할 것인지를 물었는데, 이와 관련이 없는 25퍼센트 할인이라는 내용으로 응답했으므로 오답입니다.
(C) [o] 구매 부서의 Katherine이라며 청구서를 확인할 인물을 언급했으므로 정답입니다.

06 🔊 호주식 발음 → 캐나다식 발음

Where can I get some information about tours?
(A) We have some pamphlets at the front desk.
(B) For our latest report.
(C) Sure, I can inform our manager.

front desk 안내 데스크 inform[미 infɔ́:rm, 영 infɔ́:m] 알리다

해석 제가 어디에서 견학에 대한 정보를 얻을 수 있을까요?
(A) 저희는 안내 데스크에 몇몇 소책자가 있어요.
(B) 우리의 최근 보고서에 대해서요.
(C) 물론이죠, 제가 관리자에게 알릴 수 있어요.

해설 어디에서 견학에 대한 정보를 얻을 수 있을지를 묻는 Where 의문문입니다.
(A) [o] 안내 데스크에 몇몇 소책자가 있다는 말로 안내 데스크에 있는 소책자에서 견학에 대한 정보를 얻을 수 있음을 간접적으로 전달했으므로 정답입니다.
(B) [×] 질문의 information(정보)과 관련 있는 report(보고서)를 사용하여 혼동을 준 오답입니다.
(C) [×] information – inform의 유사 발음 어휘를 사용하여 혼동을 준 오답입니다.

07 🔊 미국식 발음 → 캐나다식 발음

Who is moving into the apartment next door?
(A) It's apartment number 132.
(B) Students from a nearby university.
(C) I'll move my furniture out by Tuesday.

move into ~로 이사하다 nearby[미 nìərbái, 영 nìəbái] 근처의

해석 누가 아파트 옆집으로 이사 올 건가요?
(A) 132호예요.
(B) 근처 대학의 학생들이요.
(C) 저는 제 가구를 화요일까지 뺄 거예요.

해설 누가 아파트 옆집으로 이사 올 것인지를 묻는 Who 의문문입니다.
(A) [×] 누가 아파트 옆집으로 이사 올 것인지를 물었는데, 이와 관련이 없는 132호라는 내용으로 응답했으므로 오답입니다.
(B) [o] 근처 대학의 학생들이라며 아파트 옆집으로 이사 올 인물들을 언급했으므로 정답입니다.
(C) [×] 질문의 moving을 move로 반복 사용하여 혼동을 준 오답입니다. I'll move까지만 듣고 정답으로 고르지 않도록 주의합니다.

Where did you hear about the concert?
(A) Tickets are only $15.
(B) From my friend, Drea.
(C) It was held at Pioneer Stadium.

stadium[stéidiəm] 경기장

해석 당신은 콘서트에 대해 어디에서 들으셨나요?
(A) 입장권은 15달러밖에 하지 않아요.
(B) 제 친구 Drea로부터요.
(C) 그것은 Pioneer 경기장에서 열렸어요.

해설 콘서트에 대해 어디에서 들었는지를 묻는 Where 의문문입니다.
(A) [×] 질문의 concert(콘서트)와 관련 있는 Tickets(입장권)를 사용하여 혼동을 준 오답입니다.
(B) [○] 자신의 친구 Drea로부터라며 콘서트 소식의 출처를 언급했으므로 정답입니다.
(C) [×] 콘서트에 대해 어디에서 들었는지를 물었는데 콘서트가 열릴 만한 장소로 응답했으므로 오답입니다.

Who is editing this month's newsletter?
(A) Tom, I believe.
(B) A picture for the main story.
(C) By the end of the week.

edit[édit] 편집하다 newsletter[미 nú:zletər, 영 njú:zlètə] 소식지, 회보
main story 머리기사

해석 누가 이번 달 소식지를 편집하고 있나요?
(A) Tom일 거예요.
(B) 머리기사에 쓰일 사진이요.
(C) 이번 주말까지요.

해설 누가 이번 달 소식지를 편집하고 있는지를 묻는 Who 의문문입니다.
(A) [○] Tom일 거라며 이번 달 소식지를 편집하고 있는 인물을 언급했으므로 정답입니다.
(B) [×] 질문의 newsletter(소식지)와 관련 있는 main story(머리기사)를 사용하여 혼동을 준 오답입니다.
(C) [×] 누가 이번 달 소식지를 편집하고 있는지를 물었는데 시점으로 응답했으므로 오답입니다.

Where is Parker arriving from this evening?
(A) The passengers are now boarding.
(B) He is flying in from Berlin.
(C) At 11:40 P.M.

board[미 bɔːrd, 영 bɔːd] 탑승하다 fly in from ~에서 비행기를 타고 오다

해석 Parker는 오늘 저녁 어디에서 올 건가요?
(A) 승객들은 지금 탑승하고 있어요.
(B) 그는 베를린에서 비행기를 타고 올 거예요.
(C) 오후 11시 40분이에요.

해설 Parker가 오늘 저녁 어디에서 올 것인지를 묻는 Where 의문문입니다.
(A) [×] 질문의 arriving(오다)과 관련 있는 boarding(탑승하다)을 사용하여 혼동을 준 오답입니다.
(B) [○] 베를린에서 비행기를 타고 올 것이라며 Parker가 출발할 장소를 언급했으므로 정답입니다.
(C) [×] Parker가 오늘 저녁 어디에서 올 것인지를 물었는데 시점으로

응답했으므로 오답입니다.

Who is going to pick up lunch today?
(A) I can get it.
(B) The restaurant on the corner.
(C) Around noon.

pick up ~을 찾아오다

해석 누가 오늘 점심을 찾아올 건가요?
(A) 제가 그것을 가져올게요.
(B) 모퉁이에 있는 식당이요.
(C) 정오쯤에요.

해설 누가 점심을 찾아올 것인지를 묻는 Who 의문문입니다.
(A) [○] 자신이 그것을 가져오겠다는 말로 점심을 찾아올 인물을 전달했으므로 정답입니다.
(B) [×] 누가 점심을 찾아올 것인지를 물었는데 장소로 응답했으므로 오답입니다.
(C) [×] 누가 점심을 찾아올 것인지를 물었는데 시점으로 응답했으므로 오답입니다.

Where did James put the stapler yesterday?
(A) Have you checked his desk?
(B) The document needs to be stapled.
(C) He worked late yesterday.

stapler[미 stéiplər, 영 stéiplə] 스테이플러
staple[stéipl] 스테이플러로 고정시키다

해석 James는 어제 스테이플러를 어디에 두었나요?
(A) 그의 자리를 확인해 보셨나요?
(B) 그 서류는 스테이플러로 고정되어야 해요.
(C) 그는 어제 늦게까지 일했어요.

해설 James가 어제 스테이플러를 어디에 두었는지를 묻는 Where 의문문입니다.
(A) [○] 그의 자리를 확인해 보았는지를 되물어 모른다는 간접적인 응답을 했으므로 정답입니다.
(B) [×] stapler – stapled의 유사 발음 어휘를 사용하여 혼동을 준 오답입니다.
(C) [×] 질문의 yesterday를 반복 사용하여 혼동을 준 오답입니다.

Who is giving the presentation to the board?
(A) Sally put the boards inside.
(B) Give them to my assistant.
(C) I have no idea.

give a presentation 보고하다, 발표하다
board[미 bɔːrd, 영 bɔːd] 이사회, 판지

해석 누가 이사회에 보고할 건가요?
(A) Sally가 판지들을 안쪽에 놓았어요.
(B) 그것들을 제 비서에게 주세요.
(C) 모르겠어요.

해설 누가 이사회에 보고할 것인지를 묻는 Who 의문문입니다.
(A) [×] 질문의 board(이사회)를 '판지'라는 의미의 boards로 반복 사용하여 혼동을 준 오답입니다.

(B) [×] 누가 이사회에 보고할 것인지를 물었는데, 이와 관련이 없는 그것들을 자신의 비서에게 주라는 내용으로 응답했으므로 오답입니다.

(C) [○] 모르겠다는 말로 누가 보고할 것인지를 모른다는 간접적인 응답을 했으므로 정답입니다.

14 [호주식 발음 → 미국식 발음]

Where do we keep the spare batteries?
(A) It was better than expected.
(B) On the top shelf.
(C) An extra pen as well.

spare[미 spɛər, 영 speə] 여분의, 예비의   extra[ékstrə] 여분의, 추가의

해석 우리는 여분의 배터리를 어디에 보관하나요?
(A) 그것은 예상했던 것보다 더 좋았어요.
(B) 선반 맨 위에요.
(C) 여분의 펜도요.

해설 여분의 배터리를 어디에 보관하는지를 묻는 Where 의문문입니다.
(A) [×] batteries – better의 유사 발음 어휘를 사용하여 혼동을 준 오답입니다.
(B) [○] 선반 맨 위라며 여분의 배터리를 보관하는 위치를 언급했으므로 정답입니다.
(C) [×] 질문의 spare(여분의)와 같은 의미인 extra(여분의)를 사용하여 혼동을 준 오답입니다.

15 [미국식 발음 → 캐나다식 발음]

Who made the schedule for the seminar?
(A) Lisa Parkins, a member of the planning team.
(B) Yes, right away.
(C) If your schedule is open.

planning team 기획팀   open[미 óupən, 영 óupən] 비어 있는

해석 누가 세미나의 일정을 세웠나요?
(A) 기획팀의 사원인 Lisa Parkins요.
(B) 네, 지금 당장이요.
(C) 당신의 일정이 비어 있다면요.

해설 누가 세미나의 일정을 세웠는지를 묻는 Who 의문문입니다.
(A) [○] 기획팀의 사원인 Lisa Parkins라며 세미나의 일정을 세운 인물을 언급했으므로 정답입니다.
(B) [×] 의문사 의문문에 Yes로 응답했으므로 오답입니다.
(C) [×] 누가 세미나의 일정을 세웠는지를 물었는데, 이와 관련이 없는 상대방의 일정이 비어 있다면이라는 내용으로 응답했으므로 오답입니다.

16 [영국식 발음 → 호주식 발음]

Where can I make photocopies of these pictures?
(A) It's an original painting.
(B) Mallory is the girl in the picture.
(C) I am afraid the copy machine is broken.

make a photocopy 복사하다   original[ərídʒənl] 원본의

해석 제가 이 사진들을 어디에서 복사할 수 있나요?
(A) 그것이 원본 그림이에요.
(B) Mallory가 그 사진 속의 여자예요.
(C) 복사기가 고장 난 것 같은데요.

해설 사진들을 어디에서 복사할 수 있는지를 묻는 Where 의문문입니다.
(A) [×] 사진들을 어디에서 복사할 수 있는지를 물었는데, 이와 관련이 없는 그것이 원본 그림이라는 내용으로 응답했으므로 오답입니다.
(B) [×] 질문의 pictures를 picture로 반복 사용하여 혼동을 준 오답입니다.
(C) [○] 복사기가 고장 난 것 같다는 말로 사진들을 복사할 수 없음을 간접적으로 전달했으므로 정답입니다.

17 [캐나다식 발음 → 영국식 발음]

Who will be promoted to manager?
(A) Jeffrey Smith made an offer.
(B) It hasn't been decided.
(C) They are promoting a new product.

promote[미 prəmóut, 영 prəmə́ut] 승진하다, 홍보하다
make an offer 제의하다

해석 누가 관리자로 승진할 건가요?
(A) Jeffrey Smith가 제의했어요.
(B) 그것은 결정되지 않았어요.
(C) 그들은 신제품을 홍보하고 있어요.

해설 누가 관리자로 승진할 것인지를 묻는 Who 의문문입니다.
(A) [×] 누가 관리자로 승진할 것인지를 물었는데, 이와 관련이 없는 Jeffrey Smith가 제의했다는 내용으로 응답했으므로 오답입니다.
(B) [○] 그것은 결정되지 않았다는 말로 모른다는 간접적인 응답을 했으므로 정답입니다.
(C) [×] 질문의 promoted(승진하다)를 '홍보하다'라는 의미의 promoting으로 반복 사용하여 혼동을 준 오답입니다.

18 [미국식 발음 → 호주식 발음]

Where did you buy the sofa in your living room?
(A) I picked it up at Wilson's Furniture.
(B) We need to leave now.
(C) Two bedrooms.

living room 거실   pick up ~을 사다

해석 당신은 거실의 소파를 어디에서 샀나요?
(A) 저는 그것을 Wilson's 가구점에서 샀어요.
(B) 우리는 지금 출발해야 해요.
(C) 두 개의 침실이요.

해설 거실의 소파를 어디에서 샀는지를 묻는 Where 의문문입니다.
(A) [○] Wilson's 가구점에서 샀다며 소파를 산 장소를 언급했으므로 정답입니다.
(B) [×] 소파를 어디에서 샀는지를 물었는데, 이와 관련이 없는 지금 출발해야 한다는 내용으로 응답했으므로 오답입니다.
(C) [×] 질문의 living room(거실)과 관련 있는 bedrooms(침실)를 사용하여 혼동을 준 오답입니다.

19 [캐나다식 발음 → 미국식 발음]

Who built the new apartment complex downtown?
(A) Yes, I am moving in next week.
(B) It's a great place.
(C) Royce Construction.

move in 이사 오다

해석 누가 시내의 새로운 아파트 단지를 지었나요?
(A) 네, 저는 다음 주에 이사를 와요.
(B) 그곳은 멋진 장소예요.
(C) Royce 건설사요.

해설 누가 시내의 새로운 아파트 단지를 지었는지를 묻는 Who 의문문입니다.
(A) [x] 의문사 의문문에 Yes로 응답했으므로 오답입니다.
(B) [x] 누가 시내의 새로운 아파트 단지를 지었는지를 물었는데, 이와 관련이 없는 그곳은 멋진 장소라는 내용으로 응답했으므로 오답입니다.
(C) [o] Royce 건설사라며 시내의 새로운 아파트 단지를 지은 업체를 언급했으므로 정답입니다.

20 [♫] 호주식 발음 → 영국식 발음

Where did you spend your vacation this year?
(A) I took three weeks off this year.
(B) It was postponed because of an urgent project.
(C) No, the rate is $90 per night.

take ~ off ~ (동안)을 쉬다 postpone[미 poustpóun, 영 pəustpóun] 연기하다
urgent[미 ə́:rdʒənt, 영 ə́:dʒənt] 긴급한 rate[reit] 요금

해석 당신은 올해 휴가를 어디에서 보내셨나요?
(A) 저는 올해 3주를 쉬었어요.
(B) 그것은 긴급한 프로젝트 때문에 연기되었어요.
(C) 아니요, 요금은 하룻밤에 90달러예요.

해설 올해 휴가를 어디에서 보냈는지를 묻는 Where 의문문입니다.
(A) [x] 질문의 vacation(휴가)과 관련 있는 took three weeks off(3주를 쉬었다)를 사용하여 혼동을 준 오답입니다.
(B) [o] 긴급한 프로젝트 때문에 연기되었다는 말로 올해 휴가를 가지 않았음을 간접적으로 전달했으므로 정답입니다.
(C) [x] 의문사 의문문에 No로 응답했으므로 오답입니다. 질문의 spend(보내다)의 다른 의미인 '돈을 쓰다'와 관련 있는 $90(90달러)를 사용하여 혼동을 주었습니다.

21 [♫] 영국식 발음 → 캐나다식 발음

Who should I contact about the problem with my salary?
(A) I signed my contract.
(B) One of the clerks in accounting.
(C) I earned $2,000 last week.

contact[미 kántækt, 영 kɔ́ntækt] 연락하다 contract[kɔ́ntrækt] 계약서
clerk[미 klə:rk, 영 klɑːk] 직원, 점원 earn[미 ə:rn, 영 ə:n] 돈을 벌다

해석 제 급여 문제에 대해 누구에게 연락해야 하나요?
(A) 저는 제 계약서에 서명했어요.
(B) 회계 부서의 직원들 중 한 명이요.
(C) 저는 지난주에 2,000달러를 벌었어요.

해설 급여 문제에 대해 누구에게 연락해야 하는지를 묻는 Who 의문문입니다.
(A) [x] contact – contract의 유사 발음 어휘를 사용하여 혼동을 준 오답입니다.
(B) [o] 회계 부서의 직원들 중 한 명이라며 급여 문제에 대해 연락해야 하는 인물을 언급했으므로 정답입니다.
(C) [x] 질문의 salary(급여)와 관련 있는 earned(돈을 벌었다)를 사용하여 혼동을 준 오답입니다.

22 [♫] 호주식 발음 → 미국식 발음

Where can I get a copy of last year's budget?
(A) It's not in the budget.
(B) It was published in May.
(C) Mr. Kim has one.

budget[bʌ́dʒit] 예산(안), 운영비 publish[pʌ́bliʃ] 발행하다, 출판하다

해석 작년 예산안의 사본을 어디에서 구할 수 있나요?
(A) 그것은 예산에 포함되어 있지 않아요.
(B) 그것은 5월에 발행되었어요.
(C) Mr. Kim이 한 부 가지고 있어요.

해설 작년 예산안의 사본을 어디에서 구할 수 있는지를 묻는 Where 의문문입니다.
(A) [x] 질문의 budget을 반복 사용하여 혼동을 준 오답입니다.
(B) [x] 질문의 copy(사본)의 다른 의미인 '한 부'와 관련 있는 published(발행되다)를 사용하여 혼동을 준 오답입니다.
(C) [o] Mr. Kim이 한 부 가지고 있다는 말로 Mr. Kim으로부터 작년 예산안의 사본을 구할 수 있음을 전달했으므로 정답입니다.

23 [♫] 미국식 발음 → 캐나다식 발음

Who created the design of the new arts center?
(A) At the construction site.
(B) The painting is on display now.
(C) An architect from Halifax Building Design.

create[kriéit] 제작하다 design[dizáin] 설계도
construction[kənstrʌ́kʃən] 건설 on display 전시 중인
architect[미 ɑ́:rkətèkt, 영 ɑ́:kitekt] 건축가

해석 누가 새로운 예술 센터의 설계도를 제작했나요?
(A) 건설 현장에서요.
(B) 그 그림은 지금 전시 중이에요.
(C) Halifax 건물 설계 회사의 한 건축가요.

해설 누가 새로운 예술 센터의 설계도를 제작했는지를 묻는 Who 의문문입니다.
(A) [x] 질문의 design(설계도)과 관련 있는 construction(건설)을 사용하여 혼동을 준 오답입니다.
(B) [x] 질문의 arts center(예술 센터)와 관련 있는 on display(전시 중인)를 사용하여 혼동을 준 오답입니다.
(C) [o] Halifax 건물 설계 회사의 한 건축가라며 예술 센터의 설계도를 제작한 인물을 언급했으므로 정답입니다.

24 [♫] 영국식 발음 → 호주식 발음

Where does the school's French class take place?
(A) It is every Tuesday evening.
(B) Do you mean the beginner or intermediate class?
(C) Sorry, but only the first course.

intermediate[미 ìntərmíːdiət, 영 ìntəmíːdiət] 중급의, 중간의

해석 학교의 프랑스어 수업은 어디에서 열리나요?
(A) 매주 화요일 저녁이에요.
(B) 초급 수업이요, 아니면 중급 수업이요?
(C) 죄송하지만, 첫 번째 수업만요.

해설 학교의 프랑스어 수업이 어디에서 열리는지를 묻는 Where 의문문입니다.
(A) [x] 프랑스어 수업이 어디에서 열리는지를 물었는데 시점으로 응

답했으므로 오답입니다.
(B) [o] 초급 수업과 중급 수업 중 어느 수업을 말하는 것인지를 되물어 수업에 대한 추가 정보를 요구하는 정답입니다.
(C) [x] 질문의 class(수업)와 같은 의미인 course(수업)를 사용하여 혼동을 준 오답입니다.

25 ③ 캐나다식 발음 → 호주식 발음

> Where are those boxes going to be delivered?
> **(A) To the R&D office.**
> (B) The delivery will arrive next week.
> (C) It's in a cardboard box on the table.
>
> R&D (research and development) 연구 개발
> cardboard[미 káːrdbɔ̀ːrd, 영 káːdbɔ̀ːd] 판지의

해석 그 상자들은 어디로 배달될 건가요?
(A) 연구 개발 사무실로요.
(B) 배송품은 다음 주에 도착할 거예요.
(C) 그것은 테이블 위에 있는 판지 상자 안에 있어요.

해설 상자들이 어디로 배달될 것인지를 묻는 Where 의문문입니다.
(A) [o] 연구 개발 사무실로라며 상자들이 배달될 장소를 언급했으므로 정답입니다.
(B) [x] delivered - delivery의 유사 발음 어휘를 사용하여 혼동을 준 오답입니다.
(C) [x] 질문의 boxes를 box로 반복 사용하여 혼동을 준 오답입니다.

DAY 06 의문사 의문문 2

Course 1 When 의문문

HACKERS PRACTICE 🎧 DAY06_02   p.63

01 (B)	02 (A)	03 (B)	04 (A)
05 (C)	06 (A)	07 (C)	

01 ③ 캐나다식 발음 → 영국식 발음 / 호주식 발음 → 미국식 발음

> When does your train arrive?
> (A) At Penn Station.
> **(B) At 9:45 P.M.**
> (C) It's $125 per ticket.

해석 당신의 기차는 언제 도착하나요?
(A) Penn 역이에요.
(B) 오후 9시 45분이에요.
(C) 표 한 장당 125달러에요.

해설 기차가 언제 도착하는지를 묻는 When 의문문입니다.
(A) [x] 기차가 언제 도착하는지를 물었는데 장소로 응답했으므로 오답입니다.
(B) [o] 오후 9시 45분이라며 기차가 도착하는 시점을 언급했으므로 정답입니다.
(C) [x] 질문의 train(기차)과 관련 있는 ticket(표)을 사용하여 혼동을 준 오답입니다.

02 ③ 미국식 발음 → 호주식 발음 / 영국식 발음 → 캐나다식 발음

> When is the annual shareholders' meeting?
> **(A) Next Thursday afternoon.**
> (B) It's in the main auditorium.
> (C) I had to meet the deadline.
>
> annual[ǽnjuəl] 연례의, 매년의
> shareholders' meeting 주주총회, 주주회의
> auditorium[ɔ̀ːditɔ́ːriəm] 강당   deadline[dédlain] 마감기한

해석 연례 주주총회는 언제인가요?
(A) 다음 주 목요일 오후요.
(B) 그것은 대강당에서예요.
(C) 저는 마감기한을 맞춰야 했어요.

해설 연례 주주총회가 언제인지를 묻는 When 의문문입니다.
(A) [o] 다음 주 목요일 오후라며 연례 주주총회가 열리는 시점을 언급했으므로 정답입니다.
(B) [x] 연례 주주총회가 언제인지를 물었는데 장소로 응답했으므로 오답입니다.
(C) [x] 질문의 meeting(회의)을 '(기한 등을) 맞추다'라는 의미의 동사 meet으로 반복 사용하여 혼동을 준 오답입니다.

03 ③ 캐나다식 발음 → 미국식 발음 / 호주식 발음 → 영국식 발음

> When will the awards ceremony get underway?
> (A) It's arriving at 7 P.M.
> **(B) Once the guest speaker finishes.**
> (C) It's a great honor.
>
> awards ceremony 시상식   get underway 시작하다, 진행시키다
> once[wʌns] ~하자마자   guest speaker 초청 연사
> honor[미 ánər, 영 ɔ́nə] 영광, 명예

해석 시상식은 언제 시작하나요?
(A) 그것은 오후 7시에 도착할 거예요.
(B) 초청 연사가 끝마치자마자요.
(C) 매우 영광입니다.

해설 시상식이 언제 시작하는지를 묻는 When 의문문입니다.
(A) [x] 시간을 나타내는 7 P.M.(오후 7시)을 사용하여 혼동을 준 오답입니다.
(B) [o] 초청 연사가 끝마치자마자라며 시상식이 시작하는 시점을 언급했으므로 정답입니다.
(C) [x] 시상식이 언제 시작하는지를 물었는데, 이와 관련이 없는 매우 영광이라는 내용으로 응답했으므로 오답입니다. 질문의 awards(상)와 관련 있는 honor(영광)를 사용하여 혼동을 주었습니다.

04 ③ 호주식 발음 → 영국식 발음 / 캐나다식 발음 → 미국식 발음

> When is the store's grand opening?
> **(A) August 9.**
> (B) Over a week.
> (C) They're already on sale.
>
> grand opening 개업   on sale 판매 중인, 할인 중인

해석 가게의 개업은 언제인가요?
(A) 8월 9일이요.
(B) 1주일 동안이요.
(C) 그것들은 이미 판매 중이에요.

해설 가게의 개업이 언제인지를 묻는 When 의문문입니다.

(A) [○] 8월 9일이라며 가게의 개업 시점을 언급했으므로 정답입니다.
(B) [×] 가게의 개업이 언제인지를 물었는데 기간으로 응답했으므로 오답입니다.
(C) [×] 질문의 store(가게)와 관련 있는 on sale(판매 중인)을 사용하여 혼동을 준 오답입니다.

05 🔊 영국식 발음 → 캐나다식 발음 / 미국식 발음 → 호주식 발음

> When is the seminar going to finish?
> (A) 200 participants.
> (B) Yes, it's in Helsinki.
> (C) Around noon.
>
> participant [미 pɑːrtísəpənt, 영 pɑːtísipənt] 참석자

해석 세미나는 언제 끝날 예정인가요?
  (A) 200명의 참석자들이요.
  (B) 네, 그것은 헬싱키에서예요.
  (C) 정오쯤에요.

해설 세미나가 언제 끝날 예정인지를 묻는 When 의문문입니다.
  (A) [×] 세미나가 언제 끝날 예정인지를 물었는데 참석자 수로 응답했으므로 오답입니다.
  (B) [×] 의문사 의문에 Yes로 응답했으므로 오답입니다.
  (C) [○] 정오쯤이라며 세미나가 끝나는 시점을 언급했으므로 정답입니다.

06 🔊 호주식 발음 → 미국식 발음 / 캐나다식 발음 → 영국식 발음

> When did you start working here?
> (A) You mean, in this department?
> (B) I'm a secretary.
> (C) I work until 9 P.M. every day.
>
> department [미 dipɑ́ːrtmənt, 영 dipɑ́ːtmənt] 부서
> secretary [미 sékrətèri, 영 sékrətəri] 비서

해석 당신은 언제 이곳에서 일을 하기 시작했나요?
  (A) 이 부서에서를 말씀하시는 건가요?
  (B) 저는 비서예요.
  (C) 저는 매일 오후 9시까지 근무해요.

해설 언제 이곳에서 일을 하기 시작했는지를 묻는 When 의문문입니다.
  (A) [○] 이 부서를 말하는 건지를 되물어 상대방이 묻는 시점에 대한 추가 정보를 요구하는 정답입니다.
  (B) [×] 언제 이곳에서 일을 하기 시작했는지를 물었는데, 이와 관련이 없는 자신은 비서라는 내용으로 응답했으므로 오답입니다.
  (C) [×] 질문의 working을 work로 반복 사용하고, 시간을 나타내는 9 P.M.(오후 9시)을 사용하여 혼동을 준 오답입니다.

07 🔊 미국식 발음 → 캐나다식 발음 / 영국식 발음 → 호주식 발음

> When will I receive the furniture I ordered?
> (A) Your order will be discounted.
> (B) Five chairs and a table.
> (C) Let me ask the shipping department.
>
> order [미 ɔ́ːrdər, 영 ɔ́ːdə] 주문하다; 주문 shipping [ʃípiŋ] 배송, 운송

해석 제가 주문한 가구를 언제 받게 될까요?
  (A) 당신의 주문은 할인될 거예요.
  (B) 5개의 의자와 1개의 책상이요.
  (C) 제가 배송 부서에 물어볼게요.

해설 주문한 가구를 언제 받게 될지를 묻는 When 의문문입니다.
  (A) [×] 질문의 ordered(주문했다)를 '주문'이라는 의미의 명사 'order'로 반복 사용하여 혼동을 준 오답입니다.
  (B) [×] 질문의 furniture(가구)와 관련 있는 chairs and a table(의자와 책상)을 사용하여 혼동을 준 오답입니다.
  (C) [○] 자신이 배송 부서에 물어보겠다는 말로 모른다는 간접적인 응답을 했으므로 정답입니다.

Course 2 What · Which 의문문

HACKERS PRACTICE 🎧 DAY06_04   p.65

01 (C)	02 (A)	03 (C)	04 (B)
05 (A)	06 (A)	07 (B)	

01 🔊 영국식 발음 → 호주식 발음 / 미국식 발음 → 캐나다식 발음

> What will tomorrow's weather be like?
> (A) I like sunny days.
> (B) It's on September 24.
> (C) It's supposed to rain.
>
> be supposed to ~하기로 되어 있다

해석 내일 날씨는 어떨 것 같나요?
  (A) 저는 화창한 날이 좋아요.
  (B) 그것은 9월 24일에 열려요.
  (C) 비가 오기로 되어 있어요.

해설 내일 날씨가 어떨 것 같은지를 묻는 What 의문문입니다.
  (A) [×] 질문의 weather(날씨)와 관련 있는 sunny(화창한)를 사용하여 혼동을 준 오답입니다.
  (B) [×] 내일 날씨가 어떨 것 같은지를 물었는데 날짜로 응답했으므로 오답입니다.
  (C) [○] 비가 오기로 되어 있다는 말로 내일 날씨를 전달했으므로 정답입니다.

02 🔊 캐나다식 발음 → 영국식 발음 / 호주식 발음 → 미국식 발음

> Which tie do you think I should wear?
> (A) They all look good on you.
> (B) I'm wearing a blue suit.
> (C) Can you tie it?
>
> tie [tai] 넥타이; 매다 look good on ~에게 잘 어울리다 suit [suːt] 정장

해석 당신은 제가 어느 넥타이를 매야 한다고 생각하나요?
  (A) 그것들 모두 당신에게 잘 어울려요.
  (B) 저는 푸른색 정장을 입고 있어요.
  (C) 그것을 맬 수 있으세요?

해설 자신이 어느 넥타이를 매야 한다고 생각하는지를 묻는 Which 의문문입니다. Which tie를 반드시 들어야 합니다.
  (A) [○] 그것들 모두 상대방에게 잘 어울린다는 말로 어느 것이든 상관없다는 것을 전달했으므로 정답입니다.
  (B) [×] 질문의 wear(착용하다)와 관련 있는 suit(정장)를 사용하고, wear를 wearing으로 반복 사용하여 혼동을 준 오답입니다.
  (C) [×] 질문의 tie(넥타이)를 '매다'라는 의미의 동사로 반복 사용하여 혼동을 준 오답입니다.

03 [미국식 발음 → 호주식 발음 / 영국식 발음 → 캐나다식 발음]

What day can we go skiing next week?
(A) The mountains are covered in snow.
(B) We are staying at Henson Resort.
(C) I'm free on Thursday.

cover[미 kʌ́vər, 영 kʌ́və] 덮다, 가리다   free[fri:] 한가한, 자유로운

해석 다음 주 무슨 요일에 스키를 타러 갈까요?
(A) 그 산은 눈으로 덮여 있어요.
(B) 우리는 Henson 리조트에 머무를 거예요.
(C) 저는 목요일에 한가해요.

해설 다음 주 무슨 요일에 스키를 타러 갈 수 있을지를 묻는 What 의문문입니다. What day를 반드시 들어야 합니다.
(A) [×] 질문의 skiing(스키를 타다)과 관련 있는 snow(눈)를 사용하여 혼동을 준 오답입니다.
(B) [×] 다음 주 무슨 요일에 스키를 타러 갈지를 물었는데, 이와 관련이 없는 Henson 리조트에 머무를 것이라는 내용으로 응답했으므로 오답입니다.
(C) [○] 자신은 목요일에 한가하다는 말로 다음 주 목요일에 스키를 타러 가자는 것을 간접적으로 전달했으므로 정답입니다.

04 [캐나다식 발음 → 미국식 발음 / 호주식 발음 → 영국식 발음]

Which of these rings is the most expensive?
(A) About $8,500.
(B) The one in this case.
(C) The doorbell is ringing.

doorbell[미 dɔ́ːrbel, 영 dɔ́ːbel] 초인종

해석 이 반지들 중 어느 것이 가장 비싼가요?
(A) 약 8,500달러요.
(B) 이 케이스에 있는 것이요.
(C) 초인종이 울리고 있어요.

해설 반지들 중 어느 것이 가장 비싼지를 묻는 Which 의문문입니다. Which of these rings를 반드시 들어야 합니다.
(A) [×] 반지들 중 어느 것이 가장 비싼지를 물었는데 가격으로 응답했으므로 오답입니다. expensive(비싼)와 관련 있는 $8,500(8,500달러)를 사용하여 혼동을 주었습니다.
(B) [○] 이 케이스에 있는 것이라는 말로 가장 비싼 반지가 어느 것인지를 전달했으므로 정답입니다.
(C) [×] 질문의 rings(반지들)를 '울리다'라는 의미의 동사 ringing으로 반복 사용하여 혼동을 준 오답입니다.

05 [호주식 발음 → 영국식 발음 / 캐나다식 발음 → 미국식 발음]

What movie should we see after dinner?
(A) It's your choice.
(B) Around 8, probably.
(C) I'd like to go for pizza.

choice[tʃɔis] 선택, 결정   go for ~을 선택하다

해석 저녁 식사 후에 어떤 영화를 볼까요?
(A) 그건 당신의 선택이에요.
(B) 아마, 8시쯤이요.
(C) 저는 피자를 선택하고 싶어요.

해설 저녁 식사 후에 어떤 영화를 볼지를 묻는 What 의문문입니다. What movie를 반드시 들어야 합니다.
(A) [○] 그건 당신의 선택이라는 말로 저녁 식사 후에 볼 영화를 상대

방이 선택할 수 있음을 전달했으므로 정답입니다.
(B) [×] 저녁 식사 후에 어떤 영화를 볼지를 물었는데 시점으로 응답했으므로 오답입니다.
(C) [×] 질문의 dinner(저녁 식사)와 관련 있는 pizza(피자)를 사용하여 혼동을 준 오답입니다.

06 [영국식 발음 → 캐나다식 발음 / 미국식 발음 → 호주식 발음]

Which phone model would you like to purchase?
(A) Are any of them on sale?
(B) I will pay with a credit card.
(C) I'll return your call soon.

purchase[미 pə́ːrtʃəs, 영 pə́ːtʃəs] 구매하다   credit card 신용카드
return a call 다시 전화하다, 답례 전화를 하다

해석 당신은 어느 전화기 모델을 구매하고 싶으신가요?
(A) 그것들 중 할인 판매 중인 것이 있나요?
(B) 저는 신용카드로 지불할 거예요.
(C) 당신에게 곧 다시 전화 드릴게요.

해설 어느 전화기 모델을 구매하고 싶은지를 묻는 Which 의문문입니다. Which phone model을 반드시 들어야 합니다.
(A) [○] 그것들 중 할인 판매 중인 것이 있는지를 되물어 전화기 모델에 대한 추가 정보를 요구하는 정답입니다.
(B) [×] 질문의 purchase(구매하다)와 관련 있는 pay(지불하다)를 사용하여 혼동을 준 오답입니다.
(C) [×] 질문의 phone(전화기)과 관련 있는 call(전화)을 사용하여 혼동을 준 오답입니다.

07 [호주식 발음 → 미국식 발음 / 캐나다식 발음 → 영국식 발음]

What time is the company banquet scheduled to begin?
(A) About two hours.
(B) At 6:30 P.M.
(C) She's always on time.

banquet[bǽŋkwit] 연회   scheduled to ~으로 예정이 되어 있는
on time 시간을 어기지 않는

해석 회사 연회는 몇 시에 시작하기로 예정되어 있나요?
(A) 약 2시간이요.
(B) 오후 6시 30분이에요.
(C) 그녀는 항상 시간을 어기지 않아요.

해설 회사 연회가 몇 시에 시작하기로 예정되어 있는지를 묻는 What 의문문입니다. What time이 시간을 묻는 것임을 이해할 수 있어야 합니다.
(A) [×] 질문의 time(~시)과 관련 있는 hours(시간)를 사용하여 혼동을 준 오답입니다.
(B) [○] 오후 6시 30분이라며 연회가 시작하기로 예정되어 있는 시간을 언급했으므로 정답입니다.
(C) [×] 질문의 time을 반복 사용하여 혼동을 준 오답입니다.

HACKERS TEST ∩ DAY06_05   p.66

01 (B)	02 (B)	03 (B)	04 (B)
05 (C)	06 (A)	07 (A)	08 (A)
09 (C)	10 (B)	11 (B)	12 (B)
13 (B)	14 (C)	15 (B)	16 (C)
17 (B)	18 (B)	19 (B)	20 (A)
21 (A)	22 (C)	23 (C)	24 (C)
25 (A)			

PART 2

한 권으로 끝내는 해커스 토익 700+ (LC+RC+VOCA)

01 🔊 미국식 발음 → 영국식 발음

When are you hiring more staff?
(A) Higher than the others.
(B) Sometime this month.
(C) The interview was on Channel 16.

hire[미 haiər, 영 haiə] 고용하다   staff[미 stæf, 영 stɑːf] 직원

해석 당신은 언제 직원들을 더 고용하실 건가요?
(A) 다른 것들보다 더 높게요.
(B) 이번 달에 언젠가요.
(C) 그 인터뷰는 채널 16번에서 나왔어요.

해설 언제 직원들을 더 고용할 것인지를 묻는 When 의문문입니다.
(A) [×] hiring – Higher의 유사 발음 어휘를 사용하여 혼동을 준 오답입니다.
(B) [○] 이번 달에 언젠가라며 직원들을 더 고용할 시점을 언급했으므로 정답입니다.
(C) [×] 질문의 hiring(고용하다)과 관련 있는 interview(인터뷰)를 사용하여 혼동을 준 오답입니다.

02 🔊 영국식 발음 → 캐나다식 발음

What can I get for you to drink?
(A) In about an hour.
(B) Just water, please.
(C) It's a list of our beverages.

beverage[bévəridʒ] 음료

해석 마실 것으로 무엇을 가져다드릴까요?
(A) 약 한 시간 뒤에요.
(B) 그냥 물로 주세요.
(C) 그것은 저희 음료 목록이에요.

해설 마실 것으로 무엇을 가져다줄지를 묻는 What 의문문입니다.
(A) [×] 마실 것으로 무엇을 가져다줄지를 물었는데 시점으로 응답했으므로 오답입니다.
(B) [○] 그냥 물로 달라며 마실 것으로 가져다줄 것을 언급했으므로 정답입니다.
(C) [×] 질문의 drink(마시다)와 관련 있는 beverages(음료)를 사용하여 혼동을 준 오답입니다.

03 🔊 캐나다식 발음 → 영국식 발음

Which of the books did Sammy buy?
(A) At the library's annual sale.
(B) Only the green one, I think.
(C) Yes, this one looks better on you.

annual[ǽnjuəl] 연간의

해석 Sammy는 그 책들 중 어느 것을 구매했나요?
(A) 도서관의 연간 할인 판매에서요.
(B) 초록색 책만인 것 같아요.
(C) 네, 이것이 당신에게 더 잘 어울려요.

해설 Sammy가 그 책들 중 어느 것을 구매했는지를 묻는 Which 의문문입니다. Which of the books를 반드시 들어야 합니다.
(A) [×] Sammy가 그 책들 중 어느 것을 구매했는지를 물었는데 장소로 응답했으므로 오답입니다.
(B) [○] 초록색 책인 것 같다며 Sammy가 구매한 책을 전달했으므로 정답입니다.
(C) [×] 의문사 의문문에 Yes로 응답했으므로 오답입니다.

04 🔊 미국식 발음 → 호주식 발음

When will your office be repainted?
(A) It's light blue.
(B) As soon as everything is moved out.
(C) I'm not very artistic.

repaint[riːpéint] 다시 페인트칠하다
artistic[미 ɑːrtístik, 영 ɑːtístik] 예술적 감각이 있는

해석 당신의 사무실은 언제 다시 페인트칠이 될 것인가요?
(A) 그것은 밝은 파란색이에요.
(B) 모든 것들이 옮겨지자마자요.
(C) 저는 예술적 감각이 별로 없어요.

해설 사무실이 언제 다시 페인트칠이 될 것인지를 묻는 When 의문문입니다.
(A) [×] 질문의 repainted(다시 페인트칠이 되다)에서 연상할 수 있는 페인트 색상과 관련된 light blue(밝은 파란색)를 사용하여 혼동을 준 오답입니다.
(B) [○] 모든 것들이 옮겨지자마자라며 사무실이 다시 페인트칠이 될 시점을 언급했으므로 정답입니다.
(C) [×] 사무실이 언제 다시 페인트칠이 될 것인지를 물었는데, 이와 관련이 없는 예술적 감각이 별로 없다는 내용으로 응답했으므로 오답입니다.

05 🔊 캐나다식 발음 → 미국식 발음

What is your presentation about?
(A) On top of the cabinet.
(B) I love the present.
(C) Our quarterly profits.

quarterly[미 kwɔ́ːrtərli, 영 kwɔ́ːtəli] 분기별의
profit[미 prɑ́fit, 영 prɔ́fit] 수익

해석 당신의 발표는 무엇에 대한 것인가요?
(A) 캐비닛 맨 위에요.
(B) 저는 그 선물이 마음에 들어요.
(C) 우리의 분기별 수익이요.

해설 상대방의 발표가 무엇에 대한 것인지를 묻는 What 의문문입니다.
(A) [×] 상대방의 발표가 무엇에 대한 것인지를 물었는데 위치로 응답했으므로 오답입니다.
(B) [×] presentation – present의 유사 발음 어휘를 사용하여 혼동을 준 오답입니다.
(C) [○] 우리의 분기별 수익이라는 말로 발표가 무엇에 대한 것인지를 전달했으므로 정답입니다.

06 🔊 호주식 발음 → 영국식 발음

Which way is the hospital from here?
(A) Take this road north.
(B) I have an appointment.
(C) The clinic is very modern.

appointment[əpɔ́intmənt] (병원의) 예약
modern[미 mɑ́dərn, 영 mɔ́dən] 현대적인

해석 여기에서 병원은 어느 길로 가야 하나요?
(A) 이 길로 북쪽으로 가세요.
(B) 저는 예약이 있어요.
(C) 그 병원은 매우 현대적이에요.

해설 여기에서 병원은 어느 길로 가야 하는지를 묻는 Which 의문문입니다. Which way를 반드시 들어야 합니다.

(A) [o] 이 길로 북쪽으로 가라는 말로 병원으로 가는 길을 전달했으므로 정답입니다.

(B) [x] 질문의 hospital(병원)과 관련 있는 appointment(예약)를 사용하여 혼동을 준 오답입니다.

(C) [x] 질문의 hospital(병원)과 같은 의미인 clinic(병원)을 사용하여 혼동을 준 오답입니다.

07 영국식 발음 → 캐나다식 발음

When is the train for Cambridge leaving?
(A) It already left 15 minutes ago.
(B) For a training session.
(C) From Platform C.

training session 교육 platform[미 plǽtfɔːrm, 영 plǽtfɔːm] 승강장

해석 케임브리지행 열차는 언제 출발하나요?
(A) 그것은 이미 15분 전에 떠났어요.
(B) 교육을 위해서요.
(C) C 승강장에서요.

해설 케임브리지행 열차가 언제 출발하는지를 묻는 When 의문문입니다.
(A) [o] 그것은 이미 15분 전에 떠났다는 말로 케임브리지행 열차가 이미 출발했음을 전달했으므로 정답입니다.
(B) [x] train - training의 유사 발음 어휘를 사용하여 혼동을 준 오답입니다.
(C) [x] 케임브리지행 열차가 언제 출발하는지를 물었는데 장소로 응답했으므로 오답입니다.

08 호주식 발음 → 미국식 발음

What time does the library close?
(A) At 9:30 in the evening.
(B) Next to City Hall.
(C) It's open on national holidays.

City Hall 시청 national holiday 공휴일

해석 도서관은 언제 문을 닫나요?
(A) 밤 9시 30분이에요.
(B) 시청 옆이에요.
(C) 그곳은 공휴일에 문을 열어요.

해설 도서관이 언제 문을 닫는지를 묻는 What 의문문입니다. What time이 시간을 묻는 것임을 이해할 수 있어야 합니다.
(A) [o] 밤 9시 30분이라며 도서관이 문을 닫는 시간을 언급했으므로 정답입니다.
(B) [x] 도서관이 언제 문을 닫는지를 물었는데 장소로 응답했으므로 오답입니다.
(C) [x] 질문의 close(문을 닫다)와 반대 의미인 open(문을 연)을 사용하여 혼동을 준 오답입니다.

09 미국식 발음 → 캐나다식 발음

Which store did you buy your phone from?
(A) No, I missed your call.
(B) I keep it in the storage room.
(C) The electronics shop near Blair Park.

storage room 창고, 저장고
electronics[미 ilektrániks, 영 èlektrɔ́niks] 전자제품

해석 당신은 어느 가게에서 전화기를 구매했나요?
(A) 아니요, 저는 당신의 전화를 못 받았어요.

(B) 저는 그것을 창고에 보관해요.
(C) Blair 공원 근처의 전자제품 매장이요.

해설 전화기를 어느 가게에서 구매했는지를 묻는 Which 의문문입니다. Which store를 반드시 들어야 합니다.
(A) [x] 의문사 의문문에 No로 응답했으므로 오답입니다.
(B) [x] store - storage의 유사 발음 어휘를 사용하여 혼동을 준 오답입니다.
(C) [o] Blair 공원 근처의 전자제품 매장이라며 전화기를 구매한 가게를 언급했으므로 정답입니다.

10 영국식 발음 → 호주식 발음

When will the opera performance begin?
(A) They're at a jazz concert.
(B) Within ten minutes.
(C) Tickets are $50 each.

performance[미 pərfɔ́ːrməns, 영 pəfɔ́ːməns] 공연

해석 오페라 공연은 언제 시작하나요?
(A) 그들은 재즈 연주회에 있어요.
(B) 10분 안에요.
(C) 입장권은 한 장에 50달러예요.

해설 오페라 공연이 언제 시작하는지를 묻는 When 의문문입니다.
(A) [x] 질문의 performance(공연)와 관련 있는 concert(연주회)를 사용하여 혼동을 준 오답입니다.
(B) [o] 10분 안에라는 말로 오페라 공연이 시작할 시점을 언급했으므로 정답입니다.
(C) [x] 질문의 opera performance(오페라 공연)와 관련 있는 Tickets(입장권)를 사용하여 혼동을 준 오답입니다.

11 캐나다식 발음 → 호주식 발음

What do you want to do this weekend?
(A) It's a short drive there.
(B) I need to catch up on some work.
(C) Sure, that sounds fun.

catch up on ~을 보충하다

해석 이번 주말에 무엇을 하고 싶으세요?
(A) 그곳은 차로 가까운 거리예요.
(B) 저는 몇 가지 업무를 보충해야 해요.
(C) 물론이죠, 그것은 재미있을 것 같아요.

해설 주말에 무엇을 하고 싶은지를 묻는 What 의문문입니다.
(A) [x] 주말에 무엇을 하고 싶은지를 물었는데, 이와 관련이 없는 차로 가까운 거리에 있다는 내용으로 응답했으므로 오답입니다.
(B) [o] 몇 가지 업무를 보충해야 한다는 말로 주말에 일을 할 것임을 간접적으로 전달했으므로 정답입니다.
(C) [x] 주말에 무엇을 하고 싶은지를 물었는데, 이와 관련이 없는 그것은 재미있을 것 같다는 내용으로 응답했으므로 오답입니다.

12 미국식 발음 → 호주식 발음

Which of these cars uses the least amount of gas?
(A) About 20 to 24 liters.
(B) The red one parked by the entrance.
(C) There's a gas station on the corner.

gas[gæs] 휘발유, 가솔린 entrance[éntrəns] 입구 gas station 주유소

해석 이 차들 중 어느 것이 휘발유를 가장 적게 사용하나요?
　　(A) 약 20에서 24리터요.
　　(B) 입구 옆에 주차된 빨간 것이요.
　　(C) 모퉁이에 주유소가 있어요.

해설 차들 중 어느 것이 휘발유를 가장 적게 사용하는지를 묻는 Which 의문문입니다. Which of these cars를 반드시 들어야 합니다.
　　(A) [x] 질문의 gas(휘발유)와 관련 있는 20 to 24 liters(20에서 24리터)를 사용하여 혼동을 준 오답입니다.
　　(B) [o] 입구 옆에 주차된 빨간 것이라며 휘발유를 가장 적게 사용하는 차를 언급했으므로 정답입니다.
　　(C) [x] 질문의 cars(차들)와 관련 있는 gas station(주유소)을 사용하여 혼동을 준 오답입니다.

13 🔊 캐나다식 발음 → 미국식 발음

When is the food festival taking place?
(A) It is going to be enjoyable.
(B) On October 28.
(C) For two weeks.

take place 열리다, 개최되다　enjoyable [indʒɔ́iəbl] 재미있는, 즐거운

해석 음식 축제는 언제 열리나요?
　　(A) 그것은 재미있을 거예요.
　　(B) 10월 28일에요.
　　(C) 2주 동안이요.

해설 음식 축제가 언제 열리는지를 묻는 When 의문문입니다.
　　(A) [x] 질문의 festival(축제)과 관련 있는 enjoyable(재미있는)을 사용하여 혼동을 준 오답입니다.
　　(B) [o] 10월 28일이라며 음식 축제가 열리는 시점을 언급했으므로 정답입니다.
　　(C) [x] 음식 축제가 언제 열리는지를 물었는데 기간으로 응답했으므로 오답입니다.

14 🔊 호주식 발음 → 영국식 발음

What is the chance of rain on Saturday?
(A) I didn't work that day.
(B) Training will end on Saturday.
(C) Let me check the weather forecast.

chance [미 tʃæns, 영 tʃɑːns] 가능성　training [tréiniŋ] 교육
weather forecast 일기 예보

해석 토요일에 비가 올 가능성은 어느 정도인가요?
　　(A) 저는 그날 근무하지 않았어요.
　　(B) 교육은 토요일에 끝날 거예요.
　　(C) 제가 일기 예보를 확인해 볼게요.

해설 토요일에 비가 올 가능성이 어느 정도인지를 묻는 What 의문문입니다.
　　(A) [x] 질문의 Saturday를 나타낼 수 있는 that day(그날)를 사용하여 혼동을 준 오답입니다.
　　(B) [x] rain - Training의유사 발음 어휘를 사용하고, 질문의 Saturday를 반복 사용하여 혼동을 준 오답입니다.
　　(C) [o] 일기 예보를 확인해 보겠다는 말로 모른다는 간접적인 응답을 했으므로 정답입니다.

15 🔊 영국식 발음 → 캐나다식 발음

Which bus should I take to the convention center?
(A) She's taking a break now.
(B) Take bus 402.

↻

(C) It's on the second floor.

convention center 컨벤션 센터(회의·전시 장소가 집중된 지역 또는 종합 빌딩)

해석 컨벤션 센터로 가려면 어느 버스를 타야 하나요?
　　(A) 그녀는 지금 휴식을 취하고 있어요.
　　(B) 402번 버스를 타세요.
　　(C) 그것은 2층에 있어요.

해설 컨벤션 센터로 가려면 어느 버스를 타야 하는지를 묻는 Which 의문문입니다. Which bus를 반드시 들어야 합니다.
　　(A) [x] 질문의 take를 taking으로 반복 사용하여 혼동을 준 오답입니다.
　　(B) [o] 402번 버스를 타라는 말로 컨벤션 센터로 가는 버스를 언급했으므로 정답입니다.
　　(C) [x] 컨벤션 센터로 가려면 어느 버스를 타야 하는지를 물었는데 장소로 응답했으므로 오답입니다.

16 🔊 호주식 발음 → 미국식 발음

When can you come in for an interview?
(A) The reporter is writing it later.
(B) I'm going to apply for the job.
(C) Is Friday good for you?

apply for ~에 지원하다

해석 언제 면접을 보러 올 수 있나요?
　　(A) 기자는 그것을 나중에 쓸 거예요.
　　(B) 저는 그 직무에 지원할 거예요.
　　(C) 금요일 괜찮으신가요?

해설 언제 면접을 보러 올 수 있는지를 묻는 When 의문문입니다.
　　(A) [x] 언제 면접을 보러 올 수 있는지를 물었는데, 이와 관련이 없는 기자가 그것을 나중에 쓸 것이라는 내용으로 응답했으므로 오답입니다.
　　(B) [x] 질문의 interview(면접)와 관련 있는 apply for(~에 지원하다)를 사용하여 혼동을 준 오답입니다.
　　(C) [o] 금요일이 괜찮은지를 되물어 면접 날짜에 대한 추가 의견을 묻는 정답입니다.

17 🔊 미국식 발음 → 캐나다식 발음

What do you think about the new sick leave policy?
(A) I am not feeling well today.
(B) It will help everyone out.
(C) I thought you were a police officer.

sick leave 병가　policy [미 pɑ́ləsi, 영 pɔ́ləsi] 정책

해석 새로운 병가 정책에 대해 어떻게 생각하시나요?
　　(A) 저는 오늘 몸이 좋지 않아요.
　　(B) 그것은 모두에게 도움이 될 거예요.
　　(C) 저는 당신이 경찰관이라고 생각했어요.

해설 새로운 병가 정책에 대해 어떻게 생각하는지를 묻는 What 의문문입니다.
　　(A) [x] 질문의 sick leave(병가)와 관련 있는 not feeling well(몸이 좋지 않은)을 사용하여 혼동을 준 오답입니다.
　　(B) [o] 그것은 모두에게 도움이 될 것이라는 말로 새로운 병가 정책에 대한 의견을 전달했으므로 정답입니다.
　　(C) [x] policy - police의 유사 발음 어휘를 사용하여 혼동을 준 오답입니다.

18 3세 영국식 발음 → 호주식 발음

Which cake would you like to order for the party?
(A) It's my birthday party.
(B) What are the options?
(C) I will tell them to bring it at once.

option [미 ápʃən, 영 ɔ́pʃən] 선택할 수 있는 것, 선택 사항 at once 바로, 곧

해석 파티를 위해 어느 케이크를 주문하고 싶으신가요?
(A) 제 생일 파티예요.
(B) 선택할 수 있는 것들이 무엇인가요?
(C) 그들에게 그것을 바로 가져오라고 말할게요.

해설 파티를 위해 어느 케이크를 주문하고 싶은지를 묻는 Which 의문문입니다. Which cake를 반드시 들어야 합니다.
(A) [×] 질문의 party를 반복 사용하여 혼동을 준 오답입니다.
(B) [○] 선택할 수 있는 것이 무엇인지를 되물어 케이크에 대한 추가 정보를 요구하는 정답입니다.
(C) [×] 파티를 위해 어느 케이크를 주문하고 싶은지를 물었는데, 이와 관련이 없는 그들에게 그것을 바로 가져오라고 말하겠다는 내용으로 응답했으므로 오답입니다.

19 3세 캐나다식 발음 → 영국식 발음

When will you come back from your vacation?
(A) I'll be in China.
(B) Next Wednesday.
(C) It's a fifteen-hour flight.

vacation [veikéiʃən] 휴가   flight [flait] 비행

해석 당신은 언제 휴가에서 돌아올 건가요?
(A) 저는 중국에 있을 거예요.
(B) 다음 주 수요일이요.
(C) 그것은 15시간의 비행이에요.

해설 언제 휴가에서 돌아올 건지를 묻는 When 의문문입니다.
(A) [×] 질문의 vacation(휴가)과 관련 있는 be in China(중국에 있다)를 사용하여 혼동을 준 오답입니다.
(B) [○] 다음 주 수요일이라며 휴가에서 돌아올 시점을 언급했으므로 정답입니다.
(C) [×] 언제 휴가에서 돌아올 건지를 물었는데, 이와 관련이 없는 그것은 15시간의 비행이라는 내용으로 응답했으므로 오답입니다.

20 3세 영국식 발음 → 미국식 발음

What print shop in the area should I use?
(A) I always use the one across the street.
(B) Print a copy of the receipt.
(C) I shop for groceries every week.

receipt [risíːt] 영수증   grocery [gróusəri] 식료품

해석 지역의 어느 인쇄소를 이용해야 할까요?
(A) 저는 항상 길 건너에 있는 곳을 이용해요.
(B) 영수증 사본을 인쇄하세요.
(C) 저는 매주 식료품을 사요.

해설 지역의 어느 인쇄소를 이용해야 할지를 묻는 What 의문문입니다. What print shop을 반드시 들어야 합니다.
(A) [○] 자신은 항상 길 건너에 있는 곳을 이용한다는 말로 길 건너에 있는 곳에 가라는 것을 간접적으로 전달했으므로 정답입니다.

(B) [×] 질문의 print(인쇄)를 '인쇄하다'라는 의미의 동사로 반복 사용하고, print shop(인쇄소)과 관련 있는 copy(사본)를 사용하여 혼동을 준 오답입니다.
(C) [×] 질문의 shop(가게)을 '(물건을) 사다'라는 의미의 동사로 반복 사용하여 혼동을 준 오답입니다.

21 3세 캐나다식 발음 → 미국식 발음

Which hotel will you stay at during the conference?
(A) Michael is going instead of me.
(B) The conference call is at 3 P.M.
(C) I'll stay there for a week.

conference call 전화 회의

해석 당신은 컨퍼런스 동안 어느 호텔에 머물 건가요?
(A) Michael이 저 대신 갈 거예요.
(B) 전화 회의가 오후 3시에 있어요.
(C) 저는 그곳에 일주일 동안 머물 거예요.

해설 컨퍼런스 동안 어느 호텔에 머물 것인지를 묻는 Which 의문문입니다. Which hotel을 반드시 들어야 합니다.
(A) [○] Michael이 대신 갈 것이라는 말로 자신은 컨퍼런스에 참석하지 않아 호텔에 머물지 않을 것임을 간접적으로 전달했으므로 정답입니다.
(B) [×] 컨퍼런스 동안 어느 호텔에 머물 것인지를 물었는데, 이와 관련이 없는 전화 회의가 오후 3시에 있다는 내용으로 응답했으므로 오답입니다.
(C) [×] 질문의 stay를 반복 사용하여 혼동을 준 오답입니다.

22 3세 호주식 발음 → 영국식 발음

When is the application for the summer internship due?
(A) She is starting an internship in Denver.
(B) A number of applicants.
(C) Oh, I didn't know you were interested.

application [미 æpləkéiʃən, 영 æplikéiʃən] 지원, 신청(서)
due [미 djuː, 영 dʒuː] (언제까지 ~하기로) 되어 있는
a number of 여러, 다수의   applicant [æplikənt] 지원자

해석 하계 인턴직의 지원은 언제까지인가요?
(A) 그녀는 덴버에서 인턴직을 시작해요.
(B) 여러 지원자들이요.
(C) 아, 저는 당신이 관심이 있는지 몰랐어요.

해설 하계 인턴직의 지원이 언제까지인지를 묻는 When 의문문입니다.
(A) [×] 질문의 internship을 반복 사용하여 혼동을 준 오답입니다.
(B) [×] application – applicants의 유사 발음 어휘를 사용하여 혼동을 준 오답입니다.
(C) [○] 관심이 있는지 몰랐다는 말로 상대방이 하계 인턴직 지원에 대해 묻는 것에 놀라움을 나타내는 정답입니다.

23 3세 영국식 발음 → 캐나다식 발음

What were the results of the customer satisfaction survey?
(A) It took about 25 minutes.
(B) A customer called for you.
(C) We'll find out tomorrow.

satisfaction [미 sætisfǽkʃən, 영 sætisfǽkʃən] 만족
survey [미 sə́ːrvei, 영 sə́ːvei] (설문) 조사   find out 알게 되다

해석 고객 만족 설문 조사의 결과가 어땠나요?
(A) 그것은 25분 정도 걸렸어요.
(B) 한 고객이 당신에게 전화했어요.
(C) 우리는 내일 알게 될 거예요.

해설 고객 만족 설문 조사의 결과가 어땠는지를 묻는 What 의문문입니다.
(A) [x] 질문의 survey(설문 조사)에서 연상할 수 있는 작성 시간과 관련된 25 minutes(25분)를 사용하여 혼동을 준 오답입니다.
(B) [x] 질문의 customer를 반복 사용하여 혼동을 준 오답입니다.
(C) [o] 내일 알게 될 것이라는 말로 아직 모른다는 간접적인 응답을 했으므로 정답입니다.

24 호주식 발음 → 미국식 발음

Which of the managers should I talk to about using the company car?
(A) The talk is in Hall D.
(B) I'll leave it on my desk.
(C) Mr. Bryant can help you with that.

leave[liːv] 두다

해석 회사 차량을 사용하는 것에 대해 관리자들 중 누구와 이야기해야 하나요?
(A) 그 강연은 D 홀에서 있어요.
(B) 그것을 제 책상 위에 둘게요.
(C) Mr. Bryant가 그것에 대해 당신을 도와줄 수 있어요.

해설 회사 차량을 사용하는 것에 대해 관리자들 중 누구와 이야기해야 하는지를 묻는 Which 의문문입니다. Which of the managers를 반드시 들어야 합니다.
(A) [x] 질문의 talk(이야기하다)를 '강연'이라는 의미의 명사로 반복 사용하여 혼동을 준 오답입니다.
(B) [x] 회사 차량을 사용하는 것에 대해 관리자들 중 누구와 이야기해야 하는지를 물었는데, 이와 관련이 없는 그것을 자신의 책상에 둘 것이라는 내용으로 응답했으므로 오답입니다.
(C) [o] Mr. Bryant가 그것에 대해 당신을 도와줄 수 있다는 말로 회사 차량을 사용하는 것에 대해 이야기할 수 있는 인물을 언급했으므로 정답입니다.

25 영국식 발음 → 호주식 발음

When do you think the project will be complete?
(A) We've experienced some delays.
(B) It's in the conference room.
(C) It happens every October.

complete[kəmplíːt] 완료된, 완성된 delay[diléi] 지연, 연기

해석 프로젝트가 언제 완료될 거라고 생각하시나요?
(A) 우리는 몇 차례 지연이 있었어요.
(B) 그것은 회의실에 있어요.
(C) 그것은 10월마다 발생해요.

해설 프로젝트가 언제 완료될 것이라고 생각하는지를 묻는 When 의문문입니다.
(A) [o] 몇 차례 지연이 있었다는 말로 늦어질 것이라는 간접적인 응답을 했으므로 정답입니다.
(B) [x] 프로젝트가 언제 완료될 것이라고 생각하는지를 물었는데 장소로 응답했으므로 오답입니다.
(C) [x] 시간을 나타내는 October(10월)를 사용하여 혼동을 준 오답입니다.

DAY 07 의문사 의문문 3

Course 1 Why 의문문

HACKERS PRACTICE 🎧 DAY07_02   p.69

01 (A)	02 (A)	03 (B)	04 (C)
05 (A)	06 (B)	07 (B)	

01 미국식 발음 → 캐나다식 발음 / 영국식 발음 → 호주식 발음

Why did you take Friday off?
(A) To visit the doctor.
(B) I'm bringing it on Monday.
(C) I don't know why he did.

take ~ off ~(동안)을 쉬다

해석 당신은 왜 금요일에 쉬었나요?
(A) 의사를 방문하기 위해서요.
(B) 저는 그것을 월요일에 가져올 거예요.
(C) 저는 그가 왜 그랬는지 모르겠어요.

해설 상대방이 왜 금요일에 쉬었는지를 묻는 Why 의문문입니다.
(A) [o] 의사를 방문하기 위해서라며 금요일에 쉰 이유를 언급했으므로 정답입니다.
(B) [x] 질문의 Friday(금요일)와 관련 있는 Monday(월요일)를 사용하여 혼동을 준 오답입니다.
(C) [x] he가 나타내는 대상이 질문에 없으므로 오답입니다.

02 영국식 발음 → 호주식 발음 / 미국식 발음 → 캐나다식 발음

Why is Beth canceling our meeting?
(A) Because her schedule changed.
(B) Orders must be canceled by phone.
(C) I discussed them with our boss.

cancel[kǽnsəl] 취소하다

해석 Beth는 왜 우리의 회의를 취소하나요?
(A) 그녀의 일정이 변경되었기 때문에요.
(B) 주문은 전화로 취소되어야 해요.
(C) 저는 그것들을 우리 상사와 논의했어요.

해설 Beth가 왜 회의를 취소하는지를 묻는 Why 의문문입니다.
(A) [o] 그녀의 일정이 변경되었기 때문이라며 Beth가 회의를 취소하는 이유를 언급했으므로 정답입니다.
(B) [x] 질문의 canceling을 canceled로 반복 사용하여 혼동을 준 오답입니다.
(C) [x] 질문의 meeting(회의)과 관련 있는 discussed(논의했다)를 사용하여 혼동을 준 오답입니다.

03 캐나다식 발음 → 영국식 발음 / 호주식 발음 → 미국식 발음

Why is the new CEO visiting the office?
(A) Yes, it's a special offer.
(B) To see the board of directors.
(C) He should be arriving soon.

offer[미 ɔ́ːfər, 영 ɔ́fə] 할인, 제공 board of directors 경영진, 이사회

해석 새로운 최고 경영자가 왜 사무실을 방문할 것인가요?

(A) 네, 그것은 특별 할인이에요.
(B) 경영진을 만나기 위해서요.
(C) 그는 곧 도착할 거예요.

해설 새로운 최고 경영자가 왜 사무실을 방문할 것인지를 묻는 Why 의문문입니다.
(A) [x] 의문사 의문문에 Yes로 응답했으므로 오답입니다. office – offer의 유사 발음 어휘를 사용하여 혼동을 주었습니다.
(B) [o] 경영진을 만나기 위해서라며 새로운 최고 경영자가 사무실을 방문하는 이유를 언급했으므로 정답입니다.
(C) [x] 질문의 visiting(방문하다)과 관련 있는 arriving(도착하다)을 사용하여 혼동을 준 오답입니다.

04 🔊 미국식 발음 → 호주식 발음 / 영국식 발음 → 캐나다식 발음

Why are there balloons in the break room?
(A) Sure, that'll be fine.
(B) I go to lunch at 11.
(C) They are for Simone's birthday.

break room 휴게실

해석 왜 휴게실에 풍선들이 있나요?
(A) 물론이죠, 그것은 괜찮을 거예요.
(B) 저는 11시에 점심을 먹으러 가요.
(C) Simone의 생일을 위한 것들이에요.

해설 왜 휴게실에 풍선들이 있는지를 묻는 Why 의문문입니다.
(A) [x] 왜 휴게실에 풍선들이 있는지를 물었는데, 이와 관련이 없는 그것은 괜찮을 것이라는 내용으로 응답했으므로 오답입니다.
(B) [x] 질문의 break(휴식)와 관련 있는 lunch(점심)를 사용하여 혼동을 준 오답입니다.
(C) [o] Simone의 생일을 위한 것들이라며 휴게실에 풍선들이 있는 이유를 언급했으므로 정답입니다.

05 🔊 캐나다식 발음 → 미국식 발음 / 호주식 발음 → 영국식 발음

Why are you standing here on the corner, Jane?
(A) I am waiting for my friend.
(B) Milton Street and Vine Avenue.
(C) Just around the corner.

avenue[미 ǽvənjùː, 영 ǽvənjuː] ~가 around the corner 아주 가까운

해석 당신은 왜 이곳 모퉁이에 서 있나요, Jane?
(A) 저는 제 친구를 기다리고 있어요.
(B) Milton가와 Vine가요.
(C) 아주 가까이에요.

해설 상대방이 왜 모퉁이에 서 있는지를 묻는 Why 의문문입니다.
(A) [o] 친구를 기다리고 있다며 모퉁이에 서 있는 이유를 언급했으므로 정답입니다.
(B) [x] 질문의 corner(모퉁이)에서 연상할 수 있는 길과 관련된 Street(~가)와 Avenue(~가)를 사용하여 혼동을 준 오답입니다.
(C) [x] 질문의 corner를 반복 사용하여 혼동을 준 오답입니다.

06 🔊 호주식 발음 → 영국식 발음 / 캐나다식 발음 → 미국식 발음

Why is the printer in the copy room not working?
(A) It's next to the conference room.
(B) The printer is broken?
(C) Since sometime last week.

conference room 회의실 broken[미 bróukən, 영 brə́ukən] 고장 난

해석 복사실에 있는 인쇄기가 왜 작동하지 않나요?
(A) 그것은 회의실 옆에 있어요.
(B) 그 인쇄기가 고장 났나요?
(C) 지난주 언젠가부터요.

해설 복사실에 있는 인쇄기가 왜 작동하지 않는지를 묻는 Why 의문문입니다.
(A) [x] 질문의 room을 반복 사용하여 혼동을 준 오답입니다.
(B) [o] 그 인쇄기가 고장 났는지를 되물어 인쇄기의 상태에 대한 추가 정보를 요구하는 정답입니다.
(C) [x] 복사실에 있는 인쇄기가 왜 작동하지 않는지를 물었는데 시점으로 응답했으므로 오답입니다.

07 🔊 영국식 발음 → 캐나다식 발음 / 미국식 발음 → 호주식 발음

Why don't you see Ms. Park in the payroll department?
(A) I'm going to pay for that item.
(B) She's not here today.
(C) Yes, I can see quite well.

payroll department 경리과, 급여 지급 부서

해석 경리과의 Ms. Park을 만나보는 게 어떤가요?
(A) 저는 그 상품에 대한 금액을 지불할 거예요.
(B) 그녀는 오늘 이곳에 없어요.
(C) 네, 저는 꽤 잘 보여요.

해설 경리과의 Ms. Park을 만나보는 것이 어떤지를 묻는 Why 의문문입니다. Why don't you?가 제안하는 표현임을 이해할 수 있어야 합니다.
(A) [x] payroll – pay의 유사 발음 어휘를 사용하여 혼동을 준 오답입니다.
(B) [o] 그녀는 오늘 이곳에 없다는 말로 경리과의 Ms. Park을 만날 수 없음을 간접적으로 전달했으므로 정답입니다.
(C) [x] 질문의 see를 반복 사용하여 혼동을 준 오답입니다.

Course 2 How 의문문

HACKERS PRACTICE 🎧 DAY07_04   p.71

01 (B)	02 (B)	03 (B)	04 (C)
05 (A)	06 (B)	07 (C)	

01 🔊 호주식 발음 → 미국식 발음 / 캐나다식 발음 → 영국식 발음

How can I make this dish?
(A) It's the most famous kind of Japanese food.
(B) Just follow this recipe.
(C) I'll wash the dishes later.

dish[diʃ] 요리, 음식, 접시 recipe[미 résəpi, 영 résipi] 요리법, 조리법

해석 어떻게 이 요리를 만들 수 있나요?
(A) 그것은 가장 유명한 종류의 일본 음식이에요.
(B) 그냥 이 요리법을 따라 하세요.
(C) 제가 나중에 설거지를 할게요.

해설 어떻게 이 요리를 만들 수 있는지를 묻는 How 의문문입니다.
(A) [x] 질문의 dish(요리)와 같은 의미인 food(음식)를 사용하여 혼동을 준 오답입니다.
(B) [o] 이 요리법을 따라 하라며 요리를 만들 수 있는 방법을 언급했으므로 정답입니다.
(C) [x] 질문의 dish(요리)를 '접시'라는 의미의 dishes로 반복 사용하여 혼동을 준 오답입니다.

02 🎧 미국식 발음 → 캐나다식 발음 / 영국식 발음 → 호주식 발음

> How did your piano class go?
> (A) Many students study music.
> **(B) It went well.**
> (C) I've played for years.
>
> go well 잘 되다

해석 당신의 피아노 수업은 어땠나요?
(A) 많은 학생들이 음악을 공부해요.
(B) 잘 진행되었어요.
(C) 저는 수년간 연주해 왔어요.

해설 피아노 수업이 어땠는지를 묻는 How 의문문입니다. How ~ go가 진행 상황에 대한 의견을 묻는 것임을 이해할 수 있어야 합니다.
(A) [x] 질문의 piano(피아노)와 관련 있는 music(음악)을 사용하고, class(수업)와 관련 있는 study(공부하다)를 사용하여 혼동을 준 오답입니다.
(B) [o] 잘 진행되었다는 말로 피아노 수업에 대한 의견을 언급했으므로 정답입니다.
(C) [x] 피아노 수업이 어땠는지를 물었는데, 이와 관련이 없는 수년간 연주해 왔다는 내용으로 응답했으므로 오답입니다.

03 🎧 영국식 발음 → 호주식 발음 / 미국식 발음 → 캐나다식 발음

> How many people will attend the conference?
> (A) It's on September 21.
> **(B) Seven from each department.**
> (C) Around $200.
>
> attend[əténd] 참석하다

해석 얼마나 많은 사람들이 그 회의에 참석하나요?
(A) 그것은 9월 21일에 열려요.
(B) 각 부서에서 7명이요.
(C) 약 200달러요.

해설 얼마나 많은 사람들이 회의에 참석하는지를 묻는 How 의문문입니다. How many가 수량을 묻는 것임을 이해할 수 있어야 합니다.
(A) [x] 얼마나 많은 사람들이 회의에 참석하는지를 물었는데 날짜로 응답했으므로 오답입니다.
(B) [o] 각 부서에서 7명이라며 회의에 참석하는 인원수를 언급했으므로 정답입니다.
(C) [x] 얼마나 많은 사람들이 회의에 참석하는지를 물었는데 가격으로 응답했으므로 오답입니다.

04 🎧 캐나다식 발음 → 영국식 발음 / 호주식 발음 → 미국식 발음

> How much does this phone cost?
> (A) OK, I'll call you back.
> (B) How did you know?
> **(C) It is $125.**

해석 이 전화기는 얼마인가요?
(A) 네, 제가 다시 전화할게요.
(B) 어떻게 아셨나요?
(C) 125달러예요.

해설 전화기가 얼마인지를 묻는 How 의문문입니다. How much가 가격을 묻는 것임을 이해할 수 있어야 합니다.
(A) [x] 질문의 phone(전화기)과 관련 있는 call(전화하다)을 사용하여 혼동을 준 오답입니다.
(B) [x] 전화기가 얼마인지를 물었는데, 이와 관련이 없는 어떻게 알

앉는지를 되묻는 내용으로 응답했으므로 오답입니다.
(C) [o] 125달러라며 전화기의 가격을 언급했으므로 정답입니다.

05 🎧 미국식 발음 → 호주식 발음 / 영국식 발음 → 캐나다식 발음

> How do you like the new Thai restaurant downtown?
> **(A) I'm going there tonight.**
> (B) I've visited Bangkok many times.
> (C) I couldn't get it untied.
>
> downtown[dàuntáun] 시내의   untie[ʌntái] (매듭 등을) 풀다

해석 시내의 새 태국 음식점은 어떤 것 같나요?
(A) 저는 오늘 밤 그곳에 갈 거예요.
(B) 저는 여러 번 방콕을 방문했어요.
(C) 저는 그것을 풀 수 없었어요.

해설 시내의 새 태국 음식점이 어떤 것 같은지를 묻는 How 의문문입니다. How do you like가 의견을 묻는 것임을 이해할 수 있어야 합니다.
(A) [o] 오늘 밤 그곳에 갈 것이라는 말로 시내의 새 태국 음식점이 어떤지 아직 모른다는 간접적인 응답을 했으므로 정답입니다.
(B) [x] 질문의 Thai(태국)와 관련 있는 Bangkok(방콕)을 사용하여 혼동을 준 오답입니다.
(C) [x] Thai - untied의 유사 발음 어휘를 사용하여 혼동을 준 오답입니다.

06 🎧 캐나다식 발음 → 미국식 발음 / 호주식 발음 → 영국식 발음

> How long will we have to wait for a table?
> (A) It seats seven.
> **(B) Ask the person at the counter.**
> (C) The five-course meal.
>
> counter[미 káuntər, 영 káuntə] 계산대   meal[미 mi:l, 영 miəl] 식사

해석 테이블이 빌 때까지 얼마나 기다려야 하나요?
(A) 7명이 앉을 수 있어요.
(B) 계산대에 있는 사람에게 물어보세요.
(C) 다섯 코스짜리 식사요.

해설 테이블이 빌 때까지 얼마나 기다려야 하는지를 묻는 How 의문문입니다. How long이 기간을 묻는 것임을 이해할 수 있어야 합니다.
(A) [x] 질문의 table(테이블)과 관련 있는 seats(앉히다)를 사용하여 혼동을 준 오답입니다.
(B) [o] 계산대에 있는 사람에게 물어보라는 말로 모른다는 간접적인 응답을 했으므로 정답입니다.
(C) [x] 테이블이 빌 때까지 얼마나 기다려야 하는지를 물었는데, 이와 관련이 없는 다섯 코스짜리 식사라는 내용으로 응답했으므로 오답입니다.

07 🎧 호주식 발음 → 영국식 발음 / 캐나다식 발음 → 미국식 발음

> How often do you go to the gas station?
> (A) About 60 liters.
> (B) It costs nearly $40.
> **(C) Once a week.**
>
> gas station 주유소

해석 당신은 얼마나 자주 주유소에 가나요?
(A) 약 60리터요.
(B) 그건 거의 40달러가 들어요.
(C) 일주일에 한 번이요.

해설 얼마나 자주 주유소에 가는지를 묻는 How 의문문입니다. How often 이 빈도를 묻는 것임을 이해할 수 있어야 합니다.
(A) [×] 얼마나 자주 주유소에 가는지를 물었는데 수량으로 응답했으므로 오답입니다.
(B) [×] 얼마나 자주 주유소에 가는지를 물었는데 가격으로 응답했으므로 오답입니다.
(C) [○] 일주일에 한 번이라는 말로 주유소에 가는 빈도를 언급했으므로 정답입니다.

HACKERS TEST 🎧 DAY07_05   p.72

01 (B)	02 (A)	03 (B)	04 (A)
05 (C)	06 (B)	07 (C)	08 (A)
09 (B)	10 (B)	11 (A)	12 (A)
13 (A)	14 (A)	15 (B)	16 (A)
17 (C)	18 (C)	19 (A)	20 (C)
21 (A)	22 (B)	23 (C)	24 (A)
25 (C)			

01 🎧 영국식 발음 → 캐나다식 발음

Why was the flight canceled?
(A) It's the flight to Berlin.
(B) Because of an engine problem.
(C) I got a full refund.

refund[rí:fʌnd] 환불

해석 항공편이 왜 취소되었나요?
(A) 그것은 베를린행 항공편이에요.
(B) 엔진 문제 때문에요.
(C) 저는 전액 환불을 받았어요.

해설 항공편이 왜 취소되었는지를 묻는 Why 의문문입니다.
(A) [×] 질문의 flight를 반복 사용하여 혼동을 준 오답입니다.
(B) [○] 엔진 문제 때문이라며 항공편이 취소된 이유를 언급했으므로 정답입니다.
(C) [×] 질문의 canceled(취소되다)와 관련 있는 refund(환불)를 사용하여 혼동을 준 오답입니다.

02 🎧 호주식 발음 → 미국식 발음

How did you submit your report?
(A) By e-mail.
(B) I'm only reporting the facts.
(C) You are doing great.

submit[səbmít] 제출하다   report[미 ripɔ́:rt, 영 ripɔ́:t] 보고서; 보고하다
fact[fækt] 사실

해석 당신은 보고서를 어떻게 제출했나요?
(A) 이메일로요.
(B) 저는 사실만을 보고 드리고 있어요.
(C) 당신은 매우 잘하고 있어요.

해설 보고서를 어떻게 제출했는지를 묻는 How 의문문입니다.
(A) [○] 이메일로라며 보고서를 제출한 방법을 언급했으므로 정답입니다.
(B) [×] 질문의 report(보고서)를 '보고하다'라는 의미의 동사 reporting 으로 반복 사용하여 혼동을 준 오답입니다.
(C) [×] 보고서를 어떻게 제출했는지를 물었는데, 이와 관련 없는 상대방이 매우 잘하고 있다는 내용으로 응답했으므로 오답입니다.

03 🎧 미국식 발음 → 캐나다식 발음

Why are you quitting your job?
(A) Mr. Jin is a dentist.
(B) For a better position.
(C) You only started two months ago.

quit[kwit] 그만두다, 중지하다   position[pəzíʃən] 일자리, 직책

해석 당신은 왜 일을 그만두나요?
(A) Mr. Jin은 치과 의사예요.
(B) 더 나은 일자리를 위해서요.
(C) 당신은 두 달 전에 시작했을 뿐이잖아요.

해설 상대방이 왜 일을 그만두는지를 묻는 Why 의문문입니다.
(A) [×] 질문의 job(일)과 관련 있는 dentist(치과 의사)를 사용하여 혼동을 준 오답입니다.
(B) [○] 더 나은 일자리를 위해서라며 일을 그만두는 이유를 언급했으므로 정답입니다.
(C) [×] 질문의 quitting(그만두다)과 반대 의미인 started(시작했다)를 사용하여 혼동을 준 오답입니다.

04 🎧 영국식 발음 → 호주식 발음

How can I get a parking permit?
(A) Go talk to the building manager.
(B) I have a driver's license.
(C) There's an empty spot over there.

permit[미 pə́:rmit, 영 pə́:mit] 허가증   license[láisəns] 면허, 허가
spot[미 spɑt, 영 spɔt] 자리, 장소

해석 어떻게 주차 허가증을 받을 수 있나요?
(A) 건물 관리인에게 가서 말해 보세요.
(B) 저는 운전면허가 있어요.
(C) 저쪽에 비어있는 자리가 있어요.

해설 어떻게 주차 허가증을 받을 수 있는지를 묻는 How 의문문입니다.
(A) [○] 건물 관리인에게 가서 말해 보라는 말로 어떻게 주차 허가증을 받을 수 있는지 모른다는 간접적인 응답을 했으므로 정답입니다.
(B) [×] 질문의 parking(주차)과 관련 있는 driver(운전자)를 사용하고, permit(허가증)과 관련 있는 license(면허)를 사용하여 혼동을 준 오답입니다.
(C) [×] 어떻게 주차 허가증을 받을 수 있는지를 물었는데, 이와 관련이 없는 저쪽에 비어있는 자리가 있다는 내용으로 응답했으므로 오답입니다.

05 🎧 캐나다식 발음 → 호주식 발음

Why is the cafeteria closed today?
(A) It's not too far.
(B) I ate already.
(C) It's being repainted.

cafeteria[미 kæfətíəriə, 영 kæfətíəriə] 구내식당
repaint[미 ri:péint, 영 ri:péint] 다시 페인트칠하다

해석 오늘 구내식당이 왜 문을 닫았나요?
(A) 그렇게 멀지는 않아요.
(B) 저는 이미 먹었어요.
(C) 그곳은 다시 페인트칠이 되고 있는 중이에요.

해설 오늘 구내식당이 왜 문을 닫았는지를 묻는 Why 의문문입니다.

(A) [×] 오늘 구내식당이 왜 문을 닫았는지를 물었는데, 이와 관련이 없는 그렇게 멀지는 않다는 내용으로 응답했으므로 오답입니다.
(B) [×] 질문의 cafeteria(구내식당)와 관련 있는 ate(먹었다)를 사용하여 혼동을 준 오답입니다.
(C) [○] 그곳은 다시 페인트칠이 되고 있는 중이라며 오늘 구내식당이 문을 닫은 이유를 언급했으므로 정답입니다.

06 [3배] 미국식 발음 → 호주식 발음

How's your training going?
(A) Yes, everyone is going.
(B) I'm learning a lot.
(C) For my degree.

training[tréiniŋ] 교육, 훈련   degree[digríː] 학위, 등급

해석 교육은 어떻게 되어 가고 있나요?
(A) 네, 모든 사람이 가요.
(B) 저는 많이 배우고 있어요.
(C) 제 학위 때문에요.

해설 교육이 어떻게 되어 가고 있는지를 묻는 How 의문문입니다. How's ~ going이 진행 상황에 대한 의견을 묻는 것임을 이해할 수 있어야 합니다.
(A) [×] 의문사 의문문에 Yes로 응답했으므로 오답입니다. 질문의 going을 반복 사용하여 혼동을 주었습니다.
(B) [○] 많이 배우고 있다는 말로 교육에 대한 의견을 전달했으므로 정답입니다.
(C) [×] 질문의 training(교육)과 관련 있는 degree(학위)를 사용하여 혼동을 준 오답입니다.

07 [3배] 캐나다식 발음 → 미국식 발음

Why did you and Mr. Andreas meet on Monday?
(A) That's too early for me.
(B) After we went out for dinner.
(C) To discuss the fund-raising project.

fund-raising[fʌ́ndrèiziŋ] 모금

해석 당신과 Mr. Andreas는 왜 월요일에 만났나요?
(A) 그건 저에게는 너무 일러요.
(B) 우리가 저녁을 먹으러 나간 후에요.
(C) 모금 프로젝트에 대해 논의하기 위해서요.

해설 상대방과 Mr. Andreas가 왜 월요일에 만났는지를 묻는 Why 의문문입니다.
(A) [×] 질문의 Monday(월요일)와 관련 있는 early(이른)를 사용하여 혼동을 준 오답입니다.
(B) [×] 상대방과 Mr. Andreas가 월요일에 만난 이유를 물었는데 시점으로 응답했으므로 오답입니다.
(C) [○] 모금 프로젝트에 대해 논의하기 위해서라며 Mr. Andreas와 월요일에 만난 이유를 언급했으므로 정답입니다.

08 [3배] 호주식 발음 → 영국식 발음

How should I cut your hair?
(A) Just trim the top, please.
(B) The hairdresser is quite busy.
(C) I'd prefer a light brown color.

trim[trim] 다듬다   hairdresser[미 héərdrèsər, 영 héədrèsə] 미용사

해석 머리카락을 어떻게 잘라드릴까요?

(A) 그냥 윗머리를 다듬어 주세요.
(B) 그 미용사는 꽤 바빠요.
(C) 저는 연한 갈색이 더 좋을 것 같아요.

해설 머리카락을 어떻게 자를지를 묻는 How 의문문입니다.
(A) [○] 그냥 윗머리를 다듬어 달라는 말로 머리카락을 어떻게 자를지를 언급했으므로 정답입니다.
(B) [×] 질문의 cut ~ hair(~의 머리카락을 자르다)와 관련 있는 hairdresser(미용사)를 사용하여 혼동을 준 오답입니다.
(C) [×] 머리카락을 어떻게 자를지를 물었는데, 이와 관련이 없는 연한 갈색이 더 좋을 것 같다는 내용으로 응답했으므로 오답입니다.

09 [3배] 미국식 발음 → 캐나다식 발음

Why was Shannon late for work?
(A) She'll stay until 11 P.M.
(B) Because of rush hour traffic.
(C) The deadline already passed.

rush hour 출·퇴근 시간   traffic[trǽfik] 교통량
deadline[dédlàin] 마감기한

해석 Shannon은 왜 회사에 늦었나요?
(A) 그녀는 오후 11시까지 있을 거예요.
(B) 출근 시간의 교통량 때문에요.
(C) 마감기한이 이미 지났어요.

해설 Shannon이 왜 회사에 늦었는지를 묻는 Why 의문문입니다.
(A) [×] 질문의 late(늦은)와 관련 있는 11 P.M.(오후 11시)을 사용하여 혼동을 준 오답입니다.
(B) [○] 출근 시간의 교통량 때문이라며 Shannon이 회사에 늦은 이유를 언급했으므로 정답입니다.
(C) [×] Shannon이 왜 회사에 늦었는지를 물었는데, 이와 관련이 없는 마감기한이 이미 지났다는 내용으로 응답했으므로 오답입니다.

10 [3배] 호주식 발음 → 영국식 발음

How much is the camera discounted by?
(A) I have two of them.
(B) Around €20.
(C) For a week.

discount[diskáunt] 할인하다

해석 카메라는 얼마나 할인되나요?
(A) 저는 그것들을 두 개 가지고 있어요.
(B) 20유로 정도요.
(C) 1주일 동안이요.

해설 카메라가 얼마나 할인되는지를 묻는 How 의문문입니다. How much가 가격을 묻는 것임을 이해할 수 있어야 합니다.
(A) [×] 카메라가 얼마나 할인되는지를 물었는데, 이와 관련이 없는 그것들을 두 개 가지고 있다는 내용으로 응답했으므로 오답입니다.
(B) [○] 20유로 정도라는 말로 카메라가 할인되는 가격을 언급했으므로 정답입니다.
(C) [×] 카메라가 얼마나 할인되는지를 물었는데 기간으로 응답했으므로 오답입니다.

11 [3배] 미국식 발음 → 캐나다식 발음

Why is the IT department working overtime?
(A) Because the company network is having problems.   ○

(B) That department is in room 512.
(C) They start at 8 A.M.

---

overtime [미 óuvərtaim, 영 óuvətaim] 초과 근무

해석 IT 부서는 왜 초과 근무를 하고 있나요?
(A) 회사 네트워크에 문제가 있기 때문에요.
(B) 그 부서는 512호에 있어요.
(C) 그들은 오전 8시에 시작해요.

해설 IT 부서가 왜 초과 근무를 하고 있는지를 묻는 Why 의문문입니다.
(A) [ㅇ] 회사 네트워크에 문제가 있기 때문이라며 IT 부서가 초과 근무를 하고 있는 이유를 언급했으므로 정답입니다.
(B) [x] 질문의 department를 반복 사용하여 혼동을 준 오답입니다.
(C) [x] 질문의 working overtime(초과 근무를 하고 있다)에서 연상할 수 있는 근무 시작 시간과 관련된 start at 8 A.M.(오전 8시에 시작하다)을 사용하여 혼동을 준 오답입니다.

---

12 🔊 영국식 발음 → 호주식 발음

How often do you work from home?
(A) It depends on my schedule.
(B) Because of my long commute.
(C) The work on the home is nearly completed.

---

depend on ~에 달려 있다   commute [kəmjúːt] 통근 (거리)
complete [kəmplíːt] 완료하다

해석 당신은 얼마나 자주 집에서 일을 하시나요?
(A) 그것은 제 일정에 달려 있어요.
(B) 제 긴 통근 거리 때문에요.
(C) 그 집에 대한 작업은 거의 완료되었어요.

해설 상대방이 얼마나 자주 집에서 일을 하는지를 묻는 How 의문문입니다. How often이 빈도를 묻는 것임을 이해할 수 있어야 합니다.
(A) [ㅇ] 그것은 자신의 일정에 달려 있다는 말로 집에서 일을 하는 빈도가 일정에 따라 다름을 전달했으므로 정답입니다.
(B) [x] 얼마나 자주 집에서 일을 하는지를 물었는데 이유로 응답했으므로 오답입니다.
(C) [x] 질문의 work와 home을 반복 사용하여 혼동을 준 오답입니다.

---

13 🔊 캐나다식 발음 → 영국식 발음

Why don't you have a seat here while you wait?
(A) Thank you, I'll do that.
(B) I need to buy a new chair.
(C) Your server will be here shortly.

---

have a seat 앉다   server [미 sə́ːrvər, 영 sə́ːvə] 웨이터
shortly [미 ʃɔ́ːrtli, 영 ʃɔ́ːtli] 곧

해석 기다리시는 동안 여기 앉아 계시겠어요?
(A) 감사합니다, 그럴게요.
(B) 저는 새 의자를 사야 해요.
(C) 당신의 웨이터가 곧 여기로 올 거예요.

해설 기다리는 동안 여기 앉아 있겠냐고 묻는 Why 의문문입니다. Why don't you가 제안하는 표현임을 이해할 수 있어야 합니다.
(A) [ㅇ] 그러겠다는 말로 제안을 수락한 정답입니다.
(B) [x] 질문의 seat(자리)과 관련 있는 chair(의자)를 사용하여 혼동을 준 오답입니다.
(C) [x] 질문의 here를 반복 사용하여 혼동을 준 오답입니다.

---

14 🔊 미국식 발음 → 호주식 발음

How many pages will the catalog have?
(A) It's hard to say right now.
(B) Over an hour away.
(C) To list our products.

---

away [əwéi] (시간적·공간적으로) 떨어진 곳에
product [미 prɑ́dʌkt, 영 prɔ́dʌkt] 제품

해석 카탈로그에 몇 페이지가 들어갈 건가요?
(A) 지금 당장은 말씀드리기 어려워요.
(B) 한 시간 이상 떨어진 곳이요.
(C) 우리 제품을 목록으로 작성하기 위해서요.

해설 카탈로그에 몇 페이지가 들어갈 것인지를 묻는 How 의문문입니다. How many가 수량을 묻는 것임을 이해할 수 있어야 합니다.
(A) [ㅇ] 지금 당장은 말하기 어렵다는 말로 아직 모른다는 간접적인 응답을 했으므로 정답입니다.
(B) [x] 카탈로그에 몇 페이지가 들어갈 것인지를 물었는데 거리로 응답했으므로 오답입니다.
(C) [x] 질문의 catalog(카탈로그)와 관련 있는 To list ~ products (제품을 목록으로 작성하기 위해)를 사용하여 혼동을 준 오답입니다.

---

15 🔊 캐나다식 발음 → 미국식 발음

Why are you applying to Party Starters?
(A) It doesn't apply to beginners.
(B) To gain more experience as an event planner.
(C) My application has been sent.

---

apply [əplái] 지원하다, 적용하다   beginner [미 bigínər, 영 bigínə] 초보자
gain [gein] (경험을) 쌓다   application [미 æpləkéiʃən, 영 æplikéiʃən] 지원(서)

해석 당신은 왜 Party Starters사에 지원하나요?
(A) 그것은 초보자에게는 적용되지 않아요.
(B) 행사 기획자로서 더 많은 경험을 쌓기 위해서요.
(C) 제 지원서는 보내졌어요.

해설 왜 Party Starters사에 지원하는지를 묻는 Why 의문문입니다.
(A) [x] 질문의 applying(지원하다)을 '적용하다'라는 의미의 apply로 반복 사용하여 혼동을 준 오답입니다.
(B) [ㅇ] 행사 기획자로서 더 많은 경험을 쌓기 위해서라며 Party Starters사에 지원하는 이유를 언급했으므로 정답입니다.
(C) [x] applying - application의 유사 발음 어휘를 사용하여 혼동을 준 오답입니다.

---

16 🔊 호주식 발음 → 영국식 발음

How long did you run the advertisement?
(A) Just over three weeks.
(B) It will be a big success.
(C) On an employment Web site.

---

advertisement [미 ædvərtáizmənt, 영 ədvə́ːtismənt] 광고
success [səksés] 성공   employment [implɔ́imənt] 채용

해석 당신은 얼마나 오래 광고를 냈나요?
(A) 3주 동안만요.
(B) 그것은 큰 성공을 거둘 거예요.
(C) 채용 웹사이트에서요.

해설 얼마나 오래 광고를 냈는지를 묻는 How 의문문입니다. How long이 기간을 묻는 것임을 이해할 수 있어야 합니다.

(A) [○] 3주 동안만이라며 광고를 낸 기간을 언급했으므로 정답입니다.

(B) [×] 얼마나 오래 광고를 냈는지를 물었는데, 이와 관련이 없는 그것은 큰 성공을 거둘 것이라는 내용으로 응답으로 오답입니다.

(C) [×] 질문의 advertisement(광고)에서 연상할 수 있는 광고 매체와 관련된 Web site(웹사이트)를 사용하여 혼동을 준 오답입니다.

17 ③ 영국식 발음 → 캐나다식 발음

Why was our workshop postponed today?
(A) About company expansions.
(B) Sometime later today.
(C) An urgent meeting was called.

postpone [미 poustpóun, 영 pəustpáun] 연기하다, 미루다
expansion [ikspǽnʃən] 확장, 팽창
urgent [미 ə́ːrdʒənt, 영 ə́ːdʒənt] 긴급한   call [kɔːl] 소집하다, 부르다

해석 오늘 우리의 워크숍은 왜 연기되었나요?
(A) 회사의 확장에 대해서요.
(B) 오늘 늦게 언젠가요.
(C) 긴급회의가 소집되었어요.

해설 오늘 워크숍이 왜 연기되었는지를 묻는 Why 의문문입니다.
(A) [×] 질문의 workshop(워크숍)과 관련 있는 company(회사)를 사용하여 혼동을 준 오답입니다.
(B) [×] 오늘 워크숍이 왜 연기되었는지를 물었는데, 이와 관련이 없는 오늘 늦게 언젠가라는 내용으로 응답했으므로 오답입니다.
(C) [○] 긴급회의가 소집되었다며 워크숍이 연기된 이유를 언급했으므로 정답입니다.

18 ③ 호주식 발음 → 미국식 발음

How much was your ticket to Paris last month?
(A) It's such a romantic city.
(B) Around eight hours.
(C) I don't really remember.

romantic [미 roumǽntik, 영 rəumǽntik] 낭만적인

해석 지난달에 파리로 가는 당신의 표는 얼마였나요?
(A) 그곳은 매우 낭만적인 도시예요.
(B) 8시간 정도요.
(C) 기억이 잘 나지 않아요.

해설 지난달에 파리로 가는 상대방의 표가 얼마였는지를 묻는 How 의문문입니다. How much가 가격을 묻는 것임을 이해할 수 있어야 합니다.
(A) [×] 지난달에 파리로 가는 표가 얼마였는지를 물었는데, 이와 관련이 없는 그곳은 매우 낭만적인 도시라는 내용으로 응답했으므로 오답입니다.
(B) [×] 지난달에 파리로 가는 표가 얼마였는지를 물었는데 기간으로 응답했으므로 오답입니다. Around eight까지만 듣고 정답으로 고르지 않도록 주의합니다.
(C) [○] 기억이 잘 나지 않는다는 말로 모른다는 간접적인 응답을 했으므로 정답입니다.

19 ③ 미국식 발음 → 캐나다식 발음

Why haven't you sent me your expense report yet?
(A) Didn't you receive my e-mail yesterday?
(B) The price is reasonable.
⟳

(C) I will send my portfolio soon.

expense [ikspéns] 경비, 비용   reasonable [ríːzənəbl] 적당한
portfolio [미 pɔːrtfóuliòu, 영 pɔ̀ːtfóuliəu] 작품집

해석 왜 당신은 아직 저에게 경비 보고서를 보내지 않았나요?
(A) 어제 제 이메일을 받지 못하셨나요?
(B) 그 가격은 적당하네요.
(C) 제 작품집을 곧 보낼게요.

해설 왜 아직 경비 보고서를 보내지 않았는지를 묻는 Why 의문문입니다.
(A) [○] 어제 자신의 이메일을 받지 못했는지를 되물어 경비 보고서를 이미 보냈음을 전달했으므로 정답입니다.
(B) [×] 질문의 expense(경비)와 관련 있는 price(가격)를 사용하여 혼동을 준 오답입니다.
(C) [×] 질문의 sent를 send로 반복 사용하여 혼동을 준 오답입니다.

20 ③ 영국식 발음 → 호주식 발음

How would you like to test drive our new electric car?
(A) I am taking an eye exam.
(B) You'll like some of the car's features.
(C) That would be fantastic.

test drive 시승하다   feature [미 fíːtʃər, 영 fíːtʃə] 기능, 특징
fantastic [fæntǽstik] 환상적인, 굉장한

해석 우리의 새로운 전기 자동차를 시승해 보는 게 어떠신가요?
(A) 저는 시력 검사를 받을 거예요.
(B) 당신은 그 차의 몇몇 기능들을 좋아할 거예요..
(C) 그것은 정말 환상적이겠네요.

해설 새로운 전기 자동차를 시승하는 것이 어떤지를 묻는 How 의문문입니다. How would you like to가 의견을 묻는 것임을 이해할 수 있어야 합니다.
(A) [×] 질문의 test(시험)와 같은 의미인 exam(검사)을 사용하여 혼동을 준 오답입니다.
(B) [×] 질문의 like와 car를 반복 사용하여 혼동을 준 오답입니다.
(C) [○] 정말 환상적이겠다는 말로 전기 자동차 시승 제안에 대한 의견을 언급했으므로 정답입니다.

21 ③ 캐나다식 발음 → 영국식 발음

Why don't we go to Lake Mead this weekend?
(A) I have an assignment due on Monday.
(B) It's going to rain today.
(C) I'm not sure why they did.

assignment [əsáinmənt] 과제   due on ~까지 마감인

해석 우리 이번 주말에 미드호에 가는 게 어때요?
(A) 저는 월요일까지 마감인 과제가 있어요.
(B) 오늘은 비가 올 거예요.
(C) 저는 그들이 왜 그랬는지 모르겠어요.

해설 이번 주말에 미드호에 가는 것이 어떤지를 묻는 Why 의문문입니다. Why don't we가 제안하는 표현임을 이해할 수 있어야 합니다.
(A) [○] 월요일까지 마감인 과제가 있다는 말로 제안을 간접적으로 거절한 정답입니다.
(B) [×] 이번 주말에 미드호에 가는 것이 어떤지를 물었는데, 이와 관련이 없는 오늘은 비가 올 거라는 내용으로 응답했으므로 오답입니다.
(C) [×] 이번 주말에 미드호에 가는 것이 어떤지를 물었는데, 이와 관련이 없는 그들이 왜 그랬는지 모르겠다는 내용으로 응답했으므로 오답입니다.

22 미국식 발음 → 호주식 발음

> How much were the flowers we bought for last week's retirement party?
> (A) Five roses and ten tulips.
> **(B) I didn't pay for them.**
> (C) It was a beautiful floral arrangement.

retirement[미 ritáiərmənt, 영 ritáiəmənt] 은퇴
pay for ~의 비용을 지불하다 floral arrangement 꽃꽂이

해석 지난주의 은퇴 파티를 위해 우리가 구매한 꽃들은 얼마였나요?
(A) 장미 5송이와 튤립 10송이요.
(B) 제가 그것들의 비용을 지불하지 않았는데요.
(C) 그것은 아름다운 꽃꽂이였어요.

해설 지난주의 은퇴 파티를 위해 구매한 꽃들이 얼마였는지를 묻는 How 의문문입니다. How much가 가격을 묻는 것임을 이해할 수 있어야 합니다.
(A) [x] 질문의 flowers(꽃들)와 관련 있는 roses and ~ tulips(장미와 튤립)를 사용하여 혼동을 준 오답입니다.
(B) [o] 자신이 그것들의 비용을 지불하지 않았다는 말로 모른다는 간접적인 응답을 했으므로 정답입니다.
(C) [x] 질문의 flowers(꽃들)와 관련 있는 floral arrangement(꽃꽂이)를 사용하여 혼동을 준 오답입니다.

23 캐나다식 발음 → 미국식 발음

> Why is our delivery of office supplies not here yet?
> (A) We're supposed to be here by 9 A.M.
> (B) Only about 10 minutes.
> **(C) The shipment hasn't arrived?**

office supplies 사무용품 be supposed to ~해야 한다
shipment [ʃípmənt] 배송품

해석 우리 사무용품 배송이 왜 아직 오지 않았나요?
(A) 우리는 이곳에 오전 9시까지 와야 해요.
(B) 10분 정도만요.
(C) 배송품이 도착하지 않았나요?

해설 사무용품 배송이 왜 아직 오지 않았는지를 묻는 Why 의문문입니다.
(A) [x] 질문의 here를 반복 사용하여 혼동을 준 오답입니다.
(B) [x] 사무용품 배송이 왜 아직 오지 않았는지를 물었는데 기간으로 응답했으므로 오답입니다.
(C) [o] 배송품이 도착하지 않았는지를 되물어 문제 상황에 대한 추가 정보를 요구하는 정답입니다.

24 호주식 발음 → 영국식 발음

> How far from the conference center is the hotel you reserved?
> **(A) About four blocks.**
> (B) I think Madison Avenue is.
> (C) I am staying there all week.

reserve[미 rizə́ːrv, 영 rizə́ːv] 예약하다

해석 당신이 예약한 호텔은 컨퍼런스 센터에서 얼마나 떨어져 있나요?
(A) 네 블록 정도요.
(B) Madison가인 것 같아요.
(C) 저는 일주일 내내 그곳에 머무를 거예요.

해설 예약한 호텔이 컨퍼런스 센터에서 얼마나 떨어져 있는지를 묻는 How 의문문입니다. How far가 거리를 묻는 것임을 이해할 수 있어야 합니다.
(A) [o] 네 블록 정도라며 예약한 호텔과 컨퍼런스 센터 사이의 거리를 언급했으므로 정답입니다.
(B) [x] 예약한 호텔이 컨퍼런스 센터에서 얼마나 떨어져 있는지를 물었는데, 이와 관련이 없는 Madison가인 것 같다는 내용으로 응답했으므로 오답입니다.
(C) [x] 질문의 hotel(호텔)과 관련 있는 staying(머무를 것이다)을 사용하여 혼동을 준 오답입니다.

25 미국식 발음 → 영국식 발음

> How about ordering some takeout?
> (A) They took out the trash earlier.
> (B) It arrives in two days.
> **(C) I'm on a diet, actually.**

be on a diet 다이어트 중이다

해석 테이크아웃 음식을 주문하는 게 어때요?
(A) 그들이 더 일찍 쓰레기를 내다 놓았어요.
(B) 그것은 이틀 후에 도착해요.
(C) 사실, 저는 다이어트 중이에요.

해설 테이크아웃 음식을 주문하는 게 어떤지를 묻는 How 의문문입니다. How about이 제안하는 표현임을 이해할 수 있어야 합니다.
(A) [x] 질문의 takeout(테이크아웃 음식)을 '내다 놨다'라는 의미의 took out으로 반복 사용하여 혼동을 준 오답입니다.
(B) [x] 질문의 ordering(주문하다)에서 연상할 수 있는 배송과 관련된 arrives(도착하다)를 사용하여 혼동을 준 오답입니다.
(C) [o] 사실 다이어트 중이라는 말로 테이크아웃 음식을 주문하자는 제안을 간접적으로 거절한 정답입니다.

DAY 08 일반 의문문 및 평서문

Course 1 일반 의문문

HACKERS PRACTICE DAY08_02   p.75

01 (B)	02 (A)	03 (A)	04 (B)
05 (A)	06 (B)	07 (C)	

01 캐나다식 발음 → 미국식 발음 / 호주식 발음 → 영국식 발음

> Do you want to go to lunch?
> (A) We go there often.
> **(B) I'd love to.**
> (C) She is taking a cooking class.

해석 점심을 먹으러 가고 싶으세요?
(A) 저희는 그곳에 자주 가요.
(B) 좋아요.
(C) 그녀는 요리 수업을 수강하고 있어요.

해설 점심을 먹으러 가고 싶은지를 확인하는 일반 의문문입니다.
(A) [x] 질문의 go를 반복 사용하여 혼동을 준 오답입니다.
(B) [o] 좋다는 말로 점심을 먹으러 가고 싶음을 전달했으므로 정답입니다.
(C) [x] 질문의 lunch(점심)와 관련 있는 cooking(요리)을 사용하여 혼동을 준 오답입니다.

02 🎧 호주식 발음 → 영국식 발음 / 캐나다식 발음 → 미국식 발음

Are you attending the seminar?
(A) Yes, I'll be there.
(B) The workshop was informative.
(C) In Spencer Auditorium.

---

attend[əténd] 참석하다
informative[미 infɔ́:rmətiv, 영 infɔ́:mətiv] 유익한

해석 당신은 세미나에 참석할 건가요?
(A) 네, 저는 그곳에 갈 거예요.
(B) 그 워크숍은 유익했어요.
(C) Spencer 강당에서요.

해설 세미나에 참석할 것인지를 확인하는 일반 의문문입니다.
(A) [o] Yes로 세미나에 참석할 것임을 전달한 후, 자신은 그곳에 갈 것이라는 부연 설명을 했으므로 정답입니다.
(B) [x] 질문의 seminar(세미나)와 관련 있는 workshop(워크숍)을 사용하여 혼동을 준 오답입니다.
(C) [x] 질문의 seminar(세미나)와 관련 있는 Auditorium(강당)을 사용하여 혼동을 준 오답입니다.

03 🎧 영국식 발음 → 캐나다식 발음 / 미국식 발음 → 호주식 발음

Shouldn't we update our contact lists?
(A) Yes, they need to be revised.
(B) He will sign the contract.
(C) That date should work.

---

contact list 연락처 목록   revise[riváiz] 수정하다
contract[kɔ́ntrækt] 계약서

해석 우리의 연락처 목록을 업데이트해야 하지 않을까요?
(A) 네, 그것들은 수정되어야겠네요.
(B) 그는 계약서에 서명할 거예요.
(C) 그 날이면 되겠어요.

해설 연락처 목록을 업데이트해야 하지 않을지를 묻는 일반 의문문입니다.
(A) [o] Yes로 연락처 목록을 업데이트해야 함을 전달한 후, 그것들이 수정되어야겠다는 부연 설명을 했으므로 정답입니다.
(B) [x] contact – contract의 유사 발음 어휘를 사용하여 혼동을 준 오답입니다.
(C) [x] update – date의 유사 발음 어휘를 사용하여 혼동을 준 오답입니다.

04 🎧 호주식 발음 → 미국식 발음 / 캐나다식 발음 → 영국식 발음

Could you answer my phone?
(A) Yes, I just called.
(B) Certainly.
(C) No, I didn't.

해석 제 전화를 받아주시겠어요?
(A) 네, 제가 방금 전화를 걸었어요.
(B) 물론이죠.
(C) 아니요, 전 하지 않았어요.

해설 자신의 전화를 받아줄 수 있는지를 묻는 일반 의문문입니다.
(A) [x] 질문의 answer ~ phone(전화를 받다)과 관련 있는 called(전화를 걸었다)를 사용하여 혼동을 준 오답입니다.
(B) [o] Certainly(물론이죠)로 전화를 받아줄 것임을 전달한 정답입니다.
(C) [x] 전화를 받아줄 수 있는지를 물었는데, 이와 관련이 없는 자신

은 하지 않았다는 내용으로 응답했으므로 오답입니다.

05 🎧 미국식 발음 → 캐나다식 발음 / 영국식 발음 → 호주식 발음

Do you know where my coat is?
(A) Have you checked the closet?
(B) I'll move it for you.
(C) It looks very warm.

---

closet[미 klá:zit, 영 klɔ́zit] 옷장, 벽장

해석 제 코트가 어디에 있는지 아시나요?
(A) 옷장을 확인해 보셨나요?
(B) 제가 당신을 위해 그것을 옮겨 드릴게요.
(C) 그것은 매우 따뜻해 보여요.

해설 의문사 where를 포함하여 코트가 어디에 있는지 아는지를 묻는 일반 의문문입니다.
(A) [o] 옷장을 확인해 보았는지를 되물어 코트가 어디에 있는지 모른다는 간접적인 응답을 했으므로 정답입니다.
(B) [x] 코트가 어디에 있는지 아는지를 물었는데, 이와 관련이 없는 상대방을 위해 그것을 옮겨주겠다는 내용으로 응답했으므로 오답입니다.
(C) [x] 질문의 coat(코트)와 관련 있는 warm(따뜻한)을 사용하여 혼동을 준 오답입니다.

06 🎧 영국식 발음 → 호주식 발음 / 미국식 발음 → 캐나다식 발음

Will you lend me your pen for a moment?
(A) I already have one.
(B) Here you go.
(C) Buy more pencils also.

---

lend[lend] 빌려주다

해석 제게 잠시 당신의 펜을 빌려주시겠어요?
(A) 저는 이미 한 개가 있어요.
(B) 여기 있어요.
(C) 연필도 더 많이 사세요.

해설 잠시 펜을 빌려주겠냐고 묻는 일반 의문문입니다.
(A) [x] 잠시 펜을 빌려주겠냐고 물었는데, 이와 관련이 없는 이미 한 개가 있다는 내용으로 응답했으므로 오답입니다.
(B) [o] 여기 있다는 말로 상대방에게 펜을 빌려줄 것임을 전달했으므로 정답입니다.
(C) [x] pen – pencils의 유사 발음 어휘를 사용하여 혼동을 준 오답입니다.

07 🎧 캐나다식 발음 → 영국식 발음 / 호주식 발음 → 미국식 발음

Is the history museum going to be open today?
(A) An event on October 22.
(B) It was in the past.
(C) No, it's closed on Mondays.

---

museum[mju:zí:əm] 박물관

해석 역사박물관은 오늘 문을 여나요?
(A) 10월 22일에 열리는 행사요.
(B) 그것은 과거의 일이에요.
(C) 아니요, 그곳은 월요일에는 문을 닫아요.

해설 역사박물관이 오늘 문을 여는지를 확인하는 일반 의문문입니다.
(A) [x] 역사박물관이 오늘 문을 여는지를 물었는데, 이와 관련이 없

는 10월 22일에 열리는 행사라는 내용으로 응답했으므로 오답입니다.
(B) [×] 질문의 today(오늘)와 관련 있는 past(과거)를 사용하여 혼동을 준 오답입니다.
(C) [○] No로 역사박물관이 오늘 문을 열지 않음을 전달한 후, 월요일에는 문을 닫는다는 추가 정보를 제공했으므로 정답입니다.

Course 2 평서문

HACKERS PRACTICE 🎧 DAY08_04   p.77

01 (A)	02 (A)	03 (C)	04 (A)
05 (A)	06 (A)	07 (C)	

01 🎙 미국식 발음 → 호주식 발음 / 영국식 발음 → 캐나다식 발음

My flight arrives at 11:45 P.M.
(A) I'll pick you up then.
(B) You're an excellent pilot.
(C) The flight is full.

flight[flait] 항공편   pilot[páilət] 비행기 조종사

해석 제 항공편은 오후 11시 45분에 도착해요.
(A) 제가 그때 당신을 데리러 갈게요.
(B) 당신은 뛰어난 비행기 조종사예요.
(C) 그 항공편은 꽉 찼어요.

해설 항공편이 오후 11시 45분에 도착한다는 객관적인 사실을 전달하는 평서문입니다.
(A) [○] 그때 데리러 가겠다는 말로 오후 11시 45분에 상대방을 데리러 갈 것임을 전달했으므로 정답입니다.
(B) [×] 질문의 flight(항공편)와 관련 있는 pilot(비행기 조종사)을 사용하여 혼동을 준 오답입니다.
(C) [×] 질문의 flight를 반복 사용하여 혼동을 준 오답입니다.

02 🎙 캐나다식 발음 → 미국식 발음 / 호주식 발음 → 영국식 발음

The new TV model is very innovative.
(A) It has many new features.
(B) I didn't know you were a model.
(C) It's on a different channel.

innovative[미 ínəvèitiv, 영 ínəvətiv] 혁신적인
feature[미 fíːtʃər, 영 fíːtʃə] 기능, 특징

해석 새로운 텔레비전 모델은 매우 혁신적이에요.
(A) 그것은 여러 새로운 기능들을 갖추고 있어요.
(B) 저는 당신이 모델이었다는 걸 몰랐어요.
(C) 그것은 다른 채널에서 해요.

해설 새로운 텔레비전 모델이 매우 혁신적이라는 의견을 제시하는 평서문입니다.
(A) [○] 그것은 여러 새로운 기능들을 갖추고 있다는 말로 새로운 텔레비전 모델이 매우 혁신적이라는 의견에 동의했으므로 정답입니다.
(B) [×] 질문의 model을 반복 사용하여 혼동을 준 오답입니다.
(C) [×] 질문의 TV(텔레비전)와 관련 있는 channel(채널)을 사용하여 혼동을 준 오답입니다.

03 🎙 호주식 발음 → 영국식 발음 / 캐나다식 발음 → 미국식 발음

Clarkson Industries' profits rose by 200 percent.
(A) I'll let you know when I get it.
(B) These roses are very expensive.
(C) That's impressive.

profit[미 práfit, 영 prɔ́fit] 수익, 이윤   impressive[imprésiv] 인상적인

해석 Clarkson사의 수익이 200퍼센트 증가했어요.
(A) 제가 그것을 받으면 당신께 알려 드릴게요.
(B) 이 장미들은 매우 비싸요.
(C) 그것은 인상적이네요.

해설 Clarkson사의 수익이 200퍼센트 증가했다는 객관적인 사실을 전달하는 평서문입니다.
(A) [×] Clarkson사의 수익이 200퍼센트 증가했다고 했는데, 이와 관련이 없는 그것을 받으면 알려주겠다는 내용으로 응답했으므로 오답입니다.
(B) [×] 질문의 rose(증가했다)를 '장미'라는 의미의 명사로 반복 사용하여 혼동을 준 오답입니다.
(C) [○] 인상적이라는 말로 Clarkson사의 수익이 200퍼센트 증가한 사실에 대한 의견을 제시했으므로 정답입니다.

04 🎙 영국식 발음 → 캐나다식 발음 / 미국식 발음 → 호주식 발음

I haven't heard anything about the job I applied for.
(A) They'll contact you soon.
(B) I am looking for a job.
(C) The president's interview was brief.

apply for ~에 지원하다   brief[briːf] 짧은, 간단한

해석 저는 제가 지원했던 일자리에 대해 아무것도 듣지 못했어요.
(A) 그들이 당신에게 곧 연락할 거예요.
(B) 저는 일자리를 찾고 있어요.
(C) 회장님의 인터뷰는 짧았어요.

해설 지원했던 일자리에 대해 아무것도 듣지 못했다는 문제점을 언급하는 평서문입니다.
(A) [○] 그들이 곧 연락할 것이라는 말로 일자리에 대한 소식을 곧 듣게 될 것임을 전달했으므로 정답입니다.
(B) [×] 질문의 job을 반복 사용하여 혼동을 준 오답입니다.
(C) [×] 지원했던 일자리에 대해 아무것도 듣지 못했다고 했는데, 이와 관련이 없는 회장님의 인터뷰가 짧았다는 내용으로 응답했으므로 오답입니다.

05 🎙 호주식 발음 → 미국식 발음 / 캐나다식 발음 → 영국식 발음

It's going to be hot in Beijing during our visit.
(A) I'll have to pack some shorts, then.
(B) We visited your family.
(C) I can't eat spicy food.

shorts[미 ʃɔːrts, 영 ʃɔːts] 짧은 바지   spicy[spáisi] 매운

해석 우리가 방문하는 동안 베이징은 더울 거예요.
(A) 그렇다면, 저는 짧은 바지를 몇 벌 챙겨야겠네요.
(B) 우리는 당신의 가족을 방문했어요.
(C) 저는 매운 음식을 못 먹어요.

해설 자신들이 방문하는 동안 베이징이 더울 것이라는 문제점을 언급하는 평서문입니다.
(A) [○] 그렇다면 짧은 바지를 몇 벌 챙겨야겠다는 말로 베이징이 더

울 것이라는 문제점에 대한 대응 방안을 제시했으므로 정답입니다.
(B) [x] 질문의 visit를 visited로 반복 사용하여 혼동을 준 오답입니다.
(C) [x] 질문의 hot(더운)의 다른 의미인 '매운'과 의미가 동일한 spicy(매운)를 사용하여 혼동을 준 오답입니다.

06 🔊 미국식 발음 → 캐나다식 발음 / 영국식 발음 → 호주식 발음

> I haven't received a copy of the training schedule.
> (A) Wasn't it e-mailed to you?
> (B) The trainer is very popular.
> (C) Yes, it's interesting.

training[tréiniŋ] 교육 trainer[미 tréinər, 영 tréinə] 교관, 코치

해석 저는 교육 일정을 받지 못했어요.
(A) 당신에게 이메일로 보내지지 않았나요?
(B) 그 교관은 굉장히 인기가 있어요.
(C) 네, 그것은 재미있어요.

해설 교육 일정을 받지 못했다는 문제점을 언급하는 평서문입니다.
(A) [o] 이메일로 보내지지 않았는지를 되물어 교육 일정 발송 여부에 대한 추가 정보를 요구하는 정답입니다.
(B) [x] training – trainer의 유사 발음 어휘를 사용하여 혼동을 준 오답입니다.
(C) [x] 교육 일정을 받지 못했다고 했는데, 이와 관련이 없는 그것은 재미있다는 내용으로 응답했으므로 오답입니다.

07 🔊 영국식 발음 → 호주식 발음 / 미국식 발음 → 캐나다식 발음

> I suggest reserving a bigger venue for the workshop.
> (A) Many people attended.
> (B) He's in the IT department.
> (C) OK, I will do that right now.

venue[vénju:] 장소 department[미 dipá:rtmənt, 영 dipá:tmənt] 부서

해석 워크숍을 위해 더 큰 장소를 예약하는 것을 제안 드려요.
(A) 많은 사람들이 참석했어요.
(B) 그는 IT 부서에 있어요.
(C) 알겠어요, 제가 지금 바로 그렇게 할게요.

해설 워크숍을 위해 더 큰 장소를 예약할 것을 제안하는 평서문입니다.
(A) [x] 질문의 workshop(워크숍)과 관련 있는 attended(참석했다)를 사용하여 혼동을 준 오답입니다.
(B) [x] 워크숍을 위해 더 큰 장소를 예약하는 것을 제안했는데, 이와 관련이 없는 그가 IT 부서에 있다는 내용으로 응답했으므로 오답입니다.
(C) [o] 자신이 지금 바로 그렇게 하겠다는 말로 더 큰 장소를 예약하자는 제안을 수락한 정답입니다.

HACKERS TEST 🎧 DAY08_05 p.78

01	(C)	**02**	(B)	**03**	(A)	**04**	(C)
05	(A)	**06**	(A)	**07**	(A)	**08**	(B)
09	(A)	**10**	(C)	**11**	(A)	**12**	(A)
13	(B)	**14**	(B)	**15**	(B)	**16**	(C)
17	(A)	**18**	(C)	**19**	(B)	**20**	(B)
21	(C)	**22**	(B)	**23**	(C)	**24**	(A)
25	(B)						

01 🔊 캐나다식 발음 → 영국식 발음

> Should we stop to ask for directions?
> (A) They already read them.
> (B) It's not the first stop.
> (C) Yes, I think so.

stop[미 stɑp, 영 stɔp] 멈추다; 정거장
direction[미 dirékʃən, 영 dairékʃən] 길, 지침서

해석 길을 묻기 위해 잠시 멈춰야 할까요?
(A) 그들은 이미 그것들을 읽었어요.
(B) 첫 번째 정거장이 아니에요.
(C) 네, 그래야 할 것 같아요.

해설 길을 묻기 위해 잠시 멈춰야 할지를 확인하는 일반 의문문입니다.
(A) [x] 질문의 directions(길)의 다른 의미인 '지침서'와 관련 있는 read(읽다)를 사용하여 혼동을 준 오답입니다.
(B) [x] 질문의 stop(멈추다)을 '정거장'이라는 의미의 명사로 반복 사용하여 혼동을 준 오답입니다.
(C) [o] 그래야 할 것 같다는 말로 잠시 멈추자는 의견을 전달했으므로 정답입니다.

02 🔊 미국식 발음 → 호주식 발음

> Are you going to the conference?
> (A) It's going quite well.
> (B) I plan to.
> (C) The conference call ended two hours ago.

conference call 전화 회의

해석 당신은 회의에 가실 건가요?
(A) 그것은 꽤 잘 되어가고 있어요.
(B) 저는 그럴 계획이에요.
(C) 전화 회의는 두 시간 전에 끝났어요.

해설 회의에 갈 것인지를 확인하는 일반 의문문입니다.
(A) [x] 회의에 갈 것인지를 물었는데, 이와 관련이 없는 그것은 꽤 잘 되어가고 있다는 내용으로 응답했으므로 오답입니다.
(B) [o] 자신은 그럴 계획이라는 말로 회의에 갈 것임을 전달했으므로 정답입니다.
(C) [x] 질문의 conference를 반복 사용하여 혼동을 준 오답입니다.

03 🔊 캐나다식 발음 → 미국식 발음

> Would you like to go for coffee?
> (A) Let's go to a nearby café.
> (B) I'd like to take a taxi instead.
> (C) Coffee beans are in Aisle 1.

aisle[ail] 통로

해석 커피 마시러 가실래요?
(A) 가까운 카페로 갑시다.
(B) 저는 대신 택시를 타고 싶어요.
(C) 커피콩은 1번 통로에 있어요.

해설 커피를 마시러 갈지를 묻는 일반 의문문입니다.
(A) [o] 가까운 카페로 가자는 말로 커피를 마시러 갈 것임을 간접적으로 전달했으므로 정답입니다.
(B) [x] 커피를 마시러 갈지를 물었는데 이동 수단으로 응답했으므로 오답입니다. I'd like to까지만 듣고 정답으로 고르지 않도록 주의합니다.

(C) [×] 질문의 coffee를 반복 사용하여 혼동을 준 오답입니다.

04 호주식 발음 → 영국식 발음

Do you know who made the wedding cake?
(A) I love chocolate cakes.
(B) The bride is very beautiful.
(C) It was Urban Events Bakery.

bride[braid] 신부

해석 누가 그 결혼식 케이크를 만들었는지 아시나요?
(A) 저는 초콜릿 케이크를 좋아해요.
(B) 신부가 매우 아름다워요.
(C) Urban Events 제과점이었어요.

해설 의문사 who를 포함하여 누가 결혼식 케이크를 만들었는지 아는지를 묻는 일반 의문문입니다.
(A) [×] 질문의 cake를 cakes로 반복 사용하여 혼동을 준 오답입니다.
(B) [×] 질문의 wedding(결혼식)과 관련 있는 bride(신부)를 사용하여 혼동을 준 오답입니다.
(C) [○] Urban Events 제과점이라는 말로 결혼식 케이크를 만든 가게를 전달했으므로 정답입니다.

05 영국식 발음 → 캐나다식 발음

Weren't you in the play last night?
(A) Yes, I had the lead role.
(B) You are a basketball player.
(C) No, tomorrow is my last night.

play[plei] 연극 role[미 roul, 영 rəul] 배역, 역할

해석 어젯밤 연극에 출연하지 않으셨나요?
(A) 네, 저는 주연이었어요.
(B) 당신은 농구선수예요.
(C) 아니요, 내일이 저의 마지막 밤이에요.

해설 상대방이 어젯밤 연극에 출연하지 않았는지를 묻는 일반 의문문입니다.
(A) [○] Yes로 어젯밤 연극에 출연했음을 전달한 후, 자신이 주연이었다는 추가 정보를 제공했으므로 정답입니다.
(B) [×] play - player의 유사 발음 어휘를 사용하여 혼동을 준 오답입니다.
(C) [×] 질문의 last night(어젯밤)를 '마지막 밤'이라는 의미로 반복 사용하여 혼동을 준 오답입니다. No만 듣고 정답으로 선택하지 않도록 주의합니다.

06 호주식 발음 → 미국식 발음

Let's go to the baseball game tonight.
(A) Sorry, but I'm busy.
(B) At Ranger Stadium.
(C) Several board games are available.

stadium[stéidiəm] 경기장 available[əvéiləbl] 이용 가능한

해석 오늘 밤에 야구 경기를 보러 갑시다.
(A) 죄송하지만, 저는 바빠요.
(B) Ranger 경기장에서요.
(C) 몇몇 보드 게임이 이용 가능해요.

해설 오늘 밤에 야구 경기를 보러 가자고 제안하는 평서문입니다.
(A) [○] 바쁘다는 말로 제안을 거절한 정답입니다.
(B) [×] 질문의 baseball game(야구 경기)과 관련 있는 Stadium(경

기장)을 사용하여 혼동을 준 오답입니다.
(C) [×] 질문의 game을 games로 반복 사용하여 혼동을 준 오답입니다.

07 미국식 발음 → 캐나다식 발음

Will you be at work on Saturday morning?
(A) No, I'm taking that day off.
(B) My office is on Fourth Street.
(C) I'm the department manager.

take ~ off ~(동안)을 쉬다 department[미 dipɑ́:rtmənt, 영 dipɑ́:tmənt] 부서

해석 당신은 토요일 오전에 근무하실 건가요?
(A) 아니요, 저는 그날 쉴 거예요.
(B) 제 사무실은 4번가에 있어요.
(C) 제가 그 부서의 부장이에요.

해설 상대방이 토요일 오전에 근무할 것인지를 확인하는 일반 의문문입니다.
(A) [○] No로 토요일 오전에 근무하지 않을 것임을 전달한 후, 그날 쉴 것이라는 부연 설명을 했으므로 정답입니다.
(B) [×] 질문의 work(직장)와 관련 있는 office(사무실)를 사용하여 혼동을 준 오답입니다.
(C) [×] 토요일 오전에 근무할 것인지를 물었는데 자신의 신분으로 응답했으므로 오답입니다.

08 영국식 발음 → 미국식 발음

Are you going to the travel agency today?
(A) A few days ago.
(B) Yes. I'm leaving in a few minutes.
(C) It's a tour of a castle.

leave[li:v] 출발하다

해석 당신은 오늘 여행사에 갈 건가요?
(A) 며칠 전에요.
(B) 네. 저는 몇 분 뒤에 출발할 거예요.
(C) 그것은 성 관광이에요.

해설 오늘 여행사에 갈 것인지를 확인하는 일반 의문문입니다.
(A) [×] 오늘 여행사에 갈 것인지를 물었는데 시점으로 응답했으므로 오답입니다.
(B) [○] Yes로 오늘 여행사에 갈 것임을 전달한 후, 자신은 몇 분 뒤에 출발할 것이라는 부연 설명을 했으므로 정답입니다.
(C) [×] 질문의 travel agency(여행사)와 관련 있는 tour(관광)를 사용하여 혼동을 준 오답입니다.

09 캐나다식 발음 → 영국식 발음

Hasn't Lou given you the employee manual?
(A) He sent it to me yesterday.
(B) We can restart it manually.
(C) The new employees are arriving now.

employee manual 직원 안내서 manually[mǽnjuəli] 수동으로

해석 Lou가 당신에게 직원 안내서를 주지 않았나요?
(A) 그는 어제 제게 그것을 보냈어요.
(B) 우리는 수동으로 그것을 다시 시작할 수 있어요.
(C) 신규 직원들은 지금 오고 있어요.

해설 Lou가 직원 안내서를 주지 않았는지를 확인하는 일반 의문문입니다.

한 권으로 끝내는 해커스 토익 700+ (LC+RC+VOCA)

(A) [○] 그가 어제 그것을 보냈다는 말로 Lou가 직원 안내서를 주었음을 전달했으므로 정답입니다.

(B) [×] manual – manually의 유사 발음 어휘를 사용하여 혼동을 준 오답입니다.

(C) [×] 질문의 employee를 employees로 반복 사용하여 혼동을 준 오답입니다.

10 🔊 미국식 발음 → 영국식 발음

Do you want me to drive you home after work?
(A) That's where I live.
(B) Usually at 8 P.M.
(C) Yes, if you don't mind.

drive[draiv] (차로) 태워다 주다

해석 퇴근 후에 제가 당신을 집까지 태워다 드릴까요?
(A) 그곳은 제가 사는 곳이에요.
(B) 보통 오후 8시에요.
(C) 네, 만약 당신이 괜찮으시다면요.

해설 퇴근 후에 집까지 태워다 줄지를 묻는 일반 의문문입니다.
(A) [×] 질문의 home(집)과 관련 있는 live(살다)를 사용하여 혼동을 준 오답입니다.
(B) [×] 질문의 after work(퇴근 후에)에서 연상할 수 있는 퇴근 시간과 관련된 at 8 P.M.(오후 8시에)을 사용하여 혼동을 준 오답입니다.
(C) [○] Yes로 집까지 태워 달라고 응답했으므로 정답입니다.

11 🔊 캐나다식 발음 → 미국식 발음

Are you learning how to use the editing software?
(A) Yes, and it's easy to use.
(B) That hardware store.
(C) Get some from the editor.

edit[édit] 편집하다　hardware store 철물점
editor[미 édətər, 영 édítə] 편집자, 편집장

해석 편집 소프트웨어를 사용하는 방법을 배우고 있나요?
(A) 네, 그리고 그것은 사용하기 쉬워요.
(B) 저 철물점이요.
(C) 편집자로부터 몇 개 받으세요.

해설 편집 소프트웨어를 사용하는 방법을 배우고 있는지를 확인하는 일반 의문문입니다.
(A) [○] Yes로 편집 소프트웨어를 사용하는 방법을 배우고 있음을 전달한 후, 그것은 사용하기 쉽다는 추가 정보를 제공했으므로 정답입니다.
(B) [×] software – hardware의 유사 발음 어휘를 사용하여 혼동을 준 오답입니다.
(C) [×] editing – editor의 유사 발음 어휘를 사용하여 혼동을 준 오답입니다.

12 🔊 호주식 발음 → 캐나다식 발음

The café's lunch menu is really great.
(A) I like the food there, too.
(B) The list is on the table.
(C) You're a great cook.

해석 그 카페의 점심 메뉴는 정말 훌륭해요.
(A) 저도 그곳 음식을 좋아해요.
(B) 그 목록은 테이블 위에 있어요.

(C) 당신은 훌륭한 요리사예요.

해설 카페의 점심 메뉴가 정말 훌륭하다는 의견을 제시하는 평서문입니다.
(A) [○] 자신도 그 카페의 음식을 좋아한다는 말로 상대방의 의견에 동의했으므로 정답입니다.
(B) [×] 질문의 café(카페)와 관련 있는 table(테이블)을 사용하여 혼동을 준 오답입니다.
(C) [×] 질문의 great을 반복 사용하여 혼동을 준 오답입니다.

13 🔊 영국식 발음 → 캐나다식 발음

Did you bring a copy of your résumé with you?
(A) It is starting again next week.
(B) Was I supposed to?
(C) The scanner is down the hall.

résumé[미 rézuméi, 영 rézju:mei] 이력서
be supposed to ~해야 하다　hall[hɔːl] 복도

해석 이력서 한 부를 가져오셨나요?
(A) 그것은 다음 주에 다시 시작돼요.
(B) 그랬어야 하나요?
(C) 스캐너는 복도 끝에 있어요.

해설 이력서 한 부를 가져왔는지를 확인하는 일반 의문문입니다.
(A) [×] 질문의 résumé(이력서)와 발음이 유사한 resume(다시 시작하다)과 의미가 동일한 starting again(다시 시작하다)을 사용하여 혼동을 준 오답입니다.
(B) [○] 그랬어야 하는지를 되물어 이력서를 가져오는 것에 대한 추가 정보를 요구하는 정답입니다.
(C) [×] 이력서 한 부를 가져왔는지를 물었는데, 이와 관련이 없는 스캐너는 복도 끝에 있다는 내용으로 응답했으므로 오답입니다.

14 🔊 호주식 발음 → 미국식 발음

Are you going away for the upcoming holiday?
(A) My trip was really exciting.
(B) I haven't decided yet.
(C) We put it away already.

go away (휴가를 맞아) 어디를 가다　upcoming[ʌ́pkʌmiŋ] 다가오는
holiday[미 hάlədèi, 영 hɔ́lədei] 휴일　put ~ away ~을 치우다

해석 당신은 다가오는 휴일에 어딘가 갈 건가요?
(A) 제 여행은 정말 즐거웠어요.
(B) 아직 결정하지 못했어요.
(C) 우리는 이미 그것을 치웠어요.

해설 다가오는 휴일에 어딘가 갈 것인지를 확인하는 일반 의문문입니다.
(A) [×] 질문의 going away(어디를 가다)와 관련 있는 trip(여행)을 사용하여 혼동을 준 오답입니다.
(B) [○] 아직 결정하지 못했다는 말로 모른다는 간접적인 응답을 했으므로 정답입니다.
(C) [×] 질문의 away를 반복 사용하여 혼동을 준 오답입니다.

15 🔊 미국식 발음 → 캐나다식 발음

Could you meet me in the hotel lobby?
(A) There are no vacancies tonight.
(B) Yes, I'll be there at noon.
(C) Ask the front desk.

vacancy[véikənsi] 빈 객실　front desk 안내 데스크

해석 호텔 로비에서 저를 만나 주시겠어요?

(A) 오늘 밤에는 빈 객실이 없어요.
(B) 네, 정오에 그곳에 있을게요.
(C) 안내 데스크에 물어보세요.

해설 호텔 로비에서 자신과 만날 수 있는지를 확인하는 일반 의문문입니다.
(A) [x] 질문의 hotel(호텔)과 관련 있는 vacancies(빈 객실)를 사용하여 혼동을 준 오답입니다.
(B) [o] 정오에 그곳에 있겠다는 말로 만날 수 있음을 간접적으로 전달한 정답입니다.
(C) [x] 질문의 hotel lobby(호텔 로비)와 관련 있는 front desk(안내 데스크)를 사용하여 혼동을 준 오답입니다.

16 영국식 발음 → 호주식 발음

The new fax machine will be delivered on Tuesday.
(A) She is making a delivery.
(B) A courier service.
(C) I'll be here to sign for it.

make a delivery 배달하다, 배송하다
courier [미 kə́:riər, 영 kúriə] 택배

해석 새 팩스기는 화요일에 배송될 거예요.
(A) 그녀는 배달 중이에요.
(B) 택배 서비스요.
(C) 제가 그것에 서명하기 위해 여기 있을게요.

해설 새 팩스기가 화요일에 배송될 것이라는 객관적인 사실을 전달하는 평서문입니다.
(A) [x] delivered – delivery의 유사 발음 어휘를 사용하여 혼동을 준 오답입니다.
(B) [x] 질문의 delivered(배송되다)와 관련 있는 courier service(택배 서비스)를 사용하여 혼동을 준 오답입니다.
(C) [o] 자신이 그것에 서명하기 위해 여기 있을 것이라는 말로 새 팩스기가 화요일에 배송되면 자신이 수령할 것임을 간접적으로 전달했으므로 정답입니다.

17 캐나다식 발음 → 영국식 발음

Can Noah attend next week's advertising workshop?
(A) He'll be on a business trip then.
(B) There were excellent speakers.
(C) The shop is on the corner.

be on a business trip 출장 중이다
speaker [미 spíːkər, 영 spíːkə] 연설자, 화자

해석 Noah는 다음 주의 광고 워크숍에 참석할 수 있나요?
(A) 그는 그때 출장 중일 거예요.
(B) 뛰어난 연설자들이 있었어요.
(C) 그 가게는 모퉁이에 있어요.

해설 Noah가 다음 주의 광고 워크숍에 참석할 수 있는지를 확인하는 일반 의문문입니다.
(A) [o] 그는 그때 출장 중일 것이라는 말로 Noah가 다음 주의 광고 워크숍에 참석할 수 없음을 간접적으로 전달했으므로 정답입니다.
(B) [x] 질문의 workshop(워크숍)과 관련 있는 speakers(연설자들)를 사용하여 혼동을 준 오답입니다.
(C) [x] workshop – shop의 유사 발음 어휘를 사용하여 혼동을 준 오답입니다.

18 미국식 발음 → 호주식 발음

Is that the latest issue of *Ad Month Magazine*?
(A) It's not an issue for us.
(B) It's the oldest store in town.
(C) Yes, I got it yesterday.

issue [íʃuː] (정기 간행물의) 호, 문제

해석 그것이 *Ad Month Magazine*지의 최신 호인가요?
(A) 그것은 우리에게 문제가 되지 않아요.
(B) 그것은 마을에서 가장 오래된 가게예요.
(C) 네, 저는 어제 그걸 받았어요.

해설 그것이 *Ad Month Magazine*지의 최신 호인지를 확인하는 일반 의문문입니다.
(A) [x] 질문의 issue(호)를 '문제'라는 의미로 반복 사용하여 혼동을 준 오답입니다.
(B) [x] 질문의 latest(최신의)와 반대 의미인 oldest(가장 오래된)를 사용하여 혼동을 준 오답입니다.
(C) [o] Yes로 그것이 *Ad Month Magazine*지의 최신 호임을 전달한 후, 자신이 어제 그것을 받았다는 부연 설명을 했으므로 정답입니다.

19 캐나다식 발음 → 미국식 발음

I need to go to Brazil for business next month.
(A) Our company is doing well financially.
(B) OK, I'll tell Susan that you'll be away.
(C) Where did you travel?

do well 번창하다, 성공하다 **financially** [fainǽnʃəli] 재정적으로
away [əwéi] 부재중인

해석 저는 업무 때문에 다음 달에 브라질로 가야 해요.
(A) 우리 회사는 재정적으로 번창하고 있어요.
(B) 알겠어요, 제가 Susan에게 당신이 부재중일 거라고 말할게요.
(C) 당신은 어디를 여행했나요?

해설 자신이 업무 때문에 다음 달에 브라질로 가야 한다는 객관적인 사실을 전달하는 평서문입니다.
(A) [x] 질문의 business(업무)와 관련 있는 company(회사)를 사용하여 혼동을 준 오답입니다.
(B) [o] OK로 상대방이 다음 달에 브라질로 갈 것임을 알았음을 전달한 후, Susan에게도 이를 전달해 주겠다는 부연 설명을 했으므로 정답입니다.
(C) [x] 질문의 go to Brazil(브라질로 가다)과 관련 있는 travel(여행하다)을 사용하여 혼동을 준 오답입니다.

20 호주식 발음 → 영국식 발음

Did we receive the bill from the electric company?
(A) The electricity went out this morning.
(B) Not that I know of.
(C) Let me check the receipt.

bill [bil] 청구서 **electricity** [미 ilektrísəti, 영 èliktrísəti] 전기
go out (전기·불 등이) 나가다, 꺼지다

해석 우리가 전력 회사로부터 청구서를 받았나요?
(A) 오늘 아침에 전기가 나갔어요.
(B) 제가 알기로는 아니에요.
(C) 제가 영수증을 확인해 볼게요.

해설 전력 회사로부터 청구서를 받았는지를 확인하는 일반 의문문입니다.

(A) [×] electric – electricity의 유사 발음 어휘를 사용하여 혼동을 준 오답입니다.
(B) [○] 자신이 알기로는 아니라는 말로 청구서를 받지 않았음을 간접적으로 전달한 정답입니다.
(C) [×] receive – receipt의 유사 발음 어휘를 사용하여 혼동을 준 오답입니다. Let me check까지만 듣고 정답으로 고르지 않도록 주의합니다.

21 [영국식 발음 → 캐나다식 발음]

Are our paychecks being sent late this week?
(A) I will pay for the ticket.
(B) I just got a raise.
(C) They should've arrived already.

paycheck[미 péitʃèk, 영 péitʃek] 급료   raise[reiz] 임금 인상, 증가

해석 우리의 급료가 이번 주 늦게 보내질 건가요?
(A) 제가 표 값을 지불할게요.
(B) 저는 막 임금 인상을 받았어요.
(C) 그것들은 벌써 도착했어야 해요.

해설 급료가 이번 주 늦게 보내질 것인지를 확인하는 일반 의문문입니다.
(A) [×] paychecks – pay의 유사 발음 어휘를 사용하여 혼동을 준 오답입니다.
(B) [×] 질문의 paychecks(급료)와 관련 있는 raise(임금 인상)를 사용하여 혼동을 준 오답입니다.
(C) [○] 그것들은 벌써 도착했어야 한다는 말로 자신들의 급료가 이미 보내졌어야 함을 전달했으므로 정답입니다.

22 [호주식 발음 → 미국식 발음]

Mr. Yang wants to see the blueprints for the library soon.
(A) For a library card.
(B) They will be ready by Wednesday.
(C) I will borrow a book.

blueprint[blúːprint] 설계도, 청사진   library card (도서) 대출 카드

해석 Mr. Yang이 도서관의 설계도를 빨리 보고 싶어 하세요.
(A) 도서 대출 카드 때문에요.
(B) 그것들은 수요일까지 준비될 거예요.
(C) 저는 책을 빌릴 거예요.

해설 Mr. Yang이 도서관의 설계도를 빨리 보고 싶어 하니 준비해 달라고 요청하는 의도의 평서문입니다.
(A) [×] Mr. Yang이 도서관의 설계도를 빨리 보고 싶어 한다고 했는데, 이와 관련이 없는 도서 대출 카드 때문이라는 내용으로 응답했으므로 오답입니다.
(B) [○] 그것들은 수요일까지 준비될 것이라는 말로 요청을 수락한 정답입니다.
(C) [×] 질문의 library(도서관)와 관련 있는 book(책)을 사용하여 혼동을 준 오답입니다.

23 [미국식 발음 → 캐나다식 발음]

Should we start a customer membership program for the store?
(A) Our clients are at the airport.
(B) Yes, this item is on sale.
(C) Rachel had another suggestion.

customer[미 kʌ́stəmər, 영 kʌ́stəmə] 고객
membership[미 mémbərʃip, 영 mémbəʃip] 회원

해석 매장의 고객 회원 프로그램을 시작해야 할까요?
(A) 우리 고객들은 공항에 있어요.
(B) 네, 이 제품은 할인 중이에요.
(C) Rachel이 다른 제안을 했어요.

해설 매장의 고객 회원 프로그램을 시작해야 할지를 묻는 일반 의문문입니다.
(A) [×] 질문의 customer(고객)와 같은 의미인 clients(고객들)를 사용하여 혼동을 준 오답입니다.
(B) [×] 질문의 store(매장)와 관련 있는 item(제품)을 사용하여 혼동을 준 오답입니다.
(C) [○] Rachel이 다른 제안을 했다는 말로 고객 회원 프로그램을 시작하지 않아도 됨을 간접적으로 전달했으므로 정답입니다.

24 [영국식 발음 → 호주식 발음]

I've almost finished installing the new security software for our network.
(A) Do you think it will be done by 8 P.M.?
(B) It's much softer than I expected.
(C) We work at the same technology company.

install[instɔ́ːl] 설치하다   security[sikjúərəti] 보안, 안전

해석 저는 우리 네트워크에 새로운 보안 소프트웨어를 설치하는 것을 거의 끝냈어요.
(A) 오후 8시까지 완료될 것 같은가요?
(B) 그것은 제가 예상했던 것보다 훨씬 더 부드러워요.
(C) 우리는 같은 기술 회사에서 근무해요.

해설 새로운 보안 소프트웨어를 설치하는 것을 거의 끝냈다는 객관적인 사실을 전달하는 평서문입니다.
(A) [○] 오후 8시까지 완료될 것 같은지를 되물어 보안 소프트웨어의 설치에 대한 추가 정보를 요구하는 정답입니다.
(B) [×] software – softer의 유사 발음 어휘를 사용하여 혼동을 준 오답입니다.
(C) [×] 질문의 security software(보안 소프트웨어)와 관련 있는 technology company(기술 회사)를 사용하여 혼동을 준 오답입니다.

25 [캐나다식 발음 → 호주식 발음]

I am wondering where the meeting room is.
(A) I'll be right there.
(B) On the second floor.
(C) We can fit a dozen people.

wonder[미 wʌ́ndər, 영 wʌ́ndə] ~을 알고 싶다, 궁금해하다
dozen[dʌ́zən] 12의, 1다스의

해석 회의실이 어디에 있는지 알고 싶어요.
(A) 저는 바로 그곳에 있을 거예요.
(B) 2층이에요.
(C) 우리는 12명의 사람들에 맞출 수 있어요.

해설 회의실이 어디에 있는지 알고 싶으니 알려달라고 요청하는 의도의 평서문입니다.
(A) [×] 장소를 나타내는 right there(바로 그곳에)를 사용하여 혼동을 준 오답입니다.
(B) [○] 2층이라는 말로 회의실의 위치를 전달했으므로 정답입니다.
(C) [×] 회의실이 어디에 있는지 알려달라고 했는데 사람 수로 응답했으므로 오답입니다.

DAY 09 선택 의문문 및 부가 의문문

Course 1 선택 의문문

HACKERS PRACTICE 🎧 DAY09_02   p.81

01 (C)	02 (B)	03 (C)	04 (A)
05 (C)	06 (A)	07 (B)	

01 🔊 캐나다식 발음 → 영국식 발음 / 호주식 발음 → 미국식 발음

Do you live in London or Brighton?
(A) They're both lovely places.
(B) Brighton isn't a large city.
(C) My apartment is in London.

해석 당신은 런던에 살고 계신가요, 아니면 브라이튼에 살고 계신가요?
　　(A) 그곳들은 둘 다 아름다운 곳이에요.
　　(B) 브라이튼은 큰 도시가 아니에요.
　　(C) 제 아파트는 런던에 있어요.

해설 런던에 살고 있는지 아니면 브라이튼에 살고 있는지를 묻는 선택 의문
　　문입니다.
　　(A) [×] 질문의 London or Brighton(런던 아니면 브라이튼)과 관련
　　　　있는 places(장소)를 사용하여 혼동을 준 오답입니다.
　　(B) [×] 질문의 Brighton을 반복 사용하여 혼동을 준 오답입니다.
　　(C) [○] 자신의 아파트는 런던에 있다는 말로 런던을 선택했으므로 정
　　　　답입니다.

02 🔊 미국식 발음 → 호주식 발음 / 영국식 발음 → 캐나다식 발음

Do you want to ski or snowboard?
(A) I want the newer device.
(B) Either would be fine with me.
(C) The snow is perfect today.

device[diváis] 장비, 기기

해석 당신은 스키를 타고 싶으신가요, 아니면 스노보드를 타고 싶으신가요?
　　(A) 저는 더 최신 장비를 원해요.
　　(B) 둘 다 저에게 괜찮을 것 같아요.
　　(C) 오늘 눈이 아주 멋지네요.

해설 스키를 타고 싶은지 아니면 스노보드를 타고 싶은지를 묻는 선택 의문
　　문입니다.
　　(A) [×] 질문의 ski or snowboard(스키 아니면 스노보드)와 관련 있는
　　　　device(장비)를 사용하여 혼동을 준 오답입니다.
　　(B) [○] 둘 다 자신에게 괜찮을 것 같다는 말로 둘 다 선택했으므로 정
　　　　답입니다.
　　(C) [×] 스키를 타고 싶은지 아니면 스노보드를 타고 싶은지를 물었는
　　　　데, 이와 관련이 없는 오늘 눈이 아주 멋지다는 내용으로 응답
　　　　했으므로 오답입니다.

03 🔊 캐나다식 발음 → 미국식 발음 / 호주식 발음 → 영국식 발음

Is the bridge closed, or can I cross it?
(A) Our office closes at 5 P.M.
(B) It crosses the Han River.
(C) No, it's open now.

bridge[bridʒ] 다리   cross[미 krɔːs, 영 krɔs] 건너다, 가로지르다

해석 다리가 폐쇄되었나요, 아니면 제가 그것을 건널 수 있나요?
　　(A) 우리 사무실은 오후 5시에 문을 닫아요.
　　(B) 그것은 한강을 가로질러요.
　　(C) 아니요, 그것은 지금 개방되어 있어요.

해설 다리가 폐쇄되었는지 아니면 건널 수 있는지를 묻는 선택 의문문입니다.
　　(A) [×] 질문의 closed를 closes로 반복 사용하여 혼동을 준 오답입니다.
　　(B) [×] 질문의 bridge(다리)와 관련 있는 Han River(한강)를 사용하
　　　　고, cross를 crosses로 반복 사용하여 혼동을 준 오답입니다.
　　(C) [○] No로 다리가 폐쇄되지 않았음을 전달한 후, 다리가 지금 개방
　　　　되어 있다는 추가 정보를 제공했으므로 정답입니다.

04 🔊 호주식 발음 → 영국식 발음 / 캐나다식 발음 → 미국식 발음

Do you want to order the soup or the salad?
(A) I'll have whichever is healthier.
(B) Your order will be $12.
(C) We eat here a lot.

order[미 ɔ́ːrdər, 영 ɔ́ːdə] 주문하다; 주문
whichever[미 hwitʃévər, 영 witʃévə] 어느 것이든

해석 당신은 수프를 주문하실 건가요, 아니면 샐러드를 주문하실 건가요?
　　(A) 어느 것이든 몸에 더 좋은 것을 먹을게요.
　　(B) 당신의 주문은 12달러입니다.
　　(C) 우리는 이곳에서 자주 먹어요.

해설 수프를 주문할 것인지 아니면 샐러드를 주문할 것인지를 묻는 선택 의
　　문문입니다.
　　(A) [○] 어느 것이든 몸에 더 좋은 것을 먹을 것이라는 말로 수프와 샐러드
　　　　중 몸에 더 좋은 음식을 선택할 것임을 전달했으므로 정답입니다.
　　(B) [×] 질문의 order(주문하다)를 '주문'이라는 의미의 명사로 반복
　　　　사용하여 혼동을 준 오답입니다.
　　(C) [×] 질문의 the soup or the salad(수프 아니면 샐러드)와 관련 있
　　　　는 eat(먹다)을 사용하여 혼동을 준 오답입니다.

05 🔊 영국식 발음 → 캐나다식 발음 / 미국식 발음 → 호주식 발음

Are you going on vacation this month or next month?
(A) At the Grand Canyon Resort.
(B) I will go with my family.
(C) I leave this Saturday.

해석 당신은 휴가를 이번 달에 가시나요, 아니면 다음 달에 가시나요?
　　(A) 그랜드 캐니언 리조트에서요.
　　(B) 저는 제 가족과 갈 거예요.
　　(C) 저는 이번 주 토요일에 떠나요.

해설 휴가를 이번 달에 가는지 아니면 다음 달에 가는지를 묻는 선택 의문문
　　입니다.
　　(A) [×] 휴가를 이번 달에 가는지 아니면 다음 달에 가는지를 물었는데
　　　　장소로 응답했으므로 오답입니다.
　　(B) [×] 휴가를 이번 달에 가는지 아니면 다음 달에 가는지를 물었는
　　　　데, 이와 관련이 없는 자신의 가족과 갈 것이라는 내용으로 응
　　　　답했으므로 오답입니다.
　　(C) [○] 이번 주 토요일에 떠난다는 말로 제3의 것을 선택했으므로 정
　　　　답입니다.

06 🔊 호주식 발음 → 미국식 발음 / 캐나다식 발음 → 영국식 발음

Should I fill in both insurance forms or just this one?
(A) You don't have to fill out both.
(B) Near the top of the form.   ○

(C) My insurance agent.

insurance[inʃúərəns] 보험 · agent[éidʒənt] 중개인

해석 보험 양식을 둘 다 작성해야 하나요, 아니면 이것만 작성하면 되나요?
(A) 둘 다 작성하실 필요는 없습니다.
(B) 양식 위쪽에요.
(C) 제 보험 중개인이요.

해설 보험 양식을 둘 다 작성해야 하는지 아니면 이것만 작성하면 되는지를 묻는 선택 의문문입니다.
(A) [○] 둘 다 작성하지 않아도 된다는 말로 둘 다 선택하지 않았으므로 정답입니다.
(B) [×] 보험 양식을 둘 다 작성해야 하는지 아니면 이것만 작성하면 되는지를 물었는데 위치로 응답했으므로 오답입니다.
(C) [×] 질문의 insurance를 반복 사용하여 혼동을 준 오답입니다.

07 [미국식 발음 → 캐나다식 발음 / 영국식 발음 → 호주식 발음]

Are you going shopping, or are you going to have lunch?
(A) The mall has three floors.
(B) I have to buy some shoes.
(C) He'd rather stay home.

해석 당신은 쇼핑을 하러 갈 건가요, 아니면 점심을 먹으러 갈 건가요?
(A) 그 쇼핑몰은 3층짜리예요.
(B) 저는 신발을 좀 사야 해요.
(C) 그는 집에 있고 싶어 해요.

해설 쇼핑을 하러 갈 것인지 아니면 점심을 먹으러 갈 것인지를 묻는 선택 의문문입니다.
(A) [×] 질문의 shopping(쇼핑)과 관련 있는 mall(쇼핑몰)을 사용하여 혼동을 준 오답입니다.
(B) [○] 신발을 좀 사야 한다는 말로 쇼핑을 하러 가는 것을 간접적으로 선택했으므로 정답입니다.
(C) [×] He가 나타내는 대상이 질문에 없으므로 오답입니다.

Course 2 부가 의문문

HACKERS PRACTICE 🎧 DAY09_04   p.83

01 (B)	02 (B)	03 (A)	04 (C)
05 (A)	06 (B)	07 (C)	

01 [영국식 발음 → 호주식 발음 / 미국식 발음 → 캐나다식 발음]

You've been to Seattle, haven't you?
(A) No, I'll be in Chicago.
(B) Yes, actually I used to live there.
(C) She's never seen it.

해석 당신은 시애틀에 가본 적이 있죠, 안 그런가요?
(A) 아니요, 저는 시카고에 있을 거예요.
(B) 네, 사실 저는 그곳에 살았었어요.
(C) 그녀는 그것을 본 적이 없어요.

해설 시애틀에 가본 적이 있는지를 확인하는 부가 의문문입니다.
(A) [×] 시애틀에 가본 적이 있는지를 물었는데, 이와 관련이 없는 시카고에 있을 것이라는 내용으로 응답했으므로 오답입니다. No만 듣고 정답으로 고르지 않도록 주의합니다.
(B) [○] Yes로 시애틀에 가본 적이 있음을 전달한 후, 그곳에 살았었다는 부연 설명을 했으므로 정답입니다.
(C) [×] been – seen의 유사 발음 어휘를 사용하여 혼동을 준 오답

입니다.

02 [캐나다식 발음 → 영국식 발음 / 호주식 발음 → 미국식 발음]

We should buy a new printer, shouldn't we?
(A) I'll print out the receipt.
(B) Yes, the old one is broken.
(C) Toner is very expensive.

receipt[risíːt] 영수증

해석 우리는 새 인쇄기를 사야 해요, 안 그런가요?
(A) 제가 영수증을 인쇄할게요.
(B) 네, 예전 것이 망가졌어요.
(C) 토너는 매우 비싸요.

해설 새 인쇄기를 사야 한다는 의견에 동의를 구하는 부가 의문문입니다.
(A) [×] printer – print out의 유사 발음 어휘를 사용하여 혼동을 준 오답입니다.
(B) [○] Yes로 새 인쇄기를 사야 한다는 의견에 동의한 후, 예전 것이 망가졌다는 부연 설명을 했으므로 정답입니다.
(C) [×] 질문의 printer(인쇄기)와 관련 있는 Toner(토너)를 사용하여 혼동을 준 오답입니다.

03 [미국식 발음 → 호주식 발음 / 영국식 발음 → 캐나다식 발음]

Your department has an intern now, doesn't it?
(A) Yes, he's great.
(B) No, I'm a full-time employee.
(C) My internship will begin tomorrow.

full-time employee 정규 직원

해석 지금 당신의 부서에는 인턴사원이 있죠, 안 그런가요?
(A) 네, 그는 뛰어나요.
(B) 아니요, 저는 정규 직원이에요.
(C) 제 인턴직 근무는 내일 시작될 거예요.

해설 부서에 인턴사원이 있는지를 확인하는 부가 의문문입니다.
(A) [○] Yes로 부서에 인턴사원이 있음을 전달한 후, 그가 뛰어나다는 추가 정보를 제공했으므로 정답입니다.
(B) [×] 질문의 intern(인턴사원)과 관련 있는 full-time employee (정규 직원)를 사용하여 혼동을 준 오답입니다. No만 듣고 정답으로 고르지 않도록 주의합니다.
(C) [×] intern – internship의 유사 발음 어휘를 사용하여 혼동을 준 오답입니다.

04 [캐나다식 발음 → 미국식 발음 / 호주식 발음 → 영국식 발음]

The business lounge is next to the meeting room, isn't it?
(A) She'll repair it soon.
(B) I am starting a new business.
(C) You should ask one of the staff members.

repair[미 ripέər, 영 ripéə] 수리하다

해석 비즈니스 라운지는 회의실 옆에 있죠, 안 그런가요?
(A) 그녀가 그것을 곧 수리할 거예요.
(B) 저는 새로운 사업을 시작할 거예요.
(C) 직원들 중 한 명에게 물어보셔야 할 거예요.

해설 비즈니스 라운지가 회의실 옆에 있는지를 확인하는 부가 의문문입니다.
(A) [×] 비즈니스 라운지가 회의실 옆에 있는지를 물었는데, 이와 관련이 없는 그녀가 그것을 곧 수리할 것이라는 내용으로 응답했으므로 오답입니다.

(B) [×] 질문의 business를 반복 사용하여 혼동을 준 오답입니다.

(C) [○] 직원들 중 한 명에게 물어봐야 할 것이라는 말로 모른다는 간접적인 응답을 했으므로 정답입니다.

이 필요 없죠, 그렇죠?

05 [음성] 호주식 발음 → 영국식 발음 / 캐나다식 발음 → 미국식 발음

> Patty will become the accounting manager, won't she?
> (A) Yes, on April 1.
> (B) No, she just opened an account.
> (C) That department is on the third floor.
>
> accounting[əkáuntiŋ] 회계(부)   account[əkáunt] 계좌, 계정

해석 Patty가 회계부장이 될 것이죠, 안 그런가요?

(A) 네, 4월 1일에요.

(B) 아니요, 그녀는 막 계좌를 개설했어요.

(C) 그 부서는 3층에 있어요.

해설 Patty가 회계부장이 될 것인지를 확인하는 부가 의문문입니다.

(A) [○] Yes로 Patty가 회계부장이 될 것임을 전달한 후, 4월 1일에 될 것이라는 추가 정보를 제공했으므로 정답입니다.

(B) [×] accounting – account의 유사 발음 어휘를 사용하여 혼동을 준 오답입니다.

(C) [×] Patty가 회계부장이 될 것인지를 물었는데, 이와 관련이 없는 그 부서는 3층에 있다는 내용으로 응답했으므로 오답입니다.

06 [음성] 영국식 발음 → 캐나다식 발음 / 미국식 발음 → 호주식 발음

> Mark is organizing the investor meeting this year, isn't he?
> (A) I met him last month in Prague.
> (B) I heard he is in charge of it.
> (C) Organizational skills are very important.
>
> organize[미 ɔ́ːrɡənàiz, 영 ɔ́ːɡənaiz] 준비하다, 정돈하다
> be in charge of ~을 담당하다
> organizational[미 ɔ̀ːrɡənizéiʃənəl, 영 ɔ̀ːɡənaizéiʃənəl] 조직의

해석 Mark가 올해 투자자 회의를 준비하고 있죠, 안 그런가요?

(A) 저는 그를 지난달에 프라하에서 만났어요.

(B) 그가 그것을 담당한다고 들었어요.

(C) 조직력은 매우 중요해요.

해설 Mark가 올해 투자자 회의를 준비하고 있는지를 확인하는 부가 의문문입니다.

(A) [×] 질문의 this year(올해)와 관련 있는 last month(지난달)를 사용하여 혼동을 준 오답입니다.

(B) [○] 그가 그것을 담당한다고 들었다는 말로 Mark가 올해의 투자자 회의를 준비하고 있음을 간접적으로 전달했으므로 정답입니다.

(C) [×] organizing – Organizational의 유사 발음 어휘를 사용하여 혼동을 준 오답입니다.

07 [음성] 호주식 발음 → 미국식 발음 / 캐나다식 발음 → 영국식 발음

> You don't need any help preparing the budget for our next project, do you?
> (A) I don't have any money.
> (B) The projector isn't working right now.
> (C) Could you give me a hand?
>
> budget[bʌ́dʒit] 예산안   give a hand 도와주다

해석 당신은 우리의 다음 프로젝트를 위한 예산안을 준비하는 데 아무 도움

이 필요 없죠, 그렇죠?

(A) 저는 돈이 거의 없어요.

(B) 그 프로젝터는 지금 작동하지 않고 있어요.

(C) 당신이 저를 도와주시겠어요?

해설 다음 프로젝트를 위한 예산안을 준비하는 데 아무 도움이 필요 없는지를 확인하는 부가 의문문입니다.

(A) [×] 질문의 budget(예산안)과 관련 있는 money(돈)를 사용하여 혼동을 준 오답입니다.

(B) [×] project – projector의 유사 발음 어휘를 사용하여 혼동을 준 오답입니다.

(C) [○] 자신을 도와주겠냐고 되물어 예산안을 준비하는 데 도움이 필요하다는 것을 전달했으므로 정답입니다.

HACKERS TEST 🎧 DAY09_05   p.84

01 (B)	02 (C)	03 (A)	04 (A)
05 (C)	06 (B)	07 (A)	08 (C)
09 (A)	10 (A)	11 (B)	12 (B)
13 (C)	14 (A)	15 (A)	16 (A)
17 (C)	18 (C)	19 (B)	20 (C)
21 (A)	22 (C)	23 (C)	24 (B)
25 (C)			

01 [음성] 미국식 발음 → 캐나다식 발음

> Do you work the day or night shift?
> (A) Monday through Friday.
> (B) I normally work during the day.
> (C) I took today off.
>
> shift[ʃift] 근무 (시간)   normally[미 nɔ́ːrməli, 영 nɔ́ːməli] 보통
> take ~ off ~(동안)을 쉬다

해석 당신은 주간 근무를 하시나요, 아니면 야간 근무를 하시나요?

(A) 월요일에서 금요일까지요.

(B) 저는 보통 낮에 일을 해요.

(C) 저는 오늘 하루를 쉬었어요.

해설 주간 근무를 하는지 아니면 야간 근무를 하는지를 묻는 선택 의문문입니다.

(A) [×] 주간 근무를 하는지 아니면 야간 근무를 하는지를 물었는데 근무 요일로 응답했으므로 오답입니다.

(B) [○] 자신은 보통 낮에 일을 한다는 말로 주간 근무를 선택했으므로 정답입니다.

(C) [×] 질문의 work(근무하다)와 관련 있는 took ~ off(쉬었다)를 사용하여 혼동을 준 오답입니다.

02 [음성] 영국식 발음 → 호주식 발음

> You planned this banquet, right?
> (A) I'm planning to leave early.
> (B) Turn right down this street.
> (C) No, Mr. Morrison did.
>
> banquet[bǽŋkwit] 연회

해석 당신이 이 연회를 계획했죠, 그렇죠?

(A) 저는 일찍 떠날 예정이에요.

(B) 이 길 끝에서 우회전하세요.

(C) 아니요, Mr. Morrison이 했어요.

해설 상대방이 연회를 계획했는지를 확인하는 부가 의문문입니다.

(A) [×] planned – planning의 유사 발음 어휘를 사용하여 혼동을

준 오답입니다.
(B) [×] 질문의 right(그렇죠)를 '오른쪽으로'라는 의미의 부사로 반복 사용하여 혼동을 준 오답입니다.
(C) [ㅇ] No로 자신이 연회를 계획하지 않았음을 전달한 후, Mr. Morrison이 했다는 추가 정보를 제공했으므로 정답입니다.

03 🎧 캐나다식 발음 → 영국식 발음

Is tonight or tomorrow the play's final performance?
(A) It ends tomorrow.
(B) It lasts for about two hours.
(C) I saw it yesterday.

performance[미 pərfɔ́:rməns, 영 pəfɔ́:məns] 공연
last[미 læst, 영 lɑ:st] 계속되다, 지속되다

해석 그 연극의 마지막 공연은 오늘 밤인가요, 아니면 내일인가요?
(A) 그것은 내일 끝나요.
(B) 그것은 약 두 시간 동안 계속돼요.
(C) 저는 그것을 어제 보았어요.

해설 연극의 마지막 공연이 오늘 밤인지 아니면 내일인지를 묻는 선택 의문문입니다.
(A) [ㅇ] 내일 끝난다는 말로 내일을 선택했으므로 정답입니다.
(B) [×] 연극의 마지막 공연이 오늘 밤인지 아니면 내일인지를 물었는데, 이와 관련이 없는 그것은 약 두 시간 동안 계속된다는 내용으로 응답했으므로 오답입니다.
(C) [×] 질문의 tomorrow(내일)와 관련 있는 yesterday(어제)를 사용하여 혼동을 준 오답입니다.

04 🎧 미국식 발음 → 호주식 발음

You won't miss the deadline, will you?
(A) No, the project is almost done.
(B) I just saw her yesterday.
(C) It will be announced soon.

deadline[dédlain] 마감기한 announce[ənáuns] 공지하다

해석 당신은 마감기한을 놓치지 않을 거예요, 그렇죠?
(A) 아니요, 그 과제는 거의 끝났어요.
(B) 저는 바로 어제 그녀를 보았어요.
(C) 그것은 곧 공지될 거예요.

해설 상대방이 마감기한을 놓치지 않을 것인지를 확인하는 부가 의문문입니다.
(A) [ㅇ] No로 마감기한을 놓치지 않을 것임을 전달한 후, 그 과제가 거의 끝났다는 부연 설명을 했으므로 정답입니다.
(B) [×] her가 나타내는 대상이 질문에 없으므로 오답입니다.
(C) [×] 마감기한을 놓치지 않을 것인지를 물었는데, 이와 관련이 없는 그것은 곧 공지될 것이라는 내용으로 응답했으므로 오답입니다.

05 🎧 캐나다식 발음 → 미국식 발음

Would you like dessert or something to drink?
(A) The beach was my favorite.
(B) No, I haven't ordered yet.
(C) I'll have either a coffee or tea.

favorite[féivərit] 가장 좋아하는 것

해석 당신은 디저트나 마실 것을 원하시나요?
(A) 그 해변은 제가 가장 좋아하는 곳이었어요.

(B) 아니요, 저는 아직 주문하지 않았어요.
(C) 저는 커피나 차 중 하나를 마실게요.

해설 디저트나 마실 것 중에 무엇을 원하는지를 묻는 선택 의문문입니다.
(A) [×] 디저트나 마실 것을 원하는지를 물었는데, 이와 관련이 없는 그 해변은 자신이 가장 좋아하는 곳이었다는 내용으로 응답했으므로 오답입니다.
(B) [×] 질문의 dessert or something to drink(디저트나 마실 것)와 관련 있는 ordered(주문했다)를 사용하여 혼동을 준 오답입니다.
(C) [ㅇ] 커피나 차 중 하나를 마시겠다는 말로 마실 것을 선택했으므로 정답입니다.

06 🎧 호주식 발음 → 영국식 발음

You visited the new branch, didn't you?
(A) Two visitor passes, please.
(B) Yes, just last week.
(C) The old office equipment.

branch[미 bræntʃ, 영 brɑ:ntʃ] 지사, 지점 pass[미 pæs, 영 pɑ:s] 출입 허가증

해석 당신은 새 지사를 방문했죠, 안 그랬나요?
(A) 방문객 출입 허가증을 두 개 주세요.
(B) 네, 바로 지난주에요.
(C) 오래된 사무기기요.

해설 상대방이 새 지사를 방문했는지를 확인하는 부가 의문문입니다.
(A) [×] visited – visitor의 유사 발음 어휘를 사용하여 혼동을 준 오답입니다.
(B) [ㅇ] Yes로 새 지사를 방문했음을 전달한 후, 바로 지난주에 방문했다는 추가 정보를 제공했으므로 정답입니다.
(C) [×] 질문의 new(새로운)와 반대 의미인 old(오래된)를 사용하여 혼동을 준 오답입니다.

07 🎧 영국식 발음 → 캐나다식 발음

Would you prefer to work in marketing or advertising?
(A) I like advertising more.
(B) Yes, I have a job in that field.
(C) I saw their advertisement.

advertising[미 ǽdvərtàiziŋ, 영 ǽdvətaiziŋ] 홍보, 광고 field[fi:ld] 분야
advertisement[미 ædvərtáizmənt, 영 ədvə́:tismənt] 광고

해석 당신은 마케팅 부서에서 일하는 것이 좋으신가요, 아니면 홍보 부서에서 일하는 것이 좋으신가요?
(A) 저는 홍보 부서가 더 좋아요.
(B) 네, 저는 그 분야에서 일해요.
(C) 저는 그들의 광고를 보았어요.

해설 마케팅 부서에서 일하는 것이 좋은지 아니면 홍보 부서에서 일하는 것이 좋은지를 묻는 선택 의문문입니다.
(A) [ㅇ] 홍보 부서가 더 좋다는 말로 홍보 부서에서 일하는 것을 선택했으므로 정답입니다.
(B) [×] 질문의 work(일하다)와 관련 있는 job(일)을 사용하여 혼동을 준 오답입니다.
(C) [×] advertising – advertisement의 유사 발음 어휘를 사용하여 혼동을 준 오답입니다.

08 🎧 호주식 발음 → 미국식 발음

You sent that e-mail to our client, didn't you?
(A) No, in the mailbox.

(B) The client just arrived from Tokyo.
(C) Yes, I sent it this morning.

client[kláiənt] 고객   mailbox[미 méilbɑ:ks, 영 méilbɔks] 메일함, 우편함

해석 당신이 우리 고객에게 그 이메일을 보냈죠, 안 그랬나요?
(A) 아니요, 메일함이에요.
(B) 그 고객은 도쿄에서 막 도착했어요.
(C) 네, 저는 그것을 오늘 아침에 보냈어요.

해설 상대방이 고객에게 그 이메일을 보냈는지를 확인하는 부가 의문문입니다.
(A) [×] 질문의 e-mail(이메일)과 관련 있는 mailbox(메일함)를 사용하여 혼동을 준 오답입니다. No만 듣고 정답으로 고르지 않도록 주의합니다.
(B) [×] 질문의 sent(보냈다)와 반대 의미인 arrived(도착했다)를 사용하여 혼동을 준 오답입니다.
(C) [○] Yes로 고객에게 이메일을 보냈음을 전달한 후, 오늘 아침에 보냈다는 부연 설명을 했으므로 정답입니다.

09 ③🇺🇸 미국식 발음 → 캐나다식 발음

Do you want me to arrange chairs or hang decorations?
(A) Whichever you prefer.
(B) For a fund-raising event.
(C) Thanks for the bouquet.

arrange[əréindʒ] 배치하다   decoration[dèkəréiʃən] 장식
fund-raising[fʌndrèiziŋ] 모금

해석 제가 의자를 배치할까요, 아니면 장식을 달까요?
(A) 무엇이든 당신이 원하는 것이요.
(B) 모금 행사를 위해서요.
(C) 부케 감사해요.

해설 자신이 의자를 배치할지 아니면 장식을 달지를 묻는 선택 의문문입니다.
(A) [○] 무엇이든 당신이 원하는 것이라는 말로 둘 다 상관없음을 전달했으므로 정답입니다.
(B) [×] 질문의 arrange chairs or hang decorations(의자를 배치하거나 장식을 달기)와 관련 있는 event(행사)를 사용하여 혼동을 준 오답입니다.
(C) [×] 질문의 decorations(장식)와 관련 있는 bouquet(부케)를 사용하여 혼동을 준 오답입니다.

10 ③🇬🇧 영국식 발음 → 호주식 발음

You won't be late for your flight, will you?
(A) No, I still have plenty of time.
(B) He's going to arrive early.
(C) You'll have to book a ticket.

plenty of 많은

해석 당신은 비행기 시간에 늦지 않으실 거죠, 그렇죠?
(A) 아니요, 저는 아직 시간이 많아요.
(B) 그는 일찍 도착할 거예요.
(C) 당신은 표를 예매해야 할 거예요.

해설 비행기 시간에 늦지 않을 것인지를 확인하는 부가 의문문입니다.
(A) [○] No로 비행기 시간에 늦지 않을 것임을 전달한 후, 아직 시간이 많다는 부연 설명을 했으므로 정답입니다.
(B) [×] 질문의 late(늦은)와 반대 의미인 early(일찍)를 사용하여 혼동을 준 오답입니다.
(C) [×] 비행기 시간에 늦지 않을 것인지를 물었는데, 이와 관련 없

는 표를 예매해야 할 것이라는 내용으로 응답했으므로 오답입니다.

11 ③🇨🇦 캐나다식 발음 → 영국식 발음

Does construction on the stadium start in May or June?
(A) Where should we start?
(B) Sometime in May, I believe.
(C) The stadium is a mile away.

construction[kənstrʌ́kʃən] 건설, 건축   stadium[stéidiəm] 경기장

해석 경기장 건설은 5월에 시작하나요, 아니면 6월에 시작하나요?
(A) 어디서부터 시작해야 할까요?
(B) 5월 중인 것 같아요.
(C) 경기장은 1마일 떨어져 있어요.

해설 경기장 건설이 5월에 시작하는지 아니면 6월에 시작하는지를 묻는 선택 의문문입니다.
(A) [×] 질문의 start를 반복 사용하여 혼동을 준 오답입니다.
(B) [○] 5월 중인 것 같다는 말로 5월을 선택했으므로 정답입니다.
(C) [×] 질문의 stadium을 반복 사용하여 혼동을 준 오답입니다.

12 ③🇺🇸 미국식 발음 → 호주식 발음

You're transferring to the California office, aren't you?
(A) No, they are in Toronto.
(B) Not until this fall.
(C) Transfer at Baker Street Station.

transfer[미 trænsfə́:r, 영 trǽnsfə̀:] 전근하다, 갈아타다

해석 당신은 캘리포니아 사무실로 전근을 가죠, 안 그런가요?
(A) 아니요, 그들은 토론토에 있어요.
(B) 이번 가을이나 되어서요.
(C) Baker가 역에서 갈아타세요.

해설 상대방이 캘리포니아 사무실로 전근을 가는지를 확인하는 부가 의문문입니다.
(A) [×] 캘리포니아 사무실로 전근을 가는지를 물었는데, 이와 관련이 없는 그들은 토론토에 있다는 내용으로 응답했으므로 오답입니다. No만 듣고 정답으로 고르지 않도록 주의합니다.
(B) [○] 이번 가을이나 되어서라는 말로 이번 가을에 캘리포니아 사무실로 전근을 갈 것임을 전달했으므로 정답입니다.
(C) [×] 질문의 transferring(전근을 가다)을 '갈아타다'라는 의미의 Transfer로 반복 사용하여 혼동을 준 오답입니다.

13 ③🇨🇦 캐나다식 발음 → 미국식 발음

Can you review these customer surveys, or should I do it?
(A) Answer all the questions.
(B) You should invite John there.
(C) I'd prefer to do it myself.

review[rivjú:] 검토하다   survey[미 sə́:rvei, 영 sə́:vei] 설문 조사
invite[inváit] 초대하다

해석 이 고객 설문 조사를 검토해 줄 수 있나요, 아니면 제가 할까요?
(A) 모든 질문에 대답해 주세요.
(B) John을 그곳으로 초대하셔야 해요.
(C) 제가 직접 그것을 하고 싶어요.

해설 고객 설문 조사를 검토해 줄 수 있는지 아니면 자신이 해야 하는지를 묻는 선택 의문문입니다.
(A) [×] 질문의 surveys(설문 조사)와 관련 있는 questions(질문)를 사용하여 혼동을 준 오답입니다.
(B) [×] 고객 설문 조사를 검토해 줄 수 있는지 아니면 자신이 해야 하는지를 물었는데, 이와 관련이 없는 John을 초대해야 한다는 내용으로 응답했으므로 오답입니다.
(C) [○] 자신이 직접 그것을 하고 싶다는 말로 고객 설문 조사를 검토하는 것을 선택했으므로 정답입니다.

14 🔊 호주식 발음 → 영국식 발음

This discount coupon is currently valid, isn't it?
(A) Sorry, it appears to be expired.
(B) It's the most up-to-date product.
(C) What's the current rate of exchange?

currently[미 kэ́:rəntli, 영 kʌ́rəntli] 지금, 현재   valid[vǽlid] 유효한
expire[미 ikspáiər, 영 ikspáiə] 기한이 끝나다, 만료되다
up-to-date[ʌ̀ptədéit] 최신의   rate of exchange 환율

해석 이 할인권은 지금 유효하죠, 안 그런가요?
(A) 죄송하지만, 기한이 끝난 것 같아요.
(B) 이것은 가장 최신 제품이에요.
(C) 현재의 환율은 얼마인가요?

해설 할인권이 지금 유효한지를 확인하는 부가 의문문입니다.
(A) [○] 기한이 끝난 것 같다는 말로 할인권이 유효하지 않음을 전달했으므로 정답입니다.
(B) [×] 질문의 discount coupon(할인권)과 관련 있는 product(제품)를 사용하여 혼동을 준 오답입니다.
(C) [×] currently – current의 유사 발음 어휘를 사용하여 혼동을 준 오답입니다.

15 🔊 영국식 발음 → 캐나다식 발음

Can I use the conference room, or is it still occupied?
(A) Ms. Lee is in there right now.
(B) They occupy a building next door.
(C) The conference will be a great success.

occupy[미 ákjupài, 영 ɔ́kjəpai] 사용하다, 살다   success[səksés] 성공, 성과

해석 제가 회의실을 사용할 수 있나요, 아니면 회의실이 아직 사용 중인가요?
(A) Ms. Lee가 지금 그곳에 있어요.
(B) 그들은 옆 건물에 살아요.
(C) 회의는 매우 성공적일 거예요.

해설 회의실을 사용할 수 있는지 아니면 회의실이 아직 사용 중인지를 묻는 선택 의문문입니다.
(A) [○] Ms. Lee가 지금 그곳에 있다는 말로 회의실이 아직 사용 중임을 간접적으로 전달했으므로 정답입니다.
(B) [×] 질문의 occupied(사용 중인)를 '살다'라는 의미의 동사 occupy로 반복 사용하여 혼동을 준 오답입니다.
(C) [×] 질문의 conference를 반복 사용하여 혼동을 준 오답입니다.

16 🔊 호주식 발음 → 미국식 발음

You're the bakery's new baker, aren't you?
(A) Yes, I just started last week.
(B) He's very talented.
(C) I ordered the baked potato.

baker[미 béikər, 영 béikə] 제빵사   talented[tǽləntid] 재능 있는

해설 당신은 그 제과점의 새로운 제빵사죠, 안 그런가요?
(A) 네, 저는 지난주에 막 시작했어요.
(B) 그는 매우 재능이 있어요.
(C) 저는 구운 감자를 주문했는데요.

해설 상대방이 제과점의 새로운 제빵사인지를 확인하는 부가 의문문입니다.
(A) [○] Yes로 자신이 제과점의 새로운 제빵사임을 전달한 후, 지난주에 막 시작했다는 추가 정보를 제공했으므로 정답입니다.
(B) [×] He가 나타내는 대상이 질문에 없으므로 오답입니다.
(C) [×] baker – baked의 유사 발음 어휘를 사용하여 혼동을 준 오답입니다.

17 🔊 미국식 발음 → 캐나다식 발음

Would you like the roast chicken or the vegetarian option?
(A) On the back of the menu.
(B) Yes, the pasta is too spicy.
(C) Are there any other options?

roast[미 roust, 영 rəust] 구운
vegetarian[미 vèdʒətɛ́əriən, 영 vèdʒitéəriən] 채식주의자를 위한, 채식주의의
spicy[spáisi] 매운

해석 당신은 구운 닭고기가 좋으신가요, 아니면 채식주의자를 위한 메뉴가 좋으신가요?
(A) 메뉴판 뒤에요.
(B) 네, 그 파스타는 너무 매워요.
(C) 다른 선택 사항은 없나요?

해설 구운 닭고기가 좋은지 아니면 채식주의자를 위한 메뉴가 좋은지를 묻는 선택 의문문입니다.
(A) [×] 질문의 the roast chicken or the vegetarian option(구운 닭고기 아니면 채식주의자를 위한 메뉴)과 관련 있는 menu(메뉴판)를 사용하여 혼동을 준 오답입니다.
(B) [×] 구운 닭고기가 좋은지 아니면 채식주의자를 위한 메뉴가 좋은지를 물었는데, 이와 관련이 없는 파스타가 너무 맵다는 내용으로 응답했으므로 오답입니다.
(C) [○] 다른 선택 사항이 없는지를 되물어 제3의 것에 대한 추가 정보를 요구하는 정답입니다.

18 🔊 영국식 발음 → 호주식 발음

Parker Bash applied for a promotion, didn't he?
(A) The sales promotion ends today.
(B) Where is his office?
(C) Last month, I think.

apply for ~을 신청하다
promotion[미 prəmóuʃən, 영 prəmə́uʃən] 진급, 판촉 행사

해석 Parker Bash는 진급 신청을 했어요, 안 그랬나요?
(A) 그 판촉 행사는 오늘 끝나요.
(B) 그의 사무실은 어디인가요?
(C) 아마, 지난달에요.

해설 Parker Bash가 진급 신청을 했는지를 확인하는 부가 의문문입니다.
(A) [×] 질문의 promotion(진급)을 '판촉 행사'라는 의미로 반복 사용하여 혼동을 준 오답입니다.
(B) [×] 질문의 promotion(진급)과 관련 있는 office(사무실)를 사용하여 혼동을 준 오답입니다.
(C) [○] 지난달에라는 말로 Parker Bash가 지난달에 진급 신청을 했음을 간접적으로 전달했으므로 정답입니다.

Do you prefer cooking at home or going out to eat?
(A) She just went out.
(B) I enjoy doing both.
(C) No, I haven't eaten yet.

prefer[미 prifə́:r, 영 prifə́:] 더 좋아하다, 선호하다

해석 당신은 집에서 요리하는 것이 더 좋으신가요, 아니면 외식하는 것이 더 좋으신가요?
(A) 그녀는 방금 나갔어요.
(B) 저는 둘 다 좋아해요.
(C) 아니요, 저는 아직 식사를 하지 못했어요.

해설 집에서 요리하는 것이 좋은지 아니면 외식하는 것이 좋은지를 묻는 선택 의문문입니다.
(A) [×] 질문의 going out을 went out으로 반복 사용하여 혼동을 준 오답입니다.
(B) [○] 자신은 둘 다 좋아한다는 말로 둘 다 선택했으므로 정답입니다.
(C) [×] 질문의 eat을 eaten으로 반복 사용하여 혼동을 준 오답입니다.

The presentation will be on manufacturing costs, won't it?
(A) It costs $20.
(B) Across from our plant.
(C) It hasn't been confirmed yet.

presentation[prèzəntéiʃən] 발표, 상연
manufacturing[미 mænjufǽktʃəriŋ, 영 mænjəfǽktʃəriŋ] 제조의
confirm[미 kənfə́:rm, 영 kənfə́:m] 확정하다, 확인하다

해석 그 발표는 제조 비용에 관한 것일 거예요, 안 그런가요?
(A) 그것은 20달러예요.
(B) 우리 공장 맞은편에요.
(C) 그것은 아직 확정되지 않았어요.

해설 발표가 제조 비용에 관한 것일지를 확인하는 부가 의문문입니다.
(A) [×] 질문의 costs(비용)를 '(값이) ~이다'라는 의미의 동사로 반복 사용하여 혼동을 준 오답입니다.
(B) [×] 질문의 manufacturing(제조의)과 관련 있는 plant(공장)를 사용하여 혼동을 준 오답입니다.
(C) [○] 그것은 아직 확정되지 않았다는 말로 모른다는 간접적인 응답을 했으므로 정답입니다.

Do you want to go cycling or mountain climbing over the weekend?
(A) Both sound fun to me.
(B) It's my favorite hobby.
(C) No one in the company works on weekends.

cycling[sáikliŋ] 자전거 타기

해석 당신은 주말에 자전거를 타러 가고 싶으신가요, 아니면 등산을 가고 싶으신가요?
(A) 저는 둘 다 재미있을 것 같아요.
(B) 그것은 제가 가장 좋아하는 취미예요.
(C) 회사의 누구도 주말에 일을 하지 않아요.

해설 주말에 자전거를 타러 가고 싶은지 아니면 등산을 가고 싶은지를 묻는 선택 의문문입니다.
(A) [○] 자신은 둘 다 재미있을 것 같다는 말로 둘 다 선택했으므로 정답입니다.
(B) [×] 질문의 cycling or mountain climbing(자전거 타기 아니면 등산)과 관련 있는 hobby(취미)를 사용하여 혼동을 준 오답입니다.
(C) [×] 질문의 weekend를 weekends로 반복 사용하여 혼동을 준 오답입니다.

Clark Jones was appointed as the company's next CEO, wasn't he?
(A) The company's new name is Petertech.
(B) The CEO retired last month.
(C) I haven't heard anything about that.

appoint[əpɔ́int] 지명하다, 임명하다   retire[미 ritáiər, 영 ritáiə] 은퇴하다

해석 Clark Jones가 회사의 다음 최고 경영자로 지명되었죠, 안 그랬나요?
(A) 그 회사의 새로운 이름은 Petertech예요.
(B) 최고 경영자는 지난달에 은퇴했어요.
(C) 저는 그것에 대해 아무것도 듣지 못했어요.

해설 Clark Jones가 회사의 다음 최고 경영자로 지명되었는지를 확인하는 부가 의문문입니다.
(A) [×] 질문의 company를 반복 사용하여 혼동을 준 오답입니다.
(B) [×] 질문의 CEO를 반복 사용하고, next(다음)와 반대 의미인 last(지난)를 사용하여 혼동을 준 오답입니다.
(C) [○] 자신은 그것에 대해 아무것도 듣지 못했다는 말로 모른다는 간접적인 응답을 했으므로 정답입니다.

Have we hired a new designer, or do we need to hold more interviews?
(A) We're holding a sale.
(B) You would be perfect for the position.
(C) Didn't the HR manager tell you?

hire[미 haiər, 영 haiə] 채용하다

해석 우리는 새로운 디자이너를 채용했나요, 아니면 면접을 더 봐야 하나요?
(A) 우리는 할인 판매를 하고 있어요.
(B) 당신은 그 직책에 아주 적합할 거예요.
(C) 인사부장이 당신에게 말해주지 않았나요?

해설 새로운 디자이너를 채용했는지 아니면 면접을 더 봐야 할지를 묻는 선택 의문문입니다.
(A) [×] 질문의 hold를 holding으로 반복 사용하여 혼동을 준 오답입니다.
(B) [×] 질문의 interviews(면접)와 관련 있는 position(직책)을 사용하여 혼동을 준 오답입니다.
(C) [○] 인사부장이 말해주지 않았는지를 되물어 인사부장이 알고 있다는 것을 간접적으로 전달했으므로 정답입니다.

Our new hard drive is our best seller, isn't it?
(A) No, it's not that difficult.
(B) Yes. It's very popular.
(C) I deleted the file.

delete[dilíːt] 삭제하다

해석 새로운 하드 드라이브는 우리의 가장 잘 팔리는 상품이에요, 안 그런가요?
(A) 아니요, 그것은 그렇게 어렵지 않아요.
(B) 네. 그것은 매우 인기 있어요.
(C) 저는 그 파일을 삭제했어요.

해설 새로운 하드 드라이브가 가장 잘 팔리는 상품인지를 확인하는 부가 의문문입니다.
(A) [x] 질문의 hard drive(하드 드라이브)에서 hard의 '어려운'과 같은 의미인 difficult(어려운)를 사용하여 혼동을 준 오답입니다. No만 듣고 정답으로 고르지 않도록 주의합니다.
(B) [o] Yes로 새로운 하드 드라이브가 가장 잘 팔리는 상품임을 전달한 후, 그것이 매우 인기 있다는 부연 설명을 했으므로 정답입니다.
(C) [x] 질문의 hard drive(하드 드라이브)와 관련 있는 file(파일)을 사용하여 혼동을 준 오답입니다.

25 🌎 영국식 발음 → 미국식 발음

Margaret is giving the presentation, right?
(A) I'm getting them a present.
(B) No, it's about marketing.
(C) That's what I heard.

presentation[prèzəntéiʃən] 발표

해석 Margaret이 발표를 할 거죠, 그렇죠?
(A) 저는 그들에게 선물을 줄 거예요.
(B) 아니요, 그것은 마케팅에 관한 거예요.
(C) 제가 듣기로는 그래요.

해설 Margaret이 발표를 할 것인지를 확인하는 부가 의문문입니다.
(A) [x] presentation – present의 유사 발음 어휘를 사용하여 혼동을 준 오답입니다.
(B) [x] 질문의 presentation(발표)에서 연상할 수 있는 발표 주제와 관련된 marketing(마케팅)을 사용하여 혼동을 준 오답입니다. No만 듣고 정답으로 고르지 않도록 주의합니다.
(C) [o] 자신이 듣기로는 그렇다는 말로 Margaret이 발표를 할 것이라는 간접적인 응답을 했으므로 정답입니다.

DAY 10 전체 대화 관련 문제

Course 1 주제 및 목적 문제

HACKERS PRACTICE ∩ DAY10_02   p.89

01 (A)	02 (B)	03 (B)	04 (C)

01-02 [3에] 미국식 발음 → 호주식 발음 / 영국식 발음 → 캐나다식 발음

Questions 1-2 refer to the following conversation.

> W: Hi, Mark. This is Donna. I'd like to <u>arrange a party</u> for our boss. He became the department head last week. ⁰¹Can you <u>help me with</u> the preparations?
> M: I'd be happy to. What should I do?
> W: ⁰²Could you <u>call the company</u> that <u>catered the party</u> you organized last year? I need to know how much dinner for 50 people costs.
>
> **arrange**[əréindʒ] 준비하다   **department head** 부장
> **preparation**[prèpəréiʃən] 준비
> **cater**[미 kéitər, 영 kéitə] (사업으로 행사에) 음식을 공급하다
> **organize**[미 ɔ́ːrɡənàiz, 영 ɔ́ːɡənaiz] 준비하다, 계획하다

해석
1-2번은 다음 대화에 관한 문제입니다.

여: 안녕하세요, Mark. Donna예요. 저는 저희 상사를 위한 파티를 준비하고 싶어요. 그는 지난주에 부장이 되었어요. ⁰¹준비를 도와주실 수 있나요?
남: 기꺼이요. 제가 무엇을 하면 되나요?
여: ⁰²작년에 당신이 준비했던 파티에 음식을 공급했던 회사에 전화해 주실 수 있나요? 저는 50인분의 저녁 식사 가격이 얼마나 드는지 알아야 해요.

01
해석 전화의 목적은 무엇인가?
(A) 도움을 요청하기 위해
(B) 의견을 묻기 위해
(C) 조언을 제공하기 위해
(D) 불만을 제기하기 위해

해설 전화의 목적을 묻는 문제입니다. 여자가 "Can you help me with the preparations?"라며 준비를 도와줄 수 있는지 물었습니다. 따라서 정답은 (A) To request assistance입니다.

어휘 **assistance**[əsístəns] 도움   **submit**[səbmít] 제기하다, 제출하다

02
해석 여자는 남자에게 무엇을 해달라고 요청하는가?
(A) 가구를 구매한다.
(B) 출장 연회업체에 연락한다.
(C) 문서를 보낸다.
(D) 저녁 식사 메뉴를 변경한다.

해설 여자가 남자에게 요청하는 것을 묻는 문제입니다. 여자가 "Could you call the company that catered the party you organized ~?"라

며 남자가 준비했던 파티에 음식을 공급했던 회사에 전화해 달라고 요청하였습니다. 따라서 정답은 (B) Contact a caterer입니다.

어휘 **caterer**[미 kéitərər, 영 kéitərə] 출장 연회업체

03-04 [3에] 미국식 발음 → 영국식 발음 → 캐나다식 발음 /
영국식 발음 → 미국식 발음 → 호주식 발음

Questions 3-4 refer to the following conversation with three speakers.

> W1: ⁰³I just <u>read the review</u> of our movie, *Cosmos*. Have either of you seen it yet?
> W2: I read it this morning. Overall, it is really positive. Right, Steve?
> M: Yeah. ⁰⁴I'm happy with it. **Especially when you consider that Bill Waters wrote it.** ⁰⁴He is a <u>famous film critic</u>, and thousands of people read his articles.
> W1: Right. I'm sure it will <u>result in</u> higher ticket sales at theaters.
>
> **review**[rivjúː] 평론   **overall**[미 ð̀uvərɔ́ːl, 영 ð̀uvərɔ́ːl] 전반적으로
> **critic**[krítik] 평론가, 비평가   **article**[미 ɑ́ːrtikl, 영 ɑ́ːtikl] 기사
> **result in** ~을 가져오다, ~을 야기하다

해석
3-4번은 다음 세 명의 대화에 관한 문제입니다.

여1: ⁰³저는 방금 우리 영화 *Cosmos*의 평론을 읽었어요. 두 분 중 그것을 보신 분이 계신가요?
여2: 저는 그것을 오늘 아침에 읽었어요. 전반적으로, 매우 긍정적이더군요. 그렇죠, Steve?
남: 네. ⁰⁴저는 만족스러워요. **특히 Bill Waters가 썼다는 것을 고려했을 때요.** ⁰⁴그는 유명한 영화 평론가이고, 많은 사람들이 그의 기사를 읽으니까요.
여1: 맞아요. 저는 그 평론이 극장에서의 더 높은 티켓 판매량을 가져올 거라고 확신해요.

03
해석 대화는 주로 무엇에 대한 것인가?
(A) 티켓 할인
(B) 영화 평론
(C) 극장 개장
(D) 영화 개봉

해설 대화의 주제를 묻는 문제입니다. 여자 1이 "I just read the review of our movie"라며 방금 자신들의 영화의 평론을 읽었다고 한 뒤, 영화 평론에 관한 내용으로 대화가 이어지고 있습니다. 따라서 정답은 (B) A film review입니다.

어휘 **discount**[dískaunt] 할인   **release**[rilíːs] 개봉, 발매

04
해석 남자가 "특히 Bill Waters가 썼다는 것을 고려했을 때요"라고 말할 때 의도하는 것은 무엇인가?
(A) 그는 작품에 대해 비판적이다.
(B) 그는 대본을 수정할 것이다.
(C) 그는 기자를 존경한다.

(D) 그는 사본을 요청할 것이다.

해설 남자가 하는 말(Especially when you consider that Bill Waters wrote it)의 의도를 묻는 문제입니다. 남자가 "I'm happy with it[review of our movie]."이라며 영화의 평론이 만족스럽다고 한 뒤, "He[Bill Waters] is a famous film critic, and thousands of people read his articles."라며 Bill Waters는 유명한 영화 평론가이고 많은 사람들이 그의 기사를 읽는다고 하였습니다. 이를 통해 남자가 평론을 쓴 기자인 Bill Waters를 존경한다는 것을 전달하려는 의도임을 알 수 있습니다. 따라서 정답은 (C) He respects a writer입니다.

어휘 critical of ~에 대해 비판적인 script[skript] 대본
respect[rispékt] 존경하다, 존중하다

Course 2 화자 및 장소 문제

HACKERS PRACTICE 🎧 DAY10_04   p.91

01 (D)	02 (A)	03 (C)	04 (B)

01-02 🎙 호주식 발음 → 영국식 발음 / 캐나다식 발음 → 미국식 발음

Questions 1-2 refer to the following conversation.

M: Hello. [01]I'm staying in Suite 107, and the air conditioner in here isn't working.
W: Really? Have you tried turning the power off and then back on?
M: I already did that, but it's still not working.
W: All right. I'll tell a technician to go up and look at it immediately. If he can't get it working right away, [01/02]we'll move you to another room on the same floor.

power[미 páuər, 영 pauə] 전원, 전력 technician[tekníʃən] 기술자
immediately[imí:diətli] 지금, 즉시

해석
1-2번은 다음 대화에 관한 문제입니다.

남: 안녕하세요. [01]저는 스위트룸 107호에 머물고 있는데요, 이곳의 에어컨이 작동하지 않고 있어요.
여: 정말인가요? 전원을 껐다가 다시 켜보셨나요?
남: 이미 그렇게 해봤지만, 아직도 작동하지 않고 있어요.
여: 알겠습니다. 제가 기술자에게 지금 올라가서 그것을 살펴보라고 하겠습니다. 만약 그가 그것을 바로 작동하게 하지 못하면, 같은 층의 [01/02]다른 객실로 손님을 옮겨드리겠습니다.

01
해석 화자들은 어디에 있는 것 같은가?
(A) 여행사에
(B) 소매점에
(C) 체육관에
(D) 호텔에

해설 화자들이 있는 장소를 묻는 문제입니다. 남자가 "I'm staying in Suite 107, and the air conditioner in here isn't working."이라며 자신은 스위트룸 107호에 머물고 있으며 에어컨이 작동하지 않고 있다고 하자, 여자가 "we'll move you to another room"이라며 다른 객실로 남자를 옮겨주겠다고 한 것을 통해 화자들이 있는 장소가 호텔임을 알 수 있습니다. 따라서 정답은 (D) At a hotel입니다.

어휘 travel agency 여행사 retail store 소매점 gym[dʒim] 체육관

02
해석 여자에 따르면, 무엇이 이용 가능해질 수 있는가?
(A) 다른 객실
(B) 무료 회원권
(C) 할인된 가격
(D) 사용설명서

해설 이용 가능해질 수 있는 것을 묻는 문제입니다. 여자가 "we'll move you to another room"이라며 다른 객실로 남자를 옮겨주겠다고 한 말을 통해 다른 객실이 이용 가능해질 수 있음을 알 수 있습니다. 따라서 정답은 (A) A different room입니다.

어휘 membership[미 mémbərʃip, 영 mémbəʃip] 회원권, 회원 자격
instruction manual 사용설명서, 취급안내서

03-04 🎙 캐나다식 발음 → 미국식 발음 / 호주식 발음 → 영국식 발음

Questions 3-4 refer to the following conversation.

M: [03]Kenwood Financial. How may I help you?
W: Hello. I'm calling because I . . . uh . . . [03]I lost my credit card yesterday. I need to cancel it and get it replaced.
M: Can you provide your name and address?
W: My name is Martina Rhodes and I live at 5001 Selah Way, Danville, Vermont.
M: OK, Ms. Rhodes. Your request will take two days to process. [04]The replacement will be mailed out then.

credit card 신용카드 replace[ripléis] 교체하다, 바꾸다
replacement[ripléismənt] 교체(품) mail out 우편으로 발송하다

해석
3-4번은 다음 대화에 관한 문제입니다.

남: [03]Kenwood Financial사입니다. 어떻게 도와드릴까요?
여: 안녕하세요. 저는… 어… [03]제가 어제 신용카드를 잃어버려서 전화했어요. 그것을 취소하고 교체해야 해요.
남: 성함과 주소를 알려주시겠습니까?
여: 제 이름은 Martina Rhodes이고 저는 5001번지 Selah로, 댄빌, 버몬트주에 살아요.
남: 알겠습니다, Ms. Rhodes. 고객님의 요청이 처리되는 데 이틀이 소요될 것입니다. [04]그 후에 교체될 카드가 우편으로 발송될 것입니다.

03
해석 남자는 어디에서 일하는 것 같은가?
(A) 우체국에서
(B) 온라인 매장에서
(C) 신용카드 회사에서
(D) 투자 회사에서

해설 남자가 일하는 장소를 묻는 문제입니다. 남자가 "Kenwood Financial. How may I help you?"라며 Kenwood Financial사인데 어떻게 도와줄지를 묻자, 여자가 "I lost my credit card yesterday. I need to ~ get it replaced."라며 자신이 어제 신용카드를 잃어버려서 그것을 교체해야 한다고 한 것을 통해 남자가 일하는 곳이 신용카드 회사임을 알 수 있습니다. 따라서 정답은 (C) At a credit card company입니다.

어휘 investment[invéstmənt] 투자

04
해석 교체품에 대해 무엇이 언급되는가?
(A) 더 많은 정보를 포함할 것이다.

(B) 우편물로 보내질 것이다.
(C) 추가 요금을 필요로 할 것이다.
(D) 개선된 기능들을 포함할 것이다.

해설 교체품에 대해 언급되는 것을 묻는 문제입니다. 남자가 "The replacement will be mailed out ~."이라며 교체될 카드가 우편으로 발송될 것이라고 하였습니다. 따라서 정답은 (B) It will be sent in the mail입니다.

어휘 involve[미 inváːlv, 영 invɔ́lv] 필요로 하다, 수반하다
feature[미 fíːtʃər, 영 fíːtʃə] 기능, 특징, 특색

HACKERS TEST 🎧 DAY10_05　　　　　　　　　p.92

01 (B)	02 (D)	03 (B)	04 (D)
05 (B)	06 (B)	07 (B)	08 (D)
09 (B)	10 (D)	11 (A)	12 (D)
13 (C)	14 (A)	15 (D)	16 (B)
17 (C)	18 (B)		

01-03 🎤 호주식 발음 → 영국식 발음

Questions 1-3 refer to the following conversation.

M: ⁰¹Thank you for coming to interview for the curator position. I'm impressed with your knowledge of art and your ideas for exhibits.
W: I really appreciate the opportunity. ⁰²When will I hear back from you?
M: I'll contact all applicants this Friday. Selected applicants will be invited to a final interview next week, most likely on Wednesday. ⁰³Our president, Ms. Williams, plans to be there as well, unless something unexpected comes up.
W: All right. That works with my schedule. Thanks for the information.

curator[미 kjuəréitər, 영 kjuréitə] 큐레이터 (박물관·미술관 등의 전시 책임자)
position[pəzíʃən] 직, 직위　impressed with ~에 깊은 인상을 받은
exhibit[igzíbit] 전시(회)　appreciate[미 əpríːʃièit, 영 əpríːʃièit] 감사하다
opportunity[미 àpərtjúːnəti, 영 ɔ̀pətʃúːnəti] 기회
applicant[ǽplikənt] 지원자

해석
1-3번은 다음 대화에 관한 문제입니다.

남: ⁰¹큐레이터직을 위한 면접에 와주셔서 감사합니다. 저는 당신의 미술에 대한 지식과 전시 아이디어에 깊은 인상을 받았어요.
여: 기회를 주셔서 정말 감사드려요. ⁰²제가 언제 다시 연락을 받게 되나요?
남: 제가 이번 주 금요일에 모든 지원자들에게 연락을 드릴 거예요. 선발된 지원자들은 다음 주에 최종 면접에 오도록 요청받을 거예요, 수요일쯤이요. 예상치 못한 일이 발생하지 않는다면, ⁰³우리 관장님이신 Ms. Williams도 최종 면접에 오실 예정이에요.
여: 알겠습니다. 그것은 제 일정에 맞네요. 알려주셔서 감사합니다.

01

해석 남자는 어디에서 일하는 것 같은가?
(A) 교육 기관에서
(B) 미술관에서
(C) 콘서트홀에서
(D) 부동산 업체에서

해설 남자가 일하는 장소를 묻는 문제입니다. 남자가 "Thank you for coming to interview for the curator position. I'm impressed with ~ your ideas for exhibits."라며 큐레이터직을 위한 면접에 와

주어 감사하다고 한 뒤 여자의 전시 아이디어에 깊은 인상을 받았다고 하였습니다. 이를 통해 남자가 일하는 장소가 미술관임을 알 수 있습니다. 따라서 정답은 (B) At an art gallery입니다.

어휘 educational[èdʒukéiʃənəl] 교육의
institute[미 ínstətjùːt, 영 ínstitjùːt] 기관, 협회　art gallery 미술관
real estate 부동산

02

해석 여자는 무엇에 대해 문의하는가?
(A) 사무실이 어디에 위치해 있는지
(B) 그녀가 왜 이메일을 받지 못했는지
(C) 어떤 자격 요건이 갖춰져야 하는지
(D) 그녀가 언제 연락을 받을지

해설 여자가 문의하는 것을 묻는 문제입니다. 여자가 "When will I hear back from you?"라며 언제 다시 연락을 받게 될지를 물었습니다. 따라서 정답은 (D) When she will be contacted입니다.

어휘 requirement[미 rikwáiərmənt, 영 rikwáiəmənt] 자격 요건, 조건

03

해석 남자는 관장에 대해 무엇을 언급하는가?
(A) 그녀는 주간 회의에 참석한다.
(B) 그녀는 면접에 참석할 의향이 있다.
(C) 그녀는 공지를 했다.
(D) 그녀는 제안서를 검토했다.

해설 남자가 관장에 대해 언급하는 것을 묻는 문제입니다. 남자가 "Our president, Ms. Williams, plans to be there[final interview] as well"이라며 관장인 Ms. Williams도 최종 면접에 올 예정이라고 하였습니다. 따라서 정답은 (B) She intends to be at an interview입니다.

어휘 announcement[ənáunsmənt] 공지, 발표
proposal[미 prəpóuzəl, 영 prəpáuzəl] 제안(서)

04-06 🎤 캐나다식 발음 → 영국식 발음

Questions 4-6 refer to the following conversation.

M: I was just going over the quarterly report, and it looks like ⁰⁴sales have dropped at our clothing stores. Any idea what's going on?
W: ⁰⁵One of our competitors has started an online campaign that is attracting a lot of attention. The company uses social media sites to advertise their promotional events. It's a very effective strategy.
M: Hmm . . . Maybe we should consider doing something similar.
W: ⁰⁶Why don't we post coupons online? I'm sure that would boost sales revenues in our stores.

go over ~을 검토하다　quarterly report 분기별 보고서
competitor[미 kəmpétətər, 영 kəmpétitə] 경쟁사, 경쟁업체
attract[ətrǽkt] 끌다　attention[əténʃən] 관심, 주의
promotional[미 prəmóuʃənl, 영 prəmáuʃənl] 판촉의, 홍보의
strategy[strǽtədʒi] 전략　boost[buːst] 증대시키다, 신장시키다
revenue[미 révənjùː, 영 révənjuː] 수익, 수입

해석
4-6번은 다음 대화에 관한 문제입니다.

남: 저는 방금 분기별 보고서를 검토하고 있었는데, ⁰⁴우리 의류 매장들에서 판매량이 감소한 것처럼 보이네요. 무슨 일이 있는지 아시나요?
여: ⁰⁵우리 경쟁사들 중 한 곳에서 많은 관심을 끌고 있는 온라인 캠페인을 시작했어요. 그 회사는 판촉 행사를 광고하는 데 소셜 미디어 사이트를 활

용해요. 그것은 매우 효과적인 전략이에요.

남: 음... 우리도 비슷한 것을 하는 걸 고려해야 할 것 같네요.

여: ⁰⁶온라인으로 할인권을 게시하는 건 어때요? 저는 그것이 우리 매장들의 판매 수익을 증대시킬 거라고 확신해요.

04

해석 화자들은 주로 무엇에 대해 이야기하고 있는가?
(A) 정책 변경
(B) 기술적 오류
(C) 고객 불만
(D) 판매 실적

해설 대화의 주제를 묻는 문제입니다. 남자가 "sales have dropped at our clothing stores"라며 자신들의 의류 매장들에서 판매량이 감소했다고 한 뒤, 판매량을 증대시킬 수 있는 방법에 관한 내용으로 대화가 이어지고 있습니다. 따라서 정답은 (D) Sales results입니다.

어휘 policy[미 páləsi, 영 pɔ́ləsi] 정책 technical[téknikəl] 기술적인

05

해석 여자는 경쟁사에 대해 무엇을 말하는가?
(A) 숙련된 직원들이 있다.
(B) 온라인 마케팅을 활용한다.
(C) 값비싼 제품을 판매한다.
(D) 유명하지 않다.

해설 여자가 경쟁사에 대해 언급하는 것을 묻는 문제입니다. 여자가 "One of our competitors has started an online campaign"이라며 경쟁사들 중 한 곳에서 온라인 캠페인을 시작했다고 하였습니다. 따라서 정답은 (B) It uses online marketing입니다.

어휘 well-trained[wèltréind] 숙련된

06

해석 여자는 어떤 제안을 하는가?
(A) 관리자에게 말하기
(B) 온라인으로 할인 제공하기
(C) 고객 설문 조사 실시하기
(D) 자문 위원 고용하기

해설 여자가 제안하는 것을 묻는 문제입니다. 여자가 "Why don't we post coupons online?"이라며 온라인으로 할인권을 게시할 것을 제안하였습니다. 따라서 정답은 (B) Offering discounts online입니다.

어휘 conduct[kəndΛkt] 실시하다, 수행하다
consultant[kənsΛltənt] 자문 위원, 상담가

07-09 🎧 미국식 발음 → 캐나다식 발음

Questions 7-9 refer to the following conversation.

W: ⁰⁷Hello, Sunny Rental Agency. How can I help you today?
M: My name is Trent Zappa. ⁰⁸I'm flying to New York City in a few weeks for my older sister's wedding. I'd like to . . . ah . . . to rent a car from your company during my stay. If possible, a fuel-efficient sedan would be ideal.
W: Certainly. ⁰⁹If you tell me when, specifically, you'll be in the city, I can make the necessary arrangements.
M: I'll be there for a couple of days—June 3 and 4.

rental[réntl] 대여의, 임대의
fuel-efficient[미 fjúːəlifiʃənt, 영 fjùːəlifíʃənt] 연비가 좋은
sedan[sidǽn] 세단형 자동차
specifically[미 spisífikəli, 영 spəsífikəli] 구체적으로, 명확히

해석
7-9번은 다음 대화에 관한 문제입니다.

여: ⁰⁷안녕하세요, Sunny 대여점이에요. 오늘 어떻게 도와드릴까요?

남: 제 이름은 Trent Zappa예요. ⁰⁸저는 누나의 결혼식을 위해 몇 주 후에 뉴욕시로 갈 예정이에요. 저는... 아... 제가 머무는 동안 귀사에서 차를 대여하고 싶어요. 만약 가능하다면, 연비가 좋은 세단형 자동차가 가장 알맞을 거예요.

여: 물론입니다. ⁰⁹구체적으로, 언제 뉴욕시에 계실 것인지 말씀해 주시면, 필요한 준비를 해드리겠습니다.

남: 저는 그곳에 이틀 동안 있을 거예요—6월 3일과 4일에요.

07

해석 여자의 직업은 무엇인가?
(A) 개인 운전사
(B) 대여 담당 직원
(C) 행사 기획자
(D) 항공사 매표원

해설 여자의 직업을 묻는 문제입니다. 여자가 "Hello, Sunny Rental Agency. How can I help you today?"라며 Sunny 대여점이라고 한 뒤 어떻게 도와줄지 물은 것을 통해 여자가 대여 담당 직원임을 알 수 있습니다. 따라서 정답은 (B) Rental agent입니다.

어휘 agent[éidʒənt] 직원, 관리자

08

해석 남자는 왜 뉴욕시로 갈 것인가?
(A) 몇몇 고객들을 만나기 위해
(B) 회의에 가기 위해
(C) 오랜 친구를 방문하기 위해
(D) 결혼을 축하하기 위해

해설 남자가 뉴욕시로 갈 이유를 묻는 문제입니다. 남자가 "I'm flying to New York City ~ for my older sister's wedding."이라며 누나의 결혼식을 위해 뉴욕시로 갈 예정이라고 하였습니다. 따라서 정답은 (D) To celebrate a marriage입니다.

09

해석 여자는 남자에게 무엇에 대해 문의하는가?
(A) 호텔의 위치
(B) 여행 날짜
(C) 공항까지의 거리
(D) 서비스 요금

해설 여자가 남자에게 문의하는 것을 묻는 문제입니다. 여자가 "If you tell me when, specifically, you'll be in the city, I can make the necessary arrangements."라며 구체적으로 언제 뉴욕시에 있을 것인지 말해주면 필요한 준비를 해주겠다고 한 것을 통해, 여자가 남자에게 뉴욕 체류 날짜를 묻고 있음을 알 수 있습니다. 따라서 정답은 (B) The dates of a trip입니다.

어휘 distance[dístəns] 거리

10-12 🎧 미국식 발음 → 호주식 발음 → 영국식 발음

Questions 10-12 refer to the following conversation with three speakers.

W1: Minho and Noriko, ^{10/11}don't you think it was a great idea to hold the tennis club's charity event at this hotel?
M: The interior is more spacious than I thought it would be. I was quite impressed with the high-quality food at the dinner buffet too.
W2: I agree. The facility we've used in the past

○

is inconvenient because it's so far from the downtown area.

M: Yeah. ¹²We should mention that to the club manager before we go. I will discuss it with him.

W1: In the meantime, I'll ask the attendant to bring our car out front.

W2: Good thinking.

---

charity [tʃǽrəti] 자선 interior [미 intíəriər, 영 intíəriə] 내부, 실내 장식
spacious [spéiʃəs] 넓은 inconvenient [ìnkənvíːnjənt] 불편한
attendant [əténdənt] 안내원, 종업원

해석

10-12번은 다음 세 명의 대화에 관한 문제입니다.

여1: Minho 그리고 Noriko, ^{10/11}테니스 동호회의 자선 행사를 이 호텔에서 연 것은 정말 좋은 생각이었다고 생각하지 않으세요?

남: 제가 그럴 것이라고 생각했던 것보다 내부가 더 넓네요. 저는 저녁 뷔페의 고급 음식도 상당히 인상 깊었어요.

여2: 동의해요. 이전에 우리가 이용했던 시설은 시내 지역에서 너무 멀어서 불편해요.

남: 그래요. ¹²우리는 가기 전에 그것을 동호회 운영자에게 말해야 해요. 제가 그와 그것을 얘기해볼게요.

여1: 그동안에, 제가 안내원에게 우리 차를 앞으로 가져와달라고 요청할게요.

여2: 좋은 생각이에요.

10

해석 화자들은 어디에 있는 것 같은가?
(A) 사무실 건물에
(B) 오락 센터에
(C) 학교에
(D) 숙박 시설에

해설 화자들이 있는 장소를 묻는 문제입니다. 여자 1이 "don't you think it was a great idea to hold the tennis club's charity event at this hotel?"이라며 테니스 동호회의 자선 행사를 이 호텔에서 연 것이 정말 좋은 생각이었다고 생각하지 않는지를 물은 것을 통해 화자들이 있는 장소가 호텔임을 알 수 있습니다. 따라서 정답은 (D) At an accommodation facility입니다.

어휘 recreation [rèkriéiʃən] 오락, 휴양 academy [əkǽdəmi] 학교, 학원
accommodation [미 əkɑ̀ːmədéiʃən, 영 əkɔ̀mədéiʃən] 숙박
facility [fəsíləti] 시설

11

해석 남자는 왜 "제가 그럴 것이라고 생각했던 것보다 내부가 더 넓네요"라고 말하는가?
(A) 그가 의견에 동의한다는 것을 나타내기 위해
(B) 계획에 대한 대안을 제시하기 위해
(C) 장소가 너무 넓다는 것을 암시하기 위해
(D) 그의 동료에게 작업에 대해 안심시키기 위해

해설 남자가 하는 말(The interior is more spacious than I thought it would be)의 의도를 묻는 문제입니다. 여자 1이 "don't you think it was a great idea to hold the tennis club's charity event at this hotel?"이라며 테니스 동호회의 자선 행사를 이 호텔에서 연 것이 정말 좋은 생각이었다고 생각하지 않는지를 물은 것을 통해 남자가 여자 1의 의견에 동의한다는 것을 나타내려는 의도임을 알 수 있습니다. 따라서 정답은 (A) To indicate he agrees with an opinion입니다.

어휘 alternative [미 ɔːltə́ːrnətiv, 영 ɔːltə́ːnətiv] 대안, 대체
reassure [미 rìːəʃúər, 영 rìːəʃúə] 안심시키다, 확신시키다

12

해석 남자는 다음에 무엇을 할 것 같은가?

(A) 행사에 참석한다.
(B) 식사 선택 사항을 고른다.
(C) 서비스 요금을 낸다.
(D) 운영자에게 다가간다.

해설 남자가 다음에 할 일을 묻는 문제입니다. 남자가 "We should mention that to the club manager before we go. I will discuss it with him."이라며 가기 전에 동호회 운영자에게 말해야 한다고 하며, 그와 그것을 이야기해볼 것이라고 한 것을 통해 남자가 운영자에게 다가가서 말할 것임을 알 수 있습니다. 따라서 정답은 (D) Approach a manager입니다.

어휘 approach [미 əpróutʃ, 영 əpráutʃ] 다가가다, 접근하다

13-15 🔊 캐나다식 발음 → 영국식 발음

Questions 13-15 refer to the following conversation.

M: This is Brandon Macklin from accounting calling. ¹³I'm trying to change my phone's extension number, but I'm having some difficulties. So I'd like to get some help from an IT worker.

W: ¹⁴Unfortunately, our technicians are busy at the moment. However . . . um . . . one of our staff members should be finishing up a task soon. He should be available later this morning.

M: That would be really convenient. ¹⁵How can I arrange a time for him to visit my office?

W: ¹⁵Try calling him directly at 555-3224. That's his cell phone number. If he doesn't answer, call me again. I'll find someone else to help.

---

extension number 내선 번호 technician [teknɪ́ʃən] 기술자
at the moment 지금, 현재

해석

13-15번은 다음 대화에 관한 문제입니다.

남: 저는 회계 부서에서 전화드리는 Brandon Macklin입니다. ¹³제 전화기의 내선 번호를 바꾸려고 하는데, 어려움을 겪고 있어요. 그래서 저는 IT 부서 직원의 도움을 좀 받고 싶어요.

여: ¹⁴유감스럽게도, 저희 기술자들은 지금 바빠요. 하지만... 음... 우리 직원들 중 한 명이 곧 업무를 마무리할 거예요. 그가 오늘 오전 늦게 시간이 날 거예요.

남: 정말 괜찮겠네요. ¹⁵그가 제 사무실을 방문할 시간을 어떻게 정할 수 있나요?

여: 555-3224로 직접 ¹⁵그에게 전화해 보세요. 그것이 그의 휴대전화 번호예요. 만약 그가 전화를 받지 않는다면, 제게 다시 전화해 주세요. 도와줄 다른 사람을 찾아볼게요.

13

해석 남자는 왜 전화를 하고 있는가?
(A) 의견을 제공하기 위해
(B) 사과하기 위해
(C) 도움을 구하기 위해
(D) 손상된 기기를 보고하기 위해

해설 전화의 목적을 묻는 문제입니다. 남자가 "I'm trying to change my phone's extension number, but I'm having some difficulties. So I'd like to get some help from an IT worker."라며 전화기의 내선 번호를 바꾸는 데 어려움이 있어 IT 부서 직원의 도움을 받고 싶다고 하였습니다. 따라서 정답은 (C) To seek some assistance입니다.

어휘 feedback [fíːdbæk] 의견, 반응 seek [siːk] 구하다, 찾다

PART 3

앤 권으로 끝내는 해커스 토익 700+ (LC+RC+VOCA)

14

해석 여자는 어떤 문제를 언급하는가?
(A) 몇몇 기술자들이 시간이 없다.
(B) 수리 작업이 이루어질 수 없다.
(C) 전화기가 설치되지 않았다.
(D) 일부 직원들에게 교육이 더 필요하다.

해설 여자가 언급한 문제점을 묻는 문제입니다. 여자가 "Unfortunately, our technicians are busy at the moment."라며 유감스럽게도 기술자들이 지금 바쁘다고 하였습니다. 따라서 정답은 (A) Some technicians are unavailable입니다.

15

해석 남자는 어떻게 약속 일정을 잡을 수 있는가?
(A) 접수원에게 이메일을 보냄으로써
(B) 양식을 작성함으로써
(C) 사무실을 방문함으로써
(D) 직원에게 전화함으로써

해설 남자가 약속 일정을 잡을 수 있는 방법을 묻는 문제입니다. 남자가 "How can I arrange a time for him[one of ~ staff members] to visit my office?"라며 직원들 중 한 명이 자신의 사무실을 방문할 시간을 어떻게 정할 수 있는지 묻자, 여자가 "Try calling him"이라며 그에게 전화해 보라고 하였습니다. 따라서 정답은 (D) By calling a worker입니다.

16-18 [3번] 미국식 발음 → 호주식 발음

Questions 16-18 refer to the following conversation and map.

> W: Excuse me. I'm new to the city. ¹⁶I'm trying to get downtown. Can you give me directions to the nearest bus stop?
> M: Well, you have to walk about four blocks to reach the closest one.
> W: Really? That's quite far. I'm in a bit of a hurry because ¹⁷I'm supposed to meet my friend at the National Museum in about 30 minutes. I guess I'd better take the subway instead.
> M: Right. ¹⁸The station is just down the street . . . on the corner of Washburn Avenue and Vince Street, right next to Harris Park.
> W: Great. Thanks for your help.

---

downtown[dàuntáun] 시내로   corner[미 kɔ́ːrnər, 영 kɔ́ːnə] 모퉁이, 구석

해석

16-18번은 다음 대화와 약도에 관한 문제입니다.

여: 실례합니다. 저는 이 도시가 처음이에요. ¹⁶저는 시내로 가려고 하는데요. 가장 가까운 버스 정류장으로 가는 길을 알려주실 수 있나요?
남: 음, 가장 가까운 정류장으로 가려면 네 블록 정도는 걸으셔야 해요.
여: 정말인가요? 꽤 머네요. ¹⁷저는 약 30분 후에 국립 박물관에서 친구를 만나기로 되어 있어서 좀 서둘러야 해요. 대신 지하철을 타는 편이 나을 수도 있겠어요.
남: 맞아요. ¹⁸역이 바로 길 끝에 있어요... Washburn가와 Vince가의 모퉁이에요, Harris 공원 바로 옆이고요.
여: 그렇군요. 도와주셔서 감사해요.

	A 지점	Harris 공원	¹⁸B 지점	
Maple가		Washburn가		Vince가
	C 지점	주차장	D 지점	

16

해석 화자들은 주로 무엇에 대해 이야기하고 있는가?
(A) 교통 상황 확인하기
(B) 도심으로 이동하기
(C) 지역 공원 방문하기
(D) 버스 승차권 사기

해설 대화의 주제를 묻는 문제입니다. 여자가 "I'm trying to get downtown."이라며 시내로 가려고 한다고 한 뒤, 시내까지 가는 방법에 관한 내용으로 대화가 이어지고 있습니다. 따라서 정답은 (B) Traveling to the city center입니다.

어휘 traffic[trǽfik] 교통, 통행   travel[trǽvəl] 이동하다, 여행하다
pass[미 pæs, 영 pɑːs] 승차권, 통행권

17

해석 여자는 어디에서 친구를 만날 것인가?
(A) 미술관에서
(B) 시립 공원에서
(C) 박물관에서
(D) 쇼핑몰에서

해설 여자가 친구를 만날 장소를 묻는 문제입니다. 여자가 "I'm supposed to meet my friend at the National Museum"이라며 자신은 국립 박물관에서 친구와 만나기로 되어 있다고 하였습니다. 따라서 정답은 (C) At a museum입니다.

18

해석 시각 자료를 보아라. 지하철역은 어디에 있는가?
(A) A 지점에
(B) B 지점에
(C) C 지점에
(D) D 지점에

해설 지하철역이 있는 장소를 묻는 문제입니다. 남자가 "The station [subway station] is ~ on the corner of Washburn Avenue and Vince Street, right next to Harris Park."라며 지하철역이 Washburn가와 Vince가의 모퉁이에 있고, Harris 공원 바로 옆이라고 하였으므로, 지하철역이 B 지점에 있음을 약도에서 알 수 있습니다. 따라서 정답은 (B) At Spot B입니다.

DAY 11   세부 사항 관련 문제 1

Course 1 요청 · 제안 문제

HACKERS PRACTICE ∩ DAY11_02   p.95

01 (C)	**02** (B)	**03** (B)	**04** (A)

01-02 [3번] 호주식 발음 → 미국식 발음 / 캐나다식 발음 → 영국식 발음

Questions 1-2 refer to the following conversation.

> M: Hi, Alexandra. ⁰¹Do you want to go to the Blue Tiger concert next weekend? The band is playing on both days.
> W: Definitely. I'm busy on Saturday, but I can go on Sunday.
> M: OK. ⁰²I'll buy tickets for us online after I return home tonight.
> W: Thanks. Oh, and by the way, could you get me ⟳

an extra ticket? My sister would love to come with us, too.

definitely[미 défənitli, 영 définətli] 물론   extra[ékstrə] 추가의

해석

1-2번은 다음 대화에 관한 문제입니다.

남: 안녕하세요, Alexandra. ⁰¹다음 주말에 Blue Tiger 콘서트에 가고 싶으신가요? 그 밴드는 이틀 모두 공연할 거예요.

여: 물론이죠. 토요일에는 바쁘지만, 일요일에는 갈 수 있어요.

남: 좋아요. ⁰²제가 오늘 밤에 집에 가서 온라인으로 우리 표를 구매할게요.

여: 고마워요. 아, 그런데, 표를 추가로 한 장 더 구해줄 수 있나요? 제 여동생도 우리와 함께 가고 싶어 할 거예요.

01

해석 대화는 주로 무엇에 대한 것인가?
(A) 주말여행 가기
(B) 다가오는 콘서트 준비하기
(C) 음악 공연에 참석하기
(D) 온라인 강좌 수강하기

해설 대화의 주제를 묻는 문제입니다. 남자가 "Do you want to go to the ~ concert next weekend?"라며 다음 주말에 콘서트에 가고 싶은지 물은 뒤, 콘서트 참석에 관한 내용으로 대화가 이어지고 있습니다. 따라서 정답은 (C) Attending a musical performance입니다.

어휘 organize[미 ɔ́ːrɡənàiz, 영 ɔ́ːɡənaiz] 준비하다
upcoming[ʌ́pkʌmiŋ] 다가오는   attend[əténd] 참석하다

02

해석 남자는 무엇을 해주겠다고 제안하는가?
(A) 포스터를 인쇄한다.
(B) 표를 구매한다.
(C) 일정을 변경한다.
(D) 장소까지 운전한다.

해설 남자가 해주겠다고 제안하는 것을 묻는 문제입니다. 남자가 "I'll buy tickets for us"라며 자신이 표를 구매하겠다고 하였습니다. 따라서 정답은 (B) Purchase some tickets입니다.

어휘 venue[vénjuː] 장소

03-04 [3배] 캐나다식 발음 → 미국식 발음 / 호주식 발음 → 영국식 발음

Questions 3-4 refer to the following conversation.

> M: Could you answer any phone calls from Paula Schwartz while I'm on a business trip next week?
> W: Sure, Brad. What will she call about?
> M: Well, ⁰³she's planning to change the number of T-shirts in her order. She'll call when she knows how many she requires.
> W: OK. But ⁰⁴could you send me her phone number? I need to save it to my list of client contacts.
> M: Just give me a minute.
>
> business trip 출장   require[미 rikwáiər, 영 rikwáiə] 필요하다, 요구하다

해석

3-4번은 다음 대화에 관한 문제입니다.

남: 제가 다음 주에 출장 가 있는 동안 Paula Schwartz로부터의 전화를 받아줄 수 있나요?

여: 그럼요, Brad. 그녀가 무엇에 대해 전화할 건가요?

남: 음, ⁰³그녀는 주문한 티셔츠의 수량을 변경할 계획이에요. 얼마나 필요한

지 알게 되면 전화할 거예요.

여: 알겠어요. 그런데 ⁰⁴그녀의 전화번호를 제게 보내 주시겠어요? 제 고객 연락처 목록에 저장해야 하거든요.

남: 잠깐만요.

03

해석 Paula Schwartz는 무엇을 하려고 계획하고 있는가?
(A) 고객에게 전화한다.
(B) 주문을 업데이트한다.
(C) 항의를 제기한다.
(D) 환불을 요청한다.

해설 Paula Schwartz가 계획하고 있는 것을 묻는 문제입니다. 남자가 "she[Paula Schwartz]'s planning to change the number of T-shirts in her order"라며 Paula Schwartz가 주문한 티셔츠의 수량을 변경할 계획이라고 하였습니다. 따라서 정답은 (B) Update an order입니다.

어휘 file a complaint 항의를 제기하다   refund[ríːfʌnd] 환불

04

해석 여자는 남자에게 무엇을 해달라고 요청하는가?
(A) 연락처를 제공한다.
(B) 컴퓨터 파일을 저장한다.
(C) 데이터베이스를 검색한다.
(D) 매출 수치를 수정한다.

해설 여자가 남자에게 요청하는 것을 묻는 문제입니다. 여자가 "could you send me her[Paula Schwartz] phone number?"라며 Paula Schwartz의 전화번호를 보내달라고 요청하였습니다. 따라서 정답은 (A) Provide contact details입니다.

어휘 provide[prəváid] 제공하다   contact details 연락처
search[미 səːrtʃ, 영 səːtʃ] 검색하다   edit[édit] 수정하다, 편집하다

Course 2 언급 문제

HACKERS PRACTICE 🎧 DAY11_04   p.97

01 (D)	02 (C)	03 (C)	04 (B)

01-02 [3배] 미국식 발음 → 호주식 발음 / 영국식 발음 → 캐나다식 발음

Questions 1-2 refer to the following conversation.

> W: Hi, Paul. It's Sandra. I have to stay in Dallas for an extra day . . . until Wednesday. The author I'm getting together with, ⁰¹Oliver Yates, suddenly rescheduled our appointment. Could you contact Alliance Airlines and change my departure date?
> M: Absolutely. ⁰²Would you also like me to inform the editorial staff that you won't be attending Tuesday's meeting?
> W: Oh, I completely forgot about that. Yes, please e-mail them about that as well.
>
> get together with ~와 만나다
> reschedule[미 riːskédʒuːl, 영 riːʃédʒuːl] 일정을 변경하다
> appointment[əpɔ́intmənt] 약속
> absolutely[미 æbsəlúːtli, 영 æbsəlútli] 물론
> inform[미 infɔ́ːrm, 영 infɔ́ːm] 통지하다, 통보하다
> editorial[미 èdətɔ́ːriəl, 영 èditɔ́ːriəl] 편집의

1-2번은 다음 대화에 관한 문제입니다.

여: 안녕하세요, Paul. 저 Sandra예요. 저는 댈러스에서 하루 더 머물러야 해요... 수요일까지요. 제가 만날 작가인 ⁰¹Oliver Yates가 갑자기 우리의 약속 일정을 변경했어요. Alliance 항공사에 전화해서 제 출발 날짜를 바꿔주실 수 있나요?

남: 물론이죠. ⁰²제가 편집부 직원들에게 당신이 화요일 회의에 참석하지 않을 것이라는 것도 통지할까요?

여: 아, 저는 그것에 대해 완전히 잊고 있었네요. 네, 그것에 대해서도 직원들에게 이메일을 보내 주세요.

01

해석 Oliver Yates에 대해 무엇이 언급되는가?
(A) 그는 비행편을 예약할 것이다.
(B) 그는 회의에 참석할 것이다.
(C) 그는 댈러스에 일찍 도착했다.
(D) 그는 약속 시간을 변경했다.

해설 Oliver Yates에 대해 언급되는 것을 묻는 문제입니다. 여자가 "Oliver Yates ~ rescheduled our appointment"라며 Oliver Yates가 약속 일정을 변경했다고 하였습니다. 따라서 정답은 (D) He changed an appointment time입니다.

02

해석 남자는 무엇을 해주겠다고 제안하는가?
(A) 몇몇 서류를 검토한다.
(B) 회의 일정을 잡는다.
(C) 직원들에게 통지한다.
(D) 기술적인 문제를 해결한다.

해설 남자가 해주겠다고 제안하는 것을 묻는 문제입니다. 남자가 "Would you also like me to inform the editorial staff ~?"라며 자신이 편집부 직원들에게 여자가 화요일 회의에 참석하지 않을 것임을 통지하기를 원하는지 물었습니다. 따라서 정답은 (C) Notify staff members입니다.

어휘 notify[미 nóutəfài, 영 náutifai] 통지하다
technical[téknikəl] 기술적인, 기술의

03-04 🔊 미국식 발음 → 영국식 발음 → 캐나다식 발음 /
영국식 발음 → 미국식 발음 → 호주식 발음

Questions 3-4 refer to the following conversation with three speakers.

W1: ⁰³There are hardly any customers at our resort these days. What do you two think we should do to bring in more guests?

W2: Well, there are many online reviews stating that our rooms aren't very modern.

M: To be honest, I agree. In particular, ⁰⁴the tables and chairs in the rooms are a bit old-fashioned.

W1: All right. Thanks for your feedback. I'll discuss this with our supervisor when we meet this afternoon.

---

hardly[미 háːrdli, 영 háːdli] 거의 ~이 없다
old-fashioned[미 ðuldfǽʃənd, 영 ðuldfǽʃənd] 구식인
feedback[fíːdbæk] 의견, 반응

해석
3-4번은 다음 세 명의 대화에 관한 문제입니다.

여1: ⁰³요즘 우리 리조트에는 고객이 거의 없어요. 두 분은 우리가 더 많은 손님을 데려오기 위해 무엇을 해야 한다고 생각하세요?

여2: 음, 우리 객실이 별로 현대적이지 않다고 말하는 온라인 후기들이 많이 있어요.

남: 솔직히 말하자면, 저도 동의해요. 특히, ⁰⁴객실에 있는 탁자와 의자가 다소 구식이에요.

여1: 알겠어요. 의견을 주셔서 고마워요. 오늘 오후에 관리자와 만나면 이것에 대해 논의할게요.

03

해석 무엇이 문제인가?
(A) 불만 사항이 제기되었다.
(B) 보고서에 오류가 있다.
(C) 업체에 고객이 거의 없다.
(D) 회사에 더 많은 직원이 필요하다.

해설 문제점을 묻는 문제입니다. 여자 1이 "There are hardly any customers at our resort these days."라며 요즘 리조트에 고객이 거의 없다고 하였습니다. 따라서 정답은 (C) A business has few customers입니다.

어휘 submit[səbmít] 제기하다, 제출하다
personnel[미 pɜ̀ːrsənél, 영 pɜ̀ːsənél] 직원, 인력

04

해석 남자는 객실에 대해 무엇을 말하는가?
(A) 현대식 공예품이 있다.
(B) 구식인 가구들이 있다.
(C) 너무 작다.
(D) 관리자에 의해 점검되었다.

해설 남자가 객실에 대해 언급하는 것을 묻는 문제입니다. 남자가 "the tables and chairs in the rooms are a bit old-fashioned"라며 객실에 있는 탁자와 의자가 다소 구식이라고 하였습니다. 따라서 정답은 (B) They have outdated furnishings입니다.

어휘 artwork[미 áːrtwəːrk, 영 áːtwəːk] 공예품 outdated[àutdéitid] 구식의
furnishings[미 fáːrniʃiŋz, 영 fáːniʃiŋz] 가구, 비치 가구

HACKERS TEST 🎧 DAY11_05　　　　　　　　p.98

01 (D)	02 (C)	03 (A)	04 (B)
05 (A)	06 (C)	07 (D)	08 (B)
09 (C)	10 (B)	11 (A)	12 (D)
13 (D)	14 (A)	15 (D)	16 (C)
17 (C)	18 (D)		

01-03 🔊 캐나다식 발음 → 미국식 발음

Questions 1-3 refer to the following conversation.

M: Excuse me. I purchased this digital camera from your store on Monday. However, ⁰¹it has a small crack on the lens.

W: Let's see . . . Hmm . . . OK. I'd be happy to get you a new one. ⁰²Could I please see your receipt?

M: I thought I brought it, but it . . . um . . . it seems to be missing. Maybe I left it in my car. I'll check and be back in just a few minutes.

W: No problem. ⁰³I can go get a new device from our stockroom for you in the meantime.

---

crack[kræk] 금, 균열　receipt[risíːt] 영수증
stockroom[미 stáːkruːm, 영 stɔ́kruːm] 창고, 저장실
in the meantime 그동안에, 그 사이에

1-3번은 다음 대화에 관한 문제입니다.

남: 실례합니다. 저는 월요일에 당신의 매장에서 이 디지털 카메라를 구매했어요. 그런데, ⁰¹렌즈에 작은 금이 가 있어요.

여: 제가 한 번 보겠습니다... 음... 그렇군요. 기꺼이 새것을 드리겠습니다. ⁰²영수증을 볼 수 있을까요?

남: 가져왔다고 생각했는데, 그게... 음... 없어진 것 같네요. 아마 제 차에 두고 온 것 같아요. 확인하고 잠시 후에 다시 올게요.

여: 그렇게 하세요. 그동안에 ⁰³저는 창고에서 새 기기를 가져오겠습니다.

01

해석 남자는 카메라에 대해 무엇을 언급하는가?
(A) 너무 작다.
(B) 사용하기 어렵다.
(C) 할인 판매 중이다.
(D) 손상되었다.

해설 남자가 카메라에 대해 언급하는 것을 묻는 문제입니다. 남자가 "it [camera] has a small crack on the lens"라며 카메라의 렌즈에 작은 금이 가 있다고 하였습니다. 따라서 정답은 (D) It is damaged 입니다.

02

해석 여자는 무엇을 요청하는가?
(A) 가격표
(B) 운송 서류
(C) 구매 영수증
(D) 다른 제품

해설 여자가 요청하는 것을 묻는 문제입니다. 여자가 "Could I please see your receipt?"라며 영수증을 보여 달라고 요청하였습니다. 따라서 정답은 (C) A purchase receipt입니다.

어휘 price tag 가격표 shipping[ʃípiŋ] 운송, 선적

03

해석 여자는 다음에 무엇을 할 것 같은가?
(A) 창고에서 물건을 가져온다.
(B) 웹사이트에서 기기를 주문한다.
(C) 카메라를 수리점에 가져간다.
(D) 남자에게 배송품을 보낸다.

해설 여자가 다음에 할 일을 묻는 문제입니다. 여자가 "I can go get a new device from our stockroom"이라며 창고에서 새 기기를 가져오겠다고 하였습니다. 따라서 정답은 (A) Get an item from a storeroom입니다.

어휘 storeroom[미 stɔ́:rrùːm, 영 stɔ́:rùːm] 창고, 저장고
repair shop 수리점, 정비소

04-06 🔊 호주식 발음 → 영국식 발음

Questions 4-6 refer to the following conversation.

M: Good morning. This is Barry Freeman from Turkish Café. ⁰⁴I'm calling to adjust an order I recently placed with your company for my restaurant. The confirmation number is 44259.

W: OK. What would you like to change about the order?

M: ⁰⁵We're hosting a company banquet in two weeks, and we've got to make a large amount of food—we're serving vegetable curry. So we'll need five more boxes of mushrooms than I originally requested. ○

W: No problem. ⁰⁶I can send an updated receipt to the e-mail address you provided us.

adjust[ədʒʌ́st] 조정하다 confirmation number 예약 확인 번호
host[미 houst, 영 həust] 주최하다, 개최하다 banquet[bǽŋkwit] 연회

해석

4-6번은 다음 대화에 관한 문제입니다.

남: 안녕하세요. 저는 Turkish 카페의 Barry Freeman입니다. ⁰⁴제가 최근에 저희 식당을 위해 당신의 회사에 했던 주문을 조정하려고 전화했어요. 예약 확인 번호는 44259예요.

여: 알겠습니다. 주문에 대해 무엇을 변경하고 싶으신가요?

남: ⁰⁵저희는 2주 후에 회사 연회를 주최할 예정이어서, 많은 양의 음식을 만들어야 해요—저희는 야채 카레를 제공할 거예요. 그래서 제가 원래 요청했던 것보다 버섯 5상자가 더 필요할 거예요.

여: 문제없습니다. 저희에게 제공해 주신 ⁰⁶이메일 주소로 업데이트된 영수증을 보내 드릴게요.

04

해석 남자는 왜 전화를 하고 있는가?
(A) 메뉴에 대해 알아보기 위해
(B) 주문을 수정하기 위해
(C) 예약을 확인하기 위해
(D) 요금에 대해 문의하기 위해

해설 전화의 목적을 묻는 문제입니다. 남자가 "I'm calling to adjust an order"라며 주문을 조정하려고 전화했다고 하였습니다. 따라서 정답은 (B) To revise an order입니다.

어휘 revise[riváiz] 수정하다, 개정하다

05

해석 남자는 연회에 대해 무엇을 말하는가?
(A) 2주 후에 열릴 것이다.
(B) 인터넷에 홍보되었다.
(C) 무료로 음식을 제공받을 것이다.
(D) 지난주에 공지되었다.

해설 연회에 대해 남자가 언급하는 것을 묻는 문제입니다. 남자가 "We're hosting a company banquet in two weeks"라며 자신들은 2주 후에 회사 연회를 주최할 예정이라고 하였습니다. 따라서 정답은 (A) It will be held in a couple of weeks입니다.

어휘 a couple of 둘의 cater[미 kéitər, 영 kéitə] (행사 등에) 음식을 제공하다

06

해석 여자는 무엇을 해주겠다고 제안하는가?
(A) 주소를 제공한다.
(B) 추가 요리의 비용을 지불한다.
(C) 이메일로 영수증을 보낸다.
(D) 식당의 가격을 비교한다.

해설 여자가 해주겠다고 제안하는 것을 묻는 문제입니다. 여자가 "I can send an updated receipt to the e-mail address"라며 이메일 주소로 업데이트된 영수증을 보내 주겠다고 하였습니다. 따라서 정답은 (C) E-mail a receipt입니다.

어휘 compare[미 kəmpɛ́ər, 영 kəmpéə] 비교하다

07-09 🔊 미국식 발음 → 호주식 발음

Questions 7-9 refer to the following conversation.

W: Norman is sick today, so I have to lead the training orientation for new staff. However, ⁰⁷I can't find the employee handbooks. I'm not sure where to look. ○

PART 3

한 권으로 끝내는 해커스 토익 700+ (LC+RC+VOCA)

M: Did you check the cabinet by the front desk?

W: I did, but the handbooks aren't in there. Someone must have moved them.

M: Hmm . . . Sally Reynolds would know where they are. ⁰⁸She's the human resources manager.

W: Good point. Her department is responsible for managing those materials. ⁰⁹Could you give me her extension?

M: Sure. It's 2002.

---

cabinet[미 kǽbənit, 영 kǽbinət] 보관함　front desk 안내 데스크
extension[iksténʃən] (전화의) 내선 번호

해석

7-9번은 다음 대화에 관한 문제입니다.

여: 오늘 Norman이 아파서, 제가 신규 직원들을 위한 교육 오리엔테이션을 진행해야 해요. 하지만, ⁰⁷저는 직원 안내서를 찾을 수가 없어요. 어디를 찾아봐야 할지 모르겠어요.

남: 안내 데스크 옆에 있는 보관함을 확인해 보셨나요?

여: 확인했어요, 하지만 안내서는 그 안에 없어요. 누군가 그것들을 옮긴 것이 틀림없어요.

남: 음... Sally Reynolds가 그것들이 어디에 있는지 알 거예요. ⁰⁸그녀가 인사부장이잖아요.

여: 좋은 지적이네요. 그녀의 부서가 그 자료들을 관리하는 것을 책임지고 있으니까요. ⁰⁹그녀의 내선 번호를 알려 주실래요?

남: 그럼요. 2002예요.

07

해석 여자의 문제는 무엇인가?

(A) 그녀는 수업을 진행하는 데 도움이 필요하다.
(B) 그녀는 몸이 좋지 않다.
(C) 그녀는 오리엔테이션에 등록하는 것을 잊었다.
(D) 그녀는 물품을 찾을 수 없다.

해설 여자의 문제점을 묻는 문제입니다. 여자가 "I can't find the employee handbooks"라며 직원 안내서를 찾을 수가 없다고 하였습니다. 따라서 정답은 (D) She is unable to locate some items입니다.

어휘 sign up for ~에 등록하다　locate[미 lóukeit, 영 ləukéit] 찾다, 발견하다

08

해석 Sally Reynolds는 누구인가?

(A) 교육 강사
(B) 부서장
(C) 개인 비서
(D) 안내 데스크 직원

해설 Sally Reynolds의 신분을 묻는 문제입니다. 남자가 "She[Sally Reynolds]'s the human resources manager."라며 Sally Reynolds가 인사부장이라고 하였습니다. 따라서 정답은 (B) A department head입니다.

어휘 instructor[미 instrʌ́ktər, 영 instrʌ́ktə] 강사
assistant[əsístənt] 비서, 조수

09

해석 여자는 무엇을 요청하는가?

(A) 제품 가격
(B) 운송 날짜
(C) 전화번호
(D) 사무실 주소

해설 여자가 요청하는 것을 묻는 문제입니다. 여자가 "Could you give me her[Sally Reynolds] extension?"이라며 Sally Reynolds의 내선

번호를 알려 달라고 요청하였습니다. 따라서 정답은 (C) A phone number입니다.

10-12 ③ 영국식 발음 → 캐나다식 발음

Questions 10-12 refer to the following conversation.

W: Hey. Some of our college friends are renting a house on Myrtle Beach this weekend for a short summer trip. ¹⁰Most of us are taking a train there on Saturday morning and returning on Sunday night. Would you like to join?

M: ¹²I'd love to, but I'm supposed to meet my cousin Rachel. ¹¹I'm going to be helping her move into a new apartment in my neighborhood on Saturday.

W: Well, Thomas is driving down on Sunday morning. He has to work late the night before.

M: OK. ¹²I'll call him to see if he can give me a ride then.

---

college[미 káːlidʒ, 영 kɔ́lidʒ] 대학
neighborhood[미 néibərhùd, 영 néibəhùd] 동네, 이웃
give a ride 태워주다

해석

10-12번은 다음 대화에 관한 문제입니다.

여: 안녕하세요. 우리 대학 동기들 중 몇 명이 짧은 여름 여행을 위해 이번 주말에 Myrtle 해변에 있는 집을 빌릴 거예요. ¹⁰우리 대부분은 토요일 아침에 그곳까지 기차를 타고 가서 일요일 밤에 돌아올 거예요. 함께 갈래요?

남: ¹²가고 싶은데, 저는 사촌인 Rachel을 만나기로 했어요. ¹¹그녀가 토요일에 우리 동네의 새로운 아파트로 이사 오는 것을 제가 도와줄 거거든요.

여: 음, Thomas는 일요일 아침에 운전해서 올 거예요. 그가 전날 밤에 늦게까지 일을 해야 해서요.

남: 좋아요. ¹²제가 그에게 전화해서 그때 저를 태워줄 수 있는지 알아볼게요.

10

해석 여자는 어떻게 Myrtle 해변에 갈 것인가?

(A) 자동차로
(B) 기차로
(C) 비행기로
(D) 버스로

해설 여자가 Myrtle 해변에 갈 방법을 묻는 문제입니다. 여자가 "Most of us are taking a train there[Myrtle Beach]"라며 대부분은 Myrtle 해변까지 기차를 타고 갈 것이라고 하였습니다. 따라서 정답은 (B) By train입니다.

11

해석 Rachel에 대해 무엇이 언급되는가?

(A) 그녀는 이번 주말에 이사할 것이다.
(B) 그녀는 초과 근무를 할 것이다.
(C) 그녀는 Myrtle 해변이 있는 지역에 산다.
(D) 그녀는 휴가를 갈 계획이다.

해설 Rachel에 대해 언급되는 것을 묻는 문제입니다. 남자가 "I'm going to be helping her[Rachel] move into a new apartment ~ on Saturday."라며 Rachel이 토요일에 새로운 아파트로 이사 오는 것을 도와줄 것이라고 하였습니다. 따라서 정답은 (A) She will be moving this weekend입니다.

어휘 work overtime 초과 근무를 하다

12

해석 여자는 왜 "음, Thomas는 일요일 아침에 운전해서 올 거예요"라고 말

하는가?
(A) 지연에 대한 이유를 설명하기 위해
(B) 계획에 대한 불확실함을 나타내기 위해
(C) 그녀가 언제 출발할 것인지를 알리기 위해
(D) 교통수단 선택권을 제시하기 위해

해설 여자가 하는 말(Well, Thomas is driving down on Sunday morning)의 의도를 묻는 문제입니다. 남자가 "I'd love to, but I'm supposed to meet my cousin Rachel."이라며 가고 싶은데 사촌인 Rachel을 만나기로 했다고 한 뒤, "I'll call him[Thomas] to see if he can give me a ride then."이라며 Thomas에게 전화해서 그 때 자신을 태워줄 수 있는지 알아본다고 하였습니다. 이를 통해 여자가 교통수단 선택권을 제시하려는 의도임을 알 수 있습니다. 따라서 정답은 (D) To suggest a transportation option입니다.

어휘 uncertainty[미 ʌnsəːrtənti, 영 ʌnsəːtənti] 불확실함, 확신이 없음

13-15 🔊 호주식 발음 → 미국식 발음 → 영국식 발음

Questions 13-15 refer to the following conversation with three speakers.

> M: [13]Last week's survey showed customers don't like our soft drink's—Power Blast's—packaging.
> W1: What's the reason?
> M: [14]They said that the color and design of the label was boring.
> W1: That's a problem. We should let the other teams know.
> M: I agree. I wonder if Francine has heard about this. Ah, here she is. Francine, did you see the survey results?
> W2: Hi, you two. And yes, I did. Actually, I . . . ah . . . [15]I'm working with the marketing team members to create a more appealing packaging design.
> W1: Oh, wonderful. If you need any ideas, I'd be happy to share some that I came up with.
>
> packaging[pǽkidʒiŋ] (상품을 넣는) 용기, 포장 label[léibəl] 상표
> appealing[əpíːliŋ] 매력적인, 마음을 끄는

해석

13-15번은 다음 세 명의 대화에 관한 문제입니다.

남: [13]지난주의 설문 조사에 따르면 고객들은 우리 청량음료—Power Blast—의 용기를 좋아하지 않아요.
여1: 이유가 무엇인가요?
남: [14]그들은 상표의 색깔과 디자인이 따분하다고 했어요.
여1: 그건 문제네요. 다른 팀들에게 알려야겠어요.
남: 동의해요. Francine이 이것에 대해 들었는지 모르겠어요. 아, 그녀가 여기 있네요. Francine, 설문 조사 결과를 보았나요?
여2: 안녕하세요, 두 분. 네, 보았어요. 사실, 저는... 어... [15]저는 마케팅팀 팀원들과 함께 더 매력적인 용기 디자인을 만들기 위해 작업을 하고 있어요.
여1: 아, 잘됐네요. 만약 의견이 필요하시다면, 제가 생각한 것을 기꺼이 알려드릴게요.

13

해석 화자들은 주로 무엇에 대해 이야기하고 있는가?
(A) 음료 할인 판매
(B) 연구 프로젝트 마감기한
(C) 디자인 직무 채용
(D) 제품 용기

해설 대화의 주제를 묻는 문제입니다. 남자가 "Last week's survey showed

customers don't like our soft drink's ~ packaging."이라며 지난 주의 설문 조사에 따르면 고객들이 청량음료의 용기를 좋아하지 않는다고 한 뒤, 제품 용기에 관한 내용으로 대화가 이어지고 있습니다. 따라서 정답은 (D) Product packaging입니다.

어휘 job opening 채용, 직원 모집

14

해석 고객들에 대해 무엇이 언급되는가?
(A) 부정적인 의견을 제공했다.
(B) 소식지를 받았다.
(C) 무료 샘플을 시음했다.
(D) 여러 디자인에 대해 투표했다.

해설 고객들에 대해 언급되는 것을 묻는 문제입니다. 남자가 "They [customers] said that the color and design of the label was boring."이라며 고객들이 상표의 색깔과 디자인이 따분하다고 했다고 하였습니다. 따라서 정답은 (A) They offered negative feedback입니다.

어휘 feedback[fíːdbæk] 의견, 반응 try[trai] 시음하다, 시식하다
vote[미 vout, 영 vəut] 투표하다

15

해석 왜 몇몇 동료들이 함께 작업하고 있는가?
(A) 질문에 답변하기 위해
(B) 서류를 검토하기 위해
(C) 더 많은 자금을 획득하기 위해
(D) 디자인을 개선하기 위해

해설 몇몇 동료들이 함께 작업하고 있는 이유를 묻는 문제입니다. 여자 2가 "I'm working with the marketing team members to create a more appealing packaging design."이라며 마케팅팀 팀원들과 함께 더 매력적인 용기 디자인을 만들기 위해 작업을 하고 있다고 하였습니다. 따라서 정답은 (D) To improve a design입니다.

어휘 acquire[미 əkwáiər, 영 əkwáiə] 획득하다, 구하다
funding[fʌ́ndiŋ] 자금 improve[imprúːv] 개선하다

16-18 🔊 캐나다식 발음 → 미국식 발음

Questions 16-18 refer to the following conversation and list.

> M: Jane, is everything set up for [16]tomorrow's executive meeting? I don't want there to be any problems.
> W: Not exactly. [17]One of the speakers in Conference Room A is making a buzzing noise.
> M: Yeah, the speakers in that room are old, but we haven't gotten around to replacing them. [17]For now, you should borrow the speakers from Conference Room D. Both of them are functioning fine.
> W: They're the new, lightweight model, right?
> M: Yes. [18]I'll order a pair of those for Conference Room A as well . . . They're the lightest model available from our supplier.
>
> executive[미 igzékjutiv, 영 igzékjətiv] 임원 buzzing[bʌ́ziŋ] 윙윙거리는
> get around to ~할 시간을 내다 function[fʌ́ŋkʃən] 작동하다, 기능하다
> lightweight[láitweit] 경량의, 가벼운
> supplier[미 səpláiər, 영 səpláiə] 공급업체

해석

16-18번은 다음 대화와 표에 관한 문제입니다.

남: Jane, ¹⁶내일 있을 임원 회의를 위해 모든 게 준비되었나요? 저는 거기에 어떤 문제도 없었으면 좋겠어요.

여: 아직이요. ¹⁷A 회의실에 있는 스피커 중 하나가 윙윙거리는 소리를 내요.

남: 알아요, 그 회의실에 있는 스피커들은 오래되었지만, 그것들을 교체할 시간이 없었어요. ¹⁷우선, D 회의실에 있는 스피커를 빌려오세요. 그것들은 둘 다 제대로 작동해요.

여: 그것들은 새로 나온, 경량 모델이죠, 그렇죠?

남: 네. ¹⁸A 회의실에도 그것들을 한 세트 주문할 거예요... 그것들은 우리의 공급업체로부터 구할 수 있는 가장 가벼운 모델이거든요.

모델 번호	무게
150A	5.3 kg
172E	5.0 kg
530R	4.8 kg
¹⁸200B	4.5 kg

16

해석 남자에 따르면, 내일 무슨 일이 일어날 것인가?

(A) 제품 시연
(B) 전자제품 무역 박람회
(C) 임원 회의
(D) 교육 워크숍

해설 내일 일어날 일을 묻는 문제입니다. 남자가 "tomorrow's executive meeting"이라며 내일 있을 임원 회의라고 한 말을 통해 내일 임원 회의가 열릴 것임을 알 수 있습니다. 따라서 정답은 (C) An executive gathering입니다.

어휘 demonstration[dèmənstréiʃən] 시연, 설명 trade show 무역 박람회 gathering[gǽðəriŋ] 회의, 모임

17

해석 남자는 무엇을 제안하는가?

(A) 제대로 작동하지 않는 몇몇 기기들을 고치기
(B) 다른 회의실을 예약하기
(C) 다른 방에서 스피커를 가져오기
(D) 새로운 전자기기 공급업체에 연락하기

해설 남자가 제안하는 것을 묻는 문제입니다. 여자가 "One of the speakers in Conference Room A is making a buzzing noise."라며 A 회의실에 있는 스피커 중 하나가 윙윙거리는 소리를 낸다고 하자, 남자가 "For now, you should borrow the speakers from Conference Room D."라며 우선, D 회의실에 있는 스피커를 빌려오라고 제안하였습니다. 따라서 정답은 (C) Taking speakers from another room입니다.

어휘 malfunction[mælfʌ́ŋkʃən] 제대로 작동하지 않다

18

해석 시각 자료를 보아라. 남자는 어떤 모델을 주문할 것인가?

(A) 150A
(B) 172E
(C) 530R
(D) 200B

해설 남자가 주문할 모델을 묻는 문제입니다. 남자가 "I'll order a pair of those[speakers] ~ They're the lightest model available from our supplier."라며 스피커들을 한 세트 주문할 것이고 그것들은 공급업체로부터 구할 수 있는 가장 가벼운 모델이라고 하였으므로, 남자가 무게가 4.5kg으로 가장 가벼운 200B 모델을 주문할 것임을 표에서 알 수 있습니다. 따라서 정답은 (D) 200B입니다.

DAY 12 세부 사항 관련 문제 2

Course 1 이유 · 방법 · 정도 문제

HACKERS PRACTICE 🎧 DAY12_02   p.101

01 (C)	**02** (B)	**03** (C)	**04** (B)

01-02 🎤 캐나다식 발음 → 미국식 발음 / 호주식 발음 → 영국식 발음

Questions 1-2 refer to the following conversation.

M: Hello. ⁰¹I'm supposed to take the 8 A.M. train to Boston tomorrow. But I forgot I have a doctor's appointment tomorrow morning. ⁰¹Are there any trains that depart in the evening?

W: We have a few seats available on the train leaving at five. Will that work?

M: I'll still arrive in Boston before nine, so that's fine.

W: OK. ⁰²There is a $7 fee for changing your reservation.

be supposed to ~하기로 되어 있다
depart[미 dipá:rt, 영 dipá:t] 출발하다, 떠나다

해석

1-2번은 다음 대화에 관한 문제입니다.

남: 안녕하세요. ⁰¹저는 내일 보스턴으로 가는 오전 8시 기차를 타기로 되어 있어요. 하지만 제가 내일 오전에 진료 예약이 있다는 것을 잊고 있었네요. ⁰¹저녁에 출발하는 기차가 있나요?

여: 다섯 시에 출발하는 기차에 몇 좌석이 남아 있습니다. 괜찮으시겠어요?

남: 그래도 아홉 시 전에 보스턴에 도착할 테니까, 괜찮아요.

여: 알겠습니다. ⁰²고객님의 예약을 변경하시는 데 7달러의 요금이 있습니다.

01

해석 남자는 왜 "제가 내일 오전에 진료 예약이 있다는 것을 잊고 있었네요"라고 말하는가?

(A) 그는 행사에 참석할 수 없다.
(B) 그는 이메일을 확인하지 않았다.
(C) 그는 예약을 변경하고 싶어 한다.
(D) 그는 환불을 요청해야 한다.

해설 남자가 하는 말(I forgot I have a doctor's appointment tomorrow morning)의 의도를 묻는 문제입니다. 남자가 "I'm supposed to take the 8 A.M. train to Boston tomorrow."라며 내일 보스턴으로 가는 오전 8시 기차를 타기로 되어 있다고 한 뒤, "Are there any trains ~ in the evening?"이라며 저녁에 출발하는 기차가 있는지를 물었습니다. 이를 통해 남자가 예약을 변경하고 싶어 함을 알 수 있습니다. 따라서 정답은 (C) He wants to change a booking입니다.

02

해석 남자는 얼마를 청구받을 것인가?

(A) 5달러
(B) 7달러
(C) 8달러
(D) 9달러

해설 남자가 청구받을 금액을 묻는 문제입니다. 여자가 "There is a $7 fee for changing your reservation."이라며 예약을 변경하는 데 7달러의 요금이 있다고 하였습니다. 따라서 정답은 (B) $7입니다.

어휘 charge[미 tʃɑːrdʒ, 영 tʃɑːdʒ] 청구하다

Questions 3-4 refer to the following conversation.

M: As you know, ⁰³Mr. Johnson is retiring soon. We're going to hold a farewell party for him next Friday evening. Could you help me prepare for it?

W: Certainly. I'm not very busy today.

M: Great. I'm hoping you can find out which staff members will be coming to the party. That way, I'll be able to know how large the venue should be.

W: OK. ⁰⁴I'll ask everyone by e-mail right now.

retire[미 ritáiər, 영 ritáiə] 은퇴하다   farewell party 송별회
venue[vénjuː] 장소

해석

3-4번은 다음 대화에 관한 문제입니다.

남: 아시다시피, ⁰³Mr. Johnson이 곧 은퇴해요. 우리는 그를 위해 다음 주 금요일 저녁에 송별회를 열 예정이에요. 준비하는 것을 도와주실 수 있나요?

여: 물론이죠. 저는 오늘 그다지 바쁘지 않아요.

남: 좋네요. 당신이 어느 직원들이 파티에 올 것인지 알아봐 주시면 좋겠어요. 그렇게 하면, 장소가 얼마나 커야 하는지 알 수 있을 거예요.

여: 알겠어요. ⁰⁴지금 바로 모두에게 이메일로 물어볼게요.

03

해석 다음 주 금요일 저녁에 왜 행사가 열릴 것인가?
(A) 상을 수여하기 위해
(B) 신규 직원을 환영하기 위해
(C) 은퇴를 기념하기 위해
(D) 판촉 행사에 대해 알리기 위해

해설 다음 주 금요일 저녁에 행사가 열릴 이유를 묻는 문제입니다. 남자가 "Mr. Johnson is retiring soon. We're going to hold a farewell party for him next Friday evening."이라며 Mr. Johnson이 곧 은퇴한다고 한 뒤, 그를 위해 다음 주 금요일 저녁에 송별회를 열 예정이라고 하였습니다. 따라서 정답은 (C) To celebrate a retirement입니다.

어휘 give out ~을 수여하다   celebrate[미 séləbrèit, 영 séləbreit] 기념하다
announce[ənáuns] 알리다

04

해석 여자는 어떻게 문의를 할 것인가?
(A) 비서에게 전화함으로써
(B) 이메일을 보냄으로써
(C) 회의를 주최함으로써
(D) 공지를 게시함으로써

해설 여자가 문의를 할 방법을 묻는 문제입니다. 여자가 "I'll ask everyone by e-mail right now."라며 지금 바로 모두에게 이메일로 물어보겠다고 하였습니다. 따라서 정답은 (B) By sending an e-mail입니다.

어휘 assistant[əsístənt] 비서, 조수

Course 2 문제점 문제

HACKERS PRACTICE 🎧 DAY12_04   p.103

01 (C)	02 (D)	03 (B)	04 (A)

Questions 1-2 refer to the following conversation.

M: Excuse me. I'm looking for a new electric guitar. Do you have any here?

W: Yes, but only secondhand instruments. ⁰¹We don't have any new electric guitars in stock.

M: Hmm . . . I'd prefer a new instrument. When do you expect to get additional inventory?

W: ⁰²Our next delivery is Thursday. I'll post details about the new merchandise on our Web site once it's here, so you'll be able to check in advance.

M: Thanks. That would be great.

electric[iléktrik] 전자의, 전기의   secondhand[sèkəndhǽnd] 중고의
instrument[ínstrəmənt] 악기   in stock 재고가 있는
additional[ədíʃənəl] 추가의, 부가적인
inventory[미 ínvəntɔ̀:ri, 영 ínvəntəri] 재고(품)
merchandise[미 mə́:rtʃəndàiz, 영 mə́:tʃəndàis] 제품, 상품

해석

1-2번은 다음 대화에 관한 문제입니다.

남: 실례합니다. 저는 새 전자 기타를 사려고 합니다. 여기서 판매하나요?

여: 네, 하지만 중고 악기만 있어요. ⁰¹새 전자 기타는 재고가 없어요.

남: 음... 저는 새 악기를 사고 싶은데요. 언제 추가 재고를 받을 것으로 예상하시나요?

여: ⁰²저희의 다음 배송은 목요일이에요. 미리 확인하실 수 있도록, 새 제품이 이곳에 오면 저희 웹사이트에 그것에 대한 상세 정보를 게시해 놓을게요.

남: 감사해요. 그렇게 해주시면 좋겠어요.

01

해석 여자는 어떤 문제를 언급하는가?
(A) 악기가 손상되었다.
(B) 환불 정책이 변경되었다.
(C) 특정 종류의 제품이 재고가 없다.
(D) 공연이 취소되었다.

해설 여자가 언급한 문제점을 묻는 문제입니다. 여자가 "We don't have any new electric guitars in stock."이라며 새 전자 기타는 재고가 없다고 하였습니다. 따라서 정답은 (C) A type of item is not in stock입니다.

어휘 policy[미 pá:ləsi, 영 pɔ́ləsi] 정책, 방침

02

해석 목요일에 무슨 일이 일어날 것인가?
(A) 할인이 제공될 것이다.
(B) 영수증이 제공될 것이다.
(C) 몇몇 티켓이 판매될 것이다.
(D) 몇몇 제품이 도착할 것이다.

해설 목요일에 일어날 일을 묻는 문제입니다. 여자가 "Our next delivery is Thursday. I'll post details about the new merchandise on our Web site once it's here"라며 다음 배송은 목요일이고 새 제품이 이곳에 오면 웹사이트에 그것에 대한 상세 정보를 게시해 놓겠다고 한 것을 통해, 목요일에 새 제품이 올 것임을 알 수 있습니다. 따라서 정답은 (D) Some merchandise will arrive입니다.

어휘 receipt[risí:t] 영수증, 수령

PART 3

한 권으로 끝내는 해커스 토익 700+ (LC+RC+VOCA)

03-04 캐나다식 발음 → 미국식 발음 → 호주식 발음 /
호주식 발음 → 영국식 발음 → 캐나다식 발음

Questions 3-4 refer to the following conversation with three speakers.

M1: Harriett, do you have the contract for the Bluejay Incorporated merger?
W: Oh, no! 03It's in my briefcase. And I left that in my car.
M2: Please go and get it, then. Our supervisor wants to see it before the management meeting in 30 minutes. Right, Craig?
M1: Yeah. And 04we also have to make a copy of the contract before that meeting.

contract[kántrækt] 계약(서)
merger[미 márːdʒər, 영 máːdʒə] 합병, 인수
supervisor[미 súːpərvàizər, 영 súːpəvaizə] 관리자, 감독
management[mǽnidʒmənt] 경영(진)

해석
3-4번은 다음 세 명의 대화에 관한 문제입니다.

남1: Harriett, Bluejay사 합병에 대한 계약서를 가지고 계신가요?
여: 오, 이런! 03그건 제 서류 가방에 있어요. 그리고 저는 서류 가방을 차에 놓고 왔어요.
남2: 그러면, 가서 그것을 가져와 주세요. 우리 관리자가 30분 뒤에 있을 경영진 회의 전에 그걸 보고 싶어 하시니까요. 그렇죠, Craig?
남1: 네. 그리고 04우리도 그 회의 전에 계약서의 사본을 만들어야 해요.

03
해석 무엇이 문제인가?
(A) 제안이 거절되었다.
(B) 서류를 두고 왔다.
(C) 회의가 연기되었다.
(D) 고객이 불만족스러워한다.

해설 문제점을 묻는 문제입니다. 여자가 "It[contract]'s in my briefcase. And I left that[briefcase] in my car."라며 계약서가 서류 가방에 있으며 서류 가방을 차에 놓고 왔다고 하였습니다. 따라서 정답은 (B) A document was left behind입니다.

어휘 refuse[rifjúːz] 거절하다, 거부하다
leave behind 두고 오다, 둔 채 잊고 오다
postpone[미 poustpóun, 영 pəustpáun] 연기하다, 미루다
dissatisfied[미 dissǽtisfàid, 영 dìssǽtisfaid] 불만족스러운

04
해석 계약서에 대해 무엇이 언급되는가?
(A) 복사되어야 한다.
(B) 최근에 수정되었다.
(C) 발송되어야 한다.
(D) 오늘 서명될 것이다.

해설 계약서에 대해 언급되는 것을 묻는 문제입니다. 남자 1이 "we also have to make a copy of the contract"라며 자신도 계약서의 사본을 만들어야 한다고 하였습니다. 따라서 정답은 (A) It needs to be copied입니다.

어휘 mail out ~을 발송하다   sign[sain] 서명하다, 체결하다

---

01 (D)	02 (C)	03 (A)	04 (A)
05 (D)	06 (A)	07 (B)	08 (D)
09 (C)	10 (B)	11 (D)	12 (C)
13 (C)	14 (B)	15 (D)	16 (A)
17 (C)	18 (C)		

01-03 호주식 발음 → 미국식 발음

Questions 1-3 refer to the following conversation.

M: Hello. My name is Christian Poulter. 01I want to confirm my room reservation for June 17 and 18. 02I'm coming to Interlaken then to go hiking.
W: Yes, Mr. Poulter. You have a reservation for those two nights. Also, check-in is any time from 2 P.M. to 10 P.M. If you arrive before 2 P.M., 03we have a luggage storage room next to the dining hall. You can keep your bags there before checking in.
M: Thanks, but I don't think that will be necessary.

confirm[미 kənfɔ́ːrm, 영 kənfɔ́ːm] 확인하다
reservation[미 rèzərvéiʃən, 영 rèzəvéiʃən] 예약   hiking[háikiŋ] 등산
luggage[lʌ́gidʒ] 짐, 수하물   dining hall 식당

해석
1-3번은 다음 대화에 관한 문제입니다.

남: 안녕하세요. 제 이름은 Christian Poulter예요. 6월 17일과 18일의 01제 객실 예약을 확인하고 싶어요. 02저는 등산을 하기 위해 그때 인터라켄에 갈 예정이에요.
여: 네, Mr. Poulter. 고객님께 그 이틀 밤이 예약되어 있습니다. 또한, 체크인 시간은 오후 2시부터 오후 10시 사이에 아무 때나 가능합니다. 만약 오후 2시 전에 도착하시면, 03식당 옆에 짐 보관실이 있습니다. 체크인하기 전에 가방을 그곳에 보관하실 수 있습니다.
남: 감사해요, 하지만 그럴 필요는 없을 것 같아요.

01
해석 전화의 주된 목적은 무엇인가?
(A) 이른 도착을 계획하기 위해
(B) 객실 업그레이드를 요청하기 위해
(C) 야외 활동을 예약하기 위해
(D) 예약을 확인하기 위해

해설 전화의 목적을 묻는 문제입니다. 남자가 "I want to confirm my room reservation"이라며 자신의 객실 예약을 확인하고 싶다고 하였습니다. 따라서 정답은 (D) To check on a booking입니다.

어휘 arrange[əréindʒ] 계획하다, ~의 예정을 세우다
early arrival 이른 도착, 일찍 온 사람

02
해석 남자는 왜 인터라켄에 방문할 것인가?
(A) 시설을 건학하기 위해
(B) 그의 가족과 함께 스키를 타기 위해
(C) 등산을 하기 위해
(D) 친구를 만나기 위해

해설 남자가 인터라켄에 방문하는 이유를 묻는 문제입니다. 남자가 "I'm coming to Interlaken ~ to go hiking."이라며 등산을 하기 위해 인터라켄에 갈 예정이라고 하였습니다. 따라서 정답은 (C) To go hiking입니다.

어휘 facility[fəsíləti] 시설, 설비

03

해석 여자에 따르면, 짐은 어디에 보관될 수 있는가?
(A) 식당 옆에
(B) 안내 데스크 뒤에
(C) 로비에
(D) 계단 옆에

해설 짐이 보관될 수 있는 장소를 묻는 문제입니다. 여자가 "we have a luggage storage room next to the dining hall. You can keep your bags there"라며 식당 옆에 짐 보관실이 있으며 가방을 그곳에 보관할 수 있다고 하였습니다. 따라서 정답은 (A) By the dining hall 입니다.

04-06 🔊 캐나다식 발음 → 영국식 발음

Questions 4-6 refer to the following conversation.

> M: Kelly, are you good with electronics? I'm trying to prepare for a videoconference, but [04]I'm having trouble with our new Web camera. It won't turn on for some reason.
> W: Actually, I think the issue is your laptop. Since [05]it's a bit outdated, I don't think it will connect to that camera. It only works with newer laptop models.
> M: Oh, I didn't realize that. [06]Can you give me the camera that is sitting on the table behind you, then? I'll try that one instead.
> W: Sure . . . Here you go.
>
> electronics[미 ilektrániks, 영 èlektróniks] 전자기기
> videoconference[미 vídioukànfərəns, 영 vídiəukònfərəns] 화상회의

해석
4-6번은 다음 대화에 관한 문제입니다.

남: Kelly, 당신은 전자기기를 잘 다루나요? 저는 화상회의를 준비하려고 하는데, [04]새 화상 카메라로 문제를 겪고 있어요. 무엇 때문인지 카메라가 켜지지 않아요.
여: 사실, 문제는 당신의 휴대용 컴퓨터 같아요. [05]그건 약간 구식이라서, 그 카메라와 연동될 것 같지 않아요. 그것은 더 최신 휴대용 컴퓨터 모델에만 작동해요.
남: 아, 그런 줄은 몰랐네요. [06]그러면, 당신 뒤에 있는 탁자 위의 카메라를 주시겠어요? 그것을 대신 사용해 볼게요.
여: 물론이죠... 여기 있어요.

04

해석 무엇이 문제인가?
(A) 일부 기기가 작동하지 않는다.
(B) 일부 비품들이 분실되었다.
(C) 화상회의가 연기되었다.
(D) 전선이 충분히 길지 않다.

해설 문제점을 묻는 문제입니다. 남자가 "I'm having trouble with our new Web camera. It won't turn on"이라며 자신이 새 화상 카메라로 문제를 겪고 있다며 그것이 켜지지 않는다고 하였습니다. 따라서 정답은 (A) Some equipment is not working입니다.

어휘 equipment[ikwípmənt] 기기, 장비   supply[səplái] 비품, 용품

05

해석 남자의 휴대용 컴퓨터에 대해 무엇이 언급되는가?
(A) 내장 카메라가 있다.
(B) 화면이 작다.
(C) 전원이 나갔다.
(D) 구식 모델이다.

해설 남자의 휴대용 컴퓨터에 대해 언급되는 것을 묻는 문제입니다. 여자가 "it[laptop]'s a bit outdated"라며 남자의 휴대용 컴퓨터가 약간 구식이라고 하였습니다. 따라서 정답은 (D) It is an old model입니다.

어휘 built-in[bìltín] 내장된, 붙박이의   power[미 páuər, 영 pauə] 전원, 전력

06

해석 남자는 여자에게 무엇을 해달라고 요청하는가?
(A) 그에게 다른 모델을 준다.
(B) 사용 설명서를 찾는다.
(C) 인터넷 연결을 설정한다.
(D) 데스크톱 컴퓨터를 켠다.

해설 남자가 여자에게 요청하는 것을 묻는 문제입니다. 남자가 "Can you give me the camera that is sitting on the table behind you ~?"라며 여자의 뒤에 있는 탁자 위의 카메라를 줄 것을 요청하였습니다. 따라서 정답은 (A) Give him a different model입니다.

어휘 instruction manual 사용 설명서

07-09 🔊 호주식 발음 → 영국식 발음

Questions 7-9 refer to the following conversation.

> M: Irene, the online advertisement you made for next Tuesday's book signing looks great! [07]I think this event will be an excellent way to promote the expansion of our store.
> W: Thanks. Many customers seem excited about meeting [08]author Edward Swift. Ah, and [08]the novel he wrote has been selling well.
> M: Yeah, that's good news for the event, too. By the way, can you put signs for the event in the storefront windows?
> W: Already done. [09]I also sent an e-mail to store members reminding them to sign up for the event through our Web page.
>
> promote[미 prəmóut, 영 prəmə́ut] 홍보하다
> expansion[ikspǽnʃən] 확장   novel[미 návəl, 영 nóvəl] 소설
> sell well 잘 팔리다
> storefront[미 stɔ́ːrfrʌnt, 영 stɔ́ːfrʌnt] 가게 앞, 가게 앞에 설치된
> sign up ~에 신청하다

해석
7-9번은 다음 대화에 관한 문제입니다.

남: Irene, 당신이 다음 주 화요일의 책 사인회를 위해 만든 온라인 광고는 멋져 보여요! [07]제 생각에 이 행사는 우리 매장의 확장을 홍보하기 위한 아주 좋은 방법이 될 거예요.
여: 고마워요. 많은 고객들이 [08]Edward Swift 작가를 만나는 것에 대해 들떠 있는 것 같아요. 아, 그리고 [08]그가 쓴 소설이 잘 팔리고 있어요.
남: 네, 그것도 행사를 위한 좋은 소식이네요. 그건 그렇고, 가게 앞 창문에 행사를 위한 간판을 달아줄 수 있나요?
여: 이미 했어요. [09]저는 매장 회원들에게 우리 웹페이지를 통해 행사에 신청할 것을 상기시키는 이메일도 보냈어요.

07

해석 책 사인회는 왜 열릴 것인가?
(A) 할인 판매를 광고하기 위해
(B) 확장을 홍보하기 위해
(C) 기념일을 축하하기 위해
(D) 소설의 판매량을 증가시키기 위해

해설 책 사인회가 열리는 이유를 묻는 문제입니다. 남자가 "I think this event[book signing] will be an excellent way to promote the expansion of our store."라며 책 사인회가 매장의 확장을 홍보하기 위한 아주 좋은 방법이 될 것이라고 하였습니다. 따라서 정답은 (B) To promote an expansion입니다.

08

해석 여자는 Edward Swift에 대해 무엇을 말하는가?
(A) 그는 사은품을 나눠줄 것이다.
(B) 그는 지역 주민이다.
(C) 그는 이전에 매장을 방문했다.
(D) 그는 책을 썼다.

해설 여자가 Edward Swift에 대해 언급하는 것을 묻는 문제입니다. 여자가 "author Edward Swift"라며 Edward Swift가 작가라고 한 뒤, "the novel he[Edward Swift] wrote"라며 Edward Swift가 쓴 소설을 언급했습니다. 따라서 정답은 (D) He wrote a book입니다.

어휘 resident[미 rézədnt, 영 rézidnt] 주민, 거주민

09

해석 사람들은 어떻게 행사에 신청할 수 있는가?
(A) 이메일을 보냄으로써
(B) 직통 전화로 전화함으로써
(C) 웹사이트에 접속함으로써
(D) 직원에게 이야기함으로써

해설 사람들이 행사에 신청할 수 있는 방법을 묻는 문제입니다. 여자가 "I also sent an e-mail to store members reminding them to sign up for the event through our Web page."라며 매장 회원들에게 웹페이지를 통해 행사에 신청할 것을 상기시키는 이메일을 보냈다고 하였습니다. 따라서 정답은 (C) By going to a Web site입니다.

어휘 hot line 직통 전화, 상담 서비스
representative[rèprizéntətiv] 직원, 점원

10-12 🎧 미국식 발음 → 캐나다식 발음 → 호주식 발음

Questions 10-12 refer to the following conversation with three speakers.

> W: Welcome to Jasmine Home Goods. What can I do for you today?
> M1: ¹⁰We need 15 coffee mugs as gifts for our team members. Where are they located?
> W: They're in Aisle 4. And you're in luck. ¹¹Many of our mugs are 50 percent off today.
> M2: That's great! We checked out another shop this morning, but everything there was too expensive.
> M1: Yeah. And that store didn't have a wide variety. Oh, one more thing . . . ¹²Do you gift wrap items?
> W: We usually do. But we are out of wrapping paper at the moment, so ¹²I can't offer you that service right now.
>
> home goods 가정용품 aisle[ail] 통로, 복도
> gift wrap (선물용으로) 포장하다

해석

10-12번은 다음 세 명의 대화에 관한 문제입니다.

여: Jasmine 가정용품점에 오신 것을 환영합니다. 오늘 무엇을 도와 드릴까요?
남1: 저희 팀원들을 위한 선물로 ¹⁰커피 머그잔 15개가 필요해요. 어디에 있나요?
여: 그것들은 4번 통로에 있습니다. 그리고 고객님들께서는 운이 좋으시네요. ¹¹오늘 저희 가게의 많은 머그잔들이 50퍼센트 할인되거든요.

남2: 잘됐네요! 저희는 아침에 다른 가게도 확인해 봤는데, 거기 있는 것들은 다 너무 비쌌어요.
남1: 맞아요. 그리고 그 가게는 종류도 다양하지 않았어요. 아, 하나만 더 요... ¹²여기는 제품을 선물용으로 포장해 주나요?
여: 보통 포장해 드려요. 하지만 지금 포장지가 다 떨어져서, ¹²그 서비스를 지금 제공해 드릴 수는 없어요.

10

해석 얼마나 많은 제품이 구매될 것 같은가?
(A) 10개
(B) 15개
(C) 20개
(D) 50개

해설 구매될 제품의 개수를 묻는 문제입니다. 남자 1이 "We need 15 coffee mugs"라며 커피 머그잔 15개가 필요하다고 하였습니다. 따라서 정답은 (B) 15입니다.

11

해석 여자에 따르면, 무엇이 할인 판매 중인가?
(A) 상품권들
(B) 포장 재료들
(C) 몇몇 접시들
(D) 몇몇 컵들

해설 할인 판매 중인 것을 묻는 문제입니다. 여자가 "Many of our mugs are 50 percent off today."라며 오늘 가게의 많은 머그잔들이 50퍼센트 할인된다고 하였습니다. 따라서 정답은 (D) Some cups입니다.

어휘 plate[pleit] 접시

12

해석 여자는 어떤 문제를 언급하는가?
(A) 상품이 매진되었다.
(B) 시스템에 오류가 있다.
(C) 서비스를 이용할 수 없다.
(D) 직원이 휴가 중이다.

해설 여자가 언급한 문제점을 묻는 문제입니다. 남자 1이 "Do you gift wrap items?"라며 제품을 선물용으로 포장해 주는지를 묻자 여자가 "I can't offer you that service right now"라며 그 서비스를 지금 제공해 줄 수는 없다고 하였습니다. 따라서 정답은 (C) A service is unavailable입니다.

어휘 on leave 휴가 중인

13-15 🎧 캐나다식 발음 → 영국식 발음

Questions 13-15 refer to the following conversation.

> M: Sandra, are you free today? ¹³I can no longer attend the accounting workshop since I need to revise the expense reports. So, my spot is available if you want to go.
> W: I'd love to, but I'm too busy. ¹⁴I have to call one of our suppliers to correct a billing error. Then, I have to attend a team meeting.
> M: I see. Do you know if anyone else would be interested? An experienced accountant will be leading the event, so ¹⁵there will probably be a lot of useful information.
> W: Why don't you ask Alan? He told me he wants to participate in more workshops.
>
> accounting[əkáuntiŋ] 회계 spot[미 spɑt, 영 spɔt] 자리 ⦿

billing[bíliŋ] 청구액, 거래액 experienced[ikspíəriənst] 경험이 풍부한
accountant[əkáuntənt] 회계사 participate in ~에 참여하다

해석
13-15번은 다음 대화에 관한 문제입니다.

남: Sandra, 오늘 시간 있으세요? 저는 지출 보고서를 수정해야 해서 ¹³더 이상 회계 워크숍에 참석할 수 없어요. 그러니까, 만약 가고 싶으시다면 제 자리를 이용하실 수 있어요.

여: 그렇게 하고 싶지만, 저는 너무 바빠요. ¹⁴저는 청구액 오류를 정정하기 위해 저희 공급업체 중 한 곳에 전화해야 해요. 그다음엔, 팀 회의에 참석해야 해요.

남: 알겠어요. 관심을 가질 만한 다른 사람이 있는지 아시나요? 경험이 풍부한 회계사가 그 행사를 진행할 것이라서, ¹⁵아마 유용한 정보가 많이 있을 거예요.

여: Alan에게 물어보는 게 어때요? 그는 제게 워크숍에 더 많이 참석하고 싶다고 말했거든요.

13
해석 남자의 문제는 무엇인가?
(A) 그는 신청서를 잃어버렸다.
(B) 그는 전화 회의에 늦었다.
(C) 그는 세미나에 갈 수 없다.
(D) 그는 업무를 늦게 완료했다.

해설 남자의 문제점을 묻는 문제입니다. 남자가 "I can no longer attend the accounting workshop"이라며 더 이상 회계 워크숍에 참석할 수 없다고 하였습니다. 따라서 정답은 (C) He cannot go to a seminar입니다.

어휘 conference call 전화 회의

14
해석 여자는 청구액 오류를 어떻게 정정할 것인가?
(A) 주문서를 수정함으로써
(B) 전화를 함으로써
(C) 공급업체를 방문함으로써
(D) 서류를 제출함으로써

해설 여자가 청구액 오류를 정정할 방법을 묻는 문제입니다. 여자가 "I have to call one of our suppliers to correct a billing error."라며 청구액 오류를 정정하기 위해 공급업체 중 한 곳에 전화해야 한다고 하였습니다. 따라서 정답은 (B) By making a phone call입니다.

15
해석 남자가 "경험이 풍부한 회계사가 그 행사를 진행할 것이라서"라고 말할 때 의도하는 것은 무엇인가?
(A) 동료도 갈 것이다.
(B) 발표에 많은 사람들이 참석할 것이다.
(C) 강의에 수업료가 들 것이다.
(D) 수업이 유익할 것이다.

해설 남자가 하는 말(An experienced accountant will be leading the event)의 의도를 묻는 문제입니다. 남자가 "there will probably be a lot of useful information"이라며 아마 유용한 정보가 많이 있을 것이라고 한 것을 통해 남자가 수업이 유익할 것임을 전달하려는 의도임을 알 수 있습니다. 따라서 정답은 (D) A session will be informative입니다.

어휘 well attended 참석자가 많은
require[미 rikwáiər, 영 rikwáiə] (시간·돈이) 들다, 걸리다
informative[미 infɔ́rmətiv, 영 infɔ́ːmətiv] 유익한, 정보를 주는

16-18 [캐나다식 발음 → 미국식 발음]

Questions 16-18 refer to the following conversation and graph.

M: Did you hear that our CEO will be visiting us ¹⁶here at our mobile phone plant in three days?

W: Yes. ¹⁷Our factory produced the most units in the company—outperforming all other plants in that period. So, he wants to inspect our facility and use the findings to provide suggestions to other locations.

M: I assume he's concerned about the ones with low output.

W: Yes. Two of our factories barely met the 20,000-unit quota.

M: Anyway, we'd better prepare for the visit. Could you inspect the workstations on the second floor this afternoon?

W: ¹⁸I'm busy this afternoon, actually. I'm conducting a seminar on workplace safety. Will I have time to do it tomorrow morning?

M: That shouldn't be a problem.

outperform[미 àutpərfɔ́ːrm, 영 àutpəfɔ́ːm] 더 좋은 성과를 내다
inspect[inspékt] 점검하다, 조사하다 finding[fáindiŋ] 조사 결과, 발견(물)
concerned[미 kənsɔ́ːrnd, 영 kənsɔ́ːnd] 염려하는, 걱정하는
output[áutput] 생산량 quota[미 kwóutə, 영 kwóutə] 할당량
workstation[미 wɔ́ːrkstèiʃən, 영 wɔ́ːkstèiʃən] 작업장

해석
16-18번은 다음 대화와 그래프에 관한 문제입니다.

남: 우리 회사의 최고 경영자가 3일 후에 ¹⁶여기 우리 휴대전화 공장을 방문한다는 걸 들었나요?

여: 네. ¹⁷우리 공장이 회사에서 가장 많은 제품을 생산했고 그 기간 동안 다른 모든 공장들보다 더 좋은 성과를 냈어요. 그래서, 그는 우리 시설을 점검하고 조사 결과를 다른 지점에 제안하는 데 활용하고 싶어 해요.

남: 그가 생산량이 낮은 곳들을 염려하는 것 같네요.

여: 맞아요. 우리 공장들 중 두 곳이 간신히 20,000개의 할당량을 맞췄거든요.

남: 어쨌든, 우리는 방문을 위해 준비하는 것이 좋겠어요. 오늘 오후에 2층에 있는 작업장들을 점검해주시겠어요?

여: ¹⁸실은, 제가 오늘 오후에 바빠요. 작업장 안전에 대한 세미나를 진행할 거거든요. 내일 아침에 그걸 할 시간이 있을까요?

남: 그래도 괜찮을 거예요.

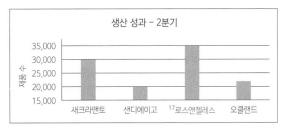

16
해석 화자들은 어디에 있는 것 같은가?
(A) 제조 시설에
(B) 가전기기 매장에
(C) 서비스 센터에
(D) 기업 본사에

해설 화자들이 있는 장소를 묻는 문제입니다. 남자가 "here at our mobile phone plant"라며 여기 휴대전화 공장이라고 한 것을 통해 화자들이 제조 시설에 있음을 알 수 있습니다. 따라서 정답은 (A) In a manufacturing facility입니다.

어휘 manufacturing[미 mænjufǽktʃəriŋ, 영 mænjəfǽktʃəriŋ] 제조(업)의
headquarters[미 hédkwɔ̀:rtərz, 영 hèdkwɔ́:təz] 본사, 본부

17

해석 시각 자료를 보아라. 화자들은 어느 지점에서 일하는가?
(A) 새크라멘토
(B) 샌디에이고
(C) 로스앤젤레스
(D) 오클랜드

해설 화자들이 일하는 지점을 묻는 문제입니다. 여자가 "Our factory produced the most units in the company—outperforming all other plants in that period"라며 자신들의 공장이 회사에서 가장 많은 제품을 생산했고 그 기간 동안 다른 모든 공장들보다 더 좋은 성과를 냈다고 하였으므로, 화자들이 생산 제품 수가 가장 많은 로스앤젤레스 지점에서 근무한다는 것을 그래프에서 알 수 있습니다. 따라서 정답은 (C) Los Angeles입니다.

18

해석 여자는 왜 오후에 바쁠 것인가?
(A) 그녀는 검사관을 견학시켜줄 것이다.
(B) 그녀는 지역 지점을 방문할 것이다.
(C) 그녀는 세미나를 진행할 것이다.
(D) 그녀는 마감일을 맞추기 위해 근무할 것이다.

해설 여자가 오후에 바쁠 이유를 묻는 문제입니다. 여자가 "I'm busy this afternoon, actually. I'm conducting a seminar"라며 실은 오늘 오후에 세미나를 진행할 것이라 바쁘다고 하였습니다. 따라서 정답은 (C) She will be leading a seminar입니다.

DAY 13 세부 사항 관련 문제 3

Course 1 특정 세부 사항 문제

HACKERS PRACTICE 🎧 DAY13_02   p.107

01 (D)	02 (C)	03 (B)	04 (A)

01-02 🔊 미국식 발음 → 캐나다식 발음 / 영국식 발음 → 호주식 발음

Questions 1-2 refer to the following conversation.

> W: I heard Mr. Jensen will retire next year. Do you know who is going to replace him?
> M: Apparently, Michaela Hernandez will. ⁰¹She's been <u>running the Los Angeles branch</u> for three years. But I guess <u>she wants to transfer</u> to New York to be closer to her family in Boston.
> W: Really? ⁰²I met her <u>while working in Portland</u> last year. She visited our branch to give a presentation.

retire[미 ritáiər, 영 ritáiə] 은퇴하다, 퇴직하다
replace[ripléis] ~의 뒤를 잇다, 대신하다
apparently[əpǽrəntli] 분명히, 명백히   run[rʌn] 경영하다, 운영하다
branch[미 bræntʃ, 영 brɑːntʃ] 지사, 지점
transfer[미 trænsfə́r, 영 trænsfə́:] 전근하다, 이동하다

해석
1-2번은 다음 대화에 관한 문제입니다.

여: Mr. Jensen이 내년에 은퇴한다고 들었어요. 누가 그의 뒤를 이을 것인지 아시나요?
남: 분명히, Michaela Hernandez일 거예요. ⁰¹그녀는 3년째 로스앤젤레스 지사를 경영해오고 있어요. 하지만 제 생각에 그녀는 보스턴에 있는 가족과 더 가까이 있기 위해 뉴욕으로 전근하고 싶어 하는 것 같아요.
여: 그래요? ⁰²저는 지난해에 포틀랜드에서 일할 때 그녀를 만났어요. 그녀가 발표를 하기 위해서 우리 지사를 방문했었거든요.

01

해석 Michaela Hernandez는 누구인가?
(A) 이사회 임원
(B) 투자자
(C) 광고주
(D) 지점장

해설 Michaela Hernandez의 신분을 묻는 문제입니다. 남자가 "She[Michaela Hernandez]'s been running the Los Angeles branch"라며 Michaela Hernandez가 로스앤젤레스 지사를 경영해오고 있다고 한 것을 통해 Michaela Hernandez가 지점장임을 알 수 있습니다. 따라서 정답은 (D) A branch manager입니다.

어휘 board[미 bɔːrd, 영 bɔːd] 이사회, 위원회
investor[미 invéstər, 영 invéstə] 투자자
advertiser[미 ǽdvərtàizər, 영 ǽdvətaizə] 광고주

02

해석 여자는 지난해에 어디에서 일했는가?
(A) 로스앤젤레스에서
(B) 보스턴에서
(C) 포틀랜드에서
(D) 뉴욕에서

해설 여자가 지난해에 일했던 곳을 묻는 문제입니다. 여자가 "I met her[Michaela Hernandez] while working in Portland last year."라며 지난해에 포틀랜드에서 일할 때 Michaela Hernandez를 만났다고 하였습니다. 따라서 정답은 (C) In Portland입니다.

03-04 🔊 미국식 발음 → 캐나다식 발음 → 영국식 발음 /
영국식 발음 → 호주식 발음 → 미국식 발음

Questions 3-4 refer to the following conversation with three speakers.

> W1: Bill and Margaret, could one of you give me a copy of our factory's production report?
> M: Here you go. I noticed that ⁰³the plant produced considerably <u>more tennis rackets</u> this quarter. But I'm not sure why.
> W1: Yes, ⁰⁴that's because we contracted a <u>different supplier</u>.
> W2: ⁰⁴Exactly. The new one delivers materials more regularly and reliably. ⁰⁴As a result, we've seen a 15 percent <u>boost in production</u>.
> M: That's quite impressive.
> W2: Yeah. Changing suppliers was the right decision.

production[prədʌ́kʃən] 생산(량)
considerably[kənsídərəbli] 상당히, 현저히
quarter[미 kwɔ́:rtər, 영 kwɔ́:tə] 분기
supplier[미 səpláiər, 영 səpláiə] 공급업체, 공급자
reliably[riláiəbli] 확실하게, 신뢰할 수 있게   boost[buːst] 증가, 향상

approve[əprúːv] 승인하다, 허가하다　shipment[ʃípmənt] 배송(품)
appreciate[미 əpríːʃieit, 영 əpríːʃieit] 감사하다

해석
3-4번은 다음 세 명의 대화에 관한 문제입니다.

여1: Bill 그리고 Margaret, 두 분 중 한 분이 제게 우리 공장의 생산 보고서 한 부를 주실 수 있나요?

남: 여기 있어요. 저는 이번 분기에 ⁰³공장에서 테니스 라켓을 상당히 더 많이 생산했다는 것을 발견했어요. 하지만 왜 그런지는 잘 모르겠어요.

여1: 네, ⁰⁴그건 우리가 다른 공급업체와 계약을 체결했기 때문이에요.

여2: ⁰⁴맞아요. 새 공급업체는 자재를 더 정기적으로 확실하게 배송해요. ⁰⁴그 결과, 우리는 생산량의 15퍼센트 증가를 경험했어요.

남: 그것은 상당히 인상적이네요.

여2: 네. 공급업체를 바꾸는 것은 올바른 결정이었어요.

03

해석 남자에 따르면, 공장에서 무엇이 만들어지는가?
(A) 사무기기
(B) 스포츠 장비
(C) 건축 자재
(D) 의류

해설 공장에서 만들어지는 것을 묻는 문제입니다. 남자가 "the plant produced ~ tennis rackets"라며 공장에서 테니스 라켓을 생산했다고 하였습니다. 따라서 정답은 (B) Sports gear입니다.

어휘 gear[미 giər, 영 giə] 장비, 용구

04

해석 여자들은 새로운 공급업체에 대해 무엇을 언급하는가?
(A) 생산량을 증가시키는 것을 도왔다.
(B) 계약에 대해 불만족스러워한다.
(C) 오늘 자재를 가져다주었다.
(D) 가격을 인상했다.

해설 여자들이 새로운 공급업체에 대해 언급하는 것을 묻는 문제입니다. 여자 1이 "that's because we contracted a different supplier"라며 테니스 라켓을 더 많이 생산한 이유가 다른 공급업체와 계약을 체결했기 때문이라고 하자, 여자 2가 "Exactly."라며 동의한 뒤, "As a result, we've seen ~ boost in production."이라며 그 결과 생산량의 증가를 경험했다고 하였습니다. 따라서 정답은 (A) It has helped increase production입니다.

어휘 be displeased with ~에 불만족스러워하다, ~에 불쾌해하다

Course 2 다음에 할 일 문제

HACKERS PRACTICE ∩ DAY13_04　　　　p.109

01 (B)	02 (D)	03 (C)	04 (B)

01-02 [음] 미국식 발음 → 호주식 발음 / 영국식 발음 → 캐나다식 발음

Questions 1-2 refer to the following conversation.

W: Thank you for calling Nexus Electronics. How can I help you?

M: I ordered a laptop from you last Thursday. However, ⁰¹when it arrived at my house, the box was crushed. Moreover, the keyboard was broken.

W: I'm sorry to hear that. I can mail you a replacement laptop for no extra charge. ⁰²I'll approve the new shipment right away.

M: Great. I'd appreciate that.

crush[krʌʃ] 뭉개다, 구기다　replacement[ripléismənt] 교체물　○

해석
1-2번은 다음 대화에 관한 문제입니다.

여: Nexus Electronics사에 전화해 주셔서 감사합니다. 어떻게 도와드릴까요?

남: 저는 지난주 목요일에 당신의 회사에서 휴대용 컴퓨터를 주문했어요. 그런데, ⁰¹그것이 집에 배달됐을 때, 상자가 뭉개져 있었어요. 게다가, 키보드는 망가져 있었어요.

여: 죄송합니다. 추가 요금 없이 교체할 휴대용 컴퓨터를 배송해 드리는 것이 가능합니다. ⁰²신규 배송을 곧바로 승인하겠습니다.

남: 좋네요. 그렇게 해주시면 감사하겠습니다.

01

해석 남자는 어떤 문제를 언급하는가?
(A) 배송품이 도착하지 않았다.
(B) 소포가 훼손되어 있었다.
(C) 고객 서비스 상담원과 이야기할 수 없었다.
(D) 상자가 잘못된 주소로 발송되었다.

해설 남자가 언급하는 문제점을 묻는 문제입니다. 남자가 "when it[laptop] arrived ~, the box was crushed. Moreover, the keyboard was broken."이라며 휴대용 컴퓨터가 배달됐을 때 상자가 뭉개져 있었으며 키보드가 망가져 있었다고 하였습니다. 따라서 정답은 (B) A package was damaged입니다.

어휘 package[pǽkidʒ] 소포, (포장용) 상자
customer representative 고객 서비스 상담원
available[əvéiləbəl] 이야기할 수 있는, 만날 수 있는

02

해석 여자는 다음에 무엇을 할 것 같은가?
(A) 일정을 확인한다.
(B) 재고 목록을 업데이트한다.
(C) 운송 요금에 대해 설명한다.
(D) 배송을 승인한다.

해설 여자가 다음에 할 일을 묻는 문제입니다. 여자가 "I'll approve the new shipment right away."라며 신규 배송을 곧바로 승인하겠다고 하였습니다. 따라서 정답은 (D) Approve a delivery입니다.

어휘 inventory[미 ínvəntɔːri, 영 ínvəntəri] 재고(품)
shipping[ʃípiŋ] 운송, 선적

03-04 [음] 미국식 발음 → 캐나다식 발음 / 영국식 발음 → 호주식 발음

Questions 3-4 refer to the following conversation.

W: Hello. ⁰³An announcement was made about my flight being delayed. What's the new departure time?

M: Ah . . . You mean Flight 345 to Philadelphia?

W: Yes. I'm concerned because I have a meeting there at 1 P.M.

M: ⁰³That flight's departure has been moved to noon because of engine problems. But maybe I can transfer you to another flight. ⁰⁴Let me check our reservation system.

delay[diléi] 지연시키다, 늦추다　departure[미 dipáːrtʃər, 영 dipáːtʃə] 출발
concerned[미 kənsə́ːrnd, 영 kənsə́ːnd] 걱정하는, 우려하는
transfer[미 trænsfə́ːr, 영 trænsfə́ː] 옮기다

3-4번은 다음 대화에 관한 문제입니다.

여: 안녕하세요. ⁰³제 항공편이 지연된 것에 대한 방송이 있었는데요. 새로운 출발 시간은 언제인가요?

남: 아... 필라델피아행 345편을 말씀하시는 건가요?

여: 네. 저는 그곳에서 오후 1시에 회의가 있어서 걱정되네요.

남: 엔진 문제 때문에 ⁰³그 항공편의 출발은 정오로 바뀌었어요. 하지만 아마 고객님을 다른 항공편으로 옮겨드릴 수 있을 거예요. ⁰⁴제가 저희 예약 시스템을 확인해 보겠습니다.

03

해석 남자는 누구인 것 같은가?

(A) 여행사 직원
(B) 관광 가이드
(C) 항공사 직원
(D) 보안 관계자

해설 남자의 신분을 묻는 문제입니다. 여자가 "An announcement was made about my flight being delayed. What's the new departure time?"이라며 항공편 지연에 대한 방송이 있었다며 새로운 출발 시간이 언제인지 묻자, 남자가 "That flight's departure has been moved to noon"이라며 변경된 항공편의 시간을 안내해 주었습니다. 이를 통해 남자가 항공사 직원임을 알 수 있습니다. 따라서 정답은 (C) An airline employee입니다.

어휘 travel agent 여행사 직원 airline[미 ɛ́ərlàin, 영 éəlain] 항공사 security official 보안 관계자

04

해석 남자는 다음에 무엇을 하겠다고 말하는가?

(A) 안내 방송을 한다.
(B) 시스템을 확인한다.
(C) 다른 표를 인쇄한다.
(D) 항공편 정보를 게시한다.

해설 남자가 다음에 할 일을 묻는 문제입니다. 남자가 "Let me check our reservation system."이라며 예약 시스템을 확인해 보겠다고 하였습니다. 따라서 정답은 (B) Check a system입니다.

HACKERS TEST 🎧 DAY13_05   p.110

01 (A)	02 (D)	03 (D)	04 (B)
05 (B)	06 (C)	07 (A)	08 (B)
09 (A)	10 (C)	11 (D)	12 (C)
13 (B)	14 (C)	15 (B)	16 (B)
17 (A)	18 (D)		

01-03 🎤 호주식 발음 → 미국식 발음

Questions 1-3 refer to the following conversation.

M: ⁰¹Welcome to Spokes Bicycle Store. Do you need help with anything?

W: Yes. I'm looking for a bike for commuting to work. I have to travel about a mile every day.

M: In that case, our hybrid bikes might be the best choice. They weigh less than mountain bikes and are more comfortable than road bikes, ⁰²making them ideal for short rides. Our selection is located near the store's entrance. ⁰³Follow me, and I'll show you our products.

commute[kəmjúːt] 통근하다   ⊙

---

hybrid[háibrid] 하이브리드(두 가지 기능이나 역할이 합쳐진 상품)의
weigh[wei] 무게가 나가다
selection[silékʃən] (선택·구매 등을 위한) 전시품

해석

1-3번은 다음 대화에 관한 문제입니다.

남: ⁰¹Spokes 자전거 매장에 오신 것을 환영합니다. 도움이 필요하신가요?

여: 네. 저는 직장 통근용 자전거를 찾고 있어요. 저는 매일 1마일 정도 이동해야 해요.

남: 그렇다면, 저희의 하이브리드 자전거가 최고의 선택일 것입니다. 그것은 산악용 자전거보다 무게가 덜 나가고 도로 자전거보다 더 편안해서, ⁰²단거리 이동에 이상적입니다. 저희의 전시품들이 매장 입구 근처에 있습니다. ⁰³저를 따라오시면, 저희 제품을 보여 드리겠습니다.

01

해석 화자들은 어디에 있는 것 같은가?

(A) 소매점에
(B) 자전거 공장에
(C) 회사 사무실에
(D) 무역 박람회에

해설 화자들이 있는 장소를 묻는 문제입니다. 남자가 "Welcome to Spokes Bicycle Store. Do you need help with anything?"이라며 Spokes 자전거 매장에 온 것을 환영한다고 하면서 도움이 필요한지 물은 것을 통해 화자들이 있는 장소가 자전거 소매점임을 알 수 있습니다. 따라서 정답은 (A) At a retail store입니다.

어휘 retail store 소매점

02

해석 남자는 왜 하이브리드 제품을 제안하는가?

(A) 다른 모델들보다 더 빠르다.
(B) 여자의 예산 내에 있다.
(C) 내구성이 높다.
(D) 단거리에 적합하다.

해설 남자가 하이브리드 제품을 제안하는 이유를 묻는 문제입니다. 남자가 "making them[hybrid bikes] ideal for short rides"라며 하이브리드 자전거가 단거리 이동에 이상적이라고 하였습니다. 따라서 정답은 (D) It is suited for short distances입니다.

어휘 durable[미 djúərəbəl, 영 dʒúərəbəl] 내구성이 있는, 튼튼한 suited for ~에 적합한, ~에 적당한

03

해석 남자는 다음에 무엇을 할 것 같은가?

(A) 제품을 테스트해본다.
(B) 몇몇 장비를 수리한다.
(C) 건물에 들어간다.
(D) 몇몇 제품을 보여준다.

해설 남자가 다음에 할 일을 묻는 문제입니다. 남자가 "Follow me, and I'll show you our products."라며 자신을 따라오면 제품을 보여 주겠다고 하였습니다. 따라서 정답은 (D) Show some merchandise입니다.

어휘 equipment[ikwípmənt] 장비, 설비 merchandise[미 mə́ːrtʃəndàiz, 영 mə́ːtʃəndàis] 제품, 상품

04-06 🎤 영국식 발음 → 캐나다식 발음

Questions 4-6 refer to the following conversation.

W: Joseph, ⁰⁴you're giving a presentation to the board members today, right? I heard you were asked to explain the new online security procedures at ⊙

their monthly meeting.

M: Right. I'm having trouble preparing for it, though. I want to make copies of some handouts, but ⁰⁵the photocopier isn't working. I'm not sure what the problem is.

W: Oh, that machine will be replaced next Monday. For now, ⁰⁶you should use the photocopier on the ninth floor instead.

M: All right. I'll head up to that floor now. Thanks.

---

give a presentation 보고하다, 발표하다 **board member** 임원
security[sikjúərəti] 보안, 안전
photocopier[미 fóutəkàpiər, 영 fə́utəukɔ̀piə] 복사기
replace[ripléis] 교체하다, 바꾸다 **head**[hed] 가다, 향하다

해석

4-6번은 다음 대화에 관한 문제입니다.

여: Joseph, ⁰⁴당신이 오늘 임원들에게 보고할 예정이죠, 그렇죠? 임원들의 월간 회의에서 새로운 온라인 보안 절차를 설명해 달라는 요청을 받았다고 들었어요.

남: 맞아요. 하지만, 그것을 준비하는 데 곤란을 겪고 있어요. 몇몇 인쇄물을 복사하고 싶은데, ⁰⁵복사기가 작동하지 않아요. 무엇이 문제인지 잘 모르겠어요.

여: 아, 그 기계는 다음 주 월요일에 교체될 거예요. 지금은, ⁰⁶9층에 있는 복사기를 대신 사용하세요.

남: 알겠어요. 지금 그 층으로 가야겠어요. 고마워요.

04

해석 남자는 어떤 행사를 준비하고 있는가?
(A) 사내 세미나
(B) 임원 회의
(C) 자선 행사
(D) 국제 컨퍼런스

해설 남자가 준비하는 행사를 묻는 문제입니다. 여자가 "you're giving a presentation to the board members today, right?"이라며 남자가 오늘 임원들에게 보고할 예정인지 물은 뒤, "I heard you were asked to explain ~ at their monthly meeting."이라며 남자가 임원들의 월간 회의에서 새로운 온라인 보안 절차를 설명해 달라는 요청을 받았다는 것을 들었다고 하였습니다. 따라서 정답은 (B) An executive meeting입니다.

어휘 **executive**[미 igzékjutiv, 영 igzékjətiv] 임원

05

해석 남자는 어떤 문제를 언급하는가?
(A) 서류가 완성되지 않았다.
(B) 기기가 작동하지 않는다.
(C) 회의가 지연되었다.
(D) 직원이 결근했다.

해설 남자가 언급하는 문제점을 묻는 문제입니다. 남자가 "the photocopier isn't working"이라며 복사기가 작동하지 않는다고 하였습니다. 따라서 정답은 (B) A device is not working입니다.

어휘 **incomplete**[ìnkəmplíːt] 완성되지 않은, 불완전한
absent[ǽbsənt] 결근한, 불참한

06

해석 여자는 무엇을 제안하는가?
(A) 추가 용지 주문하기
(B) 관리팀에 전화하기
(C) 다른 장비 사용하기
(D) 기계 다시 켜기

해설 여자가 제안하는 것을 묻는 문제입니다. 여자가 "you should use the photocopier on the ninth floor"라며 9층에 있는 복사기를 사용할 것을 제안하였습니다. 따라서 정답은 (C) Using different equipment입니다.

어휘 **additional**[ədíʃənl] 추가의 **maintenance**[méintənəns] 관리, 유지

07-09 ▣) 캐나다식 발음 → 미국식 발음 → 호주식 발음

Questions 7-9 refer to the following conversation with three speakers.

M1: ⁰⁷Are you prepared for the training session with the new employees tomorrow?

W: Yes. But it's my first time conducting an orientation workshop, and I'm rather nervous.

M2: I've led similar sessions before. So, if you want, I can review the training materials with you after my meeting with our head accountant.

M1: Oh, Kevin. Didn't you hear? ⁰⁸That meeting was canceled since expense reports for the development project aren't ready yet.

M2: I didn't realize that. I have an extra hour, then.

W: Great. ⁰⁹I'll print out my notes for the training right now.

---

training session 교육 **conduct**[kəndʌ́kt] 진행하다, 수행하다
nervous[미 nə́ːrvəs, 영 nə́ːvəs] 긴장되는, 불안한
accountant[əkáuntənt] 회계사 **expense**[ikspéns] 경비, 비용

해석

7-9번은 다음 세 명의 대화에 관한 문제입니다.

남1: ⁰⁷내일 신규 직원들의 교육을 위한 준비가 되었나요?

여: 네. 하지만 오리엔테이션 워크숍을 진행하는 것은 처음이라, 좀 긴장돼요.

남2: 저는 이전에 비슷한 교육을 진행한 적이 있어요. 그래서, 당신이 원한다면, 제가 수석 회계사와의 회의 후에 교육 자료를 함께 검토해 줄 수 있어요.

남1: 아, Kevin. 못 들었어요? 개발 프로젝트를 위한 경비 보고서가 아직 준비되지 않아서 ⁰⁸그 회의는 취소되었어요.

남2: 몰랐어요. 그러면, 저는 한 시간 여유가 생겼네요.

여: 잘됐어요. ⁰⁹교육을 위한 제 노트를 지금 인쇄할게요.

07

해석 화자들은 주로 무엇에 대해 이야기하고 있는가?
(A) 직원 교육
(B) 채용 절차
(C) 회계 시스템
(D) 비용 보고서

해설 대화의 주제를 묻는 문제입니다. 남자 1이 "Are you prepared for the training session with the new employees tomorrow?"라며 내일 신규 직원들의 교육을 위한 준비가 되었는지 물은 뒤, 직원 교육 준비에 관한 내용으로 대화가 이어지고 있습니다. 따라서 정답은 (A) A staff training session입니다.

08

해석 회의에 대해 무엇이 언급되는가?
(A) 발표를 포함할 것이다.
(B) 진행되지 않을 것이다.
(C) 한 시간 넘게 진행될 것이다.
(D) 직원 평가와 관련될 것이다.

해설 회의에 대해 언급되는 것을 묻는 문제입니다. 남자 1이 "That

meeting was canceled"라며 그 회의가 취소되었다고 하였습니다. 따라서 정답은 (B) It will not be taking place입니다.

어휘 concern[미 kənsə́:rn, 영 kənsə́:n] ~에 관련된 것이다, 걱정하다

09

해석 여자는 무엇을 할 것이라고 말하는가?
(A) 노트를 인쇄한다.
(B) 몇몇 회의 참석자들에게 연락한다.
(C) 재정 보고서를 검토한다.
(D) 프로젝트 마감기한을 변경한다.

해설 여자가 다음에 할 일을 묻는 문제입니다. 여자가 "I'll print out my notes ~ right now."라며 노트를 지금 인쇄하겠다고 하였습니다. 따라서 정답은 (A) Print some notes입니다.

10-12 [🔊] 영국식 발음 → 호주식 발음

Questions 10-12 refer to the following conversation.

W: Mr. Carlson, do customers like ¹⁰the items that were added to our menu last Sunday?
M: They do. However, ¹¹some diners have complained that the breakfast items are too expensive.
W: Really? Then maybe we should consider offering discounts on those dishes.
M: Actually, I'm already planning to do that. Starting next Monday, we're doing a daily 50 percent discount on the whole breakfast menu until 11 A.M. ¹²I'd appreciate it if you could go and tell our servers about this change now.
W: ¹²OK. I'll do that. I'll also remind them to inform our diners.

diner[미 dáinər, 영 dáinə] 손님, 식사하는 사람
complain[kəmpléin] 불평하다 remind[rimáind] 상기시키다
inform[미 infɔ́:rm, 영 infɔ́:m] 알리다, 통보하다

해석
10-12번은 다음 대화에 관한 문제입니다.

여: Mr. Carlson, 손님들이 ¹⁰지난주 일요일에 우리 메뉴에 추가된 품목들을 좋아하나요?
남: 좋아해요. 하지만, ¹¹몇몇 손님들은 아침 식사 메뉴들이 너무 비싸다고 불평했어요.
여: 정말이요? 그러면 그 요리들에 할인을 제공하는 걸 고려해봐야 할 것 같네요.
남: 사실, 저는 이미 그렇게 하려고 계획하고 있어요. 다음 주 월요일부터, 우리는 오전 11시까지 모든 아침 식사 메뉴에 50퍼센트의 평일 할인을 제공할 거예요. ¹²당신이 지금 가서 우리 서빙 직원들에게 이 변경 사항에 대해 말씀해 주시면 감사하겠어요.
여: ¹²알겠어요. 그렇게 할게요. 손님들에게 알려야 한다는 것 또한 상기시킬게요.

10

해석 지난주 일요일에 무슨 일이 일어났는가?
(A) 식당이 새롭게 문을 열었다.
(B) 추가 직원이 고용되었다.
(C) 새로운 요리가 이용 가능하게 되었다.
(D) 영업시간이 연장되었다.

해설 지난주 일요일에 일어난 일을 묻는 문제입니다. 여자가 "the items that were added to our menu last Sunday"라며 지난주 일요일에 메뉴에 추가된 품목들이라고 한 것을 통해 새로운 요리들이 이용 가능하게 되었음을 알 수 있습니다. 따라서 정답은 (C) New dishes

became available입니다.

어휘 opening hours 영업시간 extend[iksténd] 연장하다, 확장하다

11

해석 손님들은 무엇에 대해 불평했는가?
(A) 서비스의 질
(B) 이용 가능한 선택권의 수
(C) 영업시간의 길이
(D) 일부 품목들의 가격

해설 손님들이 불평한 것을 묻는 문제입니다. 남자가 "some diners have complained that the breakfast items are too expensive"라며 몇몇 손님들이 아침 식사 메뉴들이 너무 비싸다고 불평했다고 하였습니다. 따라서 정답은 (D) The price of some items입니다.

어휘 quality[미 kwɑ́:ləti, 영 kwɔ́:ləti] 질, 품질

12

해석 다음에 무슨 일이 일어날 것 같은가?
(A) 음식 품목들이 시식될 것이다.
(B) 다른 음료들이 선택될 것이다.
(C) 직원들이 정보를 얻을 것이다.
(D) 저녁 연회가 열릴 것이다.

해설 다음에 일어날 일을 묻는 문제입니다. 남자가 "I'd appreciate it if you ~ tell our servers about this change now."라며 여자에게 지금 서빙 직원들에게 이 변경 사항에 대해 말해 주면 고맙겠다고 하자, 여자가 "OK. I'll do that."이라며 그렇게 하겠다고 하였습니다. 따라서 정답은 (C) Workers will receive information입니다.

어휘 sample[미 sǽmpl, 영 sɑ́:mpl] 시식하다, 시음하다
banquet[bǽŋkwit] 연회, 축하연

13-15 [🔊] 미국식 발음 → 캐나다식 발음

Questions 13-15 refer to the following conversation.

W: Hi, Matt. ¹³I heard that you're attending the Digital Trade Show as a representative of our company. When do you leave for that?
M: It's on May 11, so I'll drive to New York on May 10.
W: Great! Then we'll have plenty of time to update the company Web site with information about our exhibit. ¹⁴Which day works best for you?
M: Actually, I'm not doing anything this afternoon, so ¹⁴let's take care of it today. ¹⁵I'm just going to call a company to book a car for my trip, and then we can get started.

trade show 무역 박람회 representative[rèprizéntətiv] 대표(자)
exhibit[igzíbit] 전시(회) take care of ~을 처리하다

해석
13-15번은 다음 대화에 관한 문제입니다.

여: 안녕하세요, Matt. ¹³당신이 우리 회사 대표로 디지털 무역 박람회에 참석할 것이라고 들었어요. 언제 떠나시나요?
남: 그건 5월 11일에 열려서, 저는 5월 10일에 뉴욕으로 운전해서 갈 거예요.
여: 잘됐네요! 그러면 회사 웹사이트에 우리의 전시에 대한 정보를 업데이트할 시간이 많이 있겠네요. ¹⁴어떤 날이 가장 좋으신가요?
남: 사실, ¹⁴저는 오늘 오후에 아무것도 안 해요, 그러니 ¹⁴오늘 처리해요. ¹⁵지금 출장을 위한 차를 예약하기 위해 업체에 전화할 건데, 그 후에 시작할 수 있어요.

13

해석 남자는 무엇에 참석할 것인가?
(A) 고객 회의
(B) 무역 박람회
(C) 박물관 전시회
(D) 회사 야유회

해설 남자가 참석할 것을 묻는 문제입니다. 여자가 "I heard that you're attending the Digital Trade Show as a representative of our company."라며 남자가 회사 대표로 디지털 무역 박람회에 참석할 것이라고 들었다고 하였습니다. 따라서 정답은 (B) A trade fair입니다.

어휘 trade fair 무역 박람회 retreat[ritrí:t] 야유회

14

해석 남자가 "저는 오늘 오후에 아무것도 안 해요"라고 말할 때 의도하는 것은 무엇인가?
(A) 그는 그의 일정을 확인하지 않았다.
(B) 그는 휴가를 냈다.
(C) 그는 업무를 할 시간이 있다.
(D) 그는 약속을 취소했다.

해설 남자가 하는 말(I'm not doing anything this afternoon)의 의도를 묻는 문제입니다. 여자가 "Which day works best for you?"라며 회사 웹사이트에 정보를 업데이트하기에 어떤 날이 가장 좋은지 묻자, 남자가 "let's take care of it today"라며 오늘 처리하자고 한 것을 통해 남자가 업무를 할 시간이 있다는 것을 전달하려는 의도임을 알 수 있습니다. 따라서 정답은 (C) He has time to work on a task입니다.

15

해석 남자는 다음에 무엇을 할 것 같은가?
(A) 차량을 찾으러 간다.
(B) 대여업체에 연락한다.
(C) 예약을 취소한다.
(D) 서류를 검토한다.

해설 남자가 다음에 할 일을 묻는 문제입니다. 남자가 "I'm just going to call a company to book a car for my trip"이라며 지금 출장을 위한 차를 예약하기 위해 업체에 전화할 것이라고 하였습니다. 따라서 정답은 (B) Contact a rental company입니다.

어휘 rental company 대여업체 look over ~을 검토하다

16-18 [호주식 발음 → 영국식 발음]

Questions 16-18 refer to the following conversation and coupon.

M: Excuse me. 16/17I'd like to purchase one ticket for the concert taking place tomorrow. 17Are there any seats available?

W: I'm afraid 17that particular performance is already sold out. However, 18there are still tickets left for the March 20 show—the day after tomorrow.

M: 18OK. I'll get a ticket for that night in the orchestra section, then. Also, I have a coupon for $10 off a performance at your concert hall, and I'd like to use it. The coupon code is 472A.

W: Hmm . . . That coupon doesn't work in our system. Please double-check that the information on it is valid.

---

performance[미 pərfɔ́:rməns, 영 pəfɔ́:məns] 공연
sold out 표가 매진된 double-check[dʌ̀bltʃék] 다시 확인하다
valid[vǽlid] 정확한, 유효한 expire[미 ikspáiər, 영 ikspáiə] 만료되다

해석

16-18번은 다음 대화와 쿠폰에 관한 문제입니다.

남: 실례합니다. 16/17내일 열리는 연주회 표를 한 장 구매하고 싶은데요. 17가능한 좌석이 있나요?

여: 죄송하지만 17그 공연은 이미 매진되었어요. 하지만, 183월 20일 공연은 아직 표가 남아 있어요—모레네요.

남: 18알겠어요. 그러면, 오케스트라석으로 그날 밤 표를 살게요. 그리고, 저는 이 콘서트홀에서 열리는 공연의 10달러 할인 쿠폰을 가지고 있어서, 그걸 사용하고 싶어요. 쿠폰 코드는 472A예요.

여: 음... 그 쿠폰은 저희 시스템에서 적용되지 않네요. 쿠폰의 정보가 정확한지 다시 한번 확인해 보세요.

쿠폰 코드: 472A

Lyle 콘서트홀
할인 쿠폰

공연 입장권 한 장에 대해 10달러 할인
오케스트라석에만 사용 가능

183월 10일에 만료됨

16

해석 남자는 무엇을 하고 싶어 하는가?
(A) 예약을 변경한다.
(B) 표를 구매한다.
(C) 일정을 확정한다.
(D) 환불을 요청한다.

해설 남자가 하고 싶어 하는 것을 묻는 문제입니다. 남자가 "I'd like to purchase one ticket"이라며 표를 한 장 구매하고 싶다고 하였습니다. 따라서 정답은 (B) Buy a ticket입니다.

어휘 confirm[미 kənfə́:rm, 영 kənfə́:m] 확정하다 refund[rí:fʌnd] 환불

17

해석 여자는 내일 공연에 대해 무엇을 말하는가?
(A) 매진되었다.
(B) 취소되었다.
(C) 무용이 포함되어 있다.
(D) 온라인으로 광고되었다.

해설 여자가 내일 공연에 대해 언급하는 것을 묻는 문제입니다. 남자가 "I'd like to purchase one ticket for the concert taking place tomorrow. Are there any seats available?"이라며 내일 열리는 연주회 표를 한 장 구매하고 싶다며 가능한 좌석이 있는지를 묻자, 여자가 "that particular performance is already sold out"이라며 그 공연은 이미 매진되었다고 하였습니다. 따라서 정답은 (A) It is sold out입니다.

어휘 feature[미 fí:tʃər, 영 fí:tʃə] 포함하다

18

해석 시각 자료를 보아라. 쿠폰은 왜 거부되는가?
(A) 다른 센터를 위한 것이다.
(B) 한 장의 표에만 사용될 수 있다.
(C) 다른 좌석 구역을 위한 것이다.
(D) 이미 만료되었다.

해설 쿠폰이 거부되는 이유를 묻는 문제입니다. 여자가 "there are still tickets left for the March 20 show—the day after tomorrow"라며 모레인 3월 20일 공연은 아직 표가 남아 있다고 하자, 남자가 "OK. I'll get a ticket for that night"이라며 3월 20일 표를 사겠다고 하였으므로, 만료일인 3월 10일이 이미 지났기 때문에 쿠폰이 거부되는 것임을 알 수 있습니다. 따라서 정답은 (D) It has already expired입니다.

어휘 reject[ridʒékt] 거부하다 section[sékʃən] 구역

Course 1 의도 파악 문제

HACKERS PRACTICE ∩ DAY14_02 p.113

01 (A)	02 (D)	03 (A)	04 (B)

01-02 🔊 영국식 발음 → 캐나다식 발음 / 미국식 발음 → 호주식 발음

Questions 1-2 refer to the following conversation.

> W: ⁰¹Would you like to eat at the Indian buffet on 12th Street tonight? It's quite tasty and inexpensive.
> M: How about Gino's Diner in Little Italy? ⁰¹I'd rather get some pasta. Plus, Gino's offers a three-course dinner special for $40 on Fridays.
> W: All right. I get off work at 4 P.M. ⁰²Let's meet up at the café next to Gino's first.
>
> inexpensive[ìnikspénsiv] 저렴한
> three-course dinner 세 코스짜리 정식 get off work 퇴근하다

해석

1-2번은 다음 대화에 관한 문제입니다.

여: ⁰¹오늘 저녁에 12번가에 있는 인도 음식 뷔페에서 식사하시겠어요? 그곳은 꽤 맛있고 저렴해요.

남: 리틀 이탈리아에 있는 Gino's 식당은 어때요? ⁰¹파스타가 먹고 싶어서요. 게다가, Gino's에서는 금요일마다 40달러에 세 코스짜리 특별 정식을 제공하거든요.

여: 좋아요. 저는 오후 4시에 퇴근해요. ⁰²우선 Gino's 식당 옆에 있는 카페에서 만나요.

01

해석 남자가 "리틀 이탈리아에 있는 Gino's 식당은 어때요"라고 말할 때 의도하는 것은 무엇인가?
(A) 그는 제안에 동의하지 않는다.
(B) 그는 여자가 오해하고 있다고 생각한다.
(C) 그는 식당이 문을 닫았다고 생각한다.
(D) 그는 결정을 내릴 수 없다.

해설 남자가 하는 말(How about Gino's Diner in Little Italy)의 의도를 묻는 문제입니다. 여자가 "Would you like to eat at the Indian buffet ~ tonight?"이라며 오늘 저녁에 인도 음식 뷔페에서 식사할 것을 제안하자, 남자가 "I'd rather get some pasta."라며 파스타가 먹고 싶다고 한 뒤 Gino's 식당에서 제공하는 식사에 대해 언급하였습니다. 이를 통해 남자가 여자의 제안에 동의하지 않음을 알 수 있습니다. 따라서 정답은 (A) He disagrees with a suggestion입니다.

어휘 disagree[dìsəgríː] 동의하지 않다
mistaken[mistéikən] 오해한, 잘못 생각하는

02

해석 여자는 무엇을 제안하는가?
(A) 배달 앱 이용하기
(B) 테이크아웃 음식 주문하기
(C) 일찍 퇴근하기
(D) 카페에서 만나기

해설 여자가 제안하는 것을 묻는 문제입니다. 여자가 "Let's meet up at the café next to Gino's first."라며 우선 Gino's 식당 옆에 있는 카페에서 만나자고 제안하는 것임을 알 수 있습니다. 따라서 정답은

(D) Meeting at a café입니다.

어휘 takeout[téikàut] 테이크아웃 음식

03-04 🔊 미국식 발음 → 캐나다식 발음 / 영국식 발음 → 호주식 발음

Questions 3-4 refer to the following conversation.

> W: Jonathan, which worksite are you assigned to today?
> M: Belleview Department Store. I clean the windows there every second Thursday of the month. Why?
> W: Well . . . the manager at Sellers Mall just called. ⁰³He asked me to send someone immediately. There's a construction site nearby, so ⁰³the building's windows are really dusty.
> M: Understood. But ⁰⁴what about Belleview Department Store?
> W: Don't worry about it. ⁰⁴I'll call them and reschedule.
>
> worksite[미 wɔ́ːrksait, 영 wɔ́ːksait] 작업장
> assign[əsáin] 배정하다, 지정하다 immediately[imíːdiətli] 즉시
> construction[kənstrʌ́kʃən] 건설, 건축 site[sait] 현장
> nearby[미 nìərbái, 영 nìəbái] 근처에, 가까이에
> dusty[dʌ́sti] 먼지가 많은, 먼지투성이의

해석

3-4번은 다음 대화에 관한 문제입니다.

여: Jonathan, 당신은 오늘 어느 작업장에 배정되었나요?

남: Belleview 백화점이요. 저는 매월 두 번째 목요일마다 그곳에서 창문을 청소해요. 왜 그러시나요?

여: 그게... Sellers 쇼핑몰의 관리자가 방금 전화했어요. ⁰³그는 저에게 누군가를 즉시 보내줄 것을 요청했어요. 근처에 건설 현장이 있어서, ⁰³그 건물의 창문에 먼지가 굉장히 많대요.

남: 알겠어요. 그런데 ⁰⁴Belleview 백화점은 어떡하죠?

여: 그것에 대해서는 걱정하지 마세요. ⁰⁴제가 그들에게 전화해서 일정을 조정할게요.

03

해석 여자는 왜 "근처에 건설 현장이 있어서"라고 말하는가?
(A) 고객의 요청에 대한 이유를 제공하기 위해
(B) 잠재적인 안전상의 문제를 지적하기 위해
(C) 쇼핑몰의 위치를 나타내기 위해
(D) 작업이 제대로 되지 않았음을 나타내기 위해

해설 여자가 하는 말(There's a construction site nearby)의 의도를 묻는 문제입니다. 여자가 "He[the manager at Sellers Mall] asked me to send someone immediately."라며 Sellers 쇼핑몰의 관리자가 누군가를 즉시 보내줄 것을 요청했다고 한 후, "the building's windows are really dusty"라며 그 건물의 창문에 먼지가 굉장히 많다고 한 말을 통해 여자가 고객의 요청에 대한 이유를 제공하려는 의도임을 알 수 있습니다. 따라서 정답은 (A) To provide the reason for a client request입니다.

어휘 point out ~을 지적하다 potential[pəténʃəl] 잠재적인, 가능성 있는
properly[미 prɑ́ːpərli, 영 prɔ́ːpəli] 제대로, 올바르게

04

해석 여자는 다음에 무엇을 할 것 같은가?
(A) 창문 공급업체를 방문한다.
(B) 백화점에 연락한다.
(C) 청소 작업팀과 만난다.
(D) 작업의 완료를 확인한다.

해설 여자가 다음에 할 일을 묻는 문제입니다. 남자가 "what about

Belleview Department Store?"라며 Belleview 백화점은 어떻게 할지 묻자, 여자가 "I'll call them and reschedule."이라며 백화점에 전화해서 일정을 조정하겠다고 하였습니다. 따라서 정답은 (B) Contact a department store입니다.

어휘 supplier[미 səpláiər, 영 səpláiə] 공급업체
crew[kru:] (함께 일을 하는) 팀 completion[kəmplíːʃən] 완료, 완성

Course 2 추론 문제

HACKERS PRACTICE 🎧 DAY14_04 p.115

01 (C)	02 (A)	03 (A)	04 (D)

01-02 🎧 캐나다식 발음 → 미국식 발음 / 호주식 발음 → 영국식 발음

Questions 1-2 refer to the following conversation.

M: ⁰¹Welcome to Green's Restaurant. Would you like to order now?
W: Yes. Can you tell me what your specials are today?
M: Certainly. We have the chef's recommended grilled fish. And ⁰²we always offer a 25 percent discount on any beverage purchased on Saturdays or Sundays.
W: I'll take the grilled fish to begin with, then, and just a glass of water to drink.

special[spéʃəl] 특별 메뉴, 정식
recommend[rèkəménd] 추천하다, 권하다 beverage[bévəridʒ] 음료

해석

1-2번은 다음 대화에 관한 문제입니다.

남: ⁰¹Green's 레스토랑에 오신 것을 환영합니다. 지금 주문하시겠어요?
여: 네. 오늘 특별 메뉴가 무엇인지 말씀해 주실 수 있나요?
남: 물론입니다. 주방장이 추천하는 생선구이가 있습니다. 그리고 ⁰²저희는 토요일 또는 일요일에 구매하시는 모든 음료에 대해 언제나 25퍼센트 할인을 제공합니다.
여: 그러면, 우선 생선구이로 하고, 마실 것은 그냥 물 한 잔으로 할게요.

01

해석 남자는 누구인 것 같은가?
(A) 요리사
(B) 판매원
(C) 종업원
(D) 디자이너

해설 남자의 신분을 묻는 문제입니다. 남자가 "Welcome to Green's Restaurant. Would you like to order now?"라며 Green's 레스토랑에 온 것을 환영한다고 하며 지금 주문할 것인지 묻는 것을 통해 남자가 종업원임을 알 수 있습니다. 따라서 정답은 (C) A server입니다.

02

해석 남자는 할인에 대해 무엇을 암시하는가?
(A) 평일에는 이용할 수 없다.
(B) 후식에 적용된다.
(C) 대규모 단체만을 위한 것이다.
(D) 쿠폰이 필요하다.

해설 남자가 할인에 대해 암시하는 것을 묻는 문제입니다. 남자가 "we always offer a 25 percent discount on any beverage purchased on Saturdays or Sundays"라며 토요일 또는 일요일에 구매하는 모든 음료에 대해 언제나 25퍼센트 할인을 제공한다고 한

것을 통해 평일에는 할인을 이용할 수 없음을 알 수 있습니다. 따라서 정답은 (A) It is not available on weekdays입니다.

어휘 apply[əplái] 적용되다, 해당되다
require[미 rikwáiər, 영 rikwáiə] 필요하다, 요구하다

03-04 🎧 미국식 발음 → 호주식 발음 / 영국식 발음 → 캐나다식 발음

Questions 3-4 refer to the following conversation.

W: What did you think of Bill's presentation this morning?
M: Oh, ⁰³I didn't realize our menswear department did so well last quarter.
W: Yeah. The suits we introduced were very popular with our customers. ⁰³Sales should increase even more when we launch our new clothing line this spring.
M: That's great. I'm assuming it will be business attire as well?
W: Actually, ⁰⁴it's a collection of casual items . . . like summer shirts and shorts.

menswear[미 ménzwer, 영 ménzweə] 남성복 do well 성공하다, 잘되다
quarter[미 kwɔ́ːrtər, 영 kwɔ́ːtə] 분기
introduce[미 ìntrədjúːs, 영 ìntrədʒúːs] (신제품을) 선보이다, 내놓다
launch[lɔ:ntʃ] 출시하다, 개시하다 business attire 비즈니스 정장
collection[kəlékʃən] (특정 계절용으로 디자인된 의류 등의) 신상품들
casual[kǽʒuəl] 평상복의

해석

3-4번은 다음 대화에 관한 문제입니다.

여: 오늘 아침 Bill의 발표에 대해 어떻게 생각하셨나요?
남: 아, ⁰³저는 지난 분기에 우리 남성복 매장이 그렇게 성공한 줄 몰랐어요.
여: 네. 우리가 선보인 정장들이 고객들에게 매우 인기가 있었어요. 이번 봄에 ⁰³우리가 새로운 의류 라인을 출시하면 매출은 한층 더 증가할 거예요.
남: 좋네요. 그것도 비즈니스 정장인가요?
여: 사실, ⁰⁴그건 평상복 품목의 신상품들이에요... 여름 셔츠와 반바지 같은 것들이요.

03

해석 남성복 매장에 대해 무엇이 암시되는가?
(A) 매출이 증가했다.
(B) 추가적인 직원 교육을 필요로 한다.
(C) 판촉 행사를 주최할 것이다.
(D) 관리자가 최근에 고용되었다.

해설 남성복 매장에 대해 암시되는 것을 묻는 문제입니다. 남자가 "I didn't realize our menswear department did so well"이라며 자신들의 남성복 매장이 그렇게 성공한 줄 몰랐다고 하자, 여자가 "Sales should increase even more when we launch our new clothing line"이라며 새로운 의류 라인을 출시하면 매출이 한층 더 증가할 것이라고 하였습니다. 이를 통해 남성복 매장의 매출이 증가했음을 알 수 있습니다. 따라서 정답은 (A) Its sales have increased입니다.

어휘 additional[ədíʃənəl] 추가적인
promotion[미 prəmóuʃən, 영 prəmə́uʃən] 판촉 행사

04

해석 여자는 새로운 의류 라인에 대해 무엇을 언급하는가?
(A) 최근에 발표되었다.
(B) 다음 달에 구매 가능해질 것이다.
(C) 다양한 비즈니스 의복으로 구성되어 있다.

해커스 토익 700+ (LC+RC+VOCA)

(D) 평상복 품목들을 포함할 것이다.

해설 여자가 새로운 의류 라인에 대해 언급하는 것을 묻는 문제입니다. 여자가 "it[new clothing line]'s a collection of casual items"라며 새로운 의류 라인은 평상복 품목의 신상품들이라고 하였습니다. 따라서 정답은 (D) It will include casual items입니다.

어휘 consist of ~으로 구성되다 outfit[áutfit] 의복, 의상

HACKERS TEST 🎧 DAY14_05   p.116

01 (C)	02 (D)	03 (C)	04 (C)
05 (B)	06 (D)	07 (C)	08 (C)
09 (A)	10 (B)	11 (A)	12 (A)
13 (C)	14 (A)	15 (D)	16 (D)
17 (D)	18 (B)		

01-03 🎧 캐나다식 발음 → 영국식 발음

Questions 1-3 refer to the following conversation.

M: Hello. This is James from Rosewood Office Supplies. I'm very sorry, but your order has been delayed. Our shipping department incorrectly labeled your package, and it was sent to the wrong location.
W: ⁰¹I can't believe that happened. I've been your customer for five years, and the service has always been perfect. Umm . . . When will my delivery arrive, then?
M: Next Tuesday. To apologize, ⁰²we'll e-mail you a code. Enter it when making your next order for a 30 percent discount.
W: OK. I will be out of town on Tuesday, so ⁰³please instruct your driver to leave the order at the front desk instead of my office.
M: Got it. And thank you for understanding.

label[léibəl] (표 등에 정보를) 적다

해석

1-3번은 다음 대화에 관한 문제입니다.

남: 안녕하세요. 저는 Rosewood 사무용품점의 James입니다. 정말 죄송하지만, 고객님의 주문이 지연되었습니다. 저희 배송 부서에서 고객님의 물품 정보를 잘못 적어서, 물품이 다른 장소로 발송되었습니다.
여: ⁰¹그런 일이 일어났다니 믿을 수가 없어요. 저는 5년 동안 그쪽의 고객이었고, 서비스는 항상 완벽했어요. 음... 그럼 제 배송품은 언제 도착하나요?
남: 다음 주 화요일입니다. 사과드리기 위해, ⁰²저희가 이메일로 코드를 보내드리겠습니다. 다음에 주문하실 때 30퍼센트 할인을 위해 그것을 입력하시면 됩니다.
여: 알겠어요. 제가 화요일에 시외에 있을 거라, ⁰³배송 기사님에게 주문품을 제 사무실 대신에 프런트에 맡겨달라고 해주세요.
남: 알겠습니다. 그리고 이해해주셔서 감사합니다.

01

해설 여자는 왜 "서비스는 항상 완벽했어요"라고 말하는가?
(A) 변경 사항을 설명하기 위해
(B) 업체를 추천하기 위해
(C) 놀라움을 표하기 위해
(D) 감사를 나타내기 위해

해설 여자가 하는 말(the service has always been perfect)의 의도를

묻는 문제입니다. 여자가 "I can't believe that happened."라며 그런 일이 일어났다니 믿을 수가 없다고 한 말을 통해 여자가 완벽했던 서비스에 문제가 일어난 것에 대해 놀라움을 표하려는 의도임을 알 수 있습니다. 따라서 정답은 (C) To express surprise입니다.

어휘 surprise[미 sərpráiz, 영 səpráiz] 놀라움, 놀라운 사건
gratitude[미 grǽtitùːd, 영 grǽtitjùːd] 감사

02

해석 남자에 따르면, 여자는 무엇을 받을 것인가?
(A) 전액 환불
(B) 품질 보증 카드
(C) 견본 세트
(D) 할인 코드

해설 여자가 받을 것을 묻는 문제입니다. 남자가 "we'll e-mail you a code. Enter it ~ for a 30 percent discount"라며 이메일로 코드를 보내줄 것이니 30퍼센트 할인을 위해 그것을 입력하면 된다고 하였습니다. 따라서 정답은 (D) A discount code입니다.

어휘 warranty[미 wɔ́ːrənti, 영 wɔ́rənti] 품질 보증

03

해석 여자는 남자에게 무엇을 해달라고 요청하는가?
(A) 배송일을 정한다.
(B) 추가 제품을 보낸다.
(C) 배송 위치를 변경한다.
(D) 연락처 정보를 제공한다.

해설 여자가 남자에게 요청하는 것을 묻는 문제입니다. 여자가 "please instruct your driver to leave the order at the front desk instead of my office"라며 배송 기사에게 주문품을 사무실 대신에 프런트에 맡겨달라고 해달라고 요청하였습니다. 따라서 정답은 (C) Change a delivery location입니다.

04-06 🎧 캐나다식 발음 → 미국식 발음

Questions 4-6 refer to the following conversation.

M: How are consumers reacting to ⁰⁴the advertisements that our firm created for Boston Camera Company?
W: The response has been mixed. Consumers seem happy with our magazine advertisements. But they do not like the television commercials, unfortunately.
M: Hmm . . . We should come up with a solution before reporting back to our client. ⁰⁵We'll need everyone to be here to brainstorm some ideas as soon as we can.
W: Right, but . . . a lot of people are out of the office at the moment. ⁰⁵Maybe we can arrange it for next week?
M: Ah, OK. In that case, ⁰⁶can you reserve a conference room for Monday?
W: ⁰⁶I'm on it.

consumer[미 kənsúːmər, 영 kənsjúːmə] 소비자, 고객
response[미 rispáːns, 영 rispɔ́ns] 반응, 대응
mixed[mikst] (의견·생각 등이) 엇갈리는, 뒤섞인
commercial[미 kəmə́ːrʃəl, 영 kəmə́ːʃəl] 광고
brainstorm[미 bréinstɔːrm, 영 bréinstɔːm] 아이디어를 생각해내다, 브레인스토밍하다 at the moment 지금

4-6번은 다음 대화에 관한 문제입니다.

남: ⁰⁴우리 회사가 Boston 카메라 회사를 위해 만든 광고에 대해 소비자들이 어떻게 반응하고 있나요?

여: 반응은 엇갈리고 있어요. 소비자들은 우리의 잡지 광고에 만족한 것 같아요. 하지만 유감스럽게도, 그들은 텔레비전 광고는 좋아하지 않아요.

남: 음... 고객에게 다시 보고하기 전에 해결책을 생각해내야겠네요. ⁰⁵할 수 있는 한 빨리 모두가 여기에 모여서 몇 가지 아이디어를 생각해내게 해야겠어요.

여: 네, 그런데... 지금 많은 사람들이 사무실 밖에 나가 있어요. ⁰⁵혹시 우리가 그걸 다음 주에 하기로 해도 될까요?

남: 아, 알겠어요. 그런 경우라면, ⁰⁶월요일로 회의실을 예약해주시겠어요?

여: ⁰⁶그럴게요.

04

해석 화자들은 어디에서 일하는 것 같은가?
(A) 출판사에서
(B) 전자기기 소매점에서
(C) 마케팅 회사에서
(D) 카메라 제조업체에서

해설 화자들이 일하는 장소를 묻는 문제입니다. 남자가 "the advertisements that our firm created"라며 자신들의 회사가 만든 광고라고 한 것을 통해 화자들이 마케팅 회사에서 근무한다는 것을 알 수 있습니다. 따라서 정답은 (C) At a marketing firm입니다.

어휘 retailer[미 rí:teilər, 영 rí:teilə] 소매점
manufacturer[미 mæ̀njufǽktʃərər, 영 mæ̀njəfǽktʃərə] 제조업체

05

해석 여자가 "지금 많은 사람들이 사무실 밖에 나가 있어요"라고 말할 때 의도하는 것은 무엇인가?
(A) 화상 회의가 더 나은 방안이다.
(B) 회의가 나중으로 일정이 잡혀야 한다.
(C) 고객의 요청이 승인될 수 없다.
(D) 더 많은 고객 의견이 필요하다.

해설 여자가 하는 말(a lot of people are out of the office at the moment)의 의도를 묻는 문제입니다. 남자가 "We'll need everyone to be here to brainstorm some ideas as soon as we can."이라며 할 수 있는 한 빨리 모두가 여기에 모여서 몇 가지 아이디어를 생각해내게 해야겠다고 하자, 여자가 "Maybe we can arrange it for next week?"이라며 혹시 그걸 다음 주에 하기로 해도 될지 물은 것을 통해 지금이 아니라 나중에 모여서 아이디어를 내야 한다는 것을 전달하려는 의도임을 알 수 있습니다. 따라서 정답은 (B) A meeting should be scheduled later입니다.

어휘 video conference 화상 회의, 영상 회의
grant[미 grænt, 영 grɑːnt] 승인하다, 허가하다

06

해석 여자는 다음에 무엇을 할 것 같은가?
(A) 발표를 한다.
(B) 동료에게 연락한다.
(C) 설문 조사를 한다.
(D) 예약을 한다.

해설 여자가 다음에 할 일을 묻는 문제입니다. 남자가 "can you reserve a conference room for Monday?"라며 월요일로 회의실을 예약해 달라고 하자, 여자가 "I'm on it."이라며 그러겠다고 하였습니다. 따라서 정답은 (D) Make a reservation입니다.

Questions 7-9 refer to the following conversation.

> M: Did you receive the e-mail with the résumés from the marketing department applicants? We'll be holding interviews starting tomorrow.
>
> W: Actually, ⁰⁷I've been having trouble accessing my company e-mail this morning. So I haven't had a chance to review them yet. ⁰⁸Could you print them out for me?
>
> M: Sure. I'll do that right now so that you can take a look at the documents. ⁰⁹They shouldn't take too long to read.
>
> W: OK. I'll read them over once I get back from lunch.
>
> M: That'd be great.

résumé[미 rézumei, 영 rézjuːmei] 이력서
applicant[ǽplikənt] 지원자, 신청자 **access**[ǽkses] 접속하다, 접근하다

해석

7-9번은 다음 대화에 관한 문제입니다.

남: 마케팅 부서 지원자들에게서 온 이력서를 포함한 이메일을 받으셨나요? 우리는 내일부터 면접을 할 거예요.

여: 사실, ⁰⁷오늘 아침에 회사 이메일에 접속하는 데 문제가 있었어요. 그래서 저는 아직 그것들을 검토할 기회가 없었어요. ⁰⁸제게 그것들을 인쇄해 주실 수 있나요?

남: 그럼요. 당신이 서류들을 살펴볼 수 있도록 지금 바로 그렇게 할게요. ⁰⁹읽는 데 시간이 아주 오래 걸리지는 않을 거예요.

여: 그렇군요. 점심 식사를 하고 돌아와서 그것들을 읽을게요.

남: 좋아요.

07

해석 여자는 어떤 문제를 언급하는가?
(A) 지원자가 시간이 되지 않는다.
(B) 인쇄기가 제대로 작동하지 않는다.
(C) 계정에 접속할 수 없다.
(D) 주문이 보류되었다.

해설 여자가 언급하는 문제점을 묻는 문제입니다. 여자가 "I've been having trouble accessing my company e-mail this morning"이라며 오늘 아침에 회사 이메일에 접속하는 데 문제가 있었다고 하였습니다. 따라서 정답은 (C) An account is inaccessible입니다.

어휘 malfunction[mælfʌ́ŋkʃən] 제대로 작동하지 않다
inaccessible[ìnəksésəbl] 접속할 수 없는 on hold 보류된, 연기된

08

해석 여자는 남자에게 무엇을 해달라고 요청하는가?
(A) 이메일을 전송한다.
(B) 면접에 참석한다.
(C) 몇몇 서류를 출력한다.
(D) 지원자에게 연락한다.

해설 여자가 남자에게 요청하는 것을 묻는 문제입니다. 여자가 "Could you print them[résumés] out for me?"라며 남자에게 이력서를 인쇄해 달라고 요청하였습니다. 따라서 정답은 (C) Print out some documents입니다.

어휘 forward[미 fɔ́ːrwərd, 영 fɔ́ːwəd] 전송하다

09

해석 남자는 서류에 대해 무엇을 암시하는가?
(A) 간결하다.

PART 3

한 권으로 끝내는 해커스 토익 700+ (LC+RC+VOCA)

(B) 오류가 있다.
(C) 수정되었다.
(D) 이해하기 어렵다.

해설 남자가 서류에 대해 암시하는 것을 묻는 문제입니다. 남자가 "They[documents] shouldn't take too long to read."라며 서류들을 읽는 데 시간이 아주 오래 걸리지는 않을 것이라고 한 것을 통해 서류들이 간결하다는 것을 알 수 있습니다. 따라서 정답은 (A) They are brief입니다.

어휘 brief[briːf] 간결한, 짧은

10-12 [3ᴹ] 영국식 발음 → 캐나다식 발음 → 호주식 발음

Questions 10-12 refer to the following conversation with three speakers.

W: Carl, something's wrong with the factory's main conveyor belt. It's moving very slowly.

M1: Again? The same thing happened before. ¹⁰Mark, didn't you call the technician last week?

M2: ¹⁰I did. The speed dial isn't working properly. And the replacement parts for it won't arrive until 5 P.M. today.

W: We have a major order due in next week. And tomorrow is a national holiday. ¹¹Even if we get the machinery operating properly tonight, our production levels are going to be affected.

M1: I know. Um . . . Is there anything we can do to produce enough units in time?

W: ¹²We'll probably need to ask our employees to work this weekend.

M2: Yes, I think so too.

---

technician[tekníʃən] 기술자, 전문가
properly[미 prάːpərli, 영 prɔ́ːpərli] 제대로, 적절히
replacement[ripléismənt] 교체, 대체
national holiday 국가의 공휴일, 국경일
operate[미 άːpəreit, 영 ɔ́pəreit] 작동하다, 조종하다
affect[əfékt] 영향을 미치다, 작용하다

해석

10-12번은 다음 세 명의 대화에 관한 문제입니다.

여: Carl, 공장의 가장 큰 컨베이어 벨트에 무언가 문제가 있어요. 그것은 아주 느리게 움직이고 있어요.

남1: 또 그런가요? 이전에 같은 일이 있었어요. ¹⁰Mark, 당신이 지난주에 기술자에게 전화하지 않았나요?

남2: ¹⁰했었어요. 속도 조절 장치가 제대로 작동하지 않고 있어요. 그리고 그것의 교체 부품은 오늘 오후 5시가 되어서야 도착할 거예요.

여: 우리는 다음 주에 마감인 대량 주문이 있어요. 그리고 내일은 공휴일이에요. ¹¹비록 우리가 그 기계를 오늘 밤에 제대로 작동하게 하더라도, 우리의 생산량이 영향을 받을 거예요.

남1: 맞아요. 음... 우리가 시간에 맞춰서 충분한 양을 생산하기 위해 할 수 있는 무언가가 있을까요?

여: ¹²우리는 아마 직원들에게 이번 주말에 근무해달라고 요청해야 할 거예요.

남2: 네, 저도 그렇게 생각해요.

10

해설 Mark는 왜 지난주에 기술자에게 전화했는가?
(A) 정전이 생산을 중단시켰다.
(B) 장비 하나가 제대로 작동하는 것을 멈췄다.
(C) 몇몇 정기 점검이 예정되어 있었다.

(D) 몇몇 공장 기계가 잘못 설치되었다.

해설 Mark가 지난주에 기술자에게 전화한 이유를 묻는 문제입니다. 남자 1이 "Mark, didn't you call the technician last week?"라며 Mark에게 지난주에 기술자에게 전화하지 않았는지 묻자, 남자 2가 "I did. The speed dial isn't working properly."라며 자신이 전화했고 속도 조절 장치가 제대로 작동하지 않고 있다고 하였습니다. 따라서 정답은 (B) A piece of equipment stopped functioning properly입니다.

어휘 power outage 정전 function[fʌ́ŋkʃən] (제대로) 작동하다 maintenance[méintənəns] 점검, 정비

11

해석 여자가 "그리고 내일은 공휴일이에요"라고 말할 때 의도하는 것은 무엇인가?
(A) 주문이 지연될 수도 있다.
(B) 축하 행사가 열릴 수도 있다.
(C) 수리가 필요하지 않을 수도 있다.
(D) 배송이 되지 않을 수도 있다.

해설 여자가 하는 말(And tomorrow is a national holiday)의 의도를 묻는 문제입니다. 여자가 "Even if we get the machinery operating properly tonight, our production levels are going to be affected."라며 비록 그 기계를 오늘 밤에 제대로 작동하게 하더라도 생산량이 영향을 받을 것이라고 한 것을 통해 여자가 주문이 지연될 수도 있음을 전달하는 의도임을 알 수 있습니다. 따라서 정답은 (A) An order may be delayed입니다.

12

해석 여자에 따르면, 직원들은 무엇을 해야 할 수도 있는가?
(A) 추가 시간을 근무한다.
(B) 점검을 한다.
(C) 다른 기기를 이용한다.
(D) 기술자에게 연락한다.

해설 직원들이 해야 할 수도 있는 것을 묻는 문제입니다. 여자가 "We'll probably need to ask our employees to work this weekend."라며 아마 직원들에게 이번 주말에 근무해달라고 요청해야 할 것이라고 하였습니다. 따라서 정답은 (A) Work extra hours입니다.

어휘 inspection[inspékʃən] 점검, 검사

13-15 [3ᴹ] 영국식 발음 → 호주식 발음

Questions 13-15 refer to the following conversation.

W: Good afternoon. ¹³Thank you for visiting Wellsburg Dry Cleaner's. What can I help you with?

M: I'm wondering if you can clean leather goods. I have a leather jacket here that I got an ink stain on last week. Do you think it can be removed?

W: That shouldn't be a problem. But ¹⁴I won't be able to get it done today. Fridays are always really busy here. However, ¹⁴I can get to it once we open again on Monday. If you're fine with that, ¹⁵I can call you as soon as I've finished.

M: I'm not in a hurry to get it back, so I don't mind waiting a few days.

---

dry cleaner 세탁소, 세탁업체 leather[미 léðər, 영 léðə] 가죽의
goods[gudz] 제품, 물품 stain[stein] 얼룩 remove[rimúːv] 제거하다

해석

13-15번은 다음 대화에 관한 문제입니다.

여: 안녕하세요. ¹³Wellsburg 세탁소를 방문해 주셔서 감사합니다. 무엇을 도와드릴까요?

남: 혹시 가죽 제품을 세탁해주실 수 있는지 알고 싶어요. 여기 지난주에 잉크 얼룩이 묻은 가죽 재킷이 있어요. 얼룩이 제거될 수 있을까요?

여: 어렵지 않을 것 같아요. 하지만 ¹⁴오늘 해드릴 수는 없을 거예요. 이곳은 금요일에 항상 매우 바쁘거든요. 하지만, ¹⁴월요일에 다시 문을 열면 해드릴 수 있어요. 만약 그게 괜찮으시다면, ¹⁵제가 끝내자마자 전화해 드릴게요.

남: 저는 그것을 빨리 돌려받아야 하는 것은 아니어서, 며칠 기다리는 것은 괜찮아요.

13

해석 이 대화는 어디에서 일어나는 것 같은가?
(A) 가정용품점에서
(B) 우체국에서
(C) 세탁 시설에서
(D) 옷 가게에서

해설 대화가 이루어지고 있는 장소를 묻는 문제입니다. 여자가 "Thank you for visiting Wellsburg Dry Cleaner's."라며 Wellsburg 세탁소에 방문해줘서 감사하다고 하였습니다. 따라서 정답은 (C) At a laundry facility입니다.

어휘 home goods 가정용품   laundry facility 세탁 시설

14

해석 업체에 대해 무엇이 암시되는가?
(A) 주말에는 문을 닫는다.
(B) 금요일마다 늦게까지 문을 연다.
(C) 새로운 직원을 고용할 것이다.
(D) 여러 개의 지점이 있다.

해설 업체에 대해 암시되는 것을 묻는 문제입니다. 여자가 "I won't be able to get it done today. Fridays are always really busy here."라며 여자의 업체는 금요일에 항상 매우 바쁘기 때문에 오늘 해줄 수는 없다고 한 뒤, "I can get to it once we open again on Monday"라며 월요일에 다시 문을 열면 해줄 수 있다고 하였습니다. 이를 통해 업체가 주말에는 문을 닫음을 알 수 있습니다. 따라서 정답은 (A) It is closed on weekends입니다.

15

해석 여자는 무엇을 해주겠다고 제안하는가?
(A) 관리자에게 이야기한다.
(B) 주문품을 배달한다.
(C) 제품을 설명한다.
(D) 고객에게 연락한다.

해설 여자가 해주겠다고 제안하는 것을 묻는 문제입니다. 여자가 "I can call you as soon as I've finished"라며 끝내자마자 남자에게 전화해 주겠다고 하였습니다. 따라서 정답은 (D) Contact a customer입니다.

어휘 demonstrate[démənstrèit] 설명하다, 보여주다

16-18 [3제] 미국식 발음 → 캐나다식 발음

Questions 16-18 refer to the following conversation.

W: This is *In-Depth Conversations*. I'm Sujin Roberts. Our guest is ¹⁶Benjamin Baxter, who has published a book titled *Capturing Attention*.

M: Thanks for having me, Ms. Roberts.

W: Your book has a lot of great marketing advice our listeners can learn from. ¹⁷What is your most important tip for business owners?   ⊙

M: Well, most importantly, you need to have something great to sell. ¹⁷You should use most of your energy to develop your product.

W: I see. What's the best place to advertise?

M: TV still gets the most viewers—by far. But ¹⁸it's not always cost-effective. I find it's more useful to focus on social media campaigns, which you can do with a much smaller budget.

---

publish[pʌ́bliʃ] 출간하다, 발행하다
cost-effective[미 kɔ̀ːstiféktiv, 영 kɔ̀stiféktiv] 비용 효율이 높은, 경제적인
campaign[kæmpéin] 광고, 조직적 활동   budget[bʌ́dʒit] 예산

해석

16-18번은 다음 대화에 관한 문제입니다.

여: *In-Depth Conversations*입니다. 저는 Sujin Roberts입니다. 저희 초대손님은 ¹⁶Benjamin Baxter이고, *Capturing Attention*이란 제목의 책을 출간하셨습니다.

남: 저를 초대해주셔서 감사합니다, Ms. Roberts.

여: 당신의 책에는 저희 청취자들이 배울 수 있는 많은 좋은 마케팅 조언이 있어요. ¹⁷사업체 소유주들을 위한 당신의 가장 중요한 조언은 무엇인가요?

남: 음, 무엇보다도, 여러분은 판매하기에 좋은 무언가가 있어야 합니다. ¹⁷여러분들의 에너지의 대부분을 제품을 발전시키는 데 써야 합니다.

여: 그렇군요. 광고를 하기에 가장 좋은 곳은 어디일까요?

남: 지금까지는 여전히 TV가 보는 사람들이 가장 많습니다. 하지만 ¹⁸그것이 항상 비용 효율이 높은 것은 아닙니다. 저는 훨씬 더 적은 예산으로 할 수 있는 소셜 미디어 광고에 중점을 두는 것이 좀 더 실용적이라고 생각합니다.

16

해석 Benjamin Baxter는 누구인가?
(A) 교수
(B) 편집자
(C) 임원
(D) 저자

해설 Benjamin Baxter의 신분을 묻는 문제입니다. 여자가 "Benjamin Baxter, who has published a book"이라며 Benjamin Baxter가 책을 출간했다고 한 것을 통해 Benjamin Baxter가 책의 저자임을 알 수 있습니다. 따라서 정답은 (D) An author입니다.

어휘 executive[igzékjətiv] 임원, 간부

17

해석 남자에 따르면, 사업체 소유주들을 위한 가장 중요한 조언은 무엇인가?
(A) 광고 예산 늘리기
(B) 제품을 더 낮은 가격에 제공하기
(C) 빈번한 고객 설문조사 하기
(D) 제품을 개선하는 것에 집중하기

해설 사업체 소유주들을 위한 가장 중요한 조언을 묻는 문제입니다. 여자가 "What is your most important tip for business owners?"라며 사업체 소유주들을 위한 가장 중요한 조언이 무엇인지 묻자, 남자가 "You should use most of your energy to develop your product."라며 에너지의 대부분을 제품을 발전시키는 데 써야 한다고 하였습니다. 따라서 정답은 (D) Focusing on improving products입니다.

어휘 increase[inkríːs] 늘리다, 인상되다   frequent[fríːkwənt] 빈번한, 잦은   improve[imprúːv] 개선하다, 향상시키다

18

해석 소셜 미디어 광고에 대해 무엇이 암시되는가?
(A) 더 적은 수의 높은 연령대의 고객들을 끌어모은다.

(B) 광고의 다른 형태들보다 더 저렴하다.
(C) 텔레비전 마케팅보다 더 많은 노력을 필요로 한다.
(D) 회사를 더 인상적이게 만들지 않는다.

해설 소셜 미디어 광고에 대해 암시되는 것을 묻는 문제입니다. 남자가
"it[TV]'s not always cost-effective. ~ it's more useful to focus
on social media campaigns, which you can do with a much
smaller budget."이라며 TV가 항상 비용 효율이 높은 것은 아니고
훨씬 더 적은 예산으로 할 수 있는 소셜 미디어 광고에 중점을 두는 것
이 좀 더 실용적이라고 하였습니다. 이를 통해 소셜 미디어 광고가 TV
광고 등의 다른 광고들보다 더 저렴함을 알 수 있습니다. 따라서 정
답은 (B) They are cheaper than other forms of advertising입니
다.

어휘 effort[미 éfərt, 영 éfət] 노력, 수고
memorable[mémərəbəl] 인상적인, 기억할 만한

DAY 15 세부 사항 관련 문제 5

Course 1 시각 자료 문제 1 (표 및 그래프)

HACKERS PRACTICE ∩ DAY15_02   p.120

| 01 (B) | 02 (C) | 03 (C) | 04 (C) |
| 05 (B) | 06 (D) | 07 (B) | 08 (B) |

01-02 [3세] 캐나다식 발음 → 영국식 발음 / 호주식 발음 → 미국식 발음

Questions 1-2 refer to the following conversation and
graph.

M: ⁰¹Are the slides prepared for Tuesday's sales
strategy presentation?
W: Not yet. When ⁰¹I was working on them this
morning, I realized that the monthly electronics
sales figures are inaccurate.
M: So, the graph you showed me this morning has an
error?
W: That's right. ⁰²Our lowest sales figure on the graph,
which is $14,000, is actually incorrect. I'm revising
the numbers now.

strategy[strǽtədʒi] 전략, 방법
electronics[미 ìlektrá:niks, 영 èlektrɔ́niks] 전자제품, 전자기기
sales figures 매출액
inaccurate[미 inǽkjərit, 영 inǽkjərət] 부정확한, 틀린

해석
1-2번은 다음 대화와 그래프에 관한 문제입니다.

남: ⁰¹화요일의 판매 전략 발표를 위한 슬라이드가 준비되었나요?
여: 아직이요. ⁰¹오늘 오전에 그것들을 작업하고 있을 때, 월별 전자제품
매출액이 부정확하다는 것을 알았어요.
남: 그러면, 오늘 아침에 당신이 제게 보여준 그래프에 오류가 있다는 건가요?
여: 맞아요. ⁰²그래프에 있는 우리의 가장 낮은 매출액 14,000달러는 사실 부
정확해요. 제가 지금 수치를 수정하고 있어요.

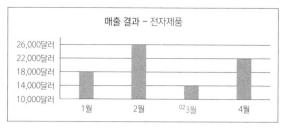

매출 결과 – 전자제품

01

해석 여자는 오늘 오전에 무엇을 했는가?
(A) 재정 보고서를 제출했다.
(B) 발표 자료를 작업했다.
(C) 예산안을 만들었다.
(D) 매출 목표를 검토했다.

해설 여자가 오늘 오전에 한 일을 묻는 문제입니다. 남자가 "Are the slides
prepared for ~ presentation?"이라며 발표를 위한 슬라이드가 준
비되었는지 묻자, 여자가 "I was working on them[slides] this
morning"이라며 오늘 오전에 슬라이드를 작업하고 있었다고 하였습니
다. 따라서 정답은 (B) Worked on a presentation입니다.

어휘 submit[səbmít] 제출하다, 제시하다   financial[fainǽnʃəl] 재정의, 금융의
budget[bʌ́dʒit] 예산(안)

02

해석 시각 자료를 보아라. 어느 달의 매출 결과가 부정확한가?
(A) 1월
(B) 2월
(C) 3월
(D) 4월

해설 매출 결과가 부정확한 달을 묻는 문제입니다. 여자가 "Our lowest
sales figure on the graph, which is $14,000, is actually
incorrect."라며 그래프에 있는 가장 낮은 매출액 14,000달러가
사실 부정확하다고 하였으므로, 매출액이 14,000달러인 3월의 결과
가 부정확하다는 것을 그래프에서 알 수 있습니다. 따라서 정답은 (C)
March입니다.

03-04 [3세] 호주식 발음 → 영국식 발음 / 캐나다식 발음 → 미국식 발음

Questions 3-4 refer to the following conversation and table.

M: Hi, Janet. ⁰³Are you ready for the interviews
tomorrow? We need to hire a great instructor for
our cooking academy.
W: Yes. I was just looking over the applicants'
résumés. We've got several qualified chefs to
choose from.
M: That's true. Oh, before I forget . . . I need to revise
the schedule. The applicant who specializes in
Italian food will come in right after lunch. As a
result, ⁰⁴all the other afternoon appointments have
been pushed back an hour.

instructor[미 instrʌ́ktər, 영 instrʌ́ktə] 강사, 교관
applicant[ǽplikənt] 지원자, 신청자
résumé[미 rézumèi, 영 rézju:mei] 이력서
qualified[미 kwáləfàid, 영 kwɔ́lifaid] 적합한, 자격 있는
specialize in ~을 전문으로 하다
push back (회의 등의 시간·날짜를 뒤로) 미루다

해석
3-4번은 다음 대화와 표에 관한 문제입니다.

남: 안녕하세요, Janet. ⁰³내일 면접을 위한 준비가 되었나요? 우리 요리 학원을 위해 훌륭한 강사를 고용해야 해요.

여: 네. 저는 막 지원자들의 이력서를 검토하고 있었어요. 선택할 수 있는 몇몇 적합한 요리사들이 있네요.

남: 맞아요. 아, 제가 잊어버리기 전에 말씀드리자면... 일정표를 수정해야 해요. 이탈리아 음식을 전문으로 하는 지원자는 점심시간 직후에 올 거예요. 그래서, ⁰⁴모든 오후 약속은 한 시간 뒤로 미뤄졌어요.

이름	시간	전문
Robert Como	오전 10시-오전 10시 50분	이탈리아 음식
Janet Durand	오전 11시-오전 11시 50분	프랑스 음식
점심시간		
⁰⁴Susan Mori	오후 1시-오후 1시 50분	일본 음식
Daniel Chavez	오후 2시-오후 2시 50분	멕시코 음식

03

해석 화자들은 주로 무엇에 대해 이야기하고 있는가?
(A) 출장 연회업체 선택하기
(B) 요리 강좌 일정 변경하기
(C) 신규 직원 찾기
(D) 학원 강사 교육하기

해설 대화의 주제를 묻는 문제입니다. 남자가 "Are you ready for the interviews tomorrow? We need to hire a great instructor"라며 여자에게 내일 면접을 위한 준비가 되었냐고 물으며 훌륭한 강사를 고용해야 한다고 한 뒤, 면접에 관한 내용으로 대화가 이어지고 있습니다. 따라서 정답은 (C) Finding a new employee입니다.

어휘 catering[kéitəriŋ] 출장 연회업

04

해석 시각 자료를 보아라. 화자들은 오후 2시에 누구를 만날 것인가?
(A) Robert Como
(B) Janet Durand
(C) Susan Mori
(D) Daniel Chavez

해설 화자들이 오후 2시에 만날 사람을 묻는 문제입니다. 남자가 "all the other afternoon appointments have been pushed back an hour"라며 모든 오후 약속이 한 시간 뒤로 미뤄졌다고 하였으므로, 화자들이 오후 1시에 만나기로 되어 있던 Susan Mori를 오후 2시에 만날 것임을 표에서 알 수 있습니다. 따라서 정답은 (C) Susan Mori입니다.

05-06 🎧 미국식 발음 → 호주식 발음 / 영국식 발음 → 캐나다식 발음

Questions 5-6 refer to the following conversation and graph.

W: Steven, there have been multiple customer complaints about our most recent smartphone model. It's a bit concerning.
M: Yeah. ⁰⁵The problem is the last software update. The number of complaints has increased for two months since its release. I'm reviewing this summary of the new software features to figure out which one might be causing the issues.
W: Hmm . . . I'd better help out to speed things up. ⁰⁶Could you e-mail me a copy of that document?
M: Sure thing.

multiple[미 mʌ́ltəpl, 영 mʌ́ltipl] 많은, 다수의
concern[미 kənsə́ːrn, 영 kənsə́ːn] 걱정스럽게 하다, 우려하게 하다
release[rilíːs] 출시, 발매 feature[미 fíːtʃər, 영 fíːtʃə] 기능, 특징
figure out ~을 알아내다, ~을 생각해내다 issue[íʃuː] 문제, 쟁점

해석
5-6번은 다음 대화와 그래프에 관한 문제입니다.

여: Steven, 우리의 최신 스마트폰 모델에 대한 많은 고객 불만이 있었어요. 조금 걱정스럽네요.

남: 맞아요. ⁰⁵문제는 마지막 소프트웨어 업데이트예요. 그것의 출시 이후 두 달 동안 불만 건수가 증가했어요. 저는 어떤 기능이 문제를 일으키고 있는 것인지 알아내기 위해 새로운 소프트웨어의 기능들의 요약본을 검토하고 있어요.

여: 음... 빨리 끝내려면 저도 도와드리는 게 좋겠네요. ⁰⁶그 서류 한 부를 제게 이메일로 보내 주실 수 있나요?

남: 물론이죠.

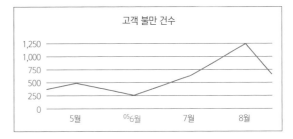

고객 불만 건수

05

해석 시각 자료를 보아라. 마지막 소프트웨어 업데이트는 언제 출시되었는가?
(A) 5월
(B) 6월
(C) 7월
(D) 8월

해설 마지막 소프트웨어 업데이트가 출시된 시기를 묻는 문제입니다. 남자가 "The problem is the last software update."라며 문제는 마지막 소프트웨어 업데이트라고 한 뒤, "The number of complaints has increased for two months since its release."라며 그것의 출시 이후 두 달 동안 불만 건수가 증가했다고 하였으므로, 마지막 소프트웨어 업데이트가 6월에 출시되었음을 그래프에서 알 수 있습니다. 따라서 정답은 (B) June입니다.

06

해석 여자는 남자에게 무엇을 해달라고 요청하는가?
(A) 몇몇 고객들에게 연락한다.
(B) 기능을 변경한다.
(C) 의견을 검토한다.
(D) 보고서를 보낸다.

해설 여자가 남자에게 요청하는 것을 묻는 문제입니다. 여자가 "Could you e-mail me a copy of that document?"라며 서류 한 부를 이메일로 보내 달라고 요청하였습니다. 따라서 정답은 (D) Send a report입니다.

07-08 🎧 캐나다식 발음 → 미국식 발음 / 호주식 발음 → 영국식 발음

Questions 7-8 refer to the following conversation and list.

M: Did you order the chairs for the new staff lounge?
W: I did, but ⁰⁷the chairs we chose are almost out of stock. We need 10, but they don't have that many in their inventory right now.
M: That's unfortunate. I guess we'll just have to wait for them to be restocked, right?
W: Well, they'll receive more chairs next Wednesday and deliver them on Thursday. So, we can finish setting up the lounge on Friday as planned.
M: Great. Then ⁰⁸can you notify the staff that the lounge will be open on Monday? ○

W: [08]I'll make an announcement now.

lounge[laundʒ] 휴게실   out of stock 재고가 없는
inventory[미 ínvəntɔ̀:ri, 영 ínvəntəri] 재고
restock[미 rì:stɑ́:k, 영 ri:stɔ́k] 다시 채우다   set up ~을 마련하다

해석
7-8번은 다음 대화와 표에 관한 문제입니다.

남: 새로운 직원 휴게실을 위한 의자들을 주문했나요?
여: 네, 하지만 [07]우리가 고른 의자는 재고가 거의 없어요. 우리는 10개가 필
요한데, 그들은 현재 재고에 그만큼 많이 가지고 있지 않아요.
남: 유감스럽네요. 제 생각엔 우리는 그저 그것들이 다시 채워질 때까지 기
다려야겠군요, 그렇죠?
여: 음, 그들은 다음 주 수요일에 의자를 더 받아서 목요일에 그것들을 배송
할 거예요. 그러니까, 우리는 계획한 대로 금요일에 휴게실을 마련하는
것을 끝낼 수 있어요.
남: 좋아요. 그러면 [08]직원들에게 휴게실이 월요일에 개방될 거라고 알려줄
수 있나요?
여: [08]지금 공지할게요.

Brady 가구점 사무용 의자 재고

제품 번호	재고량
A3349	12
[07]E2128	8
R7550	13
V6200	10

07
해석 시각 자료를 보아라. 여자는 어떤 제품을 주문했는가?
(A) A3349
(B) E2128
(C) R7550
(D) V6200

해설 여자가 주문한 제품을 묻는 문제입니다. 여자가 "the chairs we
chose are almost out of stock. We need 10, but they don't
have that many in their inventory right now."라며 자신들이 고
른 의자는 재고가 거의 없다며 10개가 필요한데 그들은 현재 재고에
그만큼 많이 가지고 있지 않다고 하였으므로, 여자가 재고량이 10개
보다 적은 E2128을 주문했음을 표에서 알 수 있습니다. 따라서 정답
은 (B) E2128입니다.

08
해석 다음에 무슨 일이 일어날 것인가?
(A) 의자가 수리될 것이다.
(B) 공지가 될 것이다.
(C) 직원들이 발표에 참석할 것이다.
(D) 사무용품들이 다시 채워질 것이다.

해설 다음에 일어날 일을 묻는 문제입니다. 남자가 "can you notify the
staff that the lounge will be open on Monday?"라며 여자에게
직원들에게 휴게실이 월요일에 개방될 거라고 알려줄 수 있는지 묻
자, 여자가 "I'll make an announcement now."라며 지금 공지하
겠다고 하였습니다. 따라서 정답은 (B) An announcement will be
made입니다.

Course 2 시각 자료 문제 2(약도 및 기타)

HACKERS PRACTICE ∩ DAY15_04   p.124

01 (A)	02 (A)	03 (B)	04 (C)
05 (C)	06 (A)	07 (C)	08 (A)

01-02 [3에] 미국식 발음 → 호주식 발음 / 영국식 발음 → 캐나다식 발음

Questions 1-2 refer to the following conversation and
menu.

W: Pardon me. There's an issue with your order.
Unfortunately, [01]we're out of black bean soup. Is
there something else we can make you?
M: That's a shame. I really want to order something
without meat. Hmm . . . I guess I'll try your other
vegetarian dish.
W: I'll put the order in right away. Do you want
something else while you wait? [02]I can bring out a
house salad—free of charge, of course.
M: OK. Thanks.

unfortunately[미 ʌnfɔ́:rtʃənətli, 영 ʌnfɔ́:tʃənətli] 안타깝게도, 불행히도
be out of ~이 떨어지다, 바닥나다   shame[ʃeim] 유감인 일, 부끄러움
vegetarian[미 vèdʒətériən, 영 vèdʒitéəriən] 채식의; 채식주의자
house salad (레스토랑의) 특선 샐러드   free of charge 무료로

해석
1-2번은 다음 대화와 메뉴에 관한 문제입니다.

여: 실례합니다. 주문에 문제가 있어요. 안타깝게도, [01]검은콩 수프가 다 떨
어졌어요. 저희가 만들어드릴 다른 무언가가 있을까요?
남: 유감이네요. 저는 고기가 없는 무언가를 정말 주문하고 싶거든요. 음... 저
는 다른 채식 요리를 시켜봐야 할 것 같네요.
여: 주문을 바로 넣어드릴게요. 기다리시는 동안 다른 무언가를 원하시나요?
물론, [02]무료로 특선 샐러드를 가져다드릴 수 있어요.
남: 좋아요. 고맙습니다.

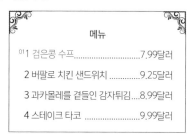

메뉴

[01]1 검은콩 수프..........................7.99달러

2 버팔로 치킨 샌드위치 9.25달러

3 과카몰레를 곁들인 감자튀김....8.99달러

4 스테이크 타코 9.99달러

01
해석 시각 자료를 보아라. 어떤 메뉴가 다 팔렸는가?
(A) 1번
(B) 2번
(C) 3번
(D) 4번

해설 다 팔린 메뉴를 묻는 문제입니다. 여자가 "we're out of black bean
soup"라며 검은콩 수프가 다 떨어졌다고 하였으므로, 1번 메뉴인 검
은콩 수프가 다 팔렸음을 알 수 있습니다. 따라서 정답은 (A) Item 1
입니다.

02
해석 여자는 무엇을 해주겠다고 제안하는가?
(A) 무료 품목을 제공한다.
(B) 디저트 메뉴를 업데이트한다.
(C) 포장용 용기를 가져온다.
(D) 식사 가격을 할인해준다.

해설 여자가 해주겠다고 제안하는 것을 묻는 문제입니다. 여자가 "I can
bring out a house salad—free of charge"라며 무료로 특선 샐러
드를 가져다줄 수 있다고 하였습니다. 따라서 정답은 (A) Provide a
free item입니다.

어휘 reduce[미 ridúːs, 영 ridʒúːs] (가격 등을) 할인하다, 낮추다, 줄이다

03-04 [음성] 영국식 발음 → 캐나다식 발음 / 미국식 발음 → 호주식 발음

Questions 3-4 refer to the following conversation and online form.

W: Hello. I'd like to <u>exchange</u> ⁰³a wool sweater I purchased from your online store last week.

M: Certainly. What seems to be the <u>problem</u>? Is it the wrong size?

W: No, that's not it. ⁰⁴There is a <u>small hole</u> in the left sleeve.

M: We'd be happy to <u>give you another sweater</u>. Just mail it back to us with a completed exchange slip in the next two weeks. You can download the form from our Web site.

exchange[ikstʃéindʒ] 교환하다 sleeve[sliːv] 소매
exchange slip 교환 명세서

해석
3-4번은 다음 대화와 온라인 양식에 관한 문제입니다.

여: 안녕하세요. ⁰³지난주에 당신의 온라인 매장에서 구매한 양모 스웨터를 교환하고 싶어요.
남: 알겠습니다. 어떤 것이 문제인 것 같나요? 사이즈가 잘못되었나요?
여: 아니요, 그게 아니에요. ⁰⁴왼쪽 소매에 작은 구멍이 있어요.
남: 기꺼이 다른 스웨터를 드리겠습니다. 2주 이내에 작성하신 교환 명세서와 함께 저희에게 스웨터를 다시 보내주시면 돼요. 양식은 저희 웹사이트에서 다운로드하실 수 있습니다.

교환 명세서		
제품명	구매 일자	반품 코드

<반품 코드>
01 - 잘못된 사이즈   02 - 잘못된 색상
⁰⁴03 - 손상된 제품   04 - 다른 제품

03
해석 여자는 지난주에 무엇을 했는가?
(A) 제품을 반품했다.
(B) 온라인 구매를 했다.
(C) 양식을 출력했다.
(D) 몇 가지 옷을 입어보았다.

해설 여자가 지난주에 한 것을 묻는 문제입니다. 여자가 "a wool sweater I purchased from your online store last week"이라며 지난주에 온라인 매장에서 구매한 양모 스웨터라고 한 것을 통해 여자가 지난주에 온라인 구매를 했음을 알 수 있습니다. 따라서 정답은 (B) Made an online purchase입니다.

어휘 purchase[미 pə́ːrtʃəs, 영 pə́ːtʃəs] 구매 try on 입어보다

04
해석 시각 자료를 보아라. 여자는 어떤 반품 코드를 사용해야 하는가?
(A) 01
(B) 02
(C) 03
(D) 04

해설 여자가 사용해야 하는 반품 코드를 묻는 문제입니다. 여자가 "There is a small hole in the left sleeve."라며 왼쪽 소매에 작은 구멍이 있다고 하였으므로, 여자가 손상된 제품에 대한 반품 코드인 03을 사용해

야 함을 온라인 양식에서 알 수 있습니다. 따라서 정답은 (C) 03입니다.

05-06 [음성] 미국식 발음 → 캐나다식 발음 / 영국식 발음 → 호주식 발음

Questions 5-6 refer to the following conversation and receipt.

W: Oh, Josh, can you look at this electronic receipt? ⁰⁵A customer just e-mailed it to me saying that <u>there's an error on it</u>. But I can't <u>figure out</u> the exact problem.

M: Sure. Well, ⁰⁶our tables were on sale when the customer made this purchase. It looks like <u>no discount was applied</u>.

W: Ah . . . you're right. We charged full price for everything. So, ⁰⁶I just need to <u>adjust the price</u> for this one item.

electronic[미 ilektrάːnik, 영 èlektrɔ́nik] 전자의
figure out ~을 알다, ~을 밝혀내다 apply[əplái] 적용하다, 신청하다
adjust[ədʒʌ́st] 조정하다, 조절하다

해석
5-6번은 다음 대화와 영수증에 관한 문제입니다.

여: 아, Josh, 이 전자 영수증 좀 봐주시겠어요? ⁰⁵한 고객이 방금 오류가 있다고 하면서 제게 그것을 이메일로 보냈어요. 하지만 정확한 문제를 알 수가 없어요.
남: 그럼요. 음, ⁰⁶고객이 이 구매를 했을 때 탁자들이 할인 판매 중이었어요. 그 할인이 적용되지 않은 것 같네요.
여: 아... 맞아요. 우리가 모든 것에 제값을 청구했어요. 그럼, ⁰⁶저는 이 한 가지 품목에 대한 가격만 조정하면 되겠네요.

Fresno 가구점	
영수증 #: 847573	구매 일자: 6월 14일
품목	**가격**
⁰⁶커피 테이블	150달러
스탠딩 램프	50달러
테이블 램프	30달러
책 선반	300달러

05
해석 여자는 어떤 문제를 언급하는가?
(A) 몇몇 제품이 고장 났다.
(B) 지불이 거절되었다.
(C) 실수를 알아낼 수 없다.
(D) 몇몇 품목들이 반품될 수 없다.

해설 여자가 언급하는 문제점을 묻는 문제입니다. 여자가 "A customer just e-mailed it[electronic receipt] to me saying that there's an error on it. But I can't figure out the exact problem."이라며 한 고객이 방금 오류가 있다고 하면서 전자 영수증을 이메일로 보냈지만 정확한 문제를 알 수가 없다고 하였습니다. 따라서 정답은 (C) A mistake cannot be determined입니다.

어휘 decline[dikláin] 거절하다, 감소하다
determine[미 ditə́ːrmin, 영 ditə́ːmin] 알아내다, 밝히다

06
해석 시각 자료를 보아라. 여자는 어떤 금액을 조정할 것인가?
(A) 150달러
(B) 50달러
(C) 30달러
(D) 300달러

PART 3

한 권으로 끝내는 해커스 토익 700+ (LC+RC+VOCA)

해설 여자가 조정할 금액을 묻는 문제입니다. 남자가 "our tables were on sale ~. It looks like no discount was applied."라며 탁자들이 할인 판매 중이었는데 그 할인이 적용되지 않은 것 같다고 하자, 여자가 "I just need to adjust the price for this one item[table]"이라며 테이블에 대한 가격만 조정하면 되겠다고 하였으므로, 여자가 커피 테이블에 매겨진 가격인 150달러를 조정할 것임을 영수증에서 알 수 있습니다. 따라서 정답은 (A) $150입니다.

07-08 🔊 캐나다식 발음 → 영국식 발음 / 호주식 발음 → 미국식 발음

Questions 7-8 refer to the following conversation and notice.

M: Did you <u>see the notice</u> in the break room?
W: Yeah. I heard that while the filters are being cleaned, the air conditioning will need to be shut off.
M: That's going to be a problem. [07]I'm meeting with an important client at 1 P.M. He'll be uncomfortable if the <u>air conditioning is turned off</u> during our meeting.
W: Right . . . I can see why that's an issue. Um, [08]why don't you <u>call the head</u> of maintenance? He might change the schedule.

notice[미 nóutis, 영 nə́utis] 공고(문), 벽보 break room 휴게실
filter[미 fíltər, 영 fíltə] 필터, 여과 장치 air conditioning 에어컨
maintenance[méintənəns] (보수) 관리, 정비

해석
7-8번은 다음 대화와 공고문에 관한 문제입니다.
남: 휴게실에 있는 공고문을 보셨나요?
여: 네. 필터가 청소되는 동안 에어컨의 전원이 꺼져야 할 것이라고 들었어요.
남: 그건 문제가 될 것 같아요. [07]저는 오후 1시에 중요한 고객을 만날 거예요. 그 회의 동안 에어컨이 꺼져 있다면 그가 불편할 거예요.
여: 맞네요... 그게 왜 문제인지 알겠어요. 음, [08]관리부장에게 전화하는 게 어때요? 그가 일정을 변경할 수 있을지도 몰라요.

에어컨 청소 – 6월 3일	
1층	오전 9시 – 오전 11시
2층	오전 11시 – 오후 1시
[07]3층	오후 1시 – 오후 3시
4층	오후 3시 – 오후 5시

07
해석 시각 자료를 보아라. 남자의 회의는 어느 층에서 있을 것인가?
(A) 1층에서
(B) 2층에서
(C) 3층에서
(D) 4층에서

해설 남자의 회의가 있을 장소를 묻는 문제입니다. 남자가 "I'm meeting with an important client at 1 P.M. He'll be uncomfortable if the air conditioning is turned off during our meeting."이라며 오후 1시에 중요한 고객을 만날 것인데 그 회의 동안 에어컨이 꺼져 있다면 그가 불편할 것이라고 하였으므로, 남자의 회의는 청소로 인해 오후 1시부터 에어컨이 꺼지는 3층에서 있을 것임을 공고문에서 알 수 있습니다. 따라서 정답은 (C) On the 3rd floor입니다.

08
해석 여자는 남자에게 무엇을 하라고 제안하는가?
(A) 부장에게 전화한다.
(B) 발표에 참석한다.
(C) 회의 일정을 변경한다.
(D) 몇몇 고객들과 이야기한다.

해설 여자가 남자에게 제안하는 것을 묻는 문제입니다. 여자가 "why don't you call the head of maintenance?"라며 관리부장에서 전화해볼 것을 제안하였습니다. 따라서 정답은 (A) Call a manager입니다.

HACKERS TEST 🎧 DAY15_05 p.126

01 (A)	02 (D)	03 (C)	04 (A)
05 (B)	06 (D)	07 (C)	08 (C)
09 (A)	10 (A)	11 (D)	12 (D)

01-03 🔊 영국식 발음 → 호주식 발음

Questions 1-3 refer to the following conversation and pie chart.

W: Wayne, your presentation at the quarterly sales meeting was very informative.
M: Thanks. [01]The executives at the meeting also seemed glad that revenue results were mostly satisfactory.
W: Yeah, except for one branch . . . Um . . . the one that didn't conduct the marketing campaign for [02]our company's recently released cookware line.
M: Right. But as the manager pointed out, [03]that branch just opened in January. There wasn't enough time to get organized for the campaign. That's why [03]it had the lowest share of customers in the second quarter.

quarterly[미 kwɔ́ːrtərli, 영 kwɔ́ːtəli] 분기별의
informative[미 infɔ́ːrmətiv, 영 infɔ́ːmətiv] 유익한
executive[미 igzékjutiv, 영 igzékjətiv] 임원
revenue[미 révənjùː, 영 révənjuː] 수익
satisfactory[미 sæ̀tisfǽktəri, 영 sæ̀tisfǽktəri] 만족스러운
except for ~을 제외하고 conduct[kəndʌ́kt] 실시하다
release[rilíːs] 출시하다 cookware[미 kúkwer, 영 kúkweə] 취사도구
share[미 ʃɛər, 영 ʃeə] 점유율, 지분

해석
1-3번은 다음 대화와 원그래프에 관한 문제입니다.
여: Wayne, 분기별 매출 회의에서 당신의 발표는 매우 유익했어요.
남: 고마워요. [01]회의 임원들 역시 수익 실적이 대체로 만족스러웠던 것에 대해 기뻐하는 것 같았어요.
여: 네, 한 지점을 제외하고는... 음... [02]최근 출시된 우리 회사의 취사도구 제품 라인의 마케팅 캠페인을 실시하지 않은 지점이요.
남: 맞아요. 하지만 지점장이 언급했듯이, [03]그 지점은 1월에 막 개업했어요. 캠페인을 위한 준비를 할 충분한 시간이 없었어요. 그것이 [03]2분기에 그곳의 고객 점유율이 가장 낮았던 이유예요.

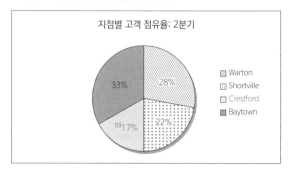

지점별 고객 점유율: 2분기
33%
28%
[03]17%
22%
Warton
Shortville
Crestford
Baytown

01

해석　남자는 회의에 대해 무엇을 말하는가?
(A) 임원들이 참석했다.
(B) 음향 시설이 필요했다.
(C) 일정이 변경되었다.
(D) 영상 회의로 진행되었다.

해설　남자가 회의에 대해 언급하는 것을 묻는 문제입니다. 남자가 "The executives at the meeting"이라며 회의의 임원들을 언급한 것을 통해 회의에 임원들이 참석했음을 알 수 있습니다. 따라서 정답은 (A) It was attended by executives입니다.

어휘　attend [əténd] 참석하다
videoconference [미 vídioukànfərəns, 영 vídiəukɔ̀nfərəns] 영상 회의

02

해석　회사는 최근에 무엇을 했는가?
(A) 현지의 회합 장소를 예약했다.
(B) 판촉 행사를 주최했다.
(C) 영업부장을 고용했다.
(D) 제품 라인을 출시했다.

해설　회사가 최근에 한 일을 묻는 문제입니다. 여자가 "our company's recently released cookware line"이라며 최근 출시된 회사의 취사도구 제품 라인이라고 한 말을 통해 회사가 최근에 제품 라인을 출시했음을 알 수 있습니다. 따라서 정답은 (D) Launched a product line입니다.

어휘　venue [vénjuː] 회합 장소
promotional [미 prəmóuʃənəl, 영 prəmə́uʃənəl] 판촉의, 홍보의
launch [lɔːntʃ] 출시하다

03

해석　시각 자료를 보아라. 어떤 지점이 1월에 개업했는가?
(A) Warton
(B) Shortville
(C) Crestford
(D) Baytown

해설　1월에 개업한 지점을 묻는 문제입니다. 남자가 "that branch just opened in January"라며 그 지점은 1월에 막 개업했다고 한 뒤, "it had the lowest share of customers in the second quarter"라며 2분기에 그곳의 고객 점유율이 가장 낮았다고 하였으므로, 고객 점유율이 가장 낮은 Crestford 지점이 1월에 개업했음을 원그래프에서 알 수 있습니다. 따라서 정답은 (C) Crestford입니다.

04-06 [3행] 캐나다식 발음 → 미국식 발음

Questions 4-6 refer to the following conversation and seating chart.

> M: Excuse me. You're showing employees to their seats, right? I'm from the accounting department, and I'm not sure where to sit.
> W: No problem. ⁰⁴Your department is seated at the table closest to the stage.
> M: OK, thanks. Oh . . . also, ⁰⁵I need to step out to call a client at 6 P.M. Will I miss the announcement for the Employee Of The Year Award?
> W: I don't think so. The president's speech regarding that starts at 5:30 P.M. and should last less than 30 minutes. Didn't you get an event schedule? ⁰⁶You can get one in the lobby of the auditorium.

accounting department 회계 부서　step out 나가다 　　　　○

award [미 əwɔ́ːrd, 영 əwɔ́ːd] 상(품)
regarding [미 rigáːrdiŋ, 영 rigáːdiŋ] ~에 대한

해석
4-6번은 다음 대화와 좌석 배치도에 관한 문제입니다.

남: 실례합니다. 당신이 직원들에게 자리를 안내하고 있죠, 그렇죠? 저는 회계 부서 소속인데, 어디에 앉아야 하는지 잘 모르겠어요.
여: 알겠습니다. ⁰⁴당신의 부서는 무대에서 가장 가까운 탁자에 앉아 있어요.
남: 그렇군요, 감사해요. 아... 그리고, ⁰⁵저는 오후 6시에 고객에게 전화하러 나가야 해요. 제가 올해의 직원상 발표를 놓치게 될까요?
여: 아닐 거예요. 그것에 대한 회장님의 연설은 오후 5시 30분에 시작해서 30분도 채 안 걸릴 거예요. 행사 일정표를 받지 않으셨나요? ⁰⁶강당 로비에서 그것을 받으실 수 있어요.

04

해석　시각 자료를 보아라. 남자의 자리는 어디에 있는가?
(A) 탁자 1에
(B) 탁자 2에
(C) 탁자 3에
(D) 탁자 4에

해설　남자의 자리가 있는 곳을 묻는 문제입니다. 여자가 "Your department is seated at the table closest to the stage."라며 남자의 부서가 무대에서 가장 가까운 탁자에 앉아 있다고 하였으므로, 남자의 자리가 탁자 1에 있음을 좌석 배치도에서 알 수 있습니다. 따라서 정답은 (A) At Table 1입니다.

05

해석　남자는 무엇을 해야 한다고 말하는가?
(A) 동료를 만난다.
(B) 전화한다.
(C) 상을 수여한다.
(D) 표를 만든다.

해설　남자가 해야 하는 것을 묻는 문제입니다. 남자가 "I need to step out to call a client"라며 고객에게 전화하러 나가야 한다고 하였습니다. 따라서 정답은 (B) Make a call입니다.

어휘　present [prizént] 수여하다, 주다

06

해석　로비에서 무엇을 받을 수 있는가?
(A) 휴대전화 충전기
(B) 주차 허가증
(C) 주소록
(D) 일정표

해설　로비에서 받을 수 있는 것을 묻는 문제입니다. 여자가 "You can get one[event schedule] in the lobby of the auditorium."이라며 강당 로비에서 행사 일정표를 받을 수 있다고 하였습니다. 따라서 정답은 (D) A schedule입니다.

어휘　charger [미 tʃɑ́ːrdʒər, 영 tʃɑ́ːdʒə] 충전기
permit [미 pə́ːrmit, 영 pə́ːmit] 허가증
directory [미 diréktəri, 영 dairéktəri] 주소록

Questions 7-9 refer to the following conversation and e-mail.

W: Good morning, Mr. Coyle. This is Patricia from the Danton Conference Center. ⁰⁷I want to notify you that we received Coretek Incorporated's registration payment for the electronics trade show.

M: I'm glad you called. There's actually a problem with our booking. ⁰⁸My manager just informed me that he'd like to attend the event, but he isn't free on the day we reserved.

W: I see. Well—⁰⁸I could move you to the following day. The booth you requested is still available.

M: Perfect. ⁰⁹Will there be an additional fee for the change?

W: No. I'll send you an updated confirmation e-mail immediately.

---

notify [미 nóutəfài, 영 nə́utifai] 알리다, 통지하다
payment [péimənt] 지불금, 대금 trade show 무역 박람회
available [əvéiləbl] 이용 가능한 additional [ədíʃənl] 추가적인

해석

7-9번은 다음 대화와 이메일에 관한 문제입니다.

여: 안녕하세요, Mr. Coyle. 저는 Danton 컨퍼런스 센터의 Patricia입니다. 전자제품 무역 박람회를 위한 ⁰⁷Coretek사의 등록 지불금을 받았다는 것을 알려드리고자 합니다.

남: 전화해 주셔서 다행이네요. 사실 저희의 예약에 문제가 있어요. ⁰⁸저희 부장님이 방금 제게 행사에 참여하고 싶다고 하셨지만, 그는 우리가 예약한 그 날 시간이 나지 않아요.

여: 그렇군요. 음—⁰⁸제가 당신의 회사를 다음 날로 옮겨드릴 수 있습니다. 당신이 요청했던 부스는 여전히 이용 가능합니다.

남: 완벽하네요. ⁰⁹변경에 대한 추가 요금이 있나요?

여: 아니요. 제가 업데이트된 확인 이메일을 즉시 보내드리겠습니다.

수신	Edward Coyle
발신	Patricia Wilkins
제목	전자제품 무역 박람회

기업명: Coretek사
지불 날짜: 5월 2일
예약 날짜: ⁰⁸5월 11일
부스 번호: 117

07

해석 전화의 목적은 무엇인가?
(A) 행사의 참여를 권장하기 위해
(B) 다가오는 전시회를 홍보하기 위해
(C) 지불금 수령을 확인시켜주기 위해
(D) 의견을 요청하기 위해

해설 전화의 목적을 묻는 문제입니다. 여자가 "I want to notify you that we received ~ registration payment"라며 등록 지불금을 받았다는 것을 알려주고자 한다고 하였습니다. 따라서 정답은 (C) To confirm receipt of payment입니다.

어휘 encourage [미 inká:ridʒ, 영 inkʌ́ridʒ] 권장하다, 장려하다
participation [미 pɑːrtìsəpéiʃən, 영 pɑːtìsipéiʃən] 참여, 참가
promote [미 prəmóut, 영 prəmə́ut] 홍보하다
confirm [미 kənfá:rm, 영 kənfá:m] 확인해주다 receipt [risíːt] 수령, 인수

08

해석 시각 자료를 보아라. 어떤 정보가 변경되었는가?
(A) Coretek사
(B) 5월 2일
(C) 5월 11일
(D) 117

해설 변경된 정보를 묻는 문제입니다. 남자가 "My manager ~ isn't free on the day we reserved."라며 부장이 행사에 참여하고 싶다고 했지만 그는 예약한 그 날 시간이 나지 않는다고 하자, 여자가 "I could move you to the following day"라며 남자의 회사를 다음 날로 옮겨줄 수 있다고 하였으므로, 예약 날짜가 5월 11일이 변경된 것임을 이메일에서 알 수 있습니다. 따라서 정답은 (C) May 11입니다.

09

해석 남자는 무엇에 대해 문의하는가?
(A) 추가 요금
(B) 시작 시간
(C) 연락처
(D) 관리자 성명

해설 남자가 문의하는 것을 묻는 문제입니다. 남자가 "Will there be an additional fee for the change?"라며 변경에 대한 추가 요금이 있는지를 물었습니다. 따라서 정답은 (A) An extra charge입니다.

어휘 charge [미 tʃɑːrdʒ, 영 tʃɑːdʒ] 요금

Questions 10-12 refer to the following conversation and sign.

M: Hey, Doreen. Sorry for being late. There's a parade on Rye Street today, so ¹⁰I took a different . . . uhm . . . longer way.

W: That's OK. How did you get here, though?

M: I went down Morrison Avenue and Granger Road since Carter Way isn't accessible.

W: Really? I thought there was a bike lane on that road too.

M: ¹¹Carter Way is under construction, so the lane is blocked off to bikers for the time being.

W: I see. Well, ¹²let's go inside the café and get some drinks. You must be hot from biking on a warm day like this!

---

parade [pəréid] 행진, 행렬 route [ruːt] 길 bike lane 자전거용 도로
under construction 공사 중인, 건설 중인

해석

10-12번은 다음 대화와 표지판에 관한 문제입니다.

남: 안녕하세요, Doreen. 늦어서 미안해요. 오늘 Rye가에 행진이 있어서, ¹⁰저는 다른... 음... 더 오래 걸리는 길로 왔어요.

여: 괜찮아요. 그런데, 여기까지 어떻게 왔어요?

남: Carter로는 출입할 수 없어서 Morrison가와 Granger로로 왔어요.

여: 그래요? 저는 Carter로에도 자전거용 도로가 있는 줄 알았는데요.

남: ¹¹Carter로는 공사 중이어서, 그 도로는 당분간 자전거를 타는 사람들에게 차단되었어요.

여: 그랬군요. 자, ¹²우리 카페로 들어가서 음료를 좀 마셔요. 오늘처럼 따뜻한 날 자전거를 타고 오느라 덥겠어요!

¹¹자전거용 도로 폐쇄됨

전방에 도로 공사 중

10

해석 남자는 왜 늦었는가?
    (A) 그는 다른 길을 이용했다.
    (B) 기차가 고장 났다.
    (C) 회의가 미뤄졌다.
    (D) 그는 교통 체증에 갇혀 있었다.

해설 남자가 늦은 이유를 묻는 문제입니다. 남자가 "I took a different ~ longer way"라며 시간이 더 오래 걸리는 다른 길로 왔다고 하였습니다. 따라서 정답은 (A) He took an alternative route입니다.

어휘 **alternative** [미 ɔːltə́ːrnətiv, 영 ɔltə́ːnətiv] 다른, 대안의
    break down 고장 나다 **stuck in traffic** 교통 체증에 갇힌

11

해석 시각 자료를 보아라. 표지판은 어디에 위치해 있을 것 같은가?
    (A) Rye가에
    (B) Granger로에
    (C) Morrison가에
    (D) Carter로에

해설 표지판이 위치해 있을 것 같은 곳을 묻는 문제입니다. 남자가 "Carter Way ~ is blocked off to bikers for the time being."이라며 Carter로는 공사 중이어서 당분간 자전거를 타는 사람들에게 차단되었다고 하였으므로, 표지판이 Carter로에 위치해 있음을 알 수 있습니다. 따라서 정답은 (D) On Carter Way입니다.

12

해석 화자들은 다음에 무엇을 할 것 같은가?
    (A) 자전거를 자물쇠로 잠근다.
    (B) 구매품을 반품한다.
    (C) 시내 지도를 검토한다.
    (D) 음식점에 들어간다.

해설 화자들이 다음에 할 일을 묻는 문제입니다. 여자가 "let's go inside the café"라며 카페로 들어가자고 한 것을 통해 화자들이 음식점에 들어갈 것임을 알 수 있습니다. 따라서 정답은 (D) Enter a dining establishment입니다.

어휘 **lock up** ~을 자물쇠로 잠그다 **purchase** [미 pə́ːrtʃəs, 영 pə́ːtʃəs] 구매(품)
    dining establishment 음식점

PART 4

DAY 16 전체 지문 관련 문제

Course 1 주제 및 목적 문제

HACKERS PRACTICE 🎧 DAY16_02   p.131

01 (A)	02 (C)	03 (B)	04 (D)

01-02 🎧 영국식 발음 / 미국식 발음

Questions 1-2 refer to the following announcement.

Attention, everyone. ⁰¹The company's overtime policy is going to be changed next month. Currently, staff members are paid extra for working more than 50 hours in one week. However, the number of hours needed for overtime pay will be lowered to 45 hours per week. ⁰²If you have any questions about this change, please send an e-mail to Minjoo in the human resources department. OK, you may return to work.

---

overtime[미 óuvərtàim, 영 óuvətaim] 초과 근무; 초과 근무의
policy[미 páləsi, 영 pɔ́ləsi] 정책 lower[미 lóuər, 영 lóuə] 낮추다, 내리다
per[미 pər:, 영 pə:] ~당, ~마다 human resources department 인사부

해석

1-2번은 다음 공지에 관한 문제입니다.

모두 주목해 주시기 바랍니다. ⁰¹회사의 초과 근무 정책이 다음 달에 변경될 예정입니다. 현재, 직원들은 한 주에 50시간 이상 근무에 대해 추가 수당을 받습니다. 하지만, 초과 근무 수당을 위해 필요한 시간은 주당 45시간으로 낮춰질 것입니다. ⁰²만약 이 변경 사항에 대해 질문이 있다면, 인사부의 Minjoo에게 이메일을 보내세요. 좋습니다, 업무를 하러 돌아가셔도 됩니다.

01

해석 화자는 주로 무엇에 대해 이야기하고 있는가?
(A) 초과 근무 정책
(B) 납부 지연
(C) 일정 변경
(D) 직원 오리엔테이션

해설 공지의 주제를 묻는 문제입니다. "The company's overtime policy is going to be changed next month."라며 회사의 초과 근무 정책이 다음 달에 변경될 예정이라고 한 뒤, 변경될 정책의 세부 사항과 관련된 내용을 언급하였습니다. 따라서 정답은 (A) An overtime policy입니다.

02

해석 청자들은 왜 Minjoo에게 이메일을 보내야 하는가?
(A) 다른 근무 시간을 요청하기 위해
(B) 그들의 참석을 확정하기 위해
(C) 추가 문의를 하기 위해
(D) 프로젝트 세부 사항을 공유하기 위해

해설 청자들이 Minjoo에게 이메일을 보내야 하는 이유를 묻는 문제입니다. "If you have any questions about this change, please send an e-mail to Minjoo"라며 만약 이 변경 사항에 대해 질문이 있다면 Minjoo에게 이메일을 보내라고 하였습니다. 따라서 정답은 (C) To

---

make further inquiries입니다.

어휘 shift[ʃift] (교대제의) 근무 시간
confirm[미 kənfá:rm, 영 kənfá:m] 확정하다, 확인하다
attendance[əténdəns] 참석 further[미 fá:rðər, 영 fá:ðə] 추가의, 그 이상의
inquiry[inkwáiəri] 문의, 질문 detail[dí:teil] 세부 사항

03-04 🎧 호주식 발음 / 캐나다식 발음

Questions 3-4 refer to the following telephone message.

Alison, this is Henry. ⁰³I'm calling to ask for a favor. Um . . . can you give a presentation to the board of directors this afternoon on our project's status? Unfortunately, I'm away at a sales conference today. ⁰⁴It doesn't end until tomorrow, so I will not be able to make it to the meeting myself. Please call me back as soon as possible to let me know if you're available. Thanks!

---

favor[미 féivər, 영 féivə] 부탁 give a presentation 보고하다, 발표하다
board of directors 이사회 status[stéitəs] (진행 과정상의) 상황
be away 부재중이다 make it 시간 맞춰 가다
available[əvéiləbl] 시간이 있는

해석

3-4번은 다음 전화 메시지에 관한 문제입니다.

Alison, Henry예요. ⁰³부탁할 것이 있어서 전화했어요. 음... 오늘 오후에 저희 프로젝트 상황에 대해 이사회에 보고를 해주실 수 있나요? 유감스럽게도, 저는 오늘 영업 컨퍼런스로 부재중이에요. ⁰⁴컨퍼런스는 내일이 되어서야 끝나서, 저는 회의 시간에 맞춰 갈 수 없을 거예요. 가능한 한 빨리 제게 다시 전화해서 시간이 있는지 알려주세요. 감사합니다!

03

해석 메시지의 목적은 무엇인가?
(A) 회의 일정을 확인하기 위해
(B) 동료의 도움을 요청하기 위해
(C) 발표 주제를 변경하기 위해
(D) 프로젝트의 진행 상황을 확인하기 위해

해설 메시지의 목적을 묻는 문제입니다. "I'm calling to ask for a favor. ~ can you give a presentation"이라며 부탁할 것이 있어서 전화했다고 한 뒤, 보고를 해줄 수 있는지 물었습니다. 따라서 정답은 (B) To request a coworker's assistance입니다.

어휘 verify[미 vérəfài, 영 vérifai] 확인하다 assistance[əsístəns] 도움

04

해석 화자는 영업 컨퍼런스에 대해 무엇을 말하는가?
(A) 이사회에 의해 준비되었다.
(B) 매우 성공적이었다.
(C) 다른 도시에서 열릴 것이다.
(D) 내일 끝난다.

해설 화자가 영업 컨퍼런스에 대해 언급하는 것을 묻는 문제입니다. "It [sales conference] doesn't end until tomorrow"라며 영업 컨퍼런스는 내일이 되어서야 끝난다고 하였습니다. 따라서 정답은 (D) It finishes tomorrow입니다.

어휘 organize[미 ɔ́:rgənàiz, 영 ɔ́:gənaiz] 준비하다

Course 2 화자 · 청자 및 장소 문제

HACKERS PRACTICE 🎧 DAY16_04　　p.133

01 (A)	02 (D)	03 (A)	04 (D)

01-02 🎧 영국식 발음 / 미국식 발음

Questions 1-2 refer to the following announcement.

> ⁰¹Attention all London Books customers! We're currently having a huge sale on science fiction novels. All books in this genre are discounted by 25 percent. This is the perfect opportunity to add to your collection. ⁰²We're also running a promotion on recipe books this weekend. If you buy two cookbooks, one will be half price. Be sure to take advantage of this great offer while it's available!

> science fiction 공상 과학　novel[미 nάvəl, 영 nɔ́vəl] 소설
> genre[미 ʒɑ́ːnrə, 영 ʒɔ́nrə] 장르, 종류　collection[kəlékʃən] 소장품, 수집품
> promotion[미 prəmóuʃən, 영 prəmə́uʃən] 판촉 행사
> recipe book 요리책　cookbook[미 kúkbùk, 영 kúkbuk] 요리책

해석

1-2번은 다음 공지에 관한 문제입니다.

⁰¹London Books의 고객 여러분 모두 주목해 주시기 바랍니다! 저희는 현재 공상 과학 소설에 대한 대대적인 할인 판매를 하고 있습니다. 이 장르의 모든 책들은 25퍼센트까지 할인됩니다. 이는 여러분의 소장품을 늘릴 완벽한 기회입니다. ⁰²저희는 또한 이번 주말에 요리책들에 대한 판촉 행사를 진행할 것입니다. 요리책 두 권을 구매하시면, 한 권은 반값이 될 것입니다. 이용할 수 있을 때 이 엄청난 할인을 꼭 활용하세요!

01

해석　공지는 누구를 대상으로 하는가?
(A) 서점 고객들
(B) 출판사 직원들
(C) 공상 과학 소설가들
(D) 컨퍼런스 참석자들

해설　청자들의 신분을 묻는 문제입니다. "Attention all London Books customers!"라며 London Books의 고객들은 모두 주목해 달라고 한 뒤, "We're currently having a huge sale on science fiction novels."라며 현재 공상 과학 소설에 대한 대대적인 할인 판매를 하고 있다고 한 말을 통해 청자들이 서점의 고객들임을 알 수 있습니다. 따라서 정답은 (A) Bookstore customers입니다.

어휘　publishing firm 출판사　attendee[미 ətèndíː, 영 ətəndíː] 참석자

02

해석　이번 주말에 무슨 일이 일어날 것인가?
(A) 매장 수리
(B) 책 사인회
(C) 작문 워크숍
(D) 판촉 할인

해설　이번 주말에 일어날 일을 묻는 문제입니다. "We're also running a promotion ~ this weekend."라며 또한 이번 주말에 판촉 행사를 진행할 것이라고 하였습니다. 따라서 정답은 (D) A promotional offer입니다.

어휘　renovation[미 rènəvéiʃən, 영 rènəvéiʃən] 수리
promotional[미 prəmóuʃənl, 영 prəməúʃənl] 판촉의
offer[미 ɔ́ːfər, 영 ɔ́fə] (짧은 기간 동안의) 할인

03-04 🎧 캐나다식 발음 / 호주식 발음

Questions 3-4 refer to the following talk.

> ⁰³Thank you for visiting Bridgeport Academy. Today, I'll discuss some of the reasons to enroll your children here. First of all, ^{03/04}our high school is well known for its academic excellence. Many of our graduates are accepted into top universities. In addition, we offer various sports and arts programs. We are particularly proud of our basketball team, which won the state championship in the tournament last week. Now, let me show you around our facilities.

> academy[əkǽdəmi] 학교, 교육기관　enroll[inróul] 입학시키다
> academic[미 æ̀kədémik, 영 æ̀kədémik] 학업의, 학문의
> graduate[grǽdʒuət] 졸업생
> accept[미 æksépt, 영 əksépt] (대학 등에)~를 입학시키다
> particularly[미 pərtíkjulərli, 영 pətíkjələli] 특히
> tournament[미 túərnəmənt, 영 túːnəmənt] 토너먼트, 선수권 대회
> facility[fəsíləti] 시설, 설비

해석

3-4번은 다음 담화에 관한 문제입니다.

⁰³Bridgeport 학교를 방문해 주셔서 감사합니다. 오늘, 저는 여러분의 자녀들을 이곳에 입학시키셔야 하는 몇 가지 이유를 말씀드리겠습니다. 먼저, ^{03/04}저희 고등학교는 학업상 우수함으로 잘 알려져 있습니다. 저희의 졸업생 중 다수가 상위 대학들에 입학합니다. 게다가, 저희는 다양한 운동 및 미술 프로그램을 제공합니다. 저희는 특히 농구팀을 자랑으로 생각하는데, 그 팀은 지난주 토너먼트에서 주 우승을 했습니다. 지금부터, 저희 시설을 둘러보시도록 여러분을 안내해 드리겠습니다.

03

해석　청자들은 어디에 있는 것 같은가?
(A) 고등학교에
(B) 종합 운동장에
(C) 미술관에
(D) 보육시설에

해설　청자들이 있는 장소를 묻는 문제입니다. "Thank you for visiting Bridgeport Academy."라며 Bridgeport 학교를 방문해 주어서 감사하다고 한 뒤, "our high school"이라며 고등학교라고 하였습니다. 따라서 정답은 (A) At a high school입니다.

어휘　art museum 미술관　daycare center 보육시설

04

해석　화자는 왜 "저희의 졸업생 중 다수가 상위 대학들에 입학합니다"라고 말하는가?
(A) 프로그램의 기간을 정당화하기 위해
(B) 더 많은 노력을 장려하기 위해
(C) 선택 사항에 대해 설명하기 위해
(D) 기관의 명성을 강조하기 위해

해설　화자가 하는 말(Many of our graduates are accepted into top universities)의 의도를 묻는 문제입니다. "our high school is well known for its academic excellence"라며 화자가 근무하는 고등학교가 학업상 우수함으로 잘 알려져 있다고 한 것을 통해, 학교의 명성을 강조하려는 의도임을 알 수 있습니다. 따라서 정답은 (D) To highlight an institution's reputation입니다.

어휘　justify[dʒʌ́stəfài] 정당화하다, 해명하다　diligence[dílidʒəns] 노력, 근면
highlight[háilàit] 강조하다　institution[ìnstətjúːʃən] 기관
reputation[미 rèpjutéiʃən, 영 rèpjətéiʃən] 명성, 평판

01 (B)	**02** (D)	**03** (B)	**04** (A)
05 (A)	**06** (D)	**07** (D)	**08** (B)
09 (D)	**10** (D)	**11** (A)	**12** (C)
13 (B)	**14** (A)	**15** (C)	**16** (D)
17 (A)	**18** (D)		

01-03 🔊 미국식 발음

Questions 1-3 refer to the following talk.

Everyone, please gather around. ⁰¹I want to introduce our magazine's newest employee, Herman Schiller. Mr. Schiller will be the new lead illustrator at our company. ⁰²He will oversee our existing visual arts team, which is responsible for creating the graphics and cover art for our monthly publications. Mr. Schiller has worked as an illustrator for over five years. I'm confident that he will become an important part of our company. ⁰³Please take some time today to say hello and make him feel welcome.

gather[미 gǽðər, 영 gǽðə] 모이다
illustrator[미 íləstrèitər, 영 íləstreitə] 삽화가
oversee[미 ðuvərsíː, 영 ðuvəsíː] 감독하다
existing[igzístiŋ] 기존의　visual arts 시각 예술　cover art 표지
publication[미 pʌ̀bləkéiʃən, 영 pʌ̀blikéiʃən] 출간물
confident[미 kʌ́nfədənt, 영 kɔ́nfidənt] 확신하는
make ~ feel welcome ~를 환영하다

해석

1-3번은 다음 담화에 관한 문제입니다.

여러분, 모여주시기 바랍니다. ⁰¹우리 잡지사의 신규 직원인 Herman Schiller를 소개해 드리려고 합니다. Mr. Schiller는 우리 회사의 새로운 수석 삽화가가 될 것입니다. ⁰²그는 기존의 시각 예술팀을 감독할 것인데, 이 팀은 우리 월간 출간물의 삽화와 표지 제작을 책임지고 있습니다. Mr. Schiller는 5년 이상 삽화가로 일해 왔습니다. 저는 그가 우리 회사의 중요한 일원이 될 것이라고 확신합니다. ⁰³오늘 시간을 내서서 인사해 주시고 그를 환영해 주시기 바랍니다.

01

해석 담화의 목적은 무엇인가?
(A) 동업자에게 감사를 표하기 위해
(B) 신규 직원을 소개하기 위해
(C) 프로젝트를 공지하기 위해
(D) 직원들로부터 조언을 구하기 위해

해설 담화의 목적을 묻는 문제입니다. "I want to introduce our magazine's newest employee"라며 잡지사의 신규 직원을 소개하려고 한다고 하였습니다. 따라서 정답은 (B) To introduce a new employee입니다.

어휘 announce[ənáuns] 공지하다, 알리다

02

해석 Mr. Schiller에 대해 무엇이 언급되는가?
(A) 그는 잡지를 창간했다.
(B) 그는 전문 사진작가이다.
(C) 그는 이 회사에서 일을 했었다.
(D) 그는 팀을 감독할 것이다.

해설 Mr. Schiller에 대해 언급되는 것을 묻는 문제입니다. "He[Mr. Schiller] will oversee our existing visual arts team"이라며 Mr. Schiller

가 기존의 시각 예술팀을 감독할 것이라고 하였습니다. 따라서 정답은 (D) He will manage a team입니다.

어휘 found[faund] 창간하다, 설립하다
professional[prəféʃənl] 전문의, 전문적인
manage[mǽnidʒ] 감독하다, 관리하다

03

해석 청자들은 무엇을 하도록 요청받는가?
(A) 새로운 이미지들을 제작한다.
(B) 신규 직원을 환영한다.
(C) 몇 가지 의견을 공유한다.
(D) 다른 회의를 연다.

해설 청자들이 요청받는 것을 묻는 문제입니다. "Please take some time today to say hello and make him[Herman Schiller] feel welcome."이라며 청자들에게 시간을 내어 인사하고 신규 직원인 Herman Schiller를 환영할 것을 요청하였습니다. 따라서 정답은 (B) Make the new worker feel welcome입니다.

04-06 🔊 캐나다식 발음

Questions 4-6 refer to the following speech.

⁰⁴I would like to welcome you all to the Canadian Accounting Conference. Over the next two days, talks will be given on subjects of interest to people working in this field. Moreover, ⁰⁵informational booths have been set up by several of the country's largest financial firms. Due to the size of this year's conference, some of our lectures and presentations will be held at the same time. To help keep track of the schedule of events, ⁰⁶I recommend picking up an event program at the welcome desk.

accounting[əkáuntiŋ] 회계　subject[미 sʌ́bdʒikt, 영 sʌ́bdʒekt] 주제, 화제
field[fiːld] 분야　informational[미 ìnfərméiʃənl, 영 infəméiʃənl] 안내의
financial[fainǽnʃəl] 금융의, 재정의　keep track of ~을 파악하고 있다

해석

4-6번은 다음 연설에 관한 문제입니다.

⁰⁴캐나다 회계 컨퍼런스에 오신 여러분 모두를 환영합니다. 앞으로 이틀 동안, 이 분야에 종사하는 분들께 흥미로운 주제들에 대한 연설이 있을 것입니다. 게다가, ⁰⁵국내에서 가장 큰 몇몇 금융 회사들의 안내 부스들이 설치되어 있습니다. 올해 컨퍼런스의 규모로 인해, 일부 강연과 발표가 동시에 열릴 것입니다. 행사 일정을 파악하시는 것을 돕기 위해, 안내 데스크에서 ⁰⁶행사 일정표를 가져가실 것을 권해 드립니다.

04

해석 청자들은 누구인 것 같은가?
(A) 회계사들
(B) 대학 강사들
(C) 컨퍼런스 주최자들
(D) 변호사들

해설 청자들의 신분을 묻는 문제입니다. "I would like to welcome you all to the Canadian Accounting Conference."라며 캐나다 회계 컨퍼런스에 온 청자들 모두를 환영한다고 한 말을 통해 청자들이 회계 분야에서 일하고 있음을 알 수 있습니다. 따라서 정답은 (A) Accountants입니다.

어휘 organizer[미 ɔ́ːrgənàizər, 영 ɔ́ːgənaizə] 주최자

05

해석 화자에 따르면, 무엇이 설치되어 있는가?
(A) 기업 부스
(B) 전시 포스터
(C) 안전 장비
(D) 추가 좌석

해설 설치되어 있는 것을 묻는 문제입니다. "informational booths have been set up by several ~ financial firms"라며 몇몇 금융 회사들의 안내 부스들이 설치되어 있다고 하였습니다. 따라서 정답은 (A) Company booths입니다.

어휘 display[displéi] 전시, 진열

06

해석 화자는 무엇을 제안하는가?
(A) 특별 강연 듣기
(B) 일정 업데이트하기
(C) 행사에 등록하기
(D) 일정표 가져오기

해설 화자가 제안하는 것을 묻는 문제입니다. "I recommend picking up an event program"이라며 행사 일정표를 가져갈 것을 권한다고 하였습니다. 따라서 정답은 (D) Getting a program입니다.

07-09 🎧 영국식 발음

Questions 7-9 refer to the following announcement.

⁰⁷Welcome to Fresh Foods Supermarket. To celebrate our 20th anniversary, ⁰⁷/⁰⁸we are offering discounts on many grocery items. ⁰⁸All specialty cheeses are currently on sale at 10 percent off, and frozen pizzas have been discounted by 15 percent. In addition, customers with a membership card can earn twice as many points as usual right now. However, ⁰⁹this offer is only valid until Friday. If you don't have a membership card, sign up for one now at the customer service desk. We thank you for shopping at Fresh Foods and hope you'll come again.

---

celebrate[미 séləbrèit, 영 séləbrèit] 기념하다 specialty[spéʃəlti] 특제품
sign up for ~을 신청하다 customer service desk 고객 서비스 데스크

해석

7-9번은 다음 공지에 관한 문제입니다.

⁰⁷Fresh Foods 슈퍼마켓에 오신 것을 환영합니다. 저희의 20주년을 기념하기 위해, ⁰⁷/⁰⁸저희는 많은 식료품 품목들에 대해 할인을 제공하고 있습니다. ⁰⁸모든 특제 치즈는 현재 10퍼센트 할인되어 판매되고 있고, 냉동 피자는 15퍼센트만큼 할인되고 있습니다. 또한, 회원 카드를 소지하신 고객들은 평상시의 2배만큼 많은 포인트를 바로 지금 얻으실 수 있습니다. 하지만, ⁰⁹이 제공은 금요일까지만 유효합니다. 만약 회원 카드가 없으시다면, 고객 서비스 데스크에서 지금 하나를 신청하세요. Fresh Foods에서 쇼핑해 주셔서 감사드리며 다시 방문해 주시기 바랍니다.

07

해석 이 공지는 어디에서 이루어지고 있는 것 같은가?
(A) 제과점에서
(B) 음식점에서
(C) 출장 연회 업체에서
(D) 식료품점에서

해설 공지가 이루어지고 있는 장소를 묻는 문제입니다. "Welcome to Fresh Foods Supermarket."이라며 Fresh Foods 슈퍼마켓에 온

것을 환영한다고 한 뒤, "we are offering discounts on many grocery items"라며 많은 식료품 품목들에 대해 할인을 제공하고 있다고 한 말을 통해 공지가 이루어지고 있는 장소가 식료품점임을 알 수 있습니다. 따라서 정답은 (D) At a grocery store입니다.

어휘 catering[kéitəriŋ] 출장 연회업체

08

해석 공지의 목적은 무엇인가?
(A) 분실물을 설명하기 위해
(B) 할인 행사를 광고하기 위해
(C) 신제품을 소개하기 위해
(D) 회사 규정을 설명하기 위해

해설 공지의 목적을 묻는 문제입니다. "we are offering discounts on many grocery items. All specialty cheeses are ~ at 10 percent off, and frozen pizzas have been discounted by 15 percent."라며 많은 식료품 품목들에 대해 할인을 제공하고 있고 모든 특제 치즈는 10퍼센트, 냉동 피자는 15퍼센트만큼 할인되고 있다고 하였습니다. 따라서 정답은 (B) To advertise a sales event입니다.

어휘 lost property 분실물

09

해석 화자에 따르면, 금요일에 무슨 일이 일어날 것인가?
(A) 제품이 출시될 것이다.
(B) 공지가 이루어질 것이다.
(C) 매장이 일찍 닫을 것이다.
(D) 판촉 행사가 끝날 것이다.

해설 금요일에 일어날 일을 묻는 문제입니다. "this offer is only valid until Friday"라며 이 제공은 금요일까지만 유효하다고 한 것을 통해 금요일에 판촉 행사가 끝날 것임을 알 수 있습니다. 따라서 정답은 (D) A promotion will conclude입니다.

어휘 promotion[미 prəmóuʃən, 영 prəmə́uʃən] 판촉 행사
conclude[kənklú:d] 끝나다, 마치다

10-12 🎧 호주식 발음

Questions 10-12 refer to the following telephone message.

---

¹⁰This is Andrew Lee from Future Computers. I'm contacting your firm regarding an incomplete order. ¹⁰Your company put in a request at our store last Friday for 20 new computer monitors. However, ¹¹five days have passed since then, and no payment has been sent. The order will be automatically canceled at 6:00 P.M. today unless payment is received. Um, this policy is clearly stated on our Web site. ¹²I'm curious whether your firm would still like to go ahead with the purchase. I can be contacted at 555-3066 to discuss the matter further.

---

regarding[미 rigá:rdiŋ, 영 rigá:diŋ] ~과 관련하여
incomplete[inkəmplí:t] 미완료의 payment[péimənt] 지불금, 지불
state[steit] 명시하다 curious[kjúəriəs] 알고 싶은

해석

10-12번은 다음 전화 메시지에 관한 문제입니다.

¹⁰저는 Future 컴퓨터점의 Andrew Lee입니다. 미완료된 주문과 관련하여 귀사에 연락을 드립니다. ¹⁰귀사는 지난주 금요일에 저희 매장에 20대의 새 컴퓨터 모니터를 신청했습니다. 그러나, ¹¹그로부터 5일이 지났지만, 지불금을 받지 못했습니다. 만약 지불금을 받지 못한다면 오늘 오후 6시에 주문은 자동으로 취소될 것입니다. 음, 이 방침은 저희 웹사이트에 명확하게 명시

PART 4

언제 어디서나 꺼내 보는 해커스 토익 700+ (LC+RC+VOCA)

되어 있습니다. ¹²귀사가 여전히 구매를 진행하고 싶은지 알고 싶습니다. 이 문제에 대해 더 이야기하시려면 555-3066으로 제게 연락 주시면 됩니다.

10
해석 화자는 어디에서 일하는 것 같은가?
(A) 광고 회사에서
(B) 서비스 센터에서
(C) 금융 회사에서
(D) 전자제품 소매점에서

해설 화자가 일하는 장소를 묻는 문제입니다. "This is Andrew Lee from Future Computers."에서 자신이 Future 컴퓨터점의 Andrew Lee 라고 한 뒤, "Your company put in a request at our store ~ for 20 new computer monitors."라며 청자의 회사가 자신의 매장에 20대의 새 컴퓨터 모니터를 신청했다고 한 것을 통해, 화자가 일하는 장소가 전자제품 소매점임을 알 수 있습니다. 따라서 정답은 (D) At an electronics retailer입니다.

어휘 retailer[미 ríːteilər, 영 ríːteilə] 소매점, 소매 상인

11
해석 지불금에 대해 무엇이 언급되는가?
(A) 수령되지 않았다.
(B) 웹사이트에서 납부되었다.
(C) 전부 환불될 수 없다.
(D) 지난주 금요일에 보내졌다.

해설 지불금에 대해 언급되는 것을 묻는 문제입니다. "five days have passed since then, and no payment has been sent"라며 주문 후 5일이 지났지만 지불금을 받지 못했다고 하였습니다. 따라서 정답은 (A) It has not been received입니다.

어휘 refund[ríːfʌnd] 환불하다

12
해석 화자는 무엇에 대해 알고 싶어 하는가?
(A) 일부 기기들이 왜 작동하지 않는지
(B) 배송품이 언제 도착할지
(C) 구매가 이루어질 것인지
(D) 배송품을 누가 받을 것인지

해설 화자가 알고 싶어 하는 것을 묻는 문제입니다. "I'm curious whether your firm would still like to go ahead with the purchase."라며 청자의 회사가 여전히 구매를 진행하고 싶은지 알고 싶다고 하였습니다. 따라서 정답은 (C) Whether a purchase will be made입니다.

13-15 [2배속] 캐나다식 발음

Questions 13-15 refer to the following talk.

---
¹³I want to clarify a few things about our refund procedure. First, you must check the product for damage. For example, inspect items of clothing for holes or rips. And ¹⁴I'd really like to emphasize this next step. You need to verify that the item being returned was purchased from our store. We've lost money in the past when employees failed to do this. Finally, have the customer sign a refund receipt. ¹⁵If you are ever uncertain, get some help. At least one floor manager will always be on duty.

---
clarify[미 klǽrəfài, 영 klǽrifài] 명확하게 하다 **refund**[ríːfʌnd] 환불
procedure[미 prəsíːdʒər, 영 prəsíːdʒə] 절차 **damage**[dǽmidʒ] 손상
inspect[inspékt] 확인하다 **rip**[rip] 찢어진 곳
verify[미 vérəfài, 영 vérifài] 확인하다   ◐

---

uncertain[미 ʌnsə́ːrtən, 영 ʌnsə́ːtən] 의문을 가지고 있는, 분명히는 모르는
on duty 근무 중인

해석
13-15번은 다음 담화에 관한 문제입니다.

¹³저는 우리의 환불 절차에 대한 몇 가지 사항을 명확하게 하고 싶습니다. 먼저, 손상에 대해 제품을 확인해야 합니다. 예를 들어, 의류 제품은 구멍이나 찢어진 곳이 있는지 확인하세요. 그리고 ¹⁴저는 정말로 이 다음 단계를 강조하고 싶습니다. 여러분은 환불되는 제품이 우리 매장에서 구매되었는지 확인해야 합니다. 자사는 과거에 직원들이 이렇게 하지 않았을 때 손해를 보았습니다. 마지막으로, 고객이 환불 영수증에 서명하도록 하세요. ¹⁵만일 의문이 있다면, 도움을 받으세요. 적어도 한 명의 층 관리자가 항상 근무하고 있을 것입니다.

13
해석 화자는 주로 무엇에 대해 이야기하고 있는가?
(A) 휴가 제도
(B) 환불 절차
(C) 교육 프로그램
(D) 안전 절차

해설 담화의 주제를 묻는 문제입니다. "I want to clarify a few things about our refund procedure."라며 환불 절차에 대한 몇 가지 사항을 명확하게 하고 싶다고 한 뒤, 매장의 환불 절차와 관련된 세부 내용을 언급하였습니다. 따라서 정답은 (B) A refund process입니다.

어휘 leave[liːv] 휴가

14
해석 화자는 무엇을 강조하는가?
(A) 제품이 그 매장의 것이어야 한다.
(B) 직원의 서명이 필요하다.
(C) 모든 구매는 최신이어야 한다.
(D) 몇몇 제품은 온라인에서만 구매 가능하다.

해설 화자가 강조하는 것을 묻는 문제입니다. "I'd really like to emphasize this next step. You need to verify that the item being returned was purchased from our store."라며 화자가 정말로 이 다음 단계를 강조하고 싶다고 하면서 환불되는 제품이 그들의 매장에서 구매되었는지 확인해야 한다고 하였습니다. 따라서 정답은 (A) An item must be from the store입니다.

15
해석 화자는 왜 "적어도 한 명의 층 관리자가 항상 근무하고 있을 것입니다"라고 말하는가?
(A) 새로운 방침을 소개하기 위해
(B) 최신 정보를 전달하기 위해
(C) 안심시켜주기 위해
(D) 다음 단계로 나아가기 위해

해설 화자가 하는 말(At least one floor manager will always be on duty)의 의도를 묻는 문제입니다. "If you are ever uncertain, get some help."라며 만일 의문이 있다면 도움을 받으라고 한 것을 통해 의문이 있을 경우 층 관리자에게 도움을 받을 수 있다고 직원들을 안심시켜주려는 의도임을 알 수 있습니다. 따라서 정답은 (C) To provide reassurance입니다.

어휘 reassurance[미 rìːəʃúrəns, 영 rìːəʃɔ́ːrəns] 안심시키기, 안심시키는 것

16-18 [3\^] 영국식 발음

Questions 16-18 refer to the following excerpt from a meeting and floor plan.

> As you know, [16]I hired several new employees for the sales department. They were supposed to join our team next week, but I've decided to delay their start date until after the company relocates in May. [17]We just don't have enough space for them here. One last thing. There's an error in the memo from human resources about the new office. The marketing team members won't be in Room 201—Um, that one will be used by accounting. Instead, [18]they'll take the room next to the elevator, directly across from the conference room.
>
> hire[미 haiər, 영 haiə] 고용하다　delay[diléi] 연기하다
> relocate[미 ri:lóukeit, 영 ri:ləukéit] 이전하다　human resources 인사부
> accounting[əkáuntiŋ] 회계(부서)

해석

16-18번은 다음 회의 발췌록과 평면도에 관한 문제입니다.

여러분이 아시다시피, [16]저는 영업부서를 위해 몇몇 신입 사원들을 고용했습니다. 그들은 다음 주에 우리 팀에 합류하기로 되어 있었지만, 저는 5월에 회사가 이전한 이후까지 그들의 근무 시작일을 연기하기로 결정했습니다. [17]이곳에는 그들을 위한 공간이 충분하지 않습니다. 마지막 안건입니다. 새로운 사무실에 대해 인사부에서 보낸 회람에 오류가 있습니다. 마케팅팀의 팀원들은 201호를 사용하지 않을 것입니다—음, 그곳은 회계부서가 사용할 것입니다. 대신, [18]그들은 엘리베이터 옆에 있고, 회의실 바로 건너편에 있는 사무실을 사용할 것입니다.

201호	회의실	202호
203호	엘리베이터	[18]204호　직원 휴게실

16

해석　청자들은 누구인 것 같은가?
(A) 기술자들
(B) 마케팅 담당 직원들
(C) 접수원들
(D) 영업 사원들

해설　청자들의 신분을 묻는 문제입니다. "I hired several new employees for the sales department. They were supposed to join our team next week"이라며 영업부서를 위해 몇몇 신입 사원들을 고용했다고 한 뒤 그들이 다음 주에 자신들의 팀에 합류하기로 되어 있었다고 하였습니다. 이를 통해 청자들이 영업부서의 직원들임을 알 수 있습니다. 따라서 정답은 (D) Sales representatives입니다.

어휘　receptionist[risépʃənist] 접수원　sales representative 영업 사원

17

해석　신입 사원들은 왜 계획된 것보다 늦게 근무를 시작할 것인가?
(A) 사무 공간이 너무 좁다.
(B) 프로젝트가 연기되었다.
(C) 사무실이 공사 중이다.
(D) 팀이 재배치되었다.

해설　신입 사원들이 계획된 것보다 늦게 근무를 시작할 이유를 묻는 문제입니다. "We just don't have enough space for them here."라며 이곳에는 그들을 위한 공간이 충분하지 않다고 하였습니다. 따라서 정

답은 (A) A work area is too small입니다.

어휘　under construction 공사 중인
reassign[rì:əsáin] 재배치하다, 다시 지정하다

18

해석　시각 자료를 보아라. 어떤 사무실이 마케팅팀에 의해 사용될 것인가?
(A) 201호
(B) 202호
(C) 203호
(D) 204호

해설　마케팅팀에 의해 사용될 사무실을 묻는 문제입니다. "they[marketing team members]'ll take the room next to the elevator, directly across from the conference room"이라며 마케팅팀의 팀원들은 엘리베이터 옆에 있고, 회의실 바로 건너편에 있는 사무실을 사용할 것이라고 하였으므로, 마케팅팀이 204호를 사용할 것임을 평면도에서 알 수 있습니다. 따라서 정답은 (D) Room 204입니다.

DAY 17　세부 사항 관련 문제 1

Course 1　요청·제안·언급 문제

HACKERS PRACTICE　🎧 DAY17_02　　　　　　p.137

01 (B)	02 (B)	03 (B)	04 (C)

01-02 [3\^] 캐나다식 발음 / 호주식 발음

Questions 1-2 refer to the following speech.

> Thank you for coming to this meeting. I want to provide an update on the repairs we've made to the apartment building since the hurricane last month. [01]All that's left to do is paint the exterior walls. This will happen on September 10. On that day, do not leave your vehicle along the side of the building. Paint might fall on your car. [02]Please make use of the underground garage.
>
> repair[미 ripéər, 영 ripéə] 보수, 수리
> exterior[미 ikstíəriər, 영 ikstíəriə] 외부의
> vehicle[미 víːikəl, 영 víəkl] 차량　along[미 əlɔ́:ŋ, 영 əlɔ́ŋ] ~을 따라
> make use of ~을 이용하다　garage[미 gərá:dʒ, 영 gǽrɑːʒ] 주차장, 차고

해석

1-2번은 다음 연설에 관한 문제입니다.

이 회의에 와주신 여러분들께 감사드립니다. 저는 지난달의 허리케인 이후에 저희가 진행한 아파트 건물 보수 작업에 관한 최신 정보를 제공해 드리고자 합니다. [01]남은 일은 외벽을 페인트칠하는 것뿐입니다. 이것은 9월 10일에 이루어질 것입니다. 그날에는, 여러분의 차량을 건물 측면을 따라 세워두지 마시기 바랍니다. 페인트가 여러분의 차에 떨어질 수도 있습니다. [02]지하 주차장을 이용해 주세요.

01

해석　화자는 아파트 건물에 대해 무엇을 말하는가?
(A) 9월 10일에 철거될 것이다.
(B) 외벽이 페인트칠될 것이다.
(C) 주차 구역이 확장될 것이다.
(D) 배달 차량들의 접근을 제한한다.

해설 화자가 아파트 건물에 대해 언급하는 것을 묻는 문제입니다. "All that's left to do is paint the exterior walls. This will happen on September 10."라며 아파트 건물에 해야 할 남은 일은 외벽을 페인트칠하는 것뿐이고 이것은 9월 10일에 이루어질 것이라고 하였습니다. 따라서 정답은 (B) Its outside walls will be painted입니다.

어휘 **demolish**[미 dimá:liʃ, 영 dimáliʃ] 철거하다, 파괴하다
limit[límit] 제한하다

02

해석 화자는 청자들에게 무엇을 해달라고 요청하는가?
(A) 옆문으로 들어간다.
(B) 특정 구역에 주차한다.
(C) 관리 사무실에 들른다.
(D) 최신 정보를 위해 일정을 확인한다.

해설 화자가 청자들에게 요청하는 것을 묻는 문제입니다. "Please make use of the underground garage."라며 지하 주차장을 이용해 달라고 요청하였습니다. 따라서 정답은 (B) Park in a certain area입니다.

어휘 **management office** 관리 사무실

03-04 [영국식 발음 / 미국식 발음]

Questions 3-4 refer to the following talk.

> May I please have everyone's attention? We'll reach Pine Forest Park very shortly. ⁰³Many of the trails in the park are very steep, so please be careful during the hike. I also recommend wearing a hat for protection against the sun. Oh . . . and halfway through our hike, we'll rest at a natural spring, where you can take photographs. If you did not bring a camera, ⁰⁴I'll gladly take your picture.
>
> **shortly**[미 ʃɔ́:rtli, 영 ʃɔ́:tli] 곧 **trail**[treil] 오솔길, 산길
> **steep**[sti:p] 가파른, 급격한 **hike**[haik] 도보여행
> **recommend**[rèkəménd] 권하다, 추천하다
> **natural**[nǽtʃərəl] 천연의, 자연의 **spring**[spriŋ] 샘

해석

3-4번은 다음 담화에 관한 문제입니다.

모두 주목해 주시겠습니까? 우리는 곧 Pine Forest 공원에 도착할 것입니다. ⁰³공원에 있는 많은 오솔길들이 매우 가파르므로, 도보여행 동안 조심하시기 바랍니다. 저는 또한 햇빛으로부터 보호하기 위해 모자를 쓰는 것을 권해 드립니다. 아... 그리고 도보여행의 중간쯤에, 천연 샘에서 휴식을 취할 것인데, 여러분은 그곳에서 사진을 찍으실 수 있습니다. 만약 카메라를 가져오지 않으셨다면, ⁰⁴제가 기꺼이 여러분의 사진을 찍어 드리겠습니다.

03

해석 화자는 Pine Forest 공원에 대해 무엇을 언급하는가?
(A) 매우 붐빈다.
(B) 가파른 오솔길이 있다.
(C) 커다란 호수가 있다.
(D) 가기 어렵다.

해설 화자가 Pine Forest 공원에 대해 언급하는 것을 묻는 문제입니다. "Many of the trails in the park are very steep"이라며 공원에 있는 많은 오솔길이 매우 가파르다고 하였습니다. 따라서 정답은 (B) It has steep trails입니다.

04

해석 화자는 무엇을 해주겠다고 제안하는가?
(A) 출발을 연기한다.

(B) 음료수를 나눠준다.
(C) 사진을 찍어준다.
(D) 다른 길을 찾는다.

해설 화자가 해주겠다고 제안하는 것을 묻는 문제입니다. "I'll gladly take your picture"라며 기꺼이 청자들의 사진을 찍어 주겠다고 하였습니다. 따라서 정답은 (C) Take photographs입니다.

어휘 **postpone**[미 poustpóun, 영 pəustpə́un] 연기하다, 미루다
departure[미 dipá:rtʃər, 영 dipá:tʃə] 출발 **pass out** ~을 나눠주다
route[ru:t] 길

Course 2 이유·방법·정도 문제

HACKERS PRACTICE ♪ DAY17_04   p.139

| 01 (B) | 02 (A) | 03 (C) | 04 (B) |

01-02 [캐나다식 발음 / 호주식 발음]

Questions 1-2 refer to the following telephone message.

> Albert, it's Vincent Shell calling. ⁰¹There has been an unexpected change to my plans. Our client asked me to remain in France for two extra days for additional meetings. Consequently, I'll miss our three o'clock presentation on Thursday. I'm sorry for the inconvenience. However, there's no need to reschedule. ⁰²I'm sure one of our other team members can give it for me. I've already e-mailed you the slideshow that I created for the presentation. Thank you.
>
> **remain**[riméin] 머무르다, 체류하다 **additional**[ədíʃənəl] 추가적인
> **consequently**[미 ká:nsəkwèntli, 영 kɔ́nsikwəntli] 그래서, 따라서
> **miss**[mis] ~을 하지 못하다
> **inconvenience**[미 ìnkənví:njəns, 영 ìnkənví:niəns] 불편
> **reschedule**[미 ri:skédʒu:l, 영 ri:ʃédʒu:l] 일정을 변경하다

해석

1-2번은 다음 전화 메시지에 관한 문제입니다.

Albert, Vincent Shell이에요. ⁰¹제 계획에 예상치 못한 변동이 생겼어요. 우리 고객이 추가 회의를 위해 제게 프랑스에 이틀 더 머물러 달라고 요청했어요. 그래서, 저는 목요일 3시 정각에 있을 우리의 발표를 하지 못할 거예요. 불편을 끼쳐서 죄송해요. 하지만, 일정을 변경할 필요는 없어요. ⁰²저는 우리의 다른 팀원들 중 한 명이 저를 대신해서 할 수 있을 거라고 확신해요. 제가 발표를 위해 만든 슬라이드 쇼는 당신께 이미 이메일로 보냈어요. 고마워요.

01

해석 화자는 왜 그의 계획을 변경했는가?
(A) 개인 휴가를 연장하기 위해
(B) 고객의 요청을 이행하기 위해
(C) 발표를 위한 시간을 내기 위해
(D) 전화 회의를 놓치지 않기 위해

해설 화자가 계획을 변경한 이유를 묻는 문제입니다. "There has been an unexpected change to my plans. Our client asked me to remain in France for two extra days for additional meetings."라며 고객이 추가 회의를 위해 프랑스에 이틀 더 머물러 달라고 요청해서 계획에 예상치 못한 변동이 생겼다고 한 것을 통해, 화자가 고객의 요청을 이행하기 위해 계획을 변경했음을 알 수 있습니다. 따라서 정답은 (B) To fulfill a client's request입니다.

어휘 **extend**[iksténd] 연장하다 **fulfill**[fulfíl] 이행하다
conference call 전화 회의

02

해석 화자가 "일정을 변경할 필요는 없어요"라고 말할 때 의도하는 것은 무엇인가?
(A) 다른 사람이 그를 대신할 것이다.
(B) 발표가 취소될 것이다.
(C) 회의가 중요하지 않다.
(D) 행사를 늦게 시작할 수 있다.

해설 화자가 하는 말(there's no need to reschedule)의 의도를 묻는 문제입니다. "I'm sure one of our other team members can give it[presentation] for me."라며 다른 팀원들 중 한 명이 자신을 대신해서 발표를 할 수 있을 거라고 확신한다고 한 것을 통해 다른 사람이 그를 대신할 것임을 전달하려는 의도임을 알 수 있습니다. 따라서 정답은 (A) Another person will replace him입니다.

어휘 **replace**[ripléis] 대신하다, 대체하다

03-04 [3인] 미국식 발음 / 영국식 발음

Questions 3-4 refer to the following broadcast.

This is Carol Ward. I'm here at one of Detroit's most unique dining establishments, Fig Leaf. ⁰³Here, customers place orders with a smartphone application right from their table. Then, a robot delivers their food from the kitchen! Owner David Maggio says this unusual style of service has many benefits. In addition to ⁰⁴reducing the average customer wait time to 10 minutes, it also has resulted in 30 percent fewer mistakes with orders.

dining[dáiniŋ] 식사 **establishment**[istæbliʃmənt] (가게·병원 등의) 시설
place an order 주문하다 **average**[ǽvəridʒ] 평균
result in 결과적으로 ~을 가져오다

해석

3-4번은 다음 방송에 관한 문제입니다.

저는 Carol Ward입니다. 저는 이곳 디트로이트의 가장 독특한 식당들 중 하나인 Fig Leaf에 와 있습니다. ⁰³여기서, 손님들이 테이블에서 바로 스마트폰 애플리케이션으로 주문합니다. 그러면, 로봇이 주방에서 음식을 배달합니다! 소유주인 David Maggio는 이 독특한 서비스 방식에 많은 이점이 있다고 말합니다. 그것은 ⁰⁴평균 고객 대기 시간을 10분으로 줄여줄 뿐만 아니라, 또한 주문과 관련하여 30퍼센트 더 적은 오류로 이어졌습니다.

03

해석 식당 손님들은 어떻게 주문할 수 있는가?
(A) 로봇에게 이야기함으로써
(B) 문자 메시지를 보냄으로써
(C) 모바일 애플리케이션을 사용함으로써
(D) 전화번호로 전화함으로써

해설 식당 손님들이 주문할 수 있는 방법을 묻는 문제입니다. "Here[one of ~ dining establishments, Fig Leaf], customers place orders with a smartphone application"이라며 Fig Leaf 식당에서는 손님들이 스마트폰 애플리케이션으로 주문한다고 하였습니다. 따라서 정답은 (C) By using a mobile application입니다.

04

해석 평균 고객 대기 시간은 얼마인가?
(A) 5분
(B) 10분

(C) 20분
(D) 30분

해설 평균 고객 대기 시간이 얼마인지를 묻는 문제입니다. "reducing the average customer wait time to 10 minutes"라며 평균 고객 대기 시간을 10분으로 줄였다고 하였습니다. 따라서 정답은 (B) 10 minutes입니다.

HACKERS TEST 🎧 DAY17_05   p.140

01	(B)	02	(A)	03	(C)	04	(A)
05	(D)	06	(B)	07	(D)	08	(D)
09	(A)	10	(C)	11	(B)	12	(B)
13	(B)	14	(D)	15	(C)	16	(C)
17	(A)	18	(C)				

01-03 [3인] 캐나다식 발음

Questions 1-3 refer to the following announcement.

Ladies and gentlemen, as noted in your programs, ⁰¹there will now be a 30-minute break before the orchestra resumes its performance. ⁰²Drinks can be purchased at the bar during the intermission. Keep in mind, however, that ⁰³beverages purchased in the lobby are not allowed in the auditorium. Please make sure to leave them behind when you take your seats at 8:25 P.M. Also, restrooms are located on either side of the main lobby. If you need any assistance during the interval, talk to one of our staff members.

program[미 próugræm, 영 próugræm] 편성표, 일정표
resume[미 rizú:m, 영 rizjú:m] 다시 시작하다
performance[미 pərfɔ́:rməns, 영 pəfɔ́:məns] 연주, 공연
purchase[미 pə́:rtʃəs, 영 pə́:tʃəs] 구입하다
intermission[미 intərmíʃn, 영 intəmíʃn] 중간 휴식
beverage[bévəridʒ] 음료 **auditorium**[ɔ̀:ditɔ́:riəm] 객석
interval[미 íntərvəl, 영 íntəvəl] 휴식 시간

해석

1-3번은 다음 공지에 관한 문제입니다.

신사숙녀 여러분, 여러분들의 편성표에 적혀 있듯이, ⁰¹지금부터 오케스트라가 연주를 다시 시작하기 전까지 30분간 휴식이 있을 예정입니다. ⁰²중간 휴식 시간 동안 판매대에서 음료를 구입하실 수 있습니다. 하지만, ⁰³로비에서 구입하신 음료는 객석에서는 허용되지 않음에 유의해 주십시오. 오후 8시 25분에 착석하실 때, 음료는 반드시 두고 오시기 바랍니다. 또한, 화장실은 중앙 로비의 양측에 위치해 있습니다. 휴식 시간 동안 도움이 필요하시다면, 저희 직원들 중 한 명에게 말씀해 주십시오.

01

해석 공지는 어디에서 이루어지고 있는가?
(A) 스포츠 경기장에서
(B) 콘서트홀에서
(C) 미술관에서
(D) 영화관에서

해설 공지가 이루어지고 있는 장소를 묻는 문제입니다. "there will now be a 30-minute break before the orchestra resumes its performance"라며 지금부터 오케스트라가 연주를 다시 시작하기 전까지 30분간 휴식이 있을 예정이라고 한 것을 통해 공지가 콘서트홀에서 이루어지고 있음을 알 수 있습니다. 따라서 정답은 (B) At a concert hall입니다.

어휘 **sports stadium** 스포츠 경기장

PART 4

해커스 토익 700+ (LC+RC+VOCA)

02

해석 화자에 따르면, 청자들은 중간 휴식 시간 동안 무엇을 할 수 있는가?
(A) 음료를 구입한다.
(B) 몇몇 연주자들을 만난다.
(C) 앞으로의 공연을 위해 예매를 한다.
(D) 공연 편성표를 요청한다.

해설 청자들이 중간 휴식 시간 동안 할 수 있는 것을 묻는 문제입니다. "Drinks can be purchased at the bar during the intermission." 이라며 중간 휴식 시간 동안 판매대에서 음료를 구입할 수 있다고 하였습니다. 따라서 정답은 (A) Purchase some drinks입니다.

03

해설 화자는 청자들에게 무엇을 해달라고 요청하는가?
(A) 돌아올 때 표를 보여준다.
(B) 휴대전화 전원을 끈다.
(C) 음료를 로비에 둔다.
(D) 귀중품을 휴대한다.

해설 화자가 청자들에게 요청하는 것을 묻는 문제입니다. "beverages purchased in the lobby are not allowed in the auditorium. Please make sure to leave them behind"라며 로비에서 구입한 음료는 객석에서는 허용되지 않는다고 한 뒤, 그것들을 반드시 두고 올 것을 요청하였습니다. 따라서 정답은 (C) Leave beverages in a lobby입니다.

어휘 present[prizént] 보여주다, 제시하다
valuables[미 vǽljuəblz, 영 vǽljəblz] 귀중품

04-06 🔊 영국식 발음

Questions 4-6 refer to the following advertisement.

> ⁰⁴Jensen Technologies is pleased to announce the release of its latest home entertainment device. The Vital Smart TV comes with several exciting features, including wireless connectivity and a built-in Web cam. And ⁰⁵until June 15, anyone who purchases this model will receive a complimentary three-month membership with Digital Content Services. This will allow you to access the latest movies and games online with your new TV. ⁰⁶Like every device we produce, the Vital Smart TV is carried by all major electronics retailers. Visit a store near you today!
>
> release[rilíːs] 출시, 발매; 출시하다
> wireless[미 wáiərlis, 영 wáiələs] 무선의　built-in[bíltin] 내장된, 붙박이의
> complimentary[미 kàmpləméntəri, 영 kɔ̀mpliméntəri] 무료의
> access[ǽkses] 이용하다, 입수하다
> carry[kǽri] (가게에서 품목을) 취급하다

해석

4-6번은 다음 광고에 관한 문제입니다.

⁰⁴Jensen Technologies사는 최신 가정용 오락 기기의 출시를 발표하게 되어 기쁩니다. Vital Smart TV에는 무선 연결 및 내장 화상 카메라를 포함한 몇몇 흥미로운 기능들이 딸려 있습니다. 그리고 ⁰⁵6월 15일까지, 이 모델을 구매하시는 모든 분들은 Digital Content Services의 무료 3개월 회원권을 받으실 것입니다. 이것은 여러분이 새 TV에서 온라인으로 최신 영화와 게임을 이용할 수 있도록 할 것입니다. ⁰⁶저희가 제조하는 모든 기기들처럼, Vital Smart TV는 모든 주요 전자제품 소매업체에서 취급됩니다. 오늘 여러분 가까이에 있는 매장을 방문하세요!

04

해석 화자는 주로 무엇에 대해 이야기하고 있는가?

(A) 새로운 제품
(B) 매장 개업
(C) 영화 개봉
(D) 임대 계약

해설 광고의 주제를 묻는 문제입니다. "Jensen Technologies is pleased to announce the release of its latest home entertainment device."라며 Jensen Technologies사는 최신 가정용 오락 기기의 출시를 발표하게 되어 기쁘다고 한 뒤, 새로운 제품과 관련된 내용을 언급하였습니다. 따라서 정답은 (A) A new product입니다.

05

해석 화자에 따르면, 6월 15일까지 무엇이 제공될 것인가?
(A) 할인
(B) 상품권
(C) 장기간 품질 보증서
(D) 회원권

해설 6월 15일까지 제공될 것을 묻는 문제입니다. "until June 15, anyone who purchases this model will receive a complimentary three-month membership"이라며 6월 15일까지 이 모델을 구매하는 모든 사람들은 무료 3개월 회원권을 받을 것이라고 하였습니다. 따라서 정답은 (D) A membership입니다.

어휘 extended[iksténdid] 장기간에 걸친

06

해석 Jensen Technologies사에 대해 무엇이 언급되는가?
(A) 올해 여러 새로운 TV 모델들을 출시했다.
(B) 기기들이 여러 업체에 의해 판매된다.
(C) 전국 각지에 소매점을 운영한다.
(D) 온라인 게임이 소비자들에게 인기가 있다.

해설 Jensen Technologies사에 대해 언급되는 것을 묻는 문제입니다. "Like every device we[Jensen Technologies] produce, the Vital Smart TV is carried by all major electronics retailers."라며 Jensen Technologies사가 제조하는 모든 기기들처럼 Vital Smart TV는 모든 주요 전자제품 소매업체에서 취급된다고 하였습니다. 따라서 정답은 (B) Its devices are sold by multiple companies입니다.

어휘 operate[미 ápərèit, 영 ɔ́pəreit] 운영하다　retail outlet 소매점

07-09 🔊 미국식 발음

Questions 7-9 refer to the following instructions.

> I have some important details regarding ⁰⁷the employee evaluations you'll complete on our company Web site. First of all, please note that the evaluation forms cannot be accessed from a mobile device. ⁰⁸The technical team manager, Roger Tan, said his staff plan to make this feature available for next quarter's evaluations. Also, don't forget to enter your five-digit worker ID code at the bottom of the form. ⁰⁹Your codes will allow management to verify who uploaded the documents. Oh, and please call my extension at 4558 with any questions about the evaluations.
>
> regarding[미 rigɑ́ːrdiŋ, 영 rigɑ́ːdiŋ] ~과 관련하여
> evaluation[미 ivæ̀ljuéiʃən, 영 ivæ̀ljuéiʃən] 평가(서), 심사
> access[ǽkses] 이용하다, 접근하다　feature[미 fíːtʃər, 영 fíːtʃə] 기능, 특징
> quarter[미 kwɔ́ːrtər, 영 kwɔ́ːtə] 분기　digit[dídʒit] 자리(수)
> verify[미 vérəfài, 영 vérifai] 확인하다, 입증하다
> extension[iksténʃən] 내선 번호

7-9번은 다음 설명에 관한 문제입니다.

⁰⁷여러분이 우리 회사 웹사이트에서 작성할 직원 평가서와 관련하여 중요한 세부 사항들이 있습니다. 가장 먼저, 평가 양식들은 모바일 기기에서는 이용할 수 없다는 것을 유념해 주시기 바랍니다. ⁰⁸기술팀의 관리자인 Roger Tan에 따르면, 그의 직원들이 다음 분기 평가에서는 이 기능을 이용할 수 있도록 할 계획이라고 합니다. 또한, 양식 맨 아래에 여러분의 다섯 자리 직원 ID 코드를 입력하는 것을 잊지 마세요. ⁰⁹여러분의 코드는 경영진이 누가 문서를 업로드했는지 확인할 수 있게 해줄 것입니다. 아, 그리고 평가와 관련된 질문이 있으시다면 제 내선 번호인 4558로 전화해 주시기 바랍니다.

07

해석 청자들은 어떻게 직원 평가서를 작성할 수 있는가?
(A) 모바일 애플리케이션을 이용함으로써
(B) 서면 양식을 작성함으로써
(C) 전화를 함으로써
(D) 온라인 페이지를 방문함으로써

해설 청자들이 직원 평가서를 작성할 방법을 묻는 문제입니다. "the employee evaluations you'll complete on our company Web site"라며 회사 웹사이트에서 작성할 직원 평가서라고 하였습니다. 따라서 정답은 (D) By visiting an online page입니다.

어휘 fill out ~을 작성하다, ~을 기입하다

08

해석 Roger Tan은 누구인가?
(A) 영업부장
(B) 보안 담당관
(C) 초청 연사
(D) 기술 직원

해설 Roger Tan의 신분을 묻는 문제입니다. "The technical team manager, Roger Tan"이라며 기술팀의 관리자인 Roger Tan이라고 한 것을 통해 Roger Tan이 기술 직원임을 알 수 있습니다. 따라서 정답은 (D) A technical worker입니다.

어휘 security[sikjúərəti] 보안, 안전

09

해석 청자들은 왜 ID 코드를 입력해야 하는가?
(A) 확인을 제공하기 위해
(B) 전자 문서를 저장하기 위해
(C) 수업에 등록하기 위해
(D) 회담에 참여하기 위해

해설 청자들이 ID 코드를 입력해야 하는 이유를 묻는 문제입니다. "Your codes[worker ID code] will allow management to verify who uploaded the documents."라며 청자들의 직원 ID 코드가 경영진이 누가 문서를 업로드했는지 확인할 수 있게 해줄 것이라고 하였습니다. 따라서 정답은 (A) To provide verification입니다.

어휘 verification[vèrəfikéiʃən] 확인, 입증 forum[fɔ́ːrəm] 회담, 토론회

10-12 🔊 호주식 발음

Questions 10-12 refer to the following speech.

Good afternoon. I'm Bradley Mendez, the facility director of Diamond Foreign Languages Academy. ¹⁰I'm pleased to be here today to celebrate your graduation. Before we begin, please note that a group picture will be taken at the end of today's ceremony. If you'd like a copy, ¹¹you should write down your name and e-mail address for our photographer. He will ⟳

e-mail the photos in about one week. And ¹²now, I ask you all to please look toward the screen behind me for a short video on our school's many achievements.

director[미 diréktər, 영 dairéktə] (고등학교의) 교장, 국장
graduation[미 grædʒuéiʃən, 영 grædʒuéiʃən] 졸업식, 학위 수여식
ceremony[미 sérəmòuni, 영 sériməni] 기념식, 예식
achievement[ətʃíːvmənt] 성과, 업적

10-12번은 다음 연설에 관한 문제입니다.

안녕하세요. 저는 Diamond 외국어 학교의 교장 Bradley Mendez입니다. ¹⁰저는 오늘 여러분의 졸업을 축하하기 위해 이 자리에 있게 되어 기쁩니다. 시작하기 전에, 오늘 기념식의 마지막에 단체 사진이 촬영될 것이라는 점을 유념해 주시기 바랍니다. 만약 한 장 원하신다면, 사진사에게 ¹¹이름과 이메일 주소를 적어 주셔야 합니다. 그가 일주일쯤 뒤에 사진을 이메일로 발송할 것입니다. 그러면 ¹²이제, 여러분 모두 우리 학교의 많은 성과에 대한 짧은 영상을 위해 제 뒤에 있는 스크린 쪽을 봐 주시기 바랍니다.

10

해석 청자들은 왜 학교에 모여 있는가?
(A) 교육에 참여하기 위해
(B) 강좌에 등록하기 위해
(C) 축하 행사에 참석하기 위해
(D) 발표를 보기 위해

해설 청자들이 학교에 모여 있는 이유를 묻는 문제입니다. "I'm pleased to be here[Diamond Foreign Languages Academy] today to celebrate your graduation."이라며 오늘 청자들의 졸업을 축하하기 위해 Diamond 외국어 학교에 있게 되어 기쁘다고 한 것을 통해 청자들이 축하 행사에 참석하기 위해 학교에 모여 있음을 알 수 있습니다. 따라서 정답은 (C) To take part in a celebration입니다.

어휘 enroll[inróul] 등록하다 celebration[sèləbréiʃən] 축하 행사

11

해석 화자는 무엇을 제안하는가?
(A) 명함 찾아가기
(B) 연락처 제공하기
(C) 카메라 플래시 끄기
(D) 기관의 웹사이트 확인하기

해설 화자가 제안하는 것을 묻는 문제입니다. "you should write down your name and e-mail address"라며 이름과 이메일 주소를 적을 것을 제안하였습니다. 따라서 정답은 (B) Providing contact information입니다.

어휘 business card 명함 contact information 연락처

12

해석 청자들은 다음에 무엇을 할 것 같은가?
(A) 강당을 나간다.
(B) 영상을 시청한다.
(C) 무대로 다가간다.
(D) 연설을 듣는다.

해설 청자들이 다음에 할 일을 묻는 문제입니다. "now, I ask you all to please look toward the screen ~ for a short video"라며 이제 모두 짧은 영상을 위해 스크린 쪽을 봐 달라고 하였습니다. 따라서 정답은 (B) View a video입니다.

어휘 exit[égzit] 나가다 auditorium[ɔ̀ːditɔ́ːriəm] 강당
approach[미 əpróutʃ, 영 əpráutʃ] 다가가다, 접근하다

Questions 13-15 refer to the following talk.

Before we end our meeting, ¹³I want to make sure no one has forgotten about the marketing workshop on June 15. The company has arranged for several experts to share their knowledge. Now, I know that it's on a Saturday . . . ¹⁴No one likes to work on the weekend, but you don't want to miss this. It'll be a great opportunity to learn some highly effective marketing strategies. The registration deadline is June 10, and space is limited to 30 participants. Um . . . ¹⁵20 people have signed up already, so don't put it off if you plan to attend next Saturday.

expert[미 ékspə:rt, 영 ékspɔ:t] 전문가 **share**[미 ʃɛər, 영 ʃeə] 공유하다
knowledge[미 nά:lidʒ, 영 nɔ́lidʒ] 경험, 지식 **effective**[iféktiv] 효과적인
registration[rèdʒistréiʃən] 등록 **sign up** ~에 등록하다
put off ~을 미루다, ~을 연기하다

해석

13-15번은 다음 담화에 관한 문제입니다.

우리가 회의를 마치기 전에, ¹³저는 6월 15일에 있을 마케팅 워크숍에 대해 아무도 잊지 않았기를 확실히 하고 싶습니다. 회사가 몇몇 전문가들이 그들의 경험을 공유할 수 있도록 준비했습니다. 자, 그게 토요일이라는 것을 알고 있습니다... ¹⁴아무도 주말에 일하고 싶어 하지 않지만, 여러분은 이것을 놓치고 싶지 않을 겁니다. 이것은 매우 효과적인 몇몇 마케팅 전략들을 배울 좋은 기회가 될 것입니다. 등록 마감기한은 6월 10일이며, 자리는 30명의 참가자로 제한되어 있습니다. 음... ¹⁵20명이 이미 등록했으니, 여러분이 다음 주 토요일에 참석할 계획이라면 미루지 마세요.

13

해석 담화의 목적은 무엇인가?
(A) 프로젝트 일정을 업데이트하기 위해
(B) 청자들에게 교육에 대해 상기시키기 위해
(C) 마케팅 캠페인에 대해 설명하기 위해
(D) 청자들에게 회사의 확장에 대해 알리기 위해

해설 담화의 목적을 묻는 문제입니다. "I want to make sure no one has forgotten about the marketing workshop"이라며 마케팅 워크숍에 대해 아무도 잊지 않았기를 확실히 하고 싶다고 한 뒤, 워크숍에 관한 내용을 언급하였습니다. 따라서 정답은 (B) To remind listeners of a training session입니다.

어휘 **remind**[rimáind] 상기시키다 **notify**[미 nóutəfài, 영 nə́utifài] 알리다
expansion[ikspǽnʃən] 확장

14

해석 화자는 왜 "자, 그게 토요일이라는 것을 알고 있습니다"라고 말하는가?
(A) 대안을 제시하기 위해
(B) 마감기한을 강조하기 위해
(C) 날짜에 대해 불평하기 위해
(D) 공감을 표하기 위해

해설 화자가 하는 말(Now, I know that it's on a Saturday)의 의도를 묻는 문제입니다. "No one likes to work on the weekend"라며 아무도 주말에 일하고 싶어 하지 않는다고 한 말을 통해 화자가 주말에 워크숍에 참석하는 것에 대해 직원들이 느낄만한 감정에 공감을 표하려는 의도임을 알 수 있습니다. 따라서 정답은 (D) To express sympathy입니다.

어휘 **alternative**[미 ɔːltə́rːnətiv, 영 ɔːltə́ːnətiv] 대안, 대체
emphasize[émfəsàiz] 강조하다 **sympathy**[símpəθi] 공감, 동정

15

해석 얼마나 많은 사람들이 다음 주 토요일의 행사에 등록했는가?
(A) 10명
(B) 15명
(C) 20명
(D) 30명

해설 다음 주 토요일의 행사에 등록한 사람들의 수를 묻는 문제입니다. "20 people have signed up already, so don't put it off if you plan to attend next Saturday."라며 20명이 이미 등록했으니 다음 주 토요일에 참석할 계획이라면 미루지 말라고 한 것을 통해 다음 주 토요일의 행사에 20명이 등록했음을 알 수 있습니다. 따라서 정답은 (C) 20입니다.

Questions 16-18 refer to the following excerpt from a meeting and graph.

I'd like to go over the results of ¹⁶the questionnaire we asked our store's customers to fill out last month. They are very happy with the store's layout. Many mentioned that they appreciated ¹⁷the increased size of our fitting rooms too. However, there were complaints about the changes to our loyalty program. Customers said that they received greater discounts under the old system. And this dissatisfaction affected our profits. Here . . . look at this. ¹⁸Sales revenue sharply declined in the month the new program was introduced, and it's remained lower since. Maybe we need to reconsider this decision.

questionnaire[미 kwèstʃənɛ́ər, 영 kwèstʃənéə] 설문지
layout[미 léiàut, 영 léiàut] 배치
appreciate[əpríːʃièit] 높이 평가하다, 고마워하다
loyalty program 회원 혜택 제도 **affect**[əfékt] 영향을 미치다
revenue[미 révənjùː, 영 révənjùː] 수익 **decline**[dikláin] 감소하다
introduce[미 ìntrədjúːs, 영 ìntrədʒúːs] 도입하다
reconsider[미 rìːkənsídər, 영 rìːkənsídə] 다시 고려하다

해석

16-18번은 다음 회의의 발췌록과 그래프에 관한 문제입니다.

저는 ¹⁶지난달에 우리가 우리 매장의 고객들에게 작성해 달라고 요청한 설문지의 결과를 살펴보려고 합니다. 고객들은 매장의 배치에 매우 만족하고 있습니다. 많은 사람들이 ¹⁷탈의실의 확장된 규모도 높이 평가한다고 언급했습니다. 하지만, 우리의 회원 혜택 제도의 변경 사항에 대해서는 불만이 있었습니다. 고객들은 이전 제도에서 더 많은 할인을 받았다고 했습니다. 그리고 이 불만은 우리의 수익에 영향을 미쳤습니다. 여기... 이것을 보세요. ¹⁸판매 수익은 새로운 제도가 도입된 달에 급격하게 감소했고, 이후로 여전히 낮아진 상태로 있습니다. 우리는 이 결정을 다시 고려해야 할 것 같습니다.

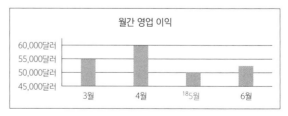

월간 영업 이익

	3월	4월	¹⁸5월	6월
60,000달러 / 55,000달러 / 50,000달러 / 45,000달러				

16

해석 매장은 최근에 무엇을 했는가?
(A) 더 많은 계산원을 고용했다.
(B) 새로운 장소로 이전했다.

(C) 설문 조사를 실시했다.

(D) 할인 행사를 열었다.

해설 매장이 최근에 한 일을 묻는 문제입니다. "the questionnaire we asked our store's customers to fill out last month"라며 지난달에 매장의 고객들에게 작성해 달라고 요청한 설문지라고 한 것을 통해 매장이 최근에 설문 조사를 실시했음을 알 수 있습니다. 따라서 정답은 (C) Conducted a survey입니다.

어휘 conduct[kəndʌ́kt] 실시하다

17

해석 남자는 탈의실에 대해 무엇을 말하는가?

(A) 확장되었다.

(B) 입구에서 가깝다.

(C) 일시적으로 폐쇄되었다.

(D) 개수가 너무 적다.

해설 남자가 탈의실에 대해 언급하는 것을 묻는 문제입니다. "the increased size of our fitting rooms"라며 탈의실의 확장된 규모라고 한 것을 통해 탈의실이 확장되었음을 알 수 있습니다. 따라서 정답은 (A) They were expanded입니다.

어휘 expand[ikspǽnd] 확장하다 shut down ~을 폐쇄하다

18

해석 시각 자료를 보아라. 새로운 회원 혜택 제도는 언제 도입되었는가?

(A) 3월에

(B) 4월에

(C) 5월에

(D) 6월에

해설 새로운 회원 혜택 제도가 도입된 시기를 묻는 문제입니다. "Sales revenue sharply declined in the month the new program was introduced, and it's remained lower since."라며 판매 수익이 새로운 제도가 도입된 달에 급격하게 감소했고 이후로 여전히 낮아진 상태로 있다고 하였으므로, 5월에 새로운 회원 혜택 제도가 도입되었음을 그래프에서 알 수 있습니다. 따라서 정답은 (C) In May입니다.

DAY 18 | 세부 사항 관련 문제 2

Course 1 특정 세부 사항 문제

HACKERS PRACTICE 🎧 DAY18_02   p.143

| 01 (D) | 02 (A) | 03 (C) | 04 (D) |

01-02 🔊 캐나다식 발음 / 호주식 발음

Questions 1-2 refer to the following talk.

> ⁰¹On this stop of the tour, we'll see the part of the factory where bottles are filled with soft drinks. When operating at full capacity, these machines can fill 10,000 containers every day. If you look to your right, you'll see empty bottles entering the room on the conveyor belt and being filled. ⁰²Now, we'll move to the next room, where you can taste some beverage samples. Please follow me.

tour[미 tuər, 영 tuə] 견학, 관광 be filled with ~으로 채워지다
soft drink 청량음료 operate[미 ápərèit, 영 ɔ́pəreit] 가동하다

full capacity 전력, 전용량 container[미 kəntéinər, 영 kəntéinə] 용기, 그릇
taste[teist] 맛보다 beverage[bévəridʒ] 음료

해석

1-2번은 다음 담화에 관한 문제입니다.

⁰¹견학 중 이번에 멈추는 곳에서, 우리는 병들이 청량음료로 채워지는 공장 구역을 구경할 것입니다. 전력으로 가동 중일 때, 이 기계들은 매일 10,000개의 용기들을 채울 수 있습니다. 여러분의 오른쪽을 보시면, 빈 병들이 컨베이어 벨트에 실려 이 장소로 들어간 후 채워지고 있는 것이 보일 것입니다. ⁰²이제, 우리는 몇몇 음료 샘플들을 맛볼 수 있는 옆 공간으로 이동하겠습니다. 저를 따라오시기 바랍니다.

01

해석 청자들은 어디에 있는 것 같은가?

(A) 체육관에

(B) 가게에

(C) 창고에

(D) 공장에

해설 청자들이 있는 장소를 묻는 문제입니다. "On this stop of the tour, we'll see the part of the factory"라며 견학 중 이번에 멈추는 곳에서 공장 구역을 구경할 것이라고 하였습니다. 따라서 정답은 (D) At a factory입니다.

어휘 warehouse[미 wérhaus, 영 wéəhaus] 창고

02

해석 청자들은 옆 공간에서 무엇을 할 수 있는가?

(A) 몇몇 샘플 음료를 맛본다.

(B) 선물을 몇 개 구매한다.

(C) 소책자를 가져온다.

(D) 영상을 본다.

해설 청자들이 옆 공간에서 할 수 있는 것을 묻는 문제입니다. "Now, we'll move to the next room, where you can taste some beverage samples."라며 몇몇 음료 샘플들을 맛볼 수 있는 옆 공간으로 이동할 것이라고 하였습니다. 따라서 정답은 (A) Try some sample drinks 입니다.

어휘 pamphlet[pǽmflət] 소책자

03-04 🔊 미국식 발음 / 영국식 발음

Questions 3-4 refer to the following telephone message.

> Hello, Frank. It's Marcie calling. I'm attending the Calvin University Career Fair on Friday, and ⁰³one of my team members was supposed to make company brochures for the event. Unfortunately, she went to Chicago for an urgent client meeting. So, uh, ⁰⁴could you possibly make the brochures instead? I'd like to use something similar to the promotional materials you created for last fall's sales expo. Please let me know sometime today whether you can complete this task.

attend[əténd] 참석하다 career fair 취업 박람회
be supposed to ~하기로 되어 있다
brochure[미 brouʃúər, 영 brə́uʃə] 소책자, 안내서
urgent[미 ə́:rdʒənt, 영 ə́:dʒənt] 급한
promotional[미 prəmóuʃənl, 영 prəmə́uʃənl] 홍보용의
material[mətíəriəl] 자료 expo[미 ékspou, 영 ékspəu] 박람회, 전람회

해석

3-4번은 다음 전화 메시지에 관한 문제입니다.

PART 4

한 권으로 끝내는 해커스 토익 700+ (LC+RC+VOCA)

안녕하세요, Frank. Marcie예요. 저는 금요일에 Calvin 대학교의 취업 박람회에 참석할 것이고, [03]제 팀원 중 한 명이 그 행사를 위해 회사 소책자를 만들기로 되어 있었어요. 유감스럽게도, 그녀는 고객과의 긴급한 회의를 위해 시카고로 떠났어요. 그래서, 어, [04]당신이 대신 소책자를 만들어 주실 수 있나요? 저는 당신이 작년 가을의 영업 박람회를 위해 만들었던 홍보용 자료들과 비슷한 것을 사용하고 싶어요. 당신이 이 업무를 완료할 수 있는지 오늘 중으로 제게 알려주세요.

03

해석 무엇이 문제인가?
(A) 행사가 취소되었다.
(B) 소책자에 오류가 있다.
(C) 동료가 시간이 없다.
(D) 고객이 불만을 제기했다.

해설 문제점을 묻는 문제입니다. "one of my team members was supposed to make company brochures for the event. Unfortunately, she went to Chicago for an urgent client meeting."이라며 자신의 팀원 중 한 명이 행사를 위해 회사 소책자를 만들기로 되어 있었지만 고객과의 긴급한 회의로 인해 시카고로 떠났다고 하였습니다. 따라서 정답은 (C) A colleague is unavailable입니다.

어휘 colleague[미 káli:g, 영 kɔ́li:g] 동료 complaint[kəmpléint] 불만

04

해석 화자는 청자에게 무엇을 해달라고 요청하는가?
(A) 명함을 준다.
(B) 포스터를 인쇄한다.
(C) 더 큰 부스를 예약한다.
(D) 인쇄물을 제작한다.

해설 화자가 청자에게 요청하는 것을 묻는 문제입니다. "could you possibly make the brochures instead?"라며 소책자들을 만들어달라고 요청하였습니다. 따라서 정답은 (D) Create some handouts입니다.

어휘 business card 명함 create[kriéit] 제작하다
handout[미 hǽndàut, 영 hǽndaut] 인쇄물, 유인물

Course 2 다음에 할 일 문제

HACKERS PRACTICE 🎧 DAY18_04   p.145

| 01 (A) | 02 (B) | 03 (B) | 04 (D) |

01-02 🎧 영국식 발음 / 미국식 발음

Questions 1-2 refer to the following telephone message.

> Jason, this is Kara. I won't be at the office until 4 P.M. I'm meeting with [01]Shawn Jameson, the CEO of Landlow Clothing. He wants to discuss the mobile application that our firm is creating for his company. I'm hoping to meet with their marketing manager as well. [02]I know we planned to discuss our quarterly budget over lunch, but we'll have to delay that until tomorrow. Sorry for the unexpected schedule change.
>
> quarterly[미 kwɔ́:rtərli, 영 kwɔ́:təli] 분기별의 budget[bʌ́dʒit] 예산
> unexpected[ʌ̀nikspéktid] 예상치 못한

해석

1-2번은 다음 전화 메시지에 관한 문제입니다.

Jason, Kara예요. 저는 오후 4시나 되어서야 사무실에 올 거예요. 저는 [01]Landlow Clothing사의 최고 경영자인 Shawn Jameson과 만날 거예요. 그는 우리 회사가 그의 회사를 위해 제작하고 있는 모바일 애플리케이션에 대해 논의하고 싶어 해요. 저는 그들의 마케팅 책임자도 만날 것으로 기대하고 있어요. [02]우리가 점심을 먹으며 분기별 예산에 대해 논의하기로 했던 것을 알지만, 그것을 내일까지 연기해야 할 것 같아요. 예상치 못한 일정 변경에 대해 사과드려요.

01

해석 Shawn Jameson은 누구인가?
(A) 기업 경영자
(B) 기술 자문 위원
(C) 마케팅 책임자
(D) 애플리케이션 설계자

해설 Shawn Jameson의 신분을 묻는 문제입니다. "Shawn Jameson, the CEO of Landlow Clothing"이라며 Shawn Jameson이 Landlow Clothing사의 최고 경영자라고 하였습니다. 따라서 정답은 (A) A company executive입니다.

어휘 executive[미 igzékjutiv, 영 igzékjətiv] 경영자, 임원
consultant[kənsʌ́ltənt] 자문 위원

02

해석 화자는 내일 무엇을 할 것 같은가?
(A) 다른 지사에 들른다.
(B) 예산에 대해 이야기한다.
(C) 서류를 수정한다.
(D) 사무 공간을 재배치한다.

해설 화자가 내일 할 것 같은 일을 묻는 문제입니다. "I know we planned to discuss our quarterly budget over lunch, but we'll have to delay that until tomorrow."라며 점심을 먹으며 분기별 예산에 대해 논의하기로 했던 것을 알지만 그것을 내일까지 연기해야 할 것이라고 하였습니다. 따라서 정답은 (B) Talk about a budget입니다.

어휘 stop by ~에 들르다
reorganize[미 riɔ́:rgənaiz, 영 ri:ɔ́:gənaiz] 재배치하다, 재편성하다

03-04 🎧 캐나다식 발음 / 호주식 발음

Questions 3-4 refer to the following announcement.

> [03]Good morning, Global Cruise Line passengers. This is your captain speaking. In one hour, we will dock in Tunis. For those interested, there are many beautiful beaches and outdoor markets that are accessible by taxi. In addition, [04]breakfast will be served in the main dining area in five minutes. Please head there now if you want to eat before we dock. Thank you for traveling with Global Cruise Line.
>
> passenger[미 pǽsəndʒər, 영 pǽsəndʒə] 승객
> captain[미 kǽptən, 영 kǽptin] 선장
> dock[미 dɑk, 영 dɔk] (배를) 정박하다, 부두에 대다
> accessible[미 æksésəbl, 영 əksésəbl] 갈 수 있는 dining area 식당

해석

3-4번은 다음 공지에 관한 문제입니다.

[03]좋은 아침입니다, Global Cruise Line의 승객 여러분. 저는 여러분의 선장입니다. 한 시간 뒤에, 저희는 튀니스에 정박할 것입니다. 관심이 있으신 분들을 위해 알려 드리자면, 택시로 갈 수 있는 많은 아름다운 해변들과 야외 시장들이 있습니다. 추가로 말씀드리자면, [04]아침 식사가 5분 후에 주 식당에서 제공될 것입니다. 부두에 정박하기 전에 식사를 원하신다면 지금 그곳으로 가시면 됩니다. Global Cruise Line사와 함께 여행해 주셔서 감사드립니다.

03

해석 화자는 누구인 것 같은가?
(A) 레스토랑 지배인
(B) 선장
(C) 택시 운전사
(D) 비행기 승무원

해설 화자의 신분을 묻는 문제입니다. "Good morning, Global Cruise Line passengers. This is your captain speaking."이라며 Global Cruise Line의 승객들에게 자신을 선장이라고 소개하였습니다. 따라서 정답은 (B) A ship captain입니다.

04

해석 5분 후에 무슨 일이 일어날 것 같은가?
(A) 직원들이 표를 확인할 것이다.
(B) 승객들이 배에 탑승할 것이다.
(C) 유람선이 항구에 도착할 것이다.
(D) 식사가 제공될 것이다.

해설 5분 후에 일어날 일을 묻는 문제입니다. "breakfast will be served ~ in five minutes"라며 아침 식사가 5분 후에 제공될 것이라고 하였습니다. 따라서 정답은 (D) A meal will be served입니다.

어휘 **board**[미 bɔːrd, 영 bɔːd] 탑승하다   **port**[미 pɔːrt, 영 pɔːt] 항구

HACKERS TEST 🎧 DAY18_05   p.146

01 (B)	02 (D)	03 (A)	04 (A)
05 (D)	06 (D)	07 (D)	08 (C)
09 (D)	10 (C)	11 (A)	12 (C)
13 (C)	14 (A)	15 (D)	16 (A)
17 (B)	18 (C)		

01-03 🎤 호주식 발음

Questions 1-3 refer to the following telephone message.

My name is George Holt, and I'm having problems with a laptop that I purchased from your store two weeks ago. The device worked well at first, but now ⁰¹it shuts down whenever I open a program. So, I am completely unable to use the device, and I'd like to have it repaired. Since ⁰²the product came with a one-year warranty, I assume that it will be fixed free of charge. ⁰³Please call me back at 555-2442 to tell me where I should mail the item.

laptop[미 lǽptɑp, 영 lǽptɔp] 휴대용 컴퓨터
shut down (기계가 작동을) 멈추다, 정지하다
completely[kəmplíːtli] 전혀, 완전히
warranty[미 wɔ́ːrənti, 영 wɔ́rənti] 품질 보증서
free of charge 무상으로, 무료   **mail**[meil] (우편으로) 보내다

해석

1-3번은 다음 전화 메시지에 관한 문제입니다.

제 이름은 George Holt이고, 당신의 매장에서 제가 2주 전에 구매한 휴대용 컴퓨터에 문제가 있습니다. 기기는 처음엔 잘 작동했지만, 지금은 ⁰¹제가 프로그램을 열 때마다 작동을 멈춥니다. 그래서, 저는 기기를 전혀 사용할 수 없고, 이것이 수리되었으면 합니다. ⁰²제품에 1년간의 품질 보증서가 딸려 있기 때문에, 저는 그것이 무상으로 수리될 거라고 생각합니다. ⁰³555-2442로 제게 다시 전화하셔서 물품을 어디로 보내야 하는지 알려주시기 바랍니다.

01

해석 화자는 무슨 문제를 언급하는가?

(A) 품질 보증서가 만료되었다.
(B) 컴퓨터가 제대로 작동하지 않고 있다.
(C) 휴대용 컴퓨터의 부속품을 잃어버렸다.
(D) 화면이 깨졌다.

해설 화자가 언급하는 문제점을 묻는 문제입니다. "it[laptop] shuts down whenever I open a program"이라며 휴대용 컴퓨터가 프로그램을 열 때마다 작동을 멈춘다고 하였습니다. 따라서 정답은 (B) A computer is malfunctioning입니다.

어휘 **expire**[미 ikspáiər, 영 ikspáiə] 만료되다
malfunction[mælfʌ́ŋkʃən] 제대로 작동하지 않다
accessory[미 æksésəri, 영 əksésəri] 부속품, 부품
crack[kræk] 깨다, 부수다

02

해석 화자에 따르면, 제품에 무엇이 포함되어 있는가?
(A) 무료 휴대용 컴퓨터 전용 가방
(B) 시용 회원권
(C) 여분의 전원 코드
(D) 1년간의 품질 보증서

해설 제품에 포함되어 있는 것을 묻는 문제입니다. "the product came with a one-year warranty"라며 제품에 1년간의 품질 보증서가 딸려 있었다고 하였습니다. 따라서 정답은 (D) A one-year warranty입니다.

어휘 **carrying case** 휴대용 컴퓨터 전용 가방   **trial**[tráiəl] 시용, 시험

03

해석 화자는 왜 청자가 자신의 전화에 답하기를 바라는가?
(A) 그는 우편 주소를 받아야 한다.
(B) 그는 운송 요금을 확인하고 싶어 한다.
(C) 그는 제품에 대해 질문이 있다.
(D) 그는 새로운 모니터를 주문하고 싶어 한다.

해설 청자가 전화에 답하기를 바라는 이유를 묻는 문제입니다. "Please call me back ~ to tell me where I should mail the item."이라며 다시 전화하여 물품을 어디로 보내야 하는지 알려달라고 하였습니다. 따라서 정답은 (A) He needs to obtain a mailing address입니다.

어휘 **obtain**[əbtéin] 받다, 입수하다

04-06 🎤 캐나다식 발음

Questions 4-6 refer to the following broadcast.

⁰⁴This is Jonathan Brady on 96.1 FM with a weather report. A storm is going to reach Miami within the next hour. Three inches of rainfall and strong winds are expected overnight. Due to the heavy rain, flooding is possible in Lincoln Creek and throughout the downtown area. ⁰⁵I encourage everyone to avoid driving near those areas if possible. Moreover, residents are advised to stay in their houses. ⁰⁶For the most up-to-date news on the situation, you can go to our Web site at www.mwkradio.com.

storm[미 stɔːrm, 영 stɔːm] 폭풍(우)   **rainfall**[réinfɔːl] 강우
flooding[flʌ́diŋ] 홍수   **creek**[kriːk] 작은 만, 시내
downtown[dàuntáun] 도심   **resident**[미 rézədnt, 영 rézidnt] 주민
up-to-date[ʌ̀ptədéit] 최신의

해석

4-6번은 다음 방송에 관한 문제입니다.

⁰⁴저는 일기 예보를 전해 드리는 FM 96.1의 Jonathan Brady입니다. 폭풍

우가 앞으로 한 시간 이내에 마이애미에 도달할 예정입니다. 3인치에 달하는 강우와 거센 바람이 오늘 밤 동안에 예상됩니다. 폭우로 인해, Lincoln 만과 도심지의 도처에 홍수가 일어날 가능성이 있습니다. 가능하다면 ⁰⁵그 지역 근처에서 운전하는 것을 피하시기 바랍니다. 또한, 주민들께서는 집 안에 머물 것을 권해 드립니다. ⁰⁶이 상황에 대한 가장 최신 뉴스를 확인하시려면, 저희 웹사이트인 www.mwkradio.com으로 가시기 바랍니다.

04
해석 화자는 누구인 것 같은가?
(A) 기상 리포터
(B) 버스 운전기사
(C) 시 공무원
(D) 웹사이트 개발자

해설 화자의 신분을 묻는 문제입니다. "This is Jonathan Brady on 96.1 FM with a weather report."라며 자신은 일기 예보를 전하는 FM 96.1의 Jonathan Brady라고 한 말을 통해 화자가 기상 리포터임을 알 수 있습니다. 따라서 정답은 (A) A weather reporter입니다.

어휘 developer[미 divéləpər, 영 divéləpə] 개발자

05
해석 화자는 무엇을 제안하는가?
(A) 고속도로에서 운전하기
(B) 홍수 방벽 준비하기
(C) 나중에 다시 청취하기
(D) 특정 지역 피하기

해설 화자가 제안하는 것을 묻는 문제입니다. "I encourage everyone to avoid driving near those areas"라며 그 지역 근처에서 운전하는 것을 피할 것을 제안하였습니다. 따라서 정답은 (D) Avoiding certain areas입니다.

어휘 highway[미 háiwèi, 영 háiwei] 고속도로
barrier[미 bǽriər, 영 bǽriə] 방벽 tune in ~을 청취하다

06
해석 화자에 따르면, 웹사이트에서 무엇이 이용 가능한가?
(A) 안전 수칙
(B) 동영상
(C) 다운로드할 수 있는 지도
(D) 최신 뉴스

해설 웹사이트에서 이용 가능한 것을 묻는 문제입니다. "For the most up-to-date news on the situation, you can go to our Web site"라며 이 상황에 대한 가장 최신 뉴스를 확인하려면 웹사이트로 가면 된다고 하였습니다. 따라서 정답은 (D) News updates입니다.

07-09 🎤 미국식 발음
Questions 7-9 refer to the following speech.

> ⁰⁷It's my pleasure to welcome you all to the Davidson City Spring Market. We hold this event yearly to encourage citizens to support local businesses. This year, ⁰⁸we have a playground for kids to enjoy as well as a variety of food and drinks! Additionally, over 100 booths have been set up. You can stop at any of them to find unique gifts for your friends or family. We're now going to welcome a very special guest to the stage. ⁰⁹Mayor Theresa Thompson, please come up here and say a few words before the market officially opens.

encourage[미 inkə́:ridʒ, 영 inkʌ́ridʒ] 권장하다, 격려하다 ◐

citizen[미 sítəzən, 영 sítizən] 시민
support[미 səpɔ́:rt, 영 səpɔ́:t] 지지하다, 지원하다
local[미 lóukəl, 영 lə́ukəl] 지역의, 현지의 set up ~을 설치하다
unique[ju:ní:k] 특별한 mayor[미 méiər, 영 mea] 시장
officially[əfíʃəli] 공식적으로

해석
7-9번은 다음 연설에 관한 문제입니다.

⁰⁷Davidson 도시 봄 시장에 오신 여러분 모두를 맞이하게 되어 기쁩니다. 저희는 시민들이 지역 사업체들을 지지하도록 권장하기 위해 이 행사를 매년 주최합니다. 올해는, 다양한 음식과 음료뿐 아니라 ⁰⁸아이들이 즐길 수 있는 놀이터가 있습니다! 게다가, 100개가 넘는 부스가 설치되어 있습니다. 그 중 어느 곳이든 들르셔서 여러분의 친구나 가족을 위한 특별한 선물을 찾으실 수 있습니다. 이제 아주 특별한 손님을 무대로 맞이하겠습니다. ⁰⁹Theresa Thompson 시장님, 이 시장이 공식적으로 열리기 전에 이곳으로 올라오셔서 몇 말씀 해주시기 바랍니다.

07
해석 연설의 목적은 무엇인가?
(A) 자선 만찬을 설명하기 위해
(B) 상인들에게 그들의 서비스에 대해 감사하기 위해
(C) 지역 사업가를 소개하기 위해
(D) 연례 행사를 설명하기 위해

해설 연설의 목적을 묻는 문제입니다. "It's my pleasure to welcome you all to the Davidson City Spring Market. We hold this event yearly to encourage citizens to support local businesses."라며 Davidson 도시 봄 시장에 온 모두를 맞이하게 되어 기쁘다고 하면서 시민들이 지역 사업체들을 지지하도록 권장하기 위해 이 행사를 매년 주최한다고 한 말을 통해 연설의 목적이 연례 행사인 Davidson 도시 봄 시장을 설명하기 위함임을 알 수 있습니다. 따라서 정답은 (D) To describe a yearly event입니다.

어휘 charity[tʃǽrəti] 자선, 자선 단체 vendor[미 véndər, 영 véndə] 상인

08
해석 무엇이 시장에서 이용 가능한가?
(A) 선물 포장 서비스
(B) 특별 할인
(C) 아이들을 위한 시설
(D) 지역 사업체 안내 책자

해설 시장에서 이용 가능한 것을 묻는 문제입니다. "we have a playground for kids to enjoy"라며 시장에 아이들이 즐길 수 있는 놀이터가 있다고 하였습니다. 따라서 정답은 (C) A facility for children입니다.

어휘 gift-wrapping[gíftræpiŋ] 선물 포장

09
해석 다음에 무슨 일이 일어날 것 같은가?
(A) 콘서트를 위한 무대가 준비될 것이다.
(B) 손님들에게 몇몇 선물이 나누어질 것이다.
(C) 음료와 간식이 제공될 것이다.
(D) 짧은 연설이 있을 것이다.

해설 다음에 일어날 일을 묻는 문제입니다. "Mayor Theresa Thompson, please ~ say a few words before the market officially opens."라며 Theresa Thompson 시장에게 이 시장이 공식적으로 열리기 전에 몇 마디 해달라고 한 것을 통해, 시장이 연설을 할 것임을 알 수 있습니다. 따라서 정답은 (D) A brief speech will be given입니다.

어휘 distribute[distríbju:t] 나누어 주다, 분배하다 beverage[bévəridʒ] 음료

Questions 10-12 refer to the following announcement.

> Before the screening of *Nowhere But Up* begins, I'd like to make an announcement. [10]Malcolm Mendez, the director of the documentary film, is in attendance tonight. He has agreed to participate in a question-and-answer session later this evening. [11]Unfortunately, Mr. Mendez cannot stay as long as originally planned due to an unexpected scheduling conflict. Nevertheless, he will still be able to take questions for about half an hour once the movie credits are finished. [12]Now, let's begin our showing of *Nowhere But Up*.
>
> screening[skríːniŋ] (영화 등의) 상영(회)   in attendance 참석한
> session[séʃən] (특정한 활동을 위한) 시간
> conflict[미 káːnflikt, 영 kɔ́nflikt] 마찰, 충돌

해석

10-12번은 다음 공지에 관한 문제입니다.

*Nowhere But Up*의 상영이 시작되기 전에, 제가 공지를 드리고자 합니다. [10]이 다큐멘터리 영화의 감독인 Malcolm Mendez가 오늘 밤 참석했습니다. 그는 오늘 밤 늦게 있을 질의응답 시간에 참석하는 것을 수락했습니다. [11]유감스럽게도, Mr. Mendez는 예기치 못한 일정 문제 때문에 원래 계획했던 것만큼 오래 머물지는 못할 것입니다. 그럼에도 불구하고, 그는 여전히 영화 크레딧이 끝나고 약 30분간은 질문을 받을 수 있을 것입니다. [12]이제, *Nowhere But Up*의 상영을 시작하겠습니다.

10

해석 Malcolm Mendez는 누구인가?
(A) 영화배우
(B) 시상자
(C) 영화감독
(D) 행사 진행자

해설 Malcolm Mendez의 신분을 묻는 문제입니다. "Malcolm Mendez, the director of the documentary film"이라며 다큐멘터리 영화의 감독인 Malcolm Mendez라고 하였습니다. 따라서 정답은 (C) A movie director입니다.

11

해석 화자는 어떤 문제를 언급하는가?
(A) 초대 손님이 일찍 떠나야 한다.
(B) 영화 평론이 부정적이었다.
(C) 상영회의 예약이 다 찼다.
(D) 강당이 문을 닫을 것이다.

해설 화자가 언급하는 문제점을 묻는 문제입니다. "Unfortunately, Mr. Mendez cannot stay as long as originally planned"라며 유감스럽게도 Mr. Mendez가 원래 계획했던 것만큼 오래 머물지는 못 할 것이라고 하였습니다. 따라서 정답은 (A) A guest must leave early입니다.

어휘 auditorium[ɔ̀ːditɔ́ːriəm] 강당, 관람석

12

해석 청자들은 다음에 무엇을 할 것 같은가?
(A) 설문지를 작성한다.
(B) 후기를 쓴다.
(C) 영화를 본다.
(D) 간식을 먹는다.

해설 청자들이 다음에 할 일을 묻는 문제입니다. "Now, let's begin our showing of *Nowhere But Up*."이라며 이제 *Nowhere But Up*의 상영을 시작하겠다고 하였습니다. 따라서 정답은 (C) View a film입니다.

어휘 questionnaire[미 kwèstʃənéər, 영 kwèstʃənéə] 설문지
refreshment[rifréʃmənt] 간식

Questions 13-15 refer to the following advertisement.

> Do you need somewhere to relax after a busy week? Then visit Shore Resort. Located 40 minutes by car from Boston, Shore Resort has a pool, an outdoor lounge, and a spa. We have only 25 rooms, and [13]they fill up fast. So, if you want to book a room, you should make a reservation at least 30 days in advance. And [14]we are offering 15 percent off the regular price in May. Don't miss out. [15]For more information, visit our Web site, www.Shore-Resort.com.
>
> relax[rilǽks] 휴식을 취하다   outdoor[미 áutdɔ̀ːr, 영 áutdɔ̀ː] 야외의
> lounge[laundʒ] (호텔 등의) 휴게실   spa[spɑː] 온천   fill up 차다
> regular price 정가

해석

13-15번은 다음 광고에 관한 문제입니다.

바쁜 한 주 후에 휴식을 취할 곳이 필요하신가요? 그렇다면 Shore 리조트를 방문하세요. 보스턴에서 차로 40분 거리에 위치한 Shore 리조트는 수영장, 야외 휴게실, 그리고 온천을 갖추고 있습니다. 저희는 단 25개의 객실만 있고, [13]객실은 빠르게 찹니다. 그러니, 객실을 예약하기를 원하시면 최소 30일 전에 예약하셔야 합니다. 그리고 [14]저희는 5월에 정가에서 15퍼센트 할인을 제공하고 있습니다. 놓치지 마세요. [15]더 많은 정보를 얻으시려면, 저희 웹사이트 www.Shore-Resort.com을 방문하세요.

13

해석 화자가 "저희는 단 25개의 객실만 있고"라고 말할 때 의도하는 것은 무엇인가?
(A) 단체 관광객들이 리조트를 방문하지 않을 수도 있다.
(B) 손님들이 조용하게 머무를 것이다.
(C) 사전 예약이 필요하다.
(D) 어떤 방들이 개조될 것이다.

해설 화자가 하는 말(We have only 25 rooms)의 의도를 묻는 문제입니다. "they fill up fast. So, if you want to book a room, you should make a reservation at least 30 days in advance"라며 객실이 빠르게 차니, 객실을 예약하기를 원하면 최소 30일 전에 예약해야 한다고 한 말을 통해 사전 예약이 필요함을 전달하려는 의도임을 알 수 있습니다. 따라서 정답은 (C) Advance reservations are needed입니다.

어휘 renovate[rénəveit] 개조하다, 수리하다

14

해석 5월에는 무슨 일이 일어날 것인가?
(A) 할인이 적용될 것이다.
(B) 리조트가 재개장할 것이다.
(C) 소책자가 출간될 것이다.
(D) 온천이 이전할 것이다.

해설 5월에 일어날 일을 묻는 문제입니다. "we are offering 15 percent off the regular price in May"라며 5월에 정가에서 15퍼센트 할인을 제공하고 있다고 하였습니다. 따라서 정답은 (A) A discount will be applied입니다.

어휘 apply[əplái] 적용하다, 신청하다

15
해석 사람들은 어떻게 Shore 리조트에 대한 더 많은 정보를 얻을 수 있는가?
(A) 문자 메시지를 보냄으로써
(B) 상담 서비스 전화에 전화함으로써
(C) 이메일을 작성함으로써
(D) 웹페이지를 방문함으로써

해설 사람들이 Shore 리조트에 대한 더 많은 정보를 얻을 수 있는 방법을 묻는 문제입니다. "For more information, visit our Web site, www.Shore-Resort.com."이라며 더 많은 정보를 얻으려면 웹사이트를 방문하라고 하였습니다. 따라서 정답은 (D) By going to a Web page입니다.

어휘 hotline[hɑ́ːtlain] 상담 서비스 전화, 직통 전화

16-18 🎧 영국식 발음
Questions 16-18 refer to the following telephone message and list.

> Hello, Mr. Lawson. This is Jacey Dolan calling from Biz Plus Office Supplies. I just want to check one detail for the order you placed with us the day before yesterday. I noticed that you requested 300 notepads, which is different from the 30 that you usually order. ¹⁶Could you call me back and confirm that you wanted these items ordered in the hundreds, not in the tens? Since ¹⁷the items will be shipped this afternoon, I hope you can get back to me sometime this morning. ¹⁸If you can only contact us after 1 P.M. today, please dial extension 120 to reach the shipping department manager directly.
>
> office supply 사무용품 notepad[미 nóutpæd, 영 náutpæd] 메모지, 메모장
> ship[ʃip] 배송하다, 선적하다 extension[iksténʃən] 내선 번호

해석
16-18번은 다음 전화 메시지와 표에 관한 문제입니다.

안녕하세요, Mr. Lawson. Biz Plus 사무용품점에서 전화 드리는 Jacey Dolan입니다. 저는 그저께 귀하께서 저희에게 주문하신 물품에 대한 한 가지 세부 사항을 확인하고자 합니다. 저는 귀하께서 메모지 300장을 요청하신 것을 보았는데, 이것은 평소에 주문하시는 30장과 다릅니다. ¹⁶제게 다시 전화하셔서 이 물품을 십 단위가 아니라 백 단위로 주문하려고 하셨던 게 맞는지 확인해 주시겠어요? ¹⁷물품이 오늘 오후에 배송될 예정이기 때문에, 오전 중으로 제게 다시 연락을 주시기 바랍니다. ¹⁸만약 귀하께서 오늘 오후 1시 이후에만 연락하실 수 있다면, 배송 부서의 부장에게 바로 연락하실 수 있도록 내선 번호 120번으로 전화주시기 바랍니다.

내선 번호	이름
100번	Jerry Chow
110번	Melinda Bright
¹⁸120번	Edward Klein
130번	Claire Preston

16
해석 화자는 청자에게 무엇을 해달라고 요청하는가?
(A) 요청된 수량을 확인한다.
(B) 쿠폰 코드를 입력한다.
(C) 배송일을 선택한다.
(D) 청구서 요금을 지불한다.

해설 화자가 청자에게 요청하는 것을 묻는 문제입니다. "Could you ~ confirm that you wanted these items ordered in the hundreds, not in the tens?"라며 물품을 십 단위가 아니라 백 단위로 주문하려고 했던 게 맞는지 확인해 달라고 요청하였습니다. 따라서 정답은 (A) Confirm a requested amount입니다.

17
해석 오늘 오후에 무슨 일이 일어날 것인가?
(A) 몇몇 물품들이 반품될 것이다.
(B) 주문품이 배송될 것이다.
(C) 일부 메모지들이 만들어질 것이다.
(D) 일정이 변경될 것이다.

해설 오늘 오후에 일어날 일을 묻는 문제입니다. "the items will be shipped this afternoon"이라며 물품이 오늘 오후에 배송될 예정이라고 하였습니다. 따라서 정답은 (B) An order will be shipped입니다.

18
해석 시각 자료를 보아라. 청자는 오후 1시 이후에 누구에게 전화해야 하는가?
(A) Jerry Chow
(B) Melinda Bright
(C) Edward Klein
(D) Claire Preston

해설 청자가 오후 1시 이후에 전화해야 할 사람을 묻는 문제입니다. "If you can only contact us after 1 P.M. today, please dial extension 120"라며 오후 1시 이후에만 연락할 수 있다면 내선 번호 120으로 전화달라고 하였으므로, 청자가 오후 1시 이후에는 Edward Klein에게 전화해야 함을 표에서 알 수 있습니다. 따라서 정답은 (C) Edward Klein입니다.

DAY 19 세부 사항 관련 문제 3

Course 1 의도 파악 문제

HACKERS PRACTICE 🎧 DAY19_02   p.149

01 (C)	02 (D)	03 (A)	04 (B)

01-02 🎧 캐나다식 발음 / 호주식 발음
Questions 1-2 refer to the following talk.

> My name is Jeff, and I'll be your guide today ⁰¹here at Lexington Incorporated's research laboratory. We'll start our tour by looking at some sketches in our design team's office. Then, we'll go to the lab for computer, phone, and tablet testing. While there, ⁰²you'll have a chance to pose questions to our head engineer, David Tao. He isn't always able to meet with tour groups. ⁰²So make sure to take advantage of this rare opportunity.
>
> research[미 rísɑːrt, 영 risɑ́ːtʃ] 연구
> laboratory[미 lǽbərətɔ̀ri, 영 ləbɔ́rətəri] 실험실 testing[téstiŋ] 시험
> pose a question 질문을 하다 take advantage of ~을 활용하다
> rare[미 rɛər, 영 reə] 드문, 희귀한
> opportunity[미 ɑ̀ːpərtjúːnəti, 영 ɔ̀pətʃúːnəti] 기회

해석

1-2번은 다음 담화에 관한 문제입니다.

제 이름은 Jeff이고, 저는 오늘 ⁰¹이곳 Lexington사의 연구 실험실에서 여러분의 가이드가 되어드릴 것입니다. 우리는 디자인 팀의 사무실에서 몇몇 스케치를 살펴보며 견학을 시작할 것입니다. 그 후에, 우리는 컴퓨터, 전화기, 그리고 태블릿 시험을 위한 실험실로 갈 것입니다. 그곳에 계시는 동안, ⁰²여러분은 저희 수석 엔지니어인 David Tao에게 질문을 할 기회를 얻게 될 것입니다. 그가 항상 견학 단체와 만날 수 있는 것은 아닙니다. ⁰²그러니 이 드문 기회를 반드시 활용하시기 바랍니다.

01

해석 담화는 어디에서 일어나고 있는가?
(A) 소매점에서
(B) 제조 공장에서
(C) 연구 시설에서
(D) 과학 박물관에서

해설 담화가 일어나고 있는 장소를 묻는 문제입니다. "here at ~ research laboratory"라며 이곳 연구 실험실이라고 하였습니다. 따라서 정답은 (C) At a research facility입니다.

어휘 retail[rí:teil] 소매의
manufacturing[미 mæ̀njufǽktʃəriŋ, 영 mæ̀njəfǽktʃəriŋ] 제조의
plant[미 plænt, 영 plɑ:nt] 공장

02

해석 화자가 "그가 항상 견학 단체와 만날 수 있는 것은 아닙니다"라고 말할 때 의도하는 것은 무엇인가?
(A) 실험실이 검사를 위해 개방될 것이다.
(B) 견학이 예상했던 것보다 더 오래 진행될 것이다.
(C) 엔지니어는 최근에 승진했다.
(D) 직원과의 시간이 높이 평가되어야 한다.

해설 화자가 하는 말(He isn't always able to meet with tour groups)의 의도를 묻는 문제입니다. "you'll have a chance to pose questions to our head engineer"라며 청자들이 수석 엔지니어에게 질문을 할 기회를 얻게 될 것이라고 한 뒤, "So make sure to take advantage of this rare opportunity."라며 이 드문 기회를 반드시 활용하라고 한 것을 통해 화자가 수석 엔지니어와의 시간이 높이 평가되어야 한다는 것을 전달하려는 의도임을 알 수 있습니다. 따라서 정답은 (D) An employee's time should be appreciated입니다.

어휘 run[rʌn] 진행되다, 계속하다

03-04 🎧 영국식 발음 / 미국식 발음

Questions 3-4 refer to the following introduction.

> Joining us next is William Peterson. Peterson has been performing as a jazz pianist for 20 years now. ⁰³Just last week, he received the prestigious Lifetime Achievement Award from the Academy of Music. But before he begins . . . he asked us to mention one thing. ⁰⁴Throughout the performance, please do not record any audio or video. Official live recordings will be available on Mr. Peterson's Web site. Thank you for understanding.
>
> perform[미 pərfɔ́:rm, 영 pəfɔ́:m] 공연하다
> prestigious[prestídʒəs] 명망 있는   mention[ménʃən] 언급하다, 말하다
> official[əfíʃəl] 공식적인, 정식의

해석

3-4번은 다음 소개에 관한 문제입니다.

다음에 우리와 함께해주실 분은 William Peterson입니다. Peterson은 재즈 피아니스트로서 지금까지 20년 동안 공연을 해오고 있습니다. ⁰³바로 지난주에, 그는 Academy of Music으로부터 명망 있는 Lifetime Achievement 상을 받았습니다. 그런데 그가 시작하기 전에... 그는 저희에게 한 가지를 언급해줄 것을 요청하셨습니다. ⁰⁴공연이 진행되는 내내, 음성을 녹음하거나 영상을 녹화하지 말아 주시기 바랍니다. 공식 라이브 영상이 Mr. Peterson의 웹사이트에서 이용 가능할 것입니다. 이해해 주셔서 감사합니다.

03

해석 지난주에 무슨 일이 일어났는가?
(A) 상이 수여되었다.
(B) 앨범이 발매되었다.
(C) 학교가 개교했다.
(D) 공연이 녹화되었다.

해설 지난주에 일어난 일을 묻는 문제입니다. "Just last week, he[Peterson] received the prestigious Lifetime Achievement Award"라며 바로 지난주에 Peterson이 명망 있는 Lifetime Achievement 상을 받았다고 하였습니다. 따라서 정답은 (A) An award was given입니다.

어휘 release[rilí:s] 발매하다, 발표하다   academy[əkǽdəmi] 학교, 학원

04

해석 화자는 왜 "공식 라이브 영상이 Mr. Peterson의 웹사이트에서 이용 가능할 것입니다"라고 말하는가?
(A) 소셜 미디어 사이트를 광고하기 위해
(B) 대안을 주기 위해
(C) 장소의 일정을 설명하기 위해
(D) 지연의 이유를 제시하기 위해

해설 화자가 하는 말(Official live recordings will be available on Mr. Peterson's Web site)의 의도를 묻는 문제입니다. "Throughout the performance, please do not record any audio or video."라며 공연이 진행되는 내내 음성을 녹음하거나 영상을 녹화하지 말아 달라고 한 것을 통해 화자가 공연 녹음이나 녹화에 대한 대안을 주려는 의도임을 알 수 있습니다. 따라서 정답은 (B) To give an alternative입니다.

어휘 alternative[미 ɔ:ltə́:rnətiv, 영 ɔ:ltə́:nətiv] 대안, 대체
venue[vénju:] 장소

Course 2 추론 문제

HACKERS PRACTICE 🎧 DAY19_04   p.151

01 (B)	02 (C)	03 (C)	04 (D)

01-02 🎧 미국식 발음 / 영국식 발음

Questions 1-2 refer to the following broadcast.

> And now for the local news . . . ⁰¹The Hamilton Art Festival will begin on Friday, July 12. This year's festival will be the largest ever, with 35 artists from the region participating. ⁰¹The money that is raised will go to local charities. Oh . . . and keep in mind that ⁰²volunteers are still needed. If you would like to help out, stop by Riverside Art Supplies to fill out a registration form.
>
> region[rí:dʒən] 지역, 지방   charity[tʃǽrəti] 자선 단체
> volunteer[미 vɑ̀ləntíər, 영 vɔ̀ləntíə] 자원봉사자   stop by ~에 들르다
> registration form 신청서

1-2번은 다음 방송에 관한 문제입니다.

이제 지역 소식입니다... ⁰¹Hamilton 예술 축제가 7월 12일 금요일에 시작됩니다. 올해의 축제는 35명의 지역 예술가들이 참여하는 가장 큰 축제가 될 것입니다. ⁰¹모인 금액은 지역 자선 단체로 전달될 것입니다. 아... 그리고 ⁰²여전히 자원봉사자들이 필요하다는 것을 잊지 마세요. 도움이 되기를 원하신다면, Riverside 미술용품점에 들르셔서 신청서를 작성하시면 됩니다.

01

해석 화자는 Hamilton 예술 축제에 대해 무엇을 암시하는가?
(A) 거의 매진되었다.
(B) 지역 단체들을 후원한다.
(C) 참가자가 거의 없다.
(D) 연기되었다.

해설 화자가 Hamilton 예술 축제에 대해 암시하는 것을 묻는 문제입니다. "The Hamilton Art Festival will begin on Friday, July 12."라며 Hamilton 예술 축제가 7월 12일 금요일에 시작된다고 한 뒤, "The money that is raised will go to local charities."라며 모인 금액은 지역 자선 단체로 전달될 것이라고 한 것을 통해 Hamilton 예술 축제가 지역 단체들을 후원함을 알 수 있습니다. 따라서 정답은 (B) It supports local organizations입니다.

어휘 support [미 səpɔ́ːrt, 영 səpɔ́ːt] (금전적으로) 후원하다
participant [미 pɑːrtísəpənt, 영 pɑːtísipənt] 참가자
postpone [미 poustpóun, 영 pəustpə́un] 연기하다

02

해석 청자들은 어떻게 자원봉사자로 등록할 수 있는가?
(A) 웹사이트에 로그인함으로써
(B) 상담 서비스에 전화함으로써
(C) 매장을 방문함으로써
(D) 양식을 이메일로 보냄으로써

해설 청자들이 자원봉사자로 등록할 수 있는 방법을 묻는 문제입니다. "volunteers are still needed. If you would like to help out, stop by Riverside Art Supplies"라며 여전히 자원봉사자들이 필요하다고 하며 도움이 되기를 원한다면 Riverside 미술용품점에 들르면 된다고 하였습니다. 따라서 정답은 (C) By visiting a store입니다.

어휘 hotline [미 hɑ́ːtlain, 영 hɔ́tlain] 상담 서비스 전화

03-04 ᴈⁿ 캐나다식 발음 / 호주식 발음

Questions 3-4 refer to the following telephone message.

This is Dean Saunders. ⁰³I'm calling regarding my latest phone bill. ⁰⁴It says that I have to pay $60, but my cell phone package is usually only $35 a month. I'm certain this is a mistake because I chose one of TeleComm's plans with unlimited talk time. What's more, I didn't exceed my data limit. So, ⁰³I'd like someone to review my records and see what the problem is.

---

regarding [미 rigɑ́ːrdiŋ, 영 rigɑ́ːdiŋ] ~과 관련하여, ~에 대해
bill [bil] 고지서, 청구서 unlimited [ʌnlímitid] 무제한의
exceed [iksíːd] 초과하다, 넘어서다

해석

3-4번은 다음 전화 메시지에 관한 문제입니다.

저는 Dean Saunders입니다. ⁰³저의 최근 전화 요금 고지서와 관련하여 전화 드립니다. ⁰⁴고지서에는 제가 60달러를 지불해야 한다고 나와 있지만, 제 휴대전화 패키지는 보통 한 달에 단 35달러입니다. 저는 TeleComm사

의 무제한 통화 시간을 제공하는 요금제 중 하나를 선택했기 때문에 이것이 오류라고 확신합니다. 게다가, 저는 제 데이터 한도를 초과하지 않았습니다. 그러므로, ⁰³누군가 제 기록을 검토하고 문제가 무엇인지 확인해 주셨으면 합니다.

03

해석 화자는 왜 전화를 하고 있는가?
(A) 데이터 요금제를 변경하기 위해
(B) 요청을 추가하기 위해
(C) 고지서에 대해 문의하기 위해
(D) 서비스 목록을 요청하기 위해

해설 전화의 목적을 묻는 문제입니다. "I'm calling regarding my latest phone bill."이라며 최근 전화 요금 고지서와 관련하여 전화한다고 한 뒤, "I'd like someone to review my records and see what the problem is"라며 누군가 자신의 기록을 검토하고 문제가 무엇인지 확인해달라고 한 것을 통해 화자가 고지서에 대해 문의하기 위해 전화하고 있음을 알 수 있습니다. 따라서 정답은 (C) To inquire about a bill입니다.

어휘 follow up ~을 추가하다, 덧붙이다

04

해석 화자는 TeleComm사에 대해 무엇을 암시하는가?
(A) 더 이상 무제한 요금제를 제공하지 않는다.
(B) 휴대전화 패키지 요금을 인상했다.
(C) 과거에 환불을 제공했다.
(D) 그에게 서비스에 대해 더 많이 청구했다.

해설 화자가 TeleComm사에 대해 암시하는 것을 묻는 문제입니다. "It[latest phone bill] says that I have to pay $60, but my cell phone package is usually only $35 a month."라며 최근 전화 요금 고지서에는 60달러를 지불해야 한다고 나와 있지만 자신의 휴대전화 패키지는 보통 한 달에 단 35달러라고 한 것을 통해 TeleComm사가 화자에게 전화 요금을 더 많이 청구했음을 알 수 있습니다. 따라서 정답은 (D) It overcharged him for a service입니다.

어휘 overcharge [미 ðuvərtʃɑ́ːrdʒ, 영 əuvətʃɑ́ːdʒ] 많이 청구하다, (금액을) 높게 매기다

HACKERS TEST ∩ DAY19_05   p.152

01 (B)	02 (D)	03 (D)	04 (A)
05 (B)	06 (B)	07 (D)	08 (B)
09 (D)	10 (A)	11 (C)	12 (D)
13 (C)	14 (A)	15 (B)	16 (D)
17 (C)	18 (D)		

01-03 ᴈⁿ 호주식 발음

Questions 1-3 refer to the following report.

Welcome back to *The Weekend Art Show*. Today we'll be discussing the work of legendary Chicago ⁰¹chef Dominique Lopez. Her food preparation and decoration techniques have become nationally famous in recent years, and her restaurant, La Fleur, offers some of the best dishes in the city. In addition, Lopez hosts renowned seminars that have helped countless amateur cooks improve their technique. ⁰²This weekend, in fact, she is conducting a full-day workshop on how to make the perfect dessert. ⁰³A few tickets are still available. Her devoted fans are likely to be interested, though. ⁰³Don't waste any ◐

---

time and hurry on over to her Web site.

legendary [미 lédʒənderi, 영 léd3əndri] 전설적인, 전설 속의
preparation [prepəréiʃən] 조리, 준비
renowned [rináund] 명성 있는, 유명한   in fact 사실은, 실제로
devoted [미 divóutid, 영 divʌútid] 헌신적인, 전념하는

해석
1-3번은 다음 보도에 관한 문제입니다.

*Weekend Art Show*에 다시 오신 것을 환영합니다. 오늘 우리는 전설적인 시카고 ⁰¹요리사인 Dominique Lopez의 업적에 대해 이야기를 나눌 것입니다. 그녀의 음식 조리와 장식 기술은 최근 몇 년 동안 전국적으로 유명해졌고, 그녀의 식당인 La Fleur는 그 도시에서 최고인 몇몇 요리들을 제공합니다. 게다가, Lopez는 취미로 요리를 하는 수많은 사람들이 그들의 기술을 향상시키는 데 도움을 주는 명성 있는 세미나들을 주최합니다. ⁰²사실, 이번 주말에 그녀는 완벽한 디저트를 만드는 방법에 대한 하루짜리 워크숍을 진행할 것입니다. ⁰³약간의 티켓이 아직 구매 가능합니다. 그렇지만, 그녀의 헌신적인 팬들이 아마 관심이 있을 것 같습니다. ⁰³시간을 끌지 마시고 그녀의 웹사이트로 서둘러 가보세요.

01
해석 Ms. Lopez는 누구인가?
(A) 미술 교수
(B) 요리사
(C) 식당 평론가
(D) 실내 장식가

해설 Ms. Lopez의 신분을 묻는 문제입니다. "chef Dominique Lopez"라며 요리사인 Dominique Lopez라고 하였습니다. 따라서 정답은 (B) A chef입니다.

어휘 reviewer [미 rivjú:ər, 영 rivjú:ə] 평론가, 비평가

02
해석 Ms. Lopez는 이번 주말에 무엇을 할 것인가?
(A) 몇몇 행사에 음식을 공급한다.
(B) 자선 행사를 주최한다.
(C) 주방을 개조한다.
(D) 워크숍을 진행한다.

해설 Ms. Lopez가 이번 주말에 할 일을 묻는 문제입니다. "This weekend, ~ she[Ms. Lopez] is conducting a full-day workshop on how to make the perfect dessert."라며 이번 주말에 Ms. Lopez가 완벽한 디저트를 만드는 방법에 대한 하루짜리 워크숍을 진행할 것이라고 한 것을 통해 Ms. Lopez가 이번 주말에 워크숍을 진행할 것임을 알 수 있습니다. 따라서 정답은 (D) Conducting a workshop입니다.

어휘 cater [미 kéitər, 영 kéitə] 음식을 공급하다, 요구를 채우다
charity gala 자선 행사

03
해석 화자가 "그렇지만, 그녀의 헌신적인 팬들이 아마 관심이 있을 것 같습니다"라고 말할 때 의도하는 것은 무엇인가?
(A) 식당이 유명해질 것으로 예상된다.
(B) 제품들이 수요가 많아질 것이다.
(C) 인터뷰가 일부 팬들의 흥미를 끌 것이다.
(D) 입장권이 빨리 팔릴 수 있다.

해설 화자가 하는 말(Her devoted fans are likely to be interested, though)의 의도를 묻는 문제입니다. "A few tickets are still available."이라며 약간의 티켓이 아직 구매 가능하다고 한 후, "Don't waste any time and hurry on over to her Web site."라며 시간을 끌지 말고 웹사이트로 서둘러 가보라고 한 것을 통해 입장권이 빨리 팔릴 수 있다는 것을 전달하려는 의도임을 알 수 있습니다. 따라서 정답은 (D) Passes could sell out quickly입니다.

어휘 appeal [əpí:l] 흥미를 끌다, 호소하다

04-06 [호주식 발음]
Questions 4-6 refer to the following telephone message.

Hello, Ms. Johnson. ⁰⁴This is Gerald Cooper, the manager of Pearson Stationery. I'm calling regarding the four . . . uh, just a minute . . . I mean, the five boxes of laser printer paper you ordered from our Web site. ⁰⁵You specified that you would like the shipment to arrive after 3:00 P.M. on Saturday. However, we only make deliveries in the mornings on weekends. ⁰⁵Would it be a problem if our driver dropped off your package at noon on Saturday? ⁰⁶Contact me at 555-4938 to let me know. I will be here until six. Thank you.

regarding [미 rigá:rdiŋ, 영 rigá:diŋ] ~에 대해
specify [미 spésəfài, 영 spésifai] 기입하다, 명시하다
shipment [ʃípmənt] 배송품   drop off ~을 가져다주다

해석
4-6번은 다음 전화 메시지에 관한 문제입니다.

안녕하세요, Ms. Johnson. ⁰⁴저는 Pearson 문구점의 점장인 Gerald Cooper입니다. 저는 네 상자의... 아, 잠시만요... 제 말은, 귀하께서 저희 웹사이트에서 주문하신 레이저 프린터 용지 다섯 상자에 대해 전화드립니다. ⁰⁵귀하께서는 토요일 오후 3시 이후에 배송품이 도착했으면 좋겠다고 기입하셨습니다. 하지만, 저희는 주말에는 오전에만 배송을 합니다. ⁰⁵저희 배송 기사가 귀하의 상품을 토요일 정오에 가져다드리면 문제가 될까요? ⁰⁶555-4938로 제게 전화하여 알려주시기 바랍니다. 저는 6시까지 이곳에 있을 것입니다. 감사합니다.

04
해석 화자는 누구인 것 같은가?
(A) 점장
(B) 배달원
(C) 비서
(D) 출판업자

해설 화자의 신분을 묻는 문제입니다. "This is Gerald Cooper, the manager of Pearson Stationery."라며 자신이 Pearson 문구점의 점장인 Gerald Cooper라고 하였습니다. 따라서 정답은 (A) A store manager입니다.

어휘 secretary [미 sékrətèri, 영 sékrətəri] 비서
publisher [미 pʌ́bliʃər, 영 pʌ́bliʃə] 출판업자

05
해석 화자가 "저희는 주말에는 오전에만 배송을 합니다"라고 말할 때 의도하는 것은 무엇인가?
(A) 고객에게 추가 금액이 청구될 것이다.
(B) 요청이 이행될 수 없다.
(C) 일정표가 잘못 인쇄되었다.
(D) 주문품이 발송되지 않았다.

해설 화자가 하는 말(we only make deliveries in the mornings on weekends)의 의도를 묻는 문제입니다. "You specified that you would like the shipment to arrive after 3:00 P.M. on Saturday."라며 청자가 토요일 오후 3시 이후에 배송품이 도착했으면 좋겠다고 기입했다고 한 뒤, "Would it be a problem if our driver dropped off your package at noon on Saturday?"라며 배송 기사가 청자의 상품을 토요일 정오에 가져다주면 문제가 될 것인지 물은 것을 통해 화자가 청자의 요청이 이행될 수 없음을 전달하려는 의도임을 알 수 있습니다. 따라서 정답은 (B) A request cannot be fulfilled입니다.

어휘 charge[미 tʃɑːrdʒ, 영 tʃɑːdʒ] (금액을) 청구하다 fulfill[fulfíl] 이행하다

06

해석 화자는 청자에게 무엇을 해달라고 요청하는가?
(A) 배송 기사에게 연락한다.
(B) 답신 전화를 한다.
(C) 웹사이트를 방문한다.
(D) 매장에 들른다.

해설 화자가 청자에게 요청하는 것을 묻는 문제입니다. "Contact me at 555-4938 to let me know."라며 555-4938로 자신에게 전화하여 알려달라고 요청하였습니다. 따라서 정답은 (B) Return a call입니다.

어휘 drop by ~에 들르다

07-09 🔊 영국식 발음

Questions 7-9 refer to the following speech.

07I hope you enjoyed the music by the various performers today. I'd like to take this opportunity to thank all of you for participating in this event. 07It was a great success, and we raised over $5,000 for the Child Literacy Foundation. I know this money will be put to good use by the organization. I would also like to express my gratitude to Merle Collins. 08He is a talented violinist whose performance was one of the highlights of the show, and 09he made a personal donation of $1,000. That's 20 percent of our total today—09Amazing. Let's give him a round of applause to show our appreciation.

foundation[faundéiʃən] 재단 gratitude[미 grǽtətjùːd, 영 grǽtitʃuːd] 감사
talented[tǽləntid] 재능 있는 donation[미 dounéiʃən, 영 dəunéiʃən] 기부
applause[əplɔ́ːz] 박수 appreciation[əprìːʃiéiʃən] 감사

해석
7-9번은 다음 연설에 관한 문제입니다.

07여러분께서 오늘 여러 연주자들의 음악을 즐기셨기를 바랍니다. 저는 이 기회를 통해 이 행사에 참석해 주신 여러분 모두에게 감사드리고자 합니다. 07이 행사는 큰 성공을 거두었고, 저희는 Child Literacy 재단을 위해 5,000달러 이상을 마련했습니다. 저는 이 기부금이 단체에 의해 좋은 곳에 쓰일 거라고 믿습니다. 저는 또한 Merle Collins에게도 감사를 표하고 싶습니다. 08그는 공연의 하이라이트 중 하나였던 연주를 한 재능 있는 바이올린 연주자이며, 091,000달러를 개인적으로 기부했습니다. 이것은 오늘 총액의 20퍼센트입니다—09놀라운 일입니다. 그에게 우리의 감사를 표하기 위해 큰 박수를 보냅시다.

07

해석 청자들은 어디에 있는 것 같은가?
(A) 재능 경연 대회에
(B) 연극 제작사에
(C) 학교 공연에
(D) 자선 콘서트에

해설 청자들이 있는 장소를 묻는 문제입니다. "I hope you enjoyed the music ~ today."라며 청자들이 오늘 음악을 즐겼기를 바란다고 한 뒤, "It was a great success, and we raised over $5,000 for the Child Literacy Foundation."이라며 행사가 큰 성공을 거두었으며 Child Literacy 재단을 위해 5,000달러 이상을 마련했다고 한 말을 통해 청자들이 있는 장소가 자선 콘서트임을 알 수 있습니다. 따라서 정답은 (D) At a charity concert입니다.

어휘 competition[미 kàːmpətíʃən, 영 kɔ̀mpətíʃən] (경연) 대회
charity[tʃǽrəti] 자선

08

해석 Merle Collins는 누구인가?
(A) 공연 주최자
(B) 음악가
(C) 재단 회원
(D) 교육자

해설 Merle Collins의 신분을 묻는 문제입니다. "He[Merle Collins] is a talented violinist"라며 Merle Collins가 재능 있는 바이올린 연주자라고 하였습니다. 따라서 정답은 (B) A musician입니다.

09

해석 화자는 왜 "이것은 오늘 총액의 20퍼센트입니다"라고 말하는가?
(A) 그녀는 정확한 금액을 확인해야 한다.
(B) 그녀는 행사의 중요성을 증명하고 싶어 한다.
(C) 그녀는 참석자의 수를 강조하고 싶어 한다.
(D) 그녀는 기부금의 규모를 강조하고 싶어 한다.

해설 화자가 하는 말(That's 20 percent of our total today)의 의도를 묻는 문제입니다. "he made a personal donation of $1,000"라며 그가 1,000달러를 개인적으로 기부했다고 한 뒤, "Amazing."이라며 놀라운 일이라고 한 말을 통해 화자가 기부금의 규모를 강조하려는 의도임을 알 수 있습니다. 따라서 정답은 (D) She wants to emphasize the size of a contribution입니다.

어휘 accuracy[미 ǽkjurəsi, 영 ǽkjərəsi] 정확(도) stress[stres] 강조하다
emphasize[미 émfəsàiz, 영 émfəsaiz] 강조하다
contribution[미 kàntrəbjúːʃən, 영 kɔ̀ntribjúːʃən] 기부금

10-12 🔊 캐나다식 발음

Questions 10-12 refer to the following announcement.

As most of you already know, 10students from a local high school are going to tour our factory today. Um, a memo about this event was sent out to everyone last Friday. They're coming here to see how a food packaging plant works. While in the facility, they must wear protective hats and gloves. 11This is an important precaution, as it will prevent the students from contaminating food with bacteria. So, remind the students that they need to keep their gear on at all times. There are no exceptions to this rule. OK, 12I'm going to go and meet the tour group now. I'll return with the students in about 20 minutes.

protective[prətéktiv] 보호용의 precaution[prikɔ́ːʃən] 예방 조치
contaminate[미 kəntǽmənèit, 영 kəntǽmineit] 오염시키다
bacteria[bæktíəriə] 세균 gear[미 giər, 영 giə] 장비

해석
10-12번은 다음 공지에 관한 문제입니다.

여러분 대부분이 이미 알고 있듯이, 10지역 고등학교의 학생들이 오늘 우리 공장을 견학할 예정입니다. 음, 이 행사에 대한 회람이 지난주 금요일에 모두에게 발송되었습니다. 그들은 식품 포장 공장이 어떻게 가동되는지를 보기 위해 이곳에 올 것입니다. 시설에 있는 동안, 그들은 안전모와 장갑을 착용해야 합니다. 11이것은 학생들이 세균으로 식품을 오염시키는 것을 방지할 것이기 때문에, 중요한 예방 조치입니다. 그러므로, 학생들에게 장비를 항상 착용하고 있어야 한다는 것을 상기시켜 주세요. 이 수칙에 대해서는 예외가 없습니다. 좋습니다, 12저는 이제 가서 견학 단체를 만나겠습니다. 학생들과 함께 20분쯤 뒤에 돌아오겠습니다.

10

해석 무엇이 공지되고 있는가?

(A) 시설 견학
(B) 직원 채용 정책
(C) 정부 시찰
(D) 직원 평가

해설 공지의 주제를 묻는 문제입니다. "students from a local high school are going to tour our factory"라며 지역 고등학교의 학생들이 공장을 견학할 예정이라고 한 뒤, 공장 견학과 관련된 내용을 언급하였습니다. 따라서 정답은 (A) A facility tour입니다.

어휘 inspection[inspékʃən] 시찰, 점검
evaluation[미 ivæljuéiʃən, 영 ivæ̀ljuéiʃən] 평가

11

해석 공장에 대해 무엇이 암시되는가?
(A) 기계가 위험할 수 있다.
(B) 동물들을 위한 식품을 생산할 수 있다.
(C) 청결한 상태로 유지되어야 한다.
(D) 제품이 전 세계적으로 판매된다.

해설 공장에 대해 암시되는 것을 묻는 문제입니다. "This[wear protective hats and gloves] is an important precaution, as it will prevent the students from contaminating food with bacteria."라며 안전모와 장갑을 착용하는 것이 학생들이 세균으로 식품을 오염시키는 것을 방지할 것이기 때문에 중요한 예방 조치라고 한 것을 통해 공장이 청결한 상태로 유지되어야 함을 알 수 있습니다. 따라서 정답은 (C) It must remain clean입니다.

12

해석 화자는 다음에 무엇을 할 것 같은가?
(A) 안전모를 착용한다.
(B) 설명을 한다.
(C) 그의 손을 씻는다.
(D) 방문 단체를 맞이한다.

해설 화자가 다음에 할 일을 묻는 문제입니다. "I'm going to go and meet the tour group now"라며 자신은 이제 가서 견학 단체를 만나겠다고 하였습니다. 따라서 정답은 (D) Greet a visiting group입니다.

어휘 put on ~을 착용하다 demonstration[dèmənstréiʃən] 설명, 시범
greet[griːt] 맞이하다, 인사하다

13-15 [음성] 미국식 발음

Questions 13-15 refer to the following advertisement.

---

¹³If you are looking to buy a new laptop, visit Digital Solutions in the Plaza Center! From July 20 to 30, all items in the store will be available at a 15 percent discount. And ¹⁴we will remain open until 10 o'clock each night during the sale, so you will have an extra hour to shop. Even if you can't make it to the store, you can still take advantage of this event. ¹⁵Orders placed through our Web site qualify for the same discount.

---

discount[dískaunt] 할인(율) extra[ékstrə] 추가적인, 여분의
make it to ~로 오다, ~에 도착하다
take advantage of ~을 이용하다, ~을 활용하다
qualify for ~의 자격이 있다, ~의 자격을 갖추다

해석

13-15번은 다음 광고에 관한 문제입니다.

¹³만약 새로운 휴대용 컴퓨터를 살 생각이시라면, Plaza 센터에 있는 Digital Solutions를 방문하세요! 7월 20일부터 30일까지, 매장 내 모든 제품이 15퍼센트 할인된 가격에 구매 가능할 것입니다. 그리고 ¹⁴저희는 할인 판매

기간 동안 매일 밤 10시 정각까지 영업할 것이므로, 쇼핑할 수 있는 추가적인 한 시간이 더 있게 될 것입니다. 매장으로 오실 수 없다고 하더라도, 여러분은 여전히 이 행사를 이용하실 수 있습니다. ¹⁵저희 웹사이트를 통한 주문은 동일한 할인을 받을 자격이 있습니다.

13

해석 광고는 주로 무엇에 대한 것인가?
(A) 전자기기 수리점
(B) 쇼핑센터
(C) 컴퓨터 소매점
(D) 인터넷 서비스 제공업체

해설 광고의 주제를 묻는 문제입니다. "If you are looking to buy a new laptop, visit Digital Solutions"라며 만약 새로운 휴대용 컴퓨터를 살 생각이라면 Digital Solutions를 방문하라고 한 것을 통해 컴퓨터 소매점이 광고되고 있음을 알 수 있습니다. 따라서 정답은 (C) A computer retailer입니다.

어휘 electronics[미 ilektrániks, 영 èlektrɔ́niks] 전자기기, 전자 기술
retailer[미 ríːteilər, 영 ríːteilə] 소매점, 소매 상인

14

해석 화자는 Digital Solutions에 대해 무엇을 암시하는가?
(A) 영업시간을 연장할 것이다.
(B) 다른 지점을 개장할 것이다.
(C) 새로운 서비스를 개발할 것이다.
(D) 이전할 것이다.

해설 화자가 Digital Solutions에 대해 암시하는 것을 묻는 문제입니다. "we[Digital Solutions] will remain open until 10 o'clock each night during the sale, so you will have an extra hour to shop"이라며 Digital Solutions는 할인 판매 기간 동안 매일 밤 10시 정각까지 영업할 것이므로 쇼핑할 수 있는 추가적인 한 시간이 더 있게 될 것이라고 한 것을 통해 Digital Solutions가 영업시간을 연장할 것임을 알 수 있습니다. 따라서 정답은 (A) It will extend its hours입니다.

어휘 extend[iksténd] 연장하다, 확장하다

15

해석 화자는 웹사이트에 대해서 무엇을 언급하는가?
(A) 7월에 개설될 것이다.
(B) 할인을 제공할 것이다.
(C) 독점 제품을 판매할 것이다.
(D) 무료 배송을 특징으로 할 것이다.

해설 화자가 웹사이트에 대해 언급하는 것을 묻는 문제입니다. "Orders placed through our Web site qualify for the same discount."라며 웹사이트를 통한 주문은 동일한 할인을 받을 자격이 있다고 한 것을 통해 웹사이트에서 할인을 제공할 것임을 알 수 있습니다. 따라서 정답은 (B) It will offer a discount입니다.

어휘 launch[lɔːntʃ] 개시하다, 출시하다
exclusive[iksklúːsiv] 독점적인, 배타적인
feature[미 fíːtʃər, 영 fíːtʃə] 특징으로 하다

16-18 [음성] 미국식 발음

Questions 16-18 refer to the following introduction.

Can I have everyone's attention before we start? It's my pleasure to introduce ¹⁶Mr. William Hoffman, who will be leading our training session today. He has 25 years of sales experience working for some of the biggest companies in North and South America. ¹⁷He is also the author of the book *How to Sell to* ⊙

Anyone, which was a bestseller for many months. Mr. Hoffman will first explain several sales techniques, and then he will give you a chance to practice them. [18]Given how many of you have joined this workshop, we will divide you into smaller groups to do this. Now, let's welcome Mr. Hoffman.

> training session 교육 과정

해석

16-18번은 다음 소개에 관한 문제입니다.

시작하기 전에 모두 주목해 주시겠습니까? 저는 오늘 [16]우리 교육 과정을 이끌어 주실 Mr. William Hoffman을 소개하게 되어 기쁩니다. 그는 북아메리카와 남아메리카의 가장 큰 회사 중 몇 곳에서 근무한 25년간의 영업 경력이 있습니다. [17]그는 *How to Sell to Anyone*이라는 책의 저자이기도 한데, 이 책은 수개월 동안 베스트셀러였습니다. Mr. Hoffman은 먼저 몇 가지 영업 기술들을 설명하고, 그다음에 여러분께 그것들을 연습할 기회를 드릴 것입니다. [18]이 워크숍에 참여한 여러분의 수를 고려하여, 연습을 하기 위해 여러분을 더 작은 그룹으로 나눌 것입니다. 이제, Mr. Hoffman을 환영해 주십시오.

16

해석 Mr. Hoffman은 누구인가?
(A) 프리랜서 편집자
(B) 회사 경영자
(C) 재무 분석가
(D) 수업 강사

해설 Mr. Hoffman의 신분을 묻는 문제입니다. "Mr. William Hoffman, who will be leading our training session"이라며 교육 과정을 이끌어 줄 Mr. William Hoffman이라고 한 것을 통해 Mr. Hoffman이 수업의 강사임을 알 수 있습니다. 따라서 정답은 (D) A course instructor입니다.

어휘 freelance[미 fríːlæns, 영 fríːlɑːns] 프리랜서의, 자유 계약자로 일하는
analyst[ǽnəlist] 분석가, 전문가
instructor[미 instrʌ́ktər, 영 instrʌ́ktə] 강사, 교관

17

해석 화자는 Mr. Hoffman에 대해 무엇을 언급하는가?
(A) 그는 남아메리카로 전근할 것이다.
(B) 그는 정부를 위해 일했다.
(C) 그는 인기 있는 책을 썼다.
(D) 그는 큰 회사를 소유하고 있다.

해설 화자가 Mr. Hoffman에 대해 언급하는 것을 묻는 문제입니다. "He[Mr. Hoffman] is also the author of the book *How to Sell to Anyone*, which was a bestseller"라며 Mr. Hoffman이 *How to Sell to Anyone*이라는 책의 저자이며 이 책은 베스트셀러였다고 하였습니다. 따라서 정답은 (C) He wrote a popular book입니다.

어휘 transfer[미 trænsfə́ːr, 영 trænsfə́ː] 전근하다 own[미 oun, 영 əun] 소유하다

18

해석 워크숍에 대해 무엇이 암시되는가?
(A) 발표자가 한 명 이상 있다.
(B) 며칠 동안 계속된다.
(C) 다양한 주제를 다룬다.
(D) 많은 참여자를 포함한다.

해설 워크숍에 대해 암시되는 것을 묻는 문제입니다. "Given how many of you have joined this workshop, we will divide you into smaller groups"라며 워크숍에 참여한 청자들의 수를 고려하여 청자들을 더 작은 그룹으로 나눌 것이라고 한 말을 통해 워크숍이 많은 참여자를 포함한다는 것을 알 수 있습니다. 따라서 정답은 (D) It

---

includes many participants입니다.

어휘 deal with ~을 다루다

DAY 20 세부 사항 관련 문제 4

Course 1 시각 자료 문제 1 (표 및 그래프)

HACKERS PRACTICE ⋂ DAY20_02   p.156

| 01 (C) | 02 (D) | 03 (C) | 04 (C) |
| 05 (A) | 06 (C) | 07 (D) | 08 (C) |

01-02 [3배] 영국식 발음 / 미국식 발음

Questions 1-2 refer to the following excerpt from a meeting and pie chart.

> This graph represents companies' shares in the <u>frozen foods market</u>. I'm pleased that [01]we've achieved the <u>second highest market share</u> among frozen foods brands. But we still have progress to make to pass the current leader, Quick Fresh. Quick Fresh has recently launched a TV advertising campaign to increase its sales. I suggest we consider doing this as well. So, [02]could you all <u>do some market research</u> so that we can create an ad concept? I'll <u>review</u> what you've found at Friday's staff meeting.

> represent[rèprizént] 나타내다, 보여주다
> share[미 ʃɛər, 영 ʃeə] 점유율   frozen food 냉동식품
> achieve[ətʃíːv] 달성하다, 얻다   pass[미 pæs, 영 pɑːs] 추월하다, 앞지르다

해석

1-2번은 다음 회의 발췌록과 원그래프에 관한 문제입니다.

이 그래프는 냉동식품 시장에서 기업들의 점유율을 나타냅니다. 저는 [01]우리가 냉동식품 브랜드 중에서 두 번째로 높은 시장 점유율을 달성하게 되어 기쁩니다. 하지만 우리는 여전히 현재의 선두주자인 Quick Fresh사를 추월하기 위해 발전을 이루어야 합니다. Quick Fresh사는 최근에 판매량을 증가시키기 위해 TV 광고 캠페인을 시작했습니다. 저는 우리도 이렇게 하기를 고려하는 것을 제안합니다. 그러므로, [02]여러분 모두 우리가 광고 콘셉트를 생각해낼 수 있도록 시장 조사를 해주시겠습니까? 제가 금요일의 직원 회의에서 여러분들이 찾아낸 것을 검토하겠습니다.

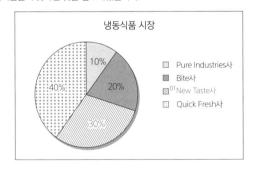

01

해석 시각 자료를 보아라. 화자는 어디에서 일하는가?
(A) Pure Industries사에서
(B) Bite사에서

(C) New Taste사에서

(D) Quick Fresh사에서

해설 화자가 일하는 곳을 묻는 문제입니다. "we've achieved the second highest market share among frozen foods brands"라며 화자의 회사가 냉동식품 브랜드 중에서 두 번째로 높은 시장 점유율을 달성하게 되었다고 하였으므로, 화자가 New Taste사에서 근무함을 원그래프에서 알 수 있습니다. 따라서 정답은 (C) At New Taste입니다.

02

해석 화자는 청자들에게 무엇을 해달라고 요청하는가?

(A) 회의실을 예약한다.

(B) 영업 컨퍼런스에 참석한다.

(C) 몇몇 장비를 주문한다.

(D) 조사를 실시한다.

해설 화자가 청자들에게 요청하는 것을 묻는 문제입니다. "could you all do some market research"라며 청자들에게 시장 조사를 해줄 것을 요청하였습니다. 따라서 정답은 (D) Conduct some research입니다.

어휘 equipment[ikwípmənt] 장비 conduct[kəndʌ́kt] 실시하다, 시행하다

03-04 [3세] 호주식 발음 / 캐나다식 발음

Questions 3-4 refer to the following talk and schedule.

03We'll now board the bus for the National Gallery. It will take about 20 minutes to reach the gallery from the hotel. That will give you some time to look over this brochure about the exhibits that I will hand out. Oh . . . and a famous artist, Linda Newman, is at the museum today. 04She will be signing autographs for tour groups. We'll have a chance to see her at the first exhibit after lunch, at 1 P.M. Alright, let's get on the bus.

board[미 bɔːrd, 영 bɔːd] 탑승하다 look over ~을 살펴보다, ~을 검토하다
autograph[미 ɔ́ːtəɡræf, 영 ɔ́ːtəɡrɑːf] 사명, 서인

해석

3-4번은 다음 담화와 일정표에 관한 문제입니다.

03우리는 이제 국립 미술관으로 가는 버스에 탑승할 것입니다. 이 호텔에서부터 미술관에 도착하기까지는 20분 정도가 걸릴 것입니다. 그것은 여러분들이 제가 나누어 드릴 전시에 대한 이 소책자를 살펴볼 시간을 줄 것입니다. 아... 그리고 유명한 예술가인 Linda Newman이 오늘 미술관에 와 있습니다. 04그녀는 관람 단체들에게 자필 서명을 해줄 것입니다. 우리는 점심 식사 후 첫 번째 전시에서 오후 1시에 그녀를 만날 기회가 있을 것입니다. 좋아요, 이제 버스에 탑승하겠습니다.

관람 일정	
유럽 풍경화	오전 10시 - 오전 10시 50분
정물화	오전 11시 - 오전 11시 50분
점심 식사	
04현대 조소	오후 1시 - 오후 1시 50분
추상 미술	오후 2시 - 오후 2시 50분

03

해석 담화는 어디에서 이루어지고 있는 것 같은가?

(A) 기차역에서

(B) 미술관에서

(C) 호텔에서

(D) 미술 학원에서

해설 담화가 이루어지고 있는 장소를 묻는 문제입니다. "We'll now board the bus ~. It will take about 20 minutes to reach the gallery from the hotel."이라며 이제 버스에 탑승할 것이고 이 호텔에서부터 미술관에 도착하기까지는 20분 정도가 걸릴 것이라고 하였습니다. 따라서 정답은 (C) At a hotel입니다.

04

해석 시각 자료를 보아라. 어떤 전시가 자필 서명하는 것을 포함할 것인가?

(A) 유럽 풍경화

(B) 정물화

(C) 현대 조소

(D) 추상 미술

해설 자필 서명하는 것을 포함할 전시를 묻는 문제입니다. "She[Linda Newman] will be signing autographs for tour groups. We'll ~ see her at the first exhibit after lunch, at 1 P.M."이라며 Linda Newman이 관람 단체들에게 자필 서명을 해줄 것이고 청자들이 점심 식사 후 첫 번째 전시에서 오후 1시에 그녀를 만날 것이라고 하였으므로, 오후 1시에 시작하는 현대 조소 전시에서 Linda Newman이 자필 서명을 해줄 것임을 일정표에서 알 수 있습니다. 따라서 정답은 (C) Modern Sculpture입니다.

어휘 landscape[lǽndskeip] 풍경화, 산수화
sculpture[미 skʌ́lptʃər, 영 skʌ́lptʃə] 조소, 조각품
abstract[미 ǽbstrækt, 영 ǽbstrækt] 추상적인

05-06 [3세] 캐나다식 발음 / 호주식 발음

Questions 5-6 refer to the following broadcast and graph.

The National Weather Service has issued a winter storm warning for Toronto. Heavy snow is expected over the next four days. 05The Toronto City Council will hire temporary laborers for snow removal. Nevertheless, residents should avoid driving unless absolutely necessary. If you must drive, please note that 06freezing rain is expected the day after we receive the heaviest snowfall. Road conditions will be extremely hazardous.

issue[íʃuː] 발령하다, 공표하다 warning[미 wɔ́ːrniŋ, 영 wɔ́ːniŋ] 경보, 주의
temporary[미 témpərèri, 영 témpərəri] 임시의 snow removal 제설
nevertheless[미 nèvərðəlés, 영 nèvəðəlés] 그렇지만, 그럼에도 불구하고
freezing rain 진눈깨비 snowfall[미 snóufɔːl, 영 snóufɔːl] 강설량
hazardous[미 hǽzərdəs, 영 hǽzədəs] 위험한

해석

5-6번은 다음 방송과 그래프에 관한 문제입니다.

국립 기상청이 토론토에 겨울 폭풍 경보를 발령했습니다. 많은 눈이 앞으로 4일 동안 예상됩니다. 05토론토 시의회는 제설을 위한 임시 작업자들을 고용할 예정입니다. 그렇지만, 주민들은 정말 필요한 경우가 아니면 운전을 하지 마시기 바랍니다. 만약 운전을 해야만 한다면, 06강설량이 최대인 날의 다음 날에 진눈깨비가 예상된다는 것을 유념하시기 바랍니다. 도로의 상태가 매우 위험할 것입니다.

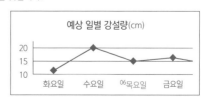

예상 일별 강설량(cm)

05

해석 화자는 토론토에 대해 무엇을 언급하는가?

(A) 임시 작업자들을 고용할 것이다.
(B) 제설 장비를 구입할 것이다.
(C) 일부 고속도로를 폐쇄할 것이다.
(D) 운전자들에게 지원을 해줄 것이다.

해설 화자가 토론토에 대해 언급하는 것을 묻는 문제입니다. "The Toronto City Council will hire temporary laborers"라며 토론토 시의회가 임시 작업자들을 고용할 예정이라고 하였습니다. 따라서 정답은 (A) It will hire temporary workers입니다.

어휘 highway[háiwèi] 고속도로 assistance[əsístəns] 지원, 도움

06

해석 시각 자료를 보아라. 진눈깨비는 언제 예상되는가?
(A) 화요일에
(B) 수요일에
(C) 목요일에
(D) 금요일에

해설 진눈깨비가 예상되는 시기를 묻는 문제입니다. "freezing rain is expected the day after we receive the heaviest snowfall"이라며 강설량이 최대인 날의 다음 날에 진눈깨비가 예상된다고 하였으므로, 강설량이 최대인 수요일 다음 날인 목요일에 진눈깨비가 예상됨을 그래프에서 알 수 있습니다. 따라서 정답은 (C) On Thursday입니다.

07-08 [3번] 미국식 발음 / 영국식 발음

Questions 7-8 refer to the following announcement and table.

> Can I have your attention, please? [07]RidgeFX, a program that many of you use, was recently upgraded to include additional design features. The IT department head will lead training sessions on the new software for everyone next Monday. You'll be divided into training groups according to team. [08]All teams will have a training session in the morning, except for the one with the most members. That team will be trained in the afternoon. I will provide more details later today.
>
> additional[ədíʃənəl] 추가적인 feature[미 fíːtʃər, 영 fíːtʃə] 기능, 특징

해석

7-8번은 다음 공지와 표에 관한 문제입니다.

주목해 주시겠습니까? [07]여러분 중 많은 분들이 사용하는 프로그램인 RidgeFX가 추가적인 디자인 기능을 포함시키기 위해 최근 업그레이드되었습니다. IT부서의 부장이 다음 주 월요일에 모두를 위해 새로운 소프트웨어에 대한 교육을 이끌 것입니다. 여러분들은 팀에 따라 교육을 받기 위한 그룹으로 나누어질 것입니다. [08]가장 많은 팀원이 있는 팀을 제외하고, 모든 팀들은 오전에 교육을 받을 것입니다. 그 팀은 오후에 교육을 받을 것입니다. 오늘 늦게 제가 더 많은 세부 사항을 알려 드리겠습니다.

팀명	직원 수
웹디자인	10명
지원	20명
[08]엔지니어링	25명
모바일 소프트웨어	15명

07

해석 RidgeFX는 왜 업그레이드되었는가?
(A) 오류를 해결하기 위해
(B) 몇몇 불만 사항을 처리하기 위해
(C) 모바일 버전을 만들기 위해
(D) 새로운 기능을 추가하기 위해

해설 RidgeFX가 업그레이드된 이유를 묻는 문제입니다. "RidgeFX ~ was recently upgraded to include additional design features."라며 RidgeFX가 추가적인 디자인 기능을 포함시키기 위해 최근 업그레이드되었다고 하였습니다. 따라서 정답은 (D) To add new features입니다.

어휘 address[ədrés] 처리하다, 다루다

08

해석 시각 자료를 보아라. 어느 팀이 오후에 교육을 받을 것인가?
(A) 웹디자인
(B) 지원
(C) 엔지니어링
(D) 모바일 소프트웨어

해설 오후에 교육을 받을 팀을 묻는 문제입니다. "All teams will have a training session in the morning, except for the one with the most members. That team will be trained in the afternoon." 이라며 가장 많은 팀원이 있는 팀을 제외하고 모든 팀들은 오전에 교육을 받을 것이며 그 팀은 오후에 교육을 받을 것이라고 하였으므로, 가장 팀원이 많은 엔지니어링 팀이 오후에 교육을 받을 것임을 표에서 알 수 있습니다. 따라서 정답은 (C) Engineering입니다.

Course 2 시각 자료 문제 2(약도 및 기타)

HACKERS PRACTICE 🎧 DAY20_04   p.160

01 (B)	02 (B)	03 (A)	04 (C)
05 (A)	06 (B)	07 (D)	08 (C)

01-02 [3번] 캐나다식 발음 / 호주식 발음

Questions 1-2 refer to the following advertisement and coupon.

> Looking for a way to beat the heat? Then visit Burger Palace Restaurant. [01]We're offering several new ice cream desserts to celebrate summer. And for a limited time, when you purchase one of our meal combos, you'll receive a free sundae. To take advantage of this offer, download a coupon from our Web site. Note that [02]this promotion is only valid at our Portland location and ends on July 4. Thank you!
>
> beat[biːt] 물리치다, 이기다
> celebrate[미 séləbrèit, 영 séləbreit] 맞이하다, 기념하다
> limited[límitid] 한정된
> sundae[sándei] 아이스크림선디(과일이나 초콜릿을 얹은 아이스크림)
> take advantage of ~을 이용하다
> promotion[미 prəmóuʃən, 영 prəmáuʃən] 판촉 행사

해석

1-2번은 다음 광고와 쿠폰에 관한 문제입니다.

더위를 물리칠 방법을 찾고 계신가요? 그렇다면 Burger Palace 레스토랑을 방문하세요. [01]저희는 여름을 맞이하여 몇 가지 새로운 아이스크림 디저트를 제공하고 있습니다. 그리고 한정된 기간 동안, 저희의 세트 메뉴 중 하나를 구매하시면, 무료 아이스크림선디 한 개를 받으실 것입니다. 이 제공을 이용하시려면, 저희 웹사이트에서 쿠폰을 다운로드하세요. [02]이 판촉 행사는 저희의 포틀랜드 지점에서만 유효하며 7월 4일에 종료된다는 것에 유의하시기 바랍니다. 감사합니다!

Burger Palace 쿠폰

무료 아이스크림선디 1개
세트 메뉴 1개 구매 필요

1234567890 1234

⁰²7월 3일 만료됨   포틀랜드 매장에서만 유효함

01

해석 화자에 따르면, 회사는 최근에 무엇을 했는가?
(A) 새로운 레스토랑을 개업했다.
(B) 메뉴 항목을 추가했다.
(C) 시설을 확장했다.
(D) 식사 가격을 내렸다.

해설 회사가 최근에 한 일을 묻는 문제입니다. "We're offering several new ice cream desserts to celebrate summer."라며 여름을 맞이하여 몇 가지 새로운 아이스크림 디저트를 제공하고 있다고 하였습니다. 따라서 정답은 (B) Added menu items입니다.

어휘 expand[ikspænd] 확장하다, 확대하다

02

해석 시각 자료를 보아라. 어떤 정보가 부정확한가?
(A) 필수 구매품
(B) 만료일
(C) 무료 제품
(D) 유효 지점

해설 부정확한 정보를 묻는 문제입니다. "this promotion ~ ends on July 4"라며 판촉 행사는 7월 4일에 종료된다고 하였으므로, 만료일 정보가 부정확함을 쿠폰에서 알 수 있습니다. 따라서 정답은 (B) Expiration date입니다.

어휘 required[미 rikwáiərd, 영 rikwáiəd] 필수인, 요구되는
expiration[èkspəréiʃən] 만료, 만기   validity[vəlídəti] 유효

03-04 [3집] 영국식 발음 / 미국식 발음

Questions 3-4 refer to the following announcement and floor plan.

OK . . . ⁰³Several student organizations are <u>touring our museum</u> tomorrow, so you'll be busy. To prevent overcrowding, please spend no more than 20 minutes at each exhibit. Also, ⁰⁴start with the exhibit <u>across from</u> the gift shop, <u>in front of</u> the ticket booth. Then, lead your group clockwise, ending with the one closest to the entrance. Oh, and the mammal exhibit was recently updated. <u>I'll distribute pamphlets</u> on the displays now for you to review.

organization[미 ɔ̀ːrgənizéiʃən, 영 ɔ̀ːgənaizéiʃən] 단체
overcrowding[미 òuvərkráudiŋ, 영 ə́uvəkráudiŋ] 혼잡, 과밀
exhibit[igzíbit] 전시   across from ~의 맞은편에
in front of ~ 앞에   clockwise[미 klɑ́ːkwaiz, 영 klɔ́kwaiz] 시계 방향으로
mammal[mæməl] 포유류

해석
3-4번은 다음 공지와 평면도에 관한 문제입니다.

좋습니다... ⁰³몇몇 학생 단체들이 내일 우리 박물관을 견학할 예정이므로, 여러분들은 바쁠 것입니다. 혼잡을 방지하기 위해, 각 전시에서 20분 이상 시간을 보내지 마세요. 그리고, ⁰⁴선물 가게 맞은편이자, 매표소 앞에 있는 전시부터 시작해 주세요. 그 다음, 여러분의 단체를 시계 방향으로 인솔하시고, 입구

에서 가장 가까운 곳에서 견학을 마쳐 주세요. 아, 그리고 포유류 전시가 최근에 업데이트되었습니다. 여러분이 검토할 수 있도록 새로운 전시에 대한 소책자를 지금 나누어 드리겠습니다.

포유류 전시		조류 전시
⁰⁴파충류 전시	선물 가게	어류 전시
매표소		입구

03

해석 화자는 누구에게 말을 하고 있는가?
(A) 안내원들
(B) 관광객들
(C) 학생들
(D) 교수들

해설 청자들의 신분을 묻는 문제입니다. "Several student organizations are touring our museum tomorrow, so you'll be busy."라며 몇몇 학생 단체들이 내일 박물관을 견학할 예정이라 청자들이 바쁠 것이라고 한 뒤, 청자들이 견학 단체들을 인솔할 때 지켜야 할 수칙들을 언급하였습니다. 이를 통해 청자들이 박물관의 안내원들임을 알 수 있습니다. 따라서 정답은 (A) Guides입니다.

04

해석 시각 자료를 보아라. 단체들은 어느 전시를 첫 번째로 관람할 것인가?
(A) 포유류 전시
(B) 조류 전시
(C) 파충류 전시
(D) 어류 전시

해설 단체들이 첫 번째로 관람할 전시를 묻는 문제입니다. "start with the exhibit across from the gift shop, in front of the ticket booth"라며 선물 가게 맞은편이자 매표소 앞에 있는 전시부터 시작해 달라고 하였으므로, 단체들이 파충류 전시를 첫 번째로 관람할 것임을 평면도에서 알 수 있습니다. 따라서 정답은 (C) The reptile exhibit입니다.

어휘 reptile[미 réptil, 영 réptail] 파충류

05-06 [3집] 미국식 발음 / 영국식 발음

Questions 5-6 refer to the following telephone message and credit card statement.

My name is Janice Walker, and I signed up for ⁰⁵the Wentworth Mall Rewards Club that <u>you launched last week</u>. Joining this loyalty program was supposed to qualify me for 10 percent off all purchases. But looking at my credit card statement, I see that ⁰⁶I was charged full price at one store. And it was for the <u>largest purchase</u> I made. I'd like you to correct this error. I'll be <u>on a business trip</u> starting tomorrow, so please call me back this afternoon.

qualify[미 kwɑ́ːləfài, 영 kwɔ́lifai] 자격을 주다
charge[미 tʃɑːrdʒ, 영 tʃɑːdʒ] 청구하다
purchase[미 pə́ːrtʃəs, 영 pə́ːtʃəs] 구매(품)   business trip 출장

해석
5-6번은 다음 전화 메시지와 신용카드 명세서에 관한 문제입니다.

제 이름은 Janice Walker이고, 저는 ⁰⁵귀사가 지난주에 출시한 Wentworth 쇼핑몰의 우대 클럽에 가입했습니다. 이 우대 프로그램에 가입하는 것은 모든 구매에 대해 제가 10퍼센트의 할인을 받을 수 있는 자격을 주도록 되어 있었습니다. 하지만 제 신용카드 명세서를 보고, ⁰⁶제가 한 매장에서 전액을

청구받았다는 것을 알게 되었습니다. 그리고 그것은 제가 한 가장 높은 금액의 구매에 대한 것이었습니다. 저는 귀사가 이 오류를 정정해 주기를 바랍니다. 저는 내일부터 출장을 갈 것이므로, 오늘 오후에 제게 다시 전화 주시기 바랍니다.

Janice Walker – 신용카드 명세서

판매자	금액
Bartleby's Books	125.00달러
[06]Hart & Crane	325.00달러
Maria's Market	65.00달러
Wentworth Clothing	75.00달러

05

해석 Wentworth 쇼핑몰 우대 클럽에 대해 무엇이 언급되는가?
(A) 새로운 프로그램이다.
(B) 아직 출시되지 않았다.
(C) 회비를 포함한다.
(D) 회원들에게 카드를 제공하지 않는다.

해설 Wentworth 쇼핑몰 우대 클럽에 대해 언급되는 것을 묻는 문제입니다. "the Wentworth Mall Rewards Club that you launched last week"이라며 청자의 회사가 지난주에 출시한 Wentworth 쇼핑몰 우대 클럽이라고 한 말을 통해, Wentworth 쇼핑몰 우대 클럽이 새로운 프로그램임을 알 수 있습니다. 따라서 정답은 (A) It is a new program입니다.

어휘 membership fee 회비

06

해석 시각 자료를 보아라. 화자는 어느 매장에서 잘못된 금액을 청구받았는가?
(A) Bartleby's Books
(B) Hart & Crane
(C) Maria's Market
(D) Wentworth Clothing

해설 화자가 잘못된 금액을 청구받은 매장을 묻는 문제입니다. "I was charged full price at one store. And it was for the largest purchase I made."라며 화자가 한 매장에서 전액을 청구받았고, 그것은 자신이 한 가장 높은 금액의 구매에 대한 것이었다고 하였으므로, 화자가 325.00달러를 지불한 Hart & Crane에서 잘못된 금액을 청구했음을 신용카드 명세서에서 알 수 있습니다. 따라서 정답은 (B) Hart & Crane입니다.

07-08 [호주식 발음 / 캐나다식 발음]

Questions 7-8 refer to the following talk and directory.

Thank you for coming to the annual International Advertising Conference. We'll have events in various rooms at Westfield Hotel today. The highlight of our day will be a speech from Melissa Grand, the CEO of Bellow Advertising Corporation. [07]This will take place at 5 P.M. in the Francesca Ballroom. After that, there will be a social gathering at the hotel's restaurant, Regina Kitchen. [08]Those interested in attending should sign up by writing their names on the form outside Hailey Hall now.

---

annual [ǽnjuəl] 연례의, 연간의

○

---

various [미 véəriəs, 영 véəriəs] 다양한, 여러 가지의
ballroom [bɔ́:lru:m] 연회장, 무도회장   gathering [gǽðəriŋ] 모임, 행사
sign up ~에 등록하다

해석
7–8번은 다음 담화와 건물 안내판에 관한 문제입니다.

연례 국제 광고 컨퍼런스에 와주셔서 감사합니다. 저희는 오늘 Westfield 호텔의 다양한 객실에서 행사를 열 것입니다. 오늘의 하이라이트는 Bellow 광고사의 CEO인 Melissa Grand의 연설이 될 것입니다. [07]이것은 오후 5시에 Francesca 연회장에서 이루어질 것입니다. 그 후에, 이 호텔의 식당인 Regina Kitchen에서 친목 모임이 있을 것입니다. [08]참석하고 싶으신 분들은 지금 Hailey 홀 밖에 있는 양식에 성함을 적어 등록해 주시기 바랍니다.

Westfield 호텔 건물 안내판	
회의실	5층
Regina Kitchen	4층
Hailey 홀	3층
[07]Francesca 연회장	2층

07

해석 시각 자료를 보아라. Melissa Grand는 어디에서 연설을 할 것인가?
(A) 5층에서
(B) 4층에서
(C) 3층에서
(D) 2층에서

해설 Melissa Grand가 연설할 장소를 묻는 문제입니다. "This[speech from Melissa Grand] will take place ~ in the Francesca Ballroom."이라며 Melissa Grand의 연설이 Francesca 연회장에서 이루어질 것이라고 하였으므로, Melissa Grand는 2층에서 연설할 것임을 건물 안내판에서 알 수 있습니다. 따라서 정답은 (D) On the 2nd floor입니다.

08

해석 몇몇 청자들은 다음에 무엇을 할 것인가?
(A) 저녁 식사를 주문한다.
(B) 소셜 미디어 사이트를 방문한다.
(C) 행사에 등록한다.
(D) 식당으로 이동한다.

해설 몇몇 청자들이 다음에 할 일을 묻는 문제입니다. 친목 모임에 대해 언급한 뒤, "Those interested in attending should sign up ~ now."라며 참석에 관심이 있는 사람들은 지금 등록해 달라고 하였습니다. 따라서 정답은 (C) Register for an event입니다.

HACKERS TEST ∩ DAY20_05   p.162

01 (D)	02 (B)	03 (A)	04 (A)
05 (C)	06 (C)	07 (C)	08 (D)
09 (B)	10 (C)	11 (D)	12 (B)

01-03 [미국식 발음]

Questions 1-3 refer to the following advertisement and sign.

Now is your chance to become a community member at Driftwood Estates, Branford's most prestigious housing development. The condominiums are almost ready, and [01]move-ins will begin on June 1. Units are selling out fast, but [02]some are still available in the $400,000 to 599,000 price range. The development ○

---

includes a swimming pool, tennis courts, and a fine-dining restaurant. If you think you might be interested, ⁰³come to our reception office to have consultation with a sales agent. It's open from 10 A.M. to 7 P.M.

prestigious[prestídʒəs] 일류의, 명망 있는
development[divéləpmənt] 주택 단지, 개발
condominium[미 kὰːndəmíniəm, 영 kɔ̀ndəmíniəm] (분양) 아파트, 콘도
reception office 접수처 **sales agent** 판매 대리인

해석

1~3번은 다음 광고와 표지판에 관한 문제입니다.

지금이 Branford의 가장 일류 주택 단지인 Driftwood Estates의 지역 주민이 될 기회입니다. 이 아파트는 준비가 거의 다 되었고, ⁰¹전입은 6월 1일에 시작될 것입니다. 아파트 세대들이 빠르게 판매되고 있지만, ⁰²일부는 400,000달러에서 599,000달러의 가격대에서 아직 구입 가능합니다. 그 주택 단지는 수영장, 테니스 코트, 고급 식당을 포함합니다. 만약 여러분이 관심이 있을 것 같다고 생각하시면, ⁰³저희 접수처에 오셔서 판매 대리인과 상담해보세요. 접수처는 오전 10시부터 오후 7시까지 운영됩니다.

Driftwood Estates의 아파트 가격	
1번 항목	⁰²2번 항목
400,000달러 미만	400,000달러에서 599,000달러
3번 항목	4번 항목
600,000달러에서 799,000달러	800,000달러 이상

01

해석 6월 1일에 무슨 일이 일어날 것인가?
(A) 스포츠 토너먼트가 시작될 것이다.
(B) 몇몇 이웃들이 파티에 참석할 것이다.
(C) 자선 경매가 열릴 것이다.
(D) 몇몇 주택 소유주들이 전입할 것이다.

해석 6월 1일에 일어날 일을 묻는 문제입니다. "move-ins will begin on June 1"라며 전입이 6월 1일에 시작될 것이라고 하였습니다. 따라서 정답은 (D) Some homeowners will move in입니다.

어휘 get underway 시작하다 charity[tʃǽrəti] 자선, 자선기금
auction[ɔ́ːkʃən] 경매

02

해석 시각 자료를 보아라. 어떤 종류의 세대들이 구입 가능한가?
(A) 1번 항목
(B) 2번 항목
(C) 3번 항목
(D) 4번 항목

해석 구입 가능한 세대의 종류를 묻는 문제입니다. "some[units] are still available in the $400,000 to 599,000 price range"라며 일부 세대가 400,000달러에서 599,000달러의 가격대에서 아직 구입 가능하다고 하였으므로, 가격이 400,000달러에서 599,000달러인 2번 세대가 구입 가능함을 표지판에서 알 수 있습니다. 따라서 정답은 (B) Category 2입니다.

03

해석 청자들은 접수처에서 무엇을 할 수 있는가?
(A) 판매원과 상담한다.
(B) 소책자를 가져간다.
(C) 견학을 신청한다.

(D) 모형을 본다.

해석 청자들이 접수처에서 할 수 있는 일을 묻는 문제입니다. "come to our reception office to have consultation with a sales agent"라며 접수처에 와서 판매 대리인과 상담해보라고 하였습니다. 따라서 정답은 (A) Consult with a salesperson입니다.

어휘 register for ~을 신청하다, ~을 등록하다

04-06 [3번] 캐나다식 발음

Questions 4-6 refer to the following telephone message and price list.

Hi, Catherine. ⁰⁴I'm calling to let you know that I made a booking with the Portland Conference Center for the seminar we're holding on June 11. The rental fee for the room was higher than expected, but ⁰⁵the room includes a projector and screen at no extra cost. And . . . Could you order some bottled water for attendees? There will be 120 participants, and we'll need two bottles for each person. So, uh . . . ⁰⁶240 in total. Please contact Pearson Beverages because that company offers significant discounts on bulk orders. Thanks.

rental[réntl] 대여, 임대 **bottled water** 병에 든 생수
attendee[미 ətèndíː, 영 ətendíː] 참석자
participant[미 pɑːrtísəpənt, 영 pɑːtísipənt] 참석자
significant[signífikənt] 상당한 **bulk order** 대량 주문

해석

4~6번은 다음 전화 메시지와 가격표에 관한 문제입니다.

안녕하세요, Catherine. 우리가 6월 11일에 주최할 세미나를 위해 Portland 컨퍼런스 센터와 ⁰⁴예약을 했다는 것을 알려드리려고 전화했어요. 회의실 대여료가 예상했던 것보다 더 비쌌지만, ⁰⁵회의실에는 추가 비용 없이 영사기와 스크린이 포함되어 있어요. 그리고... 참석자들을 위해 병에 든 생수를 주문해 주실 수 있나요? 120명의 참석자가 있을 것이고, 우리는 1인당 2병이 필요할 거예요. 그래서, 어... ⁰⁶총 240병이에요. Pearson 음료 회사가 대량 주문에 상당한 할인을 제공하니까 그 회사에 연락하세요. 고마워요.

Pearson 음료 회사	
병에 든 생수	
수량	개당 가격
1-99개	1.75달러
100-199개	1.50달러
⁰⁶200-299개	1.25달러
300개 이상	1.00달러

04

해석 화자는 왜 전화를 하고 있는가?
(A) 그가 예약을 했다는 것을 알리기 위해
(B) 청자를 행사에 참석하도록 초대하기 위해
(C) 그가 왜 세미나 일정을 변경했는지 설명하기 위해
(D) 청자에게 센터에 연락할 것을 부탁하기 위해

해석 전화의 목적을 묻는 문제입니다. "I'm calling to let you know that I made a booking"이라며 자신이 예약을 했다는 것을 알려주려고 전화했다고 하였습니다. 따라서 정답은 (A) To report that he made a reservation입니다.

어휘 reschedule[미 rìːskédʒuːl, 영 rìːʃédʒuːl] 일정을 변경하다

PART 4

해커스 토익 700+ (LC+RC+VOCA)

05

해석 화자는 회의실에 대해 무엇을 언급하는가?
(A) 할인가에 이용 가능하다.
(B) 좌석이 한정되어 있다.
(C) 무료 장비가 딸려 있다.
(D) 예상했던 것보다 크다.

해설 화자가 회의실에 대해 언급하는 것을 묻는 문제입니다. "the room includes a projector and screen at no extra cost"라며 회의실에는 추가 비용 없이 영사기와 스크린이 포함되어 있다고 하였습니다. 따라서 정답은 (C) It comes with free equipment입니다.

어휘 seating[síːtiŋ] 좌석, 자리

06

해석 시각 자료를 보라. 청자는 개당 얼마를 지불하게 될 것 같은가?
(A) 1.75달러
(B) 1.50달러
(C) 1.25달러
(D) 1.00달러

해설 청자가 개당 지불하게 될 가격을 묻는 문제입니다. "240 in total."이라며 필요한 생수가 총 240병이라고 하였으므로, 청자가 개당 지불하게 될 가격은 1.25달러임을 가격표에서 알 수 있습니다. 따라서 정답은 (C) $1.25입니다.

07-09 [3] 영국식 발음

Questions 7-9 refer to the following introduction and map.

Good morning, everyone. For today's class, we will have a guest speaker: Rosalyn Gonzalez. She's someone who's accomplished a great deal in the field of architecture. [07]Ms. Gonzalez designed Aurora Tower, a unique building adjacent to our city's harbor. Oh, and [08]she actually graduated from this university . . . that was 15 years ago now. She knows exactly what sort of challenges you're experiencing, so [09]I'd like each of you to ask a question after the talk. For now, please give her your complete attention.

accomplish[미 əkáːmpliʃ, 영 əkʌ́mpliʃ] 성취하다, 이루다
architecture[미 áːrkitektʃər, 영 áːkitektʃə] 건축, 건축학
unique[미 juníːk, 영 juːníːk] 독특한, 유일한
adjacent to ~에 인접한   attention[əténʃən] 집중, 주목

해석
7-9번은 다음 소개와 지도에 관한 문제입니다.

여러분, 안녕하세요. 오늘 수업에서, 우리는 초대 강연자인 Rosalyn Gonzalez를 모실 것입니다. 그녀는 건축 분야에서 많은 것을 성취하신 분입니다. [07]Ms. Gonzalez는 Aurora 타워를 설계했는데, 그것은 도시의 항구에 인접한 독특한 건물입니다. 아, 그리고 [08]그녀는 실제로 이 대학을 졸업했고... 그게 이제 15년 전입니다. 그녀는 여러분들이 어떤 문제들을 겪고 있는지 정확히 알고 있으므로, [09]저는 여러분 각자가 강연 후에 질문을 하기 바랍니다. 이제, 그녀에게 온전히 집중해주세요.

07

해석 시각 자료를 보라. Rosalyn Gonzalez는 어떤 건물을 설계했는가?
(A) A 건물
(B) B 건물
(C) C 건물
(D) D 건물

해설 Rosalyn Gonzalez가 설계한 건물을 묻는 문제입니다. "Ms. Gonzalez designed ~ a unique building adjacent to our city's harbor."라며 Ms. Gonzalez가 도시의 항구에 인접한 독특한 건물을 설계했다고 하였으므로, 항구 근처에 있는 C 건물을 설계했음을 지도에서 알 수 있습니다. 따라서 정답은 (C) Building C입니다.

08

해석 Rosalyn Gonzalez에 대해 무엇이 언급되는가?
(A) 그녀는 현재 도시를 위해 일한다.
(B) 그녀는 건축학 강좌를 가르친다.
(C) 그녀는 설계에 대한 상을 받았다.
(D) 그녀는 10년도 더 전에 졸업했다.

해설 Rosalyn Gonzalez에 대해 언급되는 것을 묻는 문제입니다. "she[Ms. Gonzalez] actually graduated from this university . . . that was 15 years ago now"라며 Rosalyn Gonzalez가 실제로 이 대학을 졸업했고 그게 이제 15년 전이라고 하였습니다. 따라서 정답은 (D) She graduated more than a decade ago입니다.

09

해석 화자는 청자들에게 무엇을 하라고 권하는가?
(A) 프로그램에 등록한다.
(B) 질문을 생각해본다.
(C) 녹음을 한다.
(D) 명소를 방문한다.

해설 화자가 청자들에게 권하는 것을 묻는 문제입니다. "I'd like each of you to ask a question"이라며 화자가 청자 각자가 질문을 하기 바란다고 한 것을 통해 질문을 생각해보도록 권하고 있음을 알 수 있습니다. 따라서 정답은 (B) Think of a question입니다.

어휘 landmark[미 lǽndmɑːrk, 영 lǽndmɑːk] 명소, 역사적 건물

10-12 [3] 호주식 발음

Questions 10-12 refer to the following talk and graph.

The CEO has decided to lower the company's budget for next year because of falling sales. [10]As department heads, it will be your task to reduce your teams' spending accordingly. Most departments will need to reduce monthly expenses by 10 percent. Um, there's one exception—[11]the department that already has a smaller budget than the others. Its budget will remain at $15,000 next year. I've analyzed how we can reduce spending and have sent you all the document. [12]I recommend reviewing it carefully before our regular meeting on Friday.

budget[bʌ́dʒit] 예산
accordingly[미 əkɔ́ːrdiŋli, 영 əkɔ́ːdiŋli] 그에 따라, 따라서
expense[ikspéns] 지출   exception[iksépʃən] 예외
analyze[ǽnəlàiz] 분석하다

해석
10-12번은 다음 담화와 그래프에 관한 문제입니다.

CEO가 감소하는 매출 때문에 내년을 위한 회사 예산을 줄이겠다고 결정했

습니다. [10]부서장들로서, 그에 따라 팀의 지출을 줄이는 것이 여러분의 과제
입니다. 대부분의 부서들은 월간 지출을 10퍼센트 정도 줄여야 할 것입니다.
음, [11]이미 다른 부서들보다 예산이 적은 부서는 예외입니다. 그 부서의 예산
은 내년에 15,000달러로 유지될 것입니다. 제가 지출을 줄일 수 있는 방법을
분석했으며 여러분 모두에게 그 문서를 보냈습니다. 금요일 정기 회의 전까지
이것을 꼼꼼하게 [12]검토할 것을 권합니다.

월간 운영 예산 (현 연도)

영업	
마케팅	
인사	
[11]회계	

0달러　15,000달러　20,000달러　25,000달러　30,000달러

10
해석 청자들은 누구인 것 같은가?
(A) 점원들
(B) 회사 인턴들
(C) 부서장들
(D) 이사회 회원들

해설 청자들의 신분을 묻는 문제입니다. "As department heads, it will
be your task to reduce your teams' spending accordingly."라
며 부서장들로서 그에 따라 팀의 지출을 줄이는 것이 청자들의 과제라
고 한 말을 통해 청자들이 부서장임을 알 수 있습니다. 따라서 정답은
(C) Department heads입니다.

11
해석 시각 자료를 보아라. 어느 부서가 예산이 삭감되지 않을 것인가?
(A) 영업
(B) 마케팅
(C) 인사
(D) 회계

해설 예산이 삭감되지 않을 부서를 묻는 문제입니다. "the department
that already has a smaller budget than the others. Its budget
will remain at $15,000 next year."라며 이미 다른 부서들보다 예
산이 적은 부서의 예산은 내년에 15,000달러로 유지될 것이라고 하였
으므로, 현 연도 월간 운영 예산이 15,000달러인 회계 부서의 예산이
삭감되지 않을 것임을 그래프에서 알 수 있습니다. 따라서 정답은 (D)
Accounting입니다.

12
해석 화자는 청자들에게 무엇을 하라고 제안하는가?
(A) 회의를 마련한다.
(B) 보고서를 읽는다.
(C) 관리자에게 연락한다.
(D) 발표를 한다.

해설 화자가 청자들에게 제안하는 것을 묻는 문제입니다. "I recommend
reviewing it[the document]"이라며 문서를 검토할 것을 권한다고
하였습니다. 따라서 정답은 (B) Read a report입니다.

리딩 기초 다지기

DAY 01 기초 다지기

Course 1 문장 성분 · 구와 절

HACKERS PRACTICE p.169

01 (A)	02 (D)	03 (B)	04 (E)	05 (C)
06 (A)	07 (B)	08 (A)	09 (B)	10 (B)

해석 01 관리자는 여기에 있다.

02 내 삼촌은 과학자이다.

03 Mr. Jones는 표가 필요하다.

04 직원들은 매일 일한다.

05 그 고객은 합의서에 서명을 했다.

06 인근 커피숍이 음료에 대해 할인을 제공하고 있다.

07 Mr. Quince는 Ms. White가 어디에 사는지 알지 못한다.

08 토피카행 기차는 20분만큼 지연되었다.

09 청중들은 연설이 끝났을 때 갈채를 보냈다.

10 이번 주 중으로 주문하신다면, 배송이 무료일 것이다.

Course 2 패러프레이징

HACKERS PRACTICE p.171

01 (B)	02 (B)	03 (A)	04 (B)

01

> 연례 농업 무역 박람회가 6월 5일에 Prembleton 컨벤션 센터에서 열릴 것이다. 그것은 그 지역의 150개가 넘는 생산업체 및 제조업체들에 의해 참석될 것이다.
>
> (A) 국제 기업의 생산자들이 참가할 것이다.
> (B) 농업 무역 박람회는 일 년에 한 번 열린다.

해설 답의 근거 문장은 'The annual agricultural trade show will be held'로 (B)가 정답입니다. annual(연례의)이 once a year(일 년에 한 번)라는 같은 의미의 표현으로 패러프레이징되었습니다.

어휘 annual adj. 연례의 agricultural adj. 농업의
trade show phr. 무역 박람회 producer n. 생산업체, 생산자
manufacturer n. 제조업체 region n. 지역
international adj. 국제(상)의, 국제적인

02

> 회계부 직원들은 지난 분기의 소득을 분석하고 검토하도록 요청받았다. 그들은 이번 주말까지 보고서를 제출해야 한다.
>
> (A) 회계부는 지난 분기에 큰 수익을 냈다.
> (B) 직원들은 이번 주말까지 업무를 완료해야 한다.

해설 답의 근거 문장은 'The accounting staff has been asked to analyze and review last quarter's earnings.'로 (B)가 정답입니다. The accounting staff가 Employees로 일반화되어 패러프레이징 되었습니다.

어휘 accounting n. 회계 review v. 검토하다 quarter n. 분기
submit v. 제출하다 department n. 부(서)
complete v. 완료하다; adj. 완전한 assignment n. 업무

03

> Bartletville 중앙 도서관은 월요일부터 금요일까지는 오전 9시에 열고 오후 10시에 닫는다. 하지만, 토요일, 일요일, 공휴일에는 오전 10시에 열고 오후 6시에 닫는다.
>
> (A) Bartletville 중앙 도서관은 일 년 내내 대중에게 열려 있다.
> (B) 주말에, Bartletville 중앙 도서관의 특정 시설들은 문을 닫는다.

해설 답의 근거 문장은 'The Bartletville Central Library opens at 9:00 A.M. ~ from Monday to Friday. On Saturdays, Sundays, and public holidays, ~ it opens at 10:00 A.M.'으로 (A)가 정답입니다. from Monday to Friday. On Saturdays, Sundays, and public holidays가 every day of the year로 요약되어 패러프레이징되었습니다.

어휘 facility n. 시설

04

> 많은 호텔들이 테마로 자신을 돋보이게 하려 하며, 새로 개업한 Book & Bed 역시 예외가 아니다. 2,000권 이상의 소설을 갖춘 Book & Bed는 문학을 즐기는 이들의 취향을 만족시킨다.
>
> (A) 유명한 작가들이 새로 연 호텔을 방문했다.
> (B) Book & Bed는 특정한 시장을 겨냥한 호텔이다.

해설 답의 근거 문장은 'Book & Bed caters to those who enjoy literature'로 (B)가 정답입니다. '문학을 즐기는 이들의 취향을 만족시킨다'는 내용을 근거로, '특정한 시장을 겨냥한 호텔이다'라는 새롭게 추론한 사실로 패러프레이징되었습니다.

어휘 stand out phr. 돋보이다, 두드러지다 theme n. 테마, 주제
exception n. 예외 stock v. 갖추다, 채우다; n. 재고(품)
cater to phr. ~의 취향을 만족시키다 author n. 작가, 저자
target v. 겨냥하다, 목표로 삼다 specific adj. 특정한, 구체적인

HACKERS TEST p.172

01 (D)	02 (C)	03 (B)	04 (A)
05 (B)	06 (C)	07 (A)	08 (C)

01-04

시즌 채용 증가

9월—[01]Drummond사는 전국의 자사 백화점의 수요를 충족하기 위해 다가오는 휴가철을 위한 35,000명 이상의 추가 직원을 고용할 계획이다. Drummond사의 대변인 Miriam Flacks는 회사가 실제로 8월에 채용을 시작했고 대부분의 일자리가 11월 중순까지 채워질 것으로 예상한다고 말했다. ▸

몇몇 다른 사업체들도 또한 채용 규모를 늘렸다. ⁰²우편물 배달 업체인 Parcelfast사는 회사가 많은 양의 휴가 주문품을 고객들에게 배달하는 것을 도와줄 45,000여 명을 전국적으로 고용할 것이다. 가전제품 소매업체인 Tickit사는 20,000명 이상의 시즌 매장 직원들을 모집할 것이라고 말했다. 반면, ⁰³Randon Toys사는 최종적인 채용 숫자를 발표하지는 않았지만, 자사의 가장 큰 시장 중 다섯 군데에 최소 10,000명의 직원들을 추가할 것으로 예상한다.

Lindsay Capital사의 Mark Arnott에 따르면, 채용 증가는 간단히 설명된다. "1년 중 다른 어느 때보다도 휴일 무렵에 더 많은 사람들이 쇼핑을 합니다. 그러나, ⁰⁴또 다른 요인은 지난해 동안 우리가 보은 임금 인상일 수 있습니다. 사람들은 또한 이제 쓸 돈을 더 많이 가지고 있습니다."

seasonal adj. 시즌의, 특정한 시기의, 계절의   hiring n. 채용
additional adj. 추가적인   upcoming adj. 다가오는, 곧 있을
meet v. 충족하다   demand n. 수요, 요구
spokesperson n. 대변인   expect v. 예상하다, 기대하다
scale up phr. 규모를 늘리다, 확대하다   postal adj. 우편의
nationwide adv. 전국적으로; adj. 전국적인
retailer n. 소매업체   recruit v. (직원 등을) 모집하다
meanwhile adv. 반면, 그동안에   figure n. 숫자, 수치
market n. 시장; v. 판매하다   increase n. 증가   explanation n. 설명
factor n. 요인, 요소   wage n. 임금   rise n. 인상, 증가
spend v. (돈을) 쓰다, (시간을) 보내다, 들이다

01

문제 11월에 무슨 일이 일어날 것으로 예상되는가?
(A) 몇몇 소매업체들이 다음 해를 위한 계획을 발표할 것이다.
(B) 상점의 지점망 전체에서 할인이 시작될 것이다.
(C) 몇몇 중요 직책들이 소매업체의 본사에 채워질 것이다.
(D) 백화점이 수천 명의 임시 직원들을 고용했을 것이다.

해설 답의 근거 문장은 'Drummond plans to hire more than 35,000 additional workers for the upcoming holiday season to meet demand at its department stores around the country. ~ the company actually began hiring in August and expects most jobs to be filled by mid-November.'로 (D)가 정답입니다. 35,000 additional workers for the upcoming holiday season이 thousands of temporary staff로 요약되어 패러프레이징되었습니다.

어휘 announce v. 발표하다   the coming year phr. 다음 해
launch v. 시작하다, 개시하다   branch n. 지점   position n. (일)자리
head office phr. 본사   temporary adj. 임시의

02

문제 Parcelfast사는 왜 더 많은 직원들을 고용할 계획인가?
(A) 새로운 도시들에 사무실들을 열 것이다.
(B) 경쟁사들에게 뒤처지지 않고 싶어 한다.
(C) 배송 수요가 증가할 것으로 예상한다.
(D) 최근에 다른 회사와 합병했다.

해설 답의 근거 문장은 'Postal carrier Parcelfast will hire about 45,000 people nationwide to help it deliver large numbers of holiday orders to customers.'로 (C)가 정답입니다. large numbers of holiday orders가 shipping demand로 일반화되어 패러프레이징되었습니다.

어휘 keep up with phr. ~에 뒤처지지 않다   competitor n. 경쟁사, 경쟁자
recently adv. 최근에   merge v. 합병하다   firm n. 회사

03

문제 Randon Toys사에 대해 언급된 것은?
(A) 한정된 수의 장소에서 운영한다.
(B) 10,000명 이상의 새 직원들을 고용할 수도 있다.

(C) 지난해로부터 계획을 변경하지 않았다.
(D) 대부분의 제품을 온라인 상점을 통해 판매한다.

해설 답의 근거 문장은 'Randon Toys ~ expects to add at least 10,000 workers in five of its biggest markets'로 (B)가 정답입니다. add at least 10,000 workers가 hire more than 10,000 new workers로 패러프레이징되었습니다.

어휘 limited adj. 한정된, 제한된   location n. 장소, 위치   alter v. 변경하다

04

문제 Mr. Arnott에 따르면, 채용에 대한 최근 경향의 이면에 무엇이 있을 수 있는가?
(A) 직원 급여의 증가
(B) 온라인 쇼핑의 증가하는 인기
(C) 확장을 위한 자금의 입수 가능성
(D) 시즌 광고 활동의 성공

해설 답의 근거 문장은 'another factor could be the wage rises we've seen over the past year'로 (A)가 정답입니다. the wage rises가 increase in employees' salaries로 패러프레이징되었습니다.

어휘 salary n. 급여, 연봉   availability n. 입수 가능성   capital n. 자금
expansion n. 확장   success n. 성공   effort n. 활동, 노력

05-08

수신: Ray Douglas <r.douglas@douglasbros.com>
발신: Amber Hughes <a.hughes@snippets.org>
날짜: 5월 3일
제목: Snippets와 함께 일하고 쇼핑하세요

Mr. Douglas께,

저는 저희가 시내에 Snippets라고 불리는 새로운 비영리 상점을 연다는 것을 말씀드리기 위해 귀하께 글을 씁니다. ⁰⁵저희는 주민들, 지역 단체, 사업체들에게 손상되지 않은 단추, 끈, 파지, 판지의 기부를 요청드리고 있습니다. 저희는 그것들을 저희 상점에서 공예용품으로 재판매할 계획입니다. ⁰⁶저희가 번 모든 돈은 이곳 시내의 환경 및 교육 프로젝트에 보태질 것입니다.

⁰⁷저희는 귀하의 사무실에서 귀하께서 보통 버렸을 법한 물품들을 모아 저희의 상점에 기부해 주시기를 요청드립니다. ⁰⁸저희는 귀하께 편한 장소에서 귀하께서 갖고 계실 어떠한 것이라도 수거할 준비를 할 수 있습니다.

저희의 개장은 5월 20일이 될 것입니다. 상점에 방문하셔서 Snippets에서 무엇이 구입 가능한지 확인하십시오!

Amber Hughes 드림
Snippets 총 책임자

nonprofit adj. 비영리적인   resident n. 주민   donation n. 기부
undamaged adj. 손상되지 않은   string n. 끈   scrap paper phr. 파지
resell v. 재판매하다   craft n. 공예   supply n. 용품, 공급(품)
earn v. 벌다, 얻다   put toward phr. (비용을) ~에 보태다
environmental adj. 환경적인   educational adj. 교육적인
normally adv. 보통 (때는)   throw away phr. ~을 버리다
arrange v. 준비하다   pick up phr. (물건 등을) 수거하다, 찾아가다
location n. 장소   convenient adj. 편한, 편리한
grand opening phr. 개장(식)   available adj. 구입 가능한

05

문제 사람들이 기부하는 물품에 대해 사실인 것은?
(A) 인근 공장에서 재활용될 것이다.
(B) 손상되지 않아야 한다.
(C) 온라인 상점에서 판매될 것이다.
(D) 여전히 포장이 된 채여야 한다.

해설 답의 근거 문장은 'We are asking ~ for donations of undamaged buttons, string, scrap paper, and cardboard.'로 (B)가 정답입니다. undamaged가 not be damaged로 패러프레이징되었습니다.

어휘 **nearby** adj. 인근의, 가까운 **plant** n. 공장 **packaging** n. 포장

06

문제 Snippets에 대해 언급된 것은?
(A) 지난달에 개점하였다.
(B) 정부에 의해 자금을 받는다.
(C) 지역 사회를 위해 수익을 사용할 것이다.
(D) 지역 예술가에 의해 설립되었다.

해설 답의 근거 문장은 'All the money we earn will be put toward environmental and educational projects here in town.'으로 (C)가 정답입니다. environmental and educational projects here in town이 the community로 요약되어 패러프레이징되었습니다.

어휘 **open for business** phr. 개점하다, 사업을 시작하다
fund v. 자금을 대다 **government** n. 정부 **found** v. 설립하다

07

문제 Ms. Hughes는 Mr. Douglas에게 무엇을 하기를 요청하는가?
(A) 직장에서 물품들을 모으는 것
(B) 프로젝트 제안서를 작업하는 것
(C) 지역 학교에 기부하는 것
(D) 자원봉사자 자리에 지원하는 것

해설 답의 근거 문장은 'We ask you to collect items at your office'로 (A)가 정답입니다. collect가 gather로, office가 workplace로 패러프레이징되었습니다.

어휘 **gather** v. 모으다 **workplace** n. 직장 **proposal** n. 제안서
contribute to phr. ~에 기부하다, ~에 기여하다 **local** adj. 지역의
apply for phr. ~에 지원하다 **volunteer** n. 자원봉사자
position n. (일)자리

08

문제 Mr. Douglas에 대해 암시되는 것은?
(A) 지역 공예품 상점에서 물건을 샀다.
(B) 전에 Snippets에 기부한 적이 있다.
(C) 기부 물품들을 가져다줄 필요가 없을 것이다.
(D) 비영리 단체를 위해 일한다.

해설 답의 근거 문장은 'We can arrange to pick up anything you may have at a location that's convenient for you.'로 (C)가 정답입니다. 'Mr. Douglas가 가지고 있는 어떠한 것이라도 수거할 수 있다'는 내용을 근거로, 'Mr. Douglas가 기부 물품들을 가져다줄 필요가 없을 것이다'라는 사실을 새롭게 추론하여 패러프레이징하였습니다.

어휘 **drop off** phr. (물건을 상점 등에) 가져다주다 **organization** n. 단체

DAY 02 문장 성분

Course 1 주어 · 동사

토익 실전 Check-up p.177

토익 포인트 1 ⓑ   토익 포인트 2 ⓑ
토익 포인트 3 ⓐ   토익 포인트 4 ⓑ

1 주어 자리 채우기

해설 문장에 동사(will be reviewed)만 있고 주어가 없으므로 주어 자리에 올 수 있는 명사 ⓑ regulation(규정)이 정답입니다. 동사 ⓐ regulate(규제하다)는 주어 자리에 올 수 없습니다.

해석 규정은 관리자에 의해 검토될 것이다.

어휘 review v. 검토하다

2 가짜 주어 채우기

해설 '모든 전자기기를 끄는 것이 필수적이다'라는 문장의 의미를 통해 it이 가짜 주어이고 뒤의 to 부정사(to turn off all electronic devices)가 진짜 주어임을 알 수 있습니다. 따라서 가짜 주어 역할을 하는 ⓑ It이 정답입니다. 인칭대명사 ⓐ He는 가짜 주어 역할을 할 수 없습니다.

해석 실험실 안에서는 모든 전자기기를 끄는 것이 필수적이다.

어휘 mandatory adj. 필수적인, 의무적인
turn off phr. (전기, 가스, 수도 등을) 끄다
electronic device phr. 전자기기

3 동사 자리 채우기

해설 문장에 주어(Ms. Kennedy)만 있고 동사가 없으므로 동사 evaluate (평가하다)의 3인칭 단수형 ⓐ evaluates가 정답입니다. 동명사 또는 분사 ⓑ evaluating은 동사 자리에 올 수 없습니다.

해석 Ms. Kennedy는 매년 그녀의 직원들을 평가한다.

어휘 staff n. 직원

4 명령문의 동사 자리 채우기

해설 이 문장은 주어 없이 동사원형으로 시작되는 명령문이므로 동사원형 ⓑ Ask(문의하다)가 정답입니다. to 부정사 ⓐ To ask는 명령문의 동사 자리에 올 수 없습니다.

해석 이번 달의 판촉 활동에 대해 저희 판매원들 중 아무에게나 문의하세요.

어휘 salespeople n. 판매원 promotion n. 판촉 (활동), 승진

HACKERS PRACTICE p.179

01 ⓐ [토익 포인트 1]   02 ⓑ [토익 포인트 2]
03 ⓑ [토익 포인트 3]   04 ⓑ [토익 포인트 1]
05 ⓐ [토익 포인트 3]   06 ⓑ [토익 포인트 2]
07 ⓐ [토익 포인트 1]   08 ⓐ [토익 포인트 4]
09 to verify → verify [토익 포인트 4]
10 contacting → contact [토익 포인트 3]
11 any → it [토익 포인트 2]
12 reserved → reserve [토익 포인트 3]
13 This → It [토익 포인트 2]
14 Find → Finding, To find [토익 포인트 1]
15 accumulation → accumulate [토익 포인트 3]
16 permission → permit [토익 포인트 3]

해석 01 관리자는 다음 주에 그 프로젝트 제안서를 검토할 것이다.

02 인사 부서가 새로운 직원 매뉴얼을 개발하는 것이 권장되었다.

03 Mr. Thompson은 누가 Drayvon 프로젝트를 관리할지 나중에 결정할 것이다.

04 직원 유니폼에 회사 로고의 크기를 키우는 것은 그것을 더 알아보기 쉽게 할 것이다.

05 만약 고객이 조건을 받아들인다면, 우리는 오늘 계약서를 보낼 것이다.

06 모든 관리자들이 직원 수행 평가를 하는 것은 필수다.

07 모든 직원의 컴퓨터에 새로운 보안 프로그램을 설치하는 것이 우리의 업무이다.

08 지금 등록하셔서 귀하의 받은 메일함으로 보내지는 일일 최신 정보를 받으세요.

09 수령증에 서명하여 배송품을 받았음을 확인해 주십시오.

10 호텔의 레스토랑에서 테이블을 예약하기를 원하는 손님들은 안내 데스크로 연락해야 한다.

11 시장 예측에 따르면, 올해 석유 가격이 상승할 수도 있다.

12 Ms. Hemwood는 극장의 회원이기 때문에 표를 미리 예매할 수 있다.

13 Grove로에서 주차 공간을 찾는 것은 어렵다.

14 이 도시에서 가격이 적정하게 매겨진 사무실 공간을 찾는 것이 매우 어려워지고 있다.

15 고객들은 매번 MogiShop 보상 카드를 사용할 때마다 포인트를 쌓을 수 있다.

16 직원증은 직원들이 Mason이 어디에든 주차하는 것을 허용한다.

Course 2 목적어 · 보어 · 수식어

토익 실전 Check-up p.181

토익 포인트 1 ⓐ   토익 포인트 2 ⓑ
토익 포인트 3 ⓑ   토익 포인트 4 ⓐ

1 목적어 자리 채우기

해설 동사(has)의 목적어 자리에 올 수 있는 것은 명사이므로 명사 ⓐ competition(경쟁, 대회)이 정답입니다. 형용사 ⓑ competitive는 목적어 자리에 올 수 없습니다.

해석 Frameworks사는 다른 인테리어 디자인 회사들과 많은 경쟁을 한다.

어휘 a lot of phr. 많은 firm n. 회사; adj. 단단한, 확실한

2 보어 자리 채우기

해설 be동사(are) 다음의 보어 자리에 올 수 있는 것은 명사 또는 형용사이므로 형용사 ⓑ affordable(적당한, 감당할 수 있는)이 정답입니다. 동사 ⓐ afford(~할 형편이 되다)는 보어 자리에 올 수 없습니다.

해석 온라인에서 판매되는 휴대용 컴퓨터는 쇼핑몰 상점에 있는 비슷한 제품과 비교하여 가격이 적당하다.

어휘 laptop n. 휴대용 컴퓨터 similar adj. 비슷한, 닮은

3 보어 자리 채우기

해설 'Mr. Stein의 헌신은 존경할 만하다'라는 의미로 괄호 안의 보어가 주어(Mr. Stein's commitment)를 설명해주고 있으므로 형용사 ⓑ admirable(존경할 만한)이 정답입니다. 명사 ⓐ admiration(존경)은 주어와 동격 관계가 되어 'Mr. Stein의 헌신은 존경이다'라는 어색한 문맥을 만듭니다.

해석 조직에 대한 Mr. Stein의 헌신은 존경할 만하다.

어휘 commitment n. 헌신, 약속 organization n. 조직, 단체

4 수식어 거품을 이끄는 것 채우기

해설 이 문장은 주어(All travelers)와 동사(have to pass through)를 갖춘 완전한 절이므로 (   ) at International Terminal 2는 수식어 거품으로 보아야 합니다. 따라서 수식어 거품을 이끌 수 있는 동사 arrive(도착하다)의 분사 ⓐ arriving이 정답입니다. 동사 ⓑ arrive는 수식어 거품을 이끌 수 없습니다.

해석 국제 터미널 2에 도착하는 모든 여행객들은 출입국 관리소를 통과해야 한다.

어휘 international adj. 국제의, 국제적인 pass through phr. ~를 통과하다
Immigration n. 출입국 관리소

HACKERS PRACTICE   p.183

01 ⓐ [토익 포인트 1]	**02** ⓑ [토익 포인트 1]
03 ⓐ [토익 포인트 2]	**04** ⓑ [토익 포인트 3]
05 ⓐ [토익 포인트 2]	**06** ⓐ [토익 포인트 4]
07 ⓐ [토익 포인트 1]	**08** ⓐ [토익 포인트 3]

09 expensively → expensive [토익 포인트 2]
10 receive → to receive [토익 포인트 1]
11 promise → promising [토익 포인트 3]
12 interest → interested [토익 포인트 4]
13 sessional → sessions [토익 포인트 1]
14 profitable → profit [토익 포인트 1]
15 beneficial → benefit [토익 포인트 3]
16 diligent → diligence [토익 포인트 3]

해석 **01** Ms. Alvan은 관중들에게 연설할 때 원고를 참고했다.
02 부품 배송의 장기 지연은 제조 공장에 곤경을 야기한다.
03 Mr. Loren은 팀에 훌륭한 보탬이 될 경험 많은 전문가이다.
04 안내서에 따르면, Pearson 박물관 방문은 권할 만하다.
05 그 청소 서비스업체는 모든 직원들이 철저하다는 것을 약속한다.
06 Bron's 식당의 저녁 근무 직원들은 주방이 청소되면 퇴근할 수 있다.
07 Mr. Powell은 다음 우리 제품의 공개에 발표자가 될 것이다.
08 루이지애나로 이전하는 것은 많은 직원들에게 변화였다.
09 새로운 부속 건물의 추가는 Sacred Heart 병원에게는 비쌀 수 있다.
10 Hanson 미술관은 그 프로젝트를 위해 정부의 자금 지원을 받을 것으로 예상한다.
11 그 야구팀은 챔피언전에서 이길 가능성은 전망이 좋다.
12 직업 개발 수업을 듣는 것에 관심이 있는 모든 직원들은 인사부에서 등록할 수 있다.
13 Layton 지역 문화 센터는 주민들에게 무료 요가 및 명상 수업을 제공한다.
14 Mr. Bryant는 수익을 내고 있기 때문에 그의 식당에 몇몇 테이블을 추가하는 것을 고려하고 있다.
15 야외에서 먹을 수 있는 것은 The Petunia Bar and Grill의 이점이다.
16 잠재적인 후보의 가장 중요한 자질은 성실함이다.

HACKERS TEST   p.184

PART 5				
01 (A)	**02** (C)	**03** (B)	**04** (B)	**05** (B)
06 (C)	**07** (D)	**08** (D)	**09** (B)	**10** (C)
11 (D)	**12** (C)	**13** (B)	**14** (D)	**15** (D)
16 (B)	**17** (D)	**18** (B)		

PART 6			
19 (B)	**20** (D)	**21** (C)	**22** (D)

01 보어 자리 채우기

해설 '~이 되다'라는 의미의 동사 become(became)의 보어 자리에 올 수 있는 것은 명사 또는 형용사이므로 명사 (A)와 형용사 (B)가 정답의 후보입니다. 'Ms. Wendt는 수석 회계사가 되었다'라는 의미로 주어(Ms. Wendt)와 빈칸의 보어가 동격 관계이므로 명사 (A) accountant(회계사)가 정답입니다. 형용사 (B)는 빈칸 앞의 형용사(chief)의 꾸밈을 받을 수 없습니다. 동사 또는 분사 (C)는 동사로 볼 경우 보어 자리에 올 수 없고, 분사로 볼 경우 형용사(chief)의 꾸밈을 받을 수 없으므로 답이 될 수 없습니다. 부사 (D)는 보어 자리에 올 수 없습니다.

해석 Ms. Wendt는 작년에 Ex-Tech사에 선발되었을 때 수석 회계사가 되었다.

어휘 chief adj. 수석의, (지위가) 최고인, 주요한 select v. 선발하다, 선택하다

02 동사 자리 채우기

해설 문장에 주어(The new cleaning spray)와 목적어(debris)만 있고 동사가 없으므로 동사 prevent(방지하다)의 3인칭 단수형 (C) prevents가 정답입니다. 동명사 또는 분사 (A), to 부정사 (B), 형용사 (D)는 동사 자리에 올 수 없습니다.

해석 새로운 청소 스프레이는 싱크대에 찌꺼기가 쌓이는 것을 방지한다.

어휘 debris n. 찌꺼기, 잔해 build up phr. 쌓이다 sink n. 싱크대, 개수대

03 목적어 자리 채우기

해설 동사(suggested)의 목적어 자리에 올 수 있는 동사 invest(투자하다)의 동명사 (B) investing이 정답입니다. 동사 (A), (C), (D)는 목적어 자리에 올 수 없습니다.

해석 비즈니스 라디오 프로그램에서, 금융 상담가는 주식보다는 부동산에 투자하는 것을 추천했다.

어휘 financial adj. 금융의, 재정의 property n. 부동산, 재산
rather than phr. ~보다는 stock n. 주식, 재고

04 동사 자리 채우기

해설 문장에 주어(Mr. Callahan)만 있고 동사가 없으므로 동사 organize(구성하다)의 과거형 (B) organized가 정답입니다. to 부정사 (A), 동명사 또는 분사 (C), 명사 (D)는 동사 자리에 올 수 없습니다.

해석 Mr. Callahan은 매력적인 포장 디자인을 작업할 팀을 구성했다.

어휘 attractive adj. 매력적인 package n. 포장, 소포

05 보어 자리 채우기

해설 be동사(are) 다음의 보어 자리에 올 수 있는 명사 (A)와 형용사 (B)가 정답의 후보입니다. '마케팅 수업이 유익하다'라는 의미로 빈칸이 주어(they, 즉 marketing courses)를 설명해주고 있으므로 형용사 (B) beneficial(유익한, 이로운)이 정답입니다. 명사 (A)를 쓰면 '마케팅 수업이 혜택이다'라는 어색한 문맥을 만듭니다. 부사 (C)와 '조동사 + 동사원형' (D)는 보어 자리에 올 수 없습니다.

해석 경영학 학생들은 마케팅 수업이 유익하기 때문에 그것을 듣는 것을 높이 평가한다.

어휘 **business management** phr. 경영학, 경영
appreciate v. 높이 평가하다, 고마워하다

06 수식어 거품을 이끄는 것 채우기

해설 이 문장은 주어(The schedule), 동사(is), 보어(available)를 갖춘
완전한 절이므로 _____ the department's Web site는 수식어 거품
으로 보아야 합니다. 따라서 수식어 거품을 이끌 수 있는 전치사 (C)
on(~에서)이 정답입니다. 부사 (A) yet(아직, 이제)과 (D) still(아직, 그
런데도), 접속사 (B) but(그러나)은 수식어 거품을 이끌 수 없습니다.

해석 기말고사 일정은 학부 웹사이트에서 볼 수 있다.

07 주어 자리 채우기

해설 문장에 동사(seems)만 있고 주어가 없으므로 주어 자리에 올 수 있는
명사 (D) system(체계, 제도)이 정답입니다. 부사 (A), 동사 또는 분사
(B), 형용사 (C)는 주어 자리에 올 수 없습니다.

해석 재무팀에 의하면, 새롭게 도입된 체계는 실용적으로 보인다.

어휘 **finance** n. 재무, 재정 **introduce** v. 도입하다, 소개하다
practical adj. 실용적인, 현실적인

08 수식어 거품을 이끄는 것 채우기

해설 이 문장은 주어(This demonstration)와 동사(will commence)를 갖
춘 완전한 절이므로 _____ all department managers arrive는 수식
어 거품으로 보아야 합니다. 이 수식어 거품은 동사(arrive)가 있는 거품
절이므로 거품절을 이끌 수 있는 부사절 접속사 (D) as soon as(~하자
마자)가 정답입니다. 부사 (B) meanwhile(그동안에)은 수식어 거품을
이끌 수 없습니다. 전치사 (A) throughout(~ 도처에, ~ 내내)과 (C) in
spite of(~에도 불구하고)는 거품절이 아닌 거품구를 이끕니다.

해석 이 시연은 모든 부서장들이 도착하자마자 시작될 것이다.

어휘 **demonstration** n. 시연, 설명 **commence** v. 시작되다
department manager phr. 부서장 **arrive** v. 도착하다

09 주어 자리 채우기

해설 문장에 동사(has made)만 있고 주어가 없으므로 주어 자리에 올 수
있는 명사 (B) acceptance(수락, 동의)가 정답입니다. 동사 (A)와
(D), 동사 또는 분사 (C)는 주어 자리에 올 수 없습니다.

해석 제안에 대한 고객의 수락은 회사의 임원진들을 매우 기쁘게 만들었다.

어휘 **executive** n. 임원진, 경영자

10 수식어 거품을 이끄는 것 채우기

해설 이 문장은 주어(our sales), 동사(were), 보어(very high)를 갖춘 완
전한 절이므로 _____ we did not advertise on television은 수식어
거품으로 보아야 합니다. 이 수식어 거품은 동사(did not advertise)
가 있는 거품절이므로 거품절을 이끌 수 있는 부사절 접속사 (C)
Although(비록 ~이지만)가 정답입니다. 전치사 (A)와 (D), 형용사 또
는 대명사 (B)는 거품절이 아닌 거품구를 이끕니다.

해석 비록 우리는 텔레비전에서 광고하지 않았지만, 올해 우리의 판매량은
매우 높았다.

어휘 **advertise** v. 광고하다

11 동사 자리 채우기

해설 빈칸 앞에 조동사(can)가 있으므로 동사 자리에 올 수 있는 '조동사 +
동사원형'을 만드는 동사원형 (D) choose(선택하다, 고르다)가 정답
입니다. 과거분사 (A), to 부정사 (B), 동명사 또는 현재분사 (C)는 조
동사 뒤에 올 수 없습니다.

해석 ATB 통신 회사에서, 고객들은 다양한 휴대전화 데이터 요금제 중에서
선택할 수 있다.

어휘 **a wide range of** phr. 다양한, 광범위한

12 보어 자리 채우기

해설 be동사(are) 다음의 보어 자리에 올 수 있는 형용사 (C)와 명사 (D)
가 정답의 후보입니다. '청소 서비스는 만족스럽다'라는 의미로, 보어
가 주어(The cleaning services)를 설명해주고 있으므로 형용사 (C)
satisfactory(만족스러운, 충분한)가 정답입니다. 명사 (D)는 '청소 서
비스는 만족이다'라는 어색한 문맥을 만듭니다. 동사 (A)와 (B)는 보
어 자리에 올 수 없습니다.

해석 Maids For Moving사에 의해 제공되는 청소 서비스는 대체로 만족스
럽다.

어휘 **provide** v. 제공하다, 주다

13 보어 자리 채우기

해설 be동사(is) 다음의 보어 자리에 올 수 있는 형용사 (B), 명사 (A)와
(C)가 정답의 후보입니다. '이 웹사이트의 정보는 도움이 된다'라는 의
미로, 보어가 주어(The information)를 설명해주고 있으므로 형용사
(B) helpful(도움이 되는, 유용한)이 정답입니다. 명사 (A)와 (C)는 주
어와 동격 관계가 되어 각각 '정보가 도움이다/도움이 됨이다'라는 어
색한 문맥을 만듭니다. 부사 (D)는 보어 자리에 올 수 없습니다.

해석 이 웹사이트의 정보는 디트로이트에 주택을 매입하기를 원하는 사람들
에게 도움이 된다.

어휘 **information** n. 정보 **purchase** v. 구입하다; n. 구입
helpfulness n. 도움이 됨, 유익함

14 주어 자리 채우기

해설 _____ ~ work가 이 문장의 주어이므로 주어 자리에 올 수 있는 동사
commute(통근하다, 왕복하다)의 동명사 (D) Commuting이 정답입
니다. 명사 (A)도 주어 자리에 올 수 있지만 '통근자들은 즐거움을 줄
수 있다'라는 어색한 문맥을 만듭니다. 동사 또는 분사 (B)와 형용사
(C)는 주어 자리에 올 수 없습니다.

해석 직장으로 왔다 갔다 통근하는 것이 편도 30분 이내라면 즐거움을 줄 수
있다.

어휘 **pleasant** adj. 즐거움을 주는, 유쾌한

15 수식어 거품을 이끄는 것 채우기

해설 이 문장은 주어(shoppers), 동사(hoped), 목적어(to be the first)
를 갖춘 완전한 절이므로 _____ at the entrance는 수식어 거품으로
보아야 합니다. 이 수식어 거품은 동사가 없는 거품구이므로 거품구를
이끌 수 있는 분사 (D) Gathering이 정답입니다. 동사 (A)와 (C), 형
용사 (B)는 수식어 거품을 이끌 수 없습니다.

해석 쇼핑객들은 입구에 모여서, 인기 있는 휴대전화의 최신 모델을 처음으
로 구입하기를 바라고 있었다.

어휘 **entrance** n. 입구, 입장 **latest** adj. 최신의, 최근의
popular adj. 인기 있는, 유명한

16 명령문의 동사 자리 채우기

해설 이 문장은 주어 없이 동사원형으로 시작되는 명령문이므로 동사원형
(B) secure(보호하다, 획득하다)가 정답입니다. 동명사 또는 분사 (A),
3인칭 단수형 동사 (C), 동사의 과거형 또는 형용사 (D)는 명령문의
동사 자리에 올 수 없습니다.

해석 데이터 손실을 방지하기 위해, 침입을 막는 프로그램으로 당신의 컴퓨
터를 보호하세요.

어휘 **prevent** v. 방지하다, 막다 **loss** n. 손실, 분실
protect v. 보호하다, 지키다 **intrusion** n. 침입, 침해

17 주어 자리 채우기

해설 문장에 동사(was hired)만 있고 주어가 없으므로 주어 자리에 올 수
있는 명사 (D) adviser(조언가)가 정답입니다. 동사 또는 분사 (A)는
주어 자리에 올 수 없습니다. to 부정사 (B)는 주어 자리에 올 수는 있

지만 관사나 형용사 다음에 올 수 없습니다. 동사 (C)는 주어 자리에 올 수 없습니다.

해석 새로운 마케팅 전략을 추천하기 위해 경험 있는 조언가가 고용되었다.

어휘 recommend v. 추천하다

18 보어 자리 채우기

해설 be동사(was) 다음의 보어 자리에 올 수 있는 형용사 (B), 명사 (C)와 (D)가 정답의 후보입니다. '합병 결정은 중요했다'라는 의미로, 보어가 주어(The decision)를 설명해주고 있으므로 형용사 (B) important (중요한)가 정답입니다. 명사 (C) importance(중요성)과 (D) import (수입품)는 주어와 동격 관계가 되어 각각 '합병 결정은 중요성이다/수입품이다'라는 어색한 문맥을 만듭니다. 부사 (A)는 보어 자리에 올 수 없습니다.

해석 합병 결정은 회사의 생존이 거기에 달려 있기 때문에 회사에 중요했다.

어휘 decision n. 결정, 판단 merge v. 합병하다, 병합하다 survival n. 생존 depend v. 달려 있다, 의존하다

19-22번은 다음 회람에 관한 문제입니다.

안녕하세요 여러분,

¹⁹지난 몇 달 동안 모바일 기기로 출근 게시판에 로그인하는 직원들의 사례가 있었다는 것이 몇몇 팀장들에 의해 제게 보고되었습니다. 직원들은 반드시 직장 컴퓨터를 이용해서 로그인해야 합니다. 출장 간 사람들만 휴대전화로 로그인할 수 있습니다. ²⁰이는 경영진에 의해 허용되는 유일한 예외입니다. 앞으로, 사이트로의 모바일 접속은 경영진에게서 특별 코드를 받은 사람들에게만 제한될 것입니다. ²¹모바일 기기에서의 승인되지 않은 어떠한 로그인 시도도 거부될 것입니다.

²²이 문제에 대해 질문이 있으시면, jamste@zencorp.com으로 제게 보내주시기 바랍니다.

---

report v. 보고하다, 알리다 instance n. 사례, 경우
attendance n. 출근, 출석 board n. 게시판
workplace n. 직장, 업무 현장 travel for business phr. 출장 가다
restrict v. 제한하다, 통제하다 attempt n. 시도; v. 시도하다
reject v. 거부하다, 거절하다 matter n. 문제, 일

---

19 진짜 주어 채우기

해설 이 문장에서 It은 가짜 주어로, 길이가 긴 진짜 주어 ____ ~ months 를 대신해서 쓰인 것으로 보아야 합니다. 따라서 진짜 주어로 쓰일 수 있는 that절을 만드는 (B) that이 정답입니다. 소유격 인칭대명사 (A) their, 부사 (C) then(그러고 나서)과 (D) therefore(그러므로)는 진짜 주어로 쓰일 수 없습니다.

20 알맞은 문장 고르기

해석 (A) 회사 인트라넷은 오늘부터 더 이상 접속이 불가능할 것입니다.
(B) 모든 보고서는 명시된 마감일까지 제출되어야 합니다.
(C) 여러분의 휴대전화 작동을 기록하기 위해 계정을 만드십시오.
(D) 이는 경영진에 의해 허용되는 유일한 예외입니다.

해설 빈칸에 들어갈 알맞은 문장을 고르는 문제이므로 주변이나 전체 문맥을 파악합니다. 앞부분 'Staff must sign in using their workplace computers. Only those who are traveling for business may sign in with their phones.'에서 직원들은 반드시 직장 컴퓨터를 이용해서 로그인해야 하고 출장 간 사람들만 휴대전화로 로그인할 수 있다고 했으므로 빈칸에는 회사 컴퓨터를 이용해서 로그인하지 않아도 되는 예외에 대해 설명하는 내용이 들어가야 함을 알 수 있습니다. 따라서 (D) This is the only exception permitted by the administration이 정답입니다.

어휘 accessible adj. 접근 가능한, 이용 가능한 account n. 계정, 계좌 keep track of phr. ~을 기록하다 administration n. 경영진, 행정

21 형용사 어휘 고르기 주변 문맥 파악

해설 '____한 어떠한 로그인 시도도 거부될 것이다'라는 문맥이므로 (B), (C), (D)가 정답의 후보입니다. 빈칸이 있는 문장만으로는 정답을 고를 수 없으므로 주변 문맥이나 전체 문맥을 파악합니다. 앞 문장에서 사이트로의 모바일 접속은 경영진에게서 특별 코드를 받은 사람들에게만 제한될 것이라고 했으므로, 경영진에게 승인되지 않은 로그인 시도는 거부될 것임을 알 수 있습니다. 따라서 형용사 (C) unauthorized (승인되지 않은, 허가받지 않은)가 정답입니다. (A) unused는 '사용되지 않는, 비어 있는', (B) repeated는 '거듭되는, 자주 있는', (D) random은 '임의의, 무작위의'라는 의미입니다.

22 명령문의 동사 자리 채우기

해설 please ~ at jamste@zencorp.com은 주어 없이 동사원형으로 시작되는 명령문이므로 동사원형 (D) direct(보내다)가 정답입니다. 명사, 동명사 또는 분사 (A), 명사 (B), 부사 (C)는 명령문의 동사 자리에 올 수 없습니다.

DAY 03 동사 1

Course 1 동사의 형태와 종류

토익 실전 Check-up p.187

토익 포인트 1 ⓐ	토익 포인트 2 ⓐ
토익 포인트 3 ⓐ	토익 포인트 4 ⓑ

1 조동사 다음에 동사원형 채우기

해설 빈칸 앞에 조동사(can)가 있으므로 동사원형 ⓐ register(등록하다)가 정답입니다. 동사의 과거형 ⓑ registered는 조동사 다음에 올 수 없습니다.

해석 직원들은 온라인으로 워크숍에 등록할 수 있다.

어휘 employee n. 직원, 종업원

2 'have동사 + p.p.' 채우기

해설 빈칸 앞에 have동사가 있으므로 have동사와 함께 완료형을 만드는 동사 open(열다, 개방하다)의 p.p.형 ⓐ opened가 정답입니다. 동사원형 ⓑ open은 have동사 다음에 올 수 없습니다.

해석 Mr. Creston과 그의 팀은 지난달에 세 개의 새로운 사무실을 열었다.

어휘 office n. 사무실, 사무소

3 쓰임에 맞는 동사 채우기

해설 mention(언급하다, 말하다)은 목적어를 갖는 타동사이므로 ⓐ mentioned가 정답입니다. 타동사는 전치사 없이 목적어를 바로 갖기 때문에 ⓑ mentioned about은 답이 될 수 없습니다.

해석 관리자는 대화 중에 중요한 소식을 언급했다.

어휘 supervisor n. 관리자, 감독관 important adj. 중요한, 영향력이 큰

4 쓰임에 맞는 동사 채우기

해설 괄호 뒤에 목적어(the impact)가 있으므로 타동사인 ⓑ discuss(논의하다)가 정답입니다. 자동사인 ⓐ talk는 전치사 about과 함께 쓰입니다.

해석 그들은 할인 행사의 영향을 논의하기 위해 약속을 잡았다.

어휘 appointment n. 약속 impact n. 영향, 충격

HACKERS PRACTICE
p.189

01 ⓐ [토익 포인트 1] **02** ⓐ [토익 포인트 2]
03 ⓑ [토익 포인트 2] **04** ⓑ [토익 포인트 4]
05 ⓑ [토익 포인트 3] **06** ⓑ [토익 포인트 2]
07 ⓐ [토익 포인트 4] **08** ⓑ [Day02, Course 1, 토익 포인트 1]
09 To notify → Notify [Day02, Course 1, 토익 포인트 4]
10 study → studying [토익 포인트 2]
11 completion → completed [Day02, Course 1, 토익 포인트 3]
12 deliver → delivered [토익 포인트 2]
13 talked → talked about [토익 포인트 3]
14 Inspirational → Inspiration [Day02, Course 1, 토익 포인트 1]
15 lead → led [토익 포인트 2]
16 practicing → practice [토익 포인트 1]

해석 **01** 고객들은 48시간 이내에 소프트웨어를 구입하면 할인을 받을 것이다.

02 광고주는 1월부터 태블릿 컴퓨터를 홍보해왔다.

03 창고는 내일 선적될 대량 주문을 처리하고 있다.

04 Mr. Bowman은 고객에게 투자 옵션을 설명할 계획이다.

05 그 회람은 Mr. Anderson의 승진을 알렸다.

06 성인들은 하룻밤에 6시간에서 8시간의 수면을 취하는 것이 권고된다.

07 구독자들은 그들이 *Daily News*지 웹사이트를 방문하는 것이 관찰되는 것에 동의해야 한다.

08 새로 연 사업체를 광고하는 것은 소유주들에게 힘이 들 수 있다.

09 병과 관련된 결근의 경우, 담당 관리자에게 알리십시오.

10 Eckert사는 어떻게 아시아로 영업을 확장할지 연구하고 있다.

11 그녀는 요청받은 대로 보고서를 완성했고 검토를 위해 그것을 Mr. Hartman의 책상 위에 두었다.

12 Mr. Jackson은 사무실 가구를 주문했는데, 그것은 다음 주에 배송될 것이다.

13 회계사는 낭비하는 것이 어떻게 회사에 손해를 입히고 있었는지에 대해 이야기했다.

14 그 작가의 가장 최근 소설에 대한 영감은 그녀 자신의 개인적인 경험으로부터 온 것이다.

15 Jeff Kinsey는 작년부터 홍보 부서를 이끌어왔다.

16 취업 상담자들은 구직자들이 어떻게 면접 질문에 답변할지 연습해야 한다고 말한다.

Course 2 주어와의 수일치

토익 실전 Check-up
p.191

토익 포인트 1 ⓐ	토익 포인트 2 ⓑ
토익 포인트 3 ⓑ	토익 포인트 4 ⓐ

1 주어와 수일치하는 동사 채우기

해설 주어(The video game)가 단수이므로 단수 동사 ⓐ demonstrates가 정답입니다. 괄호 앞의 LS Softworks는 회사 이름을 나타내는 고유 명사로, Softworks만 보고 복수 동사 ⓑ demonstrate를 고르지 않도록 주의합니다.

해석 LS Softworks사의 비디오 게임은 신기술의 우수함을 보여준다.

어휘 superiority n. 우수, 탁월 demonstrate v. 보여주다, 입증하다

2 부분/전체 표현 주어와 수일치하는 동사 채우기

해설 주어에 부분을 나타내는 표현(Part)이 있으므로 of 뒤의 단수 명사(the problem)에 알맞은 단수 동사 ⓑ was가 정답입니다. 복수 동사 ⓐ were는 주어에 '부분이나 전체를 나타내는 표현 + of + 복수 명사'가 왔을 때 쓰일 수 있습니다.

해석 그 문제의 일부는 사회 복지 사업에 대한 정부 자금의 부족이었다.

어휘 lack n. 부족, 결핍 government n. 정부, 정치
funding n. 자금, 재정 지원 social service phr. 사회 복지 사업

3 접속사로 연결된 주어와 수일치하는 동사 채우기

해설 주어(Some chairs or a sofa)가 접속사 or로 연결되어 있으므로 동사는 or 뒤에 오는 명사에 수일치시켜야 합니다. or 뒤에 오는 명사(a sofa)가 단수이므로 단수 동사 ⓑ is가 정답입니다. 복수 동사 ⓐ are는 주어와 수일치되지 않습니다.

해석 직원 휴게실에 의자 몇 개 또는 소파 한 개가 필요하다.

어휘 break room phr. 휴게실

4 선행사와 수일치하는 주격 관계절의 동사 채우기

해설 주격 관계사(that)의 선행사(documents)가 복수이므로 주격 관계절에는 복수 동사가 와야 합니다. 따라서 복수 동사 ⓐ contain(포함하다, 들어 있다)이 정답입니다. 단수 동사 ⓑ contains는 주격 관계사 앞에 단수 선행사가 있을 때 쓰입니다.

해석 암호는 기밀 정보를 포함하는 서류를 열람하기 위해 요구된다.

어휘 password n. 암호, 비밀번호 document n. 서류, 문서
confidential adj. 기밀의, 비밀의

HACKERS PRACTICE
p.193

01 ⓐ [토익 포인트 2] **02** ⓑ [Day02, Course 1, 토익 포인트 3]
03 ⓐ [토익 포인트 3] **04** ⓐ [Day02, Course 2, 토익 포인트 1]
05 ⓐ [토익 포인트 2] **06** ⓐ [토익 포인트 3]
07 ⓑ [토익 포인트 2] **08** ⓐ [Day02, Course 2, 토익 포인트 1]
09 qualifies → qualify [토익 포인트 1]
10 allow → allows [토익 포인트 4]
11 were → was [토익 포인트 2]
12 take → takes [토익 포인트 4]
13 applies → apply [토익 포인트 4]
14 modify → modification [Day02, Course 2, 토익 포인트 1]
15 is → are [토익 포인트 3]
16 paints → paint [토익 포인트 2]

해석 **01** 항공기에서 나가기 전에 기내용 수하물이 남겨지지 않았는지 확인하십시오.

02 위원회 회장은 자원봉사자들에게 그들의 모든 노고에 대해 감사를 표했다.

03 직원 설문 조사 및 의견은 회사에 중요한 통찰력을 갖게 해준다.

04 Mr. Pitt는 새로운 소프트웨어에 익숙해서, 교육에 참석하지 않았다.

05 취업 비자가 승인되기 전에 많은 요구 조건들이 충족되어야 한다.

06 Juno Foods는 신용카드나 현금을 받는다.

07 소비자의 50퍼센트 이상이 회사 웹사이트에서 보여지는 정보를 신뢰한다.

08 연구원들은 일부 장비를 조작하려면 허가를 받아야 한다는 것을 상기받았다.

09 사용하지 않은 휴가 기간이 있는 직원들은 연말에 추가 수당에 대한 자격이 있다.

10 Ms. Taft는 종종 Brennan 미술관을 방문하는데, 그 미술관은 일요일에 사람들이 무료로 입장하는 것을 허용한다.

11 어제까지 아무도 총지배인 자리에 선택되지 않았다.

12 최고의 사진을 찍은 참가자가 상금을 받을 것이다.

13 구독자들에게 해당되는 할인은 구매가 이루어질 때 자동으로 적용될 것이다.

14 Mr. Tang은 다가오는 이사회 회의의 일정을 수정했다.

15 Ms. Garcia와 Mr. Torres는 회사의 다가오는 광고 캠페인을 작업하고 있다.

16 나머지 직원들이 벽에 페인트를 칠하는 동안 Mr. Bing은 부엌에 수납장을 설치할 것이다.

HACKERS TEST
p.194

PART 5

01 (B)	02 (B)	03 (A)	04 (D)	05 (B)
06 (D)	07 (B)	08 (C)	09 (B)	10 (A)
11 (D)	12 (A)	13 (D)	14 (D)	15 (A)
16 (D)	17 (B)	18 (C)		

PART 6

19 (D)	20 (C)	21 (A)	22 (B)

01 주어와 수일치하는 동사 채우기

해설 문장에 주어(Mr. Peters)만 있고 동사가 없으므로 동사 (B)와 (D)가 정답의 후보입니다. 주어가 단수이므로 단수 동사 (B) sends(보내다)가 정답입니다. 복수 동사 (D)는 복수 주어와 쓰입니다. 동명사 또는 분사 (A), to 부정사 (C)는 동사 자리에 올 수 없습니다.

해석 Mr. Peters는 모금 행사를 주최할 때마다 그의 연락처 목록에 있는 모든 사람들에게 초대장을 보낸다.

어휘 invitation n. 초대장, 초대 contact list phr. 연락처 목록
organize v. 주최하다, 준비하다 fundraising n. 모금

02 쓰임에 맞는 동사 채우기

해설 '프랑크푸르트 공항에 오후 3시에 도착할 것이다'라는 의미가 되어야 하므로 동사 (B) arrive(도착하다)가 정답입니다. (A) reach도 '도달하다'라는 의미이지만 타동사이므로 전치사(at) 없이 바로 목적어를 가져야 합니다. (C) occur는 '발생하다, 일어나다', (D) follow는 '뒤따르다, 지키다'라는 의미입니다.

해석 버스 운전기사는 그들이 프랑크푸르트 공항에 예상했던 것보다 30분 이른 오후 3시에 도착할 것이라고 알렸다.

어휘 announce v. 알리다, 발표하다 expect v. 예상하다, 기대하다

03 조동사 다음에 동사원형 채우기

해설 빈칸 앞에 조동사처럼 쓰이는 표현(are able to)이 있으므로 동사원형 (A) locate(알아내다, ~의 위치를 찾아내다)가 정답입니다. 3인칭 단수형 동사 (B), 과거형 동사 또는 분사 (C), 명사 (D)는 조동사 다음에 올 수 없습니다.

해석 기술자들은 신속하게 장비 문제를 알아내고 고칠 수 있도록 고급 교육을 받는다.

어휘 technician n. 기술자, 전문가
advanced adj. (수준 등이) 고급의, 상급의 equipment n. 장비, 설비
fix v. 고치다, 정하다

04 수량 표현 주어와 수일치하는 동사 채우기

해설 관계절(in which ~ weakness)에 주어(each team member)만 있고 동사가 없으므로 동사 (B)와 (D)가 정답의 후보입니다. 주어에 단수 취급되는 수량 표현 'each + 명사(team member)'가 와 있으므로 단수 동사 (D) admits(인정하다, 받아들이다)가 정답입니다. 복수 동사 (B)는 'many/several/few/both + (of the)'와 같이 복수 취급되는

수량 표현과 쓰입니다. 명사 (A)와 부사 (C)는 동사 자리에 올 수 없습니다.

해석 마케팅팀은 각 팀원이 개인의 약점을 인정하는 훈련에 참가하고 있다.

어휘 exercise n. 훈련, 연습 weakness n. 약점, 나약함

05 수량 표현 주어와 수일치하는 동사 채우기

해설 주절(A number of ~ exposition)에 주어(A number of staff members)만 있고 동사가 없으므로 동사 (B)와 (C)가 정답의 후보입니다. 주어에 복수 취급되는 수량 표현 'a number of + 복수 명사(staff members)'가 있으므로 복수 동사 (B) represent(대표하다, 대변하다)가 정답입니다. 단수 동사 (C)는 주어와 수일치되지 않습니다. 형용사 또는 명사 (A)와 동명사 또는 분사 (D)는 동사 자리에 올 수 없습니다. 참고로, 복수 취급되는 'a number of + 복수 명사(많은 ~)'와 단수 취급되는 'the number of + 복수 명사(~의 수)'를 구별하여 알아둡니다.

해석 많은 직원들은 매년 Morel Falls에서 열리는 무역 박람회에서 회사를 대표한다.

어휘 trade exposition phr. 무역 박람회 hold v. (행사 등을) 열다, 보유하다
representative adj. 대표적인; n. 대리인, 직원

06 보어 자리 채우기

해설 선행사(outcome)를 뒤에서 꾸며주는 관계절(that ~ involved)의 동사인 be동사(was)의 보어 자리에 올 수 있는 명사 (B)와 (C), 형용사 (D)가 정답의 후보입니다. '관련된 당사자들에게 바람직한 결과'라는 의미로 보어가 선행사(outcome)를 설명해주고 있으므로 형용사 (D) desirable(바람직한, 가치 있는)이 정답입니다. 명사 (B)와 (C)는 선행사와 동격 관계가 되어 각각 '갈망/바람직함인 결과'라는 어색한 문맥을 만듭니다. 동사 (A)는 보어 자리에 올 수 없습니다.

해석 Mr. Harrison은 관련된 당사자들에게 바람직한 결과를 협상하는 것을 아주 잘 해냈다.

어휘 negotiate v. 협상하다, 교섭하다 outcome n. 결과
party n. 당사자, 일행 involve v. 관련시키다, 수반하다

07 수식어 거품을 이끄는 것 채우기

해설 이 문장은 주어(The Ultracorp conglomerate)와 동사(grew)를 갖춘 완전한 절이므로, _____ ~ operations는 수식어 거품으로 보아야 합니다. 이 수식어 거품은 동사가 없는 거품구이므로 거품구를 이끌 수 있는 동사 absorb(흡수하다, 빨아들이다)의 분사 (B) absorbing이 정답입니다. 동사 (A), (C), (D)는 수식어 거품을 이끌 수 없습니다.

해석 Ultracorp 복합 기업은 비슷한 사업을 하는 더 작은 회사들을 흡수하여 빠르게 성장했다.

어휘 conglomerate n. 복합 기업, 대기업 operation n. 사업, 운영

08 'be동사 + p.p.' 채우기

해설 '나무들은 뇌우로 인해 심하게 피해를 입었다'라는 수동의 의미이므로 빈칸 앞의 be동사(were)와 함께 수동형(be동사 + p.p.)을 만드는 동사 damage(피해를 입히다, 훼손하다)의 p.p.형 (C) damaged가 정답입니다. 명사 (A)와 (B), 형용사 (D)도 be동사(were) 다음의 보어 자리에 올 수 있지만, (A)와 (B)는 주어와 동격 관계가 되어 '나무들은 피해이다'라는 어색한 문맥을 만들고 (D)는 '나무들은 심하게 피해를 입기 쉬웠다'라는 어색한 문맥을 만듭니다.

해석 Hamilton 공원에 있는 많은 나무들은 지난밤에 발생한 강한 뇌우로 인해 심하게 피해를 입었다.

어휘 severely adv. 심하게, 엄격하게 thunderstorm n. 뇌우
occur v. 발생하다, 일어나다

09 쓰임에 맞는 동사 채우기

해설 이 문장은 주어 없이 동사원형으로 시작되는 명령문이므로 동사원

형 (A)와 (B)가 정답의 후보입니다. '답하다, 응하다'라는 의미의 respond는 목적어를 갖지 않는 자동사이므로, 빈칸 다음의 목적어 (the invitation)를 가지려면 전치사가 있어야 합니다. 따라서 전치사를 포함한 (B) respond to가 정답입니다. (A)는 respond가 '~이라고 답하다'라는 의미의 타동사로도 쓰일 수 있지만 다음에 주로 that절이나 인용구가 오고, '초대라고 답하다'라는 어색한 문맥을 만듭니다. 동명사 또는 분사 (C)와 명사 (D)는 동사 자리에 올 수 없습니다.

해석 행사 주최자들이 그에 따라 준비를 할 수 있도록 초대장에 대해 6월 1일까지 답을 해주십시오.

어휘 make arrangements phr. 준비하다
accordingly adv. 그에 따라, 따라서

10 주어 자리 채우기

해설 _____ the software가 이 문장의 주어이므로 주어 자리에 와서 목적어(the software)를 가질 수 있는 동사 update(업데이트하다)의 동명사 (A) Updating이 정답입니다. 동사 (B)는 주어 자리에 올 수 없습니다. 명사 (C)와 (D)는 주어 자리에 올 수 있지만 빈칸 뒤에 이미 명사(the software)가 있으므로 답이 될 수 없습니다.

해석 소프트웨어를 업데이트하는 것은 휴대용 컴퓨터의 속도를 높였고 배터리 수명을 상당히 향상시켰다.

어휘 increase v. 높이다, 늘리다 improve v. 향상시키다, 개선하다
considerably adv. 상당히, 많이

11 'be동사 + p.p.' 채우기

해설 '지역 축제는 BubbleFizz사와 지역 상공회의소로부터 자금을 제공받는다'라는 수동의 의미이므로 빈칸 앞의 be동사(is)와 함께 수동형(be동사 + p.p.)을 만드는 동사 fund(자금을 대다)의 p.p.형 (D) funded가 정답입니다. 명사 (A)와 (C)도 be동사(is) 다음의 보어 자리에 올 수 있지만 주어와 동격 관계가 되어 '지역 축제는 자금이다'라는 어색한 문맥을 만듭니다. -ing형 (B)는 빈칸 앞의 be동사와 능동형(be동사 + -ing)을 만들어서 '지역 축제가 자금을 대고 있다'라는 능동의 의미를 나타내므로 답이 될 수 없습니다.

해석 올해의 지역 축제는 청량음료 회사 BubbleFizz사와 지역 상공회의소로부터 자금을 제공받는다.

어휘 community n. 지역 사회, 공동체 carnival n. 축제, 카니발
soft drink phr. 청량음료 chamber of commerce phr. 상공회의소

12 동사와 수일치하는 주어 채우기

해설 문장에 동사(are)만 있고 주어가 없으므로 주어 자리에 올 수 있는 명사 (A)와 (C), 동명사 (B)가 정답의 후보입니다. 동사(are)가 복수이므로 복수 명사 (A) renovations(수리, 보수)가 정답입니다. 동명사 (B)는 단수 취급되고, 단수 명사 (C)는 단수 동사와 쓰입니다. 동사 또는 분사 (D)는 주어 자리에 올 수 없습니다.

해석 로비에서 진행되고 있는 구조상의 수리는 마감일 전에 완료될 것으로 예상된다.

어휘 structural adj. 구조상의, 구조적인 deadline n. 마감일, 마감 기한

13 조동사 다음에 동사원형 채우기

해설 빈칸 앞에 조동사(could)가 있으므로 동사원형 (D) confuse(혼란시키다, 혼동하다)가 정답입니다. 과거형 동사 또는 분사 (A), 동명사 또는 분사 (B), 명사 (C)는 조동사 다음에 올 수 없습니다.

해석 포장 체계가 어떻게 작동하는지를 신입 직원들에게 단 하루 만에 가르치는 것은 그들을 혼란스럽게 만들 수 있다.

어휘 packaging n. 포장, 소포 work v. 작동하다, 효과가 있다

14 수식어 거품을 이끄는 것 채우기

해설 이 문장은 주어(Programs), 동사(are becoming), 보어(popular)를 갖춘 완전한 절이므로 _____ ~ employees는 수식어 거품으로

보아야 합니다. 이 수식어 거품은 동사가 없는 거품구이므로 거품구를 이끌 수 있는 동사 encourage(장려하다, 격려하다)의 분사 (D) encouraging이 정답입니다. 동사 (A), (B), (C)는 수식어 거품을 이끌 수 없습니다.

해석 직원들의 신체적 건강과 행복을 장려하는 프로그램이 많은 회사에서 점점 인기 있어지고 있다.

어휘 physical adj. 신체의, 물질의 fitness n. 건강, 신체 단련
wellbeing n. 행복, 웰빙 popular adj. 인기 있는, 대중적인

15 명령문의 동사 자리 채우기

해설 이 문장은 주어가 없는 명령문이므로, 명령문의 동사로 사용되는 동사원형 (A) change(변경하다)가 정답입니다. 동사의 과거형 또는 분사 (B), 명사 또는 3인칭 단수형 동사 (C), 동명사 또는 분사 (D)는 명령문의 동사 자리에 올 수 없습니다.

해석 온라인 계정의 보안을 향상시키기 위해 정기적으로 귀하의 비밀번호를 변경하십시오.

어휘 periodically adv. 정기적으로, 주기적으로
improve v. 향상시키다, 개선하다 security n. 보안, 안전
account n. 계정

16 'be동사 + -ing' 채우기

해설 '도시 관광을 준비하고 있다'라는 진행의 의미이므로 빈칸 앞의 be동사(is)와 함께 진행형(be동사 + -ing)을 만드는 동사 arrange(준비하다, 정하다)의 -ing형 (D) arranging이 정답입니다. 동사원형 (A)와 단수 동사 (B)는 be동사 다음에 올 수 없습니다. 명사 (C)는 be동사 다음의 보어 자리에 오면 주어와 동격 관계가 되어 'Ms. Denton은 준비이다'라는 어색한 문맥을 만듭니다.

해석 Ms. Denton은 다음 주에 호텔에서 머무를 단체 방문객들을 위해 도시 관광을 준비하고 있다.

어휘 visitor n. 방문객, 손님

17 접속사로 연결된 주어와 수일치하는 동사 채우기

해설 명사절 접속사 whether가 이끄는 절(whether ~ replaced)에 주어(the tires or the steering wheel)만 있고 동사가 없으므로 동사 (B)와 (C)가 정답의 후보입니다. 주어가 접속사 or로 연결되어 있으므로 or 다음의 단수 명사(the steering wheel)에 알맞은 단수 동사 (B) needs가 정답입니다. 복수 동사 (C)는 or 다음에 복수 명사가 왔을 때 쓰입니다. 동명사 또는 분사 (A)와 to 부정사 (D)는 동사 자리에 올 수 없습니다.

해석 검사가 끝난 후에, 정비공은 타이어 또는 핸들이 교체되어야 할지 아닐지를 우리에게 알려줄 것이다.

어휘 inspection n. 검사 mechanic n. 정비공
steering wheel phr. (자동차의) 핸들 replace v. 교체하다

18 선행사와 수일치하는 주격 관계절의 동사 채우기

해설 주격 관계절(that ~ industry)에 동사가 없으므로 동사 (A)와 (C)가 정답의 후보입니다. 주격 관계사(that)의 선행사(a problem)가 단수이므로 주격 관계절에는 단수 동사가 와야 합니다. 따라서 단수 동사 (C) affects(영향을 미치다, 작용하다)가 정답입니다. 복수 동사 (A)는 주격 관계사 앞에 복수 선행사가 있을 때 쓰입니다. 동명사 또는 분사 (B)와 명사 (D)는 동사 자리에 올 수 없습니다.

해석 유가의 급격한 하락은 사실상 업계의 모든 사람들에게 영향을 미치는 문제이다.

어휘 sharp adj. 급격한, 날카로운 decline n. 하락, 감소
practically adv. 사실상, 실질적으로 industry n. 산업계, 산업

19-22번은 다음 공고에 관한 문제입니다.

버려진 개들은 도시의 거리에서 문제가 되어 왔고, 이는 주민들이 지역 정부가 조치를 취할 것을 요구하게 만들었습니다.

¹⁹공무원들은 두 가지의 해결책을 제공하는 것으로 대응했습니다. ²⁰첫 번째로, 그들은 의도적인 동물 유기에 대한 기존의 법률을 수정했고, 그러한 행위에 대한 벌금을 2천 달러로 올리고 90일까지의 징역형을 처하게 했습니다. 또한, 모든 반려동물들은 이제 전자 배지가 필요합니다. ²¹이것들은 주인이 그들을 추적할 수 있는 위치 파악 시스템 장치를 포함합니다. ²²공인된 대행사가 요금을 받고 이 배지를 발급할 것입니다.

이러한 조치들은 주인 없는 개의 수를 상당히 줄일 것으로 예상됩니다. 그동안에, 정부의 동물 관련 서비스는 계속해서 개들이 보호받고 영구 시설에 배치되도록 할 것입니다.

abandoned adj. 버려진, 황폐한 cause v. 야기하다, 초래하다
resident n. 주민, 거주자 demand v. 요구하다, 청구하다; n. 요구, 수요
take action phr. 조치를 취하다, 행동에 옮기다
official n. 공무원; adj. 공무의, 공식의 dual adj. 두 가지의, 이중의
solution n. 해결책, 해답 existing adj. 기존의, 존재하는
deliberate adj. 의도적인, 고의의 fine n. 벌금; v. 벌금을 부과하다
jail time phr. 징역형 electronic adj. 전자의, 전자 공학의
authorized adj. 공인된, 인정받은 drastically adv. 상당히, 과감하게
stray adj. 주인이 없는, 길을 잃은; n. 주인 없는 동물, 길 잃은 동물
population n. (개체 또는 인구의) 수 shelter v. 보호하다; n. 보호소, 피난처
permanent adj. 영구적인, 영속적인

---

19 동사 어휘 고르기 주변 문맥 파악

해설 '공무원들은 두 가지의 해결책을 제공하는 것으로 _____ 했다'라는 문맥이므로 (A), (B), (D)가 정답의 후보입니다. 빈칸이 있는 문장만으로는 정답을 고를 수 없으므로 주변 문맥이나 전체 문맥을 파악합니다. 앞 문단에서 버려진 개들이 문제가 되어 주민들이 지역 정부가 조치를 취할 것을 요구했다고 했으므로 주민들의 요구에 대해 공무원들이 두 가지의 해결책을 제공하는 것으로 대응했다는 것을 알 수 있습니다. 따라서 동사 respond(대응하다, 대답하다)의 p.p.형 (D) responded가 정답입니다. (A)의 decline은 '거절하다, 감소하다', (B)의 object는 '반대하다'라는 의미입니다. (C)의 address는 '처리하다, 연설하다'라는 의미의 타동사로 뒤에 목적어가 와야 합니다.

20 'have동사 + p.p.' 채우기

해설 빈칸 앞에 have동사(have)가 있으므로 have와 함께 완료형(have동사 + p.p.)을 만드는 동사 revise(수정하다, 교정하다)의 p.p.형 (C) revised가 정답입니다. 명사 (A), 동명사 또는 분사 (B), 동사원형 (D)는 have동사 다음에 올 수 없습니다.

21 알맞은 문장 고르기

해석 (A) 이것들은 주인이 그들을 추적할 수 있는 위치 파악 시스템 장치를 포함합니다.
(B) 이것들은 수의사들이 저희 주인 없는 동물들의 수를 더 줄이는 것을 돕게 할 것입니다.
(C) 도시 내의 동물 보호소에 대한 요구가 늘고 있습니다.
(D) 그 처벌은 두 번째 위반자들에게로 강화될 것입니다.

해설 빈칸에 들어갈 알맞은 문장을 고르는 문제이므로 주변 문맥이나 전체 문맥을 파악합니다. 앞 문장 'all pets now require electronic tags'에서 모든 반려동물들은 이제 전자 배지가 필요하다고 했으므로 빈칸에는 전자 배지의 기능을 설명하는 내용이 들어가야 함을 알 수 있습니다. 따라서 (A) These contain GPS devices that allow owners to track them이 정답입니다.

어휘 contain v. 포함하다, 함유하다 GPS n. 위치 파악 시스템
track v. 추적하다, 뒤쫓다 veterinarian n. 수의사

---

22 'be동사 + -ing' 채우기

해설 '공인된 대행사가 배지를 발급할 것이다'라는 진행의 의미이므로 빈칸 앞의 be동사(be)와 함께 진행형(be동사 + -ing)을 만드는 동사 issue(발급하다, 발행하다)의 -ing형 (B) issuing이 정답입니다. p.p.형 (A)도 be동사 다음에 올 수 있지만, 수동형(be + p.p.)을 만들어서 '공인된 대행사에 배지가 발급될 것이다'라는 수동의 의미를 나타내므로 답이 될 수 없습니다. 명사 (C)와 (D)도 be동사 다음의 보어 자리에 올 수 있지만 주어와 동격 관계가 되어 각각 '공인된 대행사는 발급/쟁점이다'라는 어색한 문맥을 만듭니다.

어휘 issuance n. 발급, 발행

DAY 04 동사 2

Course 1 능동태·수동태

토익 실전 Check-up   p.197

| 토익 포인트 1 ⓐ | 토익 포인트 2 ⓑ |
| 토익 포인트 3 ⓑ | 토익 포인트 4 ⓐ |

1 태에 맞는 동사 채우기

해설 괄호 뒤에 목적어(several famous landmarks)가 있으므로 능동태 동사 ⓐ visited가 정답입니다. 수동태 동사 ⓑ were visited는 뒤에 목적어가 올 수 없습니다.

해석 관광객들은 여러 유명 명소들을 방문했다.

어휘 landmark n. 명소, 주요 지형지물

2 태에 맞는 동사 채우기

해설 감정을 나타내는 타동사 interest(흥미를 일으키다)의 주어(People)가 감정을 느끼므로 수동태 동사 ⓑ were interested가 정답입니다. 능동태 동사 ⓐ interested는 주어가 감정의 원인일 때 씁니다.

해석 미술관에 있는 사람들은 새로운 전시회에 흥미가 있었다.

어휘 gallery n. 미술관 exhibit n. 전시회; v. 전시하다

3 수동태 동사 뒤에 전치사 채우기

해설 괄호 앞의 be related(is related)와 함께 '~과 관련되어 있다'라는 의미의 'be related to' 숙어를 만드는 전치사 ⓑ to가 정답입니다. 전치사 ⓐ at은 be related to 표현을 완성할 수 없습니다.

해석 탄산음료 섭취는 높은 당뇨병 발생 위험과 관련되어 있다.

어휘 consumption n. 섭취, 소비 soda n. 탄산음료
risk n. 위험, 위험 요소 diabetes n. 당뇨병

4 수동태 동사 뒤에 to 부정사 채우기

해설 괄호 앞의 be allowed(are allowed)와 함께 '~하도록 허용되다/허가받다'라는 의미의 '수동태 동사 + to 부정사' 숙어를 만드는 to 부정사 ⓐ to use가 정답입니다. 동사원형 ⓑ use는 be allowed to 표현을 완성할 수 없습니다.

해석 Presto 항공사의 승객들은 비행 중에 전자기기를 사용하는 것이 허용된다.

어휘 electronic adj. 전자의, 전자 공학의 device n. 기기, 장치
flight n. 비행, 항공편

HACKERS PRACTICE

01 ⓑ [토익 포인트 1]   **02** ⓐ [토익 포인트 2]

03 ⓑ [토익 포인트 1]   **04** ⓑ [토익 포인트 3]

05 ⓐ [토익 포인트 4]   **06** ⓑ [Day03, Course 1, 토익 포인트 4]

07 ⓐ [토익 포인트 1]   **08** ⓐ [토익 포인트 4]

09 bored → were bored [토익 포인트 2]

10 are → is [Day03, Course 2, 토익 포인트 1]

11 entitles → is entitled [토익 포인트 4]

12 was disappointed → disappointed [토익 포인트 2]

13 was hiring → was hired [토익 포인트 1]

14 permit → are permitted [토익 포인트 4]

15 accumulate → accumulates [Day03, Course 2, 토익 포인트 1]

16 paid → pay [Day03, Course 1, 토익 포인트 1]

해석 **01** Navid's 헬스클럽의 회비는 매월 부과된다.

02 연설자는 그의 첫 직장에 대한 이야기로 청중들을 즐겁게 했다.

03 이사회는 회사의 다음 사장으로 Maria Alexi를 임명하기로 결정했다.

04 대부분의 시민들은 새로 확장된 대중교통 시스템에 만족한다.

05 하급 직원들은 적어도 일주일에 한 번씩 진행 보고서를 제출하는 것을 요구받는다.

06 지역 주민들은 원자로 건설을 반대한다.

07 그 회사는 다양한 종류의 연하장을 생산한다.

08 올해의 무역 회담은 2월 7일에 열릴 것으로 예정되어 있다.

09 어제 오전의 워크숍 참석자들은 기술적인 영상만 시청했기 때문에 지루했다.

10 회계 부서는 바쁜 세금 납부 기간을 위해 임시 보조를 채용하고 있다.

11 책에 대한 그의 기여로 인해, Mr. Avery는 수익금의 1퍼센트를 받을 자격이 있다.

12 Blake사는 수익이 기대했던 것보다 낮았기 때문에 많은 투자자들을 실망시켰다.

13 Ms. Cartwright는 업계에서의 폭넓은 경험으로 인해 관리자로 고용되었다.

14 승객들은 한 개의 개인 물품과 기내용 가방을 기내에 두도록 허용된다.

15 HTI Solutions사에 의해 제공되는 신용카드는 항공 여행으로 교환될 수 있는 포인트를 적립한다.

16 우리는 청구서를 납부하는 것이 좋을 것이고, 그렇지 않으면 케이블 연결이 끊길 것이다.

Course 2 시제 · 가정법

토익 실전 Check-up

토익 포인트 **1** ⓐ   토익 포인트 **2** ⓑ

토익 포인트 **3** ⓐ   토익 포인트 **4** ⓑ

1 올바른 시제의 동사 채우기

해설 미래 시간 표현(next Monday)이 있으므로 미래 시제 ⓐ will attend가 정답입니다. 과거 시제 ⓑ attended는 과거에 일어난 일을 나타낼 때 사용됩니다.

해석 신입 직원들은 다음 주 월요일에 오리엔테이션에 참석할 것이다.

어휘 attend v. 참석하다 orientation n. 오리엔테이션, 예비 교육

2 올바른 시제의 동사 채우기

해설 '망가진 복사기를 지금 고치고 있다'라는 의미로, 지금(now) 일어나고 있는 일을 나타내고 있으므로 현재진행 시제(am/are/is + -ing)를 만드는 ⓑ is가 정답입니다. 과거 시제 ⓐ was는 과거진행 시제(was/were + -ing)를 만듭니다.

해석 기술자는 망가진 복사기를 지금 고치고 있다.

어휘 technician n. 기술자, 전문가 photocopier n. 복사기

3 올바른 시제의 동사 채우기

해설 'Ms. Petrov는 이번 주말까지 Lennoxville로 이사해 있을 것이다'라는 의미로, 미래의 특정 시점(by the end of the week)에 이미 완료되었을 일을 나타내고 있으므로 미래완료 시제 ⓐ will have moved가 정답입니다. 과거 시제 ⓑ moved는 미래의 특정 시점을 나타내는 표현과 함께 쓰일 수 없습니다.

해석 Ms. Petrov는 이번 주말까지 Lennoxville로 이사해 있을 것이다.

4 가정법 동사 채우기

해설 if절(If ~ suppliers) 다음의 절(it ~ customers)이 '주어(it) + may + 동사원형(lose)'의 형태이고, '고객을 잃을 수도 있다'라는 의미로 실현 가능성이 희박한 미래의 일을 가정하고 있으므로 가정법 미래 문장임을 알 수 있습니다. 따라서 if절은 'If + 주어(the company) + should + 동사원형(change)'의 형태가 되어야 하므로 ⓑ should가 정답입니다. ⓐ had는 p.p.형과 함께 가정법 과거완료 문장의 동사로 쓰입니다.

해석 만약 그 회사가 공급업체들을 바꾼다면, 고객을 잃을 수도 있다.

어휘 supplier n. 공급업체 lose v. 잃다 customer n. 고객

HACKERS PRACTICE

01 ⓐ [토익 포인트 1]   **02** ⓑ [토익 포인트 3]

03 ⓐ [토익 포인트 2]   **04** ⓐ [Day03, Course 2, 토익 포인트 1]

05 ⓑ [토익 포인트 1]   **06** ⓑ [토익 포인트 3]

07 ⓐ [토익 포인트 2]   **08** ⓐ [토익 포인트 4]

09 has taught → will have taught [토익 포인트 3]

10 had made → made [토익 포인트 4]

11 will meet → was meeting [토익 포인트 2]

12 rates → rate [Day03, Course 2, 토익 포인트 2]

13 has received → have received [Day03, Course 2, 토익 포인트 1]

14 was → were [토익 포인트 4]

15 will leave → left [토익 포인트 1]

16 complete → completed [Day03, Course 1, 토익 포인트 2]

해석 **01** 그 교수는 종종 10대들을 위한 방과 후 프로그램에 참여한다.

02 Pierson Clinic은 2005년 이래로 빈곤층에게 무료 의료 서비스를 제공해왔다.

03 월요일에, Mr. Shaffer는 새로운 관리자로서 출근할 것이다.

04 그 가구를 조립하기 위한 설명서는 너무 복잡하다.

05 Camberton사의 주요 시멘트 공급업체는 곧 계약을 갱신할 것이다.

06 재무 보고서가 출력되기 전에, 그것은 수 차례 수정되었다.

07 현재, 스튜디오의 프로그래머들은 새로운 비디오 게임을 개발하고 있다.

08 만약 Fortune-Tech사가 그 프로젝트에 투자했었다면 수익을 냈을 것이다.

09 Ms. Neely는 다음 달쯤에는 교육 기관에서 10년 동안 회계 수업을 가르치는 것이 된다.

10 만약 회사가 그 부동산에 대해 합리적인 제안을 한다면, 소유주는 그것을 받아들일 것이다.

11 Mr. Rogers는 내가 사무실에 도착했을 때 고객과 만나고 있었다.

12 시장 조사의 참가자 반은 그 제품을 매우 높게 평가한다.

13 Mr. Klaxton은 요리에 많은 긍정적인 평을 받아온 유명한 요리사이다.

14 만약 그 행사가 더 홍보된다면, 더 많은 참석자를 끌어모을 것이다.

15 2년 전, Mr. Jackson은 영국 정부의 외교관으로서 근무하기 위해 스페인으로 떠났다.

16 Ms. Dobbs는 교육을 마쳤고 곧 일을 시작할 것이다.

HACKERS TEST
p.204

PART 5

01 (C)	02 (A)	03 (A)	04 (B)	05 (B)
06 (B)	07 (B)	08 (B)	09 (B)	10 (B)
11 (A)	12 (A)	13 (C)	14 (D)	15 (C)
16 (C)	17 (C)	18 (D)		

PART 6

19 (D)	20 (B)	21 (B)	22 (B)

01 태에 맞는 동사 채우기

해설 주어(Many people)가 복수 명사이므로 복수 명사와 함께 쓰일 수 있는 복수 동사 (B)와 (C)가 정답의 후보입니다. '많은 사람들은 놀랐다'라는 의미로 주어(Many people)가 감정을 느끼는 주체이므로 수동태 (C) were surprised가 정답입니다. 능동태 (B)를 쓰면 '많은 사람들이 놀라게 했다'라는 어색한 문맥을 만듭니다. 단수 동사 (A)와 (D)는 복수 명사와 함께 쓸 수 없습니다.

해석 많은 사람들은 시에서 새로운 야구장을 지을 계획이라는 의회의 발표에 놀랐다.

어휘 council n. 의회 announcement n. 발표, 공지 build v. 짓다, 만들다 baseball stadium phr. 야구장

02 올바른 시제의 동사 채우기

해설 현재를 나타내는 시간 표현(As of now)이 있으므로 현재의 상태를 나타낼 때 사용되는 현재 시제 (A) occupies(차지하다, 점유하다)가 정답입니다. 과거 시제 (B), 과거완료 시제 (C), 과거진행 시제 (D)는 현재를 나타낼 수 없습니다.

해석 현재로서는 Bastion사는 Wasser 빌딩의 한 층을 차지하고 있지만, 결국에는 확장할 것이다.

어휘 as of now phr. 현재로서는 eventually adv. 결국, 마침내 expand v. 확장하다, 확대하다

03 올바른 시제의 동사 채우기

해설 that절(that ~ week)에 동사가 없으므로 동사 (A), (B), (C)가 정답의 후보입니다. '지역 정부가 다음 주에 계획을 승인해줄 것을 바라고 있다'라는 의미로, 다음 주(next week), 즉 미래에 어떤 일이 일어나기를 바라고 있으므로 미래 시제 (A) will approve가 정답입니다. 과거완료 시제 (B)와 현재완료 시제 (C)는 미래를 나타낼 수 없습니다. to 부정사 (D)는 동사 자리에 올 수 없습니다.

해석 Cowansville 주민들은 지역 정부가 다음 주에 신규 주택 개발 계획을 승인해줄 것을 바라고 있다.

어휘 resident n. 주민 government n. 정부, 정치 development n. 개발, 발전 approve v. 승인하다, 찬성하다

04 올바른 시제의 동사 채우기

해설 첫 번째 절(Mr. Quesada ~ convention)에 주어(Mr. Quesada)만 있고 동사가 없으므로 동사 (A), (B), (C)가 정답의 후보입니다. '행사 장소가 예약됐을 때쯤이면 참석자 수를 확인했을 것이다'라는 의미로,

미래의 특정 시점, 즉 행사 장소가 예약됐을 때(by the time a venue for the event is reserved)에 이미 완료되었을 일을 나타내고 있으므로 미래완료 시제 (B) will have confirmed가 정답입니다. 과거 시제 (A)와 과거진행 시제 (C)는 미래를 나타낼 수 없습니다. 명사 (D)는 동사 자리에 올 수 없습니다.

해석 행사 장소가 예약됐을 때쯤이면, Mr. Quesada는 건축가 총회의 참석자 수를 확인했을 것이다.

어휘 attendee n. 참석자, 출석자 convention n. 총회, 관습 venue n. (행사 등의) 장소, 개최 예정지 confirm v. 확인하다, 확정하다

05 목적어 자리 채우기

해설 빈칸은 동사 expect(기대하다, 예상하다)의 목적어 자리이므로 목적어 자리에 올 수 있는 to 부정사 (B) to reduce가 정답입니다. 동사 (A), (C), (D)는 목적어 자리에 올 수 없습니다.

해석 도시 설계자들은 새로운 지하철 노선 건설을 통해 시의 도로 교통량을 줄이기를 기대한다.

어휘 urban planner phr. 도시 설계자 amount n. 양, 액수 construction n. 건설, 공사

06 올바른 시제의 동사 채우기

해설 that절(that ~ accurately)에 주어(he)만 있고 동사가 없으므로 동사 (B), (C), (D)가 정답의 후보입니다. 계약을 정확하게 이해했는지 확신할 수 없었던(since he ~ accurately) 시점은 Mr. Gallagher가 변호사에게 연락했던(Mr. Gallagher contacted his attorney) 시점보다 먼저입니다. 따라서 과거 시점보다 더 과거에 일어난 일을 나타낼 때 사용되는 과거완료 시제 (B) had interpreted가 정답입니다. 현재완료 시제 (C)와 현재 시제 (D)는 과거의 특정 시점 이전의 일을 나타낼 수 없습니다. 동명사 또는 분사 (A)는 동사 자리에 올 수 없습니다.

해석 Mr. Gallagher는 그가 계약을 정확하게 이해했는지 확신할 수 없었기 때문에 그의 변호사에게 연락했다.

어휘 attorney n. 변호사, 대리인 certain adj. 확신하는, 확실한 agreement n. 계약, 합의, 동의 accurately adv. 정확하게, 정밀하게 interpret v. 이해하다, 해석하다

07 태에 맞는 동사 채우기

해설 be동사(was) 다음에 올 수 있는 -ing형 (A), p.p.형 (B), 명사 (C)가 정답의 후보입니다. 'Mr. Brookside는 상기받았다'라는 의미가 되어야 하고, 빈칸에 들어갈 동사 remind(상기시키다, 일깨우다)가 타동사인데 빈칸 뒤에 목적어가 없으므로 수동태를 만드는 p.p.형 (B) reminded가 정답입니다. -ing형 (A)는 능동태를 만들므로 답이 될 수 없습니다. 명사 (C)는 주어와 동격 관계가 되어 'Mr. Brookside는 상기시키는 것이다'라는 어색한 문맥이 됩니다. 동사 (D)는 be동사 다음에 올 수 없습니다.

해석 Mr. Brookside는 무역 박람회 때문에 다음 주에 그가 자리에 없을 것이라고 그의 고객들에게 알리라고 상기받았다.

어휘 notify v. 알리다, 통지하다 absent adj. 자리에 없는, 부재의 trade exhibition phr. 무역 박람회

08 올바른 시제의 동사 채우기

해설 '지난 3년 동안 상당히 확장되어 왔다'라는 의미로, 지난 3년 동안(over the past three years)이라는 과거 시점부터 현재 시점까지 계속되는 기간에 일어난 일을 나타내고 있으므로 현재완료 시제 (B) has expanded가 정답입니다. 현재진행 시제 (A), 미래 시제 (C), 현재 시제 (D)는 과거에서 현재까지 계속되는 일을 나타낼 수 없습니다.

해석 전자 도서관은 지난 3년 동안 상당히 확장되어 왔고 지금은 훨씬 더 다양한 자료들을 제공한다.

어휘 digital library phr. 전자 도서관 considerably adv. 상당히, 많이

a wide range of phr. 다양한   material n. 자료, 소재
expand v. 확장되다, 확대되다

09 올바른 시제의 동사 채우기

해설 '어제 들어가고 있었다'라는 의미로, 과거의 특정 시점(yesterday)에 진행되고 있던 일을 나타내고 있으므로 과거진행 시제 (B) was entering이 정답입니다. 현재 시제 (A), 현재진행 시제 (C), 현재완료 시제 (D)는 과거의 특정 시점에 진행되고 있던 일을 나타낼 수 없습니다.

해석 Mr. Campbell은 어제 들어가고 있을 때 회전문에 문제가 있음을 알아차렸다.

어휘 notice v. 알아차리다, 주목하다   revolving door phr. 회전문
enter v. 들어가다, 참가하다

10 가정법 동사 채우기

해설 if절(If ~ better) 다음의 절(the company ~ complaints)에 주어(the company)만 있고 동사가 없으므로 동사 (A), (B), (D)가 정답의 후보입니다. if절(If ~ better)이 'If + 주어(the quality) + had p.p.(had been)'의 형태이고, '만약 품질이 더 좋았었다면 더 적은 고객 항의를 받았을 것이다'라는 의미로 과거 사실의 반대를 가정하고 있으므로 가정법 과거완료 문장임을 알 수 있습니다. 따라서 if절 다음의 절은 '주어 + would/could/might/should have p.p.'의 형태가 되어야 하므로 (B) might have had가 정답입니다. 현재진행 시제 (A)는 가정법 과거완료의 동사로 쓰일 수 없습니다. 'will + 동사원형' (D)는 가정법 미래에서 쓰입니다. to 부정사 (C)는 동사 자리에 올 수 없습니다.

해석 만약 신제품의 품질이 더 좋았었다면, 회사는 더 적은 고객 항의를 받았을 것이다.

어휘 quality n. 품질, 우수함   complaint n. 항의, 불평

11 선행사와 수일치하는 주격 관계절의 동사 채우기

해설 주격 관계절(that ~ by March 9)에 동사가 없으므로 동사 (A), (C), (D)가 정답의 후보입니다. 주격 관계사(that)의 선행사(job applications)가 복수이므로 주격 관계절에는 복수 동사가 와야 합니다. 따라서 복수 동사 (A) are submitted가 정답입니다. 단수 동사 (C)와 (D)는 주격 관계사 앞의 선행사가 단수일 때 쓰입니다. 동명사 또는 분사 (B)는 동사 자리에 올 수 없습니다.

해석 오직 3월 9일까지 제출된 입사 지원서들만이 Bradbury & Associates사 채용 위원회의 검토를 받을 것이다.

어휘 job application phr. 입사 지원서, 취업 지원서
review v. 검토하다, 비평하다   committee n. 위원회

12 올바른 시제의 동사 채우기

해설 문장에 주어(The crew)만 있고 동사가 없고, 빈칸 뒤에 목적어(the tiles)가 있으므로 능동태 동사 (A)와 (C)가 정답의 후보입니다. '오늘 늦게 욕실에 타일을 추가할 것이다'라는 의미로 오늘 늦게(later today)라는 미래의 특정 시점에 진행되고 있을 일을 나타내고 있으므로 미래진행 시제 (A) will be adding이 정답입니다. 현재완료 시제 (C)는 미래를 나타낼 수 없고, 수동태 동사 (B)는 뒤에 목적어가 올 수 없습니다. 명사 (D)는 동사 자리에 올 수 없습니다.

해석 작업팀은 오늘 늦게 욕실에 타일을 추가할 것이고 목요일에 비품을 설치할 것이다.

어휘 crew n. 작업팀, 승무원   bathroom n. 욕실, 화장실
install v. 설치하다   fixture n. 비품, 설치물

13 가정법 동사 채우기

해설 if절(If ~ grow)이 'If + 주어(the city's population) + should + 동사원형(continue)'의 형태이고, '인구가 계속해서 증가한다면 더 많은 주택 단지를 건설할 것이다'라는 의미로 미래에 일어날 법한 일을 가정하고 있으므로 가정법 미래 문장임을 알 수 있습니다. 따라서 if절

다음의 절은 '주어 + will/can/may/should + 동사원형'의 형태가 되어야 하므로 (C) will construct가 정답입니다. 현재 시제 (A), 과거완료 시제 (B), 과거 시제 (D)는 가정법 미래의 동사로 쓰일 수 없습니다.

해석 만약 도시의 인구가 계속해서 증가한다면, Vero-Build사는 더 많은 주택 단지를 건설할 것이다.

어휘 population n. 인구, 주민 수   grow v. 증가하다, 자라다
residential adj. 주택지의, 거주의   complex n. 단지, 복합체

14 올바른 시제의 동사 채우기

해설 첫 번째 절(Ms. Taylor ~ month)에 주어(Ms. Taylor)만 있고 동사가 없으므로 동사 (A), (C), (D)가 정답의 후보입니다. '이번 달에 웹사이트 디자인을 작업하고 있다'라는 의미로, 이번 달(this month)이라는 현재 시점에 진행되고 있는 일을 나타내고 있으므로 현재진행 시제 (D) is working이 정답입니다. 과거완료 시제 (A)는 특정 과거 시점 이전에 일어난 일을 나타내고, 과거진행 시제 (C)는 현재를 나타낼 수 없습니다. 명사, 동명사 또는 분사 (B)는 동사 자리에 올 수 없습니다.

해석 Ms. Taylor는 이번 달에 대기업 고객을 위해 웹사이트 디자인을 작업하고 있어서, 지금 시간이 없다.

어휘 corporate adj. 기업의, 법인의   unavailable adj. 시간이 없는

15 가정법 동사 채우기

해설 if절(If ~ team) 다음의 절(she ~ efficiently)이 '주어(she) + would + 동사원형(manage)'의 형태이고, 'Ms. Scott이 마케팅팀을 담당한다면 효율적으로 운영할 것이다'라는 의미로 현재 사실의 반대를 가정하고 있으므로 가정법 과거 문장임을 알 수 있습니다. 따라서 if절은 'If + 주어(Ms. Scott) + 과거동사(be동사의 경우 were)'의 형태가 되어야 하므로 과거동사 (C) were가 정답입니다. 현재완료 시제 (A), 현재 시제 (B), 현재진행 시제 (D)는 가정법 과거의 if절의 동사 자리에 올 수 없습니다.

해석 만약 Ms. Scott이 마케팅팀을 담당한다면, 그녀는 그 팀을 효율적으로 운영할 것이다.

어휘 in charge of phr. ~을 담당해서, ~을 관리하여
manage v. 운영하다, 경영하다   efficiently adv. 효율적으로, 유효하게

16 태에 맞는 동사 채우기

해설 '새로운 고층 사무실 빌딩이 건설되었다'라는 수동의 의미이므로 수동태 (C) was built이 정답입니다. 능동태 (A), (B), (D)는 동사 build가 '건설하다'라는 의미일 때는 타동사인데 빈칸 뒤에 목적어가 없으므로 답이 될 수 없습니다.

해석 금융가 한복판에 새로운 고층 사무실 빌딩이 건설되었다.

어휘 tower n. 고층 빌딩, 타워   in the heart of phr. ~의 한복판에, ~의 한가운데에
financial district phr. 금융가

17 수식어 거품을 이끄는 것 채우기

해설 이 문장은 주어(Ms. Aileen)와 동사(will resign)를 갖춘 완전한 문장이므로 ____ she ~ or not은 수식어 거품으로 보아야 합니다. 이 수식어 거품은 동사(receives)가 있는 거품절이므로 거품절을 이끌 수 있는 부사절 접속사 (C) whether(~이든지 ~ 아닌지)가 정답입니다. 부사 (A)와 (B)는 수식어 거품을 이끌 수 없습니다. 전치사 (D)는 거품절이 아닌 거품구를 이끕니다.

해석 Ms. Aileen은 그녀가 급여 인상을 받든지 받지 않든지 다음 달에 사직할 것이다.

어휘 resign v. 사직하다, 사임하다   receive v. 받다   salary n. 급여
raise n. 인상, 증가

18 'have동사 + p.p.' 채우기

해설 빈칸 앞에 have동사(has)가 있으므로 have동사와 함께 완료형 (have + p.p.)을 만드는 동사 wide(넓히다, 확대하다)의 p.p.형 (D)

widened가 정답입니다. 형용사 (A)와 (B), -ing형 (C)는 have동사 다음에 올 수 없습니다.

해석 여론 조사는 부유층과 빈곤층 간의 격차가 이번 10년 동안 벌어져 왔다는 것을 보여준다.

어휘 poll n. 여론 조사, 투표 gap n. 격차, 간격

19-22번은 다음 이메일에 관한 문제입니다.

> 수신: <chris_rivers@globex.com>
> 발신: <b.andreson@radeelectronics.com>
>
> Mr. Rivers께,
>
> 귀하의 이메일에 감사드립니다. ¹⁹귀하께서 새 전화기에 만족하신다니 기쁩니다. 유감스럽게도, Rade Electronics사는 귀하의 전화기를 위한 케이스를 갖춰두고 있지 않습니다.
>
> ²⁰해당 모델에 적절한 스마트폰 케이스를 구하려면, 저는 귀하의 지역에 있는 Wallaby Telecom사 지점을 방문하시는 것을 권해드립니다. ²¹귀하의 편의를 위해, 제가 그들의 웹사이트에서 상점 위치를 찾아보았습니다. ²²귀하께서는 이 이메일의 첨부 파일로 지도를 찾으실 수 있을 것입니다. 귀하께서 보실 수 있듯이, 귀하의 위치에서 가장 가까운 상점이 Harold가 350번지에 있습니다.
>
> 도움이 더 필요하시다면 주저 말고 제게 알려주십시오.
>
> Bethany Anderson 드림, Rade Electronics사
>
> stock v. (상품 등을 재고에) 갖고 있다 obtain v. 구하다, 얻다
> branch n. 지점 convenience n. 편의, 편리 location n. 위치, 장소
> assistance n. 도움, 지원

19 수동태 동사 뒤에 전치사 채우기

해설 '새 전화기에 만족하다'라는 의미이고 빈칸 앞의 are pleased와 함께 '수동태 동사 + 전치사' 숙어 be pleased with(~에 만족하다, ~으로 기뻐하다)를 만드는 전치사 (D) with(~과 함께)가 정답입니다. 전치사 (A) of(~의), (B) to(~로), (C) in(~에)은 동사 please와 '수동태 동사 + 전치사' 숙어를 만들 수 없습니다.

20 형용사 어휘 고르기 주변 문맥 파악

해설 '해당 모델에 ＿＿＿한 스마트폰 케이스를 구하려면'이라는 문맥이므로 모든 보기가 정답의 후보입니다. 빈칸이 있는 문장만으로 정답을 고를 수 없으므로 주변 문맥이나 전체 문맥을 파악합니다. 앞 문장에서 이메일 수신자의 전화기를 위한 케이스를 갖춰두고 있지 않다고 했으므로, 해당 스마트폰에 적절한 케이스가 없다는 것을 알 수 있습니다. 따라서 형용사 (B) appropriate(적절한)이 정답입니다. (A) imported는 '수입된', (C) colorful은 '색채가 풍부한, 화려한', (D) expensive는 '비싼, 돈이 많이 드는'이라는 의미입니다.

21 올바른 시제의 동사 채우기 주변 문맥 파악

해설 '그들의 웹사이트에서 상점 위치를 찾아보다'라는 문맥인데, 이 경우 빈칸이 있는 문장만으로 올바른 시제의 동사를 고를 수 없으므로 주변 문맥이나 전체 문맥을 파악하여 정답을 고릅니다. 뒷부분에서 상대방의 위치에서 가장 가까운 상점이 Harold가 350번지에 있다고 했으므로, 상점 위치를 찾아본 것은 과거에 일어난 일이라는 것을 알 수 있습니다. 따라서 과거 시제 (B) looked가 정답입니다. 현재 시제 (A)와 미래 시제 (C)는 과거에 있었던 일을 나타낼 수 없고, 과거완료 시제 (D)는 특정 과거 시점 이전에 일어난 일을 나타냅니다.

어휘 look up phr. 찾아보다

22 알맞은 문장 고르기

해석 (A) 저는 귀하께서 저희 서비스에 만족하실 것으로 생각합니다.
(B) 귀하께서는 이 이메일의 첨부 파일로 지도를 찾으실 수 있을 것입니다.

(C) 그것은 그들의 모든 제품을 포함합니다.
(D) 사용자 설명서를 참조해 주십시오.

해설 빈칸에 들어갈 알맞은 문장을 고르는 문제이므로 주변 또는 전체 문맥을 파악합니다. 뒤 문장 'As you can see, the closest store to your location is on 350 Harold Street.'에서 이메일 수신자가 볼 수 있듯이 수신자의 위치에서 가장 가까운 상점은 Harold가 350번지에 있다고 했으므로 빈칸에는 수신자가 상점의 위치를 볼 수 있는 자료를 보냈다는 내용이 들어가야 함을 알 수 있습니다. 따라서 (B) You'll find the map as an attachment to this e-mail이 정답입니다.

어휘 be satisfied with phr. ~에 만족하다 attachment n. 첨부 파일, 부가(물)
feature v. 포함하다, 특징으로 삼다 refer v. 참조하다, 참고하다
manual n. 설명서

DAY 05 준동사

Course 1 to 부정사와 동명사

토익 실전 Check-up   p.207

토익 포인트 1 ⓑ	토익 포인트 2 ⓑ
토익 포인트 3 ⓐ	토익 포인트 4 ⓑ

1 to 부정사 채우기

해설 '일자리에 지원하려면 웹사이트에 등록해야 한다'라는 의미가 되어야 하므로 목적을 나타내는 to 부정사인 ⓑ to apply가 정답입니다. 동사원형 ⓐ apply는 문장에 이미 동사(must register)가 있으므로 답이 될 수 없습니다.

해석 사람들은 일자리에 지원하려면 웹사이트에 등록해야 한다.

어휘 register v. 등록하다, 기재하다 apply v. 지원하다, 신청하다

2 to 부정사 채우기

해설 동사 refuse(거절하다)는 to 부정사를 목적어로 취하는 동사이므로 to 부정사 ⓑ to pay가 정답입니다. 동명사 ⓐ paying은 동사 refuse의 목적어 자리에 올 수 없습니다.

해석 그 고객은 불만족스러운 서비스에 대해 지불하기를 거절했다.

어휘 unsatisfactory adj. 불만족스러운

3 동명사 채우기

해설 문장에 주어가 없고 동사(can be)와 보어(stressful)만 있으므로 (   ) in front of a large crowd를 주어로 보아야 합니다. 따라서 명사 역할을 하여 주어 자리에 올 수 있는 동사 speak(연설하다, 말하다)의 동명사 ⓐ Speaking이 정답입니다. 동사 ⓑ Speak은 주어 자리에 올 수 없습니다.

해석 많은 군중 앞에서 연설하는 것은 스트레스가 될 수 있다.

어휘 crowd n. 군중 stressful adj. 스트레스가 되는, 스트레스가 많은

4 동명사 채우기

해설 괄호 앞의 having difficulty와 함께 have difficulty -ing(~하는 데 어려움을 겪다) 표현을 완성하는 동명사 ⓑ connecting이 정답입니다. to 부정사 ⓐ to connect는 have difficulty -ing 표현을 완성할 수 없습니다.

해석 컴퓨터들 중 몇 대는 인터넷에 접속하는 데 어려움을 겪고 있다.

어휘 connect v. 접속하다, 연결하다

01 ⓑ [토익 포인트 1]   **02** ⓐ [토익 포인트 3]
03 ⓑ [토익 포인트 3]   **04** ⓐ [Day04, Course 2, 토익 포인트 2]
05 ⓐ [토익 포인트 1]   **06** ⓑ [토익 포인트 4]
07 ⓐ [토익 포인트 2]   **08** ⓐ [Day02, Course 1, 토익 포인트 3]
09 eat → eating [토익 포인트 4]
10 succeed → to succeed [토익 포인트 1]
11 continuing → to continue [토익 포인트 2]
12 concern → are concerned [Day04, Course 1, 토익 포인트 2]
13 choose → to choose [토익 포인트 1]
14 buy → to buy [토익 포인트 1]
15 cancel → canceled [Day03, Course 1, 토익 포인트 2]
16 receiving → to receive [토익 포인트 2]

해석 **01** Mr. Jan은 고객 불평에 대해 알리기 위해 관리자에게 전화했다.

02 대부분의 참석자들은 세미나에 참석해서 다른 사람들과 대화하는 것을 즐거워했다.

03 Ms. Harrington은 연말 직원 파티를 준비하는 것을 담당한다.

04 Mr. Rio는 그의 발표를 준비하고 있기 때문에 현재 시간이 없다.

05 새로운 언어를 배우는 가장 좋은 방법은 다른 사람들과 연습하는 것이다.

06 Ms. Dingman은 현재 고객의 문의에 답변하느라 바쁘다.

07 지역 서점들에는 그 소설책이 없기 때문에, Ms. Jones는 결국 온라인에서 그것을 주문하기로 결정했다.

08 우리는 보고서에 언급된 어떠한 제품 결함이든지 다음 달까지 해결할 것이다.

09 Mr. Kensington은 주중 근무일 동안에는 점심 식사를 근처 식당에서 먹는 것에 익숙하다.

10 Ms. Reece는 운영 관리자로서의 그녀의 역할에 있어서 성공하기 위해 매우 열심히 일했다.

11 Ms. Gable은 *PhotoLite Magazine*을 계속해서 구독하기를 원한다.

12 Bay Area의 많은 주민들이 근처 해변들의 상태에 대해 걱정스러워한다.

13 내일은 새로운 학기를 위한 강의들을 선택하는 마감일이다.

14 Ms. Lambert는 그녀의 직장을 위한 새로운 사무용 가구를 구매하기 위해 Dauphine 가구점에 방문했다.

15 제작자는 설명 없이 갑자기 그 행사를 취소했다.

16 Mr. Lee는 예산 보고서 한 부를 받을 것으로 예상한다.

Course 2 분사

토익 실전 Check-up p.211

토익 포인트 1 ⓑ   토익 포인트 2 ⓐ
토익 포인트 3 ⓐ   토익 포인트 4 ⓐ

1 분사 채우기

해설 괄호 뒤의 명사(support)를 꾸밀 수 있는 것은 형용사나 형용사 역할을 하는 분사이므로, 동사 continue(계속해서 ~하다)의 분사 ⓑ continued가 정답입니다. 동사원형 ⓐ continue는 명사를 꾸밀 수 없습니다.

해석 기부자들은 지속적인 지원에 대해 감사를 받았다.

어휘 **contributor** n. 기부자, 기고자 **support** n. 지원, 지지

2 분사 채우기

해설 이 문장은 주어(Mr. Gore), 동사(emphasizes), 목적어(the quality)를 갖춘 완전한 절이므로 (   ) ~ clients는 수식어 거품으로 보아야 합니다. 따라서 수식어 거품이 될 수 있는 분사구문((접속사 +) 분사)을 만드는 동사 speak(이야기하다, 말하다)의 분사 ⓐ Speaking이 정답입니다. 동사 ⓑ Spoke는 분사구문을 만들 수 없습니다.

해석 잠재적인 고객들에게 이야기할 때, Mr. Gore는 항상 그의 제품의 품질을 강조한다.

어휘 **potential** adj. 잠재적인, 가능성 있는
emphasize v. 강조하다, 두드러지게 하다 **quality** n. 품질, 우수함

3 현재분사와 과거분사 구별하여 채우기

해설 동사(had)의 목적어(her order)와 괄호에 들어갈 목적격 보어가 '그녀의 주문이 취소되었다'라는 의미의 수동 관계이므로 과거분사 ⓐ canceled가 정답입니다. 현재분사 ⓑ canceling은 능동 관계일 때 사용됩니다.

해석 실수를 발견한 후, Ms. Roberts는 그녀의 주문이 취소되게 했다.

어휘 **notice** v. 발견하다, 알아차리다

4 현재분사와 과거분사 구별하여 채우기

해설 수식 받는 명사(appliances)와 분사가 '손상된 기기'라는 의미의 수동 관계이므로 과거분사 ⓐ damaged가 정답입니다. 현재분사 ⓑ damaging은 능동의 의미를 나타내어 '손상시키는 기기'라는 어색한 문맥을 만듭니다.

해석 Mr. Hopps는 여러 손상된 기기를 수리한다.

어휘 **perform** v. 하다, 수행하다 **repair** n. 수리
a number of phr. 여러, 다수의 **appliance** n. 기기

HACKERS PRACTICE p.213

01 ⓑ [토익 포인트 1]   **02** ⓐ [토익 포인트 3]
03 ⓐ [토익 포인트 3]   **04** ⓑ [토익 포인트 1]
05 ⓑ [Day04, Course 1, 토익 포인트 1]   **06** ⓐ [토익 포인트 2]
07 ⓑ [Day02, Course 1, 토익 포인트 3]   **08** ⓑ [토익 포인트 3]
09 discount → be discounted [Day04, Course 1, 토익 포인트 1]
10 Returning → Returned [토익 포인트 2]
11 performed → performing [토익 포인트 3]
12 has succeeded → had succeeded [Day04, Course 2, 토익 포인트 3]
13 promised → promising [토익 포인트 4]
14 This → It [Day02, Course 1, 토익 포인트 2]
15 experiencing → experienced [토익 포인트 4]
16 preferring → preferred [토익 포인트 4]

해석 **01** 많은 직원들은 산업 기술에 대한 고급 단계 강의를 들을 자격이 있다.

02 지원하려는 후보자들은 관련 분야에 업무 경험이 있어야 한다.

03 비평가들은 그 이야기가 과장되고 대체로 부정확하다고 생각했다.

04 직원들은 관리자의 격려하는 말에 고무되었다.

05 국가 항공국은 내일 아침까지 덴버로 오고 가는 모든 항공편을 연기했다.

06 하루에 수천 번 접속되는 Leeds의 온라인 상점은 매우 인기 있다.

07 다른 사무실로 이사한 후에, Mr. Castro는 가구 몇 점을 주문했다.

08 *The Black Moon*은 몇 가지의 인상적인 특수 효과가 있는 흥미로운 액션 영화이다.

09 Electronic Superstore사의 제품들은 이번 주말에 70퍼센트까지 할인될 것이다.

10 늦게 반납되었기 때문에, 그 책은 책을 빌리려는 다른 도서관 회원

들이 이용할 수 없었다.

11 지금 그 콘서트홀에서 공연하는 밴드는 1990년대에 유명했다.

12 지난달 말까지, 시카고 공장은 생산 할당량 달성에 성공했었다.

13 다수의 새로운 기업가들에게, 체인점을 구입하는 것은 유망한 기회일 수 있다.

14 모든 거래를 전자 데이터베이스에 기록하는 것이 Ms. Ogawa의 책무이다.

15 JK Consulting사는 관리직을 위해 숙련된 전문가를 구하고 있다.

16 연회의 손님들은 그들의 선호되는 식사 선택권을 주최자들에게 알려줄 것을 요청받았다.

HACKERS TEST
p.214

PART 5

01 (C)	02 (D)	03 (D)	04 (D)	05 (A)
06 (D)	07 (C)	08 (B)	09 (C)	10 (A)
11 (B)	12 (D)	13 (D)	14 (A)	15 (B)
16 (A)	17 (A)	18 (B)		

PART 6

19 (D)	20 (A)	21 (A)	22 (D)

01 현재분사와 과거분사 구별하여 채우기

해설 빈칸 뒤의 명사(day)를 꾸밀 수 있는 형용사 역할을 하는 분사 (B)와 (C)가 정답의 후보입니다. 분사의 꾸밈을 받는 명사 day(하루, 날)와 분사가 '하루가 실망시키다'라는 의미의 능동 관계이므로 현재분사 (C) disappointing이 정답입니다. 과거분사 (B)는 수동의 의미를 나타내므로 답이 될 수 없습니다. 동사 (A)와 명사 (D)는 명사를 꾸밀 수 없습니다.

해석 비록 주식 시장에서 실망스러운 하루였지만, 대부분의 분석가들은 가격이 곧 회복될 것이라는 점에 동의했다.

어휘 stock market phr. 주식 시장, 증권 거래소 analyst n. 분석가 recover v. 회복되다, 되찾다 disappoint v. 실망시키다, 좌절시키다

02 to 부정사 채우기

해설 이 문장은 주어(management), 동사(hired), 목적어(someone)를 갖춘 완전한 절이므로 _____ ~ saying은 수식어 거품으로 보아야 합니다. 따라서 수식어 거품을 이끌 수 있는 to 부정사 (D) to interpret이 정답입니다. 명사 (A), 동사 (B), 형용사 (C)는 수식어 거품을 이끌 수 없습니다. 참고로, 이 문장에서 to 부정사는 어떤 사람을 고용한 '목적'을 나타내는 부사 역할을 하고 있음을 알아둡니다.

해석 그 대표가 주로 아랍어로 말했기 때문에, 경영진은 그가 말하는 것을 해석하기 위해 어떤 사람을 고용했다.

어휘 representative n. 대표자, 직원 primarily adv. 주로, 원래 interpret v. 해석하다, 통역하다

03 주어 자리 채우기

해설 문장에 동사(offered)와 목적어(suggestions)가 있는데 주어가 없으므로 주어 자리에 올 수 있는 명사 (D) consultant(컨설턴트)가 정답입니다. 형용사 (A), 동사 또는 분사 (B), 동사 (C)는 주어 자리에 올 수 없습니다.

해석 Mr. Craig가 고용한 컨설턴트는 어떻게 그의 직원들을 계속 의욕을 갖게 할지에 대한 제안을 했다.

어휘 suggestion n. 제안 motivated adj. 의욕을 가진, 동기 부여된

04 분사 채우기

해설 이 문장은 주어(The hospital), 동사(has adopted), 목적어(a computer program)를 갖춘 완전한 절이므로 _____ ~ records는

수식어 거품으로 보아야 합니다. 이 수식어 거품은 동사가 없는 거품구이므로 거품구를 이끌 수 있는 동사 develop(개발하다, 발전시키다)의 분사 (D) developed가 정답입니다. 동사 (A), (B), (C)는 수식어 거품을 이끌 수 없습니다.

해석 그 병원은 환자 기록을 더 잘 보존하려는 목적으로 개발된 컴퓨터 프로그램을 도입했다.

어휘 adopt v. 도입하다, 채택하다 maintain v. 보존하다, 유지하다 patient n. 환자; adj. 인내심 있는, 끈기 있는 record n. 기록

05 분사 채우기

해설 이 문장은 주어(The conference kits)와 동사(were distributed)를 갖춘 완전한 절이므로 _____ ~ information은 수식어 거품으로 보아야 합니다. 이 수식어 거품은 동사가 없는 거품구이므로 수식어 거품을 이끌 수 있는 동사 hold(포함하다, 갖고 있다)의 분사 (A) holding이 정답입니다. 동사 (B), (C), (D)는 수식어 거품을 이끌 수 없습니다.

해석 숙박 시설 및 교통 정보를 포함하는 회의 자료 세트는 참석자들에게 배부되었다.

어휘 kit n. (교재나 재료 등의) 세트 accommodation n. 숙박 시설 transport n. 교통, 수송 distribute v. 배부하다, 분배하다 participant n. 참석자

06 to 부정사 채우기

해설 이 문장은 주어(the government), 동사(has proposed), 목적어(legislation)를 갖춘 완전한 절이므로 _____ ~ hours는 수식어 거품으로 보아야 합니다. 이 수식어 거품은 동사가 없는 거품구이므로 거품구를 이끌 수 있는 to 부정사 (D) to shorten이 정답입니다. 과거분사 (A)도 거품구를 이끌 수 있지만, 빈칸 뒤에 목적어(the official working week)가 있으므로 답이 될 수 없습니다. 동사 (B)와 (C)는 수식어 거품구를 이끌 수 없습니다.

해석 더 많은 일자리를 창출하기를 바라기 때문에, 정부는 공식적인 주당 근무를 35시간으로 줄이는 법률 제정을 제안했다.

어휘 propose v. 제안하다, 제의하다 legislation n. 법률 제정, 법률 official adj. 공식의, 공무의

07 동명사 채우기

해설 빈칸 앞의 표현 be devoted to(is devoted to)에서 to는 전치사이므로 전치사의 목적어 자리에 올 수 있는 동명사 (C) providing이 정답입니다. 명사 (B)도 전치사의 목적어 자리에 올 수 있지만, 그 경우 명사(provider)와 명사(customers)가 특별한 연결이 없이 나란히 오게 되므로 답이 될 수 없습니다. 동사 (A)와 (D)는 전치사의 목적어 자리에 올 수 없습니다.

해석 Pembleton 교통 서비스는 고객들에게 운전에 있어 안전하고 편안한 대안을 제공하는 데 전념한다.

어휘 transit n. 교통, 수송 devoted to phr. ~에 전념하는, ~에 헌신적인 comfortable adj. 편안한 alternative n. 대안

08 to 부정사 채우기

해설 동사 agree(동의하다)는 to 부정사를 목적어로 취하는 동사이므로 to 부정사 (B) to follow가 정답입니다. 동사원형 (A), 수동태 동사원형 (C), 동명사 또는 분사 (D)는 동사 agree의 목적어 자리에 올 수 없습니다.

해석 모든 세입자들은 임대차 계약에 서술된 건물의 규칙에 동의해야 한다.

어휘 tenant n. 세입자 rule n. 규칙 outline v. (개요 등을) 서술하다 rental agreement phr. 임대차 계약

09 능동태와 수동태의 구별

해설 be동사(are) 다음에 와서 빈칸 앞의 부사(highly)의 꾸밈을 받을 수 있는 -ing형 (A)와 p.p.형 (C)가 정답의 후보입니다. '워크숍이 매우 높이 평가된다'라는 수동의 의미이므로 수동태를 만드는 동사 regard(평가하다, 여기다)의 p.p.형 (C) regarded가 정답입니다. -ing형 (A)는 능동태를 만드는데, 빈칸 뒤에 타동사 regard의 목적어가 없으므로 답이 될 수 없습니다. 동사 또는 명사 (B)와 (D)는 동사일 경우 각각 3인칭 단수형과 동사원형이기 때문에 be동사 다음에 올 수 없고, 명사일 경우 부사가 아닌 형용사의 꾸밈을 받습니다.

해석 Ms. Rodriguez가 소기업을 위해 회계 업무에 대해 제공하는 워크숍은 매우 높이 평가된다.

어휘 accounting n. 회계   practice n. 업무, 연습   highly adv. 높이, 대단히

10 분사 채우기

해설 빈칸 뒤의 명사(budget)를 앞에서 꾸며줄 수 있는 분사 (A) limited (제한된)가 정답입니다. 명사 (B), 명사 또는 동사 (C)와 (D)는 명사를 꾸며줄 수 없습니다.

해석 많은 기업들이 직면하는 가장 큰 문제는 대부분 제한된 예산이다.

어휘 challenge n. 문제, 도전   face v. 직면하다, 대면하다; n. 얼굴

11 to 부정사 채우기

해설 빈칸 앞의 동사(managed)의 목적어 자리에 올 수 있는 to 부정사 (B) to convey가 정답입니다. 동사 또는 분사 (A), 동사 (C)와 (D)는 목적어 자리에 올 수 없습니다.

해석 Mr. Vaughn에게 연락하려는 몇 번의 실패한 시도 후에, Ms. Dean은 간신히 그의 비서에게 메시지를 전달할 수 있었다.

어휘 failed adj. 실패한   attempt n. 시도   manage v. 간신히 ~하다
assistant n. 비서   convey v. 전달하다

12 수식어 거품을 이끄는 것 채우기

해설 이 문장은 주어(The annual report)와 동사(is being proofread)를 갖춘 완전한 절이므로 _____ it is printed는 수식어 거품으로 보아야 합니다. 이 수식어 거품은 동사(is printed)가 있는 거품절이므로 거품절을 이끌 수 있는 부사절 접속사 (A)와 (D)가 정답의 후보입니다. '출력되기 전에 교정되고 있다'라는 의미가 되어야 하므로 부사절 접속사 (D) before(~ 전에)가 정답입니다. 부사절 접속사 (A) although (비록 ~이지만)는 어색한 문맥을 만듭니다. 전치사 (B) by(~ 옆에, ~에 의해서)와 (C) during(~ 동안에)는 거품절이 아닌 거품구를 이끕니다.

해석 연례 보고서는 출력되기 전에 마지막으로 교정되고 있다.

어휘 annual adj. 연례의   proofread v. 교정하다

13 보어 자리 채우기

해설 빈칸은 동사 become(~이 되다)의 보어 자리이므로 보어 자리에 올 수 있는 명사 (A), 명사 역할을 하는 동명사 (B), 형용사 (D)가 정답의 후보입니다. '기차역 주변 지역이 붐비게 될 수 있다'라는 의미로 보어가 주어(the area)를 설명해주고 있으므로 형용사 (D) crowded (붐비는, 혼잡한)가 정답입니다. 명사 (A)와 동명사 (B)는 주어와 동격 관계가 되어 각각 '지역이 군중/붐비는 것이 될 수 있다'라는 어색한 문맥을 만듭니다. 부사 (C)는 보어 자리에 올 수 없습니다.

해석 많은 교통량과 좁은 인도 때문에, 기차역 주변 지역은 혼잡 시간 동안 붐비게 될 수 있다.

어휘 traffic n. 교통(량), 운행   narrow adj. 좁은, 한정된
sidewalk n. 인도, 보도   peak hour phr. 혼잡 시간, 피크 타임

14 올바른 시제의 동사 채우기

해설 문장에 주어(The head of the engineering department)만 있고 동사가 없으므로 동사 (A), (C), (D)가 정답의 후보입니다. '최근에 그의 팀을 도왔다'라는 의미로, 최근에(recently), 즉 과거에 있었던

일을 나타내고 있으므로 동사 assist(돕다)의 과거 시제 (A) assisted가 정답입니다. 복수 동사 (C)는 3인칭 단수 주어와 쓰일 수 없습니다. 현재 시제 (D)는 일반적인 사실이나 반복적인 행동을 나타냅니다. 동명사 또는 분사 (B)는 동사 자리에 올 수 없습니다.

해석 공학 기술 부서장은 제품의 디자인적 결함에 대한 현실적인 해결책을 제안함으로써 최근에 그의 팀을 도왔다.

어휘 engineering n. 공학 기술, 공학   practical adj. 현실적인, 실질적인
solution n. 해결책   flaw n. 결함, 결점

15 태에 맞는 동사 채우기

해설 문장에 주어(A variety of preexisting theories)만 있고 동사가 없으므로 동사 (A), (B), (C)가 정답의 후보입니다. 빈칸 뒤에 목적어(the current research)가 있고 주어가 복수 명사이므로 능동태 복수 동사 (B) guide(가이드를 제시하다, 안내하다)가 정답입니다. 참고로, a variety of(다양한)는 형용사처럼 명사 앞에 올 수 있는 수량 표현이며 복수 가산 명사 앞에 올 수 있습니다. 단수 동사 (A)는 3인칭 단수 주어와 쓰입니다. 수동태 (C)는 다음에 목적어가 올 수 없습니다. to 부정사 (D)는 동사 자리에 올 수 없습니다.

해석 다양한 기존의 이론들은 소비자 행동에 대한 현재 연구에 가이드를 제시한다.

어휘 a variety of phr. 다양한, 여러 가지의   preexisting adj. 기존의
theory n. 이론, 학설   current adj. 현재의, 지금의
behavior n. 행동, 태도

16 to 부정사 채우기

해설 이 문장은 주어(The store)와 동사(will close)를 갖춘 완전한 절이므로 _____ ~ building은 수식어 거품으로 보아야 합니다. 이 수식어 거품은 동사가 없는 거품구이므로 거품구를 이끌 수 있는 to 부정사 (A) to install이 정답입니다. 동사 (B), (C), (D)는 수식어 거품을 이끌 수 없습니다.

해석 그 상점은 건물의 앞쪽에 새 유리창을 설치하기 위해 월요일 저녁에 일찍 문을 닫을 것이다.

어휘 install v. 설치하다, 설비하다

17 to 부정사 채우기

해설 동사 need(~해야 하다, ~을 필요로 하다)는 to 부정사를 목적어로 취하는 동사이므로 to 부정사 (A) to hurry가 정답입니다. 동사 (B), (C), (D)는 동사 need의 목적어 자리에 올 수 없습니다.

해석 축구 팬들은 내일 밤 경기 티켓을 사기를 원한다면 서둘러야 한다.

어휘 football n. 축구, 축구공   hurry v. 서두르다

18 분사 채우기

해설 이 문장은 주어(A package)와 동사(was delivered)를 갖춘 완전한 절이므로 _____ ~ vase는 수식어 거품으로 보아야 합니다. 이 수식어 거품은 동사가 없는 거품구이므로 거품구를 이끌 수 있는 분사 (B) containing이 정답입니다. 동사 (A), 명사 (C)와 (D)는 수식어 거품을 이끌 수 없습니다.

해석 골동품 화병을 포함한 소포가 박물관의 큐레이터에게 직접 배달되었다.

어휘 antique adj. 골동품의; n. 골동품   containment n. 억제, 견제
container n. 용기, 그릇

19-22번은 다음 편지에 관한 문제입니다.

귀하께서 요청하신 Gespanzo 예술 센터의 교체 카드가 동봉되었습니다. ¹⁹그 카드는 귀하의 멤버십 승격을 확인해줍니다. 귀하의 새로운 다이아몬드 지위는 귀하께서 저희의 전시에 대해 할인된 입장권을 받도록 해드립니다. ²⁰추가적으로, 귀하께서는 대극장에서 상연되는 모든 공연들을 위해 미리 자리를 예약하실 수 있습니다. ○

한 권으로 끝내는 해커스 토익 700+ (LC+RC+VOCA)

²¹귀하의 후원에 저희가 얼마나 감사드리는지를 알려드리기 위해, 1월 25일 이번 주 토요일에 열릴 저희의 연례 자선 행사에 귀하를 초대하고자 합니다. ²²귀하는 행사에 1명의 손님을 무료로 데려오실 수 있습니다.

만약 카드에 대해 문의가 있으시다면, 555-6293으로 고객 관리 센터에 연락해주시기 바랍니다.

enclose v. 동봉하다   affirm v. 확인하다   status n. 지위, 신분
entitle v. ~할 수 있도록 해주다, 자격을 주다   discount v. 할인하다
admission n. 입장(권)   exhibition n. 전시   reserve v. 예약하다
in advance phr. 미리   performance n. 공연   appreciate v. 감사하다
support n. 후원, 지지   benefit n. 자선 행사, 혜택

19 명사 어휘 고르기 주변 문맥 파악

해설 '카드는 멤버십 _____을 확인해준다'는 문맥이므로 모든 보기가 정답의 후보입니다. 빈칸이 있는 문장만으로 정답을 고를 수 없으므로 주변 문맥이나 전체 문맥을 파악합니다. 앞 문장에서 교체 카드가 동봉되었다고 했고, 뒤 문장에서 새로운 다이아몬드 지위는 전시에 대해 할인된 입장권을 받도록 해준다고 했으므로 교체 카드가 더 높은 회원 지위를 확인해준다는 것을 알 수 있습니다. 따라서 명사 (D) upgrade(승격)가 정답입니다. (A) renewal은 '갱신', (B) registration은 '등록', (C) period는 '기간'이라는 의미입니다.

20 현재분사와 과거분사 구별하여 채우기

해설 이 문장은 주어(you)와 동사(may reserve)를 갖춘 완전한 절이므로 _____ ~ Grand Hall은 수식어 거품으로 보아야 합니다. 이 수식어 거품은 동사가 없는 거품구이므로 거품구를 이끌 수 있는 분사 (A)와 (B)가 정답의 후보입니다. 분사의 꾸밈을 받는 명사(performances)와 분사가 '공연들이 상연되다'라는 의미의 수동 관계이므로 과거분사 (A) presented가 정답입니다. 현재분사 (B)는 능동의 의미를 나타내므로 답이 될 수 없습니다. 동사 (C)와 (D)는 수식어 거품을 이끌 수 없습니다.

21 선행사와 수일치하는 주격 관계절의 동사 채우기

해설 주격 관계사(that)의 선행사(our annual benefit)가 단수이므로 주격 관계절(that ~ January 25)에는 단수 동사가 와야 합니다. 따라서 단수 주어와 쓰일 수 있는 동사 (A) will be held가 정답입니다. 복수 동사 (B), (C), (D)는 주격 관계사 앞에 복수 선행사가 있을 때 쓰입니다.

22 알맞은 문장 고르기

해석 (A) 저희 웹사이트는 귀하가 기부를 하실 수 있는 여러 가지 방법들을 나열하고 있습니다.
(B) 귀하의 신청서에 몇 가지 필수 정보가 누락되어 있었습니다.
(C) 저희는 귀하가 예약금을 지불해주시기를 요청드립니다.
(D) 귀하는 행사에 1명의 손님을 무료로 데려오실 수 있습니다.

해설 빈칸에 들어갈 알맞은 문장을 고르는 문제이므로 주변 문맥 또는 전체 문맥을 파악합니다. 앞 문장 'we would like to invite you to our annual benefit ~ January 25'에서 1월 25일에 열릴 연례 자선 행사에 초대하고자 한다고 했으므로 빈칸에는 행사와 관련된 내용이 들어가야 함을 알 수 있습니다. 따라서 (D) You may bring one guest to the event for free가 정답입니다.

어휘 donate v. 기부하다, 기증하다   missing adj. 누락된, 없어진, 분실한
essential adj. 필수의, 본질의   payment n. 지불, 납입
reservation n. 예약   for free phr. 무료로

DAY 06 명사와 대명사

Course 1 명사

토익 실전 Check-up   p.217

토익 포인트 1 ⓐ   토익 포인트 2 ⓑ
토익 포인트 3 ⓐ   토익 포인트 4 ⓐ

1 명사 자리 채우기

해설 문장에 주어가 없고 동사(is)만 있으므로 주어 자리에 올 수 있는 명사 ⓐ advertisement(광고)가 정답입니다. 동사 ⓑ advertise는 주어 자리에 올 수 없습니다.

해석 그 광고는 시청자들에게 인기 있다.

2 불가산 명사 채우기

해설 명사(construction)은 셀 수 없는 불가산 명사이므로 ⓑ Construction이 정답입니다. 부정관사(a)는 불가산 명사 앞에 올 수 없습니다.

해석 새로운 야구 경기장의 건설이 어제 발표되었다.

어휘 announce v. 발표하다, 알리다

3 사람명사 추상명사 구별하여 채우기

해설 '제조업자에게 돌려보내질 수 있다'라는 의미가 되어야 하므로 사람명사 ⓐ manufacturer(제조업자, 제조자)가 정답입니다. 추상명사 ⓑ manufacture(제조, 생산)를 쓰면 '제조에게 돌려보내질 수 있다'라는 어색한 문맥이 됩니다.

해석 결함 있는 제품은 제조업자에게 돌려보내질 수 있다.

어휘 defective adj. 결함 있는, 불완전한
return v. 돌려보내다, 반납하다

4 다른 명사를 수식하는 명사 채우기

해설 '접수처에 객실 열쇠를 두고 갈 수 있다'라는 의미가 되어야 하므로 괄호 뒤의 desk(데스크, 안내처)와 함께 쓰여 '접수처'라는 의미의 복합 명사를 만드는 명사 ⓐ reception(접수처)이 정답입니다. 형용사 ⓑ receptive(수용하는)를 쓰면 '수용하는 데스크/안내처'라는 어색한 문맥이 됩니다.

해석 호텔 투숙객들은 외출할 때 접수처에 객실 열쇠를 두고 갈 수 있다.

어휘 leave v. 두고 가다, 남기다   go out phr. 외출하다, 나가다

HACKERS PRACTICE   p.219

01 ⓑ [토익 포인트 1]   02 ⓐ [토익 포인트 1]
03 ⓐ [토익 포인트 3]   04 ⓐ [토익 포인트 2]
05 ⓐ [Day05, Course 1, 토익 포인트 3]   06 ⓑ [토익 포인트 2]
07 ⓐ [Day05, Course 1, 토익 포인트 2]   08 ⓐ [토익 포인트 2]
09 pleasurably → pleasure [토익 포인트 1]
10 reviewed → are reviewing [Day04, Course 2, 토익 포인트 2]
11 challenger → challenging [Day05, Course 2, 토익 포인트 1]
12 Sale → Sales [토익 포인트 4]
13 instructions → instructors [토익 포인트 3]
14 regulate → regulation [토익 포인트 1]
15 architecture → architect [토익 포인트 3]
16 Construct → Construction [토익 포인트 1]

해석 01 강사는 Ms. Kang의 수필을 대회의 출품작으로 선택했다.

02 제시간에 직장에 출근하는 것의 중요성은 아무리 말해도 과장이라 할 수 없다.

03 여권 신청 양식은 인터넷에서 다운로드될 수 있다.

04 그 상점은 휴일 시즌을 위해 진열창에 새로운 전시품을 놓았다.

05 공장 장비를 정비하는 것은 고장을 예방하는 것을 돕는다.

06 집을 어떤 색상으로 페인트칠할지 결정할 수 없으시다면, 저희 직원들이 기꺼이 추천을 해드릴 것입니다.

07 은행은 언제나 어떠한 항의에도 하루 내에 응답하기 위해 노력한다.

08 신입 직원들은 상급 직원들로부터 많은 귀중한 조언을 받았다.

09 Ms. Terrence는 Mr. Harper와 함께 일하게 되어 기뻤다고 말했다.

10 Mr. Johnson은 관리자들에게 상세한 예산안을 주었는데, 그들은 바로 지금 그것을 검토하고 있다.

11 Gaynor사의 직원들은 다음 달에 힘든 일정이 있다.

12 Preston Industries사의 판매 할당량은 겨울 시즌 초반에는 거의 달성되지 않는다.

13 단 3명의 강사들만이 여름에 수업을 할 수 있을 것이다.

14 정부는 운전면허증 취득에 관한 새로운 규정을 발표했다.

15 다음 주에, 새로운 건축가가 팀에 합류할 것이므로, 모두 그녀를 맞을 준비가 되어야 한다.

16 직원 주차장 건설은 이번 주 후반에 시작될 것이다.

Course 2 대명사

토익 실전 Check-up   p.221

토익 포인트 1 ⓐ   토익 포인트 2 ⓐ
토익 포인트 3 ⓑ   토익 포인트 4 ⓑ

1 격에 맞는 인칭대명사 채우기

해설 타동사 ask(asked)의 목적어로 쓰일 수 있는 목적격 인칭대명사 ⓐ him이 정답입니다. 주격 인칭대명사 ⓑ he는 주어 자리에 옵니다.

해석 Mr. Allen이 그 프로젝트를 완료해서, 관리자는 그에게 보고서를 작성해 달라고 요청했다.

어휘 complete v. 완료하다, 완성하다 supervisor n. 관리자, 감독관

2 지시대명사 채우기

해설 앞에서 언급된 복수 명사(shoes)를 대신할 수 있는 지시대명사 ⓐ those가 정답입니다. 지시대명사 that은 단수 명사를 대신합니다.

해석 우리 가게에서 가장 비싼 신발들은 이탈리아 제조업체의 것들이다.

3 부정형용사 채우기

해설 이 문장은 긍정문이고 '작업에 대한 약간의 의견을 요청했다'라는 의미가 되어야 하므로 '약간(의), 몇몇(의)'이라는 의미의 부정형용사 ⓑ some이 정답입니다. 목적격 인칭대명사 ⓐ them은 빈칸 뒤의 명사(feedback)를 꾸밀 수 없습니다.

해석 Mr. Watts는 그의 작업에 대한 약간의 의견을 요청했다.

어휘 feedback n. 의견, 반응

4 부정대명사 채우기

해설 '이전에 했던 다른 모든 것들'이라는 의미가 되어야 하고 괄호 앞에 복수 명사와 함께 쓰이는 all(모든)이 있으므로 '나머지 전부'라는 의미로 복수 명사를 대신하는 ⓑ the others가 정답입니다. ⓐ another는 '또 다른 하나'라는 의미로 단수 가산 명사를 대신합니다.

해석 이 업무는 당신이 이전에 했던 다른 모든 것들보다 어렵습니다.

어휘 assignment n. 업무, 임무, 과제 hard adj. 어려운, 단단한

HACKERS PRACTICE   p.223

01 ⓐ [토익 포인트 1]   **02** ⓐ [토익 포인트 1]
03 ⓑ [토익 포인트 3]   **04** ⓑ [토익 포인트 1]
05 ⓐ [Day 03, Course 1, 토익 포인트 4]   **06** ⓑ [토익 포인트 4]
07 ⓐ [Day 05, Course 1, 토익 포인트 3]   **08** ⓑ [토익 포인트 3]
09 him → his [토익 포인트 1]
10 it → itself [토익 포인트 1]
11 mine → my [토익 포인트 1]
12 other → another [토익 포인트 4]
13 for → to [Day 05, Course 1, 토익 포인트 2]
14 any → some [토익 포인트 3]
15 these → those [토익 포인트 2]
16 on → in [토익 포인트 1]

해석 01 저희는 귀하의 이력서를 면밀하게 검토했고 귀하를 면접보고자 합니다.

02 Ms. Anderson은 그녀의 휴대용 컴퓨터를 공항에 잊고 두고 왔다.

03 업계에서 가장 뛰어난 엔지니어들 중 일부가 새로운 스포츠카를 만들어내기 위해 팀을 구성했다.

04 방문 고객들이 오늘 도착할 것이라서, 그들을 태우러 가기 위해 차량이 보내졌다.

05 Volart의 재즈 공연단은 그들의 영감에 대해 이야기했다.

06 Mr. Paulson은 다른 직원들이 선반에 물품을 채우는 동안 계산대에 남아 있었다.

07 잠재적인 고객들에게 명함을 제시하는 것은 영업 회의에서 자주 행해진다.

08 관객들 중 아무도 연설자를 위한 질문이 조금도 없었다.

09 테이블에 있는 노트북이 누구의 것인지 그가 질문을 받았을 때, Mr. Lewis는 그의 것이라고 말했다.

10 거의 50년의 경력이 있는 Borton사는 고객 만족을 보장한다는 것에 대해 자사를 자랑스러워한다.

11 이번 주 중에 언제 제 사무실에 오셔서 연례 보고서 사본을 가져가세요.

12 2년 전에 개업한 이후로 성공적이었던 HNT Consulting사는 또 다른 대단한 분기를 보냈다.

13 Mr. Wynn은 연말까지는 본부로 이전하고 싶어 한다.

14 지난달에 몇몇 직원들이 휴가 중이었을 때, 사무원은 그들의 우편물을 그들의 책상에 두었다.

15 몇몇 웹사이트들은 사업에 있어 경력을 추구하는 사람들에게 지침을 제공한다.

16 캔버라의 미술관 본관 건물은 그 자체로 예술 작품이다.

HACKERS TEST   p.224

PART 5				
01 (A)	02 (D)	03 (D)	04 (A)	05 (C)
06 (C)	07 (A)	08 (D)	09 (B)	10 (A)
11 (A)	12 (B)	13 (D)	14 (A)	15 (A)
16 (B)	17 (B)	18 (B)		

PART 6			
19 (B)	20 (D)	21 (C)	22 (A)

01 사람명사와 추상명사 구별하여 채우기

해설 빈칸 앞 관사(a)와 형용사(renowned)의 꾸밈을 받을 수 있는 사람

명사 (A)와 추상명사 (B)가 정답의 후보입니다. 'Mr. Jameson은 유명한 건축가이다'라는 의미가 되어야 하므로 사람명사 (A) architect(건축가)가 정답입니다. 추상명사 (B) architecture(건축학)를 쓰면 'Mr. Jameson은 유명한 건축학이다'라는 어색한 문맥이 됩니다. 형용사 (C)와 부사 (D)는 명사 자리에 올 수 없습니다.

해석 Mr. Jameson은 혁신적인 디자인으로 여러 국제적인 상을 받은 유명한 건축가이다.

어휘 renowned adj. 유명한 win v. (상 등을) 받다, 이기다
multiple adj. 여러, 다수의 international adj. 국제적인
award n. 상 innovative adj. 혁신적인

02 격에 맞는 인칭대명사 채우기

해설 so that이 이끄는 부사절(so that ____ ~ online)에 주어가 없고 동사(can find)만 있으므로 주어 자리에 올 수 있는 부정대명사 (A)와 (C), 주격 인칭대명사 (D)가 정답의 후보입니다. '식구들은 온라인에서 그들이 서로를 찾을 수 있도록 소셜 네트워크 계정을 만들었다'라는 의미로, 빈칸에 들어갈 주어가 가리키는 것이 주절(Members ~ accounts)의 주어(Members of the O'Grady family)와 동일하므로 주격 인칭대명사 (D) they(그들)가 정답입니다. 부정대명사 (A) the others(다른 몇몇)는 이미 언급된 것 이외의 나머지를 가리킵니다. 부정대명사 (C) the one은 'I have two sisters. The one is ~ and the other is ~'와 같이 the other와 대응하여 '(양자 중의) 전자'를 가리킵니다. 재귀대명사 (B) themselves(그들 자신)는 목적어 자리에 옵니다.

해석 O'Grady 가족의 식구들은 온라인에서 그들이 서로를 찾을 수 있도록 소셜 네트워크 계정을 만들었다.

어휘 set up phr. 만들다, 설치하다 account n. 계정, 계좌

03 동명사 채우기

해설 ____ ~ techniques가 이 문장의 주어이므로 주어 자리에 올 수 있는 동명사 (D) Knowing이 정답입니다. 명사 (C)도 주어 자리에 올 수 있지만, 그 경우 명사(Knowledge)와 명사(design)가 특별한 연결이 없이 나란히 오게 되므로 답이 될 수 없습니다. 부사 (A)와 동사 (B)는 주어 자리에 올 수 없습니다.

해석 기초적인 그래픽 디자인과 전자 출판 기술을 아는 것은 이 자리에 지원하는 모든 지원자에게 이점이 될 것이다.

어휘 desktop publishing phr. 전자 출판 (데스크톱 컴퓨터와 레이저 프린터를 이용해서 출판물을 제작하는 것)
asset n. 이점, 자산 candidate n. 지원자, 후보자
apply for phr. ~에 지원하다, ~을 신청하다 knowingly adv. 고의로

04 부정형용사 채우기

해설 빈칸 뒤 명사(lawyers)를 꾸밀 수 있는 부정형용사 (A)와 소유격 인칭대명사 (B)가 정답의 후보입니다. '몇몇 변호사들과 회의를 할 것이다'라는 의미가 되어야 하므로 (A) some이 정답입니다. (B)를 쓰면 '그것의 변호사들과 회의를 할 것이다'라는 어색한 문맥이 됩니다. 부정대명사 (C)와 (D)는 부정형용사로 쓰일 수 없으므로 명사 앞에 올 수 없습니다.

해석 Ms. Henderson은 Hartford 컨벤션 센터에서 몇몇 변호사들과 회의를 할 것이다.

어휘 lawyer n. 변호사

05 격에 맞는 인칭대명사 채우기

해설 타동사 photograph(~의 사진을 찍다)의 목적어 자리에 올 수 있는 재귀대명사 (C)와 목적격 인칭대명사 (D)가 정답의 후보입니다. '관광객들은 그들 자신들의 사진을 찍는 것을 즐긴다'라는 의미로, 빈칸에 들어갈 목적어가 주어(Tourists)와 같은 대상을 지칭하고 있으므로 재귀대명사 (C) themselves가 정답입니다. 목적격 인칭대명사 (D)는 주어가 아닌 다른 대상을 가리켜 '관광객들은 그들의(자신들이 아닌

다른 사람들의) 사진을 찍는 것을 즐긴다'라는 문맥을 만드는데, them이 대신하는 명사가 문장 내에 없으므로 답이 될 수 없습니다. 소유격 인칭대명사 (A)와 주격 인칭대명사 (B)는 목적어 자리에 올 수 없습니다.

해석 관광객들은 그 지역에서 볼 수 있는 많은 사적지와 명물 옆에서 그들 자신들의 사진을 찍는 것을 즐기는 것으로 보인다.

어휘 tourist n. 관광객, 여행자 historical site phr. 사적지
attraction n. 명물, 유인, 매력

06 격에 맞는 인칭대명사 채우기

해설 '두 명의 무명작가들은 아이디어가 원래 그들의 것이었다고 주장했다'라는 의미로, 빈칸에 들어갈 인칭대명사는 3인칭 복수 명사(Two unknown authors)의 소유대명사이므로 (C) theirs가 정답입니다. (A)와 (B)는 모두 1인칭 복수의 인칭대명사이므로 인칭이 맞지 않아 답이 될 수 없습니다. 주격 인칭대명사 (D)는 보어 자리에 올 수 없습니다.

해석 두 명의 무명작가들은 유명 작가의 출판 소설의 아이디어가 원래 그들의 것이었다고 주장했다.

어휘 unknown adj. 무명의, 유명하지 않은 author n. 작가, 저자
claim v. 주장하다, 요구하다 novel n. 소설; adj. 새로운, 신기한
originally adv. 원래, 처음에

07 부정대명사 채우기

해설 형용사(cheaper)의 꾸밈을 받을 수 있는 명사 (A)와 (B)가 정답의 후보입니다. '첫 번째 후원 패키지가 너무 비싸서 더 저렴한 것을 고려해야 할 것이다'라는 의미가 되어야 하므로 정해지지 않은 단수 가산명사를 대신하는 대명사 (A) one이 정답입니다. 대명사 (B)는 관사(a)와 함께 쓰일 수 없습니다. 형용사 (C)와 전치사 또는 접속사 (D)는 명사 자리에 올 수 없습니다.

해석 첫 번째 후원 패키지가 너무 비싸서, 회사는 더 저렴한 것을 고려해야 할 것이다.

어휘 sponsorship n. 후원, 협찬 consider v. 고려하다

08 지시대명사 채우기

해설 ____ hoping to attend the strategic marketing class가 이 문장의 주어이므로 주어 자리에 올 수 있는 지시대명사 (D) Those가 정답입니다. 부정형용사 (A) Other, 관계대명사 (B) Who, 목적격 대명사 (C) Them은 주어 자리에 올 수 없습니다.

해석 전략 마케팅 수업에 참석하기를 희망하는 이들은 4월 15일 전까지 우리의 웹사이트에 등록해야 한다.

어휘 attend v. 참석하다 register v. 등록하다

09 명사 자리 채우기

해설 부정관사(a)와 전치사(for) 사이에 올 수 있는 것은 가산 명사이므로 가산 명사 (A)와 (B)가 정답의 후보입니다. 빈칸 앞에 부정관사 a가 있으므로, 부정관사 a와 함께 쓰일 수 있는 가산 명사 (B) requirement가 정답입니다. 복수 명사 (A)는 부정관사 a와 함께 쓰일 수 없고, 분사 (C)와 (D)는 명사 자리에 올 수 없습니다.

해석 컴퓨터 공학에 학위를 가지고 있는 것은 그 직업의 필요요건이다.

어휘 degree n. 학위 requirement n. 필요요건

10 명사 자리 채우기

해설 be동사(is) 뒤에 올 수 있는 명사 (A)와 p.p.형 (C)가 정답의 후보입니다. '관리자들이 논의해야 하는 첫 번째 주제는 참석자 수이다'라는 의미가 되어야 하므로 명사 (A) attendance(참석자 수)가 정답입니다. (C)를 쓰면 '첫 번째 주제가 참가되다'라는 어색한 문맥이 됩니다. 동사원형 (B)와 (D)는 be동사 뒤에 올 수 없습니다.

해석 워크숍 이전에 관리자들이 논의해야 하는 첫 번째 주제는 참석자 수

이다.

어휘 discuss v. 논의하다, 토론하다

11 격에 맞는 인칭대명사 채우기

해설 전치사(with)의 목적어 자리에 올 수 있는 목적격 인칭대명사 (A)와 소유대명사 (D)가 정답의 후보입니다. '우리와 약속을 잡다'라는 의미가 되어야 하므로 목적격 인칭대명사 (A) us(우리)가 정답입니다. 소유대명사 (D)를 쓰면 '우리의 것과 약속을 잡다'라는 어색한 문맥이 됩니다. 주격 인칭대명사 (B)는 전치사의 목적어 자리에 올 수 없습니다. 소유격 인칭대명사 (C)는 전치사의 목적어 자리에 오기 위해서는 '소유격 인칭대명사 + 명사'의 형태가 되어야 합니다.

해석 귀하의 프로젝트 비용에 대한 견적서를 원하신다면, 전화하셔서 오늘 저희와 약속을 잡으세요.

어휘 estimate n. 견적서 book v. 예약하다

12 부정형용사 채우기

해설 단수 가산 명사(floor) 앞에 올 수 있는 부정형용사 (B) another(또 다른)가 정답입니다. (A), (C), (D)는 모두 복수 명사와 함께 쓰입니다.

해석 성장에 맞추기 위해, Hepburn 백화점은 그것이 위치해 있는 건물의 또 다른 층을 매입할 계획이다.

어휘 accommodate v. 맞추다, 수용하다 locate v. 위치시키다

13 부정형용사 채우기

해설 빈칸 뒤 명사(objection)를 꾸밀 수 있는 모든 보기가 정답의 후보입니다. '약속을 연기하는 데 조금의 이의도 없다'라는 의미가 되어야 하므로 (D) any가 정답입니다. (A) both(둘 다), (B) all(모두), (C) some(몇 개의)을 쓰면 각각 'Mr. Fields는 약속을 연기하는 데 둘 다 이의가 없다/모두 이의가 없다/몇 개의 이의가 없다'라는 어색한 문맥이 됩니다.

해석 Mr. Fields는 약속을 목요일까지로 연기하는 데 조금의 이의도 없다.

어휘 objection n. 이의 postpone v. 연기하다
appointment n. 약속, 임명

14 부정대명사 채우기

해설 전치사(among)의 목적어 자리에 올 수 있는 대명사 (A), (B), (D)가 정답의 후보입니다. '그중에서도'라는 의미가 되어야 하므로 부정대명사 (A) others가 정답입니다. (B)와 (D)를 쓰면 '아무것도 없는 중에'와 '둘 중 어느 하나의 것 중에'라는 어색한 문맥이 됩니다. 부정형용사 (C)는 전치사의 목적어 자리에 올 수 없습니다.

해석 Ms. Oliver는 다양한 혜택들 때문에 그 일을 받아들였는데, 그중에서도 유동적인 업무 일정과 후한 급료 때문이었다.

어휘 accept v. 받아들이다, 수락하다 benefit n. 혜택, 수당
flexible adj. 유동적인, 융통성 있는 generous adj. 후한, 너그러운
pay n. 급료, 임금

15 to 부정사 채우기

해설 이 문장은 주어(Arlington Business Association)와 동사(is looking)를 갖춘 완전한 절이므로 _____ a new Web site for them 은 수식어 거품으로 보아야 합니다. 이 수식어 거품은 동사가 없는 거품구이므로 거품구를 이끌 수 있는 to 부정사 (A)와 분사 (B)가 정답의 후보입니다. '새로운 웹사이트를 만들어 줄 경험 많은 웹디자이너'라는 의미가 되어야 하므로 to 부정사 (A) to create가 정답입니다. 분사 (B)는 과거분사인데 빈칸 뒤에 목적어(a new Web site)가 있으므로 답이 될 수 없습니다. 명사 (C)와 동사 (D)는 수식어 거품을 이끌 수 없습니다.

해석 Arlington 사업체 협회는 그들을 위한 새로운 웹사이트를 만들어 줄 경험 많은 웹디자이너를 구하고 있다.

어휘 association n. 협회 look for phr. ~을 구하다, ~을 찾다

experienced adj. 경험 많은

16 명사 자리 채우기

해설 타동사 submit(제안하다, 제출하다)의 목적어 자리에 올 수 있는 명사 (B) nominations(임명, 지명)가 정답입니다. 동사 (A)와 (C), 동사 또는 분사 (D)는 목적어 자리에 올 수 없습니다.

해석 위원회 회원들은 의장의 사임 발표 후에 그의 후임자를 위한 임명을 제안할 것을 요청받았다.

어휘 committee n. 위원회, 위원 chairperson n. 의장, 회장
replacement n. 후임자, 대체 resignation n. 사임, 사직

17 격에 맞는 인칭대명사 채우기

해설 '그의 것을 집에 잊고 두고 오다'라는 의미로, 빈칸에 들어갈 인칭대명사는 3인칭 단수 남성 명사(Mr. Smith)의 소유대명사이므로 (B) his가 정답입니다. 3인칭 단수 여성 명사의 소유대명사 (A)는 주어(Mr. Smith)가 남성을 가리키므로 답이 될 수 없습니다. 목적격 인칭대명사 (C)와 (D)를 쓰면 'Mr. Smith는 그/그녀를 집에 잊고 두고 왔다'라는 문맥이 되는데, 문장에서 him과 her가 가리키는 대상이 없으므로 답이 될 수 없습니다.

해석 Mr. Smith는 그의 것을 집에 잊고 두고 왔기 때문에 Ms. Vargas의 휴대전화 충전기를 빌려달라고 부탁했다.

어휘 charger n. 충전기 forget v. 잊고 두고 오다, 잊다

18 재귀대명사 채우기

해설 '공장 기계를 혼자서 작동하는 것이 허용되지 않는다'라는 의미가 되어야 하므로 빈칸 앞의 전치사(on)와 함께 쓰여 'on one's own(혼자서, 혼자 힘으로)'을 만드는 (B) their own이 정답입니다. (A), (C), (D)는 재귀대명사 표현 on one's own을 만들 수 없습니다.

해석 신입 직원들은 그들이 그렇게 하도록 자격이 주어질 때까지 공장 기계를 혼자서 작동하는 것이 허용되지 않는다.

어휘 permit v. 허용하다, 허락하다 operate v. 작동하다, 운전하다
machinery n. 기계 certify v. ~의 자격을 주다

19-22번은 다음 공고에 관한 문제입니다.

대중교통 서비스 확대

[19]Glenwood 시가 성장하고 있으므로, 대중교통은 그에 따라 확대되어야 합니다. 의회는 Glenwood 시 주민들의 필요를 충족시키기 위해서는 우리의 교통 시스템에 개선이 필요하다는 결론을 내렸습니다. 이것이 성취될 수 있는 하나의 방법은 새로운 버스 노선을 만드는 것입니다. 이는 또한 오래된 노선들의 일부를 변경하는 것을 의미합니다. [20]변경은 10월 1일까지 완료되는 것으로 예정되어 있습니다. [21]또한, 시는 새로운 지하철 노선을 만들고 두 개의 기존 노선을 연장할 것입니다.

유감스럽게도, 이 작업은 도로가 파헤쳐져야 할 수도 있으므로 일상적인 통행을 방해할 것입니다. [22]노선 공사 때문에 발생하는 모든 도로 폐쇄에 대해서는 사전 공지가 게시될 것입니다.

public transit phr. 대중교통 council n. 의회, 협의회
transportation n. 교통, 수송 meet v. 충족시키다, 만나다
population n. 주민, 인구 accomplish v. 성취하다, 해내다
create v. 만들다, 창조하다 route n. 노선, 경로
mean v. 의미하다, ~이라는 뜻이다 revise v. 변경하다, 수정하다
expand v. 확대하다, 연장하다
unfortunately adv. 유감스럽게도, 불행하게도
interrupt v. 방해하다, 중단시키다 normal adj. 일상적인, 정상의
tear up phr. 파헤치다, 파기하다 advance adj. 사전의, 앞서의
occur v. 발생하다, 일어나다 construction n. 공사, 건축

19 알맞은 문장 고르기

해석 (A) 도시 변두리 근처에 새로운 공항이 건설될 것이다.

(B) Glenwood 시가 성장하고 있으므로, 대중 교통은 그에 따라 확대되어야 합니다.

(C) 늘어난 차량의 수는 주차 문제를 발생시키고 있습니다.

(D) 더 많은 교통 노선이 일시적으로 추가될 것이고, 시간이 연장될 것입니다.

해설 빈칸에 들어갈 알맞은 문장을 고르는 문제이므로 주변 문맥 또는 전체 문맥을 파악합니다. 글의 제목 'Expanded Public Transit Service'에서 대중교통 서비스를 확대한다고 했고, 뒤 문장 'The council has decided that our transportation system is in need of an upgrade in order to meet the needs of Glenwood's population.'에서 의회가 Glenwood 시 주민들의 필요를 충족시키기 위해서는 교통 시스템에 개선이 필요하다는 결론을 내렸다고 했으므로 시가 성장하고 있고 그에 따라 대중교통을 확대해야 한다는 내용이 들어가야 함을 알 수 있습니다. 따라서 (B) The city of Glenwood is growing, and public transit must expand with it이 정답입니다.

어휘 outskirts n. 변두리 grow v. 성장하다
increased adj. 늘어난, 증가된 temporarily adv. 일시적으로
extend v. 연장하다, 확장하다

20 동사와 수일치하는 주어 채우기
해설 문장에 주어가 없고 동사(are scheduled)만 있으므로 주어 자리에 올 수 있는 명사 (C)와 (D)가 정답의 후보입니다. 동사가 복수이므로 복수 명사 (D) changes(변경, 수정)가 정답입니다. 단수 명사 (C)는 단수 동사와 함께 쓰입니다. 형용사 (A)와 동사 또는 분사 (B)는 주어 자리에 올 수 없습니다.

21 형용사 어휘 고르기 주변 문맥 파악
해설 '두 개의 _____한 노선을 연장할 것이다'라는 문맥이므로 (A)와 (C)가 정답의 후보입니다. 이 경우 빈칸이 있는 문장만으로 정답을 고를 수 없으므로 주변 문맥이나 전체 문맥을 파악하여 정답을 고릅니다. 앞부분에서 오래된 노선들의 일부를 변경할 것이라고 했으므로 원래 있던 노선들을 연장할 것임을 알 수 있습니다. 따라서 형용사 (C) existing (기존의, 현재의)이 정답입니다. (A) tentative는 '임시의, 잠정적인', (B) inaccessible은 '입장이 허락되지 않는, 접근할 수 없는', (D) inoperative는 '이용할 수 없는, 작동하지 않는'이라는 의미입니다.

22 사람명사 추상명사 구별하여 채우기
해설 주격 관계절(that ~ construction)의 선행사 자리에 오면서 빈칸 앞의 street(도로, 길)과 복합 명사를 만드는 명사 (A)와 (C)가 정답의 후보입니다. '도로 폐쇄에 대해서는 사전 공지가 게시될 것이다'라는 의미가 되어야 하므로 추상명사 (A) closures(폐쇄, 종료)가 정답입니다. 사람 또는 사물명사 (C) closers(닫는 사람, 것)를 쓰면 '길 닫는 사람/것'이라는 어색한 문맥이 됩니다. 동사 (B)와 (D)는 주격 관계절의 선행사 자리에 오거나 복합 명사를 만들 수 없습니다.

DAY 07 형용사와 부사

Course 1 형용사

토익 실전 Check-up
p.227

토익 포인트 1 ⓑ   토익 포인트 2 ⓑ
토익 포인트 3 ⓐ   토익 포인트 4 ⓐ

1 형용사 자리 채우기
해설 괄호 뒤의 명사(snowstorm)를 꾸미기 위해서는 형용사가 와야 하므

로 형용사 ⓑ heavy(심한, 무거운)가 정답입니다. 명사 ⓐ heaviness는 명사를 꾸밀 수 없습니다.

해석 학교와 관공서들은 심한 눈보라로 인해 문을 닫았다.

어휘 government office phr. 관공서, 관청 snowstorm n. 눈보라

2 명사에 맞는 수량 표현 채우기
해설 단수 명사(day) 앞에 괄호가 있으므로 단수 명사 앞에 올 수 있는 수량 형용사 ⓑ every(매, 모든)가 정답입니다. ⓐ many(많은)는 복수 명사 앞에 옵니다.

해석 Mr. Conrad는 매일 출근하기 위해 지하철을 타야 해서, 연간 승차권을 샀다.

3 문맥에 어울리는 형용사 채우기
해설 'Tia's Café에 대한 호의적인 후기를 썼다'라는 의미가 되어야 하므로 형용사 ⓐ favorable(호의적인, 유리한)이 정답입니다. 형용사 ⓑ favorite은 '가장 좋아하는'이라는 의미로, 'Tia's Café에 대한 가장 좋아하는 후기를 썼다'라는 어색한 문맥을 만듭니다.

해석 비평가들은 Tia's Café에 대한 호의적인 후기를 썼다.

어휘 critic n. 비평가, 평론가

4 형용사 관용 표현 채우기
해설 '기꺼이 할인을 제공한다'라는 의미가 되어야 하므로 빈칸 앞의 are, 빈칸 뒤의 to와 함께 형용사 관용 표현 be willing to(기꺼이 ~할 의향이 있다)를 만드는 형용사 ⓐ willing이 정답입니다. 조동사, 명사, 동사 ⓑ will은 be willing to 표현을 완성할 수 없습니다.

해석 많은 회사들은 대량 구매에 대해 기꺼이 할인을 제공할 의향이 있다.

어휘 bulk adj. 대량의; n. 대량 purchase n. 구매, 구입

HACKERS PRACTICE
p.229

01 ⓐ [토익 포인트 1]   **02** ⓑ [토익 포인트 1]
03 ⓐ [Day06, Course 1, 토익 포인트 1] **04** ⓑ [토익 포인트 2]
05 ⓑ [토익 포인트 3]   **06** ⓐ [토익 포인트 3]
07 ⓐ [토익 포인트 2]   **08** ⓑ [토익 포인트 4]
09 thoroughly → thorough [토익 포인트 1]
10 few → little [토익 포인트 2]
11 economic → economical [토익 포인트 3]
12 hesitantly → hesitant [토익 포인트 1]
13 manageable → managerial [토익 포인트 3]
14 ask → to ask [Day05, Course 1, 토익 포인트 1]
15 providing → provide [Day03, Course 1, 토익 포인트 1]
16 will → willing [토익 포인트 4]

해석 **01** 관리자는 Ms. Kovac의 연례 성과 평가에서 그녀가 성실하다고 했다.

02 Colton 박물관의 방문객들은 현대 미술의 매력적인 수집품들을 볼 수 있다.

03 그 농구 선수는 지난 경기 동안의 실수에 대해 거센 비난을 받았다.

04 많은 고객들이 그 회사의 서비스에 대해 불평한다.

05 Mr. Brown은 이해심 있는 사람이므로, 그는 당신을 용서할 것입니다.

06 이미지에 대한 모든 권리는 각각의 소유주들에게 있다.

07 대회의 수상자는 매주 선정된다.

08 여권이 있는 사람들만이 해외의 임무를 맡을 자격이 있을 것이다.

09 Ms. Jones는 개발 정책에서의 최근의 변경 사항에 대한 꼼꼼한 설명을 제공했다.

10 프린터 카트리지에 잉크가 거의 남아 있지 않아서, 사무원은 다른 것을 가져왔다.

11 그 빌딩의 자재는 경제적일 뿐만 아니라 내구성도 있다.

12 Mr. Chang은 불황이 끝날 때까지 더 이상의 직원을 고용하는 것을 내키지 않아 한다.

13 Buzz사는 몇몇의 새로운 관리직에 대해 최근에 광고를 시작했다.

14 그 교수는 그의 강의 동안 학생들에게 관련된 질문을 하라고 격려한다.

15 그들의 소매 전략은 회사가 경쟁업체들보다 유리한 점을 갖게 해줄 수 있다.

16 그 이사는 회계팀의 예산 수정을 기꺼이 승인할 의향이 있다.

Course 2 부사

토익 실전 Check-up
p.231

토익 포인트 1 ⓐ	토익 포인트 2 ⓑ
토익 포인트 3 ⓑ	토익 포인트 4 ⓐ

1 부사 자리 채우기

해설 동사(be maintained)를 꾸미기 위해서는 부사가 와야 하므로 부사 ⓐ regularly(정기적으로, 규칙적으로)가 정답입니다. 형용사 ⓑ regular는 동사를 꾸밀 수 없습니다.

해석 그 복사기는 정기적으로 정비되어야 한다.

어휘 photocopier n. 복사기 maintain v. 정비하다, 유지하다

2 빈도 부사 채우기

해설 '거의 해외로 출장을 가지 않는다'라는 의미가 되어야 하므로, 괄호 앞의 빈도 부사 hardly(거의 ~않다)의 의미를 강조해주는 ⓑ ever가 정답입니다. 부정어 ⓐ never(결코 ~않다)는 hardly가 그 자체로 부정의 의미를 담고 있기 때문에 함께 쓰일 수 없습니다.

해석 Mr. Keith는 거의 해외로 출장을 가지 않는다.

어휘 overseas adv. 해외로; adj. 해외의

3 접속부사 채우기

해설 '전국에 다수의 호텔을 소유하고 있다. 더욱이, 여러 쇼핑몰들을 관리한다'라는 의미로, 괄호에 들어갈 단어가 문장(EM Development owns a number of hotels around the country.)과 문장(it manages multiple shopping centers.)을 연결하고 있으므로, 접속부사 ⓑ Moreover(더욱이)가 정답입니다. 접속부사 ⓐ Therefore는 '그러므로'라는 의미입니다.

해석 EM Development사는 전국에 다수의 호텔을 소유하고 있다. 더욱이, 여러 쇼핑몰들을 관리한다.

어휘 own v. 소유하다 a number of phr. 다수의
around the country phr. 전국에 manage v. 관리하다
multiple adj. 여러, 많은

4 의미에 맞는 부사 채우기

해설 '주민들은 대체로 이민자들이다'라는 의미가 되어야 하므로 부사 ⓐ mostly(대체로, 주로)가 정답입니다. 부사 ⓑ most는 '가장, 매우'라는 의미로 '가장 이민자들이다'라는 어색한 문맥을 만듭니다.

해석 이 동네의 주민들은 대체로 이민자들이다.

어휘 resident n. 주민 immigrant n. 이민자

HACKERS PRACTICE
p.233

01 ⓐ [토익 포인트 3]	02 ⓐ [토익 포인트 2]
03 ⓑ [토익 포인트 1]	04 ⓐ [토익 포인트 4]

05 ⓑ [Day06, Course 1, 토익 포인트 1]	06 ⓑ [토익 포인트 2]
07 ⓐ [Day06, Course 2, 토익 포인트 1]	08 ⓑ [토익 포인트 2]

09 mostly → most [토익 포인트 4]

10 submitting → to submit [Day05, Course 1, 토익 포인트 2]

11 increasing → increasingly [토익 포인트 1]

12 strong → strongly [토익 포인트 1]

13 high → highly [토익 포인트 4]

14 he → his [Day06, Course 2, 토익 포인트 1]

15 generous → generously [토익 포인트 1]

16 patience → patiently [토익 포인트 1]

해석 01 저희의 이번 주 영업 시간은 오후 10시까지 연장되었으며, 더욱이, 저희는 휴일에도 문을 열 것입니다.

02 증가하는 실업은 지난해부터 뉴스에서 종종 언급되어왔다.

03 그 쇼핑몰은 좀 더 현대적이고 안락해 보이도록 완전히 재건되었다.

04 Ms. Rogers는 그녀의 업무를 완료하기 위해 오늘 밤 회사에 늦게까지 남기로 동의했다.

05 양로원의 직원들은 의료적 요구가 있는 주민들을 돕는다.

06 Ms. Cole은 늦고 싶지 않아서 오전 8시 이후에 출근하는 경우가 거의 없다.

07 대부분의 홍보부 직원들은 2층에 책상이 있지만, 당신의 책상은 3층에 있을 것입니다.

08 관광객들은 보통 역사적으로 의미 있는 장소들을 방문한다.

09 충분하지 않은 의사소통은 사무실 환경에서 가장 문제 있는 사안이다.

10 지원자들은 그들의 이력서와 함께 집필 샘플을 제출할 필요가 있다.

11 보먼 시는 최근 몇 년간 관광객들의 인기를 점점 더 얻어왔다.

12 독자는 그 잡지에 매우 단호하게 작성된 항의 편지를 보냈다.

13 Mr. Fournier는 다음 몇 주 내에 관리 직책에 승진될 가능성이 매우 높다.

14 Keller Books사의 누군가가 Mr. Yates에게 그의 주문이 지연되었다는 것을 알리기 위해 전화했다.

15 Tricourt 협회는 그 병원에 거액의 보조금을 아주 후하게 제공했다.

16 Mr. Gordon은 뉴욕행 기차가 도착하기를 참을성 있게 기다리면서 신문을 읽었다.

HACKERS TEST
p.234

PART 5				
01 (C)	02 (A)	03 (B)	04 (B)	05 (B)
06 (D)	07 (A)	08 (D)	09 (D)	10 (B)
11 (C)	12 (C)	13 (A)	14 (A)	15 (A)
16 (C)	17 (B)	18 (B)		

PART 6			
19 (B)	20 (C)	21 (C)	22 (A)

01 보어 자리 채우기

해설 be동사(are) 다음의 보어 자리에 올 수 있는 -ing형 (A), 명사 (B), 형용사 (C)가 정답의 후보입니다. '많은 주민들이 제안에 반대한다'라는 의미로, 빈칸의 보어가 주어(A number of residents)를 설명해주고 있으므로 형용사 (C) opposed(반대하는, 대립된)가 정답입니다. (A)를 쓰면 '많은 주민들이 반대하고 있다'라는 자연스러운 문맥을 만드는 것 같지만, 동사 oppose(반대하다)는 타동사이므로 빈칸 뒤에 전

치사(to) 없이 바로 목적어가 와야 합니다. 명사 (B)는 주어와 동격 관계가 되어 '많은 주민들이 반대이다'라는 어색한 문맥을 만듭니다. 부사 (D)는 보어 자리에 올 수 없습니다.

해석 많은 주민들은 그 지역에 새로운 아파트를 짓자는 시의 제안에 반대한다.

어휘 resident n. 주민, 거주자 condominium n. 아파트, 콘도
community n. 지역, 지역 사회

02 부사 자리 채우기

해설 동사(was ~ handled)를 꾸미기 위해서는 부사가 와야 하므로 부사 (A) effectively(효율적으로, 실질적으로)가 정답입니다. 형용사 (B)와 (C), 명사 또는 동사 (D)는 동사를 꾸밀 수 없습니다.

해석 새로운 하드웨어 시스템으로의 전환은 정보 기술 부서의 모두에 의해 효율적으로 처리되었다.

어휘 transition n. 전환, 변화 handle v. 처리하다, 다루다
information technology phr. 정보 기술, 정보 통신 기술
effectual adj. 효과적인, 유효한 effective adj. 효과적인, 실질적인
effect n. 영향, 결과; v. (변화를) 초래하다

03 명사 자리 채우기

해설 전치사(of)의 목적어 자리에 올 수 있는 명사 (B) expectations(기대, 예상)가 정답입니다. 부사 (A), 형용사 (C)와 (D)는 목적어 자리에 올 수 없습니다.

해석 주최자들에게 실망스럽게도, 애틀랜타 자동차 박람회의 참석률이 기대에 못 미쳤다.

어휘 disappointment n. 실망, 낙심 organizer n. 주최자, 창시자
attendance n. 참석률, 참석자 수 fall short of phr. 못 미치다
expectant adj. 기대하고 있는 expectable adj. 예상할 수 있는

04 보어 자리 채우기

해설 be동사(is) 다음의 보어 자리에 올 수 있는 형용사 (B)와 명사 (C)가 정답의 후보입니다. '렌터카를 위해 보험을 구매하는 것이 필수적이지는 않다'라는 의미로, 보어가 진짜 주어(to purchase ~ vehicle)를 설명하고 있으므로 형용사 (B) necessary(필수적인)가 정답입니다. 명사 (C) necessity(필요)를 쓰면 주어와 동격이 되어 '렌터카를 위해 보험을 구매하는 것은 필요가 아니다'라는 어색한 문맥이 됩니다. 동사 (A)와 부사 (D)는 보어 자리에 올 수 없습니다. 참고로, 이 문장은 가짜 주어 it이 길이가 긴 진짜 주어를 대신하여 사용되었음을 알아둡니다.

해석 렌터카를 위해 보험을 구매하는 것이 필수적이지는 않지만, 그것은 강력히 권장된다.

어휘 purchase v. 구매하다 insurance n. 보험 recommend v. 권장하다

05 문맥에 어울리는 형용사 채우기

해설 be동사(be)의 보어 자리에 오면서 부사(very)의 수식을 받을 수 있는 형용사 (A)와 (B)가 정답의 후보입니다. '고급 자격을 갖춘 직원들을 고용하는 것은 회사에 매우 이득이 될 수 있다'라는 의미가 되어야 하므로 형용사 (B) profitable(이득이 되는, 수익성이 있는)이 정답입니다. (A) proficient(능숙한)를 쓰면 '고급 자격을 갖춘 직원들을 고용하는 것은 회사에 매우 능숙하다'라는 어색한 문맥을 만듭니다. 명사 (C)는 부사의 수식을 받을 수 없습니다. 부사 (D)는 부사의 수식을 받을 수 있지만 보어 자리에 올 수 없습니다.

해석 고급 자격을 갖춘 직원들을 고용하는 것은 장기적으로 봤을 때 회사에 매우 이득이 될 수 있다.

어휘 hire v. 고용하다 qualified adj. 자격을 갖춘
in the long run phr. 장기적으로 봤을 때, 결국

06 현재분사와 과거분사 구별하여 채우기

해설 빈칸 앞의 명사(branches)를 꾸밀 수 있는 분사 (A)와 (D)가 정답의

후보입니다. 분사의 꾸밈을 받는 명사 branches(지점, 지사)와 분사가 '지점이 위치해 있다'라는 의미의 수동 관계이므로 과거분사 (D) located가 정답입니다. 현재분사 (A)는 능동의 의미를 나타내므로 답이 될 수 없습니다. 동사 (B)와 (C)는 명사를 꾸밀 수 없습니다.

해석 주요 지점이 뉴욕과 샌프란시스코에 위치해 있기 때문에, Kinsi Tech 사는 전국 방방곡곡의 고객들에게 서비스를 제공한다.

어휘 branch n. 지점, 지사 from coast to coast phr. 전국 방방곡곡에
locate v. 위치시키다, ~의 위치를 찾아내다

07 태에 맞는 동사 채우기

해설 보기에 사용된 동사 divide(나누다)가 타동사인데 빈칸 뒤에 목적어 (its marketing department)가 있으므로 능동태 (A) will divide가 정답입니다. 수동태 (B), (C), (D)는 목적어와 함께 쓰일 수 없습니다.

해석 효율성을 높이기 위해서, Hudson 백화점은 마케팅 부서를 두 개의 분리된 부서로 나눌 것이다.

어휘 effectiveness n. 효율성, 효과성 separate adj. 분리된, 따로 떨어진

08 문맥에 어울리는 형용사 채우기

해설 be동사(are) 다음의 보어 자리에 올 수 있는 형용사 (A), (B), (D)가 정답의 후보입니다. '기상 조건이 좋지 않은 한'이라는 의미가 되어야 하므로 형용사 (D) favorable(좋은, 호의적인)이 정답입니다. 형용사 (A) favorite(마음에 드는, 매우 좋아하는)과 (B) favoring(유리한, 형편에 맞는)은 '기상 조건이 마음에 들지/유리하지 않은 한'이라는 어색한 문맥을 만듭니다. 부사 (C)는 be동사 다음의 보어 자리에 올 수 없습니다.

해석 기술자들은 기상 조건이 좋지 않은 한, 위성을 발사하는 것은 좋은 생각이 아니라고 경고한다.

어휘 warn v. 경고하다, 주의를 주다 launch v. 발사하다, 개시하다
satellite n. (인공) 위성, 위성 장치

09 한정사에 맞는 명사 채우기

해설 타동사(include)의 목적어 자리에 올 수 있는 것은 명사나 동명사이므로 동명사 (A), 명사 (B)와 (D)가 정답의 후보입니다. 빈칸 앞에 복수 명사 앞에 오는 수량 형용사 several(몇 개의)이 있으므로, 복수 명사 (D) facilities가 정답입니다. 동명사 (A)는 형용사의 수식을 받을 수 없습니다. 단수 명사 (B)는 several과 함께 쓰일 수 없습니다. 동사 또는 분사 (C)는 목적어 자리에 올 수 없습니다.

해석 새로운 기숙사는 학생들이 즐길 수 있는 몇 개의 오락 시설을 포함할 것이다.

어휘 dormitory n. 기숙사 recreational adj. 오락의, 휴양의

10 형용사 자리 채우기

해설 빈칸 뒤의 명사(goods)를 꾸미기 위해서는 형용사가 와야 하므로 형용사 (B) commercial(상업의, 영리적인)이 정답입니다. 명사 (A)와 (C), 동사 (D)는 명사를 꾸밀 수 없습니다.

해석 외국으로부터 상업 제품을 들여올 때 연방 정부의 규정을 따르는 것은 필수적이다.

어휘 comply with phr. ~을 따르다, ~을 지키다
federal adj. 연방 정부의, 연방제의 regulation n. 규정, 규제
import v. 들여오다, 수입하다; n. 수입, 수입품
foreign adj. 외국의, 대외적인

11 빈도 부사 채우기

해설 '주문품을 결코 받지 못했기 때문에 고객 서비스 센터에 전화했다'라는 의미가 되어야 하므로 빈도 부사 (C) never(결코 ~ 않다)가 정답입니다. (A) once는 '한 번'이라는 의미의 빈도 부사이고, '이전에'라는 의미로 시간을 나타낼 수도 있습니다. (B) ever는 '이전에', (D) after는 '그 후에, 나중에'라는 의미로 시간을 나타냅니다. 참고로, never/

hardly/rarely/seldom/barely(거의 ~ 않다) 등은 이미 부정의 뜻을 갖고 있기 때문에 not과 같은 또 다른 부정어와 함께 올 수 없음을 알아둡니다.

해석 Mr. Scranton은 그의 주문품을 결코 받지 못했기 때문에, 환불을 요청하기 위해 고객 서비스 센터에 전화했다.

어휘 refund n. 환불, 환불금

12 형용사 자리 채우기
해설 빈칸 뒤의 명사구(anti-aging products)를 꾸미기 위해서는 형용사가 와야 하므로 형용사 (C) affordable(가격이 적당한)이 정답입니다. 명사 (A), 부사 (B), 동사 (D)는 형용사 자리에 올 수 없습니다.

해석 ClearSkin사는 가격이 적당한 매우 다양한 노화 방지 제품을 제공한다.

어휘 offer v. 제공하다 a variety of phr. 다양한, 여러 가지의
anti-aging adj. 노화 방지의 product n. 제품

13 부사 자리 채우기
해설 빈칸 뒤의 형용사(complete)를 꾸밀 수 있는 것은 부사이므로 부사 (A) partially(부분적으로, 불완전하게)가 정답입니다. 형용사 (B), 명사 (C)와 동사 또는 명사 (D)는 형용사를 꾸밀 수 없습니다.

해석 Harley로에 건설되고 있는 새로운 콘서트장은 아직 부분적으로만 완성되었다.

어휘 complete adj. 완성된, 완전한 partiality n. 부분적임, 편파적임
part v. 갈라놓다; n. 부분, 부품

14 부정형용사 채우기
해설 빈칸 뒤의 명사(site)가 단수 가산 명사이고, '각각의 장소를 개별적으로 방문할 것이다'라는 의미가 되어야 하므로 부정형용사 (A) each(각각의)가 정답입니다. (B) much는 불가산 명사 앞에 오며, (C) many(많은)와 (D) a few(몇몇의)는 복수 명사 앞에 옵니다.

해석 도시 계획자는 관련된 모든 건축 법규가 지켜졌는지 확인하기 위해 각각의 장소를 개별적으로 방문할 것이다.

어휘 city planner phr. 도시 계획자

15 형용사 관용 표현 채우기
해설 be동사(is) 다음에 올 수 있는 형용사 (A), -ing형 (C), p.p.형 (D)가 정답의 후보입니다. '그는 또 다른 일 년을 계약할 것 같다'라는 문맥이고 빈칸 앞의 be동사(is), 빈칸 뒤의 to와 함께 '~할 것 같다'라는 의미의 형용사 관용 표현 be likely to를 만드는 형용사 (A) likely(~할 것 같은, 그럴듯한)가 정답입니다. -ing형 (C)와 p.p.형 (D)는 각각 진행형(be동사 + -ing)과 수동형(be동사 + p.p.)을 만드는데, 각각 '그는 계약하는 것을 좋아하는 중이다', '그는 계약하기 위해 좋아지고 있다'라는 어색한 문맥을 만듭니다. 동사 (B)는 be동사 다음에 올 수 없고, (B)가 '~과 같은'이라는 의미의 전치사로 쓰인다고 해도 '그는 계약하는 것과 같다'라는 어색한 문맥을 만듭니다.

해석 Mr. Park은 더 많은 복지 혜택이 있는 계약을 제안받았기 때문에, 그는 또 다른 일 년을 계약할 것 같다.

어휘 sign on phr. (서명하고) 계약하다

16 가정법 동사 채우기
해설 if절(If ~ change)에 주어(Mr. Andrews)만 있고 동사가 없으므로 동사 (A), (C), (D)가 정답의 후보입니다. if절 다음의 절(he ~ meeting)이 '주어(he) + would have p.p.(would ~ have missed)'의 형태이고, '일정 변경에 대해 통지를 받았더라면 이사회 회의에 불참하지 않았을 것이다'라는 의미로 과거 사실의 반대를 가정하고 있으므로 가정법 과거완료 문장임을 알 수 있습니다. 따라서 if절은 'If + 주어 + had p.p.'의 형태가 되어야 하므로 (C) had been notified가 정답입니다. 현재 시제 (A)와 'be + p.p.' 형태의 동사 (D)는 가정법 과거완료의 동사로 쓰일 수 없습니다. 명사 (B)는 동사 자리에 올 수 없습

니다.

해석 만약 Mr. Andrews가 일정 변경에 대해 통지를 받았었다면, 그는 이사회 회의에 불참하지 않았을 것이다.

어휘 miss v. 불참하다, 놓치다 notify v. 통지하다, 알리다

17 부정형용사 채우기
해설 빈칸 뒤의 명사(employees)가 복수이고 '몇몇 직원들을 식당으로 태워줄 수 있고, 나머지는 택시로 이동할 수 있다'라는 의미가 되어야 하므로 부정형용사 (B) some(몇몇의, 약간의)이 정답입니다. (A) all은 '모든'이라는 의미로 '모든 직원을 식당으로 태워줄 수 있고 나머지는 택시로 이동할 수 있다'라는 어색한 문맥을 만듭니다. (C) much(많은)와 (D) little(적은)은 불가산 명사 앞에 옵니다.

해석 Ms. Richards는 그녀의 미니밴으로 몇몇 직원들을 식당으로 태워줄 수 있고, 나머지는 택시로 이동할 수 있다고 말한다.

어휘 rest n. 나머지, 휴식

18 접속부사 채우기
해설 빈칸에 들어갈 단어는 절(Mr. Chen ~ employee)과 절(was ~ raise)을 의미적으로 연결하고 있고, '다른 어떤 직원보다 더 많이 판매해서 그 결과, 승진을 했다'라는 의미가 되어야 하므로 접속부사 (B) consequently(그 결과, 따라서)가 정답입니다. (A) however는 '그러나', (C) meanwhile은 '그동안', (D) otherwise는 '그렇지 않으면'이라는 의미입니다. 참고로, 두 번째 절(was ~ raise)의 주어는 첫 번째 절(Mr. Chen ~ employee)의 주어(Mr. Chen)와 같기 때문에 생략되고 동사(was promoted)만 남았음을 알아둡니다.

해석 Mr. Chen은 다른 어떤 직원보다 더 많이 판매해서 그 결과, 승진을 하고 임금 인상이 주어졌다.

어휘 promote v. 승진하다, 홍보하다 award v. 주다, 수여하다

19-22번은 다음 광고에 관한 문제입니다.

> Martello's 빵은 이제 당신이 있는 지역의 Price-Time 식료품점에서 살 수 있습니다! [19]다음번 방문 시에 흰 밀가루로 만든 빵, 통밀빵, 이탈리아 스타일의 빵을 확인해 보세요. 이 유명한 제과점은 최고급이고 건강에 가장 좋은 재료들을 사용하고 제품에 비타민과 미네랄을 첨가합니다. [20]그러므로, Martello's 제품들은 구매 가능한 것들 중에서 가장 영양가가 높습니다.
>
> [21]Martello's는 또한 매일 신선하게 구워지는 다양한 쿠키, 케이크, 파이를 제공합니다. 그리고 저희는 여러분의 가족이 저희의 최신 토르티야, 스위트롤, 그리고 번 또한 드셔보시는 것을 환영합니다. [22]그것들은 어떠한 식사에도 완벽한 보완이 됩니다. 가장 가까운 Price-Time 식료품점을 방문하셔서 오늘 Martello's 제품을 구입하세요.
>
> wholesome adj. 건강에 좋은, 유익한 ingredient n. 재료, 성분
> fortify v. 첨가하다, 강화하다 complement n. 보완(물), 보충(물)
> stock up on phr. 구입하다, 비축하다

19 알맞은 문장 고르기
해석 (A) 그 상점은 다음 달 말에 영업을 시작할 것입니다.
(B) 다음번 방문 시에 흰 밀가루로 만든 빵, 통밀빵, 이탈리아 스타일의 빵을 확인해 보세요.
(C) 여러분이 가장 좋아하는 모든 빵 제품에 대한 쉬운 조리법을 찾으실 것입니다.
(D) 이 시간 중에 방문하셔서 제품에 대한 특별 할인을 받으세요.

해설 빈칸에 들어갈 알맞은 문장을 고르는 문제이므로 주변 문맥이나 전체 문맥을 파악합니다. 앞 문장 'Martello's bread is now available at your local Price-Time Food Market!'에서 Martello's 빵은 이제 당신이 있는 지역의 Price-Time 식료품점에서 살 수 있다고 했으므로 빈칸에는 다음에 Price-Time 식료품점에 가면 Martello's의 제품을 찾

아보라는 내용이 들어가야 함을 알 수 있습니다. 따라서 (B) Check out white, wheat, and Italian-style breads on your next visit이 정답입니다.

어휘 white bread phr. 흰 밀가루로 만든 빵, 흰빵 wheat bread phr. 통밀빵
offer n. 할인, 제공 가격

20 접속부사 채우기 주변 문맥 파악

해설 빈칸에 들어갈 단어가 앞 문장(The famous bakery ~ vitamins and minerals.)과 빈칸이 있는 문장(Martello's products are ~ available)을 의미적으로 연결하고 있고, '최고급이고 건강에 가장 좋은 재료들을 사용하고 제품에 비타민과 미네랄을 첨가하므로, Martello's 제품들은 구매 가능한 것들 중에서 가장 영양가가 높다'라는 의미가 되어야 하므로 접속부사 (C) Therefore(그러므로)가 정답입니다. 접속부사 (A) Nonetheless는 '그럼에도 불구하고', (B) Subsequently는 '그 후에, 이어서', (D) However는 '그러나'라는 의미입니다.

21 명사 관련 어구 완성하기

해설 '다양한 쿠키, 케이크, 파이를 제공하다'라는 문맥이므로 '다양한'이라는 의미의 어구 an assortment of를 만드는 명사 (C) assortment (모음, 종합)가 정답입니다. (A) enhancement는 '향상, 상승', (B) accumulation은 '축적, 누적', (D) organization은 '조직, 준비'라는 의미입니다.

22 형용사 자리 채우기

해설 빈칸 뒤의 명사(complement)를 꾸미기 위해서는 형용사가 와야 하므로 형용사 (A) perfect(완벽한, 완전한)가 정답입니다. 명사 (B), 부사 (C), 동사 (D)는 명사를 꾸밀 수 없습니다.

DAY 08 전치사

Course 1 시간·시점·위치·방향 전치사

토익 실전 Check-up p.237

토익 포인트 1 ⓑ	토익 포인트 2 ⓑ
토익 포인트 3 ⓐ	토익 포인트 4 ⓐ

1 전치사 채우기: 장소

해설 '교육은 5층에서 실시된다'라는 의미가 되어야 하므로 표면 위나 일직선 상의 지점을 나타내는 전치사 ⓑ on(~에서)이 정답입니다. ⓐ in은 큰 공간 내의 장소를 나타냅니다.

해석 교육은 5층에서 실시된다.

어휘 training n. 교육, 훈련 conduct v. 실시하다

2 전치사 채우기: 기간

해설 '3년 이내에 이사하다'라는 의미가 되어야 하므로 기간을 나타내는 전치사 ⓑ within(~ 이내에)이 정답입니다. ⓐ from은 '~부터, ~에서'라는 의미로 시점이나 방향을 나타냅니다.

해석 Mr. Logan은 3년 이내에 프랑스로 이사할 것이다.

3 전치사 채우기: 위치

해설 '본관 뒤에 있다'라는 의미가 되어야 하므로 위치를 나타내는 전치사 ⓐ behind(~ 뒤에)가 정답입니다. ⓑ before는 '~ 전에'라는 의미로 시점을 나타냅니다.

해석 창고는 본관 뒤에 있다.

어휘 warehouse n. 창고

4 전치사 채우기: 방향

해설 '뮌헨 지사에서 전근 오는 직원'이라는 의미가 되어야 하므로 방향을 나타내는 전치사 ⓐ from(~에서, ~로부터)이 정답입니다. ⓑ along은 '~을 따라서'라는 의미입니다.

해석 뮌헨 지사에서 전근 오는 직원은 내일 도착할 것이다.

어휘 transfer v. 전근하다, 옮기다

HACKERS PRACTICE p.239

01 ⓑ [토익 포인트 3]	**02** ⓑ [토익 포인트 2]
03 ⓐ [토익 포인트 2]	**04** ⓑ [토익 포인트 4]
05 ⓐ [토익 포인트 1]	**06** ⓑ [Day07, Course 1, 토익 포인트 2]
07 ⓑ [토익 포인트 3]	**08** ⓑ [토익 포인트 4]

09 at → for [토익 포인트 2]
10 convince → convincing [Day07, Course 1, 토익 포인트 1]
11 in → to [토익 포인트 4]
12 mine → mines [Day06, Course 1, 토익 포인트 2]
13 before → after [토익 포인트 2]
14 since → from [토익 포인트 2]
15 on → at [토익 포인트 1]
16 proposing → proposed [Day05, Course 2, 토익 포인트 4]

해석 **01** 저장 공간에 있는 상자들은 습기가 있는 바닥보다 위쪽에 보관되어야 한다.
02 Humbert 대학의 많은 온라인 강좌가 1년 내내 제공된다.
03 연례 거리 축제는 6시간 동안 Bay가를 폐쇄할 것이다.
04 사무실 입구는 지하철역으로부터 길 건너편에 있다.
05 뮤지컬 공연 티켓은 온라인이나 매표소에서 구입될 수 있다.
06 지원자들은 양식의 모든 질문에 반드시 답해야만 한다.
07 Mr. Ross는 그의 가게의 정문 위에 지붕을 설치했다.
08 시는 23번 고속도로를 따라 이어지는 새로운 보행자 도로를 건설하고 있다.
09 Regina사는 다음 4일 동안 문을 닫을 것이다.
10 연구원들은 그 증거가 설득력 있다고 생각했다.
11 그 관리자는 얼마나 많은 직원들이 워크숍에 가는지 알기를 원한다.
12 지난 4년에 걸쳐 몇몇 석탄 광산들이 문을 닫았다.
13 지진 3년 후, 대부분의 건물이 다시 지어졌다.
14 그 텔레비전 광고는 5월 1일부터 5월 21일까지 몇몇 채널에서 방송될 것이다.
15 *Mind Games*의 저자가 Kendall 서점에서 책 사인회를 열 것이다.
16 GW Group사는 제안된 프로젝트에 자금을 대기 위해 개인 투자자들을 찾고 있다.

Course 2 기타 전치사 및 전치사 표현

토익 실전 Check-up p.241

토익 포인트 1 ⓐ	토익 포인트 2 ⓐ
토익 포인트 3 ⓐ	토익 포인트 4 ⓑ

1 전치사 채우기: 이유

해설 '휴일의 수요 급증 때문에 이용 가능한 방이 없다'라는 의미가 되어야 하므로 이유를 나타내는 전치사 ⓐ because of(~ 때문에)가 정답입니다. ⓑ without은 '~ 없이'라는 의미로 제외를 나타냅니다.

해석 유감스럽게도, 휴일의 수요 급증 때문에 이용 가능한 방이 없습니다.

어휘 **available** adj. 이용 가능한, 구할 수 있는 **rush** n. 수요 급증, 혼잡

2 전치사 채우기: 기타

해석 '그 지역 전역에 유적들이 있다'라는 의미가 되어야 하므로 전치사 ⓐ throughout(~ 전역에, 도처에)이 정답입니다. ⓑ as는 '~로서'라는 의미입니다.

해석 그 지역 전역에 많은 유명한 유적들이 있다.

어휘 **landmark** n. 유적, 명소 **region** n. 지역, 지방

3 두 단어 이상으로 이루어진 전치사 채우기

해설 '사무실을 책임진다'라는 의미가 되어야 하므로 괄호 앞의 in charge와 함께 '~을 책임지고 있는'이라는 의미의 in charge of를 만드는 전치사 ⓐ of가 정답입니다. ⓑ for는 '~를 향해, ~을 위해서'라는 의미로 방향이나 목적을 나타냅니다.

해석 Mr. Tate는 이사의 부재 시에 사무실을 책임진다.

어휘 **absence** n. 부재, 불참

4 '명사 + 전치사' 표현 채우기

해설 '예산 초과 문제에 대한 해결책'이라는 의미가 되어야 하므로 괄호 앞의 a solution과 함께 '~에 대한 해결책'이라는 의미의 a solution to를 만드는 전치사 ⓑ to가 정답입니다. ⓐ with는 '~과 함께'라는 의미입니다.

해석 위원회 회원들은 예산 초과 문제에 대한 해결책을 제안했다.

어휘 **council** n. 위원회, 협의회 **overspending** n. 예산 초과, 낭비

HACKERS PRACTICE p.243

01 ⓐ [토익 포인트 1] **02** ⓐ [토익 포인트 1]
03 ⓑ [토익 포인트 1] **04** ⓐ [Day07, Course 1, 토익 포인트 1]
05 ⓑ [토익 포인트 1] **06** ⓑ [Day07, Course 2, 토익 포인트 1]
07 ⓐ [토익 포인트 1] **08** ⓑ [토익 포인트 2]
09 in → to [토익 포인트 3]
10 throughout → except (for) [토익 포인트 1]
11 to → for [토익 포인트 4]
12 respond → response [Day06, Course 1, 토익 포인트 1]
13 to → for [토익 포인트 1]
14 from → of [토익 포인트 3]
15 promote → promoted [Day03, Course 1, 토익 포인트 2]
16 for → from [토익 포인트 4]

해석 **01** 급한 업무 때문에 소프트웨어 지도 시간이 연기되었다.

02 훌륭한 광고 캠페인 없이는, 새 운동화 라인은 판매가 부진할 것으로 예상된다.

03 고급 보안 시스템에도 불구하고, 컴퓨터는 여전히 침입에 취약할 수 있다.

04 직원들이 수업에 등록하는 방법에 대한 구체적인 안내서를 나눠줄 것이다.

05 대부분의 여행 웹사이트는 사람들이 호텔 객실뿐만 아니라 항공권을 예약할 수 있게 한다.

06 지속적으로 전문성 개발을 장려하는 것은 직원들의 기술을 향상시키는 데에 도움이 된다.

07 전화를 받는 것 외에, 접수원들은 파일을 관리할 책임이 있다.

08 당신은 45번 도로를 탐으로써 기차역에 빨리 도착할 수 있습니다.

09 한 비평가의 의견과 반대로, 대부분의 사람들은 그 연극이 흥미롭고 재미있다고 생각했다.

10 Lucy's Bar and Grill은 월요일을 제외하고 매일 연다.

11 직원들에게 마감일 전에 워크숍에 등록할 것이 다시 한번 상기되었다.

12 Dr. Hammerstein의 발표는 청중들로부터 열렬한 반응을 얻었다.

13 직원들은 업무와 관련된 비용에 대해서만 법인 신용카드를 사용할 수 있다.

14 Ms. Roberts는 오늘 밤 시상식에서 그녀의 팀을 대표하여 상을 받을 것이다.

15 Bexler사는 몇 가지의 제품군을 생산하지만, 각 브랜드는 개별적으로 홍보된다.

16 직원들이 3일 연속으로 결근할 경우, 증거 서류는 필수적이다.

HACKERS TEST p.244

PART 5

01 (C)	02 (D)	03 (B)	04 (B)	05 (D)
06 (C)	07 (D)	08 (A)	09 (D)	10 (A)
11 (B)	12 (C)	13 (C)	14 (A)	15 (C)
16 (A)	17 (B)	18 (D)		

PART 6

19 (B)	20 (C)	21 (B)	22 (A)

01 전치사 채우기: 시간

해설 '8월에 끝난다'라는 의미가 되어야 하므로 시간(월)을 나타내는 전치사 (C) in(~에)이 정답입니다. (A) of는 '~의'라는 의미입니다. (B) on(~에)과 (D) at(~에)도 시간을 나타내지만 on은 날짜나 요일, at은 시각이나 시점을 나타내는 표현 앞에 옵니다.

해석 Haddad 미술관의 수리는 8월에 끝날 것이다.

어휘 **renovation** n. 수리, 수선

02 '형용사 + 전치사' 표현 채우기

해설 '업무 실적은 그의 역량 수준과 일치하지 않아 왔다'라는 의미가 되어야 하므로 빈칸 앞의 형용사 consistent(일치하는)와 함께 '~과 일치하는'이라는 의미의 표현인 consistent with를 만드는 전치사 (D) with(~과 함께)가 정답입니다. (A) as는 '~로서', (B) through는 '~을 통해서', (C) under는 '~ 아래에'라는 의미로 모두 형용사 consistent와 함께 전치사 표현을 만들 수 없습니다.

해석 Mr. Wang의 업무 실적은 그의 역량 수준과 일치하지 않아 왔다.

어휘 **work performance** phr. 업무 실적 **skill level** phr. 역량 수준

03 두 단어 이상으로 이루어진 전치사 채우기

해설 '회사의 발표에 대응하여, Mr. Glass는 그의 이력서를 업데이트하기로 결정했다'라는 의미가 되어야 하므로 전치사 (B) In response to(~에 대응하여, ~에 답하여)가 정답입니다. (A) On behalf of는 '~을 대표하여', (C) As of는 '~부터, ~부로', (D) In exchange for는 '~의 대신으로'라는 의미입니다.

해석 조직을 개편할 것이라는 회사의 발표에 대응하여, Mr. Glass는 그의 이력서를 업데이트하기로 결정했다.

어휘 **announcement** n. 발표, 공고
restructure v. 조직을 개편하다, 구조를 조정하다 **résumé** n. 이력서

04 전치사 채우기: 시점

해설 '투자 회사인 Frazier Finance사에서 근무하기 전에 몇몇 은행의 고문으로 고용되어 있었다'라는 의미가 되어야 하므로 시점을 나타내는 전치사 (B) Prior to(~ 전에)가 정답입니다. (A) Along은 '~을 따라'라는 의미로 방향을, (C) Near는 '~ 근처에'라는 의미로 위치를, (D) Across from은 '~의 맞은편에'라는 의미로 위치를 나타냅니다.

해석 투자 회사인 Frazier Finance사에서 근무하기 전에, Jack Harper는

그 지역의 몇몇 은행의 고문으로 고용되어 있었다.

어휘 investment n. 투자, 투자액 employ v. 고용하다, 이용하다
advisor n. 고문, 조언자

05 형용사 관용 표현 채우기

해설 be동사(is) 다음의 보어 자리에 올 수 있는 동명사 또는 분사 (A), 명사 (B), 형용사 (D)가 정답의 후보입니다. '비디오 게임의 역사를 주제로 다룬 박물관 전시'라는 의미가 되어야 하므로 형용사 관용 표현 be devoted to(~을 주제로 다루다, ~에 헌신하다)를 만드는 형용사 (D) devoted(주제로 하는, 헌신하는)가 정답입니다. (A)는 동명사일 경우 동사 devote(헌신하다)가 타동사이기 때문에 목적어가 있어야 하고, 분사일 경우 '박물관 전시는 헌신하는 것이다'라는 어색한 문맥을 만듭니다. 명사 (B)는 선행사(A recently opened museum exhibition)와 동격 관계가 되어 '박물관 전시는 헌신이다'라는 어색한 문맥을 만듭니다. 부사 (C)는 보어 자리에 올 수 없습니다.

해석 비디오 게임의 역사를 주제로 다룬 최근 공개된 박물관 전시는 미디어의 많은 관심을 받아왔다.

어휘 exhibition n. 전시, 전시회 attention n. 관심, 주목

06 전치사 채우기: 부가

해설 이 문장은 주어(Alex)와 동사(came)를 갖춘 완전한 절이므로 _____ Ms. Garner는 수식어 거품으로 보아야 합니다. 이 수식어 거품은 동사가 없는 거품구이므로 거품구를 이끌 수 있는 전치사 (B), (C), (D)가 정답의 후보입니다. 'Ms. Garner 외에, Alex도 사무실에 왔다'라는 의미가 되어야 하므로 부가를 나타내는 전치사 (C) Besides(~ 외에)가 정답입니다. (B) Within은 '~ 내에'라는 의미로 기간이나 위치를, (D) Over는 '~ 동안, ~ 위에, ~에 관하여'라는 의미로 기간이나 위치 등을 나타냅니다. 부사 (A) Ahead(앞에, 앞으로)는 수식어 거품을 이끌 수 없고, ahead of(~ 앞에, ~보다 빨리)의 형태일 때 전치사로 쓰입니다.

해석 Ms. Garner 외에, Alex도 이번 주말에 사무실에 왔다.

어휘 weekend n. 주말

07 전치사 채우기: 제외

해설 '초반의 주가 10퍼센트 하락을 제외하면 확장은 성공적이었다'라는 의미가 되어야 하므로 제외를 나타내는 전치사 (D) Except for(~을 제외하고)가 정답입니다. (A) In charge of는 '~을 책임지고 있는'이라는 의미입니다. (B) Due to는 '~ 때문에'라는 의미로 이유를 나타내고, (C) In case of는 '~의 경우'라는 의미입니다.

해석 초반의 주가 10퍼센트 하락을 제외하면, 회사의 해외로의 확장은 전반적으로 성공적이었다.

어휘 initial adj. 초반의, 처음의 stock value phr. 주가
expansion n. 확장, 확대 overseas adv. 해외로, 국외로
overall adv. 전반적으로, 전부

08 전치사 채우기: 방향

해설 '물품들을 쓰레기통 안에 넣다'라는 의미가 되어야 하므로 전치사 (A) into(~ 안에, ~ 안으로)가 정답입니다. (B) in addition to는 '~에 더하여'라는 의미로 부가를 나타냅니다. (C) since는 '~ 이래로'라는 의미입니다. (D) in excess of는 '~을 초과하여'라는 의미입니다.

해석 재활용할 수 있는 물품들을 쓰레기통 안에 넣기 전에 그것들을 분류하는 것을 주민들에게 상기시키는 공고가 게시되었다.

어휘 remind v. 상기시키다 sort v. 분류하다, 구분하다
recyclable adj. 재활용할 수 있는 bin n. 쓰레기통

09 전치사 채우기: 이유

해설 '인적 네트워크 형성 행사의 참석 때문에 비즈니스 관계를 형성할 수 있었다'라는 의미가 되어야 하므로 이유를 나타내는 전치사 (D) due to (~ 때문에)가 정답입니다. (A) as a result(결과적으로)는 '행사 참석의 결과로 비즈니스 관계를 형성할 수 있었다'라는 자연스러운 문맥이 되

려면 as a result of의 형태가 되어야 합니다. (B) as well as는 '~뿐만 아니라', (C) regarding은 '~에 관하여'라는 의미입니다.

해석 Mr. Blanchard는 인적 네트워크 형성 행사의 참석 때문에 몇몇의 장래성 있는 비즈니스 관계를 형성할 수 있었다.

어휘 promising adj. 장래성 있는, 유망한 attendance n. 참석, 출석
networking n. 인적 네트워크 형성

10 명사 자리 채우기

해설 빈칸 앞의 형용사(printed)의 꾸밈을 받을 수 있는 것은 명사이므로 명사 (A) guides가 정답입니다. 과거분사 (B)와 동사 (C), to 부정사 (D)는 형용사의 꾸밈을 받을 수 없습니다.

해석 새로운 교육생들은 오리엔테이션의 일부로 적절한 직장 내 행동에 대해 인쇄된 지침 사항들을 제공받았다.

어휘 trainee n. 교육생, 수습 직원 proper adj. 적절한, 알맞은
conduct n. 행동, 행위; v. 하다, 행동하다

11 전치사 채우기: 목적

해설 '사무실 컴퓨터들을 위한 소프트웨어'라는 의미가 되어야 하므로 목적을 나타내는 전치사 (B) for(~을 위한)가 정답입니다. (A) outside는 '~ 밖에'라는 의미로 위치를 나타냅니다. (C) because는 '~이기 때문에', (D) even though는 '~하더라도'라는 의미의 부사절 접속사입니다.

해석 사무실 컴퓨터들을 위한 소프트웨어는 오늘 저녁때까지 설치되어야 한다.

어휘 install v. 설치하다

12 수식어 거품을 이끄는 것 채우기

해설 이 문장은 주어(The ~ SongStar)와 동사(was canceled)를 갖춘 완전한 절이므로 _____ its popularity는 수식어 거품으로 보아야 합니다. 이 수식어 거품은 동사가 없는 거품구이므로 거품구를 이끌 수 있는 전치사 (C) despite(~에도 불구하고)가 정답입니다. 부사 또는 등위접속사 (A) yet(아직, 하지만)과 접속부사 (D) however(하지만)는 수식어 거품을 이끌 수 없습니다. 부사절 접속사 (B) although(~에도 불구하고)는 거품구가 아닌 거품절을 이끕니다.

해석 리얼리티 TV쇼 SongStar는 인기에도 불구하고 10개의 시즌 이후에 지난주에 취소되었다.

어휘 popularity n. 인기, 대중성

13 전치사 채우기: 위치

해설 '창문 위에 설치된 위성 안테나'라는 의미가 되어야 하므로 위치를 나타내는 전치사 (C) above(~ 위에)가 정답입니다. (A) without은 '~ 없이', (B) following은 '~에 이어', (D) about은 '~에 대해'라는 의미입니다.

해석 집의 2층 창문 위에 설치된 위성 안테나는 폭풍 중에 심하게 파손되었다.

어휘 satellite dish phr. 위성 안테나 second-story adj. 2층의
badly adv. 심하게, 대단히 damage v. 파손시키다, 손해를 입히다
storm n. 폭풍, 폭풍우

14 두 단어 이상으로 이루어진 전치사 채우기

해설 '예상과 반대로'라는 의미가 되어야 하므로 빈칸 앞의 형용사 contrary(반대되는)와 함께 '~과 반대로'라는 의미의 표현인 contrary to를 만드는 전치사 (A) to(~로, ~쪽으로)가 정답입니다. (B) among은 '~ 사이에', (C) against는 '~에 반대하여', (D) from은 '~에서, ~로부터'라는 의미입니다.

해석 임원의 예상과 반대로, 대부분의 직원들은 경력 개발 수업을 듣는 데 관심이 있었다.

어휘 professional development class phr. 경력 개발 수업
expectation n. 예상, 기대

15 전치사 채우기: 양보

해설 이 문장은 주어(the proposed cuts)와 동사(were approved)를 갖춘 완전한 절이므로 ____ the objections ~ members는 수식어 거품으로 보아야 합니다. 이 수식어 거품은 동사가 없는 거품구이므로 거품구를 이끌 수 있는 전치사 (A), (C), (D)가 정답의 후보입니다. '회원들의 반대에도 불구하고 예산 삭감이 승인되었다'라는 의미가 되어야 하므로 양보를 나타내는 전치사 (C) Notwithstanding(~에도 불구하고)이 정답입니다. (A) Near는 '~ 가까이'라는 의미로 위치를, (D) In addition to는 '~에 더하여'라는 의미로 부가를 나타냅니다. 형용사 또는 부사 (B) Regardless(개의치 않는, 그럼에도 불구하고)는 수식어 거품을 이끌 수 없고, regardless of(~에 상관없이)의 형태일 때 전치사로 쓰입니다.

해석 여러 주요 위원회 회원들의 반대에도 불구하고, 제안된 예산 삭감이 승인되었다.

어휘 objection n. 반대, 이의 committee n. 위원회, 협의회
cut n. 삭감 budget n. 예산, 비용 approve v. 승인하다, 찬성하다

16 전치사 채우기: 기간

해설 '전자기기는 이륙 및 착륙 동안에는 전원이 꺼져 있어야 한다'라는 의미가 되어야 하므로 기간을 나타내는 전치사 (A) during(~ 동안)이 정답입니다. (B) behind는 '~ 뒤에'라는 의미로 위치를 나타냅니다. (C) among은 '~ 사이에'라는 의미로 보통 셋 이상의 사람이나 사물 앞에 쓰여 다음에 복수 명사를 취합니다. (D) into는 '~ 안으로'라는 의미로 방향을 나타냅니다.

해석 휴대용 컴퓨터나 휴대전화 등 전자기기는 이륙 및 착륙 동안에는 전원이 꺼져 있어야 한다.

어휘 electronic adj. 전자의, 전기의 device n. 기기, 장치
turn off phr. (전원을) 끄다 takeoff n. 이륙 landing n. 착륙

17 명사에 맞는 수량 표현 채우기

해설 빈칸 뒤의 불가산 명사(experience)를 꾸밀 수 있는 수량 표현 (B) Some(얼마의, 몇몇의)이 정답입니다. (A) Each(각각의)는 단수 가산 명사 앞에, (D) Both(둘 다의)는 복수 명사 앞에 옵니다. (C) Either(어느 한쪽의)를 쓰면 '어느 한쪽의 경험'이라는 어색한 문맥을 만듭니다.

해석 서비스업에서의 얼마간의 경력은 그 자리에 지원하는 데에 필수적이다.

어휘 experience n. 경력, 경험 necessary adj. 필수의, 필연적인

18 전치사 채우기: 위치

해설 '사무직원들 무리 사이에서 쿠폰과 광고지를 나누어주었다'라는 의미가 되어야 하므로 위치를 나타내는 전치사 (D) amid(~ 사이에서, ~ 한복판에서)가 정답입니다. (A) until은 '~까지'라는 의미로 시점을, (B) throughout은 '~하는 내내'라는 의미로 기간을 나타내거나 '~ 전역에, 도처에'라는 의미를 나타내며, (C) below는 '~ 아래에'라는 의미로 위치를 나타냅니다.

해석 Mr. Felding은 점심 식사를 하러 가는 사무직원들 무리 사이에서 그의 사업체에 대한 쿠폰과 광고지를 나누어주었다.

어휘 hand out phr. ~을 나누어주다 flyer n. 광고지, 전단
crowd n. 무리, 군중

19-22번은 다음 안내문에 관한 문제입니다.

당신의 새로운 Schmidt-Carr 세탁기는 고성능 기기입니다. [19]최고의 효과를 보장하기 위해, 당신의 기기를 올바르게 사용하고 관리하는 것이 중요합니다. 고려해야 할 한 가지 중요한 점은 안전입니다. [20]그러므로, 모든 사용자들은 위험한 상황을 피하려면 몇 가지 기본적인 수칙들을 따라야 합니다. ⊕

[21]첫째로, 휘발유, 식용유, 또는 알코올로 얼룩진 것들을 절대 기기에 넣지 마십시오. 이것들을 세탁하는 행위는 유독한 증기를 발생시킬 수 있습니다. 게다가, 이것들은 가연성 물질이므로, 폭발이나 화재의 위험이 있습니다. [22]그러한 것들에는, 손빨래가 최선책입니다.

---

washing machine phr. 세탁기 high-performance adj. 고성능의
equipment n. 기기, 장비 care for phr. 관리하다, 돌보다
properly adv. 올바르게, 적절하게 avoid v. 피하다, 막다
hazardous adj. 위험한 stain v. 얼룩지게 하다, 더럽히다
gasoline n. 휘발유, 가솔린 cooking oil phr. 식용유
toxic adj. 유독한, 중독의 vapor n. 증기; v. 증발하다
flammable adj. 가연성의, 인화성의 substance n. 물질
explosion n. 폭발, 폭파

19 가짜 주어 자리 채우기

해설 동사 is 앞에 문장의 주어 자리가 비어 있습니다. 빈칸 뒤에 진짜 주어(to use and care for your machine properly)가 왔으므로 가짜 주어가 될 수 있는 (B) it이 정답입니다. 대명사 (A), (C), (D)는 가짜 주어 자리에 올 수 없습니다.

20 접속부사 채우기 주변 문맥 파악

해설 빈칸에 들어갈 단어가 앞 문장(One important aspect ~ safety.)과 빈칸이 있는 문장(all users ~ hazardous situations)을 의미적으로 연결하고 있고, '고려해야 할 한 가지 중요한 점은 안전이므로, 모든 사용자들은 몇 가지 기본적인 수칙들을 따라야 한다'라는 의미가 되어야 하므로 접속부사 (C) Accordingly(그러므로)가 정답입니다. 접속부사 (A) Instead는 '대신에', (B) Meanwhile은 '그동안', (D) Otherwise는 '그렇지 않으면'이라는 의미입니다.

21 전치사 채우기: 기타

해설 '휘발유, 식용유, 또는 알코올로 얼룩진 것들을 절대 넣지 말아라'라는 의미가 되어야 하므로 전치사 (B) with(~과 함께, ~을 가지고)가 정답입니다. (A) for는 '~ 동안, ~로 향해, ~을 위해서'라는 의미로 기간, 방향, 목적을, (C) below는 '~ 아래에'라는 의미로 위치를, (D) through는 '~을 통과하여'라는 의미로 방향을 나타냅니다.

22 알맞은 문장 고르기

해석 (A) 그러한 것들에는, 손빨래가 최선책입니다.
(B) 동작이 끝나자마자, 그것들은 즉시 꺼내져야 합니다.
(C) 이는 당신의 옷이 줄어들지 않게 보장할 것입니다.
(D) 그러므로, 당신은 섬유 유연제나 얼룩 제거제를 사용하기를 원할 수도 있습니다.

해설 빈칸에 들어갈 알맞은 문장을 고르는 문제이므로 주변 문맥이나 전체 문맥을 파악합니다. 앞부분 'never put items stained (with) gasoline, cooking oil, or alcohol in the machine. The action ~ can produce toxic vapors. In addition, ~ there is a risk of explosion or fire.'에서 휘발유, 식용유, 또는 알코올로 얼룩진 것들을 절대 기기에 넣지 말라면서 그 행위는 유독한 증기를 발생시킬 수 있고 폭발이나 화재의 위험이 있다고 했으므로 빈칸에는 휘발유, 식용유, 또는 알코올로 얼룩진 것들을 어떻게 세탁해야 하는지에 대한 내용이 들어가야 함을 알 수 있습니다. 따라서 (A) For such items, hand washing is the best solution이 정답입니다.

DAY 09 접속사와 절 1

Course 1 등위접속사와 상관접속사

토익 실전 Check-up
p.247

토익 포인트 1 ⓑ   토익 포인트 2 ⓐ
토익 포인트 3 ⓐ   토익 포인트 4 ⓑ

1 등위접속사 채우기
해설 'Mr. Taylor가 전화를 받지 않아서 메시지를 남겼다'라는 의미가 되어야 하므로 등위접속사 ⓑ so(그래서)가 정답입니다. ⓐ or는 '또는'이라는 의미로 어색한 문맥을 만듭니다.
해석 Mr. Taylor가 전화를 받지 않아서, 전화를 건 사람이 메시지를 남겼다.
어휘 leave v. 남기다, 떠나다

2 접속사로 연결된 주어와 수일치하는 동사 채우기
해설 주어가 A and B(His tickets and hotel room) 형태일 때는 복수 동사를 사용하므로 복수 동사 ⓐ have가 정답입니다. 단수 동사 ⓑ has는 주어와 수일치되지 않습니다.
해석 그의 표와 호텔 객실이 예약되었다.
어휘 book v. 예약하다, 등록하다

3 상관접속사 채우기
해설 괄호 앞의 not(~이 아니다)과 함께 상관접속사 not A but B(A가 아니라 B)를 만드는 ⓐ but(하지만)이 정답입니다. ⓑ and(그리고)는 both(둘 다)와 함께 상관접속사 both A and B(A와 B 모두)를 만듭니다.
해석 그는 한 개의 언어가 아니라 세 개의 언어를 말한다.
어휘 language n. 언어, 말

4 접속사로 연결된 주어와 수일치하는 동사 채우기
해설 괄호 앞의 주어(Either posters or a banner)가 either A or B(A 또는 B 중 하나)일 때에는 동사를 B(a banner)에 수일치시켜야 하므로 단수 동사 ⓑ comes가 정답입니다. 복수 동사 ⓐ come은 주어와 수일치되지 않습니다.
해석 포스터 또는 현수막 중 하나가 협찬에 포함된다.
어휘 come with phr. ~에 포함되다, ~이 딸려오다
sponsorship n. 협찬, 후원

HACKERS PRACTICE
p.249

01 ⓐ [토익 포인트 1]   **02** ⓐ [토익 포인트 3]
03 ⓐ [토익 포인트 1]   **04** ⓑ [토익 포인트 3]
05 ⓐ [Day08, Course 1, 토익 포인트 2]   **06** ⓑ [토익 포인트 1]
07 ⓑ [Day07, Course 1, 토익 포인트 2]   **08** ⓑ [토익 포인트 1]
09 silent → silently [Day07, Course 2, 토익 포인트 1]
10 or → nor [토익 포인트 3]
11 about → for [Day08, Course 1, 토익 포인트 2]
12 is → are [토익 포인트 2]
13 then → but [토익 포인트 3]
14 are → is [토익 포인트 4]
15 and → but [토익 포인트 3]
16 need → needs [토익 포인트 2]

해석 01 도착하는 승객들은 공항에서 택시를 타거나 차량을 대여할 수 있다.
02 공장장은 그의 직원들의 안전과 생산성 모두를 보장해야 한다.
03 보고서는 오늘이 마감이었지만, 먼저 완료할 다른 일들이 너무 많이 있었다.
04 Ms. Bouma는 뛰어난 프로그래머일 뿐만 아니라 커뮤니케이션 전문가이다.
05 그 강연자는 그의 강연 끝까지 질문을 보류할 것을 모두에게 요청했다.
06 관광 산업이 번성하고 있지만, 호텔 이용률은 하락세에 있다.
07 임대료는 매월 첫째 날에 지불되어야 한다.
08 Mr. Hinkley는 Lapis사에서 계속해서 근무할 것이지만, 본사로 전근 갈 것이다.
09 도서관 이용자들은 건물 내에 있는 동안 조용히 말해야 한다.
10 그 아파트 건물의 소유주는 반려동물 소유자에게도 흡연가에게도 임대를 해주지 않을 것이다.
11 이용자들은 최소 네 시간 동안 그 웹사이트에 접속할 수 없었다.
12 파리와 마르세유는 매력적인 도시이지만, 파리는 매년 더욱 많은 방문객들을 받는다.
13 이번 달에 교육을 위해 자리를 비우는 마케팅 직원은 한 명이 아니라 두 명이다.
14 잡지도 텔레비전도 치과의 대기실에 있는 고객들에게 이용 가능하지 않다.
15 직원들은 장려금뿐만 아니라 건강 보험과 같은 혜택도 받는다.
16 부서 관리자나 국장이 휴가 신청을 승인해야 한다.

Course 2 관계절

토익 실전 Check-up
p.251

토익 포인트 1 ⓐ   토익 포인트 2 ⓐ
토익 포인트 3 ⓑ   토익 포인트 4 ⓑ

1 관계사 자리 채우기
해설 이 문장은 주어(We), 동사(ask), 목적어(customers), 목적격 보어(to fill out a survey)를 갖춘 완전한 절이므로 (　　) buy the product는 수식어 거품으로 보아야 합니다. 따라서 수식어 거품을 이끌 수 있는 관계사 ⓐ who가 정답입니다. 대명사 ⓑ they(그들, 그것들)는 수식어 거품을 이끌 수 없습니다.
해석 저희는 제품을 구매하는 고객들께 설문 조사지를 작성해 주실 것을 요청드립니다.
어휘 fill out phr. (양식을) 작성하다, 기입하다 survey n. 설문 조사지, 설문 조사

2 관계대명사 채우기
해설 선행사(The applicant)를 수식하는 관계절 ((　　) we selected)에서 동사 selected 다음에 목적어가 없으므로 목적격 관계대명사 ⓐ whom이 정답입니다. 소유격 관계대명사 ⓑ whose는 바로 다음에 꾸밈을 받는 명사가 와야 합니다.
해석 우리가 선택한 지원자는 우리의 제안을 거절했다.
어휘 applicant n. 지원자, 신청자 turn down phr. ~을 거절하다

3 관계부사 채우기
해설 선행사(the day)가 시간을 나타내므로 관계부사 ⓑ when이 정답입니다. ⓐ why는 선행사가 이유를 나타낼 때 사용됩니다.
해석 Mr. Sosa는 출장에서 돌아온 날 그 이메일을 받았다.
어휘 business trip phr. 출장

4 관계대명사와 관계부사 구별하여 채우기

해설 괄호는 명사(The new park)를 뒤에서 꾸미는 관계절을 이끄는 자리입니다. 괄호 뒤의 절(includes several sports fields)에 주어가 없으므로 주격 관계대명사 ⓑ which가 정답입니다. 관계부사 ⓐ where 뒤에는 완전한 절이 옵니다.

해석 몇 개의 스포츠 경기장을 포함하는 새로운 공원은 다음 달에 개장한다.

어휘 include v. 포함하다, 포괄하다 several adj. 몇몇의, 몇 개의
field n. 경기장, 들판

HACKERS PRACTICE
p.253

01 ⓐ [토익 포인트 2]	**02** ⓐ [토익 포인트 2]
03 ⓐ [Day08, Course 2, 토익 포인트 1]	**04** ⓑ [토익 포인트 4]
05 ⓑ [토익 포인트 2]	**06** ⓐ [토익 포인트 2]
07 ⓑ [Day05, Course 1, 토익 포인트 3]	**08** ⓑ [토익 포인트 1]

09 what → where [토익 포인트 4]
10 from → on [Day08, Course 1, 토익 포인트 1]
11 why → when [토익 포인트 3]
12 this → that 또는 which [토익 포인트 1]
13 whom → why [토익 포인트 4]
14 is → was [Day04, Course 2, 토익 포인트 1]
15 who → whose [토익 포인트 2]
16 which → how [토익 포인트 4]

해석 01 시장 선거에서 당선된 후보자는 1월 초에 취임할 것이다.
02 Mr. Gaines가 설립한 회사는, 이제 큰 수익을 내고 있다.
03 기금 모금 행사는 자원봉사자의 부족에도 불구하고 성공적이었다.
04 Starbound 여행사는 정말로 기대를 뛰어넘는 여행 패키지를 제공한다.
05 팬들은 Lucas Wright의 가장 최근 그림을 보기를 간절히 바라고 있는데, 그 작품은 Connhurst 미술관에 전시되고 있다.
06 Mr. Kent는 Ms. Meyers에게 감사해했는데, 그는 그녀에게서 교육을 받았었다.
07 Ms. Savic은 면접 질문에 빨리 대답했다.
08 동물원에 살고 있는 동물들의 수는 상당히 감소해왔다.
09 Mr. Wallace가 일하는 건물은 많은 의류 회사를 수용하고 있다.
10 작업자들이 주차장의 노면에 흰 선을 그렸다.
11 화요일 오전은 Ms. Williams가 면접을 받기를 가장 원하는 시간이다.
12 지난 월요일에 실시된 설문 조사는 대부분의 시민들이 경제에 만족한다는 것을 보여준다.
13 그 고객은 왜 계약을 취소하기로 결정했는지에 대한 이유를 대지 않았다.
14 작년에 지어진 그 주택은 고상하고 현대적으로 장식되었다.
15 그 비즈니스 잡지는 Mr. Orville에 대한 기사를 실었는데, 그의 상점은 50년 동안 영업해왔다.
16 강사는 교육생들에게 장비가 어떻게 작동되는지를 설명하고 있다.

HACKERS TEST
p.254

PART 5

01 (B)	**02** (C)	**03** (C)	**04** (D)	**05** (C)
06 (D)	**07** (C)	**08** (D)	**09** (B)	**10** (D)
11 (A)	**12** (D)	**13** (D)	**14** (A)	**15** (D)
16 (D)	**17** (C)	**18** (B)		

PART 6

19 (C)	**20** (B)	**21** (C)	**22** (C)

01 등위접속사 채우기

해설 '집 또는 사무실에서 일하다'라는 의미가 되어야 하므로 등위접속사 (B) or(또는)가 정답입니다. 참고로, 등위접속사(or)가 명사(home)와 명사(the office)를 연결하고 있음을 알아둡니다. 부사 (A) otherwise(그렇지 않으면, 다르게)와 전치사 (C) on(~ 위에), 전치사 또는 부사 (D) over(~ 동안, ~ 위에; 위에)는 두 개의 명사를 대등하게 연결할 수 없습니다.

해석 인터넷에 접속할 수 있기만 하면, 직원들은 집 또는 사무실에서 일하는 것이 허용된다.

어휘 have access to phr. ~에 접속할 수 있다, ~에 접근할 수 있다
permit v. 허용하다, 허가하다

02 관계사 자리 채우기

해설 이 문장은 주어(The benefits), 동사(include), 목적어(access ~ lounges)를 갖춘 완전한 절이므로 ____ ~ members는 수식어 거품으로 보아야 합니다. 이 수식어 거품은 동사(are)가 있는 거품절이므로 거품절을 이끌 수 있는 관계대명사 (A) whom과 (C) which가 정답의 후보입니다. 빈칸에 들어갈 관계대명사의 선행사(The benefits)가 사물이고 관계절(____ ~ members) 안에서 주어 역할을 하는 관계대명사 자리가 비어 있으므로, 선행사가 사물일 때 주격 관계대명사로 사용되는 (C) which가 정답입니다. (A) whom은 목적격 관계대명사이고 선행사가 사람일 때 사용됩니다. 인칭대명사 (B) they와 (D) them은 수식어 거품을 이끌 수 없습니다.

해석 회원들만 이용 가능한, Dale Airways사에 의해 제공되는 혜택은 귀빈실 이용을 포함한다.

어휘 benefit n. 혜택, 이점 access n. 이용, 접속 VIP lounge phr. 귀빈실

03 상관접속사 채우기

해설 빈칸 뒤의 or(또는)와 함께 상관접속사 either A or B(A 또는 B 중 하나)를 만드는 (C) either(어느 한쪽의)가 정답입니다. 형용사 또는 대명사 (A) each(각각의; 각자), (B) another(또 다른; 또 하나의 것/사람), (D) much(많은; 많음)는 or와 짝을 이루어 상관접속사를 만들 수 없습니다.

해석 Gram Magazine사의 고위 경영진은 디자이너를 더 고용하거나 삽화를 완전히 외부에 위탁할 것이다.

어휘 upper management phr. 경영진 outsource v. 외부에 위탁하다
artwork n. 삽화, 공예품 entirely adv. 완전히, 전적으로

04 관계부사 채우기

해설 선행사(Norwich)가 장소를 나타내므로 관계부사 (D) where가 정답입니다. (A) how는 방법을, (B) when은 시간을, (C) why는 이유를 나타내는 선행사 다음에 옵니다.

해석 Mr. Baxter는 노리치에서 방금 돌아왔는데, 그는 그곳으로 출장을 갔었다.

어휘 business trip phr. 출장

05 접속사로 연결된 주어와 수일치하는 동사 채우기

해설 문장에 주어(Neither the instructions nor the user guide)만 있고 동사가 없으므로 동사 (B)와 (C)가 정답의 후보입니다. 빈칸 앞의 주어가 neither A nor B(A도 B도 아닌)일 때에는 동사를 B(the user guide)에 수일치시켜야 하므로 단수 동사 (C) contains(포함하다, 함유하다)가 정답입니다. 복수 동사 (B)는 주어와 수일치되지 않습니다. 동명사 또는 분사 (A)와 명사 (D)는 동사 자리에 올 수 없습니다.

해석 설명서도 사용자 안내서도 컴퓨터를 올바르게 조립하는 데에 충분한 정보를 포함하고 있지 않다.

어휘 instructions n. 설명서, 설명 properly adv. 올바르게, 적절하게
assemble v. 조립하다, 모으다

06 관계대명사 채우기

해설 이 문장은 주어(*Bizweek*)와 동사(published), 목적어(a story)를 갖춘 완전한 절이므로 _____ ~ recession은 수식어 거품으로 보아야 합니다. 이 수식어 거품은 동사(has managed)가 있는 거품절이므로 거품절을 이끌 수 있는 관계대명사 (D) whose가 정답입니다. 인칭대명사 (A) his와 (C) he, 부정대명사 또는 부정형용사 (B) other는 수식어 거품을 이끌 수 없습니다.

해석 *Bizweek*지는 Mr. Greer에 대한 기사를 실었는데, 그의 식당은 경기 침체에도 불구하고 성공했다.

어휘 publish v. (기사 등을) 싣다, 출판하다 manage v. ~을 해내다, 경영하다 thrive v. 성공하다, 번창하다 economic recession phr. 경기 침체

07 상관접속사 채우기

해설 빈칸 뒤의 and(그리고)와 함께 상관접속사 both A and B(A와 B 모두)를 만드는 (C) both(둘 다의)가 정답입니다. 부사 (A)는 빈칸 뒤의 and와 함께 짝을 이루어 상관접속사를 만들 수 없습니다. (A)가 빈칸 뒤의 형용사(domestic)를 꾸미는 것으로 볼 경우, '국내적이기도 한 지상 서비스와 국제 화물 발송'이라는 어색한 문맥을 만듭니다. 관계부사 (B) 뒤에는 완전한 절이 와야 하므로 답이 될 수 없습니다. (D) neither는 nor와 짝을 이루어 상관접속사 neither A nor B(A도 B도 아닌)를 만듭니다.

해석 Quik Movers사는 국내 지상 서비스와 국제 화물 발송 모두에 대해 다양한 선택권을 제공한다.

어휘 option n. 선택(권), 방법 domestic adj. 국내의, 가정의 ground adj. 지상의; n. 땅 freight n. 화물, 수송 shipment n. 발송, 선적

08 명사에 맞는 수량 표현 채우기

해설 빈칸 뒤의 복수 명사(units)를 꾸밀 수 있는 수량 표현 (A)와 (D)가 정답의 후보입니다. '몇몇 기기에서 중요한 결함을 발견하다'라는 의미가 되어야 하므로 (D) some(몇몇의, 약간의)이 정답입니다. (A) any(몇몇의)는 주로 부정문, 의문문 및 조건문에서 쓰입니다. any가 '어느, 어떤'이라는 의미로 긍정문에서도 쓰일 수 있지만, 이 경우 단수 가산 명사와 함께 쓰입니다. (B) every(모든)는 단수 가산 명사 앞에, (C) less(더 적은)는 불가산 명사 앞에 옵니다.

해석 VNT Labs사는 몇몇 기기에서 중요한 결함을 발견한 후에 상점에서 자사의 모든 스마트폰을 회수하기로 결정했다.

어휘 recall v. 회수하다, 상기시키다 discover v. 발견하다, 밝히다 critical adj. 중요한, 결정적인 bug n. 결함, 오류, 벌레

09 등위접속사 채우기

해설 빈칸이 동사구(are ~ service)와 동사구(find ~ outdated)를 대등하게 연결하고 있으므로 등위접속사 (B) yet(그러나)이 정답입니다. 부사 (A) meanwhile(그동안에, 한편)과 부사절 접속사 (D) while(~하는 동안에, ~하는 반면에)은 동사구와 동사구를 대등하게 연결할 수 없습니다. (C) for도 '왜냐하면'이라는 의미의 등위접속사로 쓰일 수 있지만 오직 절과 절을 연결할 수 있고 단어나 구는 연결하지 못합니다.

해석 대부분의 Kriya 호텔 방문객들은 서비스에는 만족하지만 시설이 낡았다고 생각한다.

어휘 satisfied adj. 만족한, 충족된 facility n. 시설, 설비 outdated adj. 낡은, 시대에 뒤진

10 부사 자리 채우기

해설 동사(will be ~ rearranged)를 꾸미기 위해서는 부사가 와야 하므로 부사 (D) quickly(신속하게, 빠르게)가 정답입니다. 동사 (A), 비교급 형용사 (B), 동명사 또는 분사 (C)는 동사를 꾸밀 수 없습니다.

해석 세미나가 끝난 후에, 회의장은 저녁 연회를 준비하기 위해 신속하게 재정리될 것이다.

어휘 complete adj. 끝난, 완결된 rearrange v. 재정리하다, 다시 배열하다 in preparation for phr. ~을 준비하기 위해 banquet n. 연회, 만찬

11 관계부사 채우기

해설 이 문장은 주어(Thomas)와 동사(thinks of)를 갖춘 완전한 절이므로 _____ ~ Hawaii는 수식어 거품으로 보아야 합니다. 이 수식어 거품은 주어(his family)와 동사(traveled)를 갖춘 완전한 거품절이므로 완전한 거품절을 이끌 수 있는 관계부사 (A)와 (D)가 정답의 후보입니다. 선행사(the time)가 시간을 나타내므로 관계부사 (A) when이 정답입니다. 관계부사 (D) where는 장소를 나타내는 선행사 다음에 오고, 전치사 (B)는 거품절이 아닌 거품구를 이끕니다. 관계대명사 (C)는 다음에 주어나 목적어가 없는 불완전한 절이 옵니다.

해석 Thomas는 종종 그의 가족이 하와이로 여행 갔을 때를 생각한다.

12 접속부사 채우기

해설 빈칸에 들어갈 단어가 절(The firm ~ Johnson and Partners)과 절(all staff ~ week)을 의미적으로 연결하고 있고, '중요한 의뢰를 방금 받았고, 그러므로 모든 직원들은 추가 근무를 해달라고 요청받을 것이다'라는 의미가 되어야 하므로 접속부사 (D) therefore(그러므로)가 정답입니다. 접속부사 (A) similarly는 '비슷하게, 마찬가지로', (B) besides는 '게다가'라는 의미입니다. 부사절 접속사 (C) because(~ 때문에)는 수식어 거품절을 이끌고 다음에 주어와 동사가 옵니다.

해석 그 회사는 Johnson and Partners사로부터 중요한 의뢰를 방금 받았고, 그러므로 모든 직원들은 다음 주에 몇 시간의 추가 근무를 해달라고 요청받을 것이다.

어휘 accept v. 받다, 승낙하다 major adj. 중요한, 주요한 commission n. 의뢰, 수수료

13 접속사로 연결된 주어와 수일치하는 동사 채우기

해설 종속절(either ~ decrease)에 주어(either real estate prices or the average cost of rent)만 있고 동사가 없으므로 동사 (B)와 (D)가 정답의 후보입니다. 빈칸 앞의 주어가 either A or B(A 또는 B 중 하나)일 때에는 동사를 B(the average cost of rent)에 수일치시켜야 하므로 단수 동사 (D) needs(~해야 한다, 필요하다)가 정답입니다. 복수 동사 (B)는 주어와 수일치되지 않습니다. 동명사 또는 분사 (A)와 형용사 (C)는 동사 자리에 올 수 없습니다.

해석 많은 시민들이 부동산 가격이나 평균 임대 비용이 낮아져야 한다는 데 동의한다.

어휘 real estate phr. 부동산, 토지 average adj. 평균의, 보통의 decrease v. 낮아지다, 감소하다

14 명사 자리 채우기

해설 부정관사(an)와 전치사(for) 사이에 올 수 있는 것은 명사이므로 명사 (A) explanation(설명, 해석)이 정답입니다. 동사 (B)와 (D), 형용사 (C)는 명사 자리에 올 수 없습니다.

해석 Ms. Topham은 Shipton 쇼핑몰의 건물 디자인이 왜 그렇게 일정보다 늦어지는지에 대한 설명을 요구했다.

어휘 behind schedule phr. 일정보다 늦은

15 관계대명사 채우기

해설 이 문장은 주어(The man), 동사(gave), 목적어(her, his business card)를 갖춘 완전한 절이므로 _____ ~ event는 수식어 거품으로 보아야 합니다. 이 수식어 거품은 동사(met)가 있는 거품절이므로 거품절을 이끌 수 있는 관계대명사 (C)와 (D)가 정답의 후보입니다. 'Ms. Neilson이 행사에서 만난 남자'라는 의미가 되어야 하므로 목적격 관계대명사 (D) whom이 정답입니다. 소유격 관계대명사 (C) whose는 관계절 안에서 '~의'를 의미하며 다음에 오는 명사를 꾸미는데, 이 문장에서는 '남자의 Ms. Neilson'이라는 어색한 문맥을 만듭니다. 인칭대명사 (A) them과 지시대명사 또는 지시형용사 (B) those

는 수식어 거품을 이끌 수 없습니다.

해석 Ms. Neilson이 인적 네트워크 형성 행사에서 만난 남자는 그녀에게 그의 명함을 주었고 그에게 연락할 것을 제안했다.

어휘 business card phr. 명함

16 관계대명사 채우기

해설 이 문장은 주어(Passengers), 동사(will be able to)를 갖춘 완전한 절이므로 ____ ~ airport는 수식어 거품으로 보아야 합니다. 이 수식어 거품은 동사(check in)가 있는 거품절이므로 거품절을 이끌 수 있는 관계부사 (A), 관계대명사 (C)와 (D)가 정답의 후보입니다. ____ ~ airport가 빈칸 앞의 명사(Passengers)를 꾸미는 형용사 역할을 하고 있고 '공항에 도착하기 전에 인터넷에서 체크인하는 승객들'이라는 의미가 되어야 하므로 관계대명사 (D) who가 정답입니다. 관계부사 (A) when(~할 때)은 주어와 동사가 모두 있는 완전한 절을 이끄므로, 바로 다음에 동사(check)가 올 수 없고 주어가 와야 합니다. 관계대명사 (C) whose는 다음에 꾸밈을 받는 명사가 와야 합니다. 의문대명사 또는 의문형용사 (B) what은 수식어 거품을 이끌 수 없습니다.

해석 공항에 도착하기 전에 인터넷에서 체크인하는 승객들은 보안 검색대 입구로 바로 갈 수 있을 것이다.

어휘 security n. 보안, 경비

17 상관접속사 채우기

해설 빈칸 뒤의 but also(그러나 또한)와 함께 상관접속사 not only A but also B(A뿐만 아니라 B도)를 만드는 (C) not only(뿐만 아니라)가 정답입니다. 부사 (A) rather(오히려, 꽤)와 (D) in addition(게다가)는 but also와 함께 짝을 이루어 상관접속사를 만들 수 없습니다. (B) neither는 nor와 짝을 이루어 상관접속사 neither A nor B(A도 B도 아닌)를 만듭니다.

해석 Newbrook 출장 연회업체는 행사에 늦게 도착했을 뿐만 아니라 모든 손님들을 위한 충분한 음식을 만들지도 못했다.

어휘 catering n. 출장 연회, 음식 공급 turn up phr. 도착하다, 나타나다
fail v. ~하지 못하다, 실패하다

18 관계사 자리 채우기

해설 이 문장은 주어(The customer service workshop), 동사(is), 보어(mandatory)를 갖춘 완전한 절이므로 ____ ~ Friday는 수식어 거품으로 보아야 합니다. 이 수식어 거품은 동사(takes place)가 있는 거품절이므로 거품절을 이끌 수 있는 관계대명사 (B) which가 정답입니다. 대명사 (A) it, 의문대명사 또는 의문형용사 (C) what, 지시대명사 또는 지시형용사 (D) this는 수식어 거품을 이끌 수 없습니다.

해석 이번 금요일에 열릴 고객 서비스 워크숍은 모든 영업 직원들에게 필수적이다.

어휘 take place phr. 열리다, 일어나다 mandatory adj. 필수적인, 의무적인
representative n. 직원, 대리인

19-22번은 다음 광고에 관한 문제입니다.

매일 전국의 업체들이 엄청난 할인 판매를 하고 있습니다. ¹⁹하지만, 널리 광고되지 않는 경우에 소비자들은 그것들을 종종 놓칩니다. 거기가 바로 Bargain-A-Day사가 관여하는 곳입니다. 저희의 최신 기술의 알고리즘이 여러분의 도시의 최고의 거래들을 찾아냅니다. ²⁰저희는 그 후에 여러분에게 그것들에 대한 알림을 자동으로 보냅니다. 할인 상품들은 여러분이 필요한 것은 무엇이든지 찾는 것을 돕는 항목별로 분류됩니다. ²¹저희는 이용 가능한 최저 가격을 보장하는 가격 맞춤 보장제도 있습니다.

²²저희는 여러분이 이 기회를 이용하셔서 여러분의 도시에서 가장 좋은 가격을 즐겨보시기를 바랍니다. www.bargainaday.com을 방문하셔서 시작하십시오. ◐

---

hold a sale phr. 할인 판매하다 amazing adj. 엄청난, 놀라운
come in phr. 관여하다, 참가하다
state-of-the-art adj. 최신 기술의, 최근의
automatically adv. 자동으로, 기계적으로 notification n. 알림, 통보
bargain n. 할인 상품, 특가품 organize v. 분류하다, 정리하다
guarantee n. 보장; v. 보장하다

19 알맞은 문장 고르기

해석 (A) 그럼에도 불구하고, 회원들이 소정의 연회비를 내는 것은 불가피합니다.
(B) 할인은 오직 한정된 기간 동안만 이용할 수 있다는 것을 기억하시기 바랍니다.
(C) 하지만, 널리 광고되지 않는 경우에 소비자들은 그것들을 종종 놓칩니다.
(D) 저희 쿠폰은 Bargain-A-Day 지점 어디서든 상품으로 교환될 수 있습니다.

해설 빈칸에 들어갈 알맞은 문장을 고르는 문제이므로 주변 문맥이나 전체 문맥을 파악합니다. 앞 문장 'Every day, businesses across the nation hold amazing sales.'에서 매일 전국의 업체들이 엄청난 할인 판매를 하고 있다고 했고, 뒤 문장 'That's where Bargain-A-Day comes in.'에서 거기가 바로 Bargain-A-Day사가 관여하는 곳이라고 했으므로 빈칸에는 Bargain-A-Day사가 무엇을 하는지, 즉 전국의 업체들의 할인 판매를 광고하는 역할을 한다는 내용이 들어가야 함을 알 수 있습니다. 따라서 (C) However, consumers often miss them if they're not widely advertised가 정답입니다.

어휘 offer n. (단기) 할인 consumer n. 소비자, 고객
widely adv. 널리, 광범위하게 advertise v. 광고하다, 알리다
redeem v. (상품권 등을) 상품으로 교환하다, 상환하다

20 격에 맞는 인칭대명사 고르기 주변 문맥 파악

해설 전치사(about)의 목적어 자리에 올 수 있는 인칭대명사 (A)와 (B), 지시대명사 (C)가 정답의 후보입니다. 빈칸이 있는 문장만으로는 정답을 고를 수 없으므로 주변 문맥이나 전체 문맥을 파악합니다. 앞 문장에서 최신 기술의 알고리즘이 최고의 거래들을 찾아낸다고 했고, 빈칸에 들어갈 대명사가 앞 문장의 복수 명사 the best deals를 가리키므로 복수 인칭대명사 (B) them이 정답입니다. 인칭대명사 (A) it과 지시대명사 (C) this는 단수 대명사이므로 복수 명사를 가리킬 수 없습니다. 명사절 접속사 또는 관계대명사 (D) which는 절을 이끄는데 빈칸 뒤에 절이 없으므로 답이 될 수 없습니다.

21 관계사 자리 채우기

해설 이 문장은 주어(We), 동사(have), 목적어(a price match guarantee policy)를 갖춘 완전한 절이므로 ____ ~ available은 수식어 거품으로 보아야 합니다. 따라서 to 부정사 (A)와 수식어 거품인 관계절을 만드는 'that + 동사' (C)가 정답의 후보입니다. '가격 맞춤 보장제가 최저 가격을 보장하다'라는 의미가 되어야 하고, 빈칸의 동사 ensure(보장하다, 확실하게 하다)가 타동사인데 빈칸 뒤에 목적어(the lowest price)가 있으므로 능동태 (C) that ensures가 정답입니다. to 부정사의 수동형 (A)는 뒤에 목적어를 가질 수 없습니다. 동사 (B)와 'it + 동사' (D)는 수식어 거품이 될 수 없습니다.

22 명사 관련 어구 완성하기

해설 '이 기회를 이용하여 도시에서 가장 좋은 가격을 즐기다'라는 문맥이므로, 빈칸 앞의 take와 빈칸 뒤의 of와 함께 '~을 이용하다'라는 의미의 어구 take advantage of를 만드는 명사 (C) advantage(이점, 장점)가 정답입니다. (A) benefit은 '혜택, 이점', (B) assurance는 '보장, 확신', (D) exception은 '예외, 제외'라는 의미입니다.

GRAMMAR PART 5, 6

한 권으로 끝내는 해커스 토익 700+ (LC+RC+VOCA)

DAY 09 접속사와 절 1 **153**

DAY 10 접속사와 절 2

Course 1 부사절

토익 실전 Check-up
p.257

토익 포인트 1 ⓐ	토익 포인트 2 ⓐ
토익 포인트 3 ⓑ	토익 포인트 4 ⓐ

1 부사절 접속사 자리 채우기

해설 이 문장은 주어(Ms. Patterson), 동사(cannot do), 목적어(the assignment)를 갖춘 완전한 절이므로 (   ) ~ schedule은 수식어 거품으로 보아야 합니다. 이 수식어 거품은 동사(has)가 있는 거품절이므로 거품절을 이끌 수 있는 부사절 접속사 ⓐ because(~이기 때문에)가 정답입니다. 전치사 ⓑ because of(~ 때문에)는 거품절이 아니라 거품구를 이끕니다.

해석 Ms. Patterson은 일정이 꽉 차 있기 때문에 그 업무를 할 수 없다.

어휘 assignment n. 업무, 임무

2 부사절 접속사 채우기: 시간

해설 'Mr. Azarov는 외출한 동안 여러 통의 전화를 받았다'라는 의미가 되어야 하므로 부사절 접속사 ⓐ while(~하는 동안)이 정답입니다. ⓑ once(일단 ~하면)를 쓰면 'Mr. Azarov는 일단 외출했으면 여러 통의 전화를 받았다'라는 어색한 문맥이 됩니다.

해석 Mr. Azarov는 외출한 동안 여러 통의 전화를 받았다.

어휘 receive v. 받다, 얻다

3 부사절 접속사 채우기: 양보

해설 '비록 가격이 점점 오르고 있지만 수요는 높다'라는 의미가 되어야 하므로 양보를 나타내는 부사절 접속사 ⓑ even though(비록 ~이지만)가 정답입니다. ⓐ when은 '~할 때'라는 의미로 시간을 나타냅니다.

해석 비록 가격이 점점 오르고 있지만 지역 부동산에 대한 수요는 높다.

어휘 demand n. 수요, 요구; v. 요구하다
real estate phr. 부동산, 토지
increasing adj. 점점 오르는, 증가하는

4 부사절 접속사 채우기: 결과

해설 '높은 수익을 얻어서 몇 개의 새로운 지점을 열 수 있었다'라는 의미가 되어야 하므로 괄호 뒤의 that과 함께 부사절 접속사 such ~ that –(매우 ~해서 –하다)을 만드는 ⓐ such가 정답입니다. ⓑ as(~이기 때문에)는 that과 함께 부사절 접속사를 만들 수 없습니다.

해석 그 회사는 매우 높은 수익을 얻어서 몇 개의 새로운 지점을 열 수 있었다.

어휘 profit n. 수익, 이익

HACKERS PRACTICE
p.259

01 ⓑ [토익 포인트 1]	**02** ⓑ [토익 포인트 3]
03 ⓐ [토익 포인트 2]	**04** ⓑ [토익 포인트 3]
05 ⓑ [토익 포인트 2]	**06** ⓑ [토익 포인트 4]
07 ⓐ [토익 포인트 3]	**08** ⓑ [토익 포인트 4]

09 they → that [토익 포인트 4]
10 mistakenly → mistake [Day06, Course 1, 토익 포인트 1]
11 drops → dropped [Day03, Course 1, 토익 포인트 2]
12 him → his [Day06, Course 2, 토익 포인트 1]
13 responsibility → responsible [Day07, Course 1, 토익 포인트 4]
14 whom → who [Day09, Course 2, 토익 포인트 2]
15 in → on [토익 포인트 3]
16 even → so [토익 포인트 4]

해석 **01** 다음 회의의 안건은 회의가 열리기 전에 배부될 것이다.

02 Helmsburg 센터는 지속적으로 자금을 받는 한 계속 운영될 것이다.

03 강연자는 모든 사람들이 자리에 앉자마자 발표를 시작할 것이다.

04 두 번째 지원자는 아직 교육 중인 반면, 첫 번째 지원자는 이미 충분히 증명되었다.

05 Mr. Collins는 부서장이 자리를 비운 동안 부서를 담당할 것이다.

06 Ms. Kim은 그녀의 직원들이 계속 동기가 부여되게 하기 위해 정기적인 장려금을 준다.

07 강연자 중 한 명이 나타나지 않더라도 총회는 계속될 것이다.

08 호텔에 도착하자마자, Ms. Quincy는 매우 피곤해서 곧장 잠을 잤다.

09 바쁜 휴일 시즌에 더 많은 직원을 고용하는 것은 많은 비용이 든다는 것을 제외하면 도움이 될 것이다.

10 그 편집자는 마지막으로 문서를 교정볼 때 오류를 발견했다.

11 합병 이래로, 회사의 주가는 시장 전문가들의 예측보다 훨씬 더 낮게 떨어졌다.

12 Mr. Willis가 그의 가게를 라디오에서 홍보한 이후, 매출이 70퍼센트 상승했다.

13 주택 위원회는 폭풍우 동안 쓰러지는 모든 나무를 치워야 할 책임이 있다.

14 Mr. Jones의 세미나에 참석한 거의 모든 참석자들은 그것에 대해 긍정적으로 응답했다.

15 직원들은 오직 내일 늦게까지 남아 있는 경우에만 오늘 일찍 퇴근할 수 있다.

16 회의실은 더 많은 직원들이 편안하게 들어갈 수 있도록 확장되고 있다.

Course 2 명사절

토익 실전 Check-up
p.261

토익 포인트 1 ⓐ	토익 포인트 2 ⓑ
토익 포인트 3 ⓐ	토익 포인트 4 ⓐ

1 명사절 접속사 채우기

해설 목적어를 갖는 타동사(asked) 뒤에 절(Mr. Kline was working on)이 왔으므로, 이 절은 목적어 역할을 하는 명사절입니다. 따라서 명사절을 이끄는 명사절 접속사 ⓐ what(무엇을 ~하는지)이 정답입니다. 전치사 ⓑ about(~에 대해)은 명사절을 이끌 수 없습니다.

해석 관리자는 Mr. Kline이 무엇을 작업하고 있었는지 물었다.

어휘 supervisor v. 관리자, 감독

2 that 채우기

해설 명사(idea)와 동격을 이루는 절(people ~ ways) 사이에는 명사절 접속사가 와야 하므로 ⓑ that(~이라는 것)이 정답입니다. 대명사 ⓐ it(그것)은 명사절을 이끌 수 없습니다.

해석 사람들이 서로 다른 방식으로 배운다는 견해는 일반적으로 인정된다.

어휘 generally adv. 일반적으로, 대체로   accept v. 인정하다, 받아들이다

3 whether 채우기

해설 동사(depends) 앞에 주어(employees), 동사(are), 보어(eligible)로 이루어진 완전한 절이 와서 주어 역할을 하고 있으므로, 괄호에는 주어로 쓰이는 완전한 절을 이끌 수 있는 명사절 접속사가 와야 합니다. 따라서 주어로 쓰이는 완전한 절을 이끌 수 있는 명사절 접속사 ⓐ Whether(~인지 아닌지)가 정답입니다. 명사절 접속사 ⓑ If(~인지 아닌지)는 주어로 쓰이는 명사절을 이끌 수 없습니다.

해석 직원들이 보너스에 대한 자격이 있는지 아닌지는 그들의 실적에 달려 있다.

어휘 eligible adj. 자격이 있는, 권한이 있는
depend on phr. ~에 달려 있다, ~에 의존하다

4 의문사 채우기

해설 목적어를 갖는 타동사 explain(explains) 뒤에 주어(the building), 동사(is), 보어(inaccessible)로 이루어진 완전한 절이 와서 목적어 역할을 하고 있으므로, 괄호에는 완전한 절을 이끌 수 있는 명사절 접속사가 와야 합니다. 따라서 완전한 절을 이끌 수 있는 의문부사 ⓐ why(왜 ~하는지)가 정답입니다. 의문대명사 또는 의문형용사 ⓑ what(무엇이/어떤 ~가 ~하는지)은 다음에 주어나 목적어 등이 없는 불완전한 절이 옵니다.

해석 회람은 왜 오늘 건물에 들어갈 수 없는지를 설명한다.

어휘 explain v. 설명하다, 밝히다
inaccessible adj. 들어갈 수 없는, 접근할 수 없는

HACKERS PRACTICE p.263

01 ⓐ [토익 포인트 1]	**02** ⓑ [토익 포인트 3]
03 ⓑ [토익 포인트 1]	**04** ⓐ [토익 포인트 1]
05 ⓐ [Day09, Course 2, 토익 포인트 1]	**06** ⓑ [토익 포인트 1]
07 ⓑ [토익 포인트 3]	**08** ⓑ [토익 포인트 3]

09 how → which [토익 포인트 4]
10 Who → What [토익 포인트 4]
11 what → when [Day10, Course 1, 토익 포인트 2]
12 why → who [토익 포인트 4]
13 his → whose [Day09, Course 2, 토익 포인트 1]
14 was → were [Day03, Course 2, 토익 포인트 1]
15 besides → but also [Day09, Course 1, 토익 포인트 3]
16 which → whether [토익 포인트 3]

해석 **01** 공장 조사관은 왜 공장의 기계들이 올바르게 작동하지 않고 있었는지를 알아냈다.

02 한 고객이 온라인으로 주문된 셔츠가 반품될 수 있는지 묻기 위해 전화를 했다.

03 Mr. Tenzig의 강연에서, 그는 어떻게 그가 처음부터 다시 시작하여 회사를 세웠는지에 대해 이야기했다.

04 회사는 새로운 체중 감량 약이 성공적일 것이라고 확신했다.

05 시내에 세워진 조각상들은 시 설립자들에 대한 기념물이다.

06 Mr. Crane은 차를 어디에 주차했는지 잊어버렸다.

07 시장이 유망한지 아닌지에 상관없이 회사는 혁신을 계속할 것이다.

08 지원자는 그의 예정된 면접이 월요일까지 연기될 수 있는지 문의하고 있다.

09 귀하의 티켓은 어떤 공항 터미널에서 항공편이 출발할 것인지에 대한 정보를 포함하고 있습니다.

10 대변인이 오늘 밤에 말한 것은 내일 신문에 실릴 것이다.

11 Mr. Johansson은 최고 경영자가 로스앤젤레스 지사에 도착할 때 우리에게 연락할 것이다.

12 위원회는 누가 개회식에서 환영사를 할 것인지를 선택한다.

13 호텔 객실은 방문 고객을 위해 준비될 것인데, 그 고객의 항공편은 오늘 오후에 도착할 것이다.

14 과학 다큐멘터리는 동굴들이 어떻게 형성되었는지 상세하게 설명한다.

15 100달러 이상 주문을 하는 고객들은 할인뿐만 아니라 무료 선물도 받을 것이다.

16 설문 조사 응답자들은 그들이 정부의 새 정책들을 지지하는지 아닌지에 대해 질문을 받았다.

HACKERS TEST p.264

PART 5

01 (A)	**02** (C)	**03** (D)	**04** (A)	**05** (A)
06 (C)	**07** (D)	**08** (D)	**09** (D)	**10** (B)
11 (B)	**12** (A)	**13** (B)	**14** (B)	**15** (A)
16 (B)	**17** (B)	**18** (C)		

PART 6

19 (D)	**20** (B)	**21** (D)	**22** (A)

01 부사절 접속사 자리 채우기

해설 이 문장은 주어(Residents)와 동사(are expected)를 갖춘 완전한 절이므로 ____ ~ neighbors는 수식어 거품으로 보아야 합니다. 이 수식어 거품은 동사(do not disturb)가 있는 거품절이므로 거품절을 이끌 수 있는 부사절 접속사 (A) so that(~할 수 있도록)이 정답입니다. 전치사 (B) such as(~과 같은)와 (D) instead of(~ 대신에)는 거품절이 아니라 거품구를 이끕니다. (C) but also(그러나 또한)는 not only와 함께 상관접속사 not only A but also B(A뿐만 아니라 B도)를 만듭니다.

해석 Fulton 타워의 주민들은 이웃을 방해하지 않기 위해 오후 11시 이후에는 조용히 할 것이 요구된다.

어휘 resident n. 주민, 거주자 expect v. 요구하다, 기대하다
quiet adj. 조용한, 고요한 disturb v. 방해하다, 혼란시키다
neighbor n. 이웃 (사람)

02 명사절 접속사 채우기

해설 목적어를 갖는 타동사(recommended) 뒤에 절(the administration ~ efficiency)이 왔으므로, 이 절은 목적어 역할을 하는 명사절입니다. 따라서 명사절을 이끄는 명사절 접속사 (B)와 (C)가 정답의 후보입니다. '자문 위원은 경영진이 새로운 데이터 관리 시스템을 도입하는 것을 제안했다'라는 의미가 되어야 하므로 (C) that(~라는 것)이 정답입니다. (B) if(~인지 아닌지)는 '새로운 데이터 관리 시스템을 도입할지 안 할지를 제안했다'라는 어색한 문맥을 만듭니다. 전치사 (A) about(~에 대해)은 명사절을 이끌 수 없고, 부사절 접속사 (D) while(~하는 동안, ~한 반면에)은 명사절이 아닌 부사절을 이끕니다. 참고로, 이 문장에서는 주절(The consultant recommended)에 제안을 나타내는 동사(recommend)가 왔으므로 that절(____ ~ efficiency)에 동사원형(implement)이 왔음을 알아둡니다.

해석 자문 위원은 효율성을 높이기 위해 경영진이 새로운 데이터 관리 시스템을 도입하는 것을 제안했다.

어휘 recommend v. 제안하다, 추천하다 administration n. 경영진, 경영
implement v. 도입하다, 실행하다 management n. 관리, 경영
efficiency n. 효율(성), 능률

03 명사절 접속사 채우기

해설 동사 determine(알아내다, 결정하다)이 '알아내다, 밝히다'라는 의미일 때에는 목적어를 갖는 타동사이고, determine 뒤에 절(job incentives ~ productive)이 왔으므로, 이 절은 목적어 역할을 하는 명사절입니다. 따라서 명사절을 이끄는 명사절 접속사 (D) if(~인지 아

닌지)가 정답입니다. 지시대명사 또는 지시형용사 (A) those와 수량
형용사 또는 대명사 (C) all(모든, 모든 것)은 명사절을 이끌 수 없습니
다. 부사절 접속사 (B) as(~이기 때문에, ~할 때)는 '업무 장려금이 사
무실 직원들이 더 생산적이 되도록 고무하기 때문에/고무할 때 결심
했다'라는 어색한 문맥을 만듭니다.

해석 인사 부서는 업무 장려금이 사무실 직원들이 더 생산적이 되도록 고무
하는지 아닌지를 알아내기를 원한다.

어휘 **human resources department** phr. 인사 부서
incentive n. 장려금, 보상물   **spur** v. 고무하다, 격려하다
productive adj. 생산적인, 건설적인

04 격에 맞는 인칭대명사 채우기

해설 전치사(as)의 목적어 자리에 올 수 있는 소유대명사 (A), 목적격 인칭
대명사 (B), 재귀대명사 (C)가 정답의 후보입니다. 'Mr. Vega의 워크
숍 일정이 그녀의 것과 거의 동일하다'라는 의미가 되어야 하므로 소
유대명사 (A) hers가 정답입니다. 목적격 인칭대명사 (B) her와 재
귀대명사 (C) herself는 각각 'Mr. Vega의 워크숍 일정이 그녀와/그
녀 자신과 같다'라는 문맥으로 해석상 그럴듯해 보이지만, 두 가지 대
상을 비교할 때에는 동등한 것들끼리 해야 하기 때문에 Ms. Paulson
과 Mr. Vega를 비교하거나 Ms. Paulson's workshop schedule과
Mr. Vega's workshop schedule을 비교해야 합니다. 주격 인칭대명
사 (D) she는 목적어 자리에 올 수 없습니다.

해석 Ms. Paulson은 Mr. Vega의 워크숍 일정을 보았고 그녀의 것과 거의
동일하다는 것을 알았다.

어휘 **realize** v. 알다, 깨닫다   **nearly** adv. 거의, 가까이

05 올바른 시제의 동사 채우기

해설 미래의 특정 시점(by the time ~ analyst) 이전에 발생한 동작이 미래
의 특정 시점까지도 계속 진행되는 것을 나타낼 때 쓰이는 미래완료 시
제 (A) will have worked가 정답입니다. 참고로, by the time과 같이
시간을 나타내는 부사절 접속사가 이끄는 절에서는 미래를 나타내기
위해 미래 시제 대신 현재 시제를 사용하므로 현재 시제(becomes)
가 사용되었음을 알아둡니다. 현재완료 시제 (B)는 과거에 발생한 일
이 현재까지 영향을 미치는 것이 지속될 때 사용됩니다. 과거 시제
(C)는 이미 끝난 과거의 동작이나 상태를 표현할 때 사용됩니다. 미
래 시제 (D)는 미래의 상황에 대한 추측이나 의지를 표현할 때 사용됩
니다.

해석 Mr. Jenkins가 선임 분석가가 될 때쯤이면 그는 4년째 일하는 것이 될 것
이다.

어휘 **senior** adj. 선임의, 고위의   **analyst** n. 분석가

06 부사절 접속사 채우기: 시간

해설 이 문장은 주어(Employee satisfaction surveys), 동사(have
shown), 목적어(a marked improvement)를 갖춘 완전한 절이므
로 _____ ~ implemented는 수식어 거품으로 보아야 합니다. 이 수
식어 거품은 동사(was implemented)가 있는 거품절이므로 거품절
을 이끌 수 있는 부사절 접속사 (A)와 (C)가 정답의 후보입니다. '새로
운 복리 후생 제도가 시행된 이래로 현저한 향상을 보여왔다'라는 의
미가 되어야 하므로 시간을 나타내는 부사절 접속사 (C) since(~한 이
래로)가 정답입니다. 참고로, 부사절 접속사 since가 사용된 경우 주
절의 동사는 현재완료 시제인 경우가 많음을 알아둡니다. (A) in the
event는 '~의 경우'라는 의미로 조건을 나타내는데, 앞으로 일어날 상
황에 대처할 일을 계획하고 있을 때 쓰입니다. 전치사 (B) within(~ 내
에)과 (D) during(~ 동안)은 거품절이 아니라 거품구를 이끕니다.

해석 직원 만족도 설문 조사는 새로운 복리 후생 제도가 시행된 이래로 현저
한 향상을 보여왔다.

어휘 **satisfaction** n. 만족, 충족   **marked** adj. 현저한, 두드러진
improvement n. 향상, 증진
benefits package phr. 복리 후생 제도, 복지 혜택

implement v. 시행하다, 실행하다

07 부사절 접속사 채우기: 조건

해설 '직원들은 관리자가 미리 공지를 받은 경우에만 연중 어느 때라도 휴
가를 갈 수 있다'라는 의미가 되어야 하므로 조건을 나타내는 부사
절 접속사 (D) as long as(오직 ~하는 경우에만)가 정답입니다. (A)
as much as는 '~하는 만큼'이라는 의미입니다. (B) except that은
'~을 제외하고'라는 의미로 제외를, (C) so that은 '~할 수 있도록'이
라는 의미로 목적을 나타냅니다.

해석 모든 PINOX사 직원들은 오직 그들의 관리자가 미리 공지를 받은 경우
에만 연중 어느 때라도 휴가를 갈 수 있다.

어휘 **go on a vacation** phr. 휴가를 가다   **supervisor** n. 관리자, 감독
notify v. 공지하다   **in advance** phr. 미리

08 명사절 접속사 채우기

해설 형용사 certain(확신하는, 확실한)은 명사절을 취하는 형용사이므로 명
사절(_____ ~ ideas)을 이끌 수 있는 명사절 접속사 (A)와 (D)가 정
답의 후보입니다. 명사절이 주어(it), 동사(will be), 보어(able)를 갖
춘 완전한 절이므로 완전한 절을 이끄는 (D) that(~라는 것)이 정답입
니다. (A) who(누가 ~하는지) 다음에는 주어나 목적어가 없는 불완전
한 절이 옵니다. 접속사 (B) yet(그러나)과 (C) but(그러나)은 첫 번째
절(Belmont Corporation is certain)과 두 번째 절(it ~ ideas)을 대
등하게 연결할 수 있지만 'Belmont사는 확신하지만 회사를 인수할 수
있을 것이다'라는 어색한 문맥을 만듭니다.

해석 Belmont사는 혁신적인 사업 아이디어가 있는 소규모의 기술 회사를
인수할 수 있을 것이라고 확신한다.

어휘 **acquire** v. 인수하다, 얻다   **innovative** adj. 혁신적인, 획기적인

09 관계대명사 채우기

해설 _____ ~ Asia가 빈칸 앞의 명사(author)를 꾸미는 형용사 역할을 하
고 있고 '아시아에서 살았던 자신의 경험에 대해 쓴 베스트셀러 작가'
라는 의미가 되어야 하므로 관계대명사 (A), (B), (D)가 정답의 후보
입니다. 빈칸에 들어갈 관계대명사가 관계절 내에서 주어 역할을 하고
있으므로 주격 관계대명사 (D) who가 정답입니다. 목적격 관계대명
사 (A) whom은 관계절 내에서 목적어 역할을 하고, 소유격 관계대명
사 (B) whose는 '~의'라는 의미로 다음에 꾸밈을 받는 명사가 옵니
다. 명사절 접속사 (C) whoever(누가 ~하는지)는 명사 역할을 하는
명사절을 이끕니다.

해석 라디오 아나운서는 아시아에서 살았던 자신의 경험에 대해 쓴 베스트
셀러 작가를 인터뷰했다.

어휘 **commentator** n. 아나운서, 논평가   **experience** n. 경험; v. 경험하다

10 명사절 접속사 채우기

해설 동사 ask(묻다)는 목적어를 두 개 갖는 4형식 동사로도 쓰이므로 빈칸
을 포함한 절(_____ ~ any)은 ask의 목적어 자리에 온 명사절로 보아
야 합니다. 따라서 명사절을 이끄는 명사절 접속사 (A)와 (B)가 정답
의 후보입니다. 빈칸 뒤의 절이 주어(her dish), 동사(contained), 목
적어(any)를 갖춘 완전한 절이므로 완전한 절을 이끄는 명사절 접속
사 (B) whether(~인지 아닌지)가 정답입니다. (A) which(어느 것/사
람이 ~하는지)는 다음에 주어나 목적어가 없는 불완전한 절이 오고, 의
문형용사일 때에는 뒤에 나오는 명사를 꾸밉니다. 부사절 접속사 (C)
however(어떻게 ~할지라도)와 형용사 또는 대명사 (D) either(어느
한쪽의; 어느 한쪽)는 명사절을 이끌 수 없습니다.

해석 Ms. Patterson은 견과류 알레르기가 있어서, 종업원에게 그녀의 요리
가 견과류를 포함하는지 아닌지 물어보았다.

어휘 **nut** n. 견과, 나무 열매   **dish** n. 요리, 접시
contain v. 포함하다, 함유하다

11 부사절 접속사 채우기: 양보

해설 이 문장은 주어(Mr. Sean), 동사(received), 목적어(a great performance evaluation)를 갖춘 완전한 절이므로 ____ ~ times는 수식어 거품으로 보아야 합니다. 이 수식어 거품은 동사(was)가 있는 거품절이므로 거품절을 이끌 수 있는 부사절 접속사 (A)와 (B)가 정답의 후보입니다. '비록 여러 번 지각했지만 우수한 업무 평가를 받았다'라는 의미가 되어야 하므로 양보를 나타내는 부사절 접속사 (B) even though(비록 ~이지만)가 정답입니다. (A) in order that은 '~하기 위해서'라는 의미로 목적을 나타냅니다. 전치사 (C) in preparation for(~에 대비하여)와 (D) as of(~ 일자로, ~ 현재)는 거품절이 아닌 거품구를 이끕니다.

해석 Mr. Sean은 비록 여러 번 지각했지만 우수한 업무 평가를 받았다.

어휘 evaluation n. 평가, 사정

12 명사절 접속사 채우기

해설 목적어를 두 개 갖는 동사 show(showed)의 두 번째 목적어(____ cheese is made)가 주어(cheese)와 동사(is)로 이루어진 절이므로, 목적어 자리에 오는 명사절을 이끌 수 있는 명사절 접속사 (A) how(어떻게 ~하는지)가 정답입니다. 명사절 접속사 (B)도 명사절을 이끌 수 있지만 그 자체가 주어의 역할을 하는데 명사절 내에 이미 주어(cheese)가 있으므로 답이 될 수 없습니다. 전치사 (C)와 (D)는 명사절을 이끌 수 없습니다.

해석 요리 강사는 학생들에게 어떻게 치즈가 만들어지는지를 보여줬다.

어휘 culinary adj. 요리의, 부엌의

13 부사절 접속사 채우기: 결과

해설 '그 프로젝트의 성공을 매우 확신해서 돈을 투자했다'라는 의미가 되어야 하므로 빈칸 뒤의 that과 함께 부사절 접속사 so ~ that(매우 ~해서 –하다)을 만드는 (B) so가 정답입니다. 부사 또는 형용사 (A) even(더욱, ~까지도; 평평한, 공정한)은 that과 함께 부사절 접속사를 만들 수 없습니다. (C) who는 관계대명사로서 관계절을 이끌거나, 명사절 접속사로서 명사절을 이끕니다. 부사절 접속사 (D) as는 '~이기 때문에, ~할 때'라는 의미로 이유나 시간을 나타냅니다.

해석 Mr. Marcus는 그 프로젝트의 성공을 매우 확신해서 자신의 돈을 그것에 투자했다.

어휘 invest v. 투자하다, 쓰다

14 부사절 접속사 자리 채우기

해설 이 문장은 주어(they), 동사(will be charged), 목적어(late fees and interest)를 갖춘 완전한 절이므로 ____ ~ date는 수식어 거품으로 보아야 합니다. 이 수식어 거품은 동사(fail)가 있는 거품절이므로 거품절을 이끌 수 있는 부사절 접속사 (B) If(만일 ~라면)가 정답입니다. 부사 (A) Otherwise(그렇지 않으면, 다르게)와 (D) Thus(그러므로, 이렇게)는 수식어 거품을 이끌 수 없습니다. 전치사 (C) Following(~에 이어, ~ 후에)은 거품절이 아니라 거품구를 이끕니다.

해석 만일 대출자가 만기일까지 단기 대출금을 갚지 못한다면, 그들은 연체료와 이자를 청구받을 것이다.

어휘 borrower n. 대출자, 차용자 fail v. ~하지 못하다, 실패하다
repay v. 갚다, 상환하다 loan n. 대출금, 융자
due date phr. 만기일, 지급일 charge v. 청구하다; n. 요금, 부채
late fee phr. 연체료, 지체료 interest n. 이자, 이율

15 주어와 수일치하는 동사 채우기

해설 문장에 주어(The report)만 있고 동사가 없으므로 동사 (A), (B), (C)가 정답의 후보입니다. 주어가 단수이므로 단수 동사 (A) describes(설명하다, 서술하다)가 정답입니다. 복수 동사 (B)와 (C)는 주어와 수일치되지 않습니다. 참고로, 주어와 동사 사이에 있는 수식어 거품(on the firm's current marketing projects)은 동사의 수 결정에 아무런 영향을 주지 않으므로 주의합니다. 부사 (D)는 동사 자리에

올 수 없습니다.

해석 회사의 현재 마케팅 프로젝트에 대한 보고서는 성공적인 것으로 증명된 다양한 광고 전략을 설명한다.

어휘 current adj. 현재의, 지금의 various adj. 다양한, 많은
strategy n. 전략, 계획 prove v. 증명하다, 입증하다

16 명사절 접속사 채우기

해설 목적어를 갖거나 다음에 전치사 about/of가 오는 동사 know(알다, 이해하다) 뒤에 절(cell phone rang during the meeting)이 왔으므로, 이 절은 목적어 역할을 하는 명사절입니다. 따라서 명사절을 이끄는 명사절 접속사 (B)와 (C)가 정답의 후보입니다. 빈칸이 뒤에 나온 명사(cell phone)를 꾸미고 ____ cell phone이 명사절의 주어 역할을 하면서 '누구의 휴대전화가 울렸는지 알지 못했다'라는 의미가 되어야 하므로 의문사 (B) whose가 정답입니다. (C) that은 '휴대전화가 울렸다는 것을 알지 못해서 전화가 소리 나지 않게 할 것을 상기시켰다'라는 어색한 문맥을 만듭니다. 부정형용사 (A) any(어떤)와 (D) other(다른 몇몇)는 명사절을 이끌 수 없습니다. (A) any와 (D) other가 빈칸 다음의 단수 가산 명사 cell phone(휴대전화)를 꾸미는 것으로 볼 수도 있지만, other는 복수 명사를 수식하고 any는 '어떤 휴대전화가 울렸다는 것을 알지 못해서 전화가 소리 나지 않게 할 것을 상기시켰다'라는 어색한 문맥을 만듭니다.

해석 관리자는 회의 중에 누구의 휴대전화가 울렸는지 알지 못해서 근무 중에 전화가 소리 나지 않게 할 것을 모두에게 상기시켰다.

어휘 remind v. 상기시키다, 되새기다 silence v. 조용하게 하다; n. 정적, 고요

17 부사절 접속사 채우기: 시간

해설 '태국으로 떠나기 전에 여권과 관광 비자가 유효한지 확인했다'라는 의미가 되어야 하므로 시간을 나타내는 부사절 접속사 (B) Before(~하기 전에)가 정답입니다. (A) Unless는 '~하지 않는 한'이라는 의미로 조건을, (D) Although는 '비록 ~이지만'이라는 의미로 양보를 나타냅니다. (C) While은 '~하는 동안, ~한 반면에'라는 의미로 시간이나 양보를 나타냅니다.

해석 Ms. Hill은 태국으로 떠나기 전에, 여권과 관광 비자가 유효한지 확인했다.

어휘 ensure v. 확실하게 하다, 보장하다 passport n. 여권, 입장 허가증
valid adj. 유효한, 타당한

18 부사절 접속사 채우기: 양보

해설 이 문장은 주어(The Carson Hotel), 동사(continues), 목적어(to charge its standard rates)를 갖춘 완전한 절이므로 ____ ~ prices는 수식어 거품으로 보아야 합니다. 이 수식어 거품은 동사(have instituted)가 있는 거품절이므로 거품절을 이끌 수 있는 부사절 접속사 (C) whereas(~한 반면에)가 정답입니다. (A) why는 관계부사로 볼 경우 앞에 이유를 나타내는 선행사가 와야 하고, 의문사로 볼 경우 명사 역할을 하는 명사절을 이끕니다. 비교급 표현 (B) rather than(~보다)과 전치사 (D) despite(~에도 불구하고)는 거품절이 아니라 거품구를 이끕니다.

해석 Carson 호텔은 계속해서 기본 요금을 청구하는 반면에, 다른 호텔들은 여름 가격을 도입했다.

어휘 institute v. 도입하다, 시행하다

19-22번은 다음 공고에 관한 문제입니다.

Ready-to-Wear 패션사의 가을 행사가 Camden 빌딩의 옥상 정원에서 열릴 것임을 알리게 되어 기쁩니다. [19]이 프로그램은 지난 시즌에서 가장 많이 이야기된 쇼이기 때문에 올해의 중요한 패션 행사로 홍보되고 있습니다.

[20]저희는 신규 디자이너들과, Ann Mobley와 Peter Wells와 같은 ◐

베테랑 디자이너 모두의 가을 의류를 공개할 것입니다. ²¹여러분들은 또한 요즘 가장 촉망받는 많은 패션 모델들도 보시게 될 것입니다. 게다가, 여러분은 업계의 가장 유명한 인사들 중 몇몇과 어울릴 기회를 가지실 것입니다.

쇼는 10월 15일에 열릴 것입니다. ²²행사 티켓은 지금 30달러에서부터 판매되고 있습니다. 오늘 저희 웹사이트를 방문하시고 "가을 패션 행사"를 클릭하셔서 자리를 예약하십시오.

rooftop n. 옥상, 지붕 **program** n. 프로그램, 일정
promote v. 홍보하다 **affair** n. 행사, 일 **mingle** v. 어울리다, 섞이다
name n. 유명 인사, 이름

19 부사절 접속사 채우기: 이유

해설 이 문장은 주어(The program)와 동사(is being promoted)를 갖춘 완전한 절이므로 _____ ~ show는 수식어 거품으로 보아야 합니다. 이 수식어 거품은 동사(was)가 있는 거품절이므로 거품절을 이끌 수 있는 부사절 접속사 (A), (C), (D)가 정답의 후보입니다. '이 프로그램은 지난 시즌에서 가장 많이 이야기된 쇼이기 때문에 올해의 중요한 패션 행사로 홍보되고 있다'라는 의미가 되어야 하므로 이유를 나타내는 부사절 접속사 (D) since(~이기 때문에)가 정답입니다. (A) until은 '~할 때까지'라는 의미로 시간을, (C) even though는 '비록 ~이지만'이라는 의미로 양보를 나타냅니다. 전치사 (B) because of(~ 때문에)는 거품절이 아니라 거품구를 이끕니다.

20 올바른 시제의 동사 채우기 전체 문맥 파악

해설 '신규 디자이너들과 베테랑 디자이너 모두의 가을 의류를 공개하다'라는 문맥인데, 이 경우 빈칸이 있는 문장만으로 올바른 시제의 동사를 고를 수 없으므로 주변 문맥이나 전체 문맥을 파악하여 정답을 고릅니다. 앞 문단에서 Ready-to-Wear 패션사의 가을 행사가 열릴 것임을 알리게 되어 기쁘고 이 프로그램이 올해의 중요한 패션 행사로 홍보되고 있다고 했으므로, 가을 의류를 공개하는 행사가 열리는 것이 미래 상황이라는 것을 알 수 있습니다. 따라서 미래 시제 (B) will present가 정답입니다. 과거 시제 (A), 현재완료 시제 (C), 현재 시제 (D)는 미래 상황을 나타낼 수 없습니다.

어휘 **present** v. 공개하다, 선물하다

21 알맞은 문장 고르기

해석 (A) 이것은 참석자 전체 목록과 행사 일정표를 포함합니다.
(B) 그 컬렉션 의상은 10월 1일에 일부 소매점에서 구입할 수 있을 것입니다.
(C) 그의 수상 작품은 더 젊은 디자이너들에게 큰 영향을 줍니다.
(D) 여러분들은 또한 요즘 가장 촉망받는 많은 패션 모델들도 보시게 될 것입니다.

해설 빈칸에 들어갈 알맞은 문장을 고르는 문제이므로 주변 문맥 또는 전체 문맥을 파악합니다. 앞 문장 'We (will present) fall clothing lines by both new designers and veterans'에서 신규 디자이너들과 베테랑 디자이너 모두의 가을 의류를 공개할 것이라고 했고, 뒤 문장 'Moreover, you'll have the opportunity to mingle with some of the biggest names in the industry.'에서 게다가 업계의 가장 유명한 인사들 중 몇몇과 어울릴 기회를 가질 것이라고 했으므로, 빈칸에는 행사를 참석하는 것의 장점을 언급하는 내용이 들어가야 함을 알 수 있습니다. 따라서 (D) You'll also see many of today's most promising fashion models가 정답입니다.

어휘 **participant** n. 참석자, 참가자 **selected** adj. 선택된, 선발된
retail outlet phr. 소매점, 소매 판매점 **influence** n. 영향, 영향을 주는 것
promising adj. 촉망받는, 유망한

22 'be동사 + p.p.' 채우기

해설 빈칸 앞에 현재진행 시제의 수동형(be동사 + being p.p.)을 만드는 are being이 있으므로 동사 sell(판매하다)의 p.p.형 (A) sold가 정답

입니다. -ing형 (B), 동사원형 (C), to 부정사 (D)는 are being 다음에 올 수 없습니다.

DAY 11 특수 구문

Course 1 비교 구문

토익 실전 Check-up   p.267

토익 포인트 1 ⓑ   토익 포인트 2 ⓐ
토익 포인트 3 ⓐ   토익 포인트 4 ⓑ

1 원급 표현 채우기

해설 괄호 뒤에 형용사(professional)와 as가 왔으므로 원급 표현(as + 형용사/부사 + as)을 만드는 ⓑ as가 정답입니다. ⓐ more(더욱)는 비교급(형용사/부사의 비교급 + than)을 만듭니다.

해석 Mr. Jenkins는 전화상에서 들렸던 것만큼 전문적이다.

어휘 **professional** adj. 전문적인, 직업의
sound v. ~처럼 들리다, ~인 것 같다

2 비교급 표현 채우기

해설 괄호 앞에 비교급을 강조하는 표현(much)이 있고, 괄호 뒤에 비교급을 만드는 표현 than이 있으므로, 형용사 profitable(수익성이 있는)의 비교급 ⓐ more profitable이 정답입니다. 원급 ⓑ profitable은 than과 함께 쓰일 수 없습니다. 참고로, 비교급을 강조하는 표현에 much, even, still, far 등이 있음을 알아둡니다.

해석 Mr. Smith의 사업은 전보다 훨씬 더 수익성이 있다.

어휘 **business** n. 사업, 거래

3 최상급 표현 채우기

해설 괄호 뒤의 qualified, of the group과 함께 최상급 표현 '형용사/부사의 최상급 + of ~/in ~/that절'을 만드는 ⓐ most가 정답입니다. ⓑ much(훨씬)는 일반적으로 비교급을 강조할 때 쓰입니다.

해석 Ms. Alvares는 그 그룹에서 가장 자격을 갖춘 후보이다.

어휘 **qualified** adj. 자격을 갖춘 **candidate** n. 후보(자)

4 비교급 표현 채우기

해설 괄호 뒤에 than이 있으므로 비교급인 ⓑ later가 정답입니다. no later than은 '늦어도 ~까지'라는 뜻의 표현임을 알아둡니다. 원급 ⓐ late는 than과 함께 쓰일 수 없습니다.

해석 쇼핑 센터 건설은 늦어도 6월 3일까지는 시작할 것이다.

어휘 **construction** n. 건설, 공사

HACKERS PRACTICE   p.269

01 ⓑ [토익 포인트 3]   **02** ⓑ [토익 포인트 1]
03 ⓐ [토익 포인트 2]   **04** ⓑ [Day09, Course 1, 토익 포인트 1]
05 ⓐ [토익 포인트 1]   **06** ⓐ [토익 포인트 4]
07 ⓐ [Day08, Course 1, 토익 포인트 1]
08 ⓐ [Day10, Course 1, 토익 포인트 2]
09 harder → hardest [토익 포인트 3]
10 imaginative → more imaginative [토익 포인트 2]
11 elegance → elegant [토익 포인트 1]
12 much → many [토익 포인트 1]

13 and → than [토익 포인트 2]

14 hotter → hottest [토익 포인트 3]

15 another → other [토익 포인트 4]

16 with → of [Day08, Course 2, 토익 포인트 4]

해석 **01** 고객들은 Yerba 시장이 도시에서 가장 신선한 토마토를 판매한다는 것에 동의한다.

02 이사회는 새로운 벤처 사업에 대해 최고 경영자만큼 긍정적이다.

03 그 지역의 부동산 가격은 몇 년 전보다 훨씬 높다.

04 의류를 반품하는 고객들은 영수증을 가지고 있어야 하고 가격표가 붙어있다는 것을 확실히 해야 한다.

05 뉴스에 따르면, 작년의 폭풍우 동안 그랬던 것만큼 이번 주에 비가 많이 올 것이다.

06 우리는 직접 만나기보다는 화상 회의를 마련할 것이다.

07 Ms. Kim은 현재 업무차 런던에 있는데, 금요일까지는 돌아올 것이다.

08 경영진이 신입 직원을 몇 명 채용할 때까지, 사무실은 인원이 부족할 것이다.

09 Mr. Adams는 그의 부서에서 가장 열심히 일하는 직원이므로, 승진할 자격이 있다.

10 홍보 부장은 다른 사람들보다 더 창의적인 지원자들을 찾고 있다.

11 수리 후에, 그 호텔은 궁전만큼 우아했다.

12 올해의 퍼레이드는 작년에 그랬던 것만큼 많은 관광객들을 끌어모았다.

13 유동적인 일정을 가진 직원들은 그렇지 않은 사람들보다 더 생산적이다.

14 기상 캐스터는 10년이 넘는 기간 중 시에서 오늘이 가장 더운 날이 될 것이라고 말했다.

15 배송 영수증은 Ms. Clowery 외에 다른 사람에 의해 서명될 수 없다.

16 Cavalier 제도는 한 해의 시기와 상관없이 인기 있는 관광지다.

Course 2 병치 · 도치 구문

토익 실전 Check-up   p.271

토익 포인트 1 ⓑ   토익 포인트 2 ⓐ

토익 포인트 3 ⓐ   토익 포인트 4 ⓐ

1 병치 구문 채우기

해설 등위접속사(and) 앞에 형용사(attentive)가 있으므로 and 뒤에도 형용사가 와야 합니다. 따라서 형용사 ⓑ hospitable(친절한, 환대하는)이 정답입니다. 부사 ⓐ hospitably는 등위접속사가 같은 품사끼리 연결해야 하므로 답이 될 수 없습니다.

해석 후기들에 그 호텔의 직원들이 세심하고 친절하다고 나와 있다.

어휘 say v. ~라고 나와 있다, 말하다   attentive adj. 세심한, 배려하는

2 도치 구문 채우기

해설 주어(Ms. Campbell)와 동사(had visited)가 도치된 절 앞에서 도치 구문을 이끌 수 있는 부정어 ⓐ Never(결코 ~ 않다)가 정답입니다. ⓑ Ever(이제까지)는 비교급이나 최상급에서 강조할 때 쓰입니다.

해석 Ms. Campbell은 결코 그렇게 아름다운 호텔을 방문한 적이 없었다.

3 도치 구문 채우기

해설 이 문장은 'Only + 부사구(after returning home)'가 문장 앞에 와서 주어(Mr. Carter)와 동사(did ~ (   ))가 도치된 문장입니다.

괄호 앞에 주어와 do동사(did)가 있으므로 주어 다음의 일반동사 자리에는 동사원형이 와야 합니다. 따라서 동사원형 ⓐ check(확인하다, 점검하다)가 정답입니다. 동사의 과거형 또는 분사 ⓑ checked는 도치 구문에서 do동사 다음의 동사원형 자리에 올 수 없습니다.

해석 집에 돌아온 후에야 Mr. Carter는 이메일을 확인했다.

어휘 return v. 돌아오다, 돌려주다

4 도치 구문 채우기

해설 주어(Ms. Benoit)와 동사(is)가 도치된 절에서 도치 구문을 이끌 수 있는 ⓐ so(~도 역시 그러하다)가 정답입니다. 부사 ⓑ then(그리고 나서)은 도치 구문을 이끌 수 없습니다.

해석 Mr. Sanchez는 기꺼이 늦게까지 남을 것이고, Ms. Benoit도 역시 그렇다.

어휘 willing adj. 기꺼이 ~하는, 자발적인

HACKERS PRACTICE   p.273

01 ⓐ [토익 포인트 1]   **02** ⓑ [토익 포인트 2]

03 ⓐ [토익 포인트 1]   **04** ⓑ [토익 포인트 3]

05 ⓐ [Day09, Course 1, 토익 포인트 3]   **06** ⓐ [토익 포인트 1]

07 ⓑ [Day10, Course 1, 토익 포인트 4]   **08** ⓐ [토익 포인트 2]

09 becomes → become [토익 포인트 3]

10 such → so [토익 포인트 4]

11 cancel → canceled [토익 포인트 2]

12 by → to [Day08, Course 2, 토익 포인트 3]

13 she did → did she [토익 포인트 3]

14 either → neither [토익 포인트 4]

15 apologizes → apologized [토익 포인트 1]

16 are → is [Day03, Course 2, 토익 포인트 1]

해석 **01** 휴일 동안, 그 상점은 가격을 낮추고 영업시간을 연장한다.

02 회사는 이렇게 큰 성장을 해본 적이 결코 없었다.

03 대부분의 사람들은 그 등산 코스가 힘들지만 가치가 있다고 생각한다.

04 새로운 소프트웨어가 설치된 후에야 Ms. Howell은 그녀의 일을 시작할 수 있었다.

05 스포츠 경기장으로 가는 가장 빠른 방법은 택시나 지하철을 타는 것이다.

06 워크숍에 등록하고 그곳까지 교통편이 필요한 사람들은 Mr. Dillan에게 이야기해야 한다.

07 관리자가 교통 체증에 갇혀 있었기 때문에 오전 회의가 연기되었다.

08 Mr. Kim이 막 강연을 시작하자마자 누군가가 질문을 했다.

09 최근에서야 그 회사는 최고의 휴대용 컴퓨터 소매 업체가 되었다.

10 봄이 왔고, 보다 따뜻한 날씨를 위한 최신 패션 디자인도 그러했다.

11 이사 회의가 몇몇 이사들의 결석으로 인해 취소되는 적은 거의 없다.

12 Landcom사의 새로운 휴대전화들은 가격에 있어 Bridge Mobile사의 휴대전화들과 비슷하다.

13 Ms. Sullivan은 그녀가 사무실에 돌아온 후에야 우리가 음식 공급 업체에 전화하기를 원했다.

14 Mr. Ramirez는 새로운 초밥 식당을 아직 가보지 않았고, Ms. Powell도 그렇지 않았다.

15 Mr. Larson은 늦은 것에 대해 사과했고 다시는 그런 일이 일어나지 않을 것이라고 약속했다.

16 고객들의 가장 흔한 불만은 판매직원들이 충분하지 않다는 것이다.

PART 5				
01 (C)	02 (C)	03 (A)	04 (C)	05 (D)
06 (D)	07 (C)	08 (B)	09 (D)	10 (A)
11 (D)	12 (C)	13 (D)	14 (B)	15 (A)
16 (B)	17 (D)	18 (B)		

PART 6			
19 (C)	20 (A)	21 (D)	22 (B)

01 비교급 표현 채우기

해설 명사(share)를 꾸미기 위해서는 형용사가 와야 하므로 형용사 (A), 형용사의 비교급 (C), 형용사의 최상급 (D)가 정답의 후보입니다. 빈칸 뒤에 비교급을 만드는 표현 than(~보다)이 있으므로 형용사 large(큰, 많은)의 비교급 (C) larger가 정답입니다. 최상급 (D)와 원급 (A)는 than과 함께 쓰일 수 없습니다. 부사 (B)는 명사를 꾸밀 수 없습니다.

해석 Dozier Technology사는 지금 갖고 있는 것보다 더 큰 시장 점유율을 갖기 위해 새로운 스마트폰 모델을 출시할 계획이다.

어휘 release v. 출시하다, 개시하다   share n. 점유율, 몫

02 원급 표현 채우기

해설 빈칸 앞과 뒤에 as가 왔으므로 원급 표현(as + 형용사/부사 + as)을 만드는 부사 (A)와 형용사 (C)가 정답의 후보입니다. 빈칸은 be 동사(are) 뒤의 보어 자리이므로 보어 자리에 올 수 있는 형용사 (C) accurate(정확한, 정밀한)이 정답입니다. 부사 (A)는 보어 자리에 올 수 없습니다. 명사 (B)와 (D)는 'as + many/much/few/little 명사 + as(~만큼 많은/적은 -)'의 형태로 쓰입니다.

해석 건물을 설계할 때, 모든 치수가 가능한 한 정확한지 확인하는 것은 건축가의 책임이다.

어휘 responsibility n. 책임, 책무   architect n. 건축가, 설계자
dimension n. 치수, 크기   possible adj. 가능한, 있을 수 있는
accuracy n. 정확(성), 정밀성   accurateness n. 정확함, 틀림없음

03 도치 구문 채우기

해설 주어(they)와 동사(have been scanned)가 도치된 절(have they ~ system) 앞에서 도치 구문을 이끌 수 있는 부정어 (A) nor(~도 아니다)가 정답입니다. 부사 또는 접속사 (B) yet은 도치 구문을 이끌 수 없습니다. (C) even(더욱)은 비교급을 강조할 때 쓰입니다. 형용사 또는 대명사 (D) either(어느 한쪽의, 어느 한쪽)는 either A or B(A 또는 B 중 하나)의 형태로 자주 쓰입니다.

해석 Shen 빌딩의 설계도는 이사에게 이메일로 보내지지 않았고, 시스템에 스캔되지도 않았다.

어휘 blueprint n. 설계도, 계획

04 형용사 자리 채우기

해설 빈칸 뒤의 명사(impact)를 꾸미기 위해서는 형용사가 와야 하므로 형용사 (C) measurable(상당히 중요한, 잴 수 있는)이 정답입니다. 명사 (A), 부사 (B), 동사 또는 명사 (D)는 명사를 꾸밀 수 없습니다.

해석 Gren사와 전략적 협력 관계를 맺는 것은 회사의 성과에 상당히 중요한 영향을 끼쳤다.

어휘 establish v. (관계를) 맺다, 설립하다   impact n. 영향
performance n. 성과, 달성   measurement n. 측정, 치수
measure n. 측정, 치수, 수단; v. 측정하다

05 도치 구문 채우기

해설 첫 번째 절(had ~ baggage)은 부정어(Hardly)가 절 앞에 와서 주어(Ms. Fox)와 동사(had ____)가 도치된 절입니다. 빈칸 앞에 have 동사(had)가 있으므로 빈칸에는 have동사 다음의 일반동사가 와야

합니다. 따라서 have동사 다음의 일반동사 자리에 올 수 있는 동사 collect(가져오다, 모으다)의 p.p.형 (D) collected가 정답입니다. 동사원형 (A), to 부정사 (B), 동명사 또는 분사 (C)는 have동사 다음의 일반동사 자리에 올 수 없습니다.

해석 Ms. Fox는 막 그녀의 수하물을 찾자마자 그녀의 이름이 쓰여진 표지판을 들고 있는 운전기사를 발견했다.

어휘 hardly adv. 막 ~하자마자   baggage n. 수하물

06 상관접속사 채우기

해설 빈칸 앞의 not only(뿐만 아니라)와 함께 상관접속사 'not only A but (also) B(A뿐만 아니라 B도)'를 만드는 (D) but(그러나)이 정답입니다. 부사 (A) nor(~도 아니다)는 상관접속사 neither A nor B(A도 B도 아닌)를 만들거나, 문장 맨 앞에 와서 주어와 동사를 도치시킵니다. 접속사 (B) and는 '그리고'라는 의미의 등위접속사로 쓰이거나, 상관접속사 both A and B(A와 B 모두)를 만듭니다. 접속사 (C) or는 '또는'이라는 의미의 등위접속사로 쓰이거나, 상관접속사 either A or B(A 또는 B 중 하나)를 만듭니다.

해석 Mr. Saucedo는 잡지를 위한 기사를 쓸 뿐만 아니라 기고 작가들에게 위탁된 기사도 편집한다.

어휘 article n. 기사, 글   edit v. 편집하다, 수정하다
outsource v. (외부에) 위탁하다, 외주 제작하다
contribute v. 기고하다, 기부하다

07 원급 표현 채우기

해설 빈칸 앞과 뒤에 as가 왔으므로 원급 표현(as + 형용사/부사 + as)을 만드는 부사 (B)와 형용사 (C)가 정답의 후보입니다. 빈칸은 be 동사(was) 뒤의 보어 자리이므로 보어 자리에 올 수 있는 형용사 (C) prepared(준비된, 대비된)가 정답입니다. 명사 (A)는 'as + many/much/few/little + 명사 + as(~만큼 많은/적은 -)'의 형태로 쓰입니다. 부사 (B)와 동사 (D)는 보어 자리에 올 수 없습니다.

해석 일주일 이상의 연습 후에, Mr. Bennet은 그가 될 수 있는 만큼 면접 준비가 되었다고 결론을 내렸다.

어휘 practice n. 연습, 실행

08 비교급 표현 채우기

해설 동사(study)를 꾸미기 위해서는 부사가 와야 하므로 부사의 비교급 (B)와 부사 (D)가 정답의 후보입니다. 빈칸 뒤에 비교급을 만드는 표현 than(~보다)이 왔으므로 부사 independently(독립적으로, 자주으로)의 비교급 (B) more independently가 정답입니다. 원급 부사 (D)는 비교급 표현을 만들 수 없습니다. 형용사 (A)와 명사 (C)는 동사를 꾸밀 수 없습니다.

해석 연구원들은 성취가 높은 대부분의 대학교 학생들이 많은 그들의 또래들보다 더 독립적으로 공부하는 경향이 있다는 것을 발견했다.

어휘 researcher n. 연구원, 조사관   discover v. 발견하다, 찾다
tend to phr. ~하는 경향이 있다   peer n. 또래, 동년배

09 최상급 표현 채우기

해설 빈칸 뒤의 명사(part)를 꾸미면서 빈칸 앞의 the, 빈칸 뒤의 of the race와 함께 최상급 표현 '형용사/부사의 최상급 + of ~'를 만드는 형용사 easy(쉬운)의 최상급 (D) easiest가 정답입니다. 명사 또는 동사 (A), 명사 (B), 부사 (C)는 명사를 꾸밀 수 없습니다.

해석 마라톤에 참가하는 대부분의 주자들은 10마일 지점을 경주에서 가장 쉬운 부분으로 여기는데, 이는 대부분이 내리막길이기 때문이다.

어휘 runner n. 주자, 달리는 사람   participate v. 참가하다, 참여하다
consider v. 여기다, 고려하다   mark n. 지점, 표시

10 부사절 접속사 채우기: 시간

해설 이 문장은 주어(The CEO), 동사(will give), 목적어(the keynote

speech)를 갖춘 완전한 절이므로 ____ ~ him은 수식어 거품으로 보아야 합니다. 이 수식어 거품은 동사(introduces)가 있는 거품절이므로 거품절을 이끌 수 있는 부사절 접속사 (A), (B), (C)가 정답의 후보입니다. '그를 소개한 후에 기조연설을 할 것이다'라는 의미가 되어야 하므로 시간을 나타내는 부사절 접속사 (A) after(~ 후에)가 정답입니다. (B) since(~한 이래로, ~이기 때문에)와 (C) in order that (~할 수 있도록)을 쓰면 각각 '그를 소개한 이래로/소개하기 때문에)/소개할 수 있도록 기조연설을 할 것이다'라는 어색한 문맥을 만듭니다. 전치사 (D) during(~ 동안)은 거품절이 아니라 거품구를 이끕니다.

해석 그 최고경영자는 경영학 교수가 그를 소개한 후에 기조연설을 할 것이다.

어휘 keynote speech phr. 기조연설

11 whether (or not) 채우기

해설 타동사 know(알다)의 목적어 자리에 온 절(he can get ~ convention)을 이끌 수 있는 명사절 접속사 (D) whether(~인지 아닌지)가 정답입니다. 전치사 (A)와 (B)는 절을 목적어로 가질 수 없습니다. 부사절 접속사 (C) once(일단 ~하면)를 쓰면 '일단 전액 환불을 받으면 그는 알고 싶어 한다'라는 어색한 문맥을 만듭니다.

해석 Mr. Donati는 만약 그가 회의의 일주일 전에 등록을 취소하면 전액 환불을 받을 수 있는지 없는지를 알고 싶어 한다.

어휘 full refund phr. 전액 환불 registration n. 등록 convention n. 회의, 협의회

12 최상급 표현 채우기

해설 빈칸 뒤의 명사(startups)를 꾸미기 위해서는 형용사가 와야 하므로 형용사의 비교급 (A)와 최상급 (C)가 정답의 후보입니다. 빈칸 앞의 the, 빈칸 뒤의 of the year와 함께 최상급 표현 '형용사/부사의 최상급 + of ~'를 만드는 형용사 successful(성공한, 성공적인)의 최상급 (C) most successful이 정답입니다. 비교급 (A)는 최상급 표현을 만들 수 없습니다. 명사 (B)와 (D)는 명사를 꾸밀 수 없습니다.

해석 매년, Turner Business Journal지는 그해의 가장 성공한 신생 기업 세 곳에 영예를 주기 위해 시상식을 연다.

어휘 awards ceremony phr. 시상식 honor v. 영예를 주다, 존경하다 startup n. 신생 기업, 활동 개시

13 도치 구문 채우기

해설 and 다음의 주어(the fitness center)와 동사(will)가 도치된 절에서 도치 구문을 이끌 수 있는 (C)와 (D)가 정답의 후보입니다. 첫 번째 절 (the hotel pool ~ June 1)에서 부정어(not)가 쓰였고 '호텔 수영장은 6월 1일까지 준비되지 않을 것이고 피트니스 센터도 그렇지 않을 것이다'라는 의미가 되어야 하므로 (D) neither(~도 그렇지 않다)가 정답입니다. (C) so(~도 그러하다)는 앞에 긍정문이 나왔을 때 '~도 그렇다'라는 의미로 쓰입니다. 대명사 (A) none(아무도 ~ 않다)과 접속사 또는 부사 (B) as(~하는 동안에, ~듯이)는 도치 구문을 이끌 수 없습니다.

해석 공사 지연으로 인해, 호텔 수영장은 6월 1일까지 준비되지 않을 것이고 피트니스 센터도 그렇지 않을 것이다.

어휘 construction n. 공사, 건설 delay n. 지연, 연기

14 관계사 자리 채우기

해설 이 문장은 주어(The tourist), 동사(recorded), 목적어(over two hours of footage)를 갖춘 완전한 절이므로, ____ ~ home은 수식어 거품으로 보아야 합니다. 이 수식어 거품은 동사(shared)가 있는 거품절이므로 거품절을 이끌 수 있는 관계부사 (A), 관계대명사 (B)와 (D)가 정답의 후보입니다. 빈칸 앞의 선행사(footage)가 사물이므로 선행사가 사물일 때 사용되는 관계대명사 (B) which가 정답입니다. 관계부사 (A) how는 the way와 같이 선행사가 방법을 나타내는 표현일 때 사용되고, 관계대명사 (D) who는 선행사가 사람일 때 사용됩니다. 명사절 접속사 (C) what은 거품절이 아니라 문장에서 주어,

목적어, 보어 역할을 하는 명사절을 이끕니다.

해석 그 관광객은 2시간이 넘는 장면을 녹화했는데, 그녀는 집에 돌아오자마자 그것을 친구들과 공유했다.

어휘 record v. 녹화하다, 기록하다 footage n. 장면, 화면 share v. 공유하다, 나누다

15 형용사 자리 채우기

해설 빈칸 뒤의 명사(salesperson)를 꾸미기 위해서는 형용사가 와야 하므로 형용사 (A) competitive(경쟁력이 있는)가 정답입니다. 동사 (B)와 명사 (D)는 명사를 꾸밀 수 없습니다. to 부정사 (C)는 명사를 꾸밀 수 있지만 명사 앞이 아니라 뒤에서 꾸밉니다.

해석 Ms. Bergmann은 언제나 그녀의 동료들을 능가하는 매우 경쟁력이 있는 판매원이다.

어휘 extremely adv. 매우, 극도로 salesperson n. 판매원 surpass v. 능가하다, 뛰어넘다

16 비교급 표현 채우기

해설 '10월 1일부터 직항편을 더 이상 제공하지 않는다'라는 의미가 되어야 하므로 빈칸 앞에 no와 함께 쓰여 no longer(더 이상 ~ 않다)를 만드는 (B) longer가 정답입니다. 원급 형용사 (A), 명사 (C), 최상급 형용사 (D)는 비교급 표현 no longer를 만들 수 없습니다.

해석 10월 1일부터, Beta 항공사는 도쿄에서부터 베를린까지의 직항편을 더 이상 제공하지 않을 것이다.

어휘 direct flight phr. 직항편

17 도치 구문 채우기

해설 이 문장은 'Only + 부사구(in the last year)'가 문장 앞에 와서 주어 (Bonnie's Bakery)와 동사(did ____)가 도치된 문장입니다. 빈칸 앞에 주어와 do동사(did)가 있으므로 주어 다음의 일반동사 자리에는 동사원형이 와야 합니다. 따라서 동사원형 (D) begin(시작하다)이 정답입니다. 동사의 과거형 (A), p.p.형 (B), 동명사 또는 분사 (C)는 도치 구문에서 do동사 다음의 동사원형 자리에 올 수 없습니다.

해석 작년에서야 Bonnie's Bakery는 24시간 동안 계속해서 영업하기 시작했다.

어휘 stay v. 계속해서 ~하다, 남다

18 도치 구문 채우기

해설 주어(Telelink)와 동사(has)가 도치된 절에서 도치 구문을 이끌 수 있는 (B) so(~도 역시 그러하다)가 정답입니다. 형용사 또는 대명사 (A) such(그러한; 그러한 것)는 도치 구문을 이끌 수 없습니다. (C) why는 명사절 접속사로서 명사절을 이끌거나, 관계부사로서 관계절을 이끕니다. 인칭대명사 (D) he가 빈칸에 와서 has가 동사, Telelink가 목적어인 것으로 볼 수도 있지만, 'GC Telecom사는 가격을 낮추었고 그는 Telelink사를 가지고 있다'라는 어색한 문맥을 만듭니다.

해석 GC Telecom사가 가격을 10퍼센트 낮추었고, Telelink사도 그렇게 했다.

어휘 lower v. 낮추다, 내리다

19-22번은 다음 광고에 관한 문제입니다.

[19]Leganza Linens사는 편안한 담요, 시트, 그리고 다른 침구 용품의 Comfabulous 라인으로 유명합니다. [20]이 제품들은 100퍼센트 특제 이집트산 목화로 만들어지는 것으로 유명하고, 부드러우면서도 관리하기도 쉽다는 것이 보증됩니다. [21]그래도, 저희 고객들 중 일부는 한층 더 따뜻한 것을 요청해왔습니다.

이제, Leganza사는 Comfabulous 전기담요를 소개하게 되어 기쁩니다. 이 이불은 시리즈의 다른 제품들의 모든 편안한 부드러움에, 전열까지 추가로 제공합니다. [22]더욱이, 그것은 기계로 세탁될 수 있는 ⟳

분리 가능한 침구 커버를 포함합니다. Comfabulous 전기담요를 오늘 사용해 보세요!

cozy adj. 편안한, 아늑한 blanket n. 담요, 덮개
supply n. 용품, 비품 extra-fine adj. 특제의, 상등의
cotton n. 목화, 솜 guarantee v. 보증하다, 보장하다
maintain v. 관리하다, 유지하다 introduce v. 소개하다, 도입하다
electric adj. 전기의, 전기를 이용하는 comforter n. 이불, 위안을 주는 것
luxurious adj. 편안한, 호화로운 smoothness n. 부드러움, 평온
electric heat phr. 전열 feature v. 포함하다, 특징으로 삼다
cover n. (위에 덮는) 침구, 덮개

19 형용사 어휘 고르기

해설 'Leganza Linens사는 Comfabulous 라인으로 유명하다'라는 문맥이므로 형용사 (C) renowned(유명한, 명성 있는)가 정답입니다. (A) relevant는 '관련 있는, 적절한'이라는 의미로 전치사 to와 함께 쓰입니다. (B) receptive는 '수용적인, 잘 받아들이는', (D) reasonable은 '합리적인, 타당한'이라는 의미입니다.

20 병치 구문 채우기

해설 상관접속사 both A and B(A와 B 모두)의 and 뒤에 원급 형용사 (easy)가 있으므로 and 앞에도 원급 형용사가 와야 합니다. 따라서 원급 형용사 (A) soft(부드러운)가 정답입니다. 부사 (B), 형용사의 비교급 (C), 형용사의 최상급 (D)는 상관접속사가 같은 형태끼리 연결해야 하므로 답이 될 수 없습니다.

21 알맞은 문장 고르기

해석 (A) 이 특별 할인은 12월 내내 이용 가능합니다.
(B) 회색과 검은색 담요들은 매진되었기 때문에, 빨간색이 구매 가능한 유일한 선택 사항입니다.
(C) 요컨대, 그 라인은 더 현대적인 스타일로 다시 디자인되었습니다.
(D) 그래도, 저희 고객들 중 일부는 한층 더 따뜻한 것을 요청해왔습니다.

해설 빈칸에 들어갈 알맞은 문장을 고르는 문제이므로 주변 문맥 또는 전체 문맥을 파악합니다. 앞 문장 'The products are ~ made from 100 percent, extra-fine Egyptian cotton'에서 제품들이 100퍼센트 특제 이집트산 목화로 만들어진다고 했고, 뒤 문단 'Now, Leganza ~ introduce the Comfabulous electric blanket ~ with the addition of electric heat.'에서 이제 Leganza사가 전열까지 추가로 제공하는 Comfabulous 전기담요를 소개한다고 했으므로, 빈칸에는 기존 제품들에 더해 전기담요를 소개하는 이유를 언급하는 내용이 들어가야 함을 알 수 있습니다. 따라서 (D) Still, some of our customers have been asking for something even warmer가 정답입니다.

어휘 comtemporary adj. 현대적인, 동시대의 even adv. 한층 (더), 훨씬

22 접속부사 채우기 주변 문맥 파악

해설 빈칸에 들어갈 단어가 앞 문장(This comforter ~ electric heat.)과 빈칸이 있는 문장(it ~ machine-washed)을 의미적으로 연결하고 있고, '이 이불은 모든 편안한 부드러움에 전열까지 추가로 제공하고, 더욱이 분리 가능한 침구 커버를 포함한다'라는 의미가 되어야 하므로 접속부사 (B) Furthermore(더욱이)가 정답입니다. 접속부사 (A) Instead는 '대신에', (C) Next는 '다음에', (D) Consequently는 '결과적으로'라는 의미입니다.

DAY 12 문맥 파악 문제

Course 1 단어 고르기 문제

HACKERS TEST
p.280

01 (D)	02 (C)	03 (B)	04 (A)	05 (C)
06 (A)	07 (A)	08 (D)		

01-04번은 다음 이메일에 관한 문제입니다.

> 수신: Adrian Korlova <a.korlova@forwardcookware.com>
> 발신: Julia Morgan <j.morgan@forwardcookware.com>
> 제목: Keith Andreas와의 행사
> 날짜: 4월 22일
>
> Adrian께,
>
> 우리가 마지막으로 대화했을 때, 제가 유명한 비즈니스 연사 Keith Andreas가 하는 강연에 갈 것이라고 말한 것을 기억할 것입니다. ⁰¹그 강연은 시내의 Haverford 예술회관에서 수요일 저녁 7시 30분에 열릴 것입니다. 하지만, 제가 참석할 수 있을 것 같지 않습니다. ⁰²저는 그날 저녁에 중요한 고객에게 저녁 식사를 대접해야 합니다. ⁰³안타깝게도, 일정을 재조정할 방법이 없습니다. 대신에 당신이 그 행사 표를 가지시겠습니까?
>
> Mr. Andreas는 비즈니스 리더십에 관해 많은 책을 썼고 당신과 저 같은 중간 관리자를 대상으로 수많은 강연을 해왔습니다. ⁰⁴그러므로, 저는 그 강연이 가치 있을 것이라고 생각합니다.
>
> 당신이 그 행사에 참여할 수 있다면, 무엇이 다뤄졌는지 제가 읽을 수 있도록 메모를 좀 해주실 수 있겠습니까? 그날 저녁에 시간이 되는지 알려주십시오.
>
> Julia Morgan 드림
>
> talk n. 강연, 대화 famous adj. 유명한
> make it phr. (모임 등에) 참석하다, 가다 unfortunately adv. 안타깝게도
> instead adv. 대신에 a number of phr. 많은 numerous adj. 수많은
> lecture n. 강연, 강의 target v. ~을 대상으로 하다, 겨냥하다
> attend v. 참여하다 take a note phr. 메모하다

01 올바른 시제의 동사 채우기 주변 문맥 파악

해설 문장에 동사가 없으므로 동사 (A), (C), (D)가 정답의 후보입니다. 빈칸이 있는 문장만으로는 올바른 시제의 동사를 고를 수 없으므로 주변 문맥이나 전체 문맥을 파악합니다. 뒤 문장에서 강연에 참석할 수 있을 것 같지 않다고 했으므로 강연이 아직 열리지 않았음을 알 수 있습니다. 따라서 미래 상황에 대한 예상을 나타내는 미래 시제 (D) will happen이 정답입니다. 과거 시제 (A)는 과거에 이미 끝난 동작이나 상태를 나타냅니다. 미래완료 시제 (C)는 미래의 특정 시점 이전에 발생한 동작이 미래의 특정 시점에 완료될 것임을 나타냅니다. to 부정사 (B)는 동사 자리에 올 수 없습니다.

02 알맞은 문장 고르기

해석 (A) 아마 당신은 행사에 저와 동행하는 것에 관심이 있을 것입니다.
(B) 강연을 위한 표는 아직 웹사이트에서 구매할 수 있습니다.
(C) 저는 그날 저녁에 중요한 고객에게 저녁 식사를 대접해야 합니다.
(D) 저는 당신이 그 행사에 참석하는 데 흥미가 있을 것이라고 확신합

니다.

해설 빈칸에 들어갈 알맞은 문장을 고르는 문제이므로 주변 문맥 또는 전체 문맥을 파악합니다. 앞 문장 'I don't think I'll be able to make it'에서 강연에 참석할 수 있을 것 같지 않다고 했으므로 빈칸에는 그 이유에 대한 내용이 들어가야 함을 알 수 있습니다. 따라서 (C) I have to take an important client out for dinner that evening이 정답입니다.

어휘 accompany v. ~와 동행하다 purchase n. 구매
take out phr. (식당 등에) 데리고 나가) 대접하다

03 to 부정사 채우기

해설 명사 뒤에서 명사를 꾸미기 위해서는 형용사 역할을 하는 분사 또는 to 부정사가 와야 하므로 과거분사 (A), to 부정사 (B), 현재분사 (C)가 정답의 후보입니다. '일정을 재조정할 방법'이라는 의미가 되어야 하므로 to 부정사 (B) to reschedule이 정답입니다. 과거분사 (A)를 쓰면 '일정이 재조정된 방법'이라는 어색한 문맥이 됩니다. 현재분사 (C)를 쓰면 '일정을 재조정하는 방법'이라는 의미로 해석상 그럴듯해 보이지만, 방법(way) 자체가 스스로 일정을 재조정한다는 어색한 문맥이 됩니다. 동사 (D)는 명사를 꾸밀 수 없습니다.

04 형용사 어휘 고르기 주변 문맥 파악

해설 '그러므로 강연이 ＿＿＿할 것이라고 생각한다'라는 문맥이므로 모든 보기가 정답의 후보입니다. 앞 문장에서 Mr. Andreas는 비즈니스 리더십에 관해 많은 책을 썼고 수신자와 발신자와 같은 중간 관리자를 대상으로 수많은 강연을 했다고 했으므로 강연이 가치 있을 것임을 알 수 있습니다. 따라서 형용사 (A) worthwhile(가치 있는)이 정답입니다. (B) lengthy는 '오랜, 긴', (C) improvised는 '즉석에서 지어진', (D) exclusive는 '독점적인'이라는 의미입니다.

05-08번은 다음 기사에 관한 문제입니다.

> ⁰⁵Madgerville 교통국은 혼잡 시간대의 시간 간격이 더 짧은 지하철 및 버스 교통편을 제공할 것이다. 11월부터 시작해서, 열차들은 레드 라인과 블루 라인의 역에 3분이 아니라 2분 30초마다 도착할 것이다. ⁰⁶마찬가지로, 이용 가능한 버스도 혼잡 시간대 동안에 7퍼센트 정도가 늘어날 것이다.
>
> 이 변경 사항들을 위해, 시는 추가 차량들을 구매하고 있다. ⁰⁷이것들은 철도 장비 회사인 Falu사의 8대의 새 열차들과 125대의 새 버스들을 포함할 것이다. 이는 교통국의 차고의 확장도 필요로 할 것이다. ⁰⁸약 2억 5천만 달러가 그 계획을 위해 예산이 세워졌다.
>
> transportation n. 교통, 운송 service n. (교통 기관의) ~편, 공급
> availability n. 이용 가능성, 유용성 expansion n. 확장, 확대

05 형용사 어휘 고르기 주변 문맥 파악

해설 '혼잡 시간대의 ＿＿＿한 지하철 및 버스 교통편을 제공할 것이다'라는 문맥이므로 모든 보기가 정답의 후보입니다. 이 경우 빈칸이 있는 문장만으로 정답을 고를 수 없으므로 주변 문맥이나 전체 문맥을 파악하여 정답을 고릅니다. 뒤 문장에서 열차들이 역에 3분이 아니라 2분 30초마다 도착할 것이라고 했으므로 열차의 배차 간격이 더 짧아질 것임을 알 수 있습니다. 따라서 형용사 (C) frequent(시간 간격이 더 짧은, 잦은)가 정답입니다. (A) affordable은 '(가격이) 알맞은, 입수 가능한', (B) precise는 '정확한, 정밀한', (D) uniform은 '일정한, 고른'이라는 의미입니다.

06 접속부사 채우기 주변 문맥 파악

해설 빈칸에 들어갈 단어가 앞 문장(Starting ~ minutes.)과 빈칸이 있는 문장(bus availability ~ peak hours)을 의미적으로 연결하고 있고, '열차들이 3분이 아니라 2분 30초마다 도착할 것이고, 마찬가지로 이용 가능한 버스도 7퍼센트 정도가 늘어날 것이다'라는 의미가 되어야 하므로 접속부사 (A) Likewise(마찬가지로)가 정답입니다. 접속부사 (B) Nevertheless는 '그럼에도 불구하고', (C) Specifically는 '특히, 구체적으로', (D) Accordingly는 '그러므로'라는 의미입니다.

07 지시대명사 채우기 주변 문맥 파악

해설 문장의 주어 자리에 올 수 있는 모든 보기가 정답의 후보입니다. 앞 문장에서 시가 추가 차량들을 구매하고 있다고 했고, 빈칸에 들어갈 대명사가 앞 문장의 복수 명사 additional vehicles를 가리켜서 '추가 차량들이 8대의 새 열차들과 125대의 새 버스들을 포함할 것이다'라는 의미가 되어야 하므로 지시대명사 (A) These가 정답입니다. 대명사 (B) Such(그러한 것)와 (C) Most(대부분)를 쓰면 각각 '그러한 것과/대부분이 8대의 새 열차들과 125대의 새 버스들을 포함할 것이다'라는 어색한 문맥을 만듭니다. 부정대명사 (D) Any(몇몇, 약간)는 주로 부정문, 의문문, 조건문에 쓰입니다.

08 알맞은 문장 고르기

해석 (A) 거의 사용되지 않는 몇몇 노선들은 변경되거나 완전히 중단될 것이다.
(B) 따라서 월간 승차권의 가격은 인하될 것이다.
(C) 많은 시민들은 차이가 이미 뚜렷하다고 말해왔다.
(D) 약 2억 5천만 달러가 그 계획을 위해 예산이 세워졌다.

해설 빈칸에 들어갈 알맞은 문장을 고르는 문제이므로 주변 문맥 또는 전체 문맥을 파악합니다. 앞부분 'To make the changes, the city is purchasing additional vehicles.', 'This will call for an expansion of the department's garages.'에서 변경 사항들을 위해 시가 추가 차량들을 구매하고 있고 교통국의 차고의 확장도 필요로 할 것이라고 했으므로, 빈칸에는 추가 차량 구매 및 차고 확장에 필요한 비용을 언급하는 내용이 들어가야 함을 알 수 있습니다. 따라서 (D) Approximately $250 million has been budgeted for the project가 정답입니다.

어휘 entirely adv. 완전히, 전적으로 transit n. 교통 체계, 수송 noticeable adj. 뚜렷한, 두드러진 approximately adv. 약, 거의 budget v. 예산을 세우다; n. 예산

Course 2 문장 고르기 문제

HACKERS TEST
p.284

01 (C)	02 (B)	03 (C)	04 (C)	05 (B)
06 (A)	07 (A)	08 (C)		

01-04번은 다음 기사에 관한 문제입니다.

> **Huntington의 제3회 연례 독립 출판 박람회**
>
> Huntington—⁰¹100명 이상의 작가, 그림 소설가, 저작권 대행업체들이 Huntington의 제3회 연례 독립 출판 박람회에 참석할 것이다. ⁰²5월 3일부터 7일까지 Moira Lambert 문화 회관에서 열리기로 예정된 이 박람회는 대중들이 자비로 출판하는 작가들을 만나고 사인이 된 그들의 책을 구매할 기회가 될 것이다.
>
> ⁰³이 행사는 또한 작가 지망생들에게도 도움이 될 것이다. 베스트셀러인 *Stolen Knight* 시리즈의 작가인 Tara Holten과 같이 자비 출판계의 유명한 인물들이 인정받는 출판사의 도움 없이 성공하는 방법에 대한 발표를 할 것이다.
>
> ⁰⁴티켓은 Lambert 센터 매표소에서 구매 가능하다. 전체 프로그램 ➡

일정표에 대해서는, www.huntingtonipf.com을 방문하면 된다.

literary agency phr. 저작권 대행업, 저작권 대리점
cultural center phr. 문화 회관
self-published adj. 자비로 출판한, 자비 출판의
prove v. ~이 되다, 증명하다 aspiring adj. 장차 ~가 되려는, 야심이 있는
figure n. 인물, 숫자 established adj. 인정받는, 설립된
publishing house phr. 출판사

01 올바른 시제의 동사 채우기 주변 문맥 파악

해설 '작가, 그림 소설가, 저작권 대행업체들이 제3회 연례 독립 출판 박람회에 참석하다'라는 문맥인데, 이 경우 빈칸이 있는 문장만으로 올바른 시제의 동사를 고를 수 없으므로 주변 문맥이나 전체 문맥을 파악하여 정답을 고릅니다. 뒤 문장에서 박람회가 5월 3일부터 7일까지 열리기로 예정되어 있다고 했으므로, 박람회에 참석하는 것이 미래 상황이라는 것을 알 수 있습니다. 따라서 미래 시제 (C) will participate가 정답입니다. 과거 시제 (A), 현재 시제 (B), 현재완료진행 시제 (D)는 미래 상황을 나타낼 수 없습니다.

02 현재분사와 과거분사 구별하여 채우기

해설 빈칸 뒤의 명사(copies)를 꾸밀 수 있는 분사 (B)와 (C)가 정답의 후보입니다. 분사의 꾸밈을 받는 명사 copies(부, 권)와 분사가 '책에 사인이 되다'라는 의미의 수동 관계이므로 과거분사 (B) signed가 정답입니다. 현재분사 (C)는 능동의 의미를 나타내므로 답이 될 수 없습니다. 명사 (A)와 명사 또는 동사 (D)는 명사를 꾸밀 수 없습니다.

03 명사 어휘 고르기 주변 문맥 파악

해설 '이 _____는 작가 지망생들에게도 도움이 될 것이다'라는 문맥이므로 모든 보기가 정답의 후보입니다. 이 경우 빈칸이 있는 문장만으로 정답을 고를 수 없으므로 주변 문맥이나 전체 문맥을 파악하여 정답을 고릅니다. 뒤 문장에서 자비 출판계의 유명한 인물들이 인정받는 출판사의 도움 없이 성공하는 방법에 대한 발표를 할 것이라고 했으므로 이 행사, 즉 제3회 연례 독립 출판 박람회가 작가 지망생들에게도 도움이 될 것임을 알 수 있습니다. 따라서 명사 (C) event(행사, 사건)가 정답입니다. (A) policy는 '정책, 제도', (B) manual은 '안내서, 설명서', (D) video는 '영상, 비디오'라는 의미입니다.

04 알맞은 문장 고르기

해석 (A) 이 박람회는 그 지역에서 열리는 그 유형의 첫 번째 박람회이다.
(B) 그 책의 속편은 이번 여름에 출간될 것이다.
(C) 티켓은 Lambert 센터 매표소에서 구매 가능하다.
(D) 포스터, 만화책, 문구류는 이미 매진되었다.

해설 빈칸에 들어갈 알맞은 문장을 고르는 문제이므로 주변 문맥 또는 전체 문맥을 파악합니다. 앞부분에서 박람회의 일정 및 프로그램 등을 설명했고, 뒤 문장 'For the full program schedule, visit www.huntingtonipf.com.'에서 전체 프로그램 일정표에 대해서는 www.huntingtonipf.com을 방문하면 된다고 했으므로, 빈칸에는 박람회 참석 방법을 언급하는 내용이 들어가야 함을 알 수 있습니다. 따라서 (C) Tickets are available at the Lambert Center box office가 정답입니다.

어휘 sequel n. 속편, 후속 상황 box office phr. 매표소, 극장가 stationery n. 문구류, 문방구

05-08번은 다음 공고에 관한 문제입니다.

> **Bentworth 아파트**
> **주민들께 공지**
>
> ⁰⁵건물 관리소는 오늘 아침 수도 회사에게 연락을 받았습니다. 그들은 내일 오전 9시부터 오후 4시까지 건물의 수도 공급이 중단될 것이라고 통지했습니다. 공공 설비 작업자들이 물의 흐름을 개선하기 위해 일부 파이프를 교체할 것입니다. ⁰⁶건물의 배관이 이미 작년에 새로운 ➡

것으로 바뀌었음을 알고 있습니다. 그러나, 이는 문제를 완전히 해결하지는 못했습니다. 어쨌든, 모두가 최선을 다해 대비해주셔야 할 것입니다. ⁰⁷사용할 물을 용기에 채워 놓으실 것을 권장드립니다. ⁰⁸이 상황이 불편할 수 있을 것임을 이해하지만, 높아진 수압은 그럴 가치가 있게 해줄 것이라고 확신합니다.

---

suspend v. 중단하다 replace v. 교체하다 section n. 일부, 부분
improve v. 개선하다 plumbing n. 배관
fail to phr. ~하지 못하다, ~에 실패하다 resolve v. 해결하다
completely adv. 완전히 in any case phr. 어쨌든
do one's best phr. 최선을 다하다 situation n. 상황
water pressure phr. 수압

05 'be동사 + p.p.' 채우기

해설 be동사(was) 뒤에 올 수 있는 명사 (A)와 (D), p.p.형 (B), -ing형 (C) 모두가 정답의 후보입니다. 빈칸 뒤에 목적어가 없고 '건물 관리소는 오늘 아침 수도 회사에게 연락을 받았다'라는 의미가 되어야 하므로 수동형 'be동사 + p.p.'를 만드는 동사 contact(연락하다)의 p.p.형 (B) contacted가 정답입니다. 명사 (A)와 (D)를 쓰면 각각 '건물 관리소는 수도 회사에 의한 연락이었다/연락처였다'라는 어색한 문맥을 만듭니다. -ing형 (C)는 능동의 의미를 만드는데 빈칸 뒤에 목적어가 없으므로 답이 될 수 없습니다.

06 동사 어휘 고르기 주변 문맥 파악

해설 '건물의 배관은 이미 작년에 _____되었다'라는 문맥이므로 모든 보기가 정답의 후보입니다. 빈칸이 있는 문장만으로 정답을 고를 수 없으므로 주변 문맥이나 전체 문맥을 파악합니다. 뒤 문장에서 그러나 이는 문제를 완전히 해결하지는 못하였다고 했으므로 배관에 대한 조치가 취해졌었음을 알 수 있습니다. 따라서 동사 update(새로운 것으로 바꾸다, 개선하다)의 p.p.형 (A) updated가 정답입니다. (B)의 situate는 '위치시키다', (C)의 propose는 '제안하다', (D)의 initiate는 '착수하다, 개시하다'라는 의미입니다.

07 알맞은 문장 고르기

해석 (A) 사용할 물을 용기에 채워 놓으실 것을 권장드립니다.
(B) 그 후 건물은 평소와 같은 시간에 열고 닫을 것입니다.
(C) 그들은 무엇이 건물의 누수를 일으키고 있는지 찾아볼 것입니다.
(D) 물 사용 정도를 낮추기 위해 새로운 정책이 시행될 것입니다.

해설 빈칸에 들어갈 알맞은 문장을 고르는 문제이므로 빈칸의 주변 문맥이나 전체 문맥을 파악합니다. 앞부분에서 내일 오전 9시부터 오후 4시까지 건물의 수도 공급이 중단될 것이라고 했고, 앞 문장 'everyone should probably do their best to get ready'에서 모두가 최선을 다해 대비해주어야 한다고 했으므로 빈칸에는 수도 공급 중단을 대비하여 무엇을 준비해야 할지에 대한 내용이 들어가야 함을 알 수 있습니다. 따라서 (A) It is recommended that you fill water containers for your use가 정답입니다.

어휘 fill v. 채우다 container n. 용기, 그릇 cause v. 일으키다, 야기하다
leak n. 누수, 누출 implement v. 시행하다 usage n. 사용

08 형용사 자리 채우기

해설 빈칸이 be동사(be) 뒤에 있으므로 be동사 다음의 보어 자리에 올 수 있는 명사 (A), 분사 (B), 형용사 (C)가 정답의 후보입니다. '이 상황이 불편할 수 있겠지만'이라는 의미가 되어야 하므로 형용사 (C) inconvenient (불편한)가 정답입니다. 복수 명사 (A)는 주어(this situation)가 단수 명사이므로 보어도 단수 명사가 되어야 하므로 답이 될 수 없습니다. 과거분사 (B)를 쓰면 '이 상황이 불편함을 느끼다'라는 어색한 문맥이 됩니다. 부사 (D)는 보어 자리에 올 수 없습니다.

DAY 13 질문 유형 1

Course 1 주제 찾기 문제

전략 적용 해석   p.288

공고

공고

건물의 대회의실에서 새로 채용된 사원을 환영하기 위한 모임이 열릴 예정입니다. 이 모임은 5월 10일 토요일 오전 11시 30분에서 오후 1시까지 열릴 것입니다. 참석은 선택적이지만, 모든 분들이 참여하시기를 장려합니다. 회사에서 점심을 제공할 것입니다.

hired adj. 채용된   take place phr. 열리다, 개최되다
optional adj. 선택적인   encourage v. 장려하다, 격려하다
participate v. 참여하다

문제   공고는 무엇에 대한 것인가?
    (A) 직원 출근에 대한 정책
    (B) 고위 간부를 축하하는 기념 행사
    (C) 신입 사원을 위한 환영식

어휘   policy n. 정책   attendance n. 출근, 참여   celebration n. 기념 행사
in honor of phr. ~을 축하하는, ~을 기념하여
executive n. (기업 등의) 간부

HACKERS PRACTICE   p.289

패러프레이징 연습
01 (A)   **02** (B)
유형 연습
03 (B)   **04** (B)

01

Miller & Sons사는 회사 안내서에 정책들의 개요를 제공한다. 그러나, 회사는 또한 각 직원에게 개인 맞춤형 교육을 해주는 것이 회사의 성공에 필수적이라는 것을 인지한다.

(A) Miller & Sons사는 교육에 대한 각 직원의 개별적 요구에 초점을 맞추는 것이 옳다고 생각한다.
(B) 회사 안내서를 따르는 것은 Miller & Sons사에서 성공하는 비결이다.

해설   답의 근거 문장은 'it also recognizes that giving each employee personalized training is vital to its success'로 (A)가 정답입니다. giving each employee personalized training이 addressing each worker's individual need for instruction으로 바뀌어 표현되었습니다.

어휘   overview n. 개요   corporate adj. 회사의   manual n. 안내서, 소책자
recognize v. 인지하다, 깨닫다   personalized adj. 개인 맞춤의
vital adj. 필수적인   believe in phr. ~이 옳다고 생각하다
address v. ~에 초점을 맞추다   individual adj. 개별적인, 개인적인

02

East Sky 항공사는 왕복 항공권에 대한 요금을 낮췄을 때 매출 증가를 경험했다. 그때부터, 다른 항공사들은 계속해서 경쟁력을 갖추기 위한 노력으로 똑같이 해왔다.

(A) East Sky 항공사는 할인된 요금을 제공하기 위해 다른 항공사들과 제휴를 맺었다.
(B) 항공사들은 경쟁에 뒤지지 않기 위해 가격을 낮추기 시작했다.

해설   답의 근거 문장은 'other airlines have done the same in an effort to remain competitive'로 (B)가 정답입니다. in an effort to remain competitive가 in order to keep up with the competition으로 바뀌어 표현되었습니다.

어휘   boost n. 증가, 상승   reduce v. 낮추다, 감소시키다   fare n. 요금
round-trip adj. 왕복의   in an effort to phr. ~하기 위한 노력으로
remain v. 계속 ~이다   competitive adj. 경쟁력 있는
partner v. 제휴하다   discount v. 할인하다
keep up with phr. ~에 뒤지지 않다

03 이메일

축하드립니다! 당신의 제안서를 이사회에 보여드렸고 그들은 그것을 수락했습니다. 그들을 설득하는 것은 어렵지 않았습니다. 그들은 당신이 포함시켰던 직원 건강 프로그램의 이점을 설명한 연구를 마음에 들어 했습니다. 직원들을 위해 오늘부터 그것들에 대한 업무를 시작하시기 바랍니다. 이사회가 6개월 뒤 프로그램에 대한 보고서를 원할 것이므로 모든 결과를 반드시 기록해 주십시오.

proposal n. 제안서   accept v. 수락하다   convince v. 설득하다
include v. 포함하다   describe v. 설명하다   advantage n. 이점
wellness n. 건강   keep track of phr. 기록하다, ~을 계속 파악하다
result n. 결과

문제   이메일에서 주로 논의되는 것은 무엇인가?
    (A) 이사회 임원의 제안서
    (B) 직원 건강 프로그램
    (C) 고객 서비스 보고서

해설   주제 찾기 문제 이메일에서 주로 논의되는 것을 묻는 주제 찾기 문제입니다. 'They liked the studies ~ that describe the advantages of employee wellness programs. You can start working on them for the staff from today.'에서 이사회가 직원 건강 프로그램의 이점을 설명한 연구를 마음에 들어 했고 직원들을 위해 오늘부터 그것들에 대한 업무를 시작하라고 했으므로 (B) A staff wellness program이 정답입니다.

04 광고

경영진 모임 투자 세미나

상을 받은 이 세미나에서, 저희는 여러분에게 주식 시장에서의 투자의 기초와 장기간 동안 부를 형성하는 강력하면서 안정적인 포트폴리오를 유지하는 방법을 가르쳐드릴 것입니다. 이 기술들을 이용하여, 여러분은 퇴직을 위한 저축액을 최대화할 수 있을 것입니다.   ⊙

---

executive n. 경영진, 임원 fundamental n. 기초, 원칙
portfolio n. 포트폴리오, 투자 자산 구성
maximize v. 최대화하다, 극대화하다 savings n. 저축한 돈, 예금
retirement plan phr. 퇴직자 연금 제도, 개인 퇴직금 적립 계획

문제 광고되고 있는 것은 무엇인가?
(A) 퇴직자 연금 제도
(B) 주식 시장 교육
(C) 부동산 워크숍

해설 주제 찾기 문제 광고되고 있는 것을 묻는 주제 찾기 문제입니다. 'At this award-winning seminar, we'll teach you the fundamentals of investing in the stock market and how to maintain a strong and stable portfolio'에서 상을 받은 이 세미나에서 주식 시장에서의 투자의 기초와 강력하면서 안정적인 포트폴리오를 유지하는 방법을 가르쳐줄 것이라고 했으므로 (B) A stock market lesson이 정답입니다.

패러프레이징
seminar 세미나 → lesson 교육

Course 2 목적 찾기 문제

전략 적용 해석   p.290

이메일

수신: Jasper Conway <j.conway@zumail.com>
발신: Excel 문구사 <orders@excel.com>

Mr. Conway께,

귀하의 주문품의 도착일을 알려드리기 위해 글을 씁니다. 지난주 금요일에 귀하가 구매한 Hillman 스탠딩 책상은 오늘 배송될 것입니다. 배달은 3월 14일에 완료될 것으로 예상됩니다. 다음의 번호를 이용하여 배송품을 추적하실 수 있습니다: TS441928.

notify v. 알려주다, 통지하다 arrival n. 도착 purchase v. 구매하다
ship v. 배송하다 delivery n. 배달(품) complete v. 완료하다
track v. 추적하다 shipment n. 배송품

문제 이메일의 목적은 무엇인가?
(A) 납입에 대한 후속 조치를 취하기 위해
(B) 배송 정보를 제공하기 위해
(C) 서비스 제공업체를 추천하기 위해

어휘 follow up on phr. ~에 대한 후속 조치를 취하다 payment n. 납입, 지불
recommend v. 추천하다

HACKERS PRACTICE   p.291

패러프레이징 연습
01 (A)   02 (B)
유형 연습
03 (A)   04 (A)

01

회계사 직무가 채워졌다는 것을 알려드리게 되어 유감입니다. 후에 비슷한 일자리가 열릴 경우를 대비하여 귀하의 지원서를 보관하고 있겠습니다.

(A) 지원자는 회계 분야의 추후 일자리에 대해 고려될 수도 있다.
(B) 지원자는 예정된 일자리 면접에 대해 더 안내를 받을 것이다.

해설 답의 근거 문장은 'I will hold on to your application in case a

similar position opens up later.'로 (A)가 정답입니다. a similar position opens up later가 a future job in accounting으로 바뀌어 표현되었습니다.

어휘 accountant n. 회계사 fill v. (어떤 일자리에 사람을) 채우다
hold on to phr. ~을 보관하다, ~을 고수하다 application n. 지원(서)
in case phr. ~할 경우를 대비하여 similar adj. 비슷한
position n. 일자리, 직무 consider v. 고려하다

02

수요일에, Avery사는 터키의 철강 제조업체인 Zorko사를 매입했다고 발표했다. 그 결과, Avery사의 주가는 주당 67.20달러로 증가했다.

(A) 회사가 터키로 본부를 이전할 것이다.
(B) 매입 소식이 공개된 후에 회사의 주가가 올랐다.

해설 답의 근거 문장은 'As a result, Avery's stock price increased to $67.20 per share.'로 (B)가 정답입니다. stock price가 share values로, increased가 rose로 바뀌어 표현되었습니다.

어휘 steel n. 철강 stock price phr. 주가 share n. 주, 주식, 몫
headquarters n. 본부 rise v. 오르다, 증가하다
purchase n. 매입, 구매 go public phr. 공개되다

03 광고

Gregor Diamante가 LaSalle가에 Diamante's라는 새로운 식당을 개업했습니다. 피자에서부터 파스타까지 정통 이탈리아식 요리를 제공하며 이 식당은 적당한 가격에 편안한 밤 외출을 하려는 사람들에게 완벽합니다. 예약이 가능하며, 복장 규정은 반정장입니다.

authentic adj. 정통의, 진짜인 seek to phr. ~하려고 하다, 시도하다
night out phr. 밤 외출 affordable adj. (가격이) 적당한
permit v. 가능하게 하다, 허락하다 semi-formal adj. 반정장의

문제 광고의 목적은 무엇인가?
(A) 이탈리아식 식당을 광고하기 위해
(B) 지역 식료품점을 설명하기 위해
(C) 포도밭 견학을 소개하기 위해

해설 목적 찾기 문제 광고의 목적을 묻는 목적 찾기 문제입니다. 'Gregor Diamante has opened a new restaurant on LaSalle Street called Diamante's. Offering authentic Italian cuisine'에서 Gregor Diamante가 LaSalle가에 Diamante's라는 새로운 식당을 개업했고 정통 이탈리아식 요리를 제공한다고 한 후 식당에 대해 소개하고 있으므로 (A) To publicize an Italian restaurant이 정답입니다.

어휘 neighborhood n. 지역, 근처 grocery store phr. 식료품점
vineyard n. 포도밭

04 편지

지역 부동산업자 협회를 대표하여, 저희는 귀하께서 저희 단체에 가입하기로 결정하셔서 기쁩니다. 회원으로서, 귀하는 교육 기회와 제휴업체의 할인 프로그램을 포함하여, 귀하가 이 직종에서 성공하는 것을 돕도록 고안된 다수의 서비스에 대한 접근권을 얻을 것입니다. 이것들과 다른 혜택에 대한 더 자세한 정보를 위해 동봉된 문서를 확인하십시오.

on behalf of phr. ~을 대표하여 regional adj. 지역의
realtor n. 부동산업자 association n. 협회 delight v. 기쁘게 하다
an array of phr. 다수의 design v. 고안하다 succeed v. 성공하다
profession n. 직종, 직업 opportunity n. 기회 document n. 문서
benefit n. 혜택

문제 편지는 왜 쓰였는가?

(A) 회원 혜택을 소개하기 위해
(B) 회사의 서비스를 홍보하기 위해
(C) 회사 정책을 설명하기 위해

해설 목적 찾기 문제 편지가 쓰인 이유를 묻는 목적 찾기 문제입니다. 'As a member, you will gain access to an array of services designed to help you succeed in this profession, including learning opportunities and discount programs from partner firms.'에서 회원으로서 교육 기회와 제휴업체의 할인 프로그램을 포함하여 이 직종에서 성공하는 것을 돕도록 고안된 다수의 서비스에 대한 접근권을 얻을 것이라고 했으므로 (A) To introduce some membership benefits가 정답입니다.

HACKERS TEST
p.292

01 (C)	02 (B)	03 (C)	04 (C)	05 (D)
06 (A)	07 (C)			

01-03번은 다음 이메일에 관한 문제입니다.

수신: Ricardo Flores <rflores@learnspanish.org>
발신: Brenda Dean <bdean@fastmail.com>
02날짜: 3월 2일
제목: 문의

Mr. Flores께,

제 이름은 Brenda Dean이고, 저는 Penbrook Financial Analysts사의 직원입니다. 제 회사는 많은 해외 고객들과 일해서, 저는 때때로 그들과 직접 만나기 위해 해외로 비행기를 타고 가야 합니다.

024월 1일에, 저는 그곳에 있는 우리의 몇몇 제휴업체와 이야기하기 위해 콜롬비아에 갈 예정인데, 그들과 효과적으로 의사소통하기 위해서는 01유창한 스페인어를 하는 방법을 알아야 할 것입니다. 저는 상당한 양의 스페인어를 알고 있지만, 그곳에 가기 전에 제 실력을 향상시키고 싶습니다.

01/03저는 The Long Island Gazette 신문에서 귀하의 스페인어 과외 광고를 보았고, 01귀하의 서비스가 아직 이용 가능한지 알아보기 위해 글을 씁니다. 만약 가능하다면, 저는 스페인어 회화에 대한 2주짜리 집중 수업을 수강하고 싶습니다. 저는 오후 6시 이후부터 저녁에 시간이 되며, 주말에는 하루 종일 됩니다. 관심이 있으시다면, 이메일로 답장을 주십시오.

귀하로부터 답변이 오기를 기대하겠습니다.

Brenda Dean 드림

foreign adj. 해외의 overseas adv. 해외로 in person phr. 직접
fluent adj. 유창한 communicate v. 의사소통하다
effectively adv. 효과적으로 fair adj. 상당한 amount n. 양
improve v. 향상시키다 intensive adj. 집중적인
conversational adj. 회화의, 대화의

01 주제/목적 찾기 문제

문제 Ms. Dean은 왜 Mr. Flores에게 글을 썼는가?

(A) 일자리를 위한 지원자의 신원 조사를 하기 위해
(B) 프로젝트를 위한 재정적인 원조를 얻기 위해
(C) 언어 강사의 서비스에 대해 문의하기 위해
(D) 해외 출장을 위한 일정을 준비하기 위해

해설 Ms. Dean이 Mr. Flores에게 글을 쓴 목적을 묻는 목적 찾기 문제입니다. 특별히 이 문제는 지문의 중반과 후반에 목적 관련 내용이 언급되었음에 주의합니다. 'I'll need to know how to speak fluent Spanish'에서 유창한 스페인어를 하는 방법을 알아야 할 것이라고 했고, 'I saw your advertisement for Spanish tutoring ~ and I'm

writing to see if your services are still available.'에서 스페인어 과외 광고를 보았는데 서비스가 아직 이용 가능한지 알아보기 위해 글을 쓴다고 했으므로 (C) To ask about the services of a language instructor가 정답입니다.

어휘 screen v. (직원에 대해) 신원 조사를 하다 financial adj. 재정적인
assistance n. 원조, 도움 organize v. 준비하다, 조직하다

02 육하원칙 문제

문제 Ms. Dean은 다음 달에 무엇을 할 것인가?

(A) 평가 보고서를 작성한다
(B) 출장을 간다
(C) 호텔 객실을 예약한다
(D) 언어 수업에 등록한다

해설 Ms. Dean이 다음 달에 무엇(What)을 할 것인지를 묻는 육하원칙 문제입니다. 질문의 핵심 어구인 Ms. Dean do next month와 관련하여, 'DATE: March 2'에서 이메일이 쓰여진 날짜가 3월 2일임을 알 수 있고, 'On April 1, I'm going to Colombia to speak with several of our partners there'에서 4월 1일에 제휴업체와 이야기하기 위해 콜롬비아에 갈 예정이라고 했으므로 (B) Go on a business trip이 정답입니다.

어휘 evaluation n. 평가 business trip phr. 출장 reserve v. 예약하다
enroll in phr. ~에 등록하다

03 육하원칙 문제

문제 Ms. Dean은 Mr. Flores의 광고를 어디에서 보았는가?

(A) 웹사이트에서
(B) 지역 TV 광고 방송에서
(C) 인쇄물에서
(D) 게시판에서

해설 Ms. Dean이 Mr. Flores의 광고를 어디(Where)에서 보았는지를 묻는 육하원칙 문제입니다. 질문의 핵심 어구인 Ms. Dean see Mr. Flores' advertisement와 관련하여, 'I saw your advertisement ~ in the newspaper'에서 신문에서 광고를 봤다고 했으므로 (C) In a publication이 정답입니다.

패러프레이징
the newspaper 신문 → a publication 인쇄물

어휘 commercial n. 광고 방송; adj. 상업의 publication n. 인쇄물
bulletin board phr. 게시판

04-07번은 다음 공고에 관한 문제입니다.

RIVERDALE 동물 병원

여름이 다가왔고 귀하의 반려동물과 함께 태양 아래에서 즐거움을 만끽할 때입니다! 하지만 밖으로 나가기 전에, 귀하와 반려동물이 안전한지 확인하세요. 05태양열에 의해 초래된 높은 기온은 반려동물의 건강을 해칠 수 있습니다. 04동물 건강 세미나에 참석함으로써 그들을 보호하는 방법을 배우세요.

06Riverdale 동물 병원은 동물 건강 세미나를 매주 토요일 오전 10시부터 오후 12시까지 정기적으로 개최합니다. 그것들은 여러 가지 중요하고 관련된 주제를 다룹니다. 06입장은 무료이며 각 참가자는 기초적인 동물 건강 관리에 대한 인쇄된 안내서를 받게 됩니다. 더불어, 07참가자들은 여러 가지의 멋진 경품들 중 하나를 탈 수 있는 월간 추첨 행사에도 참여하게 됩니다. 이번 달에는, 편리한 손목 끈이 있는 여행용 반려동물 물병을 드립니다!

참석하고 싶으시다면, www.riverdalepet.com에서 온라인으로 등록하세요.

temperature n. 기온, 온도 cause v. 초래하다, 야기하다
heat n. 열 harm v. 해치다 health n. 건강 protect v. 보호하다 ●

join v. 참석하다, 합쳐지다 regularly adv. 정기적으로
hold v. (행사 등을) 개최하다, 열다 cover v. 다루다, 포함시키다
a variety of phr. 여러 가지의 relevant adj. 관련된
participant n. 참가자 basic adj. 기초적인, 기본적인
draw n. 추첨, 제비뽑기 give away phr. (선물로) 주다, 상을 수여하다
handy adj. 편리한 wrist strap phr. 손목 끈 take part phr. 참석하다
register v. 등록하다

04 주제/목적 찾기 문제

문제 공고는 주로 무엇에 대한 것인가?
(A) 월간 입양 캠페인
(B) 시설의 최신 서비스
(C) 반려동물을 보살피는 것에 대한 강연
(D) 동물에게 발생하는 질병

해설 공고가 주로 무엇에 대한 것인지를 묻는 주제 찾기 문제이므로 지문의 앞부분을 주의 깊게 확인합니다. 'Learn how to protect them by joining an Animal Health Seminar.'에서 동물 건강 세미나에 참석함으로써 반려동물들을 보호하는 방법을 배우라고 한 뒤, 세미나 관련 정보를 제공하고 있으므로 (C) A talk about caring for pets가 정답입니다.

어휘 adoption n. 입양, 채택 facility n. 시설 talk n. 강연, 담화
care for phr. 보살피다 sickness n. 질병
affect v. (질병이) 발생하다, 영향을 끼치다

05 육하원칙 문제

문제 공고에 따르면, 무엇이 반려동물에게 위험을 가할 수 있는가?
(A) 드문 운동
(B) 부족한 영양
(C) 불충분한 휴식
(D) 극심한 더위

해설 무엇(what)이 반려동물에게 위험을 가할 수 있는지를 묻는 육하원칙 문제입니다. 질문의 핵심 어구인 pose a hazard to pets와 관련하여, 'High temperatures caused by the heat of the sun can harm your pets' health.'에서 태양열에 의해 초래된 높은 기온이 반려동물의 건강을 해칠 수 있다고 했으므로 (D) Extreme heat이 정답입니다.

패러프레이징
pose a hazard 위험을 가하다 → harm 해치다
High temperatures 높은 기온 → Extreme heat 극심한 더위

어휘 pose v. (위험 등을) 가하다, (문제 등을) 제기하다 hazard n. 위험
infrequent adj. 드문 poor adj. 부족한, 가난한 nutrition n. 영양
inadequate adj. 불충분한, 부적당한 rest n. 휴식 extreme adj. 극심한

06 육하원칙 문제

문제 무엇이 매주 Riverdale 동물 병원에서 주어지는가?
(A) 무료 안내서
(B) 약 한 상자
(C) 할인 쿠폰
(D) 반려동물 사료 한 봉지

해설 무엇(What)이 매주 Riverdale 동물 병원에서 주어지는지를 묻는 육하원칙 문제입니다. 질문의 핵심 어구인 given away each week at Riverdale Pet Hospital과 관련하여, 'Riverdale Pet Hospital regularly holds Animal Health Seminars every Saturday'에서 Riverdale 동물 병원이 동물 건강 세미나를 매주 토요일에 정기적으로 개최한다고 한 후, 'Entrance is free and each participant is given a printed guide to basic animal health care.'에서 입장은 무료이며 각 참가자는 기초적인 동물 건강 관리에 대한 인쇄된 안내서를 받게 된다고 했으므로 (A) A free brochure가 정답입니다.

패러프레이징
printed guide 인쇄된 안내서 → brochure 안내서

07 육하원칙 문제

문제 월간 추첨 행사는 누구를 위해 열리는가?
(A) 회원 카드를 소지한 고객들
(B) 지역 시설의 자원봉사자들
(C) 세미나의 참석자들
(D) 반려동물 프로그램의 후원자들

해설 월간 추첨 행사가 누구(whom)를 위해 열리는지를 묻는 육하원칙 문제입니다. 질문의 핵심 어구인 the monthly draw being held와 관련하여, 'participants are entered into a monthly draw'에서 참가자들이 월간 추첨 행사에 참여하게 된다고 했으므로 (C) Participants in a seminar가 정답입니다.

어휘 volunteer n. 자원봉사자 sponsor n. 후원자

DAY 14 질문 유형 2

Course 1 육하원칙 문제

전략 적용 해석   p.294

회람

회람
최신 휴가 정책이 회사 인트라넷에 업로드되었습니다. 이는 직원들이 받을 수 있는 휴무 일수의 변경과 통지 기간에 관한 지침을 포함합니다. 질문이 있으시다면, 인사부서의 Mr. Stanley에게 연락하십시오.

be entitled to phr. ~을 받을 수 있는, ~의 자격이 되는
guideline n. 지침 notice n. 통지, 공지 period n. 기간

문제 Mr. Stanley는 누구인가?
(A) 사업 자문가
(B) 고객 서비스 직원
(C) 인사부서 직원

어휘 consultant n. 자문가, 상담가 representative n. 직원, 대표(자)

HACKERS PRACTICE   p.295

패러프레이징 연습
01 (A)   02 (B)
유형 연습
03 (A)   04 (C)

01

임대차 계약에 명시되어 있듯이, 부지 내에서 반려동물을 기르거나 흡연을 하는 것은 엄격히 금지되어 있습니다. 이 규정을 따르지 않는 것은 벌금을 야기할 것입니다.
(A) 주민들은 임대차 계약의 규정을 위반하는 것에 대해 돈을 지불하게 될 것이다.
(B) 세입자들은 흡연을 하거나 반려동물을 키우는 것을 허가받으려면 추가 요금을 내야 할 것이다.

해설 답의 근거 문장은 'Disregarding these regulations will result in fines.'로 (A)가 정답입니다. Disregarding these regulations will result in fines가 pay for breaking the rules로 바뀌어 표현되었습니다.

state v. 명시하다 **lease** n. 임대차 계약 **premises** n. 부지, 구내 **strictly** adv. 엄격히 **prohibit** v. 금지하다 **disregard** v. 따르지 않다, 무시하다 **regulation** n. 규정 **result in** phr. ~을 야기하다, ~을 낳다 **fine** n. 벌금 **resident** n. 주민, 거주자 **break** v. (규칙 등을) 위반하다 **rental contract** phr. 임대차 계약 **tenant** n. 세입자 **extra** n. 추가 요금 **allow** v. 허가하다, 허락하다

02

> 5월 11일에, BGR 은행은 Gitwoll 금융 회사와의 합병을 완료할 것이다. 이 기간 동안, 직불 카드와 인터넷 뱅킹 서비스는 이용이 불가능할 것이다.
>
> (A) BGR 은행의 서비스는 Gitwoll 금융 회사와 합병하고 나면 더 이상 이용이 불가능할 것이다.
> (B) BGR 은행은 사업상 거래를 마무리 짓는 동안 일시적으로 몇 가지 서비스를 중단할 것이다.

해설 답의 근거 문장은 'BGR Bank will be completing its merger with Gitwoll Financial. During this period, debit cards and Internet banking services will be unavailable.'로 (B)가 정답입니다. unavailable이 suspending으로, completing its merger가 finalizing a business deal로 바뀌어 표현되었습니다.

어휘 **complete** v. 완료하다 **merger** n. 합병 **debit card** phr. 직불 카드 **unavailable** adj. 이용 불가능한 **temporarily** adv. 일시적으로, 임시로 **suspend** v. 중단하다 **finalize** v. 마무리 짓다

03 주문서

이름	Marianne Verns	주소	321호, 355번지 Haskill가, Ripley, 미시간 주 43159
주문일	4월 25일		
물품	크기	수량	단가	계
Amore 티셔츠	미디엄	1	20.00달러	20.00달러
추가 요청 사항	귀하의 웹사이트에서는 몇몇 물품들은 선물 포장이 가능하다고 언급하고 있으나, 저는 주문 페이지에서 그 선택 사항을 찾을 수 없었습니다. 저는 물품이 포장되기를 원합니다.			

quantity n. 수량, 분량 **mention** v. 언급하다 **wrap** v. 포장하다

문제 Ms. Verns의 주문에 무슨 문제가 있었는가?
(A) 포장 선택 사항이 보이지 않았다.
(B) 거래가 완료될 수 없었다.
(C) 배송 주소가 저장되지 않았다.

해설 육하원칙 문제 Ms. Verns의 주문에 무슨(What) 문제가 있었는지를 묻는 육하원칙 문제입니다. 질문의 핵심 어구인 problem ~ Ms. Verns have with her order와 관련하여, 'Your Web site mentions that some items can be gift-wrapped, but I could not find the option on the order page.'에서 웹사이트에서는 몇몇 물품들은 선물 포장이 가능하다고 언급하고 있으나 Ms. Verns가 주문 페이지에서 그 선택 사항을 찾을 수 없었다고 했으므로 (A) A packaging option was not visible to her가 정답입니다.

어휘 **visible** adj. 보이는 **transaction** v. 거래

04 광고지

> 3월 10일 이번 주 목요일부터, 저희는 아래에 나열된 새로운 60분짜리 스파 패키지의 20퍼센트 할인을 즐기실 수 있도록 여러분을 초대합니다 (행사 가격이 나와 있습니다). ⟳

> Tranquility 패키지: 180달러에 얼굴 관리 그리고 세이지 보디 스크럽
> Soul 패키지: 250달러에 전신 마사지, 매니큐어, 그리고 페디큐어
>
> 할인은 4월 30일까지 이용 가능합니다. 이 행사를 이용하시려면, www.tsdspas.com에서 온라인으로 등록하시거나 저희의 Kendall Square 본점에 555-0767로 전화해 주십시오.

list v. 나열하다; n. 목록 **promotional** adj. 행사의, 홍보의 **facial** adj. 얼굴의 **treatment** n. 관리, 치료, 처리 **offer** n. 할인; v. 제공하다 **take advantage of** phr. ~을 이용하다 **register** v. 등록하다

문제 광고지에 따르면, 고객들은 어떻게 할인을 받을 수 있는가?
(A) Kendall Square 지점을 방문함으로써
(B) 본사에 이메일을 보냄으로써
(C) 웹사이트에서 등록함으로써

해설 육하원칙 문제 고객들이 어떻게(how) 할인을 받을 수 있는지를 묻는 육하원칙 문제입니다. 질문의 핵심 어구인 customers obtain a discount와 관련하여, 'To take advantage of this promotion, register online at www.tsdspas.com'에서 이 행사를 이용하려면 www.tsdspas.com에서 온라인으로 등록하라고 했으므로 (C) By signing up on a Web site가 정답입니다.

Course 2 Not/True 문제

전략 적용 해석　　　　　　　　　　　　　p.296

광고

> ### 사무용품 세일
>
> Ben's 사무용품점이 할인 행사를 엽니다. 엄선된 품목들에 대한 저렴한 가격들을 확인해 보십시오. 할인은 6월 30일에 종료됩니다.
>
> – 모든 연필과 펜 25퍼센트 할인
> – 접착식 메모지 20퍼센트 할인
> – 모든 봉투 15퍼센트 할인
>
> **envelope** n. 봉투

문제 연필에 대해 언급된 것은?
(A) 6월 30일 이후에는 없을 것이다.
(B) 할인된 가격에 판매될 것이다.
(C) 고객들에게 무료로 주어질 것이다.

어휘 **stock** v. (상품을 갖추고) 있다 **reduce** v. (가격을) 할인하다, 낮추다 **price** n. 가격 **for free** phr. 무료로

HACKERS PRACTICE　　　　　　　　　　p.297

패러프레이징 연습
01 (B)　　　**02** (B)
유형 연습
03 (C)　　　**04** (B)

01

> 기타 레슨을 전문으로 하는 음악가 Corey Lermin이 초보자들에게 악기를 연주하는 방법을 가르치기 위해 지난주에 스튜디오를 열었습니다. 문의하시려면, 555-6892로 전화하십시오.
>
> (A) Corey Lermin이 지난주에 스튜디오에서 첫 음악 공연을 했다.
> (B) 초보자들은 Corey Lermin의 새 스튜디오에서 기타를 연주하는 방법을 배울 수 있다.

해설 답의 근거 문장은 'Specializing in lessons for the guitar, musician Corey Lermin opened a studio last week to teach newcomers how to play the instrument.'로 (B)가 정답입니다. newcomers가 Beginners로, to play the instrument가 to play the guitar로 바뀌어 표현되었습니다.

어휘 specialize in phr. ~을 전문으로 하다   newcomer n. 초보자, 신입
instrument n. 악기, 기구   performance n. 공연   beginner n. 초보자

02

> Ms. Phelps가 귀하께서 요청하신 대로 웹사이트를 업데이트하는 것을 끝냈습니다. 그것은 이번 주말의 행사를 위한 연설자들의 최종 명단을 보여줍니다. 그녀는 행사 사진을 다음 주에 추가할 것입니다.
>
> (A) Ms. Phelps는 연설자 명단을 완성하기 위해 일주일이 더 필요하다.
> (B) 행사 동안 촬영된 사진들이 다음 주에 온라인에 게시될 것이다.

해설 답의 근거 문장은 'She will add pictures from the event next week.'로 (B)가 정답입니다. pictures from the event가 Photographs taken during an event로 바뀌어 표현되었습니다.

어휘 speaker n. 연설자   finalize v. 완성하다, 마무리 짓다

03 공고

> 지역 주민들을 위해 토지 개발업체 Handley사와의 모임이 준비되었습니다. 이 모임은 Handley사가 그 지역에 지을 아파트 단지와 관련된 것입니다. B회의에서, Handley사는 건물들의 위치를 포함하여, 작업과 관련된 몇 가지 주제에 대해 논의할 것입니다. A회의는 2월 8일 일요일 오후 7시에 Harmony 기념관에서 열릴 것입니다. C참석하는 모든 분들은 제안된 프로젝트에 대해 자유롭게 질문할 수 있습니다.
>
> gathering n. 모임   developer n. 개발업체, 개발자
> organize v. 준비하다   local n. 지역 주민   concern v. ~과 관련되다
> location n. 위치   propose v. 제안하다

문제 회의에 대해 언급되지 않은 것은?
(A) 주말 동안 열릴 것이다.
(B) 건물 장소에 대한 논의를 포함할 것이다.
(C) 지역의 모든 주민들에 의해 참석될 것이다.

해설 Not/True 문제 질문의 핵심 어구인 the meeting과 관련된 내용을 지문에서 찾아 각 보기와 대조하는 Not/True 문제입니다. (A)는 'The meeting will be held on Sunday'에서 회의가 일요일에 열릴 것이라고 했으므로 지문의 내용과 일치합니다. (B)는 'At the meeting, Handley plans to discuss ~ the location of the buildings.'에서 회의에서 Handley사가 건물들의 위치에 대해 논의할 것이라고 했으므로 지문의 내용과 일치합니다. (C)는 'Everyone attending is welcome to ask questions'에서 참석하는 모든 사람들이 자유롭게 질문할 수 있다고 했지 지역의 모든 주민들이 참석할 것이라는 의미는 아니므로 지문의 내용과 일치하지 않습니다. 따라서 (C) It will be attended by every resident in the area가 정답입니다.

패러프레이징
Sunday 일요일 → weekend 주말
the location of the buildings 건물들의 위치
→ building sites 건물 장소

04 편지

> Mr. Gresham께,
>
> 호주 야생 동물 관리단에 기부해 주신 것에 감사드립니다. 저희 단체는 귀하와 같은 헌신적인 회원들의 후원이 없다면 존재할 수 없을 것입 ⟳

니다. B귀하는 저희 단체의 정기적인 기부자이기 때문에, A이 편지에 무료 호주 야생 동물 관리용 달력을 동봉합니다.

Bruce Niles 드림, 호주 야생 동물 관리단

> donation n. 기부   wildlife n. 야생 동물   conservancy n. 관리단
> organization n. 단체, 기구   exist v. 존재하다   support n. 후원, 지지
> dedicated adj. 헌신적인, 전념하는   regular adj. 정기적인
> donor n. 기부자

문제 Mr. Gresham에 대해 언급된 것은?
(A) 최근에 달력을 주문했다.
(B) 단체에 정기적으로 기부한다.
(C) 유명한 과학자이다.

해설 Not/True 문제 질문의 핵심 어구인 Mr. Gresham과 관련된 내용을 지문에서 찾아 각 보기와 대조하는 Not/True 문제입니다. (A)는 'we are enclosing a free ~ calendar with this letter'에서 편지에 달력을 동봉한다고 했지 최근에 달력을 주문했다는 의미는 아니므로 지문의 내용과 일치하지 않습니다. (B)는 'you are a regular donor to our organization'에서 Mr. Gresham이 단체의 정기적인 기부자라고 했으므로 지문의 내용과 일치합니다. 따라서 (B) He donates regularly to a group이 정답입니다. (C)는 지문에 언급되지 않은 내용입니다.

패러프레이징
organization 단체 → a group 단체

HACKERS TEST
p.298

01 (A)	02 (B)	03 (D)	04 (D)	05 (B)
06 (D)	07 (C)	08 (D)		

01-04번은 다음 편지에 관한 문제입니다.

> Chiaroscuro 사진 동호회
> 85호, 377번지 Westminster로
> 랭커스터, 잉글랜드, LE5109
>
> 6월 1일
>
> 회원분들께,
>
> 다음 두 달은 우리의 회원분들께 매우 흥미진진할 것으로 보입니다. 시의 관광청이 사진 경연 대회를 열 예정입니다. 01-A/04-A대회를 위해, Lancaster의 전문 사진가들과 비전문 사진가들 모두 시의 홍보용 사진을 찍을 것이 요청됩니다. 04-A출품작들이 수령되면, 최고의 것들이 04-A시청 옆의 04-A/CFulmore 미술관에 전시될 것입니다. 이 행사와 관련하여, 04-B몇몇 이전 수상자들이 미술관에서 강연을 하는 것에 동의하였고, 사진가 지망생들에게 그들의 기술을 향상시키는 기회를 줄 것입니다. 아래는 일정표입니다:
>
> | 주제 | 강연자 | 날짜 & 시간 |
> |------|--------|-------------|
> | 여행 사진 | Isabelle Robey | 6월 15일 화요일 오후 7시 |
> | 02야외 환경에서의 인물 사진 | 02Jeanette Dennis | 6월 24일 목요일 오후 7시 |
> | 풍경 구성하기 | Wilbur Smithey | 7월 3일 토요일 오후 2시 |
> | 자연광 이용하기 | Hana Takagi | 7월 12일 월요일 오후 8시 |
>
> 물론, 저는 모든 분들이 03 7월 26일에 미술관에서 열리는 시상식에 참석하실 수 있기를 바랍니다. 오후 1시에 시작하여, 수상자들의 이름이 발표될 것입니다. 그들 각각은 오후 2시 30분에 질의응답 시간에 참석하게 될 것입니다. 전 시상식은 오후 4시에 끝날 것입니다. 더 세부적인 사항들이 공지되면 그것들을 회원분들께 보내드리겠습니다.
>
> Alvin Markham 드림, 회장
> Chiaroscuro 사진 동호회   ⟳

photography n. 사진 club n. 동호회
promise v. ~일 것으로 보이다, 약속하다 tourism office phr. 관광청
competition n. 경연 대회 professional adj. 전문의, 프로의
promotional adj. 홍보의 entry n. 출품작, 입장
on display phr. 전시된 in connection with phr. ~과 관련하여
past adj. 이전의, 과거의 agree v. 동의하다 deliver v. (강연, 연설 등을) 하다
aspiring adj. ~을 지망하는 opportunity n. 기회 improve v. 향상시키다
portrait n. 인물 사진, 초상화 outdoor adj. 야외의
setting n. 환경, 배경 compose v. 구성하다

01 Not/True 문제

문제 사진 경연 대회에 대해 사실인 것은?
(A) 참가는 비전문가들에게 열려 있다.
(B) 소액의 참가비가 있다.
(C) 상은 상금의 형태를 취할 것이다.
(D) 수상자들은 우편으로 공지 받을 것이다.

해설 질문의 핵심 어구인 the photography competition과 관련된 내용을 지문에서 찾아 각 보기와 대조하는 Not/True 문제입니다. (A)는 'For the contest, both professional and non-professional photographers ~ are invited to take promotional pictures of the city.'에서 대회를 위해 전문 사진가들과 비전문 사진가들 모두 시의 홍보용 사진을 찍을 것이 요청된다고 했으므로 지문의 내용과 일치합니다. 따라서 (A) Participation is open to amateurs가 정답입니다. (B), (C), (D)는 지문에 언급되지 않은 내용입니다.

패러프레이징
non-professional photographers 비전문 사진가들 → amateurs 비전문가들

어휘 amateur n. 비전문가, 아마추어 entrance fee phr. 참가비, 입장료
cash prize phr. 상금

02 육하원칙 문제

문제 누가 인물 사진을 찍는 것에 대한 강연을 할 것인가?
(A) Isabelle Robey
(B) Jeanette Dennis
(C) Wilbur Smithey
(D) Hana Takagi

해설 누가(Who) 인물 사진을 찍는 것에 대한 강연을 할 것인지를 묻는 육하원칙 문제입니다. 질문의 핵심 어구인 give a lecture on taking pictures of people과 관련하여, 'Portraits in outdoor settings', 'Jeanette Dennis'에서 야외 환경에서의 인물 사진의 강연자가 Jeanette Dennis라고 했으므로 (B) Jeanette Dennis가 정답입니다.

패러프레이징
pictures of people 인물 사진 → Portraits 인물 사진

03 육하원칙 문제

문제 시상식은 언제 열릴 것인가?
(A) 6월 15일에
(B) 6월 24일에
(C) 7월 12일에
(D) 7월 26일에

해설 시상식이 언제(When) 열릴 것인지를 묻는 육하원칙 문제입니다. 질문의 핵심 어구인 the awards show be held와 관련하여, 'the awards ceremony on July 26'에서 시상식이 7월 26일이라고 했으므로 (D) On July 26가 정답입니다.

04 Not/True 문제

문제 Fulmore 미술관에 대해 언급되지 않은 것은?
(A) 시청 근처에 위치해 있다.
(B) 이전 대회 수상자들의 강연을 열 것이다.
(C) 지역 사진 전시회를 포함할 것이다.
(D) 회원들에게 무료 입장을 제공한다.

해설 질문의 핵심 어구인 the Fulmore Art Gallery와 관련된 내용을 지문에서 찾아 각 보기와 대조하는 Not/True 문제입니다. (A)는 'the Fulmore Gallery next to City Hall'에서 시청 옆에 Fulmore 미술관이 있다고 했으므로 지문의 내용과 일치합니다. (B)는 'several past winners have agreed to deliver lectures at the art gallery'에서 몇몇 이전 수상자들이 미술관에서 강연을 하는 것에 동의하였다고 했으므로 지문의 내용과 일치합니다. (C)는 'For the contest, ~ photographers from Lancaster are invited to take promotional pictures of the city. ~ the best ones will be put on display in the Fulmore Gallery'에서 대회를 위해 사진가들이 시의 홍보용 사진을 찍을 것이 요청되고, 최고의 것들이 Fulmore 미술관에 전시될 것이라고 한 것에서 Fulmore 미술관이 Lancaster 지역의 사진 전시회를 포함할 것임을 알 수 있으므로 지문의 내용과 일치합니다. (D)는 지문에 언급되지 않은 내용입니다. 따라서 (D) It offers free entrance to its members가 정답입니다.

05-08번은 다음 브로슈어에 관한 문제입니다.

Baylor 수족관

Ventura 여행사는 Baylor 수족관의 자랑스러운 제휴업체입니다. [05-A]이 시설은 Louisville 지역에서 가장 큰 수족관입니다. [05-B]이곳은 또한 켄터키 주에서 바닷물고기와 민물고기를 모두 선보이는 유일한 곳입니다. 저희 여행사는 여러분이 가족과 함께 들르셔서 매혹적인 수중 동물의 세계에 대해 더 많이 배우는 것을 추천드립니다.

[07-D]인기 구경거리

상어 탱크: 바다의 가장 사나운 포식자를 관람하십시오. 탱크는 배암상어, 청새리상어, 그리고 귀상어를 포함합니다.

아마존 강 모험: 세계에서 가장 큰 강에 사는 야생 민물고기의 독특한 종과 풍부한 다양성을 탐험하십시오.

잠수함: 수족관의 세계 2차 대전 미국 잠수함의 실물 크기 복제품 견학을 위해서는 꼭 미리 등록하십시오.

[07-B]정규 영업 시간:
월요일–금요일: 오전 9시부터 오후 5시
토요일–일요일: 오전 8시부터 오후 6시

특별 행사:
매주 월요일 오후 2시: 수달 쇼
매주 수요일과 금요일 오후 1시: 잠수함 견학
[06]매주 토요일 오후 4시: 돌고래 쇼

[07-A]입장료:
일반 입장료: 10달러
학생: 신분증 지참 시 8달러
경로: 7달러

수족관 회원 및 4세 미만의 어린이들은 무료로 입장됩니다.

[08]더 많은 정보를 위해서는, inquiries@venturatrav.com으로 저희에게 이메일을 보내주십시오.

aquarium n. 수족관 facility n. 시설, 기관
feature v. (특별히) 선보이다, 특징으로 삼다 saltwater adj. 바닷물의
freshwater adj. 민물의 recommend v. 추천하다
stop by phr. 들르다 fascinating adj. 매혹적인, 황홀한
aquatic adj. 수중의, 물에서 사는 attraction n. 인기 구경거리, 명소
fierce adj. 사나운 predator n. 포식자 include v. 포함하다
adventure n. 모험 explore v. 탐험하다 unique adj. 독특한
species n. 종 (생물 분류의 기초 단위) rich adj. 풍부한
diversity n. 다양성 wildlife n. 야생 동물 populate v. 살다, 거주하다
submarine n. 잠수함 sign up phr. 등록하다
ahead of time phr. 미리 full-scale adj. 실물 크기의
reproduction n. 복제품 regular adj. 정규의, 보통의
entrance n. 입장 fee n. 요금 general adj. 일반적인, 전반적인
admission n. 입장(료) identification n. 신분증
senior n. 경로, 연장자, 상급자 for free phr. 무료로

05 Not/True 문제

문제 Baylor 수족관에 대해 언급된 것은?
(A) 지역에서 가장 인기 있는 행선지이다.
(B) 바다에 사는 동물들을 전시한다.
(C) 최근에 새로운 인기 구경거리를 추가했다.
(D) 구내식당에서 간식을 판매한다.

해설 질문의 핵심 어구인 Baylor Aquarium과 관련된 내용을 지문에서 찾아 각 보기와 대조하는 Not/True 문제입니다. (A)는 'This facility is the largest aquarium in the ~ area.'에서 지역에서 가장 큰 수족관이라고 했지 가장 인기 있다고 하지는 않았으므로 지문의 내용과 일치하지 않습니다. (B)는 'It ~ feature both saltwater and freshwater fish.'에서 바닷물고기와 민물고기를 모두 선보인다고 했으므로 지문의 내용과 일치합니다. 따라서 (B) It showcases animals that live in the sea가 정답입니다. (C)와 (D)는 지문에 언급되지 않은 내용입니다.

어휘 destination n. 행선지 region n. 지역
showcase v. 전시하다, 소개하다 cafeteria n. 구내식당

06 육하원칙 문제

문제 방문객들은 언제 돌고래 쇼를 볼 수 있는가?
(A) 월요일마다
(B) 수요일마다
(C) 금요일마다
(D) 토요일마다

해설 방문객들이 언제(When) 돌고래 쇼를 볼 수 있는지를 묻는 육하원칙 문제입니다. 질문의 핵심 어구인 visitors see the dolphin show와 관련하여, 'Saturdays at 4 P.M.: Dolphin Show'에서 매주 토요일 오후 4시에 돌고래 쇼가 있다고 했으므로 (D) On Saturdays가 정답입니다.

07 Not/True 문제

문제 브로슈어에 제공되지 않은 것은?
(A) 입장료
(B) 개관 시간
(C) 시설에 오는 길
(D) 인기 구경거리에 대한 설명

해설 브로슈어에 대해 묻는 Not/True 문제입니다. 이 문제는 질문에 핵심 어구가 없으므로 각 보기와 관련된 내용을 브로슈어에서 확인합니다. (A)는 'Entrance Fees: General admission, Students, Seniors'에서 일반, 학생, 경로 입장료를 제공하고 있으므로 지문의 내용과 일치합니다. (B)는 'Regular Hours: Monday-Friday, Saturday-Sunday'에서 요일별 영업 시간을 언급하고 있으므로 지문의 내용과 일치합니다. (C)는 지문에 언급되지 않은 내용입니다. 따라서 (C) Directions to a facility가 정답입니다. (D)는 'Attractions: Shark Tank, Amazon River Adventure, Submarine'에서 인기 구경거리들 각각에 대한 설명을 제공하고 있으므로 지문의 내용과 일치합니다.

08 육하원칙 문제

문제 사람들은 어떻게 Baylor 수족관에 대한 더 많은 정보를 얻을 수 있는가?
(A) 시설의 웹사이트에 로그인함으로써
(B) 관광객 안내 센터를 방문함으로써
(C) 영업 시간 중에 시설에 전화함으로써
(D) Ventura 여행사에 메시지를 보냄으로써

해설 사람들이 어떻게(How) Baylor 수족관에 대한 더 많은 정보를 얻을 수 있는지를 묻는 육하원칙 문제입니다. 질문의 핵심 어구인 people get more information about Baylor Aquarium과 관련하여, 'For more information, e-mail us'에서 더 많은 정보를 위해서는 저희, 즉 Ventura 여행사에 이메일을 보내달라고 했으므로 (D) By sending a message to Ventura Travel이 정답입니다.

패러프레이징
e-mail 이메일을 보내다 → sending a message 메시지를 보내는 것

어휘 establishment n. 시설 tourist n. 관광객

DAY 15 질문 유형 3

Course 1 추론 문제

전략 적용 해석   p.300

이메일

> Mr. Pugsley께,
>
> 저희 회사는 휴대전화 마이크로칩의 새로운 공급업체를 찾고 있었으며, Mervone사의 R5G 칩이 저희에게 필요한 사양을 가지고 있다고 결론지었습니다. 저희는 대량 주문을 하고자 합니다. 만약 귀사가 관심이 있다면, 회의를 마련할 수 있도록 최대한 빨리 555-2323으로 제게 연락해주십시오.
>
> Joan Marshfield 드림, 연구 부장, Saxonia사

look for phr. 찾다, 구하다 **conclude** v. 결론짓다
specification n. 사양 **require** v. 필요하다
set up phr. ~을 마련하다

문제 Mervone사에 대해 암시되는 것은?
(A) 무선 단말기 부품을 만든다.
(B) 최근에 새로운 시장에 진입했다.
(C) Saxonia사에 제품 목록을 우편으로 보냈다.

HACKERS PRACTICE   p.301

패러프레이징 연습
01 (A)   **02** (B)
유형 연습
03 (B)   **04** (A)

01

> 주문서에 귀하의 완전한 주소를 포함해야 한다는 것을 유념하십시오. 그렇지 않으면, 귀하는 가장 가까운 우체국에 소포를 가지러 가셔야 할 것입니다.

(A) 불완전한 주소가 적힌 소포는 가장 가까운 우체국으로 보내질 것이다.
(B) 소포를 위한 주문서는 가까운 우체국 어디서든지 가져갈 수 있다.

해설 답의 근거 문장은 'Otherwise, you will have to collect the package at the nearest post office.'로 (A)가 정답입니다. the nearest post office가 the closest post office로 바뀌어 표현되었습니다.

어휘 complete adj. 완전한 collect v. ~을 가지러 가다, 수집하다
package n. 소포, 포장물 parcel n. 소포, 꾸러미

02

> 만약 귀하께서 관광청에 도움을 주는 데 관심이 있는 주민이시라면, 지원서를 작성해주십시오. 귀하의 어떠한 관련 경험 및 기술이라도 목록에 포함해주셔야 합니다. ○

(A) 관광청의 회원 신청서가 이용 가능하다.
(B) 주민들은 관련 배경 정보를 포함하는 양식을 작성함으로써 지원할 수 있다.

해설 답의 근거 문장은 'You should list any of your relevant experience and skills.'로 (B)가 정답입니다. relevant experience and skills가 relevant background information으로 바뀌어 표현되었습니다.

어휘 resident n. 주민 lend a hand phr. 도움을 주다
fill out phr. (양식 등을) 작성하다, 채우다
application n. 지원(서), 신청(서) relevant adj. 관련된
experience n. 경험 skill n. 기술 available adj. 이용 가능한
include v. 포함하다 background n. 배경
information n. 정보

03 공고

어린이날을 기념하여, Mariposa 문화센터는 11월 20일 오후 4시에 세미나를 개최할 것입니다. "자녀에게 말을 거는 방법: 모든 부모가 가져야 할 대화의 기술"이라고 제목이 붙여진 이 세미나는, 유명한 심리학자 Dr. Marsha Peterson에 의해 진행될 것입니다. 좌석을 예약하시려면, 555-3209로 센터에 연락해주십시오.

in celebration of phr. ~을 기념하여, ~을 인정하여
Children's Day phr. 어린이날 entitle v. ~이라고 제목을 붙이다
conversational adj. 대화의 famous adj. 유명한
psychologist n. 심리학자

문제 공고는 누구를 대상으로 하는 것 같은가?
(A) 아동 심리 전문가
(B) 어린 자녀들의 부모
(C) 어린이들과 일하는 센터 직원

해설 추론 문제 공고의 대상을 추론하는 문제입니다. 'The seminar, entitled "How to Talk to Your Kids: Conversational Skills Every Parent Should Have," will be led'에서 "자녀에게 말을 거는 방법: 모든 부모가 가져야 할 대화의 기술"이라고 제목이 붙여진 세미나가 진행될 것이라고 했으므로 자녀를 둔 부모들을 대상으로 하는 공고임을 추론할 수 있습니다. 따라서 (B) Parents of young children이 정답입니다.

어휘 professional n. 전문가

04 이메일

Ms. Ming께,

제가 최근에 구매한 Vermillion Red 그래픽 카드에 대한 제 의견을 듣고 싶어 하신다는 것을 확인했습니다. 그 그래픽 카드는 성능을 고려했을 때 뛰어난 가치를 지녔습니다. 귀하가 업무를 위해 가정용 컴퓨터에서 사용하시는 영상 편집 소프트웨어와 함께 사용하신다면, 그 카드는 귀하가 기대하는 품질을 제공할 수 있다고 생각합니다. 다른 질문이 있으시다면 알려주십시오.

John Cortes 드림

considering prep. ~을 고려하면 performance n. 성능, 성과

문제 Ms. Ming에 대해 암시되는 것은?
(A) 그녀는 영상을 편집하기 위해 그녀의 컴퓨터를 사용한다.
(B) 그녀는 이전에 한 번도 그래픽 카드를 구매한 적이 없다.
(C) 그녀는 성공한 영화 제작자이다.

해설 추론 문제 질문의 핵심 어구인 Ms. Ming에 대해 추론하는 문제입니다. 'the video editing software you use on your home PC for

어휘 edit v. 편집하다 successful adj. 성공한, 성공적인
producer n. 제작자

Course 2 문장 위치 찾기 문제

전략 적용 해석 p.302

공고

모든 동호회 회원들은 주목해주십시오! —[1]—. 실내 테니스 코트가 수리로 인해 5월 12일부터 18일까지 폐쇄될 것입니다. —[2]—. 그동안에는, 모두 야외 코트를 사용하는 것이 권고됩니다. —[3]—.

indoor adj. 실내의 in the meantime phr. 그동안에 advise v. 권고하다

문제 [1], [2], [3]으로 표시된 위치 중, 다음 문장이 들어갈 곳으로 가장 적절한 것은?
"그러므로, 이번 주 동호회 대회는 다음 주로 미뤄졌습니다."
(A) [1]
(B) [2]
(C) [3]

어휘 competition n. 대회, 경기

HACKERS PRACTICE p.303

패러프레이징 연습
01 (B)   **02** (A)
유형 연습
03 (C)   **04** (C)

01

만약 귀하의 신용카드가 분실되었다면, 승인되지 않은 사용을 방지하기 위해 은행에 최대한 빨리 알려주십시오. 그렇지 않으면, 귀하는 발생시키지 않은 대금을 지불하도록 요구받을 수 있습니다.

(A) 새 신용카드를 활성화하기 위해 은행에 전화하는 것이 필요하다.
(B) 카드 소지자들은 분실된 신용카드에서 발생한 대금에 대해 책임을 질 수도 있다.

해설 답의 근거 문장은 'you may be required to pay for charges you did not make'로 (B)가 정답입니다. be required to pay for charges가 be responsible for charges로 바뀌어 표현되었습니다.

어휘 inform v. 알리다 prevent v. 방지하다, 예방하다
unauthorized adj. 승인되지 않은 otherwise adv. 그렇지 않으면
be required to phr. ~하도록 요구받다 charge n. 대금, 요금
activate v. 활성화하다 responsible adj. 책임을 지는

02

Herqwell사의 정수 물병은 각각의 교체 필터가 단돈 2달러의 비용만 들기 때문에 인기가 있다. 그러나 시간이 지나면, 필터가 자주 교체되어야 하기 때문에 비용이 빠르게 늘어난다.

(A) Herqwell사의 정수 물병은 궁극적으로는 보이는 것보다 더 비싸다.
(B) 시장의 모든 정수기 중에서, Herqwell사의 것이 가장 가격이 적당하다.

해설 답의 근거 문장은 'But over time, its costs add up quickly because the filters frequently need to be replaced.'로 (A)가 정답입니다. costs add up이 expensive로 바뀌어 표현되었습니다.

어휘 **replacement** n. 교체 **cost** v. 비용이 들다; n. 비용
mere adj. 단지, 오직 **over time** phr. 시간이 지나면
add up phr. 늘어나다 **frequently** adv. 자주
ultimately adv. 궁극적으로, 결국 **affordable** adj. 가격이 적당한

03 기사

이번 주 초에, Fontaineville의 소방서는 시에 의해 구매된 두 대의 새 소방차와 장비용 화물차를 배송받았다. ─[1]─. 그 트럭들은 소방서의 전체 비상 차량을 최신의 것으로 교체하기 위한 노력의 일환인데, 그 비상 차량들 중 많은 것들이 구식이다. ─[2]─. 현재, 서의 직원들은 새 차량을 위해 교육을 받아야 한다. ─[3]─.

equipment n. 장비 **purchase** v. 구매하다 **effort** n. 노력
update v. 최신의 것으로 교체하다, 갱신하다
fleet n. (한 회사 소유의) 전체 차량 **vehicle** n. 차량
outdated adj. 구식의, 낡은 **currently** adv. 현재

문제 [1], [2], [3]으로 표시된 위치 중, 다음 문장이 들어갈 곳으로 가장 적절한 것은?

"그것이 완료되면, 그 차량들이 사용되기 시작할 것이다."

(A) [1]
(B) [2]
(C) [3]

해설 문장 위치 찾기 문제 지문의 흐름상 주어진 문장이 들어가기에 가장 적절한 곳을 고르는 문제입니다. Once that is complete, the vehicles will begin to be used에서 그것이 완료되면 그 차량들이 사용되기 시작할 것이라고 했으므로, 주어진 문장 앞에 대명사 that (그것)이 가리키는 것과 차량들을 사용하기 위해 현재 진행되고 있는 것에 관한 내용이 있을 것임을 예상할 수 있습니다. [3]의 앞 문장인 'Currently, the department's staff members need to take training courses for the new vehicles.'에서 현재 서의 직원들은 새 차량을 위해 교육을 받아야 한다고 했으므로 [3]에 주어진 문장이 들어가면 그것, 즉 현재 받고 있는 교육이 끝나면 그 차량들이 사용되기 시작할 것이라는 자연스러운 문맥이 된다는 것을 알 수 있습니다. 따라서 (C) [3]이 정답입니다.

04 공고

참고: Sheridan 콘서트홀은 시설로 가져오신 그 어떤 물품의 분실이나 도난에 책임을 지지 않습니다. ─[1]─. 손님들께서는 본인의 귀중품에 신경을 쓰시기를 정중히 요청드립니다. 물건을 잃어버리셨다면, 로비에 있는 분실물 보관소 카운터에서 확인해 보십시오. ─[2]─. 부피가 큰 물품들에 대해서는, 홀에서 휴대품 보관 서비스를 제공합니다. ─[3]─. 물품을 저희 직원에게 주시면, 공연 후 귀하의 소지품을 되찾기 위한 표를 제공받으실 것입니다.

responsible adj. 책임이 있는 **loss** n. 분실 **theft** n. 도난, 절도
take care of phr. 신경을 쓰다, 돌보다 **valuables** n. 귀중품
misplace v. 물건을 둔 곳을 잊다, 잘못 두다
lost-and-found n. 분실물 보관소
coat-check service phr. 휴대품 보관 서비스 **retrieve** v. 되찾다
belongings n. 소지품 **performance** n. 공연

문제 [1], [2], [3]으로 표시된 위치 중, 다음 문장이 들어갈 곳으로 가장 적절한 것은?

"그곳에 겉옷, 우산, 그리고 큰 가방이나 짐을 맡기실 수 있습니다."

(A) [1]
(B) [2]

(C) [3]

해설 문장 위치 찾기 문제 지문의 흐름상 주어진 문장이 들어가기에 가장 적절한 곳을 고르는 문제입니다. You may leave outerwear, umbrellas, and large bags or packages there에서 그곳에 겉옷, 우산, 그리고 큰 가방이나 짐을 맡길 수 있다고 했으므로, 주어진 문장 앞에 물품을 맡길 수 있는 장소에 관한 내용이 있을 것임을 예상할 수 있습니다. [3]의 앞 문장인 'the hall does offer a coat-check service'에서 홀에서 휴대품 보관 서비스를 제공한다고 했으므로, [3]에 주어진 문장이 들어가면 홀에서 제공하는 휴대품 보관 서비스를 이용하면 그곳에 물품들을 보관할 수 있다는 자연스러운 문맥이 된다는 것을 알 수 있습니다. 따라서 (C) [3]이 정답입니다.

HACKERS TEST   p.304

01 (C)	02 (D)	03 (C)	04 (C)	05 (A)
06 (A)	07 (C)			

01-03번은 다음 기사에 관한 문제입니다.

Mark Timan을 위한 앞으로의 중요한 일

Mark Timan의 거대 금융 기업은 플로리다와 하와이에 있는 리조트의 개발과 함께 부동산 업계에서 시작되었다. 그러나, 토지 가치의 심각한 하락은 그로 하여금 Partizone사라고 하는 인터넷 회사에 투자하게 만들었다. ─[1]─. ⁰¹Partizone사의 웹사이트는 항공편, 호텔, 그리고 렌터카를 위한 선도적인 예약 도구가 되었다. Mr. Timan의 리조트와의 결합 상품과 함께, 두 사업은 곧 번창했다. 그것들은 업계의 선두 주자가 되었고 Mr. Timan을 억만장자로 만들었다. ─[2]─.

이 성공의 역사를 고려해 볼 때, 업계는 Mr. Timan이 모든 것을 팔겠다고 발표했을 때 놀라워했다. ─[3]─. ⁰³그는 "저는 나이가 들고 있고, 제 아이들과 시간을 더 많이 보내고 싶습니다. 그러나 사업이 커질수록, 그것은 제 시간을 더 많이 차지합니다."라고 말했다.

─[4]─. 그러나, 이것이 그가 완전히 은퇴한다는 것을 의미하지는 않는다. "아니요, 저는 업계에서 계속 활동하고 싶습니다"라고 여전히 활기 넘치는 Timan이 말했다. "저는 자금 조달에 중점을 두기 시작했습니다. ⁰²저는 막 생겨난 신생 기업들에 투자해보고 싶습니다. 그러한 가능성과 관련하여 제가 이미 접촉한 유망한 회사들을 몇 군데가 있습니다. 그러나, 저는 멀리서 조언하며, 덜 관여할 것입니다."

financial adj. 금융의, 재정의 **empire** n. 거대 기업 **severe** adj. 심각한
drop n. 하락 **value** n. 가치 **invest** v. 투자하다 **leading** adj. 선도적인
tie-in n. 결합 상품, 파생 상품 **flourish** v. 번창하다 **billionaire** n. 억만장자
take up phr. 차지하다 **completely** adv. 완전히 **retire** v. 은퇴하다
active adj. 활동하는, 활동적인 **energetic** adj. 활기 넘치는, 활동적인
promising adj. 유망한 **reach out to** phr. ~에 접촉하다, 접근하다
involve v. 관여시키다 **from a distance** phr. 멀리서

01 추론 문제

문제 Partizone사에 대해 암시되는 것은?
(A) 주로 사업가들을 위한 것이다.
(B) 서비스에 대해 상을 받았다.
(C) 여행 예약을 하는 데 이용된다.
(D) 원래 부동산을 팔기 위한 것이었다.

해설 질문의 핵심 어구인 Partizone에 대해 추론하는 문제입니다. 'Partizone's Web site became the leading booking tool for flights, hotels, and rental cars.'에서 Partizone사의 웹사이트가 항공편, 호텔, 그리고 렌터카를 위한 선도적인 예약 도구가 되었다고 했으므로 Partizone사가 여행 예약을 하는 데 이용된다는 사실을 추론할 수 있습니다. 따라서 (C) It is used for making travel bookings가 정답입니다.

booking ~ for flights, hotels, and rental cars 항공편, 호텔, 그리고 렌터카를 위한 예약 → travel bookings 여행 예약

02 추론 문제

문제 Mr. Timan은 가까운 미래에 무엇을 할 것 같은가?
(A) 해외 주택에 투자한다
(B) 경영 수업을 가르친다
(C) 기업의 회장이 된다
(D) 새 사업체에 자금을 댄다

해설 질문의 핵심 어구인 Mr. Timan ~ do in the near future에 대해 추론하는 문제입니다. 'I'd like to invest in fresh start-up companies. There are a few promising ones I've reached out to about that possibility already.'에서 자신, 즉 Mr. Timan이 막 생겨난 신생 기업들에 투자해보고 싶고 그러한 가능성과 관련하여 이미 접촉한 유망한 회사들 몇 군데가 있다고 했으므로 Mr. Timan이 가까운 미래에 새 사업체에 자금을 댈 것이라는 사실을 추론할 수 있습니다. 따라서 (D) Fund a new business가 정답입니다.

패러프레이징
invest in fresh start-up companies 막 생겨난 신생 기업들에 투자하다 → Fund a a new business 새 사업체에 자금을 대다

어휘 housing n. 주택 abroad adv. 해외에 corporate adj. 기업의 chairperson n. 회장 fund v. 자금을 대다

03 문장 위치 찾기 문제

문제 [1], [2], [3], [4]로 표시된 위치 중, 다음 문장이 들어갈 곳으로 가장 적절한 것은?
"비록 이유를 언급하기 꺼렸지만, Mr. Timan은 인터뷰 동안 그의 결심에 대해 설명했다."
(A) [1]
(B) [2]
(C) [3]
(D) [4]

해설 지문의 흐름상 주어진 문장이 들어가기에 가장 적절한 곳을 고르는 문제입니다. Though reluctant to discuss his reasons, Mr. Timan explained his decision during an interview에서 비록 이유를 언급하기 꺼렸지만 Mr. Timan이 인터뷰 동안 그의 결심에 대해 설명했다고 했으므로, 주어진 문장 뒤에 Mr. Timan의 결심에 대해 설명한 내용이 있을 것임을 예상할 수 있습니다. [3]의 뒤 문장인 'He said, "I am getting older, and I'd like to spend more time with my children. But as the business gets bigger, it takes up more of my time."'에서 Mr. Timan이 나이가 들고 있고 아이들과 시간을 더 많이 보내고 싶지만 사업이 커질수록 그것이 자신의 시간을 더 많이 차지한다고 했으므로, [3]에 주어진 문장이 들어가면 Mr. Timan이 인터뷰에서 아이들과 더 많은 시간을 보내기 위해 모든 것을 팔기로 했다는 그의 결심에 대해 설명하는 자연스러운 문맥이 된다는 것을 알 수 있습니다. 따라서 (C) [3]이 정답입니다.

어휘 reluctant adj. 꺼리는, 주저하는

04-07번은 다음 회람에 관한 문제입니다.

⁰⁴수신: 지역 사회 지원 활동부
발신: Kevin Miles, AAHS 회장
날짜: 6월 22일
제목: 연회

아시다시피, AAHS의 연례 연회가 다가오고 있습니다. ⁰⁴이 행사에서, 모든 주요 기부자들은 우리 역사 협회가 이룬 진전에 대한 일련의 보고를 들으면서 세 코스짜리 식사를 대접받을 것입니다.

기부자들이 이번 행사에 반드시 참석할 수 있도록 하기 위해, 우리는 ↻

그들에게 우편으로 초대장을 보내야 합니다. ―[1]―. 앞으로 며칠 동안, 여러분들이 그들 각각에게 개별 서신을 보내주시기를 바랍니다. ―[2]―. ⁰⁷저는 여러분들께 지난 한 해 동안 우리 협회에 500달러 이상을 기부한 모든 분들의 명단을 제공해드렸습니다. ―[3]―.

⁰⁵여러분의 서신에, 다음의 정보를 포함해주십시오: 연회는 7월 10일에 열릴 것입니다. ⁰⁵복장 규정은 정장입니다. 주요 보고는 우리 역사 협회 이사회의 회원에 의해 이루어질 것이며 ⁰⁶우리가 어떻게 초기 미국 골동품 수집을 확대해 왔는지에 초점을 둘 것입니다. ―[4]―. 각 서신과 함께, 협회 앞으로 보내지는 우표를 붙인 봉투와 기부자들이 그들의 저녁 식사 선호 사항과 몇 명의 손님을 데려올 것인지를 나타낼 수 있는 카드를 동봉해 주십시오. 기부자들은 이 카드를 작성하여 우리가 제공한 봉투에 담아 다시 우편으로 보내주어야 합니다.

outreach n. 지원 활동 approach v. 다가오다 donor n. 기부자
treat v. 대접하다 a series of phr. 일련의 talk n. 보고, 연설
progress n. 진전, 진척 historical adj. 역사의, 역사적인
society n. 협회, 사회 make it to phr. ~에 참석하다, ~에 도착하다
formal adj. (옷차림이) 정장인, 격식을 차린
board of trustees phr. 이사회 focus on phr. 초점을 두다, 집중하다
expand v. 확대하다 antique n. 골동품 along with phr. ~과 함께
stamped adj. 우표를 붙인 address to phr. ~ 앞으로 보내다
preference n. 선호 사항, 선택 bring v. 데려오다

04 추론 문제

문제 회람은 누구를 대상으로 하는 것 같은가?
(A) 문화 협회의 기부자들
(B) 이사회 회원들
(C) 역사 협회의 직원들
(D) 출장 음식 서비스의 고객들

해설 지문 곳곳에 퍼져 있는 여러 가지 단서를 종합하여 회람의 대상을 추론하는 문제입니다. 'To: Community outreach department'에서 회람의 수신자가 지역 사회 지원 활동부라고 했고, 'At this event, all of our major donors will be ~ listening to a series of talks about the progress our historical society has made.'에서 행사에서 모든 주요 기부자들이 자신들의 역사 협회가 이룬 진전에 대한 일련의 보고를 들을 것이라고 한 후, 필요한 업무들을 설명하고 있으므로 역사 협회의 지역 사회 지원 활동부에 소속된 직원들을 대상으로 하는 회람임을 추론할 수 있습니다. 따라서 (C) Staff at a history society가 정답입니다.

05 육하원칙 문제

문제 초대받은 기부자들은 무엇을 하도록 요구되는가?
(A) 행사를 위한 적절한 옷을 입는다
(B) 전화로 참석을 확정한다
(C) 저녁 6시까지 행사장에 도착한다
(D) 행사에 카드를 가져온다

해설 초대받은 기부자들이 무엇(What)을 하도록 요구되는지를 묻는 육하원칙 문제입니다. 질문의 핵심 어구인 the invited donors required to do와 관련하여, 'In your letters, please include the following information'에서 기부자들에게 보낼 서신에 다음 정보를 포함해달라고 한 후, 'The dress code is formal.'에서 복장 규정이 정장이라고 했으므로 (A) Wear suitable clothing for the occasion이 정답입니다.

패러프레이징
dress 복장 → clothing 옷

어휘 suitable adj. 적절한, 적당한 occasion n. 행사, 경우 confirm v. 확정하다, 확인하다 attendance n. 참석, 출석

06 추론 문제

문제 단체에 대해 암시되는 것은?
(A) 골동품들을 모은다.

(B) 연회를 일 년에 네 번 연다.
(C) 최근에 신임 회장을 고용했다.
(D) 월 단위로 전시품을 교체한다.

해설 질문의 핵심 어구인 the organization에 대해 추론하는 문제입니다. 'we've expanded our collection of early American antiques'에서 우리, 즉 역사 협회가 초기 미국 골동품 수집을 확대해 왔다고 했으므로, 단체가 골동품들을 모은다는 사실을 추론할 수 있습니다. 따라서 (A) It gathers antiques가 정답입니다.

패러프레이징
expanded ~ collection of ~ antiques 골동품 수집을 확대했다 → gathers antiques 골동품들을 모으다

어휘 **quarterly** adv. 일 년에 네 번; adj. 분기별의 **rotate** v. 교체하다, 회전하다 **exhibit** n. 전시품 **on a monthly basis** phr. 월 단위로

07 문장 위치 찾기 문제

문제 [1], [2], [3], [4]로 표시된 위치 중, 다음 문장이 들어갈 곳으로 가장 적절한 것은?

"그들의 주소 또한 그것에 포함되어 있습니다."

(A) [1]
(B) [2]
(C) [3]
(D) [4]

해설 지문의 흐름상 주어진 문장이 들어가기에 가장 적절한 곳을 고르는 문제입니다. Their addresses are also included on it에서 그들의 주소 또한 그것에 포함되어 있다고 했으므로, 주어진 문장 앞에 대명사 Their(그들)와 it(그것)이 가리키는 내용이 있을 것임을 예상할 수 있습니다. [3]의 앞 문장인 'I have provided you with a list of all the people who donated $500 or more to our society over the past year.'에서 지난 한 해 동안 협회에 500달러 이상을 기부한 모든 사람들의 명단을 제공했다고 했으므로, [3]에 주어진 문장이 들어가면 그들, 즉 기부자들의 주소가 그것, 즉 명단에 포함되어 있다는 자연스러운 문맥이 된다는 것을 알 수 있습니다. 따라서 (C) [3]이 정답입니다.

DAY 16 질문 유형 4

Course 1 의도 파악 문제

전략 적용 해석 p.306

메시지 대화문

Leo Rossi	오전 11:01

Mr. Holbrook이 집에 계시지 않네요. 귀하께서 배송해달라고 요청하신 소포를 어떻게 할까요?

Cathy Schneider	오전 11:05

건물 관리인에게 맡겨주시겠어요? 그가 처리할 수 있어요.

Leo Rossi	오전 11:06

알겠어요. 그렇게 해드릴게요.

parcel n. 소포 **building manager** phr. 건물 관리인
take care of phr. ~을 처리하다, ~를 돌보다

문제 오전 11시 6분에, Mr. Rossi가 "I can do that for you"라고 썼을 때, 그가 의도한 것은?
(A) Ms. Schneider의 집에 소포를 둘 것이다.
(B) 소포를 건물 관리인에게 맡길 것이다.

(C) Mr. Holbrook의 사무실에서 기다릴 것이다.

어휘 **drop off** phr. (물건 등을) 맡기다

HACKERS PRACTICE p.307

패러프레이징 연습
01 (A)   **02** (A)
유형 연습
03 (A)   **04** (B)

01

중앙은행은 경제를 활성화하기 위해 이자율을 더 낮출 수도 있다고 발표했다. 지난주의 몇몇 대기업의 낮은 수익 보고가 이 결정의 원인이 되었다.

(A) 실망스러운 수익 결과는 낮은 이자율을 초래할 수 있다.
(B) 이자율에 대한 결정은 경제가 나아지는 것을 막았다.

해설 답의 근거 문장은 'Last week's reports of poor earnings by several major firms contributed to this decision.'으로 (A)가 정답입니다. poor earnings가 Disappointing earnings로 바뀌어 표현되었습니다.

어휘 **interest rate** phr. 이자율 **stimulate** v. 활성화시키다, 자극하다 **earnings** n. 수익, 소득 **contribute** v. ~의 원인이 되다, 기여하다 **disappointing** adj. 실망스러운 **result** n. 결과 **prompt** v. 초래하다, 촉발하다 **decision** n. 결정 **prevent** v. 막다, 예방하다

02

Luxen 자동차 회사의 공장이 Gerringville에 문을 열 것이라는 소식은 지역 주민들로부터 환영을 받았다. 그들은 그것이 경제적으로 취약한 그 지역에 상당수의 일자리를 창출할 것이라고 기대한다.

(A) Gerringville 지역 주민들은 Luxen 자동차 회사의 새 공장이 그들의 지역에 이익을 줄 것이라고 생각한다.
(B) Gerringville에서 Luxen 자동차 회사를 위해 환영식이 열릴 것이다.

해설 답의 근거 문장은 'They expect it will create quite a few jobs in the economically weak area.'로 (A)가 정답입니다. create quite a few jobs in the economically weak area가 benefit ~ region으로 바뀌어 표현되었습니다.

어휘 **resident** n. 주민 **create** v. 창출하다, 창조하다 **quite a few** phr. 상당수의 **economically** adv. 경제적으로 **weak** adj. 취약한, 부실한 **celebration** n. 의식, 축하 행사

03 메시지 대화문

Linda Graham	오전 10:28

직원 파티를 위해 주문하신 케이크가 준비되었습니다. 언제든지 가져가실 수 있습니다.

Dave Poplar	오전 10:32

제가 지금 근무 중입니다. 배달 서비스는 제공하지 않으시죠, 그렇죠?

Linda Graham	오전 10:33

죄송하지만 하지 않습니다. 하지만 저희는 오후 8시까지 엽니다.

Dave Poplar	오전 10:34

좋아요. 오늘 오후에 일찍 들를게요.

pick up phr. 가져가다, 찾아오다 **stop by** phr. 들르다

문제 오전 10시 33분에, Ms. Graham이 "But we are open until 8 P.M."이라고 썼을 때, 그녀가 의도한 것은?
(A) 근무 후에 방문할 충분한 시간이 있을 것이다.
(B) 추가 케이크가 나중에 구매될 수 있다.
(C) 배달이 고객에게 최선의 선택일 것이다.

해설 의도 파악 문제 Ms. Graham이 의도한 것을 묻는 문제이므로, 질문의 인용구(But we are open until 8 P.M.)가 언급된 주변 문맥을 확인합니다. 'I'm at work at the moment. You don't offer a delivery service, do you?'에서 Dave Poplar가 지금 근무 중이라며 배달 서비스는 제공하지 않는지를 묻자, Ms. Graham이 'I'm afraid not.'에서 죄송하지만 하지 않는다고 하자, Dave Polar가 'OK. I'll stop by early this afternoon.'에서 오늘 오후에 일찍 들르겠다고 한 것을 통해, 근무 후에 와도 가게가 열려 있다고 한 것임을 알 수 있습니다. 따라서 (A) There will be enough time to visit after work가 정답입니다.

04 메시지 대화문

Cindy Kane	오후 4:20
Mr. Wilson이 화요일 아침에 상담을 하고 싶어 해요. 두 분 중 한 분이 그를 만날 수 있을까요? 그는 우리의 가장 큰 고객 중 한 분이에요.	
Kathy Jones	오후 4:23
저는 그날 아침에 약속이 있어서, 못할 거예요.	
James Wong	오후 4:25
제가 처리할 수 있을 것 같아요. 11시까지는 다른 예정된 것이 없어요.	
Cindy Kane	오후 4:26
고마워요, Mr. Wong.	

consultation n. 상담 appointment n. 약속
manage v. 처리하다, 관리하다

문제 오후 4시 25분에, Mr. Wong이 "I don't have anything else scheduled until 11"이라고 썼을 때, 그가 의도한 것은?
(A) 회의에 참석할 수 있을 것이다.
(B) 상담을 위해 고객을 만날 수 있다.
(C) Ms. Kane이 부재중인 동안 사무실을 관리할 것이다.

해설 의도 파악 문제 Mr. Wong이 의도한 것을 묻는 문제이므로, 질문의 인용구(I don't have anything else scheduled until 11)가 언급된 주변 문맥을 확인합니다. 'Mr. Wilson wants to have a consultation on Tuesday morning. Could either of you meet him?'에서 Cindy Kane이 Mr. Wilson이 화요일 아침에 상담을 하고 싶어 하는데 두 사람 중 한 명이 그를 만날 수 있을지 묻자, Mr. Wong이 'I should be able to manage that.'에서 자신이 처리할 수 있을 것 같다고 한 것을 통해, Mr. Wong이 상담을 위해 고객을 만날 수 있다는 것을 알 수 있습니다. 따라서 (B) He can meet a client for a consultation이 정답입니다.

어휘 attend v. 참석하다 conference n. 회의 be away phr. 부재중인

Course 2 동의어 문제

전략 적용 해석   p.308

기사

Nevertire사의 위기
당국은 Nevertire사의 전천후 타이어가 더운 날씨에서 변형되는 경향이 있는 것이 정말 맞다고 밝혔다. 그러므로, 그것들은 차량 사고를 일으킬 가능성이 있다. 이 사태에 대한 Nevertire사의 대응이 회사의 명성에 매우 중요할 것으로 예상된다. ↻

determine v. 밝히다, 확정하다 all-weather adj. 전천후의
wheel n. 타이어, 바퀴 indeed adv. 확실히, 정말로 tendency n. 경향
deform v. 변형되다 potential n. 가능성, 잠재력 cause v. 일으키다
accident n. 사고 response n. 대응, 반응
critical adj. 매우 중요한, 비판적인 reputation n. 명성

문제 1문단 세 번째 줄의 단어 "matter"는 의미상 -와 가깝다.
(A) 물건
(B) 요소
(C) 상황

HACKERS PRACTICE   p.309

패러프레이징 연습
01 (B)   **02 (A)**
유형 연습
03 (C)   **04 (B)**

01

매년 열리는, 직물 산업 박람회는 의류 소매업체들에 전 세계의 공급업체들을 만날 기회를 제공합니다. 수백만 달러에 달하는 거래들이 종종 행사에서 성사됩니다.
(A) 산업 박람회가 2년마다 패션업계의 일류 모델들을 유치한다.
(B) 박람회에서 성사된 거래들의 합쳐진 가격은 총계가 주로 수백만 달러이다.

해설 답의 근거 문장은 'Deals totaling millions of dollars are often made at the event.'로 (B)가 정답입니다. Deals totaling millions of dollars are often made가 The combined value of the deals ~ totals millions of dollars로 바뀌어 표현되었습니다.

어휘 fabric n. 직물 trade fair phr. 산업 박람회 retailer n. 소매업체
supplier n. 공급업체 total v. ~에 달하다, 총계가 ~가 되다; adj. 총계의
attract v. 유치하다, 끌어들이다

02

Mr. Tim의 지도 하에, West Pharma사는 수익을 내는 회사로 성장했다. 전 글로벌 사업 본부장인 Mark Metzner가 CEO로서의 그의 자리를 이을 것이다.
(A) Mr. Metzner가 성공적인 회사의 대표로서 Mr. Tim을 대신할 것이다.
(B) Mr. Tim은 West Pharma사의 글로벌 사업 본부장으로서 매우 생산적이었다.

해설 답의 근거 문장은 'Mark Metzner, the former head of global operations, will succeed him as the CEO'로 (A)가 정답입니다. succeed가 replace로, CEO가 head로 바뀌어 표현되었습니다.

어휘 profitable adj. 수익을 내는 succeed v. (~의 자리·지위 등의 뒤를) 잇다
replace v. 대신하다 successful adj. 성공적인
extremely adv. 매우 productive adj. 생산적인

03 회람

여러분이 아시다시피, 직원은 매년 사내 관계를 관리하는 방법에 대한 한 시간의 교육에 참석하는 것이 요구됩니다. 교육은 생산적으로 갈등을 중재하고 동료들과 좋은 관계를 유지하는 방법에 초점을 맞출 것입니다.
저는 여러분 각자가 교육에 최소한 두 가지의 질문을 가지고 오기를 바랍니다. 올해의 연설가인 Harold Bridge는 IT 산업에서 15년 이상 ↻

근무해왔고, 저는 그가 여러분들의 모든 문의 사항에 대해 설득력 있는 답변을 가지고 있을 것이라고 확신합니다. 모두 그곳에서 뵙기를 기대합니다.

attend v. 참석하다 interoffice adj. 사내의 relationship n. 관계
productively adv. 생산적으로 mediate v. 중재하다 conflict n. 갈등
colleague n. 동료 at least phr. 최소한 compelling adj. 설득력 있는
inquiry n. 문의 사항

문제 1문단 세 번째 줄의 단어 "maintain"은 의미상 –와 가장 가깝다.
(A) 일으키다
(B) 주장하다
(C) 유지하다

해설 동의어 찾기 문제 maintain을 포함하는 문장 'The session will focus on ~ how to maintain good relations with one's colleagues.'에서 maintain이 '유지하다'라는 뜻으로 사용되었습니다. 따라서 '유지하다'라는 뜻을 가진 (C) keep이 정답입니다.

04 공고

저희는 고객분들의 쇼핑 경험을 크게 향상시키기 위해 소매 공간을 확장할 것입니다. 이렇게 하기 위해서, 저희는 남성 의류와 스포츠 의류 구역을 임시로 폐쇄해야 할 것입니다. 여러분의 안전을 위해, 이 구역 중 어떤 곳에도 들어가지 말아주십시오. 각각의 구역은 표지판과 주황색 공사 테이프로 표시될 것입니다. 질문이 있으시다면 매장 직원과 상담하십시오. 여러분의 지지에 감사드립니다.

expand v. 확장하다 retail n. 소매 enhance v. 향상시키다
temporarily adv. 임시로 close off phr. 폐쇄하다
section n. 구역, 분야 safety n. 안전 mark v. 표시하다
sign n. 표지판, 표시

문제 1문단 첫 번째 줄의 단어 "dramatically"는 의미상 –와 가장 가깝다.
(A) 표현적으로
(B) 상당히
(C) 활동적으로

해설 동의어 찾기 문제 dramatically를 포함하는 문장 'We are expanding our retail space to dramatically enhance the shopping experience for customers.'에서 dramatically가 '크게'라는 뜻으로 사용되었습니다. 따라서 '상당히'라는 뜻을 가진 (B) substantially가 정답입니다.

HACKERS TEST
p.310

01 (B)	02 (D)	03 (A)	04 (C)	05 (A)
06 (D)	07 (B)			

01-04번은 다음 온라인 채팅 대화문에 관한 문제입니다.

Hannah Miller　　　　　　　　　　　　　오전 11:02
인터넷을 하다가 Enviro-Ware라는 회사를 발견했어요. 02-A그들의 모든 상품은 재활용된 종이 재료로 만들어져요. 우리의 현재 공급업체에서 교체하는 것을 고려 중이에요.

Glenn Friedman　　　　　　　　　　　　오전 11:13
저는 지금 그 회사의 웹사이트를 보고 있어요. 02-D종류도 여러 가지가 있네요. 01환경친화적인 컵을 사용하는 것은 상품의 좋은 장점이 될 수 있어요.

Olivia Liu　　　　　　　　　　　　　　　오전 11:15
하지만 02-B그들의 컵은 우리가 현재 사용하는 것보다 비용이 15퍼센트 더 들어요.

Hannah Miller　　　　　　　　　　　　　오전 11:17
03사이트에 대량 주문의 가격 책정에 대해 논의할 수 있다고 나와 있어요. 그리고 저는 마케팅에 좋을 것이라는 Glenn의 말에 동의해요.

Glenn Friedman　　　　　　　　　　　　오전 11:18
02-C제가 여기서 보니까 우리의 사양에 맞도록 제품이 디자인되게 할 수도 있는 것 같아요. 그들에게 우리 회사 로고가 박힌 견본 몇 개를 요청해야겠어요.

Hannah Miller　　　　　　　　　　　　　오전 11:19
좋은 생각이네요. 그건 우리가 컵을 평가해볼 기회를 줄 거예요. 03만약 우리가 견본이 마음에 들면, 제가 가격에 대해 무엇을 할 수 있는지 알아볼게요.

Olivia Liu　　　　　　　　　　　　　　　오전 11:22
04냅킨과 접시의 견본도 받는 게 어때요? 우리가 지금 사용하는 것들은 재활용 재료로 만들어지지 않아요.

Hannah Miller　　　　　　　　　　　　　오전 11:23
그것도 할게요. 고마워요, 그리고 여러분께 계속 상황을 알려드릴게요.

recycle v. 재활용하다 switch v. 교체하다
selection n. (상품의) 종류, 선택
environmentally friendly phr. 환경친화적인
selling point phr. (상품이 지닌) 장점, 상품의 강조점, 판매에 유리한 점
cost v. 비용이 들다 currently adv. 현재 bulk adj. 대량의
pricing n. 가격 책정 specification n. 사양, 설명서
keep ~ updated phr. ~에게 계속 상황을 알려주다

01 육하원칙 문제

문제 Mr. Friedman은 왜 Enviro-Ware사의 컵에 관심이 있는가?
(A) 환경친화업체들의 후원사이다.
(B) 마케팅에 도움이 될 수 있다고 생각한다.
(C) 회사가 돈을 절약하게 될 것이라고 생각한다.
(D) 상품 견본에 만족한다.

해설 Mr. Friedman이 왜(Why) Enviro-Ware사의 컵에 관심이 있는지를 묻는 육하원칙 문제입니다. 질문의 핵심 어구인 Mr. Friedman interested in Enviro-Ware's cups와 관련하여, 'Using environmentally friendly cups could be a good selling point.'에서 환경친화적인 컵을 사용하는 것은 상품의 좋은 장점이 될 수 있다고 했으므로 (B) He thinks they could help with marketing이 정답입니다.

패러프레이징
be a good selling point 상품의 좋은 장점이 되다
→ help with marketing 마케팅에 도움이 되다

어휘 supporter n. 후원자, 지지자 be satisfied with phr. ~에 만족하다

02 Not/True 문제

문제 Enviro-Ware사에 대해 언급되지 않은 것은?
(A) 상품이 종이로 만들어진다.
(B) 가격이 현재의 공급업체보다 더 높다.
(C) 고객들을 위해 몇몇 물품들을 주문 제작한다.
(D) 적은 종류의 상품만을 제공한다.

해설 질문의 핵심 어구인 Enviro-Ware와 관련된 내용을 지문에서 찾아 각 보기와 대조하는 Not/True 문제입니다. (A)는 'All their products are made of recycled paper materials.'에서 그들, 즉 Enviro-Ware사의 모든 상품은 재활용된 종이 재료로 만들어진다고 했으므로 지문의 내용과 일치합니다. (B)는 'their cups cost 15 percent more than the ones we currently use'에서 Enviro-Ware사의 컵은 현재 사용하는 것보다 비용이 15퍼센트 더 든다고 했으므로 지문의 내용과 일치합니다. (C)는 'I see here we can also have products designed to our specifications.'에서 여기, 즉 Enviro-Ware사의 사이트에서 보니까 사양에 맞도록 제품이 디자인되게 할 수도 있다

고 했으므로 지문의 내용과 일치합니다. (D)는 'They've got a wide selection'에서 Enviro-Ware사에 상품 종류가 여러 가지가 있다고 했으므로 지문의 내용과 일치하지 않습니다. 따라서 (D) It offers only a small selection of products가 정답입니다.

패러프레이징
products 상품 → merchandise 상품
cost 15 percent more 비용이 15퍼센트 더 들다 → prices are higher 가격이 더 높다
have products designed to ~ specifications 사양에 맞도록 제품이 디자인되게 하다 → customizes some items 몇몇 물품들을 주문 제작하다

어휘 customize v. 주문 제작하다

03 추론 문제

문제 Ms. Miller는 무엇을 하려고 하는 것 같은가?
  (A) 주문에 대한 할인 요청하기
  (B) 최근의 온라인 주문 취소하기
  (C) 회사 로고 디자인 변경하기
  (D) 서비스 후기 제출하기

해설 질문의 핵심어구인 Ms. Miller intend to do에 대해 추론하는 문제입니다. 'The site indicates that they can discuss bulk order pricing.'에서 Hannah Miller가 사이트, 즉 Enviro-Ware사의 사이트에 대량 주문의 가격 책정에 대해 논의할 수 있다고 나와 있다고 한 후, 'If we like the samples, I'll see what I can do about the price.'에서 만약 견본이 마음에 들면 자신이 가격에 대해 무엇을 할 수 있는지 알아보겠다고 했으므로, Ms. Miller가 주문에 대한 가격 책정을 논의하려고 한다는 사실을 추론할 수 있습니다. 따라서 (A) Request a discount on an order가 정답입니다.

어휘 alter v. 변경하다, 바꾸다

04 의도 파악 문제

문제 오전 11시 23분에, Ms. Miller가 "I'll do that as well"이라고 썼을 때, 그녀가 의도한 것은?
  (A) 로고가 박힌 컵 몇 개를 구매할 것이다.
  (B) Ms. Liu에게 주문서를 보낼 것이다.
  (C) 다른 종류들의 제품 견본을 요청할 것이다.
  (D) 협상에 대한 최신 정보를 제공할 것이다.

해설 Ms. Miller가 의도한 것을 묻는 문제이므로, 질문의 인용구(I'll do that as well)가 언급된 주변 문맥을 확인합니다. 'What about getting napkin and plate samples, too?'에서 Olivia Liu가 냅킨과 접시의 견본도 받는 게 어떠냐고 묻자, Ms. Miller가 'I'll do that as well'(그것도 할게요)이라고 한 것을 통해, Ms. Miller가 냅킨과 접시의 제품 견본도 추가로 요청할 것임을 알 수 있습니다. 따라서 (C) She will ask for other types of product samples가 정답입니다.

05-07번은 다음 브로슈어에 관한 문제입니다.

Proship 호화 유람선 여행

Proship사인, 저희는 미국 전역과 그 너머의 사람들에게 가장 높은 품질의 유람선 여행을 제공하는 것으로 명성이 있습니다. 저희는 신혼 부부, 은퇴자, 그리고 피서객들을 30년 동안 카리브 해의 섬들로 모셔 왔습니다. 저희는 또한 1990년대 중반에 지중해 투어를 시작했고, 심지어 세상의 마지막 거대 황무지를 탐험하는 남극행 유람선 여행도 시작했습니다.

이제 저희는 또 다시 확장합니다. [05]4월부터 시작하여, Proship사는 카리브 해로의 유람선 단기 전세 여행을 준비할 것입니다. [07-D]마이애미에 있는 저희의 항구에서 출발하여, 저희는 여러분을 바하마, 터크스케이커스, 자메이카, 도미니카 공화국, 푸에르토리코로 모셔드릴 수 있습니다. 이 유람선 여행은 [06]목적이 잊지 못할 직원 야유회를 여는 것이든 ◑

잠재적인 고객을 즐겁게 하고 발표를 하는 것이든 어떤 회사에게라도 완벽할 것입니다.

저희 직원과의 상담을 통해 업무와 즐거움 모두에 충분한 시간을 보장하는 완벽한 일정을 준비하실 수 있습니다. 여러분의 여가 시간은 해변의 마을들을 방문하는 것, 해안에서의 스쿠버다이빙, 혹은 그저 해변에서 휴식을 취하는 것을 포함할 수 있습니다. 다시 진지해질 때가 되면, [07-B]저희의 유람선들은 회의 공간을 위한 몇몇 선택사항들을 갖고 있습니다. 선박들은 또한 무선 인터넷과 영사기 시스템을 갖추고 있습니다. 그동안, 저희의 요리사들은 귀하께서 협상, 논의, 팀워크 활동, 혹은 귀하가 하고 싶어 하시는 어떠한 것에 대해서라도 잘 준비가 되어 있도록 하기 위해 지역 해산물을 포함한 맛있는 음식을 요리하고 있을 것입니다.

그러므로 선택권과 가격을 논의하기 위해 저희에게 555-9682로 전화 주셔서, 다음 사업 회의를 일생일대의 여행으로 만드십시오.

---

cruise n. 유람선 여행 reputation n. 명성 retiree n. 은퇴자
explore v. 탐험하다 wilderness n. 황무지 planet n. 세상, 행성
arrange v. 준비하다, 마련하다 chartered adj. 전세 낸, 공인된
unforgettable adj. 잊지 못할 retreat n. 야유회
entertain v. 즐겁게 하다 potential adj. 잠재적인 itinerary n. 여행 일정
consultation n. 상담 ensure v. 보장하다 pleasure n. 즐거움, 휴식
leisure n. 여가 seaside n. 해변 coast n. 해안
serious adj. 진지한, 심각한 be equipped with phr. 장비를 갖추다
projector n. 영사기 negotiation n. 협상 discussion n. 논의

---

05 주제/목적 찾기 문제

문제 광고되고 있는 것은 무엇인가?
  (A) 여행사의 새로운 유람선 여행
  (B) 선박 박물관에서의 전시회
  (C) 보트 투어를 예약하는 웹사이트
  (D) 보트 장비를 판매하는 상점

해설 광고되고 있는 것을 묻는 주제 찾기 문제입니다. 특별히 이 문제는 지문의 중반부에 주제 관련 내용이 언급되었음에 주의합니다. 'Starting in April, Proship will be arranging short chartered business cruises to the Caribbean.'에서 4월부터 시작하여 Proship사가 카리브 해로의 유람선 단기 전세 여행을 준비할 것이라고 한 후, 여행의 경유지나 유람선의 시설 등에 대해 소개하고 있으므로 (A) A travel agency's new cruises가 정답입니다.

어휘 exhibit n. 전시회

06 동의어 찾기 문제

문제 2문단 네 번째 줄의 단어 "aim"은 의미상 -와 가장 가깝다.
  (A) 설계
  (B) 믿음
  (C) 수업
  (D) 목적

해설 aim을 포함하는 구절 'whether your aim is to hold an unforgettable staff retreat or to entertain and make a presentation to potential clients'에서 aim이 '목적'이라는 뜻으로 사용되었습니다. 따라서 '목적'이라는 뜻을 가진 (D) intention이 정답입니다.

07 Not/True 문제

문제 선박들에 대해 언급된 것은?
  (A) 24시간 운영하는 식당 시설을 제공한다.
  (B) 발표를 위한 장비를 갖추고 있다.
  (C) 운동실이 개선되었다.
  (D) 항로가 바하마에서 시작된다.

해설 질문의 핵심 어구인 the ships와 관련된 내용을 지문에서 찾아 각 보기와 대조하는 Not/True 문제입니다. (A)는 지문에 언급되지 않

은 내용입니다. (B)는 'our cruise ships have several options for meeting spaces. The boats are also equipped with wireless Internet and projector systems.'에서 유람선들은 회의 공간을 위한 몇몇 선택사항들을 갖고 있으며, 무선 인터넷과 영사기 시스템도 갖추고 있다고 했으므로 지문의 내용과 일치합니다. 따라서 (B) They are equipped for presentations가 정답입니다. (C)는 지문에 언급되지 않은 내용입니다. (D)는 'Leaving from our port in Miami, we can take you to the Bahamas'에서 마이애미에 있는 항구에서 출발하여 바하마로 데려다준다고 했지 바하마에서 항로가 시작된다고 하지는 않았으므로 지문의 내용과 일치하지 않습니다.

어휘 **route** n. 항로, 경로

DAY 17 지문 유형 1

Course 1 이메일 및 편지 (E-mail & Letter)

HACKERS TEST   p.314

01 (C)	02 (B)	03 (B)	04 (C)	05 (B)

01-03번은 다음 편지에 관한 문제입니다.

Grandmercia International

402A호, 100번지 Upscale 대로, 밀워키, 미네소타 주
전화: 555-2344 팩스: 555-2343 http://www.grandmercia.com/

4월 18일

Crystal Rose 투자 회사
Mr. Bernard O'Donnell
인사 관리 부장
87번지 Werchester로, 세인트폴, 미네소타

Mr. O'Donnell께,

[01]Ms. Katherine Coolidge가 귀하의 호평받는 단체에 입사를 지원한 것과 관련하여 귀하에게 편지를 써 달라고 저에게 요청했습니다. Ms. Coolidge와 저는 10년 넘게 함께 일해왔고, 저는 그녀의 역량과 직업의식을 열렬히 증언할 수 있습니다. 그녀는 Grandmercia사에서 저와 함께 금융 상품 영업부에서 시작했고 자동차 산업의 고객 연구부 직책으로 빠르게 올라갔습니다. 그녀와 함께 일한 모든 시간 동안, 그녀는 하루도 결근하지 않았고, 성격상 시간을 엄수하고 성실했습니다.

[03]저는 그녀가 Crystal Rose 투자 회사에서 더 큰 경력의 발전을 추구하기 위해 이곳 Grandmercia사에서의 현재 자리를 자발적으로 떠나는 것임을 알고 있습니다. [02]저는 그녀가 요청받는 어떠한 업무든 완수할 수 있을 것이라고 확신합니다. 이 추천서에 대해 어떠한 질문이라도 있다면 제게 555-2348로 언제든지 연락해주십시오.

Caleb Thickett 드림
선임 분석가, Grandmercia International사

in regard to phr. ~에 관련하여 **application** n. 지원
employment n. 입사, 취업 **esteemed** adj. 호평받는
enthusiastically adv. 열렬히, 열광적으로 **testify** v. 증언하다, 증명하다
competence n. 역량 **work ethic** phr. 직업의식
automotive adj. 자동차의 **characteristically** adv. 성격상, 특질적으로
punctual adj. 시간을 엄수하는 **diligent** adj. 성실한
be aware that phr. ~을 알고 있다
of one's own accord phr. 자발적으로 **advancement** n. 발전, 진보
confident adj. 확신하는 **carry out** phr. 완수하다, 수행하다
inquiry n. 질문, 문의 **recommendation** n. 추천(서)

01 주제/목적 찾기 문제

문제 편지의 목적은 무엇인가?
(A) 면접 결과를 제공하기 위해
(B) 공석에 지원하기 위해
(C) 입사 지원자를 추천하기 위해
(D) 급여 세부 사항에 대해 문의하기 위해

해설 편지의 목적을 묻는 목적 찾기 문제입니다. 'Ms. Katherine Coolidge has asked that I write to you in regard to her application for employment with your esteemed organization.'에서 Ms. Katherine Coolidge가 입사 지원과 관련하여 편지를 써 달라고 요청했다고 한 후, Ms. Coolidge와의 업무 경험 및 장점을 설명하고 있으므로 (C) To recommend a job candidate가 정답입니다.

어휘 **vacant** adj. (일자리 등이) 빈, 결원의 **recommend** v. 추천하다
candidate n. 지원자, 후보자 **salary** n. 급여

02 동의어 찾기 문제

문제 2문단 세 번째 줄의 어구 "carry out"은 의미상 -와 가깝다.
(A) 가져오다
(B) 완료하다
(C) 주문하다
(D) 우회시키다

해설 carry out을 포함하는 문장 'I am confident that she will be able to carry out any task required of her.'에서 carry out이 '완수하다'라는 뜻으로 사용되었습니다. 따라서 '완료하다'라는 뜻을 가진 (B) complete이 정답입니다.

03 추론 문제

문제 Crystal Rose 투자 회사의 일자리에 대해 암시되는 것은?
(A) 5년 간의 사전 업무 경력을 요구한다.
(B) Ms. Coolidge에게 더 좋은 기회를 제공한다.
(C) 매우 힘이 드는 회사 부서에 있다.
(D) Mr. Thickett의 직장보다 더 높은 급여를 준다.

해설 질문의 핵심 어구인 the position at Crystal Rose Investments에 대해 추론하는 문제입니다. 'I am aware that she is leaving her current position ~ in order to seek further career advancement at Crystal Rose Investments.'에서 Ms. Coolidge가 Crystal Rose 투자 회사에서 더 큰 경력의 발전을 추구하기 위해 현재 자리를 떠나는 것임을 안다고 했으므로 Crystal Rose 투자 회사의 일자리가 Ms. Coolidge에게 경력상 더 좋은 기회라는 사실을 추론할 수 있습니다. 따라서 (B) It offers better opportunities for Ms. Coolidge가 정답입니다.

04-05번은 다음 두 이메일에 관한 문제입니다.

수신: Maureen Huddleston <huddleston@midproductions.com>
발신: Abed Khan <abed_khan@uni-direct.com>
제목: 최종 디자인
날짜: 4월 4일
첨부: 유니폼 디자인

Ms. Huddleston께,

Uni-direct를 선택해주셔서 감사합니다. 당신의 취미 야구팀 유니폼의 디자인을 첨부했습니다. 이전 해들의 주문들과 마찬가지로, 팀의 빨간색 및 파란색 로고가 셔츠의 오른쪽 소매에 있을 것입니다. 또한, [04]당신이 요청한 대로 땀에 강한 새로운 직물로 그것들을 만들게 되어 기쁩니다.

유니폼은 각각 95달러일 것입니다. 저희는 당신이 50퍼센트의 착수금을 지불하자마자 그것들을 만들기 시작할 것입니다. 또한, [05]60달러의 비용으로, 저희는 배송을 해드릴 수 있습니다. 추가 문의가 있으시면 제게 알려 주십시오.

Abed Khan 드림

recreational adj. 취미의, 여가의 previous adj. 이전의, 앞의
jersey n. (운동 경기용) 셔츠 resistant adj. ~에 강한, 잘 견디는
fabric n. 직물, 천 deposit n. 착수금, 보증금

수신: Abed Khan <abed_khan@uni-direct.com>
발신: Maureen Huddleston <huddleston@midproductions.com>
제목: 제 주문
날짜: 4월 5일

Mr. Khan께,

저는 어제 유니폼을 주문했습니다. 귀사가 디자인을 제시해주셔서 매우 기쁘다고 말씀드리고 싶습니다.

그러나, 저는 다음 시즌에 저희 팀에 두 명이 더 합류한다는 것을 방금 알게 되었습니다. 주문에 두 장의 라지 사이즈 유니폼을 추가할 수 있을까요? 저는 추가 착수금을 드릴 수 있습니다. 혹은, 제 잔금에 그 비용을 추가하실 수 있고, 이것은 ⁰⁵제가 5월 6일에 당신의 매장에서 물건을 찾아갈 때 지불하겠습니다. 감사합니다.

Maureen Huddleston 드림

come up with phr. ~을 제시하다, 제안하다
pick up phr. (맡겨 놓은 물건 등을) 찾아가다

04 육하원칙 문제

문제 유니폼의 특징은 무엇인가?
(A) 긴소매 셔츠
(B) 등에 있는 팀 로고
(C) 특수 직물
(D) 빨간색 및 파란색 모자

해설 유니폼의 특징이 무엇(What)인지를 묻는 육하원칙 문제이므로 질문의 핵심 어구인 a feature of the uniforms와 관련된 내용이 언급된 첫 번째 이메일을 확인합니다. 첫 번째 이메일의 'make them out of the new sweat-resistant fabric that you requested'에서 이메일 수신자가 요청한 대로 땀에 강한 새로운 직물로 그것들, 즉 유니폼을 만든다고 했으므로 (C) A special material이 정답입니다.

패러프레이징
fabric 직물 → material 직물

05 추론 문제 연계

문제 Ms. Huddleston에 대해 암시되는 것은?
(A) 환불을 원한다.
(B) 60달러의 서비스 비용을 지불하지 않을 것이다.
(C) 라지 사이즈의 유니폼을 입는다.
(D) 추가 착수금을 지불했다.

해설 두 지문의 내용을 종합적으로 확인한 후 추론해서 풀어야 하는 연계 문제입니다. 질문의 핵심 어구인 Ms. Huddleston이 작성한 두 번째 이메일을 먼저 확인합니다.
두 번째 이메일의 'I pick up the items at your store on May 6'에서 Ms. Huddleston이 5월 6일에 매장에서 물건을 찾아갈 것이라는 첫 번째 단서를 확인할 수 있습니다. 그런데 제품 수령 방법에 대한 정보가 제시되지 않았으므로 Ms. Huddleston에게 보내진 첫 번째 이메일에서 관련 내용을 확인합니다. 첫 번째 이메일의 'for a $60 fee, we can deliver'에서 60달러의 비용으로 배송을 해줄 수 있다고 했으므로 배송 비용이 60달러라는 두 번째 단서를 확인할 수 있습니다. Ms. Huddleston이 5월 6일에 매장에서 물건을 찾아갈 것이라는 첫 번째 단서와 배송 비용이 60달러라는 두 번째 단서를 종합할 때, Ms. Huddleston은 60달러의 서비스 비용을 지불하지 않을 것이라는 사실을 추론할 수 있습니다. 따라서 (B) She will not pay a $60 service fee가 정답입니다.

Course 2 메시지 대화문 (Text Message Chain)

HACKERS TEST

p.318

01 (C)	02 (D)	03 (C)	04 (B)	05 (D)
06 (C)				

01-02번은 다음 메시지 대화문에 관한 문제입니다.

Samson Pandia 오후 4:22
채널 22번에서 아침 뉴스 보도를 보셨나요? ⁰²Membangan사가 정부의 새 건설 프로젝트에 대한 견적을 제시하지 않기로 결정한 것으로 보이던데요.

Micah Lesmono 오후 4:24
네, 봤어요. 좋은 소식이네요. ⁰²우리가 경쟁해야 하는 회사가 단 하나만 남게 됐네요.

Samson Pandia 오후 4:26
맞아요, 하지만 그들은 이 업계에 오랫동안 있었어요, 45년 넘게요.

Micah Lesmono 오후 4:27
그래도, 저는 우리의 가능성에 자신 있어요. ⁰¹T.M. 건설 회사는 오늘날의 빠른 속도의 환경에 비해 너무 느리다는 평판을 키웠죠.

Samson Pandia 오후 4:28
동의해요. ⁰¹그들은 또한 우리가 가지고 있는 기술처럼 새로운 건축 기술을 통합할 수 없었어요.

Micah Lesmono 오후 4:29
당신의 설계 제안서와 프로젝트를 제시간에 완료하는 우리 회사의 실적을 고려해보면, 우리의 전반적인 가능성이 확실히 매우 좋아요.

Samson Pandia 오후 4:30
음, 곧 알게 되겠네요!

quote n. 견적 compete with phr. ~와 경쟁하다
reputation n. 평판, 명성 integrate v. 통합하다
track record phr. 실적 overall adj. 전반적인

01 추론 문제

문제 작성자들은 어디에서 일하는 것 같은가?
(A) 텔레비전 방송국에서
(B) 관공서에서
(C) 건설 회사에서
(D) 운송 대행사에서

해설 질문의 핵심 어구인 the writers ~ work에 대해 추론하는 문제입니다. 'T.M. Construction has developed a reputation for being too slow for today's fast-paced environment.'에서 T.M. 건설회사가 오늘날의 빠른 속도의 환경에 비해 너무 느리다는 평판을 키웠다고 했고, 'They also have not been able to integrate new building technologies like we have.'에서 그 회사는 작성자들이 가지고 있는 기술처럼 새로운 건축 기술을 통합할 수 없었다고 했으므로 작성자들은 건설 회사에서 일한다는 사실을 추론할 수 있습니다. 따라서 (C) At a construction firm이 정답입니다.

어휘 transportation n. 운송, 수송 agency n. 대행사, (정부) 기관

02 의도 파악 문제

문제 오후 4시 24분에, Ms. Lesmono가 "That's good news"라고 썼을 때, 그녀가 의도한 것은?
(A) 그녀의 동료 중 한 명이 승진될 것이다.
(B) 프로젝트가 그녀의 그룹에 배정되었다.
(C) 동료들이 행사에서 상을 받을 것이다.
(D) 한 회사의 철수가 그녀의 회사에 이득이 된다.

해설 Ms. Lesmono가 의도한 것을 묻는 문제이므로, 질문의 인용구(That's good news)가 언급된 주변 문맥을 확인합니다. 'It seems that Membangan has decided not to offer a quote for the government's new construction project.'에서 Samson Pandia가 Membangan사가 정부의 새 건설 프로젝트에 대한 견적을 제시하지 않기로 결정한 것으로 보인다고 하자, Ms. Lesmono가 'That's good news'(좋은 소식이네요)라고 한 후, 'That leaves only one other company that we need to compete with.'에서 경쟁해야 하는 회사가 단 하나만 남게 됐다고 한 것을 통해, Membangan사의 철수가 Ms. Lesmono의 회사에 이득이 된다는 것을 알 수 있습니다. 따라서 (D) A firm's withdrawal benefits her company가 정답입니다.

어휘 **assign** v. 배정하다 **award** v. 상을 주다 **withdrawal** n. 철수

03-06번은 다음 온라인 채팅 대화문에 관한 문제입니다.

Alfreda Hailey   오전 11:38
03/05-B연구 관리자직을 위해 우리가 면접을 본 최종 지원자들에 대해 어떻게 생각하셨나요? 03내일까지 그들에게 답을 주고 싶어요.

Jerome Bartha   오전 11:40
04저는 Ben Trenton이 더 좋은 학력을 갖췄다고 생각하지만, 04/05-BStefania Lucci가 우리가 물어본 질문들에 더 잘 대처했어요. 그녀가 제 선택이에요.

Dane Nielsen   오전 11:41
동의해요. 05-AStefania는 또한 우호적이었고 만남 동안에 의사소통하기가 쉬웠어요. 그것들은 지도자에게 좋은 자질이에요.

Alfreda Hailey   오전 11:43
의견 감사해요. 저도 두 분 모두에게 동의해요. 05-C그녀에게 공식 제의를 하고 싶다고 인사 부서에 알릴게요.

Jerome Bartha   오전 11:43
06그녀가 회사에 큰 보탬이 될 거라고 생각해요.

Dane Nielsen   오전 11:44
제 생각이 바로 그거예요. 또한, 05-DBen Trenton은 현재 일하고 있지만, 그녀는 그렇지 않아요. 그녀는 어느 때라도 시작할 수 있어요.

Alfreda Hailey   오전 11:45
좋아요. 하지만 그녀가 제의를 받아들이지 않을 경우에는, 두 분 모두 그 대신에 Ben Trenton이 괜찮으신가요?

Dane Nielsen   오전 11:46
저는 괜찮아요.

Jerome Bartha   오전 11:47
저도 마찬가지예요.

---

applicant n. 지원자 **interview** v. 면접을 보다
educational adj. 교육의 **qualification** n. 자격
handle v. 대처하다, 다루다 **friendly** adj. 우호적인, 친절한
communicate v. 의사소통하다 **input** n. 의견, 조언
official adj. 공식적인 **addition** n. 보탬 것, 추가
in case phr. ~할 경우에 **instead** adv. 그 대신에

03 육하원칙 문제

문제 Ms. Hailey는 무엇을 하기를 바라는가?
(A) 아침 회의 동안 최종 지원자들을 선정한다
(B) 직원을 연구직으로 승진시킨다
(C) 내일까지 후보자들에게 결정에 대해 알린다
(D) 인사 부서에 몇 가지 계약서를 가져다준다

해설 Ms. Hailey가 무엇(What)을 하기를 바라는지를 묻는 육하원칙 문제입니다. 질문의 핵심 어구인 Ms. Hailey hope to do와 관련하여, 'What did you think of the final applicants ~? I'd like to give

them an answer by tomorrow.'에서 최종 지원자들에 대해 어떻게 생각했는지 물으며 내일까지 그들에게 답을 주고 싶다고 했으므로 (C) Notify candidates of a decision by tomorrow가 정답입니다.

패러프레이징
give ~ an answer 답을 주다 → Notify ~ of a decision 결정에 대해 알리다
applicants 지원자들 → candidates 후보자들

04 추론 문제

문제 Mr. Trenton에 대해 암시되는 것은?
(A) 직원 추천 제도에 참여했다.
(B) Ms. Lucci보다 더 좋은 학력을 갖췄다.
(C) 오늘 아침 면접에 늦었다.
(D) 수석으로 졸업했다.

해설 질문의 핵심 어구인 Mr. Trenton에 대해 추론하는 문제입니다. 'I thought Ben Trenton had the stronger educational qualifications, but Stefania Lucci handled the questions we asked her better.'에서 Ben Trenton이 더 좋은 학력을 갖췄다고 생각했지만 Stefania Lucci가 물어본 질문들에 더 잘 대처했다고 했으므로 Ben Trenton이 Stefania Lucci보다 학력이 더 좋다는 사실을 추론할 수 있습니다. 따라서 (B) He has a better academic background than Ms. Lucci가 정답입니다.

어휘 **referral** n. 추천, 위탁

05 Not/True 문제

문제 Ms. Lucci에 대해 언급되지 않은 것은?
(A) 관리 직무에 적합한 자질을 갖추고 있다.
(B) 연구 부서의 일자리에 지원하고 있다.
(C) 공식적인 고용 제의를 받을 것이다.
(D) 현재 다른 회사에 고용되어 있다.

해설 질문의 핵심 어구인 Ms. Lucci와 관련된 내용을 지문에서 찾아 각 보기와 대조하는 Not/True 문제입니다. (A)는 'Stefania was also friendly and simple to communicate with during the meeting. Those are good qualities for a leader.'에서 Stefania가 우호적이었고 만남 동안에 의사소통하기 쉬웠으며 그것들은 지도자에게 좋은 자질이라고 했으므로 지문의 내용과 일치합니다. (B)는 'What did you think of the final applicants ~ for the research manager job?'에서 연구 관리직 최종 지원자들에 대해 어떻게 생각했는지를 묻자, 'Stefania Lucci handled the questions ~ better.'에서 Stefania Lucci가 질문들에 더 잘 대처했다고 했으므로 지문의 내용과 일치합니다. (C)는 'I'll notify the human resources department that we'd like to make her an official offer.'에서 그녀, 즉 Stefania Lucci에게 공식 제의를 하고 싶다고 인사 부서에 알리겠다고 했으므로 지문의 내용과 일치합니다. (D)는 'Ben Trenton is currently working, but she is not'에서 Ben Trenton은 현재 일하고 있지만 Stefania Lucci는 그렇지 않다고 했으므로 지문의 내용과 일치하지 않습니다. 따라서 (D) She is currently employed at another company가 정답입니다.

06 의도 파악 문제

문제 오전 11시 44분에, Mr. Nielsen이 "That's what I think"라고 썼을 때, 그가 의도한 것은?
(A) Mr. Trenton이 일자리에 임명되어야 한다고 생각한다.
(B) 몇몇 후보자들과 후속 면접을 하고 싶어 한다.
(C) Ms. Lucci가 직무에 가장 알맞은 후보자라는 것에 동의한다.
(D) 지원자에게 주어진 제의에 만족한다.

해설 Mr. Nielsen이 의도한 것을 묻는 문제이므로, 질문의 인용어구(That's what I think)가 언급된 주변 문맥을 확인합니다. 'I think she'd be a great addition to the company.'에서 Jerome Bartha가 그녀, 즉 Ms. Lucci가 회사에 큰 보탬이 될 것이라고 생각한다고 하자, Mr. Nielsen

이 'That's what I think'(제 생각이 바로 그거예요)라고 한 것을 통해 Mr. Nielsen이 Ms. Lucci가 가장 알맞은 후보자라는 것에 동의한다는 것을 알 수 있습니다. 따라서 (C) He agrees that Ms. Lucci is the ideal candidate for the job이 정답입니다.

어휘 **appoint** v. 임명하다, 지명하다 **follow-up** adj. 후속의
ideal adj. 가장 알맞은, 이상적인

DAY 18 지문 유형 2

Course 1 양식 (Forms)

HACKERS TEST   p.322

01 (D)	02 (D)	03 (D)	04 (D)	05 (B)
06 (C)				

01-04번은 다음 일정표에 관한 문제입니다.

8월 16일 Meadows 시민 회관에서
**제25회 Graceville 스포츠 유명 인사 만찬 및 경매에
함께하십시오**

Graceville 스포츠 유명 인사 만찬 및 경매는 자원봉사자들이 준비한 스포츠를 기념하는 행사입니다. ⁰¹이 행사는 Graceville 아동 센터를 후원하여 매년 개최됩니다. Graceville 아동 센터는 장애를 가진 청소년들에게 필수적인 치료를 받을 기회를 제공합니다.

오후 6시	**출장 요리 만찬** 만찬은 Commons 레스토랑에 의해 제공될 것입니다.
오후 7시	⁰²**연사 발표** 야구 명예의 전당에 오른 투수 Stephen Fisher와 올림픽 국가 대표 하키팀 주장 Hal Wheaton을 포함합니다.
오후 7시 30분	⁰³**경매** www.gracevillescda.com에서 판매를 위한 물품들을 미리 보십시오.

일반석 티켓은 20달러이며 맨 위층 관람석 구역에 있는
일반 좌석을 포함합니다.
고급석 티켓은 30달러이며 1층의 좌석을 포함합니다.
⁰⁴행사 티켓은 www.gracevillscda.com/events에서만
구매 가능합니다.

더 많이 알아보고 싶으시다면, 555-5782로 전화해주십시오.

후원: Ingram 은행 | Mason 출판사 | Sport Select사 |
Allied 식료품점

auction n. 경매 **volunteer** n. 자원봉사자
organize v. 준비하다, 조직하다 **celebrate** v. 기념하다 **access** n. 기회
vital adj. 필수적인 **care** n. 치료, 돌봄 **disabled** adj. 장애를 가진
gallery n. 맨 위층 관람석 **premier** adj. 고급의, 최고의
exclusively adj. ~만, 오로지, 독점적으로

---

01 육하원칙 문제
문제 누가 이 행사로부터 이익을 얻을 것인가?
(A) 지역 스포츠팀들
(B) 스포츠 상 수상자들
(C) 고등학교 학생들
(D) 장애가 있는 아이들

해설 누가(Who) 이 행사로부터 이익을 얻을 것인지를 묻는 육하원칙 문제입니다. 질문의 핵심 어구인 benefit from the event와 관련하여, 'It is held each year in support of the Graceville Children's Center. The Graceville Children's Center provides access to vital care for disabled youth.'에서 이 행사는 Graceville 아동 센터를 후원하여 매년 개최되며, Graceville 아동 센터는 장애를 가진 청소년들에게 필수적인 치료를 받을 기회를 제공한다고 했으므로 이 행사에서 이익을 얻을 사람이 장애가 있는 아이들임을 알 수 있습니다. 따라서 (D) Kids with disabilities가 정답입니다.

패러프레이징
disabled youth 장애를 가진 청소년들 → Kids with disabilities 장애가 있는 아이들

02 추론 문제
문제 초청 연사에 대해 암시되는 것은?
(A) 스포츠 기념품을 기부할 것이다.
(B) 이전에 그 행사에서 연설을 했었다.
(C) 무료 시연을 할 것이다.
(D) 잘 알려진 스포츠 유명인들이다.

해설 질문의 핵심 어구인 the invited speakers에 대해 추론하는 문제입니다. 'Speaker Presentations, Including Baseball Hall of Fame pitcher Stephen Fisher and captain of the Olympic national hockey team Hal Wheaton.'에서 연사 발표는 야구 명예의 전당에 오른 투수 Stephen Fisher와 올림픽 국가 대표 하키팀 주장 Hal Wheaton을 포함한다고 했으므로 초청 연사는 잘 알려진 스포츠 유명인들이라는 사실을 추론할 수 있습니다. 따라서 (D) They are well-known sports personalities가 정답입니다.

어휘 **give away** phr. 기부하다, 나누어 주다 **memorabilia** n. 기념품, 수집품
well-known adj. 잘 알려진, 유명한 **personality** n. 유명인

03 추론 문제
문제 행사 중 무슨 일이 일어날 것 같은가?
(A) 공연이 열릴 것이다.
(B) 고별사가 있을 것이다.
(C) 상이 나누어질 것이다.
(D) 물품들이 경매에 부쳐질 것이다.

해설 질문의 핵심 어구인 happen during the event에 대해 추론하는 문제입니다. 'Auction, Preview items for sale at www.gracevillescda.com.'에서 경매가 있을 것이고 www.gracevillescda.com에서 판매를 위한 물품들을 미리 보라고 했으므로 행사 중 물품들이 경매에 부쳐질 것이라는 사실을 추론할 수 있습니다. 따라서 (D) Items will be put up for sale이 정답입니다.

어휘 **performance** n. 공연 **farewell speech** phr. 고별사
award n. 상; v. 수여하다 **give out** phr. 나누어주다
put up for sale phr. 경매에 부치다, 팔려고 내놓다

04 육하원칙 문제
문제 손님들은 참석하기 위해 무엇을 해야 하는가?
(A) 자선 기부를 한다
(B) 확인증을 발송한다
(C) 협회 사무실에 전화한다
(D) 기관 웹페이지를 방문한다

해설 손님들이 참석하기 위해 무엇(What)을 해야 하는지를 묻는 육하원칙 문제입니다. 질문의 핵심 어구인 guests do to attend와 관련하여, 'Tickets for the event are available exclusively at www.gracevillscda.com/events.'에서 행사 티켓은 www.gracevillscda.com/events에서만 구매 가능하다고 했으므로, 손님들은 참석하기 위해 기관 웹페이지를 방문해서 티켓을 구매해야 함을 알 수 있습니다. 따라서 (D) Visit an establishment's Web page가 정답입니다.

어휘 **charitable** adj. 자선의 **send in** phr. 발송하다 **association** n. 협회
establishment n. 기관, 설립

05-06번은 다음 웹페이지와 이메일에 관한 문제입니다.

| 홈 | 정보 | 지금 등록하기 | 위치 |

시장성이 있는 실무 능력을 얻는 데 관심이 있지만 대학에 다시 갈 시간은 없으십니까? Kinski Institute가 도와드리기 위해 여기에 있습니다. 저희는 오늘날의 글로벌 시장에서 여러분이 경쟁할 수 있도록 해줄 다양한 자격증 프로그램들을 제공합니다.

저희의 다가오는 수업들은 다음과 같습니다:

프로그램	강사	날짜	가격
비즈니스 커뮤니케이션	Franklin Ward	10월 31일–12월 2일	250달러
05비영리 단체 운영	05Toby French	11월 1일–12월 6일	280달러
마케팅 관리	Melinda Jackson	11월 5일–1월 11일	310달러
재무 회계	Emily Pearce	1월 2일–1월 27일	340달러

등록하시려면, 여기를 클릭하십시오. 저희는 신용카드만 받습니다. 환불은 제공하지 않습니다. 질문이 있으시다면, customersupport@kinski.com으로 이메일을 보내시거나 555-1412로 전화해주십시오.

enroll v. 등록하다 **be interested in** phr. ~에 관심이 있다
gain v. 얻다 **marketable** adj. 시장성이 있는 **a range of** phr. 다양한
certificate n. 자격증 **compete** v. 경쟁하다 **marketplace** n. 시장
nonprofit n. 비영리 단체 **management** n. 운영, 관리, 경영
financial accounting phr. 재무 회계 **accept** v. 받다, 수락하다
refund n. 환불

수신: 고객 지원 <customersupport@kinski.com>
발신: Bill Dixon <bdixon@fastmail.com>
날짜: 8월 12일
제목: 최근의 결제

지원 부서 직원분께,

제 이름은 Bill Dixon이고, 05/06-A저는 비영리 단체 운영 경험을 얻는 것을 고려하고 있는 IT 전문가입니다. 05어제 저는 귀사의 수업 중 한 개에 등록했지만, 만료된 신용카드로 인해 제 결제가 진행되지 않았다고 통지하는 이메일을 방금 받았습니다. 하지만, 제 신용카드는 12월이나 되어야 만료됩니다. 다시 한번 확인해주시고 진행하는 방법을 알려주시겠습니까? 또한, 제 친구 06-AErin Johnson이 비즈니스 커뮤니케이션 강좌에 등록하고 싶어 하지만, 06-C그녀는 그녀 명의의 신용카드를 가지고 있지 않습니다. 그녀 대신 제가 결제해도 괜찮을까요?

도움 감사드립니다.

Bill Dixon 드림

specialist n. 전문가 **look to** phr. ~을 고려하다 **experience** n. 경험
receive v. 받다 **inform** v. 통지하다 **expire** v. 만료되다
proceed v. 진행하다

05 추론 문제 연계

문제 Mr. Dixon은 누구의 수업에 등록했을 것 같은가?
(A) Franklin Ward
(B) Toby French
(C) Melinda Jackson
(D) Emily Pearce

해설 두 지문의 내용을 종합적으로 확인한 후 추론해서 풀어야 하는 연계

문제입니다. 질문의 핵심 어구인 class ~ Mr. Dixon probably sign up for와 관련된 내용이 언급된 두 번째 지문인 Mr. Dixon이 작성한 이메일을 확인합니다.

두 번째 지문인 이메일의 'I'm ~ looking to gain nonprofit management experience. Yesterday, I signed up for one of your classes'에서 Mr. Dixon이 비영리 단체 운영 경험을 얻는 것을 고려하고 있어서 어제 수업 중 한 개에 등록했다고 했으므로 Mr. Dixon이 비영리 단체 운영 관련 수업에 등록했다는 첫 번째 단서를 확인할 수 있습니다. 그런데 비영리 단체 운영 수업을 누가 진행하는지가 제시되지 않았으므로 웹페이지에서 관련 내용을 확인합니다. 첫 번째 지문인 웹페이지의 'Nonprofit Management, Toby French'에서 비영리 단체 운영 수업은 Toby French가 진행한다는 두 번째 단서를 확인할 수 있습니다.

Mr. Dixon이 비영리 단체 운영 관련 수업에 등록했다는 첫 번째 단서와 비영리 단체 운영 수업은 Toby French가 진행한다는 두 번째 단서를 종합할 때, Mr. Dixon이 Toby French의 수업에 등록했다는 사실을 추론할 수 있습니다. 따라서 (B) Toby French가 정답입니다.

06 Not/True 문제

문제 Ms. Johnson에 대해 언급된 것은?
(A) Mr. Dixon과 동일한 강좌를 듣기를 원한다.
(B) 그녀의 지불 정보가 갱신되었다.
(C) 신용카드를 가지고 있지 않다.
(D) 그녀의 업무 경력은 비즈니스 커뮤니케이션 분야이다.

해설 질문의 핵심 어구인 Ms. Johnson과 관련된 내용을 지문에서 찾아 각 보기와 대조하는 Not/True 문제이므로 Ms. Johnson이 언급된 두 번째 지문인 이메일을 확인합니다. (A)는 'I'm ~ looking to gain nonprofit management experience.'에서 자신, 즉 Mr. Dixon이 비영리 단체 운영 경험을 얻는 것을 고려하고 있다고 했고, 'Erin Johnson wants to sign up for the business communication course'에서 Erin Johnson이 비즈니스 커뮤니케이션 강좌에 등록하고 싶어 한다고 했으므로 지문의 내용과 일치하지 않습니다. (B)는 지문에 언급되지 않은 내용입니다. (C)는 'she doesn't have her own credit card'에서 그녀, 즉 Ms. Johnson은 그녀 명의의 신용카드를 가지고 있지 않다고 했으므로 지문의 내용과 일치합니다. 따라서 (C) She does not possess a credit card가 정답입니다. (D)는 지문에 언급되지 않은 내용입니다.

패러프레이징
doesn't have ~ own credit card 자신 명의의 신용카드를 가지고 있지 않다 → does not possess a credit card 신용카드를 가지고 있지 않다

어휘 **possess** v. 가지다, 소유하다

Course 2 광고 (Advertisement)

HACKERS TEST   p.326

| 01 (C) | 02 (C) | 03 (C) | 04 (B) | 05 (D) |

01-03번은 다음 광고에 관한 문제입니다.

01사람들에게 말하는 데 재능이 있으십니까?
ShareUs 텔레마케팅 회사에서
업무에 사용하십시오!

ShareUs는 다양한 회사들을 위한 텔레마케팅 캠페인을 운영합니다. 저희의 고객들은 Greendom 식료품 회사, Fanatic 커피숍, 그리고 Huffman 백화점을 포함하지만 이에 국한되지는 않습니다.

전문 학위나 사전 경력이 요구되지는 않습니다. 지원자들이 필요한 모든 것은 외향적인 성격, 긍정적인 태도, 그리고 전화로 정중하게 말

할 수 있는 능력뿐입니다. 신입 사원 수준의 업무는 전화 업무를 처리하는 것에 제한됩니다. [02]회사에 최소한 2년 동안 머무른 직원들은 전화 서비스 관리직이나 기록 보관 같은 다른 부서로의 내부 고용을 통해 승진의 가능성을 누릴 수 있습니다.

* [03]ShareUs사가 현재 직원을 모집하고 있는 곳:
Elmwood, 앨버타주—2자리
Marston, 서스캐처원주—5자리
Pasquer, 온타리오주—4자리

ShareUs사는 언제나 지원서를 검토할 의향이 있습니다. 회사 웹사이트인 www.shareusrecruit.com을 통해 언제든지 자유롭게 지원하십시오. 지원서 양식을 작성하기만 하면, 여러분은 흥미로운 새 경력에 가까워지게 될 것입니다.

gift n. 재능 telemarketing n. 텔레마케팅, 전화 판매 run v. 운영하다
diverse adj. 다양한 client n. 고객 include v. 포함하다
limit v. 국한시키다, 제한하다 specialized adj. 전문적인, 전문화된
degree n. 학위, 정도 prior adj. 사전의 experience n. 경력, 경험
applicant n. 지원자 outgoing adj. 외향적인, 사교적인
personality n. 성격 positive adj. 긍정적인 attitude n. 태도
ability n. 능력 politely adv. 정중하게, 예의 바르게
duty n. 할 일, 직무, 의무 entry n. 입문 handle v. 처리하다, 다루다
stay v. 머무르다 prospect n. 가능성, 가망 advancement n. 승진
management n. 관리 internal adj. 내부의 hiring n. 고용
department n. 부서 currently adv. 현재
recruit v. (직원을) 모집하다 be willing to phr. (기꺼이) ~할 의향이 있다
fill out phr. (양식 등을) 작성하다, 채우다
on one's way to phr. ~에 가까워지다 interesting adj. 흥미로운
career n. 경력

01 주제/목적 찾기 문제

문제 광고되고 있는 것은 무엇인가?
(A) 고객 서비스에 관한 세미나
(B) 고객을 위한 판촉 할인 행사
(C) 서비스 공급업체의 일자리
(D) 회사의 새로운 지점들

해설 광고되고 있는 것이 무엇인지를 묻는 주제 찾기 문제이므로 지문의 앞부분을 주의 깊게 확인합니다. 'Do you have a gift for talking to people? Put that to work! At ShareUs Telemarketing'에서 사람들에게 말하는 데 재능이 있다면 ShareUs 텔레마케팅 회사에서 업무에 사용하라고 한 뒤 일자리에 필요한 요건이나 업무 내용 등을 설명하고 있으므로 (C) A job with a service provider가 정답입니다.

어휘 promotional adj. 판촉의, 홍보의 location n. 지점, 위치

02 동의어 찾기 문제

문제 2문단 네 번째 줄의 단어 "prospects"는 의미상 –와 가장 가깝다.
(A) 관점
(B) 준비
(C) 가능성
(D) 제안

해설 prospects를 포함하고 있는 구절 'Employees who stay with the company for at least two years enjoy prospects for advancement'에서 prospects가 '가능성'이라는 뜻으로 사용되었습니다. 따라서 '가능성'이라는 뜻을 가진 (C) possibilities가 정답입니다.

03 추론 문제

문제 ShareUs사에 대해 암시되는 것은?
(A) 본사를 옮길 계획이다.
(B) 기술 지원을 전문으로 한다.
(C) 여러 지점에서 직원을 모집하고 있다.
(D) 유급 교육 기간을 제공할 것이다.

해설 질문의 핵심 어구인 ShareUs에 대해 추론하는 문제입니다. 'Places where ShareUs is currently recruiting: Elmwood, Alberta—2 positions, Marston, Saskatchewan—5 positions, Pasquer, Ontario—4 positions'에서 ShareUs사가 현재 앨버타주의 Elmwood, 서스캐처원주의 Marston, 온타리오주의 Pasquer에서 직원을 모집하고 있다고 했으므로 ShareUs사가 여러 지점에서 직원을 모집하고 있다는 사실을 추론할 수 있습니다. 따라서 (C) It is recruiting staff in different locations가 정답입니다.

어휘 different adj. 여러, 각각 다른 period n. 기간
paid adj. 유급의, 보수가 주어지는

04-05번은 다음 광고, 송장, 후기에 관한 문제입니다.

GREEN-CARE사의 잔디 관리에 대한 최신의 혁신을 소개합니다!

Green-Care사의 GC-24 잔디 깎는 기계는 자체적으로 추진되고 어떠한 지형에도 적합한 바퀴를 가지고 있어서, 언덕이나 다른 경사지의 잔디를 깎기 쉽게 합니다. 배터리로 움직이며 빠르게 충전됩니다! 그뿐 아니라, 모든 Green-Care사의 제품들은 무료 수리 또는 교체에 대한 6개월짜리 품질 보증서가 딸려옵니다. [04]아래의 쿠폰을 가져오셔서 이 달의 특별 할인을 이용해보세요.

할인 쿠폰
[04]GC-24 잔디 깎는 기계 구매에 대한 25달러 할인
고객당 한 개 제한. 할인은 9월 30일에 만료됩니다.

---

introduce v. 소개하다 innovation n. 혁신
lawn mower phr. 잔디 깎는 기계
self-propelled adj. 자체적으로 추진하는 wheel n. 바퀴
suitable adj. 적합한, 적절한 terrain n. 지형 grass n. 잔디
hill n. 언덕 incline n. 경사(지) recharge v. 충전하다
come with phr. ~이 딸려오다 warranty n. 품질 보증서
repair n. 수리 replacement n. 교체
take advantage of phr. ~을 이용하다

Garrison Garden Supplies사: 543번지 West로, 샌드포인트, 아이다호주 83864
[04]고객: Mr. Westley Beecher, 827번지 Dearborn가, 샌드포인트, 아이다호주 83864
주문 번호: B-3948374

제품	가격	수량	합계
Green-Care사 GC-24 잔디 깎는 기계	375.00달러	1	375.00달러
		[04]할인	−25.00달러
		합계	350.00달러

[05-A]상품: Green-Care사 GC-24 잔디 깎는 기계
[05-A]회원: Westley Beecher

[05-D]저는 넉 달 전에 이 잔디 깎는 기계를 구매했습니다. 이 기계는 조작하기 쉽고 놀랄 만큼 강력한 모터를 갖추고 있습니다. [05-A]충전 과정은 빠르고, 보통 한 시간 이내로 걸립니다. 그러나, 제가 처음에 이것을 받았을 때, 제 기계는 한 번의 충전당 약 10분밖에 지속되지 않았습니다. [05-B]저는 그것을 제조사에 다시 보냈고, 그들은 그것을 수리해 주었습니다. 그리고 이제 [05-C]배터리는 한 시간 이상 지속됩니다. 저렴한 가격을 고려하면, Green-Care사 GC-24 잔디 깎는 기계는 가격 대비 가치가 상당합니다.

operate v. 조작하다, 작동하다 surprisingly adv. 놀랄 만큼, 대단히
process n. 과정 last v. 지속되다 charge n. 충전; v. 충전하다
considering prep. ~을 고려하면 cost n. 가격, 비용
value n. 가격 대비 가치

04 추론 문제 연계

문제 Mr. Beecher는 Garrison Garden Supplies사에 무엇을 주었을 것 같은가?

(A) 고객 만족 설문 조사
(B) 할인 쿠폰
(C) 회원권 카드
(D) 상품 구매 영수증

해설 세 지문 중 두 지문의 내용을 종합적으로 확인한 후 추론해서 풀어야 하는 연계 문제입니다. 질문의 핵심 어구인 Mr. Beecher가 Garrison Garden Supplies사를 통해 주문한 물품에 대한 송장인 두 번째 지문을 먼저 확인합니다.

두 번째 지문인 송장의 'Customer: Mr. Westley Beecher', 'Discount, −$25.00'에서 Mr. Beecher가 25.00달러를 할인받았다는 첫 번째 단서를 확인할 수 있습니다. 그런데 어떻게 할인을 받았는지가 제시되지 않았으므로 광고에서 관련 내용을 확인합니다. 첫 번째 지문인 광고의 'Bring the coupon below to take advantage of this month's special offer.'에서 아래의 쿠폰을 가져와서 이달의 특별 할인을 이용해보라고 했고, 쿠폰의 '$25 off your purchase of a GC-24 Lawn Mower'에서 쿠폰을 통해 GC-24 잔디 깎는 기계 구매에 대해 25달러를 할인받을 수 있다고 했으므로 광고의 쿠폰을 가져가면 25달러를 할인받을 수 있다는 두 번째 단서를 확인할 수 있습니다. Mr. Beecher가 25달러를 할인받았다는 첫 번째 단서와 광고의 쿠폰을 가져가면 25달러 할인을 받을 수 있다는 두 번째 단서를 종합할 때, Mr. Beecher는 Garrison Garden Supplies사에 할인 쿠폰을 주었다는 사실을 추론할 수 있습니다. 따라서 (B) A discount coupon이 정답입니다.

05 Not/True 문제

문제 Mr. Beecher에 대해 사실이 아닌 것은?

(A) 그의 잔디 깎는 기계는 재충전 가능한 배터리를 사용한다.
(B) 최근에 전자 기기를 수리받았다.
(C) 그의 기계는 한 번에 한 시간 이상 작동한다.
(D) 반년 동안 잔디 깎는 기계를 소유해왔다.

해설 질문의 핵심 어구인 Mr. Beecher와 관련된 내용을 지문에서 찾아 각 보기와 대조하는 Not/True 문제이므로 Mr. Beecher가 작성한 세 번째 지문인 후기를 확인합니다. (A)는 'Product: Green-Care GC-24 Lawn Mower', 'Member: Westley Beecher'에서 Mr. Beecher가 Green-Care사 GC-24 잔디 깎는 기계를 소유하고 있고, 'The recharging process is fast, usually taking under an hour.'에서 충전 과정이 빠르고 보통 한 시간 이내로 걸린다고 했으므로 지문의 내용과 일치합니다. (B)는 'I sent it back to the manufacturer, and they repaired it for me.'에서 자신은 그것, 즉 잔디 깎는 기계를 제조사에 다시 보냈고 그들이 그것을 수리해 주었다고 했으므로 지문의 내용과 일치합니다. (C)는 'the battery lasts for over an hour'에서 배터리가 한 시간 이상 지속된다고 했으므로 지문의 내용과 일치합니다. (D)는 'I purchased this mower four months ago.'에서 자신, 즉 Mr. Beecher가 넉 달 전에 이 잔디 깎는 기계를 구매했다고 했으므로 지문의 내용과 일치하지 않습니다. 따라서 (D) He has owned a lawn mower for half a year가 정답입니다.

패러프레이징
repaired 수리했다 → got ~ fixed 수리받았다
for over an hour 한 시간 이상 → an hour or more 한 시간 이상

어휘 electronic adj. 전자의, 전자 장비와 관련된

DAY 19 지문 유형 3

Course 1 기사 및 안내문 (Article & Information)

HACKERS TEST

01 (B)	02 (A)	03 (D)	04 (A)	05 (C)
06 (D)				

01-04번은 다음 안내문에 관한 문제입니다.

> ### 새 세입자들을 위한 안내문
>
> 세입자로서, 부동산 소유주와의 잠재적인 임대차 계약 관련 논쟁으로부터 여러분 자신을 보호하는 것이 중요합니다. [01]오슬로 세입자 자문 위원회는 부동산을 임차하는 것을 고려하고 있는 사람들을 위해 다음과 같은 조언을 제공합니다:
>
> - 서명이 된 서면 계약서를 반드시 받으십시오. 문서는 여러분 것 한 부와 부동산 소유주의 것 한 부씩 최소한 두 부를 작성하십시오. 많은 경우에, 계약 조건은 분쟁을 처리하기 위해 사용될 것이므로, 서명하기 전에 주의 깊게 읽으십시오.
> - 보호를 위해, [02]법은 임대주들이 모든 숙박 시설 보증금을 별도의 보통 예금 계좌에 보관할 것을 요구합니다. 세입자들은 이 보증금의 증명에 대한 권리가 있습니다. 따라서, 지불 시에 반드시 영수증을 요청하십시오.
> - [04-C]물품 목록을 요청하시고 그 목록이 해당 세대의 모든 물품들에 대한 정확한 세부 사항을 포함하는지 꼭 확인하십시오. 눈에 보이는 모든 손상의 사진을 찍으십시오. 그것들은 임대차 계약 종료 시에 [03]여러분의 임차 보증금에서 제해질 수도 있는 손해 배상 청구로부터 여러분 자신을 보호하기 위해 사용될 수도 있습니다.
> - 소유주가 있는 동안, [04-B]모든 배관 및 조명 장치를 테스트하셔서 그것들이 작동하는지 꼭 확인하십시오. 추가로, [04-D]모든 문과 창문의 잠금장치가 제대로 작동하는지 확인하십시오.
>
> 만약 임차하는 동안 어떠한 문제에 부딪힌다면, 세입자 자문 위원회에 555-7156으로 연락하십시오.

tenant n. 세입자　potential adj. 잠재적인
lease n. 임대차 계약; v. 임대하다　disagreement n. 논쟁, 의견 차이
advisory adj. 자문의, 고문의　committee n. 위원회
property n. 부동산, 건물　sign v. 서명하다　contract n. 계약(서)
document n. 문서　owner n. 소유주　terms n. 조건
settle v. 처리하다, 중재하다, 합의를 보다　dispute n. 분쟁, 논쟁
carefully adv. 주의 깊게, 신중하게　safekeeping n. 보호, 보관
accommodation n. 숙박 시설, 주거 시설　deposit n. 보증금, 예금
savings account phr. 보통 예금 (계좌)
entitle v. ~에 대한 권리가 있다, 자격이 있다　inventory n. 물품 목록, 재고
contain v. 포함하다　accurate adj. 정확한　unit n. 세대, 가구
visible adj. 눈에 보이는　damage n. 손상, 훼손　claim n. 청구
proprietor n. 소유주　present adj. 있는, 존재하는　plumbing n. 배관
fixture n. 장치, 기구　work v. 작동하다　lock n. 잠금장치
functional adj. 제대로 작동하는　encounter v. 부딪히다, 마주하다

01 주제/목적 찾기 문제

문제 안내문의 목적은 무엇인가?

(A) 오래된 건물의 수리 작업을 설명하기 위해
(B) 임차를 계획하고 있는 사람들에게 조언을 해주기 위해
(C) 세입자들에게 새로운 법을 알리기 위해
(D) 곧 있을 건설 작업을 알리기 위해

해설 안내문의 목적을 묻는 목적 찾기 문제이므로 지문의 앞부분을 주의 깊게 확인합니다. 'The Oslo Tenants Advisory Committee offers the following advice to those who are considering renting a

DAY 19 지문 유형 3　**187**

property:'에서 오슬로 세입자 자문 위원회가 부동산을 임차하는 것을 고려하고 있는 사람들을 위해 다음과 같은 조언을 제공한다고 한 뒤, 임차 시 주의해야 할 사항을 나열하고 있으므로 (B) To provide advice to people planning on renting이 정답입니다.

어휘 alert v. 알리다, 주의를 환기시키다

02 육하원칙 문제

문제 건물 소유주들은 세입자들에게 무엇을 줄 것이 요구되는가?
(A) 보증금 수령 증명서
(B) 여분의 문 열쇠
(C) 저장 공간의 잠금장치
(D) 비상 연락처

해설 건물 소유주가 세입자에게 무엇(What)을 줄 것이 요구되는지를 묻는 육하원칙 문제입니다. 질문의 핵심 어구인 building proprietors required to give tenants와 관련하여, 'the law requires that landlords keep all accommodation deposits in a separate savings account. Tenants are entitled to proof of this deposit. Accordingly, make sure to ask for a receipt'에서 법은 임대주들이 모든 숙박 시설 보증금을 별도의 보통 예금 계좌에 보관할 것을 요구하며 세입자들은 이 보증금의 증명에 대한 권리가 있으므로 반드시 영수증을 요청하라고 했으므로 건물 소유주인 임대주들이 세입자들에게 보증금 수령 영수증을 주어야 함을 알 수 있습니다. 따라서 (A) A proof of deposit receipt가 정답입니다.

어휘 extra adj. 여분의 storage n. 저장, 보관 emergency n. 비상 (사태)

03 추론 문제

문제 보증금에 대해 추론될 수 있는 것은?
(A) 소유주들은 그것을 지역 은행에 보관해야 한다.
(B) 한 달 치 임차료보다 많아서는 안 된다.
(C) 세입자가 통지 없이 나갈 경우 임차료를 지불하는 데 쓰일 것이다.
(D) 건물 소유주들은 손상 비용을 상쇄하기 위해 그것을 사용할 수 있다.

해설 질문의 핵심 어구인 deposits에 대해 추론하는 문제입니다. 'damage claims that can be taken from your rental deposit'에서 임차 보증금에서 제해질 수도 있는 손해 배상 청구가 언급되었으므로 건물 소유주들은 손상 비용을 상쇄하기 위해 보증금을 사용할 수 있다는 사실을 추론할 수 있습니다. 따라서 (D) Building owners may use them to cover the costs of damage가 정답입니다.

어휘 cover v. 상쇄하다 cost n. 비용, 가격

04 Not/True 문제

문제 안내문이 세입자들에게 확인하도록 권하지 않는 정보는?
(A) 환기 장치가 막히지 않았다는 것
(B) 건물에 수돗물이 나온다는 것
(C) 물품 목록이 정확하게 기록되어 있다는 것
(D) 문에 제대로 작동하는 잠금장치가 있다는 것

해설 질문의 핵심 어구인 information ~ tenants check와 관련된 내용을 지문에서 찾아 각 보기와 대조하는 Not/True 문제입니다. (A)는 지문에 언급되지 않은 내용입니다. 따라서 (A) That the ventilation system is not blocked가 정답입니다. (B)는 'test all plumbing ~ to make sure they work'에서 모든 배관 장치를 테스트해서 작동하는지 꼭 확인하라고 했으므로 지문의 내용과 일치합니다. (C)는 'Ask for an inventory list and make sure that it contains accurate details'에서 물품 목록을 요청하고 그 목록이 정확한 세부 사항을 포함하는지 꼭 확인하라고 했으므로 지문의 내용과 일치합니다. (D)는 'ensure that the locks on all doors ~ are functional'에서 모든 문의 잠금장치가 제대로 작동하는지 확인하라고 했으므로 지문의 내용과 일치합니다.

패러프레이징
contains accurate details 정확한 세부 사항을 포함하다

→ is correctly recorded 정확하게 기록되다
locks on all doors ~ are functional 모든 문의 잠금장치가 제대로 작동하다 → the doors have working locks 문에 제대로 작동하는 잠금장치가 있다

어휘 ventilation n. 환기 block v. 막다 inventory n. 물품 목록

05-06번은 다음 기사와 이메일에 관한 문제입니다.

정수장 완공 임박

05-A/B도시 교외의 Divot로에 위치한 Elkwood의 새로운 수도 관리 시설이 05-B최종 공사 단계의 끝부분에 가까워지고 있다. 그 작업을 감독하고 있는 HMC Contractors사의 소유주인 Roger Hanks는 정수장이 5월 8일에 가동될 준비가 될 것이라고 말한다. 05-D720만 달러 짜리 시설의 건설은 재산세 인상에서 자금이 제공되었고 2년 이상 걸렸다. 05-C새 정수장은 Blake가에 있는 기존의 것과 함께 도시의 수도를 처리할 것이다. 이 정수장이 가동되면, 빠르게 성장하고 있는 Elkwood 서부에 서비스를 제공하고, 모든 시민들에게 깨끗한 수돗물 공급을 보장하는 데 도움을 줄 것이다. 06시는 곧 개장식 날짜를 발표할 것인데, 이 행사는 Arlene Jennings 시장의 짧은 연설을 포함할 것이다.

water purification plant phr. 정수장 completion n. 완공, 완료 treatment n. 관리, 치료 facility n. 시설 locate v. 위치시키다 outskirts n. 교외, 변두리 construction n. 공사, 건설 phase n. 단계 oversee v. 감독하다, 감시하다 operation n. 가동, 운영 fund v. 자금을 제공하다; n. 자금 property tax phr. 재산세 serve v. (서비스 등을) 제공하다, 봉사하다 tap water phr. 수돗물 shortly adv. 곧 announce v. 발표하다 launch n. 개시, 시작, 착수 ceremony n. 행사 include v. 포함하다 speech n. 연설

수신 Leann Edison <ledison@elkwoodcity.gov>
발신 Melvin O'Rourke <meorourke@elkwoodcity.gov>
날짜 5월 2일
제목 업무

안녕하세요, Leann.

06우리는 예상했던 것보다 늦은 5월 10일에 새 관리 시설을 열 것 같습니다. 그래서 우리는 5월 9일로 시스템 검사 일정을 변경해야 할 것입니다. 이는 그 날짜에 일시적인 수도 중단이 있을 것임을 뜻합니다. 저는 당신이 이 변경 사항에 대한 공고를 가능한 한 빨리 준비해주시기를 바랍니다. 완료되고 나면, 검토를 위해 제게 사본 한 부를 보내주시겠습니까? 오후 4시 전에 해주시기 바랍니다.

Melvin 드림

reschedule v. 일정을 변경하다 temporary adj. 일시적인 interruption n. 중단 prepare v. 준비하다 review n. 검토

05 Not/True 문제

문제 기사에서 정수장에 대해 언급되지 않은 것은?
(A) 도시 변두리에 위치할 것이다.
(B) HMC Contractors사에 의해 건설되고 있다.
(C) 기존의 시설을 대체할 것이다.
(D) 재산세를 인상하는 것을 필요로 했다.

해설 질문의 핵심 어구인 the water treatment plant와 관련된 내용을 기사에서 찾아 각 보기와 대조하는 Not/True 문제이므로 기사에서 관련 내용을 확인합니다. (A)는 'Elkwood's new water treatment facility, located on the outskirts of the city'에서 도시 교외에 위치한 Elkwood의 새로운 수도 관리 시설이라고 했으므로 지문의 내용과 일치합니다. (B)는 'Elkwood's new water treatment facility ~ is nearing the end of the final construction phase. ~ HMC Contractors, is overseeing the project'에서 Elkwood의 새로운 수도 관리 시설이 최종 공사 단계의 끝부분에 가까워지고 있고 HMC

Contractors사가 그 작업을 감독하고 있다고 했으므로 지문의 내용과 일치합니다. (C)는 'The new plant will join the existing one ~ in treating the city's water.'에서 새 정수장이 기존의 것과 함께 도시의 수도를 처리할 것이라고 했으므로 지문의 내용과 일치하지 않습니다. 따라서 (C) It will replace an existing plant가 정답입니다. (D)는 'Construction of the ~ facility was funded by a property tax increase'에서 시설의 건설은 재산세 인상에서 자금이 제공되었다고 했으므로 지문의 내용과 일치합니다.

패러프레이징
outskirts 교외 → edge 변두리
construction 공사 → being built 건설되다
property tax increase 재산세 인상 → raising property taxes 재산세를 인상하는 것

어휘 replace v. 대체하다, 교체하다 existing adj. 기존의, 존재하는

06 추론 문제 연계

문제 Ms. Jennings는 언제 연설을 할 것 같은가?
(A) 5월 2일에
(B) 5월 8일에
(C) 5월 9일에
(D) 5월 10일에

해설 두 지문의 내용을 종합적으로 확인한 후 추론해서 풀어야 하는 연계 문제입니다. 질문의 핵심 어구인 Ms. Jennings가 언급된 첫 번째 지문인 기사를 먼저 확인합니다.

첫 번째 지문인 기사의 'The city will shortly announce a date for a launch ceremony, which will include a short speech by Mayor Arlene Jennings.'에서 시가 곧 개장식 날짜를 발표할 것인데, 이 행사는 Arlene Jennings 시장의 짧은 연설을 포함할 것이라고 했으므로 개장식 날에 Ms. Jennings가 연설을 할 것이라는 첫 번째 단서를 확인할 수 있습니다. 그런데 개장식이 언제인지가 제시되지 않았으므로 이메일에서 관련 내용을 확인합니다. 두 번째 지문인 이메일의 'It sounds like we are going to launch the new treatment facility ~ on May 10.'에서 5월 10일에 새 관리 시설을 열 것 같다는 두 번째 단서를 확인할 수 있습니다.

개장식 날에 Ms. Jennings가 연설을 할 것이라는 첫 번째 단서와 5월 10일에 새 관리 시설을 열 것 같다는 두 번째 단서를 종합할 때, Ms. Jennings는 5월 10일에 연설을 할 것이라는 사실을 추론할 수 있습니다. 따라서 (D) On May 10가 정답입니다.

Course 2 공고 및 회람 (Notice & Memo)

HACKERS TEST   p.334

01 (B)	02 (D)	03 (A)	04 (A)	05 (D)

01-03번은 다음 회람에 관한 문제입니다.

수신 Karpour사 전 직원
발신 Simone Kingsley, 관리부 비서
날짜 1월 10일
제목 교체 기간

01/03관리팀은 다시 한번 사무실의 비품 목록을 검토하고 손상된 물품들을 교체할 시기가 왔다고 발표했습니다. 이 평가는 3년마다 진행됩니다. 이것은 모든 직원들이 새 비품을 받을 것이라는 의미가 아님을 유념해 주십시오. 반드시 진행되어야 할 절차가 있습니다.

첫째로, 직원들은 반드시 신청서를 작성해야 합니다. 이것은 직원의 이름, 사무실 번호, 그리고 교체되어야 할 물품의 자산 번호를 포함한 짧은 설명을 요구합니다. 사무실의 모든 물품에는 이 정보가 적혀 있습니다. 만약 자산 번호가 발견될 수 없다면, 그 물품은 누군가의 개인적인 구매품일 가능성이 높으며 회사에 의해 교체될 수 없습니다.

02양식이 작성되면, 그것은 여러분이 속한 부서의 비서에게 제출되어야 하고, 그분이 저희에게 전해줄 것입니다. 그러면 누군가가 검사를 하기 위해 여러분께 연락할 것입니다. 만약 물품이 충분히 낡았다고 판단되면, 신청이 승인될 것입니다. 많은 직원들이 신청을 할 것으로 예상되기 때문에, 전체 교체 작업 과정은 약 한 달이 걸릴 것입니다. 양식 작성 완료 기한은 1월 30일입니다.

administrative adj. 관리의, 행정의 secretary n. 비서
replacement n. 교체 period n. 기간 review n. 검토
inventory n. (물품) 목록, 재고 furniture n. 비품, 가구
in disrepair phr. 손상된, 황폐한 assessment n. 평가
occur v. 진행되다, 발생하다, 일어나다 furnishings n. 비품
process n. 절차, 과정 follow v. 따르다 fill out phr. (양식 등을) 작성하다
request n. 신청, 요청 require v. 요구하다 description n. 설명, 묘사
include v. 포함하다 asset n. 자산, 재산 piece n. 물건 (한 개), 조각
label v. (표 같은 것에 정보를) 적다 likely adj. ~할 가능성이 높은
personal adj. 개인적인 purchase n. 구매(품)
be eligible to phr. ~할 수 있는, ~할 자격이 있는
complete v. (서식을 빠짐없이) 작성하다 turn in phr. 제출하다
inspection n. 검사 determine v. 판단하다, 결정하다
sufficiently adv. 충분히 approve v. 승인하다 expect v. 예상하다
entire adj. 전체의 approximately adv. 약, 대략 deadline n. 기한

01 주제/목적 찾기 문제

문제 회람은 주로 무엇에 관한 것인가?
(A) 신입 직원을 위한 사무실 휴무 정책
(B) 주기적인 사무용품 교체
(C) 다가오는 인근 건물로의 이사
(D) 보안 절차 변경

해설 회람이 주로 무엇에 관한 것인지를 묻는 주제 찾기 문제이므로 지문의 앞부분을 주의 깊게 확인합니다. 'The administration team has announced that it is time once again to review the office's inventory of furniture and replace items that are in disrepair. This assessment occurs every three years.'에서 관리팀은 다시 한번 사무실의 비품 목록을 검토하고 손상된 물품들을 교체할 시기가 왔다고 발표했으며 이 평가는 3년마다 진행된다고 했으므로 (B) A periodic replacement of office supplies가 정답입니다.

패러프레이징
occurs every three years 3년마다 진행되다 → periodic 주기적인

어휘 leave n. 휴무, 휴가 periodic adj. 주기적인
office supplies phr. 사무용품 move n. 이사, 이전 security n. 보안

02 육하원칙 문제

문제 직원들은 무엇을 할 것으로 예상되는가?
(A) 지난 구매품들의 기록을 회수한다.
(B) 사무실 비품에 자산 코드를 붙인다.
(C) 이번 주말 전에 업무를 끝낸다.
(D) 부서 직원에게 완성된 신청서를 준다.

해설 직원들이 무엇(What)을 할 것으로 예상되는지를 묻는 육하원칙 문제입니다. 질문의 핵심 어구인 employees expected to do와 관련하여, 'Once the form has been completed, it must be turned in to your department secretary'에서 양식이 작성되면 그것은 여러분, 즉 직원들이 속한 부서의 비서에게 제출되어야 한다고 했으므로 (D) Give completed forms to a department staff member가 정답입니다.

패러프레이징
be turned in to ~ department secretary 부서의 비서에게 제출되다 → Give ~ to a department staff member 부서 직원에게 주다

어휘 office equipment phr. 사무실 비품 assignment n. 업무

03 추론 문제

문제 Karpour사에 관해 사실일 것 같은 것은?

(A) 3년 이상 영업해 왔다.
(B) 그 지역에 많은 건물을 가지고 있다.
(C) 대량 구매를 이용할 것이다.
(D) 7월에 비품을 교체할 것이다.

해설 질문의 핵심 어구인 Karpour에 대해 추론하는 문제입니다. 'The administration team has announced that it is time once again to review the office's inventory of furniture and replace items that are in disrepair. This assessment occurs every three years.'에서 관리팀은 다시 한번 사무실의 비품 목록을 검토하고 손상된 물품들을 교체할 시기가 왔다고 발표했으며, 이 평가는 3년마다 진행된다고 한 내용을 통해 3년 전에 사무실의 비품을 교체하기 위한 평가를 진행한 적이 있음, 즉 Karpour사가 3년 이상 영업해 왔다는 사실을 추론할 수 있습니다. 따라서 (A) It has been in operation for over three years가 정답입니다.

어휘 operation n. 영업

04-05번은 다음 공고와 두 이메일에 관한 문제입니다.

⁰⁴이것은 Blaine 제조 회사를 위해 경비를 제공하도록 배정된 모든 Steadfast사 경비 요원을 위한 공고입니다. 11월 2일부터, 교대 근무 일정이 상당히 변경될 것입니다. Blaine 제조 회사의 경영진은 Steadfast사에 우리의 교대 근무 시간을 하루에 10시간으로 연장해줄 것을 요청하였고, 우리는 주 4일 근무를 대가로 그에 따르기로 동의했습니다. ⁰⁴Waterside 창고, Lockhart Industries사, 그리고 Henderson 공장 또한 교대 근무 시간을 연장하는 것을 고려하고 있지만, 최종적으로 계획된 바는 없습니다. 질문이 있으시면, 행정 관리자 Al Johnson(ajohnson@steadfast.com)에게 연락해주십시오.

announcement n. 공고 **guard** n. 경비 요원, 경호원 **assign** v. 배정하다, 배치하다 **security** n. 경비, 보안 **shift** n. 교대 근무 **substantially** adv. 상당히, 많이 **extend** v. 연장하다 **comply** v. 따르다, 준수하다 **in exchange for** phr. ~을 대가로 **consider** v. 고려하다 **plan** n. 계획 **administrative** adj. 행정의

수신 Al Johnson <ajohnson@steadfast.com>
발신 Brian Swift <bswift@steadfast.com>
날짜 10월 8일
제목 교대 근무 시간 변경

Mr. Johnson께,

Blaine 제조 회사의 일정 변경에 대한 공고를 읽었습니다. 저는 원래 그 교대 근무가 제게 가족을 돌볼 시간을 주었기 때문에 그곳에서의 일을 맡았습니다. 물론, ⁰⁵하루에 10시간씩 한 주당 4일을 근무하는 것에 몇몇 장점이 있지만, 저는 원래의 일정을 선호합니다. 제가 다른 회사에서 근무하도록 배정해주실 수 있는 방법이 있는지요?

Brian Swift 드림

take care of phr. ~을 돌보다, ~을 처리하다 **advantage** n. 장점, 이점

수신 Brian Swift <bswift@steadfast.com>
발신 Al Johnson <ajohnson@steadfast.com>
날짜 10월 10일
제목 회신: 교대 근무 시간 변경

안녕하세요, Brian.

연락 주셔서 감사합니다. 당신의 요청에 대해, 가능한 해결책을 찾았습니다. 당신이 우리의 다른 경비 요원들 중 한 명인 ⁰⁵Ahmed Sadik과 교대 근무를 바꿀 수 있을 것 같습니다. ⁰⁵그는 현재 Nuscope Industries사를 위해서 그들의 Cannondale 공장에서 매주 다섯 ○

번의 8시간 교대 근무를 하고 있습니다. 그가 당신과 업무를 바꾸고 싶다고 했습니다. 이 조정이 괜찮은지 제게 알려주십시오.

Al Johnson 드림

reach out phr. 연락을 취하다, 접근하다 **solution** n. 해결(책) **switch** v. 바꾸다, 전환하다 **arrangement** n. 조정, 준비

04 추론 문제

문제 Steadfast사에 대해 암시되는 것은?

(A) 여러 회사들에 경비를 제공한다.
(B) 직원 수를 줄였다.
(C) 보안용 제품들을 생산한다.
(D) 본사가 이전되었다.

해설 질문의 핵심 어구인 Steadfast Company에 대해 추론하는 문제이므로, 첫 번째 지문인 Steadfast사가 낸 공고를 먼저 확인합니다. 공고의 'This is an announcement for all Steadfast Company guards assigned to provide security for Blaine Manufacturing.'에서 Blaine 제조 회사를 위해 경비를 제공하도록 배정된 모든 Steadfast사 경비 요원을 위한 공고라고 했고, 'Waterside Warehouse, Lockhart Industries, and Henderson Milling are also considering extending shifts'에서 Waterside 창고, Lockhart Industries사, 그리고 Henderson 공장 또한 교대 근무 시간을 연장하는 것을 고려하고 있다고 했으므로, Steadfast가 Blaine 제조 회사, Waterside 창고, Lockhart Industries사, Henderson 공장 등의 여러 회사들에 경비를 제공한다는 사실을 추론할 수 있습니다. 따라서 (A) It provides security for multiple companies가 정답입니다.

어휘 multiple adj. 여러 headquarters n. 본사 relocate v. 이전하다

05 추론 문제 연계

문제 Mr. Sadik에 대해 암시되는 것은?

(A) Cannondale 공장까지 통근 시간이 길다.
(B) 이전 상사에게 추천을 받았다.
(C) 돌볼 가족이 전혀 없다.
(D) 주 4일 근무를 선호한다.

해설 세 지문 중 두 지문의 내용을 종합적으로 확인한 후 추론해서 풀어야 하는 연계 문제입니다. 질문의 핵심 어구인 Mr. Sadik이 언급된 세 번째 지문인 두 번째 이메일을 먼저 확인합니다.

'Ahmed Sadik. He currently does five eight-hour shifts each week ~. He has expressed that he would like to switch assignments with you.'에서 Ahmed Sadik이 현재 매주 다섯 번의 8시간 교대 근무를 하고 있는데 당신, 즉 Mr. Swift와 업무를 바꾸고 싶다고 했다는 첫 번째 단서를 확인할 수 있습니다. 그런데 Mr. Sadik이 Mr. Swift와 업무를 바꾸고 싶다고 한 배경이 무엇인지가 제시되지 않았으므로 첫 번째 이메일에서 관련 내용을 확인합니다. 'working four days a week ~ has some advantages, but I prefer the original schedule. Is there any way you could assign me to work at another company?'에서 한 주당 4일을 근무하는 것에 몇몇 장점이 있지만 자신, 즉 Mr. Swift가 원래의 일정을 선호하므로 다른 회사에서 근무하도록 배정해줄 수 있는지 물었으므로 Mr. Swift가 한 주당 4일을 근무하는 일정보다는 원래의 일정을 선호하며 근무 일정을 변경하고 싶어 한다는 두 번째 단서를 확인할 수 있습니다. Mr. Sadik이 Mr. Swift와 업무를 바꾸고 싶다고 했다는 첫 번째 단서와 Mr. Swift가 한 주당 4일을 근무하게 되었다는 두 번째 단서를 종합할 때, Mr. Sadik이 주 4일 근무를 선호한다는 것을 추론할 수 있습니다. 따라서 (D) He prefers to have a four-day work week이 정답입니다.

패러프레이징
working four days a week 한 주당 4일을 근무하는 것
→ a four-day work week 주 4일 근무

어휘 commute n. 통근 (시간); v. 통근하다

DAY 20 다중 지문

Course 1 이중 지문 (Double Passages)

HACKERS TEST   p.338

01 (A)	02 (B)	03 (B)	04 (B)	05 (A)

01-05번은 다음 두 이메일에 관한 문제입니다.

수신 Lucy Cruz <lcruz@carlington.edu.au>
발신 Andrea Goodman <agoodman@carlington.edu.au>
제목 가져가실 책들
날짜 11월 12일

Ms. Cruz께,

⁰¹귀하께서 예약하신 다음의 책들이 이제 대여가 가능함을 알려드리기 위해 글을 씁니다.

- Barbara Mahoney, *Modern Human Behavior*
- Stanley Bradburn, *An Introduction to Psychology*
- Robert Chin, *Statistical Methods in Sociology*

이 책들은 오전 9시에서 오후 6시 사이 아무 시간에나 Carlington 대학 도서관 건물의 안내 데스크에서 가져가실 수 있습니다. 만일 귀하께서 내일까지 예약하신 책들을 가져가지 못하실 경우, ^{02-B/C}한 권당 50센트의 요금으로 일주일 동안 저희가 보관해드릴 수 있습니다. 만약 책들이 그때까지 가져가 지지 않을 경우, 저희는 그 책들을 다른 대출자들이 대여 가능하게 할 것입니다.

⁰⁴저희의 기록은 또한 귀하께서 지금까지 60센트의 벌금이 있는 반납 기한이 지난 책 한 권을 가지고 있다고 보여줍니다. 제목은 Thomas Sanderson이 지은 *The Politics of Globalization*이고, 11월 9일 금요일이 기한이었습니다. 귀하께서 예약하신 서적들을 찾으러 오실 때 이 책을 가져와 주시기 바랍니다.

추가적인 질문이 있으시다면 알려주십시오.

Andrea Goodman 드림
도서관 서비스 부서, 캔버라 Carlington 대학교

collect v. 가져가다, 수집하다   reserve v. 예약하다   hold v. 보관하다
overdue adj. 기한이 지난   title n. 서적   due adj. 기한인, 예정된
bring v. 가져오다   pick up phr. (어디에서) ~을 찾다

수신 Andrea Goodman <agoodman@carlington.edu.au>
발신 Lucy Cruz <lcruz@carlington.edu.au>
제목 회신: 가져가실 책들
날짜 11월 12일

Ms. Goodman께,

제가 예약한 서적들이 가져갈 준비가 되었음을 알려주셔서 감사합니다. 하지만, ⁰⁴저는 제가 반납 기한이 지난 책을 가지고 있다는 주장에 반대해야 할 것 같습니다. ^{04/05}저는 그것을 반납 기한인 날짜에 반납했다고 확신하는데, ⁰⁴그때는 제가 도서관에 마지막으로 갔던 때입니다. 저는 정문 바로 안에 있는 반납 상자에 그것을 넣었습니다. ⁰³아마 직원이 상자를 비울 때 잘못 스캔되었고, 그리고 그것이 바로 제 계정에 반납 기한이 지난 것으로 반영된 이유인 것 같습니다.

⁰⁵직원 중 한 분이 시간을 내서 그 책이 현재 책꽂이에 있는지 다시 한번 확인해주시면 감사하겠습니다. 저는 내일 오후 예약된 책들을 가지러 도서관에 갈 것인데, 그때는 이 상황이 해결되어 있으면 좋겠습니다.

Lucy Cruz 드림

object v. 반대하다; n. 물건   claim n. 주장, 청구
return v. 반납하다, 돌아오다   empty v. 비우다; adj. 빈
reflect v. 반영하다, 반사하다   double-check v. 다시 한번 확인하다
shelf n. 책꽂이   situation n. 상황   resolve v. 해결하다

01 주제/목적 찾기 문제

문제 첫 번째 이메일의 한 가지 목적은 무엇인가?
(A) 출판물이 이용 가능함을 알리기 위해
(B) 회원에게 기부를 요청하기 위해
(C) 도서관 이용자들을 행사에 초대하기 위해
(D) 연체료 액수의 변동을 설명하기 위해

해설 첫 번째 이메일의 목적을 묻는 목적 찾기 문제이므로 첫 번째 이메일을 확인합니다. 첫 번째 이메일의 'I'm writing to let you know that the following books you reserved are now available.'에서 예약한 책들이 이제 대여가 가능함을 알려드리기 위해 글을 쓴다고 했으므로 (A) To announce the availability of some publications가 정답입니다.

패러프레이징
books 책들 → publications 출판물

어휘 late fee phr. 연체료

02 Not/True 문제

문제 도서관 책들에 대해 언급된 것은?
(A) 최근에 다른 층으로 옮겨졌다.
(B) 적은 요금으로 보관될 수 있다.
(C) 일주일까지 대여될 수 있다.
(D) 주말에 반납될 수 없다.

해설 질문의 핵심 어구인 library books와 관련된 내용을 지문에서 찾아 각 보기와 대조하는 Not/True 문제이므로 도서관의 책과 관련된 내용이 언급된 첫 번째 이메일을 확인합니다. (A)는 지문에 언급되지 않은 내용입니다. (B)는 'we can hold them for one week at a cost of 50 cent per book'에서 한 권당 50센트의 요금으로 일주일 동안 보관해 줄 수 있다고 했으므로 지문의 내용과 일치합니다. 따라서 (B) They can be placed on hold for a small fee가 정답입니다. (C)는 'we can hold them for one week'에서 도서관에서 책들을 일주일 동안 보관해줄 수 있다고 했지 일주일까지 대여될 수 있다는 의미는 아니므로 지문의 내용과 일치하지 않습니다. (D)는 지문에 언급되지 않은 내용입니다.

어휘 place on hold phr. 보관하다   borrow v. 대여하다, 빌리다

03 동의어 문제

문제 두 번째 이메일에서, 1문단 네 번째 줄의 단어 "reflected"는 의미상 -와 가장 가깝다.
(A) 생각되다
(B) 나타나다
(C) 동반되다
(D) 반복되다

해설 두 번째 이메일의 reflected를 포함하고 있는 문장 'Perhaps it was not scanned correctly when staff emptied the box, and that is why it is reflected as overdue on my account.'에서 reflected가 '반영되다'라는 뜻으로 사용되었는데, 이는 계정에 반영되어 나타났다는 의미를 나타냅니다. 따라서 '나타나다'라는 뜻을 가진 (B) shown이 정답입니다.

04 추론 문제 연계

문제 Ms. Cruz에 대해 암시되는 것은?
(A) 대학에서 심리학을 전공하고 있다.
(B) 금요일에 마지막으로 도서관에 방문했다.
(C) 보통 오후에 도서관에 간다.
(D) 시간제로 대학교 도서관에서 근무한다.

해설 두 지문의 내용을 종합적으로 확인한 후 추론해서 풀어야 하는 연계 문
제입니다. 질문의 핵심 어구인 Ms. Cruz가 작성한 두 번째 이메일을
먼저 확인합니다.
'I must object to the claim that I have an overdue book. I am
sure that I returned it on the date it was due, which was the
last time I was at the library.'에서 Ms. Cruz가 마지막으로 도서관
에 갔던 때인 책의 반납 기한인 날짜에 그것을 반납했다고 확신하기 때
문에 반납 기한이 지난 책이 있다는 주장에 반대한다는 첫 번째 단서를
확인할 수 있습니다. 그런데 마지막으로 도서관에 갔던 때가 언제인지
가 제시되지 않았으므로 첫 번째 이메일에서 관련 내용을 확인합니다.
'Our records also show you have a book that is overdue ~ it
was due on Friday'에서 Ms. Cruz가 기한이 지난 책 한 권을 가지
고 있는데 금요일이 반납 기한이었다는 두 번째 단서를 확인할 수 있습
니다.
Ms. Cruz가 도서관에 마지막으로 갔던 때인 책의 반납 기한인 날짜
에 그것을 반납했다고 확신하기 때문에 반납 기한이 지난 책이 있다
는 주장에 반대한다는 첫 번째 단서와 Ms. Cruz가 반납 기한이 지난
책 한 권을 가지고 있는데 금요일이 기한이었다는 두 번째 단서를 종
합할 때, Mr. Cruz는 마지막으로 금요일에 도서관에 방문했다는 사실
을 추론할 수 있습니다. 따라서 (B) She last visited the library on
Friday가 정답입니다.

어휘 **major in** phr. ~을 전공하다

05 육하원칙 문제

문제 Ms. Cruz는 도서관 직원에게 무엇을 해줄 것을 부탁하는가?
(A) 그녀가 반납한 책을 찾아보는 것
(B) 내일 그녀에게 알림을 보내는 것
(C) 그녀를 위해 추가적인 책을 예약하는 것
(D) 그녀의 예약 중 한 개를 취소하는 것

해설 Ms. Cruz가 도서관 직원에게 무엇을(What) 해줄 것을 부탁하는
지를 묻는 육하원칙 문제이므로 질문의 핵심 어구인 Ms. Cruz ask
the library staff to do와 관련된 내용이 언급된 두 번째 이메일을
확인합니다. 두 번째 이메일의 'I am sure that I returned it'에서
그녀가 책을 반납했다고 확신한다고 했고, 'I would appreciate it
if a member of staff would take the time to double-check
whether the book is currently on the shelf.'에서 직원 중 한 명이
시간을 내서 그 책이 현재 책꽂이에 있는지 다시 한번 확인해주면 감
사하겠다고 했으므로 (A) Search for a book she returned가 정답
입니다.

어휘 **search for** phr. ~을 찾아보다 **reminder** n. 알림, 상기시키는 것
additional adj. 추가적인

Course 2 삼중 지문 (Triple Passages)

HACKERS TEST p.342

01 (C)	02 (C)	03 (A)	04 (C)	05 (D)

01–05번은 다음 브로슈어, 고객 후기, 이메일에 관한 문제입니다.

당신 자신에게 Merrytime 유람선 여행을 선물하세요. 예약하시려면,
www.mtcruises.com을 방문하세요.

노선	객실 유형		
	디럭스	풍경 전망	스위트룸
Merrytime Blue 시애틀에서 01-A알래스카주 앵커 리지로	200달러 부터	410달러 부터	560달러 부터
01-B Merrytime Beachcomber 마이애미에서 01-A바하마 나소로	250달러 부터	400달러 부터	620달러 부터 ◯

01-C/02 Merrytime Sky 샌디에이고에서 01-A/02멕시코 마사틀란으로	01-C180달 러부터	380달러 부터	580달러 부터
01-B Merrytime Salsa 마이애미에서 01-A푸에르토리 코 폰세로	250달러 부터	400달러 부터	620달러 부터

01-D*5퍼센트 할인을 위해 4월 1일까지 예약하세요.

treat v. 대접하다, 한턱내다 **cabin** n. 객실, 선실 **vista** n. 풍경, 경치

https://www.cruisebeat.com

상품 검색기 | 여행 후기 | 블로그

02이름: Maxine Roscoe
후기 날짜: 4월 21일
평점: ★★★★☆

후기

03-C/04저희는 Trip Away Travel(www.tripaway.com) 덕분에 지난
주에 첫 Merrytime 유람선 여행을 갔습니다. 02선내에서의 음식은
훌륭했고 멕시코에서는 더 좋았습니다. 제 가장 큰 불만은 03-A공공
구역이 밤에 너무 시끄러웠다는 점입니다. 다행히도, 편안한 객실이
저희가 방해받지 않고 잘 수 있게 보장해주었습니다. 저는 기꺼이 다
시 그것을 할 것입니다.

제출하기

thanks to phr. ~ 덕분에, ~ 때문에 **on board** phr. 선내의, 탑승한
comfortable adj. 편안한, 쾌적한 **ensure** v. 보장하다, 확실히 ~하다
undisturbed adj. 방해받지 않은, 평온한 **submit** v. 제출하다, 항복하다

수신: Maxine Roscoe <m.roscoe@happymail.com>
발신: Cruise Beat <moderator@cruisebeat.com>
제목: 귀하의 후기
날짜: 4월 22일

Ms. Roscoe께,

귀하의 유람선 여행 후기를 제출해주셔서 감사합니다. 안타깝게도,
04/05그것이 저희 사이트의 규정을 위반했기 04때문에 게시될 수 없습니
다. 05다음을 살펴봐 주시기 바랍니다.

04모든 후기들은:
· 관련 있어야 함: 유람선 여행과 관련 없는 정보는 포함하지 마십시오.
· 직접 경험해야 함: 후기는 당신의 개인적인 경험에 대한 것이어야
  합니다.
· 비영리적이어야 함: 후기들은 어떠한 외부 서비스들의 추천도 포함
  하지 않아야 합니다.
· 현재의 것이어야 함: 후기들은 유람선 여행 3개월 이내에 작성되어
  야 합니다.

Michael Miranda 드림, Cruise Beat 관리자

violate v. 위반하다, 침해하다 **relevant** adj. 관련 있는, 적절한
firsthand adj. 직접 경험한, 직접 얻은
non-commercial adj. 비영리적인 **current** adj. 현재의, 지금의
moderator n. 관리자, 조정자

01 Not/True 문제

문제 Merrytime Cruises사에 대해 사실이 아닌 것은?
(A) 최소 네 곳의 다른 목적지로 여행한다.
(B) 같은 도시에서 출발하는 두 가지의 여행이 있다.
(C) 각 객실에 200달러 이상의 요금을 부과한다.
(D) 제한된 시간 동안의 판촉 할인을 제공하고 있다.

해설 질문의 핵심 어구인 Merrytime Cruises와 관련된 내용을 지문에서 찾아 각 보기와 대조하는 Not/True 문제이므로 첫 번째 지문인 Merrytime Cruises사의 브로슈어를 확인합니다. (A)는 'to Anchorage, Alaska', 'to Nassau, Bahamas', 'to Mazatlan, Mexico', 'to Ponce, Puerto Rico'에서 알래스카주 앵커리지, 바하마 나소, 멕시코 마사틀란, 푸에르토리코 폰세로 여행하는 것임을 알 수 있으므로 지문의 내용과 일치합니다. (B)는 'Merrytime Beachcomber, Miami', 'Merrytime Salsa, Miami'에서 Merrytime Beachcomber와 Merrytime Salsa 노선이 마이애미에서 출발하는 것임을 알 수 있으므로 지문의 내용과 일치합니다. (C)는 'Merrytime Sky', 'From $180'에서 Merrytime Sky 노선은 요금이 180달러부터라고 했으므로 지문의 내용과 일치하지 않습니다. 따라서 (C) It charges a fee of $200 or more for each cabin이 정답입니다. (D)는 '*Book by April 1 for 5 percent off'에서 5퍼센트 할인을 위해 4월 1일까지 예약하라고 했으므로 지문의 내용과 일치합니다.

패러프레이징
by April 1 4월 1일까지 → a limited-time 제한된 시간
5 percent off 5퍼센트 할인 → offer 할인

어휘 destination n. 목적지, 도착지 originate v. 시작하다, 일어나다
charge v. 부과하다, 청구하다 promotional adj. 판촉의, 할인의

02 추론 문제 연계

문제 Ms. Roscoe는 어떤 배에서 여행했을 것 같은가?
(A) Merrytime Blue
(B) Merrytime Beachcomber
(C) Merrytime Sky
(D) Merrytime Salsa

해설 세 지문 중 두 지문의 내용을 종합적으로 확인한 후 추론해서 풀어야 하는 연계 문제입니다. 질문의 핵심 어구인 Ms. Roscoe가 작성한 두 번째 지문인 고객 후기를 먼저 확인합니다.
'Name: Maxine Roscoe', 'The food on board was excellent and got even better in Mexico.'에서 Maxine Roscoe가 선내에서의 음식이 훌륭했고 멕시코에서는 더 좋았다고 했으므로 Maxine Roscoe가 멕시코로 여행을 갔다는 첫 번째 단서를 확인할 수 있습니다. 그런데 멕시코로 가는 배가 어떤 것인지가 제시되지 않았으므로 브로슈어에서 관련 내용을 확인합니다. 'Merrytime Sky', 'to Mazatlan, Mexico'에서 Merrytime Sky 노선이 멕시코 마사틀란으로 간다는 두 번째 단서를 확인할 수 있습니다.
Maxine Roscoe가 멕시코로 여행을 갔다는 첫 번째 단서와 Merrytime Sky 노선이 멕시코 마사틀란으로 간다는 두 번째 단서를 종합할 때, Maxine Roscoe가 멕시코로 가는 Merrytime Sky의 배에서 여행했다는 사실을 추론할 수 있습니다. 따라서 (C) Merrytime Sky가 정답입니다.

03 Not/True 문제

문제 Ms. Roscoe에 대해 언급된 것은?
(A) 배의 숙박 시설에 대해 만족했다.
(B) 출장의 일부로써 유람선을 타고 여행했다.
(C) 이전에 Merrytime 유람선을 한 번 타봤다.
(D) 배의 오락 선택 사항들에 만족하지 않았다.

해설 질문의 핵심 어구인 Ms. Roscoe와 관련된 내용을 지문에서 찾아 각 보기와 대조하는 Not/True 문제이므로 Ms. Roscoe가 작성한 두 번째 지문인 고객 후기를 확인합니다. (A)는 'the public areas got too loud at night. Luckily, our comfortable cabin ensured we slept undisturbed'에서 공공 구역이 밤에 너무 시끄러웠지만 다행히도 편안한 객실이 자신, 즉 Ms. Roscoe가 방해받지 않고 잘 수 있게 보장해주었다고 한 것에서 Ms. Roscoe가 배의 객실에 대해 만족했음을 알 수 있으므로 지문의 내용과 일치합니다. 따라서 (A) She was pleased with the ship's accommodations가 정답입니다. (B)는 지문에 언급되지 않은 내용입니다. (C)는 'We went on our

first Merrytime Cruise last week'에서 Ms. Roscoe가 지난주에 첫 Merrytime 유람선 여행을 갔다고 했으므로 지문의 내용과 일치하지 않습니다. (D)는 지문에 언급되지 않은 내용입니다.

패러프레이징
cabin 객실 → accommodations 숙박 시설

어휘 business trip phr. 출장 entertainment n. 오락, 즐거움

04 추론 문제 연계

문제 Ms. Roscoe의 후기와 관련된 문제는 무엇이었던 것 같은가?
(A) 관련 있는 정보를 포함하지 않았다.
(B) 그녀 자신의 휴가에 대해 언급하지 않았다.
(C) 제3의 업체를 추천했다.
(D) 유람선 여행 후 너무 늦게 게시되었다.

해설 세 지문 중 두 지문의 내용을 종합적으로 확인한 후 추론해서 풀어야 하는 연계 문제입니다. 질문의 핵심 어구인 the issue with Ms. Roscoe's review와 관련된 내용이 언급된 세 번째 지문인 이메일을 먼저 확인합니다.
'it cannot be posted because it violated our site's rules'에서 그것이 자신들의 사이트, 즉 Ms. Roscoe의 후기가 Cruise Beat 사이트의 규정을 위반했기 때문에 게시될 수 없다고 했고, 'All reviews must be: · Relevant ~, · Firsthand ~, · Non-commercial: ~ should not include recommendations of any outside services., · Current ~'에서 모든 후기들이 관련 있고, 직접 경험하고, 비영리적이어서 어떠한 외부 서비스들의 추천도 포함하지 않아야 하고, 현재의 것이어야 한다고 했으므로, Ms. Roscoe의 후기가 관련 있고, 직접 경험하고, 비영리적이고, 현재의 것이어야 한다는 규정 중 일부를 지키지 않았다는 첫 번째 단서를 확인할 수 있습니다. 그런데 Ms. Roscoe의 후기가 어떤 규정을 지키지 않았는지가 제시되지 않았으므로 고객 후기에서 관련 내용을 확인합니다. 'We went on our first Merrytime Cruise ~ thanks to Trip Away Travel (www.tripaway.com).'에서 자신, 즉 Ms. Roscoe가 Trip Away Travel(www.tripaway.com) 덕분에 첫 Merrytime 유람선 여행을 갔다고 했으므로, Ms. Roscoe가 다른 사이트인 Trip Away Travel을 언급했다는 두 번째 단서를 확인할 수 있습니다.
Ms. Roscoe의 후기가 관련 있고, 직접 경험하고, 비영리적이고, 현재의 것이어야 한다는 규정 중 일부를 지키지 않았다는 첫 번째 단서와 Ms. Roscoe가 다른 사이트인 Trip Away Travel을 언급했다는 두 번째 단서를 종합할 때, Ms. Roscoe의 후기가 외부 서비스의 추천을 포함하지 않아야 한다는 규정을 지키지 않은 문제가 있었다는 사실을 추론할 수 있습니다. 따라서 (C) It recommended a third-party business가 정답입니다.

어휘 refer to phr. ~을 언급하다, 나타내다 third-party adj. 제3의

05 육하원칙 문제

문제 Mr. Miranda는 Ms. Roscoe에게 무엇을 해달라고 요청하는가?
(A) 계정을 닫는다
(B) 양식에 서명한다
(C) 사진을 포함한다
(D) 규정을 살펴본다

해설 Mr. Miranda가 Ms. Roscoe에게 무엇을(What)을 해달라고 요청하는지를 묻는 육하원칙 문제이므로 질문의 핵심 어구인 Mr. Miranda가 작성한 세 번째 지문인 이메일을 확인합니다. 이메일의 'it violated our site's rules. Please review the following.'에서 그것, 즉 Ms. Roscoe의 후기가 사이트의 규정을 위반했으므로 다음을 살펴봐 달라고 하면서 규정들을 나열했으므로 (D) Review a policy가 정답입니다.

패러프레이징
rules 규정 → policy 규정

어휘 account n. 계정, 계좌

VOCABULARY [PART 5,6]

DAY 01 [어휘] 명사 1

토익 실전 문제   p.347

01 (D)	02 (B)	03 (B)	04 (A)	05 (B)
06 (D)	07 (B)	08 (D)	09 (B)	10 (D)

01 명사 어휘 고르기
해설 '환불을 제공하지는 않지만 상점 적립금을 제공한다'라는 문맥이므로 명사 (D) refunds(환불, 환불금)가 정답입니다. (A) proof는 '증거', (B) condition은 '조건, 상태', (C) instructions는 '설명, 지시'라는 의미입니다.
해석 Stop-Mart는 물건을 반품하기를 원하는 고객들에게 환불을 제공하지는 않지만, 상점 적립금을 제공한다.
어휘 return v. 반품하다, 보답하다   store credit phr. 상점 적립금

02 명사 어휘 고르기
해설 '관광 산업에서의 성장 덕분에 고용이 급격하게 증가해왔다'라는 문맥이므로 명사 (B) Employment(고용, 직장)가 정답입니다. (A) Announcement는 '발표', (C) Arrangement는 '준비', (D) Treatment는 '대우, 처치'라는 의미입니다.
해석 관광 산업에서의 성장 덕분에 전국적으로 고용이 급격하게 증가해 왔다.
어휘 dramatically adv. 급격하게, 극적으로
nationwide adv. 전국적으로; adj. 전국적인
thanks to phr. ~ 덕분에, ~ 때문에   industry n. 산업, 기업

03 명사 어휘 고르기
해설 '사업체 계좌와 개인 금융 계좌 간에 분리가 필요하다'라는 문맥이므로 명사 (B) separation(분리)이 정답입니다. (A) devotion은 '헌신, 전념', (C) continuation은 '지속, 연속', (D) deposit은 '예금, 보증금'이라는 의미입니다.
해석 Mr. Anderson의 회계사는 그의 사업체 계좌와 개인 금융 계좌 간에 분리가 필요하다고 그에게 강력히 충고했다.
어휘 accountant n. 회계사   warn v. 강력히 충고하다, 경고하다
financial adj. 금융의, 재정의   account n. 계좌, 계정

04 명사 어휘 고르기
해설 '구독자들은 청구서를 컴퓨터로 받고 싶다면 계정에서 설정을 변경해야 할 것이다'라는 문맥이므로 명사 (A) subscribers(구독자)가 정답입니다. (B)의 manufacturer는 '제조자, 제조업체', (C)의 monitor는 '컴퓨터 모니터, 감시 장치', (D)의 programmer는 '프로그래머'라는 의미입니다.
해석 CableTyme의 구독자들은 청구서를 컴퓨터로 받고 싶다면 계정에서 설정을 변경해야 할 것이다.
어휘 setting n. 설정, 환경   account n. 계정, 계좌   receive v. 받다
bill n. 청구서, 계산서   electronically adv. 컴퓨터로

05 명사 어휘 고르기
해설 '새로운 직원들이 공장에 고용될 것으로 예상된다'라는 문맥이므로 명사 (B) personnel(직원들, 인원)이 정답입니다. (A)의 position은 '직위,

일자리', (C)의 component는 '부품, 요소', (D)의 improvement는 '개선'이라는 의미입니다.
해석 1,000명이 넘는 새로운 직원들이 여름이 끝나기 전에 Frenton Industries사의 최신 공장에 고용될 것으로 예상된다.
어휘 expect v. 예상하다, 기대하다   hire v. 고용하다
latest adj. 최신의, 최근의

06 명사 어휘 고르기
해설 '매달 보통 예금 계좌에 입금하는 것은 사람들이 은퇴를 대비하는 데 도움이 될 수 있다'라는 문맥이므로 명사 (D) retirement(은퇴)가 정답입니다. (A) comparison은 '비교, 비유', (B) implementation은 '이행, 성취', (C) appreciation은 '감사, 감상, 인정'이라는 의미입니다.
해석 많은 금융 전문가들은 매달 보통 예금 계좌에 입금하는 것은 사람들이 은퇴를 대비하는 데 도움이 될 수 있다고 말한다.
어휘 expert n. 전문가, 권위자   savings account phr. 보통 예금(계좌)
prepare v. 대비하다, 준비하다

07 명사 어휘 고르기
해설 '캘리포니아로의 회사 본사의 이전은 내년에 이루어질 것으로 예상된다'라는 문맥이므로 명사 (B) relocation(이전, 재배치)이 정답입니다. (A) outcome은 '결과, 성과', (C) warranty는 '보증(서)', (D) compensation은 '보상'이라는 의미입니다.
해석 지난주에 발표된 회람에 따르면, 캘리포니아로의 회사 본사의 이전은 내년에 이루어질 것으로 예상된다.
어휘 memo n. 회람, 메모   release v. 발표하다   headquarters n. 본사
likely adj. ~할 것으로 예상되는   take place phr. 이루어지다, 개최되다

08 명사 어휘 고르기
해설 '이미 인기 있는 점심 식사 장소가 되고 있기 때문에 새 제과점에 대한 전망은 낙관적이다'라는 문맥이므로 명사 (D) outlook(전망, 관점)이 정답입니다. (A) force는 '힘, 영향력', (B) registration은 '등록', (C) tradition은 '전통'이라는 의미입니다.
해석 이미 인기 있는 점심 식사 장소가 되고 있기 때문에 Ms. Jonson의 새 제과점에 대한 전망은 낙관적이다.
어휘 positive adj. 낙관적인, 긍정적인   popular adj. 인기 있는, 대중적인
spot n. 장소, 지점

09 유사의미 명사 중에서 고르기
해설 '새 기차 터미널이 완공되면 승객의 양이 두 배가 될 것으로 기대된다'라는 문맥이므로 명사 (B) volume(양)이 정답입니다. (D) size는 '크기'라는 의미로, 사람이나 사물의 크기 또는 옷이나 신발 등의 치수를 나타냅니다. (A) increase는 '증가', (C) belief는 '믿음'이라는 의미입니다.
해석 새 기차 터미널이 완공되면 승객의 양이 두 배가 될 것으로 기대된다.
어휘 double v. 두 배가 되다; adj. 두 배의   complete v. 완공하다, 완료하다

10 명사 어휘 고르기
해설 '거의 6년 동안 같은 직위에 있어왔기 때문에 승진할 자격이 있다고 생각한다'라는 문맥이므로 명사 (D) promotion(승진)이 정답입니다. (A) combination은 '결합', (B) location은 '위치', (C) distribution은 '분배, 분포'라는 의미입니다.

해석 Ms. Weller는 거의 6년 동안 같은 직위에 있어왔기 때문에 그녀는 승진할 자격이 있다고 생각한다.

어휘 nearly adv. 거의, 간신히 deserve v. ~을 받을 자격이 있다, ~할 만하다

DAY 02 [어휘] 명사 2

토익 실전 문제   p.349

01 (C)	02 (C)	03 (A)	04 (D)	05 (A)
06 (C)	07 (D)	08 (C)	09 (C)	10 (D)

01 명사 어휘 고르기

해설 '연체 거래가 있는 고객들에게 독촉장을 보낸다'라는 문맥이므로 명사 (C) reminders(독촉장, 상기시켜 주는 메모)가 정답입니다. (A)의 benefit은 '혜택', (B)의 souvenir는 '기념품', (D)의 favor는 '호의'라는 의미입니다.

해석 JenTel사는 연체 거래가 있는 고객들에게 독촉장을 보내서, 이자가 적용되기 전에 지불할 것을 촉구한다.

어휘 overdue adj. 연체의 account n. 거래, 계좌 urge v. 촉구하다 interest n. 이자

02 명사 어휘 고르기

해설 '해외 이체와 같은 특정한 거래에 대해 수수료를 청구한다'라는 문맥이므로 명사 (C) transactions(거래)가 정답입니다. (A)의 statement는 '진술', (B)의 quarter는 '4분의 1, 분기', (D)의 analysis는 '분석'이라는 의미입니다. 참고로, analysis의 복수형은 analyses임을 알아둡니다.

해석 First National 은행은 해외 통화 이체와 같은 특정한 거래에 대해 수수료를 청구한다.

어휘 charge v. 청구하다 fee n. 수수료, 요금 certain adj. 특정한 transfer n. 이체 currency n. 통화, 화폐 overseas adv. 해외로

03 명사 어휘 고르기

해설 '수익성이 있을 것이기 때문에 귀중한 자산이다'라는 문맥이므로 명사 (A) asset(자산)이 정답입니다. (B) charge는 '요금', (C) lease는 '임대', (D) reward는 '보상'이라는 의미입니다.

해석 Bertel사가 작년에 취득한 부동산은 일단 그것이 개발되면 수익성이 있을 것이기 때문에 귀중한 자산이다.

어휘 property n. 부동산, 재산 acquire v. 취득하다, 얻다 profitable adj. 수익성이 있는 once conj. 일단 ~하면

04 명사 어휘 고르기

해설 '전화를 통해 상품을 판매하는 절차를 설명했다'라는 문맥이므로 명사 (D) procedure(절차, 방법)가 정답입니다. (A) relationship은 '관계', (B) loyalty는 '충성', (C) recruitment는 '채용'이라는 의미입니다.

해석 교육 동안에, 감독관은 전화를 통해 상품을 판매하는 절차를 설명했다.

어휘 supervisor n. 감독관 explain n. 설명하다 merchandise n. 상품

05 명사 어휘 고르기

해설 '가격 견적을 현장에서 제공할 수 있다고 명시한다'라는 문맥이므로 명사 (A) estimates(견적)가 정답입니다. (B)의 conflict는 '갈등', (C)의 donation은 '기부', (D)의 creation은 '창조'라는 의미입니다.

해석 웹사이트는 Crystal 건축사가 주택 작업을 위한 가격 견적을 현장에서 제공할 수 있다고 명시한다.

어휘 state v. 명시하다 on-site adj. 현장의 residential adj. 주택의. 거주의

06 명사 어휘 고르기

해설 '면접관들은 종종 그들의 가장 뛰어난 성과가 무엇이었는지 물어본다'라는 문맥이므로 명사 (C) accomplishment(성과)가 정답입니다. (A) background는 '배경', (B) operation은 '영업, 사업', (D) effect는 '효과'라는 의미입니다.

해석 잠재적인 직원들에 대한 식견을 갖기 위해, 면접관들은 종종 그들의 가장 뛰어난 성과가 무엇이었는지 물어본다.

어휘 gain insight into phr. ~에 대한 식견을 갖다

07 명사 어휘 고르기

해설 '점진적인 가치 향상은 그 주식에 투자하는 것을 가치 있게 만들었다'라는 문맥이므로 명사 (D) enhancement(향상)가 정답입니다. (A) calculation은 '계산', (B) classification은 '분류', (C) appearance는 '외관'이라는 의미입니다.

해석 수년에 걸친 PanAmerican 출판사의 점진적인 가치 향상은 그 주식에 투자하는 것을 가치 있게 만들었다.

어휘 gradual adj. 점진적인 invest v. 투자하다 stock n. 주식 worthwhile adj. 가치가 있는

08 유사의미 명사 중에서 고르기

해설 '전문 사진작가로서 인정을 받았다'라는 문맥이므로 명사 (C) recognition(인정, 승인)이 정답입니다. (B) permission도 '허가, 승인'이라는 의미이지만, 행동 등에 대한 허락, 즉 무언가를 할 수 있도록 권한이 있는 사람으로부터 받은 권리나 능력을 나타냅니다. (A) description은 '묘사', (D) communication은 '소통'이라는 의미입니다.

해석 Ms. Bueller는 열심히 일하고 강력한 온라인 인지도를 구축함으로써 전문 사진작가로서 인정을 받았다.

어휘 attain v. 얻다, 달성하다 presence n. 인지도

09 명사 어휘 고르기

해설 '위원회의 그 누구도 확장 제안에 반대하지 않았다'라는 문맥이므로 명사 (C) objection(반대)이 정답입니다. (A) indication은 '암시', (B) elevation은 '승진', (D) aspiration은 '열망'이라는 의미입니다.

해석 위원회의 그 누구도 확장 제안에 반대하지 않아서, 프로젝트는 빠르면 이번 여름에 시작할 것이다.

어휘 board n. 위원회 expansion n. 확장 proposal n. 제안

10 명사 어휘 고르기

해설 '공장 관리자들은 그들의 재량에 따라 임시 직원들을 고용할 수 있다'라는 문맥이므로 명사 (D) discretion(재량)이 정답입니다. (A) observation은 '관찰', (B) resistance는 '저항', (C) dependence는 '의존'이라는 의미입니다. 참고로, at one's discretion(~의 재량에 따라)을 관용구로 알아둡니다.

해석 공장 관리자들은 인사부서를 거치기보다 그들의 재량에 따라 임시 직원들을 고용할 수 있다.

어휘 hire v. 고용하다 temporary adj. 임시의 rather than phr. ~보다 go through phr. (절차나 방법 등을) 거치다

VOCABULARY PART 5,6 한 권으로 끝내는 해커스 토익 700+ (LC+RC+VOCA)

토익 실전 문제
p.351

| 01 (C) | 02 (D) | 03 (B) | 04 (C) | 05 (D) |
| 06 (C) | 07 (A) | 08 (B) | 09 (D) | 10 (B) |

01 명사 어휘 고르기

해설 '일자리에 지원하고 싶은 모든 사람들은 웹사이트에 기술된 절차를 따라야 한다'라는 문맥이므로 명사 (C) process(절차, 과정)가 정답입니다. (A) management는 '관리', (B) exhibition은 '전시, 전시회', (D) objective는 '목적'이라는 의미입니다.

해석 Mercer사의 일자리에 지원하고 싶은 모든 사람들은 웹사이트에 기술된 절차를 따라야 한다.

어휘 apply for phr. 지원하다 position n. 일자리 follow v. 따르다
outline v. 기술하다, 서술하다

02 명사 어휘 고르기

해설 '지역 생태계를 지키는 것이 그들의 최우선순위이다'라는 문맥이므로 명사 (D) priority(우선순위, 우선 사항)가 정답입니다. (A) space는 '공간', (B) proposition은 '제의', (C) foundation은 '토대, 창설'이라는 의미입니다.

해석 시 공무원들은 지역 생태계를 지키는 것이 그들의 최우선순위라고 말하면서, Peterson Electrical사의 확장 계획을 거부했다.

어휘 city official phr. 시 공무원 reject v. 거부하다, 반대하다
local ecosystem phr. 지역 생태계

03 명사 어휘 고르기

해설 '주최 측에 연락하여 참석 확인을 해주어야 한다'라는 문맥이므로 명사 (B) confirmation(확인, 확정)이 정답입니다. (A) consideration은 '고려, 사려', (C) involvement는 '관련', (D) realization은 '깨달음'이라는 의미입니다.

해석 낙농업자 학회의 참석자들은 주최 측에 연락하여 참석 확인을 해주어야 한다.

어휘 dairy farmer phr. 낙농업자 organizer n. 주최자, 기획자
attendance n. 참석

04 명사 어휘 고르기

해설 '런던 지사로의 전근을 받아들였다'라는 문맥이므로 명사 (C) transfer(전근, 이동)가 정답입니다. (A) revision은 '수정', (B) factor는 '요인', (D) itinerary는 '여행 일정'이라는 의미입니다.

해석 Ms. Pullman은 연봉에 있어서 상당한 인상을 받는 대가로 Devplan사의 런던 지사로의 전근을 받아들였다.

어휘 accept v. 받아들이다 in exchange for phr. ~의 대가로
substantial adj. 상당한, 실질적인 increase n. 인상, 증가
pay package phr. 연봉

05 유사의미 명사 중에서 고르기

해설 '언어 장벽에도 불구하고 회의가 순탄하게 진행되었다'라는 문맥이므로 명사 (D) barrier(장벽, 장애)가 정답입니다. (C) restraint도 '규제'라는 의미이지만, 무언가를 제한하거나 통제하는 행위 또는 감정이나 행동에 대한 통제를 나타냅니다. (A) expression은 '표현', (B) development는 '발전'이라는 의미입니다.

해석 언어 장벽에도 불구하고, Mr. Vaughn은 중국 지사 직원들과의 회의가 순탄하게 진행되었다고 생각했다.

어휘 despite prep. ~에도 불구하고 go smoothly phr. 순탄하게 진행되다

06 명사 어휘 고르기

해설 '신규 구독자들에게 잡지의 무료 발행호를 받게 할 자격을 줄 것이다'라는 문맥이므로 명사 (C) issue(발행물, 호)가 정답입니다. (A) exception은 '예외', (B) application은 '지원, 지원서', (D) installation은 '설치'라는 의미입니다.

해석 4월 동안 *Wildflower Today*지를 신청하는 것은 신규 구독자들에게 잡지의 무료 발행호를 받게 할 자격을 줄 것이다.

어휘 sign up for phr. ~을 신청하다 earn v. ~에게 –을 받게 할 자격을 주다

07 명사 어휘 고르기

해설 '일하는 시간과 버는 금액 간의 불일치를 발견하다'라는 문맥이므로 명사 (A) discrepancy(불일치, 차이)가 정답입니다. (B) collaboration은 '공동 작업', (C) translation은 '번역', (D) supplement는 '보충'이라는 의미입니다.

해석 일하는 시간과 버는 금액 간의 불일치를 발견하는 직원들은 즉시 회계팀에 알려야 한다.

어휘 accounting n. 회계팀 immediately adv. 즉시

08 명사 어휘 고르기

해설 '교내 뮤지컬 동아리의 특별 공연에 초대한다'라는 문맥이므로 명사 (B) performance(공연, 수행)가 정답입니다. (A) adjustment는 '적응', (C) negotiation은 '협상', (D) attachment는 '첨부'라는 의미입니다.

해석 Rambat 대학교는 모든 교수진, 학생들, 그리고 졸업생들을 교내 뮤지컬 동아리의 특별 공연에 초대한다.

어휘 faculty n. 교수진 alumni n. 졸업생들

09 명사 어휘 고르기

해설 '공사를 완료하는 것의 실현 가능성은 불확실하다'라는 문맥이므로 명사 (D) feasibility(실현 가능성, 실행 가능성)가 정답입니다. (A) function은 '기능', (B) assembly는 '의회', (C) occupation은 '직업'이라는 의미입니다.

해석 6월 1일까지 박물관의 공사를 완료하는 것의 실현 가능성은 마감 기한들이 이미 지켜지지 못했기 때문에 불확실하다.

어휘 in doubt phr. 불확실하다 miss v. (기한 등을) 지키지 못하다, 놓치다

10 명사 어휘 고르기

해설 '해외 지사로 발령받은 모든 직원들에게 생활 수당을 제공한다'라는 문맥이므로 명사 (B) allowance(수당, 허용)가 정답입니다. (A) admission은 '입장', (C) demand는 '요구, 수요', (D) purpose는 '목적'이라는 의미입니다.

해석 Bouvier 통신사는 해외 지사로 발령받은 모든 직원들에게 생활 수당을 제공한다.

어휘 assigned to phr. ~로 발령받다 overseas adj. 해외의; adv. 해외로

DAY 04 [어휘] 명사 4

토익 실전 문제
p.353

| 01 (D) | 02 (C) | 03 (B) | 04 (B) | 05 (A) |
| 06 (C) | 07 (A) | 08 (D) | 09 (B) | 10 (A) |

01 명사 어휘 고르기

해설 '전형적인 문의에 대한 답변을 제공한다'라는 문맥이므로 명사 (D)

inquiries(문의)가 정답입니다. (A)의 notification은 '알림', (B)의 example은 '예시', (C)의 behavior는 '행동'이라는 의미입니다.

해석 실시간 채팅 서비스를 운영하는 것에 더하여, Zap Electronics사는 자주 묻는 질문 페이지에서 전형적인 문의에 대한 답변을 제공한다.

어휘 live chat phr. 실시간 채팅　typical adj. 전형적인
　　　FAQ phr. 자주 묻는 질문(Frequently Asked Questions)

02 명사 어휘 고르기

해설 '때아닌 기온 차이로 인해 평소보다 더 적은 수확량을 거두어들였다'라는 문맥이므로 명사 (C) variations(차이)가 정답입니다. (A)의 reward는 '보상', (B)의 validation은 '확인', (D)의 exchange는 '교환'이라는 의미입니다.

해석 지역 채소 생산업체들은 이번 여름에 때아닌 기온 차이로 인해 평소보다 더 적은 수확량을 거두어들였다.

어휘 producer n. 생산업체　harvest n. 수확(량)
　　　unseasonable adj. 때아닌, 계절에 맞지 않는
　　　temperature n. 기온, 온도

03 명사 어휘 고르기

해설 '승강기를 정비하다'라는 문맥이므로 명사 (B) maintenance(정비, 보수 관리)가 정답입니다. (A) advancement는 '진보', (C) direction은 '방향', (D) appreciation은 '감상, 감탄'이라는 의미입니다.

해석 Sutton 건물에 있는 승강기는 직원들이 정비를 실시하고 있기 때문에 오늘 늦은 오후까지 이용할 수 없을 것이다.

어휘 unavailable adj. 이용할 수 없는　perform v. 실시하다, 수행하다

04 명사 어휘 고르기

해설 '시 당국에 의해 철저한 점검을 받아야 한다'라는 문맥이므로 명사 (B) authorities(당국, 권한)가 정답입니다. (A)의 evaluation은 '평가', (C)의 availability는 '유효성', (D)의 quotation은 '인용'이라는 의미입니다.

해석 식당을 운영하고자 하는 모든 사람들은 시 당국에 의해 철저한 점검을 받아야 한다.

어휘 undergo v. 받다　thorough adj. 철저한　inspection n. 점검, 검사

05 명사 어휘 고르기

해설 '올해 생산 비용을 20퍼센트만큼 감소시키기로 결정했다'라는 문맥이므로 명사 (A) resolution(결정, 결심)이 정답입니다. (B) situation은 '상황', (C) transition은 '변화', (D) reservation은 '예약'이라는 의미입니다.

해석 Arva 제조 회사의 집행 위원회는 올해 생산 비용을 20퍼센트만큼 감소시키기로 결정했다.

어휘 executive committee phr. 집행 위원회　reduce v. 감소시키다
　　　production n. 생산　cost n. 비용

06 명사 어휘 고르기

해설 '일자리의 세부 항목을 위해 회사 웹사이트를 참고하다'라는 문맥이므로 명사 (C) specifications(세부 항목)가 정답입니다. (A)의 implication은 '함축', (B)의 assortment는 '모음', (D)의 occasion은 '때, 경우'라는 의미입니다.

해석 지원자들은 일자리의 세부 항목을 위해 회사 웹사이트를 참고하는 것이 권장된다.

어휘 advise v. 권장하다, 조언하다　consult v. 참고하다, 상담하다

07 명사 어휘 고르기

해설 '프로젝트 진행 상황을 계속해서 정기적으로 확인한다'라는 문맥이므로 명사 (A) progress(진행 상황, 과정)가 정답입니다. (B) condition은 '조건', (C) production은 '생산', (D) environment는 '환경'이라

는 의미입니다.

해석 Ms. Petraki는 신입 사원이기 때문에, 관리자는 그녀의 프로젝트 진행 상황을 계속해서 정기적으로 확인한다.

어휘 regularly adv. 정기적으로　check on phr. ~을 확인하다

08 명사 어휘 고르기

해설 '상세한 보도로 기록적인 시청률을 달성했다'라는 문맥이므로 명사 (D) coverage(보도, 범위)가 정답입니다. (A) storage는 '창고', (B) engagement는 '약속', (C) combination은 '조합'이라는 의미입니다.

해석 24시간 뉴스 채널인 NTTV는 지방 선거에 대한 상세한 보도로 기록적인 시청률을 달성했다.

어휘 record adj. 기록적인　rating n. 시청률, 평가　detailed adj. 상세한
　　　provincial adj. 지방의　election n. 선거

09 유사의미 명사 중에서 고르기

해설 '결함이 있거나 오작동하는 상품의 교체가 일주일까지 지연될 것이다'라는 문맥이므로 명사 (B) replacement(교체, 교체품)가 정답입니다. (D) renovation도 '수리, 수선'이라는 의미이지만, 기존의 것, 특히 오래된 집, 건물, 방 등을 더 좋은 상태가 되도록 보수하고 고치는 것을 나타냅니다. (A) discharge는 '방출', (C) recommendation은 '추천'이라는 의미입니다.

해석 재고의 부족으로, 결함이 있거나 오작동하는 상품의 교체가 일주일까지 지연될 것이다.

어휘 lack n. 부족, 결핍　inventory n. 재고　faulty adj. 결함이 있는
　　　malfunctioning adj. 오작동하는　delay v. 지연시키다, 미루다

10 명사 어휘 고르기

해설 '정보가 제3자에게 공개되는 일은 없을 것이다'라는 문맥이므로 명사 (A) disclosure(공개, 폭로)가 정답입니다. (B) caution은 '주의', (C) execution은 '실행', (D) measure는 '조치'라는 의미입니다.

해석 Hollman's Store는 고객들에 의해 제공된 정보가 제3자에게 공개되는 일은 없을 것이라고 보장한다.

어휘 guarantee v. 보장하다　provide v. 제공하다　third party phr. 제3자

DAY 05 [어휘] 명사 5

토익 실전 문제　　　　　　　　　　　　　　　p.355

01 (D)	02 (D)	03 (D)	04 (C)	05 (D)
06 (B)	07 (C)	08 (C)	09 (B)	10 (D)

01 명사 어휘 고르기

해설 '전문성과 뛰어난 실적은 긍정적인 평판에 기여했다'라는 문맥이므로 명사 (D) reputation(평판)이 정답입니다. (A) characteristic은 '특징', (B) selection은 '선택', (C) expectation은 '기대'라는 의미입니다.

해석 Ms. Stein의 전문성과 뛰어난 실적은 고객들 사이에서의 긍정적인 평판에 기여했다.

어휘 professionalism n. 전문성　performance n. 실적

02 명사 어휘 고르기

해설 '요리 도전의 참가자가 되고 싶은 누구나 신청할 수 있다'라는 문맥이므로 명사 (D) contestant(참가자)가 정답입니다. (A) symbol은 '상징', (B) reference는 '언급', (C) specialist는 '전문가'라는 의미입니다.

해석 다가오는 Drummondville 요리 도전의 참가자가 되고 싶은 누구나 온라인으로 신청할 수 있다.

어휘 upcoming adj. 다가오는 register v. 신청하다, 등록하다

03 명사 어휘 고르기

해설 '널리 배부되지 않아서 많은 사람들은 온라인으로 기사를 읽는다'라는 문맥이므로 명사 (D) distribution(배부, 유통, 분포)이 정답입니다. (A) exclusion은 '제외', (B) inspiration은 '영감', (C) transportation은 '교통'이라는 의미입니다.

해석 일간 신문인 *The Impreda Gazette*지는 널리 배부되지 않아서, 많은 사람들이 온라인으로 기사를 읽는다.

어휘 wide adj. 넓은

04 유사의미 명사 중에서 고르기

해설 '항공사에 채식 기내식에 대한 특별 요청을 했다'라는 문맥이므로 명사 (C) request(요청, 신청)가 정답입니다. (A) claim도 '청구, 신청'이라는 의미이지만, 보상금과 같이 받을 권리가 있는 돈 등에 대한 청구를 나타냅니다. (B) problem은 '문제', (D) policy는 '정책'이라는 의미입니다.

해석 티켓을 예약할 때, Ms. Lucas는 항공사에 채식 기내식에 대한 특별 요청을 했다.

어휘 vegetarian adj. 채식의, 채식주의 in-flight adj. 기내의

05 명사 어휘 고르기

해설 '지원서의 제출 마감 기한은 10월 5일이다'라는 문맥이므로 명사 (D) submission(제출)이 정답입니다. (A) motivation은 '동기', (B) satisfaction은 '만족', (C) promotion은 '승진'이라는 의미입니다.

해석 Hall 광고사의 지사장 자리에 대한 지원서의 제출 마감 기한은 10월 5일이다.

어휘 application n. 지원서 regional director phr. 지사장

06 명사 어휘 고르기

해설 '마지막 과제를 완료하는 것에 도움이 필요한 학생들은 언제든지 교수와 상담할 수 있다'라는 문맥이므로 명사 (B) assignment(과제)가 정답입니다. (A) commitment는 '헌신', (C) appointment는 '약속', (D) incident는 '사건'이라는 의미입니다.

해석 마지막 과제를 완료하는 것에 도움이 필요한 학생들은 설명과 조언을 위해 언제든지 Oldman 교수와 상담할 수 있다.

어휘 consult v. 상담하다 clarification n. 설명 advice n. 조언, 충고

07 명사 어휘 고르기

해설 '그 기계는 현재 최대 생산 능력으로 작동하고 있다'라는 문맥이므로 명사 (C) capacity((생산) 능력, 용량)가 정답입니다. (A) defect는 '결함', (B) report는 '보고', (D) addition은 '추가'라는 의미입니다.

해석 그 기계는 현재 최대 생산 능력으로 작동하고 있어서 더 생산하도록 설정된다면 오작동할 수 있다.

어휘 machinery n. 기계 currently adv. 현재 operate v. 작동하다 malfunction v. 오작동하다

08 명사 어휘 고르기

해설 '주택 부족은 시의회가 새 주택 개발을 승인하도록 했다'라는 문맥이므로 명사 (C) shortage(부족, 결핍)가 정답입니다. (A) portion은 '일부', (B) separation은 '분리', (D) prediction은 '예측'이라는 의미입니다.

해석 Abiline의 주택 부족은 시의회가 새 주택 개발을 승인하도록 했다.

어휘 housing n. 주택 city council phr. 시의회 approve v. 승인하다 residential adj. 주택의 development n. 개발

09 명사 어휘 고르기

해설 '진행 중인 논쟁의 해결책을 생각해내기 위해 전문 협상가를 고용했다'라는 문맥이므로 명사 (B) negotiator(협상가, 교섭자)가 정답입니다. (A) debater는 '토론자', (C) supplier는 '공급자', (D) patron은 '후원자'라는 의미입니다.

해석 Shelby사와 Entemann Associates사는 그들의 진행 중인 논쟁의 해결책을 생각해내기 위해 전문 협상가를 고용했다.

어휘 professional adj. 전문적인 ongoing adj. 진행 중인 dispute n. 논쟁

10 명사 어휘 고르기

해설 '댐 건설을 막기 위해 탄원서를 썼다'라는 문맥이므로 명사 (D) petition(탄원서)이 정답입니다. (A) contribution은 '공헌', (B) memorial은 '기념비', (C) preference는 '선호'라는 의미입니다.

해석 지역 환경 단체들은 Wahatchee 강 옆의 댐 건설을 막기 위해 탄원서를 썼다.

어휘 environmental adj. 환경의

DAY 06 [어휘] 동사 1

토익 실전 문제
p.357

| 01 (C) | 02 (C) | 03 (D) | 04 (C) | 05 (A) |
| 06 (C) | 07 (A) | 08 (A) | 09 (B) | 10 (A) |

01 동사 어휘 고르기

해설 '비록 대부분의 직원들이 오후 6시에 사무실을 떠나지만, 몇몇 사람들은 잠시 동안 남아 있는다'라는 문맥이므로 동사 (C) remain(남아 있다, 계속 ~이다)이 정답입니다. (A) pause는 '잠시 멈추다, 주저하다', (B) occupy는 '차지하다, 사용하다', (D) result는 '(결과로서) 발생하다, 일어나다'라는 의미입니다.

해석 비록 대부분의 직원들이 오후 6시에 사무실을 떠나지만, 몇몇 사람들은 다음 날의 업무를 앞서 진행하기 위해 잠시 동안 남아 있는다.

어휘 get ahead phr. ~을 앞서다

02 동사 어휘 고르기

해설 '주가의 하락이 크게 가속화되었다'라는 문맥이므로 동사 accelerate(가속화하다, 촉진하다)의 과거형 (C) accelerated가 정답입니다. (A)의 release는 '발표하다, 방출하다', (B)의 motivate는 '동기부여하다, 이유가 되다', (D)의 integrate는 '통합하다, 완성하다'라는 의미입니다.

해석 Diablo Holdings사의 문제에 관한 소문이 퍼져서, 주가의 하락이 크게 가속화되었다.

어휘 rumor n. 소문 spread v. 퍼지다, 확산되다 decline n. 하락, 감소 stock price phr. 주가 greatly adv. 크게

03 동사 어휘 고르기

해설 '건설을 시작하는 것에 대한 승인을 받았다'라는 문맥이므로 동사 (D) commence(시작하다, 착수하다)가 정답입니다. (A) trust는 '신뢰하다', (B) collect는 '수집하다'라는 의미입니다. (C) embark(착수하다)도 해석상 그럴듯해 보이지만, embark가 '착수하다'라는 의미로 쓰일 때에는 자동사이기 때문에 뒤에 전치사 on이 와야 합니다.

해석 Wallaceburg Transit사는 새로운 지하철 노선의 건설을 시작하는 것에 대한 승인을 받았다.

어휘 grant v. 주다 approval n. 승인

04 동사 어휘 고르기

해설 '생산을 극대화하려는 노력으로 최신식의 기계가 주문되었다'라는 문맥이므로 동사 (C) maximize(극대화하다)가 정답입니다. (A) alternate는 '교체하다', (B) inspire는 '(자신감을 갖도록 누군가를) 격려하다', (D) designate는 '지정하다'라는 의미입니다.

해석 생산을 극대화하려는 노력으로 최신식의 기계가 공장을 위해 주문되었다.

어휘 state-of-the-art adj. 최신식의   order v. 주문하다
in an effort to phr. ~하려는 노력으로

05 동사 어휘 고르기

해설 '더 많은 책무를 처리할 수 있다는 것을 상사에게 증명하다'라는 문맥이므로 동사 (A) prove(증명하다, 입증하다)가 정답입니다. (B) fulfill은 '이행하다, 달성하다', (C) hire는 '고용하다', (D) reform은 '개혁하다'라는 의미입니다.

해석 Ms. Morrison은 그녀가 직장에서 더 많은 책무를 처리할 수 있다는 것을 상사에게 증명하기로 결심했다.

어휘 be determined to phr. ~하기로 결심하다   handle v. 처리하다, 다루다
responsibility n. 책무, 책임   at work phr. 직장에서

06 동사 어휘 고르기

해설 '회사들이 현재 직면하고 있는 문제들을 다뤘다'라는 문맥이므로 동사 address(다루다, 처리하다)의 과거형 (C) addressed가 정답입니다. (A)의 restrict는 '제한하다', (B)의 oblige는 '의무적으로 ~하게 하다', (D)의 retain은 '유지하다'라는 의미입니다.

해석 전화 회담 동안에, 최고 경영자는 모든 석유와 천연가스 회사들이 현재 직면하고 있는 문제들을 다뤘다.

어휘 conference call phr. 전화 회담   challenge n. 문제
face v. 직면하다

07 동사 어휘 고르기

해설 '수리가 이번 주 말에는 끝날 것이라고 보장했다'라는 문맥이므로 동사 guarantee(보장하다, 약속하다)의 과거형 (A) guaranteed가 정답입니다. (B)의 nominate는 '지명하다', (C)의 eliminate는 '제거하다', (D)의 advise는 '조언하다'라는 의미입니다.

해석 Frampton 건설사의 직원은 수리가 이번 주 말에는 끝날 것이라고 보장했다.

어휘 representative n. 직원, 대표   renovation n. 수리, 보수

08 동사 어휘 고르기

해설 '지난 20년 동안 저축했던 돈으로 집을 사기를 바라고 있다'라는 문맥이므로 동사 (A) acquire((사거나 받아서) 획득하다, 얻다)가 정답입니다. (B) compose는 '구성하다', (C) elevate는 '승진시키다', (D) insert는 '삽입하다'라는 의미입니다.

해석 Mr. Pelton과 그의 아내는 지난 20년 동안 저축했던 돈으로 그들의 첫 번째 집을 사기를 바라고 있다.

어휘 save up phr. 저축하다

09 유사의미 동사 중에서 고르기

해설 '인터넷을 통해 물품을 구매하는 것이 더 인기 있어지고 있다'라는 문맥이므로 동사 purchase(구매하다)의 동명사 (B) Purchasing이 정답입니다. (A)의 renew도 '갱신하다, 새로 교체하다'라는 의미이지만, 이미 갖고 있던 것을 새롭게 하거나 연장하는 것을 나타냅니다. (C)의 record는 '녹음하다', (D)의 portray는 '묘사하다'라는 의미입니다.

해석 향상된 온라인 보안 덕분에 신용카드를 사용해서 인터넷을 통해 물품을 구매하는 것은 더 인기 있어지고 있다.

어휘 popular adj. 인기 있는, 대중적인   thanks to phr. ~ 덕분에

improve v. 향상시키다   security n. 보안

10 동사 어휘 고르기

해설 '열기와 강한 바람을 견딜 준비가 되어야 한다'라는 문맥이므로 동사 (A) endure(견디다, 인내하다)가 정답입니다. (B) initiate는 '시작하다', (C) pressure는 '압박하다', (D) persist는 '지속하다'라는 의미입니다.

해석 부산 마라톤의 모든 주자들은 마라톤 코스에서의 열기와 강한 바람을 견딜 준비가 되어야 한다.

어휘 be prepared to phr. ~할 준비가 되다   heat n. 열기

DAY 07 [어휘] 동사 2

토익 실전 문제
p.359

01 (D)	02 (D)	03 (A)	04 (B)	05 (A)
06 (C)	07 (D)	08 (A)	09 (A)	10 (B)

01 동사 어휘 고르기

해설 '입국 심사 구역으로 가기 전에 그들의 짐을 되찾는 것이 요구된다'라는 문맥이므로 동사 (D) reclaim(되찾다)이 정답입니다. (A) refund는 '환불하다', (B) reduce는 '줄이다', (C) reflect는 '반영하다'라는 의미입니다.

해석 입국 심사 구역으로 가기 전에, 승객들은 도착 터미널에서 그들의 짐을 되찾는 것이 요구된다.

어휘 proceed v. 가다, 진행하다   immigration n. 입국, 이주
luggage n. 짐, 수하물   arrival n. 도착

02 동사 어휘 고르기

해설 '고객들은 개인 정보가 제3자에 의해 사용되는 것을 허락하는 데에 동의해야 한다'라는 문맥이므로 동사 (D) consent(동의하다)가 정답입니다. (A) regard는 '여기다, 간주하다', (B) assess는 '평가하다', (C) handle은 '처리하다, 다루다'라는 의미입니다.

해석 고객들은 그들이 알려주는 어떠한 개인 정보든 제3자에 의해 사용되는 것을 허락하는 데에 동의해야 한다.

어휘 allow v. 허락하다, 허가하다   personal adj. 개인의
reveal v. 알리다, 밝히다   third party phr. 제3자

03 동사 어휘 고르기

해설 '디자이너 가방은 사치품으로 분류된다'라는 문맥이므로 동사 classify(분류하다)의 p.p.형 (A) classified가 정답입니다. (B)의 compensate는 '보상하다', (C)의 substitute는 '대신하다', (D)의 adopt는 '채택하다'라는 의미입니다.

해석 디자이너 가방은 사치품으로 분류되므로 추가 세금의 대상이다.

어휘 luxury item phr. 사치품   be subject to phr. ~의 대상이다
additional adj. 추가의

04 동사 어휘 고르기

해설 '지하철 운전사는 열차가 다시 운행하기 시작할 것이라고 승객들을 안심시켰다'라는 문맥이므로 동사 assure(안심시키다)의 과거형 (B) assured가 정답입니다. (A)의 forecast는 '예측하다, 예보하다'라는 의미로 해석상 그럴듯해 보이지만, 바로 다음에 대상이 아닌 예측하는 내용이 와야 합니다. (C)의 recruit는 '모집하다, 뽑다', (D)의 deviate는 '벗어나다, 일탈하다'라는 의미입니다.

해석 지하철 운전사는 잠시 동안의 지연 후에 열차가 다시 운행하기 시작할

VOCABULARY PART 5, 6

한 권으로 끝내는 해커스 토익 700+ (LC+RC+VOCA)

것이라고 승객들을 안심시켰다.

어휘 **operator** n. 운전사, 조작자 **passenger** n. 승객
run v. 운행하다, 다니다 **brief** adj. 잠시 동안의, 짧은
delay n. 지연, 연기

05 동사 어휘 고르기

해설 '지각은 한 달에 두 번 이상 용인되지 않을 것이다'라는 문맥이므로 동사 tolerate(용인하다)의 p.p.형 (A) tolerated가 정답입니다. (B)의 attempt는 '시도하다', (C)의 misplace는 '잘못 두다, 둔 곳을 잊다', (D)의 innovate는 '혁신하다'라는 의미입니다.

해석 Thompson 가구사의 새로운 출근 규정하에, 지각은 한 달에 두 번 이상 용인되지 않을 것이다.

어휘 **attendance** n. 출근, 참석 **tardiness** n. 지각, 지체

06 동사 어휘 고르기

해설 '모든 산업 공장들은 점검을 받을 것이다'라는 문맥이므로 동사 (C) undergo(받다)가 정답입니다. (A) enroll(등록시키다)도 해석상 그럴 듯해 보이지만, 목적어로 등록시키는 대상이 와야 합니다. (B) submit은 '제출하다', (D) attach는 '첨부하다'라는 의미입니다.

해석 Harper Valley에 있는 모든 산업 공장들은 새로운 환경 관련 법안이 승인된 후에 점검을 받을 것이다.

어휘 **industrial** adj. 산업의, 공업의 **plant** n. 공장, 시설
environmental adj. 환경의 **pass** v. (법안을) 승인하다, 합격하다

07 동사 어휘 고르기

해설 '잠재적인 후보자들은 지원서에 그들의 입사 가능 상태를 명시하는 것이 요구된다'라는 문맥이므로 동사 (D) indicate(명시하다)가 정답입니다. (A) entitle은 '자격을 주다', (B) propose는 '제안하다', (C) negotiate는 '협상하다'라는 의미입니다.

해석 일자리에 대한 잠재적인 후보자들은 지원서에 그들의 입사 가능 상태를 명시하는 것이 요구된다.

어휘 **potential** adj. 잠재적인 **candidate** n. 후보자, 지원자

08 동사 어휘 고르기

해설 'The Floodgates가 올해에 가장 높이 평가되는 영화들 중의 하나였다'라는 문맥이므로 동사 rate(평가하다)의 p.p.형 (A) rated가 정답입니다. (B)의 mean은 '의미하다', (C)의 summarize는 '요약하다', (D)의 solve는 '해결하다'라는 의미입니다.

해석 Ms. Connors는 The Floodgates가 올해에 가장 높이 평가되는 영화들 중의 하나였기 때문에 그것을 보기로 결정했다.

어휘 **highly** adv. 높이, 매우

09 유사의미 동사 중에서 고르기

해설 '사람들이 기부할 수 있는 지역 사회 내의 많은 자선 기관들'이라는 문맥이므로 동사 (A) donate(기부하다)가 정답입니다. (C) support도 '지지하다, 후원하다'라는 의미이지만, donate가 'donate (+ 기부하는 것/금액) + to + 기부를 받는 대상'의 형태로 쓰이는 것과 달리 'support + 지지를 받는 대상'의 형태로 쓰이기 때문에 바로 다음에 지지를 받는 대상이 와야 합니다. (B) obtain은 '얻다', (D) invite는 '초대하다, 부탁하다'라는 의미입니다.

해석 Mowatsville 시청의 웹사이트는 사람들이 기부할 수 있는 지역 사회 내의 많은 자선 기관들을 열거한다.

어휘 **town hall** phr. 시청 **list** v. 열거하다, 목록을 작성하다
charitable adj. 자선의 **organization** n. 기관, 조직
community n. 지역 사회

10 동사 어휘 고르기

해설 'Freebird 항공사 멤버십이 만료되어 사용할 수 없게 될 것이다'라는

문맥이므로 동사 (B) expire(만료되다)가 정답입니다. (A) succeed는 '성공하다', (C) decrease는 '감소하다', (D) extend는 '연장하다'라는 의미입니다.

해석 귀하의 Freebird 항공사 멤버십은 14일 이내에 회비가 납입되지 않는 한 만료되어 사용할 수 없게 될 것입니다.

어휘 **unusable** adj. 사용할 수 없는, 쓸모없는
unless conj. ~하지 않는 한, ~한 경우 외에는

DAY 08 [어휘] 동사 3

토익 실전 문제 p.361

01 (D)	**02** (B)	**03** (C)	**04** (C)	**05** (B)
06 (C)	**07** (B)	**08** (D)	**09** (A)	**10** (B)

01 동사 어휘 고르기

해설 '몇몇 직원들은 새로운 지하철 노선을 건설하는 것이 비용이 너무 많이 들 것이라고 주장한다'라는 문맥이므로 (D) argue(주장하다)가 정답입니다. (A) execute는 '실행하다', (B) generate는 '발생시키다', (C) reserve는 '예약하다'라는 의미입니다.

해석 교통 당국의 몇몇 직원들은 새로운 지하철 노선을 건설하는 것이 비용이 너무 많이 들 것이라고 주장한다.

어휘 **transportation** n. 교통, 수송 **authority** n. 당국
costly adj. 비용이 많이 드는

02 동사 어휘 고르기

해설 '최고 경영자가 Ms. Jones를 의장으로 임명했다'라는 문맥이므로 동사 appoint(임명하다)의 과거형 (B) appointed가 정답입니다. (A)의 discover는 '발견하다', (C)의 achieve는 '달성하다, 이루다', (D)의 influence는 '영향을 끼치다'라는 의미입니다.

해석 Candy Clothing사의 최고 경영자는 Ms. Jones를 이사회의 새 의장으로 임명했다.

어휘 **board of directors** phr. 이사회 **chairperson** n. 의장, 회장

03 동사 어휘 고르기

해설 '도로 공사로부터 교통을 우회시키다'라는 문맥이므로 동사 (C) divert(우회시키다, 다른 곳으로 돌리다)가 정답입니다. (A) reveal은 '드러내다, 폭로하다', (B) expend는 '(시간, 노력 등을) 소비하다', (D) affiliate는 '제휴하다'라는 의미입니다.

해석 진행 중인 도로 공사로부터 교통을 우회시키기 위해 Florin가 옆쪽에 표지판이 설치되었다.

어휘 **sign** n. 표지판, 간판 **place** v. 설치하다, 두다 **traffic** n. 교통, 통행
ongoing adj. 진행 중인 **roadwork** n. 도로 공사

04 동사 어휘 고르기

해설 '매우 중요한 회의 중이어서 어떠한 이유로든 방해받지 않아야 한다'라는 문맥이므로 동사 disrupt(방해하다)의 p.p.형 (C) disrupted가 정답입니다. (A)의 corrupt는 '부패시키다', (B)의 complain은 '불평하다, 항의하다', (D)의 remind는 '상기시키다'라는 의미입니다.

해석 Mr. Harris는 지금 고객과 매우 중요한 회의 중이어서 어떠한 이유로든 방해받지 않아야 한다.

어휘 **at the moment** phr. 지금 **reason** n. 이유

05 동사 어휘 고르기

해설 '영화가 너무 긴 것으로 판명된다면 불필요한 몇몇 부분은 생략될 수

있다'라는 문맥이므로 동사 omit(생략하다)의 p.p.형 (B) omitted가 정답입니다. (A)의 cater는 '(사업으로 행사에) 음식을 공급하다', (C)의 deserve는 '~을 받을 자격이 있다', (D)의 afford는 '~할 수 있다, ~할 여유가 있다'라는 의미입니다.

해석 영화가 너무 긴 것으로 판명된다면 그 신작 영화의 불필요한 몇몇 부분은 편집 과정 중에 생략될 수 있다.

어휘 nonessential adj. 불필요한, 중요하지 않은 editing n. 편집 prove v. 판명되다, 증명되다

06 동사 어휘 고르기
해설 '직원들의 전반적인 능률을 평가하다'라는 문맥이므로 동사 (C) assess(평가하다)가 정답입니다. (A) minimize는 '최소화하다', (B) commit는 '전념하다, 헌신하다', (D) abolish는 '폐지하다'라는 의미입니다.

해석 Vermaco사는 다음 분기에 직원들의 전반적인 능률을 평가하기 위해 자문 위원을 고용할지도 모른다.

어휘 overall adj. 전반적인, 종합적인 efficiency n. 능률, 효율 quarter n. 분기, 4분의 1

07 동사 어휘 고르기
해설 '제품과 서비스를 설명하기 위해 잠재 고객들을 위한 설명회를 열 것이다'라는 문맥이므로 동사 (B) demonstrate(설명하다)가 정답입니다. (A) dedicate는 '전념하다', (C) house는 '수용하다, 장소를 제공하다', (D) allocate는 '할당하다'라는 의미입니다.

해석 Alida Technologies사는 자사의 제품과 서비스를 설명하기 위해 잠재 고객들을 위한 설명회를 열 것이다.

어휘 information session phr. 설명회 potential adj. 잠재적인, 가능성이 있는

08 동사 어휘 고르기
해설 '제조 비용이 지정되었던 금액을 초과했다'라는 문맥이므로 동사 exceed(초과하다)의 과거형 (D) exceeded가 정답입니다. (A)의 examine은 '조사하다', (B)의 emerge는 '나타나다', (C)의 expect는 '예상하다, 기대하다'라는 의미입니다.

해석 제조 비용이 지정되었던 금액을 초과했을 때 회사 예산은 조정되었다.

어휘 corporate adj. 회사의 budget n. 예산, 비용 adjust v. 조정하다 manufacturing n. 제조 (공업) designate v. 지정하다, 지명하다

09 동사 어휘 고르기
해설 '시의 첫 번째 멕시코 식당을 설립했다'라는 문맥이므로 동사 establish (설립하다)의 과거형 (A) established가 정답입니다. (B)의 deposit는 '두다, 맡기다', (C)의 decide는 '결정하다', (D)의 incur는 '초래하다'라는 의미입니다.

해석 Manuel Rivera는 거의 50년 전에 시의 첫 번째 멕시코 식당을 Northside 쇼핑몰에 설립했다.

어휘 nearly adv. 거의, 간신히

10 유사의미 동사 중에서 고르기
해설 'Herald 은행의 몇몇 계좌들은 지불이 중단되었다'라는 문맥이므로 동사 suspend((지불 등을) 중단하다, 정지하다)의 p.p.형 (B) suspended가 정답입니다. (A)의 cancel(취소하다)은 어떠한 일이 더는 일어나거나 연장되지 않도록 취소하는 것을 의미하는데, 'until further notice'에서 추후 공지가 있을 때까지라고 했으므로 완전히 취소하는 것이 아니라 그때까지 잠시 중단된다는 문맥임을 알 수 있습니다. (C)의 move는 '이동시키다, 움직이다', (D)의 formalize는 '공식화하다, 형식을 갖추다'라는 의미입니다.

해석 의심스러운 거래의 발생으로 인해, Herald 은행의 몇몇 계좌들은 추후 공지가 있을 때까지 지불이 중단되었다.

어휘 occurrence n. 발생, 출현 suspicious adj. 의심스러운, 의심 많은 transaction n. 거래, 매매 further adj. 추후의 notice n. 공지

DAY 09 [어휘] 동사 4

토익 실전 문제
p.363

| 01 (B) | 02 (B) | 03 (A) | 04 (C) | 05 (B) |
| 06 (B) | 07 (D) | 08 (A) | 09 (D) | 10 (C) |

01 동사 어휘 고르기
해설 '판매가 처음에는 강세를 보였지만, 최근 몇 달 동안 감소하기 시작했다'라는 문맥이므로 동사 (B) decline(감소하다)이 정답입니다. (A) expand는 '확대하다, 확장하다', (C) forward는 '전송하다', (D) supplement는 '보충하다, 추가하다'라는 의미입니다.

해석 XCR 스마트폰의 판매가 처음에는 강세를 보였지만, 최근 몇 달 동안 감소하기 시작했다.

어휘 initially adv. 처음에, 원래 strong adj. 강세의, 강한

02 동사 어휘 고르기
해설 '다양한 기금 모금 운동을 통해 Brownsville 지역사회에 봉사해오고 있다'라는 문맥이므로 동사 serve(봉사하다)의 -ing형 (B) serving이 정답입니다. (A)의 achieve는 '달성하다, 획득하다', (C)의 organize는 '조직하다, 준비하다', (D)의 operate는 '경영하다'라는 의미입니다.

해석 Lennox 재단은 50년 동안 다양한 기금 모금 운동을 통해 Brownsville 지역사회에 봉사해오고 있다.

어휘 foundation n. 재단, 설립 various adj. 다양한, 여러 가지의 fundraising adj. 기금 모금의, 모금 활동의 effort n. (모금 등의) 운동, 노력

03 동사 어휘 고르기
해설 '새로운 공원은 등산 코스와 과수원을 포함할 것이다'라는 문맥이므로 동사 (A) feature(특별히 포함하다)가 정답입니다. (B) decorate는 '장식하다, 꾸미다', (C) realize는 '깨닫다, 인식하다', (D) envision은 '마음속에 그리다, 상상하다'라는 의미입니다.

해석 Walvington의 새로운 공원은 이번 가을에 대중에 개방될 때 등산 코스와 과수원을 포함할 것이다.

어휘 trail n. 코스, 오솔길 orchard n. 과수원 public n. 대중, 공중

04 동사 어휘 고르기
해설 '운영 비용을 최소화한다면 많은 돈을 절약할 것이다'라는 문맥이므로 동사 minimize(최소화하다)의 3인칭 단수형 (C) minimizes가 정답입니다. (A)의 acclaim은 '환호하다', (B)의 intensify는 '강화하다, 증대하다', (D)의 calculate는 '계산하다'라는 의미입니다.

해석 Sanger Manufacturing사의 모든 부서가 운영 비용을 최소화한다면 많은 돈을 절약할 것이다.

어휘 operating adj. 운영상의, 조작상의

05 유사의미 동사 중에서 고르기
해설 '개인 서류를 위해 사무실 복사기를 사용하는 것에 대한 금지를 공지했다'라는 문맥이므로 동사 announce(공지하다)의 과거형 (B) announced가 정답입니다. (D)의 inform도 '알려주다, 통지하다'라는 의미이지만, announce가 'announce + 공지 내용 + to + 공지를 받는 대상'의 형태로 쓰이는 것과 달리, 'inform + 공지를 받는 대상 + of + 공지 내용'의 형태로 쓰이기 때문에 바로 다음에 공지를 받는 대상이 와야 합니다. (A)의 descend는 '내려가다', (C)의 utilize는 '이용하다, 활용하다'라는 의미입니다.

해석 인사부서는 개인 서류를 위해 사무실 복사기를 사용하는 것에 대한 금지를 공지했다.

어휘 human resources department phr. 인사부서
ban n. 금지; v. 금하다 photocopier n. 복사기
document n. 서류, 문서

06 동사 어휘 고르기

해설 '새로운 회의실을 추가하는 것은 회의를 위한 충분한 공간이 있는 것을 보장할 것이다'라는 문맥이므로 동사 (B) ensure(보장하다, 반드시 ~하게 하다)가 정답입니다. (A) enlarge는 '확대하다, 확장하다'라는 의미입니다. (C) accomplish는 '성취하다, 완수하다'라는 의미로 해석상 그럴듯해 보이지만, 목표 등을 성취한다는 것을 나타내고 accomplish the goal of having enough space와 같은 형태로 쓰여야 합니다. (D) permit는 '허용하다'라는 의미로 해석상 그럴듯해 보이지만, 다음에 -ing형이나 '목적어 + to do' 등의 형태가 와야 합니다.

해석 3층에 새로운 회의실을 추가하는 것은 회의를 위한 충분한 공간이 있는 것을 보장할 것이다.

어휘 addition n. 추가, 부가 conference n. 회의, 학회
enough adj. 충분한, ~하기에 족한 space n. 공간, 장소

07 동사 어휘 고르기

해설 'BGW 산업 은행과 National One사는 치열한 협상 후에 작년에 합병했다'라는 문맥이므로 동사 merge(합병하다)의 과거형 (D) merged가 정답입니다. (A)의 modify는 '수정하다', (B)의 acquire는 '획득하다', (C)의 accumulate는 '모으다'라는 의미입니다.

해석 BGW 산업 은행과 National One사는 몇 달간의 치열한 협상 후에 작년에 합병했다.

어휘 intense adj. 치열한, 강렬한 negotiation n. 협상, 교섭

08 동사 어휘 고르기

해설 '국가가 더 개방된 무역 망을 추구하기로 결정했다'라는 문맥이므로 동사 (A) pursue(추구하다, 계속하다)가 정답입니다. (B) conform은 '따르다, 순응하다', (C) suspect는 '의심하다, 추측하다', (D) exchange는 '교환하다, 교체하다'라는 의미입니다.

해석 일반 대중의 격렬한 반대에도 불구하고, 국가는 더 개방된 무역 망을 추구하기로 결정했다.

어휘 resistance n. 반대, 저항 general adj. 일반의, 보통의
trade n. 무역, 거래 network n. 망, 연결된 조직

09 동사 어휘 고르기

해설 '재고 시스템에 문제가 있다는 것을 알아냈다'라는 문맥이므로 동사 determine(알아내다)의 과거형 (D) determined가 정답입니다. (A)의 proceed는 '진행하다, 나아가다', (B)의 use는 '사용하다', (C)의 spend는 '(시간이나 돈 등을) 쓰다, 들이다'라는 의미입니다.

해석 재고 목록을 검토한 후에, Mr. Jacobs는 재고 시스템에 문제가 있다는 것을 알아냈다.

어휘 examine v. 검토하다, 조사하다 stock n. 재고, 재고품
inventory n. 재고, 물품 목록

10 동사 어휘 고르기

해설 '국가의 경제적 위기는 수십 년 전의 정부 정책의 결과라고 주장한다'라는 문맥이므로 동사 contend(주장하다)의 3인칭 단수형 (C) contends가 정답입니다. (A)의 found는 '설립하다, 세우다', (B)의 reduce는 '줄이다', (D)의 guarantee는 '보장하다'라는 의미입니다.

해석 그녀의 책 *Stacked*에서, Ms. Atwood는 국가의 경제적 위기는 수십 년 전의 정부 정책의 결과라고 주장한다.

어휘 crisis n. 위기, 고비 result n. 결과, 결말 government n. 정부, 정치
decade n. 10년

DAY 10 [어휘] 형용사 1

토익 실전 문제
p.365

01 (B)	02 (D)	03 (B)	04 (A)	05 (C)
06 (D)	07 (B)	08 (B)	09 (D)	10 (C)

01 형용사 어휘 고르기

해설 '그 비용이 불합리하게 과도하다고 생각했다'라는 문맥이므로 형용사 (B) excessive(과도한, 매우 많은)가 정답입니다. (A) attentive는 '주의 깊은, 세심한', (C) verifiable은 '증명할 수 있는', (D) spacious는 '(공간이) 넓은'이라는 의미입니다.

해석 건설 도급업자는 Mr. Norman을 위해 비용 견적을 냈는데, Mr. Norman은 그 비용이 불합리하게 과도하다고 생각했다.

어휘 contractor n. 도급업자, 계약자 quote v. 견적을 내다, 인용하다
unreasonably adv. 불합리하게, 터무니없이

02 형용사 어휘 고르기

해설 '작물들을 해충과 병에 더 강하게 만들다'라는 문맥이므로 형용사 (D) resistant(~에 강한, 저항하는)가 정답입니다. (A) significant는 '중요한, 의미 있는'이라는 의미입니다. (B) acceptable은 '받아들일 수 있는, 용인할 수 있는'이라는 의미로 해석상 그럴듯해 보이지만, 선물이나 제안 등을 받아들일 수 있거나 어법이나 행위 등을 용인할 수 있다는 것을 나타냅니다. (C) thorough는 '빈틈없는, 철저한'이라는 의미입니다.

해석 NRT Agricultural사는 작물들을 해충과 병에 더 강하게 만들 새로운 기술을 개발하고 있다.

어휘 develop v. 개발하다, 발전시키다 crop n. 작물, 수확물
pest n. 해충, 유해물 disease n. 병, 질환

03 형용사 어휘 고르기

해설 '수정된 제안서는 모든 변경 사항들을 포함한다'라는 문맥이므로 형용사 (B) revised(수정된)가 정답입니다. (A) acute는 '예리한', (C) aspiring은 '장차 ~이 되려는', (D) domestic은 '국내의'라는 의미입니다.

해석 수정된 제안서는 지난 회의 때 고객과 합의된 모든 변경 사항들을 포함한다.

어휘 proposal n. 제안(서) include v. 포함하다
agree v. 합의하다, 동의하다

04 형용사 어휘 고르기

해설 'Cardinal 대학교로부터 명망 있는 상을 받았다'라는 문맥이므로 형용사 (A) prestigious(명망 있는)가 정답입니다. (B) grateful은 '고마워하는', (C) keen은 '예민한', (D) complicated는 '복잡한'이라는 의미입니다.

해석 유전학 연구팀은 Cardinal 대학교로부터 후한 보조금을 포함하는 명망 있는 상을 받았다.

어휘 genetic adj. 유전학의, 유전의 award n. 상; v. 수여하다, 주다
generous adj. 후한, 관대한
grant n. 보조금, 허가; v. 수여하다, 승인하다

05 유사의미 형용사 중에서 고르기

해설 '남은 빈자리가 없을 수도 있다'라는 문맥이므로 형용사 (C) vacant(빈, 사람이 없는)가 정답입니다. (A) hollow도 '속이 빈'이라는 의미이지만, 사물의 속이 텅 비어 있는 것을 나타냅니다. (B) insincere는 '거짓의', (D) updated는 '갱신된'이라는 의미입니다.

해석 회계 심포지엄의 참석자들은 강연장에 일찍 도착하지 않으면 남은 빈

자리가 없을 수도 있다.

어휘 **attendee** n. 참석자, 출석자 **accounting** n. 회계, 경리
symposium n. 심포지엄, 학술 토론회

06 형용사 어휘 고르기

해설 '종합 자동차 보험 증서는 절도도 보상한다'라는 문맥이므로 형용사 (D) comprehensive(종합적인)가 정답입니다. (A) fortunate는 '운이 좋은', (B) incoming은 '새로 선출된', (C) wholesome은 '건강에 좋은'이라는 의미입니다.

해석 종합 자동차 보험 증서는 다른 운전자나 자연재해에 의해 야기된 어떠한 피해뿐만 아니라 절도도 보상한다.

어휘 **insurance policy** phr. 보험 증서, 보험 증권 **theft** n. 절도, 도둑질
damage n. 피해, 손상 **cause** v. 야기하다; n. 원인, 이유
natural disaster phr. 자연재해, 천재

07 형용사 어휘 고르기

해설 '유행을 따르고 가격이 알맞은 옷을 판매한다'라는 문맥이므로 형용사 (B) affordable(가격이 알맞은, 저렴한)이 정답입니다. (A) former는 '이전의, (둘 중에서) 전자의', (C) receptive는 '수용하는, 잘 받아들이는'이라는 의미입니다. (D) instant는 '즉각적인, 즉시의'라는 의미로 해석상 그럴듯해 보이지만, 주로 명사 앞에 와서 무언가가 즉시 일어난다는 것을 나타냅니다.

해석 Slick World는 유행을 따르고 가격이 알맞은 옷을 판매하기 때문에 예산이 한정된 고객들은 이곳에서 쇼핑하는 것을 즐거워할 것이다.

어휘 **on a budget** phr. 예산이 한정된
fashionable adj. 유행을 따르는, 유행하는

08 형용사 어휘 고르기

해설 '전 세계의 다양한 종류의 음식이 판매될 것이다'라는 문맥이므로 형용사 (B) diverse(다양한)가 정답입니다. (A) positive는 '긍정적인', (C) correct는 '적절한, 정확한', (D) technical은 '기술적인, 전문적인'이라는 의미입니다.

해석 전 세계의 다양한 종류의 음식이 Blumburg 국제 요리 축제에서 판매될 것이다.

어휘 **on sale** phr. 판매되는 **culinary** adj. 요리의, 음식의

09 형용사 어휘 고르기

해설 '현재의 시스템의 가장 큰 문제는 문서를 찾는 데에 시간이 너무 오래 걸린다는 것이다'라는 문맥이므로 형용사 (D) current(현재의)가 정답입니다. (A) steady는 '꾸준한', (B) eager는 '열렬한', (C) captivating은 '매혹적인'이라는 의미입니다.

해석 현재의 서류 정리 시스템의 가장 큰 문제는 문서를 찾는 데에 시간이 너무 오래 걸린다는 것이다.

어휘 **filing** n. 서류 정리 **document** n. 문서, 서류

10 형용사 어휘 고르기

해설 '모든 지원자들은 복잡한 채용 절차를 거쳐야 한다'라는 문맥이므로 형용사 (C) elaborate(복잡한)가 정답입니다. (A) accountable은 '책임이 있는', (B) invalid는 '무효한', (D) interested는 '관심 있어 하는'이라는 의미입니다.

해석 모든 지원자들은 몇 차례의 면접과 시험을 포함하는 복잡한 채용 절차를 거쳐야 한다.

어휘 **candidate** n. 지원자, 후보자 **undergo** v. (과정 등을) 거치다, 겪다, 받다
hiring n. 채용 **procedure** n. 절차

DAY 11 [어휘] 형용사 2

토익 실전 문제   p.367

01 (B)	02 (D)	03 (C)	04 (A)	05 (B)
06 (A)	07 (D)	08 (D)	09 (C)	10 (D)

01 형용사 어휘 고르기

해설 '동업자가 회사를 떠난 이후 유일한 소유주가 되었다'라는 문맥이므로 형용사 (B) sole(유일한)이 정답입니다. (A) idle은 '사용되지 않는', (C) ample은 '충분한', (D) complex는 '복잡한'이라는 의미입니다.

해석 Mr. Brooks는 그의 동업자가 작년에 회사를 떠난 이후 Vera 여행사의 유일한 소유주가 되었다.

02 형용사 어휘 고르기

해설 '저소득 가정들에게 더 큰 경제적인 보호를 제공하다'라는 문맥이므로 형용사 (D) economic(경제적인)이 정답입니다. (A) statistical은 '통계적인', (B) hesitant는 '주저하는', (C) mechanical은 '기계의'라는 의미입니다.

해석 새로운 세법 제정은 저소득 가정들에게 더 큰 경제적인 보호를 제공할 것으로 기대된다.

어휘 **legislation** n. 법률 제정, 법률 **expect** v. 기대하다, 예상하다
low-income adj. 저소득의, 저수입의 **security** n. 보호, 안전

03 형용사 어휘 고르기

해설 '쿠폰은 입장의 50퍼센트 할인에 대해 유효하다'라는 문맥이므로 형용사 (C) valid(유효한, 타당한)가 정답입니다. (A) legitimate는 '합법적인, 정당한', (B) definite는 '확실한, 분명한', (D) popular는 '인기 있는'이라는 의미입니다.

해석 각 쿠폰은 Fountain 공원 입장의 50퍼센트 할인에 대해 유효하다.

어휘 **admission** n. 입장, 인정

04 형용사 어휘 고르기

해설 '시험을 잘 못 본 것은 그에게 매우 좌절스러웠다'라는 문맥이므로 형용사 (A) frustrating(좌절스러운)이 정답입니다. (B) hopeful은 '희망에 찬, 기대하는', (C) negligible은 '(무시해도 될 정도로) 적은, 사소한', (D) bright는 '밝은, 희망적인'이라는 의미입니다.

해석 Mr. Philips는 회계 시험을 위해 매우 열심히 공부했기 때문에 시험을 잘 못 본 것은 그에게 매우 좌절스러웠다.

어휘 **poorly** adv. 잘 못하게, 좋지 못하게 **accounting** n. 회계

05 형용사 어휘 고르기

해설 '신용카드에 더하여, 대안적인 지불 방법을 받아들인다'라는 문맥이므로 형용사 (B) alternative(대안적인)가 정답입니다. (A) coordinated는 '통합된', (C) admirable은 '감탄할 만한, 존경스러운', (D) insistent는 '지속적인'이라는 의미입니다.

해석 신용카드에 더하여, 많은 사업체들은 스마트폰 애플리케이션을 통한 대안적인 지불 방법을 받아들인다.

어휘 **method** n. 방법, 체계

06 형용사 어휘 고르기

해설 '국제적으로 유명한 바이올리니스트가 특별 공연을 할 것이다'라는 문맥이므로 형용사 (A) renowned(유명한, 명성 있는)가 정답입니다. (B) immediate는 '즉각적인, 당장의', (C) modest는 '보통의, 겸손한', (D) parallel은 '평행의, 비슷한'이라는 의미입니다.

해석 국제적으로 유명한 바이올리니스트 Margaret Collins가 이번 주 금요

일에 특별 공연을 할 것이다.

어휘 performance n. 공연

07 형용사 어휘 고르기

해설 '새 교육 프로그램이 직원들을 그들의 업무에 더 능숙하게 해주기를 기대한다'라는 문맥이므로 형용사 (D) proficient(능숙한)가 정답입니다. (A) advisable은 '권할 만한', (B) solid는 '견고한', (C) considerate는 '사려 깊은'이라는 의미입니다.

해석 경영진은 새 교육 프로그램이 직원들을 그들의 업무에 더 능숙하게 해주기를 기대한다.

어휘 management n. 경영진

08 형용사 어휘 고르기

해설 '비평가들은 강렬한 공연 후에 Colin Wench에 대한 찬사에 대해 압도적으로 긍정적이었다'라는 문맥이므로 형용사 (D) lively(강렬한, 활기찬)가 정답입니다. (A) present는 '현재의, 참석한', (B) flawed는 '결함이 있는', (C) remote는 '외진, 먼'이라는 의미입니다.

해석 비평가들은 Pewter 센터에서의 강렬한 공연 후에 가수 Colin Wench에 대한 찬사에 대해 압도적으로 긍정적이었다.

어휘 overwhelmingly adv. 압도적으로 praise n. 찬사, 칭찬
performance n. 공연, 연주

09 유사의미 형용사 중에서 고르기

해설 '신입 직원들은 입문 회의에 참석해서 회사의 연혁에 대해 배울 것이다'라는 문맥이므로 형용사 (C) introductory(입문의, 서론의)가 정답입니다. (A) original도 '최초의, 원래의'라는 의미이지만, 무언가가 처음으로 만들어지거나 처음에 존재했던 것을 나타냅니다. (B) obvious는 '분명한, 확실한', (D) authentic은 '진짜인, 정확한'이라는 의미입니다.

해석 모든 신입 직원들은 입문 회의에 참석해서 회사의 연혁에 대해 배우고 시설을 견학할 것이다.

어휘 attend v. 참석하다, 다니다 history n. 연혁, 역사 tour v. 견학하다

10 형용사 어휘 고르기

해설 '디자인의 전통적인 기준과 뚜렷하게 다른 매우 혁신적인 결과를 만들어내다'라는 문맥이므로 형용사 (D) conventional(전통적인, 관습적인)이 정답입니다. (A) double은 '두 배의', (B) intense는 '강렬한', (C) voluntary는 '자발적인'이라는 의미입니다.

해석 Kaplan 건축사는 디자인의 전통적인 기준과 뚜렷하게 다른 매우 혁신적인 결과를 만들어내는 것으로 유명하다.

어휘 innovative adj. 혁신적인, 획기적인 differ v. 다르다
sharply adv. 뚜렷하게, 급격하게 standard n. 기준, 수준

DAY 12 [어휘] 형용사 3

토익 실전 문제 p.369

| 01 (D) | 02 (C) | 03 (B) | 04 (D) | 05 (B) |
| 06 (D) | 07 (B) | 08 (D) | 09 (A) | 10 (B) |

01 형용사 어휘 고르기

해설 '적절한 시간 내에 그들의 업무를 완료하다'라는 문맥이므로 형용사 (D) appropriate(적절한)이 정답입니다. (A) esteemed는 '존중받는, 호평받는', (B) undecided는 '정해지지 않은', (C) imaginary는 '가상의'라는 의미입니다.

해석 Ms. Morrell은 그녀의 직원들이 적절한 시간 내에 그들의 업무를 완료하기를 기대한다.

어휘 complete v. 완료하다, 완성하다 assignment n. 업무, 과제
time frame phr. 시간, 기간

02 형용사 어휘 고르기

해설 '퇴임하는 최고 경영자를 대신할 잠재적인 후보자를 찾다'라는 문맥이므로 형용사 (C) potential(잠재적인)이 정답입니다. (A) continuous는 '끊임없는, 연속적인', (B) adverse는 '반대의', (D) upcoming은 '다가오는'이라는 의미입니다.

해석 이사회는 퇴임하는 최고경영자 Charles Bayliss를 대신할 몇 명의 잠재적인 후보자를 찾았다.

어휘 identify v. 찾다, 확인하다 candidate n. 후보자, 지원자
replace v. 대신하다, 대체하다 outgoing adj. 퇴임하는, 떠나가는

03 형용사 어휘 고르기

해설 '온라인 후기를 읽는 것은 많은 소비자들이 제품들에 대해 아는 것이 매우 많아지도록 만들었다'라는 문맥이므로 형용사 (B) knowledgeable(아는 것이 많은, 총명한)이 정답입니다. (A) unconscious는 '무의식적인', (C) valuable은 '소중한'이라는 의미입니다. (D) impressive는 '인상적인, 감명 깊은'이라는 의미로 해석상 그럴듯해 보이지만, 소비자들이 깊은 인상을 준다는 문맥을 만들기 때문에 답이 될 수 없습니다.

해석 온라인 후기를 읽는 것은 많은 소비자들이 현재 시장에 나와 있는 제품들에 대해 아는 것이 매우 많아지도록 만들었다.

어휘 review n. 후기, 비평 consumer n. 소비자
extremely adv. 매우, 극히 currently adv. 현재
on the market phr. 시장에 나와 있는

04 형용사 어휘 고르기

해설 '시험 결과를 보고하는 데에 있어서 시간을 엄수하기 때문에 많은 의료 시설에 의해 이용된다'라는 문맥이므로 형용사 (D) punctual(시간을 엄수하는)이 정답입니다. (A) evident는 '(사실이나 상황 등이) 자명한', (B) undetermined는 '미결의, 결단을 못 내리는', (C) deficient는 '부족한, 결함 있는'이라는 의미입니다.

해석 Tristream 연구소는 시험 결과를 보고하는 데에 있어서 시간을 엄수하기 때문에 디트로이트의 많은 의료 시설에 의해 이용된다.

어휘 laboratory n. 연구소, 실험실 medical adj. 의료의, 의학의
result n. 결과, 결실

05 유사의미 형용사 중에서 고르기

해설 '가장 까다로운 수술 절차를 수행하는 것에도 도움이 될 수 있다'라는 문맥이므로 형용사 (B) delicate(까다로운, 다루기 어려운, 세심한)가 정답입니다. (C) cautious도 '주의하는, 조심스러운'이라는 의미이지만, 행동이나 생각이 조심스럽고 신중한 것을 나타냅니다. (A) perceptive는 '통찰력 있는', (D) noble은 '고귀한, 숭고한'이라는 의미입니다.

해석 고도로 진보한 로봇 장비는 의사들이 가장 까다로운 수술 절차를 수행하는 것에도 도움이 될 수 있다.

어휘 advanced adj. 진보한, 고급의 equipment n. 장비, 용품
surgical adj. 수술의, 외과의 procedure n. 절차, 방법

06 형용사 어휘 고르기

해설 '많은 숙고 후에 신중한 선택을 했다'라는 문맥이므로 형용사 (D) deliberate(신중한)이 정답입니다. (A) fragile은 '(물건 등이) 부서지기 쉬운', (B) vast는 '거대한', (C) sociable은 '사교적인'이라는 의미입니다.

해석 많은 숙고 후에, Tyvercorp사의 이사회는 해외에 있는 모든 지점들을 닫는다는 신중한 선택을 했다.

어휘 consideration n. 숙고, 고려 board of directors phr. 이사회
overseas adj. 해외에 있는, 외국의

07 형용사 어휘 고르기

해설 '모든 백열전구는 에너지 사용에 관한 한 좀 더 효율적인 것으로 교체될 것이다'라는 문맥이므로 형용사 (B) efficient(효율적인)가 정답입니다. (A) pleasurable은 '즐거운', (C) decent는 '품위 있는', (D) hospitable은 '친절한, 환대하는'이라는 의미입니다.

해석 사무실에 있는 모든 백열전구는 에너지 사용에 관한 한 좀 더 효율적인 것으로 교체될 것이다.

어휘 light bulb phr. 백열전구
when it comes to phr. ~에 관한 한, ~에 대해서라면

08 형용사 어휘 고르기

해설 '국내에서 가장 오래된 신문 중 하나로서 대부분의 사람들에 의해 신뢰할 수 있는 정보의 출처로 여겨진다'라는 문맥이므로 형용사 (D) reliable(신뢰할 수 있는, 믿을 만한)이 정답입니다. (A) reluctant는 '꺼리는, 마지못한'이라는 의미입니다. (B) reliant는 '의존하는, 의지하는'이라는 의미로 해석상 그럴듯해 보이지만, 정보의 출처가 무엇에 의존/의지한다는 문맥을 만들기 때문에 답이 될 수 없습니다. (C) relative는 '관계 있는, 상대적인'이라는 의미입니다.

해석 국내에서 가장 오래된 신문 중 하나로서, *The Porter Gazette*지는 대부분의 사람들에 의해 신뢰할 수 있는 정보의 출처로 여겨진다.

어휘 newspaper n. 신문, 신문지 source n. 출처, 원천

09 형용사 어휘 고르기

해설 '이번 분기 장려금 보너스는 2주분의 급여에 상당했다'라는 문맥이므로 형용사 (A) equivalent(상당하는, 동등한)가 정답입니다. (B) average는 '평균인, 보통의', (C) advantageous는 '유리한, 이로운', (D) composed는 '구성된'이라는 의미입니다.

해석 Ms. Bloom의 이번 분기 장려금 보너스는 2주분의 급여에 상당했다.

어휘 quarter n. 분기, 4분의 1 pay n. 급여, 보수

10 형용사 어휘 고르기

해설 '회의실 수리에 예상 밖의 지연에 대해 사과하다'라는 문맥이므로 형용사 (B) unanticipated(예상 밖의)가 정답입니다. (A) accurate는 '정확한', (C) advisory는 '자문의', (D) optional은 '선택적인'이라는 의미입니다.

해석 건설 회사는 회의실 수리에 예상 밖의 지연에 대해 사과하기 위해 Mr. Harper에게 전화했다.

어휘 construction n. 건설, 공사 apologize v. 사과하다, 사죄하다
delay n. 지연, 연기 renovation n. 수리, 수선

DAY 13 [어휘] 형용사 4

토익 실전 문제   p.371

01 (B)	02 (B)	03 (A)	04 (D)	05 (A)
06 (B)	07 (C)	08 (C)	09 (D)	10 (C)

01 형용사 어휘 고르기

해설 '주가는 상당한 액수가 하락했다'라는 문맥이므로 형용사 (B) substantial(상당한, 튼튼한)이 정답입니다. (A) vague는 '모호한', (C) selective는 '선택하는, 까다로운', (D) frequent는 '잦은, 빈번한'이라는 의미입니다.

해석 HRS 은행의 주가는 좋지 않은 분기별 실적을 발표한 다음 날에 상당한 액수가 하락했다.

어휘 value n. 가치; v. 가치 있게 여기다 stock n. 주식, 재고
decrease v. 하락하다, 감소하다 amount n. 액수, 양
quarterly adj. 분기별의 result n. 실적, 성적, 결과

02 형용사 어휘 고르기

해설 '몇 달간의 성실한 노력 후에 첫 번째 온라인 회사를 설립할 수 있었다'라는 문맥이므로 형용사 (B) diligent(성실한, 부지런한)가 정답입니다. (A) tender는 '다정한, 부드러운', (C) remote는 '먼, 동떨어진', (D) capable은 '유능한, 능력 있는'이라는 의미입니다.

해석 몇 달간의 성실한 노력 후에, Ms. Parker는 그녀의 첫 번째 온라인 회사를 설립할 수 있었다.

어휘 effort n. 노력, 수고 set up phr. 설립하다, 수립하다
business n. 회사, 사업

03 형용사 어휘 고르기

해설 '문서 정리원으로서의 자신의 직업이 따분하다고 생각했다'라는 문맥이므로 형용사 (A) mundane(따분한, 일상적인)이 정답입니다. (B) confident는 '자신감 있는', (C) sensational은 '선풍적인', (D) duplicate는 '사본의, 똑같은'이라는 의미입니다.

해석 Mr. Jensen은 문서 정리원으로서의 자신의 직업이 따분하다고 생각했고 보다 성취감을 주는 직업을 구하기로 결정했다.

어휘 filing clerk phr. 문서 정리원 look for phr. ~을 구하다, ~을 찾다
fulfilling adj. 성취감을 주는

04 형용사 어휘 고르기

해설 '모든 지원자들 중에서 선호되는 후보자였다'라는 문맥이므로 형용사 (D) preferred(선호되는, 우선의)가 정답입니다. (A) rewarding은 '보람 있는, 보답하는', (B) exhibited는 '공개된, 전시된', (C) comparable은 '비슷한, 비교할 만한'이라는 의미입니다.

해석 모든 지원자들 중에서, Mr. Nolan은 그 직무에 선호되는 후보자였다.

어휘 applicant n. 지원자, 신청자 candidate n. 후보자, 지원자

05 형용사 어휘 고르기

해설 '엄격한 규정들이 누리는 것을 방해하다'라는 문맥이므로 형용사 (A) rigorous(엄격한, 철저한)가 정답입니다. (B) cooperative는 '협력하는, 협조하는', (C) productive는 '생산적인', (D) durable은 '오래가는, 내구성이 있는'이라는 의미입니다.

해석 주민들은 국립 공원의 엄격한 규정들이 그들이 그 지역을 누리는 것을 방해한다고 항의했다.

어휘 resident n. 주민, 거주자 complain v. 항의하다, 불평하다
national park phr. 국립 공원 regulation n. 규정, 규제
prevent v. 방해하다, 예방하다

06 유사의미 형용사 중에서 고르기

해설 '청구서의 금액을 제시간에 지불하지 못한 고객들은 늦은 납입에 대한 연체료의 대상이 될 것이다'라는 문맥이므로 형용사 (B) late(늦은)가 정답입니다. (D) recent(최근의)는 기간이 얼마 지나지 않은 과거를 의미합니다. (A) financial은 '재정적인', (C) reasonable은 '합리적인'이라는 의미입니다.

해석 청구서의 금액을 제시간에 지불하지 못한 고객들은 늦은 납입에 대한 연체료의 대상이 될 것이다.

어휘 fail v. ~하지 못하다, 실패하다 bill n. 청구서
be subject to phr. ~의 대상이다 fine n. 연체료, 벌금
payment n. 납입

07 형용사 어휘 고르기

해설 '연구가 중요한 신약 개발로 이어질 수 있기 때문에 전망이 밝다'라는 문맥이므로 형용사 (C) promising(전망이 밝은, 유망한)이 정답입니다. (A) visible은 '눈에 보이는, 명백한', (B) revolving은 '회전하는', (D) preliminary는 '예비의'라는 의미입니다.

해석 HL 연구소의 연구는 중요한 신약 개발로 이어질 수 있기 때문에 전망이 밝다.

어휘 lead v. 이어지다, 이끌다 development n. 개발 medication n. 약

08 형용사 어휘 고르기

해설 '특정한 1차 작물들은 기상 상태에 매우 민감하다'라는 문맥이므로 형용사 (C) sensitive(민감한, 예민한)가 정답입니다. (A) coherent는 '일관성 있는, 논리 정연한', (B) applicable은 '해당되는, ~에 적용할 수 있는', (D) mature는 '성숙한, 숙성한'이라는 의미입니다.

해석 설탕을 포함하여, 특정한 1차 작물들은 장기적인 가뭄과 같은 기상 상태에 매우 민감하다.

어휘 certain adj. 특정한, 확실한 commodity n. 1차 상품, 필수품 crop n. 작물, 수확물 prolonged adj. 장기적인, 연장하는 drought n. 가뭄, 고갈

09 형용사 어휘 고르기

해설 '매출액이 이전의 모든 기록들을 깼을 때 그것은 분석가들의 예상을 넘은 것이었다'라는 문맥이므로 형용사 (D) previous(이전의)가 정답입니다. (A) imminent는 '임박한, 절박한', (B) conclusive는 '(의심할 여지 없이) 결정적인, 단호한', (C) massive는 '거대한, 대규모의'라는 의미입니다.

해석 FGP Group사의 첫 번째 분기 매출액이 이전의 모든 기록들을 깼을 때 그것은 분석가들의 예상을 넘은 것이었다.

어휘 sales n. 매출액, 매상 exceed v. 넘다, 초과하다, 초월하다 expectation n. 예상, 기대 analyst n. 분석가 break a record phr. 기록을 깨다

10 형용사 어휘 고르기

해설 '음식들이 꽤 맛있지만 너무 비싸다'라는 문맥이므로 형용사 (C) overpriced(너무 비싼)가 정답입니다. (A) indirect는 '간접적인', (B) active는 '활동적인, 적극적인', (D) liberal은 '관대한, 진보적인'이라는 의미입니다.

해석 비록 El Señor에서 제공되는 음식들은 꽤 맛있지만, 그곳이 있는 지역에서는 너무 비싸다.

어휘 serve v. 제공하다 neighborhood n. 지역, 인근

DAY 14 [어휘] 부사 1

토익 실전 문제
p.373

01 (C)	02 (C)	03 (D)	04 (C)	05 (C)
06 (A)	07 (D)	08 (A)	09 (A)	10 (B)

01 부사 어휘 고르기

해설 '마지막 몇 페이지가 의도적으로 비어 있다'라는 문맥이므로 부사 (C) intentionally(의도적으로, 고의로)가 정답입니다. (A) fluently는 '유창하게, 우아하게', (B) incorrectly는 '부정확하게, 부적절하게', (D) casually는 '우연히, 약식으로'라는 의미입니다.

해석 Jones Brothers 백화점의 교육용 안내 책자의 마지막 몇 페이지는 필기를 위해 의도적으로 비어 있다.

어휘 department store phr. 백화점 manual n. 안내 책자, 안내서 blank adj. 비어 있는; n. 빈칸, 여백 note-taking n. 필기

02 부사 어휘 고르기

해설 '배달원들은 종종 접수처에 소포를 갖다 놓는다'라는 문맥이므로 부사 (C) occasionally(종종, 가끔)가 정답입니다. (A) virtually는 '사실상, 실질적으로', (B) initially는 '처음에, 원래', (D) publicly는 '공개적으로, 공식적으로'라는 의미입니다.

해석 배달원들은 종종 접수처에 소포를 갖다 놓지만 수령인이 부재중일 때에만 그렇게 한다.

어휘 drop off phr. 갖다 놓다, 내려놓다 package n. 소포 reception desk phr. 접수처, 프런트 recipient n. 수령인, 수취인 unavailable adj. 부재의, 이용할 수 없는

03 부사 어휘 고르기

해설 '훌륭하게 꾸며진 연립 주택을 둘러보도록 안내했다'라는 문맥이므로 부사 (D) superbly(훌륭하게, 최고로, 최상으로)가 정답입니다. (A) vacantly는 '멍하니, 공허하게', (B) consequently는 '그 결과, 따라서', (C) jealously는 '질투하여, 빈틈없이'라는 의미입니다.

해석 Gulfstate Homes의 부동산 중개인은 몇 명의 잠재적인 구매자들이 훌륭하게 꾸며진 연립 주택을 둘러보도록 안내했다.

어휘 real estate agent phr. 부동산 중개인 show A around B phr. A가 B를 둘러보도록 안내하다 townhouse n. 연립 주택

04 부사 어휘 고르기

해설 '컨설턴트는 생산성이 향상될 것이라고 정확하게 예측했다'라는 문맥이므로 부사 (C) accurately(정확하게, 정밀하게)가 정답입니다. (A) inconclusively는 '결론을 내지 못하고, 결론 없이', (B) commonly는 '흔히', (D) vastly는 '광대하게, 크게'라는 의미입니다.

해석 컨설턴트는 새로운 사무실 시스템 덕분에 JN사의 생산성이 향상될 것이라고 정확하게 예측했다.

어휘 predict v. 예측하다, 예견하다 productivity n. 생산성, 생산력 improve v. 향상되다, 개선되다

05 부사 어휘 고르기

해설 '많은 주식들을 유심히 지켜본다'라는 문맥이므로 부사 (C) closely(유심히, 면밀히)가 정답입니다. (A) expensively는 '비싸게, 비용을 들여', (B) accidentally는 '우연히, 잘못하여', (D) rightly는 '올바르게, 당연히'라는 의미입니다.

해석 Mr. Roberts는 어떠한 가격의 변동이라도 추적 관찰하기 위해 많은 주식들을 유심히 지켜본다.

어휘 follow v. 지켜보다, 뒤를 잇다 stock n. 주식, 재고 monitor v. 추적 관찰하다, 모니터하다 fluctuation n. 변동, 오르내림

06 유사의미 부사 중에서 고르기

해설 '보고서를 작업하는 것을 즉시 시작하라고 지시받았다'라는 문맥이므로 부사 (A) immediately(즉시, 즉각)가 정답입니다. (C) briefly도 '잠시, 간략하게'라는 의미이지만, 무언가가 아주 짧은 기간 동안 일어나는 것을 가리키거나, 상황이나 사실을 요약하여 간단하고 짧게 나타낼 때 쓰입니다. (B) clearly는 '분명히, 알기 쉽게', (D) seemingly는 '외관상으로, 겉보기에'라는 의미입니다.

해석 이번 주 말까지가 기한이기 때문에 Ms. Hymer는 고객 만족도 보고서를 작업하는 것을 즉시 시작하라고 지시받았다.

어휘 satisfaction n. 만족, 충족 due adj. 만기의, 지불 기일이 된

07 부사 어휘 고르기

해설 '저녁에 서서히 맑아질 것이다'라는 문맥이므로 부사 (D) gradually

(서서히, 차츰)가 정답입니다. (A) knowingly는 '고의로, 빈틈없이', (B) internally는 '내부에, 내면적으로', (C) smoothly는 '부드럽게, 순조롭게'라는 의미입니다.

해석 일기 예보관들은 오후 내내 하늘에 구름이 낄 것이지만 그리고 나서 저녁에 서서히 맑아질 것이라고 말한다.

어휘 weather forecaster phr. 일기 예보관 cloudy adj. 구름이 낀, 흐린

08 부사 어휘 고르기

해설 '가치는 현저하게 하락한다'라는 문맥이므로 부사 (A) markedly(현저하게, 두드러지게)가 정답입니다. (B) strictly는 '엄격하게, 철저하게', (C) densely는 '밀집하여, 짙게', (D) independently는 '독립적으로'라는 의미입니다.

해석 새 자동차의 가치는 첫 번째 소유주에 의해 사용된 후에 현저하게 하락한다.

어휘 automobile n. 자동차

09 부사 어휘 고르기

해설 '고객으로부터 일상적으로 하루에 수백 통의 전화를 받는다'라는 문맥이므로 부사 (A) routinely(일상적으로)가 정답입니다. (B) severely는 '심하게', (C) carefully는 '조심스럽게', (D) securely는 '단단히'라는 의미입니다.

해석 Sensenet사의 지원 센터는 기술적인 문제를 다루며 고객으로부터 일상적으로 하루에 수백 통의 전화를 받는다.

어휘 handle v. 다루다 technical adj. 기술적인 receive v. 받다

10 부사 어휘 고르기

해설 '화재 경보 작동은 단지 훈련의 일부였다'라는 문맥이므로 부사 (B) merely(단지, 그저)가 정답입니다. (A) supremely는 '극도로, 대단하게', (C) openly는 '공개적으로, 공공연히', (D) solidly는 '견고하게, 단결하여'라는 의미입니다.

해석 Wentfield 타워에서의 화재 경보 작동은 단지 훈련의 일부였다는 것이 나중에 밝혀졌다.

어휘 reveal v. 밝히다, 폭로하다 activation n. 작동, 활성화 fire alarm phr. 화재 경보 drill n. 훈련, 연습

DAY 15 [어휘] 부사 2

토익 실전 문제
p.375

| 01 (A) | 02 (A) | 03 (C) | 04 (D) | 05 (B) |
| 06 (A) | 07 (C) | 08 (A) | 09 (B) | 10 (C) |

01 부사 어휘 고르기

해설 '정기적으로 직원들에게 설문지를 작성할 것을 요청한다'라는 문맥이므로 부사 (A) periodically(정기적으로, 주기적으로)가 정답입니다. (C) rigidly는 '엄격하게, 단호하게'라는 의미로 해석상 그럴듯해 보이지만, 쉽게 의견을 굽히지 않거나 태도 또는 생각을 바꾸지 않는다는 것을 나타냅니다. (B) significantly는 '상당히, 크게', (D) truthfully는 '정직하게, 참되게'라는 의미입니다.

해석 Hooper Tech사는 직업 만족도 수준을 평가하기 위해 정기적으로 직원들에게 설문지를 작성할 것을 요청한다.

어휘 complete v. 작성하다, 완료하다 survey n. 설문지, 설문 조사 assess v. 평가하다, 가늠하다 satisfaction n. 만족, 충족

02 부사 어휘 고르기

해설 '회사의 성공이 이전 최고 경영자에 의해 이루어진 기여와 밀접하게 관련되어 있다'라는 문맥이므로 부사 (A) inseparably(밀접하게, 불가분하게)가 정답입니다. (B) accidentally는 '우연히, 잘못하여', (C) artificially는 '인위적으로', (D) repeatedly는 '되풀이하여, 여러 차례'라는 의미입니다.

해석 Averco사 직원들의 생각 속에는, 회사의 성공이 이전 최고 경영자에 의해 이루어진 기여와 밀접하게 관련되어 있다.

어휘 success n. 성공, 성과 link v. 관련시키다, 연결시키다 contribution n. 기여, 공헌 former adj. 이전의

03 유사의미 부사 중에서 고르기

해설 '기온은 일반적으로 3월이 되어서야 오르기 시작한다'라는 문맥이므로 부사 (C) generally(일반적으로, 대체로)가 정답입니다. (A) totally는 '완전히, 모두'라는 의미이지만, 무언가가 절대적이거나 정도가 최고치라는 것을 나타냅니다. (B) deliberately는 '의도적으로, 고의로', (D) conditionally는 '조건부로, 가정적으로'라는 의미입니다.

해석 기온은 일반적으로 3월이 되어서야 오르기 시작하지만, 올해는 봄이 일찍 온 것 같다.

어휘 temperature n. 기온, 온도 rise v. 오르다, 올라가다 appear v. ~인 것 같다, 나타나다

04 부사 어휘 고르기

해설 '기한 전에 프로젝트를 거의 완료하지 못했다'라는 문맥이므로 부사 (D) barely(거의 ~하지 못한)가 정답입니다. (A) calmly는 '고요하게, 침착하게', (B) extremely는 '극도로', (C) gratefully는 '감사하여, 기꺼이'라는 의미입니다.

해석 업무가 너무 많아서 그 팀은 기한 전에 프로젝트를 거의 완료하지 못했다.

05 부사 어휘 고르기

해설 '기부된 자금은 오직 명시된 활동들을 위해서만 쓰여야 한다'라는 문맥이므로 부사 (B) exclusively(오직 ~만, 독점적으로)가 정답입니다. (A) impressively는 '인상적으로, 인상 깊게', (C) reluctantly는 '마지못해, 싫어하며', (D) decently는 '점잖게, 단정하게'라는 의미입니다.

해석 기부된 자금은 오직 명시된 활동들을 위해서만 쓰여야 하고 다른 목적을 위해서는 쓰일 수 없다.

어휘 donate v. 기부하다 fund n. 자금 specified adj. 명시된 activity n. 활동 purpose n. 목적

06 부사 어휘 고르기

해설 '교통 법규를 정확하게 따르는 운전자들이 훨씬 더 적은 사고를 겪는다'라는 문맥이므로 부사 (A) precisely(정확하게, 신중하게)가 정답입니다. (B) outwardly는 '겉으로는, 외부적으로', (C) tentatively는 '잠정적으로', (D) courteously는 '예의 바르게, 친절하게'라는 의미입니다.

해석 연구들은 교통 법규를 정확하게 따르는 운전자들이 그렇지 않은 사람들보다 훨씬 더 적은 사고를 겪는다는 것을 밝혀냈다.

어휘 study n. 연구, 공부 follow v. 따르다, 따라가다 traffic rule phr. 교통 법규 accident n. 사고, 재해

07 부사 어휘 고르기

해설 'Ms. Knight는 기념일 연회를 준비하는 것에 대해 대부분의 책임을 지고 있었다'라는 문맥이므로 부사 (C) largely(대부분, 주로)가 정답입니다. (A) gently는 '다정하게, 부드럽게', (B) slightly는 '약간', (D) plentifully는 '많이, 풍부하게'라는 의미입니다.

해석 비록 몇몇 지원자들이 그녀를 도와주기는 했지만, Ms. Knight는 기념일 연회를 준비하는 것에 대해 대부분의 책임을 지고 있었다.

어휘 volunteer n. 지원자, 자원봉사자 responsible adj. ~을 책임지고 있는, ~의 원인인

organize v. 준비하다, 조직하다 **anniversary** n. 기념일
banquet n. 연회, 축하연

08 부사 어휘 고르기

해설 '모든 신용카드 청구서의 금액을 정확히 제시간에 납부하는 것이 권장된다'라는 문맥이므로 부사 (A) promptly(정확히 제시간에, 지체없이)가 정답입니다. (B) primarily는 '주로, 원래', (C) financially는 '재정적으로, 재정상', (D) temporarily는 '일시적으로, 임시로'라는 의미입니다.

해석 연체료를 피하려면 모든 신용카드 청구서의 금액을 정확히 제시간에 납부하는 것이 권장된다.

어휘 **advisable** adj. 권장할 만한, 타당한 **bill** n. 청구서, 계산서
avoid v. 피하다, 막다 **late charge** phr. 연체료

09 부사 어휘 고르기

해설 '더 많은 직원들을 고용하는 것은 우선순위 목록에서 상대적으로 상위에 있다'라는 문맥이므로 부사 (B) relatively(상대적으로, 비교적)가 정답입니다. (A) successfully는 '성공적으로, 용케', (C) separately는 '따로따로, 별개로', (D) expertly는 '전문적으로, 훌륭하게'라는 의미입니다.

해석 더 많은 직원들을 고용하는 것은 우리의 우선순위 목록에서 상대적으로 상위에 있으므로 곧 면접이 있을 것이다.

어휘 **hire** v. 고용하다, 빌리다 **priority** n. 우선순위, 우선 사항
hold v. (회의, 시합 등을) 열다, 보유하다

10 부사 어휘 고르기

해설 '골프장을 건설하는 것은 불필요하며 그 자금은 다른 곳에 쓰여야 한다'라는 문맥이므로 부사 (C) elsewhere(다른 곳에서, 다른 경우에)가 정답입니다. (A) excessively는 '심히, 지나치게', (B) sometimes는 '가끔, 때때로', (D) considerably는 '상당히, 많이'라는 의미입니다.

해석 Valeville 주민들은 도시에 골프장을 건설하는 것은 불필요하며 그 자금은 다른 곳에 쓰여야 한다고 생각한다.

어휘 **resident** n. 주민, 거주자 **unnecessary** adj. 불필요한, 쓸데없는
fund n. 자금, 기금 **spend** v. (돈을) 쓰다, (시간을) 들이다

DAY 16 [어휘] 부사 3

토익 실전 문제

p.377

| 01 (D) | 02 (B) | 03 (C) | 04 (C) | 05 (A) |
| 06 (B) | 07 (C) | 08 (D) | 09 (A) | 10 (D) |

01 부사 어휘 고르기

해설 '이전에 Second Street 식료품 잡화점이라고 불렸던 Melman's 슈퍼마켓'이라는 문맥이므로 부사 (D) formerly(이전에, 예전에)가 정답입니다. (A) distinctly는 '뚜렷하게', (B) strictly는 '엄격하게', (C) regularly는 '규칙적으로'라는 의미입니다.

해석 이전에 Second Street 식료품 잡화점이라고 불렸던 Melman's 슈퍼마켓은 그 도시에서 신선한 과일과 채소의 가장 큰 공급업체이다.

어휘 **supplier** n. 공급업체 **fresh** adj. 신선한

02 유사의미 부사 중에서 고르기

해설 '개인 컴퓨터가 최초로 소개된 이후 엄청난 기술의 진보가 이루어져왔다'라는 문맥이므로 부사 (B) first(최초로)가 정답입니다. (D) once는 '한 번, 이전에'라는 의미이지만, 어떠한 사건이나 행동 등이 한 번만 일어나거나, 과거의 언젠가를 나타냅니다. (A) always는 '항상', (C)

lately는 '최근에'라는 의미입니다.

해석 수십 년 전에 개인 컴퓨터가 최초로 소개된 이후 엄청난 기술의 진보가 이루어져 왔다.

어휘 **stride** n. 진보 **personal** adj. 개인의 **decade** n. 10년

03 부사 어휘 고르기

해설 '계획했던 것보다 상당히 더 오래 지속되었다'라는 문맥이므로 부사 (C) considerably(상당히, 훨씬)가 정답입니다. (A) readily는 '손쉽게', (B) carelessly는 '부주의하게', (D) traditionally는 '전통적으로'라는 의미입니다.

해석 Ms. Sullivan의 은퇴 연설은 그녀가 계획했던 것보다 상당히 더 오래 지속되었는데 이는 그녀가 그렇게 많은 박수갈채를 받으리라고 기대하지 않았기 때문이다.

어휘 **retirement** n. 은퇴 **applause** n. 박수갈채

04 부사 어휘 고르기

해설 '보고서는 전부 독일어로 쓰여 있었다'라는 문맥이므로 부사 (C) entirely(전부, 완전히)가 정답입니다. (A) deeply는 '깊게', (B) honestly는 '솔직히, 정말로', (D) continually는 '계속적으로'라는 의미입니다.

해석 보고서는 전부 독일어로 쓰여 있어서, Ms. Vine은 그것을 번역시킬 필요가 있었다.

어휘 **translate** v. 번역하다

05 부사 어휘 고르기

해설 '비록 신발이 알맞게 잘 맞았지만, 구매하지 않기로 했다'라는 문맥이므로 부사 (A) reasonably(알맞게, 적절히)가 정답입니다. (B) constantly는 '지속적으로', (C) previously는 '이전에', (D) numerously는 '수없이 많이'라는 의미입니다.

해석 비록 신발이 알맞게 잘 맞았지만, Mr. Perkins는 그것을 구매하지 않기로 했다.

어휘 **fit** v. 잘 맞다

06 부사 어휘 고르기

해설 '있을 것이라고 생각했던 바로 그곳에서 발견되었다'라는 문맥이므로 부사 (B) exactly(바로, 정확히, 틀림없이)가 정답입니다. (A) frankly는 '솔직하게', (C) mostly는 '대부분', (D) sharply는 '급격하게, 날카롭게'라는 의미입니다.

해석 Mr. Hawthorne의 잃어버린 지갑은 그가 그것이 있을 것이라고 생각했던 바로 그곳에서 발견되었다.

어휘 **missing** adj. 잃어버린 **find** v. 발견하다

07 부사 어휘 고르기

해설 '일반적으로 주말에는 일하지 않지만 아픈 동료를 대신하기 위해 근무를 했다'라는 문맥이므로 부사 (C) typically(일반적으로, 전형적으로)가 정답입니다. (A) utterly는 '완전히'라는 의미로 해석상 그럴듯해 보이지만, 정도나 양이 최대라는 것을 나타냅니다. (B) correctly는 '바르게', (D) potentially는 '잠재적으로'라는 의미입니다.

해석 Ms. Rivers는 일반적으로 주말에는 일하지 않지만 아픈 동료를 대신하기 위해 토요일 교대 근무를 했다.

어휘 **shift** n. 교대 근무 **fill in for** phr. ~를 대신하다

08 부사 어휘 고르기

해설 '음식이 과도하게 양념이 되었다고 불평하곤 했었다'라는 문맥이므로 부사 (D) overly(과도하게, 지나치게)가 정답입니다. (A) secretly는 '비밀스럽게', (B) gladly는 '기쁘게', (C) purposefully는 '목적의식이 있게'라는 의미입니다.

해석 손님들이 Mamma Mia의 음식이 과도하게 양념이 되었다고 불평하곤

했었지만, 그들은 이제 그것이 너무 밍밍하다고 말한다.

어휘 diner n. 손님들 seasoned adj. 양념을 한
bland adj. 밍밍한, 자극적이지 않은

09 부사 어휘 고르기

해설 '주차 공간이 빠르게 가득 찰 것이니 일찍 도착해달라'라는 문맥이
므로 부사 (A) rapidly(빠르게, 급속히)가 정답입니다. (B) rarely는
'드물게', (C) belatedly는 '늦게, 시대에 뒤지게', (D) curiously는
'신기한 듯이'라는 의미입니다.

해석 주차 공간이 빠르게 가득 찰 것이니, 반드시 아침 일찍 회의 장소에 도
착해주십시오.

어휘 parking spot phr. 주차 공간 conference n. 회의
venue n. (행사 등의) 장소

10 부사 어휘 고르기

해설 '궂은 날씨는 음악 축제의 취소를 초래할 뻔했다'라는 문맥이므로 부사
(D) nearly(~할 뻔하다, 거의)가 정답입니다. (A) perfectly는 '완벽하
게', (B) realistically는 '현실적으로', (C) majorly는 '주로'라는 의미
입니다.

해석 궂은 날씨는 공원에서 하는 신시내티의 다가오는 음악 축제의 취소를
초래할 뻔했다.

어휘 inclement adj. (날씨가) 궂은 cancelation n. 취소

DAY 17 [어구] 형용사 관련 어구

토익 실전 문제　　　　　　　　　　　　　　p.379

01 (B)	02 (D)	03 (C)	04 (D)	05 (A)
06 (D)	07 (C)	08 (B)	09 (A)	10 (C)

01 형용사 관련 어구 완성하기

해설 '무료 배송을 받을 자격이 있을 것이다'라는 의미가 되어야 하므로 빈
칸 앞과 뒤의 be, to와 함께 '~할 자격이 있다'라는 의미의 어구인 be
eligible to를 만드는 형용사 (B) eligible(자격이 있는)이 정답입니
다. (A) complimentary는 '무료의', (C) standard는 '표준의', (D)
productive는 '생산적인'이라는 의미입니다.

해석 Thompson사의 온라인 세일 동안 100달러 이상을 쓰는 고객들은 무
료 배송을 받을 자격이 있을 것이다.

어휘 free shipping phr. 무료 배송

02 형용사 관련 어구 완성하기

해설 '기본적인 웹 서핑과 이메일 보내기에는 적합하다'라는 의미가 되어야
하므로 빈칸 앞과 뒤의 is, for와 함께 '~에 적합하다'라는 의미의 어
구인 be adequate for를 만드는 형용사 (D) adequate(적합한, 충분
한)가 정답입니다. (A) elaborate는 '정교한', (B) skilled는 '숙련된',
(C) unable은 '~할 수 없는'이라는 의미입니다.

해석 VTV 인터넷의 가장 덜 비싼 서비스는 기본적인 웹 서핑과 이메일 보내
기에는 적합하지만, 비디오 다운로드에는 그렇지 않다.

어휘 costly adj. 비싼

03 형용사 관련 어구 완성하기

해설 '정부의 승인을 부여받았기 때문에 수입세가 면제된다'라는 의미가 되
어야 하므로 빈칸 앞과 뒤의 is, from과 함께 '~이 면제되다'라는 의미
의 어구인 be exempt from을 만드는 형용사 (C) exempt(면제된)
가 정답입니다. (A) fulfilled는 '충실한', (B) unique는 '독특한', (D)

proper는 '적절한'이라는 의미입니다.

해석 정부의 승인을 부여받았기 때문에, Grayson & Kline사는 수입세가 면
제된다.

어휘 grant v. 부여하다 consent n. 승인, 동의 import n. 수입
tax n. 세금

04 형용사 관련 어구 완성하기

해설 '추정상 그들이 어겼다는 환경법을 알지 못했다'라는 의미가 되어야 하
므로 빈칸 앞과 뒤의 was, of와 함께 '~을 알지 못하다'라는 의미의 어
구인 be unaware of를 만드는 형용사 (D) unaware(알지 못하는)가
정답입니다. (A) unanimous는 '만장일치의', (B) absolute는 '완전
한', (C) negative는 '부정적인'이라는 의미입니다.

해석 Santos Industries사는 추정상 그들이 어겼다는 환경법을 알지 못했다
고 주장했다.

어휘 claim v. 주장하다 supposedly adv. 추정상, 아마
break v. (규칙 등을) 어기다

05 형용사 관련 어구 완성하기

해설 '주가 또한 올라갈 것 같다'라는 의미가 되어야 하므로 빈칸 앞과 뒤의
is, to와 함께 '~할 것 같다'라는 의미의 어구인 be likely to를 만드는
형용사 (A) likely(~할 것 같은, 그럴듯한)가 정답입니다. (B) detailed
는 '자세한', (C) slight는 '약간의', (D) active는 '활발한'이라는 의
미입니다.

해석 만약 천연가스에 대한 수요가 증가한다면, 그것을 생산하는 회사의 주
가 또한 올라갈 것 같다.

어휘 stock value phr. 주가 rise v. 올라가다

06 형용사 관련 어구 완성하기

해설 'EZ-Grabs사의 편의점 직원들은 저녁 교대 근무를 할 용의가 있어야
한다'라는 의미가 되어야 하므로 빈칸 앞과 뒤의 be, to와 함께 '~할
용의가 있다'라는 의미의 어구인 be willing to를 만드는 형용사 (D)
willing(기꺼이 하는)이 정답입니다. (A) lasting은 '지속하는', (B)
ongoing은 '계속 진행 중인', (C) similar는 '비슷한'이라는 의미입
니다.

해석 EZ-Grabs사의 편의점 직원들은 때때로 저녁 교대 근무를 할 용의가 있
어야 한다.

어휘 convenience store phr. 편의점 shift n. 교대 근무
on occasion phr. 때때로, 가끔

07 형용사 관련 어구 완성하기

해설 '과태료의 대상이다'라는 의미가 되어야 하므로 빈칸 앞과 뒤의 are,
to와 함께 '~의 대상이다'라는 의미의 어구인 be subject to를 만드
는 형용사 (C) subject(~될 수 있는)가 정답입니다. (A) worthy는 '가
치 있는', (B) questionable은 '의심스러운', (D) important는 '중요
한'이라는 의미입니다.

해석 안전 수칙을 준수하지 못한 음식 공급업체들은 과태료의 대상이며 주
의 식품 감사원에 의한 폐점 가능성이 있다.

어휘 follow v. 준수하다, 지키다 closure n. 폐점, 폐쇄
inspection board phr. 감사원

08 형용사 관련 어구 완성하기

해설 '새로운 영화를 틀림없이 볼 것이다'라는 의미가 되어야 하므로 빈
칸 앞과 뒤의 are, to와 함께 '틀림없이 ~할 것이다'라는 의미의 어
구인 be bound to를 만드는 형용사 (B) bound(~할 가능성이 큰)가
정답입니다. (A) impartial은 '공정한', (C) serious는 '진지한', (D)
absent는 '결석한'이라는 의미입니다.

해석 *Ghost Hunter* 영화 시리즈의 오랜 팬들은 이번 주에 영화관에서 새
로운 영화를 틀림없이 볼 것이다.

어휘 **longtime** adj. 오랜, 오랫동안의

09 형용사 관련 어구 완성하기

해설 '연간 회계 감사와 관련된 모든 기록'이라는 의미가 되어야 하므로 빈 칸 앞과 뒤의 were, to와 함께 '~과 관련 있다'라는 의미의 어구인 be pertinent to를 만드는 형용사 (A) pertinent(관련 있는)가 정답 입니다. (B) patient는 '참을성 있는', (C) precious는 '귀중한', (D) pleased는 '기쁜, 기뻐하는'이라는 의미입니다.

해석 회계팀은 부서 사무관에게 연간 회계 감사와 관련된 모든 재정적인 기 록을 모을 것을 요청했다.

어휘 **accounting team** phr. 회계 팀 **annual audit** phr. 연간 회계 감사

10 형용사 관련 어구 완성하기

해설 '고품질이면서 합리적으로 가격이 매겨진 LED 텔레비전 제조에 전념 한다'라는 의미가 되어야 하므로 빈칸 앞과 뒤의 is, to와 함께 '~에 전 념하다'라는 의미의 어구인 be dedicated to를 만드는 형용사 (C) dedicated(전념하는)가 정답입니다. (A) exclusive는 '독점적인', (B) duplicate는 '복제의, 똑같은', (D) concentrated는 '집중적인'이라 는 의미입니다.

해석 Fanli Electronics사는 고품질이면서 합리적으로 가격이 매겨진 LED 텔레비전 제조에 전념한다.

어휘 **manufacture** n. 제조; v. 제조하다
reasonably adv. 합리적으로, 타당하게 **priced** adj. 값이 붙은

DAY 18 [어구] 동사 관련 어구

토익 실전 문제

p.381

| 01 (C) | 02 (D) | 03 (D) | 04 (A) | 05 (B) |
| 06 (A) | 07 (A) | 08 (B) | 09 (D) | 10 (D) |

01 동사 관련 어구 완성하기

해설 '시계를 고급 보석류와 관련시켜 생각하게 만드는 것이다'라는 문맥이 므로 빈칸 뒤의 전치사 with와 함께 'A를 B와 관련시켜 생각하다'라 는 의미의 어구인 associate A with B를 만드는 동사 (C) associate (관련시켜 생각하다)가 정답입니다. (A) appreciate는 '인정하다', (B) cooperate는 '협력하다', (D) imitate는 '모방하다'라는 의미입니다.

해석 TK Watches사의 마케팅 계획의 목적은 소비자들이 그들의 시계를 고 급 보석류와 관련시켜 생각하게 만드는 것이다.

어휘 **timepiece** n. 시계 **high-end** adj. 고급의 **jewelry** n. 보석류

02 동사 관련 어구 완성하기

해설 '웨딩드레스는 매우 다양한 사이즈로 나온다'라는 문맥이므로 동사 어 구 (D) come in((상품 등이 여러 종류로) 나오다)이 정답입니다. (A) get across는 '(의미 등이) 전달되다, 이해되다', (B) move on은 '넘 어가다', (C) add up은 '말이 되다, 앞뒤가 맞다'라는 의미입니다.

해석 Bridal Heaven이 들여놓은 대부분의 웨딩드레스는 매우 다양한 사이 즈로 나온다.

어휘 **stock** v. 들여놓다, 사들이다, 비축하다

03 동사 관련 어구 완성하기

해설 '본사의 건설에 5,000만 달러를 할당해왔다'라는 문맥이므로 뒷 부분의 전치사 for와 함께 'B에 A를 할당하다'라는 의미의 어구인 designate A for B를 만드는 동사 designate(할당하다, 지명하다) 의 p.p.형 (D) designated가 정답입니다. (A)의 serve는 '제공하다',

(B)의 imply는 '암시하다, 포함하다', (C)의 adapt는 '적응하다'라는 의미입니다.

해석 Yeats 석유 화학은 새로운 본사의 건설에 5,000만 달러를 할당해왔다.

어휘 **petrochemical** n. 석유 화학 **construction** n. 건설
headquarters n. 본사, 본부

04 동사 관련 어구 완성하기

해설 '대통령이 사회를 볼 것이라고 보도되었다'라는 문맥이므로 빈칸 뒤의 전치사 over와 함께 '사회를 보다'라는 의미의 어구인 preside over 를 만드는 동사 (A) preside(사회를 보다, 주재하다)가 정답입니다. (B) perceive는 '인식하다', (C) foresee는 '예견하다', (D) reach는 '도 달하다'라는 의미입니다.

해석 Wilson 대통령이 직접 국립 공원의 개회식 사회를 볼 것이라고 보도되 었다.

어휘 **inaugural** adj. 개회의, 취임의 **national park** phr. 국립 공원

05 동사 관련 어구 완성하기

해설 '여행 산업의 성공은 정부의 능력에 달려 있다'라는 문맥이므로 '~에 달려 있다'라는 의미의 동사 어구인 depend on의 3인칭 단수형 (B) depends on이 정답입니다. (A)의 meet with는 '~와 만나다', (C) 의 narrow down은 '범위를 좁히다', (D)의 carry out은 '수행하다' 라는 의미입니다.

해석 여행 산업의 성공은 외국인 관광객들을 유치시키는 정부의 능력에 달 려 있다.

어휘 **attract** v. 유치하다, 매료하다 **foreign** adj. 외국의

06 동사 관련 어구 완성하기

해설 '상원 의원은 지방 검사를 그의 수년간의 봉사에 대해 칭찬했다'라 는 문맥이므로 뒷부분의 전치사 for와 함께 'A를 B에 대해 칭찬하다' 라는 의미의 어구인 commend A for B를 만드는 동사 commend (칭찬하다, 추천하다)의 과거형 (A) commended가 정답입니다. (B)의 assume은 '가정하다', (C)의 specify는 '명시하다', (D)의 stimulate는 '자극하다'를 의미합니다.

해석 시상식 연회에서, 상원 의원 Freya Jones는 지방 검사 Harold Moffat 를 그의 수년간의 봉사에 대해 칭찬했다.

어휘 **senator** n. 상원 의원 **district attorney** phr. 지방 검사

07 동사 관련 어구 완성하기

해설 '모든 종류의 제품을 팔지만 프랑스식 파이를 전문으로 한다'라는 문 맥이므로 빈칸 뒤의 전치사 in과 함께 '~을 전문으로 하다'라는 의미의 어구인 specialize in을 만드는 동사 (A) specializes(전문으로 하다, 전공하다)가 정답입니다. (B)의 offer는 '제공하다', (C)의 improve는 '개선하다', (D)의 deserve는 '~할 만하다'라는 의미입니다.

해석 Sweet Sensations 제과점은 모든 종류의 제품을 팔지만, 프랑스식 파 이를 전문으로 한다.

어휘 **goods** n. 제품

08 동사 관련 어구 완성하기

해설 '세미나 참석자들은 문제를 제기하면서 토론에 참여할 것이 권해진다' 라는 문맥이므로 빈칸 뒤의 전치사 in과 함께 '~에 참여하다'라는 의 미의 어구인 participate in을 만드는 동사 (B) participate(참여하다, 참가하다)가 정답입니다. (A) divide는 '나누다', (C) conform은 '따 르다', (D) deny는 '거절하다'라는 의미입니다.

해석 세미나 참석자들은 문제를 제기하면서 토론에 참여할 것이 권해진다.

어휘 **encourage** v. 권하다, 격려하다 **pose** v. 제기하다, 주장하다

09 동사 관련 어구 완성하기

해설 '사이버 범죄자들이 기밀 정보를 훔치는 것을 예방하기 위해 설치되었다'라는 문맥이므로 뒷부분의 전치사 from과 함께 'A가 B하는 것을 예방하다'라는 의미의 어구인 prevent A from B를 만드는 동사 (D) prevent(예방하다, 막다)가 정답입니다. (A) guarantee는 '보장하다', (B) describe는 '묘사하다', (C) challenge는 '도전하다'라는 의미입니다.

해석 온라인 보안 프로그램은 사이버 범죄자들이 기밀 정보를 훔치는 것을 예방하기 위해 설치되었다.

어휘 install v. 설치하다 steal v. 훔치다 confidential adj. 기밀의

10 동사 관련 어구 완성하기

해설 '고해상도의 날씨 지도를 제공하다'라는 문맥이므로 뒷부분의 전치사 with와 함께 'A에게 B를 제공하다'라는 의미의 어구인 provide A with B를 만드는 동사 provide(제공하다, 공급하다)의 동명사형 (D) providing이 정답입니다. (A)의 interfere는 '방해하다', (B)의 develop는 '발전하다', (C)의 accept는 '받아들이다'라는 의미입니다.

해석 다음 달부터, NFRNews.com은 독자들에게 고해상도의 날씨 지도를 제공하는 것을 시작할 것이다.

어휘 high-resolution adj. 고해상도의 weather n. 날씨

DAY 19 [어구] 명사 관련 어구

토익 실전 문제　　　　　　　　　　p.383

01 (B)	02 (B)	03 (D)	04 (A)	05 (A)
06 (D)	07 (C)	08 (B)	09 (D)	10 (C)

01 명사 관련 어구 완성하기

해설 '실업률은 공장들의 폐쇄의 결과이다'라는 문맥이므로 빈칸 앞의 관사 a와 빈칸 뒤의 전치사 of와 함께 '~의 결과'라는 의미의 어구인 a consequence of를 만드는 명사 (B) consequence(결과)가 정답입니다. (A) practice는 '관행', (C) reinforcement는 '강화', (D) suggestion은 '제안'이라는 의미입니다.

해석 Grettington의 높은 실업률은 최근 그 지역의 몇몇 대형 공장들의 폐쇄의 결과이다.

어휘 unemployment n. 실업 rate n. 비율 recent adj. 최근의 closure n. 폐쇄

02 명사 관련 어구 완성하기

해설 '의무적인 규제는 지난달 가뭄이 시작된 이후로 실행되었다'라는 문맥이므로 빈칸 뒤의 전치사 on과 함께 '~에 대한 규제'라는 의미의 어구인 restrictions on을 만드는 명사 (B) restrictions(규제)가 정답입니다. (A)의 invitation은 '초대', (C)의 difference는 '차이', (D)의 organization은 '조직'이라는 의미입니다.

해석 물 사용에 대한 의무적인 규제는 지난달 가뭄이 시작된 이후로 실행되었다.

어휘 mandatory adj. 의무적인 be in effect phr. 실행되다 drought n. 가뭄

03 명사 관련 어구 완성하기

해설 '세부 사항에 대한 주의로 유명하다'라는 문맥이므로 빈칸 뒤의 전치사 to와 함께 '~에 대한 주의'라는 의미의 어구인 attention to를 만드는 명사 (D) attention(주의, 주목)이 정답입니다. (A) potential은

'잠재력', (B) contribution은 '기부', (C) decrease는 '감소'라는 의미입니다.

해석 세부 사항에 대한 주의로 유명한 Technica Gear사는 비할 데 없는 품질의 의류를 제조한다.

어휘 detail n. 세부 사항 manufacture v. 제조하다 apparel n. 의류, 의복 incomparable adj. 비할 데 없는

04 명사 관련 어구 완성하기

해설 '개발에서 프로젝트 관리로의 변화를 시도하다'라는 문맥이므로 빈칸 뒤의 전치사 from, to와 함께 'A에서 B로의 변화'라는 의미의 어구인 transition from A to B를 만드는 명사 (A) transition(변화)이 정답입니다. (B) statement는 '발표', (C) measurement는 '측량', (D) discussion은 '논의'라는 의미입니다.

해석 석사 학위를 취득하는 것은 Ms. Vega가 개발에서 프로젝트 관리로의 변화를 시도할 수 있게 할 것이다.

어휘 master's degree phr. 석사 학위 attempt v. 시도하다 management n. 관리, 경영

05 명사 관련 어구 완성하기

해설 '고객들의 관점을 얻기 위해 설문 조사를 실시한다'라는 문맥이므로 빈칸 뒤의 전치사 on과 함께 '~에 대한 관점'이라는 의미의 어구인 perspective on을 만드는 명사 (A) perspective(관점, 시각)가 정답입니다. (B) accessibility는 '접근', (C) similarity는 '유사성', (D) referral은 '소개, 위탁'이라는 의미입니다.

해석 마케팅 부서는 회사 상품의 품질에 대한 고객들의 관점을 얻기 위해 설문 조사를 실시한다.

어휘 survey n. 설문 조사

06 명사 관련 어구 완성하기

해설 '신분 확인 명찰을 의무적으로 착용하는 것을 포함한 보안 강화'라는 문맥이므로 빈칸 뒤의 명사 badges와 함께 '신분 확인 명찰'이라는 의미의 어구인 identification badge를 만드는 명사 (D) identification(신분, 신원)이 정답입니다. (A) transportation은 '대중교통', (B) interaction은 '상호 작용', (C) accommodation은 '거처, 숙소'라는 의미입니다.

해석 신분 확인 명찰을 의무적으로 착용하는 것을 포함한 보안 강화는 올해 시행될 것이다.

어휘 obligatory adj. 의무적인 implement v. 시행하다

07 명사 관련 어구 완성하기

해설 '법인 카드 정책을 준수하도록 기대된다'라는 문맥이므로 빈칸 뒤의 전치사 with와 함께 '~의 준수'라는 의미의 어구인 compliance with를 만드는 명사 (C) Compliance(준수, 따름)가 정답입니다. (A) Preference는 '선호', (B) Expansion은 '확장', (D) Estimation은 '판단'이라는 의미입니다.

해석 모든 직원들은 회사 법인 카드 정책을 준수하도록 기대된다.

어휘 corporate credit card phr. 법인 카드 be expected of phr. ~을 하도록 기대되다

08 명사 관련 어구 완성하기

해설 '최고 작품이라고 일컬으며 감탄을 표했다'라는 문맥이므로 빈칸 뒤의 전치사 for와 함께 '~에 대한 감탄'이라는 의미의 어구인 admiration for를 만드는 명사 (B) admiration(감탄, 존경)이 정답입니다. (A) comparison은 '비교', (C) influence는 '영향', (D) reception은 '접수처'라는 의미입니다.

해석 비평가들은 가수 Tara Queen의 최신 앨범이 지금까지 그녀의 최고 작품이라고 일컬으며 감탄을 표했다.

어휘 call v. 일컫다, 부르다 to date phr. 지금까지

09 명사 관련 어구 완성하기

해설 '우려를 표명했다'라는 문맥이므로 빈칸 뒤의 전치사 about과 함께 '~에 대한 우려'라는 의미의 어구인 concern about을 만드는 명사 (D) concerns(우려, 걱정)가 정답입니다. (A)의 procedure는 '절차', (B)의 experiment는 '실험', (C)의 collection은 '수집품'이라는 의미입니다.

해석 최고 경영자는 주주 회의에서 감소하는 주가에 대한 우려를 표명했다.

어휘 stock n. 주식 decline v. 감소하다 shareholder n. 주주

10 명사 관련 어구 완성하기

해설 '토지의 일부를 구매할 계획이다'라는 문맥이므로 빈칸 앞의 관사 a와 빈칸 뒤의 전치사 of와 함께 '~의 일부'라는 의미의 어구인 a portion of를 만드는 명사 (C) portion(일부, 몫)이 정답입니다. (A) division은 '분할', (B) formation은 '형성', (D) trade는 '거래'라는 의미입니다.

해석 Fremway 제조업은 Millville 쇼핑몰이 있었던 토지의 일부를 구매할 계획이다.

어휘 purchase v. 구매하다 property n. 토지

DAY 20 [어구] 짝을 이루는 표현

토익 실전 문제　　　　　　　　　　p.385

01 (D)	02 (B)	03 (C)	04 (C)	05 (C)
06 (C)	07 (A)	08 (B)	09 (A)	10 (B)

01 짝을 이루는 표현 완성하기

해설 '유기농 식품 산업은 꾸준한 성장을 하고 있다'라는 의미가 되어야 하므로 빈칸 앞의 형용사 steady(꾸준한, 안정된)와 함께 '꾸준한 성장'이라는 의미의 어구인 steady growth를 만드는 명사 (D) growth(성장, 증가)가 정답입니다. (A) reach는 '도달, 범위'라는 의미입니다. (B) extension은 '확장'이라는 의미로 해석상 그럴듯해 보이지만, 무언가를 길게 만드는 것을 가리키거나, 다른 무언가에서부터 발전된 것이라는 뜻에서 '확대'라는 의미를 나타냅니다. '확대'라는 의미를 나타낼 경우 '(명사) of (명사)'의 형태로 쓰입니다. (C) range는 '범위, 다양성'이라는 의미입니다.

해석 유기농 식품 산업은 화학 성분이 없는 농산물에 대한 수요 증가 덕분에 꾸준한 성장을 하고 있다.

어휘 organic adj. 유기농의 thanks to phr. ~ 덕분에 increase n. 증가 demand n. 수요, 요구 produce n. 농산물

02 짝을 이루는 표현 완성하기

해설 '방문하는 투자가들을 위한 준비를 해달라고 요청하다'라는 의미가 되어야 하므로 빈칸 앞의 동사 make(만들다)와 함께 '준비하다'라는 의미의 어구인 make arrangements를 만드는 명사 (B) arrangements(준비, 마련)가 정답입니다. (A)의 assembly는 '조립', (C)의 speculation은 '추측', (D)의 contribution은 '기여'라는 의미입니다.

해석 Mr. Goldfinch가 방문하는 몇몇 투자가들을 위한 준비를 해달라고 비서에게 요청했을 때, 그녀는 그들을 위해 시내의 호텔을 예약했다.

어휘 investor n. 투자가 book v. 예약하다

03 짝을 이루는 표현 완성하기

해설 '몇 주간의 협상 후에, 두 최고 경영자는 상호적으로 이득이 되는 제휴에 동의했다'라는 의미가 되어야 하므로 빈칸 뒤의 형용사 beneficial (이득이 되는, 유익한)과 함께 '상호적으로 이득이 되는'이라는 의미의 어구인 mutually beneficial을 만드는 부사 (C) mutually(상호적으로, 공통으로)가 정답입니다. (D) tightly는 '단단히, 팽팽하게'라는 의미로 해석상 그럴듯해 보이지만, 무언가가 움직이지 않게 꽉 고정되어 있는 것을 나타냅니다. (A) skillfully는 '능숙하게', (B) fluently는 '유창하게'라는 의미입니다.

해석 몇 주간의 협상 후에, 두 최고 경영자는 양쪽 회사 모두에 상호적으로 이득이 되는 제휴에 동의했다.

어휘 negotiation n. 협상

04 짝을 이루는 표현 완성하기

해설 '진행 중인 보수의 결과로 근무 환경이 불편했다'라는 의미가 되어야 하므로 빈칸 앞의 명사 work(직장)와 함께 '근무 환경'이라는 의미의 어구인 work environment를 만드는 명사 (C) environment(환경, 주위)가 정답입니다. (A) machine은 '기계', (B) payment는 '지불', (D) constraint는 '제약'이라는 의미입니다.

해석 진행 중인 보수의 결과로 근무 환경이 불편했기에, 직원들은 집에서 일하는 것이 허용된다.

어휘 unpleasant adj. 불편한, 불쾌한 ongoing adj. 진행 중인 permit v. 허용하다

05 짝을 이루는 표현 완성하기

해설 '매력적인 성과금을 제공함으로써 판매 실적을 신장시키기 위해 노력한다'라는 의미가 되어야 하므로 빈칸 앞의 형용사 sales(판매)와 함께 '판매 실적'이라는 의미의 어구인 sales performance를 만드는 명사 (C) performance(실적, 성과)가 정답입니다. (A)의 function은 '기능', (B) correspondence는 '일치', (D) endorsement는 '지지'라는 의미입니다.

해석 Mercer 제약 회사의 임원들은 직원들에게 매력적인 성과금을 제공함으로써 판매 실적을 신장시키기 위해 노력한다.

어휘 executive n. 임원, 간부 endeavor v. 노력하다, 애쓰다 boost v. 신장시키다 incentive n. 성과금

06 짝을 이루는 표현 완성하기

해설 '건물에 대한 점검을 실시하다'라는 의미가 되어야 하므로 빈칸 앞의 동사 conduct(실시하다)와 함께 '점검을 실시하다'라는 의미의 어구인 conduct an inspection을 만드는 명사 (C) inspection(점검, 검사)이 정답입니다. (A) interruption은 '방해', (B) application은 '지원', (D) admission은 '허가'라는 의미입니다.

해석 경영진은 건물에 대한 점검을 실시하고 발견할 수 있는 어떠한 결함이든지 수리하기 위해 전문가들을 고용할 것이다.

어휘 defect n. 결함

07 짝을 이루는 표현 완성하기

해설 '끊임없이 주도성을 발휘하기 때문에 승진에 대해 고려되고 있다'라는 의미가 되어야 하므로 빈칸 앞의 동사 displays(보여주다, 전시하다)와 함께 '주도성을 발휘하다'라는 의미의 어구인 display initiative를 만드는 명사 (A) initiative(주도성)가 정답입니다. (B) exhibition은 '전시', (C) quantity는 '양', (D) system은 '체계'라는 의미입니다.

해석 Mr. Gordon은 끊임없이 주도성을 발휘하기 때문에 관리직으로의 승진에 대해 고려되고 있다.

어휘 promotion n. 승진 managerial adj. 관리의 consistently adv. 끊임없이

08 짝을 이루는 표현 완성하기

해설 '작업 환경을 개선하는 조치를 취하다'라는 의미가 되어야 하므로 빈칸 앞의 동사 take(취하다, 잡다)와 함께 '조치를 취하다'라는 의미의 어구 take measures를 만드는 명사 (B) measures(조치, 측정)가 정답입니다. (A)의 facility는 '시설', (C)의 section은 '구역', (D)의 design은 '설계'라는 의미입니다.

해석 능률 자문 위원은 공장 관리자에게 근로자들을 위해 작업 환경을 개선하는 조치를 취하라고 조언했다.

어휘 **consultant** n. 자문 위원 **improve** v. 개선하다
condition n. 환경, 조건

09 짝을 이루는 표현 완성하기

해설 '가수의 팬들은 그의 다음 앨범을 간절히 기다린다'라는 의미가 되어야 하므로 빈칸 뒤의 동사 await(기다리다, 대기하다)와 함께 '간절히 기다리다'라는 의미의 어구인 eagerly await를 만드는 부사 (A) eagerly(간절히, 열심히)가 정답입니다. (B) visually는 '시각적으로', (C) loosely는 '느슨하게', (D) defiantly는 '반항적으로'라는 의미입니다.

해석 호평받는 가수 Lawrence Stevens의 팬들은 그의 다음 앨범을 간절히 기다리는데, 그 앨범은 1주일 뒤에 공개되기로 예정되어 있다.

어휘 **acclaimed** adj. 호평 받는, 칭찬을 받는
be set to phr. ~하기로 예정되어 있다

10 짝을 이루는 표현 완성하기

해설 '다른 공급 업체들과 경쟁하기 위해 속도를 높여서 더 빨리 장기 계약을 따내기 시작해야 한다'라는 의미가 되어야 하므로 빈칸 앞의 동사 quicken(빠르게 하다, 활기를 띠게 하다)과 함께 '속도를 높이다'라는 의미의 어구인 quicken the pace를 만드는 명사 (B) pace(속도, 보조)가 정답입니다. (A) quest는 '탐구, 탐색', (C) march는 '행진', (D) lead는 '선두, 우세'라는 의미입니다.

해석 Wentworth Natural Gas사는 다른 공급 업체들과 경쟁하기 위해 속도를 높여서 더 빨리 장기 계약을 따내기 시작해야 한다.

어휘 **long-term** adj. 장기의

MEMO

MEMO

327만이 선택한 외국어학원
1위 해커스어학원

토익 단기졸업 달성을 위한 해커스 약점관리 프로그램

자신의 약점을 정확히 파악하고 집중적으로 보완하는 것이야말로
토익 단기졸업의 필수코스입니다.

토익종합반
**수강생
0원**

취약점
분석표 제공

STEP 01
약점체크 모의고사 응시

*비매품

최신 토익 출제경향을 반영한
약점체크 모의고사 응시

STEP 02
토익 취약점 분석표 확인

파트별 취약점 분석표를 통해
객관적인 실력 파악

STEP 03
개인별 맞춤 보완문제 증정

최대
180제
제공

*PDF

영역별 취약 부분에 대한
보완문제로 취약점 극복

지금 바로 신청하고
토익 취약점 완벽 극복 ▶

5천 개가 넘는
해커스토익 무료 자료!

대한민국에서 공짜로 토익 공부하고 싶으면 | 해커스영어 Hackers.co.kr ▾ | 검색

RC 정수진 **RC 이상길**

토익 강의 무료

베스트셀러 1위 토익 강의 150강 무료 서비스,
누적 시청 1,900만 돌파!

토익 실전 문제 무료

토익 RC/LC 풀기, 모의토익 등
실전토익 대비 문제 제공!

LC 한승태 **RC 김동영**

최신 특강 무료

2,400만뷰 스타강사의
압도적 적중예상특강 매달 업데이트!

고득점 달성 비법 무료

토익 고득점 달성팁, 파트별 비법,
점수대별 공부법 무료 확인

**전원
무료**
*미션 달성 시

가장 빠른 정답까지!

615만이 선택한 해커스 토익 정답!
시험 직후 가장 빠른 정답 확인

더 많은
토익 무료자료 보기 ▶